ISBN 978-0-428-62392-0
PIBN 11249949

FB &c Ltd, Dalton House, 60 Windsor Avenue, London, SW19 2RR.
Company number 08720141. Registered in England and Wales.

For support please visit www.forgottenbooks.com

STATE OF WISCONSIN.

GOVERNOR'S MESSAGE

AND

ACCOMPANYING DOCUMENTS

DELIVERED TO THE

LEGISLATURE IN JOINT CONVENTION,

Thursday, January 15, 1874.

VOL. I.

BY AUTHORITY.

MADISON:
ATWOOD & CULVER, STATE PRINTERS AND STEREOTYPERS.
1874.

DOCUMENTS.

1. Report of the Secretary of State.
2. " " " as Insurance Commissioner.
3. " " State Treasurer.
4. " " Commissioner of School and University Lands.
5. " " Superintendent of Public Instruction.

GOVERNOR'S MESSAGE.

Fellow Citizens of the Senate and Assembly:

You have assembled under peculiar circumstances. An era of apparent prosperity without parallel in the previous history of the nation, has been succeeded by financial reverses affecting all classes of industry, and largely modifying the standard of values. The financial classes of Wisconsin are entitled to commendation for the foresight which has enabled them measurably to resist the current of disaster. The prudence and integrity of our business men in the principal cities generally, and the vast extent of our natural resources, have also contributed largely to the restoration of mutual confidence, and averted many of the evils apparent elsewhere. To a great extent, however, this condition of things is the legitimate consequence of a healthy reaction, and may be regarded as comparatively permanent.

Accompanying these financial disturbances, has come an imperative demand from the people for a purer political morality, a more equitable apportionment of the burdens and blessings of government and a more rigid economy in the administration of public affairs. It does not become me to discuss, in this place, either the direct or remote influences which have led to this reasonable demand. We have to deal with facts as they are admitted to exist, and to apply such remedies, within the sphere of our constitutional duty, as your legislative experience and wisdom may suggest. In the execution of the popular will in this particular, it is certain that no evasion and no compromise will be patiently tolerated.

ANNUAL REPORTS OF TREASURER AND SECRETARY.

The fiscal year ended on the 30th day of September last. The Treasurer and Secretary of State have furnished you full details of expenditure for the support of the state government during the year. I commend the several items of this expenditure to your critical examination, with a view to positive legislation in behalf of retrenchment.

TOTAL RECEIPTS AND DISBURSEMENTS.

The total receipts into the state treasury during the year, including all sources of income, were $1,774,558.55. The total disbursements, for all purposes, were $1,798,023.14. The balance in the treasury at the commencement of the fiscal year was $239,109.11. The excess of total disbursements over total receipts during the year was $23,464.59, thus leaving in the treasury, to the credit of all funds, $215,644.52. The excess of total disbursements over total receipts was due to an excess of expenditure from the general fund, as will be seen by facts hereinafter stated.

THE GENERAL FUND RECEIPTS.

The total receipts of the general fund during the fiscal year were $1,095,872.29. Of this sum, the amount of $781,875.60 was derived from direct state tax upon the assessed valuation of property. $210,374.99 from taxes on the gross receipts of railroad companies, $63,299.93 from taxes on fire and life insurance companies, and the balance from miscellaneous sources.

GENERAL FUND DISBURSEMENTS.

The total disbursements from the general fund during the fiscal year were $1,191,966.01, an excess of $96,093.72 above the receipts. Deducting from this excess of expenditure the balance in the general fund at the commencement of the fiscal year—September 30, 1872—and the deficiency in this fund for the year ending September 30, 1873, is found to be $66,923.80. The total disbursements were divided among the several classes of current expenditure, as follows: Salaries and permanent appropriations, $261,572.36; legislative expenses, $103,730.22; state prison and charitable institutions, $501,246.83; miscellaneous, $325,416.60.

The deficiency in the general fund, of $66,923.80, is an overpayment, in excess of all proper resources for current expenditures, from the trust funds of the state, and is, in fact, an increase of the state debt to the precise amount of the sum thus abstracted from those funds. I am not aware of any law authorizing this increase of debt, or the diversion of the trust funds from their legitimate and proper purposes, beyond that law of necessity which leaves the state government no alternative in the administration of public affairs, but to misappropriate moneys held in trust and sacredly set apart for purposes of charity and education, rather than to permit dishonor to come upon the current obligations of the treasury. If an individual, appointed to protect the property interests of orphan minors or insane persons, were to divert to his private uses the resources entrusted to his keeping, his conduct would find no apology in law or morals. The relation of the state to its trust funds is not essentially different, and its violation of good faith not less reprehensible. The practice is especially demoralizing and dangerous as a precedent. It is possible that the past action of the state in borrowing from the school and other trust funds, under special circumstances, and by an exercise of legislative power, deemed to have been authorized by the constitution, may be regarded as affording some sanction for the present procedure. It must be admitted, however, that the special exigency under which the indebtedness to the trust fund was originally created, has wholly disappeared, and that the existing practice has no real justification, resulting, as it does, from special appropriations, made by the legislature, in excess of the revenues provided to meet them. No question as to the profit and expediency of a further loan from the trust funds to the state can, under present circumstances, be entertained. It is sufficient for us to know that an increase of the state debt beyond its present limits is prohibited by the constitution we have sworn to support; that this prohibition was wisely intended as a restraint upon the legislature, and a protection to the people, and that it cannot be honestly evaded nor safely defied.

Inasmuch as the disbursements from the general fund during the last quarter of the calendar year—being the first quarter of the present fiscal year—are compensated by no corresponding receipts into that fund during the same quarter, the deficiency which existed on the 30th of September last, is much larger at the present date. In his annual report, the secretary of state estimated that this deficiency on the first day of January instant, would reach the sum of $168,621.26. I recommend such legislation as shall rapidly repair the present deficiency and prevent, in the future, the continuation of those practices which necessitate this legislation.

THE STATE DEBT.

The legal debt of the state, denominated the "bonded and irreducible debt," at the close of the fiscal year, was $2,252,057. Of this sum $2,233,900 consists of certificates of indebtedness to the various trust funds, $18,100 of outstanding bonds, and $57 of currency certificates.

THE TRUST FUNDS.

The total productive accumulations of all the trust funds of the state, on the 30th of September, 1873, were $3,870,653.71, showing an increase during the last fiscal year of $94,468.56. At the same date these funds were thus divided:

School Fund	$2,510,181 12
University Fund	216,519 38
Agricultural College Fund	225,309 73
Normal School Fund	918,643 48

STATE TAX.

The state tax levied for 1871 was $629,143.10; for 1872, $765,291.55; for 1873, $671,582.37. The rate per cent. of this tax upon the assessed valuation for the three years named, respectively is as follows: 1871, 1 38-100 mills; 1872, 1 96-100 mills;

1873, 1 72-100 mills. The assessed valuation for 1873 was $390,454,875.

Under existing laws, taxes on railway companies are added to the tax on the assessed valuation of other property, and form a considerable portion of the annual revenue. Whether the amount paid by these companies fully accords with the principles of justice and the requirements of our state constitution, is to me a matter of grave doubt, and deserves your earnest and careful consideration. The facts set forth and the suggestions made by the Secretary of State on this subject, in his annual report, should not escape your attention.

Another matter of great importance to our people, claims your consideration in this immediate connection. I refer to the taxation of telegraph and express companies. I know of no sufficient reason why these foreign corporations should not be made fully amenable to the laws of the state which furnishes them protection, and be required to bear a full proportion of the burdens of government. It is a notorious fact that the owners of stock in these companies, enjoying special privileges, realize large incomes from their investments within the state, and that their business here is prosecuted to the practical exclusion of private enterprise in the same direction, on the part of our own citizens. While not questioning the fact of their necessity and utility, I am not prepared to concede that the benefits they confer are so far in excess of those conferred by other corporations, as to entitle them to any exemption from the ordinary obligations of corporations under similar circumstances.

TIME OF PAYING TAXES.

It is worthy of serious reflection, whether the time now provided by law for the payment of taxes could not be changed with great advantage to tax-payers. Every prudent business man equalizes his payments with reference to his available resources. In business circles custom requires the adjustment of annual balances in January. It is, apparently, unfortunate that the payment of taxes should be added to all the other pecuniary burdens of the population at this period of the year, especially as the state derives no benefit from any accumulation of surplus funds in the treasury. In the state of Ohio the law provides for semi-annual payments—in June and December I am informed by executive authority that no inconvenience has been experienced in that state from this arrangement, since, the first year or two of its operation. Should the present annual system continue, the alternative question should be carefully considered, whether the state ought not to derive a considerable income during portions of the year from the use of its surplus funds. In the city of Milwaukee interest is required and received on all deposits by the city treasurer, calculated upon daily balances. I learn that the receipts of that city from this source the present year will exceed $15,000, and that the method is regarded as wholly safe, and otherwise satisfactory.

SOURCES OF RETRENCHMENT.

The condition of the general fund, already explained, and the existing depression in business enterprises, admonish us to consider well the sources of retrenchment. It does not become me to prescribe the details of legislation immediately committed to your charge by the constitution. I venture, however, to direct your attention to several items of expenditure, more or less subject to public criticism, some of which would seem to justify legislative action for the benefit of the treasury.

The compensation of all state officers should be accurately limited and defined, and all fees, without exception, should be paid into the treasury. I do not know that the ability and responsibility expected from the heads of the executive departments, are now too liberally paid for; but any current impression that the salaries of these officers are uncertain in amount, excites public suspicion, oftentimes unjust to the officers themselves, and certainly demoralizing in its influence upon officers of inferior responsibility throughout the state. Any precedent or example tending to encourage the morbid spirit of speculation on the public resources should be scrupulously comdemned and avoided.

The clerical force of the several departments of the state government, should be paid a reasonable compensation for the labor performed, and no more, thus measurably providing an antidote against the existing greed for public office.

Constructive compensation, by way of perquisites, and the employment of supernumeraries, are palpable violations of public faith, and deserve the severest reprobation. It is the scandal of our state, that while the total salaries and mileage of the members of the legislature, as provided by law, amount to about $50,000 per annum, the legislative expenses, for employes, printing, postage and stationery, during the few weeks the legislature is in session, average about an equal sum. It may be claimed that the amount misappropriated in this and other similar cases is comparatively insignificant. But I know of no departure from public rectitude which can be mathematically measured.

It appears from the report of the Secretary of State, that the total amount paid from the general fund during the last fiscal year for printing and publishing, including $7,301.64 for the Legislative Manual, reached $95,516.61. I am not prepared to say that the cost of this work was too much for the quantity, nor do I recommend any deduction from the just wages of mechanical labor in this or any other department. The cost of this service, however, has become a great burden upon the treasury, being for the past year nearly one-twelfth of the entire disbursements from the general fund,—a cost apparently disproportionate to the public benefits rendered. While the ample publicity of the laws should be provided for through the established channels of communication with the public, I submit for your consideration, the propriety of adopting measures for the abolition of all expenditures in this department not absolutely essential to official business and public information.

GEOLOGICAL SURVEY.

The geological survey, heretofore provided by law, has been prosecuted during the past year at a cost of $8,280. I feel assured of valuable results from this work, both to the cause of general science and the material progress of the state. The vast and undeveloped resources of Wisconsin warrant a reasonable expenditure in this enterprise. The benefits which accrue from a work of this kind depend upon the thoroughness and completeness with which it is done. It is very important for this fact to be kept constantly in mind, but in view of the existing pecuniary embarrassment of tax-payers and the deficiency in the state treasury, it is no less important that the present undertaking be prosecuted with the strictest possible economy consistent with the end to be attained.

IMMIGRANT COMMISSIONER.

While I am not convinced that the office of Immigrant Commissioner can be prudently dispensed with, it is yet possible that a reduction in the expenditures of that office could be safely provided for, without prejudice to the interests committed to his charge. The growth and prosperity of our state is very largely due to the justly liberal provisions of our constitution in respect to immigrants from foreign nations, and neither in the light of public policy nor of a just hospitality can we refuse any action necessary to insure ample guidance and protection to those from abroad seeking happier homes on our bountiful soil.

REGISTRY OF ELECTORS.

The law providing for the registry of electors is costly, cumbrous and inefficient. In towns and cities alike, it is obnoxious to the people. The purity of our elections is to be sacredly guarded under all circumstances, but I trust that the wisdom of the legislature is competent to devise more simple and effective means to that end. Neither in this nor in any other state in the Union has experience demonstrated that security from fraud and corruption at elections is necessarily contingent upon a complicated elective machinery. The imposition of superabundant conditions upon the exercise of the elective franchise often opens the way for the very evils intended to be prevented, is uniformly odious to the mass of electors of honorable intent, and is manifestly in violation of the spirit, if not the actual letter of our constitution.

In the consideration of this general subject, I urge a more liberal regard for the rights and conveniences of workingmen in our large cities. Under existing laws, the polls at every general election open at 9 o'clock in the forenoon and close at sundown, and every elector employed at day wages is thus practically debarred from the privilege of exercising the elective franchise, except through the charity of his employer or at the cost of a pecuniary penalty equaling his wages for the whole or a portion of a day. This is a gross and manifest injustice. In the exercise of the right of suffrage no unnecessary discrimination or restraint should be tolerated. At the ballot box all men are equal, and it is my deliberate conviction that public expense is increased, the opportunity for fraud favored, and a full and fair expression of public opinion restrained, in the more populous districts, by the brevity of time now allotted for depositing votes and recording the names of electors.

EDUCATION.

I congratulate you upon the progress of our educational institions, public and private. It is conceded that upon the wide and thorough diffusion of knowledge depends, in great degree, the happiness of our people and the preservation of our liberal system of government. To this end, both the nation and the state have made provision for generous aid from the public property, and I bespeak a conscientious guardianship of the trust committed to your hands. Whether the results rightfully to be expected from the extensive resources at the command of the state have been fully attained, is a legitimate subject of inquiry and discussion. A frequent comparison of the faculties afforded for instruction in this and neighboring States, and of the cost at which those facilities were secured would doubtless prove profitable and tend to induce still greater progress and economy. For nothing else are the people more willing, nor can they better afford to give liberally of their substance, than for purposes of education, if they are only assured that the means contributed will be wisely and economically used. Of our public school system in this State we have reason to be proud, but it is yet far from being perfect and comes far short of what it may be made. The common schools are doing an indispensable work. The Normal Schools, now organized, are accomplishing all that is at present required of them, and doing it efficiently. The State University is rapidly growing in pop ular favor and is taking rank among the first educational institutions of the country. While all this is true, it is yet clear that there is a want of perfect gradation from the common schools to the University, which last should stand as the "crowning head" of the system. Whether the "missing link" or links are to be supplied through the agency of county academies or of the Normal Schools or of both, is a question which is forcing itself upon the attention of the people of the state and is well worthy of your earnest attention.

I shall be happy to concur in any appropriate legislation tending to more perfectly unify the public school system of the state.

CENTENNIAL EXPOSITION.

In 1876, one hundred years will have elapsed since the Declaration of American Independence. Congress, by an act, approved March 3, 1871, made provision for duly celebrating the 100dth anniversary, by holding, in the city of Philadelphia, an "International Exhibition of Arts, Manufactures and Products of the Soil and Mine," in which will be represented "the natural resources of the country and their development, and its progress in those arts which benefit mankind, in comparison with those of older nations." The act provided for the appointment, by the President, in each state and territory, of one commissioner and one alternate commissioner, to carry out the objects of this law. This centennial commission was organized on the 4th of March, 1872, and has held several meetings and made considerable progress with the work committed to its charge. It has decided that the Exposition shall continue for six months, commencing on the 19th day of April, and ending on the 19th day of October, 1876. The plans for the buildings have been adopted. On the 4th of July last, the President of the United States issued a proclamation, announcing this national celebration, and commending it to the people of this country and to those of all Nations. Several responses from foreign nations have already been received, signifying their intention to be represented. It seems fitting that such a celebration of this important event should be held, and it is hoped it will be carried out in a manner worthy of a great and enlightened nation.

Wisconsin should not be less interested in this matter than her sister states. She has vast resources that should be represented. The Centennial Commission has indicated, through circulars sent to the Executive office, that the greatest success in this work will be attained through state boards of managers, appointed by state authority, each to be composed of men thoroughly familiar with the capabilities of the state it represents; and responsible for the exhibition made under its direction. It will have to care for the interests of its own state, and of its citizens in all matters relating to the Exposition. Such board of managers would seem well calculated to effect the object in view; and the subject of providing for its appointment is respectfully submitted to the careful consideration of the Legislature.

FREE PASSES.

I recommend the enactment of a law forbidding the acceptance or use of free passes, or any other gift, immunity or compensation, by any state officer, from any railroad or other public corporation, existing under the laws of this state. With the abolition of free passes and weekly adjournments from Friday to Monday night, may not the average session be shortened fully thirty days?

CHARITABLE INSTITUTIONS.

I commend to your continued sympathy and care, those unfortunate persons whom the custom of civilized nations and the dictates of humanity have made a public charge. The general duty of the state in this respect is clear and well defined, under existing laws. The provision already made and the capital already invested in this direction are of munificent proportions, and afford creditable proof of the noble impulses of our people. The sum disbursed for these purposes during the past year, including an item of $45,550.47 for the State Prison, exceeded half a million dollars, or nearly one half the total receipts into the gen fund, and a considerable balance of past appropriations yet mains unexpended. A material modification of the amoun these expenditures, hereafter, probably will be found consis with a bountiful charity. The adaption of means to ends in department demands more than ordinary prudence and caut The good accomplished is to be measured by the actual blessi conferred, rather than by the size of the buildings erected, or the magnitude of the appropriations paid from the treasury. A dereliction of duty in this department is not merely an off against the public, but a robbery of the poor and helpless, which there can be no justification. A general supervisior the management of these institutions is now mainly exercised a State Board of Charities. While I am constrained to say this agency has not wholly met, thus far, the expectations of people, I am not quite prepared to recommend its discontinua The amount already invested in our charitable institutions, the heavy annual appropriations actually necessary for t maintenance, warrant the legislature in creating or retaining agencies which are calculated to secure the greatest wisdom economy in the use of these disbursements. My own observat has led me to believe that the want of power to act, to inve gate and correct abuses, and of a more definite responsibility the chief cause of the inefficiency of this Board as now organi I respectfully submit this subject for your careful consideratior

THE STATE PRISON.

The management of the state prison, especially demands y scrutiny. Contrary to the experience of many of the most lightened states of the Union, the punishment of our criminals a source of continued depletion to the public treasury. ' criminals confined in this institution are mostly able-bodied ma in the prime of life, capable of earning much more than the a age of men, and the fact is incomprehensible that they sho prove a perpetual burden upon the tax payers. I can see no g reason why this Institution, under proper management, sho not be made nearly or quite self-sustaining, when the Penit tiaries of so many states in the Union are a source of revenue to the public treasury. It is claimed by those who have made a careful comparison of the statistics that the inmates of our state prison cost us more *per capita*, than do the inmates of any of the charitable institutions of the state. For this condition of things there seems to be neither justification nor excuse. The continuance of an enlightened policy toward the prisoners, looking to the protection of society rather than to a malicious punishment of the guilty, will not tend to retard that reform in this direction which is now so imperatively demanded.

TEMPERANCE LAW.

Our government was wisely instituted for the protection of society, and is not an appropriate instrumentality for the dissemination of religious doctrine or for the definition and enforcement of private morality. Our state constitution clearly recognizes personal liberty as among the inherent rights of man, and the obligations imposed upon us in this regard characterize all free government wherever instituted. The precise line of division between the freedom of the individual and the rights of society may sometimes be difficult of definition. But the general restrictions upon the exercise of legislative power in this direction, are not the less positive and obligatory. The natural inclination of all classes of people, is to invoke the power of the government as a remedy for all evils, real or imaginary, and the greatest danger lies in the direction of too liberal concessions to these demands. There is, in fact, no aggregation of popular evils more to be apprehended, than a government loaded with a superabundance of arbitrary powers, and burdened with the self-imposed responsibility of righting all the wrongs of which society complains. Inordinate expenditure and taxation, popular discontents and disrespect of all the obligations of law, are the natural and direct fruits of these arbitrary interferences with the social habits, private enterprises or religious beliefs of the people.

Some of the provisions of the existing temperance law, manifestly conflict with these views, and are believed to be inefficient for the accomplishment of the laudable purposes contemplated.

Think as we may and say what we will upon the abstract q tion of temperance legislation, there is little doubt tha majority of the people of this state are opposed to the pe form of the so-called "Graham Law." I therefore, recomm such a modification of existing legislation on this subject as s dispense with these obnoxious provisions, without in any deg impairing the appropriate power of the state to regulate restrain the traffic in intoxicating liquors, or to punish offe against society originating in this cause.

BANKS AND BANKING.

Some legislation is desirable for the better protection deposits in banks, both corporate and private. The gen banking law of the state was framed mainly with refere to securing notes of circulation which have been taxed out existence by federal legislation. While these monied instituti are organized for an entirely different purpose, the statu relating to them have undergone no thorough revision. T depositor in a state bank has no adequate security against lo his faith in the integrity and capacity of its officers is really only guarantee.

The capital stock of such a corporation may be swallowed in reckless speculation, its funds may be stolen and squander by those who are placed to guard them, and its creditors have sure means of learning its true condition until it has failed a its books are in the hands of an assignee. The regular reports interested officials is not a sufficient guarantee of the soundn of a banking institution, nor is fictitious stock a proper foundati for public credit. The people should be protected from all su irresponsible institutions by the positive and wholesome restrai of statutory enactments.

I would therefore recommend that the general banking laws so amended as to increase the liability of stockholders; and th all persons doing a banking business in the state, whether corp rate or private, except corporations organized under acts of co gress, be placed under the supervision of state authority and son system of inspection adopted by which the public may be acc rately informed as to the amount of cash capital, the nature of the investments and the character of the securities.

Such a statement of the affairs of a bank, by a competent and trustworthy officer of the state, supplementing the regular semi-annual report now required, would afford all the protection against fraud and mismanagement that the people can reasonably ask at your hands.

CHEAP TRANSPORTATION BY WATER.

The relation of our state to national commerce is peculiar. More than three-fifths of the Wisconsin boundary is washed by navigable water, conceded to be under the special care of the federal government. Our principal interior streams are also navigable, dividing their bounty between the Gulf of Mexico and the Atlantic ocean, on a line nearly equi-distant between Lake Michigan and the Mississippi river.

I concede that the moneys paid into the federal treasury belong to the people of the whole Union, and we can rightfully claim the intervention of the federal government for any strictly local objects. But as to the duty of the general government to improve natural channels of commerce, clearly pertaining to the general welfare and necessary to inter-state commerce, there can be no reasonable ground for doubt. More than fifty years ago, President Monroe commended to congress the propriety of improving the navigation of western rivers between their highest navigable points, for the purpose of facilitating "intercourse between the Atlantic and the western country." The government has hitherto most signally failed to fulfill the measure of its obligation in this particular. Congress has made large and uniform concessions to special industries fostered by eastern capital, and those industries have been largely sustained by indirect taxation upon western labor and the products of our fertile soil. Equity, as well as the discharge of a clear constitutional duty, requires a different estimate and apportionment of federal obligations in future, to the end that the blessings of government to our agricultural and commercial population may better accord with its cost. It is impracticable in this place to explore or explain all the mysteries of taxation upon western labor and productions. But the d and indirect contributions of Wisconsin to the federal trea are believed to equal six or eight millions of dollars per an in addition to taxes indirectly imposed for the protection of sp industries, constituting no part of the national revenue. It i vious that for the most of this taxation we are unlikely to d any adequate return, except so far as our ability to bear the den is enlarged by an increase of those facilities of transport now demanded by the general interests of both eastern and ern trade and commerce.

I congratulate you upon what has been already achieve these particulars, having a direct relation to the prosperity of own people. During the year ending on the 30th of June the total sum of $142,187.56 was expended by the federal go ment for the improvement of harbors at Menomonee, Green Sheboygan, Port Washington, Milwaukee, Racine and Ken A considerable sum has also been expended on these harbor ring the current fiscal year, and the work will probably be co ued the ensuing year, in accordance with the recomme tions of assistant engineer W. H. Hearding, under whose imn ate and efficient direction these improvements were prosec during the past season. The aggregate exports and impor and from these harbors are now immense, the export Milwaukee alone exceeding three million tons, and those of other ports named being proportionately large. The ben which accrue to the federal government and to the people these expenditures on our lake shore are general and permar while the expenditures are limited and temporary.

THE MISSISSIPPI RIVE R.

An amount comparatively moderate has also been expende the government the past calendar year on the Mississippi riv points antiguous to our state, or otherwise directly relating t trade and commerce of Wisconsin. Practical and judicious r ures for the continuous improvement of this national water co from the head of navigation to the mouth of the river, des and must command the support of our representatives in con and the approbation of our people. An important portion of our state is now dependent upon the facilities afforded by this river for the export of its products and for its future growth in population and wealth, and a much larger portion may justly anticipate more important results from additional facilities for transportation by means of this river hereafter.

In this connection I would also call your attention to the importance of a slack water communication between the Mississippi and St. Croix rivers. Such an improvement would hasten the rapid development of our own state and would prove equally beneficial to other northern states bordering on the Mississippi. A memorial to congress on this subject might serve to call the attention of that body to the nature and importance of this route.

FOX AND WISCONSIN RIVERS.

Intimately connected with the question of cheap transportation, is the commendable undertaking of congress to complete a practical and permanent water route between the Mississippi river and the great lakes, by means of the Fox and Wisconsin rivers. For the first time the national government assumed the active and exclusive responsibility of this important national enterprise in October, 1872. At that time the work was transferred from the Green Bay and Mississippi Canal Company to the United States government, and during the past year the improvement has been effectively prosecuted under the immediate direction of assistant United States Engineer, Capt. John Nader. In his recent report of progress, Col. Houston, in general charge of this improvement, states that there is no public work more national in its character than this; that by this route the products of the southwest will find cheap transportation to the sea board, and the lumber and iron of the northwest to the Mississippi Valley, and that "there is no other route which will meet the necessities of so large a section of the United States at so small an expense." Capt. Nader estimates that the whole work may be completed in accordance with the plan early in the year 1876, and at an expense to the natio trifling in comparison with the benefits anticipated.

CHEAP TRANSPORTATION BY LAND.

The permanent improvement of natural water channels of national character, doubtless furnishes a partial solution of tl question of cheap transportation. But the problem is one vital significance in all its phases, and also must be fearlessly ai intelligently considered in relation to land carriage, with a view every possible relief from existing evils. Wisconsin has a territ rial area approximating that of all the New England states coı bined, and its soil abounds with many sources of agricultural a mineral wealth, now comparatively valueless, because of the c stacles to a quick and cheap transit of freight to distant marke Every reduction in the cost of exchanges between the produc and the consumer necessarily enhances the value of every acre our territory, and induces a corresponding investment of capi and labor in the development of our material prosperity. T serious consideration of this matter can no longer be pruden postponed. The agricultural classes, upon whom rest the heav burdens of government, and who are ordinarily the last to cla or receive special protection at the hands of the legislative pow are but reasonable in their demand for security in the fut against the wrongs of the past, and for such intervention on part of their representatives as shall secure that just reward intelligent labor already generally assured to the American peo in nearly all other departments of labor and enterprise. We c not be blind to the general truth, that classes favored by gove ment, or conspicuous in the management of corporate intere have become possessed of wealth far in excess of human want, the natural fruits of human industry, while the average farme our state scarcely realizes the ordinary wages of his hard and p tracted daily labor, and is compelled to rely upon the indirect fluences of immigration, mostly from foreign nations, for any able increase in his landed possessions. Certain it is, that W consin, with large and constant accessions to her private cap and working population, with a soil naturally productive beyond the average of American states, and with an amoun exports large in proportion to her population, should have reac at this time a rank in the scale of material progress much hig than that she now occupies.

I doubt the propriety of appeals to the federal government for relief from abuses in the operations of railways. Apart from the question of constitutional power, always worthy of grave consideration in connection with internal enterprises of this kind, it must be confessed that experience has not given occasion for unlimited confidence in the ability, purity or impartiality of congress in the management of enterprises of this class.

Fortunately no doubt can exist as to the plenary power of our own state over corporations of its own creation. By constitutional provision all existing enactments on the subject may be altered or repealed.

The duty of the legislature to exercise this power to the full extent of preventing or abolishing the evils of monopoly and extortion, is equally clear. A corporation which conspires to plunder the people by whose consent it exists, betrays its trust and justly forfeits its claim to existence.

It must be admitted, however, that railway companies are necessary to the prosperity and development of the state, and that in the discharge of their honorable obligations to the public, they are entitled to the gratitude and positive and uniform protection of legislative authority. In this matter the people will make no peace with enemies, but they seek no war with friends. While they are willing to encourage to the fullest extent the development of the railway system of our state, they cannot submit to manifest injustice, nor permit the abuse of chartered privileges.

The great problem then is, how shall the state afford proper protection and encouragement to all its varied industries, and, at the same time mete out equal and exact justice to all its citizens?

The precise manner in which the state can best exercise its power for the protection of the people against the abuses of railway corporations, is a question not now presented for the first time. There is no aspect of the subject which has not been the occasion of rigid investigation by the wisest statesmen of this country and Europe, and there is no conceivable expedient of legislation which has not been resorted to on both continents for the attainment of the most desirable results. In a matter so complicated and important, it cannot be expected of me to recommend or the legislature to adopt, specific measures of relief, w much research and mature deliberation. Permit me to suggest, however, a few general propositions of a practical c ter, as a basis of legislative action :

1. Railway companies are entitled to a full return of all expenditures for running and repairing roads, with a fair ir on the capital so invested in the construction and outfit of roads; and this interest on the capital so invested should b ficient in amount to encourage the continuous employment o ital in the same direction, and in the construction of new ar dependent lines.

2. Every stockholder in a railway company is entitled to portionate consideration for his investment, and no action majority of the stockholders in any company should be pern to jeopardize the equitable rights of the minority, or to den minority an equitable representation in boards of direction.

3. The privileges of railway companies should be defi limited to the purposes of their organization, as carriers of pa gers and freight, and any interference with private interests enterprise increasing the cost of shipment, transshipment, or age of freight, should be rigidly forbidden.

4. Discriminations among shippers, as to time or cost, shou prohibited and punished.

5. Running connections between connecting roads on eq ble terms, should be enforced.

6. It should be made a penal offense for any officer of a rai corporation to contract, as such officer, directly or indirectly, himself or with any company in which said officer has any d or indirect interest.

7. The business meetings of all corporations, a majorit whose property lies within the state, should be held within state, and the officers of such corporations should be resident the state.

8. Classifications of freight, and rates of fare and freight, wi the state, should be subject to revision and modification by authority.

9. Consolidations and combinations between companies own parallel lines of railway should be forbidden.

10. In the authorization of new lines, preference should be given, other things being equal, to those proposed lines which favor the growth and prosperity of home markets and home commerce.

In the enforcement of the policy indicated in the propositions above stated, many obvious difficulties are attendant upon a direct exercise of state authority, by the application of unyielding rules of law. In many of the states, efforts have been made to avoid statutory complications by the appointment of commissioners, vested with more or less authority to hear and determine complaints, and to restrain or abolish abuses. I am constrained to say, that this experiment has not thus far realized all the beneficial results anticipated. In many cases, however, commissions of this kind have largely contributed to a better understanding between the people and the railways, and have made public a fund of information, without which comprehensive and efficient legislation is compartively impossible. Such a commission in our state, if intelligently constituted, would undoubtedly contribute much toward the ultimate solution of all the questions at issue. No recommendation for the postponement or evasions of direct and immediate legislation, as far as practicable, should be implied from this suggestion. This commission should be designed as the supplement, and not as the substitute, of legislative authority, and its powers should comprehend no power which can be efficiently exercised by the legislature itself. In brief, no responsibility as to the main question involved can be justly or safely avoided, and in submitting the foregoing propositions and suggestions, I most earnestly assure the legislature of the hearty co-operation of the executive department, within the sphere of its constitutional duty, in every measure for the more complete protection of the public from the evils complained of.

In this place, permit me to say that the importance of this topic of transportation is not exaggerated by those who have forced it upon public attention. Wisconsin is essentially an agricultural state. Of the total assessed value of the state at the present time, nearly one-half consists of land, exclusive of city and village lots. But a small fraction of this vast land empire is yet under cultivation, and the portion which has been improved is susceptible of an almost incalculable increase in production and value. thousands of men and women in the larger cities of the (are clamoring for employment and for bread, millions o and fertile acres within our territory still await the pro power of impartial laws and the investment of enlightene I would not depreciate the value of a prosperous comm our growing manufactures, or of our extensive mineral still hidden in the earth and impatiently awaiting develo under the magic influences of industry and capital. No s the union can boast of resources more rich and varied chemist ever compounded with nicer adjustment than Prov has apportioned within our state, the ingredients of soil, c timber, minerals, water-powers—all the opportunities for m ical and manufacturing industry. But all these sources of are directly or remotely related to or dependent upon the opment and prosperity of agriculture. From the soil we i is primarily derived all that constitutes our independence an gress and the happiness of our people. Without these n products of the earth we should have little to boast of i branch of industry. The art of agriculture is the parent arts and its products the foundation of all wealth, but it is th a due proportion of acres to workshops—of brainwork to si of labor to science, that the resources of our state can be fully developed, and the material prosperity of her people surely secured. If agriculture, then, be the bed-rock upon all other industries rest, the farmers of Wisconsin feel that have rights which legislators are bound to respect. State, co and local societies are doing much to encourage this branch dustry, and I recommend that the same legislative aid at which has heretofore been granted to the state and county o zations be still continued.

Not alone because of its intrinsic importance does interest demand your special protection and defense. farming population of our state are far removed fron centers of political power. Their occupation, thus far, been wholly individualized. Unlike great monied int which are organized and cohesive, they are never four the lobbies of our legislature. They employ no attorne infest your presence and to corrupt the fountains of law. They seek no private avenues to the public treasury. They ask no special enactments for the benefit of the few at the expense of the many. They enter into no combinations for the subversion of the principles of mutual justice and equality between man and man. Submissive to the stern decree which compels them to lives of hard but cheerful toil, they trust alone to the fidelity of their sworn representatives. To violate this confidence and permit the workingmen of our state to become the prey of the professional sharper and spoilsman of the lobbies, would be not merely a technical violation of our oath of office, but a surrender of every honorable attribute of our manhood.

COMPLAINTS OF PUBLIC CORRUPTION.

It must be admitted that the popular complaints of public corruption manifest in the country at the present time are not without substantial foundation. These complaints do not originate altogether in specific assaults upon the public treasury, or special and definite violations of the popular rights by the legislative power. They relate to the whole social and political structure. The period of our civil war was succeeded by public debt, and public debt has been accompanied by inordinate expenditures for the support of the government. A secondary result is the effort to place the interest of partisan organizations above the claims of good government, and to protect favored classes at the common expense.

Private life never fails to profit by public example. Greed for office, social extravagance, immorality, contempt for honest labor, corporate extortion and the efforts of the speculative classes to amass and enjoy wealth not honestly earned, are evils which have ensued in their logical order.

I am not unconscious of the difficulties attendant upon the endeavor to resist established currents of thought and reverse rules of action invested with the sanctity of long practice and precedent. We shall not be likely to forget, however, that the responsibility of our state in respect to the issues now absorbing public attention is much enhanced by the fact that our people were among the first to realize the magnitude of those issues, and to demand formal recognition of them by their representatives in power. T influences of your action and example, therefore, are not whol limited to your immediate constituency, but in an important d gree possesses a national aspect. It is for us to determine wheth the purposes of government are superior to the purposes of part whether honesty and intelligence or personal avarice and imp tunity, constitute qualifications for office; whether legislatu shall intelligently reflect the popular will, or become the inst ments of the impertinent, the importunate, the mercenary and t corrupt.

POLITICAL ORGANIZATIONS.

It is true that political organizations are necessary to the trium of right over wrong; but let us also remember that developm and progress are dictated by the law of God; that all parties th are blind to this decree must decay and die; that a political pa sanship which renders the public good subservient to the s cess of party, or which requires electors under any circumstan to elevate vice and ignorance to public station, as a party obli tion, is to be deplored and condemned; that the honors and em uments of office rightfully belong to those who have earned th by lives of personal honesty and intelligent industry, and that greatest reward of political service is the consciousness of havi faithfully discharged a public duty. No political organizat which fails to recognize these principles of action is worthy of eration.

CONCLUSION.

In conclusion, it becomes me to acknowledge to you, th have entered upon the duties of the executive department w much diffidence, and with great distrust in my own ability, with a firm belief that I shall not be denied your generous co sel and hearty co-operation, and that the guidance and blessin an all-wise Providence will attend all our endeavors to prom the public good.

WILLIAM R. TAYLO

MADISON, January 15, 1874.

ANNUAL REPORT

OF THE

SECRETARY OF STATE

OF THE

STATE OF WISCONSIN,

For the Fiscal Year ending September 30, 1873.

OFFICE OF THE SECRETARY OF STATE,
MADISON, October 10, 1873.

To His Excellency, C. C. WASHBURN,
Governor of Wisconsin:

SIR: As required by law, I have the honor to submit a statement of the several funds, revenues and expenditures of the state for the fiscal year ending on the 30th day of September, 1873, together with such abstracts, tables and matters of general interest, as pertain to the office of the Secretary of State.

The balance in the treasury, belonging to the several funds, on the 30th day of September, 1872, was $239,109.11.

The balance in the treasury, belonging to the several funds, on the 30th day of September, 1873, was $215,644.52.

The receipts into and disbursements from the treasury, including balances in the General Fund, Trust Funds and other funds specified, during the past year, were as follows:

RECEIPTS AND DISBURSEMENTS.

RECEIPTS.		
General Fund	$1,095,872 29	
School Fund	103,818 93	
School Fund Income	179,762 87	
University Fund	9,728 12	
University Fund Income	42,716 38	
Agricultural College Fund	13,560 70	
Agricultural College Fund Income	12,558 85	
Normal School Fund	86,687 54	
Normal School Fund Income	71,369 10	
Drainage Fund	93,636 46	
Delinquent Tax Fund	27,047 10	
Commissioners' Contingent Fund	323 75	
River Falls Normal School Building Fund	5,000 00	
St. Croix and Lake Sup'r R. R. Tresp's Fund	18,891 04	
Sturgeon Bay Canal Lands Trespass Fund	12,710 62	
North Wisconsin Railroad Aid Fund	875 00	
	$1,774,558 55	
DISBURSEMENTS.		
General Fund		$1,191,966
School Fund		52,743
School Fund Income		185,136
University Fund		10,100
University Fund Income		42,716
Agricultural College Fund		10,000
Agricultural College Fund Income		12,558
Normal School Fund		52,97
Normal School Fund Income		55,36
Drainage Fund		125,25
Delinquent Tax Fund		27,75
Deposit Fund		66
Commissioners' Contingent Fund		27
Oshkosh Normal School Building Fund		3,84
St. Croix and Lake Sup'r R. R. Tresp's Fund		5,38
Sturgeon Bay Canal Land Trespass Fund		20,40
North Wisconsin Railroad Aid Fund		87
	$1,774,558 55	$1,798,02
Balance, September 30, 1872	239,109 11	
Balance, September 30, 1873		215,64
	$2,013,667 66	$2,013,6

Detailed statements, properly classified, as audited by this partment, will be found in the appendix to this report, ma "A," to which attention is respectfully invited.

The following is a statement of the receipts and disbursements during the last fiscal year of the

GENERAL FUND.

RECEIPTS.			
From counties, state tax	$781,875 60		
From counties, suit tax	3,805 00		
		$785,680 60	
Railroad companies, taxes		210,374 99	
Plankroad companies, taxes		247 68	
Fire ins. Co's, license, taxes, fees	$48,578 54		
Life insurance companies, license	14,721 39		
		63,299 93	
Bonds receivable		410 00	
Miscellaneous		35,859 09	
Total receipts			$1,095,872 29
DISBURSEMENTS.			
1st. *Salaries and Permanent Appropriations.*			
Governor's office		$7,100 00	
Secretary's office		3,200 00	
Treasurer's office		3,400 00	
Attorney General's office		2,600 00	
State Superintendents' office		5,650 00	
Office of Sup't of Public Property		3,200 00	
State Library		1,945 36	
State Historical Society		6,300 00	
Supreme Court		13,769 00	
Circuit Courts		30,433 33	
Wisconsin Supreme Court Reports		26,325 00	
Interest on State indebtedness		157,649 67	
			$261,572 36
2nd. *Legislative Expenses.*			
Senate—Salaries	$11,625 00		
Mileage	852 00		
Employes	10,971 00		
		$23,448 00	
Assembly—Salaries	$35,350 00		
Mileage	2,604 50		
Employes	12,895 00		
		50,849 50	
Contesting seats in Assembly		403 63	
Printing for Legislature		11,603 39	
Legislative Manual		7,301 64	
Postage for Legislature		4,124 20	
Stationery for Legislature		985 00	
Gas		1,589 76	
Visiting Com. on Benevolent Inst.		500 00	
Dells Investigating Committee		177 60	
Soldiers' Orphans' Home Inv. Com.		53 40	
Newspapers		2,694 10	
			$103,730 22

General Fund Disbursements—continued.

3d. State Prison and Charitable Institutions.		
State Prison	$45,550 47	....
Hospital for the Insane, Madison	119,438 15	....
Northern Wisconsin Hospital for the Insane	198,677 21	....
Institute for the Blind	20,875 00	....
Institute for the Deaf and Dumb	23,737 25	....
Industrial School for Boys	65,715 00	....
Soldiers' Orphans' Home	27,253 75	....
		$501,246 8
4th. Miscellaneous.		
Clerk hire—Secretary's office.... $13,599 99	....	....
Treasurer's office.... 7,705 00	....	....
Land office 15,487 00	....	....
	$36,791 99	....
Labor about capitol	3,518 85	....
Engineers and firemen, heating apparatus	2,621 50	....
State carpenters	1,799 75	....
Night watchmen	1,422 25	....
Janitor and messenger services	7,934 00	....
Laborers improving park	1,708 19	....
Contingent expenses	11,631 10	....
Publishing laws of general interest	12,473 40	....
Publishing private and local laws	1,056 40	....
Publishing notices and proclamations	325 10	....
Advertising sales of land	1,352 90	....
Printing	61,403 78	....
Postage	4,006 30	....
Real estate returns	432 96	....
Normal Institutes	2,043 16	....
State Board of Charities and Reform	1,872 20	....
Militia	2,154 57	....
Park fence	27,986 76	....
Park improvement	1,639 65	....
Capitol improvement	26,832 24	....
Presidential electors	296 80	....
County Agricultural Societies	3,600 00	....
Superior harbor protection	4,229 14	....
Immigration Commissioner	5,190 98	....
Land protection	5,981 92	....
Appraising lands	10 00	....
Examiners of state teachers	175 85	....
Geological survey	8,280 00	....
State Board of Equalization	79 00	....
Fish culture	368 80	....
Bounty on wild animals	6,585 00	....
Special appropriations	32,983 12	....
Miscellaneous	46,729 44	....
		825,4
Total receipts	$1,095,872 29	
Total disbursements	....	$1,191,9
Balance, September 30, 1872	29,169 92	....
Overpayment, September 30, 1873	66,923 80	....
	$1,191,966 01	$1,191,

STATEMENT *exhibiting the principal appropriations made for 1873, and balances thereof remaining unexpended.*

	Balances due on Appropriations Sept. 30, 1872.	Appropriations, 1873.	Paid up to Sept. 30, 1873.	Remaining unexpended, Sept. 30, 1873.
State Prison..........	$6,065 47	$45,735 00	$45,550 47	$6,250 00
Hospital for the Insane (Madison)..........	17,550 00	85,822 00	89,885 25	13,486 75
Northern Wis. Hospital for the Insane...	140,927 21	69,000 00	198,677 21	11,250 00
Institute for the Blind.	5,250 00	20,750 00	20,875 00	5,125 00
Institute for Deaf and Dumb	9,487 25	28,500 00	23,737 25	14,250 00
Ind'l School for Boys.	7,300 00	64,500 00	58,550 00	13,250 00
Soldiers' Orph' Home.	15,000 00	22,000 00	27,000 00	10,000 00
	$201,579 93	$336,307 00	$464,275 18	$73,611 75

THE STATE DEBT.

The bonded and irreducible indebtedness of the State on the 30th day of September, 1873, was as follows:

State bonds outstanding..................................	$18,100
Certificates of indebtedness..................................	2,233,900
Currency certificates..................................	57
Total..................................	$2,252,057

The following table shows the amount of the war bonds issued and outstanding, September 30, 1873:

Date of authorizing act.	For what purpose the debt was created.	AMOUNT OF INDEBTEDNESS.		PRINCIPAL.
		Issued.	Outstanding.	When payable.
April 16, 1861	War Loan.........	$200,000	....	Jan. 1, 1867
May 27, 1861	... do	100,000	$100	July 1, 1877
May 27, 1861	....do	100,000	....	July 1, 1878
May 27, 1861	....do	100,000	....	July 1, 1879
May 27, 1861	.. do	100,000	12,000	July 1, 1880
May 27, 1861	....do	100,000	....	July 1, 1881
May 27, 1861	....do	100,000	....	July 1, 1882
May 27, 1861	....do	100,000	....	Jnly 1, 1883
May 27, 1861	....do	100,000	1,000	July 1, 1884
May 27, 1861	... do	100,000	....	July 1, 1885
May 27, 1861	....do	100,000	4,000	July 1, 1886
April 7, 1862	General Fund	50,000	....	Apr. 1, 1867
April 7, 1862	War Loan.........	100,000	....	July 1, 1887
April 7, 1862	....do	100,000	1,000	July 1, 1888
M'ch 28, 1863	General Fund	50,000	....	Apr. 1, 1868
	Total	$1,500,000	$18,100	

It will be seen that there is still outstanding of the war bonds, the sum of $18,100. These bonds bear interest at the rate of six per cent. per annum, payable semi-annually, on the first days of January and July, in each year, in the city of New York.

The commissioners of school and university lands were directed by the legislature to invest the principal of the trust funds, so far as necessary, in the war bonds. For the loans thus made, they were required to issue certificates of indebtedness to the appropriate funds, bearing seven per cent. interest per annum, payable on the 31st day of May, in each year.

The aggregate amount of such loans and of the certificates o[f] indebtedness, issued therefor to each of the trust funds, up to September 30, 1873, will be seen from the following statement:

School Fund	$1,559,70
University Fund	111,00
Agricultural College Fund	50,60
Normal School Fund	512,60
Total	$2,233,90

SCHOOL FUND.

The School Fund is composed of:

1. Proceeds of lands granted by the United States for support of schools.
2. All moneys accruing from forfeiture or escheat and trespass penalties [o]
school land.
3. All fines collected in the several counties for breach of the penal laws.
4. All moneys paid as an exemption from military duty; and
5. Five per cent, on sale of government lands.

RECEIPTS.		
Sales of land	$21,458 14	....
Dues on certificates	38,709 02	....
Loans, payments on mortgages	15,314 84	....
Penalties and forfeitures	145 81	....
Taxes	133 01	....
Fines	822 10	....
United States, 5 per cent on sales of public lands in Wis., for year ending Dec. 31, 1873	27,216 01	....
Transferred from General Fund, to correct error	20 00	....
	$103,818 93	....
DISBURSEMENTS.		
Milwaukee water bonds	....	$40,000
Madison city board of education loan	....	12,500
Refunded for overpayment	....	248
	$103,818 93	$52,748
Balance, September 30, 1872	5,265 65	....
Balance, September 30, 1873	....	56,341
	$109,084 58	$109,08[4]

The amount of the productive School Fund on the 30th day of September, 1872 and 1873, respectively, was as follows:

	1872.	1873.
Amount due on certificates of sales...........	$515,606 52	$506,031 20
Amount due on loans........................	264,464 76	261,449 92
Certificates of indebtedness..................	1,559,700 00	1,559,700 00
United States bonds.........................	43,000 00	43,000 00
Milwaukee water bonds....................	100,000 00	140,000 00
	$2,482,771 28	$2,510,181 12

Showing an increase in the productive fund of $27,408.84 during the past year.

SCHOOL FUND INCOME.

RECEIPTS.		
Interest on principal due on lands..............	$55,646 24	....
Interest on certificates of indebtedness..........	109,179 00	....
Interest, as per chapter 79, general laws of 1866..	7,088 36	....
Interest on United States bonds..............	2,925 07	....
Interest on Milwaukee water bonds.............	3,500 00	....
Commissi'n on purchase of Milwaukee water bonds	800 00	....
Sale of Webster's Dictionaries..................	624 00	....
	$179,762 67	....
DISBURSEMENTS.		
Apportionment by State Superintendent.........	....	$181,268 79
G. & C. Merriam, Webster's Dictionaries........	....	3,200 00
Refunded for overpayment.....................	....	668 19
	$179,762 67	$185,136 98
Balance, September 30, 1872....................	19,663 63	....
Balance, September 30, 1873....................	....	14,289 32
	$199,426 30	$199,426 30

UNIVERSITY FUND.

This fund consists of the proceeds of the sales of land granted by congress for the support of a State University.

RECEIPTS.		
Sales of lands	$3,972 56	....
Dues on certificates	4,271 00	....
Loans	1,460 50	....
Taxes	8 27	....
Penalties	15 79	....
	$9,728 12	....
DISBURSEMENTS.		
Milwaukee water Bonds	....	$10,000
Refunded for overpayment	....	100
	$9,728 12	$10,100
Balance, September, 30, 1872	2,837 82	....
Balance, September, 30, 1873	....	2,465
	$12,565 94	$12,565

The amount of productive University Fund on the 30th day September, 1872 and 1873, respectively, was as follows:

	1872.	*1873.*
Amount due on certificates of sales	$63,484 38	$64,48
Amount due on mortgages	13,499 50	12,03
Certificates of indebtedness	111,000 00	111,00
Dane county bonds	19,000 00	19,00
Milwaukee water bonds	....	10,00
	$206,983 88	$216,51

Showing an increase in the productive fund during the past of $9,535 50.

UNIVERSITY FUND INCOME.

RECEIPTS.		
Interest on principal due on lands	$5,443 82	....
Interest on certificates of indebtedness	7,770 00	....
Interest on Dane county bonds	1,330 00	....
General Fund app'n, chap. 82, G. L., 1867	7,303 76	....
General Fund app'n, chap. 100, G. L., 1872	10,000 00	....
Tuition fees of students	9,825 00	....
Rent, interest, farm products and sale of lots	1,093 30	....
Commission on purchase of Mil. water bonds	200 00	....
Laboratory bills	250 00	....
	$42,716 88	....
DISBURSEMENTS.		
Paid treasurer of State University	....	$42,113 85
Refunded for overpayments	....	602 53
	$42,716 88	$42,716 88

AGRICULTURAL COLLEGE FUND.

This fund consists of the proceeds of the sales of 240,000 acres of lands granted by Congress to the State for the support of an institution of learning, where shall be taught the principles of agriculture and the arts. The interest on the productive fund forms the income.

RECEIPTS.		
Sales of land	$7,254 93	....
Dues on certificates	4,614 80	....
Loans	1,677 67	....
Penalties	13 30	....
	$13,560 70	....
DISBURSEMENTS.		
Milwaukee water bonds purchased	....	$10,000 00
Balance, Sept. 30, 1872	2,483 44	....
Balance, Sept. 30, 1873	....	6,044 14
	$16,044 14	$16,044 14

The amount of productive fund, September 30, 1872 and 1873, respectively, was as follows:

	1872.	*1873.*
Dues on certificates of sales	$133,894 20	$144,823 40
Dues on loans	11,564 00	9,886 33
Certificates of indebtedness	50,600 00	50,600 00
Dane county bonds	6,000 00	6,000 00
United States bonds	4,000 00	4,000 00
Milwaukee water bonds	....	10,000 00
	$206,058 20	$225,309 73

Showing an increase in this fund during the year of $19,251.53.

AGRICULTURAL COLLEGE FUND INCOME.

RECEIPTS.		
Interest on principal due on lands	$7,868 08	....
Interest on certificates of indebtedness	3,798 67	....
Interest on Dane county bonds	420 00	....
Interest on United States bonds	272 10	....
Com. on purchase of Milwaukee water bonds	200 00	....
	$12,558 85	....
DISBURSEMENTS.		
Paid Treasurer of State University	....	$12,524 32
Refunded for overpayment	....	34 53
	$12,558 85	$12,558 85

NORMAL SCHOOL FUND.

This fund is composed of the proceeds of the sale of lands set apart for the support of Normal Schools, by chapter 537, laws of 1865.

RECEIPTS.		
Sales	$68,947 95	....
Dues	6,109 00	....
Loans	11,551 00	....
Penalties	79 59	....
	$86,687 54	....
DISBURSEMENTS.		
Milwaukee water bonds, purchased	....	$40,000 00
Madison City Board of Education, loan	....	12,500 00
Refunded for overpayment	....	478 26
	$86,687 54	$52,978 26
Balance, September 30, 1872	7,669 86	....
Balance, September 30, 1873	....	41,884 14
	$94,357 40	$94,357 40

The amount of productive funds on the 30th day of September, 1872 and 1873, respectively, was as follows:

	1872.	1873.
Amount due on certificates of sales	$58,055 74	$55,731 43
Amount due on mortgages	146,716 05	147,812 05
Certificates of indebtedness	512,600 00	512,600 00
United States bonds	43,000 00	43,000 00
Milwaukee city water bonds	100,000 00	140,000 00
Town bonds	20,000 00	20,000 00
	$880,371 79	$918,643 48

Showing an increase in the productive fund of $38,271.69 during the past year.

The total productive accumulations of all the trust funds of the state, on the 30th day of September, 1873, were $3,870,653.71, showing an increase during the last fiscal year of $94,468.56.

The amount belonging to each fund, on the same day, was as follows:

School Fund	$2,510,181 12
University Fund	216,519 88
Agricultural College Fund	225,309 73
Normal School Fund	918,648 48
Total	$3,870,658 71

NORMAL SCHOOL FUND INCOME.

RECEIPTS.		
Interest on principal due on lands	$14,160 26	....
Interest on certificates of indebtedness	35,882 00	....
Tuition fees, Platteville Normal School	3,225 88	....
Tuition fees, Whitewater Normal School	2,237 36	....
Tuition fees, Oshkosh Normal School	2,832 55	....
Interest on United States bonds	2,925 08	....
Interest on Milwaukee water bonds	3,500 00	....
Commission on purchase of Mil. water bonds	800 00	....
Interest on Troy town bonds	140 00	....
Interest on Fall River town bonds	350 00	....
Interest on Kinnickinnic town bonds	105 00	....
Interest on Clifton town bonds	105 00	....
Transf'd from General Fund, for normal institutes	2,000 00	....
Transf'd from Oshkosh Normal Sch'l Build'g F'd	3,105 97	....
	$71,369 10	....
DISBURSEMENTS.		
Expense of regents	....	$453 00
Platteville Normal School	....	14,982 19
Whitewater Normal School	....	16,538 22
Oshkosh Normal School	....	17,363 13
Institutes	....	2,538 64
Expenses	....	3,360 20
Refunded for overpayment	....	133 24
	$71,369 10	$55,368 62
Balance, Sept. 30, 1872	38,668 87	....
Balance, Sept. 30, 1873	....	54,669 35
	$110,037 97	$110,037 97

DRAINAGE FUND.

This fund consists of the proceeds of the sale of lands set apart as drainage lands, by virtue of chapter 537, laws of 1865, the amount of which is to be annually apportioned to the several counties in which such lands lie, in proportion to the amount of sales in each county, respectively.

RECEIPTS.		
Interest	$1,378 06	....
Sales	89,751 87	....
Dues	2,472 00	....
Penalties	37 03	....
Taxes	2 50	....
	$93,636 46	....
DISBURSEMENTS.		
Apportionment to counties	....	$124,343 91
Refunded for overpayments	....	911 48
	$93,636 46	$125,255 39
Balance, September 30, 1872	55,041 12	....
Balance, September 30, 1873	....	23,422 19
	$148,677 58	$148,677 58

DELINQUENT TAX FUND.

RECEIPTS.		
Taxes collected on state lands	$27,047 09	....
DISBURSEMENTS.		
Paid counties, for taxes collected	....	$27,621 69
Refunded for overpayments	....	132 06
	$27,047 10	$27,753 75
Balance, September 30, 1872	5,793 56	....
Balance, September 30, 1873	....	5,086 91
	$32,840 66	$32,840 66

DEPOSIT ACCOUNT.

On the sale of land forfeited to the state, and the payment of the amount due the state, and all costs and penalties accrued, if any balance remain, the amount of such balance is deposited in the state treasury to the credit of the person entitled thereto, and is denominated the Deposit Account.

DISBURSEMENTS.		
C. B. McArthur	$145 96	....
D. R. Bailey	522 87	....
		$668 8
Balance, September 30, 1872	$7,467 09	....
Balanee, September 30, 1873	....	6,798 2
	$7,476 09	$7,467 0

COMMISSIONERS' CONTINGENT FUND.

RECEIPTS.		
Fees	$323 75	....
DISBURSEMENTS.		
S. S. Barlow, Att'y Gen., expenses to Washington	....	$200
T. W. Gibbs, expenses	....	34
Seifert & Gugler, maps and town plats	....	42
	$323 75	$276
Balance, September 30, 1872	1,311 86	....
Balance, September 30, 1873	....	1,359
	$1,635 61	$1,635

OSHKOSH NORMAL SCHOOL BUILDING FUND.

DISBURSEMENTS.		
Bell & Rogers, building material	....	$739
Transferred to Normal School Fund Income	....	3,105
Balance, September 30, 1872	$3,845 16	....
	$3,845 16	$3,845

RIVER FALLS NORMAL SCHOOL BUILDING FUND.

RECEIPTS.		
Pierce county donation	$5,000 00	....
Balance, September 30, 1872	20,000 00	....
Balance, September 30, 1873	....	$25,000 00
	$25,000 00	$25,000 00

ST. CROIX AND LAKE SUPERIOR R. R. TRESPASS FUND.

RECEIPTS.		
Samuel Harriman, State Agent, trespass on lands	$18,891 04	....
DISBURSEMENTS.		
Samuel Boulter, examining lands and scaling logs	....	$528 02
S. B. Dresser, protecting railroad lands	....	1,112 50
Flint & Weber, advertising	....	9 50
Charles W. Folsom, advertising	....	6 50
Sam'l Harriman, State Agent, salary	....	2,000 00
Charles E. Wilson, advertising	....	5 00
H. A. Taylor & Co., advertising	....	24 00
J. L. Tyler, examining trespasses on railroad lands	....	176 75
A. C. Van Meter, advertising	....	21 90
E. E. Blanding, surveying and scaling	....	108 00
C. H. Pratt, labor	....	157 25
A. B. Eastman, advertising	....	15 40
O. F. Jones, advertising	....	4 00
John H. Knight, maps of R. R. lands	....	57 00
H. A. Taylor & Co., printing	....	25 70
H. Woodruff, advertising	....	9 00
M. Fields, maps	....	4 00
Chas S. Mayo & Co., letter press for land agent	....	13 40
Richard Peters, labor	....	77 62
Alfred Pierce, looking after trespassers	....	317 95
Richard Relf, plats	....	6 00
J. R. Smith, examining timber	....	36 00
E. W. Anderson, advertising	....	4 95
James Edwards, protecting lands	....	25 00
Baker & Wilson, legal services	....	500 00
S. S. & H. O. Fifield, advertising	....	12 00
Peter McRorie, labor	....	16 00
Wm. Young, labor	....	100 00
Seward & Taylor, advertising	....	7 60
	$18,891 04	$5,381 04
Balance, September 30, 1872	30,354 46	....
Balance, September 30, 1873	....	43,864 46
	$49,245 50	$49,245 50

STURGEON BAY CANAL LAND TRESPASS FUND.

RECEIPTS.		
Treasurer Sturgeon Bay and Lake Michigan Ship Canal and Harbor Company—trespass on lands.	$12,710 62	....
DISBURSEMENTS.		
Treasurer Sturgeon Bay and Lake Michigan Ship Canal and Harbor Company....................	....	$20,408 99
Balance, September 30, 1872........	7,698 37	....
	$20,408 99	$20,408 99

NORTH WISCONSIN RAILROAD AID FUND.

RECEIPTS.		
Town of Stanton, interest to Jan. 1, 1873..........	$437 50	....
Town of Star Prairie, interest to Jan. 1, 1873......	437 50	....
	$875 00	....
DISBURSEMENTS.		
First National Bank, Hudson	....	$875 00

ALLOTMENT FUND.

Balance, September 30, 1872.....................	$1,843 30	....
Balance, September 30, 1873.....................	....	$1,843 30

CLERK HIRE.

STATEMENT, *showing the names of the clerks employed in the office of the Secretary of State for the year ending September 30, 1873, with the amount paid each, and the particular service rendered by each.*

CLERKS IN OFFICE OF SECRETARY OF STATE.

Levi Alden, printing clerk	$1,800 00
James Bennett, proof reader	1,083 33
David O. Bebb, insurance clerk	1,650 00
Wm. N. Coles, recording marriages	866 66
C. C. Dow, book-keeper, trust funds	1,500 00
John T. Jones, recording marriages	1,625 00
Charles F. Legate, platting	1,100 00
Robert Monteith, recording clerk	1,500 00
D. H. Tullis, book-keeper	1,800 00
Wm. H. Williams, insurance clerk, part of year	675 00
Total	$13,599 99

STATE OF WISCONSIN —*Dane County*—ss.

Ll. Breese, being duly sworn, says that the foregoing list contains the names of all the clerks employed in the office of the Secretary of State during the year ending September 30, 1873, as he verily believes; that the amount was actually paid to each clerk as stated, and that the same was necessarily expended to enable him to properly discharge the duties of the office of Secretary of State.

LL. BREESE,
Secretary of State.

Sworn to and subscribed before me, this 10th day of October, 1873.

JOHN S. DEAN,
Notary Public, Dane county, Wis.

STATE TAX.

The following is a statement showing the amount of the state tax for the year 1873, as provided by law; and giving the estimates for deficiencies, as authorized by chapter 153, General Laws of 1869:

1. State tax, as provided by chapter 225, Laws of 1873	$221,110 00
2. Interest on certificates of indebtedness and state bonds	157,459 00
3. Interest on School Fund, per chapter 79, General Laws, 1866.	7,088 36
4. Annual appropriation to the State University, per chapter 82, General Laws of 1867	7,303 76
5. Annual appropriation to the State University, per chapter 100, Laws of 1872	10,000 00
6. Estimated deficiency for last quarter of 1873, per chapter 153, General Laws of 1869	168,621 26
Total state tax	$571,582 38

The deficiency above stated was estimated as follows:

1. Deficiency in the General Fund, Sept. 30, 1873	$66,923 80
2. Salaries of state officers and judges for the last quarter of 1873.	18,000 00
3. Appropriations to penal and benevolent institutions remaining unexpended, Sept. 30, 1873	73,611 75
4. Other appropriations remaining unexpended, Sept. 30, 1873	14,689 32
5. Clerk hire, labor, printing, gas, postage and incidental expenses for last quarter of 1873	38,079 77
	$211,304 64
Less balance, tax paid by C. & N. W. R. R. Co., Oct. 7, 1873	42,683 38
Total deficiency	$168,621 26

The deficiency for the year 1873 was owing to large special appropriations made by the last legislature, in excess of the revenues provided to meet them.

It will be seen that the aggregate amount of the state tax for the present year is $671,582.38; the rate per centum upon the state assessment being 1 72–100 mills upon the dollar. To this was added, for the purposes stated, the following amounts:

Due from counties to the Industrial School for Boys	$8,188 50
Due from counties to the Hospitals for Insane..................	34,381 67
Due on State Tax of 1872 from Iowa county.....................	22,407 76
Loans to school districts over due..............................	36,550 25

A detailed statement showing the amount of each of these items charged to the appropriate county, will be seen by reference to appendix marked "B."

The following comparative table shows the valuation of real and personal property, as determined by the State Board of Assessment, the amount of the state tax levied and the rate per centum thereof upon such valuation, for the last five years:

For.	Valuation.	State Tax.	Rate per cent.
1869..................	$242,641,124	$515,961 13	$2\frac{1}{8}$ mills.
1870	455,900,800	720,323 24	$1\frac{58}{100}$ mills.
1871..................	455,900,800	629,143 10	$1\frac{38}{100}$ mills.
1872..................	390,454,875	765,291 55	$1\frac{96}{100}$ mills.
1873..................	390,454,875	671,582 38	$1\frac{72}{100}$ mills

ESTIMATES OF REVENUES AND EXPENDITURES,

For the year commencing January 1, 1875.

The Secretary of State is required by law to submit with his annual report a detailed estimate of the expenditures to be defrayed from the treasury for the ensuing year.

The expenditures for the year 1874 were estimated by the legislature of 1873, and the necessary amount of tax was levied to meet them. This tax has been apportioned among the several counties, and will be received into the treasury during the months of January and February, 1874.

The following estimates, therefore, are submitted, as being necessary to meet the expenditures of the State government, for the year commencing January 1, 1875, and the revenues should be provided by the next legislature:

EXPENDITURES.		
1. *Salaries and Permanent Appropriations.*		
Governor's office	$6,600 00	
Lieutenant Governor	1,000 00	
Secretary of State's office	3,200 00	
State Treasurer's office	3,400 00	
Attorney General's office	2,600 00	
State Superintendent's office	5,700 00	
Superintendent of Public Property's office	2,000 00	
State Library and Librarian	2,100 00	
Supreme Court salaries	18,000 00	
Circuit Court salaries	32,000 00	
Supreme Court Reporter	1,000 00	
State Historical Society	6,300 00	
Supreme Court Reports	12,000 00	
State University	10,000 00	
Immigration Commissioner's office	5,000 00	
		$105,900 00
2. *Legislative Expenses.*		
Salaries of members	$46,975 00	
Mileage of members	3,450 00	
Officers and employes	24,000 00	
Printing and other incidentals	39,000 00	
		113,425 00
3. *Interest.*		
Interest on the State debt	$157,459 00	
Interest on School Fund	7,088 36	
Interest on University Fund	7,303 76	
		171,851 12
4. *State Prison and Charitable Institutions.*		
State Prison	$15,000 00	
Wisconsin State Hospital for the Insane	60,000 00	
Northern Hospital for the Insane	60,000 00	
Institute for the Blind	20,000 00	
Institute for the Deaf and Dumb	35,000 00	
Industrial School for Boys	37,000 00	
Soldiers' Orphans' Home	18,000 00	
Supporting orphans in Normal Schools	2,400 00	
		247,400 00
5. *Clerks and Employes.*		
Secretary of State's office	$13,600 00	
Treasurer's office	7,700 00	
Land office	15,000 00	
Supreme court	700 00	
Janitors and messengers	8,000 00	
Laborers, engineers and firemen	9,000 00	
Clerks protecting state lands	6,000 00	
Geological Survey	13,000 00	
		$73,000 00

Estimates of Revenues and Expenditures—continued.

Expenditures—continued.		
6. *Miscellaneous.*		
Printing under contract	$45,000 00	
Advertising and publishing laws	15,000 00	
Stationery	10,000 00	
County Agricultural societies	4,000 00	
Gas and fuel	10,000 00	
Postage	4,000 00	
Bounties on wild animals	7,000 00	
Contingent expenses and appropriations	50,000 00	
		145,000 00
Total		$856,576 12
REVENUES.		
Railroad companies, licenses	260,000 00	
Insurance companies, taxes and licenses	65,000 00	
Telegraph and plankroads	3,800 00	
Hawkers' and peddlers' licenses	7,000 00	
Tax on suits	3,800 00	
Miscellaneous	20,000 00	
Total	$359,600 00	
Tax authorized by existing laws:		
Interest on the state debt $157,459 00		
Interest on School Fund 7,088 36		
Interest on University Fund 7,303 76		
Annual appropriation to State University 10,000 00		
	$181,851 12	541,451 12
To be provided for by the next legislature		$315,125 00

In the foregoing statement, the ordinary expenses of the State government, and of the penal and charitable institutions of the State, for the year 1875, only, have been estimated.

The revenues and expenditures estimated for the year 1874, may be found on pages 326–328, Senate Journal of 1873. If the legislature of 1874 should exceed those estimates of expenditures, in making appropriations, a corresponding deficiency in the general fund will be the result. Should the erection of a south wing to the Northern Hospital for the Insane, or any other improvement, during 1874, not provided for in the estimates in the journal referred to, be determined upon, the general fund will be overdrawn at the end of the year. Unless this is done, it is confidently believed that the tax, which has already been apportioned among the counties, and the other estimated revenues from railroad companies and from other sources, will be ample to meet all demands upon the treasury dur- the year 1874.

To meet the expenditures herewith submitted, for the year 1875, it will be necessary for the legislature, at its next session, to authorize the levy of a state tax.

It is expected that the revenues which will be received from the sources indicated in the foregoing statement will, if the rate of taxes upon corporations are not reduced, exceed the estimates made. Apart from the direct tax levied uniformly upon the state assessment, the principal items of revenue are derived from railroad and insurance companies. The estimated receipts from insurance companies is but $1,700, and from railroad companies but $6,942, more than the amounts actually received from them during the present year. With the present rapid growth and development of the state, it is but reasonable to presume that the business of these corporations will also increase, so that the amount which will be realized from them will largely exceed the estimates.

The estimates for expenditures are regarded ample for the purposes named. The items enumerated under divisions 1, 2 and 3 of expenditures, are mostly permanent and specific appropriations authorized by statutes, amounting in the aggregate to $391,176.12. So long as these laws remain unchanged, there can be no question as to the amount required for those purposes.

In class 4 of expenditures, under the heading, "State Prison and Charitable Institutions," some regard was had to future probabilities. The amount recommended for the support of the Prison is considerably reduced from the amount of appropriations heretofore made. This was done for the reason that the greater facilities for manufacturing, secured by the rebuilding of the shops, will enable it to increase the business so that larger profits in the aggregate may be expected, and the Prison become more nearly self-sustaining.

In addition to $60,000 each, estimated for the two Hospitals for the Insane, an amount of about $25,000 for each, it is expected, will be received from counties on account of inmates therefrom supported and treated in such Hospitals; making a total to be received by each of these institutions, of $85,000, which is undoubtedly a liberal estimate for current expenses. But if additional building or other permanent improvements be ordered, additional revenue must be provided.

The items classed under divisions 5 and 6 of expenditures have been estimated upon the basis of past experience, and are believed to be sufficient for the purposes named, the sum of $50,000 having been added for contingent expenses and appropriations.

These estimates have been prepared with special care, and it is confidently expected that the amount of $315,125, in addition to the revenues to be received from other sources, will meet all demands upon the general fund for the year 1875.

ASSESSMENT OF PROPERTY FOR TAXATION.

Appendix "C" herewith submitted, gives a tabulated abstract of the assessment of real and personal property by the city and town assessors, as returned to this office by the clerks of the several counties, for the year 1873.

Reports have beeen received from all of the counties except from Barron and Crawford.

By adding the valuation of property as assessed in Barron county, in 1871, which is the last received, amounting to $316,015; and that of Crawford county for 1872, amounting to $2,358,435, to the valuation of the present year, it will make an aggregate for the whole state of $343,294,702, which is an increase over the previous year of $5,296,848.

The average assessed valuation of live stock and farming lands, as will be seen by the table in question, was as follows: horses, $45.51; neat cattle, $11.61; mules and asses, $48.87; sheep and lambs, $1.64; swine, $2.13; farming lands, $8.14.

The average valuation of live stock was 53 cents per head, or 5.41 per cent., and of farming lands, 11 cents per acre, or 1.33 per cent. less than for the previous year.

The average price for which real estate was sold during the year ending September 1, 1873, as shown by the returns made to this office by registers of deeds, was $11.18 per acre; the average assessed valuation of the same lands, for 1872, was $6.06 per acre, or only 54.20 per cent. of the consideration in the deeds.

The reports of town, city and village assessments still show that nearly every class of taxable property is assessed largely below its actual cash value. This is illegal and wrong. The law requires every assessor to value all taxable property at its "full value which could ordinarily be obtained for the same at private sale, and which the owner, if he desired to sell, would accept in full payment thereof." The assessor takes a solemn oath to perform this duty faithfully, yet it is shown by the reports that real estate has been sold during the year for 5.12 per acre more than the assessed valuation. The same difference will undoubtedly be found to exist with respect to other classes of property. The tendency to this error may be partly, if not wholly, accounted for by the mistaken notion that if the aggregate city or town assessment be made small, the amount of state and county taxes to be apportioned to such city or town will be correspondingly small.

The remarks made upon this subject in the report of this department for 1871, are herein repeated:

"Nor is it right to suppose that the amount of state and county taxes apportioned to any city or town is determined by the valuation made by the city or town assessor. The state and county taxes are apportioned upon the basis of the state and county assessments respectively. The State Board of Assessment is not only a board of equalization, as formerly, but the theory of the present law is, that the State Board shall make their assessment irrespective of the city or town valuations, basing their action upon such statistics of population and other statistical information as shall be prepared for them by the Secretary of State. The city and town assessments are valuable for the purposes of state and county assessments principally, as furnishing the *number* of articles of each class of assessable property, and not so much for their valuation. If the state and county boards were furnished the correct *number* of taxable articles, the work of these boards would be comparatively easy. Should it be found by the state board that the state average, according to the city or town assessment, is too low, they would raise it to what they thought would be the true cash value; and every county, city and town would be assessed precisely the same, whether their local valuations were made at one-fifth of the state average, or otherwise. County assessments also are made according to the same rules. Thus it will be seen that the local valuations have nothing to do in determining the amount of state and county taxes apportioned to the several cities and towns. This being so, it must be admitted that there is nothing for a city or town to gain by under-valuing property, while such a practice is a gross violation of law, and works great injustice by reducing the aggregate assessed valuation of property, and correspondingly increasing the percentage of taxation. It has also the effect of keeping out and driving away capital from the state, thereby crippling its industries and retarding its growth."

TABLE *showing the comparative number, value and average value of property in the years* 1872 *and* 1873; *also the increase or decrease of each class.*

ARTICLES.	NUMBER.		Increase in 1873.	VALUE.		AVERAGE VALUE		Increase in 1873.
	1872.	1873.		1872.	1873.	1872.	1873.	
Horses	286,860	285,672	*1,188	$18,308,814	$18,001,691	46.39	$45.51	*$307,123
Cattle	803,042	831,957	28,915	10,036,126	9,661,082	12.50	11.61	*375,044
Mules and asses	5,671	5,977	306	291,935	292,111	51.48	48.87	176
Sheep and lambs	1,049,041	1,130,722	81,681	2,038,565	1,858,105	1.94	1.64	*180,460
Swine	613,240	555,133	*58,107	1,287,994	1,179,859	2.10	2.18	*108,135
Wagons, carriages, etc	163,210	168,368	5,158	3,878,525	3,909,994			31,469
Shares of bank stock		43,519		3,483,904	3,433,559			*50,345
Watches	19,022	18,635	*387	422,866	415,917			*6,949
Pianos and melodeons	9,738	10,992	1,254	972,665	1,039,805			67,140
Merchants' and manufacturers' stock				21,808,680	21,666,817			*141,863
Other personal property				23,671,754	24,155,003			483,249
Total value of personal property				$81,201,828	$80,613,943			*$587,885
Lands	21,041,544	21,348,760	307,216	173,516,806	173,722,348	8.25	8.14	205,542
City and village lots				83,279,220	86,283,961			3,004,741
Total				$337,997,854	$340,620,252			$2,622,398

*Decrease.

RAILROADS.

Ten railroad companies have been incorporated under the general laws of this State during the year ending September 30, 1873. A list of the same may be found in appendix marked "R."

An abstract of the business of the several railroads operated in the State, for the year ending December 31, 1872, will be found in appendix "D."

By reference to the following comparative table, it will be seen that three hundred and twenty-five miles of new roads were constructed during the calendar year 1872, being seventy-seven miles more than the number built the preceding year.

A brief summary, compiled from the reports filed by the companies for the year 1872, makes the following exhibit:

Length of roads operated in Wisconsin, miles	1,810
Capital stock paid up	$63,520,241 82
Total cost of roads and equipments	104,373,614 86
Dividends paid	2,233,254 77
Receipts—	
From passengers	$5,295,623 75
From mails	319,795 80
From express	370,687 31
From freights	12,486,675 01
From other sources	286,117 83
Total	$18,758,899 70
Gross earnings in Wisconsin	$8,595,518 36
Expenditures	18,317,972 45
Losses from casualties	11,798 94
Indebtedness	54,676,067 67
Freights, in tons	4,565,640
Number of cattle and horses transported	217,161
Number of hogs and sheep transported	597,587
Number of passengers transported	3,582,109
Number of persons killed	35
Number of persons injured	101

The following comparative table was arranged from the reports for the years 1871 and 1872:

	1871.	*1872.*	Increase.
Length of roads in Wisconsin in miles............	1,485	1,810	325
Receipts	$16,998,073 30	$18,758,899 70	$1,760,826 40
Earnings in Wisconsin....	7,623,904 60	8.595,518 36	971,613 76
Expenditures	20,449,170 44	18,317,972 45	*2,131,197 99
Freight in tons...........	3,597 191	4.565,640	968,449
Number of cattle and horses transported	130,131	217,161	87,030
Number of hogs and sheep transported	575,927	597,537	21,610
Number of passengers transported................	3,200,904	3,582,109	381,205
Number of persons killed .	23	35	12
Number of persons injured	29	101	72

*Decrease.

STATISTICS OF TAXES.

Section 1 of chapter 150 of the general laws of 1872, makes it the duty of every town, city and village clerk, in each year, at the time he is required by law to deliver the tax roll to the treasurer of his town, city or village, as the case may be, to make out and transmit to the county clerk of his county, a statement showing the amount of taxes levied therein, specifying each object for which the same was authorized, including the amount levied for highway and street purposes.

Section 2 of the same act requires the clerk of each county to record such statement in a book having suitable headings, and to transmit an abstract thereof to the Secretary of State, on or before the third Monday of January, in each year.

Section 3 provides that the Secretary of State shall make a condensed statement of said reports by counties, and include the same in his annual report.

Partial returns have been received from all the counties, except from Clark and Crawford. The reports from nine of the counties were found to be very incomplete; the remaining forty-seven appear to be full and approximately accurate.

The following statement shows the purposes for which the taxes were levied, and the aggregate amount of each kind of tax, for the year 1872, the aggregate local valuation being $331,747,446, as appears from such returns:

Purposes for which tax was levied.	Amount of tax.	Per cent. of tax.
State tax	$781,774 00	.2356
County tax	1,777,051 00	.5357
County school tax	257,875 00	.0777
Town taxes	2,447,067 00	.7376
School district taxes	1,263,605 00	.3809
Road district taxes	867,759 00	.2616
Totals	$7,395,131 00	2.2291

It will be seen by the foregoing statement, that the aggregate amount of taxes reported as having been levied for all purposes, for the year 1872, except specific taxes upon corporations, was $7,395,131 which is 2 cents and $2\frac{3}{10}$ mills on the dollar of the reported local valuation. While the complete returns would considerably augment this amount, yet, it is believed, that the ratio of aggregate valuation to taxes, or the per cent. would not be materially changed, as the increase would affect both the valuation and taxes in about the same proportion.

The purposes for which the county taxes were levied were as follows:

For the support of the poor	$142,619
For county buildings	74,233
For railroad aid	543,631
For roads and bridges	71,472
For salaries of county officers	205,308
For court expenses	110,624
For jail expenses, including sheriffs' accounts	86,566
For all other county expenses	906,760
Total	$2,141,213

This statement is taken from table No. 2, in appendix "E," and was made out from the records of the county clerks, and shows the amount to be $364,162, larger than the amount given in table No. 1 of the same appendix, which was based upon the reports of the town and city clerks. The amount given by the county clerks is supposed to be complete, so far as those counties reporting are concerned, while the other, in table No. 1, is but partial. The classification above made is also far from being accurate, as will appear by reference to said table No. 2, many of the county clerks having grouped all county expenses into one item.

By reference to table No. 1 in the appendix named, it will be seen that the town tax was levied for the following town purposes:

For current or ordinary expenses	$767,079
For school purposes	344,718
For the support of the poor	57,069
For other purposes	1,278,201
Total	$2,447,067

TAXATION OF RAILROAD PROPERTY.

To secure a correct comparative valuation of every class of taxable property, is one of the most difficult as well as important subjects connected with the administration of state affairs. The theory of the present law relating to this matter is, that all property, with certain exceptions, should be assessed at the value that could ordinarily be obtained therefor at private sale. The constitution provides, that the rule of taxation shall be uniform. The meaning of this language must be, that the *valuation* of taxable property, as well as the rate of taxes to be levied thereon, should be determined by the same test or standard; and that all property of every description, in any way subject to taxation, should be valued and taxed according to the same rule. Without observing this uniformity, it is nearly, if not quite, impossible to secure equality and fairness in the distribution of the burdens of taxation.

Instead of applying this uniform rule to the taxation of railroad property, lying within this state, the legislature has imposed a specific tax of three per cent. upon the gross earnings.

The aggregate amount of the gross earnings, reported by all of the companies, operating lines within this state, for the year ending December 31, 1872, was $8,595,518.36; yielding in revenue to the state, at 3 per cent., the amount of $257,865.55.

The question is, whether this amount is the same percentage of the actual or full value of this class of property, that other taxes are of other classes of property upon which they are levied. If less, it is not enough, if more, it is too much.

Three methods suggest themselves by which the correct valuation of railroad property for the purposes of taxation may be determined:

1. By taking the actual cost of the roads and equipments.

2. By adding to the total indebtedness of the roads, the aggregate market or quoted value of their stocks.

3. By taking an amount, the interest of which, at 7 per cent., or any other assumed rate, would produce a sum equal to the net earnings.

The cost of the roads and their equipments, lying wholly, and the proportionate cost of those lying partially, within the State, reporting to this department, is stated at $61,459,374.81, or $35,566.36 per mile, which is $19,550 per mile less than the average cost of roads and equipments in the United States. It is admitted that this cost may be either more or less than the actual value according to the peculiar circumstances of each road. If a road be economically built, prudently managed and located so as to command sufficient business to make it a profitable investment, it would be worth its cost or even more, but if the reverse be true, depreciation would be the result.

Assuming that the roads in Wisconsin are worth what they cost, and by taking 2.23 per cent., which is the rate found levied upon other property, as the correct tax ratio, it will appear that railroad property, at the same rate, should pay $1,370,544.06, which is over five times the amount now received by the State from this source.

Or, if only one-half of the cost be taken as the correct valuation, the State would even then realize, at the rate named, the sum of $685,272.03, which is $427,406.48 more than what is now realized, and is equal to 7.97 per cent. of the gross earnings.

By the second process mentioned, the valuation may be determined by adding to the proportion for this State of the total indebtedness of the companies, the same proportion of the aggregate market value of their stocks.

This indebtedness for Wisconsin is computed at $36,610,352.80; the proportion of the reported capital paid up for the State being $35,574,792.08. Assuming that this stock is worth but 40 per cent. of this amount, which is doubtless far below the average market quotations, the full value would then be $14,229,916.83, which if added to the indebtedness, would aggregate $50,840,269.63.

By levying upon this valuation the percentage (2.23) paid by other property, the result would give a tax of $1,133,738, which is equal to over 13 per cent. of the gross earnings.

Again, let it be supposed that the true value of the roads does not exceed the amount of their indebtedness,—that they are encumbered for all they are worth,—still it is found that they would, at the above rate, be required to pay a tax of $816,410.87, which would be equal to over 9 per cent. of the gross earnings. It certainly seems reasonable to suppose that the value of the roads must be equal, at least, to the amount loaned upon them, otherwise, they could not pay operating expenses and interest, which would result in a change of ownership and management.

The other way proposed by which the correct valuation may be determined is: Having the net earnings, to assume a rate of interest which would be a fair net income, and find the principal.

The total net earnings in Wisconsin is found to be $3,830,128.47.

This income based upon 7 per cent. interest would represent a capital of $54,716,121; or, based upon 10 per cent., would show an amount of $38,301,284.70. The former amount taken as the true valuation, would yield a tax, at the rate given, of $1,220,169.50 and the latter, the sum of $854,118.65; the one being 14.20 per cent., the other, 9.94 per cent. of the gross earnings.

The total revenue or tax which would accrue to the state by averaging the foregoing amounts would be $1,013,375.52, which is 11.79 per cent. of the gross earnings.

If this amount were annually paid into the state treasury, it would be more than sufficient to defray all of the expenses of the state government, including the penal and all the charitable institutions. It is therefore recommended that a law be enacted making it the duty of the State Board of Assessment to assess annually all railroad property lying within this state, according to the same rule that other property is now assessed; and providing that the Secretary of State shall annually ascertain the rate of taxation paid by other property, and shall levy the same rate upon the assessed valuation of railroad property so determined by said board; and providing, further, that the amount of the tax so determined shall be paid into the state treasury.

INDEBTEDNESS OF COUNTIES, CITIES AND TOWNS.

Chapter 110 of the general laws of 1872 provides, that each county, city, town and village clerk, whenever so requested by the

Secretary of State, shall furnish a full and complete statement of the financial condition thereof, showing the bonded indebtedness, the purposes for which the same was incurred, accrued interest thereon remaining unpaid, and all other forms of indebtedness.

Reports have been received from all of the counties, except from Clark and Crawford.

Table No. 1, appendix "F," shows the amount of bonded and other indebtedness, and the purposes for which the same was incurred in cities, towns, villages and school districts.

Table No. 2 of the same appendix gives the bonded and other indebtedness of counties, and the purposes for which the same was authorized.

The items in table No. 1, were incurred as follows:

BONDED INDEBTEDNESS.

For railroad aid	$3,837,672	
For roads and bridges	103,752	
For interest unpaid	109,970	
For other purposes	1,724,222	
Total bonded indebtedness		$5,775,616
All other indebtedness		117,475
Indebtedness of school districts		271,268
Total		$6,164,359

The indebtedness of counties, as given in table No. 2, is classified as follows:

For railroad aid	$2,008,732	
For roads and bridges	12,000	
For interest unpaid	18,819	
For other purposes	625,420	
Total bonded indebtedness		$2,664,971
All other indebtedness		50,699
Total		$2,715,670

By adding the debt of the counties, as exhibited in table No. 2, to that of the cities, towns and villages found in table No. 1, the aggregate indebtedness, so far as reported, is shown to be $8,880,029, which is 2.68 per cent. of the local valuation of property, for the year 1872, as appears from table No. 1, of appendix "E." The whole amount of railroad aid reported is $5,846,404. It may be added, that if full returns were made, it is believed, these figures would be considerably increased.

SALES OF REAL ESTATE.

The following table shows the average price paid per acre for farming lands, and the price paid for city and village lots sold and recorded, during the year ending September 1, 1873, and the average value of the same property, as determined by the city and town assessors, for the year 1872; together with the ratio of the price, or consideration in the deeds, to such assessed valuation:

Counties.	Farming Lands.			City and Village Lots.		
	Average consideration per acre.	Average assessment per acre.	Ratio of consideration to assessment.	Average consideration per lot.	Average assessment per lot.	Ratio of consideration to assessment
Adams	$9 80	$2 29	.23	$114 58	$58 75	.513
[1] Ashland	....	....	.....	....	....	.....
[1] Barron	....	....	.....	....	....	.....
Bayfield	2 08	2 05	.99	58 46	44 04	.753
[1] Brown	....	....	.....	....	....	.....
Buffalo	7 72	2 24	.29	342 08	116 75	.341
[1] Burnett	....	....	.....	....	....	.....
Calumet	20 31	5 18	.26	357 16	99 18	.278
Chippewa	5 29	2 08	.39	792 69	467 79	.590
Clark	6 49	3 90	.60	386 22	250 25	.648
Columbia	16 69	11 45	.69	444 71	312 25	.703
Crawford	5 68	3 53	.62	141 87	95 03	.670
Dane	21 11	13 97	.66	862 60	631 42	.732
Dodge	29 64	20 50	.69	327 24	186 09	.569
Door	10 73	5 72	.53	317 67	137 97	.434
[1] Douglas	....	....	.....	....	....	.....
Dunn	8 00	3 28	.41	418 86	226 36	.540
Eau Claire	8 48	5 36	.63	501 07	550 37	1.098
Fond du Lac	40 79	18 32	.45	884 35	416 94	.471
Grant	13 75	8 82	.64	315 21	186 59	.592
Green	20 51	15 28	.74	425 69	314 25	.738
Green Lake	18 98	12 45	.66	256 82	200 21	.780
Iowa	13 47	8 15	.61	324 31	160 30	.494
Jackson	6 23	1 90	.30	288 40	204 33	.708
Jefferson	32 33	17 80	.55	575 39	348 63	.606
Juneau	9 31	4 21	.45	221 27	203 89	.921
Kenosha	37 81	18 60	.49	696 71	302 78	.435
Kewaunee	10 22	1 45	.14	178 20	23 82	.134
La Crosse	13 52	7 72	.57	523 14	330 29	.631
La Fayette	25 40	11 25	.44	377 48	198 46	.526
Manitowoc	25 16	6 71	.29	399 64	309 85	.775
Marathon	2 16	1 30	.65	196 20	79 86	.407
Marquette	8 25	2 50	.30	....	....	.....
Milwaukee	64 68	36 83	.57	1,012 08	704 28	.696
Monroe	10 12	4 39	.43	450 10	261 61	.581
Oconto	7 64	2 56	.34	297 45	187 67	.631

[1] No report.

Sales of Real Estate, etc—continued.

Counties.	Farming Lands.			Village and City Lots.		
	Average consideration per acre.	Average assessment per acre.	Ratio of consideration to assessment.	Average consideration per lot.	Average assessment per lot.	Ratio of consideration to assessment.
Outagamie	$15 80	$6 60	.42	$670 84	$380 80	.567
Ozaukee	28 52	15 79	.55	198 16	94 06	.475
[1] Pepin..........	......	......	.....	......	......	....
Pierce	10 82	6 26	.58	406 06	221 10	.544
Polk..............	6 17	3 05	.49	138 17	61 46	.445
Portage...........	5 09	1 65	.32	215 86	109 12	.506
Racine............	33 86	22 76	.67	735 11	477 10	.649
Richland	7 47	4 33	.58	178 66	108 81	.598
Rock	32 18	21 20	.66	852 20	574 30	.674
St. Croix	8 93	5 34	.60	378 03	221 54	.586
Sauk	10 90	5 42	.50	393 64	218 87	.556
Shawano..........	4 70	1 27	.27	260 41	136 45	.524
Sheboygan	21 69	12 96	.60	367 09	185 73	.506
Trempealeau	8 03	4 15	.52	285 48	154 30	.540
Vernon	7 75	4 30	.57	140 95	75 79	.588
Walworth	30 34	22 88	.75	541 29	392 02	.724
Washington	34 28	16 48	.48	388 28	238 98	.614
Waukesha	39 72	28 55	.72	655 77	438 42	.669
Waupaca	2 15	85	.40	274 45	136 89	.498
Waushara	9 19	3 19	.35	391 48	121 46	.310
Winnebago	32 59	19 03	.58	522 16	335 73	.643
Wood	4 93	2 25	.46	504 07	173 49	.344
	$11 18	$6 06	.54	$551 11	$353 31	.642

[1] No report.

A full statement, giving the aggregates upon which the foregoing averages and ratios are based, for each county, will be found in appendix "G."

It will be noticed that the average price per acre for which farming lands were sold during the year was $11.18, while the assessed valuation per acre of the same property was only $6.06. The average price of city and village lots sold was $551.11 per lot; the average assessed valuation of the same lots being $353.31.

The average ratio of the price to the assessed valuation of farming lands was 54 per cent.; the same ratio in the case of city and village lots being 64 per cent.

If the compilation of these statistics were continued fo r a num ber of years, they would be of great value to state, county and local boards of assessment, in determining the valuation of real estate, especially of farming lands.

EXEMPT PROPERTY.

By the provisions of chapter 205, laws of 1873, it was made the duty of all assessors throughout the State, when making out the assessment rolls, to enter on blanks, furnished for the purpose, a correct and pertinent description of all real and personal property, with the exceptions made in the first section of the act, in their respective towns or wards not liable to taxation, together with a statement of its value, and for what purpose used; and to be guided in their work as nearly as practicable by existing laws relating to the assessment of property for taxation.

At the time appointed for the return of the assessment rolls, the lists so made were to have been returned to the county clerks, who, on or before the first day of October, were required to transmit a duplicate thereof to the Secretary of State.

The third section of the act referred to, provides that the Secretary of State shall compile, in suitable form, the information so by him received, and shall include a condensed statement thereof in his annual report.

Both county clerks and assessors were furnished in due time with suitable blanks, as contemplated by the law.

Reports were received from forty-two counties, sixteen having failed to respond.

Appendix "H" shows by counties the amounts of the different classes of exempt property thus received.

Great difficulty was experienced in making any classification of the property reported, and the one made in the table referred to is far from being satisfactory. In many instances, churches, parsonages, cemeteries and schools were put down upon the lists in one item, without separating the different classes, or designating the legal name of the corporation owning and controlling the property. It became, therefore, impossible to properly classify them. In a very few cases, it was found that a valuation was put upon the railroad track, while the law expressly provided, that the number of miles only should be reported.

The reports from several of the counties, as may be seen by referrence to the appendix, are quite incomplete, a number of the towns having failed to make returns.

Under the heading, "State Property," is included all of the trust funds, the Capitol, Insane Asylum and the State University, and all other State property located in Dane county.

The number of miles of railroad track reported is 1,279, against 1,810, reported by the companies themselves, in January, 1873.

The aggregate valuation of all exempt property, reported under this act, is $22,591,254, which is equal to 7.89 per cent. of all the taxable property assessed in the same counties, in 1873. Had the reports from those counties been complete, it is believed, that it would be equal to about 8 per cent. of all taxable property. If the amount of railroad property, which is included, and which is indirectly taxed, were deducted, this per centage would be reduced over one-fourth, making the net about 6 per cent.

Appendix "H" will show the following classification of exempt property:

United States	property	$1,069,454
State	do	6,538,168
County	do	1,217,000
Town, city and village	do	727,612
Common school	do	2,099 752
Colleges and academies	do	899,105
Churches	do	4,000,515
*Railroad	do	5,749,495
All other	do	790,158
Total		$22,591,254

COUNTY AGRICULTURAL SOCIETIES.

Appendix "I" gives a summary of the reports of the several County Agricultural Societies of the State, for the year ending February 1, 1873.

The number of societies reporting, and having held fairs, during the year, was 36.

* Railroad track not valued, except in very few instances.

The following statement shows the receipts and disbursements for the same period:

RECEIPTS.		
From the state	$3,600 00	....
Membership	7,196 40	....
Admission fees	20,000 53	....
Entries	2,490 00	....
Subscriptions	3,069 45	....
Other sources	10,015 41	....
Total		$46,371 79
DISBURSEMENTS.		
Premiums	$22,526 80	....
Expenses of fairs	9,384 19	....
Pay of secretaries	1,001 24	....
Other expenses	13,991 59	....
Total		$46,903 82

MARRIAGES, BIRTHS AND DEATHS.

Appendix marked "K" shows the number of marriages, births and deaths returned to this office, and recorded, during the year ending December 31, 1872, to have aggregated as follows:

Marriages	9,062
Births	8,172
Deaths	1,928

Reports of marriages have been received from every county cept from Ashland, Bayfield, Douglas and St. Croix. Eighteen counties have reported births, and fifteen, deaths.

INCORPORATIONS.

A list of companies incorporated under the laws of the state for manufacturing and other purposes, during the year ending September 30, 1873, will be found under Appendix "L," the number being fifty-four against twenty-five incorporated the preceding year.

RELIGIOUS SOCIETIES.

Appendix "M" shows the number of religious societies filing proof of their organization during the past fiscal year, to have been four.

ELECTIONS.

Appendix "N" gives a tabular statement showing the votes polled at the general election, held on the fifth day of November, 1872, for electors of President and Vice President of the United States; and on the proposition to amend the constitution of this State, increasing the number of Justices of the Supreme Court.

Appendix "O" shows the number of votes polled, at an election held on the first day of April, 1873, for associate Justice of the Supreme Court.

Appendix "P" exhibits the number of votes polled, at an election held on the first day of April, 1873, for judges of the third and tenth judicial circuits.

Appendix "Q" gives a statement of accounts audited under chapter 48, General Laws of 1866.

MISCELLANEOUS.

For the purpose of equalizing taxation and increasing the public revenues, attention is again invited to the subject of imposing a specific tax upon the gross earnings of express and telegraph companies.

As these are foreign corporations, realizing large incomes from their business within the state, it is but simple justice that they should be required to contribute their just proportion towards defraying the expenses of the state government.

It is, therefore, recommended that a law be enacted levying a tax upon these corporations, as above suggested, and repealing the law now in force relating to the taxation of telegraph companies.

In closing this, my fourth and last annual report of this department, I deem it a duty as well as a pleasure to acknowledge the constant fidelity and unremitting interest shown in the affairs of the office by all of those associated with me during my official term soon to close; and for the willingness, ability and promptness with which they have always discharged every duty entrusted to their care.

All of which is respectfully submitted.

LL. BREESE,
Secretary of State.

APPENDIX.

APPENDIX "A."

DETAILED STATEMENT.

OF THE

RECEIPTS AND DISBURSEMENTS OF THE SEVERAL FUNDS

FOR THE FISCAL YEAR ENDING SEPTEMBER 30, 1878.

GENERAL FUND RECEIPTS.

RECEIPTS FROM COUNTIES.	*State Tax.*	*Suit Tax.*	
Adams ....county..............	$2,594 82	$15 00	....
Ashland..........do...............	980 00		...
Barron ....do...............	1,134 41		...
Bayfield..........do...............	752 53	11 00	....
Brown ....do...............	12,922 92	35 00	....
Buffalo. ....do	4,370 79	47 00	....
Burnett ....do...............	769 24		...
Calumet..........do...............	6,684 30		...
Chippewa ....do...............	18,720 78		...
Clark ....do...............	5,534 36	68 00	....
Columbia ....do...............	21,519 57	87 00	....
Crawford. ....do...............	7,428 34	51 00	....
Dane.............do...............	49,885 89	809 00	....
Dodge............do...............	32,068 17		...
Door.............do...............	1,808 00	49 00	....
Douglas..........do...............	1,855 92	18 00	....
Dunn ....do...............	5,892 29	76 00	....
Eau Claire....... do...............	6,820 88	110 00	....
Fond du Lac......do...............	32,866 33	51 00	....
Grant ....do...............	29,642 37		...
Green ....do...............	20,214 81	26 00	....
Green Lake ......do...............	9,816 48	61 00	....
Iowa ....do...............	74 68		...
Jackson..........do...............	4,187 01	48 00	....
Jefferson ....do...............	22,644 86	63 00	....
Juneau ....do...............	5,023 50	80 00	....
Kenosha ....do...............	12,775 63	35 00	....
Kewaunee... .....do...............	1,493 53	27 00	....
La Crosse ....do...............	12,818 37	76 00	....
La Fayette........do...............	16,448 45	113 00	....
Manitowoc ....do...............	15,905 78	76 00	....
Marathon ... .do...............	8,378 83	80 00	....
Marquette........do...............	2,843 38	12 00	....
Milwaukee ....do...............	102,236 49	256 00	....
Monroe ....do...............	8,615 78	134 00	....
Oconto...........do...............	11,039 42		....

GENERAL FUND RECEIPTS.

Receipts from Counties—continued.	*State Tax.*	*Suit Tax.*	
Outagamie......county.	$13,524 02	$103 00	....
Ozaukee.........do...............	6,953 26	35 00	....
Pepin ....do...............	1,615 00	10 00	....
Pierce ....do...............	7,813 92	29 00	....
Polk............do...............	2,362 79	43 00	....
Portage.. ....do...............	5,834 16	82 00	....
Racine..........do...............	20,809 58	44 00	....
Richland ....do...............	7,772 07	36 00	....
Rock ....do...............	41,263 37	145 00	....
St. Croix.........do...............	8,741 89	144 00	....
Sauk ....do...............	17,486 96	44 00	....
Shawano.........do...............	3,106 66	16 00	....
Sheboygan.......do...............	17,779 28	37 00	....
Trempealeau.....do...............	4,905 58	20 00	....
Vernon .... do...............	11,281 78	48 00	....
Walworth........do...............	27,519 91	92 00	....
Washington .....do...............	13,266 61	39 00	....
Waukesha ....do...............	26,484 63	65 00	....
Waupaca ....do...............	7,654 18	60 00	....
Waushara ....do...............	4,032 23	12 00	....
Winnebago ......do...............	29,530 63	125 00	....
Wood....... ....do	3,378 18	17 00	....
	$781,875 60	$3,805 00	$785,680 60

RAILROADS.—THREE PER CENT. TAX.

Chicago and Northwestern Railroad Company....	$42,683 37	....
Green Bay and Lake Pepin Railroad Company....	846 02	....
Mineral Point Railroad Company...............	3,315 95	....
Milwaukee and Northern Railroad Company.....	3,625 21	....
Milwaukee and Lake Shore Railroad Company...	478 21	....
Milwaukee and St. Paul Railroad Company	135,989 79	....
Northern Wisconsin Railroad Company..........	167 85	....
Prairie du Chien and McGregor Railroad Comp'y	103 62	....
Sheboygan and Fond du Lac Railroad Company..	4,221 58	....
Western Union Railroad Company.............	10,047 40	....
Wisconsin Central Railroad Company...........	3,506 70	....
West Wisconsin Railroad Company	5,389 29	....
		210,374 99

PLANK AND OTHER ROADS.

Fond du Lac Gravel Road Company	$95 95	....
Milwaukee and Green Bay Plankroad Company .	12 00	....
Milwaukee and Janesville Plankroad Company...	53 00	....
Milwaukee and Washington Plankroad Company .	5 93	....
Milwaukee and Brookfield McAdamized Road Co.	32 57	....
Sheboygan and Calumet Plankroad Company	48 23	....
		247 68

INSURANCE COMPANIES.—TAXES AND LICENSE.

Fire.

Allemannia Fire Insurance Company, Pittsburg, Pa	$683 40	....
Atlantic Insurance Company, Brooklyn, N. Y	519 10	....

"A."—*Receipts and Disbursements of the Several Funds*—con.

GENERAL FUND RECEIPTS.

Insurance Companies—Fire—continued.		
Ætna Insurance Company, Hartford, Conn.	$8,187 87	....
Amazon Insurance Company, Cincinnati, Ohio	600 67	....
American Central Insurance Co., St. Louis, Mo.	183 36	....
Alemannia Fire Insurance Co., Cleveland, Ohio.	157 12	....
American Ins. Co., Chicago, Illinois	795 62	....
Arctic Fire Insurance Company, N. Y	186 08	....
Atlas Insurance Company, Hartford, Conn	500 00	....
Brewers' Fire Ins. Co. of America, Milwaukee, Wis.	1,244 15	....
Brewers' and Maltsters' Insurance Company, N. Y.	223 80	....
Black River Insurance Company, Watertown, N.Y.	67 74	....
Concordia Mutual Fire Insurance Co., Mil., Wis	299 12	....
Commerce Insurance Company, Albany, N. Y.	81 66	....
Continental Insurance Company, N. Y.	870 48	....
Capital City Insurance Company, Albany, N. Y.	14 13	....
Commercial Union Assurance Co., London, Eng.	336 50	....
Connecticut Fire Ins. Company, Hartford, Conn	113 00	....
Dodge Co. Mutual Insurance Company, Waupun.	701 43	....
Detroit Fire and Marine Ins. Co., Detroit, Mich	201 88	....
Fairfield Co. Fire Ins. Co., South Norwalk, Conn	500 00	....
Franklin Fire Insurance Company, Phil., Penn.	820 54	....
Fireman's Fund Ins. Co., San Francisco, Cal	214 20	....
Farmers' Insurance Company, Freeport, Ill	201 06	....
Fire Association, Phil., Penn	500 00	....
German Insurance Company, Erie, Penn.	598 47	....
Germania Fire Insurance Company, N. Y.	375 43	....
German American Insurance Company, N. Y	284 62	....
Germantown Far. Mut. Ins. Co., Germantown, Wis	577 93	....
Globe Insurance Company, Chicago, Ill	112 70	....
German Insurance Company, Freeport, Ill.	500 00	....
Girard Fire and Marine Ins. Co., Phil., Penn	617 14	....
Herman Farmers' Mut. Ins. Co., Herman, Wis.	111 80	....
Home Insurance Company, N. Y.	2,595 25	....
Hartford Fire Insurance Company, Hartford, Conn.	1,818 09	....
Hanover Fire Insurance Company, N. Y	375 43	....
Hoffman Fire Insurance Company, N. Y	49 86	....
Hekla Insurance Company, Madison, Wis.	328 32	....
Home Insurance Company, Columbus, Ohio	201 00	....
Howard Insurance Company, New York	126 99	....
Hamburg-Bremen Fire Ins. Co., Hamburg, Ger	59 15	....
Hartford Steam Boiler Inspection and Ins. Co.	81 16	....
Humboldt Insurance Company, Newark, N. J	500 00	....
Insurance Co. of North America, Phil., Penn.	1,344 02	....
Lancashire Insurance Company, Manchester, Eng.	548 13	....
London Assurance Corporation, Eng.	650 98	....
Lorillard Insurance Company, New York	84 28	....
Liverpool and London and Globe Ins. Co., Liv., Eng	588 60	....
Milwaukee Mechanics' Mut. Insurance Company.	3,001 79	....
Mercantile Insurance Company, Cleveland, Ohio.	129 67	....
Madison Mutual Insurance Company	1,918 05	....
Merchants' Insurance Company, Providence, R. I.	93 37	....
Mechanics and Traders' Fire Ins. Co., New York.	288 23	....
Manhattan Fire Insurance Company, New York.	238 47	....
Meriden Fire Insurance Company, Meriden, Conn.	526 18	....
Mercantile Mut Insurance Company, New York.	376 17	....
Millville Mut. Marine and Fire Ins. Co., N. J.	500 00	....
National Fire Insurance Company, Hartford, Conn	198 93	....

"A."—*Receipts and Disbursements of the Several Funds*—con.

GENERAL FUND RECEIPTS.

Insurance Companies—Fire—continued.		
Northwestern National Ins. Co., Milwaukee.......	$2,463 29	....
Niagara Fire Ins. Co., N. Y....................	375 43	....
North Missouri Ins. Co., Macon, Mo.............	633 82	....
North British and Mercantile Ins. Co., Lond. & Ed	848 99	....
Narragansett F. & M. Ins. Co., Providence, R. I...	16 46	....
New Orleans Mutual Insurance Association.......	916 67	....
National Fire and Marine Ins. Co., Phila., Pa.....	500 00	....
Orient Insurance Company, Hartford, Conn.......	166 74	....
Orient Mutual Insurance Company, New York....	314 38	....
Penn Fire Insurance Co., Phila., Pa.............	708 01	....
Phœnix Insurance Company, Hartford, Conn.....	1,097 24	....
Phenix Insurance Company, Brooklyn, N. Y.....	685 62	....
Pennsylvania Fire Insurance Co., Phila., Penn....	938 19	....
Pacific Mutual Ins. Co., New York	383 27	....
Providence Washington Ins. Co., Prov., R. I......	41 63	....
Royal Insurance Co., Liverpool, Eng............	600 88	....
Republic Fire Insurance Co., New York..........	375 43	....
State Insurance Company, Hannibal, Mo..........	63 26	....
St. Paul F. & M. Insurance Co., St. Paul, Minn....	609 26	....
St. Nicholas Insurance Co., New York	74 48	....
Springfield Fire & Marine Insurance Co., Mass...	179 98	....
Star Fire Insurance Co., New York	79 37	....
Standard Fire Insurance Co., New York..........	114 98	....
Sun Insurance Company, Cleveland, Ohio........	43 03	....
St. Joseph F. & M. Insurance Co., St. Joseph, Mo.	500 00	....
Traders' Insurance Co., Chicago, Ill............	141 15	....
Tradesmen's Fire Insurance Co., New York......	151 10	....
U. S. Branch Imperial Fire Ins. Co., London, Eng.	1,012 18	....
U. S. Branch Queen Ins. Co., Liverpool, Eng......	395 54	....
Union Insurance Company, Bangor, Me..........	112 16	....
Vernon Co. Scandinavian Mut.F Ins. Co.,Chaseb'rg	6 12	....
Watertown Fire Insurance Co., Watertown, N. Y..	31 65	....
Williamsburg City Fire Ins. Co., Brooklyn, N. Y..	71 02	....
Western Assurance Co., Toronto, Canada.........	599 75	....
Life.		
Ætna Life Insurance Co., Hartford, Conn.........	$300 00	....
Berkshire Life Insurance Co., Pittsfield, Mass.....	300 00	....
Brooklyn Life Insurance Co., N. Y..............	300 00	....
Chicago Life Insurance Co	300 00	....
Continental Life Insurance Co., New York........	300 00	....
Charter Oak Life Insurance Co., Hartford, Conn..	300 00	....
Connecticut Mut. Life Ins. Co., Hartford, Conn ...	300 00	....
Equitable Life Assur'ce Soc. of the U. States, N.Y.	300 00	....
Germania Life Insurance Co., New York.........	300 00	....
Globe Mutual Life Insurance Co., New York.....	300 00	....
Missouri Mutual Life Insurance Co., St. Louis....	375 00	....
Mutual Benefit Life Insurance Co., Newark, N. J.	300 00	....
Mutual Life Insurance Co., Chicago............	300 00	....
Mutual Life Insurance Co., New York	300 00	....
Manhattan Life Insurance Co., New York........	300 00	....
Missouri Valley Life Ins. Co., Leavenworth, Kan..	300 00	....
Metropolitan Life Insurance Co., New York......	300 00	....
Massachusetts Mut. Life Ins. Co., Springfield, Mass.	300 00	....
National Life Insurance Co., Chicago............	300 00	....

"A."—*Receipts and Disbursements of the Several Funds*—con.

GENERAL FUND RECEIPTS.

Insurance Companies—Life—continued.		
Northwestern Mut. Life Insurance Co., Milwaukee.	$4,146 39	....
New England Mutual Life Insurance Co., Boston..	300 00	....
New York Life Insurance Co., New York.........	300 00	....
National Life Ins. Co. of U. S. A., Washington....	300 00	....
New Jersey Mut. Life Ins. Co. Newark, N. J.. ...	300 00	....
North America Life Insurance Co., New York ...	300 00	....
Protection Life Insurance Company, Chicago, Ill..	300 00	....
Phœnix Mutual Life Ins. Co., Hartford, Conn.....	300 00	....
Republic Life Insurance Company, Chicago......	300 00	....
Railway Passengers Assurance Co., Hartford, Conn.	300 00	....
Security Life Insurance and Annuity Co., N. Y...	300 00	....
St. Louis Mut. Life Ins. Co., St. Louis, Mo........	300 00	....
Teutonia Life Insurance Company, Chicago	300 00	....
Travelers Life Insurance Comp'y, Hartford, Conn.	300 00	....
Universal Life Insurance Company, New York....	300 00	....
Western New York Life Ins. Co., Batavia, N. Y...	300 00	....
Washington Life Insurance Company, New York.	300 00	....
		$63,299 93
BONDS RECEIVABLE.		
Bank of Sheboygan............................	$310 00	....
Farmers and Mechanics' Bank of Fond du Lac ...	100 00	....
		410 00
MISCELLANEOUS.		
Hawkers and peddlers...........................	$7,188 29	....
Income Penalty..................................	6,304 26	....
Sale of Marathon County Lands.................	6,498 55	....
Ll. Breese, Secretary of State, surplus fees	6,761 50	....
Ll. Breese, Secretary of State, notary fees	1,882 00	....
Ll. Breese, Sec'y of State, sale of documents	37 10	....
U. S. Marshal, boarding U. S. prisoners..........	1,420 87	....
Northwestern Telegraph Company..............	3,522 00	....
C. C. Washburn, commr's of deeds in other states.	258 00	....
A. A. Meredith, Superintendent of Public Property, public property sold	409 55	....
Callaghan & Co., Wisconsin Reports............	765 00	....
Soldiers' Orphans' Home, overpayment refunded..	200 00	....
H. S. Sackett, on account of uncurrent money	400 00	....
Atwood & Culver, refunded for overpayment on voucher 1532................................	509 41	....
D. J. Pulling, salary refunded..................	147 85	....
B. F. Cram, Qr. M. Gen., transportation on arms refunded	12 60	....
State banks, printing bank report..............	37 50	....
T. D. Lang, treas. agt., J. Kline's peddler's license, money refunded	6 66	....
Luce & Burt, overpaym't for advert'g refunded ...	2 95	....
		35,859 09
Total receipts............................		$1,095,872 29

GENERAL FUND DISBURSEMENTS.

SALARIES AND PERMANENT APPROPRIATIONS.			
Governor's Office—			
C. C. Washburn, Governor, salary..	$5,000 00	....	....
M. H. Pettit, Lt. Governor, salary..	500 00	....	....
Chas. J. Martin, Gov. Priv. Sec. sal'y	1,600 00	....	....
		$7,100 00	....
Secretary's Office—			
Ll. Breese, Secretary of State, salary.	$1,200 00	....	....
John S. Dean, Ass't. Sec. State, sal'y	2,000 00	....	....
		3,200 00	....
Treasurer's Office—			
Henry Bætz, State Treasurer, salary.	$1,400 00	....	....
Wm. Ketcham, Ass't Treas'r, salary.	2,000 00	....	....
		3,400 00	....
Attorney General's Office—			
S. S. Barlow, Attorney Gen'l, salary.	$2,000 00	....	....
P. L. Spooner, Ass't At'y G'l, salary.	600 00	....	....
		2,600 00	....
State Superintendent's Office—			
Samuel Fallows, State Sup't, salary.	$1,200 00	....	....
Samuel Fallows, State Sup't. traveling expenses...	1,500 00	....	....
Samuel Fallows, State Sup't, clerk hire.......	1,000 00	....	....
John B. Pradt, Asst. State Superintendent, salary................	1,800 00		....
Annual appropriation for books ...	150 00	....	....
		5,650 00	....
Office Superintend't of Public Property—			
A. A. Meredith, Superintend't Public Property, salary	$1,000 00	....	....
A. A. Meredith, Superintendent of Pub. Prop. purchasing stationery.	1,000 00	....	....
H. H. Himebaugh, Asst. Superintendent of Public Property, salary.	1,200 00	....	....
		3,200 00	....
State Library—			
O. M. Conover, Librarian, salary ..	$1,000 00	....	....
O. M. Conover, books............	500 00	....	....
Stevens & Haynes, books..........	375 36	....	....
J. F. McMullen, books............	70 00	....	....
		1,945 36	....
State Historical Society—			
L. C. Draper, Secretary, salary.....	$1,200 00	....	....
D. S. Durrie, Librarian, salary.....	1,600 00	....	....
Annual appropriation for books ...	3,500 00	....	....
		$6,300 00	....
Supreme Court—			
L. S. Dixon, Chief Justice, salary ..	$4,000 00	....	....
Orsamus Cole, Asso. Justice, salary.	4,000 00	....	....
Wm. P. Lyon, Asso. Justice, salary.	4,000 00	....	....
O. M. Conover, Reporter, salary ...	1,000 00	....	....
La Fayette Kellogg, Clerk.........	593 00	....	....
Thos. McGrath, Crier............	162 00	....	....
C. H. Beyler, Crier...............	14 00	....	....
		$13,769 00	....

GENERAL FUND DISBURSMENTS.

Salaries and Permanent Appropriations—continued.			
Circuit Courts, salaries—			
Robert Harkness, judge 1st circuit	$2,500 00		
David W. Small, judge 2d circuit	2,500 00		
David J. Pulling, judge 3d circuit	2,733 33		
Eli C. Lewis, judge 3d circuit	200 00		
Campbell McLean, judge 4th circuit	2,500 00		
Joseph T. Mills, judge 5th circuit	2,500 00		
Romanzo Bunn, judge 6th circuit	2,500 00		
Geo. W. Cate, judge 7th circuit	2,500 00		
H. L. Humphrey, judge 8th circuit	2,500 00		
Alva Stewart, judge 9th circuit	2,500 00		
E. Holmes Ellis, judge 10th circuit	2,500 00		
Solon H. Clough, judge 11th circuit	2,500 00		
H. S. Conger, judge 12th circuit	2,500 00		
		$30,433 33	
Wisconsin Reports—			
O. M. Conover	$12,375 00		
Callaghan & Co	13,950 00		
		26,325 00	
Interest on State Indebtedness—			
State bonds	$1,020 00		
C'rtific's of indebt'nes belonging to—			
School Fund	109,179 00		
University Fund	7,770 00		
Agricultural College Fund	3,798 67		
Normal School Fund	35,882 00		
		157,649 67	
			$261,572 36

LEGISLATIVE EXPENSES.

Members of Senate—	*Salary.*	*Mileage.*		
Robert H. Baker	$350 00	$25 00		
Orrin Bacon	350 00	6 00		
William Blair	350 00	15 00		
Orlando Brown	350 00	51 00		
Samuel D. Burchard	350 00	30 00		
Francis Campbell	350 00	28 00		
Frederick W. Cotzhausen	350 00	20 00		
Horatio N. Davis	350 00	10 00		
Romanzo E. Davis	350 00	1 60		
Henry L. Eaton	350 00	10 00		
....do....Pres't, *pro tem.*	75 00			
Walter S. Green	350 00	17 00		
William H. Hiner	350 00	23 60		
Gideon C. Hixon	350 00	28 00		
John C. Holloway	350 00	19 00		
Joseph E. Irish	350 00	60 00		
John A. Johnson	350 00			
Evan O. Jones	350 00	22 00		
George Kreiss	350 00	26 40		
Myron P. Lindsley	350 00	37 00		
Francis Little	350 00	13 20		
John L. Mitchell	350 00	20 00		
Myron H. McCord	350 00	45 00		
Robert McCurdy	350 00	28 00		

GENERAL FUND DISBURSEMENTS.

Legislative Expenses—con.				
Members of Senate—con.	*Salary.*	*Mileage.*		
William Nelson	$350 00	$30 00		
Patrick H. O'Rourk	350 00	32 00		
Samuel Pratt	350 00	16 00		
Robert L. D. Potter	350 00	45 00		
John B. Quimby	350 00	6 60		
Adam Schantz	350 00	28 00		
Carl H. Schmidt	350 00	38 00		
Thomas B. Scott	350 00	50 00		
Joseph G. Thorpe	350 00	43 00		
Joseph Wagner	350 00	27 60		
	$11,625 00	$852 00		
			$12,477 00	
Senate Employes—				
J. H. Waggoner, chief clerk		$432 00		
Sid. A. Foster, assistant clerk		360 00		
T. S. Ansley, book-keeper		360 00		
Srank Abbott, enrolling clerk		288 00		
T. H. Vedder, transcribing clerk		288 00		
Charles A. Booth, engrossing clerk		288 00		
E. Emonson, sergeant-at-arms		360 00		
Stephen Coburn, 1st asst. sergt-at-arms		288 00		
Hugh Longstaff, 2d do		208 00		
P. H. Parsons, postmaster		288 00		
Wm. D. Harshaw, assistant postmaster		252 00		
Hugh Longstaff, doorkeeper		70 00		
Walter Cook, assistant doorkeeper		252 00		
W. F. Bingham do		252 00		
W. H. Hals do		252 00		
John Z. Rittman do		252 00		
G. Jones, gallery doorkeeper		252 00		
S. S. Miller, gallery doorkeeper		252 00		
Frank J. Wood, night watch		210 00		
O. M. Pettit, governor's attendant		252 00		
Charles A. Irish, clerk's messenger		144 00		
Adolph Hastreiter, messenger		144 00		
Arthur Johnson do		144 00		
Freddie Richards do		144 00		
Willie Bintliff do		144 00		
Eddie McCurdy do		144 00		
Johnnie Veeder do		144 00		
Charlie Fellows do		144 00		
Frank Bolting do		144 00		
Freddie Davis do		144 00		
John Anderson, flagman		252 00		
R. J. Flint, clerk joint com. on claims		288 00		
Ole Hage, clerk judiciary committee		288 00		
C. C. Rogers, clerk of com. to inv. S.O.H		248 00		
Frank Scott, clerk of com. on eng. bills		288 00		
E. V. Whiton, clk of com, on enld. bills		288 00		
J. H. Foster, proof reader		288 00		
Wm. Hughes, committee room attend't		252 00		
Rev. J. E. Irish, chaplain		50 00		
Peter Labonde, porter		252 00		
F. W. Parmeter, ass't transcribing cl'k		288 00		

GENERAL FUND DISBURSEMENTS.

Legislative Expenses—continued.

Senate Employes—continued.			
G. N. Wood, night watch	$42 00		
D. C. Donaldson, com. room attend't	252 00		
E. H. Smith, extra clerk (in 1872)	2 00		
Daniel Fitzpatrick, messenger	144 00		
F. J. Wood, extra clerk, (1872)	50		
Lizzie W. Camack, extra clerk	55 00		
Sarah Church ....do	4 00		
C. H. Derrickson ....do	4 00		
Libbie Dann ....do	4 00		
H. H. Himebaugh ....do	16 50		
Kate Kavenaugh ....do	25 00		
Joseph Keyes ....do	11 50		
Carrie McCord ....do	2 00		
Emily A. Meyers ....do	45 00		
Willie Main ....do	8 00		
Robert Monteith ....do	12 00		
Mary Smith ....do	55 00		
Geo. W. Stoner ....do	50 00		
Mary Wang ....do	60 50		
J. H. Waggoner, organizing senate	50 00		
J. H. Waggoner, transcrib'g senate journ	250 00		
J. H. Waggoner, indexing senate journal	200 00		
		$10,971 00	

Members of Assembly.	*Salary.*	*Mileage.*		
Henry D. Barron, speaker	$850 00			
Henry D. Barron	850 00	$68 00		
James H. Allen	850 00	26 00		
Wm. H. Armstrong	850 00	26 00		
Sherman Bardwell	850 00	57 00		
Wm. P. Bartlett	850 00	48 80		
Wm. H. Bartran	850 00	42 00		
John A. Becher	850 00	20 00		
Moritz N. Becker	850 00	20 00		
Alderbert E. Bleekman	850 00	23 00		
Julius Bodenstab	850 00	33 00		
Henry C. Brace	850 00	20 00		
Samuel S. Brannan	850 00	8 00		
Seth W. Button	850 00	36 00		
Charles A. Cady	850 00	12 60		
Columbus Caldwell	850 00	43 00		
Charles E. Chamberlin	850 00	26 00		
Dustin G. Cheever	850 00	11 00		
Satterlee Clark	850 00	30 00		
David R. Clements	850 00	40 00		
William H. Clise	850 00	19 50		
Hiram H. Cornwell	850 00	2 00		
Joseph C. Curtis	850 00	37 00		
Peter Daane, Jr.	850 00	30 00		
John W. Davis	850 00	20 00		
Orsamus S. Davis	850 00	39 00		
Patrick Devy	850 00	8 00		
Dennis Dewane	850 00	41 00		
Carlos L. Douglass	850 00	15 00		
Peter Doyle	850 00	19 00		
John Elkins	850 00	25 00		

GENERAL FUND DISBURSEMENTS.

Legislative Expenses—con.				
Members of Assembly—con.	*Salary.*	*Mileage.*	....	....
John M. Evans	$350 00	$4 80	....	....
Asahel Farr	350 00	27 00	....	....
Truman M. Fay	350 00	25 00	....	....
Eugene K. Felt	350 00	12 40	....	....
Apollos D. Foote	350 00	39 00	....	....
Carlton Foster	350 00	40 60	....	....
Wilfred C. Fuller	350 00	30 00	....	....
David C. Fulton	350 00	63 20	....	....
Charles R. Gibbs	350 00	10 00	....	....
Ferdinand Gnewuch	350 00	17 00	....	....
Horace E. Houghton	350 00	58 80	....	....
Richard W. Hubbell	350 00	46 40	....	....
Christopher Hutchinson	350 00	22 00	....	....
Norman L. James	350 00	12 40	....	....
Peter Jerman	350 00	30 00	....	....
John Kellogg	350 00	11 00	....	....
Charles S. Kelsey	350 00	12 00	....	....
Otto Kerl	350 00	8 60	....	....
Robert Lees	350 00	51 80	....	....
Frank Leland	350 00	16 00	....	....
Rensselaer M. Lewis	350 00	25 00	....	....
Alonzo A. Loper	350 00	25 60	....	....
John Luchsinger	350 00	5 20	....	....
Thomas Lynch	350 00	35 20	....	....
Thomas McConnell	350 00	40 80	....	....
James McGrath	350 00	20 00	....	....
Alexander McMellan	350 00	28 00	....	....
Ed. E. Merrett	350 00	40 00	....	....
John Montieth	350 00	18 00	....	....
Henry F. C. Nichols	350 00	18 00	....	....
James W. Ostrander	350 00	10 00	....	....
Henry L. Palmer	350 00	20 00	....	....
Francis G. Parks	350 00	18 00	....	....
Henry A. Patterson	350 00	8 00	....	....
James H. Persons	350 00	60 00	....	....
Daniel L. Plumer	350 00	60 00	....	....
John L. Porter	350 00	7 40	....	....
Albert E. Pound	350 00	50 80	....	....
Otto Puhlman	350 00	32 00	....	....
Geo. W. Putnam	350 00	15 40	....	....
Joseph Rankin	350 00	39 00	....	....
David Rhoda	350 00	11 00	....	....
Corydon L. Rich	350 00	47 00	....	....
Richard Richards	350 00	26 00	....	....
William Robinson	350 00	10 00	....	....
John A. Rœmer	350 00	25 40	....	....
Wm. E. Rowe	350 00	6 00	....	....
John Runkel	350 00	20 00	....	....
Jacob Sander	350 00	20 00	....	....
Casper M. Sanger	250 00	20 00	....	....
Hiram W. Sawyer	350 00	30 00	....	....
David F. Sayre	350 00	6 00	....	....
Galen B. Seaman	350 20	20 00	....	....
Dennis Short	350 00	33 00	....	....

GENERAL FUND DISBURSEMENTS.

Legislative Expenses—con.				
Members of Assembly—con.	*Salary.*	*Mileage.*		
De Wayne Stebbins	$350 00	$44 20		
Casper H. Steinfort	350 00	16 00		
John B. Stemper	350 00	22 00		
Thomas G. Stevens	350 00	24 00		
Henry J. Tate	350 00	30 00		
Oliver W. Thornton	350 00	4 00		
Thomas Tobin	350 00	22 00		
Isaac W. Van Schaick	350 00	20 00		
Levi B. Vilas	350 00			
Thomas Wall	350 00	40 60		
Baruch S. Weil	350 00	30 00		
Gottlob E. Weiss	350 00	20 00		
Alson Wood	350 00	39 00		
John Young	350 00	10 00		
Adolph Zimmerman	350 00	23 00		
Charles R. Zorn	350 00	35 00		
	$35,350 00	2,604.50		
			$37,954 50	
Assembly Employes—				
E. W. Young, chief clerk		$432 00		
Fred. A. Dennett, assistant clerk		360 00		
Roger C. Spooner, book-keeper		360 00		
Amos Hitchcock, enrolling clerk		288 00		
Mrs. R. A. Vilas, engrossing clerk		288 00		
Miss Fannie Russell, transcribing clerk		288 00		
O. C. Bissell, sergeant-at-arms		360 00		
W. H. Bell, 1st asst. ... do		288 00		
Rich'd Pritchard, 2d asst. do		288 00		
M. Herrick ... postmaster		288 00		
W. W. Baker, 1st asst .. do		252 00		
Chas. Volner, 2d asst .... do		252 00		
John Gale, door keeper		252 00		
Geo. W. Baker ... do		252 00		
S. G. Parkhurst .. do		252 00		
W. W. Phelps .... do		252 00		
John Bowen, gallery attendant		252 00		
H J. Stordock ..... do		252 00		
Geo. W. Williams, committee room att.		252 00		
M. S. Bowler ... do		252 00		
Ethan Griffith ... do		252 00		
Geo. Slingsby ... do		252 00		
Eugene J. Cole ... do		252 00		
O. M. Oleson, wash room attendant		210 00		
Charles Sellers, fireman		252 00		
Z. B. Russell ... do		252 00		
Fred. Bright, night watch		252 00		
H. O. Hermenson, porter		252 00		
Willie Holmes, speaker's messenger		144 00		
Frank R. Norton, clerk's .... do		144 00		
Eddie B. Weeks, serg't-at-arms' mess'r		144 00		
Charles Murphy, messenger		144 00		
Frank Porter ... do		144 00		
Henry Cutler ... do		144 00		

GENERAL FUND DISBURSEMENTS.

Legislative Expenses—continued.			
Assembly Employes—			
Ed. Hubbell .... messenger	$144 00	....	....
Edwin Rowcliff .... do	144 00	....	....
Cassius Paine .... do	144 00	....	....
John Lannan .... do	144 00	....	....
Willie Rudd .... do	144 00	....	....
Charles Wootton .... do	144 00	....	....
Julian French .... do	144 00	....	....
Charles Rothe .... do	144 00	....	....
Mike Comford .... do	144 00	....	....
John Oleson .... do	144 00	....	....
Fred. Hawley .... do	144 00	....	....
E. L. Blood, clerk of committee	128 00	....	....
Rev. Richard Dodson, chaplain	25 00	....	....
Rev. J. M. Thuringer .... do	25 00	....	....
Rev. H. Stone Richardson ... do	25 00	....	....
Rev. C. H. Richards .... do	25 00	....	....
Rev. P. S. Mather .... do	25 00	....	....
Rev. F. Gotschalk .... do	25 00	....	....
Henrietta Bevitt .... extra clerk	4 00	....	....
F. W. Case .... do	160 00	....	....
Sarah Church .... do	30 50	....	....
Libbie Dann .... do	21 00	....	....
C. H. Derrickson .... do	22 00	....	....
J. B. Egger .... do	10 00	....	....
Sadie J. Francomb .... do	175 00	....	....
Fannie E. Hopkins .... do	209 50	....	....
E. L. Hills .... do	40 00	....	....
H. H. Himebaugh .... do	4 00	....	....
Clara Hyer .... do	6 50	....	....
Mary E. Judkins .... do	45 50	....	....
Kate Kavenaugh .... do	253 00	....	....
Joseph Keyes .... do	63 50	....	....
Carrie McCord .... do	51 00	....	....
Will E. Maine .... do	141 50	....	....
Ann Norton .... do	142 50	....	....
Theo. Northrop .... do	48 50	....	....
Geo. W. Wheeler .... do	144 00	....	....
C. E. Rogers .... do	52 50	....	....
Elizabeth Richardson .... do	58 50	....	....
J. M. Sharp .... do	128 00	....	....
W. H. Thomas .... do	47 00	....	....
A. S. Reynolds .... do	2 00	....	....
E. W. Young, organizing Assembly	50 00	....	....
E. W. Young, transcribing Assembly Journal	275 00	....	....
E. W. Young, indexing Assembly Journal	250 00	....	....
		$12,895 00	....
Contesting Seats—Assembly—			
Hiram R. Bond	$175 63	....	....
George E. Weiss	228 00	....	....
		403 63	....

GENERAL FUND DISBURSEMENTS.

Legislative Expenses—continued.			
Printing for Legislature—			
Atwood & Culver—			
Printing for Legislature	$2,738 26		
Senate daily slips	985 41		
Senate bills	1,365 29		
Assembly daily slips	1,436 47		
Assembly bills	2,724 23		
and binding Ass. Jour.	1,456 84		
and binding Sen. Jour.	952 89		
		$11,603 39	
Legislative Manual—			
Atwood & Culver, printing	$2,181 97		
H. B. Hall, port. of O. C. Johnson	40 15		
Seifert, Gugler & Co., engravings	785 00		
A. J. Turner, compiling	500 00		
A. J. Turner, 1,826 copies furnished	3,715 02		
West. B'k N. C., engrav'g title page	79 50		
		7,301 64	
Postage for Legislature—			
Madison Post Office		4,124 20	
Stationery for Legislature—			
Sup't Public Property		985 00	
Gas for Legislature—			
Madison Gas Co		1,589 76	
Visiting Committee on Reformatory and Benevolent Institutions—			
D. G. Cheever	$100 00		
J. E. Irish	100 00		
C. S. Kelsey	100 00		
J. L. Mitchell	100 00		
Joseph Rankin	100 00		
		500 00	
Dells Investigating Committee (1872)—			
F. J. Blair........witness	$14 00		
George Bremmer....do	15 60		
A. B. Braley........do	2 10		
S. D. Burchard......do	2 10		
Charles Burchard....do	8 40		
Orrin Bacon........do	2 10		
J. A. Bate...........do	14 00		
Satterlee Clark......do	2 10		
A. Farr.............do	18 20		
J. C. Gregory........do	2 10		
Joseph Harris.......do	24 00		
G. C. Hazelton......do	2 10		
G. C. Hixon.........do	2 10		
Valentine Knoell....do	5 20		
Aug. Kropf.........do	2 10		
E. W. Keyes........do	2 10		
Thad. C. Pound.....do	22 00		
Sam'l Pratt..........do	2 10		
M. H. Pettit.........do	6 00		

"A."—*Receipts and Disbursements of the Several Funds*—con.

GENERAL FUND DISBURSEMENTS.

Legislative Expenses—continued.			
Dells Investigating Com.—(1872)—con.			
H. L. Palmer,....witness	$8 10		
Wm. Rusch,........do	8 60		
Wm. E. Smith, ...do	2 10		
O. R. Smith,........do	2 10		
Geo. B. Smith,......do	2 10		
J. G. Thorpe,.......do	6 20		
		$177 60	
Soldiers' Orphans' Home Investigating Committee—			
James Batholemew, witness	$6 40		
R. M. Bashford,.......do	2 10		
S. H. Carpenter,......do	2 10		
M. H. Inse, livery	22 00		
Maggie McIntire, witness	14 50		
A. C. Parkinson, ...do	2 10		
Geo. Raymer, ...do	2 10		
W. H. Worden......do	2 10		
		53 40	
Newspapers for Members—			
Atwood & Culver	$1,023 10		
Allen & Hicks	6 00		
Bashford & Wells	27 50		
E. B. Bolens	2 00		
W. H. Belden	4 00		
D. Blumenfeld	3 50		
Brannan & Turner	1 00		
W. H. Bennett	5 50		
C. M. Bright	1 00		
Fred. Borcherdt	1 50		
Brackett & Hunner	6 50		
D. W. Ballou	50		
Henry C. Bowen	4 75		
John R. Bohan	1 50		
C. E. Baker,	6 00		
E. R. Curtiss	23 50		
Cramer, Aikens & Cramer	91 75		
C. J. Cooper	50		
W. W. Coleman	26 00		
Democrat Co	188 75		
P. V. Deuster	84 00		
H. L. Devereux	50		
Sid A. Foster	50		
F. Fleischer	4 50		
Flint & Weber	1 00		
Gazette Printing Co	4 00		
T. J. Gilmore	1 00		
Geo. C. Ginty	1 50		
John P. Hume	4 50		
John Hotchkiss	8 00		
H. J. Hoffman	75		
Johnson, Anderson & Lawson	2 50		
J. H. Johnnson	9 00		
R. H. Johnson	1 50		
Chas. Kohlman	1 00		

"A."—*Receipts and Disbursements of the Several Funds*—con.

GENERAL FUND DISBURSEMENTS.

Legislative Expenses—continued.			
Newspapers for Members—con.			
Chas. Laselle & Co.	$12 00		
Leonard Lottridge	67 50		
McConnell & Smith	179 75		
Milwaukee News	118 60		
Massing & Sitzman	12 00		
Moseley & Bro.	205 85		
H. W. Meyer	1 00		
J. L. & Geo. Marsh	2 00		
Ed. E. Merrett	1 50		
Morrow & Bro.	3 65		
W. J. Park & Co.	152 00		
Porsch & McKenney	4 25		
W. H. Peck	5 00		
Pease & Goodell	50		
J. W. Reynolds	50		
Robinson & Bro	1 00		
Ryan & Bro	1 00		
H. N. Ross	2 00		
John N. Read	2 50		
Carl H. Schmidt	15 00		
J. Y. Scammon	131 00		
Mauritz Schoeffler	24 00		
Symes & Peck	48 00		
Sherman & Gowdy	2 00		
Sentinel Printing Co.	117 75		
F. W. Sackett	2 00		
H. A. Taylor	1 00		
John Turner	50		
M. G. & W. H. Tousley	50		
Wm. L. Utley	1 50		
A. Wibbert	2 50		
J. I. Wirick	1 50		
C. D. Wells	2 00		
W. J. Wrigglesworth	4 00		
J. H. Waggoner	3 00		
E. T. Wrigglesworth	5 00		
Watrous, Kutchin & Co.	5 15		
Walker & Bissell	11 00		
Z. C. & H. M. Wentworth	1 00		
Carl Zillier	3 00		
		$2,694 10	
Total Legislative expenses			$103,730 22
STATE PRISON AND CHARITABLE INSTITUTIONS.			
State Prison, current expenses	$24,815 47		
State Prison, indebtedness	20,735 00		
		$45,550 47	
Hosp. for Insane (Madison), expenses	$58,000 25		
Hosp. for Insane ....do....ass'd co's	29,552 90		
Hosp. for Insane ....do....repairs ..	25,875 00		
Hosp. for Insane ....do....workshop and water supply	6,000 00		
		$119,428 15	

GENERAL FUND DISBURSEMENTS.

State Prison and Charitable Institutions—continued.			
Institute for the Blind, expenses	$15,500 00		
Institute for the Blind, pur'se of land	5,375 00		
		$20,875 00	
Institute for Deaf and Dumb, expens's		23,787 25	
Industrial School for Boys, expenses	$35,050 00		
Ind. Sch. for Boys, assessed on co's	7,165 00		
Ind. School for Boys, improvements	23,500 00		
		65,715 00	
Soldiers' Orphans' Home, expenses	$25,000 00		
Soldiers' Orphans' Home, repairs	2,000 00		
James Bintliff, trustee, expenses	74 50		
C. K. Pier, trustee, expenses	155 00		
Milton Montgomery, trustee, exp's	19 25		
A. J. Ward, trustee, expenses	5 00		
		27,253 75	
Northern Hospital for the Insane—			
Current expenses	$33,750 00		
Lighting, furniture and fixtures	15,000 00		
Purchase of land	2,000 00		
Water supply, ice house and fixtures	19,000 00		
Improvements on ground	5,000 00		
Henry Allen, Artesian well	987 50		
Chas. F. Barron, Freight	308 33		
Jno. Davis & Co., heating apparatus	2,013 21		
John Davis & Co., contractors	6,337 54		
E. M. Danforth, building comm's	404 75		
Fish, Stevens, Sorenson, & Frederickson, contractors	39,148 20		
John Fellenz, contractor	275 56		
Field, Leiter & Co., merchandise	3,051 55		
Hill & Williams, sewerage	881 16		
D. W. Maxon, building comm'r	218 10		
A. M. Skeels	380 80		
McFetridge, Burchard & Co., bl'k'ts	3,053 20		
Henry Oscar, furniture	247 81		
Reynolds & Fellenz, contractors	43,047 90		
James Reynolds, drainage, pipe and cesspools	1,021 50		
Jas. Reynolds, setting steam boilers	581 01		
Jas. Reynolds, digging well	1,400 00		
S. V. Shipman, architect	2,004 85		
A. T. Stewart, mattresses	1,985 28		
James H. Walker, gas works	2,000 00		
Wm. Walters, office rent	40 00		
Treas. Hosp., bal. of building fund	14,539 46		
		198,677 21	
			$501,246 83
MISCELLANEOUS—*Clerk hire.*			
Office of Secretary of State—			
Levi Alden	$1,800 00		
James Bennett	1,083 33		
David O. Bebb	1,650 00		
Wm. N. Cole	866 66		
C. C. Dow	1,500 00		

GENERAL FUND DISBURSEMENTS.

Miscellaneous—Clerk-hire—con.			
Office of Secretary of State—con.			
John T. Jones	$1,625 00		
Charles F. Legate	1,100 00		
Robert Monteith	1,500 00		
D. H. Tullis	1,800 00		
Wm. H. Williams	675 00		
		$13,599 99	
State Treasurer's office—			
Fred Hineman	$1,200 00		
E. L. Hills	300 00		
A. Menges	1,800 00		
W. H. Phipps	1,600 00		
C. E. W. Struve	1,500 00		
E. G. Lindeman, messenger	940 00		
Ed. Rullman, night watch	365 00		
		7,705 00	
Land office—			
W. K. Barney	$1,300 00		
B. F. Cram	1,800 00		
H. H. Davenport	541 00		
E. C. De Moe	1,399 00		
C. M. Foresman	1,600 00		
T. W. Gibbs	1,999 00		
Chas. P. Jacobs	1,001 00		
Julius Lasche	1,300 00		
E. S. McBride	1,500 00		
A. Michelet	1,800 00		
James Ross	1,200 00		
Chas. Young	497 00		
		$14,937 00	
P. L. Spooner, clerk, commissioner of school and university lands		550 00	
			$36 791 99
LABOR ABOUT CAPITOL.			
John Benson		$638 75	
E. O. Hammer		638 75	
Mary Benson		179 35	
Mrs. C. Ryan		40 00	
A. Fink		638 75	
H. H. Himebaugh		125 00	
Geo. W. Baker		320 25	
Thos. Welsh		638 75	
Mary Ryan		16 25	
Mary McCarty		5 00	
Bridget Welsh		13 75	
James Lewis		264 25	
			3,518 85
HEATING APPARATUS.			
Edwin Culver, engineer		$912 50	
B. Sanderson, engineer		417 50	
Dennis O'Keefe, fireman		699 50	
Wm. Shine, fireman		592 00	
			2,621 50

GENERAL FUND DISBURSEMENTS.

***Miscellaneous*—continued.**		
STATE CARPENTERS.		
D. H. Wright	$939 00	
Louis Gootman	860 75	
		$1,799 75
NIGHT WATCHMEN.		
Eugene Bowen	$730 00	
Peter Delmar	692 25	
		1,422 25
JANITOR AND MESSENGER SERVICES.		
C. H. Beyler, supreme court room and state library	$676 50	
Jacob Jenny, governor's office	855 00	
Wm. J. Jones, office of supt. of public property	875 00	
Michael Lynch ...do	638 75	
F. Kohn, agricultural rooms	638 75	
Daniel Kessler, state superintendent's office	792 00	
H. W. Lovejoy, land office	638 75	
T. McGrath, supreme court room and state library	264 25	
E. R. Reed, historical rooms	638 75	
Mark Smith, secretary's office	638 75	
Andrew Peterson, state treasurer's office	638 75	
William Sauthoff, attorney general's office	638 75	
		7,934 00
LABORERS IMPROVING PARK.		
Samuel Andrews	$2 25	
Wm. Burke	17 85	
Pat Cunningham	97 48	
Mat Cronan	17 85	
John Collins	29 40	
Byron Culken	7 50	
John Comford	21 00	
Pat Conlin	23 88	
Pat Caffray	5 25	
J. H. Carr	28 50	
Pat Coyle	5 00	
Pat Dasey	104 98	
Wm. Darmody	9 15	
John Delaney	5 68	
T. Dempsey	45 15	
John Devlin	7 50	
John Daley	17 10	
Barney Foley	108 58	
John Garritz	9 60	
Charles Hughes	12 75	
Pat Higgins	16 35	
J. D. Kelley	53 55	
Martin Kelley	6 60	
Phil Karan	17 85	
J. H. Lowde	9 26	
Ed. Lally	5 10	
M. J. Link	10 50	
Mike Lawless	6 60	
John McKenna	65 40	
C. McClellen	22 65	

"A."—*Receipts and Disbursements of the Several Funds*—con.

GENERAL FUND DISBURSEMENTS.

Miscellaneous—continued.		
Laborers Improving Park—continued.		
Mike Moressey	$176 55	
Morris Morressey	88 66	
Barney Martagh	16 35	
Mike O'Callaghan	111 22	
Mike O'Harrie	28 32	
P. O'Laughlin	18 50	
Mat O'Harrie	17 85	
Tim Purcell	78 50	
Thos. Purcell	42 00	
W. C. Pierce	9 00	
H. H. Rand	180 62	
John Ryan	5 25	
Mike Smith	35 10	
Mike Shanley	3 60	
John Seal	34 50	
James Shotley	45 90	
John Tobin	10 50	
John Wesley	26 16	
		$1,708 19
CONTINGENT EXPENSES.		
American Express Company, express charges	$1 75	
Bunker & Vroman, lumber	426 68	
Charles E. Bross, express charges	440 10	
J. H. D. Baker, merchandise	3 50	
Andrew Bishop, relaying street crossing	12 25	
Clark & Mills, Merchandise	33 33	
Chicago & Northwestern Railroad Co., freight	13 25	
C. C. Church, lumber	15 80	
J. B. Ditto, asphaltum walks in park	1,820 50	
Dan. Delany, brooms	88 75	
Dunning & Sumner, merchandise	839 83	
W. J. & F. Ellsworth, brooms	7 50	
Faley & Lynch, mason work in capitol	79 88	
James E. Fisher, furniture and repairs	509 00	
Fish & Stevens, repairing well in park	28 75	
Fish & Stevens, mason work in capitol	55 43	
J. L. Fulton, repairing walks in park	886 40	
Reuben L. Garlick, crockery	78 75	
Samuel Gardiner, merchandise	54 08	
Huntley & Wootton, salt	3 25	
Hart. St'm B'r Insp. & Ins. Co., insuring boilers	78 75	
John N. Jones, iron wedges	1 50	
Sarah E. Jones, hemming towels	6 90	
Jacob Jenny, inking ribbon, Gov. office	2 00	
H. F. Jewett, pump	116 00	
S. Klauber & Co., merchandise	87 87	
Agnes Kessler, repairing chairs	9 75	
Klauber & Adler, merchandise	16 03	
Daniel Lavin, cleaning well	15 00	
B. & P. Lawrence, merchandise	455 96	
Madison Gas Co., removing lamp posts in park	49 19	
Madison Gas Co., materials, and laying gas pipes	898 90	

"A."—*Receipts and Disbursements of the Several Funds*—con.

GENERAL FUND DISBURSEMENTS.

***Miscellaneous*—continued.**

***Contingent Expenses*—continued.**

Madison Gas Co., gas lamps for park gates	$214 51	....
Madison Gas Co., lamp posts in capitol park......	80 12	....
E. Morden, repairing pumps	17 25	....
Moseley & Bro., merchandise..................	24 65	....
Milwaukee and St. Paul Railroad Co., freight	35 60	....
Madison Manufacturing Co, lamp posts, park gates.	302 40	....
R. G. Norton, repairing clocks................	28 75	....
Newton & Donovan, blacksmithing.............	49 55	....
Tim Purcell, labor with team..................	528 50	....
W. J. Park & Co, merchandise..................	67 59	....
Thos. Regan, gas and steam fittings and repairs....	1,425 15	....
Carl Schmidt, repairing locks	76 00	....
John M. Sumner, hardware.....................	340 10	....
Stark Bros., merchandise......................	36 05	....
Sorrenson & Frederickson, lumber...............	25 10	....
Joseph Schweinem, ice.........................	144 00	....
S. V. Shipman, architect about capitol...........	94 02	....
State Superintendent, dictionary for Sec'y office..	8 00	....
E. Sharpe, plastering in assembly chamber.......	585 00	....
C. R. Stein, lumber	32 58	....
W. P. Towers, painting	1,424 48	....
United States Express Company, express charges.	126 05	....
Vroman & Frank, hardware	175 52	....
Hannah Welsh, soap	18 00	....
Western Bank Note Company, bunting flag	56 00	....
Western Bank Note Co., engraving letter heads...	140 00	....
		$11,631 10

PUBLISHING GENERAL LAWS.

Atwood & Culver, publishing laws in state paper.	$1,553 40	....
E. W. Anderson	60 00	....
Allen & Hicks................................	60 00	....
Atwood & Culver	60 00	....
T. C. Aukeny.................................	60 00	....
Booth & Stone................................	60 00	....
Brannan & Turner	60 00	....
Bunnell & Son................................	60 00	....
G. F. Brigham................................	60 00	....
H. D. Bath	60 00	....
Booth & Gardner..............................	60 00	....
C. M. Bright.................................	60 00	....
Fred Borcherdt...............................	60 00	....
C. H. Boynton	60 00	....
E. B. Bolens.................................	60 00	....
J. J. Beeson	60 00	....
M. Bohan.....................................	60 00	....
D. W. Ballou.................................	60 00	....
D. Blumenfeld................................	60 00	....
Brackett & Hunner	60 00	....
Fred Burkhard	60 00	....
Emma Brown...................................	60 00	....
W. H. Bennett................................	60 00	....
J. R. Bohan	60 00	....

GENERAL FUND DISBURSEMENTS.

Publishing General Laws—continued.		
John N. Brundage	$60 00	....
Byron & Schnitzler	60 00	....
Chas. J. Cooper	60 00	....
E. D. Coe	60 00	....
W. F. Carney	60 00	....
Crucius & Kleinpel	60 00	....
J. H. Culbertson	60 00	....
Chambers & Ingersol	60 00	....
A. C. Croft	60 00	....
Cramer, Aikens & Cramer	60 00	....
A. P. Colby	60 00	....
Silas Chapman	60 00	....
John Cover	60 00	....
C. & S. Corning	60 00	....
W. W. Coleman	60 00	....
N. V. Chandler	60 00	....
Democrat Co	60 00	....
Geo. C. Duffee	60 00	....
De Groff & Rockwell	60 00	....
H. L. Devereux	60 00	....
J. R. Decker	60 00	....
P. V. Deuster	60 00	....
Carl de Haas & Son	60 00	....
Fernandez & O'Bryan	60 00	....
Theo. Friedlander	60 00	....
Chas. H. Fullerton	60 00	....
F. Fleischer	60 00	....
Flint & Weber	60 00	....
S. S. & H. O. Fifield	60 00	....
S. S. Fifield	60 00	....
Sid. A. Foster	60 00	....
E. E. Gordon	60 00	....
Gazette Printing Co	60 00	....
A. T. Glaze	60 00	....
John Gingle	60 00	....
Geo. C. Ginty	60 00	....
H. J. Hoffman	60 00	....
John P. Hume	60 00	....
John Hotchkiss	60 00	....
Hughs & Allen	60 00	....
M. Hirsch	60 00	....
Hoskinson & Follett	60 00	....
I. A. Hoxie	60 00	....
W. D. Hoard	60 00	....
H. Harris	60 00	....
A. D. Harger	60 00	....
J. W. Hall	60 00	....
Haight & Yeomans	60 00	....
A. Heidkamp	60 00	....
Paul Hein	60 00	....
Hauser & Storey	60 00	....
H. G. Ingersol	60 00	....
C. L. Ingersol	60 00	....
Chas. Jonas	60 00	....
O. F. Jones	60 00	....
David Junor	60 00	....

GENERAL FUND DISBURSEMENTS.

Publishing General Laws—continued.		
Griff. O. Jones	$60 00	
R. H. Johnson	120 00	
Geo. S. Kaime	60 00	
J. C. Keeney	60 00	
J. G. Knight	60 00	
G. W. & M. B. Kimball	60 00	
E. O. Kimberly	60 00	
J. H. Keyes	60 00	
Chas. Kohlman	60 00	
Frank Leland	60 00	
Joseph Leicht	60 00	
Luce & Burt	60 00	
Leonard Lottridge	60 00	
J. S. Lightner	60 00	
Chas. A. Leith	60 00	
Fr. Oscar Lincke	60 00	
Hays McKinley	60 00	
D. McBride & Son	60 00	
S. W. Martin	60 00	
M. D. Merrill	60 00	
Milwaukee News Co	60 00	
F. J. Mills	60 00	
H. W. Meyer	60 00	
Ed. E. Merritt	60 00	
Massing & Sitzman	60 09	
J. L. & Geo. Marsh	60 00	
W. S. Munroe	60 00	
Morrow & Bro	60 00	
A. Morse & Son	60 00	
Chas. E. Mears	60 00	
E. B. Northrop	60 00	
L. B. Noyes	60 00	
Wm. Nelson	60 00	
T. G. Olmsted	60 00	
Oliver Brothers	60 00	
J. H. Potter	60 00	
A. F. Pratt	60 00	
H. B. Philleo	60 00	
Pierce & Waterman	60 00	
H. S. Pierpont	60 00	
Pease & Goodell	60 00	
W. H. Peck	60 00	
C. J. Pratt	60 00	
P. M. Pryor	60 00	
P. R. Proctor	60 00	
Porsch & McKenney	60 00	
Read & Miller	60 00	
Ratcliff & Hopkins	60 00	
Ryan & Bro	60 00	
Rounds & Morley	60 00	
J. W. Reynolds	60 00	
Robinson & Bro	60 00	
Read & Bullard	60 00	
M. P. Rindlaub	60 00	
N. N. Ross	60 00	
R. B. Rice	60 00	

GENERAL FUND DISBURSEMENTS.

Publishing General Laws—continued.		
John N. Read	$60 00	
Richards & Powers	60 00	
Albert Reinhart	60 00	
Valentine Ringle	120 00	
A. C. Sandford	60 00	
Smith & Warren	60 00	
A. C. Sholes	60 00	
F. W. Sackett	120 00	
J. N. Stone	60 00	
N. Smith	60 00	
Spencer & Gaynor	60 00	
Symes & Peck	60 00	
Martin C. Short	60 00	
C. Swayze	60 00	
Charles G. Starks	60 00	
Frank Streeter	60 00	
Sherman & Gowdy	60 00	
Carl H. Schmidt	60 00	
Mauritz Scheoffler	60 00	
J. C. Thompson	60 00	
John Turner	60 00	
M. G. & W. H. Tousley	60 00	
H. A. Taylor & Co	60 00	
Wm. L. Utley	60 00	
John Ulrich	60 00	
G. Veeder	60 00	
A. C. Van Metre	60 00	
J. I. Wirick	60 00	
A. D. Wright	60 00	
J. H. Waggoner	60 00	
C. D. Wells	60 00	
Z. C. & L. H. Wentworth	60 00	
Jas. A. Wells	60 00	
D. W. Wilson	60 00	
J. N. Webster	60 00	
Watrous & Kutchin	60 00	
Walker & Bissell	60 00	
Frank O. Wisner	60 00	
A. O. Wilson	60 00	
W. J. Wrigglesworth	120 00	
Charles B. Walworth	30 00	
Worcester & Gorham	60 00	
Carl Zillier	60 00	
		$13,478 40
PUBLISHING PRIVATE AND LOCAL LAWS.		
Allen & Hicks	$1 20	
C. W. Anderson	6 00	
Brannan & Turner	7 20	
C. M. Bright	1 20	
Fred Borcherdt	18 00	
C. H. Boynton	129 60	
Brackett & Hunner	4 80	
W. H. Bennett	132 00	
Cramer, Aikens & Cramer	84 80	
M. C. Carney	1 20	

"A."—*Receipts and Disbursements of the Several Funds*—con.

GENERAL FUND DISBURSEMENTS.

Publishing Private and Local Laws—continued.		
Chas. J. Cooper	$3 00	
De Groff & Rockwell	2 40	
Flint & Weber	3 60	
S. S. & H. O. Fifield	6 60	
Gazette Printing Co	6 60	
Geo. C. Ginty	187 40	
A. T. Glaze	7 20	
John P. Hume	1 20	
John Hotchkiss	1 20	
Hughes & Allen	7 20	
Hoskinson & Follett	22 20	
J. W. Hall	4 80	
Haight & Yoemans	2 40	
W. D. Hoard	2 40	
Hoskinson & Follett	4 20	
David Junor	3 00	
R. H. Johnson	62 20	
G. W. & M. B. Kimball	1 80	
Joseph Leicht	1 20	
Leonard Lottridge	2 40	
Hays McKinley	3 00	
D. McBride & Son	3 00	
J. L. & Geo. Marsh	1 80	
Chas. E. Mears	7 20	
Ed. E. Merritt	1 80	
E. B. Northrop	9 00	
Wm. Nelson	1 80	
H. B. Philleo	30 00	
C. J. Pratt	132 60	
Pease & Goodell	1 80	
J. W. Reynolds	4 20	
H. N. Ross	4 20	
N. Smith	71 40	
J. N. Stone	21 60	
Sentinel Printing Co	21 00	
H. A. Taylor & Co	11 40	
Wm. L. Utley	5 40	
J. I. Wirick	1 20	
J. H. Waggoner	2 40	
C. B. Walworth	81 00	
Watrous, Kutchin & Co	12 00	
W. J. Wrigglesworth	7 20	
Worcester & Gorham	2 40	
		$1,056 40
ADVERTISING SALES OF LAND.		
Allen & Hicks	$18 80	
Atwood & Culver	47 85	
E. W. Anderson	11 75	
C. M. Bright	27 60	
J. M. Brackett	42 70	
Fred. Borcherdt	12 00	
Wm. H. Bennett	9 40	
Brannan & Turner	10 00	
Booth & Stone	9 50	
Chas. J. Cooper	32 60	

GENERAL FUND DISBURSEMENTS.

Advertising Land Sales—continued.		
Cramer, Aikens & Cramer	$13 60	
John Cover	25 85	
O. R. Dahl	5 50	
De Graff & James	30 05	
Flint & Weber	19 05	
Sid. A. Foster	14 10	
Sam. S. Fifield	18 80	
Geo. C. Ginty	89 85	
Gazette Printing Co	84 50	
J. W. Hall	89 00	
H. Harris	25 75	
Hughes & Allen	9 40	
Hoskinson & Follett	11 75	
M. Hirsch	9 40	
Haight & Yeomans	18 60	
John P. Hume	30 05	
J. E. Ingraham	22 00	
D. Junior	20 15	
R. H. Johnson	23 00	
Kimball & Moore	62 00	
G. W. & M. B. Kimball	9 40	
Luce & Burt	10 00	
D. McBride & Son	85 60	
M. H. McCord	51 50	
Ed. E. Merritt	21 90	
J. L. Marsh & Co	9 40	
Chas. E. Mears	26 00	
W. S. Munroe	27 70	
E. B. Northrop	21 50	
Wm. Nelson	47 60	
Pierce & Waterman	21 15	
Pease & Goodell	32 40	
J. M. Reed	14 10	
Republican & Leader	37 50	
H. N. Ross	18 60	
Sentinel Printing Co	20 95	
Stone & Beach	27 00	
N. Smith	12 50	
H. A. Taylor & Co	69 05	
John Turner	21 15	
J. I. Wyrick	25 85	
Waggoner & Stevens	20 00	
W. J. Wrigglesworth	11 75	
J. H. Waggoner	18 60	
Watrous, Kutchin & Co	18 60	
		$1,852 90
Atwood & Culver, pub. notices and proclamations		825 10
PRINTING.		
Atwood & Culver—		
Printing blanks for secretary of state	$2,692 06	
........do........ state treasurer	711 40	
........do........ state superintendent	1,868 84	
........do........ supreme court	248 16	
........do........ attorney general	4 88	
........do........ comm'rs S. & U. lands	1,526 44	

GENERAL FUND DISBURSEMENTS.

Printing—continued.		
Atwood & Culver—		
Printing blanks for Board of Charities & Reform	$212 61	....
........do.........State Historical Society....	40 44	....
........do.........Governor................	342 60	....
........do.........Commissioner Immigration	2 94	....
........do.........Commissioner of Insurance.	550 73	....
........do.........Supt. Public Property......	167 72	....
........do.........Qr. Master and Adj. General	48 74	....
....do.........Treasury Agent............	63 88	....
Printing Report Com's School and Uni. Lands .	115 91	....
........do......Northern Wis. Hosp. for Insane	74 72	....
........do......State Treasurer..............	220 91	....
........do......Institute for Deaf and Dumb ..	195 56	....
........do......Industrial School for Boys	190 90	....
........do......Institute for the Blind.........	144 38	....
... .do......Hospital for the Insane, Madi'n	229 76	....
........do......Academy of Science..........	642 25	....
........do......State Prison	458 14	....
........do......Qr. Master and Adj. Generals ..	109 00	....
........do......Secretary of State............	575 52	....
........do......Soldiers' Orphans' Home......	197 64	....
........do......Regents of the University.....	424 68	....
........do......State Superintendent..........	5,482 21	....
........do......Board of Charities and Reform	1,709 73	....
........do......Commissioner of Insurance....	2,191 11	....
........do......State Historical Society	1,491 35	....
....do......State Agricultural Society.....	5,463 15	....
Printing Transactions State Agricultural Soc'y.	3,836 80	....
....do...Governor's Message and Documents ..	3,147 28	....
....do...School code	2,637 17	....
....do...Election registers....................	7,953 75	....
....do...Assessment laws	212 70	....
....do...Laws of 1873........................	12,445 72	....
....do...Blank books—marriages, births and deaths, furnished counties..........	3,272 50	....
		$61,403 78
POSTAGE.		
Madison Post Office, stamps for Governor	$193 73	....
....do.... Secretary of State.	591 74	....
....do.... State Treasurer...	709 05	....
....do....State Superintend't	943 28	....
....do.... Attorney General.	36 18	....
....do ... Land Department.	234 00	....
....do.... Insurance Depart.	141 20	....
....do.... Supt. Pub. Prop..	118 10	....
....do ... Supreme Court...	171 06	....
....do.... State Hist. Soc'y..	522 85	....
....do.... State B. C. & Ref.	86 00	....
....do ... Adjutant General.	15 00	....
....do.... Treasury Agent ..	67 25	....
Box rent and unpaid postage.	176 86	....
		$4,006 30
REAL ESTATE RETURNS.		
Charles Bowler	$32 24	....
C. W. Brown..................................	10 56	....

GENERAL FUND DISBURSEMENTS.

Real Estate Returns—continued.		
Henry Colonius	$24 32	....
Ernst Clarenback	18 00	....
C. A. Capron	5 44	....
Arthur Connelly	9 84	....
Ben. Evans	10 40	....
Wm. Gudden	33 92	....
T. J. Hutton	15 84	....
John Kelley, Jr.	8 00	....
H. B. Lowe	12 00	....
Matthew McCord	7 92	....
Richard Mutz	31 20	....
Aug. Meyer	16 80	....
T. C. L. Mackay	10 32	....
C. A. Noyes, Jr.	26 80	....
F. A. Noll	4 40	....
Mair Pointon	28 16	....
C. H. Pierce	3 84	....
W. H. Packard	13 52	....
D. B. Sommers	13 44	....
Gilbert Tennant	7 60	....
C. E. Tanbery	28 48	....
W. A. Vaughan	6 56	....
L. Wachinheimer	21 76	....
James Woodhouse	13 20	....
R. R. Young	18 40	....
		$432 96
NORMAL INSTITUTES.		
Hosea Barnes	$152 90	....
V. V. Barnes	59 76	....
Chas. W. Clinton	58 05	....
A. Earthman	144 15	....
W. H. Holford	25 25	....
A. J. Hutton	185 95	....
J. B. Holbrook	51 10	....
Michael Kirwan	48 00	....
D. McGregor	151 20	....
A. F. North	140 00	....
Geo. Patton	5 00	....
J. C. Pickard	174 80	....
W. D. Parker	148 55	....
B. M. Reynolds	136 85	....
O. R. Smith	143 00	....
O. Salisbury	75 15	....
E. H. Sprague	131 65	....
Geo. Skewes	91 00	....
J. H. Terry	7 80	....
J. B. Thayer	85 00	....
A. O. Wright	83 00	....
		2,043 16
STATE BOARD OF CHARITIES AND REFORM.		
Samuel D. Hastings, secretary, salary	$1,500 00	....
Samuel D. Hastings, secretary's expenses	172 70	....
Samuel D. Hastings, expense of board	59 20	....
W. Merrill, expenses of board	4 00	....

GENERAL FUND DISBURSEMENTS.

State Board of Charities and Reform—continued.		
W. C. Allen, member of board, expenses	$35 35	
H. H. Giles, member of board, expenses	30 75	
Mrs. M. C. Lynde, member of board, expenses	50 70	
Willard Merrill, member of board, expenses	19 50	
		$1,872 20
MILITIA.		
N. W. Dean, storing caissons	$38 55	
Angus McDonald, state armorer	1,019 50	
Chas. J. Martin, military secretary	400 00	
John Pincheon, hauling arms	2 00	
A. Scott, freight and cartage on arms	58 81	
Aug. Herfurth, powder for salutes	30 00	
Charles May, repairing artillery	267 50	
Milwaukee & St. Paul R'y Co., freight on arms	28 95	
W. A. Oppell, food for eagles	30 05	
Isaac Van Wie, storing caissons	8 75	
Chicago & N. W. R'y Co., freight on arms	12 60	
Chas. A. DeVillius, freight on arms	11 06	
Robt. Monteith, Adj. Gen., mileage inspecting mil.	236 10	
R. D. Pike, freight on arms	15 70	
		2,154 57
PARK FENCE.		
Chicago & N. W. R'y Co., freight	$22 75	
L. P. Drake, surveying	25 00	
Deiner & Robinson, gate post caps	500 00	
Fish & Stevens, curbing and paving around fence	5,598 31	
J. B. Gavin, patterns for lamp posts	55 00	
Gould Bros. & Dibble, figures for park gate posts	825 00	
Madison Manufacturing Company, iron work	9,610 40	
Tim Purcell, grading street around park fence	400 00	
Tim Purcell, labor	46 60	
Thos. J. Shummin, Jr., stone work	9,023 25	
Singer & Talcott, stone	1,380 45	
S. V. Shipman, architect	500 00	
		27,986 76
PARK IMPROVEMENT.		
J. B. Ditto, asphaltum walks and drives	$862 29	
L. P. Drake, laying out walks and drives	75 00	
Geo. P. Delaplaine, park commission expenditures	697 36	
John N. Jones, tools for park commissioners	5 00	
		1,639 65
CAPITOL IMPROVEMENT.		
James Z. V. Blaney, analyzing artesian well water	$50 00	
Park commissioners, work and material	1,170 47	
Democrat Co., advertising	34 50	
Fish & Stevens, coal vault	6,554 56	
J. L. Fulton, concrete walks and drives	7,781 13	
Gazette Printing Co., advertising	32 75	
Tim Purcell, digging well	240 00	
Sentinel Printing Co., advertising	6 50	
S. V. Shipman, architect	950 00	
John Davis & Co., water-works	2,871 00	

GENERAL FUND DISBURSEMENTS.

Capitol Improvement—continued.		
Fish & Stevens, wa'r w'ks, well, pump and house..	$4,036 98	....
Fish & Stevens, labor and material..............	19 95	....
Samuel Gardiner, electrical apparatus............	2,550 00	....
John N. Jones, tools	37 58	....
Thomas Regan, water works....................	496 82	....
		$26,832 24
PRESIDENTIAL ELECTORS.		
H. D. Barron	$75 30	....
Wm. E. Cramer	22 50	....
F. Fleischer	30 50	....
Geo. E. Hoskinson..............................	40 50	....
Fred. Hilgen...................................	26 50	....
Ed. E. McFetridge..............................	32 50	....
J. S. Nickles..................................	14 50	....
Geo. E. Swain..................................	15 50	....
O. B. Thomas...................................	22 50	....
G. Van Steenwyk	16 50	....
		296 80
COUNTY AGRICULTURAL SOCIETIES.		
Adams County Agricultural Society..............	$100 00	....
Buffalo..............do.........................	100 00	....
Columbia ....do.........................	100 00	....
Crawford.............do.........................	100 00	....
Dane.................do.........................	100 00	....
Dodge ....do.........................	100 00	....
Door.................do.........................	100 00	....
Fond du Lac ....do.........................	100 00	....
Grant ....do.........................	100 00	....
Green ....do.........................	100 00	....
Green Lake...........do.........................	100 00	....
Iowa.................do.........................	100 00	....
Jackson..............do.........................	100 00	....
Jefferson ....do.........................	100 00	....
Juneau...............do.........................	100 00	....
Kenosha ....do.........................	100 00	....
La Crosse ....do.........................	100 00	....
La Fayette...........do.........................	100 00	....
Marathon ....do.........................	100 00	....
Marquette ....do.........................	100 00	....
Monroe ....do.........................	100 00	....
Outagamie ....do.........................	100 00	....
Ozaukee..............do.........................	100 00	....
Pierce...............do.........................	100 00	....
Portage ....do.........................	100 00	....
Racine ....do.........................	100 00	....
Richland.............do.........................	100 00	....
Rock.................do.........................	100 00	....
Sauk.................do.........................	100 00	....
Sheboygan ....do.........................	100 00	....
Trempealeau ....do.........................	100 00	....
Vernon...............do.........................	100 00	....
Walworth ....do.........................	100 00	....
Washington ....do.........................	100 00	....
Waukesha.............do.........................	100 00	....
Winnebago............do.........................	100 00	....
		$3,600 00

GENERAL FUND DISBURSEMENTS.

SUPERIOR HARBOR PROTECTION.		
W. H. Newton, protecting Superior harbor	$2,178 62	
Atwood & Culver, printing brief	21 25	
H. S. Orton, attorney fees	1,000 00	
H. N. Sitzer........do	236 75	
Enoch Totten, services and disbursements	573 52	
C. C. Washburn, governor, expenses	219 00	
		$4,229 14
IMMIGRATION COMMISSION.		
O. C. Johnson, commissioner	$2,500 00	
O. C. Johnson, postage and express charges	218 86	
John T. Jones, Welsh pamphlets	350 00	
Seifert, Gugler & Co., maps, engravings, ex. chges.	263 00	
J. A. Becher, German pamphlets and translating	500 00	
G. De Nevin, French pamphlets	75 00	
Wilson & Jurgens, freight	18 78	
F. M. Wallem, pamphlets	615 34	
F. A. Herscher, translating pamphlets	50 00	
Johnson, Anderson & Larson, advertising	100 00	
Tobias Jacobson, agent	56 25	
F. M. Wallem, advertising	50 00	
J. A. Becher, lithographing	150 00	
Peter Langland, agent (Chicago)	243 75	
		5,190 98
LAND PROTECTION.		
D. E. Catlin	$1,200 00	
O. R. Dahl	1,999 92	
John Reynolds	2,732 00	
		5,931 92
APPRAISING LAND.		
Wm. Montague	$5 00	
O. W. Spaulding	5 00	
		10 00
EXAMINERS OF STATE TEACHERS.		
Martha E. Hazard	$55 25	
Alexander Kerr	59 60	
I. N. Stewart	61 00	
		175 85
GEOLOGICAL SURVEY.		
John Murrish	$780 00	
I. A. Lapham	7,500 00	
		8,280 00
STATE BOARD OF EQUALIZATION.		
J. H. Waggoner, secretary	$50 00	
Charles Young, messenger	9 00	
W. J. Force	20 00	
		79 00
FISH CULTURE.		
I. A. Lapham, expense procuring fish eggs	$26 70	
Wayne Ramsay........do..........do	341 60	
		368 30

GENERAL FUND DISBURSEMENTS.

BOUNTY ON WILD ANIMALS.		
M. F. Adams	$20 00	
A. P. Andrews	5 00	
Elias Anderson	25 00	
Fred Aherns	5 00	
Solomon Aikens	5 00	
Henry Acker	8 00	
Hiram Allen	10 00	
Calvin Anderson	15 00	
Christian Ableman	5 00	
J. W. Austin	5 00	
R. J. Atwood	5 00	
Josiah Adams	9 00	
A. Anderson	5 00	
Jacob Allinger	85 00	
J. S. Andrews	5 00	
Edgar Abbott	8 00	
Wallace Andrew	15 00	
Franklin Adams	40 00	
James H. Adee	5 00	
Wm. Alverson	5 00	
A. A. Arms	5 00	
Henry Archer	8 00	
Philip Apple	5 00	
Matthew T. Adams	5 00	
Amos Arnold	5 00	
M. T. Adams	20 00	
Henry Althens	10 00	
John Basner	5 00	
D. F. Bestor	85 00	
Wm. Brawner	5 00	
B. F. Bentley	5 00	
Seth Barns	5 00	
James Brown	10 00	
Peter T. Butness	5 00	
John Bell	6 00	
James Brothers	8 00	
David Brittz	8 00	
A. Blont	5 00	
Simon Bartness	5 00	
A. Burt	5 00	
L. H. Boughton	15 00	
Ira Blood	15 00	
R. J. Burcham	12 00	
A. H. Best	8 00	
M. E. Bradley	5 00	
W. J. Bear	5 00	
Frank Bigelow	5 00	
M. R. Burcham	8 00	
Thos. Bright	9 90	
John Bradley	8 00	
G. Bishop	8 00	
John Blair	8 00	
Lewis Beach	8 00	
Joseph Blain	5 00	
V. R. Barnard	5 00	
Henry Borst	10 00	

GENERAL FUND DISBURSEMENTS.

Bounty on Wild Animals—continued.		
Samuel Barrett	$5 00	
J. W. Bentis	5 00	
Jesse Blanco	5 00	
Orin Byington	5 00	
M. H. Brownell	5 00	
John Bowles	5 00	
A. N. Brackett	35 00	
N. Brery	75 00	
Robt. H. Bennetto	40 00	
D. F. Bestor	5 00	
L. H. Boughton	10 00	
Chancy Blancher	5 00	
J. E. Borah	8 00	
Frank Bogar	8 00	
James Bolster	25 00	
A. Bonner	25 00	
Alfred Bliss	20 00	
Chas. Bowen	20 00	
Herman Bishop	40 00	
John L. Bennett	10 00	
Jas. H. Buckley	5 00	
Fred Burges	5 00	
N. N. Berge	5 00	
V. R. Brainard	5 00	
Stephen Burris	10 00	
Richard Brown	8 00	
David Bestor	5 00	
F. J. Bevry	5 00	
Alfred Bonner	25 00	
G. S. Burdick, Jr	5 00	
L. H. Coe	18 00	
G. W. Collins	10 00	
Geo. O. Colburn	8 00	
Darwin Costley	8 00	
G. F. Cook	15 00	
Michael Cassiday	8 00	
S. A. Colegrove	8 00	
Harry Coats	5 00	
W. W. Chinnock	25 00	
J. J. Cooper	5 00	
B. J. Coyhis	8 00	
Geo. Clarage	10 00	
Willis Cool	8 00	
S. R. Canon	5 00	
W. D. Campbell	5 00	
Wm. Cannon	5 00	
G. W. Conlee	10 00	
Wm. Craham	5 00	
T. N. Canon	5 00	
Wm. Cowper	5 00	
C. F. Curtiss	5 00	
J. A. Coats	5 00	
Edward Combs	25 00	
Wm. Cragg	25 00	
David Conway	10 00	
Thos. Crisman	8 00	

"A."—*Receipts and Disbursements of the Several Funds*—con.

GENERAL FUND DISBURSEMENTS.

Bounty on Wild Animals—continued.		
John Corydon	$5 00	
David Chidister	5 00	
Jos. Cook	10 00	
W. W. Chennock	10 00	
Joseph Cragg	5 00	
Wm. Canan	8 00	
C. D. Cook	5 00	
James Crossen	5 00	
Wm. Cragg	6 00	
O. S. Cook	8 00	
O. V. Davis	5 00	
Stewart Daniels	5 00	
W. H. Davis	18 00	
Joseph Dennis	5 00	
A. S. Davis	8 00	
Henry Dooley	5 00	
F. De Voe	5 00	
Lucean Dewey	21 00	
J. H. Densmore	5 00	
R. E. Doty	5 00	
Patrick Dorsey	8 00	
John Davis	8 00	
Wm. Ducher	8 00	
Joseph Dixon	15 00	
David Downer	5 00	
Frank Dun Levy	5 00	
J. H. Densmore	5 00	
N. Darling	35 00	
Dewit Dennis	5 00	
Wm. Davis	85 00	
Benj. Dearmond	10 00	
W. S. Dunbar	10 00	
John Dish	5 00	
Joseph Dennis	5 00	
Joseph Dixon	14 00	
Francis Durn	8 00	
Lucean Dewey	8 00	
Alfred Divall	10 00	
David Day	5 00	
W. J. Davis	5 00	
T. Erickson	10 00	
Thos. Eaton	5 00	
Luke Elam	20 00	
Alief Emerson	5 00	
Otto Esser	5 00	
L. Edgcomb	10 00	
Nathan Elliott	5 00	
Albert Ellis	5 00	
L. Edgcomb	10 00	
W. J. Evans	40 00	
Christian Engroff	5 00	
J. Eckelkrout	10 00	
S. R. Eldredge	40 00	
J. S. Eastman	20 00	
Andrew Everson	85 00	
Henry Evans	55 00	

GENERAL FUND DISBURSEMENTS.

Bounty on Wild Animals—continued.

Wm. Egan	$5 00	
Geo. Englert	20 00	
Geo. B. Evans	10 00	
D. E. Evans	5 00	
Luke Elam	5 00	
Louis Fredler	5 00	
A. Fry	5 00	
John Farneau	5 00	
L. H. Fessenden	5 00	
W. M. Fleek	10 00	
L. D. Fitcroft	3 00	
Knud Fingerson	5 00	
Edwin France	84 00	
Daniel Fitzgerald	10 00	
John Foley	3 00	
James Finnegan	5 00	
Madison Frazier	85 00	
Edwin France	105 00	
Chas. Frazier	25 00	
Jonathan Fitchett	5 00	
Robert Finley	5 00	
Sam'l Fitzgerald	20 00	
Oscar Freeman	5 00	
M. L. Graham	5 00	
E. Grimes	10 00	
Henry Gortz	3 00	
Frank Gatwinkle	5 00	
H. F. Goff	5 00	
Henry Gutwinkle	10 00	
Joseph Graves	5 00	
Miles Griswald	5 00	
Gulick Gulickson	5 00	
Andrew Gulickson	3 00	
Thos. Goodyear	5 00	
Louis Gregor	25 00	
George Gerrard	10 00	
Nathan George	5 00	
John A. George	30 00	
John Gray	10 00	
J. L. Gillespie	163 00	
Frank Goodwin	3 00	
R. B. Gillespie	15 00	
E. George	5 00	
David George	5 00	
Chas. Geissbachler	3 00	
H. C. Gleason	3 00	
Isaac Garinger	5 00	
Herman Gilson	5 00	
W. H. Gilbert	5 00	
Albrecht Gartman	5 00	
Byron Gilman	12 00	
James Gibbon	5 00	
Honest John (Indian)	5 00	
August Haack	5 00	
Gustav Huber	6 00	
C. Hutchinson	5 00	

GENERAL FUND DISBURSEMENTS.

Bounty on Wild Animals—continued.		
Casper Hatter	$10 00	
Edward Hodget	5 00	
R. J. Henry	5 00	
W. S. Hamilton	8 00	
S. B. Hewitt, Jr.	20 00	
H. Hupel	8 00	
J. V. Huntsinger	5 00	
James Hough	5 00	
W. Hamilton	8 00	
T. C. Hyatt	5 00	
M. L. Howe	5 00	
C. Haskell	15 00	
Benj. Hodgson	5 00	
Hiram Hudson	5 00	
B. F. Hobert	5 00	
J. Hutchinson, Jr	5 00	
Joseph Hutchinson	5 00	
James Hough	5 00	
P. D. Heckerson	8 00	
Ole T. Hegna	8 00	
Henry Hanson	8 00	
Jerman Hendee	5 00	
A. Harrington	8 00	
Ole Halvorson	5 00	
Hans Hanson	10 00	
G. W. Hitchens	8 00	
Lewis Halverson	5 00	
Charles Hall	10 00	
H. Harnden	5 00	
W. H. Halbert	8 00	
Jacob Hill	5 00	
James Hunter	5 00	
Joshua Hicks	10 00	
Wm. P. Hall	5 00	
Ole Halverson	10 00	
W. H. Hatrick	5 00	
Malcom Horton	15 00	
W. S. Hamilton	5 00	
Rudolph Horsley	5 00	
A. Harrington	5 00	
David Henry	25 00	
J. Heath and J. Hitchen	45 00	
Wm. Houghton	85 00	
Wm. R. Heath	10 00	
Patrick Hickey	5 00	
Tory Hanson	5 00	
James Heath	83 00	
W. S. Hamilton	18 00	
Hiram Hill	25 00	
Thos. Hore	5 00	
Edmund Holly	15 00	
J. Hoover	8 00	
Ole Iverson	10 00	
Indian (Charlie)	5 00	
Holmes Ives	80 00	
Edward Inman	80 00	

GENERAL FUND DISBURSEMENTS.

Bounty on Wild Animals—continued.

B. Johnson	$5 00	
Isaac Jenkins	5 00	
Geo. F. Jackson	5 00	
Knud Johnson	9 00	
Wm. Jack	12 00	
Wm. M. Johnson	10 00	
Oliver Johnson	8 00	
R. L. Joiner	9 00	
J. R. Jones, Jr.	10 00	
Sam'l Johnson	5 00	
Ole Johnson	5 00	
John Johnson	5 00	
John E. Jones	5 00	
Frank Jones	40 00	
J. R. Jones	5 00	
Knud Johnson	45 00	
A. C. Joslin	5 00	
Martin Jones	5 00	
John R. Jones	10 00	
L. T. Jay	5 00	
Geo. Kelly	6 00	
H. F. Kenslee	5 00	
K. Knudson	20 00	
Stephen Kellogg	8 00	
Wm. P. Kelly	5 00	
D. Kingsley	5 00	
J. Kellar	25 00	
Ole Kringle	12 00	
Jonathan Keyser	5 00	
James Kitchen	80 00	
Jacob Kundert	5 00	
Myron Keys	5 00	
Nicholas Kenyon	5 00	
Oley Knudson	8 00	
H. Knutson	5 00	
K. Knutson	5 00	
Peter Lasher	8 00	
Frank Lewis	8 00	
E. Love	6 00	
C. Lever	5 00	
E. Lamphere	10 00	
L. Lamphere	6 00	
Jonas Love	2 00	
Zac Love	8 00	
W. H. Lobdell	5 00	
John Lane	8 00	
Geo. Leach	5 00	
Rufus Lord	6 00	
Matthew Leach	5 00	
Orsamus Larson	5 00	
Chas. Luck	5 00	
E. Lamphere	8 00	
L. Lamphere	10 00	
Peter Ludinger	5 00	
Patrick Langan	20 00	
Conrad Lees	85 00	

"A"—*Receipts and Disbursements of the Several Funds*—con.

GENERAL FUND DISBURSEMENTS.

Bounty on Wild Animals—continued.		
L. D. Layton	$30 00	
Joachim Legler	5 00	
Franz Lanstedt	5 00	
Johanna Lynch	5 00	
Emerson Little	6 00	
B. McDermot	5 00	
W. McBoyle	3 00	
O. J. McGillon	5 00	
John McKenzie	9 00	
J. M. McClune	5 00	
Michael McKinnan	5 00	
Chas. A. McBride	5 00	
Geo. E. McIntosh	9 00	
Charles McCarty	8 00	
Gardner McLean	5 00	
Patrick McDermot	5 00	
Thos. McCarty	3 00	
Louis McKahan	5 00	
Jas. McConnell	15 00	
Seth Moor	5 00	
A. Motley	5 00	
C. F. Marden	8 00	
Wm. Muzzy	5 00	
Peter A. Meickle	8 00	
Benj. Maxwell	24 00	
Felix Maguire	15 00	
Benj. Monteith	8 00	
Spencer Monroe	5 00	
A. E. Morrison	8 00	
John Morrison	8 00	
James Moore	3 00	
John Marlett	5 00	
Daniel Morris	5 00	
Wm. L. Mathewson	8 00	
J. J. Mathewson	8 00	
Henry Miller	8 00	
A. E. Mathewson	15 00	
John Mashagne	6 00	
A. W. Moore	8 00	
Christopher Matson	5 00	
P. C. Moulton	6 00	
Edward Metcalf	10 00	
Joseph Meyer	5 00	
John Mashane	3 00	
Halver Martinson	8 00	
John Morrison	8 00	
John Metcalf	5 00	
Jas. A. Mosher	5 00	
A. C. Morrison	5 00	
Peter A. Mickle	51 00	
P. D. Minor	5 00	
J. E Mathews	10 00	
Lars P. Moe	15 00	
Michael Maring	40 00	
J. A. Mathews & E. A. Graves	30 00	
J. A. Meacham	25 00	

GENERAL FUND DISBURSEMENTS.

Bounty on Wild Animals—continued.		
Wm. Merrill	$5 00	
Albert Mathews	10 00	
Thos. C. Morrow	40 00	
W. H. Moore	20 00	
Michael Minle	5 00	
Edward Morrison	8 00	
Peter A. Mickle	8 00	
Lyman Norton	20 00	
W. Nicholdson	5 00	
G. E. Norton	12 00	
W. S. Newland	8 00	
Nels E. Nelson	15 00	
J. B. Newkirk	8 00	
Knud Neilson	5 00	
Fred. Nipple	85 00	
Henry Nold	5 00	
F. A. Oscar	5 00	
John P. Oleson	43 00	
Andrew Oleson	8 00	
Lyman Ormsby	3 00	
Ole T. Oleson	15 00	
Martin O'Brien	6 00	
John Oleson	5 00	
Michael Oleson	8 00	
Ole Oleson	50 00	
Wm. Ostrander	5 00	
Ou Au (Indian)	5 00	
John O'Riley	40 00	
Charles Pompert	10 00	
J. W. Pennister	5 00	
Wm. M. Prentice	10 00	
James D. Pittullo	6 00	
John Plimpton	5 00	
R. J. Pearce	5 00	
Chauncey Pierce	5 00	
John V. Person	8 00	
W. H. Peck	6 00	
A. Perkinson	9 00	
Henry W. Pradt	80 00	
Evan Peterson	5 00	
Elijah Powell	6 00	
John Powell	5 00	
E. R. Peck	5 00	
John Parks	3 00	
Wallace Porter	5 00	
David Primmer	5 00	
Justin Pierce	85 00	
Sylvanus Powell	75 00	
A. L. Palmer	25 00	
Smith Pierce	5 00	
Robert Pollard	85 00	
John Plimpton	10 00	
Geo. Paylor	25 00	
John V. Persons	5 00	
Michael Quinn	25 00	
Edward Rogers	5 00	

"A."—*Receipts and Disbursements of the Several Funds*—con.

GENERAL FUND DISBURSEMENTS.

Bounty on Wild Animals—continued.

Cossett Riley	$15 00	
E. E. Renn	8 00	
David Row	5 00	
John W. Roberts	5 00	
Abram Rood	15 00	
John Reynolds,	5 00	
Howard Ropp	5 00	
Thos. Rowe	5 00	
L. B. Ripley	5 00	
John Rowley	5 00	
Robert Rogers	6 00	
Winsten Remy	5 00	
John A. Ruble	5 00	
L. F. Rowell	10 00	
John C. Rowell	8 00	
J. O. Rundahl	8 00	
Geo. W. Rutter	8 00	
Charles Randall	6 00	
Wm. Roache	6 00	
M. Rouse	10 00	
John Roach	8 00	
J. Raisbeck	45 00	
Joshua Reese	5 00	
Michael Ryan	20 00	
Thos. Robson	5 00	
Wm. Ramsey, Sen	5 00	
Robert Ray	15 00	
Cosset Riley	15 00	
Pierce Roberts	25 00	
John Reel	5 00	
Wm. Reynolds	8 00	
James O. Rundall	8 00	
G. Rumage	12 00	
H. Robinson	5 00	
John Sleep	5 00	
Herman Stone	20 00	
J. W. Stanson	5 00	
B. F. Stewart	8 00	
Patrick Sheaman	5 00	
Lyman Smelk	5 00	
Evan Stocksith	9 00	
Adam Smith	6 00	
Patrick Smith	20 00	
Jesse Scott	8 00	
W. A. Smith	5 00	
Jacob Silbraugh	8 00	
Ole Syverson	6 00	
Robert Stone	5 00	
C. H. Sager	5 00	
Thomas Studley	10 00	
Edward Seeber	8 00	
F. W. Sylvester	8 00	
J. L. Stubondy,	5 00	
W. T. Sterling	5 00	
Isham Stevens	5 00	
John Stenner	5 00	

GENERAL FUND DISBURSEMENTS.

Bounty on Wild Animals—continued.		
Thos. Sutcliff	$5 00	
Samuel Searls	5 00	
Nathan Skeels	6 00	
Geo. Sterliug	8 00	
W. L. Sheely	6 00	
G. Schimmick	3 00	
Evan Stockset	3 00	
Patrick Smith	10 00	
A. F. Smith	3 00	
Peter Schneider	5 00	
H. O. Sullivan	10 00	
James Smith	5 00	
Michael Simer	5 00	
Taylor Swan	5 00	
Ferdinand Schneiber	5 00	
Mason Sparrow	5 00	
Wm. Shurtliff	30 00	
H. M. Sheldon	35 00	
Samuel Sherman	5 00	
W. A. Sexton	5 00	
J. P. Smith	30 00	
W. S. Stroud	5 00	
A. K. Stow	5 00	
James Smith	10 00	
Daniel Staples	5 00	
Geo. W. Sparrow	35 00	
Casper Salmon	70 00	
Arthur Sylvester	25 00	
Thos. Solan	40 00	
John Smith	45 00	
Henry Stucky	3 00	
Alfred Scidmore	6 00	
M. J. Swart	25 00	
Daniel St. Otis	5 00	
Herman Stone	10 00	
W. A. Sholts	20 00	
Anton Shulka	30 00	
John Sheffler	5 00	
E. Turner	5 00	
H. M. Terens	5 00	
B. F. Taylor	9 00	
W. W Trimmer	30 00	
C. E. Thomas	5 00	
N. S. Taylor	9 00	
Thomas Tibbitts	5 00	
G. W. Thorpe	5 00	
K. Turner	3 00	
Evan Thomas	5 00	
Francis Thompson	5 00	
C. Thompson	5 00	
Morris Terberry	5 00	
Daniel Taylor	3 00	
Kennister Turner	6 00	
E. Tichenor	5 00	
Thomas Tibbitts	10 00	
Mark Townsend	5 00	

GENERAL FUND DISBURSEMENTS.

Bounty on Wild Animals—continued.

E. Taylor	9 00	
K. Turner	8 00	
Evan Thomas	10 00	
Geo. Theobald	5 00	
C. H. Thomas	8 00	
Patrick Turrey	8 00	
J. S. Tucker	5 00	
Samuel Truax	5 00	
Oscar Tyru	5 00	
Martin Thoreson	5 00	
Ephraim Thompson	58 00	
Charles Terwillegar	5 00	
J. C. Thompson	10 00	
H. Y. Underhill	20 00	
John Voss	5 00	
O. D. Vincent	50 00	
R. Van Buskirk	5 00	
Bartley Welsh	5 00	
Jesse Walker	15 00	
D. C. Ware	55 00	
Reuben Warren	8 00	
Alex. Wood	8 00	
Daniel Weaver	8 00	
Joseph Wanyeck	8 00	
A. H. Wells	5 00	
Richard Wilson	5 00	
H. C. Webb	8 00	
Wm. Withy	8 00	
Leader Willard	8 00	
H. White	10 00	
R. B Whitehouse	10 00	
Dennis West	5 00	
Wayne Williams	8 00	
John Wayne	8 00	
Wm. Wilson	40 00	
Daniel Weaver	5 00	
Jesse Walker	5 00	
F. A. Wood	40 00	
Albert Wood	30 00	
J. S. Woolstone	25 00	
T. J. Wilcox	20 00	
A. Warrenton	5 00	
Z. Waite	5 00	
Fernando Walker	5 00	
M. Wadzanski	8 00	
Waponsa, (Indian)	5 00	
W. W. Williams	20 00	
G. Wilson	25 00	
Geo. Ward	45 00	
Ephraim Wilson	10 00	
Handley White	5 00	
C. J. Wannenker	5 00	
Chas. Walker	5 00	
J. Wintushin	5 00	
Chas. Webb	5 00	
Abram Yeomans	20 00	

GENERAL FUND DISBURSEMENTS.

Bounty on Wild Animals—continued.		
Alex. Young	$5 00	....
Henry Zweefer	10 00	....
Andrew Zimmer	5 00	....
		$6,535 00
SPECIAL APPROPRIATIONS.		
Nelson Boutin, suppressing riot—Ashland Co	$1,527 00	....
Thos. Kopff, assistant surgeon, 3d Wis. volunteers	339 00	....
State agricultural society	2,000 00	....
David Taylor, compilation of laws	675 00	....
W. W. Tredway, securing war claims	50 00	....
Roger Spooner, assignee of E. A. Spencer, index to laws	4,000 00	....
University fund income, chapter 82, general laws, 1867	7,303 76	....
University fund income, chapter 100, general laws 1872	10,000 00	....
School fund income, chapter 79, general laws 1866	7,088 36	....
		32,983 12
MISCELLANEOUS.		
Superintendent of public property, stationery	$10,000 00	....
Volunteer aid	1,365 32	....
C. C. Washburn, governor's contingent fund	600 00	....
C. C. Washburn, governor, relief of sufferers by fire	7,610 16	....
Lucius Fairchild, services and expenses Fox and Wis. rivers improvement appropriation	2,000 00	....
D. K. Noyes, treasury agent	480 34	....
T. D. Lang, treasury agent	1,997 50	....
Treasurer of Soldiers' Orphans' Home—pupils in normal schools	939 94	....
Conklin & Gray, coal for 1872 and 1873	11,834 70	....
Jacob Cline, peddler's license money refunded	20 00	....
Wis. state horicultural society, engravings for report	220 50	....
Transferred to normal school fund income, for normal institutes	2,000 00	....
Refunded income penalty	44 57	....
A. J. Cramer, refunded for overpayment Mil. Mechanics' Mut. Ins. Co	303 79	....
State prison commissioner, boarding U. S. prisoners	1,420 87	....
Madison Gas Co.; gas	5,871 75	....
Transferred to school fund to correct error	20 00	....
		46,729 44
Total disbursements	....	$1,191,966 01

SCHOOL FUND.

RECEIPTS.		
Sales of land	$21,458 14	....
Dues on certificates	38,709 02	....
Loans, payments on mortgages	15,314 84	....
Penalties and forfeitures	145 81	....
Taxes	183 01	....
Fines	822 10	....
United States, 5 per cent. on sales of public lands in Wisconsin, for year ending Dec. 31, 1872	27,216 01	....
Transfered from General Fund, to correct error	20 00	....
Total receipts		$103,818 93
DISBURSEMENTS.		
Commiss'rs of public debt, Mil. water bonds	$40,000 00	....
Loaned to Madison city board of education	12,500 00	....
Refunded for overpayment	243 37	....
Total disbursements		$52,743 37

SCHOOL FUND INCOME.

RECEIPTS.		
Interest on principal due on lands	$55,646 24	....
Interest on certificates of indebtedness	109,179 00	....
Interest per chapter 79, general laws of 1866	7,088 36	....
Interest on U. S. bonds	2,925 07	....
Interest on Milwaukee water bonds	3,500 00	....
Commission on purchase of Milwaukee water b's	800 00	....
Sale of Webster's dictionaries	624 00	....
Total receipts		$179,762 67
DISBURSEMENTS.		
School Apportionment.		
Adams......County	$1,074 36	....
Barron ......do	135 24	....
Bayfield ......do	73 92	....
Brown ......do	4,570 86	....
Buffalo......do	1,997 10	....
Burnett ......do	123 48	....
Calumet......do	2,285 64	....
Chippewa ....do	1,208 72	....
Clark ......do	664 44	....
Columbia ....do	4,665 78	....
Crawford.....do	2,658 60	....
Dane.........do	8,938 44	....
Dodge ....do	7,624 26	....
Door.........do	955 92	....
Douglas......do	152 04	....
Dunn ....do	1,664 88	....
Eau Claire ...do	1,488 02	....
Fond du Lac..do	8,043 42	....
Grant........do	6,514 62	....
Green ....do	3,759 42	....
Green Lake.. do	2,161 32	....
Iowa.........do	4,370 94	....
Jackson......do	1,522 08	....
Jefferson .....do	6,122 34	....
Juneau.......do	2,235 24	....
Kenosha .....do	2,049 18	....
Kewaunee....do	1,924 44	....
La Crosse ....do	3,297 00	....
La Fayette ...do	3,960 45	....
Manitowoc ...do	6,544 02	....
Marathon.....do	1,095 06	....
Marquette....do	1,457 82	....
Milwaukee...do	14,709 24	....
Monroe ......do	3,009 30	....
Oconto.......do	1,310 82	....
Outagamie ...do	3,589 34	....
Ozaukee .....do	3,048 36	....
Pepin........do	882 84	....
Pierce ....do	1,979 88	....
Polk ....do	728 70	....

SCHOOL FUND INCOME DISBURSEMENTS.

School Apportionment—continued.		
Portage ... County	$1,859 84	
Racine ...... do	4,119 78	
Richland ..... do	2,845 92	
Rock .... do	6,015 24	
St. Croix .... do	1,819 02	
Sauk .... do	4,057 20	
Shawano .... do	585 90	
Sheboygan .. do	5,811 42	
Trempealeau do	1,937 46	
Vernon ..... do	3,385 20	
Walworth ... do	3,964 80	
Washington . do	4,336 92	
Waukesha ... do	4,602 36	
Waupaca .... do	2,707 74	
Waushara ... do	1,996 68	
Winnebago .. do	6,079 08	
Wood .... do	697 20	
		$181,268 79
G. and C. Merriam, Webster's Dictionaries		3,200 00
Refunded for over payments		668 19
Total disbursements		$185 136 98

UNIVERSITY FUND.

RECEIPTS.		
Sales of land	$3,972 56	
Dues on certificates	4,271 00	
Loans	1,460 50	
Taxes	8 27	
Penalties	15 79	
Total receipts		$9,728 12
DISBURSEMENTS.		
Comm'rs of public debt, Milwaukee water bonds	$10,000 00	
Refunded for overpayments	100 51	
Total disbursements		$10,100 51

UNIVERSITY FUND INCOME.

RECEIPTS.		
Interest on principal due on lands	$5,443 82	
Interest on certificates of indebtedness	7,770 00	
Interest on Dane county bonds	1,330 00	
General Fund appropriation, Chapter 82, General Laws of 1867	7,303 76	
General Fund appropriation, Chapter 100, General Laws of 1872	10,000 00	
Tuition fees of students	9,325 00	
Rent, interest, farm products and sale of lots	1,093 80	
Commission on purchase of Milwaukee water bonds	200 00	
Laboratory bills	250 00	
Total receipts		$42,716 38
DISBURSEMENTS.		
Henry Bætz, Treasurer of State University	$42,113 85	
Refunded for overpayments	602 53	
Total disbursements		$42,716 38

AGRICULTURAL COLLEGE FUND.

RECEIPTS.		
Sales of land	$7,254 93	
Dues on certificates	4,614 80	
Loans	1,677 67	
Penalties	13 30	
Total receipts		$13,560 70
DISBURSEMENTS.		
Milwaukee water bonds, purchased		$10,000 00

AGRICULTURAL COLLEGE FUND INCOME.

RECEIPTS.		
Interest on principal due on lands	$7,868 08	....
Interest on certificates of indebtedness	3,798 67	....
Interest on Dane county bonds	420 00	....
Interest on U. S. bonds	272 10	....
Commission on Mil. water bonds purchased	200 00	....
Total receipts		$12,558 85
DISBURSEMENTS.		
Henry Bætz, Treasurer of State University	$12,524 32	....
Refunded for overpayment	34 53	....
Total disbursements		$12,558 85

NORMAL SCHOOL FUND.

RECEIPTS.		
Sales	$68,947 95	....
Dues	6,109 00	....
Loans	11,551 00	....
Penalties	79 59	....
Total receipts		$86,687 54
DISBURSEMENTS.		
Milwaukee water bonds, purchased	40,000 00	....
Madison city board of education—loan	$12,500 00	....
		$52,500 00
Refunded for overpayments	....	478 26
Total disbursements	....	$52,978 26

NORMAL SCHOOL FUND INCOME.

RECEIPTS.		
Interest on principal due on lands	$14,160 26	
Interest on certificates of indebtedness	35,882 00	
Tuition fees—Platteville Normal School	3,225 88	
Whitewater .....do	2,237 36	
Oshkosh .... do	2,832 55	
Interest on U. S. bonds	2,925 08	
Interest on Milwaukee water bonds	3,500 00	
Commission on purchase of...do	800 00	
Interest on Troy town bonds	140 00	
Interest on Fall River town bonds	350 00	
Interest on Kinnickinnic..do	105 00	
Interest on Clifton ....do	105 00	
Transferred from Gen. Fund for normal institutes	2,000 00	
Transferred from Oshkosh Normal School Building Fund, to close that fund	3,105 97	
Total receipts		$71,869 10
DISBURSEMENTS.		
Expense of Regents.		
W. H. Chandler	$21 50	
J. H. Evans	51 20	
R. Graham	41 40	
S. P. Gary	49 15	
J. I. Lyndes	52 60	
W. E. Smith	33 50	
Wm. Starr	62 00	
T. D. Weeks	28 90	
A. H. Weld	90 00	
W. C. Whitford	22 75	
		$453 00
Platteville Normal School.		
C. A. Adams....teacher	$720 00	
E. A. Charlton....do	2,250 00	
E. Curtis ....do	630 00	
T. J. Colburn.....do	363 00	
Geo. Beck........do	1,350 00	
D. McGregor .....do	1,350 00	
Eva M. Mills......do	630 00	
D. Gray Purman..do	1,350 00	
Helen E. Charlton.do	150 00	
J. H. Evans, supplies	2,055 57	
Goodell & Drinkall, supplies	6 90	
E. A. Charlton.... ...do	58 25	
W. D. Parker, visitor, expenses	39 85	
C. M. Treat...........do	35 65	
Samuel Fallows ......do	10 15	
Alexander Kerr... ...do	24 50	
Mason & Hamlin, organ	138 84	
J. H. Evans, repairs	382 69	
L. L. Goodell, janitor	550 00	

NORMAL SCHOOL FUND INCOME DISBURSEMENTS.

Platteville Normal School—continued.		
G. A. Libby, labor and material	$316 80	
W. E. & G. B. Carter, in case of Mrs. Chapman	50 78	
Coats & Thompson, building material	160 02	
J. H. Evans, cabinet	47 88	
Geo. Mathews, fire extinguisher	80 00	
J. Nellegar & Co., apparatus	247 24	
Wm. Starr, reference library	104 48	
J. H. Evans, text books	590 14	
J. H. Evans, addition to building	1,200 00	
S. H. Shellenger, librarian	100 00	
		$14,982 19
Whitewater Normal School.		
Oliver Arey, teacher	$2,250 00	
H. E. G. Arey, do	900 00	
T. C. Chamberlin, do	1,620 00	
Mary DeLany, do	500 00	
S. E. Eldridge, do	680 00	
C. A. Lilly, do	680 00	
M. Montague, do	200 00	
S. S. Rockwood, do	1,400 00	
Wm. J. Showers, do	50 00	
M. A. Terry, do	520 00	
Martha J. Bent, do	162 50	
Albert Salesbury, do	450 00	
Wm. J. Showers, librarian	50 00	
J. D. Vincent, janitor	550 00	
Oliver Arey, supplies	525 41	
Day & O'Connor, supplies	311 07	
T. D. Weeks, supplies	728 10	
W. A. De La Matyr, visitor, expenses	25 10	
Alex. F. North, do do	9 00	
J. W. Bashford, do do	17 75	
A. G. Chamberlin, building material	111 70	
N. M. Littlejohn, do do	74 44	
J. H. Goodearl, do do	74 45	
Wm. De Wolf, hardware	160 78	
Hoffman, Billings & Co., heating apparatus	70 50	
G. A. Libby, do do	622 77	
Mason & Hamlin, organ	138 33	
F. M. Wilkinson, inspecting boilers	70 05	
Winchester & Partridge, grate	85 92	
J. H. Evans, cabinet	29 70	
H. H. Greenman, music teacher	480 00	
E. S. Redington & Co., coal	1,866 26	
C. M. Sikes, drayage	133 27	
L. Stadtmuller, cabinet	100 00	
Tuttle & Shaffer, building material	39 23	
J. Nellegar & Co., apparatus	20 69	
Wm. Starr, reference library	113 20	
E. D. Coe, printing	170 00	
G. W. Hersee, repairing pianos	8 00	
M. M. Leahy, heating apparatus	650 00	
		16,538 22

NORMAL SCHOOL FUND INCOME DISBURSEMENTS.

Oshkosh Normal School.		
G. S. Albee ....teacher	$2,250 00	
F. E. Albee.......do	540 00	
H. E. Bateman....do	720 00	
H. C. Bowen......do	1,350 00	
Robert Graham...do	1,620 00	
M. S. Hills ....do	720 00	
M. E. Hazard.....do	630 00	
Mary H. Ladd....do	720 00	
Anna W. Moody..do	900 00	
Rose C. Swart....do	630 00	
M. Hosford, librarian	90 00	
E. Baker, janitor	765 00	
Ginn Bros.......books	47 00	
Harper & Bros....do	12 80	
P. B. Hulse.......do	81 50	
John H. Rolphe ..do	27 50	
Wilson, Kemble & Co., books	9 30	
A. Ethridge............do	14 04	
Mackmullen & Co ......do	24 00	
G. R. Lampard, music books	76 00	
John Magill, janitor	25 00	
Allen & Hicks, printing	224 00	
Rounds & Morley, printing	2 75	
S. P. Gary, wood	806 67	
Geo. Williams & Co., wood	549 56	
Geo. Williamson & Co., wood	225 00	
S. P. Gary, supplies	1,653 37	
Ivison, Blakeman, Taylor & Co., books	254 60	
J. B. Lippencott, books	12 60	
Mason & Hamlin, organs	300 00	
J. Nellegar & Co., apparatus	880 53	
J. C. Pickard, visitor	14 55	
B. M. Reynolds.do	31 50	
A. O. Wright...do	37 20	
H. C. Bowen, supplies	30 00	
Drandorf & Co., supplies	51 73	
J. H. Evans, cabinet	28 40	
Geo. Root & Son, music books	132 90	
A. H. Andrews, furnishing	240 24	
W. J. Button, books	32 01	
L. C. Cooley, apparatus	110 00	
Wm. Starr, reference library	332 95	
S. P. Gary, new roof for building	166 95	
Wilder & Davis, liquid slating	43 48	
		$17,363 13
Institutes.		
R. Graham	$783 80	
J. W. Bashford	15 00	
Etta J. Carle	20 00	
T. C. Chamberlin	23 00	
A. Earthman	159 65	
N. H. Holden	20 00	
J. K. Hoffman	26 15	
Charles H. Mears	32 65	
M. Montague	52 00	

NORMAL SCHOOL FUND INCOME DISBURSEMENTS.

Institutes—continued.		
T. V. Maguire	$50 00	
A. F. North	35 00	
W. D. Parker	52 90	
Geo. Skewes	65 00	
O. J. Taylor	47 25	
A. O. Wright	5 00	
M. Lynch	37 00	
T. D. Mills	18 35	
J. B. Pradt	21 75	
Wm. Starr	65 78	
F. S. Belden	52 44	
A. H. Cookey	20 00	
D. McGregor	288 50	
B. M. Reynolds	48 00	
A. Salisbury	478 12	
O. R. Smith	25 55	
C. M. Treat	20 00	
I. N. Stewart	71 15	
J. H. Terry	9 60	
		$2,538 64
EXPENSES.		
Samuel Fallows, secretary of board of regents	$187 50	
Seifert, Gugler & Co., views normal school build'gs	20 00	
Fallows & Pradt, advertising	75 00	
Samuel Fallows, telegraphing	5 88	
Atwood & Rublee, printing	30 00	
W. H. Chandler, expenses of committee	202 75	
Silas Chapman, maps	10 00	
Samuel Fallows, expenditures for board	10 45	
Gary & Harmon, insurance	1,650 00	
W. J. Park, stationery for institutes	75 32	
Wm. Starr, expenses of committee	1,000 00	
Seifert, Gugler & Co., diplomas	25 80	
Stadman, Brown & Lyon, books for regents	48 00	
Wm. Starr, historical atlas	20 00	
		$3,360 20
Refunded for overpayment		133 24
Total disbursements		$55,368 62

DRAINAGE FUND.

RECEIPTS.		
Interest	$1,373 06	
Sales	89,751 87	
Dues	2,472 00	
Penalty	37 03	
Taxes	2 50	
Total receipts		
DISBURSEMENTS.		
Apportionment to Counties.		
Adams county	$1,611 34	
Ashland do	8,346 23	
Barron do	415 96	
Bayfield do	700 00	
Brown do	366 30	
Buffalo do	542 26	
Burnett do	3,486 37	
Chippewa do	16,522 76	
Clark do	3,891 89	
Columbia do	724 27	
Crawford do	66 12	
Dane do	1,071 44	
Dodge do	148 93	
Door do	1,978 87	
Douglas do	2,504 89	
Dunn do	573 66	
Eau Claire do	538 03	
Fond du Lac do	189 93	
Grant do	153 31	
Green do	2 80	
Green Lake do	459 04	
Jackson do	8,844 46	
Jefferson do	417 33	
Juneau do	2,698 95	
Kewaunee do	352 28	
La Crosse do	479 87	
Manitowoc do	381 62	
Marathon do	27,683 59	
Marquette do	924 66	
Monroe do	3,720 78	
Oconto do	9,943 39	
Outagamie do	23 30	
Pepin do	261 82	
Pierce do	3 15	
Polk do	299 93	
Portage do	2,821 28	
Rock do	18 90	
Sauk do	136 25	
St. Croix do	13 72	

DRAINAGE FUND DISBURSEMENTS.

Apportionment to counties—continued.		
Shawano county	$2,994 70	
Trempealeau do	787 08	
Walworth ...do	48 27	
Washington. do	3 36	
Waukesha...do	44 10	
Waupaca....do	2,054 68	
Waushara ...do	1,469 75	
Winnebago..do	1,399 53	
Wood ......do	12,222 76	
		$124,343 91
Refunded for overpayments		911 48
Total disbursements		$125,255 39

DELINQUENT TAX FUND.

RECEIPTS.		
Taxes on state lands		27,047 09
DISBURSEMENTS.		
Adams.......county	$220 14	
Ashland... ....do	303 90	
Barron......... do	216 06	
Bayfield........do	643 49	
Brown ....do	155 30	
Buffalo.........do	239 68	
Burnett ....do	23 63	
Calumet........do	183 15	
Chippewa ......do	1,307 83	
Clark.. ....do	759 86	
Columbia ......do	300 83	
Crawford ......do	124 98	
Dane...........do	247 61	
Dodge . ...do	15 99	
Door...........do	845 72	
Douglas........do	174 24	
Dunn.. ....do	346 88	
Eau Claire......do	164 59	
Fond du Lac....do	12 83	
Grant ....do	93 57	
Green Lake.....do	142 78	
Iowa ....do	74 68	
Jackson ....do	730 87	
Jefferson ....do	14 15	
Juneau.........do	349 69	
Kewaunce ......do	381 81	

"A."—*Receipts and Disbursements of the Several Funds*—con.

DELINQUENT TAX FUND DISBURSEMENTS.

Disbursements—continued.		
La Crosse ....county	142 68	....
La Fayette......do	66 23	....
Manitowoc .....do	415 87	....
Marathon ......do	2,908 02	....
Marquette......do	109 82	....
Milwaukee .....do	101 10	....
Monroe ....do	608 46	....
Oconto ....do	1,332 34	....
Outagamie .....do	993 99	....
Pepin ....do	57 04	....
Pierce..........do	2,008 20	....
Polk ....do	1,174 10	....
Portage ....do	567 09	....
Richland. ......do	489 10	....
Rock............do	82 73	....
St. Croix ....do	2,094 82	....
Sauk ....do	190 12	....
Shawano ....do	$2,385 68	....
Sheboygan......do	60 80	....
Trempealeau ...do	255 43	....
Vernon ....do	595 90	....
Waukesha......do	40 43	....
Waupaca ....do	582 95	....
Waushara.......do	273 18	....
Winnebago......do	48 86	....
Wood ....do	2,012 64	....
		$27,621 69
Refunded for overpayments	....	132 06
Total disbursements	....	$27,753 75

APPENDIX "B."

STATEMENT *of the Valuation of the Taxable Property of the Several Counties of the State of Wisconsin, as determined by the State Board of Assessors for the year* 1872, *and the Apportionment of the State Tax to be Levied for the year* 1873.

COUNTIES.	Valuation by State Board, 1872.	STATE TAX FOR 1873.			Total.	Due on Loans to School Districts.
		Per cent. on Valuation, 1 72-100 mills.	Industrial School for Boys.	Hospitals for the Insane.		
Adams	$1,176,613	$2,023 77	....	$855 58	$2,879 35	$129 22
Ashland	500,000	860 00	....	....	860 00	
Barron	578,779	995 50	....	....	995 50	....
Bayfield	383,942	660 38	....	....	660 38	....
Brown	6,254,662	10,758 02	$430 00	714 90	11,902 92	298 00
Buffalo	2,093,702	3,601 17		303 47	3,904 64	1,120 00
Burnett	318,922	548 55	....	190 14	738 69	1,707 51
Calumet	3,272,849	5,628 44	104 00	257 54	5,989 98	....
Chippewa	9,398,909	16,166 12		288 81	16,454 93	589 00
Clark	3,642,208	6,264 60	....	112 78	6,377 38	842 72
Columbia	10,419,911	17,922 25	210 50	1,086 81	19,219 56	....
Crawford	3,395,534	5,840 32	312 00	479 24	6,631 56	1,729 78
Dane	24,393,808	41,957 35	414 00	2,310 14	44,681 49	369 50
Dodge	15,571,449	26,782 89	342 00	1,558 99	28,683 88	1,057 65
Door	603,648	1,038 27	....	311 32	1,349 59	....
Douglas	900,955	1,549 64	....	96 36	1,646 00	605 00
Dunn	2,974,863	5,116 76	....	136 37	5,253 13	21 00
Eau Claire	3,267,076	5,620 40	....	456 60	6,077 00	2,200 00

"B."—*Valuation of the Taxable Property in the Several Counties*—continued.

Counties.	Valuation by State Board, 1872.	State Tax for 1873.			Total.	Due on Loans to School Districts.
		Per cent. on Valuation, 1 72-100 mills.	Industrial School for Boys.	Hospitals for the Insane.		
Fond du Lac	$15,733,756	$27,062 06	$1,249 00	$1,555 56	$29,866 62	$224 80
Grant	14,465,860	24,880 42	208 00	1,216 70	26,305 12	3,096 68
Green	9,997,160	17,195 13	226 00	699 42	18,120 55	2,500 50
Green Lake	4,707,085	8,096 19	250 00	618 11	8,964 30	620 00
Iowa*	9,100,057	15,652 10	70 50	857 04	16,579 64	374 27
Jackson	1,927,125	3,314 66	....	319 45	3,634 11	1,041 84
Jefferson	10,859,305	18,678 00	403 00	1,096 83	20,177 83	2,246 00
Juneau	2,396,525	4,122 02	52 00	467 60	4,641 62	114 00
Kenosha	6,227,415	10,711 15	236 00	242 57	11,189 72	....
Kewaunee	608,405	1,046 46	....	119 79	1,166 25	....
La Crosse	6,279,701	10,801 00	160 00	611 41	11,572 50	513 00
La Fayette	7,961,681	13,694 09	52 00	594 24	14,340 33	1,149 00
Manitowoc	7,544,207	12,976 04	198 50	1,175 30	14,349 84	1,260 00
Marathon	4,135,741	7,113 47	52 00	147 57	7,313 04	2,225 25
Marquette	1,204,665	2,072 02	52 00	482 32	2,606 34	116 50
Milwaukee	50,757,658	87,303 17	435 50	2,754 47	90,493 14	682 93
Monroe	4,194,781	7,215 02	102 00	385 92	7,702 94	327 18
Oconto	5,506,186	9,470 64	99 50	359 61	9,929 75	....
Outagamie	6,694,468	11,514 49	60 50	513 86	12,088 85	250 00
Ozaukee	3,367,485	5,792 08	....	594 27	6,386 35	....
Pepin	763,776	1,313 69	....	99 57	1,413 26	....
Pierce	3,943,335	6,782 54	27 00	169 80	6,979 34	325 41
Polk	1,122,482	1,930 67	....	325 16	2,255 83	135 00
Portage	2,830,158	4,867 87	27 50	307 62	5,202 99	470 00
Racine	10,161,083	17,477 06	296 00	746 46	18,519 52	....

Richland	3,862,591	6,643 66	34 00	332 34	7,010 00	202 23
Rock	20,167,738	34,688 49	321 50	1,301 02	36,401 01	1,198 00
St. Croix	4,326,317	7,441 09	14 50	234 22	7,679 81	152 50
Sauk	8,386,997	14,425 63	249 00	615 58	15,290 21	1,070 00
Shawano	1,379,156	2,372 15	....	182 38	2,554 53	125 62
Sheboygan	8,621,242	14,828 54	263 00	925 05	16,016 59	2,710 00
Trempealeau	2,347,412	4,037 55	52 00	300 48	4,390 03	142 00
Vernon	5,587,970	9,611 81	....	564 94	10,176 25	1,470 97
Walworth	13,582,761	23,362 35	161 00	605 73	24,129 08	....
Washington	6,419,906	11,042 24	....	731 53	11,773 77	713 69
Waukesha	12,859,426	22,118 21	329 00	1,084 49	23,531 70	....
Waupaca	3,670,062	6,312 51	....	434 84	6,747 35	242 00
Waushara	1,983,551	3,411 71	108 00	86 10	3,605 81	21 00
Winnebago	14,078,844	24,215 61	587 00	1,335 66	26,138 27	160 50
Wood	1,543,470	2,654 77	....	357 61	3,012 38	....
Total	$390,454,875	$671,582 38	$8,188 50	$34,381 67	$41 135	$36,550 25

* This county is in arrears $22,407.76, which amount was added to the tax of the county and certified to the county clerk.

APPENDIX "C"

Abstract *of the Assessment Rolls of the Several Counties in the State of Wisconsin, as returned to the Secretary of State for the year* 1873, *under the provisions of chapter* 106 *of the general laws of* 1869, *giving also the average value of stock and real estate by counties, and for the State at large.*

Counties.	Horses.			Neat Cattle.			Mules and Asses.		
	No.	Value.	Average Value.	No.	Value.	Average Value.	No.	Value.	Average Value.
Adams	1,706	$56,521	$33 13	7,531	$79,354	$10 53	71	$2,452	$34 53
Ashland	838	7,535	90 78	82	4,045	49 32	10	1,350	135 00
[1]Barron	.....	.....	.....	.....	.....	.....	.....	.....	.....
Bayfield	35	2,460	70 29	39	1,[illegible]	49 36	.....	.....	.....
Brown	4,347	96,057	22 10	9,547	82,748	8 66	35	845	24 14
Buffalo	3,608	127,700	35 39	14,736	132,284	8 98	139	5,348	38 47
Burnett	90	3,918	43 53	1,148	13,629	11 87	3	135	45 00
Calumet	3,290	100,848	30 65	10,821	97,491	9 00	65	1,374	21 14
Chippewa	1,719	62,141	36 15	5,033	62,006	12 31	49	2,283	46 59
Clark	806	51,370	63 73	2,766	63,405	22 92	82	3,980	48 53
Columbia	9,987	416,445	41 70	24,792	260,377	10 50	128	5,750	44 92
[1]Crawford	.....	.....	.....	.....	.....	.....	.....	.....	.....
Dane	19,127	[illegible]3,712	49 34	46,415	531,637	11 45	316	16,997	53 78
Dodge	13,131	608,809	46 36	85,590	422,324	11 87	151	7,644	50 62
Door	807	38, 54	47 77	2,806	38.881	13 85	37	2,315	62 56
Douglas	62	3,360	54 19	59	1,255	21 27	.....	.....	.....
Dunn	2,544	134,481	52 86	10,636	145,963	13 72	201	11,574	57 58
Eau Claire	2,716	206,533	76 04	6,665	91,176	13 68	72	6,470	89 86
Fond du Lac	11,753	529,504	45 05	33,440	362,224	10 83	148	6,642	44 88

Grant	15,737	711,369	45 20	40,209	480,299	11 92	429	20,545	48 60
Green	9,204	390,277	42 40	20,019	330,685	11 70	179	8,319	46 47
Green Lake	4,693	211,159	44 99	12,930	140,287	10 84	40	1,855	46 37
Iowa	9,598	371,130	38 67	31,452	358,332	11 28	193	8,005	41 48
Jackson	2,618	106,485	40 78	8,348	90,047	10 78	97	4,758	49 05
Jefferson	8,486	386,075	45 60	26,317	323,300	12 30	178	8,799	49 43
Juneau	3,154	149,681	47 42	10,001	124,570	12 45	78	4,090	52 43
Kenosha	4,256	208,069	48 89	15,648	216,081	13 81	57	2,501	43 88
Kewaunee	486	19,876	40 90	2,418	27,390	11 33	8	520	65 00
La Crosse	4,586	254,641	55 53	12,771	142,951	11 19	142	9,126	64 26
La Fayette	10,267	378,360	36 85	30,168	294,924	9 77	441	17,803	40 36
Manitowoc	5,773	121,336	21 02	18,137	121,814	6 71	44	768	17 45
Marathon	984	87,449	38 05	6,028	54,651	9 07	12	330	27 50
Marquette	2,447	90,284	36 87	10,493	98,629	9 39	27	958	35 48
Milwaukee	8,792	512,986	58 34	11,057	181,469	16 41	86	4,550	52 90
Monroe	4,695	178,828	38 09	14,758	153,336	10 32	154	7,020	45 58
Oconto	1,527	77,385	50 68	2,305	47,062	20 42	62	2,815	45 40
Outagamie	4,037	161,273	39 94	13,913	145,638	10 47	63	2,950	46 83
Ozaukee	3,868	114,334	29 56	11,549	97,333	8 43	27	775	28 70
Pepin	1,153	71,456	61 97	4,162	58,885	14 15	29	1,707	58 86
[2]Pierce	3,148	177,127	56 26	11,750	149,798	12 75	66	4,820	73 03
Polk	740	41,690	56 33	4,595	73,110	15 91	34	2,095	61 61
Portage	2,204	103,519	46 96	9,601	123,888	12 90	94	4,103	43 65
Racine	5,853	277,409	47 39	18,588	211,764	11 39	84	4,470	53 21
Richland	4,901	190,640	38 90	15,468	151,569	9 80	192	7,184	37 42
Rock	15,035	763,623	50 78	31,499	419,426	13 79	308	16,107	53 16
St. Croix	4,020	202,780	50 41	10,455	122,033	11 67	130	7,013	53 94
Sauk	7,668	337,457	44 01	23,326	249,931	10 71	165	7,593	46 03
Shawano	659	28,858	43 78	3,053	33,645	11 02	7	240	34 29
Sheboygan	7,397	317,250	42 88	28,993	356,412	12 29	106	4,523	41 88
Trempealeau	3,848	194,635	50 58	14,313	182,513	12 75	123	7,461	60 65
Vernon	5,894	284,889	48 33	19,634	228,693	11 65	121	5,483	45 31
Walworth	10,265	646,278	62 95	24,507	399,135	16 29	163	10,455	64 14

[1] No report.

[2] One Town not reported.

"C."—*Abstract of Assessment Rolls of the Several Counties*—continued.

Counties.	Horses.			Neat Cattle.			Mules and Asses.		
	No.	Value.	Average Value.	No.	Value.	Average Value.	No.	Value.	Average Value.
Washington	7,120	$263,735	$37 04	20,056	$185,772	$9 26	96	$3,650	$38 02
Waukesha	9,209	529,668	57 52	21,245	343,769	16 18	146	9,225	63 18
Waupaca	3,318	116,700	35 17	12,859	132,058	10 26	61	2,255	36 97
Waushara	3,209	111,575	34 77	12,026	115,533	9 61	107	4,262	39 83
Winnebago	7,631	444,530	58 25	23,716	270,136	11 39	126	7,305	57 97
Wood	651	27,077	41 59	2,401	29,040	12 09	5	515	103 00
Totals	285,672	$13,001,691	$45 51	831,957	$9,661,082	$11 61	5,977	$292,111	$48 87

"C."—*Abstract of Assessment Rolls of the Several Counties*—continued.

Counties.	Sheep and Lambs.			Swine.			Wagons, Carriages and Sleighs.	
	No.	Value.	Average Value.	No.	Value.	Average Value.	No.	Value.
Adams	7,014	$8,097	$1 15	3,406	$4,793	$1 41	1,012	$16,335
Ashland				14	60	4 29	87	1,273
[1]Barron								
Bayfield				2	16	8 00	24	895
Brown	5,403	3,423	63	4,874	4,997	1 02	3,560	49,754
Buffalo	8,295	9,781	1 18	7,076	9,112	1 28	1,951	24,059
Burnett	249	297	1 19	298	594	1 99	69	1,450
Calumet	10,774	10,888	1 01	5,582	6,560	1 17	2,401	24,716
Chippewa	1,614	1,773	1 10	2,337	2,942	1 26	1,190	22,062
Clark	822	1,214	1 47	745	2,239	3 00	982	22,426
Columbia	56,206	81,651	1 45	14,437	33,424	2 31	4,532	104,833
[1]Crawford								
Dane	64,241	112,383	1 75	34,888	86,246	2 47	9,108	253,266
Dodge	67,650	100,382	1 62	18,797	39,749	2 11	8,087	164,070
Door	560	791	1 41	1,185	2,334	1 97	929	18,860
Douglas	9	8	89	4	15	3 75	35	655
Dunn	5,766	8,954	1 55	4,990	10,176	2 04	1,849	45,121
Eau Claire	1,701	2,700	1 59	2,237	7,500	3 35	1,628	60,643
Fond du Lac	78,589	117,016	1 49	12,217	27,265	2 23	6,691	159,926
Grant	20,901	36,478	1 75	55,542	124,495	2 24	7,344	186,434
Green	27,203	53,736	1 97	33,246	82,982	2 49	3,622	89,384
Green Lake	39,848	63,867	1 60	6,109	12,891	2 11	2,622	59,190
Iowa	11,325	18,300	1 61	40,167	63,020	1 57	4,175	104,771
Jackson	5,136	6,017	1 17	2,531	5,289	2 08	1,323	24,810
Jefferson	48,513	83,953	1 74	15,469	33,643	2 17	5,014	112,999

[1] No report.

"B."—*Abstract of the Assessment Rolls of the Several Counties*—continued.

Counties.	Sheep and Lambs.			Swine.			Wagons, Carriages and Sleighs.	
	No.	Value.	Average Value.	No.	Value.	Average Value.	No.	Value.
Juneau	9,171	$12,617	$1 37	5,945	$9,579	$1 61	1,975	$41,564
Kenosha	49,801	101,630	2 05	6,408	17,145	2 67	2,185	62,108
Kewaunee	265	415	1 57	746	627	84	326	3,965
La Crosse	10,646	16,196	1 52	5,599	10,387	1 85	2,338	68,809
La Fayette	14,690	22,620	1 54	38,331	77,361	2 01	4,082	85,838
Manitowoc	16,198	12,584	78	7,478	10,639	1 42	4,639	40,407
Marathon	2,231	1,734	77	1,851	2,061	1 11	1,015	14,214
Marquette	17,168	20,699	1 20	5,185	8,410	1 62	1,488	31,951
Milwaukee	6,684	11,677	1 74	5,881	15,759	2 67	7,474	338,161
Monroe	15,412	17,550	1 13	8,470	13,343	1 57	2,827	55,246
Oconto	442	584	1 32	787	2,401	3 05	1,376	35,624
Outagamie	18,002	21,090	1 17	6,937	9,496	1 37	3,237	52,357
Ozaukee	6,446	8,335	1 29	5,314	9,044	1 70	2,702	38,091
[1]Pepin	2,107	3,768	1 79	2,110	4,453	2 11	956	17,543
[1]Pierce	6,161	10,896	1 77	5,361	10,822	2 02	1,975	44,331
Polk	922	1,484	1 61	1,112	3,408	3 06	592	13,549
Portage	10,267	10,908	1 06	4,421	7,822	1 77	2,023	36,189
Racine	38,086	61,091	1 60	6,529	18,762	2 87	3,278	82,611
Richland	25,172	31,846	1 26	16,916	23,210	1 37	2,100	42,478
Rock	46,381	97,417	2 10	27,320	85,450	3 12	7,819	243,187
St. Croix	1,891	2,720	1 44	3,484	8,914	2 56	2,290	55,204
Sauk	23,302	31,164	1 33	18 553	32,414	1 75	4,847	102,122
Shawano	1,248	1,212	97	1,841	1,599	87	840	11,847
Sheboygan	38,843	58,604	1 38	9,457	18,808	1 98	5,423	98,482
Trempealeau	11,734	18,436	1 57	5,190	7,554	1 45	1,844	39,154
Vernon	25,231	33,289	1 32	17,801	25,185	1 41	3,083	57,065

Walworth	94,418	241,293	2 55	21,420	72,314	3.37	5,242	187,213
Washington	28,599	29,216	1 24	12,502	21,712	1.73	5,278	75,167
Waukesha	77,033	152,087	1 97	16,925	51,738	3.05	6,390	173,070
Waupaca	14,997	16,087	1 61	5,045	9,089	1.80	2,702	38,490
Waushara	16,685	17,988	1 08	6,115	8,862	1.45	1,772	27,788
Winnebago	43,046	64,718	1 50	7,038	19,587	2.78	5,488	150,578
Wood	624	541	86	908	1,553	1.71	633	12,450
Totals	1,130,722	$1,858,105	$1.64	555,133	$1,179,859	$2.13	168,368	$3,909,994

[1] One town not reported.

"C."—*Abstract of Assessment Rolls of the Several Counties*—continued.

Counties.	Watches. No.	Watches. Value.	Pianos and Melodeons. No.	Pianos and Melodeons. Value.	Shares of Bank Stock. No.	Shares of Bank Stock. Value.	Value of merchants and manufacturers' stock.	Value of all other personal property.	Total value of all personal property aforesaid.
Adams	90	$747	32	$1,815	....	....	$15,517	$84,170	$219,301
Ashland	40	1,702	9	1,400	1	$1,000	31,883	30,970	81,218
[1]Barron	....	....	....	....	....	....	....	....	....
Bayfield	37	1,647	13	2,890	....	901	9,820	14,510	34,564
Brown	320	7,978	185	15,910	2,067	118,870	369,681	186,179	936,442
Buffalo	80	588	28	1,093	3	1,150	35,521	1,652	406,788
Burnett	13	123	....	....	....	....	3,100	2,549	25,795
Calumet	152	869	41	1,625	....	....	49,809	57,388	351,577
Chippewa	101	2,890	24	1,936	....	....	135,175	88,299	411,507
Clark	115	2,913	44	4,207	....	....	78,223	51,676	281,653
Columbia	545	11,770	387	31,259	750	55,000	397,963	595,610	[illegible],062
[1]Crawford	....	....	....	....	....	....	....	....	....
Dane	1,175	28,085	562	57,827	2,766	289,375	777,290	1,623,189	4,720,107
Dodge	619	13,140	511	[illegible]	1,569	121,589	298,228	898,034	2,721,[illegible]
Door	81	1,354	10	1,100	1	2,560	46,342	40,127	188,227
Douglas	30	905	12	710	....	....	....	2,757	9,665
Dunn	194	3,143	50	3,945	....	....	44,000	216,527	968,884
Eau Claire	266	8,600	123	24,555	600	60,000	769,101	341,153	1,578,431
Fond du Lac	796	15,845	585	47,948	2,099	78,243	625,[illegible]	878,650	2,848,431
Grant	834	12,710	363	[illegible]	500	31,250	414,444	793,554	2,838,028
Green	400	6,509	255	20,213	1,400	90,200	201,867	589,859	1,873,081
Green Lake	376	3,511	275	15,494	....	....	122,840	263,847	894,891
Iowa	308	5,115	173	9,793	....	....	165,[illegible]	318,676	1,417,338
Jackson	131	3,439	60	4,296	....	8,327	153,888	121,635	528,886
Jefferson	428	6,524	362	26,847	1,350	144,505	376,000	488,767	1,991,912
Juneau	314	5,764	112	8,725	1	2,000	215,808	167,166	741,559
Kenosha	456	11,918	244	26,034	525	35,000	208,306	428,074	1,316,866

[illegible]nee	......	......	8	685	......	......	49,467	8,579	111,524
La Crosse	289	10,958	194	22,696	750	72,000	474,148	409,933	1,591,835
La [illegible]e	805	5,434	220	18,208	......	14,500	105,557	262,052	1,277,716
Manitowoc	51	810	60	1,549	400	14,163	287,658	192,034	808,762
Marathon	110	2,694	52	2,603	......	6,840	10,000	34,111	836,687
Marquette	75	729	52	2,748	1	400	21,306	25,183	291,247
Milwaukee	1,784	70,286	1,491	253,105	15,480	1,035,000	8,959,647	4,945,724	16,328,364
Monroe	371	6,193	166	9,745	......	30,400	187,851	182,622	842,134
[illegible]o	90	3,042	56	6,890	5	1,400	505,805	100,511	783,519
Outagamie	164	8,370	101	9,662	1,126	84,875	201,122	109,545	801,878
[2] Ozaukee	38	563	36	2,433	......	375	49,475	115,108	435,866
[1] Pepin	117	1,317	32	1,665	4	1,000	35,424	43,498	240,716
Pierce	251	8,290	88	6,063	......	6,085	99,290	155,301	667,828
Polk	71	912	30	1,835	1	350	18,438	36,219	193,090
Portage	210	3,961	94	11,210	......	......	208,620	106,695	616,915
Racine	335	11,976	321	33,375	3,502	263,812	493,120	942,475	2,400,865
Richland	309	3,118	100	4,014	2	4,891	70,616	138,161	667,727
Rock	1,540	39,995	809	74,424	2,730	307,500	782,400	1,793,096	4,622,625
St. [illegible]oix	274	5,044	125	10,632	750	42,500	133,067	204,725	795,232
Sauk	716	10,632	266	18,620	......	35,900	204,525	406,020	1,436,378
Shawano	51	1,145	13	734	......	......	9,482	1,752	90,014
Sheboygan	391	5,053	241	18,187	35	15,000	246,865	475,283	1,609,467
[illegible]au	129	1,738	68	4,845	......	7,342	47,041	174,101	684,820
Vernon	269	2,749	51	2,459	......	......	70,358	227,643	937,763
W[illegible]worth	890	21,734	574	53,445	2,000	125,150	347,838	1,299,991	8,404,846
Washington	161	2,648	156	6,779	......	710	110,844	401,484	1,101,717
Waukesha	588	14,888	364	31,988	500	50,000	335,296	1,091,060	2,782,789
Waupaca	272	3,086	145	6,422	33	3,765	129,723	78,320	535,954
Waushara	107	1,283	46	1,718		......	33,979	38,259	861,247
Winnebago	697	17,719	510	47,245	2,050	250,056	1,188,404	1,717,689	4,177,967
Wood	79	1,766	63	5,495	489	19,575	143,[illegible]26	42,911	284,669
Totals	18,635	$415,917	10,992	$1,039,805	43,519	$3,433,559	$21,666,817	$24,155,008	$[illegible],613,948

[1] No report.

[2] One town not reported.

"C."—*Abstract of Assessment Rolls of the Several Counties*—continued.

Counties.	Land.			Value of City and Village Lots.	Total Value of all Real Estate.	Total Value of all Property.
	Number of Acres.	Value.	Average Value.			
Adams	313,989	$648,775	$2 06	$21,261	$670,036	$889,387
Ashland	255,368	819,822	3 21	154,197	974,019	1,055,287
[1]Barron	....	....	....	....	....	....
Bayfield	....	548,388	....	68,815	612,203	646,767
Brown	295,484	891,081	3 02	2,314,757	3,205,838	4,142,280
Buffalo	274,317	635,560	2 32	187,651	773,211	1,181,999
Burnett	103,600	207,200	2 00	....	207,200	232,995
Calumet	200,432	1,746,836	8 71	74,797	1,821,633	2,173,210
Chippewa	1,687,123	4,232,555	2 51	350,866	4,583,421	4,994,928
Clark	392,310	1,517,289	3 86	19,511	1,536,800	1,818,453
Columbia	485,616	5,735,207	11 81	1,360,212	7,095,419	9,069,501
[1]Crawford	....	....	....	....	....	....
Dane	746,670	11,215,195	15 02	3,654,508	14,869,703	19,589,810
Dodge	549,068	10,099,868	18 39	2,509,381	12,609,249	15,330,358
Door	201,922	726,909	3 60	48,565	775,474	963,701
Douglas	174,147	515,768	2 96	764,474	1,280,242	1,289,907
Dunn	306,417	1,344,988	4 39	210,866	1,555,354	2,539,238
Eau Claire	221,825	1,608,603	7 25	2,134,771	3,743,374	5,321,805
Fond du Lac	448,939	7,680,683	17 11	4,089,321	11,770,004	14,618,485
Grant	729,177	6,282,669	8 62	1,365,543	7,648,212	10,486,240
Green	366,971	5,329,889	14 52	1,057,774	6,387,663	8,260,694
Green Lake	218,581	2,937,596	13 44	725,195	3,662,791	4,557,682
Iowa	481,239	3,628,728	7 54	646,986	4,275,714	5,693,052
Jackson	316,504	714,705	2 26	266,494	981,199	1,510,085
Jefferson	341,227	6,132,797	17 97	1,815,062	7,947,859	9,989,771
Juneau	299,686	1,033,041	3 45	491,493	1,524,534	2,266,098
Kenosha	171,788	3,610,252	21 02	748,043	4,358,295	5,675,161

Kewaunee	126,571	406,241	3 21	....	406,241	517,765
La Crosse	260,409	1,761,477	6 76	1,989,626	3,751,108	5,842,988
La Fayette	397,818	4,484,689	11 27	363,205	4,847,894	6,125,610
Manitowoc	369,484	2,362,718	6 40	1,519,162	3,881,880	4,685,642
Marathon	1,219,871	1,619,187	1 33	118,418	1,732,555	2,069,242
Marquette	266,892	739,940	2 77	55,930	795,870	1,087,117
Milwaukee	140,838	5,839,285	41 46	33,258,910	39,098,195	55,426,559
Monroe	435,068	1,601,066	3 68	577,192	2,178,258	3,020,392
Oconto	1,079,529	2,005,375	1 86	757,065	2,762,440	3,545,959
Outagamie	345,158	2,620,587	7 59	1,362,154	3,982,741	4,784,119
Ozaukee	146,890	2,544,802	17 32	268,163	2,812,965	3,248,831
[2]Pepin	105,486	458,220	4 34	91,128	549,348	790,059
Pierce	340,554	1,792,652	5 26	317,456	2,110,108	2,777,931
Polk	315,108	957,437	3 04	84,293	1,041,730	1,284,820
Portage	428,608	1,017,144	2 37	456,343	1,473,487	2,090,402
Racine	208,490	4,385,977	21 04	2,884,677	7,270,654	9,671,519
Richland	318,803	1,669,548	5 24	160,520	1,830,068	2,497,795
Rock	451,087	10,672,121	23 65	4,046,094	14,718,215	19,340,840
St. Croix	388,619	2,306,559	5 94	598,113	2,904,672	3,699,904
Sauk	517,880	3,374,513	6 52	844,049	4,218,562	5,654,940
Shawano	416,380	767,078	1 84	....	767,078	857,092
Sheboygan	322,983	5,292,751	16 39	1,562,201	6,854,952	8,464,419
Trempealeau	300,751	1,208,460	4 02	161,325	1,369,785	2,054,605
Vernon	466,002	2,189,788	4 70	143,962	2,333,750	3,271,518
Walworth	349,000	8,659,318	24 81	1,763,534	10,422,852	13,827,698
Washington	258,773	4,387,983	16 96	308,549	4,696,532	5,798,249
Waukesha	348,524	10,022,708	28 76	1,301,546	11,324,254	14,107,048
Waupaca	416,972	1,381,363	2 99	458,226	1,839,589	2,375,543
Waushara	378,740	1,801,570	3 48	74,310	1,875,880	1,787,127
Winnebago	271,853	5,314,697	19 55	5,522,172	10,836,869	15,014,836
Wood	378,470	737,740	1 95	210,600	948,340	1,233,009
Totals	21,348,760	$173,722,348	$8 14	$86,283,961	$260,006,309	$340,620,252

[1] No report.

[2] One town not reported.

APPENDIX "D."

ABSTRACT *from Reports of Railroads operated in Wisconsin for* 1872, *made in conformity with the provisions of Chapter* 91, *Laws of* 1858.

NAME OF COMPANY.	Capital Stock subscribed.	Capital Stock paid.	Length of road operated in Wisconsin.	Length of road operated elsewhere.	Whole length of road.	Total cost of road and equipment.	Dividends declared.
Chicago and Northwestern	....	$36,242,743 82	$418\frac{64}{100}$	$996\frac{36}{100}$	1,415	$54,415,471 66	$2,001,746 06
Green Bay and Lake Pepin	$927,300 00	728,000 00	40	....	40	1,239,993 01	....
LaCrosse, Trempealeau and Prescott	50,000 00	....	29	....	29	1,424,091 51	....
Madison and Portage	[1]........	[1]........	39	....	39	[1]........	....
Milwaukee, Lake Shore and Western	3,000,000 00	1,250,000 00	43	....	43	[2]........	....
Milwaukee and Northern	1,733,000 00	1,530,300 00	$92\frac{83}{100}$	....	$92\frac{83}{100}$	3,249,050 00	....
Milwaukee and St. Paul	12,432,198 00	12,432,198 00	622	....	622	25,533,979 61	231,508 71
Mineral Point	....	1,200,000 00	49	....	49	1,200,000 00	....
Prairie du Chien and McGregor	100,000 00	55,000 00	$1\frac{3}{4}$	$\frac{1}{4}$	2	51,110 00	....
St. Croix and Lake Superior	315,500 00	315,500 00	[3]........	....	....	[2]........	....
Sheboygan and Fond du Lac	1,389,500 00	1,359,500 00	$78\frac{4}{10}$	....	$78\frac{4}{10}$	2,[illegible]0,299 00	....
Superior and St. Croix	734,000 00	[4]407,000 00	[3]........	....	....	[2]........	....
Western Union	4,000,000 00	4,000,000 00	$85\frac{2}{10}$	$130\frac{3}{10}$	$215\frac{5}{10}$	7,594,[illegible]5 42	....
West Wisconsin	4,000,000 00	4,000,000 00	197	....	197	3,060,135 11	....
Wisconsin Central	[4]........	[4]........	$114\frac{2}{10}$	....	$114\frac{2}{10}$	3,645,[illegible]9 54	....
	$28,681,498 00	$63,520,241 82	$1,810\frac{3}{100}$	$1,126\frac{91}{100}$	$2,936\frac{93}{100}$	$104,373,614 86	$2,233,254 77

[1] Road operated by Mil. and S. P. R. R. Co., and items not given.
[2] Road in process of construction.
[3] Not given.
[4] Includes $350,000 00 in bonds of Douglas county.

"D."—*Abstract from Reports of Railroads Operated in Wisconsin in* 1872—continued.

Name of Company.	Receipts.					
	Passengers.	Mails.	Express.	Freights.	Other Sources.	Total.
Chicago and Northwestern	$3,478,216 52	$211,400 17	$232,493 82	$8,160,179 17	$189,774 30	$12,272,063 98
Green Bay and Lake Pepin	8,199 53	....	....	24,016 97	....	32,216 50
La Crosse, Trempealeau and Prescott	79,510 85	700 00	6,482 49	132,974 43	5 34	219,673 11
Madison and Portage	16,177 08	1,675 00	495 13	19,755 70	138 69	38,241 60
Milwaukee, Lake Shore and Western	5,149 25	....	....	10,791 14	....	15,940 39
Milwaukee and Northern	57,251 89	838 92	1,258 69	61,413 05	77 89	120,840 44
Milwaukee and St. Paul	[1]1,149,486 44	78,436 55	108,758 39	3,075,454 98	72,974 74	4,485,111 10
Mineral Point	17,693 67	2,585 24	1,800 00	92,964 15	....	115,043 06
Prairie du Chien and McGregor	83 60	....	....	3,864 00	....	3,947 60
Sheboygan and Fond du Lac	55,198 69	4,272 00	836 65	65,513 56	....	125,820 90
Western Union	208,056 56	9,020 00	12,000 00	603,098 97	14,935 68	847,111 21
West Wisconsin	165,263 67	7,727 92	5,013 75	183,795 55	4,198 93	365,999 82
Wisconsin Central	55,836 00	3,140 00	1,548 39	52,853 34	4,012 26	116,889 99
	$5,295,623 75	$319,795 80	$370,687 31	$12,486,675 01	$286,117 83	$18,758,899 70

[1] Includes gross earnings Milwaukee and Northern Railway from Jan. 1 to March 21, 1872. Also earnings of Oshkosh and Miss. River Railroad.

"D."—*Abstract from Reports of Railroads Operated in Wisconsin in* 1872—continued.

Name of Company.	Gross Earnings in Wisconsin.	Amount Due Company.	Expenditures.				
			Repairs.	Building.	Engines.	Cars.	Fuel.
Chicago and Northwestern	$2,625,885 23	....	....	....	....	....	....
Green Bay and Lake Pepin	32,216 50	....	[1]$10,000 00	[1]$4,000 00	$60,000 00	$42,883 95	[1]$10,800 00
La Crosse, Trempeal'u and Pres't.	216,673 11	....	....	....	....	....	....
Madison and Portage	38,241 60	....	7,267 70	13 63	308 89	417 90	4,539 33
Mil'kee Lake Shore and Western	15,940 39	....	[2]........	....	....	....	....
Milwaukee and Northern	120,840 44	....	16,017 29	3,261 79	289 42	....	4,639 50
Milwaukee and St. Paul	4,485,111 10	$868,767 49	519,047 57	44,128 47	161,795 08	386,535 75	351,217 50
Mineral Point	110,531 56	....	29,457 05	472 59	....	[3]23,257 69	7,907 22
Pr. du Chien and McGregor	3,454 15	....	250 00	....	....	....	....
St. Croix and Lake Superior	[4]........	....	....	....	....	....	....
Sheboygan and Fond du Lac	125,820 90	....	22,134 11	1,359 94	12,192 80	9,704 58	10,483 65
Superior and St. Croix	[4]........	....	....	....	....	....	....
Western Union	334,913 57	184,879 71	137,299 43	9,978 03	92,453 39	78,628 96	83,097 09
West Wisconsin	365,999 82	15,818 79	56,040 97	4,911 08	16,284 19	13,742 14	29,081 70
Wisconsin Central	116,889 99	....	18,374 89	1,367 74	1,953 65	3,695 84	5,494 50
Totals	$8,595,518 36	$1,069,465 99	$815,889 01	$69,493 27	$345,277 42	$558,866 31	$507,260 49

[1] Estimated. [2] Road in process of construction and items not given. [3] Includes engines. [4] Items not reported.

"D."—*Abstract from Reports of Railroads Operated in Wisconsin in 1872*—continued.

Name of Company.	EXPENDITURES—*continued.*						
	Wages of Employes.	Salaries of Officers.	Other operating expenses.	Taxes.	Interest.	New Construction.	Dividends.
Chicago and Northwestern		[1] $6,568,845 77	[7] $847,735 56	$330,150 35	$1,254,252 26	$4,696,067 79	$2,001,746 06
Green Bay and Lake Pepin	[2] $34,776 00	12,000 00			47,812 46	1,357,500 00	
La Crosse, Tremp. & Prescott		[1] 47,479 01	1,077 23	14 00	100,000 00	15,639 22	
Madison and Portage	[3]			645 34			
Mil. Lake Shore and Western	[4]						
Milwaukee and Northern	13,780 09	3,367 60			74,560 00		
Milwaukee and St. Paul	[3]	[3]	[5] 417,150 14	148,668 05	967,175 00	606,806 25	231,508 71
Mineral Point	25,830 52	9,900 00		3,064 43	32,000 00		
Prairie du Chien & McGregor	500 00						
SaintCroix and Lake Superior	[6]						
Sheboygan and Fond du Lac	20,294 46	2,500 00		2,354 27	80,690 00		
Superior and St. Croix	5,974 18	[6]					
Western Union	[3]	[3]		31,233 66	125,682 41	71,761 13	
West Wisconsin	148,662 53	25,260 00		11,149 51		414,789 68	
Wisconsin Central	[8] 26,027 01			3,519 40			
	$275,344 79	$6,669,352 38	$765,962 93	$530,799 01	$2,682,172 13	$7,162,584 07	$2,233,254 77

[1] Includes the six preceding items.
[2] Estimated.
[3] Included in other items.
[4] Road in process of construction and items not given.
[5] Paid on indebtedness.
[6] Items not reported.
[7] Including $123,517 50 for losses, expenses and renewals on account of the Chicago fire.
[8] Including officers' salaries.

"D"—*Abstracts from Reports of Railroads operated in Wisconsin in* 1872—continued.

Name of Company.	Expenditures—continued.		Losses from Casualties.	Indebtedness.	Freights in Tons.			
	Other Purposes.	Total.			Lumber.	Wheat.	Oats, Rye and Barley.	Corn.
Chicago and Northwestern....	[1]$1,392,976 15	$16,591,793 94	....	$22,492,457 80	256,386	384,655	111,416	125,859
Green Bay and Lake Pepin....	....	1,579,772 41	....	2,546,000 00	7,185	273	199	122
La Crosse, Tremp, and Presc'tt	....	164,209 46	....	1,424,091 51	4,068	12,639	1,314	83
Madison and Portage..........	16,859 18	30,051 97	....	....	3,372	5,274	138	167
Mil., L. Shore and Western ...	....	....	....	3,000,000 00	[3].......	....	....	....
Milwaukee and Northern......	31,900 00	147,815 69	....	1,718,750 00	3,658	5,395	45	361
Milwaukee and St. Paul.......	1,075,626 39	4,909,658 91	$6,441 61	13,122,500 00	102,034	259,116	7,670	5,115
Mineral Point	6,138 92	137,528 42	....	320,000 00	2,060	6,295	8,667	27
Prairie du Chien and McGregor	....	750 00	....	....	....	....	....	....
St. Croix and Lake Superior...	[3]...............	....	....	132,000 00	[3].......	....	....	....
Sheboygan and Fond du Lac..	....	161,713 81	....	1,595,689 47	13,428	5,720	79	171
Superior and St. Croix	....	5,974 18	[2]...........	....	....	....	....	....
Western Union...............	285,957 11	916,091 21	5,140 08	3,684,578 89	36,353	30,689	17,219	39,039
West Wisconsin..............	127,633 02	847,554 82	217 25	4,640,000 00	57,479	14,870	273	1,378
Wisconsin Central............	11,356 78	71,789 31	....	....	5,286	77	486	549
Total	$2,948,447 55	$25,564,704 13	$11,798 94	$54,676,067 67	491,309	725,003	147,506	172,821

[1] Losses, expenses and renewals, occasioned by "Chicago fire," rental of leased lands and new rolling stock.
[2] Business done by construction train and no report made. [3] Items not reported.

"D."—*Abstracts from Reports of Railroads Operated in Wisconsin in 1872*—continued.

Name of Company.	Freights (in tons)—*continued.*								No. of Horses and Cattle.	No. of Hogs and Sheep.
	Flour.	Farm Implements.	Lead.	Iron.	Coal.	Merchandise.	Miscellaneous.	Total.		
Chicago and Northwestern	20,180	39,928	....	539,584	198,460	384,280	[1]544,813	2,605,561	182,044	359,842
Green Bay and Lake Pepin	146	12	....	45	297	1,049	1,924	11,251	....	....
La Crosse, Trempealeau and Prescott	10,653	726	....	14	....	6,270	89,854	125,575	....	....
Madison and Portage	21	176	....	....	....	198	1,433	10,779	....	....
Milwaukee and Northern	5,202	95	....	11	325	4,619	3,425	23,136	....	....
Milwaukee and St Paul	65,678	10,381	880	119,874	22,766	130,816	572,444	1,296,774	24,075	126,715
Mineral Point	859	682	1,789	15,450	2,383	5,179	8,540	51,931	5,374	32,796
Prairie du Chien and McGregor	....	....	....	....	....	....	21,622	21,622	....	....
Sheboygan and Fond du Lac	3,811	423	....	....	2,164	5,467	[2]14,911	46,174	389	354
Western Union	4,310	7,899	....	1,186	18,895	18,122	62,547	236,259	5,161	77,832
West Wisconsin	3,762	1,072	530	682	1,291	14,917	22,859	119,113	94	344
Wisconsin Central	683	47	....	109	211	5,527	4,490	17,465	24	154
Total	115,305	61,441	3,199	676,955	246,792	576,444	1,348,862	4,565,640	217,161	597,537

[1] Includes lead.

[2] Includes dressed hogs and cement.

"D."—*Abstracts from Reports of Railroads Operated in Wisconsin in* 1872—continued.

Name of Company.	Number of Through Passengers.	Number of Way Passengers.	Total.	Rate per Mile for Through Passengers.	Rate per Mile for Way Passengers.	Number of Passengers Killed.	Number of Employes Killed.	Number of others Killed.	Total.
Chicago and Northwestern.....	1,655,078	797,019	2,452,097	\$0 08$\frac{11}{100}$	\$0 02$\frac{43}{100}$	7	......	......	7
Green Bay and Lake Pepin.....	1,460	5,157	6,617	03$\frac{75}{100}$	04	......	......	......	......
La Crosse, Trempealeau & Presct	48,358	7,468	55,826	03$\frac{50}{100}$	05	......	......	......	......
Madison and Portage	13,636	....	13,636	04$\frac{89}{100}$	....	1	......	......	1
Milwaukee and Northern	131	40,797	40,928	04	04	......	......	......	......
Milwaukee and St. Paul........	70,017	541,413	611,430	03$\frac{43}{100}$	03$\frac{43}{100}$	1	14	5	20
Mineral Point	5,681	11,845	17,026	05	05	......	......	......	......
Prairie du Chien and McGregor.	836	....	836	05	....	......	......	......	......
Sheboygan and Fond du Lac...	608	65,277	65,885	03$\frac{70}{100}$	04$\frac{33}{100}$	1	......	......	1
Western Union	2,418	188,324	190,742	03$\frac{87}{100}$	03$\frac{87}{100}$	4	1	......	5
West Wisconsin	1,154	89,151	90,305	03$\frac{46}{100}$	04$\frac{54}{100}$	......	1	......	1
Wisconsin Central	36,781	....	36,781	04$\frac{246}{1000}$	....	......	......	......	......
Total	1,836,158	1,745,951	3,582,109	\$0 03$\frac{36}{100}$	\$0 04$\frac{6}{100}$	14	16	5	35

"D."—*Abstracts of Reports of Railroads Operated in Wisconsin in 1872*—continued.

NAME OF COMPANY.	Number of Passengers Injured.	Number of employes Injured.	Number of others Injured.	Total.	Total number killed and injured.	CAUSES OF DEATHS AND INJURIES. Lying on track.	Getting on train.	Getting off train.	Crossing track.	Falling off train.	Coupling cars.	Trains running off track.	Walking on track.	Other causes.
Chicago and Northwestern	5	1	.....	6	13	.....	.....	.....	.....	.....	.....	.....	.....	.....
Green Bay and Lake Pepin	.....	.....	.....	.....	.....	.....	.....	.....	.....	.....	.....	.....	.....	.....
La Crosse, Trempealeau and Prescott	.....	1	.....	1	1	.....	.....	.....	.....	.....	1	.....	.....	.....
Madison and Portage	.....	.....	.....	.....	.....	.....	.....	.....	.....	.....	.....	.....	.....	1
Milwaukee and Northern	.....	.....	.....	.....	.....	.....	.....	.....	.....	.....	.....	.....	.....	.....
Milwaukee and St. Paul	25	8	11	44	64	3	6	7	1	1	7	.....	7	32
Mineral Point	.....	.....	.....	.....	.....	.....	.....	.....	.....	.....	.....	.....	.....	.....
Prairie du Chien and McGregor	.....	.....	.....	.....	.....	.....	.....	.....	.....	.....	.....	.....	.....	.....
Sheboygan and Fond du Lac	.....	2	.....	2	3	.....	.....	.....	.....	.....	2	.....	.....	1
Western Union	9	3	.....	12	17	.....	3	1	.....	.....	3	5	3	2
West Wisconsin	1	1	.....	2	3	.....	.....	.....	.....	.....	2	.....	.....	1
Wisconsin Central	.....	.....	.....	.....	.....	.....	.....	.....	.....	.....	.....	.....	.....	.....
Totals	40	16	11	67	101	13	9	8	1	1	15	5	10	37

"D"—*Abstracts from Reports of Railroads operated in Wisconsin in* 1872—continued.

A COMPARATIVE TABLE SHOWING THE BUSINESS OF THE RAILROAD COMPANIES FOR 1871 AND 1872.

	CHICAGO AND NORTHWESTERN.		GREEN BAY AND LAKE PEPIN.		LA CROSSE, TREMPEALEAU AND PRESCOTT.	
	1871.	*1872.*	*1871.*	*1872.*	**1871.*	*1872.*
Length of road in Wisconsin. ... Miles	373 $\frac{4}{10}$	418 $\frac{64}{100}$	40	40	....	29
Dividends	$2,508,780 20	$2,001,746 06	....	....	....	....
Receipts	11,008,280 46	12,272,063 98	....	$32,216 50	....	$219,678 11
Gross earnings in Wisconsin	2,144,047 97	2,625,885 23	....	....	....	219,673 11
Indebtedness	22,159,397 08	22,492,457 80	$640,000	2,546 000 00	....	1,424,091 56
Expenditures	14,311,634 12	9,345,062 26	....	1,579,772 41	....	164,209 46
Losses from casualties	....	....	....	....	....	....
Freights ... Ton	2,631,868	2,605,561	....	11,251	....	125,575
Cattle and horses transported ... No.	104,892	182,044	....	....	....	....
Hogs and sheep transported ... No.	327,923	359,842	....	....	....	....
Passengers ... No.	2,339,545	2,452,097	....	6,617	....	55,826
Killed—passengers ... No.	....	7	....	....	....	....
Injured—passengers ... No.	....	....	....	....	....	....
Employes and others killed ... No.	4	5	....	....	....	1
Employes and others injured ... No.	6	1	....	....	....	....

*No report.

"D."—*Abstracts from Reports of Railroads Operated in Wisconsin in 1872.—Comparative Table*—continued.

		MADISON AND PORTAGE.		MILWAUKEE, LAKE SHORE AND WESTERN.		MILWAUKEE AND NORTHERN.	
		1871.	*1872.*	**1871.*	*1872.*	*1871.*	*1872.*
Length of road in Wisconsin	**Miles**	39	39	....	43	$18\frac{73}{100}$	$92\frac{88}{100}$
Dividends		....	....	....	....	....	....
Receipts		$25,294 20	$38,241 60	....	$15,940 39	$7,822 14	$120,840 44
Gross earnings in Wisconsin		25,294 20	38,241 60	....	15,940 39	7,822 14	....
Indebtedness		627,000 00	....	....	3,000,000 00	408,430 00	1,718,750 00
Expenditures		4,729 72	30,051 97	....	....	....	147,815 69
Losses from casualties		....	....	....	....	....	....
Freight	Tons	351	10,779	....	....	....	23,136
Cattle and horses transported	No.	....	8	....	....	....	....
Hogs and sheep transported	No.	....	62	....	....	....	....
Passengers	No.	....	13,636	....	....	....	40,928
Killed—passengers	No.	....	1	....	....	....	....
Injured—passengers	No.	....	....	....	....	....	....
Employes and others killed	No.	....	....	....	....	....	....
Employes and others injured	No.	....	....	....	....	....	....

* No report.

"D."—*Abstracts from Reports of Railroads Operated in Wisconsin in* 1872—*Comparative Table*—continued.

	MILWAUKEE AND ST. PAUL.		MINERAL POINT.		PRAIRIE DU CHIEN AND McGREGOR.	
	1871.	*1872.*	*1871.*	*1872.*	*1871**	*1872.*
Length of road in Wisconsin. Miles.	622	622	49	49		2
Dividends	$463,017 42	$231,508 71				
Receipts	4,766,599 53	4,485,111 10	$98,066 90	$115,043 06		$8,947 15
Gross earnings in Wisconsin	4,766,599 53	4,485,111 10	94,221 14	110,531 56		8,454 15
Indebtedness	13,122,500 00	13,122,500 00	320,000 00	320,000 00		
Expenditures	4,627,903 03	4,909,658 91	118,133 78	137,528 42		750 00
Losses from casualties	9,559 11	6,441 61				
Freights. Tons	1,055,680	1,296,774	20,521	51,931		836
Cattle and horses transported.. No.	16,628	24,075	4,208	5,374		
Hogs and sheep transported ... No.	121,573	126,715	38,436	32,796		
Passengers ... No.	583,788	611,430	16,554	17,026		
Killed—passengers ... No.		1				
Injured—passengers ... No.	2	25				
Employes and others killed ... No.	12	19				
Employes and others injured.. No.	12	19				

*No Report.

"D."—*Abstracts from Reports of Railroads Operated in Wisconsin in 1872—Comparative Table*—continued.

	ST. CROIX AND LAKE SUPERIOR.		SHEBOYGAN AND FOND DU LAC.		SUPERIOR AND ST. CROIX.	
	**1871.*	*1872.*	*1871.*	*1872.*	**1871.*	*1872.*
Length of road in Wis. .Miles.	....	....	43	$78\frac{54}{100}$	....	....
Dividends	....	....	....	....	....	....
Receipts	....	....	$77,809 28	$125,820 90	....	....
Gross earnings in Wisconsin	....	....	77,809 28	125,820 90	....	....
Indebtedness	....	$132,000 00	1,220,000 00	1,595,689 47	....	....
Expenditures	....	....	450,660 70	161,713 81	....	$5,974 18
Losses from casualties	....	....	....	....	....	....
Freights ...Tons.	....	....	34,821	46,174	....	....
Cattle and horses transp'd. No.	....	....	28	389	....	....
Hogs and sheep transp'ed. No.	....	....	149	354	....	....
Passengers ...No.	....	....	32,318	65,885	....	....
Killed—passengers ...No.	....	....	....	1	....	....
Injured—passengers ...No.	....	....	....	....	....	....
Employes and others kil'd. No.	....	....	1	....	....	....
Employes and others inj'd. No.	....	....	....	2	....	....

*No report.

"D."—*Abstracts from Reports of Railroads Operated in Wisconsin in* 1872—*Comparative Table*—continued.

	WESTERN UNION.		WEST WISCONSIN.		WISCONSIN CENTRAL.	
	1871.	*1872.*	*1871.*	*1872.*	*1871.*	*1872.*
Length of road in Wis......Miles.	$85\frac{3}{10}$	$85\frac{2}{10}$	157	197	62.88	$114\frac{2}{10}$
Dividends....................	....	....	....	....	....	....
Receipts.....................	$842,169 22	$847,111 21	$159,664 64	$365,999 82	$12,366 93	....
Gross earnings in Wisconsin	336,078 77	334,913 57	159,664 64	365,999 82	12,366 93	$116,889 99
Indebtedness.................	3,571,020 51	3,684,578 89	3,700,000 00	4,640,000 00	....	....
Expenditures.................	800,298 18	916,091 21	129,820 43	847,554 82	5,990 48	71,789 81
Losses from casualties...........	4,309 00	5,140 08	19 00	217 25	....	....
Freights..................Tons.	234,867	236,259	33,808	119,113	1,881	17,465
Cattle and horses transported..No.	4,331	5,161	34,079	94	12	24
Hogs and sheep......do .....No.	87,732	77,332	....	344	41	154
Passengers..........do......No.	190,059	190,742	....	90,805	$4,571\frac{1}{2}$	86,781
Killed—passengers..........No.	3	4	....	....	....	....
Injured— ...do.............No.	6	9	....	1	....	....
Employes and others killed...No.	2	1	....	1	....	....
Employes and others injured .No.	1	3	2	1	....	....

CHICAGO AND NORTHWESTERN RAILWAY COMPANY.

ANNUAL REPORT of the Operations of the CHICAGO AND NORTHWESTERN RAILWAY COMPANY, being a railroad company in the states of Illinois, Iowa, Michigan and Wisconsin, during the year ending on the 31st day of December, 1872, made to the stockholders of said company, in accordance with the provisions of chapter 91 of the General Laws of 1858.

	Miles.
I. Whole length of road operated by this company in Wisconsin and elsewhere, December 31, 1872	1,415
458 5/10 miles of which in the states of Illinois, Iowa and Wisconsin are perpetually leased to this company.	
Length of double track	30
Length of other lines operated by this company in Wisconsin, as follows:	
Wisconsin Division, from Sharon to Menomonee river.	220 5/10
Kenosha ....do......Genoa to Kenosha	27 5/10
Madison .. ..do......Beloit to Elroy	121 7/10
Galena..........do......Genoa to Geneva Lake	8 7/10
Milwaukee .....do......State Line to Milwaukee	40 44/100
Weight of rail per yard, 40 @ 60 pounds.	

II. Amount of capital stock subscribed .. Amount of capital stock paid	....	$36,242,743 82
III. Cost of road to December 31, 1871, and equipment to June 1, 1874	$48,721,484 71	.. ..
For right of way, included in above	....	....
For bridging .... do	....	....
For grading ....do	....	....
For iron ....do	....	....
For buildings ....do	....	....
For engines and cars, prior to June 1, 1864, included in above	....	....
For engines and cars purchased and built, June 1, 1864, to Dec. 31, 1871.	5,693,986 95	....
Costing in all		$54,415,471 66
IV. Amount of indebtedness—		
First mortgage	$21,073,000 00	....
Second mortgage	1,130,000 00	....
Third mortgage	9,500 00	....
Floating debt	279,957 80	....
		$22,492,457 80

'D"—*Abstracts from Reports of Railroads operated in Wisconsin in* 1872—continued.

Name of Company.	Expenditures—continued. Other Purposes.	Expenditures—continued. Total.	Losses from Casualties.	Indebtedness.	Freights in Tons. Lumber.	Freights in Tons. Wheat.	Freights in Tons. Oats, Rye and Barley.	Freights in Tons. Corn.
Chicago and Northwestern....	[1]$1,392,976 15	$16,591,793 94	....	$22,492,457 80	256,386	384,655	111,416	125,859
Green Bay and Lake Pepin....	....	1,579,772 41	....	2,546,000 00	7,185	273	199	122
La Crosse, Tremp, and Presc'tt	....	164,209 46	....	1,424,091 51	4,068	12,639	1,314	83
Madison and Portage..........	16,859 18	30,051 97	....	....	3,372	5,274	138	167
Mil., L. Shore and Western ...	....	....	....	3,000,000 00	[2]........	....	....	....
Milwaukee and Northern......	31,900 00	147,815 69	....	1,718,750 00	3,658	5,395	45	361
Milwaukee and St. Paul.......	1,075,626 39	4,909,658 91	$6,441 61	13,122,500 00	102,034	259,116	7,670	5,115
Mineral Point................	6,138 92	137,528 42	....	320,000 00	2,060	6,295	8,667	27
Prairie du Chien and McGregor	....	750 00	....	....	....	....	....	....
St. Croix and Lake Superior...	[3]...............	....	....	132,000 00	[3]........	....	....	....
Sheboygan and Fond du Lac..	....	161,713 81	....	1,595,689 47	13,428	5,720	79	171
Superior and St. Croix	....	5,974 18	[2]............	....	....	....	....	....
Western Union...............	285,957 11	916,091 21	5,140 08	3,684,578 89	36,353	30,689	17,219	39,039
West Wisconsin..............	127,633 02	847,554 82	217 25	4,640,000 00	57,479	14,870	273	1,378
Wisconsin Central...........	11,356 78	71,789 31	....	....	5,286	77	486	549
Total	$2,948,447 55	$25,564,704 13	$11,798 94	$54,676,067 67	491,309	725,003	147,506	172,821

[1] Losses, expenses and renewals, occasioned by "Chicago fire," rental of leased lands and new rolling stock.
[2] Business done by construction train and no report made. [3] Items not reported.

"D."—*Abstracts from Reports of Railroads Operated in Wisconsin in 1872*—continued.

Name of Company.	Freights (in tons)—*continued.*								No. of Horses and Cattle.	No. of Hogs and Sheep.
	Flour.	Farm Implements.	Lead.	Iron.	Coal.	Merchandise.	Miscellaneous.	Total.		
Chicago and Northwestern	20,180	39,928	....	539,584	198,460	384,280	[1] 544,813	2,605,561	182,044	359,842
Green Bay and Lake Pepin	146	12	....	45	297	1,049	1,924	11,251	....	....
La Crosse, Trempealeau and Prescott	10,653	726	....	14	....	6,270	89,854	125,575	....	....
Madison and Portage	21	176	....	....	....	198	1,433	10,779	....	....
Milwaukee and Northern	5,202	95	....	11	325	4,619	3,425	23,136	....	....
Milwaukee and St Paul	65,678	10,381	880	119,874	22,766	130,816	572,444	1,296,774	24,075	126,715
Mineral Point	859	682	1,789	15,450	2,383	5,179	8,540	51,931	5,374	32,796
Prairie du Chien and McGregor	....	....	....	....	....	....	21,622	21,622	....	....
Sheboygan and Fond du Lac	3,811	423	....	....	2,164	5,467	[2] 14,911	46,174	389	354
Western Union	4,310	7,899	....	1,186	18,895	18,122	62,547	236,259	5,161	77,332
West Wisconsin	3,762	1,072	530	682	1,291	14,917	22,859	119,113	94	344
Wisconsin Central	683	47	....	109	211	5,527	4,490	17,465	24	154
Total	115,305	61,441	3,199	676,955	246,792	576,444	1,348,862	4,565,640	217,161	597,537

[1] Includes lead.

[2] Includes dressed hogs and cement.

"D."—*Abstracts from Reports of Railroads Operated in Wisconsin in* 1872—continued.

NAME OF COMPANY.	Number of Through Passengers.	Number of Way Passengers.	Total.	Rate per Mile for Through Passengers.	Rate per Mile for Way Passengers.	Number of Passengers Killed.	Number of Employes Killed.	Number of others Killed.	Total.
Chicago and Northwestern	1,655,078	797,019	2,452,097	\$0 03$\frac{11}{100}$	\$0 02$\frac{43}{100}$	7	......	......	7
Green Bay and Lake Pepin	1,460	5,157	6,617	03$\frac{75}{100}$	04	......	......	......	...
La Crosse, Trempealeau & Presct	48,358	7,468	55,826	03$\frac{50}{100}$	05	......	......	......	...
Madison and Portage	13,636	....	13,636	04$\frac{39}{100}$	....	1	......	......	1
Milwaukee and Northern	131	40,797	40,928	04	04	......	......	......	...
Milwaukee and St. Paul	70,017	541,413	611,430	03$\frac{43}{100}$	03$\frac{43}{100}$	1	14	5	20
Mineral Point	5,681	11,345	17,026	05	05	......	......	......	...
Prairie du Chien and McGregor	836	....	836	05	....	......	......	......	...
Sheboygan and Fond du Lac	608	65,277	65,885	03$\frac{70}{100}$	04$\frac{33}{100}$	1	......	......	1
Western Union	2,418	188,324	190,742	03$\frac{87}{100}$	03$\frac{87}{100}$	4	1	......	5
West Wisconsin	1,154	89,151	90,305	03$\frac{46}{100}$	04$\frac{54}{100}$	......	1	......	1
Wisconsin Central	36,781	....	36,781	04$\frac{246}{1000}$	....	......	......	......	...
Total	1,836,158	1,745,951	3,582,109	\$0 03$\frac{26}{100}$	\$0 04$\frac{6}{100}$	14	16	5	35

"D."—*Abstracts of Reports of Railroads Operated in Wisconsin in 1872*—continued.

Name of Company.	Number of Passengers Injured.	Number of employes Injured.	Number of others Injured.	Total.	Total number killed and injured.	CAUSES OF DEATHS AND INJURIES. Lying on track.	Getting on train.	Getting off train.	Crossing track.	Falling off train.	Coupling cars.	Trains running off track.	Walking on track.	Other causes.
Chicago and Northwestern	5	1	......	6	13	......	......	......	......	......	......	......	......	......
Green Bay and Lake Pepin	......	......	......	......	......	......	......	......	......	......	......	......	......	......
La Crosse, Trempealean and Prescott	......	1	......	1	1	......	......	......	......	......	1	......	......	......
Madison and Portage	......	......	......	......	......	......	......	......	......	......	......	......	......	1
Milwaukee and Northern	......	......	......	......	......	......	......	......	......	......	......	......	......	......
Milwaukee and St. Paul	25	8	11	44	64	8	6	7	1	1	7	......	7	32
Mineral Point	......	......	......	......	......	......	......	......	......	......	......	......	......	......
Prairie du Chien and McGregor	......	......	......	......	......	......	......	......	......	......	......	......	......	......
Sheboygan and Fond du Lac	......	2	......	2	3	......	......	......	......	......	2	......	......	1
Western Union	9	3	......	12	17	......	3	1	......	......	3	5	3	2
West Wisconsin	1	1	......	2	3	......	......	......	......	......	2	......	......	1
Wisconsin Central	......	......	......	......	......	......	......	......	......	......	......	......	......	......
Totals	40	16	11	67	101	13	9	8	1	1	15	5	10	37

"D"—*Abstracts from Reports of Railroads operated in Wisconsin in* 1872—continued.

A COMPARATIVE TABLE SHOWING THE BUSINESS OF THE RAILROAD COMPANIES FOR 1871 AND 1872.

	CHICAGO AND NORTHWESTERN.		GREEN BAY AND LAKE PEPIN.		LA CROSSE, TREMPEALEAU AND PRESCOTT.	
	1871.	*1872.*	*1871.*	*1872.*	**1871.*	*1872.*
Length of road in Wisconsin....Miles	373 4/10	418 64/100	40	40	....	29
Dividends	$2,508,780 20	$2,001,746 06	....	....	....	....
Receipts	11,008,280 46	12,272,063 98	....	$32,216 50	....	$219,673 11
Gross earnings in Wisconsin	2,144,047 97	2,625,885 23	....	....	....	219,673 11
Indebtedness	22,159,397 03	22,492,457 80	$640,000	2,546 000 00	....	1,424,091 56
Expenditures	14,311,634 12	9,345,062 26	....	1,579,772 41	....	164,209 46
Losses from casualties	....	....	....	....	....	....
Freights....Ton	2,631,868	2,605,561	....	11,251	....	125,575
Cattle and horses transported....No.	104,892	182,044	....	....	....	....
Hogs and sheep transported....No.	327,923	359,842	....	....	....	....
Passengers....No.	2,339,545	2,452,097	....	6,617	....	55,826
Killed—passengers....No.	....	7	....	....	....	....
Injured—passengers....No.	....	....	....	....	....	....
Employes and others killed....No.	4	5	....	....	....	1
Employes and others injured....No.	6	1	....	....	....	....

*No report.

"D."—*Abstracts from Reports of Railroads Operated in Wisconsin in 1872.—Comparative Table*—continued.

		MADISON AND PORTAGE.		MILWAUKEE, LAKE SHORE AND WESTERN.		MILWAUKEE AND NORTHERN.	
		1871.	*1872.*[1]	**1871.*	*1872.*	*1871.*	*1872.*
Length of road in Wisconsin	Miles	89	89		43	$13\frac{74}{100}$	$92\frac{44}{100}$
Dividends							
Receipts		$25,294 20	$38,241 60		$15,940 39	$7,822 14	$120,840 44
Gross earnings in Wisconsin		25,294 20	38,241 60		15,940 39	7,822 14	
Indebtedness		627,000 00			3,000,000 00	408,430 00	1,718,750 00
Expenditures		4,729 72	30,051 97				147,815 69
Losses from casualties							
Freight	Tons	351	10,779				23,136
Cattle and horses transported	No.		8				
Hogs and sheep transported	No.		62				
Passengers	No.		13,636				40,928
Killed—passengers	No.		1				
Injured—passengers	No.						
Employes and others killed	No.						
Employes and others injured	No.						

*No report.

"D."—*Abstracts from Reports of Railroads Operated in Wisconsin in* 1872—*Comparative Table*—continued.

	MILWAUKEE AND ST. PAUL.		MINERAL POINT.		PRAIRIE DU CHIEN AND McGREGOR.	
	1871.	*1872.*	*1871.*	*1872.*	*1871**	*1872.*
Length of road in Wisconsin. Miles.	622	622	49	49	....	2
Dividends	$463,017 42	$231,508 71	....	....	....	....
Receipts	4,766,599 53	4,485,111 10	$98,066 90	$115,043 06	....	$3,947 15
Gross earnings in Wisconsin	4,766,599 53	4,485,111 10	94,221 14	110,531 56	....	3,454 15
Indebtedness	13,122,500 00	13,122,500 00	320,000 00	320,000 00	....	....
Expenditures	4,627,903 03	4,909,658 91	118,133 78	137,528 42	....	750 00
Losses from casualties	9,559 11	6,441 61	....	....	....	....
Freights Tons	1,055,680	1,296,774	20,521	51,931	....	836
Cattle and horses transported.. No.	16,628	24,075	4,208	5,374	....	....
Hogs and sheep transported ... No.	121,573	126,715	38,436	32,796	....	....
Passengers ... No.	583,783	611,430	16,554	17,026	....	....
Killed—passengers ... No.	....	1	....	....	....	....
Injured—passengers ... No.	2	25	....	....	....	....
Employes and others killed ... No.	12	19	....	....	....	....
Employes and others injured.. No.	12	19	....	....	....	....

*No Report.

"D."—*Abstracts from Reports of Railroads Operated in Wisconsin in 1872—Comparative Table*—continued.

	ST. CROIX AND LAKE SUPERIOR.		SHEBOYGAN AND FOND DU LAC.		SUPERIOR AND ST. CROIX.	
	**1871.*	*1872.*	*1871.*	*1872.*	**1871.*	*1872.*
Length of road in Wis. . Miles.	....	....	43	$78\frac{14}{16}$	....	....
Dividends	....	....	....	....	....	....
Receipts	....	....	$77,809 28	$125,820 90	....	....
Gross earnings in Wisconsin	....	....	77,809 28	125,820 90	....	....
Indebtedness	....	$132,000 00	1,220,000 00	1,595,689 47	....	....
Expenditures	....	....	450,660 70	161,713 81	....	$5,974 18
Losses from casualties	....	....	....	....	....	....
Freights . . . Tons.	....	....	34,821	46,174	....	....
Cattle and horses transp'd. No.	....	....	23	389	....	....
Hogs and sheep transp'ed. No.	....	....	149	354	....	....
Passengers . . . No.	....	....	32,318	65,885	....	....
Killed—passengers . . . No.	....	....	....	1	....	....
Injured—passengers . . . No.	....	....	....	....	....	....
Employes and others kil'd. No.	....	....	1	....	....	....
Employes and others inj'd. No.	....	....	....	2	....	....

*No report.

Number of passengers killed—con.		
Number of employes killed........	None.	....
No. of passengers and others injured	None.	....
Number of employes injured......	None.	....
		....
XIV. The cause of death is as follows: "Crazy man," escaped from his keepers and jumped from train while moving at full speed	One.	....
		....

XV. Of the foregoing accidents none have arisen from carelessness or negligence of employes on the road.

The employes from whose carelessness or negligence such accidents have arisen, retained in the service of the corporation, are as follows: none.

State of Wisconsin—County of Milwaukee—ss.

We, R. D. Jennings, Treasurer, and H. C. Atkins, Superintendent of the Madison and Portage Railroad Company, do each of us solemnly swear, that the foregoing report has been made from the best sources of information at our disposal, and that the several matters therein set forth are correct and true, to the best of our knowledge, information and belief. So help us God.

R. D. JENNINGS, *Treasurer*.
H. C. ATKINS, *Superintendent*.

Subscribed and sworn to before me, this 10th day of February, 1873.
D. C. Green, *Notary Public*, Milwaukee, Co., Wis.

MILWAUKEE, LAKE SHORE AND WESTERN RAILROAD COMPANY.

Annual Report of the operations of the Milwaukee, Lake Shore and Western Railroad Company, being a railroad company in the state of Wisconsin, during the year ending on the thirty-first day of December, 1872, made to the stockholders of said company, in accordance with the provisions of chapter 91 of the general laws of 1858.

	Miles
I. Whole length of road operated by this company in Wisconsin and elsewhere	43
Length of double track	3
Roads in Wisconsin—	
Length of main line from Manitowoc to Appleton...........	43
Weight of rail per yard, 50 to 60 pounds.	

"D"—*Abstract of Railroads—M., L. S. & W. R. R. Co.*—con.

II. Amount of capital stock subscribed	....	$3,000,000 00
Amount of capital stock paid	....	1,250,000 00
III. Cost of road and equipment	Road in process of construction.	
For right of way		
For bridging		
For grading		
For iron		
For buildings		
For engines and cars		
For other purposes	....	....
IV. Amount of indebtedness	....	....
First mortgage	$3,000,000	....
Second mortgage	....	....
Third mortgage	....	....
Floating debt	....	....
V. Receipts from the following sources:		
From passengers	$5,149 25	....
From mails	....	....
From express companies	....	....
From freight	10,791 14	....
From interest	....	....
From other sources	....	....
		$15,940 39
VI. Amount of gross earnings in the state of Wisconsin	....	$15,940 39
VII. Expenditures	Road incomplete and in process of construction.	
For repairs of road		
For buildings		
For engines		
For cars		
For fuel		
For wages of employes		
For salaries exceeding one thousand dollars		
For taxes		
For interest on		
For indebtedness		
For new construction		
For dividends		
For other purposes		
VIII. Amount due the corporation	....	....
IX. Loss to the company from casualty	....	....

"D"—*Abstract of Railroads—M., L. S. & W. R. R. Co.*—con.

X. Amount of freight reduced to tons, except animals— Lumber, Wheat, Oats, Corn, Flour, Farming implements, Lead, Iron, Coal, Merchandise, Miscellaneous, Cattle, Hogs and sheep	Business done by construction train. No regular business carried on.	
XI. Number of through passengers— Number of way passengers, Rate per mile of through passengers, Rate per mile of way passengers	Road operated by contractors.	
XII. Number of dividends declared	....	....
When made	....	....
How paid	....	....
XIII. Number of passengers and others killed	....	....
Number of employes killed	....	....
Number of passengers and others injured	....	....
Number of employes injured	....	....

STATE OF WISCONSIN—COUNTY OF MANITOWOC—ss.

We, C. Luling, secretary, C. C. Barnes, treasurer, and H. G. H. Reed, Superintendent of the Milwaukee, Lake Shore and Western Railroad Company, do each of us solemnly swear, that the foregoing report has been made from the best sources of information at our disposal, and that the several matters therein set forth are correct and true, to the best of our knowledge, information and belief. So help us God.

C. LULING, *Secretary*.
C. C. BARNES, *Treasurer*.
H. G. H. REED, *Superintendent*.

Subscribed and sworn to before me this 11th day of September, 1873,
GEO. B. BURNET, Notary Public.

MILWAUKEE AND NORTHERN RAILWAY COMPANY.

Annual Report of the operations of the Milwaukee and Northern Railway Company, being a Railroad Company in the State of Wisconsin, during the year ending on the thirty-first day of December, 1872, made to the Stockholders of said Company, in accordance with the provisions of Chapter 91 of the General Laws of 1858.

	Miles.
I. Whole length of road operated by this Company in Wisconsin and elsewhere	$92\frac{43}{100}$
Length of double track	....
Roads in Wisconsin:—	
Length of main line from Schwartzburg to Menasha	$92\frac{43}{100}$
Length of other lines operated by this Company in Wisconsin, as follows:	
Milwaukee & St. Paul railroad, from Milwaukee to Schwartzburg	$6\frac{17}{100}$
Weight of rail per yard, 56 pounds.	

II. Amount of capital stock subscribed including Shawano Co. subscription	$1,783,000 00	....
Amount of capital stock paid	1,530,000 00	....
III. Cost of road and equipment—		
For right of way; For bridging; For grading; For iron; For buildings; For engines and cars; For other purposes — Road built by contract at a given rate per mile.		$8,249,050 00
IV. Amount of indebtedness:		
First mortgage	$1,625,000 00	....
Second mortgage	....	....
Third mortgage	....	....
Floating debt subject to adjustment by bonds under contract	93,750 00	....
		$1,718,750 00
V. Receipts from the following sources:		
From passengers	$57,251 89	....
From mails	838 92	....
From express companies	1,258 69	....
From freight	61,413 05	....
From interest	....	....
From other sources	77 89	....
		$120,840 44

"D."—*Abstract of Railroads—M. & N. R'y. Co.*—continued.

VI. Amount of gross earnings in the State of Wisconsin	....	....
VII. Expenditures:		
For repairs of road	$16,017 29	....
For buildings	3,261 79	....
For engines	289 42	....
For cars	....	....
For fuel	4,639 50	....
For wages of employes	13,780 09	....
For salaries exceeding one thousand dollars	3,367 60	....
For taxes	....	....
For interest on funded debt	74,560 00	....
For indebtedness	....	....
For new construction	....	....
For dividends	....	....
For other purposes	31,900 00	....
		$147,815 69
VIII. Amount due the corporation	....	....
IX. Loss to the company from casualty	....	....
X. Amount of freight reduced to tons except animals:	TONS.	LBS.
Lumber	3,658	1,460
Wheat	5,895	1,820
Oats	45	530
Corn	361	1,070
Flour	5,202	50
Farming implements	95	960
Lead	....	50
Iron	11	1,748
Coal	325	....
Merchandize	4,619	1,865
Miscellaneous	3,425	1,540
Cattle	....	....
Hogs and sheep	....	....
XI. Number of through passengers from December 1st	131	....
Number of way passengers from March 22d	40,797	....
Rate per mile of through passengers	4c	....
Rate per mile of way passengers	4c	....
XII. Number of dividends declared	....	....
When made	....	....
How paid	....	....
XIII. Number of passengers and others killed	....	....
Number of employes killed	....	....
Number of passengers and others injured	....	....
Number of employes injured	....	....
XIV. The cause of death is as follows:		
The cause of injuries is as follows:		

XV. Of the foregoing accidents, none have arisen from carelessness or negligence of employees on the road.

The employes from whose carelessness or negligence such accidents have arisen, retained in the service of the Corporation, are as follows; None.

STATE OF WISCONSIN—COUNTY OF MILWAUKEE—ss.

We, Wm. Taintor, Secretary and Treasurer, and Jared W. Crippen, Superintendent of Milwaukee and Northern Railway Company, do each of us solemnly swear, that the foregoing report has been made from the best sources of information at our disposal, and that the several matters therein set forth are correct and true, to the best of our knowledge, information and belief. So help us God.

WM. TAINTOR, *Secretary and Treasurer.*
J. W. CRIPPEN, *Superintendent.*

Subscribed and sworn to before me, this 10th day of February, 1873.
F. B. VAN VALKENBURG, *Notary Public.*

MINERAL POINT RAILROAD.

ANNUAL REPORT of the operations of the MINERAL POINT RAILROAD, of Mineral Point, Wisconsin, being a Railroad Company in the State of Wisconsin, during the year ending on the thirty-first day of December, 1872, made to the stockholders of said company, in accordance with the provisions of Chapter 91 of the General Laws of 1858.

	Miles.
I. Whole length of road operated by this company, from Mineral Point to Warren, Ill	83
Length of double track	......
Length of main line from Mineral Point to State line, in Wis.	81
Length of other lines operated by this company in Wisconsin, is as follows:	
Dubuque, Platteville and Milwaukee Railroad, from Calamine, Wis., to Platteville, Wis.	18
Weight of rail per yard, 57 pounds.	

II. Amount of capital stock subscribed	....	....
Amount of capital stock paid	$1,200,000 00	$1,200,000 00
III. Cost of road and equipment:		
For right of way	....	....
For bridging	....	....
For grading	....	....
For iron	....	....
For buildings	....	....
For engines and cars	....	....
For other purposes	....	....
		$1,200,000 00

"D."—*Abstract of Railroads—Mineral Point R. R. Co.*—con.

IV. Amount of indebtedness:		
First mortgage	$320,000 00	
Second mortgage		
Third mortgage		
Floating debt		
		$320,000 00
V. Receipts from the following sources:		
From passengers	$17,698 67	
From mails	2,585 24	
From express companies	1,800 00	
From freight	92,964 15	
From interest		
From other sources		
		$115,043 06
VI. Amount of gross earnings in the State of Wisconsin		$110,531 56
VII. Expenditures:		
For repairs of road	$29,457 05	
For buildings	472 59	
For engines and cars		
For fuel	23,257 69	
For wages of employes	7,907 22	
For salaries exceeding one thousand	25,330 52	
dollars	9,900 00	
For taxes	3,064 43	
For interest on first mortgage bonds	32,000 00	
For indebtedness		
For new construction		
For dividends		
For other purposes	6,138 92	
		$137,528 42
VIII. Amount due the corporation		
IX. Loss to the company from casualty		
X. Amount of freight reduced to tons, except animals:		
Lumber	2,060,872	feet
Wheat	6,295	tons
Oats	8,667	tons
Corn	27	tons
Flour	859	tons
Cattle	5,374	head
Hogs and sheep	32,796	head
Farming implements	682	tons
Lead	1,789	...do
Zinc ore	15,450	...do
Coal	2,383	...do
Merchandise	5,179	...do
Miscellaneous	8,540	...do
XI. Number of through passengers	5,681	
Number of way passengers	11,345	
Rate per mile of through passengers	5 c.	
Rate per mile of way passengers	5 c.	

XII. Number of dividends declared	....	....
When made	....	....
How paid	....	....
XIII. Number of passengers and others killed	....	....
Number of employes killed	....	....
Number of passengers and others injured	....	....
Number of employes injured	....	....
XIV. The cause of death is as follows:		
The cause of injuries is as follows:		

XV. Of the foregoing accidents, —— have arisen from carelessness or negligence of employes on the road.

The employes from whose carelessness or negligence such accidents have arisen, retained in the service of the corporation, are as follows:

STATE OF WISCONSIN—COUNTY OF IOWA—ss.

We, Calvert Spensley, Auditor, and Geo. W. Cobb, Superintendent of the Mineral Point Railroad, do each of us solemnly swear, that the foregoing report has been made from the best sources of information at our disposal, and that the several matters therein set forth are correct and true, to the best of our knowledge, information and belief. So help us God.

CALVERT SPENSLEY, *Auditor*,
GEO. W. COBB, *Superintendent*.

Subscribed and sworn to before me, this 22d day of January, 1873.

CYRUS LANYON, *Notary Public*.

MILWAUKEE AND ST. PAUL RAILWAY COMPANY.

ANNUAL REPORT of the MILWAUKEE AND ST. PAUL RAILWAY COMPANY, being a railroad company in the State of Wisconsin, during the year ending on the thirty-first day of December, 1872, made to the stockholders of said company, in accordance with the provisions of chapter 91 of the general laws of 1858.

	Miles.
I. Whole length of road operated by this company	622
Length of double track	.....
Length of main line from Milwaukee to La Crosse, in Wisc'n	196
Length of main line from Milwaukee to Prairie du Chien	193
Length of other lines operated by this company in Wisconsin, as follows:	
La Crosse Division, from Watertown to Madison	38
Northern.........do.... Milwaukee to Portage	96
Northern.........do.... Horicon to Berlin	43
Northern.........do.... Rush Lake to Winneconne	14
Prairie du Chien..do.... Milton to Monroe	42
Weight of rail per yard, 60 pounds.	

"D."—*Abstract of Railroads—Mil. & St. P. R'y Co.*—continued

II. Amount of capital stock subscribed		$12,432,198 00	....
Amount of capital stock paid		12,432,198 00	$12,432,198 00
Cost of road and equipment—			
For right of way... For bridging... For grading... For iron... For buildings... For engines and cars	By purchase	$18,891,568 66	....
	By construction and equipment	6,642,410 95	....
For other purposes		....	....
			$25,533,979 61
IV. Amount of indebtedness—			
First mortgage		$10,447,000 00	....
Second mortgage		2,527,000 00	....
Real estate purchase money bonds		148,500 00	....
Floating debt, none.			
			$13,122,500 00
V. Receipts from the following sources—			
From passengers		$1,149,486 44	....
From mails		78,436 55	....
From express companies		108,758 39	....
From freight		3,075,454 98	....
From interest		....	....
From other sources		72,974 74	....
			$4,485,111 10
VI. Amount of gross earnings in the State of Wisconsin		....	$4,485,111 10
VII. Expenditures—			
For repairs of roads		$519,047 57	....
For buildings		44,128 47	....
For engines		161,795 08	....
For cars		386,585 75	....
For fuel		351,217 50	....
For wages of employes, $1,979,028 26, included in other items.			
For salaries of officers, exceeding one thousand dollars, $20,500, in above items.			
For taxes		148,668 05	....
For interest on bonds		967,175 00	....
For indebtedness		417,150 14	....
For new construction		606,806 25	....
For dividends		281,508 71	....
For other purposes		1,075,626 89	....
			$4,909,658 91
VIII. Amount due the corporation		....	$868,767 49
IX. Loss to the company from casualty		....	$6,441 61
X. Amount of freight reduced to tons, except animals—		Tons.	No.
Lumber		102,034	....
Wheat		259,116	....
Oats		7,670	....
Corn		5,115	....

"D."—*Abstract of Railroads—Mil. & St. P. R'y Co*—continued.

		Tons.	No.
	Amount of freight etc.—con.		
	Flour	65,678	
	Cattle	18,057	34,075
	Hogs and sheep	22,175	126,715
	Farming implements	10,881	
	Lead	880	
	Iron	33,833	
	Iron ore	86,041	
	Coal	22,766	
	Merchandize	130,816	
	Miscellaneous	572,444	
XI.	Number of through passengers	70,017	
	Number of way passengers	541,418	
	Rate per mile of through pass'gers / Rate per mile of way passengers	3 $\frac{44}{100}$ cts.	
XII.	Number of dividends declared	1	
	When made	Aug. 5, 1872	
	How paid, in cash	$231,508 71	
XIII.	Number of passengers killed	1	
	Number of persons other than passengers and employes killed	5	
	Number of employes killed	14	
			20
	Number of passengers injured	25	
	Number of persons other than passengers and employes injured	11	
	Number of employes injured	8	
			44
			64
XIV.	The cause of death is as follows: 3 getting on train while in motion, 3 getting off train while in motion, 2 coupling cars, 2 lying on track, 1 working cars on track, 2 collision, 1 walking on track, 1 getting truck on track, 2 explosion of engine boiler, 1 crossing track, 1 falling from train while in motion, 1 struck by spout at iron net	20	
	The cause of injuries is as follows: 6 walking on track, 4 getting off train while in motion, 3 getting on train while in motion, 2 falling on track, 5 coupling cars, 1 lying on track, 23 train running off track	44	
			64

XV. Of the foregoing accidents, none have arisen from carelessness or negligence of employes on the road.

The employes from whose carelessness or negligence such accidents have arisen, retained in the service of the corporation, are as follows: none.

STATE OF WISCONSIN—COUNTY OF MILWAUKEE—ss.

We, Royal D. Jennings, Secretary and Treasurer, and S. S. Merrill, General Manager of the Milwaukee and Saint Paul Railway Company, do each of us solemnly swear, that the foregoing report has been made from the best sources of information at our disposal, and that the several matters therein set forth are correct and true, to the best of our knowledge, information and belief. So help us God.

R. D. JENNINGS, *Secretary and Treasurer.*
S. S. MERRILL, *Gen'l Manager.*

Subscribed and sworn before me, this 10th day of February, 1872.

D. C. GREEN, *Notary Public*, Mil. Co., Wis.

PRAIRIE DU CHIEN AND McGREGOR RAILWAY COMPANY.

ANNUAL REPORT of the operations of the PRAIRIE DU CHIEN AND McGREGOR RAILWAY COMPANY, being a railroad company in the state of Wisconsin, from the first to the thirty-first day of December, 1872, made to the stockholders of said company, in accordance with the provisions of chapter 119 of the general laws of 1872.

	Miles.
I. Whole length of road operated by this company	2
Length of double track	......
Length of main line from Prairie du Chien to State Line, in Wisconsin	1¼
Weight of rail per yard, 56 pounds.	

"D."—*Abstract of Railroads—P. du C. & McG. R'y Co.*—con.

II. Amount of capital stock subscribed	....	$100,000 00
Amount of capital stock paid	....	55,000 00
III. Cost of road—		
For right of way	610 00	....
For bridging	30,000 00	....
For grading	500 00	....
For iron	20,000 00	....
For buildings	....	....
For engines and cars (provided by Milwaukee and Saint Paul Railway Company)	....	....
For other purposes	....	....
		$51,110 00
IV. Amount of indebtedness	None.	....
First mortgage	....	....
Second...do	....	....
Third ....do	....	....
Floating debt	....	....
		....
V. Receipts from the following sources—		
From passengers	$83 60	....
From mails	....	....
From express companies	....	....
From freight	3,864 00	....
From interest	....	....
From other sources	....	....
		$3,947 60
VI. Amount of gross earnings in the state of Wisconsin	....	$3,454 15
VII. Expenditures—		
For repairs of road	$250 00	....
For buildings	....	....
For engines	....	....
For cars	....	....
For fuel	....	....
For wages of employes	500 00	....
For salaries exceeding one thousand dollars	....	....
For taxes	....	....
For interest on	....	....
For indebtedness	....	....
For new construction	....	....
For dividends	....	....
For other purposes	....	....
		....
VIII. Amount due the corporation	....	....
IX. Loss to the company from casualty	....	....

	Tons.	Lbs.
X. Amount of freight reduced to tons, except animals......	21,622	....
Lumber........................	....	....
Wheat........................	....	....
Oats........................	....	....
Corn........................	....	....
Flour........................	....	....
Cattle........................	....	....
Hogs and Sheep........................	....	....
Farming implements........................	....	....
Lead........................	....	....
Iron........................	....	....
Coal........................	....	....
Merchandize........................	....	....
Miscellaneous........................	....	....
XI. Number of through passengers........	836	....
Number of way passengers........	....	....
Rate per mile of through passengers..	5 cents.	....
Rate per mile of way passengers.....	....	....
XII. Number of dividends declared........	....	....
When made........................	....	....
How paid........................	....	....
XIII. Number of passengers and others killed	....	....
Number of employes killed........	....	....
Number of passengers and others injured........	....	....
Number of employes injured........	....	....
XIV. The cause of death is as follows:		
The cause of injuries is as follows:		

XV. Of the foregoing accidents, —— have arisen from carelessness or negligence of employes on the road.

The employes from whose carelessness or negligence such accidents have arisen, retained in the service of the corporation, are as follows:

STATE OF WISCONSIN—COUNTY OF CRAWFORD—ss.

We, Peter Doyle, Secretary and Treasurer, and James Lawler, Superintendent of the Prairie du Chien and McGregor Railway Company, do each of us solemnly swear, that the foregoing report has been made from the best sources of information at our disposal, and that the several matters therein set forth are correct and true, to the best of our knowledge, information and belief. So help us God.

PETER DOYLE, *Secretary and Treasurer.*
JAMES LAWLER, *Superintendent.*

Subscribed and sworn to before me, this 25th day of January, 1873.

JAC. RAFFAUF, *Notary Public.*

ST. CROIX AND LAKE SUPERIOR RAILROAD COMPANY.

ANNUAL REPORT of the Operations of the ST. CROIX AND LAKE SUPERIOR RAILROAD COMPANY, being a railroad company in the State of Wisconsin, during the year ending on the thirty-first day of December, 1872, made to the stockholders of said company, in accordance with the provisions of chapter 91 of General Laws of 1858.

	Miles.
I. Whole length of road operated by this company in Wisconsin and elsewhere	None.

II. Amount of capital stock subscribed	$815,500 00	....
Amount of capital stock paid	815,500 00	....
III. Cost of road equipment—		
For right of way	The road having been purchased for a gross sum, these different items cannot be accurately given by the present officers.	....
For bridging		....
For grading		....
For engines and cars		....
For other purposes		....
For iron		....
For buildings		....
		....
IV. Amount of indebtedness—		
First mortgage	$82,000 00	....
Second mortgage	... .	....
Third mortgage	....	....
Floating debt, about	$100,000 00	....
		$182,000 00
V. Recipts from the following sources:		
From passngers	....	....
From mails	....	....
From express companies	....	....
From freight	....	....
From interest	....	....
From other sources	....	....
		....
VI. Amount of gross earnings in the state of Wisconsin	....	....
VII. Expenditures—		
For repairs of road	....	....
For buildings	....	....
For engines	....	....
For cars	....	....
For fuel	....	....
For wages of employes	....	....
For salaries exceeding one thousand dollars	....	....

"D."—*Abstract of Railroads—St. C. & L. S. R. R. Co.*—con.

Expenditures—continued.		
For taxes	....	....
For interest on	....	....
For indebtedness	....	....
For new construction	....	....
For dividends	....	....
For other purposes	....	....
		....
VIII. Amount due the corporation	....	....
IX. Loss to the company from casualty	....	....
X. Amount of freight reduced to tons, except animals—	....	....
Wheat	....	....
Lumber	....	....
Oats	....	....
Corn	....	....
Flour	....	....
Farming implements	....	....
Lead	....	....
Iron	....	....
Coal	....	....
Merchandize	....	....
Miscellaneous	....	....
Cattle	....	....
Hogs and sheep	....	....
		....
XI. Number of through passengers	....	....
Number of way passengers	....	....
Rate per mile of through passengers	....	....
Rate per mile of way passengers	....	....
		....
XII. Number of dividends declared	....	....
When made	....	....
How paid	....	....
		....
XIII. Number of passengers and others killed	....	....
Number of employes killed	....	....
Number of passengers and others injured	....	....
Number of employes injured	....	....
		....
XIV. The cause of death is as follows:		
The cause of injuries is as follows:		

XV. Of the foregoing accidents, —— have arised from carelessness or negligence of employes on the road.

The employes from whose carelessness or negligence such accidents have arisen, retained in the service of the corporation, are as follows:

"D."—*Abstract of Railroads—St. C. & L. S. R. R. Co.*—con.

STATE OF NEW YORK—COUNTY OF NEW YORK—ss.

We, ROBERT J. BEACH, Secretary, LUDLOW PATTON, Treasurer, and ——— ——— Superintendent of the St. Croix and Lake Superior Railroad Company, do each of us solemnly swear, that the foregoing report has been made from the best sources of information at our disposal, and that the several matters therein set forth are correct and true, to the best of our knowledge, information and belief. So help us God.

ROBT. J. BEACH, *Secretary.*
LUDLOW PATTON, *Treasurer.*

Subscribed and sword to before me, this 20th day of January, 1873.
CHAS. NETTLETON, *Commissioner* in New York.

SHEBOYGAN AND FOND DU LAC RAILROAD COMPANY.

ANNUAL REPORT of the operations of the SHEBOYGAN AND FOND DU LAC RAILROAD, being a Railroad Company in the State of Wisconsin, during the year ending on the thirty-first day of December, 1872, made to the Stockholders of said Company, in accordance with the provisions of Chapter 91 of the General Laws of 1858.

	MILES.
I. Whole length of road operated by this Company in Wisconsin and elsewhere	$78\frac{4}{10}$
Weight of rail per yard, 45 to 56 pounds.	

II. Amount of capital stock subscribed	$1,389,500 00	
Amount of capital stock paid	1,359,500 00	
III. Cost of road and equipment	$2,960,299 00	
For right of way		
For bridging		
For grading		
For iron		
For buildings		
For engines and cars		
For other purposes		
		$2,960,299 00
IV. Amount of indebtedness:		
First mortgage	$1,509,000 00	
Second mortgage		
Third mortgage		
Floating debt	86,689 47	
		$1,595,689 47
V. Receipts from the following sources:		
From passengers	$55,198 69	
From mails	4,272 00	
From express companies	836 65	
From freight	65,513 56	
From interest		
From other sources		
		$125,820 90

"D."—*Abstract of Railroads—S. & F. R. R.*—continued.

VI. Amount of gross earnings in the State of Wisconsin		$125,820 90
VII. Expenditures:		
For repairs of road	$22,134 11	
For buildings	1,359 94	
For engines	12,192 80	
For cars	9,704 58	
For fuel	10,488 65	
For wages of employes	20,294 46	
For salaries exceeding one thousand dollars	2,500 00	
For taxes	2,364 27	
For interest on bonds	80,690 00	
For indebtedness		
For new construction		
For dividends		
For other purposes		
		$161,718 81
VIII. Amount due the corporation		
IX. Loss to the company from casualty		
X. Amount of freight reduced to tons except animals:	TONS.	
Lumber	13,428	
Wheat	5,720	
Oats	79	
Corn	171	
Flour	3,811	
Farming implements	428	
Salt and cement	2,651	
Dressed hogs	227	
Coal	2,164	
Merchandize	5,467	
Miscellaneous	12,033	
Cattle ... Head	389	
Hogs and sheep ... do	354	
XI. Number of through passengers	608	
Number of way passengers	65,277	
Rate per mile of through passengers	3 7/10c	
Rate per mile of way passengers	4 1/3 c	
XII. Number of dividends declared		
When made		
How paid		
XIII. Number of passengers and others killed	1	
Number of employes killed		
Number of passengers and others injured		
Number of employes injured	2	
XIV. The cause of death is as follows:		
Boy about 12 years of age killed while cars were being switched at Ripon, running between cars	1	
The cause of injuries is as follows:		
Hand injured while coupling cars	2	

XV. Of the foregoing accidents, none have arisen from carelessness or negligence of employees on the road.

The employes from whose carelessness or negligence such accidents have arisen, retained in the service of the Corporation, are as follows: None.

STATE OF WISCONSIN—COUNTY OF ——,—ss.

We, Edwin Slade, Secretary, A. G. Ruggles, Treasurer, and Brandon Mozley, Superintendent of the Sheboygan and Fond du Lac Railroad Company, do each of us solemnly swear, that the foregoing is a true copy of the annual report made to the Stockholders of said Company, for the year ending December 31, 1872; that said report has been made from the best sources of information at our disposal, and that the several matters therein set forth are correct and true, to the best of our knowledge, information and belief. So help us God.

EDWIN SLADE, *Secretary.*
——— ———, *Treasurer.*
B. MOZLEY, *Superintendent.*

Subscribed and sworn to before me, this 19th day of September, 1873.
J. B. PERRY, *Notary Public.*

SUPERIOR AND ST. CROIX RAILROAD COMPANY.

ANNUAL REPORT of the operations of the SUPERIOR and ST. CROIX RAILROAD COMPANY, being a railroad company in the State of Wisconsin, during the year ending on the 31st day of December, 1872, made to the stockholders of said company, in accordance with the provisions of chapter 91 of the General Laws of 1858.

I. Whole length of road operated by this company in Wisconsin and elsewhere—none reported.

II. Amount of capital stock subscribed	$734,000 00	
*Amount of capital stock paid	407,000 00	
III. Cost of road and equipment—		
For right of way	$1,044 72	
For bridging	6,484 95	
For grading	12,361 04	
For ties	12,199 90	
For buildings		
For engines and cars		
For other purposes	18,935 21	
		$51,025 82

*Of "amount of capital stock paid," three hundred and fifty thousand dollars is in the bonds of Douglas county, upon subscription of the county to the stock of the company in like amount. This report also covers a distance of about nine miles in the state of Minnesota, organized under the name of the Superior & Northwestern Railroad, and connecting the Superior & St. Croix Railroad with the North Pacific Railroad, the expenditures on account of which last portion are comparatively unimportant, sufficient accuracy being observed in accrediting the whole to the Superior and St. Croix Railroad Company.

"D."—*Abstract of Railroads—S. & St. Croix R. R. Co.*—con.

IV.	Amount of indebtedness—	None.	
	First mortgage		
	Second mortgage		
	Third mortgage		
	Floating debt		
V.	Receipts from the following sources—		
	From passengers		
	From mails		
	From express companies		
	From freight		
	From interest		
	From other sources		
VI.	Amount of gross earnings in the state of Wisconsin		
VII.	Expenditures—		
	For repairs of road		
	For buildings		
	For engines		
	For cars		
	For fuel		
	For wages of employes	$5,974 18	
	For salaries exceeding one thousand dollars		
	For taxes		
	For interest on		
	For indebtedness		
	For new construction		
	For dividends		
	For other purposes		
			$5,974 18
VIII.	Amount due the corporation		
IX.	Loss to the company from causalty		
X.	Amount of freight reduced to tons, except animals—		
	Lumber		
	Wheat		
	Oats		
	Corn		
	Flour		
	Farming implements		
	Lead		
	Iron		
	Coal		
	Merchandise		
	Miscellaneous		
	Cattle		
	Hogs and sheep		
XI.	Number of through passengers		
	Number of way passengers		

Rate per mile of through passengers	....	....
Rate per mile of way passengers...	....	....
		....
XII. Number of dividends declared	....	....
When made...............	....	....
How paid......................	....	....
		....
XIII. No. of passengers and others killed...	....	....
Number of employes killed	....	....
Number of passengers and others injured	....	....
Number of employes injured......	....	....
		....
XIV. The cause of death is as follows; The cause of injuries is as follows:		

XV. Of the foregoing accidents, —— have arisen from carelessness or negligence of employes on the road. The employes from whose carelessness or negligence such accidents have arisen, retained in the service of the corporation, are as follows:

STATE OF WISCONSIN—COUNTY OF DOUGLASS—ss.

We, Hiram Hayes, Secretary and acting Treasurer and —— Superintendent, of the Superior and St. Croix Railroad Company, do each of us solemnly swear, that the foregoing report has been made from the best sources of information at our disposal, and that the several matters therein set forth are correct and true, to the best of our knowledge, information and belief. So help us God.

HIRAM HAYES, *Secretary and Acting Treasurer.*

Subscribed and sworn to before me, this 16th day of January, 1873.

WM. R. PERRY, *Notary Public.*

WESTERN UNION RAILROAD COMPANY.

ANNUAL REPORT of the operations of the WESTERN UNION RAILROAD COMPANY, being a railroad company in the State of Wisconsin, during the year ending on the thirty-first day of December, 1872, made to the stockholders of said company, in accordance with the provisions of Chapter 91 of the General Laws of 1858.

		Miles.
I.	Whole length of road operated by this company in Wisconsin and elsewhere	$215\frac{5}{10}$
	Length of double track	.....
	Roads in Wisconsin—	
	Length of main line from Racine to Beloit	$68\frac{7}{10}$
	Length of other lines operated by this company in Wisconsin, as follows:	
	Eagle Branch Railroad, from Elkhorn to Eagle	$16\frac{5}{10}$
	Total length of roads in Wisconsin	$85\frac{2}{10}$
	Weight of rail per yard, 56 pounds.	

II.	Amount of capital stock subscribed		....	$4,000,000 00
	Amount of capital stock paid		....	4,000,000 00
III.	Cost of road and equipment:			
	For right of way	By purchase.	....	....
	For bridging		$7,000,000 00	....
	For grading	By construction and equipment.	....	....
	For iron		....	....
	For buildings		594,045 42	....
	For engines and cars		....	....
	For other purposes		....	....
				$7,594,045 42
IV.	Amount of indebtedness:			
	First mortgage		$3,275,000 00	....
	Second mortgage		....	....
	Third mortgage		....	....
	Floating debt		409,578 89	....
				$3,684,578 89
V.	Receipts from the following sources:			
	From passengers		$208,056 56	....
	From mails		9,020 00	....
	From express companies		12,000 00	....
	From freight		603,098 97	....
	From interest		....	....
	From other sources		14,935 68	....
				$847,111 21
VI.	Amount of gross earnings in the state of Wisconsin, $\frac{852}{2155}$ of $847,111.21		....	$334,913 57

VII. Expenditures:		
For repairs of road	$187,299 43	
For buildings	9,978 08	
For engines	92,453 39	
For cars	78,628 96	
For fuel	83,097 00	
For wages of employes included in other items, $377,226.36.		
For salaries exceeding one thousand dollars, as above, $14,120.00.		
For taxes	31,233 66	
For interest on bonded and floating debt	125,682 41	
For indebtedness		
For new construction	71,761 18	
For dividends		
For other purposes	285,957 11	
		$916,091 21
VIII. Amount due the corporation		$184,879 71
IX. Loss to the company from casualty		$5,140 08
X. Amount of freight reduced to tons, except animals—	TONS. LBS.	No.
Lumber	36 353	
Wheat	30,689	
Oats	17,219	
Corn	39,039	
Flour	4,310	
Farming implements	7,899	
Lead		
Iron	1,186	
Coal	18,895	
Merchandise	18,122	
Miscellaneous	62,547	
Cattle	2,580	5,161
Hogs and sheep	7,733	77,332
XI. Number of through passengers	2,418	
Number of way passengers	188,824	
Rate per mile of through passengers } Rate per mile of way passengers }	.03$\frac{87}{100}$	
XII. Number of dividends declared	None.	
When made		
How paid		
XIII. Number of passengers and others kill'd	4	
Number of employes killed	1	
Number of passengers and others injured	9	
Number of employes injured	3	

XIV. The cause of death is as follows:

1 fell between cars; 1 getting on train while in motion; 1 walking on track; 1 getting off; breakman fell off train.

The cause of injuries is as follows:

5, train running off track; 2 walking on track, (1 deaf); 2 getting on train while in motion; 3 coupling.

XV. Of the foregoing accidents, none have arisen from carelessness or negligence of employes on the road.

The employes from whose carelessness or negligence such accidents have arisen, retained in the service of the corporation, are as follows: none.

State of Wisconsin—County of Racine—ss.

We, Darwin R. May, Secretary and Treasurer, and Daniel A. Olin, Superintendent of the Western Union Railroad Company, do each of us solemnly swear, that the foregoing is a true copy of the annual report made to the stockholders of said company for the year ending December 31, 1872; that said report has been made from the best sources of information at our disposal, and that the several matters therein set forth are correct and true, to the best of our knowledge, information and belief. So help us God.

D. R. MAY, *Secretary and Treasurer*,
D. A. OLIN, *Superintendent*.

Subscribed and sworn to before me, this 17th day of March, 1873.

W. T. EMERSON, *Notary Public*.

WEST WISCONSIN RAILWAY COMPANY.

Annual Report of the Operations of the West Wisconsin Railway Company, being a railroad company in the state of Wisconsin, during the year ending on the 31st day of December, 1872, made to the stockholders of said company, in accordance with the provisions of chapter 91 of the General Laws of 1858.

	Miles.
I. Whole length of road operated by this company in Wisconsin and elsewhere	197
Length of side track	6
Roads in Wisconsin—	
Length of main line from Hudson to Elroy	178
Length of other lines operated by this company in Wisconsin, as follows:	
North Wisconsin Railroad, from North Wisconsin Junction to New Richmond	14
Weight of rail per yard, 50 and 55 pounds.	

II. Amount of capital stock subscribed	$4,000,000 00	
Amount of capital stock paid	4,000,000 00	
III. Cost of road and equipment—		
For right of way	$42,563 57	
For bridging	253,855 26	
For grading	681,681 51	
For iron	1,319,400 00	
For buildings	50,672 42	
For engines and cars	376,410 54	
For fencing	23,605 00	
For track laying, ballasting, cross ties, etc	187,887 90	
For other purposes	124,558 91	
		$3,060,135 11

IV. Amount of indebtedness	$4,640,000 00	
First mortgage		
Second mortgage		
Third mortgage		
Floating debt		
V. Receipts from the following sources:		
From passengers	$165,263 67	
From mails	7,727 92	
From express companies	5,013 75	
From freight	183,795 55	
From interest		
From other sources	4,198 93	
		$365,999 82
VI. Amount of gross earnings in the state of Wisconsin		$365,999 82
VII. Expenditures—		
For repairs of road	$56,040 97	
For buildings	4,911 08	
For engines	16,284 19	
For cars	13,742 14	
For fuel	29,081 70	
For wages of employes (included in items of expenditures)	148,662 53	
For salaries exceeding $1,000 (included in items of expenditures)	25,260 00	
For taxes	11,149 51	
For interest on		
For indebtedness		
For new construction	414,789 68	
For dividends		
For other purposes	127,633 02	
		$847,554 82
VIII. Amount due the corporation		$15,818 79
IX. Loss to the company from casualty		$217 25

	TONS.	LBS.	
X. Amount of freight reduced to tons, except animals—			
Lumber	57,479		
Wheat	14,870		
Oats	273		
Corn	1,378		
Flour	3,762		
Farming implements	1,072		
Lead	530		
Iron	682		
Coal	1,291		
Merchandise	14,917		
Miscellaneous	22,859		
Cattle ... head	94		
Hogs and sheep ... head	344		

XI. Number of through passengers	1,154	
Number of way passengers	89,151	
Rate per mile of thro' passengers	.03 46/100	
Rate per mile of way passengers	.04 54/100	

XII. Number of dividends declared........	....	....
When made	....	....
How paid	....	....
		....
XIII. Number of pass'gers and others killed.	None.	....
Number of employes killed	One.	....
Number of passengers and others injured...........	One.	....
Number of employes injured......	One.	....
		....

XIV. The cause of death is as follows:

Brakeman crushed, coupling cars.

The cause of injuries is as follows: Passenger in caboose injured by an engine running into freight train.

Brakeman's hand crushed, coupling cars.

XV. Of the foregoing accidents, none have arisen from carelessness or negligence of employes on the road. The employes from whose carelessness or negligence such accidents have arisen, retained in the service of the corporation, are as follows: None.

STATE OF WISCONSIN—COUNTY OF ST. CROIX—ss.

We, F. E. Trowbridge, secretary and treasurer, and Wm. G. Swan, superintendent of the West Wisconsin Railway Company, do each of us solemnly swear, that the foregoing is a true copy of the annual report made to the stockholders of said company, for the year ending December 31, 1872; that said report has been made from the best sources of information at our disposal, and that the several matters therein set forth are correct and true, to the best of our knowledge, information and belief. So help us God.

F. E. TROWBRIDGE, *Secretary and Treasurer*
WM. G. SWAN, *Superintendent.*

Subscribed and sworn to before me, this 26th day of September, 1873.

D. M. WHITE, *Notary Public.*

WISCONSIN CENTRAL RAILROAD COMPANY.

ANNUAL REPORT of the operations of the PHILLIPS AND COLBY CONSTRUCTION Co. in building and operating the WISCONSIN CENTRAL RAILROAD, being a railroad company in the state of Wisconsin, during the year ending on the thirty-first day of December, 1872, made to the stockholders of said company in accordance with the provisions of chapter 91 of the general laws of 1858.

		Miles.
I. Whole length of road operated by this company		$114\frac{3}{10}$
Length of double track		......
Length of track laid from Appleton to Salem in Wisconsin	$119\frac{5}{10}$	$125\frac{5}{10}$
Length of track laid from Ashland (Lake Superior) to White River	6	
Weight of rail per yard, 57 pounds.		

II. Amount of capital stock subscribed	....	....
Amount of capital stock paid	....	....
III. Cost of road and equipment (figures below cover finished and unfinished portions of road)—		
For right of way and real estate	$18,911 28	....
For bridging and timber, plank and piling	258,998 32	....
For grading and masonry	608,849 31	....
For iron rails and fastenings and frogs and switches (partly on hand)	1,432,439 35	....
For buildings, fixtures and water stations	98,905 52	....
For engines and cars	432,932 78	....
For other purposes	799,402 98	....
		$3,645,439 54
IV. Amount of indebtedness	....	....
First mortgage	....	....
Second mortgage	....	....
Third mortgage	....	....
Floating debt	....	....
		....
V. Receipts from the following sources:		
From passengers	$55,336 00	....
From mails	3,140 00	....
From express companies	1,548 39	....
From freight	52,853 34	....
From interest	....	....
From other sources	4,012 26	....
		....
VI. Amount of gross earnings in the state of Wisconsin	116,889 99	....

"D"—*Abstract of Railroads—W. C. R. R. Co.*—con.

VII. Expenditures for operating—		
For repairs of road	$18,374 89	
For repairs of buildings	1,367 74	
For repairs of engines	1,953 65	
For repair of cars	3,695 34	
For fuel consumed	5,494 50	
For wages of employes / For salaries exceeding one thousand dollars—exceeding foregoing	26,027 01	
For taxes	3,519 40	
For interest on		
For indebtedness		
For new construction		
For dividends		
For other purposes	11,356 78	
		$71,789 31
VIII. Amount due the corporation		
IX. Loss to the company from casualty		
X. Amount of freight reduced to tons, except animals—	TONS.	LBS.
Lumber	5,286	111
Wheat	77	1,888
Oats	486	1,550
Corn	549	1,410
Flour	683	227
Cattle and horses 24		39,000
Hogs and sheep 154		40,568
Farming implements	47	1,310
Lead		
Iron	109	1,696
Coal	211	1,000
Merchandise	5,527	925
Miscellaneous	4,490	1,817
XI. Number of through passengers / Number of way passengers	36,781	
Rate per mile of through passengers	.04 44/100	
Rate per mile of way passengers		
XII. Number of dividends declared		
When made		
How paid		
XIII. Number of passengers and others killed		
Number of employes killed		
Number of passengers and others injured		
XIV. The cause of death is as follows:		
The cause of injuries is as follows:		

XV. Of the foregoing accidents, none have arisen from carelessness or negligence of employes on the road.

The employes from whose carelessness or negligence such accidents have arisen, retained in the service of the corporation, are as follows:

STATE OF MASSACHUSETTS—COUNTY OF SUFFOLK—ss.

I, Charles L. Colby, secretary and treasurer, do solemnly swear that the foregoing report has been made from the best sources of information at our disposal, and that the several matters therein set forth are correct and true, to the best of my knowledge, information and belief. So help me God.

CHAS. L. COLBY,
Secretary and Treasurer.

Subscribed and sworn to before me, this 26th day of February, 1873.

W. H. H. ANDREWS, *Justice of the Peace.*

TABLE I.—APPENDIX "E."

TABULAR STATEMENT *showing the Valuation of all Property, as Valued by the Town Assessors, together with all Taxes Levied thereon, as Returned to the Secretary of State, for the year* 1872, *as provided by Chapters* 110 *and* 150, *General Laws of* 1872.

COUNTIES.	Assessed Valuation of all Property.	State Tax.	County Tax.	County School Tax.	TOWN TAXES.				Total Town Taxes.	School District Taxes.	Road District Taxes.	Total Taxes.
					Current Expenses.	School Purposes.	Support of Poor.	Other Purposes.				
[2]Adams	$787,565	$2,262	$9,399	$896	$1,531	$100	....	$673	$2,304	$7,659	$3,364	$25,884
Ashland	608,724	1,826	4,870	609	3,253	3,715	$609	609	8,186	....	1,826	17,317
Barron	1,448,228	1,135	15,550	250	1,250	7,033	600	1,580	10,463	....	4,740	32,138
Bayfield	605,316	753	1,800	....	600	2,400	300	8,400	11,700	....	....	14,258
Brown	4,446,167	12,923	83,248	3,839	16,834	14,629	120	62,559	94,142	23,854	15,600	233,606
Buffalo	1,170,088	4,371	9,011	3,473	7,110	500	375	3,304	11,289	21,685	10,169	59,998
Burnett	219,863	769	3,578	219	578	....	347	....	925	1,514	2,500	9,505
Calumet	1,655,032	6,684	8,388	2,012	2,749	....	874	10,882	14,505	15,286	12,376	59,251
[2]Chippewa	5,088,458	18,214	29,061	870	12,599	973	2,349	700	16,621	16,251	24,736	105,758
[3]Clark	....	....	....	....	....	....	....	....	....	....	....	....
Columbia	9,421,569	21,520	24,530	5,723	11,619	7,030	....	23,458	42,107	38,474	26,819	159,173
[3]Crawford	....	....	....	....	....	....	....	....	....	....	....	....
Dane	19,950,266	49,883	41,255	8,705	30,636	14,668	50	55,796	101,150	52,551	53,464	307,008
Dodge	14,770,177	32,070	43,390	6,849	24,232	12,943	3,226	7,177	47,578	45,931	31,099	206,917
[2]Door	213,329	527	5,679	255	1,100	....	100	200	1,400	3,253	2,907	14,021
Douglas	1,117,864	1,856	12,320	136	1,500	....	1,000	7,000	9,500	7,250	7,500	38,562
Dunn	2,350,630	5,892	24,205	1,798	14,892	925	490	600	16,907	22,747	11,131	82,680
Eau Claire	4,947,096	6,820	14,000	1,475	24,651	....	425	1,459	26,535	33,652	14,273	96,755
Fond du Lac	14,791,972	32,866	47,273	7,440	47,050	41,878	85	82,816	170,779	36,998	33,850	329,201
Grant	10,400,157	29,282	38,114	5,835	10,620	....	2,895	24,362	37,877	59,444	29,607	190,159

[1]Green	8,565,880	20,915	20,676	3,510	9,677	....	....	1,209	10,886	36,806	22,157	114,250
Green Lake	[1]4,704,201	9,787	11,698	2,006	1,095	1,092	100	183	2,420	1,092	786	27,789
Iowa	5,720,855	22,424	498,159	4,986	9,692	150	....	77,411	87,253	29,784	10,855	652,911
[3]Jackson	1,488,868	4,187	8,636	1,840	4,256	2,544	2,169	875	9,844	18,551	12,856	55,414
Jefferson	9,621,828	21,718	28,780	5,565	28,245	12,598	....	8,856	49,699	36,440	27,423	169,625
[illegible]au	2,247,628	5,023	9,467	3,087	8,178	211	894	2,887	12,170	20,616	11,248	61,611
[3]Kenosha	5,097,639	12,775	11,115	6,325	2,378	....	1,447	1,055	4,880	13,502	9,640	58,287
[illegible]ee	564,000	1,495	12,000	1,860	1,250	....	350	1,948	3,543	3,775	3,140	25,818
La Crosse	5,267,176	12,818	23,223	3,951	2,810	30,644	9,903	25,642	68,999	17,017	11,120	187,128
La Fayette	6,320,910	16,448	17,969	3,673	8,478	155	1,940	8,299	13,872	40,872	20,701	118,535
Manitowoc	4,319,115	14,886	38,025	10,555	6,292	975	2,825	45,114	55,206	39,852	39,933	197,957
Marathon	1,826,016	9,127	13,695	9,127	16,046	1,798	913	1,926	20,683	23,000	16,885	92,517
Marquette	854,159	2,612	7,773	1,690	2,882	....	465	567	3,914	3,300	6,597	30,886
Milwaukee	53,332,294	102,237	215,341	53,809	184,708	77,515	... ...	460,450	722,668	29,048	17,898	1,141,001
Monroe	3,219,518	8,747	24,000	2,766	1,900	150	....	17,071	19,121	28,399	19,762	102,795
[illegible]o	3,238,703	11,445	16,255	1,087	18,550	12,190	2,573	19,926	53,289	14,181	6,240	102,447
Outagamie	4,654,522	12,892	35,526	5,126	16,114	10,818	2,564	22,778	51,774	19,697	12,496	137,511
[illegible]aukee	3,389,827	6,953	11,500	2,859	5,004	2,000	64	8,081	15,699	13,887	13,005	63,303
Pepin	838,182	1,615	9,000	660	1,357	200	....	....	1,557	8,065	3,648	24,545
Pierce	2,631,467	7,814	18,000	1,633	8,367	105	....	4,302	12,774	26,158	13,912	80,291
[2]Polk	988,523	2,358	2,960	1,474	4,784	1,487	339	2,379	8,989	11,108	10,067	36,951
Portage	1,762,404	5,315	18,572	1,438	16,547	....	375	8,250	20,172	19,807	9,212	74,516
Racine	9,523,275	20,810	19,530	7,465	27,348	15,000	2,070	46,490	90,908	20,791	16,248	175,752
Richland	2,457,307	7,772	8,500	3,560	2,911	476	1,014	5,019	9,420	20,128	6,854	56,234
Rock	20,028,201	41,263	52,256	11,266	28,632	15,000	....	40,422	79,054	60,112	26,854	270,805
St. Croix	3,538,184	8,444	14,654	1,744	9,934	3,385	....	6,531	19,850	4,584	9,082	58,358
Sauk	5,590,776	17,487	26,235	3,701	5,847	3,850	4,076	18,705	32,478	41,410	27,895	149,206
Shawano	584,669	2,922	10,379	1,604	10,357	3,558	....	3,379	17,294	9,280	3,451	44,930
Sheboygan	7,951,743	17,779	51,522	5,382	17,329	3,755	3,192	32,674	56,950	27,153	28,673	187,459
Trempealeau	2,013,586	4,905	2,600	2,432	3,081	330	1,700	2,522	7,633	19,144	12,270	48,984
Vernon	3,232,701	11,282	21,428	3,650	6,767	420	....	3,253	10,440	25,471	21,196	93,467
Walworth	14,067,895	27,520	14,987	3,703	9,623	....	100	9,370	19,093	52,609	25,647	143,559
[2]Washington	4,958,527	10,475	11,601	4,279	7,229	1,949	181	3,516	12,875	14,200	19,406	72,836
Waukesha	13,155,741	26,485	23,292	4,138	9,039	....	....	4,399	13,438	38,255	38,250	143,858

[1]According to report of secretary of state. [2]Report incomplete. [3]No report.

"E."—TABLE I.—*Statement showing Valuation of all Property, by Town Assessors, etc.*—continued.

COUNTIES.	Assessed Valuation of all Property.	State Tax.	County Tax.	County School Tax.	TOWN TAXES.				Total Town Taxes.	School District Taxes.	Road District Taxes.	Total Taxes.
					Current Expenses.	School Purposes.	Support of Poor.	Other Purposes.				
Waupaca	$2,414,529	$7,645	$15,635	$3,460	$9,640	$684	$1,370	$16,449	$28,143	$24,012	$12,723	$91,618
[1]Waushara ...	1,614,067	4,033	8,596	3,126	4,740	140	1,300	1,084	7,264	15,180	10,068	48,267
Winnebago ..	14,735,584	27,508	29,795	18,699	39,871	26,145	200	77,389	143,605	35,652	21,262	276,521
Wood	1,240,000	3,400	8,000	805	8,322	9,600	1,150	6,820	25,892	9,128	2,888	50,118
Totals ...	$331,747,446	$781,774	$1,777,051	$257,875	$767,079	$344,718	$57,069	$1,278,201	$2,447,067	$1,263,605	$867,759	$7,395,181

[1] Report incomplete.

TABLE II—APPENDIX "E."—continued.

TABULAR STATEMENT *Showing the Purposes for which the County Taxes in the several Counties in the State of Wisconsin, were levied, as returned to the Secretary of State, for the year* 1872, *as provided by Chapters* 110 *and* 150, *General Laws of* 1872.

COUNTIES.	Support of poor.	County buildings.	Railroad aid or indebtedness.	Roads and bridges.	Salaries of county officers.	Court expenses.	Jail expenses, including sheriff's account.	All other county expenses.	Total taxes levied.
Adams	$3,498							[1] $7,351	$10,849
Ashland					$1,000			3,870	4,870
Barron	300			$10,000				5,250	15,550
Bayfield					600			1,200	1,800
Brown	6,000		$23,558	10,000				[1] 43,690	83,248
Buffalo				2,700	3,500	$1,200	$1,300	1,100	9,800
Burnett		$500			1,500			1,578	3,578
Calumet								[1] 8,000	8,000
Chippewa	3,000			3,000	5,400	4,000	2,500	[2] 11,980	[2] 29,880
[3] Clark									
Columbia	6,500							[1] 18,030	24,530
[3] Crawford									
Dane	12,000				9,800	12,000		6,200	40,000
Dodge	5,000	7,400			9,700	4,000	2,400	14,118	42,618
Door				9,090	[4] 5,400	[5] 300	[6] 500	[7] 1,839	17,129
Douglas				1,120	3,000	500	500	7,200	12,320
Dunn		6,359						19,105	25,464

[1] All county purposes.
[2] Including $89.80 for old indebtedness.
[3] Not reported.
[4] General fund.
[5] Stationery.
[6] County Superintendent salary.
[7] To pay outstanding orders.

"E."—TABLE II.—*Purposes for which the County Taxes in the Several Counties were Levied.*—continued.

COUNTIES.	Support of Poor.	County buildings.	Railway aid or indebtness.	Roads and bridges.	Salaries of county officers.	Court expenses.	Jail expenses including Sheriff's account.	All other county expenses.	Total taxes levied.
Eau Claire	....	....	....	....	$6,200	[1] $2,000	[1] $3,000	[1] $4,275	$15,475
Fond du Lac	$10,000	$500	....	....	7,000	10,724	4,258	296,723	329,205
Grant	1,355	7,004	....	$3,000	4,800	4,000	2,118	6,223	28,500
Green	3,000	1,550	[2] $3,510	[3] 1,169	4,200	3,000	800	7,028	24,257
Green Lake	2,000	200	....	....	2,300	2,000	....	7,796	14,296
Iowa	2,000	150	[4] 466,049	....	4,250	5,000	1,500	19,200	498,149
Jackson	1,000	....	....	1,500	3,950	1,000	....	1,186	8,636
Jefferson	6,000	5,025	....	....	5,100	2,000	3,388	7,695	29,208
Juneau	1,121	1,020	....	....	4,400	....	....	3,932	10,473
Kenosha	600	400	....	....	3,400	2,000	3,000	1,815	11,215
Kewaunee	....	[5] 12,000	....	....	....	....	....	....	12,000
La Crosse	....	....	....	3,000	5,850	....	....	14,373	23,223
La Fayette	1,500	....	....	1,000	6,000	....	[6] 5,000	[7] 4,469	17,969
Manitowoc	....	....	11,000	....	7,900	1,700	6,000	9,600	36,200
Marathon	....	....	....	....	....	....	....	[8] 16,234	16,234
Marquette	287	....	....	700	3,150	627	618	4,660	10,042
Milwaukee	30,000	....	....	....	18,000	15,000	18,000	134,137	215,137
Monroe	3,000	1,000	....	....	5,050	3,000	....	11,950	24,000
Oconto	....	....	....	....	....	....	....	[8] 16,000	16,000
Outagamie	2,000	1,000	....	13,000	4,650	2,500	2,000	9,850	35,000
Ozaukee	900	....	....	....	5,150	760	8,273	545	15,628
Pepin	....	....	....	....	....	....	....	[8] 9,659	9,659
Pierce	....	....	....	....	....	....	....	[8] 18,000	18,000
Polk	....	....	....	....	....	....	....	[8] 3,000	3,000
Portage	....	....	[9] 8,000	700	4,400	....	....	7,402	20,502
Racine	1,800	....	....	....	3,100	2,000	....	11,100	18,000
Richland	....	....	....	1,500	2,450	1,100	....	3,450	8,500

Rock	9,000	19,000	....	....	6,360	8,000	2,500	17,834	62,684
St. Croix	....	35	....	....	3,300	2,000	....	9,165	14,500
Sauk	6,000	4,000	....	....	5,600	2,200	2,000	6,200	26,000
Shawano	....	....	....	3,500	....	....	....	10,730	14,230
Sheboygan	3,858	....	17,500	....	5,800	2,000	5,307	17,057	51,522
Trempealeau	....	....	....	....	....	....	....	[8]2,600	2,600
Vernon	8,100	1,500	....	6,498	4,200	2,000	1,200	2,935	21,428
Walworth	5,000	....	....	....	4,750	2,500	2,491	3,762	18,503
Washington	1,200	....	....	....	3,900	1,500	3,000	24,140	33,740
Waukesha	4,000	590	[10]2,014	....	5,750	1,513	3,863	5,052	22,782
Waupaca	2,000	....	....	....	5,400	....	....	8,235	15,635
Waushara	....	....	....	....	3,050	1,000	1,050	3,400	8,500
Winnebago	5,600	5,000	....	....	6,058	7,500	....	6,842	31,000
Wood	....	....	12,000	....	....	....	....	[8]8,000	20,000
Totals	$142,619	$74,233	$543,631	$71,472	$205,308	$110,624	$86,566	$906,760	$2,141,213

[1] Estimated.
[2] School tax.
[3] Deliquent county tax.
[4] Levied but not collected.
[5] Including all other purposes.
[6] Including court expenses.
[7] Including debt of towns to county.
[8] All county purposes.
[9] Interest due in 1873.
[10] For county poor.

TABLE No. I.—APPENDIX "F."

TABULAR STATEMENT *showing the Bonded and other Indebtedness of the Towns, Cities and Villages in the Several Counties in the State of Wisconsin as returned to the Secretary of State for the year* 1872, *as provided by Chapter* 110, *G. L. of* 1872.

COUNTIES.	BONDED INDEBTEDNESS.				All other indebtedness.	Indebtedness of School Dis.	Total Indebtedness.
	Railroad aid.	Roads and bridges.	Other Purposes.	Interest unpaid.			
[1]Adams					$6	$772	$778
Ashland							
Barron							
Bayfield							
Brown	$135,279	$6,562	$16,882		9,167	24,000	191,890
Buffalo		3,475		$348	1,500	2,250	7,573
Burnett							
Calumet	75,000					2,100	77,100
[1]Chippewa		1,499		5,343			6,842
[4]Clark							
Columbia	72,300	1,500		7,459	5,112	17,297	103,668
[4]Crawford							
Dane	16,500	600	225,000	805		3,250	246,155
Dodge	[2]		7,800		772	10,106	[2]18,678
[1]Door					503	39	542
Douglas	[3]350,000				12,000		362,000
Dunn							
Eau Claire		20,000	6,500		203	13,525	40,228
Fond du Lac	307,991			1,819		22,400	332,210
Grant	118,000	600			126	14,976	133,702

Green					40	7,499	7,539
Green Lake	[5]242,856				942	159	243,957
Iowa					449	10,850	11,299
Jackson	[7]900,477		5,000	2,157	500	10,042	[7]918,176
[1]Jefferson					44		44
[1]Juneau							
Kenosha							
[1]Kewaunee	36,000				436	333	36,769
La Crosse		185			688	18,384	19,257
La Fayette	113,000	10,000			1,041	18,000	142,041
Manitowoc					4,704	8,000	12,704
Marathon[2]							
[1]Marquette							
Milwaukee	200,000		1,204,000		2,259	5,652	1,411,911
Monroe	13,000		6,550	673	257	1,113	21,593
Oconto							
Outagamie	19,000		8,704	1,840	287		29,831
Ozaukee	12,000	[6]11,000					23,000
Pepin							
Pierce			13,000	455	4,599	341	18,395
[1]Polk							
[1]Portage	37,444	117			631		38,192
Racine	65,500	3,000	207,628	50,000			326,128
Richland						2,000	2,000
Rock	221,900	10,980	15,300	2,574	191	37,420	288,365
St. Croix	25,000	600	7,025	1,960	17,592	250	52,427
Sauk	125,000			10,844	2,396	11,112	148,852
[1]Shawano					2,542	1,453	3,995
Sheboygan	277,625			480		10,000	288,105
Trempealeau							
Vernon					1,812	8,260	10,072
Walworth	62,400	259	51	1,449	15,819	3,600	83,069
[1]Washington	30,000			1,800		3,886	35,686

[1] Returns incomplete.
[2] See Jefferson county.
[3] Contested.
[4] No reports.
[5] Estimated.
[6] Of which $9,000 is for harbor aid.
[7] Including $750,000 R. R. aid indebtedness of the city of Watertown, two wards of which are in Dodge county.

"F."—Table No. I—*Statement showing the Bonded and other Indebtedness of Towns, etc.*—continued.

Counties.	Bonded Indebtedness.				All other indebtedness.	Indebtedness of School Districts.	Total indebtedness.
	Railroad aid.	Roads and Bridges.	Other purposes.	Interest unpaid.			
[1]Waukesha	....	....	....	....	....	....	....
Waupaca	$165,000	....	....	$7,200	$1,867	$200	$174,267
Waushara	....	....	....	....	561	300	861
[1]Winnebago	201,400	$32,975	$782	13,273	16,240	1,699	266,369
Wood	20,000	400	....	....	12,689	....	33,089
	$3,837,672	$103,752	$1,724,222	$109,970	$117,475	$271,268	$6,164,359

[1]Returns incomplete.

TABLE No. II—APPENDIX "F."

TABULAR STATEMENT *showing the Bonded and other Indebtedness of the several Counties in the State of Wisconsin, as returned to the Secretary of State, for the year* 1872, *as provided by chapter* 110, *General Laws of* 1872.

COUNTIES.	BONDED INDEBTEDNESS.				Total Bonded Indebtedness.	All other Indebtedness.	Total Indebtedness.
	Railroad Aid.	Roads and Bridges.	Interest Unpaid.	Other Purposes.			
Adams	....	....	....	....	....	....	....
Ashland	....	....	....	....	....	....	....
Barron	....	....	....	....	....	....	....
Bayfield	....	....	....	....	....	....	....
Brown	$154,500	....	....	[1] $13,500	$168,000	....	$168,000
Buffalo	....	....	....	....	....	....	....
Burnett	....	....	....	....	....	....	....
Calumet	....	....	....	....	....	....	....
Chippewa	....	....	$4,980	[1] 56,000	60,980	....	60,980
[3] Clark	....	....	....	....	....	....	....
Columbia	....	....	....	....	....	....	....
[3] Crawford	....	....	....	....	....	....	....
Dane	....	....	....	[2] 25,000	25,000	....	25,000
Dodge	....	....	....	....	....	....	....
Door	....	....	....	....	....	$1,839	1,839
Douglas	350,000	....	....	....	350,000	6,334	356,334
Dunn	....	....	....	6,800	6,800	....	6,800
Eau Claire	....	....	....	[1] 3,000	3,000	....	3,000

[1] Court house bonds.

[2] Agricultural college bonds.

[3] No reports.

"F."—Table II.—*Statement showing Bonded and other Indebtedness of Counties, etc.*—continued.

Counties.	Bonded Indebtedness.				Total Bonded Indebtednes.	All other Indebtedness.	Total Indebtedness.
	Railroad Aid.	Roads and Bridges.	Interest Unpaid.	Other Purposes.			
Fond du Lac	$307,992		$1,818		$309,810		$309,810
[3]Grant							
Green						$7,539	7,539
[3]Green Lake							
Iowa	[1] 500,000				[1] 500,000	12,100	512,100
Jackson	[2] 35,000		7,125		42,125		42,125
[3]Jefferson							
Juneau						5,543	5,543
[3]Kenosha							
[3]Kewaunee							
[3]La Crosse							
La Fayette						1,100	1,100
Manitowoc	150,000				150,000		150,000
Marathon		$12,000			12,000		12,000
[3]Marquette							
Milwaukee				$481,120	481,120		481,120
[3]Monroe							
Oconto						12,680	12,680
[3]Outagamie							
[3]Ozaukee							
[3]Pepin							
[3]Pierce							
[3]Polk							
Portage	100,000				100,000		100,000
[3]Racine							
[3]Richland							

Rock			4,000	40,000	44,000		44,000
[3]St. Croix							
[3]Sauk							
Shawano						8,564	8,564
Sheboygan	156,240		896		157,136		157,136
[illegible]							
[3]Vernon							
[3]Walworth							
Washington	55,000				55,000		55,000
[3] [1] [illegible]							
[3] [illegible]							
[3] [1] [illegible]ra							
[3]Winnebago							
[illegible]d	200,000				200,000		200,000
Totals	$2,008,732	$12,000	$18,819	$625,420	$2,664,971	$50,699	$2,715,670

[1] Estimated. [2] Contested. [3] No reports.

APPENDIX "G."

Tabular Statement *showing the Sales of Real Estate, Made and Recorded in the Several Counties, in the State of Wisconsin, during the Year ending September* 1, 1873, *as Returned to the Secretary of State, according to the provisions of Chapter* 210, *Laws of* 1873.

Counties.	No. of Acres.	Considerations in Deed.	Average per Acre.	Assessed Value.	Average per Acre.	Ratio of Consideration to Assessment.	No. of City and Village Lots.	Consideration in Deed.	Average per Lot.	Assessed Value.	Average per Lot.	Ratio of Consideration to Assessment.
Adams	18,982	$137,062	$9 80	$32,071	$2 29	.23	12	$1,375	$114 58	$705	$58 75	.513
[1]Ashland												
[1]Barron												
Bayfield	50,612	105,393	2 08	104,005	2 05	.99	97	5,670	58 46	4,272	44 04	.758
[1]Brown												
Buffalo	18,148	140,050	7 72	40,550	2 24	.29	65	22,235	342 08	7,588	116 75	.341
[1]Burnett												
Calumet	12,771	259,411	20 31	66,188	5 18	.26	44	15,715	357 16	4,364	99 18	.278
Chippewa	106,872	563,318	5 29	221,165	2 08	.39	114	90,367	792 69	53,328	467 79	.590
Clark	47,772	310,286	6 49	186,546	3 90	.60	41	15,835	386 22	10,260	250 25	.648
Columbia	20,443	341,179	16 69	234,144	11 45	.69	238	105,808	444 71	74,315	312 25	.703
Crawford	10,904	61,920	5 68	38,472	3 53	.62	155	21,990	141 87	14,730	95 03	.670
Dane	23,870	503,793	21 11	332,081	13 97	.66	378	326,056	862 60	238,676	631 42	.732
Dodge	30,827	913,623	29 64	632,040	20 50	.69	672	219,902	327 24	125,055	186 09	.569
Door	15,419	165,379	10 73	88,241	5 72	.53	30	9,530	317 67	4,139	137 97	.434
[1]Douglas												
Dunn	14,511	116,078	8 00	47,601	3 28	.41	108	45,237	418 86	24,447	226 36	.540
Eau Claire	9,536	80,854	8 48	51,072	5 36	.63	452	226,482	501 07	248,765	550 37	1.098
Fond du Lac	23,050	940,241	40 79	422,355	18 32	.45	710	627,886	884 35	296,030	416 94	.471
Grant	33,574	451,543	13 75	296,042	8 82	.64	211	66,510	315 21	39,870	186 59	.592

Green	20,828	427,861	20	51	318,329	15	28	.74	276	117,488	425	60	86,738	314	25	.738
Green Lake	7,204	138,096	18	98	90,844	12	45	.66	228	58,555	256	83	45,648	200	21	.780
Iowa	23,515	308,178	18	47	184,509	8	15	.61	80	28,864	324	81	14,267	160	30	.494
Jackson	33,887	211,180	6	28	64,062	1	90	.30	97	27,975	288	40	19,820	204	33	.708
Jefferson	17,390	578,882	32	33	318,385	17	80	.55	361	207,717	575	39	125,856	348	68	.606
Juneau	18,437	171,614	9	31	77,674	4	21	.45	164	36,288	221	27	33,438	208	89	.921
Kenosha	9,245	348,512	37	81	171,986	18	60	.49	235	163,728	696	71	71,154	302	78	.435
Kewaunee	17,072	174,491	10	22	24,740	1	45	.14	208	37,066	178	20	4,956	23	82	.134
La Crosse	8,731	118,069	13	52	67,380	7	72	.57	505	264,184	523	14	166,798	330	29	.631
La Fte	15,147	384,749	25	40	170,392	11	25	.44	129	48,695	377	48	25,601	198	46	.526
Moc	20,846	482,786	23	16	139,955	6	71	.29	318	127,158	399	64	98,582	309	85	.775
Marathon	199,752	430,671	2	16	260,863	1	30	.65	117	22,955	196	20	9,344	79	86	.407
Marquette	7,309	60,290	8	25	18,307	2	50	.30	...	...	...	...	...	...	...	...
Milwaukee	2,375	153,496	64	63	87,382	36	88	.57	1,751	1,772,149	1,012	08	1,233,193	704	28	.696
[1] Me	15,811	159,946	10	12	69,434	4	39	.43	179	80,568	450	10	46,829	261	61	.581
Onto	9,640	73,609	7	64	24,706	2	56	.34	218	64,824	297	45	40,913	187	67	.631
Outagamie	8,844	139,713	15	80	58,410	6	60	.42	125	83,855	670	84	47,537	380	30	.567
Oaukee	12,818	365,660	28	52	202,339	15	79	.55	211	41,812	198	16	19,847	94	06	.475
Pin	...	...	...	...	...	...	...	...	...	...	...	...	...	...	...	...
Pierce	17,265	186,818	10	82	108,120	6	26	.58	84	34,111	406	08	18,570	221	10	.544
Polk	6,638	40,986	6	17	20,225	3	05	.49	24	3,316	138	17	1,475	61	46	.445
Portage	10,007	50,958	5	09	16,532	1	65	.32	281	60,657	215	86	30,668	109	12	.506
Racine	6,800	230,231	33	86	154,782	22	76	.67	354	260,228	735	11	[illegible]	477	10	.649
Richland	21,997	164,848	7	47	95,383	4	33	.58	99	17,192	173	66	10,277	103	81	.598
Rock	14,336	461,307	32	18	303,973	21	20	.66	478	407,350	852	20	274,514	574	30	.674
St. Cix	24,415	218,106	8	93	130,405	5	34	.60	193	72,959	378	03	42,757	221	54	.586
Sk	28,200	307,502	10	90	152,706	5	42	.50	150	59,046	393	64	32,831	218	87	.556
Sho	48,677	228,764	4	70	61,655	1	27	.27	103	26,822	260	41	14,054	136	45	.524
Sheboygan	16,353	354,728	21	69	211,994	12	96	.60	374	137,290	367	09	69,462	185	73	.506
Tu	10,324	82,864	8	03	42,855	4	15	.52	33	9,421	285	48	5,092	154	30	.540
Vernon	26,371	204,310	7	75	113,564	4	30	.57	63	8,880	140	95	,745	75	79	.538
Walworth	18,586	563,930	30	34	425,223	22	88	.75	334	180,798	541	29	130,938	392	02	.724
Washington	5,510	188,904	34	28	90,811	16	48	.48	55	21,355	388	28	13,105	238	28	.614
Waukesha	11,398	452,782	39	72	325,370	28	55	.72	130	85,250	655	77	56,995	438	42	.669

[1] No report.

"G."—*Statement showing the Sales of Real Estate Made and Recorded in the Several Counties*—con.

Counties.	No. of acres.	Considerations in Deed.	Average per acre.	Assessed value.	Average per Acre.	Ratio of Consideration to Assessment.	No. of City and Village Lots.	Consideration in Deed.	Average per lot.	Assessed Value.	Average per lot.	Ratio of Consideration to Assessment.
Waupaca	88,359	$190,351	$2 15	$75,138	$ 85	.40	368	$101,197	$274 45	$50,376	$136 89	.498
Waushara	17,979	165,252	9 19	57,355	3 19	.35	61	23,880	391 48	7,409	121 46	.310
Winnebago	8,859	288,718	32 59	168,557	19 03	.58	1,109	579,074	522 16	372,330	335 78	.643
Wood	12,195	60,087	4 93	27,453	2 25	.46	43	21,675	504 07	7,460	173 49	.344
Totals	1,274,501	$14,252,873	$11 18	$7,723,771	$6 06	.54	12,874	$7,094,970	$551 11	$4,548,481	$353 31	.642

APPENDIX "H."

Tabular Statement *showing the Amount of the Different Classes of Property not liable to Taxation in the Several Counties under existing Laws, returned to the office of the Secretary of State, as provided by Chapter 205, Laws of* 1873.

Counties.	U. S. property.	State property.	County property.	Town, city and village property.	Common school property.	College and academy property.	[1]Church property.	[2]Railroad property.	All other property.	Total property.	Miles of railroad.
Adams	$735	$1,274	$4,055	$140	$5,835	....	$953	$785	$63	$13,840	......
Ashland	....	....	....	4,100	3,500	....	2,500	95,400	....	105,500	18
[3] Barron	....	....	....	....	....	....	....	....	....	....	......
Bayfield	....	....	....	290	1,800	....	2,900	....	....	4,990	......
[3] Brown	....	....	....	....	....	....	....	....	....	....	......
[4] Buffalo	....	....	7,050	770	22,590	....	28,215	....	50	58,675	......
[1] [illegible]tt	....	22,006	400	....	1,100	....	1,100	....	....	24,606	......
[5] Calumet	....	....	3,000	300	17,410	....	12,520	[5]50,405	850	84,485	21½
[3] [illegible]a	....	....	....	....	....	....	....	....	....	....	......
[5] Clark	....	....	....	....	....	....	....	....	....	....	......
[illegible]ia	805	859	26,790	19,575	83,377	$805	140,465	60,695	19,785	353,156	83¾
[3] Crawford	....	....	....	....	....	....	....	....	....	....	......
Dane	389,000	[7]5,400,749	61,770	51,642	172,351	8,000	306,035	222,350	406,048	7,017,940	86 5/12
[6] Dodge	....	100,055	....	5,594	67,922	11,500	76,055	221,187	13,580	495,893	55½
Door	10,000	....	3,800	100	4,200	....	5,325	....	150	23,575	......
Douglas	....	....	....	....	....	....	2,305	....	....	2,305	......
Dunn	....	....	....	....	5,640	....	16,375	126,349	50	148,414	6
Eau Claire	63,780	5,825	30,817	15,045	62,903	....	55,885	1,478,973	....	1,713,228	41

[1] [illegible]luding parsonages, church schools and cemeteries.
[2] Excluding value of railroad track.
[3] No report.
[4] Eight towns not reported.
[5] Railroad track partly valued.
[6] Railroad depots and shops not all valued.
[7] Including school, university and other trust funds.

“H.”—*Statement showing the Amount of Exempt Property, etc.*—continued.

COUNTIES.	U. S. property.	State property.	County property.	Town, city and village property.	Common school property.	College and academy property.	[1]Church property.	[2]Railroad property.	All other property.	Total property.	Miles of railroad.
[3] Fond du Lac	....	....	$7,360	$39,500	$121,298	$48,300	$268,905	$212,653	$31,551	$729,567	64
[4] Grant	....	....	....	....	....	....	....	....	....	....	....
[3] Green	....	....	29,400	19,898	85,195	....	99,094	[3] 40,500	16,705	290,792	22½
[5] Green Lake	....	$520	6,500	14,345	41,375	....	57,805	90,000	2,983	213,528	15¼
[6] Iowa	$15	....	9,480	11,275	44,208	....	89,135	....	2,290	156,403	21¾
Jackson	....	....	2,639	2,600	36,786	....	20,500	235,710	....	298,235	72
Jefferson	....	....	....	17,600	87,060	33,000	149,170	190,000	32,930	509,760	63⅛
Juneau	....	....	8,573	6,503	20,900	....	18,999	2,000	6,700	63,675	55¾
[7] Kenosha	....	....	7,500	13,465	17,480	....	35,300	3,000	3,460	80,205	32¼
[7] Kewaunee	....	220	600	51	8,100	....	8,941	....	2,600	20,512	....
La Crosse	....	....	21,000	11,095	44,535	....	106,044	79,115	10,560	272,349	46 18/80
[4] La Fayette	....	....	....	....	....	....	....	....	....	....	....
[8] Manitowoc	1,050	....	17,500	23,690	16,096	....	24,860	140,000	5,916	228,612	47
[9] Marathon	....	....	5,000	1,000	15,292	....	9,950	....	10,000	41,242	....
Marquette	....	....	4,000	615	3,600	....	11,010	....	....	19,225	....
Milwaukee	580,050	1,150	681,080	359,845	185,965	19,800	1,363,220	851,105	38,000	4,080,215	58½
Monroe	4,320	....	13,000	10,565	20,040	....	18,025	[3] 161,705	3,417	231,072	68
[4] Oconto	....	....	....	....	....	....	....	....	....	....	....
Outagamie	....	....	....	120	4,089	....	4,340	29,903	680	9,229	7
[6] Ozaukee	2,000	....	1,000	1,840	17,315	....	27,971	16,300	980	81,009	14
Pepin	6,192	....	8,000	1,620	12,263	....	5,030	....	2,560	51,970	....
Pierce	....	....	2,590	50	7,005	....	12,915	....	1,170	23,730	....
Polk	....	....	1,750	1,255	8,710	....	3,331	....	....	15,046	....
[4] Portage	....	....	....	....	....	....	....	....	....	....	....
Racine	....	....	19,400	38,870	75,985	135,000	190,700	[3] 775,475	108,365	1,348,295	54
[4] Richland	....	....	....	....	....	....	....	....	....	....	....
Rock	2,000	102,100	116,455	21,210	179,740	58,700	269,465	486,500	11,807	1,242,977	117 17/80

[6]St. Croix											
Sauk	2,627	2,830	35,436	140	78,028		65,580	17,000	4,855	207,891	50¼
[4]Shawano											
[4]Sheboygan											
[7]Trempealeau											
Vernon			10,050		48,851		21,695		3,960	79,056	
Walworth		200,000	23,950	6,200	105,465	11,000	164,400	8,000	14,950	583,965	58¾
Washington			7,000	200	80,011		42,116	[3]39,000	1,261	119,588	86½
Waukesha		150,000	26,055	3,700	201,150	78,000	140,625	78,200	13,308	691,088	82½
[4]Waupaca											
Waushara	6,880	580	2,000	1,050	15,455		7,370		8,970	42,305	
Winnebago		550,000	12,000	22,254	123,727		113,886	37,185	9,604	868,656	40 11/16
[4]Wood											
Totals	$1,069 454	$6,538,168	$1,217,000	$727,612	$2,099,752	$399,105	$4,000,515	$5,749,495	$790,153	$22,591,254	1,279½

[1]Including parsonages, church schools and cemeteries.
[2]Railroad property.
[3]Railroad track partly valued.
[4]No report.
[5]Except the town of St. Marie.
[6]Railroad depots and shops all not valued.
[7]Two towns not reported.
[8]Six towns not reported.
[9]Partly estimated, returns being incomplete.

APPENDIX "I."

Synopsis *of the Annual Reports of County Agricultural Societies for the year* 1873.

Counties.	When Fair was held.	Where held.	Receipts.						
			From State.	Membership.	Admission Fee.	Entries.	Subscriptions.	Other Sources.	Totals.
Adams	Oct. 2, 3, 1872	Friendship	$200 00	$41 00			$226 00	$51 50	$518 50
Buffalo	Oct. 9–11, 1872	Lincoln		250 00	$50 95	$75 70		300 00	676 65
Columbia	Sep. 18–20, 1872	Portage	100 00	294 00	186 71		211 50	69 00	861 21
Crawford	Oct. 8, 9, 1872	Prairie du Chien	100 00	10 00	113 05	45 20		51 62	319 87
Dane	Sep. 16–19, 1872	Madison	100 00	98 00	1,691 36	697 75	643 75	1,782 09	5,012 95
Dodge	Sep. 13–15, 1872	Juneau	100 00		295 10	36 00		30 00	461 10
Door	Sep. 27, 28, 1872	Sturgeon Bay	100 00	61 00	9 25	4 00	36 00	46 99	257 24
Fond du Lac	Sep. 10–12, 1872	Fond du Lac	100 00		879 63	179 00		645 35	1,808 98
Grant	Sep. 18–20, 1872	Lancaster	100 00	181 00	581 80	40 50		136 45	1,039 75
Green	Sep. 12–14, 1872	Monroe	110 00		665 00			166 00	931 00
Green Lake	Sep. 10–13, 1872	Berlin	100 00		744 70				844 70
Iowa	Sep. 18–20, 1872	Dodgeville	100 00	305 00	388 25			273 56	1,066 81
Jackson	Sep. 18–20, 1872	Black River Falls	100 00	120 00	185 40	15 00	225 00	500 00	1,145 40
Jefferson	Sep. 17–20, 1872	Jefferson	100 00	476 00	428 13	48 00	228 00	337 00	1,617 13
Juneau	Sep. 17–19, 1872	Mauston	100 00	279 00	102 20	32 00		137 00	650 20
Kenosha	Sep. 17–19, 1872	Bristol	100 00	246 00	406 75	38 00		196 46	987 21
La Crosse	Sep. 17–19, 1872	Salem	100 00	504 00	159 00	3 90		105 40	872 30
La Fayette	Sep. 12–14, 1872	Darlington	100 00		647 95	112 80		174 40	1,035 15
Marathon	Sp. 30, O't. 1, 1872	Wausau	100 00		76 80			375 00	551 80
Marquette	Oct. 2, 3, 1872	Westfield	100 00	78 00	19 50	4 00			201 50
Monroe	Sep. 11–13, 1872	Sparta	100 00					432 50	532 50

Outagamie	Sept. 18–20, 1872	Appleton	100 00	136 00	472 55	....	....	....	708 55
Ozaukee	Oct. 7, 8, 1872	Cedarburg	100 00	122 00	33 45	....	....	5 00	260 45
Pierce	Oct. 10, [illegible]72	Prescott	100 00	110 00	141 25	....	500 00	63 44	913 69
Portage	Sept. 19–21, 1872	Amherst	100 00	520 00	183 51	18 80	410 00	8 00	1,229 31
Racine	Sept. 11–12, 1872	Burlington	100 00	1,795 40	....	225 00	....	1,638 97	3,759 37
Richland	[illegible]t. 2–4, 1872	[illegible]d Center	100 00	23 00	425 75	159 00	8 00	40 00	750 75
Rock	[illegible]pt. 17–20, 1872	[illegible]ille	100 00	64 00	2,986 85	100 50	....	788 13	3,989 48
Sauk	Sept. 17, 18, 1872	[illegible]o	100 00	10 00	404 05	88 00	....	95 50	697 55
Sheboygan	Sept. 18, 19, 1872	[illegible]ygan Falls	100 00	425 00	74 45	29 10	....	25 00	653 55
Trempealeau	Oct. 1, 2, 3, 1872	[illegible]ille	100 00	214 00	250 80	45 00	12 75	47 82	670 37
Vernon	Oct. 1–4, 1872	Vernon	100 00	1 00	493 00	90 00	....	90 00	774 00
Walworth	Oct. 1–4, 1872	[illegible]rn	100 00	709 00	1,823 00	55 00	....	561 09	3,248 09
Washington	Oct. 2–4, 1872	[illegible]t Bend	100 00	69 00	146 15	88 75	456 50	440 24	1,250 64
Waukesha	[illegible]	[illegible]a	100 00	45 00	658 49	91 00	116 95	162 90	1,169 34
Winnebago	Sp. [illegible]	Oshkosh	100 00	10 00	4,281 70	223 00	....	295 00	4,909 70
Totals	....	....	$3,600 00	$7,196 40	$20,000 53	$2,490 00	$3,069 45	$10,015 41	$46,371 79

"I."—*Synopsis of the Annual Reports of County Agricultural Societies*—continued.

Counties.	Expenditures.					On Hand.
	Premiums.	Expenses of Fair.	Secretary's Office.	Other Expenses.	Total.	
Adams	$163 38	$15 00	$10 00	$377 50	$565 88	$24 07
Buffalo	130 00	125 00	....	1,038 00	1,293 00	....
Columbia	570 00	181 85	67 45	134 60	953 90	296 70
Crawford	140 80	111 01	....	....	251 81	68 06
Dane	2,891 50	1,053 98	154 75	949 80	5,050 03	40 09
Dodge	178 80	205 28	....	85 00	469 08	24 03
Door	165 50	47 36	85	....	213 71	43 58
Fond du Lac	930 95	673 03	100 00	100 00	1,803 98	....
Grant	591 50	265 59	25 00	300 00	1,182 09	155 93
Green	525 13	305 87	....	100 00	931 00	....
Green Lake	618 70	236 00	25 00	....	879 70	....
Iowa	425 00	488 73	155 91	....	1,069 64	....
Jackson	428 25	50 00	4 20	725 00	1,207 45	44 25
Jefferson	725 29	263 00	52 10	561 23	1,601 62	65 84
Juneau	413 50	64 64	20 50	140 84	639 48	126 10
Kenosha	496 42	212 37	25 00	162 20	897 99	88 22
La Crosse	479 50	250 00	25 00	75 00	829 50	42 80
La Fayette	568 25	168 90	40 00	260 67	1,037 82	....
Marathon	448 00	40 43	4 35	190 08	682 86	....
Marquette	131 50	....	10 00	50 00	191 50	10 00
Monroe	290 00	125 00	....	161 47	576 47	....
Outagamie	297 80	255 88	....	169 00	722 68	....
Ozaukee	151 00	41 50	30 00	....	222 50	37 95
Pierce	150 75	77 66	....	865 12	1,093 53	....
Portage	226 75	66 80	60 00	1,209 03	1,562 58	....
Racine	1,554 89	....	....	1,711 05	3,265 94	488 48

Richland	289 50	89 50	1 30	349 00	729 30	21 45
Rock	1,516 14	670 67	....	1,723 82	3,990 63	....
Sauk	438 50	95 30	5 00	162 33	701 18	....
Sheboygan	485 25	168 40	17 88	74 85	696 38	....
[illegible]u	245 50	140 25	15 00	387 18	787 88	52 39
Vernon	458 25	265 14	30 00	....	753 30	20 61
[illegible]th	1,361 00	400 00	122 00	1,365 09	[illegible]8 09	....
Washington	423 50	275 14	....	273 82	972 46	278 18
Waukesha	720 00	118 96	....	339 96	1,178 92	1 42
Winnebago	2,864 00	1,836 00	....	....	4,700 00	377 00
Totals	$22,526 80	$9,384 19	$1,001 24	$13,991 59	$46,908 82	$2,297 05

"I."—*Synopsis of the Annual Reports of County Agricultural Societies*— continued.

Counties.	Officers.		
	President.	Secretary.	Treasurer.
Adams	V. E. Smith	David Schofield	A. F. Hill
Buffalo	Robert Henry	John Hunner	J. W. DeGraff
Columbia	A. G. Cook	L. H. Doyle	J. Q. Adams
Crawford	Joseph Atherton	Ira B. Brunson	Lawrence Case
Dane	W. R. Taylor	O. S. Willey	Geo. A. Mason
Dodge	M. E. Babcock	E. B. Bolens	David Barber
Door	Geo. Pinney	R. M. Wright	James R. Mann
Fond du Lac	E. S. Hammond	Dana C. Lamb	A. B. Taylor
Grant	John B. Callis	F. A. Burr	W. W. Robe
Green	T. H. Eaton	Wm. W. Wright	Wm. Brown
Green Lake	S. W. Mather	L. C. Potter	Scott B. Rogers
Iowa	Joel Whitman	John Ralph	John Ellwood
Jackson	Wm. T. Price	F. H. Allen	Oliver O'Hearn
Jefferson	O. C. Olin	D. E. Baker	Jas. Barr
Juneau	Luther Beckwith	F. S. Veeder	M. Temple
Kenosha	J. M. Kellogg	H. H. Tarbell	L. W. Thayer
La Crosse	Wm. Van Zandt	A. J. Philips	F. W. Stiles
La Fayette	S. Warden	H. L. Brown	Wm. J. Bird
Marathon	W. C. Silverthorn	M. M. Charles	Jacob Kolter
Marquette	James Graham	S. A. Pease	W. F. Stebbins
Monroe	J. A. Clark	E. Nutting	Fred. B. Tyler
Outagamie	A. P. Lewis	L. L. Randall	P. S. Bennett
Ozaukee	A. M. Alling	Wm. Vogenitz	Theodore Fricke
Pierce	H. A. Jay	Wm. Howe	A. Gray
Portage	C. Couch	J. H. Felch	Enoch Webster
Racine	N. D. Fratt	A. L. Lawton	W. E. Chapman

Richland	J. B. McGraw	J. H. Waggoner	D. L. Downs.
Rock	Seth Fisher	R. J. Richardson	C. Miner.
Sauk	H. H. Potter	John M. True	T. T. English.
Sheboygan	Enos Eastman	Jno. E. Thomas	B. F. Heald.
Trempealeau	Joshua Rhodes	Chas. E. Perkins	Douglas Arnold.
Vernon	F. K. Van Wagner	Geo. W. Nuzum	C. M. Butt.
Walworth	P. G. Harrington	S. G. Kent	Hollis Latham.
Washington	Peter Fraser	Albert Semler	Franz Lorenz.
Waukesha	Isaac Kain	Frank H. Putney	A. M. Tyler.
Winnebago	J. M. Ball	James Brainard	R. D. Torrey.

APPENDIX "K."

Abstract *of Marriages, Births and Deaths Reported, Recorded and Indexed, in the Office of the Secretary of State, for the year ending December* 31, 1872.

Counties.	Marriages.	Births.	Deaths
Adams	89	....	.....
Barron	19	....	.....
Brown	227	33	.....
Buffalo	74	7	.....
Burnett	5	....	.....
Calumet	255	22	15
Chippewa	88	....	.....
Clark	43	....	.....
Columbia	243	....	.....
Crawford	170	....	.....
Dane	405	....	.....
Dodge	329	44	34
Door	43	39	2
Dunn	125	....	.....
Eau Claire	152	....	.....
Fond du Lac	406	66	13
Grant	312	....	.....
Green	183	8	2
Green Lake	85	....	.....
Iowa	146	18	2
Jackson	90	....	.....
Jefferson	283	87	33
Juneau	95	....	.....
Kenosha	100	....	.....
Kewaunee	83	....	.....
La Crosse	247	....	.....
La Fayette	134	....	.....
Manitowoc	171	276	52
Marathon	63	....	.....
Marquette	45	....	.....
Milwaukee	1,076	1,449	1,118
Monroe	119	....	.....
Oconto	66	....	.....
Outagamie	128	....	.....
Ozaukee	255	3,387	584
Pepin	66	....	.....
Pierce	133	....	.....
Polk	48	12	4
Portage	59	....	.....
Racine	233	....	.....
Richland	149	....	.....
Rock	373	262	16
Sauk	170	....	.....
Shawano	31	....	.....
Sheboygan	175	2,428	27
Trempealeau	91	....	.....

"K"—*Marriages, Births and Deaths*—con.

Counties.	Marriages.	Births.	Deaths.
Vernon	159	....	......
Walworth	201	83	10
Washington	232	7	......
Waukesha	174	8	16
Waupaca	111	....	......
Waushara	72	....	......
Winnebago	340	....	......
Wood	11	....	......
Totals	9,082	8,172	1,923

APPENDIX "L."

LIST OF INCORPORATIONS *organized under the general laws of this State, during the year ending Sept.* 30, 1873.

Kenosha Insulator Company.
The Hudson Manufacturing Company.
Waterhouse Manufacturing Company.
Kickapoo Valley Iron Mining Company.
Esdaile Manufacturing Company.
Edward P. Allis Iron Company.
The Janesville Water Power Company.
F. B. Gardner Company.
Bayfield Gas Light Company.
The Ashland Lumber Company.
Menominee Barge Line Company.
The Green Bay Silver Mining Company.
Lodi Valley Cheese Factory.
The Oakton Springs Company.
Sunny Side Mining Company.
Manufacturing Association of Ripon.
The Milwaukee Manufacturing Company.
The Northern Mining Land and Iron Company.
The Little Suamico Lumber and Manufacturing Company.
The Philip Best Brewing Company.
Wauwatosa Cheese Company.
The Sturgeon Bay Company.
Green and Button Company.
Meridian Mill Company.
German Protestant Printing Association.
The Wauzeka Manufacturing Company.
The Pewaukee Cheese Manufacturing Company.
The Omro Woolen Manufacturing Company.
Ames Wood Pulp Company.
German Catholic Printing Society.
Hitchcock Cranberry Company.
Eclipse Wind Mill Company.
Two Rivers Sash, Door and Blind Works.
Wisconsin River Lumber Company.
The Marshall Brothers Church Organ Manufacturing Company.
The Ripon Industrial Aid Company.
Racine Dredge Company.
The Wisconsin Mineral Land and Mining Company.
The Ripon Horticultural Association.
Ripon Boot and Shoe Company.
The Clintonville Extract Company.
Great Western Compound Company.
McLean Manufacturing Company.
The Weed Lumber Company.
Northwestern Lumber Company.
Weed & Gumaer Manufacturing Company.
Dexterville Manufacturing and Boom Company.
Scranton Manufacturing and Boom Company.
The Minerva Furnace Company.

Ripon Packing Company.
The Waukesha Hotel Company.
Winchester and Partridge Manufacturing Company.
Appleton Paper Manufacturing Company.
The A. C. Conn Company.

APPENDIX "M."

List of Religious Societies *organized under the general laws of this State during the year ending September* 30, 1873.

Bridge Street Methodist Church of Beloit.
The First Scandinavian Evangelical Lutheran Congregation of Chippewa Falls.
Freie Evangelisch Protestantisch Gemeinde of Eau Claire.
Our Savior's Danish Lutheran Church of Neenah.

APPENDIX "N."

TABULAR STATEMENT *of the Votes polled for Electors of President and Vice President of the United States, and on the Proposition to amend the Constitution, at a General Election held in the several Towns, Wards and Election Precincts in the State of Wisconsin, on the Tuesday succeeding the first Monday, being the fifth day of November, A. D.* 1872.

COUNTIES.	ELECTORS OF PRESIDENT AND VICE PRESIDENT.									
	William E. Cramer.	F. Fleischer.	Jerome S. Nickles.	Geo. G. Swain.	Ormsby B. Thomas.	Frederick Hilgen.	Edward C. McFetridge	George E. Hoskinson.	Romanzo Bunn.	Henry D. Barron.
Adams	885	885	885	885	885	885	885	885	885	885
Ashland	86	86	86	86	86	86	86	86	86	86
Barron	120	120	120	120	120	120	120	120	120	128
Bayfield	89	89	89	89	89	89	89	89	89	89
Brown	2,693	2,694	2,694	2,694	2,694	2,695	2,694	2,692	2,694	2,694
Buffalo	843	843	843	843	843	843	843	843	843	843
Burnett	160	160	160	160	160	160	160	160	160	160
Calumet	756	756	757	757	757	757	757	757	757	757
Chippewa	1,025	1,025	1,024	1,024	1,024	1,024	1,025	1,025	1,025	1,024
Clark	801	801	801	801	801	801	801	801	801	801
Columbia	3,070	3,070	3,070	3,070	3,070	3,070	3,070	3,070	3,070	3,070
Crawford	1,162	1,162	1,162	1,162	1,161	1,162	1,162	1,162	1,163	1,163
Dane	5,141	5,139	5,141	5,141	5,142	5,142	5,142	5,143	5,142	5,143
Dodge	3,051	3,051	3,051	3,051	3,051	3,051	3,051	3,051	3,051	3,051
Door	873	873	873	873	873	873	873	873	873	873
Douglas	72	72	72	72	72	72	72	72	72	72
Dunn	1,390	1,390	1,390	1,390	1,390	1,390	1,390	1,390	1,390	1,390

Eau Claire	1,616	1,616	1,615	1,615	1,615	1,615	1,615	1,615	1,615	1,615
Fond du Lac	4,292	4,292	4,292	4,292	4,292	4,292	4,292	4,292	4,292	4,292
Grant	4,307	4,307	4,307	4,307	4,307	4,307	4,307	4,307	4,307	4,307
Green	2,450	2,450	2,450	2,450	2,450	2,450	2,450	2,450	2,450	2,450
Green Lake	1,541	1,541	1,541	1,541	1,541	1,541	1,541	1,541	1,541	1,541
Iowa	2,078	2,078	2,078	2,078	2,078	2,078	2,078	2,078	2,078	2,078
Jackson	956	956	956	956	956	956	956	956	956	956
Jefferson	2,580	2,580	2,579	2,579	2,579	2,579	2,579	2,579	2,579	2,579
Juneau	1,421	1,421	1,421	1,421	1,421	1,421	1,421	1,421	1,421	1,421
Kenosha	1,408	1,408	1,408	1,408	1,408	1,408	1,408	1,408	1,408	1,408
Kewaunee	508	508	508	508	508	508	508	508	508	508
La Crosse	2,177	2,180	2,180	2,178	2,179	2,179	2,178	2,179	2,178	2,178
La Fayette	2,080	2,081	2,080	2,081	2,081	2,081	2,081	2,081	2,081	2,081
Manitowoc	2,289	2,289	2,289	2,289	2,289	2,289	2,289	2,280	2,289	2,289
Marathon	491	491	491	491	491	491	491	491	491	491
Marquette	643	643	643	643	643	643	643	643	643	643
Milwaukee	5,833	5,833	5,834	5,834	5,882	5,887	5,835	5,834	5,834	5,834
Monroe	2,117	2,117	2,117	2,117	2,117	2,117	2,117	2,117	2,117	2,117
Oconto	1,076	1,076	1,077	1,077	1,077	1,068	1,077	1,075	1,076	1,076
Outagamie	1,535	1,535	1,535	1,535	1,535	1,535	1,535	1,535	1,535	1,535
Ozaukee	574	574	574	574	574	574	574	574	574	574
Pepin	644	644	644	644	644	644	644	644	644	644
Pierce	1,460	1,460	1,460	1,460	1,460	1,460	1,460	1,460	1,460	1,460
Polk	659	659	659	659	659	659	659	659	659	655
Portage	1,536	1,536	1,536	1,536	1,536	1,536	1,536	1,536	1,536	1,536
Racine	2,880	2,880	2,880	2,880	2,880	2,880	2,880	2,880	2,880	2,880
Richland	1,675	1,675	1,675	1,675	1,675	1,675	1,675	1,675	1,675	1,675
Rock	5,138	5,138	5,138	5,138	5,138	5,138	5,138	5,138	5,138	5,138
St. Croix	1,373	1,373	1,373	1,373	1,373	1,373	1,373	1,373	1,373	1,373
Sauk	2,702	2,702	2,702	2,702	2,702	2,702	2,702	2,702	2,702	2,702
Shawano	416	416	416	416	416	416	416	416	416	416
Sheboygan	2,687	2,687	2,687	2,687	2,687	2,687	2,687	2,685	2,686	2,687
Trempealeau	1,457	1,457	1,457	1,457	1,457	1,457	1,457	1,457	1,456	1,457
Vernon	2,445	2,445	2,445	2,445	2,445	2,445	2,445	2,445	2,445	2,445
Walworth	3,512	3,512	3,512	3,512	3,512	3,512	3,512	3,512	3,512	3,512
Washington	947	947	947	947	947	947	947	947	947	947

"N."—*Votes Polled for Electors of President and Vice President, etc.*—continued.

Counties.	Electors of President and Vice President.									
	William E. Cramer.	F. Fleischer.	Jerome S. Nickles.	Geo. G. Swain.	Ormsby B. Thomas.	Frederick Hilgen.	Edward C. McFetridge	George E. Hoskinson.	Romanzo Bunn.	Henry D. Barron.
Waukesha	2,671	2,671	2,670	2,671	2,671	2,671	2,671	2,671	2,671	2.671
Waupaca	2,050	2,050	2,050	2,050	5,050	2,050	2,050	2,050	2,050	2,050
Waushara	1,708	1,708	1,708	1,708	1,708	1,708	1,708	1,708	1,708	1,708
Winnebago	4,280	4,280	4,280	4,280	4,280	4,280	4,280	4,280	4,280	4,280
Wood	563	563	563	563	563	563	563	563	563	563
Total	104,987	104,990	104,989	104,989	104,988	104,990	104,992	104,986	104,989	104,988

"N."—*Votes Polled for Electors of President and Vice President, etc.*—continued.

Counties.	Electors of President and Vice President, etc.—continued.											Amendment to the Constitution.	
	John Black.	Mons Anderson.	Wyman Spooner.	Amasa G. Cook.	George H. Klug.	Samuel Rindskopf	Robert H. Hotchkiss	Anton Klaus.	Milton Montgomery.	Matthew Wadleigh.	Scattering.	For Amending Constitution increasing Justices of the Supreme Court.	Against Amending Constitu'n increasing Justices of the Supreme Court.
Adams	233	233	233	233	233	233	233	233	233	233	1	158	62
Ashland	43	43	43	43	43	43	43	43	43	43	.....	....	....
Barron	38	38	38	38	38	38	38	38	38	86	.....	....	....
Bayfield	42	42	42	42	42	42	42	42	42	42	.....	42	....
Brown	2,185	2,185	2,186	2,186	2,186	2,185	2,186	2,172	2,186	2,186	21	568	949
Buffalo	862	861	862	862	862	862	862	861	861	862	30	104	659
Burnett	7	7	7	7	7	7	7	7	7	7	.....	9	125
Calumet	1,313	1,313	1,313	1,313	1,313	1,313	1,313	1,312	1,313	1,313	5	31	42
Chippewa	751	750	750	750	750	750	750	750	751	751	.....	101	48
Clark	118	118	118	119	119	119	119	119	119	119	2	14	1
Columbia	1,835	1,835	1,835	1,835	1,835	1,835	1,835	1,835	1,835	1,835	11	522	1,208
Crawford	1,151	1,151	1,151	1,151	1,151	1,151	1,151	1,151	1,151	1,151	14	121	33
Dane	4,782	4,783	4,783	4,783	4,782	4,782	4,782	4,782	4,783	4,782	8	1,407	1,942
Dodge	5,622	5,622	5,622	5,622	5,623	5,623	5,623	5,622	5,622	5,622	3	451	854
Door	214	214	214	214	214	214	214	214	214	214	.....	....	....
Douglas	96	96	96	96	96	96	96	96	96	96	.....	7	4
Dunn	498	498	498	498	498	498	498	498	498	498	2	393	300
Eau Claire	816	816	818	818	818	818	818	818	818	818	.....	286	86
Fond du Lac	4,429	4,430	4,430	4,430	4,430	4,429	4,430	4,430	4,430	4,430	19	708	2,229
Grant	2,319	2,318	2,319	2,319	2,319	2,319	2,319	2,319	2,319	2,319	17	813	3,068
Green	1,246	1,246	1,246	1,246	1,246	1,246	1,246	1,246	1,246	1,246	33	276	1,418
Green Lake	1,045	1,045	1,045	1,045	1,045	1,045	1,045	1,045	1,045	1,045	1	154	830
Iowa	1,978	1,978	1,978	1,978	1,978	1,978	1,978	1,978	1,978	1,978	16	146	101
Jackson	858	858	858	858	858	858	858	858	858	858	.....	185	324
Jefferson	3,559	3,559	3,559	3,559	3,559	3,559	3,559	3,559	3,559	3,559	78	308	472

"N."—*Votes Polled for Electors of President and Vice President, etc.*—continued.

COUNTIES.	ELECTORS OF PRESIDENT AND VICE PRESIDENT, ETC.—continued.											AMENDMENT OF THE CONSTITUTION.	
	John Black.	Mons Anderson.	Wyman Spooner.	Amasa G. Cook.	George H. King.	Samuel Rindskopf	Robert H. Hotchkiss	Anton Klaus.	Milton Montgomery.	Matthew Wadleigh.	Scattering.	For Amending Constitution increasing Justices of the Supreme Court.	Against Amending Constitut'n increasing Justices of the Supreme Court.
Juneau	1,068	1,068	1,068	1,068	1,068	1,068	1,068	1,068	1,068	1,068	.....	443	315
[illegible]ha	1,215	1,215	1,215	1,215	1,215	1,215	1,215	1,215	1,215	1,215	.....	217	826
Kewaunee	1,012	1,012	1,012	1,012	1,012	1,012	1,012	1,012	1,012	1,012	.....	....	....
La Crosse	1,801	1,965	1,966	1,966	1,966	1,966	1,966	1,966	1,966	1,966	19	380	514
La Fayette	1,908	1,909	1,908	1,907	1,907	1,907	1,908	1,908	1,908	1,908	99	135	600
Manitowoc	2,677	2,677	2,677	2,677	2,677	2,677	2,677	2,677	2,677	2,677	.....	1,017	287
[illegible]n	911	911	911	911	911	911	911	911	911	911	38	....	....
Marquette	910	910	910	910	910	910	910	910	910	910	.....	51	355
[illegible]kee	8,514	8,512	8,515	8,512	8,511	8,510	8,511	8,511	8,512	8,512	7	330	829
Monroe	1,425	1,425	1,425	1,425	1,425	1,425	1,425	1,415	1,425	1,425	14	795	384
Oconto	396	396	388	395	395	396	395	396	395	395	25	112	3
Outagamie	1,970	1,970	1,970	1,970	1,970	1,970	1,970	1,969	1,970	1,970	5	885	132
[illegible]aukee	1,594	1,594	1,594	1,594	1,594	1,594	1,594	1,594	1,594	1,594	101	124	29
Pepin	272	272	272	272	272	272	272	272	272	272	5	112	336
[illegible]ie	634	634	634	634	634	634	634	634	634	634	41	119	463
Polk	189	189	189	189	189	189	189	189	189	188	1	89	322
Portage	798	798	798	798	798	798	798	798	798	798	.....	140	9
Racine	2,100	2,100	2,100	2,100	2,100	2,100	2,100	2,100	2,100	2,100	1	38	50
Richland	999	999	999	999	999	999	999	999	999	999	53	83	1,874
Rock	1,740	1,740	1,740	1,740	1,740	1,740	1,740	1,740	1,740	1,740	21	1,000	2,515
St. Croix	1,190	1,190	1,190	1,190	1,190	1,190	1,190	1,190	1,190	1,190	.....	25	70
Sauk	1,354	1,354	1,354	1,354	1,354	354	1,354	1,354	1,354	1,354	2	932	914
[illegible]ho	464	464	464	464	464	464	464	464	464	464	.....	....	71
Sheboygan	2,948	2,948	2,948	2,848	2,948	2,948	2,947	2,950	2,948	2,948	2	153	305
Trempealeau	417	417	417	417	417	417	417	417	417	417	1	178	101

Vernon	542	549	542	542	542	542	549	542	542	542	7	710	1,507
Walworth	1,499	1,499	1,500	1,499	1,499	1,499	1,499	1,499	1,499	1,499	19	709	409
Washington	2,727	2,727	2,727	2,727	2,727	2,726	2,727	2,726	2,727	2,727	......	4	80
Waukesha	2,720	2,720	2,721	2,720	2,720	2,720	2,720	2,720	2,720	2,720	8	174	66
Waupaca	945	945	945	945	945	945	945	945	945	945	1	191	682
Waushara	889	889	889	889	889	889	889	889	889	889	28	158	1,471
Winnebago	2,969	2,969	2,969	2,969	2,969	2,969	2,969	2,969	2,969	2,969	......	163	111
Wood	473	473	473	473	473	473	473	473	473	473	80	6	9
Totals	86,310	86,477	86,474	86,476	86,474	86,472	86,475	86,460	86,477	86,474	884	16,273	29,755

APPENDIX "O."

Tabular Statement *of the votes polled for Associate Justice of the Supreme Court of the State of Wisconsin, at an Election held in the several towns, wards, and election precincts in the said State, on Tuesday, the first day of April,* 1873.

Counties.	Associate Justice Supreme Court.	
	Orasmus Cole.	Scattering.
Adams	981	......
Ashland	160	......
Barron	254	......
Bayfield	157	......
Brown	3,709	......
Buffalo	1,833	......
Burnett	111	4
Calumet	1,732	......
Chippewa	1,219	......
Clark	622	......
Columbia	2,263	1
Crawford	1,911	2
Dane	4,922	2
Dodge	2,795	122
Door	847	4
Douglas	13	......
Dunn	1,556	2
Eau Claire	2,066	......
Fond du Lac	6,720	12
Grant	2,939	......
Green	2,031	1
Green Lake	1,584	309
Iowa	2,556	......
Jackson	865	2
Jefferson	3,757	18
Juneau	2,239	......
Kenosha	1,578	......
Kewaunee	619	1,201
La Crosse	3,111	......
La Fayette	2,755	......
Manitowoc	1,255	......
Marathon	1,294	......
Marquette	1,040	......
Milwaukee	10,185	2
Monroe	2,342	......
Oconto	723	......
Outagamie	3,448	......
Ozaukee	1,646	4
Pepin	616	17
Pierce	2,028	......
Polk	771	......
Portage	1,527	......

"O."—*Votes Polled for Associate Justice*—continued.

Counties.	Associate Justice Supreme Court.	
	Orasmus Cole.	Scattering.
Racine	2,943	......
Richland	1,946	1
Rock	3,016	......
St. Croix	2,097	......
Sauk	3,129	......
Shawano	762	5
Sheboygan	2,341	......
Trempealeau	1,474	3
Vernon	2,445	2
Walworth	1,458	6
Washington	1,909	......
Waukesha	3,365	......
Waupaca	2,552	......
Waushara	1,404	2
Winnebago	4,390	1
Wood	815	2
Total	120,776	1,725

APPENDIX "P."

Tabular Statement *of the Votes polled for Judge of the Circuit Court of the Third Judicial Circuit, in the State of Wisconsin, at a special election held in the several towns, wards and election precincts in the several counties comprising said judicial circuit, on Tuesday, the first day of April, A. D.* 1873.

Counties.	D. J. Pulling.	Scat'g.
Dodge	4,573	122
Green Lake	1,864	29
Marquette	1,008	......
Ozaukee	1,388	212
Washington	2,427	......
Winnebago	4,891	1
Total	16,131	364

Tabular Statement *of the Votes polled for Judge of the Tenth Judicial Circuit of the State of Wisconsin, at an election held in the several towns, wards and election precincts in the several counties comprising said judicial circuit, on Tuesday, the first day of April, A. D.*, 1873.

Counties.	E. H. Ellis.	Scat'g.
Brown	3,737	.....
Door	848	4
Oconto	721	.....
Outagamie	3,401	.....
Shawano	762	5
Total	9,469	9

APPENDIX "Q."

Accounts Audited *under Chapter* 48, *Section* 4 *of the General Laws of* 1866, *during the year ending Sept.* 30, 1873, *except ordinary labor about the Capitol.*

Date.	To whom.	For what.	Amount.
1872.			
Oct. 2	Bunker & Vroman	Lumber	$90 06
Oct. 16	Jas. B. Ditto	Asphaltum walk	1,820 50
Oct. 17	Conklin & Gray	Coal	5,868 95
Oct. 28	Thos. Regan	Gas fixtures, plumbing, etc.	192 18
Nov. 2	John M. Sumner	Hardware and labor	42 81
Nov. 2	Charles Smith	Rep'g locks and making keys.	39 10
Nov. 2	Tim Purcell	Labor in capitol park	199 00
Nov. 9	Mrs. H. Welsh	Soft soap	10 00
Nov. 11	Dan'l Delaney	Brooms	8 00
Nov. 13	Fahey & Lynch	Mason work	79 38
Nov. 15	Huntley & Wootton	Salt	3 25
Nov. 20	Jas. E. Fisher	Furniture and upholstering	107 00
Nov. 26	R. G. Norton	Repairing clocks	23 75
Nov. 26	John N. Jones	Iron wedges	1 50
Nov 29	Tim Purcell	Labor with team	21 75
3	W. J. Park & Co	Wrapping paper	30 04
4	Newton & Donovan	Blacksmithing	4 50
9	W. P. Towers	Painting and glazing	185 26
16	Stark Brothers	Toweling	36 05
18	Sarah E. Jones	Hemming towels	6 90
19	E. Worden	Repairing pump	17 75
20	Mad. C. G. L. & C. Co.	Removing lamps in park, etc.	49 19
26	John M. Sumner	Hardware and tinware	46 66
28	Sorrenson & Fred'kson.	Lumber, etc	25 10
Dec. 30	Jas. E. Fisher	Upholstering, etc	87 00
1873.			
Jan. 3	Dunning & Sumner	Oils, paints, etc	271 81
Jan. 3	Klauber & Adler	Merchandise	87 87
Jan. 3	Bunker & Vroman	Lumber	224 60
Jan. 4	W. P. Towers	Varnishing, painting, etc	488 60
Jan. 6	Vroman, Frank & Co.	Hardware, etc	84 58
Jan. 8	Newton & Donovan	Blacksmithing	7 75
Jan. 8	Moseley & Bro	Vellum	13 50
Jan. 8	Thos. Regan	Labor, gas and steam fixtures.	285 54
Jan. 9	Dan'l Delaney	Rrooms	24 00
Jan. 11	Jos. Schweinem	Ice	144 00
Jan. 21	W. B'k Note & Eng. Co.	Flag for dome	56 00
Jan. 22	R. L. Garlick	Crockery	78 75
Jan. 29	S. V. Shipman	Architectural designs	94 02
Jan. 31	T. Purcell	Hauling water	112 00
Feb. 4	John M. Sumner	Hardware, tinware, etc	127 76
Feb. 6	W. B'k Note & Eng. Co.	Steel plate letter heads	70 00
Feb. 12	Jacob Jenny	Ink, ribbon and dates	2 00
Feb. 25	Jas. E. Fisher	Cabinet ware	27 00
Feb. 28	Tim Purcell	Hauling water	82 25
Mar 6	Newton & Donovan	Blacksmithing	6 00
M	Carl Schmidt	Keys, repairing locks, etc	36 90
M 12	W. J. Park & Co	Manilla paper, cord, etc	24 75
Mar. 24	Daniel Laven	Cleaning the well in park	15 00

"Q."—*Accounts Audited under Chap.* 48, *G. L.*, 1866, *etc.*—con.

Date	To whom.	For what.	Amount.
1874.			
Apr. 7	T. Purcell	Labor with team	$80 50
Apr. 8	John M. Sumner	Hardware, etc	40 54
Apr. 12	W. P. Towers	Painting and glazing	47 58
Apr. 14	Clark & Mills	Soap, matches, etc	33 33
Apr. 30	Agnes Kessler	Bottoming chairs	9 75
May 2	Newton & Donovan	Blacksmithing	9 25
May 8	Silas Chapman	Maps of Wisconsin	60 00
May 8	Tim Purcell	Labor with team	28 00
May 8	Madison G.L.& Coke Co.	Labor, pipe, etc	287 67
May 9	J. H. D. Baker	Willow baskets	3 50
May 13	H. J. Jewett	Iron pump for well, etc	116 00
May 14	Dunning & Sumner	Oils, paints, glass, etc	68 02
May 17	Fish & Stevens	Mason work in well	28 75
May 17	W. P. Towers	Painting	100 00
May 23	Mil. &. St. P. R'y Co.	Freight	3 35
May 24	Dan Delaney	Brooms	6 75
June 3	Hartford S. B. Ins. Co.	Insuring Boilers in Capitol	78 75
June 4	Vroman, Frank & Co	Hardware, etc	90 94
June 6	W. J. Park & Co	Manilla paper, etc	12 80
June 12	John M. Sumner	Hardware, etc	51 13
June 27	Mrs. H. Welsh	Soft soap	8 00
June 27	J. E. Fisher	Cabinet work	48 00
July 1	Supt. Pub. Property	Webster' Dictionary	8 00
July 2	Newton & Donovan	Blacksmithing	13 95
July 2	Moseley & Brother	Manilla paper	11 15
July 8	Mil. & St. P. R'y Co.	Freight on twine	32 25
July 8	Bunker & Vroman	Lumber	112 02
July 9	Klauber & Adler	Merchandise	16 03
July 10	B. & P. Lawrence	Wrapping paper and twine	455 96
July 14	Ch. & N. W. R'y Co	Freight on twine	13 25
July 19	C. C. Church	Basswood lumber	15 80
July 23	W. J. & F. Ellsworth	Brooms	7 50
July 23	W. B'k N. & Eng. Co	Eng. letter headings	70 00
July 23	Thos. Regan	Plumbing, gas fitting, etc	106 92
July 23	Andrew Bishop	Laying street crossing	12 25
Aug. 14	W. P. Towers	Painting and glazing	608 04
Aug. 25	E. Sharp & Son	Plastering in assem'y chamber	235 00
Aug. 29	Samuel Gardiner	Zinc and carbon plates	32 63
Aug. 27	...do .....do	Sulphuric acid	21 45
Aug. 28	Christian R. Stein	Lumber	32 58
Aug. 30	John Comford	Labor with team	21 00
Aug. 30	Tim Purcell	Labor grading in park	31 50
Sept. 3	Madison G.L.& Coke Co.	Changing lamps in park	30 12
Sept. 3	John M. Sumner	Hardware and labor	31 20
Sept. 4	Newton & Donovan	Blacksmithing	8 10
Sept. 5	Thos. Regan	Labor and gas fixtures	271 74
Sept. 5	Thos. Regan	Pipe and steam fitting	568 77
Sept. 6	J. L. Fulton	Rep'g and relaying old walks	386 40
Sept. 6	Wm. T. Fish & Co.	Mason work	55 43
Sept. 8	Conklin & Gray	Coal	5,944 75
Sept. 22	Conklin & Gray	Br. Hill coal	21 00
Sept. 26	J. E. Fisher	Cabinet work and upholstery	240 00
			$22,038 76

A. A. MEREDITH,
Superintendent Public Property.

APPENDIX "R."

LIST OF RAILROAD COMPANIES *organized under the laws of this state, during the year ending September* 30, 1873.

Prairie du Chien and McGregor Railway Company.
The Chicago and Tomah Railroad Company.
The Chippewa and Red Cedar River Railroad Company.
Michigan and Wisconsin Pacific Railway.
Wisconsin and Lake Superior Railway Company.
La Crosse Transit Railroad Company.
Wisconsin Midland Railway Company.
Wisconsin Railway Company.
The Chippewa Falls and Western Railway Company.
Portage and Superior Railroad Company.

DOCUMENT 2.

FOURTH

ANNUAL REPORT

OF THE

SECRETARY OF STATE

AS EX-OFFICIO

COMMISSIONER OF INSURANCE

OF THE

STATE OF WISCONSIN.

May 1, 1873.

PART I.—FIRE AND MARINE INSURANCE.

MADISON, WIS.:
ATWOOD & CULVER, PRINTERS AND STEREOTYPERS.
1873.

INDEX.

PART I—FIRE AND MARINE COMPANIES.

STATISTICAL TABLES.

STATEMENTS OF COMPANIES.

WISCONSIN STOCK COMPANIES.

WISCONSIN MUTUAL COMPANIES.

COMPANIES OF OTHER STATES.

COMPANIES OF FOREIGN COUNTRIES.

FOURTH ANNUAL REPORT

OF THE

SECRETARY OF STATE,

As Ex-Officio

COMMISSIONER OF INSURANCE.

PART I.

Fire and Marine Insurance.

STATE OF WISCONSIN,

OFFICE OF SECRETARY OF STATE,

DEPARTMENT OF INSURANCE,

MADISON, May 1, 1873.

To the Honorable the Legislature of the State of Wisconsin:

In compliance with the requirements of law, the Secretary of State, as *ex-officio* Commissioner of Insurance, has the honor to submit this, the Fourth Annual Report of the Insurance Department, comprising such suggestions and tables as are deemed of general interest and utility, together with abstracts of annual statements of the several fire companies that transacted business in this state, and reported to this department for the year ending December 31, 1872.

COMPANIES WITHDRAWN.

The following companies, licensed for 1872, having failed to file annual statements, and otherwise to comply with the requirements of law, are not authorized to transact business for the current year:

Companies Licensed *in* 1872, *but not authorised to transact business in* 1873:

German Mutual, Milwaukee.
Andes, Cincinnati, O.
Commercial Fire, New York.
Eastern, Bangor, Maine.
Firemen's, New York.

International, New York.
National, Bangor, Maine.
National, Boston, Mass.
People's Fire, Worcester, Mass.
Triumph, Cincinnati, Ohio.

Union, San Francisco, Cal.

Some of the above companies are still solvent, and transacting business elsewhere. Others, having suffered heavy losses both in the Chicago fire of 1871, and in that of Boston of 1872, were compelled to wind up their affairs.

COMPANIES ADMITTED.

The following table gives the name, location, date of admission and the amount of the capital stock of companies of other states and foreign countries, admitted to transact business in this state since the first day of May, 1872, the date of the last annual report of this department:

Companies Admitted *since date of last Report.*

Name of Company.	Location.	Date of Admission.	Capital.
Allemannia Fire	Pittsburg, Pa	Oct. 28, 1872	$150,000
Atlantic	Brooklyn, N. Y	Oct. 22, 1872	200,000
Black River	Watertown, N. Y	June 5, 1872	250,000
[1]Capital City	Albany, N. Y	Aug. 27, 1872	150,000
Eastern	Bangor, Me	June 25, 1872	225,000
Fairfield County Fire	South Norwalk, Conn	Oct. 1, 1872	200,000
German	Freeport, Ill	Mar. 1, 1873	200,000
German	Erie, Pa	June 26, 1872	200,000
Manhattan Fire	New York	May 13, 1873	250,000
Meriden Fire	Meriden, Conn	Oct. 23, 1872	200,000
National Fire and Marine	Philadelphia, Pa	May 1, 1873	200,000
New Orleans Mutual	New Orleans, La	Apr. 3, 1873	607,777
Penn Fire	Philadelphia, Pa	Nov. 11, 1872	156,650
[1]Providence Washington	Providence, R. I	Apr. 29, 1873	200,000
Saint Joseph Fire and Marine	St. Joseph, Mo	Apr. 12, 1873	200,000
State	Hannibal, Mo	June 3, 1872	210,007
Traders	Chicago, Ill	Aug. 15, 1872	500,000
Watertown Fire	Watertown, N. Y	July 31, 1872	200,000
Hamburg-Bremen Fire	Hamburg, Germany	June 14, 1872	162,000
Lancashire	Manchester, G. B	Oct. 28, 1872	730,700
London Assurance Corporation	London, G. B	Nov. 13, 1872	[2]2,465,513
Western Assurance	Toronto, Canada	Nov. 21, 1872	200,451

[1] Re-admitted. [2] Converted into Federal currency, at $5.50 to the pound sterling.

COMPANIES NOW LICENSED.

Up to the date of this report, eighty-eight fire and marine insurance companies have been authorized to transact business in Wisconsin for the current year, making eleven more than the number licensed at the same date the year previous. Of this number ten are organized under the laws of this state, three being joint stock, and seven mutual. Sixty-eight were admitted from other states, and ten from foreign countries.

SUMMARY OF BUSINESS.

The amount of capital stock represented by these companies December 31, 1872, was $32,780,973; gross assets, $100,746,703; amount at risk, $4,748,386,895; gross liabilities, including reinsurance reserve, $56,476,025; net assets, $69,616,130; the ratio of net assets to amount at risk, 1.47 per cent. The amount of surplus held by the companies for the indemnity of policy holders was $44,270,678. This is over and above every liablity, (except capital stock,) including reinsurance reserve; the net surplus, including the capital stock liability, was $11,489,705. The amount of risks written during the year was $6,198,362,050; premiums received, $55,290,609; expenses, $16,594,851; losses paid, $44,527,208. The average ratio of expenses to premiums received, is 30.01 per cent; of losses to premiums received, 80.53; showing an aggregate loss on the business of the year of $5,831,450, which is 10.54 per cent. of the premiums received.

Six of the ten foreign companies report only their American business; their business outside the United States, and their general financial condition on December 31, 1872, not having been reported in time to be used here.

A TABLE *giving the aggregate capital, amount at risk, assets, liabilities and surplus of all companies transacting business in Wisconsin, for the year ending December 31, 1872.*

	Capital Paid.	Amt. at risk Dec. 31, 1872.	Net Assets.	Per ctg. of as'ts. to amt. of risk.	Gross Assets.	[1] Gross Liabilities.	Surplus as to policy holders.	Net Surplus.	[1] Per centage
Wisconsin Joint Stock Companies	$483,506	$23,683,581	$810,396	3.43	$871,895	$295,544	$576,351	$93,775	19.43
Wisconsin Mutual Companies	[2] 1,168,106	89,645,143	[2] 1,888,708	2.05	[2] 1,855,285	568,355	1,286,880	123,774	10.64
Companies of other States	26,719,374	3,087,604,810	47,688,515	[3] 1.53	59,848,049	30,298,535	29,549,514	2,830,140	10.59
Companies of Foreign Countries	4,415,987	1,607,518,911	19,288,212	[4] .80	38,171,594	25,318,591	12,853,003	8,442,016	[5] 130.17
Totals	$32,780,973	$4,748,886,895	$69,616,130	1.47	$100,746,708	$56,476,035	$44,270,673	$11,489,705	35.05

[1] Of net surplus to capital.
[2] Including premium notes.
[3] Average excluding the New Orleans Mutual.
[4] Average excluding the London Assurance Corporation.
[5] Of foreign companies reporting capital.

A TABLE *showing the aggregate mean amount at risk, premiums received, cash income, expenses, losses paid; and expense and loss ratios of all companies transacting business in Wisconsin for the year ending December 31, 1872.*

	Mean Amount at Risk.	Premiums Received.	Cash Income.	Expenses.	Losses Paid.	PERCENTAGE OF			
						Expenses to		*Losses to*	
						Prems. Rec'd.	Cash Income.	M'n amt at risk.	Prems. Rec'd.
Wisconsin Joint Stock Companies	$16,768,500	$527,526	$569,573	$161,348	$271,083	30.59	28.33	1.62	51.38
Wisconsin Mutual Companies	88,394,995	355,776	409,300	161,439	263,649	45.38	39.44	.30	74.10
Companies of other States	2,781,406,719	39,446,258	42,677,919	11,660,758	31,545,279	29.56	27.32	[1] 1.13	79.97
Companies of Foreign Countries	1,472,706,918	14,961,055	17,020,446	4,611,306	12,447,247	30.82	27.09	[2] .77	83.20
Totals	$4,359,274,132	$55,290,609	$60,677,238	$16,594,851	$44,527,208	30.01	27.35	1.02	80.53

[1] Omitting the New Orleans Mutual.
[2] Omitting the London Assurance Corporation.

It will be observed that the ratio of expenses to premiums received is a trifle larger for last year than for the year previous, while the ratio of losses to such premiums is less, being 80.53 per cent. in 1872, against 97.19 in 1871. The high loss ratio is largely due to Chicago losses which were not paid until the beginning of 1872, but more particularly to later losses in Boston. While these great calamities, quickly following one the other, may have important lessons to fire underwriters, it can hardly be claimed by any one that the experience as to cost of insurance for the past two years should be taken as a proper criterion for the adjustment of future premiums. Yet it is evident it should secure greater care in the selection and distribution of risks, and above all, teach the importance of accumulating a large reserve fund.

BUSINESS IN WISCONSIN.

The amount of risks written in this state during the year ending December 31, 1872, by the eighty-eight companies reporting to this department is $142,351,376; premiums received, $1,910,677; losses paid, $922,637. The ratio of losses to risks written is .65 per cent. against .58 in 1871, and .80 in 1870; the ratio of losses to premiums received being 48.29 per cent., against 49.65, in 1871, and 72.44, in 1870.

The excess of premiums received over losses paid in Wisconsin is $988,040. If thirty per cent. of the aggregate premiums received, which is the expense ratio in the country at large, be deducted from this amount, the sum of $414,837, or 21.71 per cent. of all the premiums received is left as net profits on the aggregate business in Wisconsin for 1872, against $304,753, or 21.22 per cent. for the previous year, showing a net gain of $110,084, or .49 per cent.

The foregoing results will appear more in detail by reference to the following comparative table, showing the business in Wisconsin for the past three years.

	No. of comp's	Risks written.	Premiums received.	Losses paid.	Percentage of Losses.	
					To risks written.	To prem's received.
1872.						
Wisconsin Joint Stock Companies.	3	$17,580,664	$210,438	$63,516	.36	30.18
Wisconsin Mutual Companies...	7	25,264,861	358,394	252,988	1.04	71.78
Companies of other States........	68	84,478,871	1,129,565	496,392	.59	43.95
Companies of Foreign Countries .	16	15,127,040	204,289	99,746	.66	48.88
Totals........................	88	$142,351,376	$1,910,677	$888,687	.65	46.29
1871.						
Wisconsin Joint Stock Companies.	3	$14,942,041	$128,753	$37,286	.25	26.84
Wisconsin Mutual Companies....	8	21,023,229	273,060	281,023	1.34	103.28
Companies of other States........	60	75,054,421	896,219	385,387	.51	43.00
Companies of Foreign Countries..	6	11,064,674	129,126	9,434	.10	7.31
Totals	77	$122,084,404	$1,436,197	$713,060	.58	49.65
1870.						
Wisconsin Joint Stock Companies.	3	$13,450,970	$97,961	$36,193	.27	36.95
Wisconsin Mutual Companies...	8	28,809,559	339,474	234,096	.81	68.96
Companies of other States........	74	100,257,448	1,136,170	868,654	.87	76.45
Companies of Foreign Countries..	4	4,654,978	48,787	36,270	.78	74.44
Totals	89	$147,172,955	$1,622,392	$1,175,213	.80	72.44

ANNUAL STATEMENTS.

It is made the duty of the Secretary of State, as Commissioner of Insurance, to prepare and furnish to each of the companies transacting business in this state, printed forms of annual statements; and to make such changes therein from time to time as shall to him seem best adapted to secure a correct and uniform exhibit of the condition of such companies.

To this end, the uniform blank, as amended by the last National Insurance Convention, was adopted. Considerable difficulty was experienced in securing on all points a strict compliance with its requirements, many of the companies preferring to follow their own views with reference to the points involved, rather than adhere to the blank.

While the blank under heading No. 17, "assets," calls for "gross premiums in due course of collection," and under heading No. 20, "liabilities," for a corresponding entry for commissions, many of the companies have reported the former as "gross," without a corresponding liability charge under the latter. Others reported the former as "net."

It is thought that while these premiums which have not been transmitted to the home office, and consequently the agent not having performed all his duties so as to entitle him to his commission, while the transaction between the local agent and the company remains thus incomplete, the best way is to carry the "gross premiums," reported to the company by the agent to "assets," and the commission thereon due him on the completion of his work to "liabilities." This appears to have been the view of the subject which was taken by the National Convention. If this item is reported "gross," it is very plain that the agent's commission should be entered under heading No. 20, "liabilities." But whether these uncollected premiums should be reported as "gross" or "net" is not as important as it is that the statements be made uniform. If some companies report this item as "gross" and others as "net", it becomes impossible to exhibit correctly their relative condition. One important object to be gained by uniform statements is, that every feature of the condition and management of the companies may be subjected to the same test, thereby enabling the public to decide upon their relative security and merit.

By reference to the detailed statements, it will also be observed that the companies have not made a uniform exhibit of their income account, some construing items Nos. 1 to 5, inclusive, to mean all premiums upon the risks written during the year, and which have been reported up to December 31, whether such premiums had been received in cash at the home office or not, assuming that whenever a policy is delivered, the premiums have been paid to the local agent, and that such supposed payment is a "receipt in cash" of such premiums by the company within the meaning of the blank. Others understand these items as embracing only such premiums as had been received *in cash* at the home office on or before December 31, and that item No. 6 "Income," which is to be carried inside, should be understood to include all premiums which had not been so received. The latter construction was adopted by this Department. Every effort was made to secure uniformity in the exhibit of these items. This involved a tedious and protracted correspondence, in which an effort was made to show the reasonableness of the construction given to the blank, and the importance of uniformity.

The success was but partial. The result is that in the tables of this report, there can be no fair relative showing of the cash income of the companies, some having included those premiums, while others excluded them, reporting nothing as cash except what had been actually received into the treasury of the company at the home office in money, on or before December 31. Much, it is true, has been done within the past two or three years to secure uniform statements, still it is equally true that there is much yet to be accomplished. This can only be brought about by the co-operation of the state officials having charge of the subject, and of the companies themselves. True statements rendered upon uniform blanks, bringing thereby the companies in their methods and management under proper and uniform tests, will do much, not only to simplify the duties of supervising officers, but also to secure soundness of organization and proper management.

WISCONSIN COMPANIES.

The number of companies organized under the laws of this state which have reported and have been licensed by this department for the current year is ten, three of which are joint stock and seven mutual. The German Mutual, of Milwaukee, ceased doing business during the past year. Its outstanding risks were all reinsured in good and responsible companies.

The cash capital of the stock companies was increased during the year as follows:

Brewers' Fire Insurance Company of America, Milwaukee	$17,000
Hekla Fire Insurance Company, Madison	21,881
Northwestern National Insurance Company, Milwaukee	48,000

EXAMINATION OF COMPANIES.

At the request of the officers, a personal examination was made of the following companies; their affairs and condition being found correctly shown by their statements herein published:

Brewers' Fire Insurance Company of America, Milwaukee.
Milwaukee Mechanics' Mutual, Milwaukee.
Northwestern National, Milwaukee.

BUSINESS OF WISCONSIN COMPANIES.

The following is a condensed summary of the business of Wisconsin companies as exhibited by their statements for the year ending December 31, 1872: Risks written, $70,423,455; risks in force December 31, $113,268,674; net assets, $2,644,103; reinsurance reserve, $780,942; ratio of net assets to mean amount at risk, 2.33 per cent. The mean amount at risk was $105,163,495; cash premiums received, $883,302; expenses, $322,787; losses paid, $534,680. The ratio of expenses to premiums received was 36.54 per cent., and of losses to premiums received, 60.53 per cent., the ratio of the aggregate expenditures to the premiums received being 97.07 per cent., leaving a margin for profits of about $25,835, or three per cent. of the premiums. In addition to this, the stock companies received, principally from interest on their investments, the sum of $42,047. The mutual companies realized, also, mainly from the same source, the sum of $53,524. This is the first time in five years that the premium receipts of the Wisconsin companies have exceeded their expenses and losses, the ratio of expenditures to premiums for the four previous years having been as follows: In 1871, 187.39 per cent.; in 1870, 106.09 per cent.; in 1869, 104.93 per cent.; and in 1868, 144.86 per cent.

It will be seen by the following table that the expense ratio has gradually decreased during each of the five years mentioned. The same is also true of the loss ratio, except for the year 1869.

A COMPARATIVE TABLE *showing the risks written, risks in force Dec. 31, net assets, reinsurance reserve, and the ratio of net assets to mean amount at risk of Wisconsin companies.*

No. of Cos.	Year.	Risks written during the year.	Risks in force Dec. 31st.	Net Assets.	Reinsurance Reserve.	Percentage of net assets to amount at risk.
10	1872	$70,423,455	$113,268,674	$2,644,103	$780,942	2.33
11	1871	47,887,187	97,926,441	2,472,392	618,641	2.59
10	1870	40,685,510	118,694,814	2,911,012	560,899	2.45
8	1869	37,580,219	111,278,195	2,744,425	365,589	2.47
8	1868	34,222,655	116,040,746	2,818,140	76,591	2.43
9	1867	23,796,348	95,995,511	2,499,176	70,802	2.60
		$254,222,874	$653,204,811	$16,084,948	$2,262,414	2.46

A COMPARATIVE *table giving the mean amount at risk, cash premiums received, expenses, losses paid, and the ratio of expenses to premiums, and of losses to premiums and to mean amount at risk of Wisconsin Companies on December 31, for the last five years:*

No of Cos.	Year.	Mean Amount at risk.	Cash Premiums.	Expenses.	Losses Paid.	PER CENTAGE.		
						Expenses to Premiums.	*Losses.* To Premiums.	*Losses.* To mean am't at risk.
10	1872	$105,168,495	$833,808	$302,797	$504,680	36.54	60.53	.51
11	1871	113,659,436	518,615	217,948	744,588	42.42	144.98	.66
10	1870	124,226,469	427,998	196,941	271,435	44.12	61.97	.24
8	1869	108,704,758	367,686	168,515	217,219	45.84	59.09	.19
8	1868	106,912,129	367,367	198,121	180,185	53.94	90.92	.17
		$548,582,311	$2,569,908	$1,100,610	$1,948,007	42.88	75.80	.36

The cash income of all the state companies, except two, exceeds their expenditures. In other words, they have made money. The profits made by the stock companies aggregate $137,192, or 24.09 per cent. of their cash income.

Five of the mutual companies aggregate a profit of $49,263, or 22.82 per cent. The average ratio of expenditures to cash income of the other two mutual companies is 133.63 per cent., which is a loss of $65,051, or 33.63 per cent. This is partly accounted for by the fact that both companies carried over from the year before large amounts of unmatured losses caused by the forest fires of October, 1871.

PREMIUMS, ASSETS AND INVESTMENTS.

The following comparative table gives a classification of the gross assets of Wisconsin companies for the last four years:

	1872.	1871.	1870.	1869.
STOCK COMPANIES.				
Loans on bonds and mortgages........	$58,961	$31,418	$2,000	....
Stocks and bonds	570,397	411,064	252,126	$127,024
Other loans........	3,600	1,451	....	3,100
Cash........	108,464	95,597	75,150	62,[illegible]
Interest due and accrued	5,658	1,900	70	....
Unpaid premiums	104,591	35,300	18,929	4,449
Miscellaneous	26,059	18,190	536	3,563
	$872,760	$874,800	$374,884	$310,395
Doubtful assets........	965	1,200	....	....
Totals	$871,825	$873,600	$374,884	$310,395
MUTUAL COMPANIES.				
Real estate	$35,966	$38,889	$19,019	$9,075
Loans on bonds and mortgages........	33,694	36,327	27,209	41,765
Stocks and bonds	306,064	238,077	186,837	218,163
Other loans........	13,909	15,[illegible]	....	14,[illegible]
Cash........	68,063	146,716	79,137	66,865
Interest due and accrued	8,694	9,311	12,436	....
Unpaid premiums........	175,584	208,369	252,314	269,597
Premium notes........	1,180,894	1,340,[illegible]	1,883,073	1,924,658
Miscellaneous........	7,436	69,053	70,674	6,815
	$1,859,185	$2,107,815	$2,565,788	$2,553,117
Doubtful assets........	3,950	55,963	....	....
Totals	$1,855,235	$2,051,853	$2,565,788	$2,553,117

It appears from this table that the assets of the stock companies have increased from $310,395, in 1869, to $871,825 in 1872.

It is believed that they are securely invested, and can readily be made available.

The exhibit of the assets of the mutual companies is not so favorable. Their aggregate assets have decreased within the period named from $2,553,117 to $1,855,235. This, however, is found upon examination to be more apparent than real. The amount of decrease as shown above is $697,882. But it is found that this shrinkage is limited altogether to the item of premium notes. In 1869, the mutual companies, being eight in number, had $1,924,658, of this kind of assets; while on December 31, 1872, the seven companies report but $1,180,894, showing a decrease of $743,764. The amount of premium notes retired by the German Mutual, of Milwaukee, which ceased doing business, was but about $35,000.

Throwing out all of the premium notes, it will then appear that the remaining assets of these companies in 1872 are larger by

$45,882, than in 1869. It also appears that they have now in the aggregate, excluding premium notes, more good assets in proportion to the amount at risk than they had at any time during the period covered by the foregoing table.

While the condition of the mutual companies, in view of the unprecedented losses of the past few years, is, on the whole, favorable, yet it is a fact that the gain in the accumulated assets is hardly what could be desired. The expenses and losses of some of these companies for many years, excluding assessments, have exceeded their cash income. This must be the result of one or more of the following causes: extravagant expenses, taking hazardous risks, the credit system, or too low rates of premiums.

It is perfectly plain that if insurance, or anything else, is sold at less than cost, the business must soon stop.

If the cost cannot be reduced, then it is clear that the price must be raised—that the premium rates must be increased. To replenish their assets by assessments upon their policy-holders every few years, it will be conceded by the most intelligent underwriters, would be as impracticable and ruinous to the companies themselves, as it would be unequal and therefore unjust to the insured. Experience clearly teaches that this cannot be done except under the most extraordinary and unforeseen circumstances.

If permanent success would be attained, the same general principles governing other business enterprises must be applied to mutual fire insurance. Their business affairs must be so managed that their income will exceed their expenditures.

Respectfully submitted,

LL. BREESE,

Secretary of State, and ex-officio

Commissioner of Insurance.

STATISTICAL TABLES.

TABLE No. I.—Assets.

Name of Company.	Real Estate.	Loans on Bonds and Mortgages.	Stocks, Bonds and Securities.	Loans on Collaterals.	All other Loans.	Cash in Office and Bank.	Interest Due and Accrued.	Premiums Unpaid.	Miscellaneous.	Deductions for Doubtful Assets.	Total Assets.
Wisconsin Joint Stock.											
Brewers' Fire Ins. Co. of America	....	$8,000	$321,294	....	....	$53,156	$538	$86,509	$1,980	$980	$490,547
Hekla	....	45,961	1,058	....	$3,600	7,752	1,120	8,109	408	25	67,998
Northwestern National	....	....	248,050	....	....	47,556	4,000	59,978	23,706	....	383,285
Totals	....	$53,961	$570,397	....	$3,600	$108,464	$5,658	$104,591	$26,089	$955	$871,835
Wisconsin Mutual.											
Concordia Mutual Fire	....	$9,700	$5,600	....	....	$12,095	$347	$3,599	[6] $17,947	....	[6] $49,118
Dodge County Mutual	$5,100	1,178	....	....	$250	12,524	97	72,148	[7] 69,897	$3,950	[7] 157,944
Germantown Farmers' Mutual	6,500	28,108	....	....	10,282	6,456	3,489	13,809	[8] 144,846	....	[8] 213,490
Herman Farmers' Mutual	....	6,800	....	....	2,335	1,990	644	3,508	[9] 20,897	....	[9] 36,174
Madison Mutual	19,820	10,202	125,000	....	....	11,486	3,693	66,540	[10] 595,989	....	[10] 832,660
Milwaukee Mechanics' Mutual	4,546	6,616	175,464	....	....	23,501	479	15,880	[11] 338,806	....	[11] 565,242
Vernon County Scandinavian Mut. F.	....	....	....	....	1,042	50	45	150	....	....	1,287
Totals	$35,966	$62,604	$306,064	....	$13,909	$68,082	$8,694	$175,584	$1,188,382	$3,950	$1,855,285
Companies of other States.											
Ætna, Conn	$405,000	$98,330	$3,668,251	$57,140	....	$228,632	$30,980	$928,098	....	....	$5,396,381
Alemannia Fire, O	....	235,195	....	....	$6,328	54,060	36,370	70,633	$35	....	402,596
Allemannia Fire, Pa	....	176,275	135	....	16,191	37,722	3,467	20,150	30	....	253,970
Amazon, O	....	619,572	248,411	95,117	....	18,582	29,683	98,962	37,371	$57,418	1,070,280
American, Ill	7,000	175,647	126,757	65,200	....	14,438	3,907	80,508	64,876	....	538,333
American Central, Mo	....	....	341,800	....	....	183,352	....	62,292	7,500	....	544,944
[1] Arctic Fire, N. Y	12,500	38,000	153,525	....	....	35,151	1,097	12,430	27,765	....	275,468
Atlantic, N. Y	....	85,300	170,318	55,909	....	20,165	455	21,131	....	....	303,264
Black River, N. Y	15,000	177,878	56,625	....	....	98,095	10,868	14,434	4,722	....	377,622
Brewers' and Maltsters', N. Y	....	22,000	139,500	5,300	....	19,139	887	81,798	15,754	....	284,378
Capital City, N. Y	....	....	169,940	2,000	....	2,316	5,050	3,805	600	....	183,711
Commerce, N. Y	45,000	....	308,750	....	....	31,287	260	19,481	500	....	400,158
Connecticut Fire, Conn	....	....	554,580	94,985	....	84,308	....	64,862	....	....	798,665
Continental, N. Y	628,000	458,300	579,468	41,270	....	389,766	17,221	168,799	3,488	....	2,284,308

Detroit Fire and Marine, Mich.		144,860	62,150			12,851	3,810	33,808	9,895		267,349
[2] Fairfield County Fire, Conn.	26,738	164,470	122,400	26,047	9,500	19,225	3,859	21,286	3,018		297,218
[3] Farmers, Ill		107,000	6,548			1,673	6,812	4,200	3,000		132,[illegible]
[4] Fireman's Fund, Cal.	165,000	146,761	131,113	15,500		41,490	4,175	88,514	82,668		619,281
Franklin Fire, Pa	65,000	2,569,684	160,008	128,750		151,108	44,464	291,798	2,869		3,363,671
German, Pa		157,940	22,000	14,500	[12] 3,280	108,529	13,458	36,670	2,595		358,896
German, Ill	10,000	197,540	4,000			29,291	1,500	18,795	2,118	4,850	268,394
German American, N. Y			973,400	243,850		40,842		110,998	10,000		1,379,090
Germania Fire, N. Y	49,396	494,900	475,100	12,250		167,184	9,061	91,075	14,492		1,318,378
Girard Fire and Marine, Pa	183,000	194,850	215,842	9,150	1,591	50,075	2,548	54,330	12,558	58	653,321
Globe, Ill		225,000	50,000		8,445	17,478	12,216	94,995	3,500		341,634
Hanover Fire, N. Y	2,726	147,700	514,114	34,500		59,142	9,579	102,229	16,450		886,540
Hartford Fire, Conn	448,176	457,250	974,781			92,388	42,139	156,856	32,857		2,204,397
Hartford Steam B'r Insp. & Ins. Conn		32,800	118,070			4,246	3,966	11,496	2,400		173,998
[5] Hoffman Fire, N. Y		166,750	68,800			1,356	5,243	48,706	2,500		288,355
Home, O	1,728	372,633	62,205	32,728	16,245	25,276	24,746	192,140	73,088		800,734
Home, N. Y		1,910,765	1,725,965	94,124		204,284	52,735	295,111	163,925		4,446,859
Howard, N. Y	125,000	68,900	373,808	1,000		16,441	4,810	16,888	7,117		608,264
Insurance Company of N. A., Pa	35,000	878,250	1,288,438	58,696		177,115	10,370	809,372	24,496		3,276,739
Lorillard, N. Y	5,083	258,100		5,000		91,188	9,084	29,083			397,433
Manhattan Fire, N. Y		105,068	242,660	20,886		67,730	5,000	52,480			493,769
Mechanics and Traders Fire, N. Y		334,409	68,275	12,741		47,290	2,188	74,841			589,735
Mercantile, O		100,800	117,862	16,000		21,482	4,900	27,696	6,614		295,304
Mercantile Mutual, N. Y			468,215	27,000	150,000	58,718	6,084	594,886	133,662	24,950	1,408,565
Merchants, R. I			352,150			71,969	5,471	10,444	[13] 45,695		485,729
Meriden Fire, Conn		10,400	61,009	124,730		42,720	6,816	5,649	1,808		253,137
Narragansett F. & M., R. I		120,785	222,994			58,496	2,649	110,629	16,012	5,000	563,565
National Fire, Conn		135,000	340,721	52,890		169,342	8,213	35,000			742,166
National F. & M., Pa	75,667	87,150	95,426	4,788	7,668	59,267	2,998	82,449	4,008		419,521
New Orleans Mutual, La	168,205	189,104	115,758	221,297	68,901	117,665		510,116			1,391,041
Niagara Fire, N. Y	22,726	154,000	745,600	195,050		17,007	11,657	116,948	1,550		1,264,538
North Missouri, Mo	37,000	175,662	152,485	20,259	6,531	78,425	7,061	265,458	10,797		753,678
Orient, Conn		157,956	292,597	180,866		80,729	10,554	75,000	8,818		705,520
Orient Mutual, N. Y			749,684	30,000		359,148	13,510	279,800	[14] 608,539		[14] 2,065,661
Pacific Mutual, N. Y			467,828	195,450		92,642	2,197	214,987	[15] 56,988	9,000	[15] 1,081,092
Penn Fire, Pa	13,300	95,946	15,888	18,687		32,674	3,525	54,691	3,342		288,058

[1] Statement of assets March 1, 1878.
[2] Statement of assets February 28, 1878.
[3] Statement of assets March 8, 1878.
[4] For the year ending Jan'y 28, 1878.
[5] An assessm't of $100,000 was paid in cash January 20, 1878.
[6] Of which $17,247 is premium notes.
[7] Of which $68,393 is premium notes and assessment thereon.
[8] Of which $144,046 is premium notes.
[9] Of which $20,507 is premium notes.
[10] Of which $592,994 is premium notes and assessment thereon.
[11] Of which $337,617 is premium notes.
[12] Judgment notes.
[13] Uncollected assessment.
[14] Including $549,795 notes taken in advance for premiums.
[15] Of which $19,000 is subscription notes.

TABLE No. 1—Assets—continued.

Name of Company.	Real Estate.	Loans on Bonds and Mortgages.	Stocks, Bonds and Securities.	Loans on Collaterals.	All other Loans.	Cash in Office and Bank.	Interest due and accrued.	Premiums unpaid.	Miscellaneous.	Deductions for doubtful assets.	Total Assets.
Companies of other States—con.											
[1] Pennsylvania Fire, Pa.	$60,000	$480,967	$401,700	$7,950		$113,209	$12,097	$114,182			$1,188,895
Phenix, N. Y.	295,000	370,895	679,210	87,800		145,494	13,995	365,488	$117,781	$4,345	2,001,313
Phœnix, Conn.	79,013	19,386	1,148,695	35,000		107,192	2,942	196,189			1,582,647
Providence Washington, R. I.			50,500			69,314	8,294	21,591	106,295		250,854
Republic Fire, N. Y.	73,976	48,700	338,386	56,000		15,942	8,846	57,096	[4] 186,467		[4]775,348
Saint Joseph Fire and Marine, Mo.		116,400	21,650	94,800	45,902	67,016		82,737	1,200		299,705
Saint Nicholas, N. Y.	25,000	51,400	110,000	21,650		17,409	2,312	21,285	12,564		261,690
Saint Paul Fire and Marine, Minn.	98,814	111,697		295,928		107,586	14,270	62,489	5,395		626,128
Springfield Fire and Marine, Mass.	100,000	219,667	345,892	148,498		171,076	7,177	80,472	3,080		1,070,742
Standard Fire, N. Y.		58,400	276,750	92,400		8,913	646	16,202	5,299		458,612
Star Fire, N. Y.		212,895	11,500	54,100		53,759	2,771	21,968	3,500		360,418
State, Mo.	14,444	168,979	23,333	39,187		85,941	14,180	41,801	13,810		346,675
Sun, O.		90,295	161,050	35,300		27,787	8,608	20,604	4,615		343,189
Traders, Ill.		30,111	500,500			25,451	699	15,942	15,689		588,842
Tradesmen's Fire, N. Y.		148,948	97,010	16,000		61,994	4,657	98,666	1,000		357,500
Union, Me.		175,600	85,965	94,400		66,566	1,260	248,589	7,640	602	609,368
Watertown Fire, N. Y.		240,342	45,950	61,875		49,351	7,895	33,478	6,000		444,891
Williamsburg City Fire, N. Y.	40,000	306,550	107,444	35,870		35,696	5,396	56,284	8,213		595,883
Totals	$3,268,396	$15,176,283	$22,668,799	$3,047,098	$340,507	$4,962,967	$587,347	$7,900,840	$2,012,210	$106,218	$59,848,049
Companies of Foreign Countries.											
Commercial Union (U. S. B.), G. B.			$342,000			$150,185		$13,838	$9,936		$515,909
Hamburg-Bremen Fire, Germany.		$258,598	253,091			180,618		21,718	73,106		781,196
Imperial Fire (U. S. Branch) G. B.			1,049,788	$100,000		15,105		188,664			1,348,507
Lancashire (U. S. Branch), G. B.			229,500			21,810		101,897			358,207
Liver. & Lon. & Globe (Am. B.) G. B.	$447,917	1,065,400	1,580,430	600		756,299	$85,304	348,804	35,918		4,195,773

[2] London Assurance Corporation. G. B.	....	9,398,498	4,810,136	198,383	56,097	259,469	14,388	397,147	398	....	15,095,501
North British & Mercantile (U. S. Branch) G. B.	....	....	1,298,740	....	....	284,977	12,500	101,750	9,880	....	1,701 447
Queen (U. S. Branch) G. B.	....	....	608,080	....	....	38,115	....	13,918	4,000	....	659,078
[3] Royal G. B	1,095,608	412,648	5,311,275	4,858,167	410,469	771,556	....	128,811	....	....	12,957,504
Western Assurance, Canada	24,375	71,558	940,137	....	....	84,690	5,147	97,280	12,056	$1,640	588,543
Totals	$1,567,895	$11,130,687	$15,658,097	$5,149,090	$446,556	$8,685,874	$37,614	$1,337,768	$145,659	$1,640	$38,171,584

[1] Supplementary statement made by this Co., Feb. 4, 1873, shows that the capital had been repaired to the amount of $84,133, leaving deficiency of $49,009.

[2] Converted into federal currency at $5.50 to the pound sterling.

[3] Statement for the year ending June 30, 1872; converted into federal currency at $5.50 to the pound sterling.

[4] Of which $180,000 is assessment on capital stock, which was paid in cash, January 17, 1873.

TABLE No. II.—Liabilities.

Name of Company.	Net claims for losses.	Reinsurance Fund. Fire and Inland.	Reinsurance Fund. Marine.	Dividends.	Borrowed Money.	All other claims.	Total Liabilities.	Capital Stock.	Net surplus over capital.	Deficiency in capital.
Wisconsin Joint Stock.										
Brewers' Fire Insurance Company of America	$36,237	$144,959	....	....	....	....	$181,196	$200,000	$39,351	....
Hekla	20	20,654	....	....	....	$3,428	94,097	47,006	....	$3,110
Northwestern National	21,750	68,501	....	....	....	....	90,251	235,500	57,534	....
Totals	$58,007	$234,114	....	....	....	$3,428	$365,544	$482,506	$96,885	$3,110
Wisconsin Mutual.										
Concordia Mutual Fire	....	$18,758	....	....	....	$592	$19,350	[6] $24,667	[8] $5,101	....
Dodge County Mutual	$2,735	71,813	....	....	....	1,476	76,024	[7] 58,067	[9] 28,158	....
Germantown Farmers' Mutual	....	49,300	....	....	....	....	49,300	[7] 144,046	[9] 20,144	....
Herman Farmers' Mutual	742	5,427	....	....	....	74	6,243	[7] 20,597	[9] 9,334	....
Madison Mutual	11,977	220,394	....	....	....	1,279	233,650	[7] 588,112	[9] 15,918	....
Milwaukee Mechanics' Mutual	2,620	180,601	....	....	....	....	183,221	[7] 387,617	[9] 44,404	....
Vernon County Scandinavian Mutual Fire	....	535	....	....	....	32	567	....	[10] 720	....
Totals	$18,074	$546,828	....	....	....	$3,453	$568,355	$1,163,106	$123,774	....
Companies of other States.										
Ætna, Conn	$988,871	$2,042,590	....	....	$401,672	$500	$3,433,633	$2,000,000	$12,748	....
Alemannia Fire, O	17,549	96,936	....	....	....	16,141	130,626	250,000	21,970	....
Allemannia Fire, Pa	1,730	58,222	....	....	....	....	59,952	150,000	44,018	....
Amazon, O	159,337	447,546	....	....	....	4,935	611,818	500,000	....	$41,538
American, Ill	58,560	187,127	....	....	....	44,131	289,818	200,000	48,490	....
American Central Mo	37,499	197,390	....	....	....	....	234,889	275,000	35,055	....
[1] Arctic Fire, N. Y	8,614	53,022	....	$127	....	1,964	63,727	200,000	11,741	....
Atlantic, N. Y	33,827	55,014	....	....	....	....	88,841	200,000	14,428	....
Black River, N. Y	70,467	63,058	....	....	....	....	133,525	250,000	....	5,908
Brewers and Maltsters, N. Y	47,000	74,074	....	....	....	757	121,831	200,000	....	37,458
Capital City, N. Y	4,650	11,071	....	....	....	1,121	16,842	150,000	16,869	....
Commerce, N. Y	54,585	123,899	....	....	....	3,917	182,401	200,000	17,757	....
Connecticut Fire, Conn	50,595	130,645	....	....	25,000	9,730	215,970	500,000	12,735	....
Continental, N. Y	380,198	801,175	....	[11] 35,151	....	14,570	1,231,094	1,000,000	56,158	....

Detroit Fire and Marine, Mich	12,948	92,089				807	96,772	150,000	[8]1,077	
[2]Fairfield County Fire, Conn	21,985	72,961					95,946	200,000	1,578	
[3]Farmers, Ill	6,985	27,671			10,000	2,742	47,378	100,000		
[4]Fireman's Fund, Cal	58,411	178,609	$12,906	226		60,349	224,801	200,000		12,146
Franklin Fire, Pa	865,421	878,131	[11]1,290,500	120	96,879	12,940	2,688,991	400,000	394,660	5,580
German, Pa	45,090	102,368				5,500	158,958	200,000	944	
German, Ill	4,484	24,843				1,502	30,889	200,000	27,565	
German American, N. Y	59,337	282,955				2,067	344,289	1,000,000	34,761	
Germania Fire, N. Y	273,443	449,407				10,276	739,125	500,000	74,258	
Girard Fire and Marine, Pa	9,900	197,874				11,286	219,060	300,000	134,261	
Globe, Ill	11,750	29,191			20,000	4,999	65,940	300,000		24,306
Hanover Fire, N. Y	166,377	455,990					692,367	250,000	14,178	
Hartford Fire, Conn	313,108	920,175			115,000		1,348,278	1,000,000		143,881
Hartford Steam Boiler Insp. and Ins., Conn	649	25,139					25,788	120,000	26,218	
[5]Hoffman Fire, N. Y	98,284	96,115				3,214	192,618	200,000		[9]104,258
Home, Ohio	147,975	330,766				24,480	508,221	250,000	47,513	
Home, N. Y	587,989	1,686,244		2,975			2,277,158	2,500,000		330,299
Howard, N. Y	5,633	100,229				57	105,919	500,000	3,045	
Insurance Co. of North America, Pa	784,968	906,048	489,615	2,500		[11]812,879	2,446,010	500,000	330,729	
Lorillard, N. Y	21,500	64,554					86,054	300,000	11,379	
Manhattan Fire, N. Y	45,000	148,475					198,475	250,000	50,294	
Mechanics and Traders Fire, N. Y	34,200	118,706				2,337	155,243	200,000	184,492	
Mercantile, Ohio	35,350	41,987		54		814	78,205	200,000	17,099	
Mercantile Mutual, N. Y	185,410		323,368	12,372	95,218	24,040	640,408	1,000,000		231,848
Merchants, R. I	206,780	86,579	27				293,336	200,000		7,607
Meriden Fire, Conn	21,732	40,507				1,233	68,472	200,000		10,335
Narragansett Fire and Marine, R. I	121,910	134,581				15,013	271,454	250,000	12,111	
National Fire, Conn	69,585	163,101					222,686	500,000	9,480	
National Fire and Marine, Pa	22,210	96,421	[11]1,178			16,490	136,299	300,000		16,778
New Orleans Mutual, La	107,500	234,505	1,425	7,147			350,577	907,717	132,747	
Niagara Fire, N. Y	246,700	386,000		85			632,735	500,000	181,808	
North Missouri, Mo	61,478	330,578	5,94			15,539	413,514	350,000		9,836
Orient, Conn	51,958	145,409			60,000	15,125	272,492	500,000		66,972
Orient Mutual, N. Y	148,801		334,614	[12]1,511	[14]868,441	8,689	857,056	[16]1,068,625	115,000	
Pacific Mutual, N. Y	108,000		100,396	[13]12,075	[15]60,718	17,855	299,044		[10]722,048	

[1]Statement of liabilities, March 1, 1873.
[2]Statement of liabilities, February 28, 1873.
[3]Statement of liabilities, March 8, 1873.
[4]For the year ending Jan. 28, 1873.
[5]An assessment of $100,000 was paid in cash, January 20, 1873.
[6]Of which $17,247 is premium notes.
[7]Premium notes.
[8]Over capital and premium notes.
[9]Over premium notes.
[10]Over liabilities.
[11]Amount reclaimable on perpetual fire risks.
[12]And scrip ordered redeemed.
[13]Scrip ordered redeemed.
[14]Balances of notes taken in advance for premiums.
[15]Of which $718 is balances of subscription notes.
[16]Permanent reserve fund.

Table No. II. — Liabilities — continued.

Name of Company.	Net claims for losses.	Reinsurance Fund. Fire and Inland.	Reinsurance Fund. Marine.	Dividends.	Borrowed Money.	All other claims.	Total liabilities.	Capital stock.	Net surplus over capital	Deficiency in capital.
***Companies of other States* — continued.**										
Penn Fire, Pa.	$38,075	$49,810	.....	.....	.....	$14,198	$87,068	$156,650		$5,680
[1] Pennsylvania Fire, Pa.	190,738	321,489	[4]$382,735	$688	.....	26,888	922,467	400,000	.....	[1] 183,142
Phenix, N. Y.	367,473	473,207	100,725	.....	.....	.....	941,405	1,090,000	$59,906	.....
Phœnix, Conn.	185,721	784,905	.....	.....	$160,000	.....	1,070,696	600,000	.....	87,979
Providence Washington, R. I.	16,893	30,317	.....	.....	.....	500	47,709	200,000	3,145	.....
Republic Fire, N. Y.	235,431	290,682	.....	.....	.....	5,458	461,571	300,000	18,772	.....
Saint Joseph F. & M., Mo.	6,618	51,004	.....	.....	.....	5,547	63,168	200,000	38,542	.....
Saint Nicholas, N. Y.	41,100	61,741	.....	.....	.....	.....	102,841	150,000	8,779	.....
Saint Paul Fire & Marine, Minn.	28,382	173,570	.....	.....	.....	.....	201,952	400,000	94,171	.....
Springfield F. & M., Mass.	151,241	408,078	.....	.....	.....	10,880	570,199	500,000	548	.....
Standard Fire, N. Y.	177,705	72,481	.....	.....	.....	4,987	255,178	200,000	8,489	.....
Star Fire, N. Y.	42,651	118,567	.....	.....	.....	2,988	158,451	200,000	1,967	.....
State, Mo.	58,918	88,048	.....	.....	.....	.....	146,956	210,007	.....	10,988
Sun, O.	58,000	85,101	.....	.....	.....	.....	143,101	200,000	38	.....
Traders, Ill.	8,266	62,573	796	.....	.....	6,688	78,200	500,000	10,142	.....
Tradesmen's Fire, N. Y	78,155	108,877	.....	88	.....	4,484	186,604	150,000	20,886	.....
Union, Me.	128,270	125,548	124,878	.....	20,440	209	398,826	200,000	10,542	.....
Watertown Fire, N. Y.	3,300	120,281	.....	.....	.....	.....	123,581	200,000	121,310	.....
Williamsburg City Fire, N. Y.	139,291	171,782	.....	498	.....	8,612	330,188	250,000	25,150	.....
Totals	$8,257,298	$16,694,900	$3,118,814	$75,681	$1,373,368	$778,594	$30,298,535	$37,782,999	$3,058,344	$1,291,890
Companies of Foreign Countries.										
Commercial Union (U. S. Branch) G. B.	$101,813	$202,168	.....	.....	.....	$1,667	$305,648	.....	$[4] 210,266	.....
Hamburg-Bremen Fire, Germany	11,107	180,424	.....	$96,578	.....	301,839	469,943	$160,000	151,183	.....
Imperial Fire (U. S. Branch) G. B.	358,532	682,449	.....	.....	.....	29,100	1,070,081	.....	[4] 278,426	.....
Lancashire (U. S. Branch) G. B.	69,686	165,282	.....	.....	.....	15,285	250,265	.....	[4] 109,942	.....
Liverpool & London & Globe (Am. Branch) G. B.	814,457	1,656,727	[4] $998,045	.....	[4] $106,471	50,000	2,923,700	.....	[4]1,972,072	.....

[3] London Assurance Corporation, G. B	495,400	397,012	245,140	1,297	[6]3,174,618	19,858	2,272,710	2,465,518	3,297,275	....
North British and Mercantile (U. S. Branch), G.B	302,559	576,198	....	....	....	....	1,295,757	....	[4]473,690	....
Queen (U. S. Branch), G. B	46,413	240,181	[5]12,267	....	....	2,971	301,752	....	[4]397,396	....
[3] Royal, G. B	157,402	1,574,260	[5]26,445	5,973	[6]7,491,550	....	2,185,680	1,590,098	2,211,851	....
Western Assurance, Canada	93,989	188,655	16,768	1,409	....	4,296	366,110	200,451	97,989	....
Totals	$2,441,868	$6,163,301	$596,685	$35,249	$15,702,084	$375,016	$25,318,591	$4,415,987	$5,442,016	....

[1] Supplementary statement made by this company February 4, 1878, shows that the capital had been repaired to the amount of $84,138, leaving deficiency of $49,009.

[2] Converted into federal currency at $5.50 to the pound sterling.

[3] For the year ending June 30th, 1872. Converted into federal currency at $5.50 to the pound sterling.

[4] Over liabilities.

[5] Amount reclaimable on perpetual fire risks.

[6] Liabilities of other departments.

TABLE No. III—Income.

Name of Company.	Net Cash Premiums.	Interest and Dividends.	From all other Sources.	Total cash Income.	Cash Income over Expend'res	Expenditures over Cash Income.	Premiums unpaid.	Received from Stockholders.
Wisconsin Joint Stock.								
Brewers' Fire Insurance Company of America	$368,078	$26,536	....	$394,684	$71,667	....	$36,509	$28,200
Hekla	13,983	4,357	$110	18,400	10,770	....	8,109	....
Northwestern National	[3]245,515	11,094	....	[3]256,589	[3]54,755	....	20,336	....
Totals	$527,526	$41,987	$110	$569,573	$187,192	....	$64,954	$28,200
Wisconsin Mutual.								
Concordia Mutual Fire	$16,844	$1,210	....	$18,054	$10,359	....	$3,599	$1,150
Dodge County Mutual	55,562	1,878	[3]$5,500	[3]62,940	....	$12,466	38,473	[5]3,840
Germantown Farmers' Mutual	23,316	2,809	....	26,125	7,430	....	18,809	[4]44,675
Herman Farmers' Mutual	4,484	1,019	....	5,503	2,389	....	3,508	[5]6,811
Madison Mutual	99,646	15,091	[4]15,774	[4]130,511	....	52,585	84,461	[5]125,681
Milwaukee Mechanics' Mutual	155,818	9,516	677	166,011	29,027	....	15,189	[5]65,907
Vernon County Scandinavian Mutual Fire	106	50	....	156	58	....	150	....
Totals	$355,776	$31,573	$21,951	$409,300	$49,263	$65,051	$109,189	$267,564
Companies of other States.								
Ætna, Conn.	[6]$4,727,485	$308,436	$11,627	[6]$5,042,498	....	$682,792	....	....
Alemannia Fire, O.	255,470	7,051	716	263,237	....	26,473	$70,628	$85,681
Allemannia, Fire, Pa.	68,446	17,394	20,000	105,840	$40,049	....	20,150	100,000
Amazon, O.	1,151,833	44,616	25,582	1,222,031	388,415	....	98,962	....
American, Ill.	432,748	10,531	10,508	453,787	....	6,965	[12]898,177	50,000
American Central, Mo.	478,818	19,470	....	498,288	80,962	....	62,292	....
Arctic Fire, N. Y.	135,264	16,422	230	151,916	....	44,208	7,879	....
Atlantic, N. Y.	145,037	17,141	....	162,178	83,294	....	21,131	....
Black River, N. Y.	117,371	3,176	460	121,007	35,096	....	14,434	62,500
Brewers & Maltsters, N. Y.	198,659	12,094	1,935	212,688	....	62,096	81,793	....
Capital City, N. Y.	19,385	5,277	....	24,662	....	6,251	3,805	50,000
Commerce, N. Y.	211,735	21,707	2,793	236,235	....	19,809	19,421	....
Connecticut Fire, Conn.	205,431	49,579	....	255,010	23,691	....	64,862	....
Continental, N. Y.	1,549,155	83,594	24,712	1,657,459	....	786,151	168,799	400,000

Detroit F. & M., Mich.	[7] 198,898	13,748	2,681	[7] 281,208		8,444	16,409	
Fairfield County Fire, Conn.	[8] 148,974	18,898	2,322	[8] 164,434	26,196			
Farmers, Ill.	58,469	6,308	777	65,549		10,589	[13] 75,648	
[1] Fireman's Fund, Cal.	476,668	33,096	16,454	596,218		144,212	22,514	
Franklin Fire, Pa.	1,399,674	202,469	3,086	1,606,179		64,580	221,798	[13] 156,012
German, Pa.	251,340	5,896		267,236	26,265		36,695	
German, Ill.	[9] 75,016	576	274	[9] 75,866	[9] 23,365		8,069	10,100
German American, N. Y.	580,348	65,787		586,135	243,699		110,998	
Germania Fire, N. Y.	888,419	64,381	18,595	921,395	10,069		91,075	250,000
Girard F. & M., Pa.	364,596	21,781	6,985	393,312	86,998		54,380	[18] 5,663
Globe, Ill.	[10] 58,095			[10] 58,095		38,396		43,350
Hanover Fire, N. Y.	802,942	48,862		851,104	11,465		102,239	
Hartford Fire, Conn.	2,138,307	85,326	5,602	2,229,235		610,571	156,856	
Hartford Steam Boiler Insp. & Ins., Conn.	100,458	9,967	45,096	155,521	645		11,496	
Hoffman Fire, N. Y.	200,180	12,334	6,082	218,596		54,174	48,706	
Home, O.	559,464	34,808		594,267		176,484	212,359	
Home, N. Y.	[11] 3,142,306	253,390	5,998	[11] 3,401,694		253,072	3,629	
Howard, N. Y.	227,679	28,102	5,200	260,981		80,842	16,888	
Insurance Co. of N. A., Pa.	2,877,216	161,404		3,038,620		690,488	809,872	[12] 53,415
Lorillard, N. Y.	148,750	11,667		160,417		40,684	29,083	100,000
Manhattan Fire, N. Y.	299,166	10,990		310,156	127,482		52,480	
Mechanics & Traders Fire, N. Y.	257,017	28,246		285,263	3,497		74,841	
Mercantile, O.	156,447	12,213		168,660	24,816		27,696	
Mercantile Mutual, N. Y.	1,304,678	33,622		1,338,300		80,247	594,886	
Merchants, R. I.	168,080	25,160		193,240		19,295	10,444	[18] 100,000
Meriden Fire, Conn.	[14] 80,934	4,225		[14] 85,159	[14] 40,288			200,000
Narragansett, F. & M., R. I.	336,632	57,834		394,466		213,666	110,629	
National Fire, Conn.	[15] 332,299	34,527	69	[15] 366,895	[15] 66,604			150,000
National F. & M., Pa.	[16] 198,868	6,502	3,468	[16] 208,838	[16] 114,706			300,000
New Orleans Mutual, La.	1,062,837	76,131		1,138,968	409,807			
Niagara Fire, N. Y.	728,265	73,372	5,507	807,144	7,399		116,948	
North Missouri, Mo.	675,211	16,864	2,165	694,240	126,028		223,762	150,000
Orient, Conn.	[17] 814,391	31,614		[17] 846,005	35,156			
Orient Mutual, N. Y.	1,145,408	40,254	4,405	1,190,067	9,668		279,800	

[1] For the year ending Jan. 28, 1878.
[2] Of which $39,637 is in course of collection.
[3] Of which $5,350 is from assessment of pre'm notes.
[4] Of which $15,174 is from assessm't of pre'm notes.
[5] Premium notes.
[6] Of which $928,098 is in course of collection.
[7] Of which $17,484 is in course of collection.
[8] Of which $34,422 is in course of collection.
[9] Of which $6,426 is in course of collection.
[10] Of which $24,995 is in course of collection.
[11] Of which $295,111 is in course of collection.
[12] Including instalment notes.
[13] Deposit premium on perpetual fire risks.
[14] Of which $5,649 is in course of collection.
[15] Of which $35,000 is in hands of agents.
[16] Of which $82,449 is in hands of agents.
[17] Of which $75,000 is in course of collection.
[18] Assessment on capital stock.

Table No. III.—Income—continued.

Name of Company.	Net Cash Premiums.	Interest and Dividends.	From all other Sources.	Total Cash Income.	Cash income over Expendit's.	Expenditures over Cash Income.	Premiums unpaid.	Received from Stockholders.
***Companies of other States*—continued.**								
Pacific Mutual, N. Y	$589,686	$34,966	$107,894	$672,476	....	$8,696	$178,018	....
Penn Fire, Pa	40,724	150	....	40,874	$13,882	....	54,691	$18,868
Pennsylvania Fire, Pa	490,412	75,756	13,827	579,995	....	180,476	114,188	[5]32,555
Phenix, N. Y	1,533,459	67,639	15,850	1,616,948	47,419	....	181,061	....
Phœnix, Conn	[2,3]1,525,188	88,645	890	[3]1,614,717	....	249,506	....	....
Providence Washington, R. I	59,753	7,887	141	67,781	....	29,296	....	209,485
Republic Fire, N. Y	448,568	22,633	13,259	484,460	70,971	....	....	....
Saint Joseph F. & M., Mo	122,264	21,752	650	144,666	47,877	....	32,787	60,450
Saint Nicholas, N. Y	166,770	11,727	....	178,497	3,290	....	....	....
Saint Paul F. & M., Minn	347,556	36,869	12,088	396,463	82,608	....	68,489	....
Springfield F. & M., Mass	[4]684,185	56,180	3,600	[4]693,965	....	122,950	....	150,000
Standard Fire, N. Y	159,117	26,380	....	185,497	....	152,785	16,202	150,000
Star Fire, N. Y	245,422	23,277	173	268,872	....	66,405	21,963	50,000
State, Mo	196,706	9,155	17,592	223,453	....	3,596	41,501	34,456
Sun, O	150,663	19,187	....	169,850	....	123	20,604	50,000
Traders', Ill	245,473	14,526	1,199	261,198	72,400	....	15,942	....
Tradesmen's Fire, N. Y	210,806	26,486	29,196	266,488	....	134,605	28,666	75,000
Union, Me	395,836	47,104	....	442,940	....	10,406	....	41,825
Watertown Fire, N. Y	214,965	19,258	....	234,223	53,528	....	33,478	....
Williamsburg City Fire, N. Y	390,338	29,419	456	420,213	27,290	....	56,234	....
Totals	$39,446,262	$2,780,783	$450,984	$42,677,919	$2,525,823	$5,079,011	$5,855,061	$3,069,665
Companies of Foreign Countries.								
Commercial Union (U. S. Branch), G. B	$444,886	....	....	$444,886	....	$109,013	$13,888	[7]$229,445
Hamburg-Bremen Fire, Germany	229,968	$19,210	$2,016	251,194	$49,944	....	....	....
Imperial Fire (U. S. Branch), G. B	1,422,154	1,921	....	1,424,075	....	880,111	183,664	[7]526,584
Lancashire (U. S. Branch), G. B	288,628	....	....	288,628	12,485	....	101,897	....
Liverpool and London and Globe (Am. Branch), G. B.	[8]3,501,946	154,914	76,941	[8]3,733,101	....	751,898	....	[7]1,088,632

[1] London Assurance Corporation, G. B.	1,616,166	881,688	974,949	8,118,846	989,967			
North British and Mercantile (U. S. Branch), G. B.	1,747,858	72,708	4,384	1,894,380		197,889		[7]898,383
Queen (U. S. Branch), G. B.	1,080,758	16,855		1,096,993		540,449	18,913	[7]541,583
[2]Royal, G. B.	4,850,686	180,974	8,681	4,440,338	788,596			[6]5,558
Western Assurance, Canada.	489,818	28,783		513,051		58,116	97,280	88,848
Totals	$14,961,055	$1,091,377	$988,014	$17,090,446	$1,057,999	$1,982,418	$410,529	$2,778,417

[1]Converted into federal currency at $5.50 to the pound sterling.
[2]For the year ending June 30, 1872. Converted into federal currency at $5.50 to the pound sterling.
[3]Of which $196,189 is in course of collection.
[4]Of which $89,478 is in course of collection.
[5]Of which $842,804 is in course of collection.
[6]Deposit premium on perpetual fire risks.
[7]Received from home office.

[8]Deposit premium on perpetual fire risks.

TABLE No. IV.—Expenditures.

Name of Company.	Losses Paid.	Dividends.	Commissi'n and Brokerage.	Salaries of officers and employes.	Taxes. State and National.	All other payments.	Total expenditures.
Wisconsin Joint Stock.							
Brewers Fire Ins. Co. of America	$129,557	....	$46,217	$15,000	$5,747	$26,446	$222,967
Hekla	2,119	....	2,791	1,585	220	915	7,630
Northwestern National	139,357	....	29,790	13,016	3,929	15,692	201,784
Totals	$271,033	....	$78,798	$29,601	$9,896	$43,053	$432,381
Wisconsin Mutual.							
Concordia Mutual Fire	$1,601	....	$2,646	$1,704	$350	$1,394	$7,695
Dodge County Mutual	50,902	....	13,235	4,500	1,284	5,585	75,406
Germantown Farmers' Mutual	12,252	....	....	2,827	495	3,121	18,695
Herman Farmers' Mutual	1,575	....	968	238	137	186	3,114
Madison Mutual	122,909	....	26,608	22,930	1,143	9,511	183,096
Milwaukee Mechanics' Mutual	74,330	....	33,685	11,708	5,857	11,409	136,984
Vernon County Scandinavian Mutual Fire	10	....	....	49	13	26	98
Totals	$263,649	....	$77,152	$43,946	$9,159	$31,182	$425,088
Companies of other States.							
Ætna, Connecticut	$4,567,014	....	$677,256	$359,108	97,452	$24,465	$5,725,290
Alemannia Fire, Ohio	198,082	....	62,746	5,086	5,808	17,998	289,710
Allemannia Fire, Pennsylvania	28,615	$10,000	13,270	5,638	1,436	6,832	65,791
Amazon, Ohio	544,061	45,000	108,243	84,362	11,876	100,054	888,616
American, Illinois	116,531	10,458	224,010	69,297	4,910	35,546	460,752
American Central, Missouri	245,298	446	85,690	34,096	11,121	40,675	417,326
Arctic Fire, New York	106,811	26,450	21,808	19,573	6,928	15,560	196,134
Atlantic, New York	38,687	....	12,053	23,630	2,630	1,954	78,954
Black River, New York	36,098	....	19,998	14,944	4,586	10,983	85,909
Brewers and Maltsters, New York	198,759	....	33,945	30,873	2,260	8,947	274,784
Capital City, New York	18,991	....	2,070	4,138	231	5,488	30,918
Commerce, New York	176,689	10,000	31,159	15,585	9,761	12,850	256,044

Connecticut Fire, Conn.	145,800	30,000	31,448	12,268	6,745	5,874	231,319
Continental, N. Y.	1,747,397	[3] 74,980	273,438	161,354	43,985	142,683	2,443,840
Detroit, F. & M., Mich.	182,658	....	20,695	18,815	1,336	11,318	239,695
Fairfield County Fire, Conn.	78,097	18,000	94,510	5,548	1,091	11,069	188,336
Farmers, Ill.	26,177	....	26,647	13,598	420	9,095	75,871
[1] Fireman's Fund, Cal.	499,128	....	68,362	34,047	6,728	62,091	670,420
Franklin Fire, Pa.	1,051,723	[2] 130,576	202,695	184,396	41,504	58,867	1,669,759
German, Pa.	76,744	20,071	47,259	3,168	5,490	11,239	168,971
German, Ill.	8,473	10,100	17,747	11,042	1,084	4,055	52,501
German American, N. Y.	178,764	....	88,205	31,515	7,617	46,335	342,436
Germania Fire, N. Y.	546,700	50,000	128,212	53,455	19,017	118,949	911,333
Girard, F. & M., Pa.	154,106	30,000	50,260	14,164	14,875	42,909	306,314
Globe, Ill.	68,959	....	3,958	11,715	1,161	15,708	96,491
Hanover Fire, N. Y.	517,741	400,000	117,610	46,045	20,196	98,047	889,689
Hartford Fire, Conn.	2,233,552	....	311,379	112,289	45,698	136,953	2,839,806
Hartford Steam Boiler Insp. & Ins., Conn.	18,236	31,000	34,805	8,096	2,707	60,062	154,876
Hoffman Fire, N. Y.	177,181	20,050	31,116	19,466	5,954	19,008	272,770
Home, O.	581,906	....	82,697	52,479	18,748	29,231	770,751
Home, N. Y.	2,582,732	122,435	478,845	200,751	66,207	208,796	3,654,766
Howard, N. Y.	263,857	....	25,636	23,666	11,395	17,267	341,823
Insurance Co. of N. A., Pa.	2,968,639	97,500	398,295	60,000	74,731	184,948	3,739,108
Lorillard, N. Y.	187,266	....	19,481	22,500	6,323	15,581	201,101
Manhattan Fire, N. Y.	94,267	....	58,114	18,425	....	21,868	182,674
Mechanics and Traders Fire, N. Y.	178,558	40,000	29,424	19,344	7,281	7,159	281,766
Mercantile, O.	104,061	9,946	10,795	10,737	2,188	6,617	144,344
Mercantile Mutual, N. Y.	1,113,669	35,878	92,321	129,004	15,164	32,511	1,418,547
Merchants, R. I.	146,636	20,000	27,276	10,180	6,951	1,490	212,535
Meriden Fire, Conn.	20,177	....	12,483	4,779	2,536	4,896	44,871
Narragansett F. & M., R. I.	528,466	....	45,495	25,560	8,611	....	608,132
National Fire, Conn.	174,509	20,000	49,519	28,262	2,594	25,287	300,291
National F. & M., Pa.	26,659	....	17,470	14,604	3,165	27,234	89,132
New Orleans Mutual, La.	172,651	492,206	....	55,759	8,554	....	729,161
Niagara Fire, N. Y.	549,869	52	109,907	37,381	23,609	78,927	799,745
North Missouri, Mo.	300,614	....	155,204	28,211	8,122	76,061	568,212
Orient, Conn.	196,574	....	47,362	23,805	7,935	35,183	310,849
Orient, Mutual, N. Y.	892,674	[5] 131,295	57,218	64,357	12,440	22,420	1,180,404
Pacific Mutual, N. Y.	440,574	[5] 108,985	25,930	55,156	8,936	46,591	681,172

[1] For the year ending January 28, 1873.
[2] Including interest to scrip holders and scrip redeemed.
[3] In gold.
[4] Including rent.
[5] Interest to scrip holders and scrip redeemed.

Table No. IV.—Expenditures—continued.

Name of Company.	Losses paid.	Dividends.	Commis'ns and Brokerage.	Salaries of officers and employes.	Taxes. State and National.	All other payments.	Total Expenditures.
***Companies of Other States*—continued.**							
Penn Fire, Pa	$810	....	$7,748	$1,457	$1,137	$15,900	$27,052
Pennsylvania Fire, Pa	539,091	$59,317	127,719	14,831	2,842	2,671	768,471
Phenix, N. Y	1,028,584	100,000	199,160	101,408	32,844	111,574	1,569,589
Phœnix, Conn	1,497,848	....	297,818	56,179	45,256	127,122	1,864,288
Providence Washington, R. I	78,947	....	7,978	4,152	811	5,195	97,077
Republic Fire, N. Y	249,146	....	65,219	29,137	11,696	58,361	418,489
Saint Joseph Fire and Marine, Mo	55,786	....	20,807	17,978	2,778	....	97,289
Saint Nicholas, N. Y	104,340	15,000	26,694	14,098	2,917	12,884	175,297
Saint Paul Fire and Marine, Minn	186,945	20,000	55,869	12,264	2,221	35,916	313,855
Springfield Fire and Marine, Mass	600,489	40,256	95,126	29,973	19,280	21,792	816,915
Standard Fire, N. Y	244,445	30,500	12,875	22,175	4,798	23,439	338,232
Star Fire, N. Y	284,079	20,000	11,598	16,626	6,398	46,648	385,277
State, Mo	128,200	....	42,105	25,592	1,871	29,281	227,049
Sun, O	106,733	20,000	15,478	23,479	4,258	....	169,948
Traders, Ill	158,048	....	14,211	10,889	....	10,650	188,798
Tradesmen's Fire, N. Y	315,699	21,322	21,079	26,090	3,735	13,168	401,093
Union, Me	358,481	12,308	58,040	10,698	5,125	18,694	458,346
Watertown Fire, N. Y	68,170	28,000	37,658	18,260	10,887	18,785	180,685
Williamsburg City Fire, N. Y	248,429	25,000	51,716	30,086	7,897	29,815	392,893
Totals	$31,545,279	$2,026,071	$5,592,150	$2,696,721	$850,400	$2,521,487	$45,231,108
Companies of Foreign Countries.							
Commercial Union, (U. S. Branch) G. B	$451,150	....	$88,977	$5,297	$8,475	....	$553,899
Hamburg-Bremen Fire, Germany	91,585	$13,120	60,435	36,110	....	....	201,250
Imperial Fire (U. S. Branch), G. B	1,267,659	....	209,950	44,375	34,514	$197,688	1,754,186
Lancashire (U. S. Branch), G. B	160,269	....	57,000	....	4,318	4,551	226,138
Liverpool and London and Globe (Am. Branch), G. B	3,631,589	....	474,985	57,907	48,812	271,806	4,484,999

[1] London Assurance Corporation, G. B.	1,134,364	501,798	165,112	181,808	15,144	708,774	2,330,979
North British and Mercantile (U. S. Branch), G. B.	1,530,548	....	[illegible]	111,064	96,306	87,994	2,082,144
Queen, (U. S. Branch), G. B.	1,336,394	....	142,398	35,170	68,740	40,965	1,577,449
[2] Royal, G. B.	2,397,426	265,004	548,497	319,840	....	261,998	3,707,749
Western Assurance, Canada	456,361	16,470	52,456	16,748	....	94,112	588,167
Totals	$12,447,947	$886,317	$2,054,001	$706,818	$179,209	$1,671,783	$17,944,870

[1] Converted into Federal currency at $5.50 to the pound sterling. [2] For the year ending June 30, 1879. Converted into Federal currency at $5.50 to the pound sterling.

TABLE No. V.

Name of Company.	Net risks in force Dec. 31, 1871.	Risks written during the year.	Net risks in force Dec. 31, 1872.	Losses incurred during the year.	Business in Wisconsin in 1872.		
					Risks writt'n	Premiums received.	Losses paid.
Wisconsin Joint Stock.							
Brewers Fire Insurance Company of America	$4,259,126	$17,375,686	$14,776,787	$123,505	$3,635,406	$55,652	$16,540
Hekla	788,308	1,069,198	1,741,171	2,119	1,009,198	13,983	2,119
Northwestern National	4,866,083	24,343,561	7,105,573	85,930	12,886,060	140,848	44,857
Totals	$9,913,469	$42,788,445	$23,623,531	$211,554	$17,530,664	$210,483	$63,516
Wisconsin Mutual.							
Concordia Mutual Fire	$998,118	$1,151,670	$1,920,851	$1,601	$1,151,670	$16,844	$1,601
Dodge County Mutual	12,364,650	3,086,065	11,460,297	33,364	3,086,065	55,563	50,903
Germantown Farmers' Mutual	6,594,789	1,958,770	6,685,818	12,323	1,958,770	28,316	12,323
Herman Farmers' Mutual	904,728	442,986	1,206,044	1,972	442,986	4,484	1,575
Madison Mutual	46,208,646	[a]11,286,677	45,934,025	106,258	9,890,669	118,112	122,909
Milwaukee Mechanics' Mutual	20,083,668	9,722,887	22,375,080	53,599	8,630,686	147,830	78,664
Vernon County Scandinavian Mutual Fire	50,948	48,955	63,598	10	48,955	256	10
Totals	$87,144,847	$27,696,010	$89,645 143	$210,321	$25,204,801	$366,394	$262,983
Companies of other States.							
Ætna, Conn	$290,084,987	$443,992,046	$319,295,153	$4,527,919	$13,430,167	$159,394	$74,791
Alemannia Fire, Ohio	7,377,912	18,457,100	10 726,757	227,131	349,172	7,856	4,396
Allemannia Fire, Pa	4,986,054	5,680,311	6,687,514	28,615	76,100	1,947	....
Amazon, Ohio	11,236,983	95,754,925	52,873,342	673,725	1,928,430	30,083	17,078
American, Ill	48,685,499	41,454,571	83,229,947	137,423	4,129,645	39,781	8,398
American Central, Mo	10,968,349	41,469,447	24,746,787	294,723	485,428	6,668	4,469
Arctic Fire, N. Y	11,220,245	15,370,018	11,724,394	187,714	596,064	6,801	....
Atlantic, N. Y	....	23 116,160	15,125,120	72,515	54,700	955	....
Black River, N. Y	....	10,554,229	7,505,966	106,565	169,025	3,387	....
Brewers and Maltsters', N. Y	9,341,197	41,185,400	16,437,741	254,206	1,236,456	11,190	4,996
Capital City, N. Y	1,259,987	2,963,864	2,479,695	11,298	51,275	707	....
Commerce, N. Y	21,997,258	21,190,614	21,537,163	208,149	401,885	4,088	36

Connecticut Fire, Conn	³6,000,018	26,480,000	29,499,900	194,200	312,000	5,650	800
Continental, N. Y	177,348,898	281,882,295	159,810,150	1,352,097	5,645,951	42,594	12,204
Detroit Fire and Marine, Mich	10,388,606	17,633,079	11,380,187	118,498	861,264	10,091	788
Fairfield County Fire, Conn	5,342,721	14,105,651	11,365,485	135,298			
Farmers, Ill	9,289,736	4,086,186	11,962,416	94,104	907,400	10,058	4,730
¹ Fireman's Fund, Cal	25,158,107	89,217,884	25,804,299	383,000	761,540	10,710	6,400
Franklin Fire, Pa	149,782,455	119,534,942	142,331,895	1,156,768	1,366,648	26,088	10,008
German, Pa	3,643,978	15,350,900	11,688,508	125,834	181,189	3,289	
German, Ill	5,106,075	4,696,255	7,853,869	12,518			
German American, N. Y		65,165,259	49,088,891	233,104	748,748	14,281	1,168
Germania Fire, N. Y	92,449,498	94,281,586	101,189,767	764,268	1,047,158	18,772	12,780
Girard Fire and Marine, Pa	23,112,125	29,556,128	34,678,229	152,156	386,785	3,904	1,366
Globe. Ill	97,808	2,885,290	2,274,980	65,711	202,929	5,695	5,898
Hanover Fire, N. Y	72,894,685	100,127,198	88,470,677	620,681	1,047,158	18,772	12,780
Hartford Fire, Conn	150,000,000	150,888,916	157,830,750	1,655,617	5,812,380	90,904	38,560
Hartford Steam Boiler Inspection and Insurance, Conn	8,721,270	12,258,954	11,854,076	16,977	355,850	2,841	480
Hoffman Fire, N. Y	10,409,085	28,598,298	17,491,587	262,058	210,600	2,498	298
Home. O	52,336,498	40,938,689	48,916.405	588,311	833,688	10,080	1,905
Home, N. Y	294,852,308	346,086,172	340,149,668	2,331,445	8,584,635	129,763	49,435
Howard, N. Y	25,044,578	33,955,669	27,595,649	77,247	552,685	6,350	3,897
Insurance Company of North America, Pa	149,450,216	294,940,864	182,688,902	3,691,797	3,687,420	69,075	47,894
Lorillard, N. Y		22,096,094	14 211,817	158,766	359,196	4,214	1,475
Manhattan Fire, N. Y		32,912,888	21,765,562	139,287	807,567	11,674	172
Mechanics and Traders' Fire, N. Y	23,797,875	49,647,458	25,883,579	205,568	1,560,392	14,161	1,447
Mercantile, O	5,274,208	12,985,680	5,185,299	137,616	694,991	6,438	1,264
Mercantile Mutual, N. Y	13,663,446	96,672,449	17,207,960	1,127,277	1,649,692	18,809	11,869
Merchants', R. I	13,652,067	17,620,491	12,663,874	329,567	414,258	4,669	858
Meriden Fire, Conn		6,332,250	5,816,262	41,908	102,425	1,309	
Narragansett Fire and Marine, R. I	22,368,882	27,002,010	20,559,741	578,428	70,600	898	2,338
National Fire, Conn	1,670,767	28,256,279	24,127,945	244,094	882,541	9,947	2,720
National Fire and Marine, Pa	137,586	12,150,631	10,992,670	48,869			
New Orleans Mutual, La							
Niagara Fire, N. Y	71,752,018	88,422,087	71,457,051	731,169	1,047,158	18,772	12,780
North Missouri, Mo	8,050,083	45,499,976	27,208,914	350,089	1,336,161	31,698	16,200
Orient, Conn		25,280,094	19,254,008	248,532	510,641	8,337	3,654
Orient Mutual, N. Y	19,551,285	137,416,461	20,600,498	839,990	2,163,339	15,719	92
Pacific Mutual, N. Y	7,468,399	68,644,958	6,762,128	414,974	3,013,990	19,163	6,591

¹ For the year ending January 28, 1873. ² And restored. ³ In force February 1, 1873.

TABLE No. V.—continued.

NAME OF COMPANY.	Net risks in force Dec. 31, 1871.	Risks written during the year.	Net risks in force Dec. 31, 1872.	Losses incurred during the year.	BUSINESS IN WISCONSIN IN 1872. Risks written	Premiums received.	Losses paid.
Companies of other States—continued.							
Penn Fire, Pa.	....	$5,086,043	$4,915,088	$34,360	$101,000	$3,767	....
Pennsylvania Fire, Pa.	$38,085,188	58,544,617	60,980,711	739,091	904,768	14,606	$3,657
Phenix, N. Y.	83,085,487	175,104,588	101,086,778	1,215,894	2,350,060	34,281	16,469
Phenix, Conn.	128,670,169	118,578,128	132,802,967	1,283,434	3,741,417	54,869	24,544
Providence Washington, R. I.	*58,585	6,893,161	5,248,390	....	....	....	....
Republic Fire, N. Y.	40,089,681	46,812,885	40,856,441	452,564	1,047,158	18,772	12,760
Saint Joseph Fire and Marine, Mo.	4,133,000	9,650,238	7,781,508	59,837	....	....	....
Saint Nicholas, N. Y.	14,346,995	20,507,868	17,065,601	139,616	240,000	3,721	5,418
Saint Paul Fire and Marine, Minn.	9,838,194	27,057,008	20,512,894	184,058	2,097,410	30,468	8,896
Springfield Fire and Marine, Mass.	55,885,756	58,280,712	67,277,611	616,198	688,990	8,989	7,411
Standard Fire, N. Y.	21,362,126	27,984,793	17,488,068	411,199	518,920	5,749	9,554
Star Fire, N. Y.	21,848,289	28,798,721	24,244,787	297,807	298,450	3,968	3,708
State, Mo.	6,441,340	11,897,847	9,342,188	129,169	320,575	3,168	....
Sun, Ohio	12,966,447	14,646,394	13,775,951	165,000	348,250	2,152	1,728
Traders, Ill.	....	28,174,180	9,950,590	294,465	1,102,168	7,058	....
Tradesmen's Fire, N. Y.	25,367,974	25,905,895	28,385,657	384,216	578,006	7,555	9,414
Union, Maine	17,129,958	25,169,121	19,794,877	353,481	665,392	5,608	1,522
Watertown Fire, N. Y.	21,656,100	29,430,500	38,362,500	66,470	210,300	1,582	....
Williamsburg City Fire, N. Y.	30,484,881	47,640,682	41,867,365	353,863	269,787	3,551	6,176
Totals	$2,387,581,376	$3,842,941,686	$3,027,604,310	$33,211,672	$84,478,871	$1,129,565	$496,392
Companies of Foreign Countries.							
Commercial Union (U. S. Branch), G. B.	$17,770,885	$48,117,314	$32,860,838	$508,060	$1,302,943	$16,825	$6,239
Hamburg-Bremen Fire, Germany	57,027,858	76,967,768	41,044,567	91,585	291,450	2,958	....
Imperial Fire (U. S. Branch), G. B.	74,185,086	174,758,823	116,720,112	1,667,298	3,761,617	50,609	38,697
Lancashire (U. S. Branch), G. B.	....	35,830,596	30,462,068	229,967	378,055	2,406	....
Liverpool and London and Globe (Am. Branch), G. B.	268,349,404	429,588,988	278,869,431	3,967,000	1,845,900	26,989	12,811

[1] London Assurance Corporation, G. B.	....	....	....	....	669,350	7,549	....
North British & Mercantile (U. S. Branch) G. B.	115,776,766	199,454,897	144,202,849	1,655,490	2,716,696	42,199	16,296
Queen (U. S. Branch) G. B.	47,675,958	107,596,965	50,076,336	1,367,639	1,836,690	19,777	12 994
[2] Royal, G. B.	720,664,450	1,151,697,150	892,222,300	2,397,456	2,477,059	30,944	17,717
Western Assurance, Canada	15,951,462	36,105,945	39,054,597	....	368,090	4,958	....
Totals	$1,807,431,857	$2,284,996,909	$1,607,518,911	$11,909,390	$15,187,040	$204,285	$99.746

[1] Converted into federal currency at $5.50 to the pound sterling, except business in Wisconsin.

[2] For the year ending June 30, 1872. Converted into federal currency at $5.50 to the pound sterling. Business in Wisconsin for the year ending December 31, 1872.

[3] In force May 1, 1872.

TABLE NO. VI.

Name of Company.	Capital Paid.	Amount at Risk Dec. 31, 1872.	Net Assets.	Percent. Net Ast's to Amt at Risk.	Gross Assets.	Gross Liabilities.	Surplus as regards Policy holders.	Net surplus or impairm't of Capital.	[10] Per centage
Wisconsin Joint Stock.									
Brewers Fire Ins. Co. of America	$200,000	$14,776,787	$384,310	2.60	$420,547	$181,196	$239,351	$39,351	19.68
Heckla	47,006	1,741,171	64,550	3.71	67.996	24,097	43,896	— 3,110	6.62
Northwestern National	235,500	7,105,573	361,535	5.09	383,235	90,251	293,084	57,584	24.43
Totals	$482,506	$23,623,531	$810,395	3.43	$871,835	$295,544	$576,281	$93,775	19.43
Wisconsin Mutual.									
Concordia Mutual Fire	[1] $34,667	$1,920,351	[3] $48,536	2.53	[3] $49,118	$19,350	$29,768	$5,101	20.68
Dodge County Mutual	[2] 53,067	11,460,227	[3] 153,063	1.34	[3] 157,244	76,094	81,220	28,153	53.05
Germantown Farmers' Mutual	[2] 144,046	6,685,818	[3] 213,490	3.19	[3] 213,490	49,300	164,190	20,144	13.98
Herman Farmers' Mutual	[2] 20,597	1,206,044	[3] 35,358	2.93	[3] 36,174	6,243	29,931	9,334	45.32
Madison Mutual	[2] 583,112	45,984,095	[3] 819,494	1.78	[3] 832,680	233,650	599,030	15,918	2.73
Milwaukee Mechanics' Mutual	[2] 337,617	22,375,080	[3] 562,622	2.51	[3] 565,242	183,221	382,021	44,404	13.15
Vernon County Scandinavian Mutual Fire	....	63,598	1,255	1.97	1,287	567	720	720	....
Totals	$1,163,106	$89,645,143	$1,833,708	2.05	$1,855,235	$568,355	$1,286,880	$123,774	10.64
Companies of other States.									
Ætna, Conn.	$2,000,000	$319,295,158	$4,055,338	1.27	$5,396,381	$3,383,633	$2,012,748	$12,748	.63
Alemannia Fire, O.	250,000	10,726,757	368,906	3.44	402,596	130,626	271,970	21,970	8.79
Allemannia Fire, Pa.	150,000	6,687,514	252,240	3.77	253,970	59,952	194,018	44,018	29.35
Amazon, O	500,000	52,873,842	906,008	1.71	1,070,280	611,818	458.462	— 41,538	8.31
American, Ill	200,000	88,229,947	435,617	.52	538,338	289,838	248,490	48,490	24.25
American Central, Mo.	275,000	24,746,737	307,445	2.05	544,944	234,889	310,055	35,055	12.75
[4] Arctic Fire, N. Y	200,000	11,724,824	[4] 264,763	2.26	[4] 275,468	[4] 63,727	211,741	11,741	5.87
Atlantic, N. Y	200,000	15,125,120	269,437	1.78	303,264	88,841	214,423	14,423	7.21
Black River, N. Y	250,000	7,505,966	307,155	4.09	377,692	133,595	244,097	— 5,903	2.36
Brewers' & Maltsters, N. Y	200,000	16,437,741	236,616	1.44	284,373	121,831	162,542	— 37,458	18.73
Capital City, N. Y	150,000	2,479,625	177,940	7.18	183,711	16,842	166,869	16,869	11.25
Commerce, N. Y	200,000	21,587,163	341,656	1.59	400,158	183,401	217,757	17,757	8.88

Connecticut Fire, Conn.	500,000	32,499,900	642,380	2.36	728,635	215,900	512,735	12,735	2.55
Continental, N. Y.	1,000,000	189,316,150	1,354,338	.95	2,334,250	1,281,094	1,053,156	53,156	5.32
Detroit Fire and Marine, Mich.	150,000	11,396,187	254,099	2.24	267,849	96,772	171,077	21,077	14.05
[5] Fairfield County Fire, Conn.	200,000	11,365,495	[5] 275,333	2.42	[5] 297,218	[5] 95,946	201,272	1,272	.64
[6] Farmers, Ill.	100,000	11,962,416	[6] 109,535	.92	[6] 129,232	[6] 47,378	81,854	— 18,146	18.15
[7] Fireman's Fund, Cal.	300,000	25,804,299	486,235	1.86	619,221	324,801	294,420	— 5,580	1.86
Franklin Fire, Pa.	400,000	143,331,895	1,597,811	1.11	3,423,671	2,628,991	794,680	394,680	81.17
German, Pa.	200,000	11,683,502	306,306	2.60	353,896	152,952	200,944	944	.47
German, Ill.	200,000	7,352,399	252,408	3.43	258,394	30,829	227,565	27,565	13.78
German American, N. Y.	1,000,000	49,083,391	1,317,716	2.68	1,379,090	344,329	1,034,761	34,761	3.48
Germania Fire, N. Y.	500,000	101,189,767	1,028,660	1.01	1,313,378	739,125	574,253	74,253	14.85
Girard Fire and Marine, Pa.	300,000	34,678,289	632,135	1.82	653,321	219,060	434,261	134,261	44.75
Globe, Ill.	300,000	2,274,980	304,885	13.40	341,634	65,940	275,694	— 24,306	8.10
Hanover Fire, N. Y.	250,000	83,470,677	720,163	.86	886,540	622,367	264,173	14,173	5.67
Hartford Fire, Conn.	1,000,000	157,830,750	1,776,294	1.13	2,204,397	1,348,278	856,119	— 143,881	14.39
Hartford Steam Boiler Insp. and Ins., Conn.	120,000	11,854,076	173,349	1.46	173,998	25,788	148,210	28,210	23.51
[5] Hoffman Fire, N. Y.	200,000	17,491,537	191,857	1.10	298,355	202,613	95,742	— 104,258	52.13
Home, O.	250,000	48,916,405	626,279	1.28	800,734	503,221	297,513	47,513	19.01
Home, N. Y.	2,500,000	340,149,868	3,855,945	1.13	4,446,859	2,277,158	2,169,701	— 330,299	13.21
Howard, N. Y.	500,000	27,595,649	608,274	2.19	608,964	105,919	503,045	3,045	.61
Insurance Co. of North America, Pa.	500,000	182,688,902	2,176,322	1.19	3,276,739	2,446,010	830,729	330,729	66.15
Lorillard, N. Y.	300,000	14,211,817	375,933	2.65	397,433	86,054	311,379	11,379	3.79
Manhattan Fire, N. Y.	250,000	21,765,562	448,769	2.06	498,769	198,475	300,294	50,294	20.12
Mechanics' and Traders' Fire, N. Y.	200,000	25,883,579	508,198	1.94	539,735	155,243	384,492	184,492	92.25
Mercantile, O.	200,000	5,185,299	259,086	5.00	295,804	78,205	217,099	17,099	8.55
[8] Mercantile Mutual, N. Y.	[9] 1,000,000	17,207,980	1,091,525	6.34	1,408,565	640,408	768,157	— 231,843	23.18
Merchants, R. I.	200,000	12,668,874	278,999	2.20	485,729	293,336	192,393	— 7,607	3.80
Meriden, Fire, Conn.	200,000	5,816,262	230,172	3.96	253,137	63,472	189,665	— 10,335	5.17
Narragansett Fire and Marine, R. I.	250,000	20,559,741	326,642	1.98	533,565	271,454	262,111	12,111	4.84
National Fire, Conn.	500,000	24,127,945	672,581	2.79	742,166	232,686	509,480	9,480	1.90
National Fire and Marine, Pa.	300,000	10,992,670	379,643	3.45	419,521	136,299	283,222	— 16,778	5.59
New Orleans Mutual, La.	907,717	....	1,276,394	....	1,391,041	350,577	1,040,464	132,747	14.62
Niagara Fire, N. Y.	500,000	71,457,051	1,017,808	1.42	1,364,538	682,735	681,803	181,803	36.36
North Missouri, Mo.	350,000	27,208,914	676,661	2.49	752,678	412,514	340,164	— 9,836	2.81
Orient, Conn.	500,000	19,254,006	578,437	3.00	705,520	272,492	433,028	— 66,972	13.39

[1] Capital paid, $7,490, and premium notes, $17,247.
[2] Premium notes.
[3] Including premium notes.
[10] Of net surplus, or impairment of capital, to capital.
[4] Statement of assets and liabilities March 1, 1873.
[5] Statement of assets and liabilities Feb. 28, 1873.
[6] Statement of assets and liabilities March 8, 1873.
[7] For the year ending January 28, 1873.
[8] An assessment of $100,000 was paid in cash, Jan. 20, 1873.
[9] Capital stock reduced to $500,000, Feb. 25, 1873.

Table No. VI—continued.

Name of Company.	Capital Paid.	Am't at Risk Dec. 31, 1872.	Net Assets.	Percent. Net As'ts to Am't at Risk.	Gross Assets.	Gross Liabilities.	Surplus as regards Policy Holders.	Net Surplus or Impairm't of Capital.	[11] Percentage
Companies of other States—continued.									
Orient Mutual, N. Y.	....	$30,600,488	$1,518,239	7.35	[3]$2,035,681	$857,056	$1,178,625	[4]$1,178,625	....
Pacific Mutual, N. Y.	....	6,762,128	822,444	1.22	[3]1,021,092	299,044	722,048	[5]722,048	....
Penn Fire, Pa.	$156,650	4,915,088	200,780	4.09	238,058	87,088	150,970	— 5,680	3.63
[1]Pennsylvania Fire, Pa.	400,000	60,980,711	588,347	.96	1,189,325	922,467	266,858	— 133,142	33.29
Phenix, N. Y.	1,000,000	101,036,778	1,638,840	1.62	2,001,313	941,405	1,059,908	59,908	5.99
Phœnix, Conn.	600,000	132,892,967	1,296,986	.98	1,582,647	1,070,626	512,021	— 87,979	14.66
Providence Washington, R. I.	200,000	5,248,390	233,463	4.45	250,854	47,709	203,145	3,145	1.57
Republic Fire, N. Y.	300,000	40,856,441	534,454	1.31	775,343	461,571	313,772	13,772	4.59
Saint Joseph Fire and Marine, Mo.	200.000	7,731,502	287,546	3.72	299,705	63,163	236,542	36,542	18.27
Saint Nicholas, N. Y.	150,000	17,055,601	220,590	1.29	261,620	102,841	158,779	8,779	5.85
Saint Paul Fire and Marine, Minn.	400,000	20,512,894	597,741	2.91	696,123	201,952	494,171	94,171	6.04
Springfield Fire and Marine, Mass	500,000	67,277,611	908,621	1.35	1,070,742	570,199	500,543	543	.11
Standard Fire, N. Y.	200,000	17,438,068	275,289	1.58	458,612	255,173	203,439	3,439	1.72
Star Fire, N. Y.	200,000	24,244,787	315,584	1.30	360,418	158,451	201,967	1,967	.98
State, Mo.	210,007	9,342,188	287,762	3.08	346,675	146,956	199,719	— 10,288	4.90
Sun, O.	200,000	13,775,951	285,139	2.07	348,139	148,101	200,038	38	.02
Traders', Ill.	500,000	9,950,590	573,443	5.76	588,342	78,200	510,142	10,142	2.03
Tradesmens' Fire, N. Y.	150,000	26,385,657	274,773	1.04	357,500	186,604	170,896	20,896	13.93
Union, Me.	200,000	19,794,877	460,456	2.33	609,438	398,896	210,542	10,542	5.27
Watertown Fire, N. Y.	200,000	38,363,500	441,591	1.15	444,891	123,581	321,310	121,310	60.66
Williamsburg City Fire, N. Y.	250,000	41,667,365	446,932	1.07	595,338	320,188	275,150	25,150	10.06
Totals	$26,719,374	$3,027,604,310	$47,688,815	[6]1.58	$59,848,049	$30,298,535	$29,549,514	$2,880,140	10.59
Companies of Foreign Countries.									
Commercial Union, (U. S. Branch,) G. B.	....	$32,860,888	$412,429	1.26	$515,909	$305,643	$210,266	[4]$210,266	....
Hamburg-Bremen Fire, Germany	$160,000	41,044,567	491,607	1.20	781,126	469,943	311,183	151,183	94.49
Imperial Fire, (U. S. Branch,) G. B.	....	116,720,112	960,975	.82	1,348,507	1,070,081	278,426	[5]278,426	....
Lancashire, (U. S. Branch,) G. B.	....	30,462,068	268,294	.88	353,907	250,965	102,942	[5]102,942	....
Liverpool & London & Globe, (Am. Br.) G. B.	....	278,869,421	2,928,799	1.05	4,195,773	2,923,700	1,272,073	[5]1,272,073	....

[9] London Assurance Corporation, G. B.	2,465,513	....	6,464,948	....	16,085,501	9,272,710	5,868,791	3,357,278	128.17
North British and Mercantile (U. S. B.), G. B.	....	144,202,849	1,348,868	.94	1,791,447	1,288,787	472,680	[5] 472,690	....
Queen (U. S. Branch), G. B.	....	50,076,286	597,457	1.19	659,078	301,753	307,386	[5] 357,326	....
[10] Royal, G. B.	1,590,026	691,292,200	5,376,134	.60	12,297,504	6,185,680	3,801,874	2,311,851	129.11
Western Assurance, Canada	280,451	22,054,587	483,866	1.97	585,542	305,110	298,435	97,968	12.95
Totals	$4,415,987	$1,097,513,911	$19,288,212	[7] .80	$88,171,594	$25,818,591	$12,858,006	$8,442,016	[9] 130.17

[1] Supplementary statement made by this company, Feb. 4, 1873, shows that the capital stock had been repaired to the amount of $84,138, leaving deficiency of $49,009.

[2] Including $549,735 in notes taken in advance for premiums.

[3] Including $19,000 in notes taken in advance for premiums.

[4] Surplus over liabilities, of which $1,068,635 is permanent reserve fund.

[5] Surplus over liabilities.

[6] Average, excluding the New Orleans Mutual.

[7] Average, excluding the London Assurance Corporation.

[8] Average of foreign companies reporting capital.

[9] Converted into federal currenty at $5.50 to the pound sterling.

[10] For the year ending June 30, 1873. Converted into federal currency at $5.50 to the pound sterling.

[11] Of net surplus or impairment of capital, to capital.

TABLE No. VII.

NAME OF COMPANY.	Mean Amount at risk.	Premiums Received.	Cash Income.	Expenses.	Losses Paid.	PER CENTAGE OF — Expenses to — Premiums received.	Expenses to — Cash Income.	Losses to — Mean am't at risk.	Losses to — Premiums received.
Wisconsin Joint Stock.									
Brewers Fire Ins. Co. of America	$9,517,958	$268,078	$294,684	$93,410	$129,557	34.84	31.70	1.36	48.38
Hekla	1,264,739	13,983	18,400	5,511	2,119	39.55	29.95	.17	15.21
Northwestern National	5,985,803	[3] 245,515	[3] 256,539	62,427	139,357	25.42	24.33	2.33	56.76
Totals	$16,768,500	$527,596	$569,578	$161,348	$271,033	30.59	28.33	1.62	51.38
Wisconsin Mutual.									
Concordia Mutual Fire	$1,456,735	$16,844	$18,054	$6,094	$1,601	36.18	33.75	.11	9.50
Dodge County Mutual	11,912,438	55,562	[14] 62,940	24,504	50,902	44.10	38.98	.42	91.61
Germantown Farmers' Mutual	6,640,304	23,316	26,125	6,378	12,328	27.33	24.39	.19	52.85
Herman Farmers' Mutual	1,055,386	4,484	5,508	1,539	1,575	34.32	27.97	.15	35.12
Madison Mutual	46,068,835	99,646	[15] 130,511	60,187	122,909	60.40	46.12	.27	123.35
Milwaukee Mechanics' Mutual	21,204,374	155,818	166,011	62,654	74,330	40.21	37.74	.35	47.70
Vernon County Scandinavian Mutual Fire	56,923	106	156	88	10	83.02	56.41	.02	9.43
Totals	$88,394,995	$355,776	$409,300	$161,439	$263,649	45.38	39.44	.30	74.10
Companies of other States.									
Ætna, Conn	$304,690,070	[4] $4,727,435	[4] $5,042,498	$1,158,276	$4,567,014	24.50	22.97	1.50	96.61
Alemannia Fire, O.	9,052,334	255,470	263,237	91,626	198,082	35.87	34.81	2.19	77.54
Allemannia Fire, Pa.	5,811,784	68,446	105,840	27,176	28,615	39.70	25.68	.49	41.81
Amazon, O.	32,055,162	1,151,883	1,222,081	249,535	544,081	21.66	20.42	1.70	47.24
American, Il	65,957,723	432,748	453,787	333,763	116,531	77.18	73.55	.18	29.73
American Central, Mo	17,857,548	478,818	496,288	171,582	245,298	35.83	34.43	1.37	51.23
Arctic Fire, N. Y	11,472,320	135,264	151,916	63,863	106,811	47.21	42.04	.93	78.96
Atlantic, N. Y	[2] 15,125,120	145,067	162,178	40,267	38,687	27.76	24.83	.26	26.67
Black River, N. Y	[2] 7,505,966	117,371	121,007	49,811	36,096	42.44	41.16	.48	30.76
Brewers and Maltsters, N. Y	12,889,469	198,659	212,686	76,026	198,759	38.27	35.74	1.54	100.05
Capital City, N. Y	1,869,736	19,385	24,662	11,922	18,991	61.50	48.34	1.02	97.97
Commerce, N. Y	21,767,257	211,785	236,255	60,395	[illegible]	28.76	29.36	.81	83.45

Connecticut Fire, Conn	15,949,959	308,431	355,010	55,819	145,560	47.17	91.99	.95	79.84
Continental, N. Y	188,380,581	1,549,153	1,687,439	681,355	1,747,287	40.11	57.49	.85	113.80
Detroit Fire and Marine, Mich	10,867,397	[5]198,898	[8]201,238	47,044	122,658	28.76	21.25	1.68	91.88
Fairfield County Fire, Conn	8,854,073	[6]148,274	[6]164,434	42,211	78,097	28.47	25.67	.95	88.68
Farmers, Ill	10,686,071	58,489	65,549	49,684	36,177	84.99	75.81	.85	44.77
[1]Fireman's Fund, Cal	25,478,708	476,668	586,218	171,388	499,192	35.98	38.54	1.96	104.78
Franklin Fire, Pa	146,532,175	1,399,674	1,605,179	487,461	1,051,728	34.83	30.37	.78	75.14
German, Pa	7,668,710	261,340	257,298	67,156	76,744	26.72	26.11	1.00	30.58
German, Ill	6,292,952	[7]75,016	[7]75,886	33,928	8,473	45.28	44.73	.14	11.29
German American, N. Y	[2]49,088,391	589,348	586,125	166,678	172,764	28.42	28.78	.85	23.80
Germania Fire, N. Y	96,819,687	836,419	921,395	314,696	546,700	37.58	34.15	.56	65.21
Girard Fire and Marine, Pa	28,895,698	364,596	398,812	122,308	154,106	33.52	31.07	.53	42.27
Globe, Ill	1,186,366	[4]58,095	[4]58,095	32,532	68,959	56.00	56.00	5.39	110.09
Hanover Fire, N. Y	78,147,681	802,942	851,104	281,898	517,741	35.14	33.12	.66	64.54
Hartford Fire, Conn	158,915,375	2,136,307	2,289,295	606,264	2,232,558	28.35	27.20	1.45	104.45
Hartford Steam Boiler Insp. and Ins., Conn	10,287,678	100,458	155,581	105,640	18,236	105.16	67.98	.18	18.15
Hoffman Fire, N. Y	12,950,311	200,180	218,596	75,589	177,181	37.74	34.56	1.27	88.51
Home, Ohio	50,626,417	559,464	594,287	188,845	581,906	33.75	31.78	1.15	104.01
Home, N. Y	317,500.988	[9]3,142,806	[9]3,401,694	949,599	2,588,728	30.28	27.92	.81	82.19
Howard, N. Y	26,320,111	237,679	260,951	77,966	263,857	34.24	29.87	1.00	115.89
Insurance Co. of North America, Pa	166,067,059	2,877,216	3,086,690	662,974	2,968,629	23.04	21.82	1.79	103.18
Lorillard, N. Y	[2]14,211,817	148,750	160,417	63,885	137,266	42.91	39.79	.97	92.28
Manhattan Fire, N. Y	[2]21,765,562	299,166	310,156	88,407	94,297	29.55	28.50	.43	31.51
Mechanics and Traders Fire, N. Y	24,840,727	257,017	285,263	63,208	178,558	24.59	22.16	.71	69.47
Mercantile, Ohio	5,289,758	156,447	166,660	30,337	104,061	19.39	17.99	1.99	66.52
Mercantile Mutual, N. Y	15,425,706	1,304,678	1,386,300	269,000	1,113,669	20.62	20.10	7.21	85.36
Merchants, R. I	12,157,961	166,089	196,240	45,897	146,638	27.31	23.75	1.11	87.24
Meriden Fire, Conn	[3]5,816,282	[10]80,984	[10]85,159	24,694	20,177	30.51	29.00	.35	24.96
Narragansett Fire and Marine, R. I	21,464,286	366,622	394,466	79,666	528,466	28.67	20.20	2.46	156.29
National Fire, Conn	12,899,356	[11]332,299	[11]366,895	105,782	174,509	31.88	28.88	1.35	52.52
National Fire and Marine, Pa	5,565,104	[12]196,868	[12]208,838	62,478	26,659	32.22	30.65	.48	13.75
New Orleans Mutual, La	....	1,062,837	1,138,968	64,304	172,651	6.05	5.65	....	16.24
Niagara Fire, N. Y	71,604,535	728,265	807,144	249,824	549,869	34.30	30.95	.77	75.50
North Missouri, Mo	17,629,473	675,211	694,940	267,598	300 614	39.63	38.55	1.71	44.52
Orient, Conn	[2]19,254,006	[13]314,391	[13]346,005	114,275	196,574	36.35	33.08	1.02	62.53

[1]For the year ending January 28, 1873.
[2]In force December 31, 1872.
[3]Of which $39,687 is in course of collection.
[4]Of which $228,098 is in course of collection.
[5]Of which $17,484 is in course of collection.
[6]Of which $34,428 is in course of collection.
[7]Of which $6,426 is in course of collection.
[8]Of which $24,995 is in course of collection.
[9]Of which $295,111 is in course of collection.
[10]Of which $5,649 is in course of collection.
[11]Of which $35,000 is in hands of agents.
[12]Of which $32,449 is in hands of agents.
[13]Of which $75,000 is in course of collection.
[14]Of which $5,350 is from ass'm't of prem. notes.
[15]Of which $15,174 is from ass'm't of prem. notes.

Table No. VII—continued.

Name of Company.	Mean Amount at Risk.	Premiums Received.	Cash Income.	Expenses.	Losses paid.	Percentage of Expenses to Premiums Received.	Percentage of Expenses to Cash Income.	Percentage of Losses to Mean Am't at Risk.	Percentage of Losses to Premiums Received.
***Companies of other States*—continued.**									
Orient Mutual, N. Y.	$20,075,877	$1,145,488	$1,190,067	$156,435	$892,674	13.66	13.15	4.45	77.94
Pacific Mutual, N. Y.	7,115,261	499,686	672,476	136,613	440,574	25.79	20.31	6.19	88.17
Penn Fire, Pa	[3] 4,915,098	40,794	40,874	26,288	810	64.44	64.20	.02	1.99
Pennsylvania Fire, Pa.	48,098,980	490,412	579,995	162,088	539,091	33.05	27.94	1.28	109.98
Phenix, N. Y.	91,581,148	1,588,459	1,616,948	445,995	1,028,584	28.08	27.58	1.12	66.75
Phœnix, Conn.	128,281,583	[4] 1,595,189	[4] 1,614,717	486,875	1,407,848	29.92	28.26	1.10	88.31
Providence Washington, R. I.	2,652,498	59,758	67,781	18,180	78,947	30.34	26.75	2.98	13.21
Republic Fire, N. Y.	40,448,081	448,588	484,480	164,342	249,146	36.64	33.92	.62	55.54
Saint Joseph Fire and Marine, Mo.	5,922,251	122,264	144,666	41,563	55,726	33.99	28.73	.94	45.58
Saint Nicholas, N. Y.	15,706,258	166,770	178,497	55,867	104,840	33.50	31.30	.66	62.57
Saint Paul Fire and Marine, Minn.	14,280,544	347,556	396,468	106,910	186,945	30.76	26.97	1.25	53.79
Springfield Fire and Marine, Mass.	61,581,682	[5] 634,185	[5] 698,965	176,170	600,489	27.78	25.20	.98	94.69
Standard Fire, N. Y.	19,400,098	159,117	185,497	62,287	244,445	39.77	34.13	1.26	153.62
Star Fire, N. Y.	22,046,586	245,422	268,872	81,198	234,079	33.09	30.20	1.06	95.38
State, Mo.	7,891,784	196,706	228,452	98,849	128,200	50.25	44.24	1.62	65.17
Sun, O	18,382,199	150,683	169,880	43,210	106,738	28.68	25.44	.60	70.83
Traders, Ill.	[3] 9,950,590	245,473	261,198	35,750	153,048	14.56	13.69	1.54	62.35
Tradesmen's Fire, N. Y.	25,876,816	210,806	266,488	64,072	315,699	30.39	24.04	1.22	149.76
Union, Maine.	18,462,414	395,886	442,940	87,557	353,481	22.12	19.77	1.91	89.30
Watertown Fire, N. Y.	30,009,800	214,985	234,268	85,595	68,170	39.79	36.51	.21	29.39
Williamsburg City Fire, N. Y.	36,176,128	392,288	420,218	119,464	248,439	30.61	28.43	.69	63.65
Totals	$2,781,406,719	$39,446,228	$42,677,919	$11,660,758	$31,545,279	29.56	27.32	[7] 1.13	79.97
Companies of Foreign Countries.									
Commercial Union (U. S. Branch), G. B.	$25,315,887	$444,686	$444,686	$102,749	$451,150	23.10	23.10	1.78	101.41
Hamburg-Bremen Fire, Germany	49,086,209	229,968	251,194	96,545	91,585	41.99	38.43	.18	39.88
Imperial Fire (U. S. Branch), G. B.	95,452,589	1,429,154	1,424,075	486,597	1,267,659	34.23	34.16	1.33	89.14
Lancashire (U. S. Branch), G. B.	[3] 30,468,095	238,686	238,686	65,859	160,259	27.60	27.60	.53	67.16
Liverpool and London and Globe (Am. B'h), G. B.	205,609,416	[6] 3,501,346	[6] 3,758,101	858,460	3,681,589	24.38	22.86	1.85	104.78

[1] London Assurance Corporation, G. B.	....	1,616,189	3,112,846	1,124,779	1,134,234	60.60	36.12	....	70.19
North British and Mercantile (U. S. Branch), G. B	129,990,314	1,747,[illegible]	1,694,389	491,690	1,580,646	25.14	25.95	1.18	57.60
Queen (U. S. Branch), G. B.	48,876,154	1,080,7[illegible]	1,066,909	251,148	1,296,294	24.60	24.28	2.71	129.98
[2] Royal, G. B	805,943,395	4,250,[illegible]	4,440,888	1,045,300	2,397,436	24.59	23.54	.30	56.40
Western Assurance, Canada	19,017,994	489,318	518,051	98,316	456,381	19.07	18.19	2.40	58.97
Totals.	$1,472,708,918	$14,961,055	$17,080,446	$4,611,306	$13,447,247	30.33	27.09	[8] .77	83.20

[1] Converted into federal currency at $5.50 to the pound sterling.
[2] For the year ending June 30, 1872. Converted into federal currency at $5.50 to the pound sterling.
[3] In force Dec. 31, 1872.
[4] Of which $196,189 is in course of collection.
[5] Of which $80,472 is in course of collection.
[6] Of which $243,804 is in course of collection.
[7] Omitting the New Orleans Mutual.
[8] Omitting the London Assurance Corporation.

STATEMENTS

OF

Fire and Marine Insurance Companies.

WISCONSIN JOINT STOCK COMPANIES.

BREWERS' FIRE INSURANCE COMPANY OF AMERICA.

MILWAUKEE, WIS.

[Incorporated in 1868. Commenced business in 1869.]

JACOB OBERMANN, *President.* JOSEPH SCHLITZ, *Secretary.*

I. CAPITAL.

Capital authorized	$1,000,000 00
Capital actually paid up in cash	200,000 00

II. ASSETTS.

Loans on bond and mortgage, (first liens)	$8,000 00
Interest accrued on bond and mortgage loans	150 00
Stocks and bonds, market value	331,293 74
Cash in the company's principal office and in bank	53,155 46
Interest due and accrued, not included in market value	388 11
Gross premiums in due course of collection	36,509 34
All other pro,erty belonging to the company, viz: Due for reinsurance on losses paid, $1,230; office furniture, $750; total	1,980 00
Gross amount of all the assets of the company	$431,476 67
Amount which should be deducted from the above assets, on account of bad and doubtful debts and securities, viz: from item No. 19	930 00
Aggregate of all the assets of the company, stated at their actual value	$430,546 67

III. LIABILITIES.

Losses adjusted and unpaid	$13,937 46	....
Losses unadjusted, including all reported and supposed losses	24,800 00	....
Total gross amount of claims for losses	$38,737 46	....
Deduct salvage thereon	2,500 00	....
Net amount of unpaid losses and claims		$36,237 46
Reinsurance at 50 per cent. of prem. on fire risks, under one year	$141,905 75	....
Reinsurance *pro rata*, on fire risks running more than one year	3,052 68	....
Amt. required to safely reinsure all outstanding risks		144,958 43
Total liabilities, except capital stock		$181,195 89

Capital stock actually paid up in cash	$400,000 00
Surplus beyond capital stock	30,350 78
Aggregate and of all liabilities, including capital stock and net surplus	$430,546 67

IV. INCOME DURING THE YEAR.

Gross premiums received in cash, fire	$386,847 21	
Deduct re-insurance, rebate and retd. prems	18,768 86	
Net cash received for premiums		$368,078 35
Gross premiums, remaining unpaid	$36,509 35	
Received for interest on bonds and mortgages		140 00
Received for int. and dividends on stocks and bonds, and from other sources		26,416 14
Received for calls on capital, $6,200; for increased capital, 17,000; total, $23,200		
Aggregate amount of income received during the year in cash		$394,634 49

V. EXPENDITURES DURING THE YEAR.

Gross amount paid for losses, fire	$131,401 70	
Deduct re-insurance	1,845 00	
Net amount paid during the year for losses		$129,556 70
Paid for commissions and brokerage		46,217 47
Salaries and all other charges of officers, clerks, agents and all other employes		15,000 00
Paid for state, national and local taxes		5,747 16
All other payments, viz: traveling, adjusting, printing, stationery, advertising, office furniture and agency expenses		26,446 11
Aggregate amount of expenditures during the year, in cash		$222,967 44

VI. MISCELLANEOUS.

	Fire Risks.	Premiums thereon.
In force December 31, 1871	$4,259,128	$88,142 93
Written during 1872	17,375,686	325,514 37
Total	$21,634,814	$413,657 30
Deduct those terminated	6,858,027	125,266 67
Net amount in force December 31, 1872	$14,776,787	$288,390 63
In force, having not more than one year to run	$14,433,737	$288,811,51
Having more than one year and not more than three years to run	295,750	3,575 88
Having more than three years to run	47,300	890 24
Net amount in force	$14,776,787	$288,390 63

General Interrogatories.

Total premiums received from the organization of the company to date	$406,990 38
Total losses paid from the organization of the company to date	368,441 54
Total dividends declared since the company commenced business	6,699 06
Total amount of losses incurred during the year	128,504 63
Total amount of the company's stock owned by the directors, at par value	78,000 00
Total amount loaned to stockholders, not officers	2,000 00

Business in the State of Wisconsin during the Year 1872.

Risks taken, fire	$3,635,406 09
Premiums received	55,651 80
Losses paid on risks taken	16,589 74
Losses incurred during the year, in Wisconsin	15,914 74
Taxes on premiums, paid to the State of Wisconsin	81 87
Taxes on premiums, paid to fire departments in Wisconsin	391 30

HEKLA INSURANCE COMPANY.

MADISON, WIS.

[Incorporated in 1871. Commenced business in 1871.]

MONS ANDERSON, *President*. HALLE STEENLAND, *Secretary*.

I. CAPITAL.

Capital authorized	$500,000 00
Capital actually paid up in cash	47,006 06

II. ASSETS.

Loans on bond and mortgage, (first liens)	$44,461 26
Loans on bond and mortgage, (first liens), upon which more than one year's interest is due	1,500 00
Interest accrued on bond and mortgage loans	1,120 89
Stocks and bonds, market value	1,058 00
Cash in company's principal office, and in bank	7,752 26
Gross premiums in due course of collection	3,186 92
Bills receivable, not matured, taken for fire risks	2,027 31
Bills receivable, taken for fire risks, past due	2,894 79
All other property belonging to the company, viz., office furniture	408 50
Gross amount of all the assets of the company	$68,017 89
Amount which should be deducted from the above assets, on account of bad and doubtful debts and securities	25 00
Aggregate of all the assets of the company, stated at their actual value	$67,992 89

III. LIABILITIES.

Net amount of unpaid losses and claims		$880 00
Reinsurance at 50 per cent. of prem., on fire risks, under one year	$260 50	
Reinsurance, *pro rata*, on fire risks running more than one year	20,398 60	
Am't required to safely reinsure all outstanding risks		20,653 59
Due and accrued for salaries, rent and other expenses		1,885 39
All other demands against the company, viz.: Due agents, $1,272.52; due E. Olson, $985.32; total		1,537 84
Total liabilities, except capital stock		$34,096 73
Capital stock actually paid up in cash		47,006 06
Aggregate amount of all liabilities, including capital stock		$71,102 79

IV. INCOME DURING THE YEAR.

Gross premiums received in cash, fire	$7,235 70	
Gross cash received on bills and notes taken for premiums	6,946 19	
Gross cash received for premiums	$14,181 89	
Deduct re-insurance, rebate and returned premiums	248 25	
Net cash received for premiums		$13,933 64
Received for interest from all sources		4,356 73
Income received from all other sources		109 71
Gross premiums, remaining unpaid	$8,109 02	
Aggregate amount of income received during the year in cash		$18,400 08

V. EXPENDITURES DURING THE YEAR.

Gross amount paid for losses, fire	$2,119 45	
Net amount paid during the year for losses		$2,119 45
Paid for commissions and brokerage		2,790 73
Salaries and all other charges of officers, clerks, agents and all other employes		1,585 15
Paid for state, national and local taxes		219 79

All other payments, viz: sundry expenses, $266 80; traveling expenses, $175 45; printing, stationery and advertising, $472 29; total	914 54
Aggregate amount of expenditures during the year, in cash	$7,639 66

VI. MISCELLANEOUS.

	Fire Risks.	Premiums thereon.
In force, December 31, 1871	$788,308 00	$11,378 44
Written during 1872	1,009,198 00	14,447 34
Total	$1,797,506 00	$25,825 78
Deduct those terminated	56,335 30	608 99
Net amount in force, Dec. 31, 1872	$1,741,170 70	$25,218 79
In force, not having more than one year to run	$69,542 00	$610 96
Having more than one year and not more than three years to run	174,747 00	2,134 61
Having more than three years to run	1,496,881 70	22,473 22
Net amount in force	$1,741,170 70	$25,218 79

GENERAL INTERROGATORIES.

Total premiums received from the organization of the company to date	$25,856 23
Total losses paid from the organization of the company to date	2,944 45
Total amount of losses incurred during the year	2,119 45
Total amount of the company's stock owned by the directors, at par value	40,400 00
Total dividends payable in stock	1,459 83
Total amount loaned to officers and directors	650 00
Total amount loaned to stockholders, not officers	12,368 58
Amount deposited in different states and countries, for the security of policy holders, Wisconsin	10,140 00

NORTHWESTERN NATIONAL INSURANCE COMPANY.

MILWAUKEE, WIS.

[Incorporated in 1869. Commenced business in 1869.]

ALEXANDER MITCHELL, *President*. FRANK H. WHIPP, *Secretary, pro tem.*

I. CAPITAL.

Capital authorized	$1,000,000 00
Capital actually paid up in cash	235,500 00

II. ASSETS.

Stocks and bonds, market value	$248,050 00
Cash in the company's principal office, and in bank	37,465 19
Cash in hands of agents	10,091 07
Interest due and accrued, not included in market value	4,000 00
Gross premiums in due course of collection	39,636 95
Bills receivable, not matured, taken for fire, marine and inland risks	19,718 77
Bills receivable, taken for fire, marine and inland risks, past due	617 00
All other property belonging to the company, viz.: salvage on losses paid, $7,008.16; due from stockholders, $3,550; office furniture, $2,500; reinsurance due on losses paid, $10,648.22; total	23,706 38
Aggregate of all the assets of the company, stated at their actual value.	$383,285 36

III. LIABILITIES.

Losses unadjusted, including all reported and supposed losses..	$25,625 00	....
Losses resisted, including interest, costs and expenses.........	7,500 00	....
Total gross amount of claims for losses......................	$33,125 00	....
Deduct reinsurance and salvage thereon	11,375 00	....
Net amount of unpaid losses and claims.................		$21,750 00
Reinsurance at 50 per cent. of premium, on fire risks, under one year..	$53,676 86	....
Reinsurance, *pro rata*, on fire risks running more than one year.	7,794 25	....
Reinsurance at 50 per cent. of premium on inland navigation risks	7,030 00	....
Amount required to safely reinsure all outstanding risks ...		68,501 11
Total liabilities, except capital stock..................................		$90,251 11
Capital stock actually paid up in cash..................................		235,500 00
Surplus beyond capital stock..		57,534 25
Aggregate amount of all liabilities, including capital stock and net surplus..		$383,285 36

IV. INCOME DURING THE YEAR.

	Fire.	Marine and Inland.	
Gross premium received in cash	$196,180 21	$78,158 38	....
Gross cash received on bills and notes taken for premiums	....	18,477 69	....
Gross cash received for premiums............	$196,180 21	$96,636 02	....
Deduct re-insurance, rebate and returned premiums..................................	19,561 73	27,739 03	....
Net cash received for premiums...........	$176,618 48	$68,896 99	*$245,515 47
Bills and notes received during the year for premiums, remaining unpaid...		$20,335 77	
Received for interest and dividends on stocks and bonds, and from all other sources..			$11,023 99
Aggregate amount of income received during the year in cash........			*$256,539 46

V. EXPENDITURES DURING THE YEAR.

	Fire.	Marine and Inland.	
Gross amount paid for losses..........	$96,934 50	$52,994 27	....
Deduct salvage and re-insurance	6 01	10,565 83	....
Net amount paid during the year for losses	$96,928 49	$42,428 44	$139,356 93
Paid for commmissions and brokerage			29 789 62
Salaries and all other charges of officers, clerks, agents and all other employes			13,015 24
Paid for State, National and local taxes..			3,929 38
All other payments, viz: revenue stamps, $797.80; postage, $622.22; exchange; $255.85; other expenses, $14,016.17; total			15,692 09
Aggregate amount of expenditure during the year, in cash............			$201,783 94

VI. MISCELLANEOUS.

	Fire Risks.	Premiums thereon.	Marine & Inland Risks.	Premiums thereon.
In force, December 31, 1871.........	$4,844,173	$68,023 51	$21,860	$670 78
Written during the year............	12,542,298	196,180 21	11,801,263	116,971 79
Total............................	$17,386,471	$264,203 72	$11,823,123	$117,642 57
Deduct those terminated........	10,543,698	144,422 01	11,560,323	103,582 57
Net amount in force, Dec. 31, 1872........................	$6,842,773	$119,781 71	$262,800	$14,060 00
In force, having not more than one year to run	$5,947,975	$108,808,41	$262,800	$14,060 00
Having more than one year and not more than three years to run.........................	736,943	8,324 26	....	....

*Of this amount $39,636 95 is in course of collection.

Having more than three years to run	157,855	2,654 04	....	....
Net amount in force	$6,842,773	$119,781 71	$262,800	$14,060 00

GENERAL INTERROGATORIES.

Total premiums received from the organization of the company to date	$658,088 91
Total losses paid from the organization of the company to date	451,075 61
Total amount of losses incurred during the year	85,989 56
Total amount of the company's stock owned by the directors, at par value	139,102 00
Total dividend payable in stock	37,500 00

BUSINESS IN THE STATE OF WISCONSIN, DURING THE YEAR 1872.

	Fire.	Marine and Inland.	Aggregate.
Risks taken	$5,577,654 00	$7,308,406 00	$12,886,060 00
Premiums received	78,463 39	62,385 04	140,848 43
Losses paid on risks taken	28,322 82	16,534 55	44,857 37
Losses incurred during the year, in Wisconsin	....	....	51,968 37
Taxes on premiums, paid to the State of Wisconsin	....	....	1,894 40
Taxes on premiums, paid to fire departments in Wisconsin	....	....	782 01

WISCONSIN MUTUAL COMPANIES.

CONCORDIA MUTUAL FIRE INSURANCE COMPANY.

MILWAUKEE, WIS.

[Incorporated in 1870. Commenced business in 1870.]

CHAS. EISSFELDT, *President.* GUSTAV WOLLAEGER, *Secretary.*

I. CAPITAL.

Capital authorized	$500,000 00
Capital actually paid up in cash	7,420 00

II. ASSETS.

Loans on bond and mortgage, (first liens)		$9,700 00
Interest accrued on bond and mortgage loans		247 17
Stocks and bonds, market value		5,600 00
Cash in the company's principal office and in bank		12,025 17
Gross premiums in due course of collection		3,382 25
Bills receivable, not matured, taken for fire risks		216 90
Premium notes		17,246 67
All other property belonging to the company, viz: office furniture		700 00
Stockholders' notes given for capital subscribed	$66,780	
Aggregate of all the assets of the company, stated at their actual value		$49,118 16

III. LIABILITIES.

Reinsurance at 50 per cent. of prem. on fire risks under one year	$3,236 40	
Reinsurance, *pro rata*, on fire risks running more than one year	15,521 85	
Amount required to safely reinsure all outstanding risks		$18,758 25
All other demands against the company, viz: due to agents		591 88
Total liabilities, except capital stock		$19,350 13
Capital stock actually paid up in cash and premium notes		24,666 67
Surplus beyond capital stock and premium notes		5,101 36
Aggregate amount of all liabilities including capital stock, premium notes and net surplus		$49,118 00

IV. INCOME DURING THE YEAR.

Gross premiums received in cash, fire	$16,995 23	
Gross cash rec'd on bills and notes taken for prem's	157 62	
Gross cash received for premiums	$17,152 85	
Deduct reinsurance, rebate and returned premiums	309 50	
Net cash received for premiums		$16,843 35
Received for interest on bonds and mortgaaes		1,210 21
Gross premiums remaining unpaid	$3,599 15	
Received for increased capital	1,150 00	
Aggregate amount of income received during the year in cash		$18,033 56

V. EXPENDITURES DURING THE YEAR.

Gross amount paid for losses, fire	$1,601 00	
Net amount paid during the year for losses		$1,601 00
Paid for commissions and brokerage		2,645 97
Salaries and all other charges of officers, clerks, agents and all other employes.		1,703 35
Paid for state, national and local taxes		350 27
All other payments, viz.: For stationery, printing and traveling expenses, $1,120.46; usage of office furniture, $92.30; difference in market value of U. S. bonds, $181.25; total		1,894 01
Aggregate amount of expenditures during the year, in cash		$7,694 60

VI. MISCELLANEOUS.

	Fire risks.	Premiums thereon.
In force, December 31, 1871	$993,118	$15,733 84
Written during 1872	1,151,670	19,073 55
Total	$2,144,788	$34,807 39
Deduct those terminated	224,437	3,632 65
Net amount in force, Dec. 31, 1872	$1,920,351	$31,174 74
In force, having not more than one year to run	$643,760	$10,136 43
Having more than one year and not more than three years to run	1,095,249	18,440 32
Having more than three years to run	181,342	2,597 99
Net amount in force	$1,920,351	$31,174 74

GENERAL INTERROGATORIES.

Total premiums received from the organization of the company to date	$32,616 88
Total losses paid from the organization of the company to date	2,332 90
Total amount of losses incurred during the year	1,601 00
Total amount of the company's stock owned by the directors, at par value	11,700 00

DODGE COUNTY MUTUAL INSURANCE COMPANY.

WAUPUN, WIS.

[Incorporated in 1852. Commenced business in 1852.]

WILLIAM HOBKIRK, *President.* J. A. BAKER, *Secretary.*

I. CAPITAL.

Capital authorized	Mutual.

II. ASSETS.

Value of real estate owned by the company, less incumbrances	$5,100 00
Loans on bond and mortgage, (first liens)	1,178 00
Interest accrued on bond and mortgage loans	94 35
Loan on endorsed note	250 00
Cash in the company's principal office and in bank	12,524 40
Due on assessment of premium notes	15,825 75
Interest due and accrued on collateral loans	2 25
Gross premiums in due course of collection	9,775 10

Bills receivable, not matured, taken for fire risks	22,000 00
Bills receivable, taken for fire risks, past due	40,372 73
Premium notes, subject to assessment	53,066 71
All other property belonging to the company, viz.: salvage on losses paid, $165.35; office furniture, $1,398.98; total	1,504 33
Gross amount of all the assets of the company	$161,193 63
Amount which should be deducted from the above assets, on account of bad and doubtful debts and securities, viz: from item No. 15, $3,200; No. 17, $750; total deductions	3,950 00
Aggregate of all the assets of the company, stated at their actual value	$157,243 63

III. LIABILITIES.

Losses adjusted and unpaid	$1,989 78	....
Losses unadjusted, including all reported and supposed losses	1,130 00	....
Losses resisted, including interest, costs and expenses	450 00	....
Total gross amount of claims for losses	$3,569 78	....
Deduct salvage thereon	835 00	....
Net amount of unpaid losses and claims		$2,734 78
Reinsurance at 50 per cent. of premium, on fire risks, under one year	$153 20	....
Reinsurance, *pro rata*, on fire risks running more than one year	71,659 82	....
Amount required to safely reinsure all outstanding risks		71,813 02
All other demands against the company, viz: due and to become due to agents		1,476 12
Total liabilities, except premium notes		$76,023 92
Premium notes		53,066 71
Surplus beyond premium notes		28,132 99
Aggregate amt of all liabilities, including prem. notes and net surplus		$157,243 63

IV. INCOME DURING THE YEAR.

Gross premiums received in cash, fire	$3,871 99	....
Gross cash received on bills and notes taken for premiums	61,045 11	....
Gross cash received for premiums	$64,917 10	....
Deduct reinsurance, rebate and returned premiums	9,354 84	....
Net cash received for premiums		$55,562 26
Bills and notes received during the year for premiums, remaining unpaid	$38,473 00	....
Received for interest on bonds and mortgages		$495 50
Received for interest on bills receivable, and from other sources		1,382 88
Income received from all other sources, viz.: rents, $150; assessment on premium notes, $5,349.59; total		5,499 59
Premium notes received during the year	$3,840 00	....
Aggregate amount of income received during the year in cash		$62,940 23

V. EXPENDITURES DURING THE YEAR.

Net amount paid for losses, fire (including $19,772 by northern fires of 1871)	$50,901 63
Paid for commissions and brokerage	13,235 63
Salaries and all other charges of officers, clerks, agents and all other employes	4,500 00
Paid for state, national and local taxes	1,234 02
All other payments, viz.: printing, $1,763.65; express, exchange, collections and postage, $2,490.77; stationery, house plates and advertising, $1,280.60; total	5,535 02
Aggregate amount of expenditures during the year, in cash	$75,406 35

VI. MISCELLANEOUS.

	Fire risks.	Premiums thereon.
In force, December 31, 1871	$12,364,650	$154,556 90
Written during the year	3,086,065	52,432 84
Total	$15,450,715	$206,989 74
Deduct those terminated	3,990,488	51,922 71
Net amount in force, December 31, 1872	$11,460,227	$155,067 03

In force, having not more than one year to run	$3,690,594	$49,243 66
Having more than one year and not more than three years to run	4,348,760	56,572 22
Having more than three years to run	3,420,873	49,251 15
Net amount in force	$11,460,227	$155,067 03

GENERAL INTERROGATORIES.

Total premiums received from the organization of the company to date	$574,933 92
Total losses paid from the organization of the company to date	227,238 62
Total amount of losses incurred during the year	33,864 46
Taxes on premiums, paid to the state of Wisconsin	559 47
Taxes on premiums, paid to fire departments in Wisconsin	9 74

GERMANTOWN FARMERS' MUTUAL INSURANCE COMPANY.

GERMANTOWN, WIS.

[Incorporated in 1854. Commenced business in 1854.]

GEORGE REGENFUSS, *President.* HENRY FLEISCHER, *Secretary.*

I. CAPITAL.

Capital authorized	Mutual.

II. ASSETS.

Value of real estate owned by the company, less incumbrances	$6,500 00
Loans on bond and mortgage, (first liens)	38,108 40
Interest due on bond and mortgage loans	1,688 82
Interest accrued on bond and mortgage loans	1,800 00
Loans on prommissory notes	10,282 32
Cash belonging to the company, deposited in bank	6,455 68
Gross premiums in due course of collection	13,809 45
Premium notes	144,045 69
All other property belonging to the company, viz: office furniture	800 00
Aggregate of all the assets of the company, stated at their actual value	$213,490 36

III. LIABILITIES.

Reinsurance at 50 per cent. of premium, on fire risks, under one year	$918 10	....
Reinsurance *pro rata*, on fire risks running more than one year	48,381 90	....
Amount required to safely reinsure all outsanding risks		$49,300 00
Total liabilities, except premium notes		$49,300 00
Premium notes		144,045 69
Surplus beyond premium notes		20,144 67
Aggregate amount of all liabilities, including premium notes and net surplus		$213,490 36

IV. INCOME DURING THE YEAR.

Gross premiums received in cash, fire	$94,427 88	....
Deduct reinsurance, rebate and returned premiums	1,112 15	....
Net cash received for premiums		$93,315 73

Bills and notes received during the year for premiums, remaining unpaid	13,809 45	....
Received for interest on bonds and mortgages and notes		2,809 04
Premium notes received	$44,674 69	....
Aggregate amount of income received during the year in cash		$26,124 77

V. EXPENDITURES DURING THE YEAR.

Net amount paid during the year for losses, fire	$12,322 17
Salaries and all other charges of officers, agents and all other employes	2,826 52
Paid for state, national and local taxes	425 67
All other payments	3,121 01
Aggregate amount of expenditures during the year, in cash	$18,695 37

VI. MISCELLANEOUS.

	Fire Risks.	Premiums thereon.
In force, December 31, 1871	$6,594,789	$164,941 33
Written during the year	1,953,770	30,320 64
Total	$8,548,559	$195,261 97
Deduct those terminated	1,862,741	102,617 11
Net amount in force, Dec. 31, 1872	$6,685,818	$92,644 86
In force, having not more than one year to run	$1,536,377	$21,253 48
Having more than one year and not more than three years to run	3,226,229	42,437 90
Having more than three years to run	1,923,212	28,953 48
Net amount in force	$6,685,818	$92,644 86

HERMAN FARMERS' MUTUAL INSURANCE COMPANY.

HERMAN, WIS.

[Incorporated in 1856. Commenced business in 1857.]

JOHN ZIRBEL, *President.* JOHN STEINER, *Secretary.*

I. CAPITAL.

Capital authorized	Mutual.

II. ASSETS.

Loans on bond and mortgage, (first lien)	$6,800 00
Interest accrued on bond and mortgage loans	500 00
Loans on personal security	2,335 00
Cash in the company's principal office	1,989 50
Premium notes in force	20,597 41
Interest accrued on loans	144 25
Gross premiums in due course of collection	574 24
Bills receivable, not matured, taken for fire risks	693 33
Bills receivable, taken for fire risks, past due	2,240 61
All other property belonging to the company, viz: office furniture	300 00
Aggregate of all the assets of the company, stated at their actual value	$36,174 34

III. LIABILITIES.

Losses adjusted and unpaid	$742 00	
Net amount of unpaid losses and claims		$742 00
Reinsurance at 50 per cent. of premium, on fire risks, under one year	$229 71	
Reinsurance, *pro rata*, on fire risks running more than one year,	5,197 33	
Amount required to safely reinsure all outstanding risks		5,427 04
All other demands against the company, viz: commissions to agents		73 61
Total liabilities		$6,242 65
Premium notes		20,597 41
Surplus beyond premium notes		9,334 28
Aggregate amount of all liabilities including premium notes and net surplus		$36,174 34

IV. INCOME DURING THE YEAR.

Gross premiums received in cash, fire	$2,851 81	
Gross cash received on bills and notes taken for premiums	2,114 07	
Gross cash received for premiums	$4,965 88	
Deduct reinsurance, rebate and returned premiums	481,23	
Net cash received for premiums		$4,484 15
Received for interest on bonds and mortgages		600 75
Received for interest from all other sources		418 42
Gross premiums remaining unpaid	$3,508 18	
Premium notes received	6,311 27	
Aggregate amount of income received during the year in cash		$5,508 32

V. EXPENDITURES DURING THE YEAR.

Net amount paid during the year for losses, fire	$1,574 90
Paid for commissions and brokerage	983 54
Salaries and all other charges of officers, clerks, agents and all other employes	233 27
Paid for State, National and local taxes	136 65
All other payments, viz: postage, $20 95; office sign, $14; traveling expenses, printing, stationery and advertising, $89 22; lost on notes, $61 95; total	186 12
Aggregate amount of expenditures during the year, in cash	$3,114 48

VI. MISCELLANEOUS.

	Fire Risks.	Premiums thereon.
In force, December 31, 1871	$904,728	$6,382 43
Written during the year	442,986	5,257 01
Total	$1,347,714	$11,639 44
Deduct those terminated	141,670	785 35
Net amount in force, Dec. 31, 1872	$1,206,044	$10,854 09
In force, having not more than one year to run	$72,134	$461 67
Having more than one year and not more three years to run	440,559	3,251 99
Having more than three years to run	693,351	7,140 43
Net amount in force	$1,206,044	$10,854 09

General Interrogatories.

Total premiums received from the organization of the company to date	$15,740 29
Total losses paid from the organization of the company to date	4,927 50
Total amount of losses incurred during the year	1,971 90
Total amount loaned to officers and directors	4,300 00
Taxes on premiums, paid to the State of Wisconsin	60 75

MADISON MUTUAL INSURANCE COMPANY.

MADISON, WIS.

[Incorporated in 1851. Commenced business in 1851.]

DAVID ATWOOD, *President.* D. WORTHINGTON, *Secretary.*

I. CAPITAL.

Capital actually paid up in cash	Mutual.

II. ASSETS.

Value of real estate owned by the company, less incumbrances	$19,819 84
Loans on bond and mortgage, (first liens)	6,095 55
Loans on bond and mortgage. (first liens), upon which more than one year's interest is due	4,106 50
Interest due on bond and mortgage loans	768 43
Interest accrued on bond and mortgage loans	419 57
Stocks and bonds, market value	125,000 00
Cash in company's principal office, and in bank	11,486 48
Interest due and accrued, not included in market value	2,504 58
Gross premiums in due course of collection	46,018 50
Bills receivable, taken for fire risks	20,521 98
Assessment in process of collection	9,882 77
Premium notes	583,111 48
All other property belonging to the company, viz.: Furniture and fixtures, $2,115.53; rents, $81.25; due from other sources, $747.55; total	2,944 33
Aggregate of all the assets of the company, stated at their actual value	$832,679 96

III. LIABILITIES.

Losses adjusted and unpaid	$2,206 65	
Losses unadjusted, including all reported and supposed losses	7,654 81	
Losses resisted, including interest, costs and expenses	2,115 75	
Net amount of unpaid losses and claims		$11,977 21
Reinsurance at 50 per cent. of premium, on fire risks, under one year	$1,416 67	
Reinsurance, *pro rata*, on fire risks running more than one year	218,977 33	
Amount required to safely reinsure all outstanding risks		$220,394 00
Due and accrued for salaries, rent and other expenses		703 20
All other demands against the company, viz.: Commissions to agents		575 86
Total liabilities		$233,650 27
Premium notes		583,111 48
Surplus beyond premium notes		15,918 21
Aggregate amount of all liabilities, including premium notes and net surplus		$832,679 96

IV. INCOME DURING THE YEAR.

Gross premiums received in cash, fire	$84,651 50	
Gross cash received on bills and notes taken for premiums	21,273 76	
Gross cash received for premiums	$105,925 26	
Deduct returned premiums	6,279 06	
Net cash received for premiums		$99,646 20
Bills and notes received during the year for premiums remaining unpaid	$34,460 73	
Received for interest from all sources		15,091 29
Received from assessments		15,173 43
Income received from all other sources, viz: rents, $518 65; recording fees, $86 75. Total		600 40
Received of premium notes	$125,681 48	
Aggregate amount of income received during the year in cash		$130,511 32

V. EXPENDITURES DURING THE YEAR.

Net amount paid during the year for losses, fire	$122,908 84
Paid for commissions and brokerage	26,602 87
Salaries and all other charges of officers, clerks, agents and all other employes	22,930 46
Paid for State, National and local taxes	1,142 00
Paid for collecting assessment	568 95
All other payments, viz: advertising, $2,550 52; exchange, 104 48; expense, $2,595 47; office expenses, $494 26; postage, $1,923 45; printing and stationery, $1,273 61. Total	8,941 79
Aggregate amount of expenditures during the year, in cash	$183,095 91

VI. MISCELLANEOUS.

	Fire Risks.	Premiums thereon.
In force, December 31, 1871	$46,203,646 00	$481,321 15
Written during the year and restored	11,288,677 00	132,607 89
Total	$57,492,323 00	$613,929 04
Deduct those terminated	11,558,298 00	122,399 56
Net amount in force, Dec. 31, 1872	$45,934,025 00	$491,529 48
In force, having not more than one year to run	$10,488,357 61	$107,598 78
Having more than one year and not more than three years to run	22,753,180 46	230,954 53
Having more than three years to run	12,692,486 93	152,976 22
Net amount in force	$45,934,025 00	$491,529 48

GENERAL INTERROGATORIES.

Total amount of losses incurred during the year	$106,958 23

MILWAUKEE MECHANICS' MUTUAL INSURANCE COMPANY.

MILWAUKEE, WIS.

[Incorporated in 1852. Commenced business in 1852.]

CHRISTIAN PREUSSER, *President.* ADOLF J. CRAMER, *Secretary.*

I. CAPITAL.

Capital authorized	Mutual.

II. ASSETS.

Value of real estate owned by the company, less incumbrances	$4,546 25
Loans on bond and mortgage (first liens)	6,615 39
Interest accrued on bond and mortgage loans	288 28
Stocks and bonds, market value	175,464 13
Cash in company's principal office, and in bank	23,500 90
Interest accrued, not included in market value	190 63
Gross premiums in due course of collection	15,189 84
Bills receivable, not matured, taken for fire risks	641 00
Premium notes in force	337,616 94
All other property belonging to the company, viz: office furniture	1,189 00
Aggregate of all the assets of the company, stated at their actual value	$565,241 86

III. LIABILITIES.

Losses resisted, including interest, costs and expenses	$2,620 00	
Net amount of unpaid losses and claims		$2,620 00
Reinsurance at 50 per cent of premium, on fire risks under one year	$40,619 60	
Reinsurance, *pro rata*, on fire risks running more than one year	189,981 40	
Amount required to safely reinsure all outstanding risks		180,601 00
Total liabilities		$183,221 00
Premium notes		337,616 94
Surplus beyond premium notes		44,403 92
Aggregate amt. of all liabilities including prem. notes and net surplus		$565,241 86

IV. INCOME DURING THE YEAR.

Gross premiums received in cash, fire	$157,528 59	
Gross cash received on bills and notes taken for premiums	5,883 97	
Gross cash received for premiums	$163,412 56	
Deduct reinsurance, rebate and returned premiums	7,594 39	
Net cash received for premiums		$155,818 17
Bills and notes received during the year for premiums, remaining unpaid	$15,189 84	
Received for interest on bonds and mortgages		9,516 16
Income received from all other sources, viz.: fees		676 22
Premium notes received	$85,906 94	
Aggregate amount of income received during the year in cash		$166,010 55

V. EXPENDITURES DURING THE YEAR.

Net amount paid during the year for losses, fire	$74,330 43
Paid for commissions and brokerage	33,684 67
Salaries and all other charges of officers, clerks, agents and all other employes	11,708 00
Paid for state, national and local taxes	5,856 87
All other payments, viz.: office expenses, rent, stationery, advertising, etc.	11,409 41
Aggregate amount of expenditures during the year in cash	$136,984 38

VI. MISCELLANEOUS.

	Fire risks.	Premiums thereon.
In force, December 31, 1871	$20,033,668	$306,627 30
Written during the year	9,722,887	172,717 98
Total	$29,756,555	$479,345 28
Deduct those terminated	7,370,975	124,142 75
In force, December 31, 1872	$22,385,580	$355,202 48
Deduct amount reinsured	10,500	98 75
Net amount in force	$22,375,080	$355,103 73
In force, having not more than one year to run	$5,561,200	$81,239 21
Having more than one year to run	16,824,380	273,963 27
Net amount in force	$22,385,580	$355,202 48

General Interrogatories.

Total premiums received from the organization of the company to date	$800,438 58
Total losses paid from the organization of the company to date	341,244 83
Total amount of losses incurred during the year	53,599 43

Business in the State of Wisconsin, during the Year 1872.

Risks taken	$8,630,686 00
Premiums received	147,880 13
Losses paid on risks taken	73,663 77
Losses incurred during the year, in Wisconsin	52,983 77
Taxes on premiums, paid to the state of Wisconsin	2,468 15
Taxes on premiums, paid to fire departments in Wisconsin	950 75

VERNON COUNTY SCANDINAVIAN MUTUAL FIRE INSURANCE COMPANY.

CHASEBURG, WIS.

[Incorporated in 1867. Commenced business in 1870.]

A. NELSON, *President*. OLE JOHNSON, *Secretary*.

I. CAPITAL.

Capital authorized	Mutual.

II. ASSETS.

Loans on personal security	$1,041 64
Cash in company's principal office	50 00
Interest due and accrued on loan notes	45 09
Gross premiums in due course of collection	150 00
Aggregate of all the assets of the company, stated at their actual value	$1,286 73

III. LIABILITIES.

Reinsurance, *pro rata*, on fire risks running more than one year	$534 96	
Am't required to safely reinsure all outstanding risks		$534 96
Due and accrued for salaries, rent and other expenses		31 80
Total liabilities		$566 76
Surplus beyond liabilities		719 97
Aggregate amount of all liabilities, including net surplus		$1,286 73

IV. INCOME DURING THE YEAR.

Net cash received for premiums, fire		$105 88
Gross premiums, remaining unpaid	$150 00	
Received for interest on loans		50 00
Aggregate amount of income received during the year in cash		$155 88

V. EXPENDITURES DURING THE YEAR.

Net amount paid during the year for losses, fire	$10 00
Salaries and all other charges of officers, clerks, agents and all other employes	49 25
Paid for state, national and local taxes	12 78
All other payments	26 05
Aggregate amount of expenditures during the year, in cash	$98 08

VI. MISCELLANEOUS.

	Fire Risks.	Premiums thereon.
In force, December 31, 1871	$50,248	$5 4 18
Written during the year	48,955	255 88
Total	$99,203	$760 06
Deduct those terminated	35,605	225 10
Net amount in force, December 31, 1872	$63,598	$534 96

In force, having more than one year and not more than three years to run	$24,485	$153 06
Having more than three years to run	39,113	381 90
Net amount in force	$63,598	$534 96

GENERAL INTERROGATORIES.

Total premiums received from the organization of the company to date	$1,610 51
Total losses paid from the organization of the company to date	415 80
Total amount of losses incurred during the year	10 00
Total amount loaned to officers and directors	155 00
Total amount loaned to policy holders, not officers	886 64

MUTUAL HAIL INSURANCE COMPANY,

OF MILWAUKEE, WISCONSIN.

Net assets, January 1, 1872		$1,017 69
RECEIPTS during the year—		
Cash premiums	$9,009 33	....
Premium notes	4,430 78	....
From other sources	254 70	....
		13,694 81
Total		$14,712 50
DISBURSEMENTS—		
Losses by hail, paid	$2,662 83	....
Cash premiums refunded	11 54	....
Commissions and salaries to agents	952 81	....
Revenue stamps	275 15	....
Salaries	1,667 00	....
Traveling expenses, appraisers' fees and general expenses	1,956 62	....
		7,525 95
Net assets, January 1, 1873		$7,186 55
Consisting of		
Premium notes	$4,430 78	....
Office furniture	280 00	....
Cash on hand and in bank	852 60	....
Due from agents	1,628 17	....
		$7,186 55

Number of policies issued during the year, 2434.
Amount of risks thereon, $1,430,875.18.

CARL MIEDING, *Secretary.* SAMUEL RINDSKOPF, *President.*

COMPANIES OF OTHER STATES.

ÆTNA INSURANCE COMPANY.

HARTFORD, CONN.

[Incorporated in 1819. Commenced business in 1819.]

LUCIUS J. HENDEE, *President.* JOTHAM GOODNOW, *Secretary.*

Attorney to accept service of process in Wisconsin, CHAS. W. POTTER, Milwaukee.

I. CAPITAL.

Capital authorized	$8,000,000 00
Capital actually paid up in cash	2,000,000 00

II. ASSETTS.

Value of real estate owned by the company, less incumbrances	$405,000 00
Loans on bond and mortgage, (first liens)	93,330 00
Interest accrued on bond and mortgage loans	1,589 49
Stocks and bonds, market value	3,668,250 69
Cash loans secured by collaterals	57,140 00
Cash in the company's principal office and in bank	223,632 37
Interest due and accrued, not included in market value	16,305 28
Interest due and accrued on collateral loans	3,084 94
Net premiums in due course of collection	928,097 73
Aggregate of all the assets of the company, stated at their actual value	$5,396,380 50

III. LIABILITIES.

Losses adjusted and unpaid	$286,452 79	
Losses unadjusted, including all reported and supposed losses	619,787 84	
Losses resisted, including interest, costs and expenses	32,630 45	
Net amount of unpaid losses and claims		$938,871 08
Reinsurance at 50 per cent. of prem. on fire risks, under one year	$1,226,721 54	
Reinsurance *pro rata*, on fire risks running more than one year	797,931 38	
Reinsurance at 50 per cent. of premium on inland navigation risks	17,936 72	
Amt. required to safely reinsure all outstanding risks		2,042,589 64
Due and accrued for salaries, rent and other expenses		500 00
Due and to become due for borrowed money		401,672 21
Total liabilities, except capital stock		$3,383,632 93
Capital stock actually paid in cash		2,000,000 00
Surplus beyond capital stock		12,747 57
Aggregate amount of all liabilities, including capital stock and net surplus		$5,396,380 50

IV. INCOME DURING THE YEAR.

	Fire.	Inland.	
Gross premiums received in cash	$4,581,855 08	$453,380 40	....
Deduct re-insurance, rebate and returned premiums	268,498 26	39,301 87	....
Net cash received for premiums	$4,318,356 82	$414,078 53	[1] $4,727,435 35
Received for interest on bonds and mortgages			5,173 75
Received for interest and dividends on stocks and bonds, and from all other sources			298,261 85
Income received from all other sources, viz.: rents			11,626 57
Aggregate amount of income received during the year in cash			$5,042,497 52

V. EXPENDITURES DURING THE YEAR.

	Fire.	Inland.	
Gross amount paid for losses	$4,813,989 45	$253,024 44	....
Net amount paid during the year for losses			$4,567,013 89
Paid for commissions and brokerage			677,256 81
Salaries and all other charges of officers, clerks, agents and all other employes			359,108 01
Paid for state, national and local taxes			97,451 90
All other payments, viz.: interest on borrowed money			24,465 54
Aggregate amount of expenditures during the year, in cash			$5,725,290 15

VI. MISCELLANEOUS.

	Fire risks.	Premiums thereon.	Inland risks.	Premiums thereon.
In force, December 31, 1871	$289,523,679	$3,634,186 29	$561,308	$36,169 72
Written during the year	393,824,900	4,581,855 08	50,167,146	453,380 40
Total	$683,348,579	$8,216,041 37	$50,728,454	$489,550 12
Deduct those terminated	363,500,742	4,290,655 76	49,947,138	447,949 68
In force, December 31, 1872	$319,847,837	$3,925,385 61	$781,316	$41,600 44
Deduct amount re-insured	1,200,000	13,500 00	134,000	5,727 00
Net amount in force	$318,647,837	$3,911,885 61	$647,316	$35,873 44
In force, having more than one year to run	$209,867,101	$2,453,443 08	$647,316	$35,873 44
Having more than one year and not more than three years to run	72,207,811	943,128 73	....	....
Having more than three years to run	36,572,925	515,313 80	....	....
Net amount in force	$318,647,837	$3,911,885 61	$647,316	$35,873 44

General Interrogatories.

Total premiums received from the organization of the company to date	$57,590,381 11
Total losses paid from the organization of the company to date	37,574,024 29
Total dividends declared since the company commenced business	6,169,960 00
Total amount of losses incurred during the year	4,527,918 72
Total amount of the company's stock owned by the directors, at par value	287,400 00
Total dividends payable in stock	2,805,000 00
Total amount loaned to officers and directors	8,000 00
Total amount loaned to stockholders, not officers	119,470 00
Amount deposited in different states and countries, for the security of policy holders, $50,000, deposited as follows: in the state of Tennessee, $20,000; South Carolina, $20,000; Alabama, $10,000.	

Business in the State of Wisconsin, during the Year 1872.

	Fire.	Inland.	Aggregate.
Risks taken	$7,865,050 00	$5,565,117 00	$13,430,167 00
Premiums received	116,637 63	42,756 20	159,393 83
Losses paid on risks taken	56,666 79	18,124 00	74,790 79
Losses incurred during the year, in Wisconsin			68,008 98
Taxes on premiums, paid to the state of Wisconsin			2,389 50
Taxes on premiums, paid to fire departments in Wisconsin			2,431 11

[1] Of which $928,097 73 is in course of collection.

ALEMANNIA FIRE INSURANCE COMPANY.

CLEVELAND, OHIO.

[Incorporated in 1870. Commenced business in 1870.]

DR. WM. MEYER, *President*. ISIDORE WOLF, *Ass't. Secretary*.

Attorney to accept service of process in Wisconsin, ADDISON B. MYERS, Milwaukee.

I. CAPITAL.

Capital authorized	$250,000 00
Capital actually paid up in cash	250,000 00

II. ASSETS.

Loans on bond and mortgage, (first liens)	$36,970 00
Loans on bond and mortgage, (first liens), upon which more than one year's interest is due	198,225 00
Interest due on bond and mortgage loans	34,251 50
Interest accrued on bond and mortgage loans	2,118 06
Cash in company's principal office and in bank	54,060 57
Gross premiums in due course of collection	70,622 99
Bills receivable	6,322 75
All other property belonging to the company	25 00
Aggregate of all the assets of the company, stated at their actual value	$402,595 87

III. LIABILITIES.

Losses adjusted and unpaid	$18,549 00	
Losses unadjusted, including all reported and supposed losses	10,500 00	
Total gross amount of claims for losses	$29,049 00	
Deduct reinsurance thereon	11,500 00	
Net amount of unpaid losses and claims		$17,549 00
Reinsurance at 50 per cent. of prem.; on fire risks, under one year	$84,710 50	
Reinsurance, *pro rata*, on fire risks running more than one year	12,225 25	
Amount required to safely reinsure all outstanding risks		96,935 75
Due and accrued for salaries, rent and other expenses		136 30
All other demands against the company, viz.: taxes, $1,880 80; commissions, $14,124 60; total		16,005 40
Total liabilities except capital stock		$130,626 45
Capital stock actually paid up in cash		250,000 00
Surplus beyond capital stock		21,969 42
Aggregate amount of all liabilities, including capital stock and net surplus		$402,595 87

IV. INCOME DURING THE YEAR.

Gross premiums received in cash (fire)	$340,481 57	
Deduct reinsurance, rebate and returned premiums	85,010 89	
Net cash received for premiums		$255,470 68
Received from interest and dividends from all sources		7,050 77
Income received from all other sources, viz: rents, $325; ret. com's; $390 75 total		715 75
Gross premiums remaining unpaid	$70,622 99	
Received for assessment on capital	85,681 00	
Aggregate amount of income received during the year in cash		$263,237 20

V. EXPENDITURES DURING THE YEAR.

Net amount paid during the year for losses (fire)	$198,089 90
Paid for commissions and brokerage	62,746 13
Salaries and all other charges of officers, clerks, agents and all other employes	5,086 04
Paid for state, national and local taxes	5,808 55
All other payments, viz: interest on borrowed money, $2,098 33; expenses, $15,894 25; total	17,992 58
Aggregate amount of expenditures during the year, in cash	$289,710 60

VI. MISCELLANEOUS.

	Fire Risks.	Premiums thereon.
In force, December 31, 1871	$7,377,912 35	$127,552 08
Written during 1872	18,457,100 23	340,481 57
Total	$25,835,012 58	$468,033 65
Deduct those terminated	11,375,232 48	243,925 50
In force, December 31, 1872	$14,459,780 10	$224,108 15
Deduct amount reinsured	3,733,023 00	24,712 15
Net amount in force	$10,726,757 10	$199,396 00
In force, having not more than one year to run	$7,419,547 10	$169,421 00
Having more than one year and not more than three years to run	2,562,810 00	22,247 00
Having more than three years to run	744,400 00	7,728 00
Net amount in force	$10,726,757 10	$199,396 00

General Interrogatories.

Total premiums received from the organization of the company to date	$452,310 80
Total losses paid from the organization of the company to date	368,377 06
Total amount of losses incurred during the year	227,131 20
Total amount of the company's stock owned by the directors, at par value	55,000 00
Total amount loaned to stockholders, not officers	206,000 00

Business in the State of Wisconsin, during the Year 1872.

Fire risks taken	$349,172 00
Premiums received	7,856 00
Losses paid on risks taken	4,395 82
Losses incurred during the year, in Wisconsin	4,395 82

ALLEMANNIA FIRE INSURANCE COMPANY.

Pittsburg, Pa.

[Incorporated in 1868. Commenced business in 1868.]

ROBERT C. SCHMERTZ, *President*. CHAS. F. HERROSEE, *Secretary*.

Attorney to accept service of process in Wisconsin, J. O. Myers, Milwaukee.

I. CAPITAL.

Capital authorized	$300,000 00
Capital actually paid up in cash	150,000 00

II. ASSETS.

Loans on bond and mortgage (first liens)		$176,275 44
Interest due on bond and mortgage loans		667 82
Interest accrued on bond and mortgage loans		2,799 72
Stocks and bonds, market value		135 00
Cash in the company's principal office and in bank		37,721 88
Gross premiums in due course of collection		20,149 58
Bills receivable, not matured		16,190 81
All other property belonging to the company		30 00
Stockholders' notes for capital subscribed	$50,000 00	....
Aggregate of all assets of the company, stated at their actual value		$253,969 90

III. LIABILITIES.

Losses adjusted and unpaid	$1,730 32	....
Net amount of unpaid losses and claims		$1,730 32
Reinsurance at 50 per cent. of premium, on fire risks, under one year	$40,231 68	....
Reinsurance, *pro rata*, on fire risks running more than one year	17,989 85	....
Amount required to safely reinsure all outstanding risks		58,221 53
Total liabilities, except capital stock		$59,951 85
Capital stock actually paid up in cash		150,000 00
Surplus beyond capital stock		44,018 05
Aggregate amount of all liabilities, including capital stock and net surplus		$253,969 90

IV. INCOME DURING THE YEAR.

Gross premiums received in cash (fire)	$76,025 93	....
Deduct reinsurance, rebate and returned premiums	7,579 61	....
Net cash received for premiums		$68,446 32
Received for interest on bonds and mortgages		17,393 54
Income received from all other sources		20,000 00
Gross premiums remaining unpaid	$20,149 58	....
Aggregate amount of income received during the year in cash		$105,839 86

V. EXPENDITURES DURING THE YEAR.

Net amount paid during the year for losses, (fire)	$28,614 63
Cash dividends paid	10,000 00
Paid for commissions and brokerage	13,269 81
Salaries and all other charges of officers, clerks, agents and all other employes	5,638 24
Paid for state, national and local taxes	1,435 97
All other payments	6,832 15
Aggregate amount of expenditures during the year, in cash	$65,790 80

VI. MISCELLANEOUS.

	Fire Risks.	Premiums thereon.
In force, December 31, 1871	$4,935,054 37	$72,537 74
Written, during 1872	5,680,810 65	96,175 46
Total	$10,616,365 02	$168,713 20
Deduct those terminated	3,823,101 15	50,971 18
In force, December 31, 1872	$6,793,268 87	$117,742 02
Deduct the amount reinsured	105,750 00	1,300 15
Net amount in force	$6,687,518 97	$116,441 87
In force, having not more than one year to run	$4,508,515 31	$80,462 16
Having more than one year and not more than three years to run	2,188,998 66	35,979 71
Net amount in force	$6,687,518 97	$116,441 87

General Interrogatories.

Total premiums received from the organization of the company to date	$248,141 25
Total losses paid from the organization of the company to date	80,404 63
Total dividends declared since the company commenced business	25,000 00

Total amount of losses incurred during the year	28,614 63
Total amount of the company's stock owned by the directors, at par value	42,800 00
Total amount loaned to officers and directors	10,000 00
Total amount loaned to stockholders, not officers	4,000 00

BUSINESS IN THE STATE OF WISCONSIN, DURING THE YEAR 1872.

Risks taken, (fire)	$78,100 00
Premiums received	1,946 68
Taxes on premiums, paid to the state of Wisconsin	58 40

AMAZON INSURANCE COMPANY.

CINCINNATI, OHIO.

[Incorporated in 1871. Commenced business in 1871.]

GAZZAM GANO, *President*. BYRON D. WEST, *Secretary*.

Attorney to accept service of process in Wisconsin, W. B. HIBBARD, Milwaukee.

I. CAPITAL.

Capital authorized	$500,000 00
Capital actually paid up in cash	500,000 00

II. ASSETS.

Loans on bond and mortgage, (first liens)	$619,572 00
Interest accrued on bond and mortgage loans	28,433 83
Stocks and bonds, market value	248,411 37
Cash loans secured by collaterals	95 117 00
Cash in the company's principal office and in bank	13,581 77
Interest due and accrued, not included in market value	416 02
Interest due and accrued on collateral loans	833 33
Net premiums in due course of collection	66,170 36
Bills receivable, not matured, taken for fire, marine and inland risks	27,791 36
All other property belonging to the company, viz: personal property, $10,000; agency supplies, $17,371.85	27,371 85
Gross amount of all the assets of the company	$1,127,698 89
Amount which should be deducted from the above assets, on account of bad and doubtful debts and securities	57,418 85
Aggregate of all the assets of the company, stated at their actual value	$1,070,280 04

III. LIABILITIES.

Losses adjusted and unpaid	$83,306 94	
Losses unadjusted, including all reported and supposed losses	64,030 46	
Losses resisted, including interest, costs and expenses	12,000 00	
Net amount of unpaid losses and claims		$159,336 70
Reinsurance at 50 per ct. of prem on fire risks, under one year	$326,744 70	
Reinsurance, *pro rata*, on fire risks, running more than one year	95,310 55	
Reinsurance at 50 per cent. of premium on inland navigt'n risks	25,490 53	
Amount required to safely reinsure all outstanding risks		447,545 78
Cash dividends declared to stockholders, unpaid		64 00
All other demands against the company		4,871 56
Total liabilities, except capital stock		$611,818 04
Capital stock actually paid up in cash		500,000 00
Aggregate amt. of all liabilities, including capital stock		$1,111,818 04

IV. INCOME DURING THE YEAR.

	Fire.	Marine and Inland.	
Gross premiums received in cash	$1,117,971 81	$143,525 86	....
Deduct reinsurance, rebate and returned premiums	105,914 81	3,750 00	....
Net cash received for premiums	$1,012,057 00	$139,775 86	....
			$1,151,833 86
Net premiums, remaining unpaid	....	$98,961 72	....
Received for interest on bonds and mortgages			28,056 08
Received for int. and divid's on stocks and bonds, and from all other sources			16,559 63
Income received from all other sources			25,581 45
Aggregate amount of income received during the year in cash			$1,222,030 52

V. EXPENDITURES DURING THE YEAR.

	Fire.	Marine and Inland.	
Gross amount paid for losses,	$440,956 79	$109,586 85	....
Deduct salvage and reinsurance	....	6,463 00	....
Net amount paid during the year for losses	$440,956 79	$103,123 85	....
			$544,080 64
Cash dividends paid			45,000 00
Paid for commissions and brokerage			103,242 98
Salaries and all other charges of officers, clerks, agents and all other employes			84,362 35
Paid for state, national and local taxes			11,875 99
All other payments and expenditures			100,058 79
Aggregate amount of expenditures during the year, in cash			$888,615 70

VI. MISCELLANEOUS.

	Fire Risks.	Premiums thereon.	Marine and Inland Risks.	Premiums thereon.
In force, December 31, 1871	$10,459,172	$239,829 20	777,810	$39,774 22
Written during 1872	80,809,756	1,117,971 81	14,945,169	171,317 22
Total	$91,268,928	$1,357,801 01	$15,722,979	$211,091 44
Deduct those terminated	39,825,214	592,762 15	14,144,571	156,360 39
In force, December 31, 1872	$51,443,714	$765,038 86	$1,578,408	$54,731 05
Deduct amount reinsured	91,500	928 35	57,280	3,750 00
Net amount in force	$51,352,214	$764,110 51	$1,521,128	$50,981 05
In force, having not more than one year to run	$41,836,082	$658,489 40	$1,521,128	$50,981 05
Having more than one year and not more than three years to run	5,892,782	68,139 96	....	....
Having more than three years to run	3,623,350	42,481 15	....	....
Net amount in force	$51,352,214	$764,110 51	$1,521,128	$50,981 05

General Interrogatories.

Total premiums received from the organization of the company to date	$1,639,895 60
Total losses paid from the organization of the company to date	574,609 38
Total dividends declared since the company commenced business	45,000 00
Total amount of losses incurred during the year,	673,794 70
Total amount of the company's stock owned by the directors, at par value	101,880 00
Total amount loaned to officers and directors	286,809 00
Total amount loaned to stockholders, not officers	291,200 00
Amount deposited in different states and countries, for the security of policy holders, $25,000, deposited as follows: in the state of Alabama $10,000, Mississippi, $15,000.	

Business in the State of Wisconsin, during the Year 1872.

	Fire.	Marine and Inland.	Aggregate.
Risks taken,	$1,219,199 00	$709,281 00	$1,928,480 00
Premiums received	23,489 30	6,544 18	30,033 48
Losses paid on risks taken	....	....	17,678 15

AMERICAN INSURANCE COMPANY.

CHICAGO, ILL.

[Incorporated in 1855. Commenced business in 1859.]

H. Z. CULVER, *President.* CHAS. L. CURRIER, *Secretary.*

Attorneys to accept service of process in Wisconsin, WHITFORD & HEFFRON, Beloit.

I. CAPITAL.

Capital authorized	$300,000 00
Capital actually paid up in cash	200,000 00

II. ASSETS.

Value of building owned by the company, less incumbrances		$7,000 00
Loans on bond and mortgage, (first liens)		175,646 86
Interest due on bond and mortgage loans		59 74
Interest accrued on bond and mortgage loans		2,706 04
Stocks and bonds, market value		126,757 11
Cash loans secured by collaterals		65,200 00
Cash in company's principal office and in bank		14,438 43
Interest due and accrued on collateral loans		1,141 00
Gross premiums in due course of collection		80,870 17
Bills receivable, not matured, taken for fire risks		46 82
Bills receivable, taken for fire risks, past due		85 80
All other property belonging to the company, viz: Personal property, $1,744.87; personal accounts, $6,055.67; agency, $54,520.55; rent, $40.00; office furniture and fixtures, $2,500; postage stamps, $15; total		64,876 09
Installment notes	$754,041 28	
Aggregate of all the assets of the company, stated at their actual value		$538,828 06

III. LIABILITIES.

Losses adjusted and unpaid	$27,874 17	
Losses unadjusted, including all reported and supposed losses	20,497 68	
Losses resisted, including interest, costs and expenses	10,707 97	
Net amount of unpaid losses and claims		$59,079 82
Reinsurance at 50 per cent of prem. on fire risks, under one year	$185,930 58	
Reinsurance, *pro rata*, on fire risks running more than one year	1,196 40	
Amount required to safely reinsure all outstanding risks		187,126 98
Due and accrued for salaries, rent and other expenses		33,261 33
All other demands against the company, viz: Taxes, $1,500; personal accounts, $9,369.69; total		10,869 69
Total liabilities, except capital stock		$290,337 82
Capital stock actually paid up in cash		200,000 00
Surplus beyond capital stock		48,490 24
Aggregate amount of all liabilities, including capital stock and net surplus		$538,828 06

IV. INCOME DURING THE YEAR.

Gross premiums received in cash (fire)	$434,056 20	
Gross cash received on bills and notes taken for premiums	348 91	
Gross cash received for premiums	$434,405 11	
Deduct re-insurance, rebate and returned premiums	1,657 41	
Net cash received for premiums		$432,747 70
Received for interest on bonds and mortgages		8,728 06
Received for interest and dividends on stocks and bonds, and from all other sources		1,809 31

Income received from all other sources	....	10,507 95
Gross premiums, including instalment notes, remaining unpaid	$898,177 41	....
Received for increased capital	50,000 00	....
Aggregate amount of income received during the year in cash		$453,786 96

V. EXPENDITURES DURING THE YEAR.

Net amount paid during the year for losses (fire)	$116,580 58
Cash dividends paid	10,458 00
Paid for commissions and brokerage	224,010 40
Salaries and all other charges of officers, clerks, agents and all other employes	69,296 49
Paid for state, national and local taxes	4,910 33
All other payments, viz: rents, $1,688.94; incidental expenses, $1,717.51; postage, $7,336.85; revenue, $7,857.86; advertising, $9,687.83; exchange, $130.69 express charges, $250.76; stationery and supplies, $6,694.68; discount, $286.31; total	35,546 87
Aggregate amount of expenditure during the year, in cash	$460,752 12

VI. MISCELLANEOUS.

	Fire Risks.	Premiums thereon.
In force, December 31, 1871	$48,685,499	$236,051 79
Written during 1872	41,454,571	434,405 06
Total	$90,140,070	$670,456 85
Deduct those terminated	6,836,710	302,138 45
In force, December 31, 1872	$83,303,360	$368,318 40
Deduct amount reinsured	73,413	1,657 41
Net amount in force	$83,229,947	$366,660 99
In force, having not more than one year to run	$83,050,176	$363,326 02
Having more than one year and not more than three years to run	125,126	2,113 54
Having more than three years to run	54,645	1,221 43
Net amount in force	$83,229,947	$366,660 99

General Interrogatories.

Total premiums received from the organization of the company to date	$673,460 94
Total losses paid from the organization of the company to date	218,478 62
Total dividends declared since the company commenced business	10,458 00
Total amount of losses incurred during the year	127,428 06
Total amount of the company's stock owned by the directors, at par value	148,800 00
Total amount loaned to officers and directors	143,300 00
Total amount loaned to stockholders, not officers	56,500 00

Business in the State of Wisconsin, during the Year 1872.

Fire risks taken	$41,129,645 00
Premiums received	39,781 15
Losses paid on risks taken	8,898 89
Losses incurred during the year, in Wisconsin	28,772 17
Taxes on premiums, paid to the state of Wisconsin	417 52

AMERICAN CENTRAL INSURANCE COMPANY.

St. Louis, Mo.

[Incorporated in 1853. Commenced business in 1853.]

GEO. P. PLANT, *President.* GEO. T. CRAM, *Secretary.*

Attorney to accept service of process in Wisconsin, Martin C. Cooley, Racine.

I. CAPITAL.

Capital actually paid up in cash	$275,000 00

II. ASSETS.

Stocks and bonds, market value	$341,800 00
Cash in the company's principal office and in bank	133,351 61
Net premiums in due course of collection	62,292 07
All other property belonging to the company	7,500 00
Aggregate of all assets of the company, stated at their actual value	$544,943 68

III. LIABILITIES.

Losses adjusted and unpaid	$20,000 00	
Losses unadjusted, including all reported and supposed losses	11,498 98	
Losses resisted, including interest, costs and expenses	6,000 00	
Net amount of unpaid losses and claims		$37,498 98
Reinsurance at 50 per cent. of premium, on fire risks, under one year	$156,553 54	
Reinsurance, *pro rata*, on fire risks running more than one year	40,836 70	
Amount required to safely reinsure all outstanding risks		197,389 54
Total liabilities, except capital stock		$234,888 52
Capital stock actually paid up in cash		275,000 00
Surplus beyond capital stock		35,055 16
Aggregate amount of all liabilities, including capital stock and net surplus		$544,943 68

IV. INCOME DURING THE YEAR.

	Fire.	Marine and Inland.	
Gross premiums received in cash	$448,584 75	$78,607 54	
Deduct reinsurance, rebate and returned premiums	36,531 46	11,842 38	
Net cash received for premiums	$412,053 29	$66,765 16	$478,818 45
Net premiums remaining unpaid		$62,292 07	
Received for interest and dividends on stocks and bonds, and from all other sources			19,470 02
Aggregate amount of income received during the year in cash			$498,288 47

V. EXPENDITURES DURING THE YEAR.

	Fire.	Marine and Inland.	
Gross amount paid for losses	$193,318 63	$51,978 91	
Net amount paid during the year for losses			$245,297 54
Cash dividends paid			446 45
Paid for commissons and brokerage			85,689 77

Salaries and all other charges of officers, clerks, agents and all other employes.	34,096 15
Paid for state, national and local taxes	11,120 88
All other payments, viz: postage, $3,481 80; advertising, $4,296 98; supplies, $6,994 49; rents, $2,500 20; expenses, $19,568 74; profit and loss, $3,887 88; total	40,674 99
Aggregate amount of expenditures during the year, in cash	$417,325 78

VI. MISCELLANEOUS.

	Fire risks.	Premiums thereon.	Marine and Inland.	Premiums. thereon.
In force, December 31. 1871	$10,968,349 00	$173,155 96	....	....
Written during 1872	30,333,433 00	489,331 42	$11,136,014 00	$78,697 54
Total	$41,301,782 00	$662,487 38	$11,136,014 00	$78,607 54
Deduct those terminated	15,928,095 00	283,410 17	11,136,014 00	78,607 54
In force, December, 1872	$25,373,687 00	$379,077 21	....	....
Deduct amount reinsured	626,950 00	10,258 20	....	....
Net amount in force	$24,746,737 00	$368,819 01	....	....
In force, having not more than one year to run	$20,887,415 00	$312,107 08	....	....
Having more than one year and not more than three years to run	2,297,190 00	31,377 21	....	....
Having more than three years to run	1,562,132 00	24,334 72	....	....
Net amount in force	$24,746,737 00	$368,819 01	....	....

General Interrogatories.

Total premiums received from the organization of the company to date	$2,002,116 84
Total losses paid from the organization of the company to date	1,316,561 74
Total dividends declared since the company commenced business	41,286 20
Total amount of losses incurred during the year	224,723 25
Total amount of the company's stock owned by the directors, at par value	95,500 00
Total dividends payable in stock	56,250 00

Business in the State of Wisconsin, during the Year 1872.

Fire risks taken	$485,423 00
Premiums received	6,666 16
Losses paid on risks taken	4,466 79
Losses incurred during the year, in Wisconsin	4,466 79

ARCTIC FIRE INSURANCE COMPANY.

New York.

[Incorporated in 1853. Commenced business in 1853.]

VINCENT TILYON, *President*. CHAS. BAMBURG, *Secretary*.

Attorney to accept service of process in Wisconsin, H. S. Durand, Milwaukee.

I. CAPITAL.

Capital authorized	$250,000 00
Capital actually paid up in cash	250,000 00

II. ASSETS.

Value of real estate owned by the company, less incumbrances	$14,409 17
Loans on bond and mortgage, (first liens)	45,000 00
Interest accrued on bond and mortgage loans	1,575 00
Stocks and bonds, market value	197,750 00
Cash loans secured by collatrrals	11,000 00
Cash in company's principal office and in bank	7,508 90
Interest due and accrued on collateral loans	73 77
Gross premiums in due course of collection	20,989 87
Bills receivable, not matured, taken for fire, marine and inland risks	7,619 25
Bills receivable, taken for fire, marine and inland risks, past due	510 00
All other property belonging to the company	9,834 92
Aggregate of all the assets of the company, stated at their actual value	$316,265 88

III. LIABILITIES.

Losses adjusted and unpaid	$1,541 61	
Losses unadjusted, including all reported and supposed losses	96,071 69	
Losses resisted, including interest, costs and expenses	3,375 00	
Total gross amount of claims for losses	$100,988 30	
Deduct reinsurance thereon	11,497 32	
Net amount of unpaid losses and claims		$89,490 98
Reinsurance at 50 per cent. of premium, on fire risks, under one year	$44,974 36	
Reinsurance, *pro rata*, on fire risks running more than one year	3,746 74	
Reinsurance at 50 per cent. of prem. on inland navigation risks	3,423 18	
Amount required to safely reinsure all outstanding risks		52,144 28
Cash dividends declared to stockholders, unpaid		285 00
Due and accrued for salaries, rent and other expenses		688 33
All other demands against the company, viz: commissions to agents		2,316 67
Total liabilities, except capital stock		$144,920 26
Capital stock actually paid up in cash		250,000 00
Aggregate amount of all liabilities, including capital stock		$394,920 26

IV. INCOME DURING THE YEAR.

	Fire.	Marine and Inland.	
Gross premiums received in cash	$123,549 79	$38,288 24	
Gross cash received on bills and notes taken for premiums		26,773 22	
Gross cash received for premiums	$123,549 79	$65,061 46	
Deduct reinsurance, rebate and returned premiums	18,685 07	34,662 47	
Net cash received for premiums	$104,864 72	$30,398 99	$135,263 71
Bills and notes received during the year for premiums, remaining unpaid		$7,879 25	
Received for interest on bonds and mortgages			3,465 00
Received for interest and dividends on stocks and bonds, and from all other sources			12,957 35
Income received from all other sources			229 63
Aggregate amount of income received during the year in cash			$151,915 69

V. EXPENDITURES DURING THE YEAR.

	Fire.	Marine and Inland.	
Gross amount paid for losses	$82,865 09	$42,831 56	
Deduct salvage and reinsurance	557 27	18,328 36	
Net amount paid during the year for losses	$82,307 82	$24,503 20	$106,811 02
Cash dividends paid			25,450 00
Paid for commissions and brokerage			21,808 04
Salaries and all other charges of officers, clerks, agents and all other employes			19,571 68
Paid for state, national and local taxes			6,922 68
All other payments and expenditures			15,560 18
Aggregate amount of expenditures during the year, in cash			$196,123 60

VI. MISCELLANEOUS.

	Fire risks.	Premiums thereon.	Marine and inland risks.	Premiums thereon.
In force, December 31, 1871	$11,220,245	$92,181 68	$664,107	$11,672 09
Written during 1872............	15,370,018	104,864 72	6,490,800	30,398 97
Total	$26,590,263	$197,046 40	$7,154,907	$42,071 06
Deduct those terminated...	14,114,006	95,449 18	6,951,032	31,945 15
In force, December 31, 1872.	$12,476,257	$101,597 22	$203,875	$10,125 93
Deduct amount reinsured..	751,863	4,155 00	81,925	3,279 56
Net amount in force...	$11,724,394	$97,442 22	$121,950	$6,846 37
In force, having not more than one year to run............	$11,061,057	$89,948 73	$121,950	$6,846 37
Having more than one year and not more than three years to run.....................	573,000	6,354 28	....	....
Having more than three years to run.....................	90,337	1,139 21	....	....
Net amount in force.......	$11,724,394	$97,442 22	$121,950	$6,846 37

General Interrogatories.

Total premiums received, from the organization of the company to date......	$2,533,861 00
Total losses paid, from the organization of the company to date...............	1,709,545 00
Total dividends declared since the company commenced business	477,500 00
Total amount of losses incurred during the year............	187,718 91
Total amount of the company's stock owned by the directors, at par value....	45,175 00

Business in the State of Wisconsin, during the Year 1872.

	Fire.	Marine and inland.	Aggregate.
Risks taken....................................	$452,075 00	$143,989 00	$596,064 00
Premiums received	4,064 92	2,736 54	6,801 46
Losses incurred during the year, in Wisconsin	....	....	1,000 00
Taxes on premiums, paid to the state of Wis..	....	....	515 00
Taxes on premiums, paid to fire dep'ts of Wis.	....	....	20 00

Supplemental Statement of the Condition of the

ARCTIC FIRE INSURANCE COMPANY.

Of New York.

March 1st, 1873.

I. CAPITAL.

Capital actually paid up	$200,000 00

II. ASSETS.

Value of real-estate owned by the company, less incumbrances............ ...	$12,500 00
Loans on bond and mortgage, (first liens)..	38,000 00
U. S. bonds owned, market value...	51,595 00
Cash loans secured by collaterals...	102,000 00

Cash in the company's principal office and in banks		85,150 47
Interest accrued		1,096 66
Premiums in hands of agents and office premiums		112,430 38
Bills receivable		7,479 72
Assessment due March 20, 1873		9,966 50
All other property belonging to the company		10,819 08
Aggregate of all the assets of the company, stated at their actual value		$275,467 71

III. LIABILITIES.

Net amount of unpaid losses and claims		$8,618 50
Reinsurance at 50 per cent. of premium on risks	$59,046 13	
Deduct return commissions and rebates	6,024 51	
		53,021 62
Cash dividends declared to stockholders, unpaid		127 50
Due, and to become due for reinsurance		1,964 47
Total liabilities, except capital stock		$63,727 09
Capital stock actually paid up in cash		200,000 00
Surplus beyond capital stock		11,740 62
Aggregate amount of all liabilities, including capital stock and net surplus		$275,467 71

ATLANTIC INSURANCE COMPANY.

BROOKLYN, N. Y.

[Incorporated in 1871. Commenced business in 1872.]

JOHN D. COCKS, *President.* WILLIAM D. CORNELL, *Secretary.*

Attorney to accept service of process in Wisconsin, CHAS. J. CARY, Milwaukee.

I. CAPITAL.

Capital authorized	$200,000 00
Capital actually paid up in cash	200,000 00

II. ASSETS.

Loans on bond and mortgage, (first liens)	$35,800 00
Interest accrued on bond and mortgage loans	869 83
Stocks and bonds, market value	170,312 50
Cash loans secured by collaterals	55,900 00
Cash in the company's principal office, and in bank	20,164 80
Interest due and accrued on collateral loans	85 65
Net premiums in due course of collection	21,130 67
Aggregate of all the assets of the company, stated at their actual value	$303,263 45

III. LIABILITIES.

Losses unadjusted, including all reported and supposed losses	$31,327 06	
Losses resisted, including interest, costs and expenses	2,500 00	
Net amount of unpaid losses and claims		$33,827 06
Reinsurance at 50 per cent. of prem., on fire risks, under one year	$53,087 73	

Reinsurance, *pro rata*, on fire risks running more than one year..	1,996 05	....
Amount required to safely reinsure all outstanding risks.....		55,018 78
Total liabilities except capital stock..............		$88,840 86
Capital stock actually paid up in cash...............		200,000 00
Surplus beyond capital stock..............		14,428 59
Aggregate amount of all liabilities, including capital stock and net surplus..............		$308,268 45

IV. INCOME DURING THE YEAR.

Gross premiums received in cash (fire)..............	$162,884 77	....
Deduct reinsurance, rebate and returned premiums.........	17,847 91	....
Net cash received for premiums..............		$145,086 86
Net premiums, remaining unpaid..............	$21,180 67	....
Received for interest on bonds and mortgages..............		540 50
Received for interest and dividends on stocks and bonds, and from all other sources..............		16,600 21
Aggregate amount of income received during the year in cash............		$162,177 57

V. EXPENDITURES DURING THE YEAR.

Gross amount paid for losses (fire)..............	$88,692 40	....
Deduct salvage..............	4 95	....
Net amount paid during the year for losses..............		$88,687 45
Paid for commissions and brokerage..............		12,053 06
Salaries and all other charges of officers, clerks, agents and all other employes		23,629 78
Paid for state, national and local taxes..............		2,630 00
All other payments and expenditures..............		1,958 39
Aggregate amount of expenditures during the year, in cash..............		$78,958 65

VI. MISCELLANEOUS.

	Fire Risks.	Premiums thereon.
Written during 1872..............	$23,116,160 00	$173,215 44
Deduct those terminated..............	7,928,340 00	63,481 77
In force, December 31, 1872..............	$15,187,820 00	$109,733 67
Deduct amount reinsured..............	62,700 00	793 16
Net amount in force..............	$15,125,120 00	$108,940 51
In force, having not more than one year to run..............	$14,764,270 00	$106,175 46
Having more than one year and not more than three years to run..............	322,850 00	2,281 14
Having more than three years to run..............	38,000 00	483 91
Net amount in force..............	$15,125,120 00	$108,940 51

General Interrogatories.

Total premiums received from the organization of the company to date.......	$162,884 77
Total losses paid from the organization of the company to date..............	88,687 45
Total amount of losses incurred during the year..............	72,514 58
Total amount of company's stock owned by the directors, at par value.......	75,500 00
Total amount loaned to officers and directors..............	10,000 00

Business in the State of Wisconsin, during the Year 1872.

Fire risks taken..............	$54,700 00
Premiums received..............	954 75
Taxes on premiums, paid to the state of Wisconsin..............	15 19

BLACK RIVER INSURANCE COMPANY.

WATERTOWN, N. Y.

[Incorporated in 1872. Commenced business in 1872.]

G. LORD, *Vice President.* ORIN C. FROST, *Secretary.*

Attorney to accept service of process in Wisconsin, CHAS. J. CARY, Milwaukee.

I. CAPITAL.

Capital authorized	$250,000 00
Capital actually paid up in cash	250,000 00

II. ASSETS.

Value of real estate owned by the company, less incumbrances	$15,000 00
Loans on bond and mortgage, (first liens)	177,877 80
Interest due on bond and mortgage loans	3,542 43
Interest accrued on bond and mortgage loans	7,325 42
Stocks and bonds, market value	56,625 00
Cash in the company's principal office, and in bank	98,095 43
Net premiums in due course of collection	14,433 78
All other property belonging to the company	4,721 72
Aggregate of all the assets of the company, stated at their actual value	$377,621 58

III. LIABILITIES.

Losses adjusted and unpaid	$24,262 15	
Losses unadjusted, including all reported and supposed losses	49,954 85	
Total gross amount of claims for losses	$74,217 00	
Deduct reinsurance thereon	3,750 00	
Net amount of unpaid losses and claims		$70,467 00
Reinsurance at 50 per cent. of premium, on fire risks, under one year	$59,413 44	
Reinsurance, *pro rata*, on fire risks running more than one year.	3,645 01	
Amount required to safely reinsure all outstanding risks		63,058 45
Total liabilities, except capital stock		$133,525 45
Capital stock actually paid up in cash		250,000 00
Aggregate amount of all liabilities, including capital stock		$383,525 45

IV. INCOME DURING THE YEAR.

Gross premiums received in cash, (fire)	$122,604 40	
Deduct reinsurance, rebate and returned premiums	5,233 57	
Net cash received for premiums		$117,370 83
Received for interest on bonds and mortgages		3,175 99
Income received from all other sources, viz: rents		460 00
Net premiums remaining unpaid	$14,433 78	
Received for calls on capital	62,500 00	
Aggregate amount of income received during the year in cash		$121,006 82

V. EXPENDITURES DURING THE YEAR.

Net amount paid during the year for losses, (fire)	$36,097 97
Paid for commissions and brokerage	19,997 95
Salaries and all other charges of officers, clerks, agents and all other employes	14,344 30

Paid for state, national and local taxes	4,885 67
All other payments and expenditures	10,982 70
Aggregate amount of expenditures during the year, in cash	$85,908 59

VI. MISCELLANEOUS.

	Fire Risks.	Premiums thereon.
Written during 1872	$10,554,228 73	$141,725 59
Deduct those terminated	3,015,762 57	18,296 58
In force, December 31, 1872	$7,538,466 16	123,429 01
Deduct amount reinsured	32,500 00	414 23
Net amount in force	$7,505,966 16	$123,014 78
In force, having not more than one year to run	$7,131,039 16	$118,836 78
Having more than one year and not more than three years to run	327,165 00	3,599 82
Having more than three years to run	47,762 00	578 18
Net amount in force	$7,505,966 16	$123,014 78

GENERAL INTERROGATORIES.

Total premiums received from the organization of the company to date	$141,725 59
Total losses paid from the organization of the company to date	86,097 97
Total amount of losses incurred during the year	106,564 97
Total amount of the company's stock owned by the directors at par value	113,500 00

BUSINESS IN THE STATE OF WISCONSIN, DURING THE YEAR 1872.

Fire risks taken	$169,025 00
Premiums received	3,387 04

BREWERS' AND MALTSTERS' INSURANCE COMPANY.

NEW YORK.

[Incorporated in 1871. Commenced business in 1871.]

C. W. STANDART, *President.* W. B. OGDEN, *Secretary.*

Attorney to accept service of process in Wisconsin, WM. S. HIBBARD, Milwaukee.

I. CAPITAL.

Capital actually paid up in cash	$200,000 00

II. ASSETS.

Loans on bond and mortgage, (first liens)	$32,000 00
Interest accrued on bond and mortgage loans	23 33
Stocks and bonds, market value	189,500 00
Cash loans secured by collaterals	5,300 00
Cash in the company's principal office, and in bank	19,139 43
Interest due and accrued, not included in market value	758 34

Interest due and accrued on collateral loans	105 00
Net premiums in due course of collection	29,710 59
Bills receivable, taken for fire, marine and inland risks	52,082 44
All other property belonging to the company, viz: Salvage, $12,562.05; due for reinsurance on losses paid, $989.19; office furniture, $2,203.01; total	15,754 25
Aggregate of all the assets of the company, stated at their actual value	$284,878 38

III. LIABILITIES.

Losses adjusted and unpaid	$6,629 00	
Losses unadjusted, including all reported and supposed losses	40,371 00	
Net amount of unpaid losses and claims		$47,000 00
Reinsurance at 50 per cent. of prem., on fire risks under one year	$48,976 18	
Reinsurance, *pro rata*, on fire risks running more than one year	2,987 91	
Reinsurance at 50 per cent. of prem. on inland navigation risks	22,109 68	
Amount required to safely reinsure all outstanding risks		74,073 77
Due and accrued for salaries, rent and other expenses		458 33
All other demands against the company, viz.: Return prem's		298 57
Total liabilities except capital stock		$121,830 67
Capital stock actually paid up in cash		200,000 00
Aggregate amount of all liabilities, including capital stock		$321,830 67

IV. INCOME DURING THE YEAR.

	Fire.	Marine and inland.	
Gross premiums received in cash	$155,441 76	$53,847 20	
Gross cash received on bills and notes taken for premiums		29,366 26	
Gross cash received for premiums	$155,441 76	$83,213 46	
Deduct reinsurance, rebate and returned premiums	22,045 06	17,950 81	
Net cash received for premiums	$133,396 70	$65,262 65	$198,659 35
Net premiums, remaining unpaid		$31,793 08	
Received for interest on bonds and mortgages			945 97
Received for interest and dividends on stocks and bonds, and from all other sources			11,148 31
Income received from all other sources			1,934 57
Aggregate amount of income received during the year, in cash			$212,688 20

V. EXPENDITURES DURING THE YEAR.

	Fire.	Marine and inland.	
Gross amount paid for losses	$139,096 82	$61,453 78	
Deduct salvage and reinsurance	1,069 16	722 23	
Net amount paid during the year for losses	$138,027 66	$60,731 55	$198,759 21
Paid for commissions and brokerage			33,944 84
Salaries and all other charges of officers, clerks, agents and all other employes			30,878 01
Paid for state, national and local taxes			2,260 23
All other payments, viz.: printing $5,915 79; advertising, $1,776.17; postage, $432.69; revenue stamps, $821.99; total			8,946 64
Aggregate amount of expenditures during the year, in cash			$274,788 93

VI. MISCELLANEOUS.

	Fire risks.	Premiums thereon.	Marine and inland risks.	Premiums thereon.
In force, December 31, 1871....	$8,864,087	$66,287 25	$477,160	$10,836 58
Written during 1872...........	24,088,133	159,963 34	17,097,217	152,824 90
Total......................	$32,952,220	$226,250 59	$17,574,377	$163,661 48
Deduct those terminated...	17,741,804	112,234 50	15,976,426	108,841 20
In force, December 31, 1872.	$15,210,416	$114,016 09	$1,597,951	$54,820 28
Deduct amount reinsured..	182,871	12,079 83	187,755	10,600 93
Net amount in force...	$15,027,545	$101,936 26	$1,410,196	$44,219 35
In force, having not more than one year to run............	$14,644,800	$97,952 86	$1,410,196	$44,219 35
Having more than one year and not more than three years to run....................	258,775	2,408 98	....	....
Having more than three years to run....................	123,970	1,574 42	....	....
Net amount in force.......	$15,027,545	$101,936 26	$1,410,196	$44,219 35

GENERAL INTERROGATORIES.

Total premiums received, from the organization of the company to date......	$399,480 79
Total losses paid, from the organization of the company to date..............	217,228 50
Total amount of losses incurred during the year..............................	254,225 50
Total amount of the company's stock owned by the directors, at par value...	99,200 00
Total amount loaned to stockholders, not officers............................	9,000 00

BUSINESS IN THE STATE OF WISCONSIN, DURING THE YEAR 1872.

	Fire.	Marine and inland.	Aggregate.
Risks taken..................................	$92,613 00	$1,143,848 00	$1,236,461 00
Premiums received............................	538 78	10,651 28	11,190 06
Losses paid on risks taken...	3,550 55	1,447 07	4,997 62
Losses incurred during the year, in Wisconsin.	....	....	3,089 51

CAPITAL CITY INSURANCE COMPANY.

ALBANY, N. Y.

[Incorporated in 1865. Commenced business in 1865.]

FRANK CHAMBERLAIN, *President*. JAMES F. CROSBY, *Secretary*.

Attorney to accept service of process in Wisconsin, A. W. HATCH, Milwaukee.

I. CAPITAL.

Capital authorized..	$150,000 00
Capital actually paid up in cash....................................	150,000 00

II. ASSETS.

Stocks and bonds, market value	$169,940 60
Cash loans secured by collaterals	2,000 00
Cash in the company's principal office and in bank..................	2,316 21
Interest due and accrued, not included in market value..............	5,007 05
Interest due and accrued on collateral loans........................	43 67
Gross premiums in due course of collection..........................	3,804 35
All other property belonging to the company.........................	600 00
Aggregate of all the assets of the company, stated at their actual value ..	$183,710 98

III. LIABILITIES.

Losses adjusted and unpaid	$1,503 00	....
Losses unadjusted, including all reported and supposed losses..	3,147 00	....
Net amount of unpaid losses and claims		$4,650 00
Reinsurance at 50 per cent. of premium, on fire risks, under one year...	$10,959 84	....
Reinsurance, *pro rata*, on fire risks running more than one year	111 46	....
Amount required to safely reinsure all outstanding risks ...		11,071 30
Due and accrued for salaries, rent and other expenses................		1,121 00
Total liabilities, except capital stock................................		$16,842 30

Capital stock actually paid up in cash		150,000 00
Surplus beyond capital stock		16,868 68
Aggregate amount of all liabilities, including capital stock and net surplus		$183,710 98

IV. INCOME DURING THE YEAR.

Gross premiums received in cash (fire)	$20,888 87	
Deduct reinsurance, rebate and returned premiums	1,503 73	
Net cash received for premiums		$19,385 14
Received for interest and dividends on stock and bonds, and from all other sources		5,276 50
Gross premiums remaining unpaid	$3,804 95	
Received for calls on capital	50,000 00	
Aggregate amount of income received during the year in cash		$24,661 64

V. EXPENDITURES DURING THE YEAR.

Gross amount paid for losses, (fire)	$19,694 64	
Deduct reinsurance	703 44	
Net amount paid during the year for losses		$18,991 20
Paid for commission and brokerage		2,069 66
Salaries and all other charges of officers, clerks, agents and all other employes		4,133 28
Paid for state, national and local taxes		231 20
All other payments and expenditures		5,487 73
Aggregate amount of expenditures during the year, in cash		$30,913 07

VI. MISCELLANEOUS.

	Fire Risks.	Premium thereon.
In force, December 31, 1871	$1,259,887 00	$9,975 00
Written during 1872	2,963,864 00	24,554 83
Total	$4,223,751	$34,529 83
Deduct these terminated	1,709,626	12,442 95
In force, December 31, 1872	$2,514,125 00	$22,086 88
Deduct amount reinsured	34,500 00	275 03
Net amount in force	$2,479,625 00	$21,811 85
In force, having not more than one year to run	$2,464,275 60	21,644 65
Having more than one year and not more than three years to run	15,350 00	167 20
Net amount in force	$2,479,625 00	$21,811 85

General Interrogatories.

Total premiums received, from the organization of the company to date	$314,315 68
Total losses paid, from the organization of the company to date	292,618 40
Total dividends declared since the company commenced business	98,000 00
Total amount of losses incurred during the year	11,298 39
Total amount of the company's stock owned by the directors, at par value	65,800 00
Total amount loaned to stockholders, not officers	2,000 00

Business in the State of Wisconsin, during the Year 1872.

Risks taken (fire)	$51,275 00	
Premiums received	706 66	

COMMERCE INSURANCE COMPANY.

Albany, N. Y.

[Incorporated in 1859. Commenced business in 1859.]

ADAM VAN ALLEN, *President*. RICHARD VARICK De WITT, *Secretary*.

Attorney to accept service of process in Wisconsin. A. W. Hatch, Milwaukee.

I. CAPITAL.

Capital authorized	$500,000 00
Capital actually paid up in cash	200,000 00

II. ASSETS.

Value of real estate owned by the company, less incumbrances	$45,000 00
Stocks and bonds, market value	308,750 00
Cash in the company's principal office and in bank	31,236 55
Interest due and accrued, not included in market value	250 00
Gross premiums in due course of collection	19,421 30
All other property belonging to the company, viz.: rents	500 00
Aggregate of all the assets of the company, stated at their actual value	$400,157 85

III. LIABILITIES.

Losses adjusted and unpaid	$1,500 00	
Losses unadjusted, including all reported and supposed losses.	51,985 00	
Losses resisted, including interest, costs and expenses	1,100 00	
Net amount of unpaid losses and claims		$54,585 00
Reinsurance at 50 per cent. of prem., on fire risks, under one year	$99,256 30	
Re-insurance, *pro rata*, on fire risks running more than one year	24,642 88	
Amount required to safely reinsure all outstanding risks		$123,899 18
All other demands against the company, viz.: commissions, $2,929 93; return premiums, $986 63. Total		3,916 56
Total liabilities, except capital stock		$182,400 69
Capital stock actually paid up in cash		200,000 00
Surplus beyond capital stock		17,757 16
Aggregate amount of all liabilities including capital stock and net surplus		$400,157 58

IV. INCOME DURING THE YEAR.

Gross premiums received in cash (fire)	$234,211 35	
Deduct reinsurance, rebate and returned premiums	22,475 90	
Net cash received for premiums		$211,735 45
Gross premiums remaining unpaid	$19,421 30	
Received for interest and dividends on stocks and bonds, and from all other sources		21,706 95
Income received from all other sources, viz.: rents		2,798 05
Aggregate amount of income received during the year in cash		$236,235 45

V. EXPENDITURES DURING THE YEAR.

Gross amount paid for losses (fire)	$185,139 81	
Deduct reinsurance	8,450 57	
Net amount paid during the year for losses		$176,689 24
Cash dividends paid		10,000 00
Paid for commissions and brokerage		31,159 23
Salaries and all other charges of officers, clerks, agents and all other employes		15,585 35
Paid for state, national and local taxes		9,761 11
All other payments, viz: Advertising and printing, $4,394.88; traveling and adjusting, $4,768.64; agency supplies, maps and office repairs, $2,097.98; office expenses and incidentals, $1,668.96; total		12,849 35
Aggregate amount of expenditures during the year, in cash		$256,044 28

VI. MISCELLANEOUS.

	Fire risks.	Premiums thereon.
In force, December 31, 1871	$21,997,352	$241,921 16
Written during 1872	21,190,614	236,162 82
Total	$43,187,966	$478,083 98
Deduct those terminated	21,340,707	235,766 21
In force, December 31, 1872	$21,847,259	$242,317 77
Deduct amount reinsured	310,096	3,857 69
Net amount in force	$21,537,163	$238,460 08
In force, having not more than one year to run	$18,242,620	$198,512 61
Having more than one year and not more than three years to run	2,612,889	30,366 95
Having more than three years to run	681,654	9,600 52
Net amount in force	$21,537,163	$238,460 08

General Interrogatories.

Total premiums received, from the organization of the company to date	$2,246,098 38
Total losses paid, from the organization of the company to date	1,699,960 17

Total dividends declared since the company commenced business	310,000 00
Total amount of losses incurred during the year	208,148 80
Total amount of the company's stock owned by the directors, at par value	62,375 00

Business in the State of Wisconsin, during the Year 1872.

Risks taken (fire)	$401,885 00
Premiums received	4,068 05
Losses paid on risks taken	37 50
Losses incurred during the year, in Wisconsin	550 74
Taxes on premiums paid to the state of Wisconsin	86 00
Taxes on premiums, paid to fire departments in Wisconsin	77 85

CONNECTICUT FIRE INSURANCE COMPANY.

HARTFORD, CONN.

[Incorporated in 1850. Commenced business in 1850.]

JOHN B. ELDREDGE, *President.* M. BENNETT, JR., *Secretary.*

Attorney to accept service of process in Wisconsin, F. W. JACOBI, Milwaukee.

I. CAPITAL.

Capital authorized	$500,000 00
Capital actually paid up in cash	500,000 00

II. ASSETS.

Stocks and bonds owned by the company, market value	$554,580 00
Cash loans secured by collaterals	94,985 00
Cash in the company's principal office and in bank	84,207 78
Gross premiums in due course of collection	64,869 26
Aggregate of all the assets of the company, stated at their actual value	$798,635 04

III. LIABILITIES.

Losses unadjusted, including all reported and supposed losses	$50,525 00	
Net amount of unpaid losses and claims		$50,525 00
Reinsurance at 50 per cent. of premium, on fire risks, under one year	$121,753 83	
Reinsurance, *pro rata*, on fire risks running more than one year	8,891 41	
Amount required to safely reinsure all outstanding risks		$130,645 24
Due and to become due for borrowed money		25,000 00
All other demands against the company, viz: commissions		9,729 34
Total liabilities, except capital stock		$215,899 58
Capital stock actually paid up in cash		500,000 00
Surplus beyond capital stock		82,735 46
Aggregate amount of all liabilities, including capital stock and net surplus		$798,635 04

IV. INCOME DURING THE YEAR.

Gross premiums received in cash, (fire)	$312,358 66	
Deduct reinsurance, rebate and returned premiums	8,928 81	
Net cash received for premiums		$303,430 85
Gross premiums, remaining unpaid	$64,869 26	
Received for interest and dividends from all sources		49,578 76
Aggregate amount of income received during the year in cash		$353,009 61

V. EXPENDITURES DURING THE YEAR.

Gross amount paid for losses (fire)	$147,651 80	
Deduct reinsurance	2,151 87	
Net amount paid during the year for losses		$145,499 93
Cash dividends paid		30,000 00
Paid for commissions and brokerage		31,441 76
Salaries and all other charges of officers, clerks, agents and all other employes		12,258 33
Paid for state, national and local taxes		6,745 00
All other payments, viz: interest on borrowed money, $527 78; miscellaneous expenses, $4,845 60; total		5,373 38
Aggregate amount of expenditures during the year, in cash		$231,318 40

VI. MISCELLANEOUS.

	Fire risks.	Premiums thereon.
In force, February 1, 1872	$8,000,018 00	$77,220 27
Written during 1872	23,450,000 00	277,215 92
Total	$31,450,018 00	$354,436 19
Deduct those terminated	8,550,518 00	92,071 27
In force, December 31, 1872	$22,879,500 00	$262,364 92
Deduct amount reinsured,	379,600 00	4,346 50
Net amount in force	$22,499,900 00	$258,018 42
In force, having not more than one year to run	$20,904,100 00	$243,507 67
Having more than one year and not more than three years to run.	1,055,500 00	9,795 50
Having more than three years to run	540,300 00	4,715 25
Net amount in force	$22,499,900 00	$258,018 42

GENERAL INTERROGATORIES.

Total premiums received from the reorganization of the company to date	$277,215 92
Total losses paid from the reorganization of the company to date	145,499 93
Total dividends declared since the company recommenced business	30,000 00
Total amount of losses incurred during the year	194,200 00
Total amount of the company's stock owned by the directors, at par value	140,300 00
Total amount loaned to officers and directors	3,660 00
Total amount loaned to stockholders, not officers	21,275 00

BUSINESS IN THE STATE OF WISCONSIN, DURING THE YEAR 1872.

Risks taken (fire)	$312,050 00
Premiums received	5,659 47
Losses paid on risks taken	600 00

CONTINENTAL INSURANCE COMPANY.

NEW YORK.

[Incorporated in 1852. Commenced business in 1853.]

GEO. T. HOPE, *President.* CYRUS PECK, *Secretary.*

Attorney to accept service of process in Wisconsin, C. D. ADSIT, Milwaukee.

I. CAPITAL.

Capital authorized	$1,000,000 00
Capital actually paid up in cash	1,000,000 00

II. ASSETS.

Value of real estate owned by the company, less incumbrances		$632,000 00
Loans on bond and mortgage (first liens)		452,300 00
Interest due on bond and mortgage loans		2,691 30
Interest accrued on bond and mortgage loans		12,616 39
Stocks and bonds, market value		579,468 50
Cash loans secured by collaterals		41,270 00
Cash in the company's principal office, and in bank		389,766 29
Interest due and accrued on collateral loans and other sources		1,913 41
Net premiums in due course of collection		168,798 55
All other property belonging to the company, viz: rents due and accrued		3,488 33
Installment notes taken for premiums	$836,599 84	....
Aggregate of all the assets of the company, stated at their actual value		$2,264,251 97

III. LIABILITIES.

Losses unadjusted, including all reported and supposed losses.	$409,770 58	....
Losses resisted, including interest, cost and expenses	13,000 00	....
Total gross amount of claims for losses	$422,770 58	....
Deduct reinsurance thereon	42,642 66	....
Net amount of unpaid losses and claims		$380,127 92
Reinsurance at 50 per cent. of premium, on fire risks, under one year	$560,447 68	....
Reinsurance, *pro rata*, on fire risks running more than one year	240,727 59	....
Amount required to safely reinsure all outstanding risks		801,175 27
Principal unpaid on scrip ordered redeemed		33,496 00

Cash dividends declared to stockholders, unpaid	1,794 50
Interest due and declared, remaining unpaid	14,570 08
Total liabilities, except capital stock	$1,231,096 71
Capital stock actually paid up in cash	1,000,000 00
Surplus beyond capital stock	53,158 26
Aggregate amt. of all liabilities, including capital stock and net surplus	$2,284,251 97

IV. INCOME DURING THE YEAR.

Gross premiums received in cash (fire)	$1,721,425 34	....
Deduct reinsurance, rebate and returned premiums	172,261 99	....
Net cash received for premiums		$1,549,158 35
Received for interest on bonds and mortgages		31,573 34
Rec'd for interest and dividends on stocks and bonds, and from all other sources		52,051 84
Income received from all other sources, viz.: rents, $34,125.17; premium on gold, $586.63; total		34,711 80
Net premiums remaining unpaid	$168,796 55	....
Received for calls on capital	400,000 00	....
Aggregate amount of income received during the year in cash		$1,667,489 33

V. EXPENDITURES DURING THE YEAR.

Gross amount paid for losses (fire)	$1,778,099 29	....
Deduct salvage and reinsurance	30,712 24	....
Net amount paid during the year for losses		$1,747,387 05
Cash dividends paid, $58,755.50; interest paid to scripholders, $2,947.08; total		61,702 58
Scrip or certificates of profits redeemed in cash		12,217 00
Paid for commissions and brokerage		273,482 80
Salaries and all other charges of officers, clerks, agents and all other employes		161,333 96
Paid for state, national and local taxes		42,963 27
All other payments and expenditures		142,638 46
Aggregate amount of expenditures during the year, in cash		$2,442,640 08

VI. MISCELLANEOUS.

	Fire Risks.	Premiums thereon.
In force, December 31, 1871	$177,348,892	$1,352,009 79
Written during 1872	221,862,298	1,589,491 26
Total	$399,211,190	$2,941,501 05
Deduct those terminated	206,771,492	1,397,824 41
In force, December 31, 1872	$192,439,698	$1,543,676 64
Deduct amount reinsured	3,129,548	20,109 33
Nat amount in force	$189,310,150	$1,523,567 31
In force, having not more than one year to run	$157,351,899	$1,141,004 69
Having more than one year and not more than three years to run	26,913,661	293,307 58
Having more than three years to run	8,174,138	109,364 37
Net amount in force	$192,439,698	$1,543,676 64

General Interrogatories.

Total premiums received from the organization of the company to date	$9,807,720 47
Total losses paid from the organization of the company to date	5,669,080 64
Total dividends declared since the company commenced business	2,355,028 44
Total amount of losses incurred during the year	1,852,097 25
Total amount of the company's stock owned by the directors, at par value	301,100 00
Total amount loaned to officers and directors	17,500 00
Total amount loaned to stockholders, not officers	18,720 00

Amount deposited at market value in different states and countries, for the security of policy holders, $91,012.50, deposited as follows: Virginia, $26,000; West Virginia, $25,000; Alabama, $10,000; South Carolina, $20,000; and Tennessee, $20,000.

Business in the State of Wisconsin, during the Year 1872.

Fire risks taken	$3,648,981 00
Premiums received	43,526 96
Losses paid on risks taken	12,204 43
Losses incurred during the year, in Wisconsin	14,235 08
Taxes on premiums, paid to the state of Wisconsin	1,544 68
Taxes on premiums, paid to fire departments in Wisconsin	372 83

DETROIT FIRE AND MARINE INSURANCE COMPANY.

DETROIT, MICH.

[Incorporated in 1866. Commenced business in 1866.]

CALEB VAN HUSAN, *President*. JAMES J. CLARK, *Secretary*.

Attorney to accept service of process in Wisconsin, JOS. W. HOBBINS, Madison.

I. CAPITAL.

Capital authorized	$350,000 00
Capital actually paid up in cash	150,000 00

II. ASSETS.

Loans on bond and mortgage, (first liens)	$146,850 00
Interest due on bond and mortgage loans	1,479 25
Interest accrued on bond and mortgage loans	1,555 43
Stocks and bonds, market value	62,150 00
Cash in the company's principal office, and in bank	12,251 08
Interest due and accrued, not included in market value	275 00
Gross premiums in due course of collection	17,488 84
Bills receivable, not matured, taken for fire, marine and inland risks	15,597 00
Bills receivable, taken for fire, marine and inland risks, past due	889 50
All other property belonging to the company	9,894 53
Aggregate of all the assets of the company, stated at their actual value	$267,848 63

III. LIABILITIES.

Losses unadjusted, including all reported and supposed losses	$10,948 20	....
Losses resisted, including interest, costs and expenses	2,000 00	....
Net amount of unpaid losses and claims		$12,948 20
Reinsurance at 50 per ct. of prem., on fire risks, under one year	$54,977 66	....
Reinsurance, *pro rata*, on fire risks running more than one year	19,195 98	....
Reinsurance at 50 per cent. of prem. on inland navigation risks	8,847 78	....
Amount required to safely reinsure all outstanding risks		83,021 42
Due and accrued for rent		150 00
All other demands against the company		657 26
Total liabilities, except capital stock		$96,771 88
Capital stock actually paid up in cash		150,000 00
Surplus beyond capital stock		21,076 74
Aggregate am't of all liabilities, including capital st'k and net surplus		$267,848 63

IV. INCOME DURING THE YEAR.

	Fire.	Marine and Inland.	
Gross premiums received in cash	$148,896 47	$32,435 44	....
Gross cash recd. on bills and notes taken for prems.	....	57,918 22	....
Gross cash received for premiums	$148,896 47	90,353 66	....
Deduct reinsurance, rebate and returned prems.	19,164 11	21,258 47	....
Net cash received for premiums	$129,732 36	$69,095 19	*$198,827 55
Bills and notes rec'd during the year for prem's unpaid		$16,409 50	....
Received for interest on bonds and mortgages			13,357 56
Rec'd for interest and dividends on stocks and bonds, and from all other sources			5,385 62
Income received from all other sources			3,680 79
Aggregate amount of income received during the year in cash			$221,251 52

V. EXPENDITURES DURING THE YEAR.

	Fire.	Marine and Inland.	
Gross amount paid for losses	$145,403 26	$37,248 19	
Net amount paid during the year for losses			$182,651 45
Paid for commissions and brokerage			20,685 32
Salaries and all other charges of officers, clerks, agents and all other employes			13, 14 76
Paid for state, national and local taxes			1,385 82
All other payments and expenditures			11,218 38
Aggregate amount of expenditures during the year, in cash			$229,695 73

VI. MISCELLANEOUS.

	Fire Risks.	Premiums thereon.	Marine and Inland Risks.	Premiums thereon.
In force, December 31, 1871....	$10,184,356 00	$133,933 78	$204,250 00	$11,335 00
Written during 1872......... ...	11,682,578 00	150,137 47	5,952,501 00	96,417 66
Total	$21,866,934 00	$284,071 25	$6,156,751 00	$107,752 66
Deduct those terminated...	10,870,071 00	137,245 35	5,827,427 00	90,057 10
In force, December 31, 1872	$10,996,863 00	$146,825 90	$329,324 00	$17,695 56
In force, having not more than one year to run............	$8,822,158 00	$120,187 51	$329,324 00	$17,695 56
Having more than one year, and not more than three years to run......................	2,006,665 00	24,161 64	....	....
Having more than three years to run......................	168,040 00	2,476 75	....	....
Net amount in force.........	$10,996,863 00	$146,825 90	$329,324 00	$17,695 56

General Interrogatories.

Total premiums received from the organization of the company to date.......	$1,082,472 10
Total losses paid from the organization of the company to date..............	774,228 57
Total dividends declared since the company commenced business............	77,500 00
Total amount of losses incurred during the year....	113,428 10
Total amount of the company's stock owned by the directors, at par value....	27.425 00
Total amount loaned to stockholders, not officers..............................	10,000 00

Business in the State of Wisconsin, during the Year.

	Fire.	Marine and Inland.	Aggregate.
Risks taken....................................	$462,375 00	$418,889 00	$881,264 00
Premiums received.................	5,829 71	4,261 67	10,091 38
Losses paid on risks taken.......................	....	786 46	786 46
Losses incurred during the year, in Wisconsin	....	....	786 46
Taxes on premiums, paid to the state of Wisconsin..................................	....	....	70 18
Taxes on premiums, paid to fire departments in Wisconsin	....	....	34 66

*Of which $17,488 84 is in course of collection.

FAIRFIELD COUNTY FIRE INSURANCE COMPANY.

South Norwalk, Conn.

[Incorporated in 1869. Commenced business in 1869.]

W. S. HANFORD, *President*. HENRY R. TURNER, *Secretary*.

Attorney to accept service of process in Wisconsin, James H. Dodge, Milwaukee.

I. CAPITAL.

Capital authorized	$200,000 00
Capital actually paid up in cash..	200,000 00

II. ASSETS.

Value of real estate owned by the company, less incumbrances...............	$28,640 09
Loans on bond and mortgage (first liens)..	151,395 00
Interest due on bond and mortgage loans..	2,313 33
Interest accrued on bond and mortgage loans....................................	70 00
Stocks and bonds, market value.......	28,400 00
Cash loans secured by collaterals	29,133 88
Cash in the company's principal office and in bank	9,623 79
Interest due and accrued, not included in market value........................	715 00
Interest due and accrued on collateral loans..	1,536 52
Gross premiums in due course of collection.........................	34,421 59
Bills receivable..	9,500 00
All other property belonging to the company.........................	3,240 45
Aggregate of all the assets of the company, stated at their actual value...	$298,969 59

III. LIABILITIES.

Losses adjusted and unpaid	$33,846 50	....
Losses unadjusted, including all reported and supposed losses.	35,395 00	....
Total gross amount of claims for losses	$69,241 50	....
Deduct reinsurance and salvage thereon	5,141 93	....
Net amount of unpaid losses and claims		$64,099 57
Reinsurance at 50 per cent. of prem., on fire risks, under one year	$64,718 07	....
Reinsurance, *pro rata*, on fire risks running more than one year.	8,718 95	....
Amount required to safely reinsure all outstanding risks		73,437 02
Due and accrued for salaries, rent and other expenses		250 00
All other demands against the company		5,805 38
Total liabilities, except capital stock		$143,581 97
Capital stock actually paid up in cash		200,000 00
Aggregate amount of all liabilities, including capital stock		$343,581 97

IV. INCOME DURING THE YEAR.

Gross premiums received in cash (fire)	$164,999 01	....
Deduct reinsurance, rebate and returned premiums	16,725 32	....
Net cash received for premiums		*$148,273 69
Received for interest on bonds and mortgages		9,919 14
Rec'd for int. and dividends on stocks and bonds, and from all other sources		3,909 31
Income received from all other sources		2,332 30
Aggregate amount of income received during the year in cash		$164,434 44

V. EXPENDITURES DURING THE YEAR.

Gross amount paid for losses (fire)	$78,087 31	....
Net amount paid during the year for losses		$78,087 31
Cash dividends paid		18,000 00
Paid for commissions and brokerage		24,509 56
Salaries and all other charges of officers, clerks, agents and all other employes		5,547 69
Paid for state, national and local taxes		1,091 37
All other payments and expenditures		11,061 71
Aggregate amount of expenditures during the year, in cash		$138,297 64

VI. MISCELLANEOUS.

	Fire Risks.	Premiums thereon.
In force, December, 31, 1871	$5,342,720 58	$53.302 19
Written during 1872	14,105,681 46	164,999 01
Total	$19,448,402 04	$218,301 20
Deduct those terminated	7,689,996 00	72,189 54
In force, December 31, 1872	$11,758,406 04	$146,111 66
Deduct amount reinsured	392,961 00	3,934 63
Net amount in force	$11,365,445 04	$142,177 03
In force, having not more than one year to run	$10.170,536 67	$129,426 14
Having more than one year and not more than three y'rs to run	941,790 00	10,190 67
Having more than three years to run	253,109 00	2,560 22
Net amount in force	$11,365,435 67	$142,177 03

GENERAL INTERROGATORIES.

Total premiums received from the organization of the company to date	$231,948 51
Total losses paid from the organization of the company to date	104,485 89
Total dividends declared since the company commenced business	18,000 00
Total amount of losses incurred during the year	125,297 97
Total amount of the company's stock owned by the directors, at par value	76,700 00
Total amount loaned to officers and directors	25 500 00
Total amount loaned to stockholders, not officers	29,500 00

*Of which $34,421.59 is in course of collection.

Supplementary Statement of the Condition of the

FAIRFIELD COUNTY FIRE INSURANCE COMPANY,

OF SOUTH NORWALK, CONN.,

February 28, 1878.

[Incorporated in 1869. Commenced business in 1869.]

W. S. HANFORD, *President.* HENRY R. TURNER, *Secretary.*

Attorney to accept service of process in Wisconsin, JAMES H. DODGE, Milwaukee.

I. CAPITAL.

Capital authorized	$500,000 00
Capital actually paid up in cash	200,000 00

II. ASSETS.

Value of real estate owned by the company, less incumbrances	$23,722 32
Loans on bond and mortgage, (first liens)	164,470 00
Interest due and accrued on bond and mortgage loans	3,858 14
Stocks and bonds, market value	28,400 00
Cash loans secured by collaterals	23,047 28
Cash in the company's principal office and in bank	19,922 94
Net premiums in due course of collection	21,385 53
Bills receivable	9,500 00
All other property belonging to the company	3,017 87
Aggregate of all the assets of the company, at their actual value	$297,317 58

III. LIABILITIES.

Losses adjusted and unpaid	$9,662 39	
Losses unadjusted, including all reported and supposed losses	12,322 44	
Net amount of unpaid losses and claims		$21,984 83
Amount required to safely reinsure all outstanding risks		73,960 71
Total liabilities, except capital stock		$95,945 54
Capital stock actually paid up in cash		200,000 00
Surplus beyond capital stock		1,371 98
Aggregate of all liabilities, including capital and surplus		$297,317 58

FARMERS' INSURANCE COMPANY.

FREEPORT, ILL.

[Incorporated in 1857. Commenced business in 1867.]

JOHN H. ADDAMS, *President.* L. T. LEMON, *Secretary.*

Attorney to accept service of process in Wisconsin, JOHN W. STEWART, Monroe.

I. CAPITAL.

Capital authorized	$500,000 00
Capital actually paid up in cash	100,000 00

II. ASSETS.

Loans on bond and mortgage, (first liens)		$107,000 00
Interest accrued on bond and mortgage loans		5,802 47
Stocks and bonds, market value		6,548 00
Cash in company's principal office, and in bank		1,840 50
Gross premiums in due course of collection		3,434 44
Bills receivable, not matured, taken for fire, marine and inland risks		1,483 11
Bills receivable, taken for fire, marine and inland risks, past due		3,407 98
All other property belonging to the company, viz.: personal property, $1,000; interest accrued on bills receivable, $2,070.19; total		3,070 19
Installment notes	$156,538 49	
Aggregate of all the assets of the company, at their actual value		$132,586 69

III. LIABILITIES.

Losses adjusted and unpaid	$2,858 48	....
Losses unadjusted, including all reported and supposed losses	2,366 96	....
Losses resisted, including interest, costs and expenses	1,900 00	....
Net amount of unpaid losses and claims		$7,125 44
Reinsurance at 50 per cent. of prem. on fire risks, under one y'r.	$24,455 06	....
Reinsurance, *pro rata*, on fire risks running more than one year.	3,215 93	....
Amount required to safely reinsure all outstanding risks		27,670 99
Due and accrued for salaries, rent and other expenses		2,987 32
Due and to become due for borrowed money		13,500 00
Total liabilities, except capital stock		$51,283 75
Capital stock actually paid up in cash		100,000 00
Aggregate of all liabilities, including capital		$151,283 75

IV. INCOME DURING THE YEAR.

Gross premiums received in cash (fire)	$25,581 00	....
Gross cash received on bills and notes taken for premiums	33,173 38	....
Gross cash received for premiums	$58,754 38	....
Deduct reinsurance, rebate and returned premiums	285 80	....
Net cash received for premiums		$58,468 58
Bills and notes rec'd during the year for prem's unpaid	$75,648 87	....
Received for interest on bonds and mortgages		6,233 33
Received for interest and dividends from all other sources		69 41
Income received from all other sources		777 63
Aggregate amount of income received during the year in cash		$65,548 89

V. EXPENDITURES DURING THE YEAR.

Gross amount paid for losses (fire)	$26,176 56	....
Net amount paid during the year for losses		$26,176 56
Paid for commissions and brokerage		25,647 89
Salaries and all other charges of officers and all employes		13,591 91
Paid for state, national and local taxes		429 77
All other payments, viz.: interest on borrowed money, $1,544.86; general expenses, $3,849.45; stamps, $2,274 92; printing, $1,355.93; total		9,025 16
Aggregate amount of expenditures during the year		$75,870 79

VI. MISCELLANEOUS.

	Fire risks.	Premiums thereon.
In force, December 31, 1871	$9,289,726	$47,688 22
Written during 1872	4,026,186	25,581 00
Total	$13,315,912	$73,269 22
Deduct those terminated	1,350,996	8,762 36
In force, December 31, 1872	$11,964,916	$64,506 86
Deduct amount reinsured	2,500	18 75
Net amount in force	$11,962,416	$64,488 11
In force, having not more than one year to run	$11,601,252	$58,056 26
Having more than one and not more than three years to run	166,398	2,494 38
Having more than three years to run	194,766	3,937 47
Net amount in force	$11,962,416	$64,488 11

General Interrogatories.

Total amount of losses incurred during the year	$24,108 87
Total amount of the company's stock owned by the directors, at par value	99,000 00
Total amount loaned to officers and directors	106,000 00
Total amount loaned to stockholders, not officers	1,000 00

Business in the State of Wisconsin, during the Year 1872.

Risks taken (fire)	$907,400 00
Premiums received	10,058 09
Losses paid on risks taken	4,749 58
Losses incurred during the year, in Wisconsin	6,549 08
Taxes on premiums, paid to the state of Wisconsin	180 26

Supplementary Statement of the Condition of the

FARMERS' INSURANCE COMPANY.

FREEPORT, ILL., MARCH 8, 1873.

[Incorporated in 1857. Commenced business in 1857.]

JOHN H. ADDAMS, *President.* L. T. LEMON, *Secretary.*

Attorney to accept service of process in Wisconsin, JOHN W. STEWART, Monroe.

I. CAPITAL.

Capital authorized		$500,000 00
Capital actually paid up in cash		100,000 00

II. ASSETS.

Loans on bond and mortgage, (first liens)		$107,000 00
Interest accrued on bond and mortgage loans		6,811 74
Stocks and bonds, market value		6,548 00
Cash in the company's principal office and in bank		1,671 88
Gross premiums in due course of collection, cash value		2,500 00
Bills receivable, not matured, taken for fire, marine and inland risks		1,700 00
All other property belonging to the company		3,000 00
Aggregate of all the assets of the company, at their actual value		$129,231 62

III. LIABILITIES.

Losses adjusted and unpaid	$1,340 43	
Losses unadjusted, including all reported and supposed losses	3,724 00	
Losses resisted, including interest, costs and expenses	1,900 00	
Net amount of unpaid losses and claims		$6,964 43
Reinsurance at 50 per cent. of prem. on fire risks under one year	$24,455 06	
Reinsurance, *pro rata*, on fire risks running more than one year	3,215 93	
Amount required to safely reinsure all outstanding risks		$27,670 99
Due and accrued for salaries, rent and other expenses		2,743 12
Due and to become due for borrowed money		10,000 00
Total liabilities, except capital stock		$47,377 54
Capital stock actually paid up in cash		100,000 00
Aggregate of all liabilities including capital		$147,377 54

FIREMAN'S FUND INSURANCE COMPANY.

SAN FRANCISCO, CAL.

[Incorporated in 1863. Commenced business in 1863.]

DAVID J. STAPLES, *President.* GEO. D. DORNIN, *Secretary.*

Attorney to accept service of process in Wisconsin, F. H. MAGDEBURG, Milwaukee.

I. CAPITAL.

Capital authorized	$800,000 00
Capital actually paid up in cash	300,000 00

II. ASSETS.

Value of real estate owned by the company, less incumbrances	$165,000 00
Loans on bond and mortgage, (first liens)	146,761 10
Interest due and accrued on bond and mortgage loans	874 69
Stocks and bonds, market value	131,118 46
Cash loans secured by collaterals	15,500 00
Cash in the company's principal office and in bank	41,490 36
Interest due and accrued, not included in market value	3,300 00
Gross premiums in due course of collection	22,513 43
Bills receivable, not matured, taken for fire, marine and inland risks	10,000 95
All other property belonging to the company, viz: salvage, $497 89; personal acc's, $76,808 97; furniture, $4,227 98; stamps, $538 65; suspense acc'ts, $600 00; total	82,667 49
Aggregate of all the assets of the company	$619,221 48

III. LIABILITIES.

Losses adjusted and unpaid	$11,490 50	....
Losses unadjusted, including all reported and supposed losses	54,000 00	....
Losses resisted, including interest, costs and expenses	4,500 00	....
Total gross amount of claims for losses	$69,990 50	....
Deduct reinsurance thereon	17,579 36	....
Net amount of unpaid losses and claims		$52,411 14
Reinsurance at 50 per cent. of prem., on fire risks, under one year	$158,072 08	....
Reinsurance, *pro rata*, on fire risks running more than one year,	12,255 75	....
Reinsurance at 50 per cent. of premium on inland risks	8,280 70	....
Gross premiums received on all unexpired marine risks	13,206 21	....
Amount required to safely reinsure all outstanding risks		191,814 74
Cash dividends declared to stockholders, unpaid		225 50
Eastern bills payable		78,750 00
All other demands against the company, viz: personal acc'ts, $902 10; mortgage tax, $26; marine bils payable, $671 25; total		1,599 35
Total liabilities, except capital stock		$324,800 73
Capital stock actually paid up in cash		300,000 00
Aggregate of all liabilities, including capital stock		$624,800 73

IV. INCOME DURING THE YEAR.

	Fire.	Marine and Inland.	
Gross premiums received in cash	$426,755 06	$66,133 35	....
Gross cash rec'd on bills and notes taken for prem's	....	13,098 10	....
Gross cash received for premiums	$426,755 06	$79,231 45	....
Deduct re-insurance, rebate and ret'd prem's	15,805 16	13,513 15	....
Net cash received for premiums	$410,949 90	$65,718 30	$476,668 20
Gross premiums remaining unpaid	....	$32,514 88	....
Rec'd for interest on bonds and mortgages and collaterals			33,095 85
Income received from all other sources, viz: rents, $15,844 09; tax on policies, $609 78; total			16,453 88
Aggregate amount of income received during the year in cash			$526,217 87

V. EXPENDITURES DURING THE YEAR.

	Fire.	Marine and Inland.	
Gross amount paid for losses	$477,574 73	$47,719 37	....
Deduct reinsurance	11,851 19	14,251 21	....
Net amount paid during the year for losses	$465,723 54	$33,468 16	$499,191 70
Paid for commissions and brokerage			68,369 45
Salaries and all other charges of officers, and all employes			34,047 40
Paid for state, national and local taxes			6,737 81
All other payments and expenditures			62,091 08
Aggregate amount of expenditures during the year, in cash			$670,439 89

VI. MISCELLANEOUS.

	Fire Risks.	Premiums thereon.	Marine & Inland Risks.	Premiums thereon.
In force, December 31, 1871	$24,608,962	$295,629 09	$549,145	$18,131 65
Written during the year	35,527,443	473,982 49	3,690,441	88,273 26
Total	$60,131,405	$769,611 58	$4,239,586	$106,405 91
Deduct those terminated	31,744,366	389,793 09	3,508,544	74,213 03
In force, December 31, 1872	$28,387,039	$379,818 49	$731,042	$32,190 88
Deduct amount reinsured	3,248,145	43,248 06	65,637	2,423 27
Net amount in force	$25,138,894	$336,570 43	$665,405	$29,767 61
In force, having not more than one year to run	$23,777,143	$316,144 17	$665,405	$29,767 61
Having more than one, and not more than three years to run	1,326,251	19,591 64	....	....
Having more than three years to run	35,500	834 62	....	....
Net amount in force	$25,138,894	$336,570 43	$665,405	$29,767 61

GENERAL INTERROGATORIES.

Total premiums received from the organization of the company to date	$2,265,918 00
Total losses paid from the organization of the company to date	1,178,079 00
Total dividends declared since the company commenced business	474,000 00
Total amount of losses incurred during the year	363,000 00
Total amount loaned to officers and directors	5,000 00
Amount deposited in different states, for the security of policy holders, $127,900, deposited as follows: in the state of Virginia, $7,900; Nevada, $50,000; Oregon, $50,000.	

BUSINESS IN THE STATE OF WISCONSIN, DURING THE YEAR 1873.

Fire risks taken	$761,859 90
Premiums received	10,710 84
Losses paid on risks taken	6,400 00
Losses incurred during the year, in Wisconsin	6,400 00

FRANKLIN FIRE INSURANCE COMPANY.

PHILADELPHIA, PA.

[Incorporated in 1829. Commenced business in 1829.]

ALFRED G. BAKER, *President*. THEODORE M. REGER, *Secretary*.

Attorney to accept service of process in Wisconsin, JOHN L. HATHAWAY, Milwaukee.

I. CAPITAL.

Capital authorized	$400,000 00
Capital acutally paid up in cash	$400,000 00

II. ASSETS.

Value of real estate owned by the company, less incumbrances	$65,000 00
Loans on bond and mortgage, (first liens)	$2,589,684 28
Interest due on bond and mortgage loans	943 13
Interest accrued on bond and mortgage loans	41,895 58
Stocks and bonds, market value	160,008 25
Cash loans secured by collaterals	128,750 00
Cash in the company's principal office and in bank	151,108 42
Interest due and accured, not included in market value	1,080 00
Interest due and accured on collateral loans	594 88
In hands of agents	221,798 72
All other property belonging to the company, viz: deposit premiums	2,869 00
Aggregate of all the assets of the company, at their actual value	$3,363,671 16

III. LIABILITIES.

Losses adjusted and unpaid	$125,821 30	
Losses unadjusted, including all reported and supposed losses	233,100 00	
Losses resisted, including interest, costs and expenses	6,500 00	
Net amount of unpaid losses and claims		$365,421 30
Reinsurance at 50 per cent. of prem. on fire risks, under one year	$556,810 59	
Reinsurance, *pro rata*, on fire risks running more than one year	316,370 58	
Amount required to safely reinsure all outstanding risks		873,181 17
Amount reclaimable on perpetual fire risks		1,290,499 84
Cash dividends declared to stockholders, unpaid		120 00
Due and to become due for borrowed money		96,879 00
All other demands against the company, viz: surveyors and surveys		12,989 75
Total liabilities, except capital stock		$2,638,990 56
Capital stock actually paid up in cash		400,000 00
Surplus beyond capital stock		324,680 60
Aggregate of all liabilities, including capital and surplus		$3,363,671 16

IV. INCOME DURING THE YEAR.

Gross premiums received in cash, fire	$1,545,010 71	
Deduct reinsurance, rebate and returned premiums	145,336 97	
Net cash received for premiums		$1,399,673 74
Received for interest on bonds and mortgages		166,929 88
Received for interest from all other sources		35,538 99
Income received from all other sources, viz: surveys		3,036 00
Premiums in hands of agents	$221,798 72	
Deposit premiums, received for perpetual fire risks	156,011 84	
Aggregate amount of income received during the year		$1,605,178 61

V. EXPENDITURES DURING THE YEAR.

Gross amount paid for losses (fire)	$1,051,721 60	
Net amount paid during the year for losses,		$1,051,721 60
Cash dividends paid (gold)		130,576 00
Paid for commissions and brokerage		202,694 78
Salaries and all other charges of officers, and all employes		184,395 28
Paid for state, national and local taxes		41,508 69
All other payments, viz: surveyors, $2,967: loss expenses, $16,404 83; revenue stamps, $9,552 96; miscellaneous, $29,942 55; total		58,867 34
Aggregate amount of expenditures during the year		$1,669,758 69

VI. MISCELLANEOUS.

	Fire Risks.	Premiums thereon.
In force, December 31, 1871	$149,732,454 57	$2,815,541 84
Written during the year	119,534,941 95	1,691,773 88
Total	$269,267,396 52	$4,507,315 72
Deduct those terminated	125,787,726 94	1,599,228 69
In force, December 31, 1872	$143,479,669 58	$2,908,087 03
Deduct amount reinsured	147,775 00	1,397 18
Net amount in force,	$143,331,894 58	$2,906,689 85
In force, having not more than one year to run	$61,512,493 84	$1,113,621 19
Having more than one and not more than three years to run	17,095,067 00	235,485 55
Having more than three years to run	13,040,676 00	199,162 76
Perpetual risks in force and int. prem	51,683,659 94	1,358,420 35
Net amount in force	$143,331,894 58	$2,906,689 85

General Interrogatories.

Total premiums received from the organization of the company to date	$11,084,406 50
Total losses paid from the organization of the company to date	7,611,448 96
Total dividends declared since the company commenced business	2,266,400 00
Total amount of losses incurred during the year	1,156,763 42
Total amount of the company's stock owned by the directors, at par value	51,000 00
Total amount loaned to stockholders, not officers	14,900 00
Amount deposited in different states and countries, for the security of policy holders, $45,000, deposited as follows: in Tennessee, $20,000; Alabama, $10,000; Mississippi, $15,000.	

Business in the State of Wisconsin, during the Year 1872.

Fire risks taken	$1,366,648 00	....
Premiums received	26,083 84	....
Losses paid on risks taken	10,008 45	....
Losses incurred during the year, in Wisconsin	12,208 12	....
Taxes on premiums, paid to fire departments in Wisconsin	460 46	....

GERMAN FIRE INSURANCE COMPANY.

Erie, Pa.

[Incorporated in 1867. Commenced business in 1868.]

M. SCHLAUDECKER, *President*. J. EICHENLAUB, Jr., *Secretary*.

Attorneys to accept service of process in Wisconsin, Magdeburg & Cohen, Milwaukee.

I. CAPITAL.

Capital authorized	$500,000 00
Capital actually paid up in cash	200,000 00

II. ASSETS.

Loans on bond and mortgage, (first liens)	$157,989 75
Interest due on bond and mortgage loans	9,539 18
Stocks and bonds, market value	22,000 00
Cash loans secured by collaterals	14,500 00
Cash in company's principal office, and in bank	105,589 13
Interest due and accrued, not included in market value	720 00
Interest due and accrued on collateral loans	1,014 00

Gross premiums in due course of collection		36,670 40
Bills receivable, not matured, taken for fire risks		94 50
Bills receivable, judgment notes		3,290 60
All other property belonging to the company		4,689 21
Aggregate of all the assets of the company, at their actual value		$358,896 17

III. LIABILITIES.

Losses adjusted and unpaid	$33,750 00	
Losses unadjusted, including all reported and supposed losses	15,339 72	
Total gross amount of claims for losses	$49,089 72	
Deduct reinsurance thereon	4,000 00	
Net amount of unpaid losses and claims		$45,089 72
Reinsurance at 50 per cent. of prem. on fire risks, under one year	$91,112 20	
Reinsurance, *pro rata*, on fire risks running more than one year	11,250 00	
Am't required to safely reinsure all outstanding risks		102,362 20
All other demands against the company, viz.: commissions		5,500 00
Total liabilities, except capital stock		$152,951 92
Capital stock actually paid up in cash		200,000 00
Surplus beyond capital stock		944 25
Aggregate of all liabilities, including capital and surplus		$358,896 17

IV. INCOME DURING THE YEAR.

Gross premiums received in cash, fire	$291,127 43	
Deduct reinsurance, rebate and returned premiums	39,787 37	
Net cash received for premiums		$251,340 06
Gross premiums remaining unpaid	$36,694 90	
Received for interest on bonds and mortgages		5,408 69
Received for interest and dividends from all other sources		487 15
Aggregate amount of income received during the year in cash		$257,235 90

V. EXPENDITURES DURING THE YEAR.

Gross amount paid for losses, fire	$76,743 80	
Net amount paid during the year for losses		$76,743 80
Cash dividends paid		20,071 02
Paid for commissions and brokerage		47,258 78
Salaries and all other charges of officers and all employes		3,168 13
Paid for state, national and local taxes		5,490 56
All other payments, viz: printing, advertising and supplies, $3,359.21; postage, telegraph, express and stationery, $7,379.60; rent and repairs, $500; total		11,238 81
Aggregate amount of expenditures during the year		$163,971 10

VI. MISCELLANEOUS.

	Fire Risks.	Premiums thereon.
In force, December 31, 1871	$3,643,918	$59,724 71
Written during 1872	15,350,200	330,220 40
Total	$18,994,118	$389,945 11
Deduct those terminated	6,550,216	176,245 71
In force, December 31, 1872	$12,443,902	$213,699 40
Deduct amount reinsured	760,400	13,355 00
Net amount in force, Dec. 31, 1872	$11,683,502	$200,344 40
In force, having not more than one year to run	$10,520,270	$182,224 40
Having more than one and not more than three years to run	710,204	11,372 20
Having more than three years to run	453,028	6,747 80
Net amount in force	$11,683,502	$200,344 40

General Interrogatories.

Total premiums received from the organization of the company to date	$479,736 36
Total losses paid from the organization of the company to date	88,580 74
Total dividends declared since the company commenced business	31,742 49
Total amount of losses incurred during the year	125,833 58
Total amount of the company's stock owned by the directors, at par value	166,300 00
Total dividends payable in stock	15,000 00
Total amount loaned to officers and directors	89,340 90
Total amount loaned to stockholders, not officers	72,054 75

BUSINESS IN THE STATE OF WISCONSIN, DURING THE YEAR 1872.

Fire risks taken	$181,189 00
Premiums received	3,283 39

GERMAN INSURANCE COMPANY.

FREEPORT, ILL.

[Incorporated in 1865. Commenced business in 1866.]

C. O. COLLMANN, *President*. F. GUND, *Secretary*.

Attorney to accept service of process in Wisconsin, JULIUS NATHANSON, Milwaukee.

I. CAPITAL.

Capital authorized	$500,000 00
Capital actually paid up in cash	200,000 00

II. ASSETS.

Value of real estate owned by the company, less incumbrances	$10,000 00
Loans on bond and mortgage, (first liens)	197,540 00
Interest accrued on bond and mortgage loans	970 00
U. S. 5-20 bonds, par value	4,000 00
Cash in the company's principal office and in bank	29,291 24
Interest due and accrued, not included in market value. and bills receivable.	530 00
Net premiums in due course of collection	6,426 13
Bills receivable, not matured, taken for fire, marine and inland risks	8,069 10
Bills receivable, taken for fire, marine and inland risks, past due	4,300 00
All other property belonging to the company	2,117 95
Gross amount of all the assets of the company	$263,244 42
Amount which should be deducted from the above assets, on account of bad and doubtful debts and securities, viz: from item No. 18, $3,850.10; No. 2, $1,000; total deductions	4,850 10
Aggregate of all the assets of the company	$258,394 32

III. LIABILITIES.

Losses adjusted and unpaid	$3,488 70	
Losses unadjusted, including all reported and supposed losses	1,000 00	
Net amount of unpaid losses and claims		$4,488 70
Reinsurance at 50 per cent. of prem. on fire risks, under one y'r.	$9,235 53	
Reinsurance, *pro rata*, on fire risks running more than one year.	15,607 75	
Amount required to safely reinsure all outstanding risks		24,843 28
Due and accrued for salaries, rent and other expenses		1,502 00
Total liabilities, except capital stock		$30,828 98
Capital stock actually paid up in cash		200,000 00
Surplus beyond capital stock		27,565 34
Aggregate amount of all liabilities, including capital and net surplus		$258,394 32

IV. INCOME DURING THE YEAR.

Gross premiums received in cash (fire)	$77,731 70	
Deduct reinsurance, rebate and returned premiums	2,715 81	
Net cash received for premiums		$75,015 89
Bills and notes received during the year for prem's unpaid.	$8,069 10	
Received for interest on bonds and mortgages and bills receivable		575 65
Income received from all other sources, viz.: rents		274 68
Received for increased capital	$10,100 00	
Aggregate amount of income received during the year		$75,866 22

V. EXPENDITURES DURING THE YEAR.

Gross amount paid for losses (fire)	$9,329 45	
Deduct salvage and reinsurance	856 00	
Net amount paid during the year for losses		$8,473 45
Cash dividends paid		10,100 00
Paid for commissions and brokerage		17,747 00
Salaries and all other charges of officers, and all employes		11,041 94
Paid for state, national and local taxes		1,084 04

All other payments, viz: interest on borrowed money, $92.18; revenue and postage stamps, $1,300.11; printing and stationery, $2,662.79; total......	4,055 08
Aggregate amount of expenditures during the year....................	$58,501 46

VI. MISCELLANEOUS.

	Fire risks.	Premiums thereon.
In force, December 31, 1871....................................	$5,106,075	$40,851 70
Written during 1872..	4,636,255	75,015 89
Total	$9,742,330	$115,867 59
Deduct those terminated....................................	2,388,441	62,340 93
In force, Dec. 31, 1872..	$7,353,889	$53,526 66
In force, having not more than one year to run................	$3,232,833	$18,471 06
Having more than one, and not more than three years to run..	1,941,077	10,948 70
Having more than three years to run	2,179,979	24,111 90
Net amount in force..	$7,353,889	$53,526 66

General Interrogatories.

Total premiums received, from the organization of the company to date.......	$188,291 98
Total losses paid from the organization of the company to date....	33,667 40
Total dividends declared since the company commenced business.............	10,100 00
Total amount of losses incurred during the year..............................	12,518 15
Total amount of the company's stock owned by the directors, at par value....	101,200 00
Total dividends payable in stock..	10,100 00
Total amount loaned to officers and directors..................................	20,700 00
Total amount loaned to stockholders, not officers......	84,700 00

GERMAN AMERICAN INSURANCE COMPANY.

NEW YORK.

[Incorporated in 1871. Commenced business in 1872.]

WILLIAM F. HEINS, *President.* JOHN W. MURRAY, *Secretary.*

Attorney to accept service of process in Wisconsin, J. W. HOBBINS, Madison.

I. CAPITAL.

Capital authorized............	$1,000,000 00
Capital actually paid up in cash.	1,000,000 00

II. ASSETS.

Stocks and bonds owned, market value..	$973,400 00
Cash loans secured by collaterals..	243,850 00
Cash in company's principal office and in bank................................	40,842 35
Gross premiums in due course of collection..........	110,998 12
All other property belonging to the company...................................	10,000 00
Aggregate of all the assets of the company at, their actual value..........	$1,379,090 47

III. LIABILITIES.

Losses unadjusted, including all reported and supposed losses..	$59,336 87	....
Net amount of unpaid losses and claims..........................		$59,336 87
Reinsurance at 50 per cent of prem. on fire risks under one year.	$253,623 17	....
Reinsurance, *pro rata*, on fire risks running more than one year	29,331 64	....
Amount required to safely reinsure all outstanding risks...		282,954 81
All other demands against the company.................................		2,036 87
Total liabilities, except capital stock....................................		$344,328 55
Capital stock actually paid up in cash....................................		1,000,000 00
Surplus beyond capital stock..		34,761 92
Aggregate of all liabilities including capital and surplus..............		$1,379,090 47

IV. INCOME DURING THE YEAR.

Gross premiums received in cash (fire)	$557,417 02	
Deduct re-insurance, rebate and returned premiums	37,068 60	
Net cash received for premiums		$520,348 42
Gross premiums, remaining unpaid	$110,998 12	
Received for interest and dividends from all sources		65,786 60
Aggregate amount of income received during the year in cash		$586,135 02

V. EXPENDITURES DURING THE YEAR.

Gross amount paid for losses (fire)	$177,915 86	
Deduct salvage and reinsurance	4,151 69	
Net amount paid during the year for losses		$173,764 17
Paid for commissions and brokerage		82,205 28
Salaries and all other charges of officers and all employes		31,514 56
Paid for state, national and local taxes		7,617 26
All other payments and expenditures		46,335 17
Aggregate amount of expenditures during the year		$342,436 43

VI. MISCELLANEOUS.

	Fire Risks.	Premiums thereon.
Written during 1872	$65,185 259	$618,415 14
Deduct those terminated	15,486 843	64,569 27
In force, December 31, 1872	$49,678,416	$553,845 87
Deduct amount reinsured	595,025	5,700 18
Net amount in force	$49,083,391	$548,145 69
In force, having not more than one year to run	$46,210,556	$512,947 28
Having more than one and not more than three years to run.	2,434,419	27,598 58
Having more than three years to run	1,033,441	13,305 09
Net amount in force	$49,678,416	$553,845 87

GENERAL INTERROGATORIES.

Total premiums received from the organization of the company to date	$557,417 02
Total losses paid from the organization of the company to date	173,764 17
Total amount of losses incurred during the year	233,104 04
Total amount of the company's stock owned by directors, at par value	267,000 00
Total amount loaned to stockholders, not officers	154,000 00

BUSINESS IN THE STATE OF WISCONSIN, DURING THE YEAR 1872.

Fire risks taken	$748,748 00
Premiums received	14,281 01
Losses paid on risks taken	1,168 16

GERMANIA FIRE INSURANCE COMPANY.

NEW YORK.

[Incorporated in 1859. Commenced business in 1859.]

RUD. GARRIGUE, *President.* HUGO SCHUMANN, *Secretary.*

Attorney to accept service of process in Wisconsin, GEO. E. REDFIELD, Beaver Dam.

I. CAPITAL.

Capital authorized	$500,000 00
Capital actually paid up in cash	500,000 00

II. ASSETS.

Value of real estate owned by the company, less incumbrances	$49,365 95
Loans on bond and mortgage, (first liens)	494,900 00
Interest accrued on bond and mortgage loans	9,055 96
Stocks and bonds owned, market value	475,160 00
Cash loans secured by collaterals	12,250 00
Cash in the company's principal office, and in bank	167,188 54
Interest due and accrued on collateral loans	5 30
Gross premiums in due course of collection	86,721 63

Bills receivable, not matured, taken for fire, marine and inland risks..........		2,056 52
Bills receivable, taken for fire, marine and inland risks, past due		2,296 59
All other property belonging to the company, viz.: salvage, $3,000; rents, $800; office furniture and fixtures, $10,691.98; total..............................		14,491 98
Aggregate of all the assets of the company, ...		$1,313,877 46

III. LIABILITIES.

Losses adjusted and unpaid	$118,980 91	....
Losses unadjusted, including all reported and supposed losses.	151,964 29	....
Losses resisted, including interest, costs and expenses	11,716 27	....
Total gross amount of claims for losses....................	$282,706 47	....
Deduct reinsurance and salvage thereon....	3,264 85	....
Net amount of unpaid losses and claims		$279,441 62
Reinsurance at 50 per ct. of prem. on fire risks, under one year.	$370,673 62	....
Reinsurance, *pro rata*, on fire risks, running more than one year	78,732.99	....
Amount required to safely reinsure all outstanding risks...		449,406 61
All other demands against the company, viz.: commissions..................		10,276 91
Total liabilities, except capital stock..................................		$739,194 44
Capital stock actually paid up in cash..................................		500,000 00
Surplus beyond capital stock..............		74,253 02
Aggregate am't of all liabilities, including capital and surplus........		$1,313,877 46

IV. INCOME DURING THE YEAR.

	Fire.	Marine and Inland.	
Gross cash received for premiums.............	$905,997 45	$1,151 59	....
Deduct reinsurance, rebate and ret'd prem's...	68,730 06	....	....
Net cash received for premiums	$837,267 39	$1,151 59	....
			$838,418 98
Received for interest on bonds and mortgages........................			28,116 97
Received for interest and dividends from all other sources..................			36,264 30
Income received from all other sources, viz.: rents			18,595 26
Gross premiums in course of collection		$91,074 74	....
Received for calls on capital...............................		250,000 00	....
Aggregate amount of income received during the year in cash...... .			$921,394 91

V. EXPENDITURES DURING THE YEAR.

	Fire.	Marine and inland.	
Gross amount paid for losses......................	$553,489 80	$3,730 46	....
Deduct salvage and reinsurance	10,428 66	91 84	....
Net am't paid during the year for losses...	$543,061 14	$3,638 62	....
			$546,699 76
Cash dividends paid..................			50,000 00
Paid for commissions and brokerage			122,212 04
Salaries and all other charges of officers and all employes....................			58,454 91
Paid for state, national and local taxes			19,017 52
All other payments, viz.: interest on borrowed money, $531.12; rents, $18,006.05; traveling, office and agency expenses, fire patrol, advertising, etc., $100,404.43; total.......			118,941 60
Aggregate amount of expenditures during the year, in cash...........			$911,325 83

VI. MISCELLANEOUS.

	Fire risks.	Premiums thereon.	Marine and Inland risks.	Premiums thereon.
In force, December 31, 1871......	$92,432,322	$798,484 75	$17,166	$559 98
Written during the year.........	94,113,546	905,997 45	117,980	1,151 59
Total........................	$186,545,868	$1,704,482 20	$135,146	$1,711 57
Deduct those terminated....	84,252,521	799,450 59	135,146	1,711 57
In force, December 31, 1872.	$102,293,347	$905,031 61	....	....
Deduct amount reinsured ..	1,103,580	6,218 39	....	....
Net amount in force.....	$101,189,767	$898,813 22	....	....
In force, having not more than one year to run................	$89,939,793	$741,346 94	....	....
Having more than one and not more than three years to run....	7,633,642	102,223 36	....	....
Having more than three years to run...	3,616,332	55,243 62	....	....
Net amount in force.........	$101,189,767	$898,813 22	....	....

GENERAL INTERROGATORIES.

Total premiums received from the organization of the company to date	$5,585,805 76
Total losses paid from the organization of the company to date	2,971,162 81
Total dividends declared since the company commenced business	486,000 00
Total amount of losses incurred during the year	764,238 33
Total amount of the company's stock owned by the directors, at par value	160,100 00

Amount deposited in different states and countries, for the security of policy holders, $20,000, deposited in the state of South Carolina.

BUSINESS IN THE STATE OF WISCONSIN, DURING THE YEAR 1872.

Fire risks taken	$1,047,158 00
Premiums received	18,771 51
Losses paid on risks taken	12,780 87
Losses incurred during the year, in Wisconsin	11,599 87
Taxes on premiums, paid to the state of Wisconsin	543 34

GIRARD FIRE AND MARINE INSURANCE COMPANY.

PHILADELPHIA, PA.

[Incorporated in 1853. Commenced business in 1853.]

THOMAS CRAVEN, *President*. JAS. B. ALVORD, *Secretary*.

Attorney to accept service of process in Wisconsin, JAMES B. KELLOGG, Milwaukee.

I. CAPITAL.

Capital authorised	$300,000 00
Capital actually paid up in cash	300,000 00

II. ASSETS.

Value of real estate owned by the company, less incumbrances	$183,000 00
Loans on bond and mortgage, (first liens)	121,900 00
Loans on bond and mortgage, (first liens), upon which more than one year's interest is due	2,950 00
Interest due on bond and mortgage loans	494 00
Interest accrued on bond and mortgage loans	1,781 88
Stocks and bonds, market value	215,341 95
Cash loans, secured by collaterals	9,150 00
Loans on personal security	1,581 00
Cash in the company's principal office, and in bank	50,074 76
Interest due and accrued on collateral loans	373 12
Gross premiums in due course of collection	54,329 72
Furniture and fixtures of company's office	3,000 00
Am't deposited for perpetual insurance on company's building	1,500 00
Furniture, etc., of Quaker City Bank	7,500 00
All other property belonging to the company, viz: rents	558 58
Gross amount of all the assets of the company	$653,873 96
Amount which should be deducted from the above assets, on account of bad and doubtful debts and securities, viz: from item No. 4	52 67
Aggregate of all the assets of the company	$653,821 29

III. LIABILITIES.

Losses unadjusted, including all reported and supposed losses	$11,900 00	
Deduct salvage thereon	2,000 00	
Net amount of unpaid losses and claims		$9,900 00
Reinsurance at 50 per ct. of prem. on fire risks, under one year	$149,551 42	
Reinsurance, *pro rata*, on fire risks running more than one year	48,322 62	
Amount required to safely reinsure all outstanding risks		197,874 04
Due and accrued for salaries, rent and other expenses		800 00
All other demands against the company, viz: taxes, $470 56; commissions, $9,609 57; return premiums, $405 63; total		10,485 76
Total liabilities, except capital stock		$219,059 80
Capital stock actually paid up in cash		300,000 00
Surplus beyond capital stock		134,761 49
Aggregate of all liabilities, including capital and surplus		$653,821 29

IV. INCOME DURING THE YEAR.

Gross premiums received in cash (fire)	$373,392 98	
Deduct reinsurance, rebate and returned premiums	8,796 38	
Net cash received for premiums		$364,596 60
Gross premiums, remaining unpaid	$54,389 72	
Received for interest on bonds and mortgages		7,018 75
Received for interest and dividends from all other sources		14,767 39
Income received from all other sources, viz: rents		6,985 09
Deposit premiums received for perpetual fire risks	$5,665 33	
Aggregate amount of income received during the year		$393,312 22

V. EXPENDITURES DURING THE YEAR.

Gross amount paid for losses (fire)	$160,081 98	
Deduct reinsurance	5,975 00	
Net amount paid during the year for losses		$154,106 98
Cash dividends paid		30,000 00
Paid for commissions and brokerage		50,259 46
Salaries and all other charges of officers, and all employes		14,164 31
Paid for state, national and local taxes		14,874 96
All other payments, viz: postage, $844.28; general expenses, $40,458.11; revenue stamps, $1,606.14; total		42,908 53
Aggregate amount of expenditures during the year, in cash		$306,313 54

VI. MISCELLANEOUS.

	Fire Risks.	Premiums thereon.
In force, December 31, 1871	$23,113,135	$288,271 30
Written during 1872	29,556,122	422,268 94
Total	$52,669,257	$710,589 54
Deduct those terminated	17,710,543	253,097 87
In force, December 31, 1872	$34,958,714	$457,491 67
Deduct amount reinsured	280,485	2,773 65
Net amount in force	$34,678,229	$454,718 02
In force, having not more than one year to run	$27,525,086	$310,777 48
Having more than one and not more than three years to run	3,153,845	41,089 55
Having more than three years to run	1,190,600	17,866 89
Perpetual risks in force and int. prem	3,089,183	87,757 75
Net amount in force	$34,958,714	$457,491 67

General Interrogatories.

Total premiums received from the organization of the company to date	$2,208,251 25
Total losses paid from the organization of the company to date	1,068,800 66
Total dividends declared since the company commenced business	244,381 52
Total amount of losses incurred during the year	152,156 04
Total amount of company's stock owned by the directors, at par value	118,000 00
Total amount loaned to officers and directors	22,660 00
Total amount loaned to stockholders, not officers	100 00

Business in the State of Wisconsin, during the Year 1872.

Fire risks taken	$386,735 00
Premiums received	3,904 47
Losses paid on risks taken	1,366 16
Losses incurred during the year in Wisconsin	1,366 16

GLOBE INSURANCE COMPANY.

Chicago, Ill.

[Incorporated in 1865. Commenced business in 1865.]

GEO. K. CLARK, *President*. S. P. WALKER, *Secretary*.

Attorney to accept service of process in Wisconsin, Addison B. Myers, Milwaukee.

I. CAPITAL.

Capital authorized	$1,000,000 00
Capital actually paid up in cash	200,000 00

II. ASSETS.

Loans on bond and mortgage, (first liens)	$176,000 00
Loans on bond and mortgage, (first liens), upon which more than one year's interest is due	49,000 00
Interest due and accrued on bond and mortgage loans	12,215 66
Stocks and bonds, market value	50,050 00
Cash in company's principal office and in bank	17,477 98
Gross premiums in due course of collection	24,995 41
Bills receivable	5,200 00
Ledger balances secured	3,245 30
All other property belonging to the company, viz: due for reinsurance, $2,000; office furniture, $1,500	3,500 00
Aggregate of all the assets of the company, at their actual value	$341,684 35

III. LIABILITIES.

Losses adjusted and unpaid	$11,750 30	
Net amount of unpaid losses and claims		$11,750 30
Reinsurance at 50 per cent. of prem., on fire risks, under one year	$28,795 43	
Reinsurance, *pro rata*, on fire risks running more than one year	395 86	
Amount required to safely reinsure all outstanding risks		29,191 29
Due, and to become due for borrowed money		20,000 00
All other demands against the company		4,999 08
Total liabilities except capital stock		$65,940 67
Capital stock actually paid up in cash		300,000 00
Aggregate of all liabilities, including capital		$365,940 67

IV. INCOME DURING THE YEAR.

Gross premiums received in cash (fire)	$60,038 54	
Deduct reinsurance, rebate and returned premiums	1,943 42	
Net cash received for premiums		*$58,095 12
Received from stockholders	$12,250 00	
Aggregate amount of income received during the year in cash		$58,095 12

V. EXPENDITURES DURING THE YEAR.

Gross amount paid during the year for losses, (fire)	$63,958 94	
Net amount paid during the year for losses		$63,958 94
Paid for commissions and brokerage		3,952 94
Salaries and all other charges of officers, clerks, agents and all other employes		11,714 68
Paid for state, national and local taxes		1,161 10
All other payments, viz: interest on borrowed money, $4,727 59; expenses, $10,975 88: total		15,703 47
Aggregate amount of expenditures during the year, in cash		$96,491 08

VI. MISCELLANEOUS.

	Fire Risks.	Premiums thereon.
In force, December 31, 1871	$97,802 00	$1,451 37
Written, during 1872	2,865,290 49	67,480 63
Total	$2,963,092 49	$68,932 00
Deduct those terminated	705,662 00	10,797 18
In force, December 31, 1872	$2,277,430 49	58,124 82
Deduct the amount reinsured	2,500 00	52 50
Net amount in force	$2,274,930 49	$58,082 32
In force, having not more than one year to run	$2,239,880 49	$57,490 87
Having more than one and not more than three years to run	31,550 00	556,45
Having more than three years to run	3,500 00	85 00
Net amount in force	$2,274,930 49	$58,082 32

GENERAL INTERROGATORIES.

Total premiums received from the reorganization of the company to date	$58,095 12
Total losses paid from the reorganization of the company to date	63,958 94
Total amount of losses incurred during the year	65,710 74
Total amount of the company's stock owned by the directors, at par value	167,700 00
Total amount loaned to officers and directors	91,000 00
Total amount loaned to stockholders, not officers	86,000 00

BUSINESS IN THE STATE OF WISCONSIN, DURING THE YEAR 1872.

Fire risks taken	$802,999 00	....
Premiums received*	5,635 14	....
Losses paid on risks taken	8,828 53	....

* Of which $24,995 is in course of collection.

HANOVER FIRE INSURANCE COMPANY.

OF NEW YORK.

[Incorporated in 1852. Commenced business in 1852.]

B. S. WALCOTT, *President*. I. REMSEN LANE, *Secretary*.

Attorney to accept service of process in Wisconsin, GEO. E. REDFIELD, Beaver Dam.

I. CAPITAL.

Capital authorized	$250,000 00
Capital actually paid up in cash	250,000 00

II. ASSETS.

Value of real estate owned by the company, less incumbrances	$2,725 95
Loans on bond and mortgage, (first liens)	147,700 00
Interest due on bond and mortgage loans	700 00
Interest accrued on bond and mortgage loans	856 34
Stocks and bonds, market value	514,114 25
Cash loans secured by collaterals	34,500 00
Cash in company's principal office and in bank	59,141 99
Interest due and accrued not included in market value	7,164 66
Interest due and accrued on collateral loans	857 48
Net premiums in due course of collection	97,976 28
Bills receivable, not matured, taken for fire, marine and inland risks	2,056 58
Bills receivable, taken for fire, marine and inland risks, past due	2,296 59
All other property belonging to the company, viz: Salvage, $100; rents, $404 15; office furniture, etc., $11,000; due from underwriters' agency, $4,946 26; total	16,450 40
Aggregate of all the assets of the company	$886,540 40

III. LIABILITIES.

Losses adjusted and unpaid	$39,747 27	....
Losses unadjusted, including all reported and supposed losses	121,557 39	....
Losses resisted, including interest, costs and expenses	8,337 43	....
Total gross amount of claims for losses	$169,642 09	....
Deduct reinsurance thereon	3,264 85	....
Net amount of unpaid losses and claims		$166,377 24
Reinsurance at 50 per cent of prem. on fire risks, under one year	$347,697 80	....
Reinsurance, *pro rata*, on fire risks running more than one year	108,291 87	....
Amount required to safely reinsure all outstanding risks		455,989 67
Total liabilities, except capital stock		$622,366 91
Capital stock actually paid up in cash		250,000 00
Surplus beyond capital stock		14,173 49
Aggregate of all liabilities, including capital stock and surplus		$886,540 40

IV. INCOME DURING THE YEAR.

	Fire.	Marine and Inland.	
Gross premiums received in cash	$878,835 59	$1,151 59	....
Deduct reinsurance, rebate and ret'd prem's	77,944 82	....	....
Net cash received for premiums	$801,069 77	$1,151 59	$802,242 36
Net premiums, remaining unpaid		$102,299 39	....
Received for interest on bonds and mortgages			7,764 99
Received for interest and dividends from all other sources			41,096 57
Aggregate amount of income received during the year, in cash			$851,108 92

V. EXPENDITURES DURING THE YEAR.

	Fire.	Marine and inland.	
Gross amount paid for losses	$529,787 72	$8,730 47	....
Deduct salvage and reinsurance	15,686 17	91 21	....
Net amount paid during the year for losses	$514,101 55	$8,639 26	....
			$517,740 81
Cash dividends paid			40,000 00
Paid for commissions and brokerage			117,609 78
Salaries and all other charges of officers and all employes			46,045 01
Paid for state, national and local taxes			20,196 10
All other payments and expenditures			98,047 17
Aggregate amount of expenditures during the year, in cash			$839,638 87

VI. MISCELLANEOUS.

	Fire risks.	Premiums thereon.	Marine and Inland.	Premiums. thereon.
In force, December 31. 1871	$72,807,519 17	$770,340 22	$17,166 00	$559 98
Written during 1872	100,009,218 32	887,804 37	117,980 00	1,151 59
Total	$172,816,737 49	$1,658,144 59	$135,146 00	$1,711 57
Deduct those terminated	87,448,493 50	728,860 10	135,146 00	1,711 57
In force, December 31, 1872	$85,368,243 99	$929,284 49	....	....
Deduct amount reinsured	1,897,566 89	17,305 15	....	....
Net amount in force	$83,470,677 10	$911,979 34	....	....
In force, having not more than one year to run	$66,099,425 39	$695,895 60	....	....
Having more than one year and not more than three years to run	12,808,520 86	150,212 15	....	....
Having more than three years to run	4,567,730 85	66,871 59	....	....
Net amount in force	$83,470,677 10	$911,979 34	....	....

General Interrogatories.

Total premiums received from the organization of the company to date	$4,589,469 65
Total losses paid from the organization of the company to date	2,647,164 82
Total dividends declared since the company commenced business	617,000 00
Total amount of losses incurred during the year	620,681 45
Total amount of the company's stock owned by the directors, at par value	74,650 00
Total amount loaned to stockholders, not officers	5,000 00

Business in the State of Wisconsin, during the Year 1872.

Fire risks taken	$1,047,158 00
Premiums received	18,771 51
Losses paid on risks taken	12,780 37
Losses incurred during the year, in Wisconsin	11,599 37
Taxes on premiums, paid to the state of Wisconsin	548 34

HARTFORD FIRE INSURANCE COMPANY.

Hartford, Conn.

[Incorporated in 1810. Commenced business in 1810.]

GEO. L. CHASE, *President.* J. D. BROWNE, *Secretary.*

Attorney to accept service of process in Wisconsin, David M. Belden, Milwaukee.

I. CAPITAL.

Capital actually paid up in cash	$1,000,000 00

II. ASSETS.

Value of real estate owned by the company, less incumbrances	$448,175 60
Loans on bond and mortgage, (first liens)	457,250 00
Interest accrued on bond and mortgage loans	18,087 38
Stocks and bonds, market value	974,731 21
Cash in the company's principal office, and in bank	92,387 68

State tax due from non-resident stockholders	12,790 85
Interest due and accrued not included in market value	29,072 00
Net premiums in due course of collection	156,856 20
Bills receivable, not matured	2,827 13
All other property belonging to the company	17,268 99
Aggregate of all the assets of the company, at their actual value	$3,204,396 54

III. LIABILITIES.

Losses unadjusted, including all reported and supposed losses	$301,958 25	
Losses resisted, including interest, costs and expenses	11,150 00	
Net amount of unpaid losses and claims		$313,108 25
Reinsurance at 50 per cent. of prem., on fire risks, under one year	$604,012 60	
Reinsurance, *pro rata*, on fire risks running more than one year	316,162 55	
Amount required to safely reinsure all outstanding risks		920,175 15
Due and to become due for borrowed money		115,000 00
Total liabilities except capital stock		$1,848,278 40
Capital stock actually paid up in cash		1,000,000 00
Aggregate of all liabilities, including capital		$2,848,278 40

IV. INCOME DURING THE YEAR.

Gross premiums received in cash (fire)	$2,281,750 16	
Deduct reinsurance, rebate and returned premiums	143,443 55	
Net cash received for premiums		$2,138,306 61
Gross premiums remaining unpaid	$156,856 20	
Received for interest on bonds and mortgages		20,984 25
Received for interest and dividends from all other sources		64,892 00
Income received from all other sources, viz: rents		5,602 06
Aggregate amount of income received during the year in cash		$2,229,784 92

V. EXPENDITURES DURING THE YEAR.

Gross amount paid for losses (fire)	$2,263,551 94	
Net amount paid during the year for losses		$2,263,551 94
Paid for commissions and brokerage		311,379 11
Salaries and all other charges of officers and all employes		112,229 22
Paid for state, national and local taxes		45,698 46
All other payments and expenditures		136,958 07
Aggregate amount of expenditures during the year, in cash		$2,869,805 80

VI. MISCELLANEOUS.

	Fire Risks.	Premiums thereon.
In force, December 31, 1871	$150,000,000 00	$1,802,250 00
Written during 1872	150,888,916 00	2,138,306 61
Total	$300,888,916 00	$3,940,556 61
Deduct those terminated	142,058,166 00	2,134,206 41
In force, December 31, 1872	$157,830,750 00	$1,806,350 20
In force, having not more than one year to run	$110,481,525 00	$1,264,445 14
Having more than one and not more than three years to run	31,566,150 00	361,270 04
Having more than three years to run	15,783,075 00	180,635 02
Net amount in force	$157,830,750 00	$1,806,350 20

General Interrogatories.

Total premiums received from the organization of the company to date	$38,980,294 09
Total losses paid from the organization of the company to date	16,105,885 43
Total dividends declared since the company commenced business	2,486,100 00
Total amount of losses incurred during the year	1,655,616 70
Total amount of the company's stock owned by the directors, at par value	271,300 00
Total dividends payable in stock	700,000 00

Amount deposited in different states and countries, for the security of policy holders, $150,000, deposited as follows: in Alabama, $10,000; South Carolina, $20,000; Tennessee, $20,000; Canada, $100,000.

Business in the State of Wisconsin, during the Year 1872.

Risks taken (fire)	$5,619,390 00
Premiums received	92,904 43
Losses paid on risks taken	38,589 54
Losses incurred during the year, in Wisconsin	46,719 88
Taxes on premiums, paid to the state of Wisconsin	2,303 50

HARTFORD STEAM BOILER INSPECTION AND INSURANCE COMPANY.

HARTFORD, CONN.

[Incorporated in 1866. Commenced business in 1866.]

J. M. ALLEN, *President.* THEO. H. BABCOCK *Secretary.*

Attorney to accept service of process in Wisconsin, SAML. M. OGDEN, Milwaukee.

I. CAPITAL.

Capital authorized	$1,000,000 00
Capital actually paid up in cash	120,000 00

II. ASSETS.

Loans on bond and mortgage, (first liens)		$33,800 00
Interest accrued on bond and mortgage loans		796 33
Stocks and bonds, market value		118,070 00
Cash in the company's principal office in currency		4,246 20
Interest due and accrued, not included in market value		3,190 00
Net premiums in due course of collection		11,495 61
All other property belonging to the company		2,400 00
Stockholder's notes or other obligation given for capital subscribed	$880,000 00	....
Aggregate of all assets of the company		$173,998 14

III. LIABILITIES.

Losses adjusted and unpaid	$549 48	....
Losses unadjusted, including all reported and supposed losses	100 00	....
Net amount of unpaid losses and claims		$649 48
Reinsurance at 25 per cent. of premium, on risks		25,138 61
Total liabilities, except capital stock		$25,788 09
Capital stock actually paid up in cash		120,000 00
Surplus beyond capital stock		28,210 05
Aggregate of all liabilities, including capital and surplus		$173,998 14

IV. INCOME DURING THE YEAR.

Gross premiums received in cash,	$105,225 59	....
Deduct reinsurance, rebate and returned premiums	4,767 81	....
Net cash received for premiums		$100,457 78
Net premiums, remaining unpaid	$11,495 61	....
Received for interest on bonds and mortgages		2,405 97
Received for interest and dividends, from all other sources		7,560 71
Income received from all other sources, viz: for inspection		45,096 68
Aggregate amount of income received during the year in cash		$155,521 14

V. EXPENDITURES DURING THE YEAR.

Net amount paid during the year for losses	$18,206 50
Cash dividends paid	31,000 00
Paid for commissions and brokerage	34,804 81
Salaries and all other charges of officers, and all employes	8,095 80
Paid for state, national and local taxes	2,707 12
All other payments, and expenditures	60,061 66
Aggregate amount of expenditure during the year, in cash	$154,875 89

VI. MISCELLANEOUS.

	Risks.	Premiums thereon.
In force, December 31, 1871	$8,721,270	$73,645 46
Written during 1872	12,258,954	103,524 81
Total	$20,980,224	$177,170 27
Deduct those terminated	9,136,148	76,615 82
In force, December 31, 1872	$11,844,076	$100,554 45

In force, having not more than one year to run	$11,844,076	$100,399 45
Having more than one and not more than three years to run	10,000	155 00
Net amount in force	$11,854,076	$100,554 45

GENERAL INTERROGATORIES.

Total premiums received, from the organization of the company to date	$429,265 67
Total losses paid, from the organization of the company to date	26,429 67
Total cash dividends declared since the company commenced business	29,000 00
Total amount of losses incurred during the year	16,976 65
Total amount of the company's stock owned by the directors, at par value	117,500 00
Total dividends endorsed on stock notes	20,000 00
Amount deposited in different states and countries, for the security of policy holders, $100,000, deposited in the state of Connecticut	

BUSINESS IN THE STATE OF WISCONSIN, DURING THE YEAR 1872.

Risks taken	$355,850 00
Premiums received	2,840 78
Received for inspection	1,217 47
Losses paid on risks taken	480 48
Losses incurred during the year, in Wisconsin	480 48
Taxes on premiums, paid to the state of Wisconsin	51 72

HOFFMAN FIRE INSURANCE COMPANY.

NEW YORK.

[Incorporated in 1864. Commenced business in 1864.]

MARCUS F. HODGES, *President*. OLIVER A. DRAKE, *Secretary*.

Attorney to accept service of process in Wisconsin, C. J. CARY, Milwaukee.

I. CAPITAL.

Capital actually paid up in cash	200,000 00

II. ASSETS.

Loans on bond and mortgage, (first liens)	$166,750 00
Interest accrued on bond and mortgage loans	5,242 68
Stocks and bonds, market value	63,800 00
Cash in the company's principal office and in bank	1,356 10
Gross premiums in due course of collection	48,706 34
All other property belonging to the company, viz: office furniture	2,500 00
Aggregate of all the assets of the company, at their actual value	$288,355 12

III. LIABILITIES.

Losses adjusted and unpaid	$11,223 90	
Losses unadjusted, including all reported and supposed losses	78,460 12	
Losses resisted, including interest, costs and expenses	3,600 00	
Net amount of unpaid losses and claims		$93,284 02
Reinsurance at 50 per ct. of prem's on fire risks, under one year	$91,655 91	
Reinsurance, *pro rata*, on fire risks running more than one year	4,458 70	
Amount required to safely reinsure all outstanding risks		96,114 61
Due and accrued for salaries, rent and other expenses		1,000 00
All other demands against the company		2,214 31
Total liabilities, except capital stock		$192,612 94
Capital stock actually paid up in cash		200,000 00
Aggregate amount of all liabilities, including capital stock		$392,612 94

Note.—An assessment of 50 per cent. on the capital stock of this company was all paid in cash, January 20, 1873.

IV. INCOME DURING THE YEAR.

Gross premiums received in cash (fire)	$218,254 02	
Deduct reinsurance, rebate and returned premiums	18,074 19	
Net cash received for premiums		$200,179 83
Gross premiums remaining unpaid	$48,706 34	
Received for interest on bonds and mortgages		8,073 78
Received for interest and dividends from all other sources		4,249 95
Income received from all other sources		6,082 53
Aggregate amount of income received during the year in cash		$218,586 09

V. EXPENDITURES DURING THE YEAR.

Gross amount paid for losses, (fire)	$177,332 15	....
Deduct salvage	150 71	....
Net amount paid during the year for losses		$177,181 44
Cash dividends paid		20,050 00
Paid for commissions and brokerage		31,116 17
Salaries and all other charges of officers, and all employes		19,465 61
Paid for state, national and local taxes		5,954 21
All other payments and expenditures		19,002 89
Aggregate amount of expenditures during the year, in cash		$272,470 32

VI. MISCELLANEOUS.

	Fire Risks.	Premiums thereon.
In force, December 31, 1871	$10,409,084 71	$121,966 48
Written during 1872	23,593,286 07	260,281 48
Total	$34,002,370 78	$382,247 96
Deduct those terminated	16,042,585 83	187,878 02
In force, December 31, 1872	$17,959,784 95	$194,369 94
Deduct amount reinsured	468,247 74	5,411 05
Net amount in force	$17,491,537 21	$188,958 89
In force, having not more than one year to run	$17,085,512 21	$183,811 82
Having more than one, and not more than three years to run	269,575 00	2,319 08
Having more than three years to run	136 450 00	2,827 99
Net amount in force	$17,491,537 21	$188,958 89

General Interrogatories.

Total premiums received from the organization of the company to date	$669,155 01
Total losses paid from the organization of the company to date	538,082 96
Total dividends declared since the company commenced business	20,000 00
Total amount of losses incurred during the year	262,062 29
Total amount of the company's stock owned by the directors at par value	68,350 00
Total amount loaned to officers and directors	5,000 00

Business in the State of Wisconsin, during the Year 1872.

Risks taken, (fire)	$310,690 00
Premiums received	2,498 99
Losses paid on risks taken	298 11
Losses incurred during the year, in Wisconsin	298 11
Taxes on premiums, paid to fire departments in Wisconsin	56 80

HOME INSURANCE COMPANY.

COLUMBUS, OHIO.

[Incorporated in 1863. Commenced business in 1864.]

M. A. DAUGHERTY, *President.* JACOB PEETREY, *Secretary.*

Attorney to accept service of process in Wisconsin, GEO. A. HANAFORD, Milwaukee.

I. CAPITAL.

Capital authorized	$350,000 00
Capital actually paid up in cash	250,000 00

II. ASSETS.

Value of real estate owned by the company, less incumbrances	$1,727 80
Loans on bond and mortgage (first liens)	342,593 35
Loans on bond and and mortgage (first lien), upon which more than one years interest is due	30,040 22
Interest due on bond and mortgage loans	4,550 82
Interest accrued on bond and mortgage loans	18,208 94
Stocks and bonds, market value	62,205 41
Cash loans secured by collaterals	82,798 10
Bills receivable, personal security	16,245 40
Cash in the company's principal office and in bank	25,275 96
Interest due and accured, not included in market value	174 96
Interest due and accrued on collateral loans	1,811 76

Gross premiums in due course of collection	171,920 64
Bills receivable, not matured, taken for fire, marine and inland risks	15,109 76
Bills receivable, taken for fire, marine and inland risks, past due	5,199 43
All other property belonging to the company, viz: personal property, $8,272 20; agency outfit, $15,000; reinsurance on losses paid, $49,765 68; total	73,037 88
Aggregate of all assets of the company	800,733 76

III. LIABILITIES.

Losses adjusted and unpaid	$62,974	
Losses unadjusted, including all reported and supposed losses	45,000 56	
Losses resisted, including interest, costs and expenses	40,000 00	
Net amount of unpaid losses and claims		$147,974 56
Reinsurance at 50 per cent. of prem. on fire risks, under one year	$191,042 09	
Reinsurance, *pro rata*, on fire risks running more than one year	139,723 59	
Amount required to safely reinsure all outstanding risks		$330,765 68
All other demands against the company, viz: commissions		24,480 16
Total liabilities, except capital stock		$503,220 40
Capital stock actually paid up in cash		250,000 00
Surplus beyond capital stock		47,513 36
Aggregate amount of all liabilities, including capital and surplus		$800,733 76

IV. INCOME DURING THE YEAR.

Gross premiums received in cash (fire)	$567,848 02	
Gross cash received on bills and notes taken for premiums	5,265 68	
Gross cash received for premiums	$573,113 70	
Deduct reinsurance, rebate and returned premiums	13,650 17	
Net cash received for premiums		$559,463 53
Gross premiums remaining unpaid	$212,359 00	
Received for interest on bonds and mortgages		34,803 27
Aggregate amount of income received during the year in cash		$594,266 80

V. EXPENDITURES DURING THE YEAR.

Gross amount paid for losses (fire)	$595,106 28	
Deduct reinsurance	13,200 19	
Net amount paid during the year for losses		$581,906 09
Paid for commissions and brokerage		92,696 76
Salaries and all other charges of officers, and all employes		52,478 72
Paid for state, national and local taxes		13,747 96
All other payments and expenditures		29,921 11
Aggregate amount of expenditures during the year, in cash		$770,750 64

VI. MISCELLANEOUS.

	Fire Risks.	Premiums thereon.
In force, December 31, 1871	$52,336,428 00	$378,000 00
Written during 1872	45,938,639 00	618,589 92
Total	$98,275,067 00	$996,589 92
Deduct those terminated	48,496,941 00	325,096 04
In force, December 31, 1872	$49,778,126 00	671,493 88
Deduct amount reinsured	861,721 00	9,962 52
Net amount in force,	$48,916,405 00	$661,531 36
In force, having not more than one year to run	$39,353,800 00	$530,890 88
Having more than one and not more three years to run	6,988,058 00	81,338 44
Having more than three years to run	2,574,547 00	49,302 04
Net amount in force,	$48,916,405 00	$661,531 36

General Interrogatories.

Total premiums received from the organization of the company to date	$1,909,411 93
Total losses paid from the organization of the company to date	1,387,872 97
Total dividends declared since the company commenced business	47,126 60
Total amount of losses incurred during the year	568,311 24
Total amount of the company's stock owned by the directors, at par value	60,470 00
Total dividends payable in stock	73,055 00
Total amount loaned to officers and directors	51,698 72
Total amount loaned to stock holders, not officers	190,497 64

Amount deposited in different states and countries, for the security of policy holders, $50,000, deposited in the state of Virginia $25,000; West Virginia, $25,000.

BUSINESS IN THE STATE OF WISCONSIN, DURING THE YEAR 1872.

Risks taken, (fire)	$833,688 00	....
Premiums received	10,050 23	....
Losses paid on risks taken	1,905 14	....
Losses incurred during the year, in Wisconsin	3,573 60	....
Taxes on preminms, paid to the state of Wisconsin	500 00	....
Taxes on premiums, paid to fire departments in Wisconsin	58 04	....

HOME INSURANCE COMPANY.

NEW YORK.

[Incorporated in 1853. Commenced business in 1853.]

CHARLES J. MARTIN, *President*. JOHN H. WASHBURN, *Secretary*.

Attorney to accept service of process in Wisconsin, HENRY S. DURAND, Racine.

I. CAPITAL.

Capital authorized	$2,500,000 00
Capital actually paid up in cash	2,500,000 00

II. ASSETS.

Loans on bond and mortgage, (first liens)	$1,916,765 00
Interest accrued on bond and mortgage loans	48,364 67
Stocks and bonds, market value	1,725,965 00
Cash loans secured by collaterals	94,123 49
Cash belonging to the company, deposited in bank	204,353 61
Interest due and accrued on collateral loans and bank balances	4,370 66
Net premiums in due course of collection	290,484 46
Bills receivable, not matured, taken for fire, marine and inland risks	3,093 66
Bills receivable, taken for fire, marine and inland risks, past due	998 16
Bills receivable, taken for steamer Magnet	12,500 01
Salvage and reinsurance on losses paid	72,701 64
Advanced and secured accounts	28,723 40
Leare, 185 and 187 Broadway, N. Y	30,000 00
All other property belonging to the company	20,000 00
Aggregate of all the assets of the company, at their actual value	$4,446,858 78

III. LIABILITIES.

Losses unadjusted, including all reported and supposed losses	$565,089 20	....
Losses resisted, including interest, costs and expenses	32,899 99	....
Total gross amount of claims for losses	$597,989 19	....
Deduct reinsurance thereon	10,000 00	....
Net amount of unpaid losses and claims		$587,989 19
Reinsurance at 50 per cent. of prem., on fire risks, under one year	$1,014,076 00	....
Reinsurance, *pro rata*, on fire risks running more than one year	672,168 00	....
Amount required to safely reinsure all outstanding risks		1,686,244 00
Cash dividends declared to stockholders, unpaid		2,975 00
Total liabilities except capital stock		$2,277,158 19
Capital stock actually paid up in cash		2,500,000 00
Aggregate of all liabilities, including capital		$4,777,158 19

IV. INCOME DURING THE YEAR.

Gross premiums received in cash (fire)	$3,371,860 39	....
Deduct reinsurance, rebate and returned premiums	229,554 06	....
Net cash received for premiums		*$3,142,306 33
Bills and notes rec'd during the year for prem's, unpaid	$3,698 66	....
Received for interest on bonds and mortgages		129,864 01
Received for interest and dividends from all other sources		123,525 76
Income received from all other sources, viz: rents		5,998 32
Aggregate amount of income received during the year in cash		$3,401,694 44

V. EXPENDITURES DURING THE YEAR.

Gross amount paid for losses (fire)	$2,766,432 35	....
Deduct salvage and reinsurance	168,700 47	....
Net amount paid during the year for losses		$2,598,731 88

Cash dividends paid	122,485 00
Paid for commissions and brokerage	478,844 91
Salaries and all other charges of officers, and all employes	200,750 51
Paid for state, national and local taxes	66,207 23
All other payments and expenditures	208,796 45
Aggregate amount of expenditures during the year, in cash	$3,654,765 97

VI. MISCELLANEOUS.

	Fire risks.	Premiums thereon.
In force, December 31, 1871	$294,852,308	$2,881,053 00
Written during 1872	346,036,172	3,142,306 33
Total	$640,888,480	$6,023,359 33
Deduct those terminated	299,174,423	2,829,691 41
In force, December 31, 1872	$341,714,057	$3,193,667 92
Deduct amount reinsured	1,564,389	12,475 50
Net amount in force	$340,149,668	$3,181,192 42
In force, having not more than one year to run	$251,913,955	$2,233,724 21
Having more than one and not more than three years to run.	62,714,786	655,089 06
Having more than three years to run	25,520,927	292,379 15
Net amount in force	$340,149,668	$3,181,192 42

General Interrogatories.

Total premiums received from the organization of the company to date	$28,455,872 66
Total losses paid from the organization of the company to date	18,601,499 44
Total dividends declared since the company commenced business	3,190,000 00
Total amount of losses incurred during the year	2,331,445 39
Total amount of the company's stock owned by the directors, at par value	566,300 00
Total dividends payable in stock	500,000 00
Total amount loaned to directors	76,228 49
Total amount loaned to stockholders, not officers	17,750 00

Amt. deposited in different states and countries, for the security of policy holders $194,000; deposited as follows: in the State of Virginia, $44,000; Tennessee, $20,000; Alabama, $10,000; South Carolina, $20,000; Russia, $100,000.

Business in the State of Wisconsin, during the Year 1872.

Risks taken (fire)	$8,584,635 00
Premiums received	122,762 86
Losses paid on risks taken	49,424 63
Losses incurred dusing the year in Wisconsin	44,488 52
Taxes on premiums paid to the state, and fire departments of Wisconsin	4,346 43

*Of which $395,111.30 is in course of collection.

HOWARD INSURANCE COMPANY.

New York.

[Incorporated in 1825. Commenced business in 1825.]

SAMUEL T. SKIDMORE, *President.* THEODORE KEELER, *Secretary.*

Attorney to accept service of process in Wisconsin, J. A. Helfenstein, Milwaukee.

I. CAPITAL.

Capital authorized	$500,000 00
Capital actually paid up in cash	500,000 00

II. ASSETS.

Value of real estate owned by the company, less incumbrances	$125,000 00
Loans on bond and mortgage, (first liens)	63,900 00
Interest accrued on bond and mortgage loans	1,064 19
Stocks and bonds, market value	373,808 00
Cash loans secured by collaterals	1,000 00
Cash in the company's principal office and in bank	16,440 96
Interest due and accrued, not included in market value	3,711 21
Interest due and accrued on collateral loans	85 00

Net premiums in due course of collection	16,887 87
All other property belonging to the company, viz: salvage, 1,250; rents, $866 67; office furniture, $5,000; total	7,116 67
Aggregate of all the assets of the company	$608,963 93

III. LIABILITIES.

Losses unadjusted, including all reported and supposed losses	$4,633 06	
Losses resisted, including interest, costs and expenses	1,000 00	
Net amount of unpaid losses and claims		$5,633 06
Reinsurance at 50 per cent. of prem. on fire risks under one year	$90,209	
Reinsurance, *pro rata*, on fire risks running more than one year	9,619 48	
Reinsurance at 50 per cent. of prem. on inland navigation risks	400 69	
Amount required to safely reinsure all outstanding risks		100,229 29
All other demands against the company, viz: balances due ag'ts		56 63
Total liabilities, except capital stock		$105,918 98
Capital stock actually paid up in cash		500,000 00
Surplus beyond capital stock		3,044 94
Aggregate of all liabilities, including capital and surplus		$608,963 93

IV. INCOME DURING THE YEAR.

	Fire.	Marine and Inland.	
Gross premiums received in cash	$242,629 60	$1,136 00	
Deduct reinsurance, rebate and returned prem's	16,086 67		
Net cash received for premiums	$226,542 93	$1,136 00	$227,678 93
Net premiums, remaining unpaid		$16,887 87	
Received for interest on bonds and mortgages			5,637 13
Received for interest and dividends from all other sources			22,465 02
Income received from all other sources, viz., rents			5,200 00
Aggregate amount of income received during the year in cash			$260,981 08

V. EXPENDITURES DURING THE YEAR.

Gross amount paid for losses (fire)	$263,856 59	
Net amount paid during the year for losses		$263,856 59
Paid for commissions and brokerage		25,636 21
Salaries and all other charges of officers, and all employes		23,663 43
Paid for state, national and local taxes		11,394 72
All other payments, viz: interest on borrowed money, $2,896 20; printing, advertising and supplies, $2,702 71; repairs to real estate, $559 33; other expenses, $1,109 01; total		17,267 30
Aggregate amount of expenditures during the year, in cash		$341,828 25

VI. MISCELLANEOUS.

	Fire Risks.	Premiums thereon.	Marine and Inland Risks.	Premiums thereon.
In force, December 31, 1871	$35,094,573	$161,743 82	$20,000	$1,000 00
Written during 1872	33,962,469	247,903 05	23,200	1,136 00
Total	$68,957,042	$409,646 87	$43,200	$2,136 00
Deduct those terminated	30,715,055	208,304 00	33,200	1,336 00
In force, December 31, 1872	$28,241,987	$201,342 87	$10,000	$800 00
Deduct amount reinsured	656,338	3,923 30		
Net amount in force	$27,585,649	$197,419 57	$10,000	$800 00
In force, having not more than one year to run	$26,185,628	$180,418 97	$10,000	$800 00
Having more than one and not more than three years to run	1,171,671	14,174 85		
Having more than three years to run	228,350	2,825 75		
Net amount in force	$27,585,649	$197,419 57	$10,000	$800 00

General Interrogatories.

Total premiums received from the organization of the company to date	$5,169,075 00
Total losses paid from the organization of the company to date	3,914,061 03
Total dividends declared since the company commenced business	1,668,875 00

Total amount of losses incurred during the year	77,246 51
Total amount of the company's stock owned by the directors, at par value....	78,850 00
Total amount loaned to officers and directors	1,000 00

BUSINESS IN THE STATE OF WISCONSIN, DURING THE YEAR 1872.

Risks taken (fire)	$552,685 00
Premiums received	6,349 56
Losses paid on risks taken	3,336 99
Losses incurred during the year, in Wisconsin	3,336 99
Taxes on premiums, paid to the state of Wisconsin	130 12

THE INSURANCE COMPANY OF NORTH AMERICA.

PHILADELPHIA, PA.

[Incorporated in 1794. Commenced business in 1792.]

ARTHUR G. COFFIN. *President.* MATTHIAS MARIS, *Secretary.*

Attorney to accept service of process in Wisconsin, A. H. MAIN, Madison.

I. CAPITAL.

Capital authorized	$500,000 00
Capital actually paid up	500,000 00

II. ASSETS.

Value of real estate owned by the company, less incumbrances	$35,000 00
Loans on bond and mortgage, (first liens)	878,250 00
Interest due on bond and mortgage loans	10,094 17
Stocks and bonds, market value	1,283,438 00
Cash loans secured by collaterals	58,695 23
Cash belonging to the company, deposited in bank	177,115 19
Interest due and accrued on collateral loans	276 00
Net premiums in course of transmission, (fire)	154,677 11
Net premiums in due course of collection, (marine)	196,660 13
Bills receivable, not matured, taken for marine risks	458,035 07
Premium on gold and balances due the company	24,498 01
Aggregate of all the assets of the company, at their actual value	$3,276,738 91

III. LIABILITIES.

Losses unadjusted, including all reported and supposed losses.	$771,967 91	
Losses resisted, including interest, costs and expenses	13,000 00	
Net amount of unpaid losses and claims		$784,967 91
Reinsurance at 50 per cent. of prem. on fire risks, under one year	$770,148 08	
Reinsurance, *pro rata*, on fire risks running more than one year	185,906 23	
Gross premiums on all unexpired marine risks	439,614 69	
Amount required to safely reinsure all outstanding risks...		$1,345,662 95
Amount reclaimable on perpetual fire risks		812,878 94
Cash dividends declared to stockholders, unpaid		2,500 00
Total liabilities, except capital stock		$2,446,009 80
Capital stock actually paid up in cash		500,000 00
Surplus beyond capital stock		330,729 11
Aggregate of all liabilities including capital and surplus		$3,276,738 91

IV. INCOME DURING THE YEAR.

	Fire.	Marine and Inland.	
Gross premiums received in cash	$1,822,487 82	$1,049,308 77	
Gross cash rec'd on bills and notes taken for premiums		526,446 00	
Gross cash received for premiums	$1,822,487 82	$1,575,754 77	
Deduct reinsurance, rebate and ret'd prems	125,221 97	395,805 07	
Net cash received for premiums	$1,697,265 85	$1,179,949 70	$2,877,215 55
Net premiums remaining unpaid		$309,872 81	
Received for interest on bonds and mortgages			59,999 97
Received for interest and dividends from all other sources			101,404 14
Deposit premiums, received for perpetual fire risks		$53,415 06	
Aggregate amount of income received during the year in cash			$3,088,619 66

V. EXPENDITURES DURING THE YEAR.

	Fire.	Marine and inland.	
Gross amount paid for losses	$1,982,226 67	$1,190,292 81	....
Deduct salvage and reinsurance	....	203,890 52	....
Net am't paid during the year for losses	$1,982,226,67	$986,402 29	$2,968,628 96
Cash dividends paid		....	97,500 00
Paid for commission and brokerage			343,299 58
Salaries and all other charges of officers, and all employes			60,000 00
Paid for state, national and local taxes			74,731 12
All other payments and expenditures			184,948 49
Aggregate amount of expenditures during the year, in cash			$3,729,108 15

VI. MISCELLANEOUS.

	Fire risks.	Premiums thereon.	Marine and Inland Risks.	Premiums thereon.
In force, December 31, 1871	$128,848,876	$1,458,811 52	$20,601,340	$412,746 79
Written during 1872	165,565,580	1,947,041 21	129,375,354	1,629,274 39
Total	$294,414,456	$3,405,852 73	$149,976,694	$2,042,021 18
Deduct those terminated	139,696,208	1,593,756 20	133,346,965	1,602,406 49
In force, December 31, 1872	$154,718,248	$1,812,096 53	$16,629,729	$439,614 69
In force, having not more than one year to run	$131,510,512	$1,540,282 06	$16,629,729	$439,614 69
Having more than one and not more than three years to run	15,471,824	181,209 65	....	....
Having more than three years to run	7,735,912	90,604 82	....	....
Perpetual risks in force and int. prem	11,335,925	329,346 25	....	....
Net amount in force	$166,054,173	$2,141,442 78	$16,629,729	$439,614 69

General Interrogatories.

Total premiums received from the organization of the company to date, about	$40,000,000 00
Total losses paid from the organization of the company to date, about	28,000,000 00
Total dividends declared since the company commenced business	8,300,000 00
Total amount of losses incurred during the year	3,691 796 87
Total amount of the company's stock owned by the directors, at par value 11,598 @ $10	115,980 00
Total amount loaned to officers and directors	2,500 00
Total amount loaned to stockholders, not officers	28,200 00

Business in the State of Wisconsin, during the Year 1872.

Risks taken (fire)	$3,687,420 00
Premiums received	69,076 17
Losses paid on risks taken	47,828 52
Losses incurred during the year, in Wisconsin	50,900 00
Taxes on premiums, paid to the state of Wisconsin	1,004 39
Taxes on premiums, paid to fire departments in Wisconsin	798 96

LORILLARD INSURANCE COMPANY.

New York.

Incorporated in 1871. Commenced business in 1872.

CARLISLE NORWOOD, *President.* JOHN C. MILLS, *Secretary.*

Attorney to accept service of process in Wisconsin, C. J. Cary, Milwaukee.

I. CAPITAL.

Capital authorized	$300,000 00
Capital actually paid up in cash	300,000 00

II. ASSETS.

Value of real estate owned by the company, less incumbrances	$5,083 50
Loans on bond and mortgage, (first liens)	268,100 00
Interest accrued on bond and mortgage loans	8,868 50
Cash loans secured by collaterals	5,000 00
Cash in the company's principal office and in bank	91,188 42

Interest due and accured on collateral loans		175 00
Gross premiums in due course of collection		29,088 13
Aggregate of all the assets of the company, at their actual value		$397,432 55

III. LIABILITIES.

Losses unadjusted, including all reported and supposed losses	$21,500 00	
Net amount of of unpaid losses and claims		$21,500 00
Reinsurance at 50 per cent. of prem. on fire risks under one year	62,799 12	
Reinsurance, *pro rata*, on fire risks running more than one year	1,754 59	
Amount required to safely reinsure all outstanding risks		64,553 71
Total liabilities, except capital stock		$86,053 71
Capital stock actually paid up in cash		300,000 00
Surplus beyond capital stock		11,378 84
Aggregate of all liabilities including capital stock and surplus		$397,432 55

IV. INCOME DURING THE YEAR.

Gross premiums received in cash (fire)	$165,167 19	
Deduct reinsurance, rebate and returned premiums	16,417 59	
Net cash received for premiums		$148,749 60
Gross premiums remaining unpaid	$29,088 13	
Received for interest on bonds and mortgages		11,667 59
Received for calls on capital	$100,000 00	
Aggregate amount of income received during the year, in cash		$160,417 19

V. EXPENDITURES DURING THE YEAR.

Net amount paid during the year for losses (fire)	$137,965 70
Paid for commissions and brokerage	19,481 12
Salaries and all other charges of officers, and all employes	22,500 00
Paid for state, national and local taxes	6,322 95
All other payments and expenditures	15,531 50
Aggregate amount of expenditures during the year, in cash	$201,101 27

VI. MISCELLANEOUS.

	Fire Risks.	Premiums thereon.
Written during 1878	$22,096,024	$194,250 00
Deduct those terminated	7,067,183	57,851 52
In force, December 31, 1878	$15,028,841	$136,398 48
Deduct amount reinsured	817,024	8,023 41
Net amount in force	$14,211,817	$128,375 07
In force, having not more than one year to run	$13,918,068	$125,598 24
Having more than one and not more than three years to run	293,749	2,776 83
Net amount in force	$14,211,817	$128,375 07

General Interrogatories.

Total premiums received from the organization of the company to date	$194,250 00
Total losses paid from the organization of the company to date	137,965 70
Total amount of losses incurred during the year	158,765 70
Total amount of the company's stock owned by the directors, at par value	105,000 00
Total amount loaned to stockholders, not officers	22,500 00

Business in the State of Wisconsin, during the Year 1878.

Risks taken (fire)	$309,198 00
Premiums received	4,214 12
Losses paid on risks taken	1,475 00
Losses incurred during the year in Wisconsin	1,475 00

MANHATTAN FIRE INSURANCE COMPANY.

NEW YORK.

[Incorporated in 1872. Commenced business in 1872.]

ANDREW J. SMITH, *President.* JOHN H. BEDELL, *Secretary.*

Attorney to accept service of process in Wisconsin, HENRY S. DURAND, Racine.

I. CAPITAL.

Capital authorized	$250,000 00
Capital actually paid up in cash	250,000 00

II. ASSETS.

Loans on bond and mortgage, (first liens)	$105,068 00
Interest due on bond and mortgage loans	665 00
Interest accrued on bond and mortgage loans	612 86
Stocks and bonds, market value	242,660 00
Cash loans secured by collaterals	20,655 56
Cash belonging to company, deposited in bank	67,730 88
Interest due and accrued, not included in market value	3,000 00
Interest due and accrued on collateral loans	729 14
Net premiums in course of collection	52,479 80
Aggregate of all the assets of the company, at their actual value	$498,769 19

III. LIABILITIES.

Total net amount of claims for losses		$45,000 60
Reinsurance at 50 per ct. of pre'm on fire risk under one year	$147,200 00	....
Reinsurance, *pro rata*, on fire risks running more than one year	1,275 00	....
Amount required to safely reinsure all outstanding risks		148,475 00
Total liabilities, except capital stock		$193,475 00
Capital stock actually paid up in cash		250,000 00
Surplus beyond capital stock		50,294 19
Aggregate of all liabilities, including capital and surplus		$498,769 19

IV. INCOME DURING THE YEAR.

	Fire.	Marine and Inland.	
Gross premiums received in cash	$305,598 85	$6,000 00	....
Deduct reinsurance, rebate and returned prem's	12,433 97	....	....
Net cash received for premiums	$293,165 88	$6,000 00	$299,165 88
Net premiums, remaining unpaid		$52,479 80	....
Received for interest on bonds and mortgages			1,759 68
Received for interest and dividends from all other sources			9,230 00
Aggregate amount of income received during the year in cash			$310,155 50

V. EXPENDITURES DURING THE YEAR.

Net amount paid during the year for losses (fire)	$94,266 96
Paid for commissions and brokerage	53,114 31
Salaries and all other charges of officers, and all employes	13,425 00
All other payments and expenditures	21,867 71
Aggregate amount of expenditures during the year, in cash	$182,673 98

VI. MISCELLANEOUS.

	Fire Risks.	Premiums thereon.	Marine and Inland Risks.	Premiums thereon.
Written during 1872	$32,384,806 27	$358,078 65	$527,580 00	$6,000 00
Deduct those terminated	9,823,126 60	55,460 00	527,580 00	6,000 00
In force, December 31, 1872	$22,561,681 67	$302,618 65	....	....
Deduct amount reinsured	796,120 00	6,635 00	....	....
Net amount in force	$21,765,561 67	$295,983 65	....	....

In force, having not more than one year to run..........	$21,765,561 67	$295,988 65	....	....
Having more than one and not more than three years to run..........	847,507 59	688 25	....	....
Having more than three years to run..........	274,130 00	260 85	....	....
Net amount in force..........	$22,887,199 17	$296,882 75	....	....

GENERAL INTERROGATORIES.

Total premiums received from the organization of the company to date	$364,078 65
Total losses paid from the organization of the company to date..............	94,266 96
Total amount of losses incurred during the year	139,266 96
Total amount of the company's stock owned by the directors, at par value...	78,900 00
Total amount loaned to officers and directors..............................	5,000 00
Amount deposited in different states and countries, for the security of policy holders, $32,500, deposited as follows: in the state of South Carolina, $20,000; Virginia, $12,500.	

BUSINESS IN THE STATE OF WISCONSIN, DURING THE YEAR 1872.

Risks taken..........	$807,567 00
Premiums received..........	11,078 56
Losses paid on risks taken..........	171 95
Losses incurred during the year, in Wisconsin..........	171 95

MECHANICS AND TRADERS' FIRE INSURANCE COMPANY.

NEW YORK.

Incorporated in 1853. Commenced business in 1853.

JAMES R. LOTT, *President*, JOHN M. TOMPKINS, *Secretary*.

Attorneys to accept service of process in Wisconsin, W. B. and E. C. HIBBARD, Milwaukee.

I. CAPITAL.

Capital authorized..........	$200,000 00
Capital actually paid up in cash..........	200,000 00

II. ASSETS.

Loans on bond and mortgage, (first liens)..........	$284,400 00
Interest accrued on bond and mortgage loans..........	1,950 66
Stocks and bonds..........	68,275 00
Cash loans secured by collaterals..........	12,740 68
Cash in the company's principal office and in bank..........	47,290 25
Interest due and accrued on collateral loans..........	287 00
Gross premiums in due course of collection..........	36,719 35
Bills receivable, not matured, taken for fire, marine and inland risks..........	88,121 59
Aggregate of all the assets of the company, at their actual value..........	$539,734 48

III. LIABILITIES.

Losses unadjusted, including all reported and supposed losses.	$29,300 00	....
Losses resisted, including interest, costs and expenses	4,900 00	....
Net amount of unpaid losses and claims..........		$34,200 00
Reinsurance at 50 per cent. of prem, on fire risks, under one year	$92,807 66	....
Reinsurance, *pro rata*, on fire risks running more than one year	345 72	....
Reinsurance at 50 per cent. of prem. on inland risks	25,552 47	....
Amount required to safely reinsure all outstanding risks.		$118,705 85
Due and accrued for rent..........		500 00
All other demands against the company, viz: commissions		1,837 85
Total liabilities, except capital stock		$155,243 20
Capital stock actually paid up in cash..........		200,000 00
Surplus beyond capital stock..........		184,491 28
Aggregate of all liabilities including capital and surplus..........		$539,734 48

IV. INCOME DURING THE YEAR.

	Fire.	Marine and Inland.	
Gross premiums received in cash	$206,523 65	$25,481 44	....
Gross cash rec'd on bills and notes taken for prem's	....	42,303 21	....
Gross cash received for premiums	$206,523 65	$67,784 65	....
Deduct reinsurance, rebate and ret'd prem's	6,452 64	10,788 66	....
Net cash received for premiums	$200,071 01	$56,945 99	$257,017 00
Gross premiums remaining unpaid		$74,840 94	....
Received for interest on bonds and mortgages			23,855 98
Received for interest and dividends from all other sources			4,890 00
Aggregate amount of income received during the year in cash			$285,762 98

V. EXPENDITURES DURING THE YEAR.

	Fire.	Marine and Inland.	
Gross amount paid for losses	$98,892 73	$86,154 01	....
Deduct salvage and reinsurance	....	6,488 75	....
Net amount paid during the year for losses	$98,892 73	$79,665 26	$178,557 99
Cash dividends paid			40,000 00
Paid for commissions and brokerage			29,423 66
Salaries and all other charges of officers, and all employes			19,344 56
Paid for state, national and local taxes			7,281 05
All other payments, viz.: fire patrol and underwriters' board, $1,270.52; rent, stationery, advertising, and current expenses, $5,888.34; total			7,158 86
Aggregate amount of expenditures during the year, in cash			$281,766 12

VI. MISCELLANEOUS.

	Fire Risks.	Premiums thereon.	Marine and Inland risks.	Premiums thereon.
In force, December 31, 1871	$22,894,793	$168,707 88	$903,082	$22,902 61
Written during 1872	31,889,981	204,108 73	17,757,477	100,856 97
Total	$54,784,774	$372,816 61	$18,660,559	$123,759 58
Deduct those terminated	30,087,194	185,039 03	16,997,408	64,377 00
In force, December 31, 1872	$24,697,580	$187,777 58	$1,663,151	$59,382 58
Deduct amount reinsured	289,397	1,704 22	187,755	8,277 63
Net amount in force	$24,408,183	$186,073 36	$1,475,396	$51,104 95
In force, having not more than one year to run	$24,367,845	$185,615 32	$1,475,396	$51,104 95
Having more than one and not more than three years to run	40,338	458 04	....	....
Net amount in force	$24,408,183	$186,073 36	$1,475,396	$51,104 95

General Interrogatories.

Total premiums received, from the organization of the company to date	$2,020,890 00
Total losses paid, from the organization of the company to date	1,064,762 00
Total dividends declared since the company commenced business	548,000 00
Total amount of losses incurred during the year	205,568 00
Total amount of the company's stock owned by the directors, at par value	49,725 00

Business in the State of Wisconsin, during the Year 1872.

	Fire.	Marine and Inland.	Aggregate.
Risks taken	$416,548 88	$1,143,843 00	$1,560,391 88
Premiums received	3,509 76	10,651 28	14,161 04
Losses paid on risks taken	....	1,447 07	1,447 07
Losses incurred during the year, in Wisconsin	....	....	3,082 51

MERCANTILE INSURANCE COMPANY.

Cleveland, Ohio.

[Incorporated in 1871. Commenced business in 1871.]

WILLIAM J. GORDON, *President*. GEORGE A. TISDALE, *Secretary*.

Attorney to accept service of process in Wisconsin, William P. McLaren, Milwaukee.

I. CAPITAL.

Capital authorized	$200,000 00
Capital actually paid up in cash	200,000 00

II. ASSETS.

Loans on bond and mortgage (first liens)	$100,800 00
Interest due on bond and mortgage loans	3,792 00
Interest accrued on bond and mortgage loans	399 22
Stocks and bonds, market value	117,862 00
Cash loans secured by collaterals	16,000 00
Cash in the company's principal office and in bank	21,481 51
Interest due and accrued on collateral loans	708 00
Gross premiums in due course of collection	3,163 81
Bills receivable, not matured, taken for fire, marine and inland risks	19,681 48
Bills receivable, taken for fire, marine and inland risks, past due	4,900 84
All other property belonging to the company, viz: salvage, $4,189 94; due on account, $624.18; office furniture, $1,800; total	6,614 12
Aggregate of all the assets of the company at their actual value	$295,308 63

III. LIABILITIES.

Losses unadjusted, including all reported and supposed losses	$35,350 00	....
Net amount of unpaid losses and claims		$35,350 00
Reinsurance at 50 per cent. of prem. on fire risks, under one year	$22,900 84	....
Reinsurance, *pro rata*, on fire risks running more than one year	3,216 43	....
Reinsurance at 50 per cent. of prem. on inland risks	15,869 33	....
Amount required to safely reinsure all outstanding risks		41,986 60
Cash dividends declared to stockholders, unpaid		54 00
All other demands against the company		814 03
Total liabilities, except capital stock		$78,204 63
Capital stock actually paid up in cash		200,000 00
Surplus beyond capital stock		17,099 00
Aggregate of all liabilities, including capital and net surplus		$295,308 63

IV. INCOME DURING THE YEAR.

	Fire.	Marine and Inland.	
Gross premiums received in cash	$52,618 84	$59,674 56	....
Gross cash rec'd on bills and notes taken for prem.	....	66,456 53	....
Gross cash received for premiums	$52,618 84	126,131 09	....
Deduct reinsurance, rebate and ret'd pre'ms	6,387 68	16,015 65	....
Net cash received for premiums	$46,231 16	$110,115 44	$156,446 60
Gross premiums, remaining unpaid	....	$27,696 08	....
Received for interest on bonds and mortgages			4,483 00
Received for interest and dividends from all other sources			7,730 07
Aggregate amount of income received during the year in cash			$168,659 67

V. EXPENDITURES DURING THE YEAR.

	Fire.	Marine and Inland.	
Gross amount paid for losses	$27,897 16	$84,187 59	....
Deduct salvage and reinsurance	4,333 43	3,690 10	....
Net amount paid during the year for losses	$23,563 73	$80,497 49	$104,061 22
Cash dividends paid			9,946 00
Paid for commissions and brokerage			10,794 41
Salaries and all other charges of officers, and all employes			10,736 65

Paid for state, national and local taxes	2,198 49
All other payments, viz: stationery, printing and miscellaneous expenses, $5,098 51; agency expenses, $1,518 58; total	6,617 09
Aggregate amount of expenditures during the year, in cash	$144,248 77

VI. MISCELLANEOUS.

	Fire Risks.	Premiums thereon.	Marine and Inland Risks.	Premiums thereon.
In force, December 31, 1871.....	$4,891,210 00	$26,948 57	$453,998 00	$16,459 28
Written during 1872...........	5,560,178 00	55,122 63	7,405,502 00	138,077 54
Total......................	$10,351,388 00	$82,071 20	$7,858,500 00	$154,536 82
Deduct those terminated..	5,662,783 00	31,287 82	7,267,606 00	121,698 17
In force, December 31, 1872	$4,688,605 00	$50,783 38	590,894 00	32,843 65
Deduct amount reinsured .	78,200 00	1,063 54	16,000 00	1,105 00
Net amount in force...	$4,610,405 00	$49,719 84	$574,894 00	$31,738 65
In force, having not more than one year to run	$4,007,922 00	$45,801 69	$574,894 00	$31,738 65
Having more than one, and not more than three years to run	522,350 00	3,255 38	....	....
Having more than three years to run..................	80,133 00	662 77	....	....
Net amount in force	$4,610,405 00	$49,719 84	$574,894 00	$31,738 65

General Interrogatories.

Total premiums received from the organization of the company to date.......	$898,810 31
Total losses paid from the organization of the company to date.............	104,061 22
Total dividends declared since the company commenced business............	10,000 00
Total amount of losses incurred during the year	127,616 02
Total amount of the company's stock owned by directors, at par value........	126,000 00
Total amount loaned to officers and directors................................	85,490 00
Total amount loaned to stockholders, not officers............................	25,400 00

Business in the State of Wisconsin, during the Year 1872.

	Fire.	Marine and Inland.	Aggregate.
Risks taken....................................	$196,800 00	$498,191 00	$694,991 00
Premiums received..............................	1,687 27	4,886 12	6,468 39
Losses paid on risks taken......................	....	1,268 85	1,268 85
Losses incurred during the year, in Wisconsin	....	....	3,545 20

MERCANTILE MUTUAL INSURANCE COMPANY.

New York.

[Incorporated in 1842. Commenced business in 1842.]

ELLWOOD WALTER, *President.* C. J. DESPARD, *Secretary.*

Attorney to accept service of process in Wisconsin, Wm. B. Hibbard, Milwaukee.

I. CAPITAL.

Capital authorized...	$1,000,000 00
Capital acutally paid up in cash...	$1,000,000 00

II. ASSETS.

Stocks and bonds, market value..	$468,215 00
Cash loans secured by collaterals..	27,000 00
Cash in the company's principal office and in bank...........................	53,717 25
Interest due and accrued, not included in market value	5,462 21
Interest due and accrued on collateral loans	639 05
Gross premiums in due course of collection..................................	221,551 66
Bills receivable, not matured, taken for marine and inland risks	349,469 49
Bills receivable, taken for marine and inland risks past due................	22,814 70

Bills receivable, security notes		150,000 00
All other property belonging to the company, viz.: salvage, $98,817 00; premium on gold, $8,100 16; reinsurance due, $32,945; total		138,662 16
Gross amount of all the assets of the company		$1,438,515 15
Amount which should be deducted from the above assets, on account of bad and doubtful debts and securities, viz.: from item No. 18, $13,032 58; No. 17, $11,917 63; total deductions		24,950 21
Aggregate of all the assets of the company at their actual value		$1,408,564 94

III. LIABILITIES.

Losses adjusted and unpaid	$60,771 00	
Losses unadjusted, including all reported and supposed losses	108,811 00	
Losses resisted, including interest, costs and expenses	30,828 00	
Total gross amount of claims for losses	$200,410 00	
Deduct reinsurance thereon	15,000 00	
Net amount of unpaid losses and claims		$185,410 00
Amount required to safely reinsure all outstanding risks		323,367 63
Cash dividends declared to stockholders, unpaid		12,372 32
Due and to become due for borrowed money		95,218 00
All other demands against the company, viz: taxes, $16,539 58; commissions, $2,500; reinsurances estimated, $5,000; total		24,039 58
Total liabilities, except capital stock		$640,407 53
Capital stock actually paid up in cash		1,000,000 00
Aggregate of all liabilities, including capital		$1,640,407 53

IV. INCOME DURING THE YEAR.

Gross premiums received in cash (marine and inland)	$994,876 50	
Gross cash received on bills and notes taken for prem's	563,052 35	
Gross cash received for premiums	$1,557,928 85	
Deduct reinsurance, rebate and returned premiums	253,251 08	
Net cash received for premiums		$1,304,677 77
Gross premiums remaining unpaid	$594,835 78	
Received for interest and dividends from all sources		33,622 23
Aggregate amount of income received during the year in cash		$1,338,300 00

V. EXPENDITURES DURING THE YEAR.

Gross amount paid for losses (marine and inland)	$1,367,639 23	
Deduct salvage and reinsurance	253,970 07	
Net amount paid during the year for losses		$1,113,669 16
Interest paid to stockholders		85,877 61
Paid for commissions and brokerage		92,321 16
Salaries and all other charges of officers and all employes		129,004 22
Paid for state, national and local taxes		15,163 53
All other payments and expenditures		32,511 38
Aggregate amount of expenditures during the year		$1,418,547 06

VI. MISCELLANEOUS.

	Marine and inland risks.	Premiums thereon.
In force, December 31, 1871	$13,663,446	$286,488 98
Written during 1872	96,672,449	1,525,828 50
Total	$110,335,895	$1,812,317 48
Deduct those terminated	93,127,935	1,488,949 85
Net amount in force, December 31, 1872	$17,207,960	$323,367 63

General Interrogatories.

Total premiums received from the organization of the company to date	$32,483,684 72
Total dividends declared since 1857	1,242,108 26
Total amount of losses incurred during the year	1,127,277 09
Total amount of the company's stock owned by the directors, at par value	179,000 00

Business in the State of Wisconsin, during the Year 1872.

Risks taken (marine and inland)	$1,649,692 00
Premiums received	18,808 60
Losses paid on risks taken	11,868 90

Note.—The capital stock of this company was reduced to $500,000 on the 25th day of February, 1873.

MERCHANTS' INSURANCE COMPANY.

PROVIDENCE, R. I.

[Incorporated in 1851. Commenced business in 1851.]

WALTER PAINE, *President*. CHARLES FOSTER, *Secretary*.

Attorney to accept service of process in Wisconsin, SAMUEL M. OGDEN, Milwaukee.

I. CAPITAL.

Capital authorized	$200,000 00
Capital actually paid up in cash	200,000 00

II. ASSETS.

Stocks and bonds owned by the company, market value	$352,149 50
Cash in the company's principal office, and in bank	71,969 22
Interest due and accrued, not included in market value	5,471 48
Net premiums in due course of collection	10,444 27
Bills receivable, not matured, taken for assessment	21,225 00
Uncollected assessment	24,469 63
Aggregate of all the assets of the company, at their actual value	$485,729 10

III. LIABILITIES.

Losses adjusted and unpaid	$114,449 00	....
Losses unadjusted, including all reported and supposed losses	92,281 00	....
Net amount of unpaid losses and claims		$206,730 00
Reinsurance at 50 per ct. of prem., on fire risks, under one year	$80,197 31	....
Reinsurance, *pro rata*, on fire risks running more than one year	6,381 50	....
Gross premiums on all unexpired marine risks	27 50	....
Amount required to safely reinsure all outstanding risks		86,606 31
Total liabilities, except capital stock		$293,336 81
Capital stock actually paid up in cash		200,000 00
Aggregate of all liabilities, including capital		$493,336 81

IV. INCOME DURING THE YEAR.

	Fire.	Marine and Inland.	
Gross premiums received in cash	$170,660 50	$7,919 99	....
Gross cash rec'd on bills and notes taken for prem's	4,671 20	....	....
Gross cash received for premiums	$175,331 70	$7,919 99	....
Deduct reinsurance, rebate and ret'd prem's	14,432 25	739 95	....
Net cash received for premiums	$160,899 45	$7,180 04	$168,079 49
Received for interest and dividends from all sources			25,160 06
Net premiums remaining unpaid		$10,444 27	....
Received for assessment on capital		100,000 00	....
Aggregate amount of income received during the year in cash			$193,239 55

V. EXPENDITURES DURING THE YEAR.

	Fire.	Marine and Inland.	
Gross amount paid for losses	$146,919 81	$4,997 15	....
Deduct salvage and reinsurance	1,813 10	3,465 82	....
Net amount paid during the year for losses	$145,106 71	$1,531 33	$146,638 04
Cash dividends paid			20,000 00
Paid for commissions and brokerage			27,276 70
Salaries and all other charges of officers, and all employes			10,179 75
Paid for state, national and local taxes			6,950 84
All other payments and expenditures			1,489 69
Aggregate amount of expenditures during the year, in cash			$212,535 02

VI. MISCELLANEOUS.

	Fire Risks.	Premiums thereon.	Marine & Inland Risks.	Premiums thereon.
In force, December 31, 1871	$13,615,196	$176,334 29	$36,851	$368,71
Written during the year............	15,787,281	184,341 51	1,833,210	8,884 10
Total............................	$29,402,477	$360,675 80	$1,870,061	$9,252 81
Deduct those terminated........	16,748,253	190,463 02	1,860,411	9,225 31
In force, December 31, 1872......	$12,654,224	$170,212 78	$9,650	$27 50
In force, having not more than one year to run	$11,981,328	$160,394 62	$9,650	$27 50
Having more than one, and not more than three years to run	305,538	4,682 07	....	....
Having more than three years to run	367,358	5,136 09	....	....
Net amount in force	$12,654,224	$170,212 78	$9,650	$27 50

General Interrogatories.

Total premiums received from the organization of the company to date.......	$2,797,260 18
Total losses paid from the organization of the company to date...............	2,084,918 09
Total dividends declared since the company commenced business............	412,000 00
Total amount of losses incurred during the year...........................	329,566 71
Total amount of the company's stock owned by the directors, at par value....	41,500 00

Business in the State of Wisconsin, during the Year 1872.

Fire risks taken..	$414,288 00
Premiums received	4,668 60
Losses paid on risks taken..	352 94
Losses incurred during the year, in Wisconsin....................	352 94
Taxes on premiums, paid to fire departments in Wisconsin.....	229 11

MERIDEN FIRE INSURANCE COMPANY.

Meriden, Conn.

[Incorporated in 1868. Commenced business in 1872.]

J. WILCOX, *President.* E. B. COWLES, *Secretary.*

Attorney to accept service of process in Wisconsin, Wm. B. Hibbard, Milwaukee.

I. CAPITAL.

Capital authorized..	$500,000 00
Capital actually paid up in cash.....................................	200,000 00

II. ASSETS.

Loans on bond and mortgage, (first liens)........................	$10,400 00
Interest due and accrued on bond and mortgage loans..................	268 21
Stocks and bonds owned by the company, market value	61,009 00
Cash loans secured by collaterals....................................	124,730 00
Cash in the company's principal office and in bank..................	42,730 09
Due from non-resident stockholders, for taxes paid	305 00
Interest due and accrued, not included in market value..............	150 00
Interest due and accrued on collateral loans.........................	6,407 84
Gross premiums in due course of collection..........................	5,649 24
All other property belonging to the company, viz.: office furniture	1,497 61
Aggregate of all the assets of the company, stated at their actual value...	$253,136 99

III. LIABILITIES.

Losses adjusted and unpaid...	$13,906 61	....
Losses unadjusted, including all reported and supposed losses .	$7,825 00	....
Net amount of unpaid losses and claims		$21,731 61
Reinsurance at 50 per cent. of prem., on fire risks, under one year	$38 562 35	....
Reinsurance, *pro rata*, on fire risks running more than one year,	1,944 60	
Amount required to safely reinsure all outstanding risks....		40,506 95
Due and accrued for salaries, rent and other expenses............		600 00
All other demands against the company, viz; commissions..................		633 21
Total liabilities, except capital stock		$63,471 77
Capital stock actually paid up in cash.........		200,000 00
Aggregate of all liabilities, including capital stock..................		$263,471 77

IV. INCOME DURING THE YEAR.

Gross premiums received in cash (fire)	$87,784 80	
Deduct reinsurance, rebate and returned premiums	6,850 31	
Net cash received for premiums		$80,934 49
Received for interest on bonds and mortgages		430 57
Received for interest and dividends, from all other sources		3,794 13
Received for calls on capital	$200,000 00	
Aggregate amount of income received during the year in cash		$85,159 19

V. EXPENDITURES DURING THE YEAR.

Gross amount paid for losses (fire)	$20,176 64	
Net amount paid during the year for losses		$20,176 64
Paid for commissions and brokerage		12,483 37
Salaries and all other charges of officers, and all employes		4,778 58
Paid for state, national and local taxes		2,536 49
All other payments and expenditures		4,896 33
Aggregate amount of expenditures during the year, in cash		$44,871 41

VI. MISCELLANEOUS.

	Fire risks.	Premiums thereon.
Written during 1872	$6,382,350	$87,784 80
Deduct those terminated	462,438	6,878 23
In force, December 31, 1872	$5,919,912	$80,906 57
Deduct amount reinsured	103,650	1,222 29
Net amount in force	$5,816,262	$79,684 28
In force, having not more than one year to run	$5,542,863	$77,124 71
Having more than one and not more than three years to run	69,273	772 95
Having more than three years to run	204,126	1,786 62
Net amount in force	$5,816,262	$79,684 28

General Interrogatories.

Total premiums received from the organization of the company to date	$87,784 80
Total losses paid from the organization of the company to date	20,176 64
Total amount of losses incurred during the year	41,908 25
Total amount of the company's stock owned by the directors, at par value	87,500 00
Total amount loaned to officers and directors	67,650 00
Total amount loaned to stockholders, not officers	56,980 00

Business in the State of Wisconsin, during the Year 1872.

Risks taken (fire)	$108,494 98
Premiums received	1,309 38
Paid to the state of Wisconsin, for license	300 00
Taxes on premiums, paid to fire departments in Wisconsin	26 76

NARRAGANSETT FIRE AND MARINE INSURANCE COMPANY.

Providence, R. I.

[Incorporated in 1859. Commenced business in 1864.]

HENRY HARRIS, *President*. IRA A. FOSTER, *Secretary*.

Attorney to accept service of process in Wisconsin, J. H. Crampton, Milwaukee.

I. CAPITAL.

Capital authorized	$500,000 00
Capital actually paid up in cash	250,000 00

II. ASSETS.

Loans on bond and mortgage, (first liens)	$120,784 79
Interest due on bond and mortgage loans	747 94
Interest accrued on bond and mortgage loans	1,901 09
Stocks and bonds, market value	222,996 50

Cash in the company's principal office, and in bank	58,496 01
Gross premiums in due course of collection	68,878 01
Bills receivable, not matured, taken for fire marine and inland risks	94,880 86
Bills receivable, taken for fire, marine and inland risks, past due	16,980 96
All other property belonging to the company, viz: salvage, $6,500; reinsurance, $7,012 55; office furniture, $2,500; total	16,012 55
Gross amount of all the assets of the company	$538,565 21
Amount which should be deducted from the above assets, on account of bad and doubtful debts and securities, viz: from item No. 18, $5,000	5,000 00
Aggregate of all the assets of the company, at their actual value	$533,565 21

III. LIABILITIES.

Losses adjusted and unpaid	$20,550 87	....
Losses unadjusted, including all reported and supposed losses	96,859 04	....
Losses resisted, including interest, costs and expenses	4,500 00	....
Net amount of unpaid losses and claims		$121,909 91
Reinsurance at 50 per cent. of prem. on fire risks, under one year	$109,627 14	....
Reinsurance, *pro rata*, on fire risks running more than one year	24,903 83	
Am't required to safely reinsure all outstanding risks		134,530 97
Due and accrued for salaries, rent and other expenses		2,690 85
All other demands against the company, viz: taxes, $2,060 82; commissions, $10,331 70; total		12,322 02
Total liabilities, except capital stock		$271,453 75
Capital stock actually paid up in cash		250,000 00
Surplus beyond capital stock		12,111 46
Aggregate of all liabilities, including capital and surplus		$533,565 21

IV. INCOME DURING THE YEAR.

	Fire.	Marine and Inland.	
Gross premiums received in cash	$277,406 44	$70,231 10	....
Gross cash rec'd on bills and notes taken for prem's	....	38,327 13	....
Gross cash received for premiums	$277,406 44	$108,558 23	....
Deduct reinsurance, rebate and returned prem's	19,610 54	29,722 48	....
Net cash received for premiums	$257,795 90	$78,835 75	$336,631 65
Gross premiums remaining unpaid		$110,629 33	....
Received for interest on bonds and mortgages			9,361 10
Rec'd for interest and dividends, from all other sources, and prem. on stocks sold			48,472 94
Aggregate amount of income received during the year in cash			$394,465 69

V. EXPENDITURES DURING THE YEAR.

	Fire.	Marine and Inland.	
Gross amount paid for losses	$365,058 40	$169,277 29	
Deduct salvage and reinsurance	....	5,869 44	
	$365,058 40	$163,407 85	
Net amount paid during the year for losses			$528,466 25
Paid for commissions and brokerage			45,495 26
Salaries and all other charges of officers, and all employes			25,559 60
Paid for state, national and local taxes			8,611 22
Aggregate amount of expenditures during the year, in cash			$608,132 33

VI. MISCELLANEOUS.

	Fire Risks.	Premiums thereon.	Marine and Inland Risks.	Premiums thereon.
In force, December 31, 1871	$21,310,259	$274,034 47	$1,058,573	$54,829 35
Written during 1872	21,504,653	267,431 04	5,497,357	98,811 64
Total	$42,814,912	$541,465 51	$6,555,930	$153,640 99
Deduct those terminated	22,211,671	267,945 31	6,380,330	143,633 99
In force, December 31, 1872	$20,603,241	$273,520 20	$175,600	$10,007 00
Deduct amount reinsured	43,500	380 72	175,600	10,007 00
Net amount in force	$20,559,741	$273,139 48	....	....

In force, having not more than one year to run	$16,580,456	$219,254 29	....	....
Having more than one year, and not more than three years to run	3,616,860	48,765 57	....	....
Having more than three years to run	406,025	5,500 34	....	....
Net amount in force	$20,603,241	$273,520 20	....	....

GENERAL INTERROGATORIES.

Total premiums received from the organization of the company to date	$3,378,108 65
Total losses paid from the organization of the company to date	2,717,497 73
Total dividends declared since the company commenced business	165,000 00
Total amount of losses incurred during the year	578,498 98
Total amount of the company's stock owned by the directors, at par value	82,750 00

BUSINESS IN THE STATE OF WISCONSIN, DURING THE YEAR 1872.

Fire risks taken	$70,600 00
Premiums received	898 15
Losses paid on risks taken	2,333 34
Losses incurred during the year, in Wisconsin	2,333 34
Taxes on premiums, paid to the state of Wisconsin	89 51

NATIONAL FIRE INSURANCE COMPANY.

HARTFORD, CONN.

[Incorporated in 1871. Commenced business in 1871.]

MARK HOWARD, *President.* JAMES NICHOLS, *Secretary.*

Attorney to accept service of process in Wisconsin, SAML. M. OGDEN, Milwaukee.

I. CAPITAL.

Capital authorized	$1,000,000 00
Capital actually paid up in cash	500,000 00

II. ASSETS.

Loans on bond and mortgage, (first liens)	$135,000 00
Interest accrued on bond and mortgage loans	3,665 41
Stocks and bonds, market value	340,721 00
Cash loans secured by collaterals	58,890 00
Cash in the company's principal office and in bank	169,341 60
Interest due and accrued, not included in market value	3,125 00
Interest due and accrued on collateral loans	1,422 07
In the hands of agents	35,000 00
Aggregate of all the assets of the company, at their actual value	$742,166 08

III. LIABILITIES.

Losses adjusted and unpaid	$27,539 67	....
Losses unadjusted, including all reported and supposed losses	42,044 96	....
Net amount of unpaid losses and claims		$69,584 63
Reinsurance at 50 per cent. of prem. on fire risks under one year	$132,820 33	....
Reinsurance, *pro rata*, on fire risks running more than one year	30,281 34	....
Amount required to safely reinsure all outstanding risks		$163,101 67
Total liabilities, except capital stock		$232,686 30
Capital stock actually paid up in cash		500,000 00
Surplus beyond capital stock		9,479 78
Aggregate of all liabilities including capital and surplus		$742,166 08

IV. INCOME DURING THE YEAR.

Gross premiums received in cash (fire)	$353,060 04	
Deduct reinsurance, rebate and returned premiums	20,761 53	....
Net cash received for premiums		*$332,298 51
Received for interest on bonds and mortgages		1,942 84
Received for interest and dividends from all other sources		32,584 58
Income received from all other sources		68 81
Received from stockholders	$150,000 00	....
Aggregate amount of income received during the year		$366,894 74

V. EXPENDITURES DURING THE YEAR.

Net amount paid during the year for losses (fire)	$174,509 34
Cash dividends paid	20,000 00
Paid for commissions and brokerage	49,518 45
Salaries and all other charges of officers, and all employes	28,281 75
Paid for state, national and local taxes	2,593 68
All other payments and expenditures	25,387 42
Aggregate amount of expenditures during the year, in cash	$300,290 64

VI. MISCELLANEOUS.

	Fire Risks.	Premiums thereon.
In force, December 31, 1871	$1,670,767 09	$20,695 43
Written during 1872	28,256,279 00	332,298 51
Total	$29,927 046	$352,993 94
Dedrct those terminated	5,688,095	47,807 86
In force, December 31, 1872	$24,238 951	$305,186 08
Deduct amount reinsured	111,006	1,104 22
Net amount in force	$24,127,945	$304,081 86
In force, having not more than one year to run	$21,259,521	$265,640 66
Having more than one, and not more than three years to run	1,614,511	21,036 06
Having more than three years to run	$1,253,913	17,405 10
Net amount in force	$24,127,945	$304,081 86

GENERAL INTERROGATORIES.

Total premiums received, from the organization of the company to date	$372,862 99
Total losses paid, from the organization of the company to date	174,509 34
Total dividends declared since the company commenced business	20,000 00
Total amount of losses incurred during the year	244,098 97
Total amount of the company's stock owned by the directors, at par value	128,600 00
Total amount loaned to officers and directors	13,900 60
Total amount loaned to stockholders, not officers	39,990 00

BUSINESS IN THE STATE OF WISCONSIN, DURING THE YEAR 1872.

Risks taken (fire)	$332,541 00
Premiums received	9,946 54
Losses paid on risks taken	2,719 82
Losses incurred during the year, in Wisconsin	2,719 82
Taxes on premiums, paid to fire departments in Wisconsin	33 83

*Of which amount $35,000 is in hands of agents.

NATIONAL FIRE AND MARINE INSURANCE COMPANY,

PHILADELPHIA, PA.

[Incorporated in 1869. Commenced business in 1871.]

SIMON J. STINE, *President.* W. D. HALFMANN, *Secretary.*

Attorney to accept service of process in Wisconsin, E. C. HIBBARD, Milwaukee.

I. CAPITAL.

Capital authorized	$300,000 00
Capital actually paid up in cash	300,000 00

II. ASSETS.

Value of real estate owned by the company, less incumbrances	$75,666 67
Loans on bond and mortgage, (first liens)	83,149 76
Interest accured on bond and mortgage loans	2,234 05
Stocks and bonds, market value	95,496 00
Cash loans secured by collaterals	4,788 00
Cash in the company's principal office and in bank	59,365 67
Interest due and accured not included in market value	764 30
Gross premiums in due course of collection	82,445 64
Bills receivable	7,668 33
Bonds secured by second lien	4,000 00
All other property belonging to the company	4,008 20
Aggregate of all the assets of the company, at their actual value	$419,580 68

III. LIABILITIES.

Losses adjusted and unpaid	$3,528 39	....
Losses unadjusted, including all reported and supposed losses	17,700 00	....
Losses resisted, including interest, costs and expenses	6,000 00	....
Total gross amount of claims for losses	$27,228 39	....
Deduct reinsurance thereon	5,018 00	....
Net amount of unpaid losses and claims		$22,210 39
Reinsurance at 50 per cent. of prem., on fire risks, under one year	$91,658 77	....
Reinsurance, *pro rata*, on fire risks running more than one year	4,762 32	....
Amount required to safely reinsure all outstanding risks		96,421 09
Amount reclaimable on perpetual fire risk		1,178 00
All other demands against the company, viz.: commissions		16,489 72
Total liabilities, except capital stock		$136,299 20
Capital stock actually paid up in cash		300,000 00
Aggregate amount of all liabilities, including capital		$436,299 20

IV. INCOME DURING THE YEAR.

Gross premiums received in cash (fire)	$205,119 27	....
Deduct reinsurance, rebate and returned premiums	11,251 67	....
Net cash received for premiums		*$193,867 60
Received for interest on bonds and mortgages		478 80
Received for interest and dividends from all other sources		6,024 54
Income received from all other sources, viz.: rents		3,467 81
Deposit premiums, received for perpetual fire risks	$1,178 00	
Received from stockholders, for capital	300,000 00	....
Aggregate amount of income received during the year, in cash		$203,838 25

V. EXPENDITURES DURING THE YEAR.

Gross amount paid for losses (fire)	$31,654 06	....
Deduct salvage	4,995 00	....
Net amount paid during the year for losses		$26,659 06
Paid for commissions and brokerage		17,469 95
Salaries and all other charges of officers and all employes		14,604 50
Paid for state, national and local taxes		3,164 60
All other payments and expenditures		27,234 07
Aggregate amount of expenditures during the year, in cash		$89,132 18

VI. MISCELLANEOUS.

	Fire Risks.	Premiums thereon.
In force, December 31, 1871	$137,588 00	$1,716 61
Written during 1872	12,150,580 98	203,402 66
Total	$12,288,168 98	$205,119 27
Deduct those terminated	1,201,361 57	13,937 62
In force, December 31, 1872	$11,086,807 41	$191,181 65
Deduct amount reinsured	94,137 50	1,514 27
Net amount in force,	$10,992,669 91	$189,667 38
In force, having not more than one year to run	$10,596,094 68	$182,077 55
Having more than one and not more than three years to run	229,525 00	3,236 08
Having more than three years to run	120,550 23	2,413 70
Perpetual risks in force and int. prem's	46,500 00	1,940 00
Net amount in force	$10,992,669 91	$189,667 38

General Interrogatories.

Total premiums received from the organization of the company to date	$205,119 27
Total losses paid from the organization of the company to date	26,659 06
Total amount of losses incurred during the year	48,869 39
Total amount of the company's stock owned by the directors, at par value	125,750 00
Total amount loaned to officers and directors	3,500 00
Total amount loaned to stockholders, not officers	3,535 00

*Of which $33,448 64 is in course of collection.

NEW ORLEANS MUTUAL INSURANCE COMPANY.

NEW ORLEANS, LA.

[Incorporated in 1869. Commenced business in 1869.]

CHARLES CAVAROC, *President*. GEO. LANAUX, *Secretary*.

Attorney to accept service of process in Wisconsin, DAVID M. BELDEN, Milwaukee.

I. CAPITAL.

Capital authorized	$1,000,000 00
Capital actually paid up in cash	907,717 00

II. ASSETS.

Value of real estate owned by the company, less incumbrances		$168,204 69
Loans on bond and mortgage, (first liens)		189,104 56
Stocks and bonds, market value		115,752 88
Cash loans secured by collaterals		221,296 79
Other loans, commercial paper at short date		68,901 22
Cash in the company's principal office and in bank		117,665 08
Net premiums in due course of collection		197,132 41
Premiums not matured, taken for fire, marine and inland risks		812,988 26
Stockholders' notes given for capital stock subscribed	$87,782 94	
Aggregate of all the assets of the company		$1,891,040 89

III. LIABILITIES.

Losses adjusted and unpaid	$37,300 00	
Losses unadjusted, including all reported and supposed losses	52,900 00	
Losses resisted, including interest, costs and expenses	17,300 00	
Net amount of unpaid losses and claims		$107,500 00
Reinsurance, *pro rata* on fire risks, under one year	$204,435 29	
Reinsurance, *pro rata*, on fire risks running more than one year	30,069 35	
Gross premiums on all unexpired marine risks	1,494 50	
Amount required to safely reinsure all outstanding risks		235,999 14
Cash dividends declared to stockholders, unpaid		7,147 43
Total liabilities, except capital stock		$350,576 57
Capital stock actually paid up in cash		907,717 06
Surplus beyond capital stock		182,747 26
Aggregate of all liabilities, including capital and surplus		$1,891,040 89

IV. INCOME DURING THE YEAR.

	Fire.	Marine and inland.	
Gross premiums received in cash	$539,799 88	$582,595 75	
Deduct reinsurance, rebate and ret'd prem's		54,528 74	
Net cash received for premiums	$539,799 88	$528,067 01	
			$1,062,836 88
Received for interest and dividends from all sources			76,130 80
Aggregate amount of income received during the year, in cash			$1,138,967 68

V. EXPENDITURES DURING THE YEAR.

	Fire.	Marine and inland.	
Net amount paid during the year for losses	$49,066 90	$123,582 59	
			$172,165 13
Cash dividends paid			492,205 49
Paid for commissions and brokerage			55,750 79
Salaries and all other charges of officers, and all employes			8,553 80
Aggregate amount of expenditures during the year, in cash			$729,161 89

GENERAL INTERROGATORIES.

Total premiums received, from the organization of the company to date	$2,415,960 20
Total losses paid, from the organization of the company to date	1,070,994 07
Total dividends declared since the company commenced business	224,267 49
Total amount of losses incurred during the year	280,651 49
Total amount of the company's stock owned by the directors, at par value	71,600 00
Total amount loaned to officers and directors	50,896 57

NIAGARA FIRE INSURANCE COMPANY.

NEW YORK.

[Incorporated in 1850. Commenced business in 1850.]

HENRY A. HOWE, *President.* PETER NOTMAN, *Secretary.*

Attorney to accept service of process in Wisconsin, GEO. E. REDFIELD, Beaver Dam.

I. CAPITAL.

Capital authorized	$500,000 00
Capital actually paid up in cash	500,000 00

II. ASSETS.

Value of leasehold estate owned by the company, less incumbrances	$22,725 95
Loans on bond and mortgage, (first liens)	154,000 00
Interest accrued on bond and mortgage loans	5,890 00
Stocks and bonds, market value	745,600 00
Cash loans secured by collaterals	195,050 00
Cash belonging to the company, deposited in bank	17,007 25
Interest due and accrued on collateral loans	6,267 00
Net premiums in due course of collection	116,948 05
All other property belonging to the company, viz.: rents	1,550 00
Aggregate of all the assets of the company, at their actual value	$1,264,588 25

III. LIABILITIES.

Losses unadjusted, including all reported and supposed losses	$228,088 00	....
Losses resisted, including interest, costs and expenses	18,612 00	....
Net amount of unpaid losses and claims		$246,700 00
Reinsurance at 50 per cent. of prem., on fire risks, under one year	$311,184 69	....
Reinsurance, *pro rata*, on fire risks running more than one year	74,815 31	....
Amount required to safely reinsure all outstanding risks		386,000 00
Cash dividends declared to stockholders, unpaid		35 25
Total liabilities except capital stock		$632,735 25
Capital stock actually paid up in cash		500,000 00
Surplus beyond capital stock		131,853 00
Aggregate of all liabilities, including capital and surplus		$1,264,588 25

IV. INCOME DURING THE YEAR.

	Fire.	Marine and inland.	
Gross premiums received in cash	$786,809 99	$1,151 59	....
Deduct reinsurance, rebate and returned prem's	59,696 87	....	....
Net cash received for premiums	$727,113 12	$1,151 59	$728,264 71
Net premiums remaining unpaid		$116,948 05	....
Received for interest on bonds and mortgages			11,130 00
Received for interest and dividends from all other sources			62,241 96
Income received from all other sources, viz: rents			5,507 00
Aggregate amount of income received during the year, in cash			$807,143 67

V. EXPENDITURES DURING THE YEAR.

	Fire.	Marine and inland.	
Gross amount paid for losses	$554,660 63	$3,780 47	....
Deduct salvage and reinsurance	8,430 90	91 21	....
Net amount paid during the year for losses	$546,229 73	$3,689 26	$549,868 99
Cash dividends paid			52 00
Paid for commissions and brokerage			109,906 66
Salaries and all other charges of officers, and all employes			87,381 40
Paid for state, national and local taxes			23,609 16
All other payments and expenditures			78,996 67
Aggregate amount of expenditures during the year, in cash			$799,744 88

VI. MISCELLANEOUS.

	Fire risks.	Premiums thereon.	Marine and inland risks.	Premiums thereon.
In force, December 31, 1871	$71,734,852	$573,734 66	$17,166	$559 98
Written during 1872	83,314,107	831,332 06	117,980	1,151 59
Total	$155,048,959	$1,405,066 72	$135,146	$1,711 57
Deduct those terminated...	83,591,908	633,680 22	135,146	1,711 57
In force, Dec. 31, 1872 ..	$71,457,051	$771,386 50	....	....
In force, having not more than one year to run	$58,577,699	$622,369 32	....	....
Having more than one year and not more than three years to run	9,909,514	111,199 74	....	....
Having more than three years to run	2,969,838	37,817 44	....	....
Net amount in force.......	$71,457,051	$771,386 50	....	....

General Interrogatories.

Total premiums received, from the organization of the company to date......	$6,602,588 00
Total losses paid, from the organization of the company to date...............	3,789,292 00
Total dividends declared since the company commenced business...........	1,144,000 00
Total amount of losses incurred during the year............................	751,169 00
Total amount of the company's stock owned by the directors, at par value...	200,700 00
Total amount loaned to officers and directors..................................	176,500 00
Total amount loaned to stockholders, not officers	173,800 00
Am't deposited in different states and countries, for the security of policy holders, $30,000; deposited as follows: in the State of Tennessee, $20,000; Alabama, $10,000.	

Business in the State of Wisconsin, during the Year 1872.

Risks taken (fire)...	$1,047,158 00
Premiums received..	18,771 51
Losses paid on risks taken...	12,780 37
Losses incurred during the year, in Wisconsin,.............................	11,599 37
Taxes on premiums, paid to the state of Wisconsin	543 34

NORTH MISSOURI INSURANCE COMPANY.

Macon, Mo.

[Incorporated in 1867. Commenced business in 1867.]

JOHN F. WILLIAMS, *President*. ALBERT LARRABEE, *Secretary*.

Attorney to accept service of process in Wisconsin, J. O. Myers, Milwaukee.

I. CAPITAL.

Capital authorised	$500,000 00
Capital actually paid up in cash..	350,000 00

II. ASSETS.

Value of real estate owned by the company, less incumbrances..............	$37,000 00
Loans on bond and mortgage, (first liens)...........................	175,662 26
Interest accrued on bond and mortgage loans	6,460 99
Stocks and bonds owned, market value	152,485 00
Cash loans secured by collaterals...	20,259 42
Bills receivable and call loans..	6,531 00
Cash in the company's principal office, and in bank..........................	78,494 90
Interest due and accrued, not included in market value................ ...	600 00
Gross premiums in due course of collection....................................	186,650 62
Bills receivable, not matured, taken for fire, marine and inland risks.... ...	73,015 28
Bills receivable, taken for fire, marine and inland risks, past due	5,791 90
All other property belonging to the company, viz.: salvage, $275; rents, $300; office furniture and personal property, $10,221.73; total..................	10,796 73
Aggregate of all the assets of the company, ...	$753,678 05

III. LIABILITIES.

Losses unadjusted, including all reported and supposed losses.	$55,478 18	....
Losses resisted, including interest, costs and expenses.........	6,000 00	....
Net amount of unpaid losses and claims		$61,478 18

Reinsurance at 50 per ct. of prem. on fire risks, under one year.	$244,418 97	....
Reinsurance, *pro rata*, on fire risks, running more than one year	86,153 62	....
Gross premiums on all unexpired marine risks..................	5,924 88	....
Amount required to safely reinsure all outstanding risks...		$336,497 47
All other demands against the company, viz.: commissions..................		15,588 62
Total liabilities, except capital stock...		$418,514 97
Capital stock actually paid up in cash...		350,000 00
Aggregate am't of all liabilities, including capital.....................		$768,514 97

IV. INCOME DURING THE YEAR.

	Fire.	Marine and inland.	
Gross premiums received in cash..................	$650,110 34	$84,889 52	....
Deduct reinsurance, rebate and ret'd prem's..	59,788 90	....	....
Net cash received for premiums	$590,321 44	$84,889 52	$675,210 97
Gross premiums remaining unpaid..........................		$228,761 51	....
Received for interest on bonds and mortgages..................................			10,767 26
Received for interest and dividends from all other sources			6,096 87
Income received from all other sources, viz: rents, $976.05; exchange, $1,188 91; total..			2,164 96
Received for increased capital............................		$150,000 00	....
Aggregate amount of income received during the year in cash........			$694,240 05

V. EXPENDITURES DURING THE YEAR.

	Fire.	Marine and inland.	
Gross amount paid for losses.......	$270,607 99	$32,464 53	....
Deduct salvage and reinsurance..............	2,000 00	458 39	....
Net amount paid during the year for losses	$268,607 99	$32,006 14	$300,614 13
Paid for commissions and brokerage..................			155,208 67
Salaries and all other charges of officers, and all employes..................			28,211 34
Paid for state, national and local taxes..			8,122 00
All other payments and expenditures			76,061 05
Aggregate amount of expenditures during the year, in cash...............			$568,212 19

VI. MISCELLANEOUS.

	Fire risks.	Premiums thereon.	Marine and Inland.	Premiums. thereon.
In force, December 31. 1871	$8,050,032 85	$178,297 58	....	....
Written during 1872	39,791,363 67	835,555 82	$5,636,612 50	$84,889 52
Total....................	$47,841,396 52	$1,013,853 40	$5,636,612 50	$84,889 52
Deduct those terminated... ..	20,517,611 81	376,638 95	5,546,245 50	78,964 64
In force, December 31, 1872	$27,323,784 71	$637,214 45	$90,367 00	$5,924 88
Deduct amount reinsured .	205,237 50	4,787 18	....	....
Net amount in force...	$27,118,547 21	$632,427 32	$90,367 00	$5,924 88
In force, having not more than one year to run	$21,657,981 21	$488,887 94	$90,367 00	$5,924 88
Having more than one year and not more than three years to run...	1,668,571 00	33,085 08	....	....
Having more than three years to run..................	3,791,995 00	110,554 85	....	....
Net amount in force........	$27,118,547 21	$632,427 32	$90,367 00	$5,924 88

General Interrogatories.

Total premiums received from the organization of the company to date........	$1,238,160 09
Total losses paid from the organization of the company to date..............	415,076 37
Total amount of losses incurred during the year..	360,068 90
Total amount of the company's stock owned by the directors, at par value ...	57,000 00
Total amount loaned to officers and directors..................	17,200 00

Business in the State of Wisconsin, during the Year 1872.

Fire risks taken..	$1,386,150 68
Premiums received..	31,691 52
Losses paid on risks taken..	16,199 95
Taxes on premiums, paid to the state of Wisconsin........................	395 57

ORIENT INSURANCE COMPANY.

HARTFORD, CONN.

[Incorporated in 1867. Commenced business in 1872.]

C. T. WEBSTER, *President*. GEO. W. LESTER, *Secretary*.

Attorney to accept service of process in Wisconsin, C. H. VILAS, Madison.

I. CAPITAL.

Capital authorized	$2,000,000 00
Capital actually paid up in cash	500,000 00

II. ASSETS.

Loans on bond and mortgage, (first liens)	$157,955 90
Interest due and accrued on bond and mortgage loans	5,112 68
Stocks and bonds, market value	292,597 00
Cash loans, secured by collaterals	130,365 95
Balances due from agents	5,817 78
Cash in the company's principal office, and in bank	30,728 60
Interest due and accrued, not included in market value	1,500 00
Interest due and accrued on collateral loans	2,941 69
Gross premiums in due course of collection	75,000 00
All other property belonging to the company, viz: office furniture and safe	2,500 00
Aggregate of all the assets of the company, at their actual value	$705,519 60

III. LIABILITIES.

Losses unadjusted, including all reported and supposed losses	$51,958 41	
Net amount of unpaid losses and claims		$51,958 41
Reinsurance at 50 per ct. of prem. on fire risks, under one year	$127,531 28	
Reinsurance, *pro rata*, on fire risks running more than one year	17,877 58	
Amount required to safely reinsure all outstanding risks		145,408 86
Due and accrued for salaries, rent and other expenses		2,000 00
Due and to become due for borrowed money		60,000 00
All other demands against the company, viz: commissions		13,125 00
Total liabilities, except capital stock		$272,492 27
Capital stock actually paid up in cash		500,000 00
Aggregate of all liabilities, including capital stock		$772,492 27

IV. INCOME DURING THE YEAR.

Gross premiums received in cash (fire)	$334,125 96	
Deduct reinsurance, rebate and returned premiums	19,733 99	
Net cash received for premiums		$314,391 97
Received for interest and dividends from all sources		31,613 93
Aggregate amount of income received during the year, in cash		$346,005 90

V. EXPENDITURES DURING THE YEAR.

Net amount paid for losses (fire)	$196,578 68
Paid for commissions and brokerage	47,286 69
Salaries and all other charges of officers, and all employes	23,804 61
Paid for state, national and local taxes	7,994 59
All other payments and expenditures	35,183 98
Aggregate amount of expenditures during the year	$310,848 55

VI. MISCELLANEOUS.

	Fire Risks.	Premiums thereon.
Written during the year	$25,280,024	$334,125 96
Deduct those terminated and reinsured	6,026,018	52,559 27
Net amount in force, December 31, 1872	$19,254,006	$281,566 69
In force, having not more than one year to run	$17,087,479	$255,068 57
Having more than one and not more than three years to run	1,295,507	15,394 16
Having more than three years to run	871,020	11,103 96
Net amount in force	$19,254,006	$281,566 69

GENERAL INTERROGATORIES.

Total premiums received from the organization of the company to date......	*$334,126 26
Total losses paid from the organization of the company to date..............	196,573 66
Total amount of losses incurred during the year..............................	248,522 09
Total amount of the company's stock owned by directors, at par value........	138,300 00
Total amount loaned to officers and directors..................................	55,415 90
Total amount loaned to stockholders, not officers..............................	100,405 95

BUSINESS IN THE STATE OF WISCONSIN, DURING THE YEAR 1872.

Fire risks taken	$510,641 00
Premiums received..............	8,336 79
Losses paid on risks taken	3,654 33
Losses incurred during the year, in Wisconsin	4,704 33

*Of which $75,000 is in course of collection.

ORIENT MUTUAL INSURANCE COMPANY.

NEW YORK.

[Incorporated in 1854. Commenced business in 1854.]

EUGENE DUTILH, *President*. CHARLES IRVING, *Secretary*.

Attorney to accept service of process in Wisconsin, ALFRED CHURCH, Milwaukee.

I. CAPITAL.

Capital actually paid up in cash...........	None.

II. ASSETS.

Stocks and bonds owned by the company, market value..................	$749,684 10
Cash loans secured by collaterals	30,000 00
Cash belonging to the company, deposited in bank	359,147 59
Interest due and accrued, not included in market value..............	18,509 96
Net premiums in due course of collection..............	117,560 42
Bills receivable not matured, taken for marine and inland risks..............	147,540 66
Bills receivable, taken for marine and inland risks, past due	14,699 16
Subscription notes in advance of premiums..............	549,794 65
All other property belonging to the company, viz: salvage on losses paid...	58,744 34
Aggregate of all the assets of the company, at their actual value.......	$2,035,680 88

III. LIABILITIES.

Losses adjusted and unpaid..............	$70,206 30	
Losses unadjusted, including all reported and supposed losses......	105,335 00	
Losses resisted, including interest, costs and expenses..............	19,260 00	
Total gross amount of claims for losses..............	$194,801 30	
Deduct reinsurance thereon..............	51,000 00	
Net amount of unpaid losses and claims..............		$143,801 30
Amount required to safely reinsure all outstanding risks		334,613 56
Principal unpaid on scrip ordered redeemed..............		1,511 00
Interest due and declared, remaining unpaid..............		7,297 15
Unused balances of subscription notes..............		368,441 48
All other demands against the company, viz: return premiums..............		1,391 39
Total liabilities, except capital stock..............		$857,055 88
Permanent reserve fund		1,063,625 00
Surplus beyond permanent reserve fund		115,000 00
Aggregate of all liabilities, including reserve and surplus...........		$2,035,680 88

IV. INCOME DURING THE YEAR.

	Marine and Inland.	
Gross premiums received in cash	$1,345,823 84	
Deduct reinsurance, rebate and returned premiums.........	200,415 43	
Net cash received for premiums		$1,145,408 41
Net premiums, remaining unpaid..............	$979,800 94	
Received for interest and dividends from all sources		40,253 20
Income received from all other sources		4,405 00
Aggregate amount of income received during the year		$1,190,066 61

V. EXPENDITURES DURING THE YEAR.

	Marine and Inland.	
Gross amount paid for losses	$978,839 74	
Deduct salvage and reinsurance	86,165 59	
Net amount paid during the year for losses		$892,674 15
Interest paid to scripholders		62,894 60
Scrip or certificates of profits redeemed in cash		68,400 00
Paid for commissions and brokerage		57,218 23
Salaries and all other charges of officers, and all employes		64,357 10
Paid for state, national and local taxes		12,440 11
All other payments and expenditures		22,420 19
Aggregate amount of expenditures during the year, in cash		$1,180,404 88

VI. MISCELLANEOUS.

	Marine and Inland Risks.	Premiums thereon.
Net amount in force, December, 31, 1871	$19,551,265	$348,754 26
Written during 1872	137,416,461	1,397,664 20
Total	$156,967,726	$1,746,418 46
Deduct those terminated	136,367,228	1,411,804 90
Net amount in force	$20,600,498	$334,613 56

Business in the State of Wisconsin, during the Year 1872.

Risks taken (marine and inland)	$2,163,339 04
Premiums received	15,719 15
Losses paid on risks taken	91 89
Losses incurred during the year in Wisconsin	1,805 68
Taxes on premiums paid to the state of Wisconsin	588 00

PACIFIC MUTUAL INSURANCE COMPANY.

New York.

[Incorporated in 1854. Commenced business in 1855.]

JOHN K. MYERS, *President.* THOMAS HALE, *Secretary.*

Attorney to accept service of process in Wisconsin, John L. Hathaway, Milwaukee.

I. CAPITAL.

Capital actually paid up in cash	Mutual.

II. ASSETS.

Stocks and bonds owned by the company, market value	$467,897 95
Cash loans secured by collaterals	195,450 00
Cash in the company's principal office and in bank	92,641 68
Interest due and accrued, not included in market value	1,690 00
Interest due and accrued on collateral loans	507 50
Gross premiums in due course of collection	51,078 64
Bills receivable, not matured, taken for marine and inland risks	150,204 24
Bills receivable, taken for marine and inland risks, past due	18,708 90
All other property belonging to the company, viz: Salvage and reinsurance on losses paid, $25,000; unterminated prem's, $7,479.20; premium on gold, $5,508.54; subscription notes, $19,000; total	56,987 74
Gross amount of all the assets of the company	$1,030,091 59
Amount which should be deducted from the above assets, on account of bad and doubtful debts and securities, viz: from item No. 18	9,000 00
Aggregate of all the assets of the company, at their actual value	$1,021,091 59

III. LIABILITIES.

Net amount of unpaid losses and claims	$108,000 00
Amount required to safely reinsure all outstanding risks	100,395 77
Principal unpaid on scrip ordered redeemed	12,075 00
Unused subscription notes	717 74
Interest remaining unpaid	8,212 50
Due and to become due for borrowed money	60,000 00

All other demands against the company, viz.: Commissions, $2,500; return prem's, $4,652 48; reinsurance prem., $2,490.01; total	$9,642 49
Total liabilities	$299,048 50
Surplus beyond liabilities	722,043 09
Aggregate of all liabilities including net surplus	$1,021,091 59

IV. INCOME DURING THE YEAR.

	Marine and Inland.	
Gross premiums received in cash	$362,006 28	....
Gross cash received on bills and notes taken for premiums	314,068 51	....
Gross cash received for premiums	$676,074 79	....
Deduct reinsurance, rebate and returned premiums	146,388 77	....
Net cash received for premiums		$529,686 02
Bills and notes received during the year for premiums remaining unpaid	$173,017 55	....
Received for interest and dividends from all sources		34,965 79
Income received from all other sources, viz.: bills payable, $20,000; loan notes, $76,550; sales of stocks, $11,000; scrip redeemed, $215; loss on notes, $59.62; total		107,824 62
Aggregate amount of income received during the year, in cash		$672,476 43

V. EXPENDITURES DURING THE YEAR.

	Marine and Inland.	
Gross amount paid for losses	$552,555 40	....
Deduct salvage and reinsurance	111,981 69	....
Net amount paid during the year for losses		$440,573 71
Interest paid to scripholders		39,964 80
Scrip or certificates of profits redeemed in cash		64,020 00
Paid for commissions and brokerage		25,980 53
Salaries and all other charges of officers, and all employes		55,155 83
Paid for state, national and local taxes		8,986 51
All other payments, viz: interest, $1,319.78; rent, furniture, moving, stationery, etc., $29,155.96; board of underwriters, $3,020.38; agency expenses, $13,094.92; total		46,591 04
Aggregate amount of expenditures during the year		$681,172 42

VI. MISCELLANEOUS.

	Marine and Inland Risks.	Premiums thereon.
In force, December 31, 1871	$7,468,399 00	$135,328 68
Written during 1872	68,644,958 00	673,365 08
Total	$76,113,357 00	$808,693 76
Deduct those terminated	68,989,886 00	708,297 99
In force, December 31, 1872	$7,123,471 00	$100,395 77
Deduct the amount reinsured	361,348 00	7,479 20
Net amount in force	$6,762,123 00	$92,916 57

General Interrogatories.

Total premiums received from the organization of the company to date	$12,875,172 08
Total losses paid from the organization of the company to date	7,430,068 87
Total amount of losses incurred during the year	414,973 71
Total amount loaned to directors	124,000 00

Business in the State of Wisconsin, during the Year 1872.

Risks taken (marine and inland)	$3,012,980 00
Premiums received	19,168 31
Losses paid on risks taken	6,590 95

PENN FIRE INSURANCE COMPANY.

PHILADELPHIA, PA.

[Incorporated in 1855. Commenced business in 1873.]

CHARLES H. STOKES, *President*. J. R. WARNER, *Secretary*.

Attorney to accept service of process in Wisconsin, P. C. HALE, Milwaukee.

I. CAPITAL.

Capital authorized	$500,000 00
Capital actually paid up in cash	156,650 00

II. ASSETS.

Value of real estate owned by the company, less incumbrances	$13,300 00
Loans on bond and mortgage, (first liens)	95,945 88
Interest accrued on bond and mortgage loans	2,514 73
Stocks and bonds, market value	15,887 50
Cash loans secured by collaterals	18,687 50
Cash in the company's principal office and in bank	32,674 22
Interest due and accrued, not included in market value	450 00
Interest due and accrued on collateral loans	560 62
Gross premiums in due course of collection	54,690 57
Bills receivable, not matured	357 50
All other property belonging to the company, viz: rents, $555; office furniture and supplies, $2,429.46; total	2,984 46
Aggregate of all the assets of the company	$238,052 98

III. LIABILITIES.

Losses unadjusted, including all reported and supposed losses	$23,550 00	
Deduct salvage thereon	475 00	
Net amount of unpaid losses and claims		$23,075 00
Reinsurance at 50 per cent. of prem., on fire risks, under one year	$46,374 87	
Reinsurance, *pro rata*, on fire risks running more than one year.	3,435 08	
Amount required to safely reinsure all outstanding risks		49,809 95
Due and accrued for salaries, rent and other expenses		525 00
All other demands against the company, viz.: commissions		18,762 64
Total liabilities except capital stock		$87,082 59
Capital stock actually paid up in cash		156,650 00
Aggregate of all liabilities, including capital		$243,732 59

IV. INCOME DURING THE YEAR.

Gross premiums received in cash, (fire)	$42,011 31	
Deduct reinsurance, rebate and returned premiums	1,287 23	
Net cash received for premiums		$40,724 08
Gross premiums, remaining unpaid	$54,690 57	
Received for interest and dividends, from all sources		150 00
Received for calls on capital	$18,862 50	
Aggregate amount of income received during the year, in cash		$40,874 08

V. EXPENDITURES DURING THE YEAR.

Net amount paid during the year for losses, (fire)	$809 94
Paid for commissions and brokerage	7,748 24
Salaries and all other charges of officers, and all employes	1,456 65
Paid for state, national and local taxes	1,187 73
All other payments and expenditures	15,899 75
Aggregate amount of expenditures during the year, in cash	$27,052 31

VI. MISCELLANEOUS.

	Fire Risks.	Premiums thereon.
Written during 1873	$5,086,043 29	$97,909 92
Deduct those terminated	148,700 00	710 64
In force, December 31, 1873	$4,937,343 29	$97,199 28
Deduct amount reinsured	22,305 00	497 40
Net amount in force	$4,915,038 29	$96,701 88

In force, having not more than one year to run	$4,671,420 48	$92,740 45
Having more than one, and not more than three years to run	140,095 81	2,261 76
Having more than three years to run	103,582 00	1,699 67
Net amount in force	$4,915,098 29	$96,701 88

GENERAL INTERROGATORIES.

Total premiums received from the organization of the company to date	$97,199 28
Total losses paid from the organization of the company to date	809 94
Total amount of losses incurred during the year	24,859 94
Total amount of the company's stock owned by the directors at par value	59,500 00
Total amount loaned to officers and directors	51,087 50
Total amount loaned to stockholders, not officers	825 95

BUSINESS IN THE STATE OF WISCONSIN, DURING THE YEAR 1878.

Risks taken, (fire)	$101,000 00
Premiums received	2,767 10

PENNSYLVANIA FIRE INSURANCE COMPANY.

PHILADELPHIA, PA.

[Incorporated in 1825. Commenced business in 1825.]

DAN'L SMITH, JR., *President*. WM. C. CROWELL, *Secretary*.

Attorney to accept service of process in Wisconsin, P. C. HALE, Milwaukee.

I. CAPITAL.

Capital authorized	$400,000 00
Capital actually paid up in cash	400,000 00

II. ASSETS.

Value of real estate owned by the company, less incumbrances	$80,000 00
Loans on bond and mortgage, (first liens)	480,957 00
Interest due on bond and mortgage loans	60 00
Interest accrued on bond and mortgage loans	7,748 00
Stocks and bonds, market value	401,700 00
Cash loans secured by collaterals	7,250 00
Cash in the company's principal office and in bank	118,309 46
Interest due and accrued, not included in market value	4,294 00
Gross premiums in due course of collection	114,188 00
Aggregate of all the assets of the company, at their actual value	$1,189,385 46

III. LIABILITIES.

Losses adjusted and unpaid	$103,065 00	
Losses unadjusted, including all reported and supposed losses	87,673 00	
Net amount of unpaid losses and claims		$190,738 00
Reinsurance at 50 per ct. of prem's on fire risks, under one year	$254,235 24	
Reinsurance, *pro rata*, on fire risks running more than one year	67,253 26	
Amount required to safely reinsure all outstanding risks		321,488 50
Amount reclaimable on perpetual fire risks		382,735 00
Cash dividends declared to stockholders, unpaid		682 50
All other demands against the company, viz: commissions		26,823 00
Total liabilities, except capital stock		$922,467 00
Capital stock actually paid up in cash		400,000 00
Aggregate amount of all liabilities, including capital stock		$1,322,467 00

IV. INCOME DURING THE YEAR.

Gross premiums received in cash (fire)	$532,541 95	
Deduct reinsurance, rebate and returned premiums	42,129 79	
Net cash received for premiums		$490,412 16
Gross premiums remaining unpaid	$114,188 00	
Received for interest on bonds and mortgages		32,780 04
Received for interest and dividends from all other sources		42,975 42
Income received from all other sources		13,827 11
Deposit premiums received for perpetual fire risks	$32,835 19	
Aggregate amount of income received during the year, in cash		$579,994 73

V. EXPENDITURES DURING THE YEAR.

Gross amount paid for losses (fire)	$539,771 44	
Deduct salvage and reinsurance	680 63	
Net amount paid during the year for losses		$539,090 81
Cash dividends paid		59,317 50
Paid for commissions and brokerage		127,719 42
Salaries and all other charges of officers, and all employes		14,830 58
Paid for state, national and local taxes		9,841 91
All other payments and expenditures		9,670 68
Aggregate amount of expenditures during the year, in cash		$760,470 90

VI. MISCELLANEOUS.

	Fire Risks.	Premiums thereon.
In force, December 31, 1871	$18,025,188	$216,953 50
Written during 1872	58,544,617	622,985 03
Total	$76,569,805	$839,938 53
Deduct those terminated	29,836,059	247,107 78
In force, December 31, 1872	$46,733,746	$592,830 75
Deduct amount reinsured	900,400	5,449 85
Net amount in force	$45,833,346	$587,380 90
In force, having not more than one year to run	$41,023,393	$508,470 48
Having more than one and not more than three years to run	2,011,138	31,346 05
Having more than three years to run	2,798,815	47,563 47
Perpetual risks in force and int. prem's	15,147,365	24,275 56
Net amount in force	$60,980,711	$611,655 56

General Interrogatories.

Total premiums received from the organization of the company to date	$3,366,429 00
Total losses paid from the organization of the company to date	2,253,861 44
Total dividends declared since the company commenced business	1,179,000 00
Total amount of losses incurred during the year	729,090 81
Total amount of the company's stock owned by the directors, at par value	31,000 00
Total amount loaned to officers and directors	7,250 00

Business in the State of Wisconsin, during the Year 1872.

Fire risks taken	$904,762 00
Premiums received	14,606 36
Losses paid on risks taken	2,657 17
Taxes on premiums, paid to the state of Wisconsin	20 78

Note.—A supplemental statement made by this company, February 4, 1873, shows that the capital stock had been repaired to the amount of $84,133.22.

PHENIX INSURANCE COMPANY.

Brooklyn, New York.

[Incorporated in 1853. Commenced business in 1853.]

STEPHEN CROWELL, *President.* PHILANDER SHAW, *Secretary.*

Attorneys to accept service of process in Wisconsin, Main & Spooner, Madison.

I. CAPITAL.

Capital authorized	$1,000,000 00
Capital actually paid up in cash	1,000,000 00

II. ASSETS.

Value of real estate owned by the company, less incumbrances	$225,000 00
Loans on bond and mortgage, (first liens)	370,895 00
Interest due on bond and mortgage loans	686 00

Interest accrued on bond and mortgage loans	$7,396 20
Stocks and bonds, market value	679,209 47
Cash loans secured by collaterals	87,800 00
Cash in the company's principal office and in bank	145,498 55
Interest due and accrued, not included in market value	4,418 71
Interest due and accrued on collateral loans	1,494 38
Net premiums in due course of collection	213,048 17
Bills receivable, not matured, taken for fire, marine and inland risks	181,060 81
Bills receivable, taken for fire, marine and inland risks, past due	21,374 50
All other property belonging to the company, viz: salvage, $62,220; rents $4,584 84; reinsurance, $17,961 71; bills receivable, $6,014 32; wrecking apparatus, $17,000; office furniture, safes, etc., $10,000; total	117,780 87
Gross amount of all the assets of the company	$2,005,657 66
Amount which should be deducted from the above assets, on account of bad and doubtful debts and securities, viz: from item No. 18	4,344 64
Aggregate of all the assets of the company, at their actual value	$2,001,313 02

III. LIABILITIES.

Losses adjusted and unpaid	$252,377 28	....
Losses unadjusted, including all reported and supposed losses	99,809 48	....
Losses resisted, including interest, costs and expenses	15,286 00	....
Net amount of unpaid losses and claims		$367,472 76
Reinsurance at 50 per cent. of prem. on fire risks, under one year	$405,299 51	....
Reinsurance, *pro rata*, on fire risks running more than one year	67,907 85	....
Gross premiums on all unexpired marine risks	100,724 92	....
Amount required to safely reinsure all outstanding risks		$573,932 28
Total liabilities, except capital stock		$941,405 04
Capital stock actually paid up in cash		1,000,000 00
Surplus beyond capital stock		59,907 98
Aggregate of all liabilities, including capital and surplus		$2,001,313 02

IV. INCOME DURING THE YEAR.

	Fire.	Marine and inland.	
Gross premiums received in cash	$1,302,718 36	$271,950 04	....
Gross cash rec'd on bills and notes taken for prem's	....	236,519 49	....
Gross cash received for premiums	$1,302,718 36	$508,469 53	....
Deduct reinsurance, rebate and ret'd prem's	108,998 31	168,730 23	....
Net cash received for premiums	$1,193,720 05	$339,739 30	$1,533,459 35
Bills and notes received during the year for premiums remaining unpaid		$131,060 81	....
Received for interest on bonds and mortgages			25,257 66
Received for interest and dividends from all other sources			42,381 15
Income received from all other sources, viz: rents, $7,791 65; wrecking pump earnings, $2,562 83; premium on gold, $5,495 08; total			15,849 56
Aggregate amount of income received during the year, in cash			$1,616,947 72

V. EXPENDITURES DURING THE YEAR.

	Fire	Marine and inland.	
Gross amount paid for losses	$842,342 88	$296,468 16	....
Deduct salvage and reinsurance	....	115,277 20	....
Net amount paid during the year for losses	$842,342 88	$181,190 96	$1,023,533 84
Cash dividends paid			100,000 00
Paid for commissions and brokerage			199,169 41
Salaries and all other charges of officers, clerks, agents and all other employes			101,408 48
Paid for state, national and local taxes			33,844 07
All other payments, and expenditures			111,578 51
Aggregate amount of expenditures during the year, in cash			$1,569,529 96

VI. MISCELLANEOUS.

	Fire Risks.	Premiums thereon.	Marine and inland.	Premiums thereon.
In force, December 31, 1871......	$77,979,288	$868,808 70	$4,046,144	$96,688 30
Written during the year.........	137,306,961	1,310,659 79	37,797,601	580,418 85
Total......................	$215,286,254	$2,178,468 49	$41,843,745	$687,097 15
Deduct those terminated....	117,641,544	1,244,011 56	38,009,422	586,372 23
In force, December 31, 1872.	$97,644,720	$929,451 93	$3,834,323	$100,724 92
Deduct amount reinsured ...	442,265	4,475 89	....	....
Net amount in force.....	$97,202,455	$924,976 04	$3,834,323	$100,724 92
In force, having not more than one year to run................	$83,800,427	$810,599 03	$3,834,323	$100,724 92
Having more than one and not more than three years to run....	9,364,836	70,574 60	... .	....
Having more than three years to run..........................	4,037,192	43,802 41	....	....
Net amount in force.........	$97,202,455	$924,976 04	$3,834,323	$100,724 92

General Interrogatories.

Total premiums received from the organization of the company to date.......	$15,118,166 86
Total losses paid from the organization of the company to date	8,774,916 08
Total dividends declared since the company commenced business....	1,114,000 00
Total amount of losses incurred during the year..................................	1, 315, 294 44
Total amount of the company's stock owned by the directors, at par value...	294,900 00
Total amount loaned to officers and directors..................................	117,975 00
Total amount loaned to, stock holders, not officers	11,900 00

Amount deposited in different states and countries, for the security of policy holders, $70,000, deposited as follows: in the state of Tennessee, $20,000; Mississippi $20,000; Alabama, $10,000; South Carolina, $20,000.

Business in the State of Wisconsin, during the Year 1872.

	Fire.	Marine and inland	Aggregate.
Risks taken...	$2,172,560 00	$177,500 00	$2,350,060 00
Premiums received..............................	29,425 98	4,854 90	34,280 88
Losses paid on risks taken...	13,469 42	3,000 00	16,469 42
Losses incurred during the year, in Wisconsin.........			10,406 85
Taxes on premiums, paid to the state of Wisconsin.........			718 63
Taxes on premiums, paid to fire departments in Wisconsin.........			477 63

PHŒNIX INSURANCE COMPANY.

Hartford, Conn.

[Incorporated in 1854. Commenced business in 1854.]

H. KELLOGG, *President.* — D. W. C. SKILTON, *Secretary.*

Attorney to accept service of process in Wisconsin, C. Ainsworth, Madison.

I. CAPITAL.

Capital authorized..	$2,100,000 00
Capital actually paid up in cash..	600,000 00

II. ASSETS.

Value of real estate owned by the company, less incumbrances...............	$79,012 46
Loans on bond and mortgage, (first liens)	12,336 00
Interest accrued on bond and mortgage loans....................................	330 40
Stocks and bonds, market value...	1,143,694 53
Cash loans secured by collaterals	35,000 00
Cash in the company's principal office and in bank..........................	107,192 45
Interest due and accrued on collateral loans and bank deposits..........	1,912 00
Gross premiums in due course of collection and transmission	196,186 71
Aggregate of all the assets of the company, at their actual value.........	$1,582,646 55

III. LIABILITIES.

Losses unadjusted, including all reported and supposed losses.	$177,520 78	....
Losses resisted, including interest, costs and expenses	8,200 00	....
Net amount of unpaid losses and claims		$185,720 78
Reinsurance at 50 per cent. of prem. on fire risks under one year	$542,783 00	....
Reinsurance, *pro rata*, on fire risks running more than one year	242,122 23	....
Amount required to safely reinsure all outstanding risks...		784,905 23
Due and to become due for borrowed money		100,000 00
Total liabilities, except capital stock........................		$1,070,625 96
Capital stock actually paid up in cash		600,000 00
Aggregate of all liabilities including capital...........		$1,670,625 96

IV. INCOME DURING THE YEAR.

Gross premiums received in cash (fire)............................	$1,626,522 45	....
Deduct reinsurance, rebate and returned premiums...........	101,340 88	....
Net cash received for premiums..........................		*$1,525,181 57
Received for interest on bonds and mortgages..............................		5,599 04
Received for interest and dividends, from all other sources................		83,045 94
Income received from all other sources, viz: rents		890 00
Aggregate amount of income received during the year, in cash........		$1,614,716 55

V. EXPENDITURES DURING THE YEAR.

Net amount paid during the year for losses, (fire)............................	$1,407,848 05
Paid for commissions and brokerage..	227,818 45
Salaries and all other charges of officers, and all employes.......	56,179 37
Paid for state, national and local taxes....................................	45,255 93
All other payments and expenditures..	127,121 62
Aggregate amount of expenditures during the year, in cash...........	$1,864,223 42

VI. MISCELLANEOUS.

	Fire risks.	Premiums thereon.
In force, December 31, 1871......................	$123,670,169	$1,488,110 76
Written during 1872..	118,578,128	1,525,181 57
Total	$242,248,297	$3,008,292 33
Deduct those terminated..................................	109,355,330	1,438,481 87
In force, December 31, 1872	$132,892,967	$1,569,810 46
In force, having not more than one year to run...............	$94,889,683	$1,085,566 01
Having more than one and not more than three years to run.	25,201,641	309,581 45
Having more than three years to run..................	12,801,643	174,663 00
Net amount in force..	$132,892,967	$1,569,810 46

General Interrogatories.

Total premiums received from the organization of the company to date......	$13,297,226 52
Total losses paid from the organization of the company to date................	8,642,816 18
Total dividends declared since the company commenced business.............	1,180,000 00
Total amount of losses incurred during the year................................	1,283,434 41
Total amount of the company's stock owned by the directors, at par value....	120,000 00
Amount deposited in different states and countries, for the security of policy holders, $80,000, deposited as follows: in the state of Tennessee, $20,000; Alabama, $10,000; Oregon, $50,000.	

Business in the State of Wisconsin, during the Year 1872.

Risks taken (fire)..	$3,741,417 00
Premiums received..	54,862 14
Losses paid on risks taken..	24,543 87
Losses incurred during the year, in Wisconsin................................	25,226 00
Taxes on premiums, paid to the state and fire departments of Wisconsin.. ..	1,622 66

*Of which $196,188 71 is in course of collection and transmission.

PROVIDENCE WASHINGTON INSURANCE COMPANY.

PROVIDENCE, R. I.

[Incorporated in 1799. Commenced business in 1799.]

JOHN KINGSBURY, *President*, WARREN S. GREENE, *Secretary*.

Attorney to accept service of process in Wisconsin, H. S. DURAND, Racine.

I. CAPITAL.

Capital authorized	$300,000 00
Capital actually paid up in cash	200,000 00

II. ASSETS.

Stocks and bonds owned by the company, market value	$50,500 00
Participation account of R. I. Hospital Trust Co.	100,000 00
Cash in the company's principal office and in bank	69,314 15
Interest due and accrued, not included in market value	3,224 04
Gross premiums in due course of collection	21,590 38
Bills receivable, not taken for premiums	6,225 00
Aggregate of all the assets of the company, at their actual value	$250,853 57

III. LIABILITIES.

Losses unadjusted, including all reported and supposed losses.	$16,891 81	
Net amount of unpaid losses and claims		$16,891 81
Reinsurance at 50 per cent. of prem's on fire risks, under one year	$23,817 32	
Reinsurance, *pro rata*, on fire risks running more than one year	6,499 92	
Amount required to safely reinsure all outstanding risks		30,317 24
Due and accrued for salaries, rent and other expenses		500 00
Total liabilities, except capital stock		$47,709 05
Capital stock actually paid up in cash		200,000 00
Surplus beyond capital stock		3,144 52
Aggregate of all liabilities including capital and surplus		$250,853 57

IV. INCOME DURING THE YEAR, FROM MAY 1.

Gross premiums received in cash (fire)	$62,048 05	
Deduct reinsurance, rebate and returned premiums	2,294 61	
Net cash received for premiums		$59,753 44
Received for interest and dividends from all sources		7,886 69
Income received from all other sources		140 64
Received for calls on capital, $60,000; for increased capital, $149,485; total	$209,485 00	
Aggregate amount of income received during the year, in cash		$67,780 77

V. EXPENDITURES DURING THE YEAR, FROM MAY 1.

Net amount paid during the year for losses (fire).	$78,947 94
Paid for commissions and brokerage	7,971 53
Salaries and all other charges of officers, and all employes	4,151 53
Paid for state, national and local taxes	810 61
All other payments and expenditures	5,194 97
Aggregate amount of expenditures during the year, in cash	$97,076 58

VI. MISCELLANEOUS.

	Fire Risks.	Premiums thereon.
In force, May 1, 1872	$55,585	$660 54
Written during 1872	6,896,161	62,048 05
Total	$6,951,746	$62,708 59
Dedrct those terminated	1,640,231	6,308 27
In force, December 31, 1872	$5,311,515	$56,400 32
Deduct amount reinsured	65,125	640 78
Net amount in force	$5,246,390	$55,759 54

In force, having not more than one year to run	$4,705,296	$47,634 64
Having more than one, and not more than three years to run	255,394	3,817 67
Having more than three years to run	287,700	4,307 23
Net amount in force..	$5,248,390	$55,759 54

GENERAL INTERROGATORIES.

Total amount of the company's stock owned by the directors, at par value....	$84,880 00
Total amount loaned to officers and directors..................................	6,225 00

REPUBLIC FIRE INSURANCE COMPANY.

NEW YORK.

[Incorporated in 1852. Commenced business in 1853.]

ROB'T S. HONE, *President*. DUCAN F. CURRY, *Secretary*.

Attorney to accept service of process in Wisconsin, GEO. E. REDFIELD, Beaver Dam.

I. CAPITAL.

Capital authorized	$300,000 00
Capital actually paid up in cash..	300,000 00

II. ASSETS.

Value of real estate owned by the company, less incumbrances	$78,975 05
Loans on bond and mortgage, (first liens).......................................	48,700 00
Interest accrued on bond and mortgage loans......................................	1,607 34
Stocks and bonds, market value....	333,336 00
Cash loans secured by collaterals..	55,999 67
Cash in the company's principal office and in bank..............................	15,942 11
Interest due and accrued, not included in market value..........................	2,199 59
Interest due and accrued on collateral loans.....................................	39 21
Net premiums in due course of collection...	50,171 96
Bills receivable, not matured, taken for fire, marine and inland risks	4,556 52
Bills receivable, taken for fire, marine and inland risks, past due.............	2,297 72
Assessment on capital paid in cash January 17, 1878..............................	180,000 00
All other property belonging to the company, viz., rents.........................	6,166 66
Aggregate of all the assets of the company, at their actual value.........	$775,342 73

III. LIABILITIES.

Losses adjusted and unpaid..	$180,	....
Losses unadjusted, including all reported and supposed losses .	48,599 97	....
Losses resisted, including interest, costs and expenses.........	9,555	....
Total gross amount of claims for losses..........................	$338,	....
Deduct salvage and reinsurance thereon	3,	....
Net amount of unpaid losses and claims...........................	695	$335,431 12
Reinsurance at 50 per cent. of prem., on fire risks, under one year	$176,[illegible] 43	....
Reinsurance, *pro rata*, on fire risks running more than one year,	44,136 [illegible]	
Amount required to safely reinsure all outstanding risks....		220,682 17
Interest remaining unpaid		5,457 83
Total liabilities, except capital stock		$461,571 12
Capital stock actually paid up in cash...........................		300,000 00
Surplus beyond capital stock.....................................		13,771 61
Aggregate of all liabilities, including capital and surplus............		$775,342 73

IV. INCOME DURING THE YEAR.

	Fire.	Marine and Inland.	
Gross premiums received in cash	$487,170 77	$1,629 37	....
Deduct reinsurance, rebate and ret'd prem's	39,754 31	478 04	....
Net cash received for premiums.......	$447,416 46	$1,151 33	$448,567 79

Received for interest on bonds and mortgages..................................	526 29
Received for interest and dividends from all other sources....................	22,107 00
Income received from all other sources, viz.: rents, $10,049 52; profits from investments, $3,209 17; total..	13,258 69
Aggregate amount of income received during the year, in cash........	484,459 77

V. EXPENDITURES DURING THE YEAR.

	Fire.	Marine and inland.	
Gross amount paid for losses	$250,594 61	$3,519 07	....
Deduct salvage and reinsurance	4,876 76	91 21	....
Net am't paid during the year for losses	$245,717 85	$3,427 86	$249,145 71
Paid for commissions and brokerage			65,219 31
Salaries and all other charges of officers, and all employes			29,137 00
Paid for state, national and local taxes			11,626 12
All other payments, viz.: interest on borrowed money, $611 94; rents, $5,000; office and agency expenses, including stationery, advertising, etc., $52,749 07; total			58,361 01
Aggregate amount of expenditures during the year, in cash			$413,489 15

VI. MISCELLANEOUS.

	Fire risks.	Premiums thereon.	Marine and Inland Risks.	Premiums thereon.
In force, December 31, 1871	$40,012,455	$403,436 54	$17,166	$559 98
Written during 1872	46,194,405	487,170 77	117,980	1,629 37
Total	$86,206,860	$890,607 31	$135,146	$2,189 35
Deduct those terminated	44,836,708	442,208 35	135,146	2,189 35
In force, December 31, 1872	$41,370,152	$448,398 96	....	....
Deduct amount reinsured	513,711	7,034 62	....	....
Net amount in force	$40,856,441	$441,364 34	....	....
In force, having not more than one year to run	$33,051,943	$355,792 77	....	....
Having more than one and not more than three years to run	6,142,483	59,898 74	....	....
Having more than three years to run	1,662,015	25,672 83	....	....
Net amount in force	$40,856,441	$441,364 34	....	....

General Interrogatories.

Total premiums received from the organization of the company to date	$4,084,365 96
Total losses paid from the organization of the company to date	2,323,889 31
Total dividends declared since the company commenced business	347,589 35
Total amount of losses incurred during the year	452,564 47
Total amount of the company's stock owned by the directors, at par value	88,300 00
Total amount loaned to officers and directors	20,099 67
Total amount loaned to stockholders, not officers	900 00

Business in the State of Wisconsin, during the Year 1872.

Risks taken (fire)	$1,047,158 00
Premiums received	18,771 51
Losses paid on risks taken	12,786 37
Losses incurred during the year, in Wisconsin	11,599 37
Taxes on premiums, paid to the state of Wisconsin	543 34

SAINT JOSEPH FIRE AND MARINE INSURANCE COMPANY.

St. Joseph, Mo.

[Incorporated in 1867. Commenced business in 1868.]

R. L. McLAUGHLIN, *President.* JNO. A. NICELY, *Secretary.*

Attorney to accept service of process in Wisconsin, Sam'l M. Ogden, Milwaukee.

I. CAPITAL.

Capital authorized	$400,000 00
Capital actually paid up in cash	200,000 00

II. ASSETS.

Loans on bond and mortgage, (first liens)	$116,400 00
Stocks and bonds, market value	21,650 00
Cash loans secured by collaterals	24,800 00

Cash in the company's principal office, and in bank		$57,015 76
Other loans — notes discounted		45,902 36
Gross premiums in course of collection		32,736 44
All other property belonging to the company, viz.: office furniture		1,200 00
Aggregate of all the assets of the company, at their actual value		$299,704 56

III. LIABILITIES.

Losses adjusted and unpaid	$1,011 32	....
Losses unadjusted, including all reported and supposed losses	3,600 00	....
Losses resisted, including interest, costs and expenses	2,000 00	....
Net amount of unpaid losses and claims		$6,611 32
Reinsurance at 50 per ct. of pre'm on fire risk under one year	$45,455 58	....
Reinsurance, *pro rata*, on fire risks running more than one year	5,548 21	....
Amount required to safely reinsure all outstanding risks		51,003 79
All other demands against the company, viz: commissions		5,547 28
Total liabilities, except capital stock		$63,162 39
Capital stock actually paid up in cash		200,000 00
Surplus beyond capital stock		36,542 17
Aggregate of all liabilities, including capital and surplus		$299,704 56

IV. INCOME DURING THE YEAR.

	Fire.	Marine and Inland.	
Gross premiums received in cash	$133,104 69	$13,297 21	....
Deduct reinsurance, rebate and ret'd prem's	19,198 33	4,940 00	....
Net cash received for premiums	$113,906 36	$8,357 21	$122,263 57
Gross premiums remaining unpaid		$32,736 44	....
Received for interest and dividends from all sources			21,751 87
Income received from all other sources			650 23
Received for calls on capital		$60,450 00	
Aggregate amount of income received during the year, in cash			$144,665 67

V. EXPENDITURES DURING THE YEAR.

	Fire.	Marine and Inland.	
Gross amount paid for losses	$52,813 61	$2,912 50	....
Net amount paid during the year for losses			$55,726 11
Paid for commissions and brokerage			20,807 20
Salaries and all other charges of officers, and all employes			17,977 51
Paid for state, national and local taxes			2,778 50
Aggregate amount of expenditures during the year, in cash			$97,289 32

VI. MISCELLANEOUS.

	Fire Risks.	Premiums thereon.	Marine and Inland risks.	Premiums thereon.
In force, December 31, 1871	$4,133,000	$69,606 99	....	....
Written during 1872	8,450,238	133,104 69	$1,200,000	$13,297 21
Total	$12,583,238	$201,711 68	$1,200,000	$13,297 21
Deduct those terminated	4,346,325	90,299 76	1,200,000	13,297 21
In force, December 31, 1872	$8,236,913	$111,411 92	....	....
Deduct amount reinsured	505,411	8,415 93	....	....
Net amount in force	$7,731,502	$102,995 99	....	....
In force, having not more than one year to run	$6,905,096	$90,688 46	....	....
Having more than one and not more than three years to run	701,406	9,855 36	....	....
Having more than three years to run	125,000	2,452 17	....	....
Net amount in force	$7,731,502	$102,995 99	....	....

General Interrogatories.

Total premiums received, from the organization of the company to date	$342,116 04
Total losses paid, from the organization of the company to date	146,817 92
Total amount of losses incurred during the year	59,287 43
Total amount of the company's stock owned by the directors, at par value	92,000 00
Total dividends payable in stock	60,000 00

SAINT NICHOLAS INSURANCE COMPANY.

New York.

[Incorporated in 1852. Commenced business in 1852.]

WILLIAM WINSLOW, *President.* J. DU BOIS, *Secretary.*

Attorneys to accept service of process in Wisconsin, Magdeburg & Cohen, Milwaukee.

I. CAPITAL.

Capital authorized	$150,000 00
Capital actually paid up in cash	150,000 00

II. ASSETS.

Value of real estate owned by the company, less incumbrances	$25,000 00
Loans on bond and mortgage (first liens)	51,400 00
Interest accrued on bond and mortgage loans	1,790 79
Stocks and bonds, market value	110,000 00
Cash loans secured by collaterals	21,650 00
Cash in the company's principal office and in bank	17,409 26
Interest due and accrued on collateral loans	590 60
Gross premiums in due course of collection	21,215 00
All other property belonging to the company, viz: claim for return assessment, $1,174 09; judgments, $4,000; reinsurance due, $2,890; office fixtures and furniture, $4,500; total	12,564 09
Aggregate of all the assets of the company, at their actual value	$261,619 74

III. LIABILITIES.

Losses adjusted and unpaid	$14,400 00	
Losses unadjusted, including all reported and supposed losses	25,200 00	
Losses resisted, including interest, costs and expenses	3,500 00	
Total gross amount of claims for losses	$43,100 00	
Deduct salvage thereon	2,000 00	
Net amount of unpaid losses and claims		$41,100 00
Reinsurance at 50 per cent. of prem. on fire risks, under one year	$59,086 67	
Reinsurance, *pro rata*, on fire risks running more than one year	2,654 40	
Am't required to safely reinsure all outstanding risks		61,741 07
Total liabilities, except capital stock		$102,841 07
Capital stock actually paid up in cash		150,000 00
Surplus beyond capital stock		8,778 67
Aggregate of all liabilities, including capital and surplus		$261,619 74

IV. INCOME DURING THE YEAR.

	Fire.	Marine and Inland.	
Gross premiums received in cash	$173,710 68	$1,783 11	
Deduct reinsurance, rebate and returned prem's	8,723 98		
Net cash received for premiums	$164,986 70	$1,783 11	$166,769 81
Received for interest on bonds and mortgages			2,416 42
Received for interest and dividends from all other sources			9,310 36
Aggregate amount of income received during the year, in cash			$178,496 59

V. EXPENDITURES DURING THE YEAR.

	Fire.	Marine and Inland.	
Gross amount paid for losses	$104,943 56	$1,636 24	
Deduct reinsurance	2,240 00		
Net amount paid during the year for losses	$102,703 56	$1,636 24	$104,339 80
Cash dividends paid			15,000 00
Paid for commissions and brokerage			26,094 27
Salaries and all other charges of officers, and all employes			14,021 86
Paid for state, national and local taxes			2,917 08
All other payments and expenditures			12,833 88
Aggregate amount of expenditures during the year, in cash			$175,206 79

VI. MISCELLANEOUS.

	Fire Risks.	Premiums thereon.	Marine & Inland Risks.	Premiums thereon.
In force, December 31, 1871	$14,846,925	$89,953 95	....	....
Written during the year	20,364,713	173,710 68	$142,650	$1,788 11
Total	$34,711,638	$263,664 63	$142,650	$1,788 11
Deduct those terminated	17,458,725	139,327 94	142,650	1,788 11
In force, December 31, 1872	$17,252,913	$124,336 69	....	....
Deduct amount reinsured	187,312	1,411 36	....	....
Net amount in force	$17,065,601	$122,925 33	....	....
In force, having not more than one year to run	$16,620,385	$118,173 34	....	....
Having more than one, and not more than three years to run	561,813	6,163 35	....	....
Having more than three years to run	70,715		....	....
Net amount in force	$17,252,913	$124,336 69	....	....

GENERAL INTERROGATORIES.

Total premiums received from the organization of the company to date	$1,565,607 78
Total losses paid from the organization of the company to date	949,966 29
Total dividends declared since the company commenced business	150,000 00
Total amount of losses incurred during the year	139,616 35
Total amount of the company's stock owned by the directors, at par value	61,850 00
Total amount loaned to directors	30,450 00
Total amount loaned to stockholders, not officers	1,000 00

BUSINESS IN THE STATE OF WISCONSIN, DURING THE YEAR 1872.

Fire risks taken	$240,000 00
Premiums received	3,721 42
Losses paid on risks taken	5,417 96
Losses incurred during the year, in Wisconsin	5,417 96

SAINT PAUL FIRE & MARINE INSURANCE COMPANY.

SAINT PAUL, MINN.

[Incorporated in 1865. Commenced business in 1865.]

J. C. BURBANK, *President.* C. H. BIGELOW, *Secretary.*

Attorney to accept service of process in Wisconsin, WM. B. HIBBARD, Milwaukee.

I. CAPITAL.

Capital authorized	$400,000 00
Capital actually paid up in cash	400,000 00

II. ASSETS.

Value of real estate owned by the company, less incumbrances	$98,814 14
Loans on bond and mortgage, (first liens)	111,696 78
Interest due on bond and mortgage loans	870 68
Interest accrued on bond and mortgage loans	3,935 00
Cash loans secured by collaterals	295,992 43
Cash in the company's principal office and in bank	107,585 76
Interest due and accrued on collateral loans	9,465 15
Net premiums in due course of collection	62,489 11
All other property belonging to the company, viz.: office furniture, $2,933.87; supplies, $2,460.73; total	5,394 60
Aggregate of all the assets of the company, at their actual value	$696,123 65

III. LIABILITIES.

Losses adjusted and unpaid	$15,000 00	....
Losses unadjusted, including all reported and supposed losses	13,381 25	....
Net amount of unpaid losses and claims		$28,381 25
Reinsurance at 50 per cent. of prem. on fire risks, under one year	$144,120 89	....
Reinsurance, *pro rata*, on fire risks running more than one year	29,449 31	....
Amount required to safely reinsure all outstanding risks		173,570 20
Total liabilities, except capital stock		$201,951 45

Capital stock actually paid up in cash	$400,000 00
Surplus beyond capital stock	24,171 29
Aggregate of all liabilities, including capital and surplus	$686,122 65

IV. INCOME DURING THE YEAR.

	Fire.	Marine and Inland.	
Gross premiums received in cash	$281,270 19	$54,230 52	....
Gross cash rec'd on bills and notes taken for prem's	24,699 01	....	....
Gross cash received for premiums	$305,969 20	$54,230 52	....
Deduct reinsurance, rebate and ret'd prem's	12,606 45	37 38	....
Net cash received for premiums	$293,362 75	$54,193 14	$347,555 89
Net premiums remaining unpaid	....	$62,489 11	....
Received for interest on bonds and mortgages			13,408 81
Received for interest and dividends from all other sources			23,465 53
Income received from all other sources			12,087 67
Aggregate amount of income received during the year			$396,462 90

V. EXPENDITURES DURING THE YEAR.

	Fire.	Marine and Inland.	
Net amount paid during the year for losses	$156,439 86	$30,504 50	$186,944 36
Cash dividends paid			20,000 00
Paid for commmissions and brokerage			55,808 79
Salaries and all other charges of officers, and all employes			12,264 31
Paid for state, national and local taxes			2,921 28
All other payments, viz.: advertising, $2,727.92; profit and loss, $117.05; general expenses, $33,071.12; total			35,916 09
Aggregate amount of expenditures during the year, in cash			$313,854 83

VI. MISCELLANEOUS.

	Fire Risks.	Premiums thereon.	Marine and Inland Risks.	Premiums thereon.
In force, December 31, 1871	$9,328,194 00	$154,368 00	....	....
Written during 1872	19,052,877 00	334,061 54	$8,004,126 00	$54,193 14
Total	$28,381,071 00	$488,424 54	$8,004,126 00	$54,193 14
Deduct those terminated	7,703,827 00	113,133 17	8,004,126 00	54,193 14
In force, December 31, 1872	$20,677,244 00	$375,291 37	....	....
Deduct amount reinsured	164,350 00	2,908 69	....	....
Net amount in force	$20,512,894 00	$372,382 68	....	....
In force, having not more than one year to run	$15,811,752 00	$288,241 78	....	....
Having more than one, and not more than three years to run	3,726,831 00	67,245 71	....	....
Having more than three years to run	974,311 00	16,895 19	....	....
Net amount in force	$20,512,894 00	$372,382 68	....	....

General Interrogatories.

Total premiums received from the organization of the company to date	$750,655 55
Total losses paid from the organization of the company to date	501,677 62
Total dividends declared since the company commenced business	32,000 00
Total amount of losses incurred during the year	184,052 64
Total amount of the company's stock owned by directors, at par value	278,500 00
Total amount loaned to officers and directors	190,066 43
Total amount loaned to stockholders, not officers	52,440 60

Business in the State of Wisconsin, during the Year 1872.

	Fire.	Marine and Inland.	Aggregate.
Risks taken	$1,399,692 00	$697,718 00	$2,097,410 00
Premiums received	26,251 64	4,211 59	30,463 23
Losses paid on risks taken	8,896 29	....	8,896 29
Losses incurred during the year, in Wisconsin	....	....	9,096 29
Taxes on premiums, paid to the state of Wis	....	....	158 23

SPRINGFIELD FIRE AND MARINE INSURANCE COMPANY.

SPRINGFIELD, MASS.

[Incorporated in 1849. Commenced business in 1851.]

EDMUND FREEMAN, *President*. SANFORD J. HALL, *Secretary*.

Attorney to accept service of process in Wisconsin, J. H. CRAMPTON, Milwaukee.

I. CAPITAL.

Capital authorized	$500,000 00
Capital actually paid up in cash	500,000 00

II. ASSETS.

Value of real estate owned by the company, less incumbrances	$100,000 00
Loans on bond and mortgage, (first liens)	219,666 55
Interest accrued on bond and mortgage loans	3,147 45
Stocks and bonds, market value	345,892 00
Cash loans secured by collaterals	143,428 51
Cash in the company's principal office and in bank	171,076 44
Interest due and accured, not included in market value	2,805 11
Interest due and accured on collateral loans	1,728 99
Gross premiums in due course of collection	80,473 23
All other property belonging to the company, viz: rents, $666.66; office furniture, $2,363.07; total	3,029 73
Aggregate of all the assets of the company	$1,070,742 01

III. LIABILITIES.

Losses adjusted and unpaid	$76,278 58	
Losses unadjusted, including all reported and supposed losses	73,384 19	
Losses resisted, including interest, costs and expenses	5,078 24	
Total gross amount of claims for losses	$154,741 01	
Deduct reinsurance thereon	3,500 00	
Net amount of unpaid losses and claims		$151,241 01
Reinsurance at 50 per ct. of prem., on fire risks, under one year	$277,051 97	
Reinsurance, *pro rata*, on fire risks running more than one year	131,025 99	
Amount required to safely reinsure all outstanding risks		408,077 96
All other demands against the company, viz; commissions		10,880 04
Total liabilities, except capital stock		$570,199 01
Capital stock actually paid up in cash		500,000 00
Surplus beyond capital stock		543 00
Aggregate of all liabilities, including capital and surplus		$1,070,742 01

IV. INCOME DURING THE YEAR.

Gross premiums received in cash, (fire)	$686,989 45	
Deduct reinsurance, rebate and returned prem's	52,804 51	
Net cash received for premiums		*$634,184 94
Received for interest on bonds and mortgages		11,239 88
Received for interest and dividends from all other sources		44,940 36
Income received from all other sources, viz: rents		3,600 00
Received for calls on capital	$150,000 00	
Aggregate amount of income received during the year, in cash		$693,965 18

V. EXPENDITURES DURING THE YEAR.

Gross amount paid for losses (fire)	$607,711 63	
Deduct salvage and reinsurance	7,222 32	
Net amount paid during the year for losses		$600,489 31
Cash dividends paid		40,256 40
Paid for commissions and brokerage		95,125 98
Salaries and all other charges of officers, and all employes		29,972 07
Paid for state, national and local taxes		19,279 73
All other payments and expenditures		31,791 58
Aggregate amount of expenditures during the year		$816,915 07

VI. MISCELLANEOUS.

	Fire Risks.	Premiums thereon.
In force, December 31, 1871	$55,885,756	$668,042 68
Written during 1872	58,230,712	686,989 45
Total	$114,116,468	$1,355,032 13
Deduct those terminated	46,838,857	538,876 21
In force, December 31, 1872	$67,277,611	$816,155 92
In force, having not more than one year to run	$44,851,741	$554,103 95
Having more than one, and not more than three years to run	8,970,348	108,820 78
Having more than three years to run	13,455,522	153,231 19
Net amount in force	$67,277,611	$816,155 92

GENERAL INTERROGATORIES.

Total premiums received from the organization of the company to date	$6,342,292 60
Total losses paid from the organization of the company to date	4,857,550 95
Total dividends declared since the company commenced business	857,042 06
Total amount of losses incurred during the year	616,108 42
Total amount of the company's stock owned by the directors, at par value	176,100 00
Total amount loaned to officers and directors	181,907 09
Total amount loaned to stockholders, not officers	125,035 00

BUSINESS IN THE STATE OF WISCONSIN, DURING THE YEAR 1872.

Risks taken (fire)	$683,990 00
Premiums received	8,999 19
Losses paid on risks taken	7,411 11
Losses incurred during the year, in Wisconsin	11,311 11
Taxes on premiums paid to the state of Wisconsin	221 99
Taxes on premiums, paid to fire departments in Wisconsin	278 17

*Of which $80,472 23 is in course of collection.

STANDARD FIRE INSURANCE COMPANY.

NEW YORK.

[Incorporated in 1859. Commenced business in 1859.]

WILLIAM CRIPPS, *President*. WILLIAM M. ST. JOHN, *Secretary*.

Attorney to accept service of process in Wisconsin, C. J. CARY, Milwaukee.

I. CAPITAL.

Capital authorized	$200,000 00
Capital acutally paid up in cash	200,000 00

II. ASSETS.

Loans on bond and mortgage, (first liens)	$58,400 00
Interest accrued on bond and mortgage loans	840 65
Stocks and bonds, market value	276,750 00
Cash loans secured by collaterals	92,400 00
Cash belonging to company, deposited in bank	8,913 35
Interest due and accrued on collateral loans and deposits	307 12
Gross premiums in due course of collection	16,202 38
All other property belonging to the company, viz: salvage, 1,478 84; office furniture and fixtures, $2,590 50; revenue stamps, $244; due from agents $985 58: total	5,298 92
Aggregate of all the assets of the company, at their actual value	$458,612 42

III. LIABILITIES.

Losses unadjusted, including all reported and supposed losses	$195,134 92	
Deduct reinsurance and salvage thereon	17,429 87	
Net amount of unpaid losses and claims		$177,705 05
Reinsurance at 50 per cent. of prem. on fire risks under one year	$65,947 27	
Reinsurance, *pro rata*, on fire risks running more than one year	6,533 18	
Amount required to safely reinsure all outstanding risks		72,480 45

Due and accrued for salaries, rent and other expenses	$1,066 66
All other demands against the company, viz: commissions, $3,285 66; return premiums, $634 89; total	3,920 55
Total liabilities, except capital stock	$255,172 71
Capital stock actually paid up in cash	200,000 00
Surplus beyond capital stock	3,439 71
Aggregate of all liabilities, including capital and surplus	$458,612 42

IV. INCOME DURING THE YEAR.

Gross premiums received in cash (fire)	$174,448 65	
Deduct reinsurance, rebate and ret'd pre'ms	15,331 56	
Net cash received for premiums		$159,117 09
Gross premiums, remaining unpaid	$16,202 38	
Received for interest on bonds and mortgages		3,969 09
Received for interest and dividends from all other sources		22,411 23
Received December 21, 1872, for calls on capital	$150,000 00	
Aggregate amount of income received during the year, in cash		$185,497 41

V. EXPENDITURES DURING THE YEAR.

Gross amount paid for losses (fire)	$247,166 60	
Deduct salvage and reinsurance	2,721 99	
Net amount paid during the year for losses		$244,444 61
Cash dividends paid		30,500 00
Paid for commissions and brokerage		12,875 05
Salaries and all other charges of officers, and all employes		22,175 59
Paid for state, national and local taxes		4,797 85
All other payments and expenditures		23,438 84
Aggregate amount of expenditures during the year, in cash		$338,231 94

VI. MISCELLANEOUS.

	Fire Risks.	Premiums thereon.
In force, December 31, 1871	$21,362,128 26	$161,101 45
Written during 1872	27,934,792 96	182,834 12
Total	$49,296,921 22	$343,935 57
Deduct those terminated	31,459,536 70	198,261 08
In force, December 31, 1872	$17,837,384 52	$145,674 49
Deduct amount reinsured	399,316 67	1,901 44
Net amount in force	$17,438,067 85	$143,773 05
In force, having not more than one year to run	$16,288,672 85	$131,894 53
Having more than one and not more than three years to run	743,443 00	6,229 01
Having more than three years to run	405,950 00	5,649 51
Net amount in force	$17,438,067 85	$143,773 05

General Interrogatories.

Total premiums received from the organization of the company to date	$1,440,802 85
Total losses paid from the organization of the company to date	838,272 47
Total dividends declared since the company commenced business	288,250 00
Total amount of losses incurred during the year	411,199 25
Total amount of the company's stock owned by the directors, at par value	130,850 00
Total amount loaned to officers and directors	14,600 00
Total amount loaned to stockholders, not officers	2,500 00

Business in the State of Wisconsin, during the Year 1872.

Fire risks taken	$518,990 00
Premiums received	5,748 80
Losses paid on risks taken	9,554 44
Losses incurred during the year, in Wisconsin	9,554 44
Taxes on premiums, paid to the state of Wisconsin	232 67

STAR FIRE INSURANCE COMPANY.

NEW YORK.

[Incorporated in 1864. Commenced business in 1864.]

NICHOLAS C. MILLER, *President.* JAMES M. HODGES, *Secretary.*

Attorney to accept service of process in Wisconsin, C. J. CARY, Milwaukee.

I. CAPITAL.

Capital authorized	$200,000 00
Capital actually paid up in cash	200,000 00

II. ASSETS.

Loans on bond and mortgage, (first liens)	$212,825 00
Interest due on bond and mortgage loans	1,947 75
Stocks and bonds, market value	11,500 00
Cash loans secured by collaterals	54,100 00
Cash in the company's principal office and in bank	53,758 68
Interest due and accrued on collateral loans	823 47
Gross premiums in due course of collection	21,963 30
All other property belonging to the company, viz.: salvage, $1,000 00; office furniture, maps, safes, etc., $2,500; total	3,500 00
Aggregate of all the assets of the company, at their actual value	$360,418 20

III. LIABILITIES.

Losses adjusted and unpaid	$10,000 00	
Losses unadjusted, including all reported and supposed losses	32,650 84	
Net amount of unpaid losses and claims		$42,650 84
Reinsurance at 50 per cent. of prem. on fire risks, under one year	$105,822 98	
Reinsurance, *pro rata*, on fire risks running more than one year	7,743 72	
Amount required to safely reinsure all outstanding risks		113,566 70
Due and accrued for salaries, rent and other expenses		833 33
All other demands against the company, viz: commissions		1,400 00
Total liabilities, except capital stock		$158,450 87
Capital stock actually paid up in cash		200,000 00
Surplus beyond capital stock		1,967 33
Aggregate of all liabilities, including capital and surplus		$360,418 20

IV. INCOME DURING THE YEAR.

Gross premiums received in cash (fire)	$258,796 00	
Deduct reinsurance, rebate and returned prem's	13,374 03	
Net cash received for premiums		$245,421 97
Gross premiums, remaining unpaid	$21,963 30	
Received for interest on bonds and mortgages		11,073 47
Received for interest and dividends from all other sources		12,203 68
Income received from all other sources		173 09
Received for calls on capital	$50,000 00	
Aggregate amount of income received during the year, in cash		$268,872 21

V. EXPENDITURES DURING THE YEAR.

Net amount paid during the year for losses (fire)	$234,078 80
Cash dividends paid	20,000 00
Paid for commissions and brokerage	11,532 18
Salaries and all other charges of officers, and all employes	16,625 61
Paid for state, national and local taxes	6,391 91
All other payments, viz.: office rent, stationery, etc., $10,847.14; branch offices and agency expenses, $33,638.31; stamps, $870.88; board of underwriters, $997.02; exchange, etc., $295.28; total	46,648 63
Aggregate amount of expenditures during the year, in cash	$335,277 13

VI. MISCELLANEOUS.

	Fire Risks.	Premiums thereon.
In force, December 31, 1871	$21,848,289 00	$196,260 71
Written during 1872	28,798,721 04	264,385 78
Total	$50,642,010 04	$460,636 49
Deduct those terminated	25,945,139 99	232,204 17
In force, December 31, 1872	$24,696,870 05	$228,432 32
Deduct amount reinsured	452,083 00	3,791 08
Net amount in force	$24,244,787 05	$224,641 24
In force, having not more than one year to run	$23,127,262 05	$211,645 96
Having more than one and not more than three years to run	1,067,525 00	12,498 28
Having more than three years to run	50,000 00	497 00
Net amount in force	$24,244,787 05	$224,641 24

GENERAL INTERROGATORIES.

Total premiums received from the organization of the company to date	$1,091,070 96
Total losses paid from the organization of the company to date	623,968 42
Total dividends declared since the company commenced business	120,000 00
Total amount of losses incurred during the year	267,306 57
Total amount of the company's stock owned by the directors at par value	94,000 00
Total amount loaned to directors	31,600 00
Total amount loaned to stockholders, not officers	8,850 00

BUSINESS IN THE STATE OF WISCONSIN, DURING THE YEAR 1872.

Risks taken (fire)	$299,450 00
Premiums received	3,968 44
Losses paid on risks taken	3,707 88
Losses incurred during the year in Wisconsin	3,707 88
Taxes on premiums, paid to the state of Wisconsin	128 64

STATE INSURANCE COMPANY.

HANNIBAL, MO.

[Incorporated in 1865. Commenced business in 1865.]

J. T. K. HAYWARD, *President*. JOHN N. STRONG, *Secretary*.

Attorney to accept service of process in Wisconsin, ALVIN B. ALDEN, Portage.

I. CAPITAL.

Capital authorized	$1,000,000 00
Capital actually paid up in cash	210,006 85

II. ASSETS.

Value of real estate owned by the company, less incumbrances	$14,443 73
Loans on bond and mortgage, (first liens)	152,729 36
Loans on bond and mortgage, (first liens), upon which more than one years's interest is due	11,250 00
Interest due on bond and mortgage loans	1,118 28
Interest accrued on bond and mortgage loans	9,585 61
Stocks and bonds, market value	28,832 50
Cash loans secured by collaterals	39,187 15
Cash in the company's principal office and in bank	85,940 84
Interest due and accrued, not included in market value	1,048 30
Interest due and accrued on collateral loans	2,433 18
Net premiums in due course of collection	35,837 56
Bills receivable, taken for fire, marine and inland risks	5,963 34
All other property belonging to the company, viz.: bills receivable, $4,025; personal accounts $1,584.49; office furniture and personal property, $3,400.78; judgments, $4,800; total	13,810 27
Aggregate of all the assets of the company	$346,675 07

III. LIABILITIES.

Losses adjusted and unpaid	$15,680 29	....
Losses unadjusted, including all reported and supposed losses	38,172 76	....
Losses resisted, including interest, costs and expenses	6,860 00	....
Total gross amount of claims for losses	$60,713 05	....
Deduct re-insurance thereon	1,800 00	....
Net amount of unpaid losses and claims		$58,913 05
Reinsurance at 50 per cent. of prem., on fire risks, under one year	$79,930 24	....
Reinsurance, *pro rata*, on fire risks running more than one year	8,113 23	....
Amount required to safely reinsure all outstanding risks		88,044 47
Total liabilities, except capital stock		$146,956 52
Capital stock actually paid up in cash		210,006 85
Aggregate of all liabilities, including capital		$356,963 37

IV. INCOME DURING THE YEAR.

	Fire.	Marine and Inland.	
Gross premiums received in cash	$218,463 75	$3,523 38	....
Deduct reinsurance, rebate and ret'd prem's	24,963 77	317 86	....
	$193,499 98	$3,205 52	
Net cash received for premiums			$196,705 50
Net premiums remaining unpaid		$41,800 90	....
Received for interest on bonds and mortgages			8,697 45
Received for interest and dividends, from all other sources			458 00
Income received from all other sources			17,592 17
Received for calls on capital		$34,455 64	....
Aggregate amount of income received during the year in cash			$223,453 12

V. EXPENDITURES DURING THE YEAR.

	Fire.	Marine and Inland.	
Gross amount paid for losses	$129,099 22	$866 75	....
Deduct salvage and reinsurance	1,385 43	380 87	....
	$127,713 79	$485 88	....
Net amount paid during the year for losses			$128,199 67
Paid for commissions and brokerage			42,105 43
Salaries and all other charges of officers, and all employes			25,592 00
Paid for state, national and local taxes			1,870 66
All other payments, viz: advertising, $4,278 68; revenue, $1,331 93; books, printing and stationery, $4,252 04; etc., etc.; total			29,281 64
Aggregate amount of expenditures during the year, in cash			$227,049 40

VI. MISCELLANEOUS.

	Fire Risks.	Premiums thereon.	Marine and Inland Risks.	Premiums thereon.
In force, December 31, 1871	$6,441,340	$92,540 82	....	....
Written during 1872	11,460,042	247,157 62	$437,805	$3,523 38
Total	$17,901,382	$339,698 44	$437,805	$3,523 38
Deduct those terminated	8,465,144	152,644 17	437,805	3,523 38
In force, December 31, 1872	$9,436,238	$187,054 27	....	....
Deduct amount reinsured	94,050	2,093 30	....	....
Net amount in force	$9,342,188	$184,960 97	....	....
In force, having not more than one year to run	$8,334,800	$159,860 40	....	....
Having more than one and not more than three years to run	852,942	20,421 33	....	....
Having more than three years to run	154,446	4,679 24	....	....
Net amount in force	$9,342,188	$184,960 97	....	....

General Interrogatories.

Total premiums received from the organization of the company to date	$611,561 83
Total losses paid from the organization of the company to date	280,615 12
Total amount of losses incurred during the year	139,169 29

Total amount of the company's stock owned by the directors, at par value....	$88,500 00
Total dividends payable in stock..............................	5,014 74
Total amount loaned to officers and directors..............................	61,198 58
Total amount loaned to stockholders, not officers..............................	101,910 46
Amount deposited in the state of Alabama, for the security of policy holders	10,000 00

BUSINESS IN THE STATE OF WISCONSIN, DURING THE YEAR 1872.

Risks taken (fire)..............................	$320,575 00
Premiums received..............................	3,163 10

SUN INSURANCE COMPANY.

CLEVELAND, OHIO.

[Incorporated in 1865. Commenced business in 1865.]

STILLMAN WITT, *President*. E. C. ROUSE, *Secretary*.

Attorney to accept service of process in Wisconsin, D. M. BELDEN, Milwaukee.

I. CAPITAL.

Capital authorized..............................	$200,000 00
Capital actually paid up in cash..............................	200,000 00

II. ASSETS.

Loans on bond and mortgage, (first liens)..............................	$90,225 00
Interest accrued on bond and mortgage loans..............................	3,058 00
Stocks and bonds, market value..............................	161,050 00
Cash loans secured by collaterals..............................	35,300 00
Cash in the company's principal office, and in bank..............................	27,736 33
Interest due and accrued on collateral loans..............................	555 00
Net premiums in due course of collection..............................	20,604 21
All other property belonging to the company..............................	4,615 16
Aggregate of all the assets of the company, at their actual value..........	$343,138 70

III. LIABILITIES.

Losses adjusted and unpaid..............................	$6,000 00	....
Losses unadjusted, including all reported and supposed losses.	52,000 00	....
Net amount of unpaid losses and claims..............................		$58,000 00
Reinsurance at 50 per cent. of prem. on fire risks under one year	$54,809 26	....
Reinsurance, *pro rata*, on fire risks running more than one year	30,291 85	....
Amount required to safely reinsure all outstanding risks ...		85,101 11
Total liabilities, except capital stock..............................		$143,101 11
Capital stock actually paid up in cash..............................		200,000 00
Surplus beyond capital stock..............................		37 59
Aggregate of all liabilities, including capital stock and surplus......		$343,138 70

IV. INCOME DURING THE YEAR.

Gross premiums received in cash (fire)..............................	$169,096 00	....
Deduct reinsurance, rebate and returned premiums... ...	18,412 79	....
Net cash received for premiums..............................		$150,683 21
Net premiums remaininig unpaid..............................	$20,604 21	....
Received for interest and dividends from all other sources..............		19,136 43
Received for call on capital..............................	$50,000 00	....
Aggregate amount of income received during the year, in cash.......		$169,819 64

V. EXPENDITURES DURING THE YEAR.

Net amount paid during the year for losses (fire)..............................	$106,733 23
Cash dividends paid..............................	20,000 00
Paid for commissions and brokerage..............................	15,477 45
Salaries and all other charges of officers, and all employes..............................	23,479 06
Paid for state, national and local taxes..............................	4,253 12
Aggregate amount of expenditures during the year, in cash..............	$169,942 86

VI. MISCELLANEOUS.

	Fire Risks.	Premiums thereon.
In force, December 31, 1871	$13,038,447 00	$158,676 31
Written during 1872	14,646,394 00	174,800 21
Total	$27,684,841 00	$333,476 52
Deduct those terminated	13,447,660 00	158,474 80
In force, December 31, 1872	$14,187,181 00	$178,001 72
Deduct amount reinsured	411,230 00	7,799 50
Net amount in force	$13,775,951 00	$170,202 22
In force, having not more than one year to run	$9,885,860 00	$120,856 71
Having more than one and not more than three years to run	2,627,235 00	33,160 42
Having more than three years to run	1,262,856 00	16,185 09
Net amount in force	$13,775,951 00	$170,202 22

General Interrogatories.

Total premiums received from the organization of the company to date	$752,288 00
Total losses paid from the organization of the company to date	573,845 00
Total dividends declared since the company commenced business	126,000 00
Total amount of losses incurred during the year	165,000 00
Total amount of the company's stock owned by the directors, at par value	62,000 00
Total amount loaned to officers and directors	15,000 00
Total amount loaned to stockholders, not officers	19,800 00

Business in the State of Wisconsin, during the Year 1872.

Risks taken (fire)	$348,250 00
Premiums received	2,151 64
Losses paid on risks taken	1,732 06
Losses incurred during the year, in Wisconsin	1,732 06
Taxes on premiums, paid to the state of Wisconsin	30 10

TRADERS' INSURANCE COMPANY.

CHICAGO, ILL.

[Incorporated in 1865. Commenced business, (reorganized) in 1872.]

B. P. HUTCHINSON, *President.* WM. E. ROLLO, *Secretary.*

Attorneys to accept service of process in Wisconsin, KELLOGG & HATHAWAY, Milwaukee.

I. CAPITAL.

Capital authorized	$1,000,000 00
Capital actually paid up in cash	500,000 00

II. ASSETS.

Loans on bond and mortgage, (first liens)	$30,111 10
Interest accrued on bond and mortgage loans	699 29
U. S. bonds, market value	500,500 00
Cash in the company's principal office and in bank	25,451 37
Net premiums in due course of collection	14,981 46
Bills receivable not matured, taken for fire, marine and inland risks	960 00
All other property belonging to the company, viz: salvage, $11,600; reinsurance, $2,335 91; office furniture, $1,702 97; Total	15,638 88
Aggregate of all the assets of the company, stated at their actual value	$588,342 10

III. LIABILITIES.

Losses unadjusted, including all reported and supposed losses	$8,266 00	....
Net amount of unpaid losses and claims		$8,266 00
Reinsurance at 50 per ct. of prem. on fire risks, under one year	$55,638 94	....
Reinsurance, *pro rata*, on fire risks running more than one year	3,873 00	....
Reinsurance at 50 per ct. of prem. on inland navigation risks	3,062 50	....
Gross premiums on all unexpired marine risks	728 25	....
Amount required to safely reinsure all outstanding risks		63,300 99
Due and accrued for salaries, rent and other expenses		6,633 55
Total liabilities, except capital stock		$78,200 54

Capital stock actually paid up in cash.....	$500,000 00
Surplus beyond capital stock	10,141 56
Aggregate of all liabilities, including capital and net surplus.........	$588,842 10

IV. INCOME DURING THE YEAR.

	Fire.	Marine and Inland.	
Gross premiums received in cash..................	$152,430 75	$141,130 12	....
Deduct reinsurance, rebate and retur'd prem's.	5,848 30	42,239 22	....
Net cash received for premiums...........	$146,583 45	$98,890 90	....
			$245,473 35
Net premiums remaining unpaid..............................		$15,941 46	....
Received for interest on bonds and mortgages..................................			1,680 69
Received for interest and dividends from all other sources....................			12,894 92
Income received from all other sources..			1,199 29
Aggregate amount of income received during the year, in cash............			$261,198 25

V. EXPENDITURES DURING THE YEAR.

	Fire.	Marine and Inland.	
Gross amount paid for losses......................	$116,550 06	$99,648 86	....
Deduct salvage and reinsurance...............	....	63,150 51	....
Net amount paid during the year for losses.	$116,550 06	$36,498 35	....
			$153,048 41
Paid for commissions and brokerage........			14,210 77
Salaries, and all other charges of officers, and all employes..................			10,888 95
All other payments and expenditures...			10,649 48
Aggregate amount of expenditures during the year, in cash...............			$188,797 61

VI. MISCELLANEOUS.

	Fire Risks.	Premiums thereon.	Marine and Inland Risks.	Premiums thereon.
Written during the year.......	$16,889,750	$167,412 21	$12,784,430	$142,090 12
Deduct those terminated..	6,885,350	49,892 72	12,155,790	135,965 12
In force, December 31, 1872.	$9,554,400	$117,589 49	$628,640	$6,125 00
Deduct amount reinsured .	232,450	2,168 00	....	....
Net amount in force...	$9,321,950	$115,426 49	$628,640	$6,125 00
In force, having not more than one year to run..........	$8,984,430	$111,276 49	$628,640	$6,125 00
Having more than one, and not more than three years to run......................	146,730	2,024 00	....	... .
Having more than three years to run....	198,740	2,126 00	....	....
Net amount in force.......	$9,329,900	$115,426 49	$628,640	$6,125 00

General Interrogatories.

Total premiums received from the organization of the company to date.......	$809,502 33
Total losses paid from the organization of the company to date...............	216,198 92
Total amount of losses incurred during the year..............................	224,464 92
Total amount of the company's stock owned by the directors at par value....	213,300 00

Business in the State of Wisconsin, during the Year 1872.

	Fire.	Marine and Inland.	Aggregate.
Risks taken..................................	$122,600 00	$979,568 00	$1,102,168 00
Premiums received...........................	916 66	6,140 88	7,057 54

TRADESMEN'S FIRE INSURANCE COMPANY.

NEW YORK.

[Incorporated in 1858. Commenced business in 1858.]

DAVID B. KEELER, *President*. TIMOTHY Y. BROWN, *Secretary*.

Attorney to accept service of process in Wisconsin, F. H. MAGDEBURG, Milwaukee.

I. CAPITAL.

Capital authorized	$150,000 00
Capital actually paid up in cash	150,000 00

II. ASSETS.

Loans on bond and mortgage, (first liens)	$148,943 00
Interest accrued on bond and mortgage loans	4,801 25
Stocks and bonds, market value	97,010 00
Cash loans secured by collaterals	16,000 00
Cash in the company's principal office and in bank	61,994 08
Interest due and accrued, not included in market value	215 70
Interest due and accrued on collateral loans	140 00
Gross premiums in due course of collection	28,665 66
All other property belonging to the company, viz.: salvage	1,000 90
Aggregate of all the assets of the company, at their actual value	$357,499 63

III. LIABILITIES.

Losses adjusted and unpaid	$7,	
Losses unadjusted, including all reported and supposed losses	87,075 00	
Losses resisted, including interest, costs and expenses	980 00	
Total gross amount of claims for losses	$94,855 00	
Deduct salvage and reinsurance thereon	16,700 00	
Net amount of unpaid losses and claims		$78,155 00
Reinsurance at 50 per ct. of prem's on fire risks, under one year	$96,183 75	
Reinsurance, *pro rata*, on fire risks running more than one year	7,518 95	
Reinsurance at 50 per cent. of prem. on inland risks	174 27	
Amount required to safely reinsure all outstanding risks		103,876 97
Cash dividends declared to stockholders, unpaid		87 50
Due and accrued for salaries, rent and other expenses		741 66
All other demands against the company, viz: commissions, $2,791.06; return prem's, $308.22; reinsurance prem's, $647.92; total		3,748 20
Total liabilities, except capital stock		$186,608 83
Capital stock actually paid up in cash		150,000 00
Surplus beyond capital stock		20,896 80
Aggregate of all liabilities, including capital stock and net surplus		$357,499 63

IV. INCOME DURING THE YEAR.

	Fire.	Marine and inland.	
Gross premiums received in cash	$223,705 35	$1,391 20	
Deduct reinsurance, rebate and ret'd prem's	14,151 98	139 12	
Net cash received for premiums	$209,553 37	$1,252 08	$210,805 45
Gross premiums remaining unpaid		$28,665 66	
Received for interest on bonds and mortgages			10,434 90
Received for interest and dividends from all other sources			16,050 78
Income received from all other sources, viz: prem's on securities sold			29,196 35
Received for calls on capital		$75,000 00	
Aggregate amount of income received during the year, in cash			$266,487 48

V. EXPENDITURES DURING THE YEAR.

Gross amount paid for losses (fire)	$330,771 42	
Deduct reinsurance	15,079 46	
Net amount paid during the year for losses		$315,698 96
Cash dividends paid		21,328 00
Paid for commissions and brokerage		21,079 04
Salaries and all other charges of officers, and all employes		26,090 00
Paid for state, national and local taxes		3,735 28
All other payments and expenditures		13,167 50
Aggregate amount of expenditures during the year, in cash		$401,092 78

VI. MISCELLANEOUS.

	Fire risks.	Premiums thereon.	Marine and Inland Risks.	Premiums. thereon.
In force, December, 31, 1871	$25,340,311	$182,542 07	$27,663	$577 89
Written during 1872	25,544,014	238,063 66	361,871	1,391 20
Total	$50,884,325	$420,605 73	$389,534	$1,969 09
Deduct those terminated	23,682,368	211,191 08	385,534	1,620 55
In force, December 31, 1872	$27,201,957	$209,414 65	$4,000	$348 54
Deduct amount reinsured	320,300	4,340 27	....	....
Net amount in force	$26,881,657	$205,074 38	$4,000	$348 54
In force, having not more than one year to run	$25,600,304	$194,178 59	$4,000	$348 54
Having more than one year and not more than three years to run	555,353	7,543 29	....	....
Having more than three years to run	226,000	3,352 50	....	....
Net amount in force	$26,881,657	$205,074 38	$4,000	$384 54

General Interrogatories.

Total premiums received from the organization of the company to date	$1,787,189 81
Total losses paid from the organization of the company to date	1,171,739 96
Total dividends declared since the company commenced business	186,000 00
Total amount of losses incurred during the year	334,215 83
Total amount of the company's stock owned by the directors, at par value	53,900 00

Amount deposited in different states and countries, for the security of policy holders, $10,000, deposited in the state of Alabama.

Business in the State of Wisconsin, during the Year 1872.

Fire risks taken	$378,006 00
Premiums received	7,555 45
Losses paid on risks taken	9,418 59
Losses incurred during the year in Wisconsin	9,418 59
Taxes on premiums, paid to the state of Wisconsin	309 58

UNION INSURANCE COMPANY.

Bangor, Maine.

[Incorporated in 1868. Commenced business in 1869.]

N. C. AYER, *President.* R. B. FULLER, *Secretary.*

Attorney to accept service of process in Wisconsin, W. P. McLaren, Milwaukee.

I. CAPITAL.

Capital authorized	$500,000 00
Capital actually paid up in cash	200,000 00

II. ASSETS.

Loans on bond and mortgage, (first liens)	$166,600 00
Loans on bond and mortgage, (first liens), upon which more than one year's interest is due	7,000 00
Interest accrued on bond and mortgage loans	1,260 00
Stocks and bonds, market value	85,965 00
Cash loans secured by collaterals	94,400 00
Cash in the company's principal office and in bank	66,566 58
Gross premiums in due course of collection	129,142 08
Bills receivable not matured, taken for fire, marine and inland risks	110,208 09
Bills receivable, taken for fire, marine and inland risks, past due	9,194 80
All other property belonging to the company	7,639 66
Gross amount of all the assets of the company	$609,970 73
Amount which should be deducted from the above assets on account of bad and doubtful debts and securities, viz: from item No. 18	602 26
Aggregate of all the assets of the company, at their actual value	$609,368 47

III. LIABILITIES.

Losses adjusted and unpaid	$76,160 33	
Losses unadjusted, including all reported and supposed losses	47,151 00	
Losses resisted, including interest, costs and expenses	4,958 40	
Net amount of unpaid losses and claims		$128,269 73
Reinsurance at 50 per cent. of prem. on fire risks under one year	$100,024 94	
Reinsurance, *pro rata*, on fire risks running more than one year	25,518 23	
Gross premiums on all unexpired marine risks	124,373 43	
Amount required to safely reinsure all outstanding risks		249,916 60
Due and accrued for salaries, rent and other expenses		200 00
Due and to become due for borrowed money and reinsurance		20,440 00
Total liabilities, except capital stock		$398,826 33
Capital stock actually paid up in cash		200,000 00
Surplus beyond capital stock		10,542 14
Aggregate of all liabilities, including capital and net surplus		$609,368 47

IV. INCOME DURING THE YEAR.

	Fire.	Marine and inland.	
Gross premiums received in cash	$219,075 76	$232,949 65	
Deduct reinsurance, rebate and ret'd prem's	25,104 85	31,084 52	
Net cash received for premiums	$193,970 91	$201,865 13	$395,836 04
Received for interest and dividends from all sources			47,104 34
Received from stockholders		$41,895 00	
Aggregate amount of income received during the year, in cash			$442,940 38

V. EXPENDITURES DURING THE YEAR.

	Fire	Marine and inland.	
Gross amount paid for losses	$229,402 47	$124,078 18	
Net amount paid during the year for losses			$353,480 65
Cash dividends paid			12,307 69
Paid for commissions and brokerage			53,040 22
Salaries and all other charges of officers, and all employes			16,698 33
Paid for state, national and local taxes			5,125 00
All other payments, and expenditures			18,694 31
Aggregate amount of expenditures during the year, in cash			$459,346 20

VI. MISCELLANEOUS.

	Fire risks.	Premiums thereon.	Marine and inland risks.	Premiums thereon.
In force, December 31, 1871	$15,785,163	$218,734 40	$1,344,789	$93,697 49
Written during 1872	16,749,981	219,075 76	8,419,140	232,949 65
Total	$32,535,144	$437,810 16	$9,763,929	$326,647 14
Deduct those terminated	14,504,827	186,723 82	7,999,369	202,273 71
Net amount in force	$18,030,317	$251,086 34	$1,764,560	$124,373 43

General Interrogatories.

Total premiums received, from the organization of the company to date	$1,597,947 43
Total losses paid, from the organization of the company to date	1,081,418 96
Total dividends declared since the company commenced business	88,094 64
Total amount of losses incurred during the year	358,480 65
Total amount of the company's stock owned by the directors, at par value	90,000 00
Total amount loaned to officers and directors	91,400 00
Total amount loaned to stockholders, not officers	191,600 00

Business in the State of Wisconsin, during the Year 1872.

	Fire.	Marine and inland	Aggregate.
Risks taken	$300,749 00	$364,583 00	$665,332 00
Premiums received	3,101 43	2,506 35	5,607 78
Losses paid on risks taken	1,581 71		1,581 71
Losses incurred during the year, in Wisconsin			1,581 71

WATERTOWN FIRE INSURANCE COMPANY.

Watertown, N. Y.

[Incorporated in 1867. Commenced business in 1867.]

NORRIS WINSLOW *President*. JESSE M. ADAMS, *Secretary*.

Attorney to accept service of process in Wisconsin, Jas. Fowler, Milwaukee.

I. CAPITAL.

Capital authorized	$200,000 00
Capital actually paid up in cash	200,000 00

II. ASSETS.

Loans on bond and mortgage, (first liens)	$240,341 90
Interest due on bond and mortgage loans	470 11
Interest accrued on bond and mortgage loans	5,767 41
Stocks and bonds, market value	45,950 00
Cash loans secured by collaterals	61,874 64
Cash in the company's principal office, and in bank	49,850 34
Interest due and accrued, not included in market value	681 19
Interest due and accrued on collateral loans	976 58
Gross premiums in due course of collection	33,179 87
Bills receivable, not matured, taken for fire risks	298 50
All other property belonging to the company, viz: furniture, supplies, etc	6,000 00
Aggregate of all the assets of the company, at their actual value	$444,890 54

III. LIABILITIES.

Losses unadjusted, including all reported and supposed losses	$3,300 00	
Net amount of unpaid losses and claims		$3,300 00
Reinsurance at 50 per ct. of prem., on fire risks, under one year	$31,055 00	
Reinsurance, *pro rata*, on fire risks running more than one year	89,206 15	
Amount required to safely reinsure all outstanding risks		120,261 15
Total liabilities, except capital stock		$123,561 15
Capital stock actually paid up in cash		200,000 00
Surplus beyond capital stock		121,329 39
Aggregate of all liabilities, including capital stock and surplus		$444,890 54

IV. INCOME DURING THE YEAR.

Gross premiums received in cash (fire)	$218,712 15	
Deduct reinsurance, rebate and returned premiums	3,746 96	
Net cash received for premiums		$214,965 19
Gross premiums, remaining unpaid	$33,478 37	
Received for interest on bonds and mortgages		14,954 35
Received for interest and dividends, from all other sources		4,308 24
Aggregate amount of income received during the year, in cash		$234,228 78

V. EXPENDITURES DURING THE YEAR.

Gross amount paid for losses, (fire)	$68,707 15	
Deduct reinsurance	537 50	
Net amount paid during the year for losses		$68,169 65
Cash dividends paid		32,000 00
Paid for commissions and brokerage		37,658 04
Salaries and all other charges of officers, and all employes		18,280 00
Paid for state, national and local taxes		10,896 92
All other payments and expenditures		18,785 11
Aggregate amount of expenditures during the year, in cash		$180,694 72

VI. MISCELLANEOUS.

	Fire risks.	Premiums thereon.
In force, December 31, 1871	$21,656,100	$148,455 29
Written during 1872	29,430,500	214,429 51
Total	$51,086,600	$362,884 80
Deduct those terminated	12,124,500	119,210 00
In force, December 31, 1872	$38,962,100	$243,674 80
Deduct amount reinsured	598,600	3,112 50
Net amount in force	$38,363,500	$240,562 30
In force, having not more than one year to run	$10,121,200	$62,110 00
Having more than one and not more than three years to run	27,145,500	170,460 30
Having more than three years to run	1,096,800	7,992 00
Net amount in force	$38,363,500	$240,562 30

GENERAL INTERROGATORIES.

Total premiums received from the organization of the company to date	$406,497 58
Total losses paid from the organization of the company to date	117,487 35
Total dividends declared since the company commenced business	61,000 00
Total amount of losses incurred during the year	66,469 65
Total amount of the company's stock owned by the directors, at par value	138,500 00
Total amount loaned to officers and directors	57,500 00
Total amount loaned to stockholders, not officers	20,110 00

BUSINESS IN THE STATE OF WISCONSIN, DURING THE YEAR 1872.

Risks taken (fire)	$210,300 00
Premiums received	1,582 30

WILLIAMSBURG CITY FIRE INSURANCE COMPANY.

BROOKLYN, N. Y.

[Incorporated in 1853. Commenced business in 1853.]

EDMUND DRIGGS, *President.* N. W. MESEROLE, *Secretary.*

Attorney to accept service of process in Wisconsin, F. H. MAGDEBURG, Milwaukee.

I. CAPITAL.

Capital authorized	$250,000 00
Capital actually paid up in cash	250,000 00

II. ASSETS.

Value of real estate owned by the company, less incumbrances	$40,000 00
Loans on bond and mortgage, (first liens)	275,550 00
Loans on bond and mortgage (first liens), upon which more than one year's interest is due	31,000 00
Interest due on bond and mortgage loans	3,045 00
Interest accrued on bond and mortgage loans	1,788 21
Stocks and bonds, market value	107,443 75
Cash loans secured by collaterals	38,870 00
Cash in the company's principal office and in bank	35,696 17
Interest due and accrued on collateral loans	563 04
Gross premiums in due course of collection	56,234 00
All other property belonging to the company, viz: rents, $845; furniture, $7,367 96; total	8,212 96
Aggregate of all the assets of the company	$598,333 13

III. LIABILITIES.

Losses adjusted and unpaid	$52,467 85	....
Losses unadjusted, including all reported and supposed losses.	84,423 96	....
Losses resisted, including interest, costs and expenses	2,400 00	....
Net amount of unpaid losses and claims		$139,291 81
Reinsurance at 50 per cent. of prem., on fire risks, under one year	$158,188 24	....
Reinsurance, *pro rata*, on fire risks running more than one year.	12,708 31	....
Reinsurance at 50 per cent. of prem. on inland risks	885 41	....
Amount required to safely reinsure all outstanding risks		171,781 96
Cash dividends declared to stockholders, unpaid		497 50
Due and accrued for salaries, rent and other expenses		1,588 33
All other demands against the company, viz.: commissions		7,029 25
Total liabilities, except capital stock		$320,188 85
Capital stock actually paid up in cash		250,000 00
Surplus beyond capital stock		25,149 78
Aggregate amount of all liabilities, including capital and surplus		$595,338 13

IV. INCOME DURING THE YEAR.

	Fire.	Marine and inland.	
Gross premiums received in cash	$401,570 91	$2,083 33	....
Deduct reinsurance, rebate and returned prem's	18,316 42	....	....
Net cash received for premiums	$383,254 49	$2,083 33	$385,337 82
Gross premiums remaining unpaid		$56,284 00	....
Received for interest on bonds and mortgages			27,611 01
Received for interest and dividends from all other sources			6,807 90
Income received from all other sources			456 75
Aggregate amount of income received during the year, in cash			$420,213 48

V. EXPENDITURES DURING THE YEAR.

	Fire.	Marine and inland.	
Gross amount paid for losses	$247,688 11	$1,988 87	....
Deduct salvage and reinsurance	1,198 14	....	....
Net amount paid during the year for losses	$246,489 97	$1,988 87	$248,478 84
Cash dividends paid			25,000 00
Paid for commissions and brokerage			51,716 88
Salaries and all other charges of officers, and all employes.			30,036 19
Paid for state, national and local taxes			7,897 42
All other payments and expenditures			29,814 60
Aggregate amount of expenditures during the year, in cash			$392,896 48

VI. MISCELLANEOUS.

	Fire risks.	Premiums thereon.	Marine and inland risks.	Premiums thereon.
In force, December 31, 1871	$30,454,881	$236,669 00	$30,000	$1,150 00
Written during the year	47,589,799	428,964 78	50,833	2,083 33
Total	$78,044,680	$665,633 78	$80,833	$3,233 33
Deduct those terminated	35,977,944	333,275 29	30,000	1,462 50
In force, December 31, 1872.	$42,066,736	$332,358 49	$50,833	$1,770 83
Deduct amount reinsured	250,204	2,649 70	....	....
Net amount in force	$41,816,532	$329,708 79	$50,833	$1,770 83
In force, having not more than one year to run	$39,425,423	$316,376 47	$50,833	$1,770 83
Having more than one and not more than three years to run	2,201,480	10,207 74	....	....
Having more than three years to run	439,833	5,774 28	....	....
Net amount in force	$42,066,736	$332,358 49	$50,833	$1,770 83

General Interrogatories.

Total premiums received from the organization of the company to date	$2,886,384 64
Total losses paid from the organization of the company to date	1,745,449 04
Total dividends declared since the company commenced business	360,000 00

Total amount of losses incurred during the year	$353,868 94
Tatal amount of the company's stock owned by the directors, at par value	96,850 00
Total amount loaned to officers and directors	45,050 00
Total amount loaned to stock holders, not officers	1,000 00

BUSINESS IN THE STATE OF WISCONSIN, DURING THE YEAR 1872.

Fire risks taken	$269,787 00
Premiums received	3,550 86
Losses paid on risks taken	6,176 45
Losses incurred during the year, in Wisconsin	6,176 45

COMPANIES OF FOREIGN COUNTRIES.

U. S. BRANCH OF THE COMMERCIAL UNION ASSURANCE COMPANY.

LONDON, G. B.

[Incorporated in 1861. Commenced business in U. S. in 1871.]

ALFRED GILES, *President*. **ALEX. SUTHERLAND**, *Secretary*.

Attorney to accept service of process in Wisconsin, WM. B. HIBBARD, Milwaukee.

I. CAPITAL.

Capital authorized	$12,500,000 00
Capital actually paid up in cash	1,250,000 00

II. ASSETS IN U. S.

U. S. 5-20 bonds, market value	$342,000 00
Cash in the company's principal office and in bank	150,134 93
Gross premiums in due course of collection	13,838 35
All other property belonging to the company, viz.: reinsurance due on losses paid	9,965 84
Aggregate of all the assets of the company	$515,909 12

III. LIABILITIES IN U. S.

Losses adjusted and unpaid	$35,416 68	
Losses unadjusted, including all reported and supposed losses	64,565 39	
Losses resisted, including interest, costs and expenses	5,423 40	
Total gross amount of claims for losses	$105,405 47	
Deduct reinsurance thereon	3,592 44	
Net amount of unpaid losses and claims		$101,813 03
Reinsurance at 50 per cent. of prem., on fire risks, under one year	$190,529 34	
Reinsurance, *pro rata*, on fire risks running more than one year	11,633 38	
Amount required to safely reinsure all outstanding risks		202,162 72
All other demands against the company, viz.: commissions		1,666 77
Total liabilities in U. S.		$305,642 52
Surplus beyond liabilities		210,266 60
Aggregate of all liabilities and net surplus		$515,909 12

IV. INCOME DURING THE YEAR.

Gross premiums received in cash (fire)	$499,889 09	
Deduct reinsurance, rebate and returned premiums	55,003 18	
Net cash received for premiums		$444,885 91
Gross premiums, remaining unpaid	$13,838 35	
Received for exchange on London	229,444 68	
Aggregate amount of income received during the year		$444,885 91

V. EXPENDITURES DURING THE YEAR.

Gross amount paid for losses (fire)	$456,096 62	
Deduct salvage and reinsurance	4,946 23	
Net amount paid during the year for losses		$451,150 39
Paid for commissions and brokerage		88,977 18
Salaries and all other charges of officers, and all employes		5,296 77
Paid for state, national and local taxes		8,474 91
Aggregate amount of expenditures during the year, in cash		$553,899 25

VI. MISCELLANEOUS.

	Fire Risks.	Premiums thereon.
In force, December 31, 1871	$17,770,835	$194,332 47
Written during 1872	43,117,314	514,385 57
Total	$60,888,149	$708,718 04
Deduct those terminated	27,423,787	310,059 29
In force, December 31, 1872	$33,464,362	398,658 75
Deduct amount reinsured	603,524	6,921 85
Net amount in force	$32,860,838	$391,736 90
In force, having not more than one year to run	$31,555,713	$374,136 83
Having more than one and not more than three years to run	624,875	7,495 32
Having more than three years to run	680,250	10,104 75
Net amount in force	$32,860,838	$391,756 90

General Interrogatories.

Total premiums received from the organization of the company to date	$710,128 69
Total losses paid from the organization of the company to date	565,975 65
Total amount of losses incurred during the year	398,059 61
Am't deposited in different states and countries, for the security of policy holders, $300,000 par value, deposited as follows: in the state of New York, $200,000; Ohio, $100,000.	

Business in the State of Wisconsin, during the Year 1872.

Fire risks taken	$1,302,942 75
Premiums received	16,835 11
Losses paid on risks taken	6,238 52
Losses incurred during the year, in Wisconsin	6,238 52
Taxes on premiums, paid to the state of Wisconsin	183 19

HAMBURG-BREMEN FIRE INSURANCE COMPANY.

HAMBURG, GERMANY.

[Incorporated in 1854. Commenced business in 1855.]

SENATOR DR. SCHROEDER, *President*. ALFRED KLAUHOLD, *Managing Director*.

Attorney to accept service of process in Wisconsin, HARLOW PEASE, Watertown.

I. CAPITAL.

Capital authorized	$800,000 00
Capital actually paid up in cash	160,000 00
Capital subscribed and unpaid	640,000 00

II. ASSETS.

Loans on bond and mortgage, (first liens)		$252,592 80
Stocks and bonds, market value		258,090 80
Cash in the company's principal office, and in bank		180,617 73
Gross premiums in due course of collection		21,718 07
All other property belonging to the company, viz.: marine acceptances		73,106 14
Stockholders' notes or other obligations given for capital subscribed, but not actually paid up in cash	$640,000	....
Aggregate of all the assets of the company		$781,125 54

III. LIABILITIES.

Losses adjusted and unpaid	$27,607 00	....
Deduct reinsurance thereon	16,500 00	....
Net amount of unpaid losses and claims		$11,107 00
Reinsurance at 50 per cent. of prem. on fire risks, under one year		180,428 60
Cash dividends declared to stockholders, unpaid		26,572 80
Liabilities for securities put up as deposits		200,000 00
All other demands against the company, viz: reinsurance		51,839 06
Total liabilities, except capital stock		$469,942 46
Capital stock actually paid up in cash		160,000 00
Surplus beyond capital stock		151,186 08
Aggregate of all liabilities, including capital and surplus		$781,125 54

IV. INCOME DURING THE YEAR.

Gross premiums received in cash (fire)	$420,964 68	....
Deduct reinsurance, rebate and returned premiums	190,996 68	....
Net cash received for premiums		$229,968 01
Received for interest and dividends from all sources		19,210 00
Income received from all other sources		2,016 80
Aggregate amount of income received during the year, in cash		$251,194 81

V. EXPENDITURES DURING THE YEAR.

Gross amount paid for losses (fire)	$220,716 98	....
Deduct reinsurance	129,132 35	....
Net amount paid during the year for losses		$91,584 63
Cash dividends paid		18,120 00
Paid for commissions and brokerage		60,435 21
Salaries and all other charges of officers, and all employes		36,110 42
Aggregate amount of expenditures during the year, in cash		$206,250 26

VI. MISCELLANEOUS.

	Fire Risks.	Premiums thereon.
In force, December 31, 1871	$57,027,852	$286,834 00
Written during 1872	76,967,768	420,964 68
Total	$133,995,620	$707,798 68
Deduct those terminated	66,272,085	346,946 48
In force, December 31, 1872	$67,723,535	$360,847 20
Deduct amount reinsured	26,678,968	157,656 40
Net amount in force,	$41,044,567	$203,190 80
In force, having not more than one year to run	$35,149,769	$182,709 20
Having more than one year to run	5,894,798	20,481 60
Net amount in force	$41,044,567	$203,190 80

General Interrogatories.

Total premiums received from the organization of the company to date	$2,505,712 40
Total losses paid from the organization of the company to date	1,424,123 40
Total dividends declared since the company commenced business	239,030 89
Total amount of losses incurred during the year	91,584 63
Total amount of the company's stock owned by the directors, at par value	7,769 00

Amount deposited in different states and countries, for the security of policy holders, viz: $200,000, deposited in the state of Illinois.

Business in the State of Wisconsin, during the Year 1872.

Risks taken, (fire)	$391,450 00
Premiums received	2,967 69

U. S. BRANCH OF THE IMPERIAL FIRE INSURANCE COMPANY.

London, G. B.

[Incorporated in 1808. Commenced business in 1808.]

E. M. ARCHIBALD, *Chairman Local Board.* E. W. CROWELL, *Resident Manager.*

Attorney to accept service of process in Wisconsin, James O. Gordon, Madison.

I. CAPITAL.

Capital authorised	£1,600,000 00
Capital actually paid up in cash	700,000 00

II. ASSETS IN THE UNITED STATES.

Stocks and bonds, market value	$1,049,787 50
Cash loans secured by collaterals	100,000 00
Cash in the company's principal office and in bank	15,105 50
Gross premiums in due course of collection	182,890 87
Bills receivable, not matured, taken for fire risks	774 07
Aggregate of all the assets of the company, at their actual value	$1,348,507 44

III. LIABILITIES.

Losses unadjusted, including all reported and supposed losses	$435,010 17	
Losses resisted, including interest, costs and expenses	13,950 00	
Total gross amount of claims for losses	$448,960 17	
Deduct reinsurance thereon	90,428 15	
Net amount of unpaid losses and claims		$358,532 02
Reinsurance at 50 per cent. of prem., on fire risks, under one year	$566,402 50	
Reinsurance, *pro rata*, on fire risks running more than one year	116,046 37	
Amount required to safely reinsure all outstanding risks		682,448 87
Due and accrued for salaries, rent and other expenses		1,666 67
All other demands against the company, viz.: commissions		27,433 54
Total liabilities in the U. S		$1,070,081 10
Surplus beyond liabilities		278,426 34
Aggregate am't of all liabilities, including net surplus		$1,348,507 44

IV. INCOME DURING THE YEAR.

Gross premiums received in cash (fire)	$1,681,752 15	
Deduct reinsurance, rebate and returned premiums	259,593 63	
Net cash received for premiums		$1,422,158 52
Gross premiums, remaining unpaid	$183,664 44	
Received for interest and dividends from all sources		1,921 96
Received from London office	$596,583 97	
Aggregate amount of income received during the year, in cash		$1,424,074 78

V. EXPENDITURES DURING THE YEAR.

Gross amount paid for losses (fire)	$1,284,535 88	
Deduct reinsurance	16,876 33	
Net amount paid during the year for losses		$1,267,658 55
Paid for commissions and brokerage		209,950 21
Salaries and all other charges of officers, and all employes		44,875 58
Paid for state, national and local taxes		34,518 82
All other payments and expenditures		197,687 85
Aggregate amount of expenditures during the year, in cash		$1,754,185 96

VI. MISCELLANEOUS.

	Fire Risks.	Premiums thereon.
In force, December 31, 1871	$74,185,066 00	$971,484 00
Written during 1872	174,758,393 08	1,772,081 88
Total	$248,943,409 08	$2,743,465 88
Deduct those terminated	122,671,318 34	1,270,287 02
In force, December 31, 1872	$126,272,090 69	$1,473,178 86
Deduct amount reinsured	9,551,978 52	108,280 57
Net amount in force	$116,720,112 17	$1,364,897 79
In force, having not more than one year to run	$99,188,439 93	$1,132,805 05
Having more than one and not more than three years to run	11,687,781 50	154,728 49
Having more than three years to run	5,843,890 74	77,364 25
Net amount in force	$116,720,112 17	$1,364,897 79

General Interrogatories.

Total premiums received from the organization of the company to date	$4,071,474 87
Total losses paid from the organization of the company to date	2,925,627 05
Total amount of losses incurred during the year	1,667,298 14
Amount deposited in different states and countries, for the security of policy holders	1,000,000 00

BUSINESS IN THE STATE OF WISCONSIN, DURING THE YEAR 1872.

Risks taken (fire)	$3,761,617 60
Premiums received	50,609 97
Losses paid on risks taken	38,696 86
Losses incurred during the year, in Wisconsin	35,899 75

LANCASHIRE (U. S. BRANCH) INSURANCE COMPANY.

MANCHESTER, G. B.

[Incorporated in 1852. Commenced business in 1872.]

JOSEPH L. LORD, *Resident Manager*.

Attorney to accept service of process in Wisconsin, C. D. ADSIT, Milwaukee.

I. CAPITAL.

Capital actually paid up in cash	None in U. S.

II. ASSETS.

U. S. 5-20 bonds, market value	$229,500 00
Cash belonging to the company, deposited in bank	21,809 89
Gross premiums in due course of collection	101,896 83
Aggregate of all the assets of the company, at their actual value	$353,206 72

III. LIABILITIES.

Losses adjusted and unpaid	$18,823 09	
Losses unadjusted, including all reported and supposed losses	50,875 00	
Net amount of unpaid losses and claims		$69,698 09
Amount required to safely reinsure all outstanding risks		165,282 17
All other demands against the company, viz.: commissions		15,284 52
Total liabilities		$250,264 78
Surplus beyond liabilities		102,941 94
Aggregate of all liabilities including net surplus		$353,206 72

IV. INCOME DURING THE YEAR.

Gross premiums received in cash (fire)	$266,796 48	
Deduct reinsurance, rebate and returned premiums	28,163 61	
Net cash received for premiums		$238,632 87
Gross premiums, remaining unpaid	$101,896 83	
Aggregate amount of income received during the year, in cash		$238,632 87

V. EXPENDITURES DURING THE YEAR.

Gross amount paid for losses (fire)	$161,283 94	
Deduct salvage and reinsurance	1,015 00	
Net amount paid during the year for losses		$160,268 94
Paid for commissions and brokerage		56,999 84
Paid for state, national and local taxes		4,318 43
All other payments and expenditures		4,551 08
Aggregate amount of expenditures during the year, in cash		$226,138 29

VI. MISCELLANEOUS.

	Fire Risks.	Premiums thereon.
Written during the year	$35,830,597 79	$368,682 31
Deduct those terminated	5,293,530 00	37,775 79
In force, December 31, 1872	$30,537,067 79	$330,906 52
Deduct amount reinsured	75,000 00	342 17
mount in force	$30,462,067 79	$330,564 35

GENERAL INTERROGATORIES.

Total premiums received from the organization of the company to date	$368,688 31
Total losses paid from the organization of the company to date	160,268 94
Total amount of losses incurred during the year	229,967 08
Amount deposited for the security of policy holders, in the state of N. Y.	200,000 00

BUSINESS IN THE STATE OF WISCONSIN, DURING THE YEAR 1872.

Risks taken (fire)	$378,055 00
Premiums received	2,406 47

LIVERPOOL AND LONDON AND GLOBE (AMERICAN BRANCH) INSURANCE COMPANY.

LIVERPOOL, G. B.

[Incorporated in 1836. Commenced business in the U. S. in 1851.]

ALFRED PELL, *Resident Manager*. J. E. PULSFORD, *Secretary*.

Attorney to accept service of process in Wisconsin, ROBERT ELIOT, Milwaukee.

I. CAPITAL.

Capital authorized	$[illegible],000,000 00
Capital actually paid up in cash	391,753 00

II. ASSETS.

Value of real estate owned by the company, less incumbrances	$447,916 78
Loans on bond and mortgage, (first liens)	1,065,400 00
Interest accrued on bond and mortgage loans	16,489 00
Stocks and bonds, market value	1,520,430 00
Cash loans, secured by collaterals	600 00
Cash belonging to the company, deposited in bank	756,399 47
Interest due and accrued, not included in market value	8,776 66
Interest due and accrued on collateral loans	88 38
Gross premiums in due course of collection	343,808 55
Bills receivable, not taken for dremiums	30,482 38
All other property belonging to the company, viz.: rents	5,436 23
Aggregate of all the assets of the company, at their actual value	$4,195,772 40

III. LIABILITIES.

Losses unadjusted, including all reported and supposed losses	$748,538 38	....
Losses resisted, including interest, costs and expenses	65,918 43	....
Net amount of unpaid losses and claims		$814,456 81
Reinsurance at 50 per cent. of prem., on fire risks, under one year	$1,481,495 89	....
Reinsurance, *pro rata*, on fire risks running more than one year	175,231 77	....
Amount required to safely reinsure all outstanding risks		$1,656,727 66
Amount reclaimable on perpetual fire risks		288,044 91
Liabilities etc, of life department		106,470 72
All other demands against the company, viz: commissions		58,009 60
Total liabilities		$2,923,700 10
Surplus beyond liabilities		1,272,072 30
Aggregate of all liabilities, including net surplus		$4,195,772 40

IV. INCOME DURING THE YEAR.

Gross premiums received in cash (fire)	$3,865,148 80	....
Deduct reinsurance, rebate and returned premiums	363,902 39	....
Net cash received for premiums		*$3,501,246 41
Received for interest on bonds and mortgages		84,760 57
Received for interest and dividends from all sources		70,153 22
Income received from all other sources, viz.: rents, $33,377 54; exchange, $20,481 32; life premium, $23,081 56; total		76,940 42
Deposit premiums received for perpetual fire risks	$42,743 42	....
Received from home office	1,068,681 54	....
Aggregate amount of income received during the year, in cash		$3,733,100 62

V. EXPENDITURES DURING THE YEAR.

Gross amount paid for losses (fire)	$3,649,611 71	....
Deduct salvage and reinsurance	18,072 87	....
Net amount paid during the year for losses		$3,631,538 84
Paid for commissions and brokerage		474,984 68
Salaries and all other charges of officers, and all employes		57,907 08
Paid for state, national and local taxes		48,811 67
Life expenditures and annuities		11,511 55
All other payments and expenditures		260,295 09
Aggregate amount of expenditures during the year, in cash		$4,484,998 86

VI. MISCELLANEOUS.

	Fire Risks.	Premiums thereon.
In force, December 31, 1871	$258,349,404 00	$2,849,656 61
Written during 1872	429,538,988 00	3,865,148 80
Total	$687,888,392 00	$6,714,805 41
Deduct those terminated	404,096,874 00	3,454,741 76
In force, December 31, 1872	$283,791,518 00	$3,260,063 65
Deduct amount reinsured	4,922,087 00	28,301 97
Net amount in force	$278,869,431 00	$3,231,761 68
In force, having not more than one year to run	$250,462,457 00	$2,943,198 29
Having more than one, and not more than three years to run	14,759,804 00	208,647 29
Having more than three years to run	5,731,924 00	60,222 61
Perpetual risks in force and int. prem	7,915,246 00	19,698 49
Net amount in force	$278,869,431 00	$3,231,761 68

General Interrogatories.

Total premiums received from the organization of the branch to date	$25,277,200 14
Total losses paid from the organization of the branch to date	17,015,121 43
Total amount of losses incurred during the year	3,967,060 00

Amount deposited in the different states and countries, for the security of policy holders, $825,000, deposited as follows: in the state of New York, $310,000; Massachusetts, $200,000; Ohio, $100,000; Nevada, $50,000; Oregon, $50,000; Tennessee, $20,000; South Carolina, $20,000; Alabama, $10,000; Mississippi, $20,000; Virginia, $45,000.

Business in the State of Wisconsin, during the Year 1872.

Risks taken (fire)	$1,845,900 00
Premiums received	26,980 00
Losses paid on risks taken	12,811 40

* Of which $343,808 55 is in course of collection.

LONDON ASSURANCE CORPORATION.

London, G. B.

[Incorporated in 1720. Commenced business in 1720.]

EDWIN GOWER, *Governor*. JOHN PHILIP LAWRENCE, *Secretary*.

Attorney to accept service of process in Wisconsin, Samuel M. Ogden, Milwaukee.

I. CAPITAL.

Capital actually paid up in cash	£448,275 0 0

II. ASSETS.

Loans on bond and mortgage (first liens)	£1,696,089 14 2
Stocks and bonds, market value	874,570 2 6
Cash loans secured by collaterals	85,515 00 00
Government life annuities	6,563 00 00
Cash in the company's principal office and in bank	69,529 17 10
Interest due and accrued	2,708 12 3
Gross premiums in due course of collection, and agents' balances	52,698 12 4
Bills receivable, not matured, taken for fire, marine and life risks	5,788 10 5
All other property belonging to company, viz: policy stamps	175 2 8
Aggregate of all the assets of the company, stated at their actual value	£2,744,686 11 9

III. LIABILITIES.

Net amount of losses and claims	£79,168 11 11
Amount required to safely reinsure all outstanding risks	116,755 00 00
Reinsurance and liabilities of life department	1,486,184 5 2
Cash dividends declared to stockholders, unpaid	284 00 00
All other demands against the company, viz: income tax, £126 3 4; annuities, £236 6 6; clerks' savings fund, £8,247 9 9; total	8,610 9 7
Total liabilities, except capital stock	£1,685,947 6 8
Capital stock actually paid up in cash	448,275 00 00
Surplus beyond capital stock	610,414 5 1
Aggregate of all liabilities, including capital and surplus	£2,744,636 11 9

IV. INCOME DURING THE YEAR.

	Fire.	Marine and inland.	
Gross premiums received in cash	£198,864 4 5	£125,769 8 2	
Deduct reinsurance, rebate and ret'd prems	18,403 15 9	12,874 8 10	
Net cash received for premiums	£180,460 8 8	£113,887 19 4	£293,848 8 0
Received for interest and dividends, from all sources			113,084 3 8
Income received from all other sources			159,271 3 11
Aggregate amount of income received during the year, in cash			£566,153 15 7

V. EXPENDITURES DURING THE YEAR.

	Fire.	Marine and Inland.	
Gross amount paid for losses	£117,269 11 2	£92,606 11 6	
Deduct salvage and reinsurance	579 19 10	3,044 10 3	
Net am't paid during the year for losses	£116,689 11 4	£89,562 1 3	£206,251 12 7
Cash divdends paid			107,586 0 0
Paid for commissions and brokerage			30,080 7 3
Salaries and all other charges of officers, and all employes			33,054 18 4
Paid for state, national and local taxes			2,753 9 11
All other payments and expenditures			138,675 3 6
Aggregate amount of expenditures during the year, in cash			£518,341 11 7

BUSINESS IN THE STATE OF WISCONSIN, DURING THE YEAR 1872.

Risks taken (fire)	$669,250 00
Premiums received	7,548 89
Taxes on premiums, paid to the state of Wisconsin	46 55

U. S. BRANCH OF THE NORTH BRITISH AND MERCANTILE INSURANCE COMPANY.

LONDON AND EDINBURGH, G. B.

[Incorporated in 1809. Commenced business in U. S. in 1866.]

CHAS. E. WHITE, *Associate Manager.*

Attorney to accept service of process in Wisconsin, J. H. CRAMPTON, Milwaukee.

I. ASSETS.

Stocks and bonds owned by the company, market value	$1,292,740 00
Cash in the company's principal office and in bank	284,977 02
Interest due and accrued, not included in market value	12,300 00
Balances due from agents	101,750 00
Bills receivable	2,796 77
All other property belonging to the company, viz: office furniture	6,882 79
Aggregate of all the assets of the company, at their actual value	$1,701,446 95

II. LIABILITIES.

Losses adjusted and unpaid	$157,775 64	....
Losses unadjusted, including all reported and supposed losses	194,783 50	....
Net amount of unpaid losses and claims		$352,559 14
Reinsurance at 50 per ct. of prem., on fire risks, under one year	$747,783 23	....
Reinsurance, *pro rata*, on fire risks running more than one year	128,414 64	....
Amount required to safely reinsure all outstanding risks		876,197 87
Total liabilities		$1,228,757 01
Surplus beyond liabilities		472,689 94
Aggregate of all liabilities including net surplus		$1,701,446 95

III. INCOME DURING THE YEAR.

Gross premiums received in cash (fire)	$1,910,571 20	....
Deduct reinsurance, rebate and returned premiums	163,318 03	....
Net cash received for premiums		$1,747,253 17
Received for interest and dividends from all sources		72,708 04
Income received from all other sources, viz: premium on gold		4,383 93
Received from home office	$298,333 08	....
Aggregate amount of income received during the year, in cash		$1,894,339 14

IV. EXPENDITURES DURING THE YEAR.

Net amount paid during the year for losses (fire)	$1,580,548 30
Paid for commissions and brokerage	258,385 95
Salaries and all other charges of officers and all employes	111,064 14
Paid for state, national and local taxes	39,206 18
All other payments and expenditures	87,963 81
Aggregate amount of expenditures during the year, in cash	$2,022,167 88

V. MISCELLANEOUS.

	Fire Risks.	Premiums thereon.
In force, December 31, 1871	$115,776,786 00	$1,312,330 31
Written during 1872	199,454,836 51	1,910,571 20
Total	$315,231,622 51	$3,222,901 51
Deduct those terminated	171,027,780 59	1,513,310 70
In force, December 31, 1872	$144,203,841 92	$1,709,590 81
In force, having not more than one year to run	$127,803,220 10	$1,495,566 47
Having more than one and not more than three years to run	10,895,792 47	138,994 10
Having more than three years to run	5,504,829 35	75,030 24
Net amount in force	$144,203,841 92	$1,709,590 81

General Interrogatories.

Total premiums received from the organization of the company to date	$6,226,855 74
Total losses paid from the organization of the company to date	5,669,776 42
Total amount of losses incurred during the year	1,685,490 25

Amount deposited in different states and countries, for the security of policy holders, including trust fund, $958,000, deposited as follows: in the state of Virginia, $70,000; Ohio $100,000; South Carolina, $30,000; Alabama, 10,000; Tennessee, $20,000; trust fund, $758,000.

Business in the State of Wisconsin, during the Year 1872.

Risks taken (fire)	$2,716,628 00
Premiums received	42,199 40
Losses paid on risks taken	16,297 85
Losses incurred during the year in Wisconsin	19,297 85
Taxes on premiums, paid to the state of Wisconsin	1,086 39

U. S. BRANCH OF THE QUEEN INSURANCE COMPANY.

LIVERPOOL, G. B.

[Incorporated in 1858. Commenced business in 1858.]

W. H. ROSS, *Manager*, New York.

Attorney to accept service of process in Wisconsin, C. J. CARY, Milwaukee.

I. CAPITAL.

Capital authorized	£2,000,000 00
Capital actually paid up in cash	179,800 00

II. ASSETS.

Stocks and bonds owned by the company, market value	$603,050 00
Cash belonging to the company, deposited in bank	38,114 93
Gross premiums in due course of collection	13,912 54
All other property belonging to the company	4,000 00
Aggregate of all the assets of the company, stated at their actual value	$659,077 47

III. LIABILITIES.

Losses unadjusted, including all reported and supposed losses	$69,367 88	
Losses resisted, including interest, costs and expenses	7,987 00	
Total gross amount of claims for losses	$77,354 88	
Deduct reinsurance thereon	30,941 88	
Net amount of unpaid losses and claims		$46,413 00
Reinsurance at 50 per cent. of prem., on fire risks, under one year	$369,722 05	
Reinsurance *pro rata*, on fire risks running more than one year	30,714 40	
Gross amount	$400,436 45	
Less reinsured, or on joint account	160,305 05	
Am't required to safely reinsure all outstanding risks		240,131 40
Amount reclaimable on perpetual fire risks		12,236 75
Due and accrued for salaries, rent and other expenses		1,383 33
All other demands against the company, viz.: commissions		1,587 29
Total liabilities		$301,751 77
Surplus beyond liabilities		357,325 70
Aggregate of all liabilities, including net surplus		$659,077 47

IV. INCOME DURING THE YEAR.

Gross premiums received in cash (fire)	$1,139,353 67	
Deduct reinsurance, rebate and returned premiums	118,596 11	
Net cash received for premiums		$1,020,757 56
Gross premiums remaining unpaid	$13,912 54	
Received for interest and dividends from all sources		16,235 15
Deposit premiums, received for perpetual fire risks	$6,676 60	
Received from chief office	541,523 50	
Aggregate amount of income received during the year, in cash		$1,036,992 71

V. EXPENDITURES DURING THE YEAR.

Net amount paid during the year for losses (fire)	$1,326,294 28
Paid for commissions and brokerage	148,283 14
Salaries and all other charges of officers, and all employes	33,169 57
Paid for state, national and local taxes	28,740 29
All other payments and expenditures	40,954 88
Aggregate amount of expenditures during the year, in cash	$1,577,442 16

VI. MISCELLANEOUS.

	Fire Risks.	Premiums thereon.
In force, December 31, 1871	$47,675,982	$633,923 43
Written during 1872	107,595,986	1,134,823 11
Total	$155,271,968	$1,768,746 54
Deduct those terminated	85,127,174	949,992 13
In force, December 31, 1872	$70,144,794	$818,754 41
Deduct amount reinsured	20,068,468	330,632 27
Net amount in force	$50,076,326	$488,122 14
In force, having not more than one year to run	$65,420,193	$751,772 79
Having more than one and not more than three years to run	2,173,751	28,587 71
Having more than three years to run	2,045,050	32,842 09
Perpetual risks in force, and int. prem	505,800	551 82
Gross amount in force	$70,144,794	$818,754 41

General Interrogatories.

Total premiums received, from the organization of the company to date	$2,793,863 00
Total losses paid, from the organization of the company to date	2,199,470 00
Total amount of losses incurred during the year	1,367,622 00

Total amount of the company's stock owned by the directors in U. S., at par value, £1,100.

Amount deposited in different states and countries, for the security of policy holders, $530,000; of which there is deposited as follows: in the state of Tennessee, $20,000; Alabama, $10,000; Ohio, $100,000.

Business in the State of Wisconsin, during the Year 1872.

Risks taken (fire)	$1,326,690 00
Premiums received	19,776 80
Losses paid on risks taken	12,993 58
Losses incurred during the year, in Wisconsin	12,993 58
Taxes on premiums, paid to the state of Wisconsin	789 10

ROYAL INSURANCE COMPANY.

Liverpool, G. B.

[Incorporated in 1845. Commenced business in 1845.]

JOHN H. McLAREN, *Manager*. CHARLES GEORGE FOTHERGILL, *Sub Manager*.

Attorney to accept service of process in Wisconsin, Chas. J. Cary, Milwaukee.

I. CAPITAL.

	£	s.	d.
Capital authorized	£2,000,000	0	0
Capital actually paid up in cash	289,095	0	0
Capital subscribed and unpaid	1,638,205	0	0

II. ASSETS.

	£	s.	d.
Value of real estate owned by the company, less incumbrances	£199,200	11	5
Loans on bond and mortgage, (first liens)	75,025	18	2
Stocks and bonds, market value	965,686	7	10
Cash loans secured by collaterals	882,392	2	3
Cash loans secured by life policies	74,628	19	7
Cash in the company's principal office and in bank	140,282	18	8
Gross premiums in due course of collection and balance in hands of agents and ins. companies	24,147	7	11
St'kh'ds' notes or other obligation given for capital unpaid £1,648,205			
Aggregate of all the assets of the company	£2,361,364	5	10

III. LIABILITIES.

Losses unadjusted, including all reported and supposed losses	£24,561 0 5	....
Losses resisted, including interest, costs and expenses	7,174 18 4	....
Total gross amount of claims for losses	£31,735 18 9	....
Deduct reinsurance thereon	3,117 5 11	....
Net amount of unpaid losses and claims		£28,618 12 10
Reins'ce at 50 per ct. of prem. on fire risks, under one year	£270,498 0 0	....
Reinsur'ce, *pro rata*, on fire risks, runn'g more than one year	15,731 0 0	....
Amount required to safely reinsure all outstanding risks		286,229 0 0
Amount reclaimable on perpetual fire risks		4,808 5 4
Cash dividends declared to stockholders, unpaid		1,085 19 0
Reinsurance and all other liabilities of life and other departments		1,349,372 18 2
Total liabilities, except capital stock		£1,670,114 10 4
Capital stock actually paid up in cash		289,095 0 0
Surplus beyond capital stock		402,154 15 6
Aggregate of all liabilities, including capital and net surplus		£2,361,364 5 10

IV. INCOME DURING THE YEAR.

Gross premiums received in cash (fire)	£962,558 14 3	....
Deduct reinsurance, rebate and returned premiums	189,707 4 0	....
Net cash received for premiums		£772,851 10 3
Transfer fees, £38. 7s.; returned anonymously, £1,540; total		1,578 7 0
Received for interest and dividends from all other sources	£89,091 3 4	....
Income received from all other sources, viz.: rents	9,980 6 9	....
	£99,071 10 1	....
Less amount carried to life department	66,167 3 6	....
		32,904 6 7
Deposit premiums, received for perpetual fire risks	£1,009 7 6	....
Aggregate amount of income received during the year, in cash		£807,334 3 10

V. EXPENDITURES DURING THE YEAR.

Gross amount paid for losses (fire)	£545,903 10 3	....
Deduct reinsurance	110,005 14 0	....
Net amount paid during the year for losses		£435,897 16 3
Cash dividends paid		48,182 10 0
Paid for commissions and brokerage		98,812 5 2
Salaries and all other charges of officers, and all employes		39,970 17 10
All other payments and expenditures		51,271 7 10
Aggregate amount of expenditures during the year, in cash		£674,134 17 1

VI. MISCELLANEOUS.

	Fire risks.	Premiums thereon.
Written during the year	£214,841,300	£905,066 18 11
Deduct those terminated of the year	26,855,100	113,133 7 5
In force, December 31, 1872	£187,986,200	£791,933 11 6
Deduct amount reinsured	25,945,800	115,688 10 8
Net amount in force, having not more than one year to run	£162,040,400	£676,245 0 10
In force, having not more than one year to run	£162,040,400	£676,245 0 10
Having more than one, and not more than three years to run	1,144,600	16,523 13 11
Having more than three years to run	958,800	14,938 18 2
Perpetual risks in force	125,500	....
Net amount in force	£164,269,300	£707.707 12 11

General Interrogatories.

Total premiums received, from the organization of the company to date	£8,878,555 2 10
Total losses paid, from the organization of the company to date	4,424,999 17 11
Total dividends declared since the company commenced business	702,068 2 6
Total amount of losses incurred during the year	435,897 16 3
Total amount of the company's stock owned by the directors at par value	41,511 0 0

Amount deposited in different states and countries, for the security of policy holders, deposited as follows: in the State of New York, $335,000; Ohio, $100,000; Virginia, $50,000; Alabama, $10,000; Illinois, $200,000; Canada, $150,000; Brazils, m.3,000.

BUSINESS IN THE STATE OF WISCONSIN, DURING THE YEAR 1878.

Risks taken (fire)	$2,477,052 00
Premiums received	30,048 88
Losses paid on risks taken	17,717 21
Losses incurred during the year, in Wisconsin	15,450 97
Taxes on premiums, paid to fire departments of Wisconsin	504 68

WESTERN ASSURANCE COMPANY.

TORONTO, CANADA.

[Incorporated in 1851.]

JOHN McMURRICH, *President*. FREDERICK LOVELACE, *Secretary*.

Attorneys to accept service of process in Wisconsin, HIBBARDS & VANCE, Milwaukee.

I. CAPITAL.

Capital authorised	$800,000 00
Capital actually paid up in cash	200,450 98

II. ASSETS.

Value of real estate owned by the company, less incumbrances	$24,874 73
Loans on bond and mortgage, (first liens)	68,467 58
Loans on bond and mortgage (first liens), upon which more than one year's interest is due	3,090 31
Interest accrued on bond and mortgage loans	3,397 90
Stocks and bonds, market value	240,137 07
Cash belonging to the company, deposited in bank	84,690 61
Interest due and accrued, not included in market value	1,818 88
Gross premiums in due course of collection	52,558 00
Bills receivable, taken for fire, marine and inland risks	44,668 95
All other property belonging to the company, viz: salvage	12,055 70
Gross amount of all the assets of the company	$535,182 88
Amount which should be deducted from the above assets, on account of bad and doubtful debts and securities,	1,639 82
Aggregate of all the assets of the company, at their actual value	$533,543 06

III. LIABILITIES.

Net amount of unpaid losses and claims	$93,982 45
Amount required to safely reinsure all outstanding risks	205,423 47
Cash dividends declared to stockholders, unpaid	1,408 58
All other demands against the company, viz.: commissions	4,295 69
Total liabilities, except capital stock	$305,110 14
Capital stock actually paid up in cash	200,450 98
Surplus beyond capital stock	27,981 94
Aggregate of all liabilities, including capital and surplus	$533,543 06

IV. INCOME DURING THE YEAR.

Net cash received for premiums		$489,317 74
Received for interest and dividends from all sources		23,732 94
Received for calls and for increased capital	$68,347 77	....
Aggregate amount of income received during the year, in cash		$513,050 68

V. EXPENDITURES DURING THE YEAR.

Net amount paid during the year for losses	$456,380 60
Cash dividends paid	16,470 10
Paid for commissions and brokerage	58,456 30
Salaries and all other charges of officers, and all employes	16,747 30
All other payments and expenditures	24,112 24
Aggregate amount of expenditures during the year, in cash	$566,166 54

VI. MISCELLANEOUS.

	Fire risks.	Premiums thereon.	Marine and Inland risks.	Premiums thereon.
In force, Dec. 31, 1871	$15,355,262	$91,079 29	$626,200	$14,920 00
Written during 1872	26,688,102	302,727 87	9,417,843	140,625 82
Total	$42,043,364	$393,807 16	$10,044,043	$155,545 82
Deduct those terminated..	20,351,836	248,402 94	9,118,919	132,316 30
In force December 31, 1872.	$21,691,528	$145,404 22	$925,124	$23,229 52
Deduct amount reinsured..	467,025	3,386 00	95,100	2,173 47
Net amount in force...	$21,224,503	$142,018 22	$830,024	$21,056 05
In force, having not more than one year to run..........	$20,708,138	$135,815 56	$830,024	$21,056 05
Having more than one, and not more than three years to run.................... ..	516,365	6,212 66	....	....
Net amount in force.......	$21,224,503	$142,028 22	$830,024	$21,056 05

BUSINESS IN THE STATE OF WISCONSIN, DURING THE YEAR 1872.

	Fire.	Marine and Inland.	Aggregate.
Risks taken...............	$282,823 00	$85,267 00	$368,090 00
Premiums received...........................	3,023 86	1,964 03	4,987 89

FOURTH

ANNUAL REPORT

OF THE

SECRETARY OF STATE

AS EX-OFFICIO

COMMISSIONER OF INSURANCE

OF THE

STATE OF WISCONSIN.

May 1, 1873.

PART II.—LIFE AND ACCIDENT INSURANCE.

MADISON, WIS.:
ATWOOD & CULVER, PRINTERS AND STEREOTYPERS.
1873.

INDEX.

PART II—LIFE AND ACCIDENT COMPANIES.

STATEMENTS OF COMPANIES.

WISCONSIN COMPANY.

COMPANIES OF OTHER STATES.

FOURTH ANNUAL REPORT

OF THE

SECRETARY OF STATE,

As Ex-Officio

COMMISSIONER OF INSURANCE.

PART II.

Life and Accident Insurance.

STATE OF WISCONSIN,

OFFICE OF SECRETARY OF STATE,

DEPARTMENT OF INSURANCE,

MADISON, May 1, 1873.

To the Honorable the Legislature of the State of Wisconsin:

As required by law, the Secretary of State, as *ex-officio* Commissioner of Insurance, has the honor to submit this, the fourth annual report, containing the statements of the life and accident insurance companies, reporting for the year ending December 31, 1872, and such tables and suggestions based thereon as are deemed of general interest.

In order to secure the official valuation of the policies of all the companies, the publication of this report has been delayed until the same were all received. This important information cannot possibly be had from official sources in time to publish the report by the first of May, as required by law.

COMPANIES ADMITTED.

Since the date of the last annual report, the following companies have been admitted to transact business in this state:

Excelsior, N. Y., July 24, 1872,
John Hancock Mutual, Mass., Aug. 29, 1872.
Missouri Mutual, Mo., Dec. 6, 1872.
Missouri Valley, Kansas, July 20, 1872.
New Jersey Mutual, N. J., April 26, 1873.
Western New York, N. Y., February 13, 1873.

The Missouri Mutual and the New Jersey Mutual having transacted business in the state before, were re-admitted upon complying with the requirements of the law.

COMPANIES WITHDRAWN.

Of the companies heretofore reporting, the following failed to file statements and otherwise to comply with the insurance law, and are therefore no longer authorized to transact business in this state:

Asbury, N. Y.
Economical Mutual, R. I.
Excelsior, N. Y.
Guardian Mutual, N. Y.
John Hancock Mutual, Mass.
Home, N. Y.
Hope Mutual, N. Y.
Life Association of America, Mo.
Union Mutual, Maine.

It is understood that the above companies all continue business except the following, which have re-insured: The Economical Mutual, R. I., re-insured in the Republic of Chicago; Excelsior, N. Y., in the National of the U. S. A., and the Hope Mutual in the New Jersey Mutual, N. J.

BUSINESS OF 1872.

The number of companies transacting business in this state, and reporting for the year 1872, was thirty-seven, against thirty-nine for the previous year.

The number of policies issued by these companies was 200,483; insured thereby $519,969,521; the number of policies issued by the same companies in 1871 was 190,359, insured thereby $463,194,925, showing an increase in the number of policies issued of 10,124, and in the amount of insurance of $56,774,596, or 12.26 per cent. The business of the Railway Passengers' Assurance Company is not included in these figures. Additions by dividends, old policies revived and increased are included, and are treated in the tables of this report as new business.

The aggregate insurance carried by these companies Dec. 31, 1872, was as follows: number of policies 709,277; insured thereby

$1,844,162,506; against 658,206 policies, and $1,727,775,594 insurance at the beginning of the year; showing an increase as the result of the year's business of 51,071 policies, and $116,386,912 insurance, or 6.74 per cent.

Of these companies thirty have increased the amount of their insurance $129,489,935; and seven reduced theirs $13,103,023.

The number of policies terminated by various causes during the year, was 148,932; insured thereby, $395,313,068; the number of policies terminated the previous year, was 154,414; insured thereby, $411,097,472; showing a decrease of $15,784,404, or 3.84 per cent. Still it will be seen that the ratio of terminations to new business, is 76.03 per cent.

The modes of termination were as follows: by death, $20,630,-401; by expiry, $88,258,268; by surrender, $65,351,049; by lapse, $140,063,461; by change, $21,286,673; not taken, $59,723,216. The amount lapsed and not taken, was $199,786,677, or 50.54 per cent. of the total terminations, and 38.42 of all the business of 1872, showing an improvement or decrease compared with the previous year.

FINANCIAL SUMMARY.

From the tables found in this report, it will be seen that the whole amount of gross admitted assets of the companies represented in this state on December 31, 1872, was $285,087,195; the net premium reserve, $244,293,331; surplus as regards policyholders, $31,538,151. Twenty-two companies show an aggregate net surplus of $26,660,210, and fifteen show a deficiency, after deducting capital stock, of $1,143,182.

The total income was $97,235,897. Of this amount, $88,563,314 was received in cash, and $8,672,583 in premium notes and loans. The excess of income over expenditures was $33,104,265, or 34.05 per cent. The total income of the same companies for the previous year was $91,720,067; showing an increase for 1872 of $5,515,-830, or 6.01 per cent.

The aggregate cash expenditures of these companies for the year was $57,367,773, which has been classified as follows: death losses and policy claims, $20,663,181; lapsed, surrendered and purchased policies, $7,206,927; dividends to policyholders, $14,845,173; dividends to stockholders, $367,797; commissions and salaries to agents, $6,937,935; medical examiners' fees, $557,718; salaries of officers and employes, $1,886,543; taxes, $1,070,059; all other payments, $3,832,440.

Tables carefully compiled from the annual company statements will be found herein, giving comparative ratios of the principal items above mentioned, by which the relative standing and merits of each company may be judged.

BUSINESS IN WISCONSIN.

The number of policies issued upon the lives of citizens of this state during the year, so far as reported, was 6,478; insured thereby, $11,423,411; against 6,752 policies, and $11,686,812 insurance in 1871; showing a decrease in the amount of insurance of $263,401.

The number of policies in force Dec. 31, 1872, was 26,377; insured thereby, $42,233,417.

The total premiums received, including cash and notes, was $1,669,252; losses paid, $349,557.

The following comparative table shows the total amount of premiums received, losses paid, and the ratio of losses to premiums for the last four years:

Years.	No. Co's.	Prem's rec'd.	Losses Paid	Percentage.
1872	37	$1,669,252	$349,557	20.94
1871	39	1,834,838	315,337	17.18
1870	36	1,770,060	268,755	15.18
1869	43	1,780,275	310,089	17.42

WISCONSIN COMPANY.

The Northwestern Mutual Life Insurance Company of Milwaukee, organized in 1858, is the only life company incorporated under the laws of this state. Its affairs are managed with great energy, ability and prudence; and its business continues to show substantial growth and prosperity.

The ratio of losses and claims to income was 15.76 per cent.; the average ratio for all the companies reporting being 21.94 per cent. The ratio of losses and claims to mean amount at risk was .92 per cent.; the average being 1.19 per cent. The ratio of expenses to income was 13.53 per cent., a decrease compared with the previous year, the average of all the companies reporting being 15.07 per cent.

The aggregate amount of gross admitted assets held by the company, December 31, 1872, was $12,349,811, against $10,535,472 the previous year, an increase of $1,814,339; premium reserve, American Experience Table, with four and one-half per cent., interest, $10,046,014; net surplus, $2,224,922.

The income for the year was $3,695,064; expenses, $500,082; death losses paid, $582,387; lapsed, surrendered and purchased policies, $434,343; dividends to policyholders, $449,371, leaving a balance of the income of the year over total expenditures of $1,728,881 or 46.79 per cent. of the aggregate income.

The number of policies issued during the year was 6,487; insured thereby, $14,361,933.

TABLE No. I.

RATIO *of Net Assets to Computed Premium Reserve at 4½ per cent., December* 31, 1872, *and* 1871.

NAME OF COMPANY.	Computed Premium Reserve.	Net Assets.	Net Assets, less Capital.	PERCENTAGE TO COMPUTED PREMIUM RESERVE OF			
				Net Assets.		Net Assets, less Capital.	
				1872.	*1871.*	*1872.*	*1871.*
Wis. Co.							
Northw'n Mut..	$10,046,014	$12,270,986	$12,270,986	122.15	119.42	122.15	119.42
Co's of other States.							
[1]Asbury.... ...	350,000	399,268	249,268	114.08	134.76	71.22	79.20
Brooklyn.......	1,690,785	1,889,174	1,764,174	111.73	115.16	104.34	106.56
Charter Oak....	[2]9,589,777	10,420,207	10,220,207	109.23	....	107.13	....
Chicago	212,731	245,998	120,998	115.64	....	56.88	....
Continental	5,270,367	5,793,192	5,693,192	109.92	111.17	108.02	108.87
Equitable	16,656,409	18,712,845	18,612,845	112.34	111.25	111.74	110.54
Germania	4,482,844	5,041,156	4,841,156	112.45	116.01	107.99	110.66
Globe Mut......	3,421,994	3,519,358	3,419,359	102.85	111.40	99.92	107.61
Manhattan	6,200,125	7,961,110	7,861,110	128.40	125.17	126.79	123.43
Metropolitan ...	1,199,038	1,389,702	1,189,702	115.90	113.58	99.22	113.58
[3]Missouri Mut..	263,998	295,719	170,719	112.02	....	64.67	....
[3]MissouriValley	420,776	512,390	350,140	121.77	......	83.21	....
Mutual, Ill	496,338	556,404	356,404	112.10	111.33	71.81	78.64
Mutual, N. Y...	51,667,250	57,787,403	57,787,403	111.85	....	111.85	....
National U.S.A.	1,664,168	2,451,479	1,451,479	147.31	159.40	87.22	80.89
[3]N. Jersey Mut.	1,103,152	1,173,997	1,073,997	106.42	....	97.36	....
New York.......	18,089,360	20,927,418	20,927,418	115.69	115.53	115.69	115.53
North America.	5,150,764	5,269,540	5,269,540	102.31	104.08	102.31	104.08
Phœnix Mut....	[2]6,776,117	7,878,965	7,862,965	116.28	128.47	116.04	126.64
Republic.......	773,442	1,515,044	666,434	195.88	....	86.16	....
St. Louis Mut..	5,881,186	6,200,191	6,100,191	105.42	104.88	103.72	102.92
Security........	3,025,998	3,406,665	3,296,665	112.58	115.86	108.94	111.85
Universal	883,107	1,170,616	970,616	132.56	138.94	109.91	111.63
Washington....	2,914,325	3,341,061	3,216,061	114.64	114.49	110.35	109.45
[3]Western N.Y..	112,541	195,967	70,967	174.18	....	63.06	... ...
Totals......	$158,292,601	$180,325,290	$175,813,480	113.92	116.36	111.07	112.44

[1] Has withdrawn from the state.
[2] Valuation computed by the company.
[3] Admitted into the state since date of last report.

TABLE No. II.

Ratio *of Net Assets to Computed Premium Reserve, at* 4 *per cent., Dec.* 31, 1872 *and* 1871.

Name of Company.	Computed Premium Reserve.	Net Assets.	Net Assets less Capital.	Percentage to computed prem. reserve of Net Assets.		Net Assets less Capital.	
				1872.	*1871.*	*1872.*	*1871.*
Wisconsin Co.							
Northw'rn Mut.	[1]$10,880,967	$12,270,936	$12,270,936	113.80	....	113.80	....
Co's of other States.							
Ætna	15,769,950	16,564,564	16,461,508	105.04	111.12	104.38	110.05
Berkshire	2,085,134	2,133,835	2,108,335	104.85	101.68	103.60	95.94
Charter Oak ...	10,344,286	10,420,207	10,220,207	100.73	102.81	98.80	100.57
Conn. Mut	29,128,809	34,189,088	34,189,088	117.37	122.14	117.37	122.14
Manhattan	[1]6,354,337	7,961,110	7,861,110	125.29	....	123.71	....
Mass. Mut	3,983,447	4,364,946	4,364,946	109.58	....	109.58	....
Mutual, N. Y ..	[1]54,690,333	57,787,403	57,787,403	105.66	107.72	105.66	107.72
Mut. Benefit ...	22,042,372	23,851,730	23,851,730	108.21	109.41	108.21	109.41
National, Ill ...	76,996	315,004	75,004	409.12	386.30	97.41	68.66
New Eng. Mut.	10,092,463	11,310,887	11,310,887	112.07	113.54	112.07	113.54
Phœnix Mut ...	7,295,038	7,878,965	7,862,965	108.00	....	107.79	....
Teutonia	195,399	332,797	138,590	170.32	187.43	70.93	63.42
Travelers'	1,292,586	1,907,400	1,407,400	147.56	150.71	108.88	108.40
Totals [1]	$174,131,617	$191,288,872	$189,910,109	109.85	112.10	109.06	110.44

[1] Valuation computed by the company.

TABLE No. III.

Ratio *of Premium Notes and Loans, to Net Assets.*

Name of Company.	Net Assets.	Prem. Notes and Loans.	Percentage. 1872.	Percentage. 1871
Wisconsin Co.				
Northwestern Mutual	$12,270,936	$4,296,064	35.01	38.60
Co's of other States.				
Ætna, Conn	16,564,564	5,602,200	33.82	38.99
[1]Asbury, N. Y	399,268	71,750	17.97	17.94
Berkshire, Mass	2,133,835	200,246	9.38	9.66
Brooklyn, N. Y	1,689,174	436,529	25.75	29.13
Charter Oak, Conn.	10,420,207	3,242,341	31.12	29.73
Chicago, Ill	245,998	13,183	5.36	3.79
Connecticut Mutual, Conn.	34,189,088	8,800,038	25.74	29.68
Continental, N. Y.	5,798,192	2,012,279	34.74	36.82
Equitable, N. Y	18,712,345	....	....	....
Germania, N. Y	5,041,156	....	....	....
Globe, Mutual, N. Y	3,519,858	30,948	.88	.44
Manhattan, N. Y	7,961,110	2,313,089	29.05	32.42
Massachusetts Mutual, Mass	4,364,946	952,644	21.82	22.42
Metropolitan, N. Y	1,389,702	325,588	23.43	22.09
[2]Missouri Mutual, Mo.	295,719	111,044	37.55	....
[2]Missouri Valley, Kan	512,390	....	....	....
Mutual, Ill	556,404	169,775	30.51	34.62
Mutual, N. Y	57,787,408	....	....	....
Mutual Benefit, N. J.	23,851,730	6,854,426	28.74	30.47
National, Ill	315,004	11,059	3.51	6.76
National of U. S. A., D. C	2,451,479	1,925	.08	....
New England Mutual, Mass	11,310,887	2,289,271	20.24	21.54
[2]New Jersey Mutual, N. J	1,173,997	289,528	24.66	....
New York, N. Y	20,927,413	986,244	4.71	5.28
North America, N. Y	5,269,540	981,776	18.63	18.77
Phœnix Mutual, Conn	7,878,965	3,551,237	45.07	47.92
Protection, Ill	130,559	2,622	2.01	.45
Railway Passengers', Conn	405,382	....	....	....
Republic, Ill	1,515,044	107,884	7.12	2.36
Saint Louis Mutual, Mo	6,200,191	2,718,155	43.84	33.60
Security, N. Y	3,406,665	1,978,139	58.07	58.79
Teutonia, Ill	332,797	39,269	11.81	14.19
Travelers', Conn	1,907,400	....	....	....
Universal, N. Y	1,170,616	331,089	28.28	27.66
Washington, N. Y	3,341,061	....	....	....
[2]Western New York, N. Y	195,967	22,530	11.50	....
Totals	$275,331,482	$48,798,287	[3]25.94	[3]28.91

[1] Has withdrawn from the state.
[2] Admitted into the state since date of last report
[3] Average of companies reporting premium notes and loans.

TABLE No. IV.

RATIO *of Deferred and Uncollected Premiums, to Net Assets.*

NAME OF COMPANY.	Net Assets.	Deferred Premiums.	Uncollect'd Premiums.	PERCENTAGE TO NET ASSETS OF		
				Defr'd Prem.	Uncol. Prem's	Total.
Wisconsin Co.						
Northwestern Mut.	$12,270,986	[2]$296,731	$310,181	2.42	2.53	4.95
Co's of other States.						
Ætna	16,564,564	158,361	201,109	.96	1.21	2.17
[1] Asbury	399,263	25,291	38,877	6.33	9.74	16.07
Berkshire	2,133,835	37,272	21,778	1.75	1.02	2.77
Brooklyn	1,889,174	56,155	....	2.97	.....	2.97
Charter Oak	10,420,207	165,184	101,148	1.58	.97	2.55
Chicago	245,998	22,806	18,272	9.27	7.43	16.70
Conn. Mut	34,189,088	28,429	38,013	.08	.11	.19
Continental	5,793,192	794,813	386,115	13.72	6.66	20.38
Equitable	18,712,345	[3]1,120,899	135,813	5.99	.73	6.72
Germania	5,041,156	266,535	110,847	5.29	2.20	7.49
Globe Mut	3,519,358	217,225	83,828	6.17	2.38	8.55
Manhattan	7,961,110	111,888	410,433	1.41	5.16	6.57
Mass. Mut	4,364,946	100,981	211,200	2.31	4.84	7.15
Metropolitan	1,389,702	263,708	269,174	18.98	19.37	38.35
Missouri Mut	295,719	13,969	12,399	4.72	4.19	8.91
Missouri Valley	512,890	54,434	63,247	10.62	12.34	22.96
Mutual, Ill	556,404	24,755	17,022	4.45	3.06	7.51
Mutual, N. Y	57,787,403	931,648	102,457	1.61	.18	1.79
Mut. Benefit	23,851,730	33,543	295,469	.14	1.24	1.38
National, Ill	315,004	93,063	14,895	29.54	4.73	34.27
National U. S. A	2,451,479	90,249	20,179	3.68	.82	4.50
New Eng. Mut	11,310,887	271,361	406,685	2.40	3.60	6.00
New Jersey Mut	1,173,997	94,745	116,722	8.07	9.94	18.01
New York	20,927,413	502,695	256,290	2.40	1.22	3.62
North America	5,269,540	519,461	374,114	9.86	7.10	16.96
Phœnix Mut	7,878,965	120,845	477,245	1.53	6.06	7.59
Protection	130,559	....	5,713	.....	4.38	4.38
Republic	1,515,044	49,189	49,599	3.25	3.27	6.52
St. Louis Mut	6,200,191	[4]384,895	190,211	6.20	3.07	9.27
Security	3,406,665	154,535	457,511	4.54	13.43	17.97
Teutonia	332,797	51,563	39,276	15.49	11.80	27.29
Travelers'	1,907,400	52,241	90,383	2.74	4.74	7.48
Universal	1,170,616	149,452	109,792	12.77	9.38	22.15
Washington	3,341,061	[5]191,127	50,678	5.72	1.52	7.24
Western N. Y	195,967	20,430	10,255	10.43	5.23	15.66
Totals	$275,426,100	$7,468,922	$5,496,878	2.71	2.00	4.71

[1] Has withdrawn from the state.
[2] Including $51,407, in course of transmission.
[3] Including $375,591 in course of transmission,
[4] Including $236,576 in course of transmission.
[5] Including $21,805 in course of transmission.

TABLE No. V.

RATIO *of Deferred and Uncollected Premiums, to Premium Receipts*.

NAME OF COMPANY.	Total Prem. Receipts.	Deferred Prem's.	Uncollect'd Prem's.	PERCENTAGE OF — Deferred Premiums to Prem. Rec'ts. 1872.	PERCENTAGE OF — Deferred Premiums to Prem. Rec'ts. 1871.	PERCENTAGE OF — Uncollected Premi'ms to Prem. Rec's 1872.	PERCENTAGE OF — Uncollected Premi'ms to Prem. Rec's 1871
Wisconsin Company.							
Northwestern Mutual......	$2,939,597	[4]$296,731	$310,181	10.09	18.23	10.55	9.96
Co's of other States.							
Ætna	4,751,306	158,861	201,109	3.33	3.97	4.23	4.34
[1]Asbury	195,962	25,291	38,877	12.91	34.76	19.84	17.37
Berkshire.	535,076	37,272	21,778	6.97	11.75	4.07	4.71
Brooklyn....	615,501	56,155	....	9.12	8.42	....	......
Charter Oak............ ...	3,633,434	165,134	101,148	4.54	17.82	2.78	14.14
Chicago.....................	163,912	22,806	18,272	13.91	28.62	11.15	16.56
Connecticut Mutual.........	7,715,068	28,429	38,013	.37	1.12	.49	.78
Continental.	2,537,589	794,818	386,115	31.32	45.57	15.22	14.36
Equitable..................	7,426,862	[5]1,120,399	135,813	15.09	18.48	1.83	9.62
Germania	1,525,699	266,535	110,847	17.47	27.52	7.27	8.50
Globe Mutual..............	1,337,880	217,225	83,826	16.24	21.48	6.27	4.72
Manhattan..	1,635,674	111,888	410,433	6.84	31.47	25.09	26.06
Massachusetts Mutual.....	1,320,432	100,981	211,200	7.65	37.55	15.99	23.96
Metropolitan.............	704,917	263,706	269,174	37.41	73.14	38.19	37.97
[2]Missouri Mutual..........	226,219	13,969	12,399	6.17	....	5.48	......
[2]Missouri Valley...........	286,248	54,484	63,247	19.02	....	22.10	......
Mutual, Ill.....	285,225	24,755	17,022	8.68	18.38	5.97	8.33
Mutual, N. Y	14,336,864	931,643	102,457	6.48	9.43	.71	1.01
Mutual Benefit............	5,344,940	33,543	295,469	.63	4.96	5.53	4.39
National, Ill...............	267,123	93,063	14,895	34.84	37.03	5.58	6.25
National U S. A...........	714,685	90,249	20,179	13.63	15.66	2.82	3.56
New England Mutual......	2,722,352	271,361	406,685	9.97	27.97	14.94	17.67
[2]New Jersey Mutual.......	837,455	94,745	116,722	11.31	....	13.94	....
New York	6,277,327	502,695	256,290	8.01	13.79	4.08	5.08
North America.............	1,515,473	519,461	374,114	34.28	56.50	24.69	21.46
Phœnix Mutual	2,942,490	120,345	477,945	4.09	20.30	16.22	18.11
Protection.................	66,114	....	5,713	....	13.42	8.64	13.42
Republic.	595,655	49,189	49,599	8.26	30.21	8.33	19.24
St. Louis Mutual..........	2,662,599	[6]384,395	190,211	14.44	34.95	7.14	26.02
Security	1,442,306	154,534	457,511	10.71	41.26	31.72	29.98
Teutonia..................	105,275	51,563	39,276	48.98	48.01	37.31	20.14
Travelers'	1,031,481	52,241	90,333	5.06	17.23	8.76	11.91
Universal	695,277	149,452	109,792	21.50	43.71	15.79	18.49
Washington...	1,032,413	[7]191,127	50,678	18.51	24.74	4.91	7.09
[2]Western New York..... .	88,333	20,480	10,255	23.13	....	11.61	......
Totals.................	$80,564,718	$7,468,922	$5,496,878	9.27	[3]18.76	6.82	[3]9.95

[1] Has withdrawn from the state.
[2] Admitted into the state since date of last report.
[3] Average of companies doing business in the state during 1871.
[4] Including $51,407 in course of transmission.
[5] Including $575,591 in course of transmission.
[6] Including $236,576 in course of transmission.
[7] Including $21,805 in course of transmission.

TABLE No. VI.

RATIO *of Expenses, excluding Dividends to Stockholders, to Premium Receipts.*

NAME OF COMPANY.	Gross Prem. Receipts.	Expenses.	PERCENTAGE.	
			1872.	*1871.*
Wisconsin Company.				
Northwestern Mutual	$2,989,597	$500,082	17.01	16.53
Companies of other States.				
Ætna, Conn	4,751,306	761,705	16.03	14.94
[1] Asbury, N. Y	195,962	94,491	48.22	47.41
Berkshire, Mass	535,076	92,204	17.23	24.23
Brooklyn, N. Y	615,501	197,628	32.11	29.17
Charter Oak, Conn	3,633,434	566,114	15.06	14.11
Chicago, Ill	168,912	63,339	38.64	44.20
Connecticut Mutual, Conn	7,715,068	1,023,421	13.27	14.09
Continental, N. Y	2,537,589	657,454	25.91	26.13
Equitable, N. Y	7,426,862	1,371,968	18.47	17.40
Germania, N. Y	1,525,699	288,190	18.89	21.53
Globe Mutual, N. Y	1,337,830	320,419	23.95	27.37
Manhattan, N. Y	1,635,674	306,788	18.76	16.86
Massachusetts Mutual, Mass	1,320,432	264,319	20.00	20.33
Metropolitan, N. Y	704,917	184,275	26.14	27.62
[2] Missouri Mutual, Mo.	226,219	98,121	43.37	....
[2] Missouri Valley, Kan	286,248	112,256	39.22	....
Mutual, Ill	285,225	161,123	56.49	48.27
Mutual, N. Y	14,386,864	1,351,711	9.40	9.68
Mutual Benefit, N. J	5,344,940	673,401	12.60	12.63
National, Ill	267,123	137,334	51.41	69.60
National of U. S. A., D. C	714,685	221,645	31.01	43.62
New England Mutual, Mass	2,722,352	471,250	17.31	13.36
[2] New Jersey Mutual, N. J	837,455	97,166	11.60	....
New York, N. Y	6,277,327	940,218	14.98	14.61
North America, N. Y	1,515,478	424,719	28.03	25.78
Phœnix Mutual, Conn	2,942,490	556,199	18.90	18.38
Protection, Ill	66,114	66,758	100.97	136.83
Railway Passengers', Conn	130,980	90,236	68.89	71.06
Republic, Ill	595,655	316,720	53.17	39.08
Saint Louis Mutual, Mo	2,662,599	535,138	20.10	23.77
Security, N. Y	1,442,306	342,872	23.77	28.95
Teutonia, Ill	105,275	64,424	61.20	46.71
Travelers', Conn	1,031,481	430,767	41.76	46.62
Universal, N. Y	695,277	223,232	32.11	30.56
Washington, N. Y	1,032,413	224,118	21.71	21.42
[2] Western New York, N. Y	88,333	52,880	59.86	....
Totals	$80,695,693	$14,284,695	17.70	[3] 18.30

[1] Has withdrawn from the state.
[2] Admitted into the state since date of last report.
[3] Average of companies doing business in the state during 1871.

TABLE No. VII.

RATIO *of Expenses, including Dividends to Stockholders, to Total Income.*

NAME OF COMPANY.	Total Income.	Expenses.	PERCENTAGE.	
			1872.	*1871.*
Wisconsin Company.				
Northwestern Mutual	$3,695,064	$500,082	13.53	13.65
Companies of other States.				
Ætna, Conn	6,040,946	806,769	13.36	12.82
[1] Asbury, N. Y	220,240	94,491	42.90	47.17
Berkshire, Mass	653,252	93,989	14.39	20.82
Brooklyn, N. Y	725,520	213,873	29.48	27.24
Charter Oak, Conn	4,102,917	582,114	14.19	12.96
Chicago, Ill	178,981	73,669	41.17	47.60
Connecticut Mutual, Conn	9,754,421	1,023,421	10.49	11.30
Continental, N. Y	3,082,528	664,454	21.56	24.68
Equitable, N. Y	8,420,045	1,379,840	16.39	15.63
Germania, N. Y	1,811,924	312,190	17.23	19.93
Globe Mutual, N. Y	1,535,592	331,724	21.60	25.07
Manhattan, N. Y	2,151,855	349,788	16.26	15.58
Massachusetts Mutual, Mass	1,571,461	264,319	16.82	17.27
Metropolitan, N. Y	751,004	184,275	24.54	26.22
[2] Missouri Mutual, Mo	258,555	110,281	42.65	....
[2] Missouri Valley, Kan	318,295	122,471	38.48	....
Mutual, Ill	306,887	161,123	52.50	45.88
Mutual, N. Y	17,716,095	1,351,711	7.63	7.87
Mutual Benefit, N. J	6,869,056	673,401	9.80	10.06
National, Ill	273,708	137,334	50.18	62.47
National of U. S. A., D. C	884,896	251,645	28.44	36.30
New England Mutual, Mass	3,364,283	471,250	14.01	11.12
[2] New Jersey Mutual, N. J	874,612	99,166	11.34	....
New York, N. Y	7,515,407	940,218	12.51	12.27
North America, N. Y	1,835,635	424,719	23.14	22.02
Phœnix Mutual, Conn	3,413,752	557,159	16.32	15.96
Protection, Ill	125,762	66,758	53.08	75.62
Railway Passengers', Conn	160,325	120,236	75.00	78.80
Republic, Ill	659,164	316,720	48.05	35.94
Saint Louis Mutual, Mo	3,014,665	545,138	18.08	21.34
Security, N. Y	1,576,538	357,572	22.68	22.57
Teutonia, Ill	123,575	64,444	52.15	51.92
Travelers', Conn	1,192,149	480,767	40.33	46.48
Universal, N. Y	756,107	238,632	31.56	30.63
Washington, N. Y	1,202,994	233,869	19.44	19.64
[2] Western New York, N. Y	97,737	52,880	54.10	....
Totals	$97,235,397	$14,652,492	15.07	[3]15.86

[1] Has withdrawn from the State.
[2] Admitted into the state since date of last report.
[3] Average of companies doing business in the state during 1871.

TABLE No. VIII.

RATIO *of Dividends to Policyholders, to Net Surplus and to Premium Receipts.*

NAME OF Co.	Net Surplus Dec. 31, 1871	Total Prem. Receipts.	Dividends to Policy-holders.	PERCENTAGE OF DIVIDENDS TO.			
				Net Surplus.		Prem. Rec'pts.	
				1872.	*1871.*	*1872.*	*1871*
Wisconsin Co.							
Northwestern Mutual....	$1,694,700	$2,939,597	$449,871	26.52	38.85	15.29	15.96
Co's of other States.							
Ætna	[7]1,408,981	4,751,806	1,052,021	74.67	28.45	22.14	18.98
[1]Asbury	[2]56,150	195,962	11,631	[2].......	[2].......	5.94	2.60
Berkshire	[2 7]70,737	535,076	60,012	[2].......	68.95	11.22	10.04
Brooklyn	95,426	615,501	61,610	64.56	41.69	10.01	6.50
Charter Oak	[7]51,070	3,633,434	789,711	1546.33	182.93	21.73	28.67
Chicago	[2 7]84,339	163,912	19,275	[2].......	[2].......	11.76	18.64
Conn. Mut.	[7]5,670,765	7,715,068	2,906,213	51.25	48.45	37.67	63.20
Continental	385,338	2,537,589	289,238	75.06	106.38	11.40	11.89
Equitable	1,472,112	7,426,862	1,085,754	73.75	80.80	14.62	15.69
Germania	398,491	1,525,699	222,402	55.81	29.32	14.58	9.20
Globe Mut.	201,353	1,337,330	205,720	102.17	472.85	15.38	17.90
Manhattan	1,341,303	1,635,674	364,141	27.15	24.87	22.26	22.33
Mass. Mut.	525,089	1,320,432	186,510	35.52	31.24	14.12	12.78
Metropolitan	129,809	704,917	60,640	46.71	[2].......	8.60	6.97
[6]Missouri Mut.	[4]15,093	226,219	16,354	[2].......	....	7.23	......
[6]Missouri Valley	[4]28,548	286,248	28,883	[2].......	....	10.09	......
Mutual, Ill.	[2]108,464	285,225	2,614	[2].......	[2].......	.92	9.15
Mutual, N. Y.	[7]8,636,120	14,886,864	5,259,205	144.64	62.63	36.56	26.59
Mutual Benefit	[7]1,848,860	5,344,940	1,660,427	89.81	81.85	31.07	44.66
National, Ill.	[2 7]23,678	267,123	....	....	....	....	......
National U. S. A.	[3]243,434	714,685	....	....	....	....	......
New Eng. Mut.	[7]1,217,278	2,722,352	463,383	38.07	32.83	17.02	17.68
[6]New Jersey Mut.	[3]30,066	337,455	27,121	[2].......	....	8.24	......
New York	2,436,360	6,277,327	781,602	32.08	48.65	12.45	14.09
North America	209,598	1,515,473	169,107	80.68	39.20	11.16	8.26
Phœnix Mut.	1,457,823	2,942,490	995,443	68.28	43.91	33.83	24.53
Protection	[2]14,426	66,114	....	....	....	....	......
Republic	[2 7]306,669	595,655	7,812	[2].......	[2].......	1.31	.90
St. Louis Mut.	152,685	2,662,599	124,908	81.81	103.32	4.69	13.77
Security	325,384	1,442,306	245,688	75.51	82.55	17.08	10.16
Teutonia	[2 7]48,979	105,275	2,328	[2].......	....	2.21	......
Travelers'	[7]99,284	1,031,481	2,370	2.39	2.25	.23	.33
Universal	85,176	695,277	....	....	....	....	......
Washington	233,942	1,032,418	109,096	46.63	46.38	10.57	10.64
[6]Western N. Y.	[3]18,775	88,833	8,758	[2].......	....	.99	......
Totals	....	$80,564,713	$17,669,348	....	....	[8]22.42	[8]23.22

[1] Has withdrawn from the state.
[2] Deficiency.
[3] Deficiency according to N. Y. report.
[4] Deficiency according to Mo. report.
[5] Average of companies doing business in the state during 1871.
[6] Admitted since date of last report.
[7] With premium reserve computed at 4 per cent. interest.
[8] Average of companies declaring dividends.

TABLE No. IX.

RATIO *of Policies not taken, to Policies issued during the Year.*

NAME OF COMPANY.	[5]Policies issued.		Policies not taken.		PERCENTAGE.			
					1872.		*1871.*	
	No.	Amount.	No.	Amount.	No.	Am't.	No.	Am't.
Wis. Co.								
N'western Mut...	6,487	[2]$14,361,938	957	$2,324,294	14.75	16.18	15.70	20.73
Co's of other States.								
Ætna	8,791	15,334,287	1,101	2,391,878	12.52	15.60	14.41	19.70
[1]Asbury	1,632	[2]3,264,174	403	651,074	24.69	19.95	17.96	22.54
Berkshire.... ...	767	[2]2,014,667	114	275,575	14.86	13.68	21.82	18.73
Brooklyn	1,504	[2]3,811,575	293	781,500	19.48	20.50	51.50	52.76
Charter Oak	5,929	12,246,591	1,180	2,097,625	19.90	17.13	22.69	20.39
Chicago	1,800	2,248,230	171	223,500	9.50	9.94	15.86	23.33
Conn. Mut.......	5,520	14,502,090	536	1,362,100	9.71	9.39	15.04	13.48
Continental......	12,010	[2]22,782,299	2,330	4,950,000	19.40	21.73	26.14	26.43
Equitable........	12,491	[2]51,911,079	2,129	9,446,150	17.04	18.20	17.39	16.78
Germania	2,623	[2]4,387,078	274	421,180	10.45	9.60	12.45	13.33
Globe Mut.......	3,179	[2]8,166,258	357	1,175,531	11.23	14.39	17.79	21.17
Manhattan.......	1,701	[2]4,991,710	215	492,616	12.64	9.87	16.87	14.09
Mass. Mut.	3,204	7,130,000	562	1,133,700	17.54	15.90	18.36	15.96
Metropolitan.....	8,642	11,556,663	1,930	2,129,809	22.33	18.43	24.80	33.97
[3]Missouri Mut...	1,249	[2]2,795,736	152	449,100	12.17	16.06	....	......
[3]Missouri Valley	1,199	[2]4,187,397	147	429,330	12.26	10.25	....	......
Mutual, Ill.......	2,733	4,740,094	647	1,063,206	23.68	22.43	23.14	23.75
Mutual, N. Y....	12,186	[2]59,263,961	1,161	3,200,805	9.53	5.40	18.18	13.08
Mutual Benefit...	3,172	9,573,063	364	1,044,600	11.48	10.91	10.70	9.05
National, Ill.....	4,673	6,581,600	362	570,000	7.75	8.66	10.59	8.51
National U. S. A.	3,110	6,852,715	481	925,627	15.47	13.51	21.12	21.74
New Eng. Mut...	2,799	[2]6,874,773	451	1,072,282	16.11	15.60	29.65	27.86
[3]N. Jersey Mut..	6,162	[2]12,897,940	384	910,850	6.23	7.06	....	......
New York	8,910	[2]27,096,274	871	2,883,749	9.78	10.64	15.30	13.80
North America...	2,375	[2]4,623,963	270	693,149	11.37	14.99	10.91	13.35
Phœnix Mutual..	10,690	[2]22,192,311	2,537	5,057,931	23.73	22.79	21.94	20.62
Protection	5,039	5,039,000	409	409,000	8.12	8.12	14.29	14.29
Republic	4,667	11,530,364	1,195	2,813,218	25.61	24.40	....	......
Saint Louis Mut.	6,819	19,941,117	983	2,386,181	14.42	11.97	32.73	29.00
Security	3,281	[2]7,260,311	674	1,397,538	20.54	19.25	42.87	45.42
Teutonia.........	2,969	2,415,787	539	444,500	18.15	18.40	14.36	18.20
Travelers'[5]........	34,806	109,463,221	411	622,325	1.18	.57	1.15	.56
Universal........	3,575	9,941,482	740	2,475,843	20.70	24.90	22.11	19.17
Washington	2,368	6,254,707	305	772,005	12.88	12.34	15.94	16.69
[3]Western N. Y...	1,416	[2]1,785,122	176	246,500	12.43	14.21	....	......
Totals	200,483	$519,969,521	25,811	$59,723,216	12.87	11.49	[4]16.98	[4]16.15

[1] Has withdrawn from the state.
[2] Including additions by dividends.
[3] Admitted into the state since date of last report
[4] Average of the companies doing business in the state during 1871.
[5] Including old policies revived and increased.

TABLE No. X.

RATIO *of Policies Lapsed and Surrendered during the Year, to Policies in force Dec.* 31, 1871.

NAME OF COMPANY.	Policies in Force.		Policies Lapsed and Surrendered.		PERCENTAGE.			
					1872.		*1871.*	
	No.	Amount.	No.	Amount.	No.	Am't.	No.	Am't.
Wisconsin Co.								
Nor'western Mut	34,349	$62,425,187	4,132	$7,131,142	12.03	11.42	14.76	14.56
Co's of other States.								
Ætna	47,653	101,324,862	4,714	12,095,691	9.89	11.94	13.84	16.34
[1] Asbury	2,843	5,096,345	929	1,710,116	32.68	33.56	29.23	27.72
Berkshire	4,451	10,149,905	579	1,254,180	13.01	12.36	17.09	16.53
Brooklyn	4,321	11,430,308	882	2,246,750	20.41	19.66	32.60	31.26
Charter Oak	25,449	61,634,076	3,188	7,645,777	12.53	12.41	17.08	17.34
Chicago	2,294	3,272,308	912	1,231,384	39.76	37.63	44.11	41.22
Conn. Mut	62,458	182,785,236	3,790	11,259,692	6.07	6.16	7.97	8.35
Continental	25,654	57,158,716	6,269	13,255,375	24.44	23.19	20.14	19.72
Equitable	38,827	154,331,143	5,586	23,436,739	14.39	15.19	14.93	15.68
Germania	18,507	33,099,969	1,199	1,959,320	6.48	5.92	8.61	8.64
Globe Mutual	11,599	28,451,485	1,720	4,504,488	14.83	15.83	21.23	23.15
Manhattan	13,038	42,140,907	1,031	3,082,496	7.91	7.31	11.36	10.23
Mass. Mut	14,468	33,578,515	1,173	3,047,594	8.11	9.08	8.13	8.63
Metropolitan	11,299	14,989,582	2,266	3,279,095	20.05	21.88	26.47	24.78
[2] Missouri Mut	1,631	4,466,233	414	1,035,613	25.38	23.19	....	......
[2] Missouri Valley	2,069	6,451,619	817	2,602,764	39.49	40.34	....	......
Mutual, Ill	3,273	5,067,743	1,623	2,608,123	49.59	51.47	55.24	54.54
Mutual, N. Y	73,911	228,789,408	5,979	18,053,595	8.09	7.89	10.19	9.89
Mutual Benefit	38,669	133,086,942	1,150	3,555,425	2.97	2.67	3.01	3.06
National, Ill	5,296	6,672,000	4,649	5,658,000	87.78	84.80	167.75	183.50
National U. S. A.	7,908	18,465,472	1,001	2,137,406	12.67	11.58	19.77	18.36
New Eng. Mut	22,892	67,815,733	2,617	6,777,536	11.43	9.99	12.11	10.92
[2] New Jersey Mut	3,984	8,049,052	836	1,331,064	20.98	16.54	....	......
New York	38,988	113,154,809	5,304	15,669,993	13.60	13.85	14.49	14.08
North America	14,209	37,063,467	1,735	3,950,751	12.21	10.66	12.60	11.61
Phœnix Mut	28,707	63,554,620	2,951	6,381,207	10.28	10.04	11.81	11.90
Protection	1,593	1,593,000	1,453	1,453,000	91.21	91.21	....	......
Republic	6,359	13,889,519	1,751	3,811,810	27.54	27.44	....	......
St. Louis Mut	15,884	48,978,292	5,830	19,256,939	36.70	39.32	15.36	14.16
Security	13,216	32,517,238	1,933	4,457,153	14.63	13.71	20.84	21.96
Teutonia	1,767	2,089,246	428	526,500	24.22	25.20	20.97	21.35
Travelers'	43,835	94,075,048	969	1,619,947	2.21	1.72	2.28	2.27
Universal	5,273	14,229,379	1,046	3,398,452	19.84	23.85	36.13	36.50
Washington	10,634	24,293,143	1,617	3,453,265	15.21	14.59	23.49	21.01
[2] Western N. Y	904	1,606,097	299	451,128	33.08	28.10	....	......
Totals	658,206	$1,727,775,594	82,772	$205,414,510	12.58	11.89	[3] 14.39	[3] 13.42

[1] Has withdrawn from the state.
[2] Admitted into the state since date of last report.
[3] Average of the companies doing business in the state during 1871.

TABLE No. XI.

RATIO *of Losses and Claims Paid, to Mean Amount at Risk.*

NAME OF COMPANY.	Commenced Business.	Mean Amount at Risk.	[2] Losses and Claims Paid.	PERCENTAGE. 1872.	1871
Wisconsin Co.					
Northwestern Mutual	1858	$68,300,202	$582,387	.92	.95
Co's of other States.					
Ætna, Conn	1850	100,971,318	1,407,674	1.39	1.19
[1] Asbury, N. Y	1868	5,111,742	65,142	1.27	1.22
Berkshire, Mass	1851	10,300,159	74,650	.72	1.17
Brooklyn, N. Y	1864	11,711,630	139,696	1.19	1.08
Charter Oak, Conn	1850	62,530,882	745,569	1.19	1.18
Chicago, Ill	1867	3,617,226	25,000	.69	.85
Connecticut Mutual, Conn	1846	182,256,038	2,211,992	1.21	.96
Continental, N. Y	1866	58,708,053	556,165	.95	.90
Equitable, N. Y	1859	162,887,247	1,682,682	1.03	1.06
Germania, N. Y	1860	33,850,117	452,776	1.34	1.19
Globe Mutual, N. Y	1864	29,136,085	405,936	1.39	1.21
Manhattan, N. Y	1850	42,242,260	578,012	1.36	1.11
Massachusetts Mutual, Mass	1851	33,096,261	391,680	1.18	.72
Metropolitan, N. Y	1867	17,767,962	165,000	.93	.62
[4] Missouri Mutual, Mo	1867	4,788,830	58,284	1.22	......
[4] Missouri Valley, Kan	1868	7,006,990	24,063	.34	......
Mutual, Ill	1865	5,488,965	37,841	.69	.66
Mutual, N. Y	1843	246,583,876	2,740,257	1.11	1.26
Mutual Benefit, N. J	1845	133,125,555	1,953,211	1.47	1.20
National, Ill	1870	6,795,300	116,922	1.72	.75
National of U. S. A., D. C	1868	19,359,040	190,205	.98	.49
New England Mutual, Mass	1843	66,890,129	821,897	1.23	1.20
[4] New Jersey Mutual, N. J	1865	12,977,610	95,174	.73	......
New York, N. Y	1845	115,888,707	1,426,702	1.23	1.19
North America, N. Y	1862	34,874,572	1,152,222	3.30	1.59
Phœnix Mutual, Conn	1851	67,782,443	878,499	1.30	1.15
Protection, Ill	1871	3,159,000	37,804	1.20	.16
Republic, Ill	1870	14,437,233	133,669	.93	.....
Saint Louis Mutual, Mo	1857	47,608,114	853,792	1.79	1.56
Security, N. Y	1862	31,815,400	491,895	1.55	1.46
Teutonia, Ill	1869	2,758,864	28,696	1 04	.89
Travelers', Conn	1866	104,322,077	311,875	.30	.31
Universal, N. Y	1865	15,686,133	195,942	1.25	1.41
Washington, N. Y	1860	25,122,016	267,369	1.06	1.16
[4] Western New York, N. Y	1868	2,080,994	11,851	.57	......
Totals	......	$1,785,969,050	$21,307,533	1.19	[3] 1.06

[1] Has withdrawn from the state.
[2] Including annuities and endowments.
[3] Average of companies doing business in the state during 1871.
[4] Admitted into the state since date of last report.

TABLE No. 12.

RATIO *of various items composing the Total Expenditures and Excess of Income, to Total Income.*

NAME OF COMPANY.	Total Income.	Amount for Losses and Claims.	Am't paid for lapsed, surrend'ed and purchased Policies.	Dividends to Policy holders.	Expenses, including Dividends to Stockholders.	Total Expenditures.	Excess of Income.	PERCENTAGE TO TOTAL INCOME OF: Amount paid for Losses and Claims.	Am't paid for laps'd surrendered & purchased Policies.	Dividends to Policy-holders.	Expenses, including Dividends to Stockholders.	Total Expenditures.	Excess of Income.
Wisconsin Company.													
Northwestern Mutual	$3,695,064	$582,387	$434,348	$449,371	$500,082	$1,966,188	$1,728,881	15.76	11.76	12.16	13.53	53.21	46.79
Companies of other States.													
Ætna	6,040,946	1,407,674	[2]1,375,898	1,052,021	806,769	4,642,357	1,398,589	23.30	22.78	17.41	13.36	76.85	23.15
[1] Asbury	220,240	65,142	[2]5,784	11,631	94,491	176,998	43,242	29.58	2.60	5.28	42.90	80.36	19.64
Berkshire	653,252	74,650	[2]36,425	60,012	93,989	265,076	388,176	11.43	5.58	9.18	14.39	40.58	59.42
Brooklyn	725,520	139,698	98,387	61,610	213,878	513,568	211,952	19.26	13.56	8.49	29.48	70.79	29.21
Charter Oak	4,102,917	745,569	754,970	789,711	582,114	2,872,364	1,230,553	18.17	18.40	19.25	14.19	70.01	29.99
Chicago	178,931	25,000	26,575	19,275	73,669	144,519	34,412	13.97	14.85	10.78	41.17	80.77	19.23
Connecticut Mutual	9,754,421	2,211,992	[2]678,811	2,906,213	1,023,421	6,820,437	2,933,984	22.68	6.96	29.79	10.49	69.92	30.08
Continental	3,082,528	556,165	[2]527,236	289,238	664,454	2,037,093	1,045,435	18.04	17.11	9.38	21.56	66.09	33.91
Equitable	8,420,045	1,682,682	877,855	1,065,754	1,379,840	5,026,131	3,393,914	19.98	10.43	12.89	16.39	59.69	40.31
Germania	1,811,924	452,776	105,209	222,402	312,190	1,092,577	719,347	24.99	5.81	12.27	17.23	60.30	39.70
Globe Mutual	1,535,592	405,936	65,863	205,720	331,724	1,009,243	526,349	26.44	4.29	13.39	21.60	65.72	34.28
Manhattan	2,151,855	573,012	143,835	364,141	349,788	1,430,776	721,079	26.63	6.68	16.92	16.26	66.49	33.51
Mass. Mut.	1,571,461	391,680	[2]197,446	186,510	264,319	1,039,955	531,506	24.93	12.56	11.87	16.82	66.18	33.82
Metropolitan	751,004	165,000	[2]78,430	60,640	184,275	488,345	262,659	21.97	10.44	8.08	24.54	65.03	34.97
Missouri Mutual	258,555	58,284	[2]44,143	16,354	110,281	229,062	29,493	22.54	17.07	6.33	42.65	88.59	11 41
Missouri Valley	318,295	94,063	27,321	28,883	122,471	202,738	115,557	7.56	8.58	9.07	38.48	63.69	36.31
Mutual, Ill.	306,887	37,841	[2]44,347	2,614	161,123	245,925	60,962	12.33	14.45	.86	52.50	80.14	19.86
Mutual, N. Y.	17,716,095	2,740,257	1,555,009	5,259,205	1,351,711	10,906,182	6,809,913	15.47	8.78	29.68	7.63	61.56	38.44
Mutual Benefit	6,869,056	1,953,211	286,025	1,660,427	673,401	4,573,064	2,295,992	28.44	4.16	24 17	9.80	66.57	33.43

National, Ill.	273,708	116,922	[2]4,996	....	187,384	259,252	14,456	42.72	1.82	....	50.18	94.72	5.28
National U. S. A.	884,896	190,205	51,683	....	251,645	498,533	391,363	21.49	5.84	....	28.44	55.77	44.23
New England Mutual	3,364,283	821,897	[2]452,143	463,383	471,250	2,208,678	1,155,610	24.43	13.44	13.77	14.01	65.65	34.35
New Jersey Mutual	874,612	95,174	32,488	27,121	99,166	253,899	620,713	10.88	3.71	3.10	11.34	29.08	70.97
New York	7,515,407	1,426,702	[3]1,481,790	781,602	940,218	4,680,312	2,885,095	18.96	19.72	10.40	12.51	61.61	38.39
North America	1,835,635	1,152,222	[3]131,395	169,107	424,719	1,877,443	[4]41,808	62.77	7.16	9.21	23.14	102.28	[5]2.28
Phœnix Mutual	3,413,752	878,499	[2]806,084	995,443	557,159	2,737,185	676,567	25.73	8.97	29.16	16.32	80.18	19.82
Protection	125,762	87,804	[2]835	....	66,758	105,397	20,365	30.06	.67	....	53.08	83.81	16.19
Railway Passengers'[1]	160,325	29,100	....	....	120,236	149,336	10,989	18.15	....	....	75.00	93.15	6.85
Republic	659,164	183,669	[2]52,588	7,812	316,720	510,789	148,375	20.28	7.98	1.18	48.05	77.49	22.51
St. Louis Mutual	3,014,665	853,792	[2]163,215	124,908	545,138	1,687,058	1,327,612	28.32	5.42	4.14	18.08	55.96	44.04
Security	1,576,538	491,895	202,789	245,688	357,572	1,297,894	278,644	31.20	12.86	15.59	22.68	82.33	17.67
Teutonia	123,575	28,696	[2]13,517	2,898	64,444	108,980	14,595	23.22	10.94	1.88	52.15	88.19	11.81
Travelers'[1]	1,192,149	311,875	8,006	2,370	480,767	808,018	389,131	26.16	.67	.20	40.33	67.36	32.64
Universal	756,107	195,942	[2]141,819	....	238,682	576,393	179,714	25.91	18.76	....	31.56	76.23	23.77
Washington	1,202,994	267,369	61,455	109,096	233,869	671,789	581,205	22.22	5.11	9.07	19.44	55.84	44.16
Western N. Y	97,737	11,851	[2]4,604	8,758	52,880	78,093	19,644	12.13	4.71	8.96	54.10	79.90	20.10
Totals	$97,235,997	$21,336,633	$10,473,164	$17,689,349	$14,652,492	$64,131,682	$33,104,365	21.94	10.77	18.17	15.07	65.95	34.05

[1] Has withdrawn from the state.

[2] Including premium loans voided by lapse of policies.

[3] Including premium loans voided by lapse of policies and redeemed by maker in cash.

[4] Excess of expenditures over income.

[5] Percentage of excess of expenditures over income, to income.

14 Ins.

TABLE No. XIII.—Assets.

Name of Company.	Loans on Bond and Mortgage.	Loans on Collaterals.	Prem. Notes and Loans on Policies.	Real Estate.	Stocks and Bonds.	Cash in Office and Bank.	Interest and Rents.	Unpaid and Deferred Premiums.	All other admitted Assets.	Total admitted Assets.	Unadmitted Assets.
Wisconsin Company.											
Northwestern Mutual....	$6,490,545	$741	$4,296,064	$319,258	$173,925	$97,714	$364,657	$606,912	....	$12,349,811	$84,717
Companies of other States.											
Ætna, Conn........	5,451,001	594,799	5,602,200	....	4,060,613	942,656	496,813	359,470	$47,000	17,554,558	192,512
[1]Asbury, N. Y........	6,270	22,600	71,750	....	164,575	78,128	....	64,168	....	409,491	50,568
Berkshire, Mass........	999,529	22,700	200,946	169,792	630,680	48,766	30,876	59,650	....	2,181,639	19,334
Brooklyn, N. Y........	927,835	24,200	486,529	....	240,895	124,777	41,206	56,155	6,577	1,908,174	....
Charter Oak, Conn........	4,199,738	1,107,238	3,242,841	844,281	495,775	217,406	280,233	266,282	1,635	10,655,594	144,566
Chicago, Ill........	127,460	54,150	12,183	....	....	16,404	1,708	41,078	15	253,998	575
Connecticut Mutual, Conn	17,652,992	298,508	8,600,088	1,189,972	4,687,687	1,061,133	975,580	66,442	253,844	34,236,141	....
Continental, N. Y........	880,950	108,880	2,012,279	810,000	552,727	321,551	75,577	1,180,928	....	5,942,898	465,754
Equitable, N. Y........	12,226,573	687,661	....	2,334,359	1,803,171	778,598	135,821	1,256,212	....	19,222,395	381,909
Germania, N. Y........	3,536,561	4,500	....	....	978,686	250,074	65,673	377,382	....	5,212,876	....
Globe Mutual, N. Y........	1,908,762	44,000	30,948	....	1,269,495	201,618	25,517	301,051	200	3,776,596	34,311
Manhattan, N. Y........	3,741,451	540,330	2,313,069	....	730,299	321,101	102,220	522,821	69	8,270,870	70,285
Mass'ts Mutual, Mass........	2,116,768	140,456	952,644	125,000	682,296	74,564	98,000	312,181	....	4,501,909	....
Metropolitan, N. Y........	249,700	37,496	325,563	....	230,265	21,540	25,737	532,882	200	1,423,408	79,474
Missouri Mutual, Mo........	147,020	14,880	111,044	6,134	....	15,868	9,085	26,368	....	330,404	46,240
Missouri Valley, Kan........	285,544	3,016	....	24,520	17,106	58,978	13,784	117,681	28	520,652	252,946
Mutual, Ill........	142,926	1,569	169,775	34,700	151,135	16,452	6,379	41,777	4,670	569,408	21,353
Mutual, N. Y........	47,002,804	....	....	1,814,608	6,146,005	2,159,868	753,679	1,034,100	....	58,411,059	24,100
Mutual Benefit, N. J........	10,224,308	....	6,854,426	149,062	7,898,029	508,718	584,682	329,012	....	26,486,233	118,978
National, Ill........	108,400	49,656	11,059	57,727	27,000	16,145	14,294	107,968	69	392,308	24,894
National of U. S. A., D.C.	909,912	850,000	1,925	....	532,320	78,814	84,177	110,428	....	2,517,576	29,062
New Eng. Mutual, Mass.	1,695,343	549,319	2,289,271	600,000	5,225,464	195,881	256,139	678,046	....	11,489,463	....
New Jersey Mutual, N. J.	464,323	85,480	289,528	....	79,997	81,907	23,728	211,467	14,642	1,251,072	80,342
New York, N. Y........	11,390,534	....	986,244	1,768,174	4,274,226	[2]2,242,747	112,152	758,985	....	21,533,062	....
North America, N. Y........	2,996,381	38,366	981,776	299,116	127,904	94,158	98,082	896,575	27,100	5,556,408	182,445

Phoenix Mutual, Conn.	2,975,302	101,579	3,551,297	....	588,864	118,679	101,835	597,590	....	3,085,086	96,988
Protection, Ill	112,000	....	2,628	....	4,000	10,585	16,868	5,713	....	151,788	9,298
Railway Pass'gers', Conn	45,000	5,000	....	....	374,385	18,835	787	....	....	444,007	8,785
Republic, Ill	541,922	62,146	107,884	533,333	122,425	60,530	20,708	98,788	....	1,547,686	81,696
Saint Louis Mutual, Mo	1,900,198	8,000	2,718,155	776,282	192,777	64,682	115,011	574,606	5,023	6,354,684	159,336
Security, N. Y	15,000	....	1,978,139	....	721,788	78,815	81,338	612,045	21,994	3,508,589	127,648
Teutonia, Ill	73,764	3,538	39,289	68,547	56,763	10,594	4,512	90,839	....	347,846	[3]816,791
Travelers', Conn	784,797	....	....	50,000	1,102,170	126,285	24,960	142,574	....	2,280,786	4,249
Universal, N. Y	147,759	57,000	331,089	3,500	293,750	68,704	20,820	259,244	18,200	1,195,016	59,842
Washington, N. Y	1,656,008	6,107	....	....	1,175,500	301,617	30,171	241,805	....	3,411,208	15,000
Western New York, N.Y.	132,090	....	22,580	....	....	6,298	9,061	30,685	....	200,659	12,488
Totals	$144,264,455	$5,323,980	$48,798,297	$11,448,400	$45,807,642	$10,880,680	$5,001,805	$12,965,800	$401,196	$265,067,195	$3,[illegible],881

[1] Has withdrawn from the state.

[2] And in course of transmission.

[3] Of which $205,793 is stock notes.

TABLE No. XIV.—LIABILITIES.

NAME OF COMPANY.	Losses and Policy Claims.	Net Premium Reserve at 4½ per cent.	Dividends to Policy-holders.	All other Claims.	Total Liabilities except Capital.	Surplus as to Policy-holders.	Capital stock.	Net Surplus.	Deficiency.
Wisconsin Company.									
Northwestern Mutual	$67,715	[4]$10,046,014	$76,160	$5,000	$10,194,889	$2,294,999		$2,294,999	
Companies of other States.									
Ætna, Conn	501,258	[2]15,769,950	486,094	2,706	16,759,998	794,614	$108,056	691,558	
[1]Asbury, N. Y	7,928	850,000		2,306	860,228	49,263	150,000		$100,787
Berkshire, Mass	44,754	[2]2,085,134	3,002	38	2,082,998	98,701	25,500	73,201	
Brooklyn, N. Y	19,000	1,690,785			1,709,785	198,389	125,000	73,389	
Charter Oak, Conn	235,817	[2]10,344,286			10,579,608	75,921	200,000		124,079
Chicago, Ill	8,000	212,781			220,781	33,262	125,000		91,738
Connecticut Mutual, Conn	747,058	[2]29,128,309			29,875,368	5,060,779		5,060,779	
Continental, N. Y	149,700	5,270,367			5,420,067	522,895	100,000	422,895	
Equitable, N. Y	866,077	16,656,469	75,874	68,099	17,166,459	2,055,986	100,000	1,955,986	
Germania, N. Y	92,548	4,482,844	76,246	2,926	4,654,564	556,812	200,000	356,812	
Globe Mutual, N. Y	52,852	3,421,994		204,376	3,679,222	97,364	100,000		2,636
Manhattan, N. Y	210,947	6,200,125	92,608	6,210	6,509,885	1,760,985	100,000	1,660,985	
Massachusetts Mutual, Mass	112,420	[2]3,983,447	24,548		4,120,410	381,499		381,499	
Metropolitan, N. Y	17,500	1,199,088	13,576	2,625	1,232,789	190,664	200,000		9,336
Missouri Mutual, Missouri	15,822	263,996	3,282	15,601	298,703	31,721	125,000		93,279
Missouri Valley, Kan	2,000	420,776	4,878	1,889	429,088	91,614	162,250		70,636
Mutual, Ill	12,875	496,338	124		509,337	60,066	200,000		139,934
Mutual, N. Y	552,475	51,667,260		71,181	52,290,906	6,120,153		6,120,153	
Mutual Benefit, N. J	754,225	[2]22,042,872	348,625	1,533,652	24,678,374	1,809,358		1,809,358	
National, Ill	70,119	[2]76,996		7,185	154,300	238,008	240,000		1,992
National of U. S. A., D. C	66,097	1,664,163			1,730,260	787,816	1,000,000		212,684
New England Mutual, Mass	102,730	[2]10,092,463	75,846		10,271,039	1,218,424		1,218,424	
New Jersey Mutual, N. J	50,672	1,108,158		26,408	1,185,237	70,845	100,000		29,155
New York, N. Y	474,212	18,089,360	181,437		18,695,009	2,838,053		2,838,053	
North America, N. Y	236,690	5,150,764		60,173	5,437,687	118,776		118,776	

Phœnix Mutual, Conn	156,121	[2]7,295,088	....	....	7,451,159	588,997	16,000	567,997	....
Protection, Ill	12,410	[2]45,644	....	8,814	66,868	84,915	146,500	....	61,585
Railway Passengers', Conn	38,000	[3]15,000	....	625	53,625	390,382	300,000	90,382	....
Republic, Ill	22,500	773,442	....	10,142	806,084	741,603	848,610	....	107,008
Saint Louis Mutual, Mo	154,493	5,881,186	....	....	6,035,679	319,005	100,000	219,005	....
Security, N. Y	96,500	3,025,998	....	5,374	3,127,872	380,667	110,000	270,667	....
Teutonia, Ill	10,000	[3]195,399	49	5,000	210,448	137,398	194,207	....	56,809
Travelers', Conn	138,625	[3]1,292,586	....	184,761	1,615,972	614,814	500,000	114,814	....
Universal, N. Y	24,400	883,107	....	....	907,507	287,509	200,000	87,509	....
Washington, N. Y	66,660	2,914,325	212	3,270	2,984,467	426,786	125,000	301,786	....
Western New York, N. Y	....	112,541	1,547	3,145	117,233	83,426	125,000	....	41,574
Totals	$5,680,689	$244,293,331	$1,343,523	$2,231,501	$253,549,044	$31,538,151	$6,021,128	$26,660,210	$1,143,182

[1] Has withdrawn from the state. [2] Computed at 4 per cent. interest. [3] Estimated.
The reserve actually held by this company, on the basis of the Actuaries' life table at four per cent. interest, is $10,830,967.

TABLE No. XV.—Income.

Name of Company.	Cash Premiums.	Interest, Dividends and Rents.	Cash from other Sources.	Note Income.	Total Income.	Excess of Income over Expenditures.	Per ct. of excess to Income
Wisconsin Company.							
Northwestern Mutual	$1,882,880	$755,467	....	$1,056,767	$3,695,064	$1,728,861	46.79
Companies of other States.							
Ætna, Conn.	3,390,758	1,206,666	282,974	1,160,558	6,040,946	1,398,589	23.15
[1]Asbury, N. Y.	179,822	12,626	11,650	16,640	220,240	43,243	19.64
Berkshire, Mass.	486,212	118,176	....	48,864	653,252	388,176	59.42
Brooklyn, N. Y.	540,111	101,004	9,015	75,890	726,020	211,958	29.21
Charter Oak, Conn.	[2]3,633,434	469,483	....	....	4,102,917	1,230,558	29.99
Chicago, Ill.	163,912	15,019	....	....	178,931	34,412	19.23
Connecticut Mutual, Conn.	7,487,738	2,039,358	....	227,335	9,754,431	2,933,984	30.08
Continental, N. Y.	1,765,898	526,689	18,250	772,191	3,082,598	1,045,435	33.91
Equitable, N. Y.	7,426,862	993,183	....	....	8,420,045	3,398,914	40.31
Germania, N. Y.	1,525,699	286,190	105	....	1,811,994	719,347	39.70
Globe Mutual, N. Y.	1,337,830	197,762	....	....	1,535,592	536,349	34.93
Manhattan, N. Y.	1,463,827	516,181	....	171,847	2,151,855	721,079	33.51
Massachusetts Mutual, Mass.	990,658	251,029	....	329,779	1,571,461	531,506	33.82
Metropolitan, N. Y.	541,576	46,087	....	163,341	751,004	262,659	34.97
Missouri Mutual, Mo.	163,527	25,769	6,567	62,692	258,555	29,498	11.41
Missouri Valley, Kan.	286,248	32,047	....	....	318,295	115,587	36.31
Mutual, Ill.	254,045	20,965	697	31,180	306,887	60,968	19.86
Mutual, N. Y.	14,886,864	2,829,231	....	....	17,716,095	6,809,913	38.44
Mutual Benefit, N. J.	4,544,095	1,524,116	....	800,845	6,869,056	2,295,923	33.43
National, Ill.	267,123	6,585	....	....	273,708	14,456	5.28
National of U. S. A., D. C.	714,685	157,361	12,850	....	884,896	391,363	44.23
New England Mutual, Mass.	1,764,819	641,931	....	957,533	3,364,283	1,155,610	34.35
New Jersey Mutual, N. J.	663,327	37,157	....	174,128	874,612	620,718	70.97
New York, N. Y.	5,998,628	1,204,006	34,074	283,699	7,515,407	2,885,095	38.39
North America, N. Y.	1,285,098	303,966	16,196	280,380	1,885,635	[3]41,808	42.23

Phœnix Mutual, Conn.	2,385,994	471,[illegible]	....	556,496	3,418,752	678,567	19.86
Protection, Ill.	62,714	476	59,170	3,400	125,762	20,265	16.19
Railway Passengers[1], Conn.	130,980	29,345	....	....	160,325	10,989	6.85
Republic, Ill.	480,571	53,509	10,000	115,084	659,164	148,375	29.51
Saint Louis Mutual, Mo.	1,823,065	339,300	12,766	839,564	3,014,665	1,327,612	44.04
Security, N. Y.	1,010,986	120,722	13,500	431,330	1,576,538	278,644	17.67
Teutonia, Ill.	89,059	15,645	2,655	16,216	123,575	14,595	11.81
Travelers[1], Conn.	1,061,481	151,586	9,148	....	1,192,149	289,181	32.64
Universal, N. Y.	560,067	60,830	....	135,210	756,107	179,714	23.77
Washington, N. Y.	1,032,413	166,290	2,263	[4]............	1,202,994	531,205	44.16
Western New York, N. Y.	76,204	9,404	....	12,129	97,737	19,644	20.10
Totals	$72,028,110	$16,288,941	$301,966	$8,672,583	$97,265,897	$32,104,265	34.05

[1] Has withdrawn from the state.
[2] Including note income.
[3] Excess of expenditures over income.
[4] Percentage of excess of expenditures over income, to income.

TABLE No. XVI.—Cash Expenditures.

Name of Company.	Cash for Losses and Claims.	Cash for lapsed, surrendered and purchased Policies.	Cash Dividends to Policy-holders.	Dividends to Stock-holders.	Commissions and Salaries to Agents.	Medical Examiners' Fees.	Salaries of Officers, etc.	National, State and Local Taxes.	All other Payments.	Total cash Expenditures.
Wisconsin Company.										
Northwestern Mutual	$541,288	$138,989	$68,147	....	$299,401	$19,008	$76,541	$37,496	$67,687	$1,288,406
Co's of other States.										
Ætna, Conn..	1,298,268	621,929	286,653	$45,064	409,885	25,488	64,918	108,283	158,686	3,008,619
[1]Asbury, N. Y..............	64,804	1,664	6,376	....	41,428	3,761	19,927	3,089	26,286	166,885
Berkshire, Mass..............	73,137	33,877	49,560	1,785	48,819	1,986	9,990	7,137	94,329	250,568
[illegible]n, N. Y...............	129,757	38,827	61,610	16,250	57,812	7,198	25,914	6,458	100,946	444,067
[illegible]ter Oak, Conn............	[2]745,569	[2]754,970	[2]789,711	16,000	358,182	15,057	44,070	64,294	84,581	[2]2,872,364
Chicago, Ill..	25,000	26,575	19,275	10,330	28,339	5,808	12,453	1,658	15,086	144,519
Connecticut Mutual, Conn....	2,191,992	257,818	2,638,897	....	586,408	15,142	68,496	219,647	138,788	6,112,128
Continental, N. Y............	588,560	201,778	94,225	7,000	285,265	31,616	66,585	29,968	244,020	1,499,017
Equitable, N. Y	1,682,682	877,855	1,085,754	7,852	577,047	67,888	223,837	67,838	436,378	5,036,181
Germania, N. Y...	452,776	105,209	222,402	24,000	188,607	10,331	62,198	12,443	64,616	1,092,577
[illegible], N.	405,936	65,863	205,720	11,305	149,208	12,967	71,361	13,886	72,497	1,009,243
Manhattan, N. Y..	531,033	31,248	355,098	43,000	171,998	9,434	61,949	12,078	51,404	1,287,092
Massachusetts Mutual, Mass.	377,191	96,690	55,199	....	152,629	8,550	34,726	11,794	56,620	793,399
Metropolitan, N.	160,738	31,279	34,490	....	89,443	18,958	31,453	13,221	31,905	410,777
Missouri Mutual, ...	57,061	25,702	10,065	12,160	58,769	5,617	9,408	6,156	23,176	208,129
Missouri [illegible]lley, ...	24,063	27,321	28,883	10,215	47,804	3,655	23,400	3,136	34,261	202,738
Mutual, Ill.........	36,299	37,974	1,657	....	89,648	7,147	20,338	3,530	40,470	237,058
Mutual, N. Y.....	2,740,257	1,555,009	5,259,205	....	335,015	38,507	268,708	114,639	594,847	10,906,182
[illegible]al Benefit, N.	1,824,837	168,835	1,428,518	....	406,948	20,882	65,512	84,644	95,420	4,085,586
National, Ill......	116,922	380	....	....	58,728	4,250	26,200	4,598	46,464	254,696
National of U. S. A., D. C....	190,205	51,688	....	30,000	88,147	8,486	38,936	8,388	77,698	498,588
New England Mutual, Mass..	787,554	236,627	240,900	....	164,900	11,634	50,000	23,868	220,848	1,736,381
New Jersey Mutual, N. J......	98,649	23,441	26,764	2,000	34,159	5,597	14,650	3,466	39,364	243,089

New York, N. Y.	1,409,559	1,438,452	695,598	....	412,492	55,485	129,494	59,455	308,488	4,407,794
North America, N. Y.	1,046,046	63,296	80,661	....	180,856	21,154	44,230	39,583	148,906	1,614,743
Phœnix Mutual, Conn.	831,116	32,060	943,442	960	364,684	30,821	34,516	46,339	79,849	2,363,777
Protection, Ill.	37,804	....	....	....	25,442	602	13,379	2,392	24,943	104,563
Railway Passengers', Conn.	29,100	....	....	30,000	49,870	3,431	14,055	4,350	18,530	149,336
Republic, Ill.	182,818	34,712	7,812	....	198,868	9,716	36,867	10,646	65,628	492,069
Saint Louis Mutual, Mo.	809,319	28,496	30,669	10,000	316,901	21,116	74,926	29,983	92,261	1,413,686
Security, N. Y.	468,433	85,666	83,201	14,700	188,754	13,909	28,583	13,249	96,384	994,872
[illegible], Ill.	28,042	2,471	1,485	20	26,294	5,609	13,365	2,866	16,290	96,448
Travelers', [illegible]	311,875	8,006	2,370	50,000	262,618	7,770	35,695	10,994	113,760	808,018
Universal, N. Y.	195,942	56,165	....	15,400	111,916	16,223	27,460	12,089	55,544	490,789
Washington, N. Y.	267,369	61,455	109,096	9,756	97,801	8,056	41,360	9,631	67,265	671,789
Western New York, N. Y.	11,742	655	1,796	....	38,430	5,559	4,046	2,042	2,808	67,073
Totals	$20,663,181	$7,206,927	$14,845,173	$367,797	$6,987,985	$557,718	$1,886,548	$1,070,059	$3,839,440	$57,367,773

[1] Has withdrawn from the state.

[2] Including premium loan disbursements.

TABLE No. XVII.—Premium Loan Disbursements.

Name of Company.	Cash and Note Expenditures.			Premium-Loan Disbursements.					Total Cash Expenditures	Total Expenditures
	In payment of Losses and Claims.	For lapsed, surrendr'd and purchd Policies.	Total Div'ds to Policyholders.	In paym't of Losses and Claims	In purch. of surrendr'd Policies.	Dividends to Policyholders.	Voided by Lapse of Policies.	Total Note Disbursements.		
Wisconsin Co.										
Northwestern Mutual	$588,387	$246,649	$449,871	$41,149	$112,710	$386,294	$187,694	$727,777	$1,288,406	$1,966,183
Co's of other States.										
Ætna, Conn	1,407,674	1,172,628	1,052,021	114,406	550,698	765,368	[2]208,271	1,638,738	3,008,619	4,642,357
[1] Asbury, N. Y	65,142	1,664	11,631	836		5,255	4,070	10,163	166,885	176,998
Berkshire, Mass	74,650	33,877	60,012	1,518		10,452	2,548	14,518	250,568	265,076
Brooklyn, N. Y	139,698	96,387	61,610	9,941	59,560			69,501	444,067	513,568
Charter Oak, Conn	745,569	754,970	789,711						[4]2,872,364	2,872,364
Chicago, Ill	25,000	26,575	19,275						144,519	144,519
Connecticut Mutual, Conn	2,211,992	571,906	2,906,213	20,000	314,088	267,316	106,905	708,309	6,112,128	6,820,437
Continental, N. Y	556,165	375,011	289,238	17,605	178,233	195,013	152,225	538,076	1,499,017	2,087,098
Equitable, N. Y	1,682,689	877,855	1,085,754						5,026,131	5,026,181
Germania, N. Y	452,776	105,209	292,402						1,092,577	1,092,577
Globe Mutual, N. Y	405,986	65,863	205,720						1,009,243	1,009,243
Manhattan, N. Y	578,012	148,835	364,141	41,979	[3]112,587	9,116		163,684	1,297,092	1,460,776
Massachusetts Mut., Mass	391,680	117,499	186,510	14,489	20,809	131,811	79,947	246,556	798,399	1,089,955
Metropolitan, N. Y	165,000	61,287	60,640	4,267	30,048	26,150	17,108	77,568	410,777	488,345
Missouri Mutual, Mo	58,284	35,929	16,254	1,208	10,297	6,269	8,214	25,968	208,129	290,069
Missouri Valley, Kan	24,063	27,321	28,888						202,738	202,738
Mutual, Ill	37,841	38,851	2,614	1,542	877	967	5,496	8,872	237,058	245,965
Mutual, N. Y	2,740,257	1,555,009	5,259,205						10,906,182	10,906,182
Mutual Benefit, N. J	1,953,211	286,085	1,660,427	128,374	122,190	236,914		487,478	4,085,586	4,573,064
National, Ill	116,922	380					4,616	4,616	254,686	259,262
National of U. S. A., D. C	190,205	51,688							498,538	498,538
New England Mutual, Mass	891,897	297,989	462,288	34,342	61,812	222,488	154,204	472,348	1,736,321	2,208,673
New Jersey Mutual, N. J	96,174	32,428	27,121	1,565	[5]8,997	367		10,879	242,020	252,899

New York, N. Y.	1,496,708	1,441,394	781,603	17,170	8,943	156,010	40,396	222,518	4,407,794	4,680,312
North America, N. Y.	1,158,988	67,106	169,107	106,176	8,810	88,496	64,269	268,701	1,614,742	1,877,443
Phœnix Mutual, Conn.	878,499	50,636	985,443	47,388	18,568	52,001	255,456	373,408	2,363,777	2,737,185
Protection, Ill.	87,804	....	....	....	....	....	885	885	104,562	105,397
Railway Passengers', Conn.[1]	29,100	....	....	....	....	....	....	....	149,336	149,336
Republic, Ill.	183,669	47,115	7,812	851	12,408	....	5,478	18,727	492,062	510,789
Saint Louis Mutual, Mo.	858,793	41,398	194,908	44,478	12,897	94,289	121,822	273,431	1,418,632	1,667,063
Security, N. Y.	491,895	202,739	245,668	23,462	[3]117,078	162,487	....	303,022	994,872	1,297,894
Teutonia, Ill.	28,696	4,267	2,323	654	1,796	888	9,250	12,588	96,442	108,969
Travelers,' Conn.	311,875	8,006	2,370	....	....	....	....	....	808,018	808,018
Universal, N. Y.	195,942	104,157	....	....	47,993	....	37,669	85,654	490,739	576,393
Washington, N. Y.	267,369	61,455	109,096	....	....	....	....	....	671,789	671,789
Western New York, N. Y.	11,851	655	8,758	109	....	6,962	3,949	11,090	67,078	78,098
Totals	$21,396,633	$9,007,739	$17,669,343	$673,458	$1,800,812	$2,894,170	$1,465,425	$6,763,859	$57,367,778	$64,131,632

[1] Has withdrawn from the state. [2] And lapsed. [3] And redeemed by maker in cash. [4] Including note expenditures.

TABLE No. XVIII.—Exhibit of Policies.

Name of Company.	Policies in force, Dec. 31, 1871.		[3] Policies issued during the year.		Policies terminat'd and decreased.		Reinsured.		Policies in force, Dec. 31, 1872.		Increase.		Decrease.	
	No.	Amount.	No.	Amount.	No.	Amount.	No.	Amount.	No.	Amount.	No.	Amount.	No.	Amount.
Wisconsin Co.														
Northwestern Mutual...........	34,349	$62,425,187	6,487	[2]$14,361,938	5,631	$12,611,908	....	....	35,205	$64,175,217	856	$1,750,030	....	....
Co's of other States.														
Ætna, Conn....................	47,658	101,394,862	8,791	15,334,287	6,416	16,041,376	....	....	50,098	100,617,778	2,375	....	....	$707,069
[1]Asbury, N. Y..................	2,843	5,096,345	1,632	[3]3,264,174	1,700	2,878,380	....	$355,000	2,775	5,127,139	....	30,794	68	....
Berkshire, Mass................	4,451	10,149,905	767	[2]2,014,667	739	1,639,159	10	75,000	4,469	10,450,413	18	300,508	....	....
Brooklyn, N. Y..................	4,321	11,430,308	1,504	[3]3,811,575	1,236	3,248,920	....	....	4,589	11,992,958	268	562,655	....	....
Charter Oak, Conn..............	25,449	61,634,076	5,929	12,246,591	4,622	10,452,979	...	....	26,756	63,427,688	1,307	1,793,612	....	....
Chicago, Ill.......................	2,294	3,272,308	1,800	2,948,230	1,104	1,479,884	....	78,500	2,990	3,962,149	696	689,846	....	....
Connecticut Mutual, Conn........	62,458	182,785,236	5,530	14,502,090	5,152	15,560,486	....	....	62,836	181,726,840	366	....	....	1,058,396
Continental, N. Y................	25,654	57,158,716	12,010	[3]22,782,299	9,085	19,317,625	....	376,000	28,579	60,247,390	2,925	3,088,674	....	....
Equitable, N. Y...................	38,827	154,331,143	12,491	[3]51,911,079	8,183	34,798,871	....	....	43,135	171,443,351	4,308	17,112,208	....	....
Germania, N. Y...................	18,507	33,099,969	2,683	[2]4,387,078	1,765	2,886,783	....	....	19,365	34,600,264	858	1,500,295	....	....
Globe Mutual, N. Y...............	11,599	28,451,485	3,179	[3]8,166,258	2,244	6,381,558	177	415,500	12,357	29,820,685	758	1,369,200	....	....
Manhattan, N. Y..................	13,038	42,140,907	1,701	[2]4,991,710	1,615	4,789,004	....	....	13,124	42,343,613	86	202,706	....	....
Massachusetts Mutual, Mass......	14,468	33,578,515	3,204	7,130,000	3,189	7,512,507	....	582,000	14,483	32,614,008	15	....	....	964,507
Metropolitan, N. Y...............	11,299	14,989,582	8,642	11,856,663	4,596	5,999,904	....	....	15,345	20,846,341	4,046	5,856,759	....	....
Missouri Mutual, Mo.	1,631	4,466,283	1,249	[3]2,795,736	658	1,868,541	....	292,000	2,222	5,101,498	591	635,195	....	....
Missouri Valley, Kan........	2,089	6,451,619	1,199	[2]4,187,397	975	3,076,656	....	....	2,293	7,562,360	204	1,110,741	....	....
Mutual, Ill.........................	3,278	5,067,743	2,738	4,740,094	2,297	3,714,940	48	192,670	3,666	5,900,227	388	832,484	....	....
Mutual, N. Y......................	73,911	228,789,408	12,186	[3]59,263,961	7,904	23,675,025	....	....	78,193	264,378,344	4,282	35,588,936	....	....
Mutual Benefit, N. J.............	38,668	183,086,942	3,172	9,573,068	2,415	9,495,836	....	....	39,425	183,164,169	757	77,227	....	....
National, Ill......................	5,296	6,672,000	4,673	6,581,600	5,094	6,335,000	....	....	4,875	6,918,600	....	246,600	421	....
National of U. S. A., D. C........	7,908	18,465,472	3,110	6,858,715	1,828	3,967,579	183	1,098,000	9,007	20,258,608	1,104	1,787,136	....	....
New England Mutual, Mass......	22,892	67,815,783	2,799	[2]6,874,778	3,354	8,725,981	....	....	22,337	65,964,585	....	....	555	1,851,208
New Jersey Mutual, N. J........	3,984	8,049,052	6,162	[2]12,897,940	1,278	2,780,325	....	260,500	8,873	17,906,167	4,889	9,857,115	....	....
New York, N. Y............ ...	38,988	113,154,809	8,910	[3]27,096,274	6,664	21,628,477	....	....	41,234	118,622,606	2,246	5,467,797	....	....

North America, N. Y.	14,209	37,063,467	2,375	[2]4,623,962	2,752	7,331,753	....	1,670,000	13,832	32,685,676	......	....	377	4,377,791
Phœnix Mutual, Conn.	28,707	63,554,620	10,690	[3]22,192,311	6,377	13,781,664	....	55,000	33,020	71,910,267	4,313	8,355,647	....	....
Protection, Ill.	1,593	1,593,000	5,039	5,039,000	1,907	1,907,000	....	....	4,725	4,725,000	3,132	3,132,000	....	....
Republic, Ill.	6,359	13,889,519	4,667	11,530,364	4,637	9,927,052	....	507,885	6,389	14,984,946	20	1,095,427	....	....
Saint Louis Mutual, Mo.	15,884	48,978,292	6,819	19,941,117	7,062	22,541,473	23	140,000	15,618	46,237,936	......	....	266	2,740,356
Security, N. Y.	13,216	32,517,238	3,281	[3]7,260,311	3,013	7,223,487	....	1,440,500	13,484	31,113,562	268	....	....	1,403,676
Teutonia, Ill.	1,767	2,069,246	2,969	2,415,737	1,052	1,065,500	....	21,000	3,684	3,418,483	1,917	1,329,237	....	....
Travelers', Conn.	43,835	94,075,048	34,806	109,463,221	27,837	88,791,277	37	177,886	50,767	114,569,106	6,932	20,494,058	....	....
Universal, N. Y.	5,278	14,229,379	3,575	9,941,482	2,006	6,505,875	....	522,100	6,842	17,142,886	1,569	2,913,507	....	....
Washington, N. Y.	10,634	24,293,143	2,368	6,254,707	2,035	4,596,960	....	....	10,967	25,950,890	333	1,657,747	....	....
Western New York, N. Y.	904	1,605,097	1,416	[2]1,735,122	520	773,328	2	10,000	1,798	2,556,891	894	951,794	....	....
Totals	658,206	$1,727,775,594	200,483	$519,969,521	148,932	$395,313,068	480	$8,269,541	709,277	$1,844,162,506	52,758	$129,489,935	1,687	$13,103,023

[1] Has withdrawn from the state. [2] Including additions by dividends. [3] Including old policies revived and increased.

TABLE No. XIX.—Termination of Policies.

Name of Company.	By Death. No.	By Death. Amount.	By Expiry. No.	By Expiry. Amount.	By Surrender. No.	By Surrender. Amount.	By Lapse. No.	By Lapse. Amount.	By Change. No.	By Change. Amount.	Not Taken. No.	Not Taken. Amount.	Total Terminated. No.	Total Terminated. Amount.
Wisconsin Co.														
Northwestern Mutual	301	$550,329	3	$58,830	807	$1,204,680	3,325	$5,996,469	238	$2,547,308	957	$2,324,294	5,631	$12,611,905
Co's of other States.														
Ætna, Conn	586	1,501,312	15	52,500	2,586	6,389,654	2,128	5,706,087	....	....	1,101	2,391,873	6,416	16,041,376
[1] Asbury, N. Y	28	66,607	8	13,500	5	13,500	994	1,696,616	332	437,063	403	651,074	1,700	2,878,360
Berkshire, Mass	46	109,404	....	....	76	185,830	508	1,068,350	....	....	114	275,575	[illegible]	1,639,159
Brooklyn, N. Y	57	159,750	1	2,500	276	949,200	606	1,297,550	3	58,490	298	781,500	1,236	3,248,990
Charter Oak, Conn	251	707,077	3	2,500	884	2,263,647	2,304	5,382,130	....	....	1,180	2,097,625	4,622	10,452,979
Chicago, Ill	21	25,000	....	....	152	205,674	760	1,095,710	....	....	171	228,500	1,104	1,479,884
Connecticut Mutual, Conn	814	2,402,774	12	31,000	1,534	4,666,127	2,256	6,598,565	....	504,990	536	1,362,100	5,152	15,560,486
Continental, N. Y	212	553,250	4	9,000	689	1,836,214	5,580	11,419,161	270	550,000	2,330	4,950,000	9,085	19,817,625
Equitable, N. Y	423	1,688,882	45	227,100	2,108	10,108,598	3,478	18,333,141	....	....	2,129	9,446,150	8,183	34,798,871
Germania, N. Y	266	453,116	11	23,563	515	913,459	684	1,045,861	15	29,604	274	421,180	1,765	2,886,783
Globe Mutual, N. Y	147	392,109	1	1,000	388	1,176,561	1,832	3,327,927	19	[2]808,430	357	1,175,581	2,244	6,881,558
Manhattan, N. Y	180	566,492	....	....	93	316,992	938	2,765,504	189	647,400	215	492,616	1,615	4,789,004
Massachusetts Mutual, Mass	145	358,557	501	1,154,500	298	499,094	985	2,548,500	808	1,818,156	562	1,133,700	3,199	7,512,507
Metropolitan, N. Y	125	164,000	1	5,000	304	661,249	1,962	2,617,846	274	422,000	1,930	2,129,809	4,596	5,999,904
Missouri Mutual, Mo	24	55,500	....	....	76	174,813	338	861,300	66	328,328	152	449,100	656	1,868,541
Missouri Valley, Kan	11	23,062	....	....	106	301,086	711	2,301,728	....	21,500	147	429,330	975	3,076,656
Mutual, Ill	27	43,611	....	....	285	454,109	1,338	2,154,014	....	....	647	1,063,206	2,297	3,714,940
Mutual, N. Y	761	2,407,625	....	....	[2]5,979	[2]18,053,595	....	....	3	13,500	1,161	3,200,305	7,904	23,675,095
Mutual Benefit, N. J	503	1,979,070	14	47,000	159	516,100	991	3,089,325	384	2,869,741	364	1,044,600	2,415	9,495,836
National, Ill	83	107,000	....	....	3	9,000	4,646	5,649,000	....	....	362	570,000	5,094	6,335,000
National of U. S. A., D. C	71	206,996	....	....	55	205,956	946	1,931,450	270	697,550	481	925,627	1,823	3,967,579
New England Mutual, Mass	262	778,018	24	63,200	455	1,422,848	2,162	5,354,693	....	40,000	451	1,072,222	3,354	8,736,981
New Jersey Mutual, N. J	48	100,800	5	23,000	278	665,809	563	665,755	....	414,611	384	910,850	1,278	2,780,825
New York, N. Y	481	1,508,006	8	26,500	2,612	8,492,169	2,692	7,177,894	....	1,543,229	871	2,888,749	6,664	21,636,477
North America, N. Y	188	564,578	110	562,925	61	188,107	1,674	3,762,644	449	1,540,350	270	698,149	2,752	7,351,769

Phœnix Mutual, Conn	311	768,176	1	500	106	276,497	2,845	6,104,710	577	1,578,850	2,587	5,067,981	6,377	13,761,664
Protection, Ill	45	45,000	....	....	....	....	1,458	1,458,000	....	....	409	409,000	1,907	1,907,000
Republic, Ill	42	126,318	8	48,000	339	585,540	1,412	3,296,270	1,641	3,182,706	1,195	2,818,318	4,687	9,997,063
Saint Louis Mutual, Mo	288	822,495	....	....	75	203,226	5,755	19,058,718	11	75,858	969	2,886,181	7,069	22,541,478
Security, N. Y	178	577,075	11	60,000	180	561,200	1,753	3,895,953	217	781,721	674	1,397,588	3,018	7,228,497
Teutonia, Ill	30	38,500	2	2,000	45	81,000	363	445,500	53	54,000	539	444,500	1,059	1,065,500
Travelers', Conn	182	306,147	26,135	65,818,150	51	88,522	918	1,531,425	190	494,708	411	693,326	27,887	68,791,277
Universal, N. Y	64	196,880	1	5,000	170	461,155	876	2,982,297	158	425,700	740	2,475,343	2,008	6,505,375
Washington, N. Y	110	275,690	3	6,000	495	1,170,255	1,122	2,378,000	....	....	806	772,005	2,085	4,596,960
Western New York, N. Y	9	11,700	2	3,000	27	55,628	272	395,500	34	61,000	176	246,500	520	773,328
Totals	7,222	$30,630,401	26,929	$88,258,268	22,207	$65,351,049	60,565	$140,063,461	6,198	$21,286,678	25,811	$59,728,216	148,982	$395,318,066

[1] Has withdrawn from the state. [2] And lapse. [3] And reversionary dividends canceled.

TABLE No. XX.—Business in Wisconsin.

Name of Company.	Policies in Force Dec. 31, 1871.		Policies Issued During the Year.		Policies in Force Dec. 31, 1872.		Premiums received.	Losses paid.
	No.	Amount.	No.	Amount.	No.	Amount.		
Wisconsin Company.								
Northwestern Mutual	10,668	$14,815,275	982	$1,376,781	10,296	$13,980,054	$653,219	$99,593
Companies of other States.								
Ætna, Conn	1,002	1,616,226	192	219,101	989	1,601,284	91,599	17,500
[1]Asbury, N. Y.	58	77,807	10	11,000	27	30,000	757	2,000
Berkshire, Mass	64	94,600	64	78,250	....	....	5,282	....
Brooklyn, N. Y.	....	....	....	....	....	....	....	4,200
Charter Oak, Conn	698	1,057,809	116	138,048	731	978,745	51,240	18,000
Chicago, Ill	398	451,858	714	841,000	988	1,106,858	87,104	2,000
Connecticut Mutual, Conn	1,262	3,750,000	67	82,684	1,118	1,782,234	110,420	32,050
Continental, N. Y	401	630,990	302	412,400	558	841,490	41,551	5,500
Equitable, N. Y.	782	1,593,745	112	323,600	817	1,757,345	69,928	32,000
Germania, N. Y.	620	778,614	71	92,500	639	806,548	30,249	4,566
Globe Mutual, N. Y.	....	....	33	23,896	279	367,277	14,792	8,595
Manhattan, N. Y.	77	164,950	5	9,000	68	147,662	....	....
Massachusetts Mutual, Mass	....	....	71	116,790	169	296,230	12,191	161
Metropolitan, N. Y.	74	115,800	55	59,568	81	101,000	2,822	1,000
[2]Missouri Mutual, Mo	....	....	13	12,000	12	12,000	288	....
[2]Missouri Valley, Kan	....	....	10	66,000	11	68,500	185	....
Mutual, Ill	160	248,511	155	250,240	168	259,577	11,642	1,000
Mutual, N. Y	....	....	175	348,315	2,151	4,481,280	173,407	42,861
Mutual Benefit, N. J.	178	569,600	69	104,500	219	740,320	14,230	20,000
National, Ill	634	748,000	306	398,000	....	....	4,000	3,000
National of U. S. A., D. C	148	309,986	141	231,971	247	480,707	15,152	....
New England Mutual, Mass	433	1,001,000	55	63,481	386	546,473	27,611	6,000
[2]New Jersey Mutual, N. J.	....	....	....	....	....	....	....	....
New York, N. Y.	360	900,000	83	186,500	919	1,650,400	55,916	4,500
North America, N. Y.	221	280,100	42	54,000	294	321,600	11,584	2,000

Phœnix Mutual, Conn.	979	1,514,518	299	500,495	1,489	2,219,580	97,390	9,000
Protection, Ill.			151	151,000	158	158,000	1,790	
Railway Passengers'[1], Conn.							2,330	300
Republic, Ill.			261	480,241	384	714,126	22,315	1,000
Saint Louis Mutual, Mo.	50	72,250	20	29,700	57	72,250	2,436	1,000
Security, N. Y.	62	86,000	89	118,500	126	168,235	5,737	
Teutonia, Ill.	77	74,500	129	83,500	168	125,000	3,392	
Travelers', Conn.	1,916	4,710,292	1,461	4,254,950	1,870	4,857,442	40,061	15,331
Universal, N. Y.	219	417,100	138	215,000	263	493,900	19,107	7,500
Washington, N. Y.	973	1,448,000	156	195,500	845	1,116,806	39,175	14,000
[2]Western New York, N. Y.								
Totals	22,509	$37,522,462	6,478	$11,428,411	26,377	$42,283,417	$1,669,252	$349,557

[1] Has withdrawn from the state. [2] Admitted into the state since the date of last report.

CO-OPERATIVE INSURANCE.

Two companies organized upon this plan—the National Life and the Protection Life insurance companies, of Chicago, Illinois, are transacting business in this state.

The co-operative system, adopted by them, has been regarded by many as defective and uncertain, and as not furnishing sufficient security to the policy-holders.

The legislatures of several of the states have enacted laws prohibiting the admission of such companies. A bill of similar import was introduced in the legislature of this state in 1872, but its passage was defeated. The law of this state, regulating life insurance, as it now stands, requires of each life company a guarantee capital, or actual assets, of $100,000, which shall be safely invested, before authority to transact business be given. It also provides that "the actual funds of any life insurance company doing business in this state," must be "of a net value equal to the net value of its policies, according to the American Experience Table of Mortality, with interest at four and one-half per cent."

A certificate executed by the Treasurer of the state of Illinois shows that both of these companies, with respect to capital, have complied with the law. Their policies were valued under the supervision of the Auditor of Public Accounts of the same state, who is also Superintendent of Insurance. The standard according to which the valuation was made, is the Actuaries' Table of Mortality, with interest at four per cent., which requires a larger reserve fund than the standard of this state.

The net assets of the National Life on December 31, 1872, were $315,004; the net present value of its policies, according to the above basis, as computed by the Illinois department, was $76,996; leaving a surplus as regards policyholders, of $238,008.

The net assets of the Protection Life, on the same day, were $130,559; the net present value of its policies was $45,644; leaving a surplus as regards policyholders, of $84,915.

An official examination of the assets having been made by the Superintendent of Insurance of a neighboring state, and the annual statements having been duly authenticated, it is assumed that the assets are good, and that the policy liabilities are correctly computed, according to the standard above named, and the exact conditions of the insurance contracts or policies; and that, therefore, the latter provision of the law referred to is also fully met.

Presuming the policy valuation to be accurate, then the amount of net reserve held by each company, as above stated, is also the amount of its net liability on its policies.

The ratio of net reserve to amount at risk in the National Life on December 31, 1872, was 1.11 per cent.; in the Protection Life, .97 per cent.; the average ratio in the ordinary life companies was 13.32 per cent.

One peculiarity of this class of companies is that the longer a policy runs, the less its value or liability; while the reverse is true of a policy in an ordinary life company.

The following supplemental statement, showing the amounts realized by the representatives of deceased members, etc., in this state, will throw some light upon this system and its practical operations.

SUPPLEMENTAL STATEMENT *of the* NATIONAL LIFE INSURANCE COMPANY *of Chicago, Ill.*

NAMES OF DECEASED MEMBERS RESIDING IN WISCONSIN.	Residence.	Occupation.	Age when Ins.	Date of Policy.	No. of Policy.	Insurance.	Guaranteed insurance	Prem's paid includ'g assm'ts	Date of Death.	Losses Paid.	Amt. Paid.
Adaline Abert	Milwaukee	Housewife	28	Sep. 26, 1871	10,439	$2,500	$1,000	$28 10	Apl. 8, 1872	Mch. 17, 1873	$1,000
August F. Brunotto	Milwaukee	Clerk	40	June 3, 1871	7,410	2,500	1,000	18.40	Dec. 8, 1871	May 21, 1872	1,236
Caroline H. Baecker	Watertown	Housewife	44	Sep. 3, 1872	15,664	5,000	2,000	31.00	Oct. 31, 1872	Apl. 4, 1873	2,257
Ingraham Gould	Beaver Dam	Nurseryman	60	Dec. 24, 1870 Dec. 31, 1870	3,343 3,765	5,000	2,000	47.40	July 16, 1871	Nov. 15, 1871	3,520
John Thompson	Beaver Dam	Merchant	59	Oct. 23, 1871	10,908	2,500	1,000	16.00	Jan. 30, 1872	July 22, 1872	1,000
Nathan A. Wright	Pr. du Chien	Druggist	58	Dec. 9, 1871	11,850	2,500	1,000	29.80	Sep. 11, 1872	Mch. 20, 1873	1,000
Martha Littlejohn	Fulton	Housewife	54	Oct. 3, 1871	10,574	2,500	1,000	25.40	Sep. 10, 1872	Jan. 13, 1873	1,200
Frederick Holborn	Milwaukee	Hairworker	51	June 2, 1871	7,195	2,500	1,000	31.10	Jan. 1, 1872	May 18, 1872	1,176
James Stacks	Milwaukee	Boarding House	25	Dec. 17, 1870	3,133	2,500	1,000	25.90	Oct. 8, 1871	May 22, 1872	1,000
Jerry L. Brown	Berlin	Farmer	58	Nov. 8, 1870	2,497	2,500	1,000	38.00	Nov. 18, 1871	Apl. 23, 1872	1,230
						$30,000	$12,000				$14,609

MISCELLANEOUS QUESTIONS.

How many separate classes were in existence in your company Dec. 31, 1872? **Ans. Six.**

What was the number of members in each class? Ans. Memberships on books, not all in force, **Div. D., Series 1—2,534. Div. D., Series 2—1,040. Div. C., Series** 1—1,538. Div. C., Series 2—177. Div. B., Series 1—973. Commercial League, 216.

What was the aggregate amount of insurance contemplated by each class? Ans. Divisions B., **C. and D. guaranteed insurance $1,000 each; contingent insurance, $2,500** each; Commercial League, guaranteed insurance, $4,000; contingent insurance, $10,000.

STATE OF ILLINOIS, *County of Cook,* } ss.

Benjamin Lombard, President, and H. G. Teed, Secretary **of the National Life Insurance Company of Chicago, being duly sworn, depose and say, and each for** himself, says that they are the officers of the said company, **as above described, and that the above and accompanying statement and answers are true and correct to** the best of their knowledge, information and belief.

BENJ. LOMBARD, *President.*
H. G. TEED, *Secretary.*

Sworn and subscribed before me, this 26th day of June A. D. 1873.

[SEAL.] **FRANK M. GOODRICH, a Commissioner for the State of Wisconsin, residing in Illinois.**

The above statement of the National Life shows that the policy-holders are divided into six classes; that out of $2,500, the face of the policies, $1,000 is guaranteed to every one of the insured in divisions B, C and D, and that out of $10,000 in the class called the "Commercial League," $4,000 is guaranteed.

Since the admission of this company into Wisconsin, ten of its members, who were residents of this state, have died. The aggregate insurance taken by them was $30,000; guaranteed by the company, $12,000; paid $14,609, or 48.70 per cent. of the insurance. Had the classes been full, and all the members paid their dues and assessments, the representatives of these deceased members would have received $30,000, the whole amount of insurance, as represented by the policies; as it was, less than one-half of that amount was realized.

SUPPLEMENTAL STATEMENT OF THE PROTECTION LIFE INSURANCE COMPANY *of Chicago, Ill.*

The number of members deceased in Wisconsin since the admission of the company was one, viz.: Haynes French, grain dealer of Kenosha, age when insured being sixty-four; date of policy March 1, 1873; number of policy 9,355; insurance as stated in policy $5,000; premiums received including assessments, none; date of death June 4, 1873. The premium on this policy was never received by the company and no assessments have been paid to the company by this party. We received a notification of this death on the 14th inst. but no proofs of death have been out or filed with this office; no payments having been made on this policy, we do not consider it a valid claim.

QUESTIONS.

How many separate classes were in existence in your company Dec. 31, 1872? Ans. There are no "classes" in this company; all the policy holders are together and contribute to the payment of each loss.

What was the number of members in each class? Ans. The company is not on the "class" system.

What was the aggregate amount of insurance contemplated by each class? Ans. The company issues policies for only two amounts, viz.: $2,500 and $5,000, conditioned on the number of members in the company; but each policy contains a guarantee of at least $1,000 for three years and five years respectively. We may add in further explanation of the plan of this company that all the policy holders contribute to the payment of every loss, and that the equity is established between them by each paying his proportion according to age and the amount of his policy.

We the undersigned, Vice President and Secretary of the Protection Life Insurance Company certify that the answers made to the questions asked on this sheet are true in every respect.

[SEAL.]

D. R. HARDER, *Vice President.*
MARTIN RYAN, *Secretary.*

STATE OF ILLINOIS, COUNTY OF COOK, CITY OF CHICAGO—ss:

Personally appeared before me M. J. Dunne, a Notary Public in and for said city in the county and state aforesaid, D. R. Harder, Vice President, and Martin Ryan, Secretary of the Protection Life Insurance Company of Chicago, who being severally sworn, each for himself, states on oath that the above statement subscribed by him is true in substance and fact.
Chicago, June, 19, A. D. 1873.

[SEAL.]

M. J. DUNNE,
Notary Public.

The statement of the Protection Life shows that only one of its members residing in this state has died since its admission, and that the policy of that one had lapsed for non-payment of premiums and assessments.

This company issues policies for two amounts, $2,500 and $5,000, conditioned on the number of members in the company; each policy containing a guarantee of $1,000, for three and five years respectively. For instance, a policy issued for $2,500 contains a condition "that the company guarantees the payment of at least $1,000 upon the policy for three years from the date thereof, if in force, in case of the death of the holder of the same." After the expiration of three years, or the "guarantee period," the value of the policy, or liability of the company to pay any definite sum ceases; the company agreeing to pay only what it receives from the assessment, together with the amount of the "defaulted assessments," upon policies then in force.

A failure to pay these monthly assessments and costs of collection within thirty days after the date of the notice, renders the policy "null and void and of no effect."

By reference to table No. 10, it will be seen that the amount of insurance in force, December 31, 1871, in case of the National Life, was $6,672,000; lapsed during the year 1872,* $5,658,000, or 84.80 per cent.

The amount in force at the same time in case of the Protection Life was $1,593,000; lapsed during the year, $1,453,000, or 91.21 per cent.

The average ratio of lapsed and surrendered policies to risks in force in the ordinary life companies, including the above two, was 11.89 per cent.

As nearly all of those who were members in these companies at the beginning of the year, went out, or suffered their policies to lapse before its close, and as the security of the companies and the amount of insurance which a beneficiary will realize at death, depend largely upon the number of paying members in the class, or in the company, it is manifest, to say the least, that it is a *very uncertain resource* for dependent widows and orphan children.

CONCLUDING REMARKS.

It is again recommended that the law charging life companies a license fee of $300 per annum be repealed, and that a law be enacted establishing a uniform rate per centum upon gross premium receipts.

The operation of the present law relating to this subject is very unjust. For instance, the premium receipts of one company trans-

*Of this amount $9,000 was surrendered.

acting business in this state last year were $173,407; paid for license, $300, which is but seventeen-hundredths (.17) per cent. of the premium receipts. The premium receipts of another company were $757; paid for license, $300, which is thirty-nine and sixty-three hundredths (39.63) per cent. of the premium receipts. In other words, one company, or one class of policy-holders is made to pay over two hundred and thirty-three times as much as the other.

If a uniform tax of but one per cent. upon gross premium receipts were charged, instead of $300 per company, not only would justice, both to the companies and policy-holders, be secured, but the revenue to the state from this source would also be largely increased.

Respectfully submitted,

LL. BREESE,

Secretary of State, and ex-officio
Commissioner of Insurance.

STATEMENTS

OF

Life and Accident Insurance Companies.

WISCONSIN COMPANY.

NORTHWESTERN MUTUAL LIFE INSURANCE COMPANY.

MILWAUKEE, WIS.

JOHN H. VAN DYKE, *President.* WILLARD MERRILL, *Secretary.*

[Incorporated, March 1857. Commenced business, Nov. 25, 1858.]

I. CAPITAL.

Capital authorized		Purely Mutual.
Capital actually paid up in cash		

II. ASSETS.

Loans secured by mortgages on real estate		$6,490,545 13
Loans on policies assigned to the company as collateral		741 35
Prem. notes and loans, taken for prem's on policies in force		4,296,063 51
Cash value of real estate, unincumbered		319,252 87
Cash market value of bonds and stocks		173,925 00
Cash in office of company		12,185 96
Cash deposited in banks and trust companies		85,528 33
Amount in course of transmission		51,407 30
Interest accrued on cash loans and on bonds		211,159 83
Interest accrued on premium loans and notes		151,555 74
Rents accrued for use of company's property, or under sub-lease		1,941 66
Gross premiums uncollected, not more than three months due, on policies in force Dec. 31, 1872	$387,726 59	
Gross deferred quarterly and semi-annual prem's, on policies in force Dec. 31, 1872	306,653 85	
Total	$694,380 44	
Deducted to reduce the last two items to the net value of the policies	138,876 09	
Net amount deferred and outstanding premiums		555,504 35
Total admitted assets		$12,349,810 98

ITEMS NOT ADMITTED AS ASSETS.

Agents' ledger balances	$67,817 86
Furniture, safes and fixtures	5,000 00
Other items, viz.: bills receivable	11,898 92
Total unadmitted items	$84,716 78

III. LIABILITIES.

Claims for death losses and matured endowments, in process of adjustment, or adjusted and not due	$67,715 19
*Net present value of all the outstanding policies in force on the 31st day of December, 1872, computed according to the American Experience Table of Mortality, with four and one-half per cent. interest	*10,046,014 00
Amount of all unpaid dividends of surplus, or other description of profits due policyholders	6,159 60
Accrued commissions, estimated	5,000 00
Total liabilities	$10,124,888 79

IV. INCOME.

Cash received for premiums on new policies, without deductions	$381,972 98
Cash received for renewal premiums, without deductions	1,500,856 66
Cash received for interest on cash loans	411,152 48
Cash received for interest on bonds owned and dividends on stocks	5,480 50
Cash received for interest on premium notes or loans, and deferred prem's	326,731 86
Cash received for interest on other debts due the company	2,994 30
Rents received for use of company's property, or under sub-lease	9,108 28
Gross amount of notes or other obligations taken on account of new prem's	61,890 32
Gross amount of notes or other obligations taken on account of renewal premiums	994,877 10
Total income	$3,695,064 48

V. EXPENDITURES.

Cash paid for losses and policy claims, and additions thereto	$541,287 95
Cash paid on account of policies lapsed, surrendered or purchased	133,938 64
Cash paid for dividends to policyholders	63,147 63
Cash paid for commissions to agents on first and renewal premiums	267,182 69
Cash paid for salaries and expenses of managers of agencies, and agents	32,218 27
Cash paid for medical examiners' fees, and salaries	19,007 75
Cash paid for salaries and other compensation of officers and employes	76,541 09
Cash paid for United States taxes and revenue stamps, $1,829 40; state and local taxes and fees in state where organized, $8,101 62; taxes, licenses and fees in other states, $27,564 45; total	37,495 47
Cash paid for furniture, safes and fixtures for home or agency offices	2,028 18
Cash paid on any account not itemized aboved, viz: exchange and postage, $16,193 05; advertising, printing and stationery, $27,072 25; general expenses, law, building, etc., $22,348 09; total	65,613 39
Total cash expenditures	$1,238,406 05

PREMIUM-LOAN DISBURSEMENTS.

Amount used in payment of losses and claims	41,148 84
Amount used in purchase of surrendered policies	112,710 09
Amount used in payment of dividends to policyholders	386,223 95
Amount voided by lapse of policies	187,694 07
Total expenditures	$1,966,183 00

VI. PREMIUM-NOTE ACCOUNT.

Premium notes and other premium obligations at beginning of the year		$4,022,521 75
Premium notes and other premium obligations received during the year		1,056,767 42
Total		$5,079,289 17
Deductions during the year as follows:		
Amount used in payment of losses and claims	$41,148 84	
Amount used in purchase of surrendered policies	112,710 09	
Amount used in payment of dividends to policyholders	386,223 95	
Amount voided by lapse of policies	187,694 07	
Amount redeemed by maker in cash, and changes	55,448 71	
Total reduction of premium note account		783,225 66
Balance, note assets at the end of the year		$4,296,063 51

VII. EXHIBIT OF POLICIES.

NUMBER AND AMOUNT OF POLICIES AND ADDITIONS CLASSIFIED.

Policies in force at the beginning of the year:

	No.	Amount.	No.	Amount.
Whole life policies	22,260	$42,324,093 30		
Endowment policies	11,559	19,043,255 60		
Joint lives and survivorships	521	961,338 47		
Short term and irregular policies	9	96,500 12		
			34,349	$62,425,187 49

* The reserve actually held by the company, on the basis of the Actuaries' life table at four per cent. interest, is $10,880,967.

New policies issued during the year:				
Whole life policies	4,494	$10,997,538 97	......	....
Endowment policies	1,095	1,772,730 37	......	....
Joint lives and survivorships	175	319,500 00	......	....
Short term and irregular policies	8	106,500 00	......	....
			5,772	$13,196,279 34
Old policies revived during the year:				
Whole life policies	394	$639,900 00	......	....
Endowment policies	221	337,750 00	......	....
Joint lives and survivorships	8	16,750 00	......	....
			623	994,400 00
Old policies increased during the year:				
Whole life policies	33	$23,612 42	......	....
Joint lives and survivorships	56	92,000 00	......	....
Short term and irregular policies	3	13,150 90	......	....
			92	128,763 32
Additions by dividends during the year:				
Whole life policies	......	$5,720 00	......	....
Endowment policies	......	2,407 00	......	....
Joint lives and survivorships	......	33 00	......	....
Short term and irregular policies	......	34,330 00	......	42,490 00
Totals	......	....	40,836	$76,787,120 05
Deduct policies decreased and ceased to be in force:				
Whole life policies	3,491	$8,320,012 51	......	....
Endowment policies	2,007	3,958,957 54	......	....
Joint lives and survivorships	128	264,088 47	......	....
Short term and irregular policies	5	68,844 17	......	....
			5,631	12,611,902 69
Net numbers and amounts in force Dec. 31, 1872:				
Whole life policies	23,690	$45,670,872 18	......	....
Endowment policies	10,868	17,197,175 33	......	....
Joint lives and survivorships	632	1,125,533 00	......	....
Short term and irregular policies	15	181,636 85	......	....
Totals			35,205	$64,175,217 36

Policies ceased to be in force during the year, with mode of termination:

	Number.	Amount
By death	301	$550,329 94
By expiry	3	58,899 96
By surrender	807	1,204,680 98
By lapse	3,325	5,926,461 81
By change and old policies decreased	238	2,547,307 41
Not taken	957	2,324,294 00
Totals	5,631	$12,611,902 69

Business in the State of Wisconsin during the year 1872:

Policies issued	932	$1,376,731 00
Policies in force at the end of the year	10,296	13,930,054 01
Premiums received		653,218 90
Losses paid		99,523 45

COMPANIES OF OTHER STATES.

ÆTNA LIFE INSURANCE COMPANY.

HARTFORD, CONN.

T. O. ENDERS, *President*. J. L. ENGLISH, *Secretary*.

Attorneys to accept service of process in Wisconsin, F. T. & T. C. DAY, Milwaukee.

[Incorporated in 1820. Commenced business July, 1850.]

I. CAPITAL.

Captal authorized	$150,000 00
Capital actually paid up in cash	108,056 00

II. ASSETS.

Loans secured by deeds of trust or mortgages on real estate		$5,451,001 02
Loans secured by pledge of bonds, stocks or securities, as collateral		594,799 36
Premium notes and loans taken for prem's on policies now in force		5,602,199 61
Cash market value of bonds and stocks owned by the company		4,060,612 79
Cash in office of company		79,798 19
Cash deposited in banks and trust companies		862,863 10
Interest accrued on cash loans and on bonds owned by the company		496,813 25
Gross premiums uncollected, some of which are more than three months due, on policies in force Dec. 31, 1872	$268,144 89	
Gross deferred quarterly and semi-annual prem's, on policies in force Dec. 31, 1872	211,147 84	
Total	$479,292 73	
Deducted to reduce the last two items, to the net value of the policies	119,823 18	
Net amount deferred and outstanding prem's		359,469 55
Due from other companies on account of reinsured risks		47,000 00
Total admitted assets as above		$17,554,551 87

ITEMS NOT ADMITTED AS ASSETS.

Present value of leases owned by the company	$7,539 64
Cash due from agents	30,076 81
Loans on personal security only	24,258 78
Furniture, safes and fixtures	13,693 35
Stockholders' notes (endorsed)	46,944 00
Total unadmitted items	$122,512 08

III. LIABILITIES.

Claims for death losses due and unpaid	$69,961 16
Claims for death losses and matured endowments, in process of adjustment, or adjusted and not due	329,109 00
Claims for death losses and other policy claims resisted by the company	102,168 00
Net present value of all the outstanding policies in force on the 31st day of December, 1872, computed according to the Combined Experience Table of Mortality, with four per cent. interest	15,769,950 00
Amount of all unpaid dividends of surplus, or other description of profits due policyholders	486,088 33
Printing and other bills unpaid	2,706 25
Total liabilities as to policyholders	$16,759,987 74

IV. INCOME.

Cash received for premiums on new policies and renewal prem's, without deductions	$3,578,967 34
Cash received for all other premiums	11,089 73
Cash premiums from other companies for reinsuring their risks	696 10

Cash other than prem's rec'd from co's for assuming or reinsuring their risks	$36,608 59
Cash received for interest on cash loans	547,094 93
Cash received for interest on bonds owned and dividends on stocks, and gain in securities	272,229 08
Cash received for interest on premium notes or loans	312,084 87
Cash received for interest on other debts due the company	36,145 23
Discount on claims paid in advance	2,553 45
Cash from other companies for losses or claims on policies reinsured	60,705 00
Cash income from other sources	22,268 75
Gross amount of notes or other obligations taken on account of renewal pr'ms	1,160,552 86
Total income	$6,040,945 92

V. EXPENDITURES.

Cash paid for the company's own losses and and policy claims and additions thereto	$1,293,267 93
Cash paid on account of policies lapsed, surrendered or purchased	621,928 96
Cash paid for dividends to policyholders	286,652 86
Cash paid for dividends to stockholders	45,064 00
Cash paid for premiums (less rebate or commissions) to other companies for policies reinsured	105,358 52
Cash paid for commissions to agents on first and renewal premiums	397,617 53
Cash paid for salaries and expenses of managers of agencies, and agents	11,767 26
Cash paid for medical examiners' fees	25,483 15
Cash paid for salaries and other compensation of officers and employes	64,916 35
Cash paid for United States taxes and revenue stamps, $3,109 15; state and local taxes in state where organized, $59,760 63; taxes, licenses and fees in other states, $40,013 49; of which the sum of $350 was paid in the state of Wisconsin; total	108,283 97
Cash paid for rents	11,116 20
Cash paid on any account not itemized above, viz: express, $1,776 74; telegrams, $408 57; postage, $11,495 48; advertising, $3,436 35; printing, $4,528 21; stationery, $3,115 67; legal expenses, $2,085 38; supplies, $7,218 30; incidentals, $1,481 18; state valuations, $3,105 25; profit and loss, $3,565 15; total	42,211 28
Total cash expenditures	$3,008,619 28

PREMIUM-LOAN DISBURSEMENTS.

Amount used in payment of losses and claims	114,405 97
Amount used in purchase of surrendered policies	550,693 29
Amount used in payment of dividends to policyholders	765,368 27
Amount voided by lapse of policies, and redeemed in cash	203,270 53
Total expenditures	$4,642,357 34

VI. PREMIUM-NOTE ACCOUNT.

Premium notes and other premium obligations at beginning of the year		$6,075,384 81
Premium notes and other premium obligations received during the year		1,160,552 86
Total		$7,235,937 67
Deductions during the year as follows:		
Amount used in payment of losses and claims	$114,405 97	
Amount used in purchase of surrendered policies	550,693 29	
Amount used in payment of dividends to policyholders	765,368 27	
Amount voided by lapse of policies	194,879 85	
Amount redeemed by maker in cash	8,390 68	
Total reduction of premium note account		1,633,738 06
Balance, note assets at the end of the year		$5,602,199 61

VII. EXHIBIT OF POLICIES.

NUMBER AND AMOUNT OF POLICES AND ADDITIONS CLASSIFIED.

	Number.	Amount.	Number.	Amount.
Policies in force at the end of the year:				
Whole life policies	28,415	$69,509,262 50		
Endowment policies	18,442	29,657,539 50		
Joint lives and survivorships	141	308,750 00		
Short term and irregular policies	655	1,849,310 00		
			47,653	$101,324,862 00
New policies issued during the year:				
Whole life policies	5,709	$11,274,367 00		
Endowment policies	2,741	3,086,552 00		
Short term and irregular policies	819	914,387 00		
			8,769	15,275,306 00
Old policies revived during the year:				
Whole life policies	12	$35,053 00		
Endowment policies	9	15,571 00		
Short term and irregular policies	1	1,000 00		
			22	51,624 00

Old policies increased during the year:

Whole life policies	......	$7,357 00	......	....
			......	$7,357 00
Totals	......	....	56,444	$116,659,149 00

Deduct policies decreased and ceased to be in force:

Whole life policies	3,884	$10,883,988 50	......	....
Endowment policies	2,354	4,648,238 00	......	....
Joint lives and survivorships	17	40,750 00	......	....
Short term and irregular policies	161	468,300	......	....
			6,416	16,041,373 50

Net numbers and amounts in force December 31st, 1872:

Whole life policies	30,252	$69,942,051 00	......	....
Endowment policies	18,838	28,111,324 50	......	....
Join lives and survivorships	124	268,000 00	......	....
Short term and irregular policies	814	2,296,397 00	......	....
Totals			50,028	$100,617,772 50

Policies ceased to be in force during the year, with mode of termination:

	Number.	Amount.
By death	586	$1,501,812 00
By expiry	15	52,500 00
By surrender	2,586	6,389,654 00
By lapse	2,128	5,706,037 50
Not taken	1,101	2,391,373 00
Totals	6,416	$16,041,376 50

Business in the State of Wisconsin during the year 1872:

Policies issued	192	$219,101 00
Policies in force at the end of the year	* 989	1,601,284 46
Premiums received	......	91,599 33
Losses paid	......	17,500 00

BERKSHIRE LIFE INSURANCE COMPANY.

PITTSFIELD, MASS.

THOMAS F. PLUNKETT, *President.* JAMES W. HULL, *Secretary.*

Attorney to accept service of process in Wisconsin. HENRY MARSHALL, Milwaukee.

[Incorporated, May, 1851. Commenced Business, September 3, 1851.]

I. CAPITAL.

Capital authorized	$100,000 00
Capital actually paid up in cash, $100,000, of which $74,500 is redeemed, leaving outstanding	25,500 00

II. ASSETS.

Loans secured by mortgages on real estate		$999,528 96
Loans secured by pledge of bonds, stocks or securities, as collateral		22,700 00
Premium notes and loans taken for premiums, on policies now in force		200,345 50
Cash value of real estate owned by the company, unincumbered		189,782 50
Cash market value of bonds and stocks owned by the company		630,680 00
Cash in office of company		550 55
Cash deposited in banks and trust companies		48,215 29
Interest accrued on cash loans and on bonds owned by the company		28,638 65
Interest accrued on premium loans and notes		7,387 11
Gross premiums uncollected, not more than three months due, on policies in force December 31, 1872	$24,197 82	....
Gross deferred quarterly and semi-annual premiums, on policies in force December 31, 1872	41,413 45	....
Total	$65,611 27	....
Deducted to reduce the last two items, to the net value of the policies	6,561 13	....
Net amount deferred and outstanding premiums		59,050 14
Total admitted assets		$2,181,628 70

ITEMS NOT ADMITTED AS ASSETS.

Cash in hands of officers or agents due the company	$12,669 22
Loans on personal security only	3,665 08
Furniture, safes and fixtures	3,000 00
Total unadmitted items	$19,334 25

III. LIABILITIES.

Claims for death losses and matured endowments, in process of adjustment, or adjusted and not due	$41,754 00
Claims for death losses and policy claims resisted by the company	3,000 00
Net present value of all the outstanding policies in force on the 31st day of December, 1872, computed according to the Combined Experience Table of Mortality, with four per cent. interest	2,035,134 21
Amount of all unpaid dividends of surplus, due policyholders	3,001 48
Amount of any other liability, viz.: ledger balances	38 32
Total liabilities as to policyholders	$2,082,928 01

IV. INCOME.

Cash received for premiums on new policies, without deductions	$78,606 55
Cash received for renewal premiums, without deductions	402,947 38
Cash premiums from other companies for reinsuring their risks	3,658 10
Cash received for interest on cash loans	55,699 48
Cash received for interest on bonds owned and dividends on stocks	41,501 45
Cash received for interest on premium notes or loans	11,524 05
Rents received for use of company's property, or under sub-lease	9,060 21
Discount on claims paid in advance	390 37
Gross amount of notes or other obligations taken for new premiums	3,385 00
Gross amount of notes or other obligations taken for renewal premiums	43,910 10
Gross amount of notes or other obligations taken for reinsurance	1,569 00
Total income	$658,251 69

V. EXPENDITURES.

Cash paid for the company's own losses and claims, and additions thereto	$78,136 9
Cash paid on account of policies lapsed, surrendered or purchased	83,877 68
Cash paid for dividends to policyholders	49,559 87
Cash paid for dividends to stockholders	1,785 00
Cash paid for premiums to other companies for policies reinsured	4,844 81
Cash paid for commissions to agents on first premiums	16,099 13
Cash paid for commissions to agents on renewal premiums	30,278 72
Cash paid for salaries and expenses of managers of agencies, and agents	2,441 15
Cash paid for medical examiners' fees	1,936 00
Cash paid for salaries and other compensation of officers and employes	9,989 68
Cash paid for United States taxes and revenue stamps, $120 48; state and local taxes in state where organized, $3,478 04; taxes, licenses and fees in other states, $3,559 25; total	7,187 16
Cash paid for rents	7,104 58
Cash paid on any account not itemized above, viz: printing, $1,952 47; advertising, $3,995 38; postage, $969 13; express, $170 14; stationery and incidentals, $5,285 45; total	12,392 57
Total cash expenditures	$250,563 23

PREMIUM-LOAN DISBURSEMENTS.

Amount used in payment of losses and claims	1,513 01
Amount used in payment of dividends to policyholders	10,452 18
Amount voided by lapse of policies	2,547 27
Total expenditures	$265,075 69

VI. PREMIUM-NOTE ACCOUNT.

Premium notes and other prem. obligations at beginning of the year		$170,914 53
Premium notes and other prem. obligations received during the year		48,864 10
Total		$219,778 63
Deductions during the year as follows:		
Amount used in payment of losses and claims	$1,513 01	
Amount used in payment of dividends to policyholders	10,452 18	
Amount voided by lapse of policies	2,547 27	
Amount redeemed by maker, in cash	5,020 67	
Total reduction of premium note account		19,533 13
Balance, note assets at end of the year		$200,245 50

VII. EXHIBIT OF POLICIES.

NUMBER AND AMOUNT OF POLICIES AND ADDITIONS CLASSIFIED.

	No.	Amount.
Policies in force at the beginning of the year	4,451	$10,149,905
New policies issued during the year	651	1,726,930
Old policies revived during the year	116	278,200
Additions by dividends during the year	......	9,537
Totals	5,218	$12,164,572
Deduct policies decreased and ceased to be in force	739	1,639,159
Totals at the end of the year	4,479	$10,525,413
Deduct policies reinsured	10	75,000
Net numbers and amounts in force, December 31, 1872	4,469	$10,450,413

Policies ceased to be in force during the year, with mode of termination:

	No.	Amount.
By death	46	$109,404
By surrender	76	185,830
By lapse	503	1,068,350
Not taken	114	275,575
Totals	739	$1,639,159

Business in the State of Wisconsin, during the year 1872:

Policies issued	64	$78,250 00
Premiums received	......	5,231 87

BROOKLYN LIFE INSURANCE COMPANY.

New York.

C. W. BOUCK, *President.* WILLIAM M. COLE, *Secretary.*

Attorney to accept service of process in Wisconsin, William Wright, Sparta.

[Incorporated July, 1864. Commenced business July, 1864.]

I. CAPITAL.

Capital authorized	$125,000 00
Capital actually paid up in cash	125,000 00

II. ASSETS.

Loans secured by deeds of trust or mortgages on real estate		$927,884 67
Loans secured by pledge of bonds, stocks or securities as collateral		24,200 00
Premium notes and loans, taken for premiums on policies now in force		486,528 60
Cash market value of bonds and stocks owned by the company		240,895 00
Cash in office of company		25,707 27
Cash deposited in banks and trust companies		99,070 10
Loans on policies, held as collaterals		6,576 78
Interest accrued on cash loans and on bonds owned by the company		23,500 23
Interest accrued on premium loans and notes		17,705 72
Gross deferred quarterly and semi-annual premiums, on policies in force Dec. 31, 1872	$60,938 26	....
Deduct to reduce the last item to the net value of the policies	4,783 00	....
Net amount deferred and outstanding premiums		56,155 26
Total admitted assets		$1,908,173 63

III. LIABILITIES.

Claims for death losses and matured endowments, in process of adjustment, or adjusted and not due	$17,500 00
Claims for death losses and other policy claims resisted by the company	1,500 00
Net present value of all the outstanding policies in force on the 31st day of December, 1872, computed according to the American Experience Table of Mortality, with four and one-half per cent. interest	1,690,785 00
Total liabilities as to policyholders	$1,709,785 00

IV. INCOME.

Cash received for premiums on new policies, without deductions	$100,742 50
Cash received for renewal premiums, without deductions	430,408 71
Cash received for all other premiums—extra	1,486 11
Cash premiums from other companies for reinsuring their risks	7,481 72
Cash received for interest on cash loans	56,778 96
Cash received for interest on bonds owned and dividends on stocks	11,695 07
Cash received for interest on premium notes or loans	32,599 93
Cash from other companies for losses on policies reinsured	5,000 00
Cash income from other sources, viz: prem. on gold	4,015 08
Gross amount of notes or other obligations taken for renewal premiums	75,389 63
Total income	$725,519 66

V. EXPENDITURES.

Cash paid for the company's own losses and claims, and additions thereto	$124,183 23
Cash paid to other companies for losses or claims on their policies reinsured	5,568 23
Cash paid on account of policies lapsed, surrendered or purchased	38,826 97
Cash paid for dividends to policyholders	61,610 37
Cash paid for dividends to stockholders	16,250 00
Cash paid for premiums to other companies for policies reinsured	7,497 16
Cash paid for commissions to agents on first premiums	18,444 41
Cash paid for commissions to agents on renewal premiums	24,406 46
Cash paid for salaries and expenses of managers of agencies, and agents	14,961 16
Cash paid for medical examiners' fees	7,193 39
Cash paid for salaries and other compensation of officers and employes	25,918 45
Cash paid for taxes, revenue stamps, and state licenses and fees	6,458 40
Cash paid for rents of home office and all agencies	12,036 47
Cash paid for commuting commissions	26,702 43
Cash paid for furniture, safes and fixtures for home and agency offices	4,127 98
Cash paid on any account not itemized above, viz: printing and advertising, $18,651 04; expense ac'ct, $18,162 88; law expenses, $4,318 61; interest on capital, $8,750; total	49,882 03
Total cash expenditures	$444,067 14

PREMIUM-LOAN DISBURSEMENTS.

Amount used in payment of losses and claims	9,940 49
Amount used in purchase of surrendered policies	59,559 98
Total expenditures	$513,567 61

VI. PREMIUM-NOTE ACCOUNT.

Premium notes and other prem. obligations at beginning of the year		$487,765 39
Premium notes and other prem. obligations received during the year		75,389 63
Total		$563,155 02
Deductions during the year as follows:		
Amount used in payment of losses and claims	$9,940 49	
Amount used in purchase of surrendered policies	59,559 98	
Amount redeemed by maker in cash	7,125 95	
Total reduction of premium note account		76,626 42
Balance, note assets at end of the year		$486,528 60

VII. EXHIBIT OF POLICIES.

NUMBER AND AMOUNT OF POLICIES AND ADDITIONS CLASSIFIED.

	Number.	Amount.	Number.	Amount.
Policies in force at the beginning of the year:				
Whole life policies	3,131	$8,246,220		
Endowment policies	1,185	3,170,088		
Short term and irregular policies	5	14,000		
			4,321	$11,430,308
New policies issued during the year:				
Whole life policies	1,062	$2,691,453		
Endowment policies	297	405,974		
Short term and irregular policies	13	43,000		
			1,372	3,140,427
Old policies revived during the year:				
Whole life policies	164	$449,800		
Endowment policies	63	174,500		
Short term and irregular policies	2	3,500		
			229	627,800
Old policies increased during the year:				
Whole life policies	3	$17,000		
Endowment policies		1,000		
			3	18,000

Additions by dividends during the year:

Whole life policies	......	$16,438	......	....
Endowment policies	......	8,910	......	....
			......	$25,348
Totals			5,825	$14,941,878

Deduct policies decreased and ceased to be in force:

Whole life policies	944	$2,542,450	......	....
Endowment policies	280	676,970	......	....
Short term and irregular policies	12	29,500	......	....
			1,236	3,248,920

Net numbers and amounts in force December 31st, 1872:

Whole life policies	3,386	$8,578,461	......	....
Endowment policies	1,195	3,083,497	......	....
Short term and irregular policies	8	31,000	......	....
Totals			4,589	$11,692,958

Policies ceased to be in force during the year, with mode of termination:

	Number.	Amount.
By death	57	$159,750
By expiry	1	2,500
By surrender	276	949,200
By lapse	606	1,297,550
By change and old policies decreased	3	58,420
Not taken	293	781,500
Totals	1,236	$3,248,920

Business in the State of Wisconsin during the year 1872:

Losses paid	$4,290

CHARTER OAK LIFE INSURANCE COMPANY.

HARTFORD, CONN.

JAS. C. WALKLEY, *President.* HALSEY STEVENS, *Secretary.*

Attorney to accept service of process in Wisconsin, WILSON GRAHAM, Milwaukee.

[Incorporated, May, 1850. Commenced business, Oct., 1850.]

I. CAPITAL.

Capital authorized	$200,000 00
Capital actually paid up in cash	200,000 00

II. ASSETS.

Loans secured by deeds of trust or mortgages on real estate		$4,199,782 92
Loans secured by pledge of bonds, stocks, or securities, as collateral		1,107,237 83
Premium notes and loans, taken for prem's, on policies now in force		3,242,841 12
Cash value of real estate owned by the company, unincumbered		844,380 54
Cash market value of bonds and stocks owned by the company		395,775 00
Cash in office of company		204,411 45
Cash deposited in banks and trust companies		12,994 84
Postage and revenue stamps		1,684 65
Interest accrued on cash loans and on bonds owned by the company		275,650 00
Rents accrued for use of company's property, or under sub-lease		4,583 33
Gross premiums uncollected, not more than three months due, on policies in force December 31, 1872	$112,042 47	....
Gross deferred quarterly and semi-annual premiums, on policies in force December 31, 1872	182,919 92	....
Total	$294,962 39	....
Deducted to reduce the last two items, to the net value of the policies	28,680 40	....
Net amount deferred and outstanding prem's		266,281 99
Total admitted assets		$10,655,528 67

ITEMS NOT ADMITTED AS ASSETS.

Value of agency supplies, printed matter and stationery on hand	$5,000 00
Loans on personal security only	130,313 94
Furniture, safes and fixtures	9,254 32
Total unadmitted items	$144,568 26

III. LIABILITIES.

Claims for death losses and matured endowments, in process of adjustment, or adjusted and not due	$212,817 00
Claims for death losses and other policy claims resisted by the company	22,500 00
Net present value of all the outstanding policies in force on the 31st day of December, 1872, computed according to the Combined Experience Table of Mortality, with four per cent. interest	10,344,286 00
Total liabilities as to policyholders	$10,579,603 00

IV. INCOME.

Cash received for premiums on new policies, without deductions	$442,154 73
Cash received for renewal premiums, without deductions	3,191,279 58
Cash received for int. on cash loans, bonds owned and dividends on stocks	304,208 84
Cash received for interest on premium notes or loans	135,839 07
Rents received for use of company's property, or under sub-lease	29,434 38
Total income	$4,102,916 60

V. EXPENDITURES.

Cash paid for the company's losses and claims, and additions thereto	$742,068 53
Cash paid for matured endowment	3,500 00
Cash paid on account of policies lapsed, surrendered or purchased	754,970 36
Cash paid for dividends to policyholders	789,710 97
Cash paid for dividends to stockholders	16,000 00
Cash paid for commissions to agents on first premiums	78,000 00
Cash paid for commissions to agents on renewal premiums	278,682 10
Cash paid for salaries and expenses of managers of agencies	6,500 00
Cash paid for medical examiners' fees	15,057 36
Cash paid for salaries and other compensation of officers and employes	44,089 52
Cash paid for taxes, revenue stamps and state licenses and fees	64,294 48
Cash paid for furniture, safes and fixtures for home or agency offices	3,254 32
Cash paid for all other expenses not above specified	81,326 73
Total expenditures	$2,872,364 37

VI. EXHIBIT OF POLICIES.

NUMBER AND AMOUNT OF POLICIES AND ADDITIONS CLASSIFIED.

	No.	Amount.	No.	Amount.
Policies in force at the beginning of the year:				
Whole life policies	17,288	$46,987,913 00		
Endowment policies	6,550	12,840,001 00		
Joint lives and survivorships	1,599	1,785,662 00		
Short term and irregular policies	12	20,500 00		
			25,449	$61,634,076 00
New policies issued during the year:				
Whole life policies	2,897	$6,975,081 00		
Endowment policies	941	1,512,321 00		
Joint lives and survivorships	631	608,435 00		
Short term and irregular policies	579	1,108,009 00		
			5,048	10,203,846 00
Old policies revived during the year:				
Whole life policies	584	$1,589,230 00		
Endowment policies	195	371,115 00		
Joint lives and survivorships	102	82,400 00		
			881	2,042,745 00
Totals			31,378	$73,880,667 00
Deduct policies decreased and ceased to be in force:				
Whole life policies	2,686	$7,199,035 00		
Endowment policies	1,276	2,483,455 00		
Joint lives and survivorships	497	525,740 00		
Short term and irregular policies	163	244,749 00		
			4,622	10,452,979 00

Net numbers and amounts in force December 31st, 1872:

Whole life policies	18,083	$48,358,189 00	......	....
Endowment policies	6,410	12,289,982 00	......	....
Joint lives and survivorships	1,835	1,950,757 00	......	....
Short term and irregular policies	428	888,760 00	......	....
Totals			26,756	$63,487,688 00

Policies ceased to be in force during the year, with mode of termination:

	Number.	Amount.
By death	251	$707,077 00
By expiry	3	2,500 00
By surrender	884	2,263,647 00
By lapse	2,304	5,382,130 00
Not taken	1,180	2,097,625 00
Totals	4,622	$10,452,979 00

Business in the state of Wisconsin during the year 1872:

Policies issued	116	$138,048 00
Policies in force at the end of the year	721	978,745 00
Premiums received	......	51,240 12
Losses paid	......	18,000 00

CHICAGO LIFE INSURANCE COMPANY.

CHICAGO, ILL.

WILLIAM F. TUCKER, *President.* JOHN W. CLAPP, *Secretary.*

Attorney to accept service of process in Wisconsin, SAM'L M. PARISH, Delavan.

[Incorporated February 1867. Commenced business February 1867.]

I. CAPITAL.

Capital authorized	$500,000 00
Capital actually paid up in cash	125,000 00

II. ASSETS.

Loans secured by deeds of trust or mortgages on real estate		$127,459 99
Loans secured by pledge of bonds, stocks, or securities, as collateral		54,150 00
Premium notes and loans, taken for premiums, on policies now in force		13,183 07
Cash in office of company		2,389 06
Cash deposited in banks and trust companies		14,014 86
Postage and revenue stamps		15 00
Interest accrued on cash loans and on bonds owned by the company		1,263 42
Interest accrued on premium loans and notes		489 48
Gross premiums uncollected, not more than three months due, on policies in force December 31, 1872	$19,753 62	....
Gross deferred quarterly and semi-annual premiums, on policies in force December 31, 1872	24,654 80	....
Total	$44,408 42	....
Deducted to reduce the last two items, to the net value of the policies	3,330 63	....
Net amount deferred and outstanding premiums		41,077 79
Total admitted assets		$253,992 62

ITEMS NOT ADMITTED AS ASSETS.

Furniture, safes and fixtures, 50 per cent. of cost	$575 11
Total unadmitted items	$575 11

III. LIABILITIES.

Claims for death losses and matured endowments, in process of adjustment, or adjusted and not due	$8,000 00
Net present value of all the outstanding policies in force on the 31st day of December, 1872, computed according to the American Experience Table of Mortality, with four and one-half per cent. interest	212,731 20
Total liabilities as to policyholders	$220,731 20

IV. INCOME.

Cash received for premiums on new policies, without deductions	$69,729 17
Cash received for renewal premiums without deductions	94,182 96
Cash received for interest on bonds owned and dividends on stocks	15,019 35
Total income	$178,931 48

V. EXPENDITURES.

Cash paid for the company's losses and claims, and additions thereto	$25,000 00
Cash paid on account of policies lapsed, surrendered or purchased	26,575 52
Cash paid for dividends to policyholders	19,274 60
Cash paid for dividends to stockholders	10,829 95
Cash paid for premiums to other companies for policies reinsured	1,444 16
Cash paid for commissions to agents on first premiums	10,458 00
Cash paid for commissions to agents on renewal premiums	2,586 83
Cash paid for salaries and expenses of managers of agencies, and agents	15,294 70
Cash paid for medical examiners' fees	5,802 53
Cash paid for salaries and other compensation of officers and employes	12,453 29
Cash paid for taxes, revenue stamps and state licenses and fees	1,658 49
Cash paid for rents	1,462 58
Cash paid for furniture, safes and fixtures for home or agency offices	1,150 22
Cash paid on any account not itemized above, viz: printing, $3,269 54; advertising, $3,592 76; postage, $1,403 41; exchange, $94 49; stationery, $1,047 19; freight, $235 33; sundry office expenses, $1,446 12; total	11,088 84
Total expenditures	$144,519 13

VI. EXHIBIT OF POLICIES.

NUMBER AND AMOUNT OF POLICIES AND ADDITIONS CLASSIFIED.

	No.	Amount.	No.	Amount.
Policies in force at the beginning of the year:				
Whole life policies	1,797	$2,838,952 06		
Endowment policies	497	433,350 94		
			2,294	$3,272,303 00
New policies issued during the year:				
Whole life policies	1,421	$1,883,177 00		
Endowment policies	378	362,553 00		
Short term and irregular policies	1	2,500 00		
			1,800	2,248,230 00
Totals			4,094	$5,520,533 00
Deduct policies decreased and ceased to be in force:				
Whole life policies	835	$1,221,836 98		
Endowment policies	269	258,057 00		
			1,104	1,479,888 98
Totals at the end of the year:				
Whole life policies	2,383	$3,500,302 13		
Endowment policies	606	537,846 94		
Short term and irregular policies	1	2,500 00		
			2,990	$4,040,649 07
Deduct policies reinsured:				
Whole life policies				78,500 00
Net numbers and amounts in force, December 31, 1872:				
Whole life policies	2,383	$3,421,802 13		
Endowment policies	606	537,846 94		
Short terms and irregular policies	1	2,500 00		
Total			2,990	$3,962,149 07

Policies ceased to be in force during the year, with mode of termination:

	No.	Amount.
By death	21	$25,000 00
By surrender	152	205,674 00
By lapse	760	1,025,709 98
Not taken	171	223,500 00
Totals	1,104	$1,479,888 98

Business in the State of Wisconsin, during the year 1872:

Policies issued	714	$841,000 00
Policies in force at the end of the year	963	1,106,363 00
Premiums received		37,108 98
Losses paid		2,000 00

CONNECTICUT MUTUAL LIFE INSURANCE COMPANY.

HARFORD, CONN.

JAMES GOODWIN, *President*. JACOB L. GREENE, *Secretary*.

Attorney to accept service of process in Wisconsin, H. L. PAGE, Milwaukee.

[Incorporated, July 15th, 1846. Commenced business, Dec. 15th, 1846.]

I. CAPITAL.

Capital authorized	Mutual.
Capital actually paid up in cash	

II. ASSETS.

Loans secured by deeds of trust or mortgages on real estate		$17,652,992 32
Loans secured by pledge of bonds, stocks, or securities, as collateral		298,508 28
Premium notes and loans, taken for premiums, on policies now in force		8,800,087 92
Cost of real estate owned by the company, unincumbered		1,139,972 47
Cost of bonds and stocks owned by the company		4,687,636 80
Cash in office of company		26,782 28
Cash deposited in banks and trust companies		1,084,350 58
Agents' balances		89,886 14
Interest accrued on cash loans and on bonds owned by the company		667,579 00
Interest accrued on premium loans and notes		308,001 29
Gross premiums uncollected, not more than three months due, on policies in force December 31, 1872	$57,019 07	
Gross deferred quarterly and semi-annual premiums, on policies in force December 31, 1872	42,643 37	
Total	$99,662 44	
Deducted to reduce the last two items, to the net value of the policies	33,220 81	
Net amount deferred and outstanding prem's		66,441 63
Present market value of bonds and stocks over cost		214,457 52
Total admitted assets		$34,936,141 18

III. LIABILITIES.

Claims for death losses due and unpaid, awaiting completion of proofs	$176,200 00
Claims for death losses and matured endowments, in process of adjustment, or adjusted and not due	475,353 00
Claims for death losses and other policy claims resisted by the company	95,500 00
Net present value of all the outstanding policies in force on the 31st day of December, 1872, computed according to the Combined Experience Table of Mortality, with four per cent. interest	29,128,309 00
Total liabilities as to policyholders	$29,875,362 00

IV. INCOME.

Cash received for premiums on new policies without deductions	$552,275 26
Cash received for renewal premiums without deductions	6,927,609 12
Cash received for all other premiums	7,848 45
Cash received for interest on cash loans	1,036,259 74
Cash received for interest on bonds owned and dividends on stocks	418,322 92
Cash received for interest on premium notes and loans	574,523 27
Discount on claims paid in advance	10,247 28
Gross amount of notes or other obligations taken for new prem's	54,801 00
Gross amount of notes or other obligations taken for renewal prem's	172,534 00
Total income	$9,754,420 99

V. EXPENDITURES.

Cash paid for the company's losses and claims, and additions thereto	$2,191,991 46
Cash paid on account of policies lapsed, surrendered or purchased	257,817 39
Cash paid for dividends to policyholders	2,638,897 25
Cash paid for commisions to agents on first premiums	106,168 14
Cash paid for commissions to agents on renewal premiums	480,284 98
Cash paid for medical examiners' fees	15,142 09
Cash paid for salaries and other compensation of officers and employes	63,496 36
Cash paid for taxes, revenue stamps, state licenses and fees	219,647 06
Cash paid for furniture, safes and fixtures for home or agency offices	16,786 15
Cash paid on any account not itemized above, viz: printing, stationery, rent, advertising, postage, exchange, profit and loss, total	121,997 20
Total cash expenditures	$6,112,128 08

PREMIUM-LOAN DISBURSEMENTS.

Amount used in payment of losses and claims	$20,000 10
Amount used in purchase of surrendered policies	314,087 65
Amount used in payment of dividends to policyholders	267,315 84
Amount voided by lapse of policies	106,904 87
Total expenditures	$6,820,436 54

VI. PREMIUM-NOTE ACCOUNT.

Premium notes and other premium obligations at beginning of the year		$9,285,065 38
Premium notes and other premium obligations received during the year		227,335 00
Total		$9,512,400 38
Deductions during the year as follows:		
Amount used in payment of losses and claims	$20,000 10	
Amount used in purchase of surrendered policies	314,087 65	
Amount used in payment of dividends to policyholders	267,315 84	
Amount voided by lapse of policies	106,904 87	
Amount redeemed by maker in cash	4,054 00	
Total reduction of premium note account		712,962 46
Balance, note assets at end of the year		$8,800,067 92

VII. EXHIBIT OF POLICIES.

NUMBER AND AMOUNT OF POLICIES AND ADDITIONS CLASSIFIED.

	Number.	Amount.	Number.	Amount.
Policies in force at the beginning of the year:				
Whole life policies	52,610	$157,634,976		
Endowment policies	8,499	22,205,084		
Joint lives and survivorships	1,320	2,892,936		
Short term and irregular policies	29	52,300		
			62,458	$182,785,296 00
New policies issued during the year:				
Whole life policies	4,156	$11,459,720		
Endowment policies	856	1,518,556		
Joint lives and survivorships	46	9,389		
Short term and irregular policies	3	18,000		
			5,061	13,005,665 00
Old policies revived during the year:				
Whole life policies	321	$1,133,625		
Endowment policies	114	280,700		
Joint lives and survivorships	23	65,500		
			458	1,479,825 00
Old policies increased during the year:				
Whole life policies		$13,600		
Endowment policies	1	3,000		
			1	16,600 00
Totals			67,978	$197,287,386 00
Deduct policies decreased and ceased to be in force:				
Whole life policies	4,016	$12,649,405		
Endowment policies	973	2,500,786		
Joint lives and survivorships	147	369,295		
Short term and irregular policies	16	41,000		
			5,152	15,560,486 00
Net numbers and amounts in force December 31st, 1872:				
Whole life policies	53,071	$157,592,516		
Endowment policies	8,597	21,506,504		
Joint lives and survivorships	1,142	2,596,520		
Short term and irregular policies	16	29,300		
Totals			62,826	$181,726,840 00

Policies ceased to be in force during the year, with mode of termination:

	No.	Amount.
By death	814	$2,402,774 00
By expiry	12	31,000 00
By surrender	1,534	4,666,127 00
By lapse	2,256	6,593,565 00
By change and old policies decreased		504,920 00
Not taken	536	1,362,100 00
Totals	5,152	$15,560,486 00

Business in the state of Wisconsin during the year 1872:

Policies issued	67	$88,684 00
Policies in force at the end of the year	1,118	1,782,284 00
Premiums received	......	110,419 75
Losses paid	......	82,050 00

CONTINENTAL LIFE INSURANCE COMPANY.

NEW YORK.

L. W. FROST, *President*. J. P. ROGERS, *Secretary*.

Attorney to accept service of process in Wisconsin, D. S. BURNHAM, Milwaukee.

[Incorporated March 13th, 1866. Commenced business May 10th, 1866.]

I. CAPITAL.

Capital authorized	$100,000 00
Capital actually paid up in cash	100,000 00

II. ASSETS.

Loans secured by deeds of trust or mortgages on real estate		$880,950 00
Loans secured by pledge of bonds, stocks, or other securities, as collateral		108,880 00
Premium notes and loans, taken for premiums, on policies now in force		2,012,278 70
Cash value of real estate owned by the company, unincumbered		810,000 00
Cash market value of bonds and stocks owned by the company		552,796 87
Cash in office of company		1,282 18
Cash deposited in banks and trust companies		320,318 87
Interest accrued on cash loans and on bonds owned by the company		17,682 19
Interest accrued on premium loans and notes		52,089 70
Rents accrued for use of company's property, or under sub-lease		5,905 66
Gross premiums uncollected, not more than three months due, on policies in force December 31, 1872	$424,302 14	....
Gross deferred quarterly and semi-annual premiums, on policies in force December 31, 1872	873,421 19	....
Total	$1,297,723 33	....
Deducted to reduce the last two items, to the net value of the policies	116,795 10	....
Net amount deferred and outstanding prem's		1,180,928 23
Total admitted assets		$5,942,892 40

ITEMS NOT ADMITTED AS ASSETS.

Am't invested in commuting commissions; or renewal com's purchased	$349,444 76
Cash in hands of officers or agents due the company	74,628 96
Value of agency supplies, printed matter and stationery on hand	8,500 00
Furniture, safes and fixtures	33,180 47
Total unadmitted items	$465,754 21

III. LIABILITIES.

Claims for death losses and matured endowments, in process of adjustment, or adjusted and not due	$134,700 00
Claims for death losses and other policy claims resisted by the company	15,000 00
Net present value of all the outstanding policies in force on the 31st day of December, 1872, computed according to the American Experience Table of Mortality, with four and one-half per cent. interest	5,270,367 00
Total liabilities as to policyholders	$5,420,067 00

IV. INCOME.

Cash rec'd for prem's on new policies and renewal prem's, without deductions.	$1,748,443 68
Cash premiums from other companies for reinsuring their risks	16,958 77
Cash received from other companies for assuming their risks	295,695 03
Cash received for interest on cash loans	7,001 04
Cash received for interest on bonds owned and dividends on stocks	55,490 82
Cash received for interest on premium notes or loans	129,481 65
Cash received for interest on other debts due the company	6,881 74
Rents received for use of company's property, or under sub-lease	31,495 84
Discount on claims paid in advance	642 22
Cash from other companies for losses or claims on policies reinsured.	18,250 00

Gross am't of notes or other obligations taken for new and renewal prem's..	$629,614 28
Gross am't of notes or other obligations received from companies for assuming or reinsuring their risks	132,577 02
Total income	$3,082,527 78

V. EXPENDITURES.

Cash paid for the company's own losses and claims, and additions thereto	$520,731 11
Cash paid to other companies for losses or claims on their policies reinsured by this company	15,000 00
Cash paid to annuitants	2,828 50
Cash paid on account of policies lapsed, surrendered or purchased	201,777 67
Cash paid for dividends to policyholders	94,234 65
Cash paid for dividends to stockholders	7,000 00
Cash paid for premiums to other companies for policies reinsured	12,429 05
Cash paid for commissions to agents on first and renewal premiums	201,412 55
Cash paid for salaries and expenses of managers of agencies, and agents	53,852 18
Cash paid for medical examiners' fees	31,616 28
Cash paid for salaries and other compensation of officers and employes	66,585 36
Cash paid for United States taxes and revenue stamps, $1,820.66; state and local taxes in state where organized, $9,680.33; taxes, licenses and fees in other states, $18,466.89; total	29,967 88
Cash paid for rents, at agencies	23,250 00
Cash paid for commuting commissions	117,709 74
Cash paid for furniture, safes and fixtures for home or agency offices	3,594 52
Cash paid on any account not itemized above, viz.: advertising and stationery, $35,852.65; fire insurance, $1,827.69; counsel fees, $4,149.71; postage, $1,690.20; agency expenses, $43,217.08; total	86,737 33
Total cash expenditures	$1,499,016 80

PREMIUM-LOAN DISBURSEMENTS.

Amount used in payment of losses and claims	17,605 09
Amount used in purchase of surrendered policies	173,232 87
Amount used in payment of dividends to policyholders	195,018 50
Amount voided by lapse of policies	152,224 78
Total expenditures	$2,037,098 04

VI. PREMIUM-NOTE ACCOUNT.

Premium notes and other premium obligations at beginning of the year		$1,778,163 64
Premium notes and other premium obligations received during the year		772,191 30
Total		$2,550,354 94
Deductions during the year as follows:		
Amount used in payment of losses and claims	$17,605 09	
Amount used in purchase of surrendered policies	173,232 87	
Amount used in payment of dividends to policyholders	195,018 50	
Amount voided by lapse of policies	152,224 78	
Total reduction of premium note account		538,076 24
Balance, note assets at end of the year		$2,012,278 70

VII. EXHIBIT OF POLICIES.

NUMBER AND AMOUNT OF POLICIES AND ADDITIONS CLASSIFIED.

	Number.	Amount.	Number.	Amount.
Policies in force at the beginning of the year:				
Whole life policies	15,157	$36,586,992 75		
Endowment policies	9,110	16,745,735 00		
Joint lives and survivorships	1,038	2,153,888 00		
Short term and irregular policies	349	1,672,100 00		
			25,654	$57,158,715 75
New policies issued during the year:				
Whole life policies	8,049	$16,617,157 00		
Endowment policies	3,485	5,151,485 00		
Joint lives and survivorships	441	785,833 00		
Short term and irregular policies	35	161,500 00		
			12,010	22,715,925 00
Additions by dividends during the year:				
Whole life policies		$43,146 00		
Endowment policies		21,901 00		
Joint lives and survivorships		1,327 00		
				66,374 00
Totals			37,664	$79,941,014 75

Deduct policies decreased and ceased to be in force:

Whole life policies	5,221	$11,203,812 75	......	....
Endowment policies	3,184	5,430,532 00	......	....
Joint lives and survivorships	394	686,260 00	......	....
Short term and irregular policies	286	1,392,000 00	......	....
			9,085	$19,317,624 75

Totals at the end of the year:

Whole life policies	17,985	$41,438,483 00	......	....
Endowment policies	9,411	16,488,519 00	......	....
Joint lives and survivorships	1,085	2,254,788 00	......	....
Short term and irregular policies	98	441,600 00	......	....
			28,579	$60,623,390 00
Deduct policies reinsured			......	376,000 00
Net numbers and amounts in force December 31, 1872			28,579	$60,247,390 00

Policies ceased to be in force during the year, with mode of termination:

	No.	Amount.
By death	212	$353,250 00
By expiry	4	9,000 00
By surrender	689	1,836,214 00
By lapse	5,580	11,419,160 75
By change and old policies decreased	270	550,000 00
Not taken	2,330	4,950,000 00
Totals	9,085	$19,317,624 75

Business in the state of Wisconsin during the year 1872:

Policies issued	302	$412,400 00
Policies in force at the end of the year	553	841,490 00
Premiums received		41,551 35
Losses paid		5,500 00

EQUITABLE LIFE ASSURANCE SOCIETY OF THE UNITED STATES.

New York.

WILLIAM C. ALEXANDER, *President.* SAMUEL BORROWE, *Secretary.*

Attorney to accept service of process in Wisconsin, Joseph Hamilton, Milwaukee.

[Incorporated July 25, 1859. Commenced business July 28, 1859.]

I. CAPITAL.

Capital authorized	$100,000 00
Capital actually paid up in cash	100,000 00

II. ASSETS.

Loans secured by deeds of trust or mortgages on real estate		$12,226,572 50
Loans secured by pledge of bonds, stocks or securities, as collateral		687,661 00
Cash value of real estate owned by the company, unincumbered		2,334,359 05
Cash market value of bonds and stocks owned by the company		1,808,170 80
Cash in office of company and deposited in banks and other depositories		778,598 84
Cash in course of transmission		575,591 47
Interest accrued on cash loans and bonds owned by the company		115,829 16
Rents accrued for use of company's property, or under sub lease		19,991 54
Gross premiums uncollected, for the most part not more than three months due, on policies in force Dec. 31, 1872	$181,084 59	....
Gross deferred quarterly and semi-annual premiums, on policies in force December 31, 1872	726,410 00	....
Total	$907,494 59	....
Deducted to reduce last two items to the net value of the policies	226,873 65	....
Net amount deferred and outstanding premiums		680,620 94
Total admitted assets		$19,222,394 80

ITEMS NOT ADMITTED AS ASSETS.

Present value of leases owned by the company....	$19,409 88
Cash in hands of agents due the company	169,177 58
Value of agency supplies, printed matter and stationery on hand	9,609 00
Furniture, safes and fixtures	107,558 29
Fifteen per cent. of items 12 and 13 above	136,194 19
Total unadmitted items	$381,968 94

III. LIABILITIES.

Claims for death losses due and unpaid	$65,960 60
Claims for matured endowments due and unpaid	2,326 28
Claims for death losses and matured endowments, in process of adjustment, or adjusted and not due	268,270 00
Claims for death losses and other policy claims resisted by the company.....	29,500 00
Net present value of the outstanding policies in force on the 31st day of December, 1872, computed according to the American Experience Table of Mortality, with four and one-half per cent. interest	16,658,409 00
Amount of all unpaid dividends of surplus or profits due policyholders	75,874 00
Liability under three months clause	68,099 00
Liabilities as to policyholders	$17,166,458 88

IV. INCOME.

Cash received for all premiums during the year, without deductions	$7,426,861 70
Cash received for interest on bonds owned and dividends on stocks	828,417 96
Cash received for interest on other debts due the company	60,529 38
Rents received for use of company's property, or under sub-lease	104,235 82
Total income	$8,420,044 86

V. EXPENDITURES.

Cash paid for the company's own losses and claims, and additions thereto....	$1,653,988 47
Cash paid for matured endowments	94,682 90
Cash paid to annuitants	4,010 41
Cash paid on account of policies lapsed, surrendered or purchased	877,854 59
Cash paid for dividends to policyholders	1,085,753 68
Cash paid for dividends to stockholders	7,852 09
Cash paid for premiums to other companies for policies reinsured	8,900 43
Cash paid for commissions to agents on first and renewal premiums	544,766 84
Cash paid for salaries and expenses of managers of agencies, and agents	32,280 00
Cash paid for medical examiners' fees	67,388 43
Cash paid for salaries and other compensation of officers and employes	223,337 42
Cash paid for United States taxes and revenue stamps, $4,280 51; state and local taxes in state where organized, $24,980.58; taxes, licenses and fees in other states, $38,576.68, of which the sum of $377 was paid in the state of Wisconsin; total	67,837 77
Cash paid for rents	40,869 91
Cash paid for commuting commissions	66,908 15
Cash paid on any account not itemized above, viz.: advertising and office expenses, $162,465.90; printing, stationery and agency expenses, $65,977.74; law expenses, $26,026.80; expressage, postage, exchange, etc., $65,229.24; total	319,699 68
Total expenditures	$5,096,130 59

VI. EXHIBIT OF POLICIES.

NUMBER AND AMOUNT OF POLICIES AND ADDITIONS CLASSIFIED.

	Number.	Amount.	Number.	Amount.
Policies in force at the beginning of the year:				
Whole life policies	29,972	$122,119,321	......	....
Endowment policies	8,525	31,089,943	......	....
Joint lives and survivorships	235	711,209	......	....
Short term and irregular policies	95	410,670	......	....
			38,827	$154,331,143
New policies issued during the year:				
Whole life policies	10,348	$43,473,484	......	....
Endowment policies	1,316	3,943,280	......	....
Joint lives and survivorships	81	240,914	......	....
Short term and irregular policies	33	228,000	......	....
			11,778	47,885,678
Old policies revived during the year:				
Whole life policeies	558	$2,532,460	......	....
Endowment policies	158	535,941	......	....
Joint lives and survivorships	2	2,000	......	....
Short term and irregular policies	1	5,000	......	....
			718	3,075,401

Additions by dividends during the year:

Whole life policies	......	$735,000	......	....
Endowment policies	......	213,000	......	....
Joint lives and survivorships	......	2,000	......	....
				$950,000
Totals			51,318	$206,242,223

Deduct policies decreased and ceased to be in force:

Whole life policies	6,490	$28,437,398	......	....
Endowment policies	1,568	5,801,295	......	....
Joint lives and survivorships	58	246,308	......	....
Short term and irregular policies	67	313,370	......	....
			8,183	34,798,871

Net numbers and amounts in force December 31st, 1872:

Whole life policies	34,888	$140,423,367	......	....
Endowment policies	8,425	29,980,869	......	....
Joint lives and survivorships	260	709,815	......	....
Short term and irregular policies	62	330,300	......	....
Totals			43,135	$171,443,351

Policies ceased to be in force during the year, with mode of termination:

By death	423	$1,688,882
By expiry	45	227,100
By surrender	2,108	10,108,598
By lapse	3,478	13,333,141
Not taken	2,129	9,446,150
Totals	8,183	$34,798,871

Business in the state of Wisconsin during the year 1872:

Policies issued	112	$323,600 00
Policies in force at the end of the year	817	1,757,345 00
Premiums received	......	69,928 46
Losses paid	......	32,000 00

GERMANIA LIFE INSURANCE COMPANY.

NEW YORK.

HUGO WESENDONCK, *President.* CORNELIUS DOREMUS, *Secretary.*

Attorney to accept service of process in Wisconsin, F. W. HUNDHOUSEN, Milwaukee.

[Incorporated, April 10th, 1860. Commenced business, July 17th, 1860.]

I. CAPITAL.

Capital authorized	$200,000 00
Capital actually paid up in cash	200,000 00

II. ASSETS.

Loans secured by deeds of trust or mortgages on real estate		$3,586,561 03
Loans secured by pledge of bonds, stocks, or securities, as collateral		4,500 00
Cash market value of bonds and stocks owned by the company		978,686 25
Cash in office of company		2,537 44
Cash deposited in banks and trust companies		247,537 01
Interest accrued on cash loans and on bonds owned by the company		65,672 50
Gross premiums uncollected, not more than three months due, on policies in force December 31, 1872	$133,821 90	....
Gross deferred quarterly and semi-annual premiums, on policies in force December 31, 1872	321,778 58	....
Total	$455,600 48	....
Deducted to reduce the last two items to the net value of the policies on account of those premiums	78,218 33	....
Net amount deferred and outstanding prem's		377,382 15
Total admitted assets		$5,212,876 38

III. LIABILITIES.

Claims for death losses and matured endowments, in process of adjustment, or adjusted and not due	$89,644 00
Claims for death losses and other policy claims resisted by the company	23,904 41
Net present value of all the outstanding policies in force on the 31st day of December, 1872, computed according to the American Experience Table of Mortality, with four and one-half per cent. interest	4,482,844 00
Net present value of extra risks and lapsed policies	2,985 96
Amount of all unpaid dividends of surplus, or other profits due policyhold's.	76,245 71
Total liabilities as to policyholders	$4,654,584 08

IV. INCOME.

Cash received for premiums on new policies and renewal prem's, without deductions	$1,516,537 87
Cash received for sale of annuities	717 50
Cash received for all other premiums	8,444 03
Cash received for interest on cash loans	231,745 93
Cash received for interest on bonds owned	53,772 01
Discount on claims paid in advance	602 00
Cash income from other sources, viz.: policy fees	104 98
Total income	$1,811,924 32

V. EXPENDITURES.

Cash paid for the company's own losses and claims, and additions thereto	$447,594 48
Cash paid to annuitants	5,251 38
Cash paid on account of policies lapsed, surrendered or purchased	105,208 81
Cash paid for dividends to policyholders	222,402 15
Cash paid for dividends to stockholders, and int. on capital	24,000 00
Cash paid for commissions to agents on first and renewal premiums	106,250 26
Cash paid for salaries and expenses of managers of agencies, and agents	32,356 42
Cash paid for medical examiners' fees	10,331 21
Cash paid for salaries and other compensation of officers and employes	62,198 34
Cash paid for taxes, revenue stamps, and for state licenses and fees	12,442 67
Cash paid for rents	7,030 19
Cash paid for commuting commissions	33,523 83
Cash paid on any account not itemized above, viz: printing and advertising, $12,420 78; stationery, postage, furniture, etc., $11,651 80; total	24,072 58
Total expenditures	$1,092,577 32

VI. EXHIBIT OF POLICIES.

NUMBER AND AMOUNT OF POLICIES AND ADDITIONS CLASSIFIED.

	Number.	Amount.	Number.	Amount.
Policies in force at the beginning of the year:				
Whole life policies	15,224	$27,243,540 37	......	......
Endowment policies	3,068	5,551,424 20	......	......
Joint lives and survivorships	194	277,504 68	......	......
Short term and irregular policies	26	27,500 00	......	......
			18,507	$33,099,969 25
New policies issued during the year:				
Whole life policies	1,810	$3,172,430 69	......	......
Endowment policies	683	869,764 50	......	......
Joint lives and survivorships	76	103,186 13	......	......
Short term and irregular policies	4	26,987 50	......	......
			2,573	4,172,368 82
Old policies revived during the year:				
Whole life policies	39	$71,905 61	......	......
Endowment policies	7	4,989 03	......	......
			46	76,894 64
Old policies increased during the year:				
Endowment policies	......	......	4	6,460 00
Additions by dividends during the year:				
Whole life policies	......	$112,546 00	......	......
Endowment policies	......	18,333 65	......	......
Joint lives and survivorships	......	474 60	......	......
			......	131,354 25
Totals			21,130	$37,487,046 96

Deduct policies decreased and ceased to be in force:

Whole life policies	1,279	$2,142,546 44	......	....
Endowment policies	444	673,091 94	......	....
Joint lives and survivorships	38	60,096 08	......	....
Short term and irregular policies	5	20,050 00	......	....
			1,765	$2,886,783 41

Net numbers and amounts in force, December 31st, 1872:

Whole life policies	15,795	$28,456,876 28	......	....
Endowment policies	3,313	5,777,879 44	......	....
Joint lives and survivorships	282	281,070 88	......	....
Short term and irregular policies	25	84,437 50	......	....
Totals			19,365	$34,600,263 55

Policies ceased to be in force during the year, with mode of termination:

	No.	Amount.
By death	266	$458,115 71
By expiry	11	23,563 50
By surrender	515	918,459 49
By lapse	684	1,045,860 54
By change and old policies decreased	15	29,603 75
Not taken	274	421,180 42
Totals	1,765	$2,886,783 41

Business in the state of Wisconsin during the year 1872:

Policies issued	71	$92,560 00
Policies in force at the end of the year	639	806,547 61
Premiums received	......	30,249 31
Losses paid	......	4,566 00

GLOBE MUTUAL LIFE INSURANCE COMPANY.

NEW YORK.

PLINY FREEMAN, *President*. JAMES M. FREEMAN, *Secretary*.

Attorney to accept service of process in Wisconsin, JNO. G. MCKINDLEY, Kenosha.

[Incorporated June, 1864. Commenced business June, 1864.]

I. CAPITAL.

Capital authorized	$100,000 00
Capital actually paid up in cash	100,000 00

II. ASSETS.

Loans secured by deeds of trust or mortgages on real estate		$1,908,762 35
Loans secured by pledge of bonds, stocks, or securities, as collateral		44,000 00
Premium loans, on policies now in force		30,947 89
Cash market value of bonds and stocks owned by the company		1,269,495 39
Cash in office of company		9,839 81
Cash deposited in banks and trust companies		191,773 00
Postage and revenue stamps		200 00
Interest accrued on cash loans and on bonds owned by the company		23,418 00
Interest accrued on premium loans and notes		1,608 75
Rents accrued for use of company's property, or under sub-lease		500 00
Gross premiums uncollected, not more than three months due, on policies in force December 31, 1872	$88,237 95	....
Gross deferred quarterly and semi-annual premiums, on policies in force December 31, 1872	228,657 77	....
Total	$316,895 72	....
Deducted to reduce the last two items, to the net value of the policies	15,844 78	....
Net amount deferred and outstanding premiums		301,050 94
Total admitted assets		$3,776,586 13

ITEMS NOT ADMITTED AS ASSETS.

Amount invested in commuting com's or renewal com's purchased	$640 49
Amount advanced to officers or agents to be repaid	15,022 51
Cash in hands of officers or agents due the company	1,914 45
Value of agency supplies, printed matter and stationery on hand	4,800 00
Furniture, safes and fixtures	11,933 30
Total unadmitted items	$34,310 75

III. LIABILITIES.

Claims for death losses due and unpaid	$1,261 08
Claims for death losses and matured endowments, in process of adjustment, or adjusted and not due	27,223 52
Claims for death losses and other policy claims resisted by the company	24,367 41
Net present value of all the outstanding policies in force on the 31st day of December, 1872, computed according to the American Experience Table of Mortality, with four and one-half per cent. interest	3,421,994 00
Net present value of dividend additions to policies	153,686 00
Reserved for value of lapsed policies	44,790 00
All other claims estimated	5,900 00
Total liabilities as to policyholders	$3,679,222 01

IV. INCOME.

Cash received for premiums on new policies, without deductions	$282,328 72
Cash received for renewal premiums, without deductions	1,050,111 46
Cash premiums from other companies for reinsuring their risks	5,390 21
Cash received for interest on cash loans	109,938 58
Cash received for interest on bonds owned and dividends on stocks	68,964 29
Cash received for interest on premium loans	550 00
Cash received for interest on other debts due the company	10,836 80
Rents received for use of company's property, or under sub-lease	7,076 56
Discount on claims paid in advance	385 57
Total income	$1,535,592 14

V. EXPENDITURES.

Cash paid for the company's own losses and claims, and additions thereto	$405,175 87
Cash paid to annuitants	750 00
Cash paid on account of policies lapsed, surrendered or purchased	65,862 97
Cash paid for dividends to policyholders	205,720 15
Cash paid for dividends to stockholders	11,305 00
Cash paid for premiums to other companies for policies reinsured	7,680 11
Cash paid for commissions to agents on first and renewal premiums	97,408 87
Cash paid for salaries and expenses of managers of agencies, and agents	51,804 16
Cash paid for medical examiners' fees	12,967 22
Cash paid for salaries and other compensation of officers and employes	71,860 66
Cash paid for United States taxes and revenue stamps, $694.74; state and local taxes in state where organized, $331.50; taxes, licenses and fees in other states, $12,859.84, of which the sum of $331 was paid in the state of Wisconsin; total	13,886 08
Cash paid for rents	30,588 49
Cash paid for commuting commissions	640 49
Cash paid for furniture, safes and fixtures for home or agency offices	626 02
Cash paid on any account not itemized above, viz.: agency expenses, $3,951.22; exchange and postage, $4,704.48; advertising, printing, etc., $17,462.57; office and legal expenses, $6,918.97; total	33,037 24
Total expenditures	$1,009,248 32

VI. EXHIBIT OF POLICIES.

NUMBER AND AMOUNT OF POLICIES AND ADDITIONS CLASSIFIED.

	Number.	Amount.	Number.	Amount.
Policies in force at the beginning of the year:				
Whole life policies	7,933	$21,067,236 00	......	....
Endowment policies	3,625	7,151,399 00	......	....
Joint lives and survivorships	1	3,000 00	......	....
Short term and irregular policies	40	229,850 00	......	....
			11,599	$28,451,485 00
New policies issued during the year:				
Whole life policies	2,297	$5,862,016 00	......	....
Endowment policies	383	583,409 00	......	....
Short term and irregular policies	9	55,500 00	......	....
			2,689	6,500,925 00

Old policies revived during the year:				
Whole life policies	341	$1,002,508 00	......	....
Endowment policies	131	288,800 00	......	....
Short term and irregular policies	3	3,000 00	......	....
			475	$1,289,309 00
Old policies increased during the year:				
Whole life policies	13	$30,000 00	......	....
Endowment policies	1	5,000 00	......	....
Short term and irregular policies	1	4,000 00	......	....
			15	39,000 00
Additions by dividends during the year:				
Whole life policies	......	$225,803 00	......	....
Endowment policies	......	111,223 00	......	....
			......	337,024 60
Totals			14,778	$36,617,743 00
Deduct policies decreased and ceased to be in force:				
Whole life policies	1,638	$4,750,002 00	......	....
Endowment policies	583	1,292,945 00	......	....
Short term and irregular policies	23	115,181 00	......	....
			2,244	6,881,558 00
Totals at the end of the year:				
Whole life policies	8,946	$23,487,561 00	......	....
Endowment policies	3,557	6,841,885 00	......	....
Joint lives and survivorships	1	3,000 00	......	....
Short term and irregular policies	80	177,169 00	......	....
			12,584	$30,286,185 00
Deduct policies reinsured			177	415,500 00
Net numbers and amounts in force December 31st, 1872			12,357	$29,870,685 00

Policies ceased to be in force during the year, with mode of termination:

	Number.	Amount.
By death	147	$329,109 00
By expiry	1	1,000 00
By surrender	388	1,176,541 00
By lapse	1,332	3,827,927 00
By change and old policies decreased	19	308,430 00
Not taken	357	1,175,531 00
Totals	2,244	$6,881,558 00

Business in the state of Wisconsin during the year 1872:

Policies issued	38	$23,896 00
Policies in force at the end of the year	279	367,277 28
Premiums received	......	14,791 78
Losses paid	......	8,595 00

MANHATTAN LIFE INSURANCE COMPANY.

NEW YORK.

HENRY STOKES, *President*. JACOB L. HALSEY, *Secretary*.

Attorney to accept service of process in Wisconsin, J. H. CRAMPTON, Milwaukee.

[Organized August, 1850. Commenced business August 1, 1850.]

I. CAPITAL.

Capital authorized	$100,000 00
Capital actually paid up in cash	100,000 00

II. ASSETS.

Loans secured by deeds of trust or mortgages on real estate	$3,741,451 38
Loans secured by pledge of bonds, stocks, or securities, as collateral	540,320 00
Premium notes and loans, taken for premiums, on policies now in force	2,318,068 55
Cash market value of bonds and stocks owned by the company	730,298 94
Cash in office of company	1,358 42

Cash deposited in banks and trust companies		$319,747 57
Postage and revenue stamps		69 38
Interest due and accrued on loans and bonds owned by the company		102,280 21
Gross premiums uncollected, not more than three months due, on policies in force December 31, 1872	$456,036 39	
Gross deferred quarterly and semi-annual premiums, on policies in force December 31, 1872	124,820 23	
Total	$580,856 62	
Deducted to reduce the last two items, to the net value of the policies	58,035 66	
Net amount deferred and outstanding premiums		522,820 96
Total admitted assets		$8,270,870 41

ITEMS NOT ADMITTED AS ASSETS.

Amount invested in commuting com's; or renewal com's purchased	$826,281 05
Present value of leases owned by the company	20,000 00
Cash in hands of agents due the company	15,008 46
Value of agency supplies, printed matter and stationery on hand	3,000 00
Furniture, safes and fixtures	6,000 00
Total unadmitted items	$70,284 51

III. LIABILITIES.

Claims for death losses and matured endowments, in process of adjustment, or adjusted and not due	$151,447 00
Claims for death losses and other policy claims resisted by the company	59,500 00
Net present value of all the outstanding policies in force on the 31st day of December, 1872, computed according to the American Experience Table of Mortality, with four and one-half per cent. interest	6,200,125 00
Amount of all unpaid dividends of surplus, or other profits due policyholders	92,608 08
Amount of unpaid dividends to stockholders	6,210 73
Total liabilities as to policyholders	$6,509,885 76

IV. INCOME.

Cash received for premiums on new policies and renewal prem's, without deductions	$1,457,655 18
Cash received for sale of annuities	2,798 86
Cash received for all other premiums	3,373 16
Cash received for interest on cash loans	271,021 99
Cash received for interest on bonds owned and dividends on stocks	46,449 89
Cash received for interest on premium notes or loans	177,260 50
Cash received for premium on gold	8,199 08
Discount on claims paid in advance	13,249 00
Gross amount of notes or other obligations taken for renewal premiums	171,846 96
Total income	$2,151,854 52

V. EXPENDITURES.

Cash paid for the company's own losses and claims, and additions thereto	$597,287 37
Cash paid to annuitants	3,745 31
Cash paid on account of policies lapsed, surrendered or purchased	31,248 23
Cash paid for dividends to policyholders	355,022 85
Cash paid for dividends to stockholders	43,000 00
Commissions to agents on first and renewal premiums	171,928 45
Cash paid for medical examiners' fees	9,433 50
Cash paid for salaries and other compensation of officers and employes	61,949 42
Cash paid for taxes, revenue stamps, and state licenses and fees	12,072 72
Cash paid for rents	8,000 00
Cash paid for commuting commissions	3,892 14
Cash paid on any account not itemized above, viz: interest on capital, $7,000; advertising, $13,167 23; office expenses, $13,631 01; sundry expenses, $5,713,27; total	39,511 51
Total cash expenditures	$1,267,091 50

PREMIUM-LOAN DISBURSEMENTS.

Amount used in payment of losses and claims	$41,978 68	
Amount used in purchase of surrendered policies, and voided by lapse	112,586 98	
Amount used in payment of dividends to policyholders	9,118 38	
Total premium note expenditures		163,683 99
Total expenditures		$1,430,775 49

VI. PREMIUM-NOTE ACCOUNT.

Premium notes and other premium obligations at beginning of the year......		$2,323,229 74
Premium notes and other premium obligations received during the year.....		171,846 98
Total..		$2,495,076 72
Deductions during the year as follows:		
Amount used in payment of losses and claims..................	$41,978 68	....
Amount used in purchase of surrendered policies, and voided by lapse..........	112,536 93	....
Amount used in payment of dividends to policyholders.......	9,118 38	....
Amount redeemed by maker in cash..........................	4,365 87	....
Amount in hands of agents for collection....	13,988 31	....
Total reduction of premium note account.................		181,988 17
Balance, note assets at end of the year		$2,313,088 55

VII. EXHIBIT OF POLICIES.

NUMBER AND AMOUNT OF POLICIES AND ADDITIONS CLASSIFIED.

	Number.	Amount.	Number.	Amount.
Policies in force at the beginning of the year:				
Whole life policies..........................	11,114	$37,051,643	......	....
Endowment policies..........................	1,866	4,918,764	......	....
Joint lives and survivorships..............	68	170,500	......	....
			13,068	$42,140,907
New policies issued during the year:				
Whole life policies..........................	1,277	$4,096,394	......	....
Endowment policies..........................	421	879,575	......	....
Joint lives and survivorships..............	3	11,000	......	....
			1,701	4,986,969
Additions by dividends during the year:				
Whole life policies......	....	....	......	4,741
Totals....................................			14,739	$47,132,617
Deduct policies decreased and ceased to be in force:				
Whole life policies..........................	1,227	$3,830,130	......	....
Endowment policies..........................	384	946,874	......	....
Joint lives and survivorships..............	4	12,000	......	....
			1,615	4,789,004
Net numbers and amounts in force December 31st, 1872:				
Whole life policies..........................	11,164	$37,322,648	......	....
Endowment policies..........................	1,908	4,851,465	......	....
Joint lives and survivorships..............	57	169,500	......	....
Totals....................................			13,124	$42,343,613

Policies ceased to be in force during the year, with mode of termination:

	No.	Amount.
By death..	180	$566,493
By surrender..	93	316,992
By lapse..	938	2,765,504
By change and old policies decreased........................	189	647,400
Not taken...	215	492,616
Totals..	$1,615	$4,789,004

Business in the State of Wisconsin during the year 1872:

Policies issued..	5	$9,000 00
Policies in force at the end of the year.........................	68	147,662 00

MASSACHUSETTS MUTUAL LIFE INSURANCE COMPANY.

SPRINGFIELD, MASS.

CALEB RICE, *President.* CHAS. McLEAN KNOX, *Secretary.*

Attorney to accept service of process in Wisconsin, P. M. CHILD, Milwaukee.

[Incorporated, May 15, 1851. Commenced Business, August 1, 1851.]

I. CAPITAL.

Capital authorized	Purely Mutual
Capital actually paid up in cash	

II. ASSETS.

Loans secured by deeds of trust or mortgages on real estate		$2,116,767 90
Loans secured by pledge of bonds, stocks or securities, as collateral		140,456 54
Premium notes and loans taken for premiums, on policies now in force		952,643 57
Cash value of real estate owned by the company, unincumbered		125,000 00
Cash market value of bonds and stocks owned by the company		682,296 00
Cash in office of company		54,572 84
Cash deposited in banks and trust companies		19,991 63
Interest accrued on cash loans and on bonds owned by the company		67,834 66
Interest accrued on premium loans and notes		28,569 30
Rents accrued for use of company's property, or under sub-lease		1,595 83
Gross premiums uncollected, not more than three months due, on policies in force December 31, 1872	$254,457 63	
Gross deferred quarterly and semi-annual premiums, on policies in force December 31, 1872	121,664 11	
Total	$376,121 74	
Deducted to reduce the last two items, to the net value of the policies	63,940 69	
Net amount deferred and outstanding premiums		312,181 05
Total admitted assets		$4,501,909 33

III. LIABILITIES.

Claims for death losses and matured endowments, in process of adjustment, or adjusted and not due	$67,420 00
Claims for death losses and other policy claims resisted by the company	45,000 00
Net present value of all the outstanding policies in force on the 31st day of December, 1872, computed according to the Actuaries' Table of Mortality, with four per cent. interest	3,983,446 82
Amount of all unpaid dividends of surplus, or other profits due policyholders	24,543 32
Total liabilities as to policyholders	$4,120,410 14

IV. INCOME.

Cash rec'd for prem's during the year, without deductions for expenses	$971,583 90
Cash premiums from other companies for reinsuring their risks	19,069 15
Cash received for interest on cash loans	144,807 41
Cash received for interest on bonds owned and dividends on stocks	42,929 75
Cash received for interest on premium notes or loans	55,940 28
Rents received for use of company's property, or under sub-lease	5,679 33
Discount on claims paid in advance	1,672 65
Gross am't of notes or other obligations taken for new and renewal prem's	329,778 55
Total income	$1,571,461 02

V. EXPENDITURES.

Cash paid for the company's own losses and claims, and additions thereto		$356,191 02
Cash paid to other companies for losses or claims on their policies reinsured by this company		20,000 00
Cash paid for matured policies		1,000 00
Cash paid on account of policies lapsed, surrendered or purchased		96,689 84
Cash paid for dividends to policyholders		55,198 46
Cash paid for premiums to other companies for policies reinsured		10,168 41
Cash paid for commissions to agents on first and renewal premiums		107,487 10
Cash paid for salaries and expenses of managers of agencies, and agents		45,141 79
Cash paid for medical examiners' fees		8,550 00
Cash paid for salaries and other compensation of officers and employes		34,725 97
Cash paid for United States taxes and revenue stamps, $912 15; state and local taxes in state where organized, $1,921.78; taxes, licenses and fees in other states, $8,960 47; total		11,794 40
Cash paid for rents		9,087 83
Cash paid for furniture, safes and fixtures for home or agency offices		1,125 00
Cash paid on any account not itemized above, viz.: printing, advertising, traveling expenses, legal fees, etc		36,289 06
Total cash expenditures		$793,398 88
PREMIUM-LOAN DISBURSEMENTS.		
Amount used in payment of losses and claims	$14,488 63	
Amount used in purchase of surrendered policies	20,808 90	
Amount used in payment of dividends to policyholders	131,311 68	
Amount voided by lapse of policies	79,946 84	
Total premium note expenditures		246,556 05
Total expenditures		$1,039,954 93

VI. PREMIUM-NOTE ACCOUNT.

Premium notes and other premium obligations at beginning of the year		$878,227 13
Premium notes and other premium obligations received during the year		329,778 55
Total		$1,208,005 68
Deductions during the year as follows:		
Amount used in payment of losses and claims	$14,488 63	
Amount used in purchase of surrendered policies	20,808 90	
Amount used in payment of dividends to policyholders	131,311 68	
Amount voided by lapse of policies	79,946 84	
Amount redeemed by maker in cash	3,806 06	
Total reduction of premium note account		250,362 11
Balance, note assets at end of the year		$957,643 57

VII. EXHIBIT OF POLICIES.

NUMBER AND AMOUNT OF POLICIES AND ADDITIONS CLASSIFIED.

	Number.	Amount.	Number.	Amount.
Policies in force at the beginning of the year:				
Whole life policies	9,509	$23,389,437		
Endowment policies	3,335	6,394,528		
Joint lives and survivorships	165	383,000		
Short term and irregular policies	1,459	3,411,550		
			14,468	$33,578,515
New policies issued during the year:				
Whole life policies	1,673	$4,053,365		
Endowment policies	636	1,181,740		
Joint lives and survivorships	77	182,645		
			2,386	5,417,750
Old policies revived during the year:				
Whole life policies	29	$80,000		
Endowment policies	5	10,500		
			34	90,500
Old policies increased during the year:				
Whole life policies				2,100
Additions by dividends and change to equity:				
Short term and irregular policies			784	1,619,650
Totals			17,672	$40,708,515
Deduct policies decreased and ceased to be in force:				
Whole life policies	1,657	$4,342,945		
Endowment policies	909	1,714,162		
Joint lives and survivorships	49	113,300		
Short term and irregular policies	574	1,342,100		
			3,189	7,512,507
Totals at the end of the year:				
Whole life policies	9,554	$23,181,957		
Endowment policies	3,067	5,872,606		
Joint lives and survivorships	198	452,345		
Short term and irregular policies	1,669	3,689,100		
			14,488	$33,196,008
Deduct policies reinsured				582,000
Net numbers and amounts in force December 31, 1872			14,488	$32,614,008

Policies ceased to be in force during the year, with mode of termination:

	No.	Amount.
By death	145	$358,557
By expiry	501	1,154,500
By surrender	238	499,094
By lapse	935	2,548,500
By change and old policies decreased	808	1,818,156
Not taken	562	1,133,700
Totals	3,189	$7,512,507

Business in the state of Wisconsin during the year 1872:

Policies issued	71	$118,790 00
Policies in force at the end of the year	169	296,280 00
Premiums received		12,191 88
Losses paid		160 00

METROPOLITAN LIFE INSURANCE COMPANY.

New York.

JOSEPH F. KNAPP, *President.* ROBERT A. GRANNISS, *Secretary.*

Attorney to accept service of process in Wisconsin, FREDERICK FURTHMAN, Milwaukee.

[Incorporated January, 1866. Commenced business June, 1867.]

I. CAPITAL.

Capital authorized		$200,000 00
Capital actually paid up in cash		200,000 00

II. ASSETS.

Loans secured by deeds of trust or mortgages on real estate		$249,700 00
Loans secured by pledge of bonds, stocks, or securities, as collateral		37,495 82
Premium notes and loans, taken for premiums, on policies now in force		335,582 83
Cash market value of bonds and stocks owned by the company		290,265 00
Cash in office of company, and deposited in bank		21,539 66
Postage and revenue stamps		200 00
Interest accrued on cash loans and on bonds owned by the company		7,219 83
Interest accrued on premium loans and notes		18,517 20
Home office premiums in course of collection	$110,410 24	
Gross premiums uncollected, not more than three months due, on policies in force December 31, 1872, in hands of agents	189,505 05	
Gross deferred quarterly and semi-annual premiums, on policies in force December 31, 1872	293,825 12	
Total	$593,740 41	
Deducted to reduce the last three items, to the net value of the policies	60,858 00	
Net amount deferred and outstanding premiums		532,882 41
Total admitted assets		$1,493,402 77

ITEMS NOT ADMITTED AS ASSETS.

Am't invested in commuting commissions; or renewal com's purchased	$23,333 53
Am't advanced to agents to be repaid out of future salaries or com's	23,711 02
Value of agency supplies, printed matter and stationery on hand	5,000 00
Furniture, safes and fixtures	27,429 01
Total unadmitted items	$79,473 56

III. LIABILITIES.

Claims for death losses and matured endowments, unpaid	$17,500 00
Net present value of all the outstanding policies in force on the 31st day of December, 1872, computed according to the American Experience Table of Mortality, with four and one-half per cent. interest	1,198,968 00
Amount of all unpaid dividends of surplus, or other profits due policyholders	13,576 00
Amount due on account of salaries, rents and expenses	2,695 00
Total liabilities as to policyholders	$1,232,739 00

IV. INCOME

Cash received for new and renewal premiums, without deductions for expense	$541,575 44
Cash received for interest from all sources	46,086 88
Gross amount of notes or other obligations taken for premiums	163,341 18
Total income	$751,003 50

V. EXPENDITURES.

Cash paid for the company's own losses and claims, and additions thereto	$155,723 44
Cash paid for matured endowments	5,000 00
Cash paid on account of policies lapsed, surrendered or purchased	31,279 06
Cash paid for dividends to policyholders	34,489 98
Cash paid for premiums to other companies for policies re-insured	778 30
Cash paid for commissions to agents on first and renewal premiums	69,729 04
Cash paid for salaries and expenses of managers of agencies and agents	19,714 01
Cash paid for medical examiners' fees	18,953 17
Cash paid for salaries and other compensation of officers and employes	31,453 66
Cash paid for United States taxes and revenue stamps, $4,840 25; taxes, licenses and fees, $8,380 73; total	13,220 98
Cash paid for rents	13,205 86

Cash paid on any account not itemized above, viz: legal fees, $4,079 03; stationery, printing and advertising, $9,426 96; expense account, fire insurance, exchange, expressage, etc, $3,716 97; total		$17,222 96
Total cash expenditures		$410,766 46

PREMIUM-LOAN DISBURSEMENTS.

Amount used in payment of losses and claims	$4,267 56	
Amount used in purchase of surrendered policies	30,047 71	
Amount used in payment of dividends to policyholders	26,150 03	
Amount voided by lapse of policies	17,108 00	
Total premium note expenditures		77,568 30
Total expenditures		$488,344 76

VI. PREMIUM-NOTE ACCOUNT.

Premium notes and other premium obligations at beginning of the year		$239,809 95
Premium notes and other premium obligations received during the year		163,341 18
Total		$403,151 13
Deductions during the year as follows:		
Amount used in payment of losses and claims	$4,267 56	
Amount used in purchase of surrendered policies	30,047 71	
Amount used in payment of dividends to policyholders	26,150 03	
Amount voided by lapse of policies	17,108 00	
Total reduction of premium note account		77,568 30
Balance, note assets at the end of the year		$325,582 83

VII. EXHIBIT OF POLICIES.

NUMBER AND AMOUNT OF POLICES AND ADDITIONS CLASSIFIED.

	Number.	Amount.	Number.	Amount.
Policies in force at the beginning of the year:				
Whole life policies	7,129	$10,286,285		
Endowment policies	4,117	4,618,576		
Joint lives and survivorships	51	71,221		
Short term and irregular policies	2	13,500		
			11,299	$14,989,582
New policies issued and old policies revived during the year:				
Whole life policies	6,269	$9,639,648		
Endowment policies	2,369	1,911,750		
Joint lives and survivorships	4	5,265		
			8,642	11,556,663
Totals			19,941	$26,546,245
Deduct policies decreased and ceased to be in force:				
Whole life policies	2,259	$3,390,118		
Endowment policies	2,326	2,588,786		
Joint lives and survivorships	10	16,000		
Short term and irregular policies	1	5,000		
			4,596	5,999,904
Net numbers and amounts in force December 31st, 1872:				
Whole life policies	11,139	$16,535,815		
Endowment policies	4,160	3,941,540		
Joint lives and survivorships	45	60,486		
Short term and irregular policies	1	8,500		
Totals			15,345	$20,546,341

Policies ceased to be in force during the year, with mode of termination:

	Number.	Amount.
By death	125	$164,000
By expiry	1	5,000
By surrender	304	661,249
By lapse	1,962	2,617,846
By change and old policies decreased	274	422,000
Not taken	1,930	2,129,809
Totals	4,569	$5,999,904

Business in the state of Wisconsin during the year 1872:

Policies issued	55	$59,568 00
Policies in force at the end of the year	81	101,000 00
Premiums received		2,828 15
Losses paid		1,000 00

MISSOURI MUTUAL LIFE INSURANCE COMPANY.

ST. LOUIS, MO.

B. W. ALEXANDER, *President*. BEN. WILLIAMS, *Secretary*.

Attorney to accept service of process in Wisconsin, A. W. DILLINGHAM, Madison.

[Incorporated, Aug., 1867. Commenced business, Sept., 1867.]

I. CAPITAL.

Capital authorized		$125,000 00
Capital actually paid up in cash		125,000 00

II. ASSETS.

Loans secured by deeds of trust or mortgages on real estate		$147,019 61
Loans secured by pledge of bonds, stocks or securities as collateral		14,890 07
Prem. notes and loans, taken for prem's on policies now in force		111,048 88
Cash value of real estate, owned by the company, unincumbered		6,134 30
Cash in office of company		15,883 35
Interest accrued on cash loans and on bonds owned by the company		8,965 38
Rents accrued for use of company's property, or under sub-lease		100 00
Gross premiums uncollected, not more than three months due, on policies in force Dec. 31, 1872	$13,470 32	
Gross deferred quarterly and semi-annual prem's, on policies in force Dec. 31, 1872	15,952 90	
Total	$29,423 22	
Deducted to reduce the last two items to the net value of the policies	3,659 16	
Net amount deferred and outstanding premiums		25,764 06
Due from other companies for premiums on reinsured risks		608 45
Total admitted assets		$330,424 04

ITEMS NOT ADMITTED AS ASSETS.

Amount invested in commuting com's; or renewal com's purchased	$13,131 84
Cash in hands of officers or agents due the company	14,918 30
Loans on personal security only, and bankable paper	12,214 25
Furniture, safes and fixtures	2,600 62
Other items, viz.: debts secured	3,374 79
Total unadmitted items	$46,239 80

III. LIABILITIES.

Claims for death losses and matured endowments, in process of adjustment, or adjusted and not due	$15,892 00
Net present value of all the outstanding policies in force on the 31st day of December, 1872, computed according to the American Experience Table of Mortality, with four and one-half per cent. interest	263,998 00
Amount of all unpaid dividends of surplus, or other profits due policyholders	3,281 39
Amount of unpaid dividends to stockholders	150 00
Amount of loans in excess of value of policies	12,578 24
Amount of ledger balances	2,873 08
Total liabilities as to policyholders	$298,702 71

IV. INCOME.

Cash received for premiums on new policies, without deductions	$66,342 58
Cash received for renewal premiums, without deductions for expense	97,184 52
Cash received for interest on cash loans	17,914 98
Cash received for interest on premium notes or loans	7,569 11
Rents received for use of company's property, or under sub-lease	284 90
Cash from other companies for losses on policies of this company reinsured	5,000 00
Cash income from other sources, viz: Int. dividend left on deposit	1,567 85
Gross amount of notes or other obligations taken for premiums	62,691 50
Total income	$258,554 89

V. EXPENDITURES.

Cash paid for the company's own losses and claims, and additions thereto	$54,580 47
Cash paid to other companies for losses on claims on their policies reinsured by this company	2,500 00
Cash paid on account of policies lapsed, surrendered or purchased	25,702 39

Cash paid for dividends to policyholders	$10,065 17
Interest deposits withdrawn	255 55
Total cash paid for dividends to stockholders	12,160 00
Cash paid for premiums to other companies for policies reinsured	5,294 77
Cash paid for commissions to agents on first and renewal premiums, and salaries and expenses	58,769 13
Cash paid for medical examiners' fees	5,617 12
Cash paid for salaries and other compensation of officers and employes	9,402 71
Cash paid for state and local taxes in state where organized, $3,818.89; taxes, licenses and fees in other states, $2,336.54, of which the sum of $108 was paid in the state of Wisconsin; total	6,155 43
Cash paid for rents	3,278 72
Cash paid on any account not itemized above, viz: printing, advertising, postage, revenue stamps, fire insurance, legal fees and general expenses	14,352 13
Total cash expenditures	$203,128 56

PREMIUM-LOAN DISBURSEMENTS.

Amount used in payment of losses and claims	$1,208 28	
Amount used in purchase of surrendered policies	10,227 20	
Amount used in payment of dividends to policyholders	6,289 81	
Amount voided by lapse of policies	8,213 98	
Total premium note expenditures		25,938 67
Total expenditures		$229,062 23

VI. PREMIUM-NOTE ACCOUNT.

Premium notes and other premium obligations at beginning of the year		$74,755 99
Premium notes and other premium obligations received during the year		62,691 50
Total		$137,447 49
Deductions during the year as follows:		
Amount used in payment of losses and claims	$1,208 28	
Amount used in purchase of surrendered policies	10,227 20	
Amount used in payment of dividends to policyholders	6,289 81	
Amount voided by lapse of policies	8,213 98	
Amount redeemed by maker in cash	470 00	
Total reduction of premium note account		26,403 67
Balance, note assets at the end of the year		$111,043 82

VII. EXHIBIT OF POLICIES.

NUMBER AND AMOUNT OF POLICIES AND ADDITIONS CLASSIFIED.

	No.	Amount.	No.	Amount.
Policies in force at the beginning of the year:				
Whole life policies	1,466	$4,138,145 19		
Endowment policies	142	270,558 05		
Joint lives and survivorships	21	54,029 61		
Short term and irregular policies	2	3,500 00		
			1,631	$4,446,232 85
New policies issued during the year:				
Whole life policies	1,125	$2,509,200 00		
Endowment policies	115	263,380 00		
Joint lives and survivorships	6	10,000 00		
Short term and irregular policies	3	12,000 00		
			1,249	2,794,580 00
Additions by dividends during the year:				
Whole life policies		$1,017 49		
Endowment policies		82 78		
Join lives and survivorships		56 03		
				1,156 30
Totals			2,880	$7,241,969 15
Deduct policies decreased and ceased to be in force:				
Whole life policies	582	$1,688,098 22		
Endowment policies	65	150,293 10		
Joint lives and survivorships	11	30,150 00		
			658	1,868,541 32
Totals at the end of the year:				
Whole life policies	2,009	$4,960,264 46		
Endowment policies	192	383,727 73		
Joint lives and survivorships	16	33,935 64		
Short term and irregular policies	5	15,500 00		
			2,222	$5,393,427 83

Deduct policies reinsured:

Whole life policies	......	$292,000 00
Net numbers and amounts in force December 31st, 1872:	2,222	$5,101,427 86

Policies ceased to be in force during the year, with mode of termination:

	Number.	Amount.
By death	24	$55,500 00
By surrender	76	174,313 22
By lapse	338	861,300 00
By change and old policies decreased	68	328,328 10
Not taken	152	449,100 00
Totals	658	$1,868,541 32

Business in the state of Wisconsin during the year 1872:

Policies issued	12	$12,000 00
Policies in force at the end of the year	12	12,000 00
Premiums received	......	288 27

MISSOURI VALLEY LIFE INSURANCE COMPANY.

LEAVENWORTH, KANSAS.

H. D. MACKAY, *President.* GEO. A. MOORE, *Secretary.*

Attorney to accept service of process in Wisconsin, A. S. ALLEN, Milwaukee.

[Incorporated, Aug. 28th, 1867. Commenced business, Jan. 1, 1868.]

I. CAPITAL.

Capital authorized	$430,000 00
Capital actually paid up in cash	162,250 00

II. ASSETS.

Loans secured by deeds of trust or mortgages on real estate		$285,543 97
Loans secured by pledge of bonds, stocks, or securities, as collateral		3,016 07
Cash value of real estate owned by the company, unincumbered		24,580 10
Cash market value of bonds and stocks owned by the company		17,105 65
Cash in office of company		8,388 88
Cash deposited in banks and trust companies		50,584 47
Postage and revenue stamps		28 83
Interest due and accrued on cash loans and on bonds owned by the company		13,783 77
Gross premiums uncollected, not more than three months due, on policies in force December 31, 1872	$84,207 18	....
Gross deferred quarterly and semi-annual premiums, on policies in force December 31, 1872	72,478 85	....
Total	$156,681 03	....
Deducted to reduce the last two items, to the net value of the policies	39,000 00	....
Net amount deferred and outstanding prem's		117,681 03
Total admitted assets		$520,652 22

ITEMS NOT ADMITTED AS ASSETS.

Amount invested in commuting com's, or renewal com's purchased	$55,779 73
Value of agency supplies, printed matter and stationery on hand	4,875 00
Loans on personal security only	17,870 18
Furniture, safes and fixtures	5,971 24
Loans on endorsed personal security approved by the directors	267,750 00
Total unadmitted items	$352,246 15

III. LIABILITIES.

Claims for death losses and matured endowments, in process of adjustment, or adjusted and not due	$2,000 00
Net present value of all the outstanding policies in force on the 31st day of December, 1872, computed according to the American Experience Table of Mortality, with four and one-half per cent. interest	420,776 01
Amount of all unpaid dividends of surplus, or other profits due policyhold's.	4,372 83
Amount due on account of salaries, rents and expenses	1,888 76
Total liabilities as to policyholders	$429,037 60

IV. INCOME.

Cash received for premiums on new policies, without deductions	$121,415 52
Cash received for renewal premiums, without deductions for expense	164,832 22
Cash received for interest on cash loans	29,108 07
Cash received for interest on bonds owned and dividends on stocks	2,160 00
Cash received for interest on other debts due the company	783 67
Total income	$318,294 48

V. EXPENDITURES.

Cash paid for the company's own losses and claims, and additions thereto	$24,062 79
Cash paid on account of policies lapsed, surrendered or purchased	27,821 60
Cash paid for dividends to policyholders	28,883 10
Cash paid for dividends to stockholders	10,215 00
Cash paid for commissions to agents on first premiums	30,298 41
Cash paid for commissions to agents on renewal premiums	9,830 22
Cash paid for salaries and expenses of managers of agencies, and agents	7,675 00
Cash paid for medical examiners' fees	3,654 77
Cash paid for salaries and other compensation of officers and employes	23,400 00
Cash paid for United States taxes and revenue stamps, $400 00; state and local taxes in state where organized, $177 00; taxes, licenses and fees in other states, $2,558 75; of which the sum of $179 25 was paid in the state of Wisconsin; total	3,135 75
Cash paid for rents	1,930 00
Cash paid for commuting commissions	16,785 41
Cash paid for furniture, safes and fixtures for home and agency offices	578 41
Cash paid on any account not itemized above, viz: advertising, $3,818 87; printing, stationery and supplies, $6,637 76; postage, telegrams and express, $1,387 90; sundry office and miscellaneous expenses, $3,122 85; total	14,967 38
Total expenditures	$202,737 84

VI. EXHIBIT OF POLICIES.

NUMBER AND AMOUNT OF POLICIES AND ADDITIONS CLASSIFIED.

	No.	Amount.	No.	Amount.
Policies in force at the beginning of the year:				
Whole life policies	1,244	$4,323,391		
Endowment policies	807	2,060,228		
Joint lives and survivorships	18	68,000		
			2,069	$6,451,619
New policies issued during the year:				
Whole life policies	918	$3,459,738		
Endowment policies	271	668,830		
			1,189	4,128,578
Old policies revived during the year:				
Whole life policies	4	$20,000		
Endowment policies	6	31,000		
			10	51,000
Additions by dividends during the year:				
Whole life policies		$4,346		
Endowment policies		3,317		
Joint lives and survivorships		162		
				7,825
Totals			3,268	$10,689,016
Deduct policies decreased and ceased to be in force:				
Whole life policies	606	$2,101,712		
Endowment policies	361	947,782		
Joint lives and survivorships	8	27,162		
			975	3,076,656
Net numbers and amounts in force, December 31, 1872:				
Whole life policies	1,560	$5,705,658		
Endowment policies	723	1,815,702		
Joint lives and survivorships	10	41,000		
Totals			2,293	$7,562,360

Policies ceased to be in force during the year, with mode of termination:

	No.	Amount.
By death	11	$23,062
By surrender	106	301,086
By lapse	711	2,301,728
By change and old policies decreased		21,500
Not taken	147	429,280
Totals	975	$3,076,656

Business in the state of Wisconsin, during the year 1872:

Policies issued	10	$66,000 00
Policies in force at the end of the year	11	68,500 00
Premiums received	......	135 39

MUTUAL LIFE INSURANCE COMPANY.

CHICAGO, ILL.

E. R. PAUL, *President.* STEWART MARKS, *Secretary.*

Attorney to accept service of process in Wisconsin, BEMIS MALTBY, Madison.

[Incorporated, February 16th, 1865. Commenced business, April, 1865.]

I. CAPITAL.

Capital authorized	$200,000 00
Capital actually paid up in cash	200,000 00

II. ASSETS.

Loans secured by deeds of trust or mortgages on real estate		$142,926 12
Loans secured by pledge of bonds, stocks, or securities, as collateral		1,589 15
Premium notes and loans, taken for premiums on policies now in force		169,775 11
Cash value of real estate owned by the company, unincumbered		34,700 00
Cash market value of bonds and stocks owned by the company		151,185 01
Cash in office of company		3,131 23
Cash deposited in banks and trust companies		13,320 78
Postage and revenue stamps		90 20
Cash value of adjusted claims against fire Ins. Cos.		4,300 00
Interest accrued on cash loans and on bonds owned by the company		3,353 95
Interest accrued on premium loans and notes		3,025 10
Gross premiums uncollected, not more than three months due, on policies in force December 31, 1872	$18,640 88	
Gross deferred quarterly and semi-annual premiums, on policies in force December 31, 1872	27,109 81	
Total	$45,750 69	
Deducted to reduce the last two items to the net value of the policies	3,974 07	
Net amount deferred and outstanding prem's		41,776 62
Amount due from other companies on account of reinsured risks		279 26
Total admitted assets		$569,403 53

ITEMS NOT ADMITTED AS ASSETS.

Amount invested in commuting com's or renewal com's purchased	$1,918 88
Amount advanced to officers or agents to be repaid	5,240 92
Judgments for debts rendered in favor of the company	2,054 23
Value of agency supplies, printed matter and stationery on hand	1,500 00
Loans to agents mostly secured	5,764 86
Furniture, safes and fixtures	2,000 00
Other items, viz.: balances of agents' accounts	2,874 15
Total unadmitted items	$21,353 04

III. LIABILITIES.

Claims for death losses and matured endowments, in process of adjustment, or adjusted and not due	$11,875 00
Claims for death losses and other policy claims resisted by the company	1,000 00
Net present value of all the outstanding policies in force on the 31st day of December, 1872, computed according to the American Experience Table of Mortality, with four and one-half per cent. interest	496,338 00
Amount of all unpaid dividends of surplus, or other profits due policyholders	123 66
Total liabilities as to policyholders	$509,336 66

IV. INCOME.

Cash received for premiums on new policies, without deductions	$118,871 82
Cash received for renewal premiums, without deductions	131,601 41
Cash received for all other premiums	2,880 45
Cash premiums from other companies for reinsuring their risks	684 63
Cash received for interest on cash loans	2,437 36
Cash received for interest on bonds owned	1,641 15

Cash received for interest on premium notes or loans	$15,698 06
Rents received for use of company's property, or under sub-lease	268 80
Discount on claims paid in advance	994 81
Cash income from other sources, viz.: fire insurance, $201 70; sundry items, $495 33; total	697 03
Gross amount of notes or other obligations taken for renewal premiums	31,180 09
Total income	$306,886 61

V. EXPENDITURES.

Cash paid for the company's own losses and claims, and additions thereto	$36,298 90
Cash paid on account of policies lapsed, surrendered or purchased	87,973 74
Cash paid for dividends to policyholders	1,657 49
Cash paid for premiums to other companies for policies reinsured	3,801 37
Cash paid for commissions to agents on first premiums	15,060 86
Cash paid for commissions to agents on renewal premiums	4,347 99
Cash paid for salaries and expenses of managers of agencies, and agents	70,239 52
Cash paid for medical examiners' fees	7,147 28
Cash paid for salaries and other compensation of officers and employes	20,398 27
Cash paid for United States taxes and revenue stamps, $708 20; state and local taxes in state where organized, $704 51; taxes, licenses and fees in other states, $2,116 88; of which the sum of $337 00 was paid in the state of Wisconsin; total	3,529 59
Cash paid for rents	2,446 08
Cash paid for capital stock retired	10,000 00
Cash paid for commuting commissions	1,366 63
Cash advanced to agents or officers, to be repaid	1,140 84
Cash paid for furniture, safes and fixtures for home or agency offices	566 40
Cash paid on any account not itemized above, viz.: printing, advertising, stationery, supplies, postage, general expenses and express and legal fees	21,148 36
Total cash expenditures	$237,063 32

PREMIUM-LOAN DISBURSEMENTS.

Amount used in payment of losses and claims	$1,541 54	
Amount used in purchase of surrendered policies	876 85	
Amount used in payment of dividends to policyholders	956 69	
Amount voided by lapse of policies	5,496 19	
Total premium note expenditures		8,871 27
Total expenditures		$245,934 59

VI. PREMIUM-NOTE ACCOUNT.

Premium notes and other prem. obligations at beginning of the year		$147,854 51
Premium notes and other prem. obligations received during the year		31,180 09
Total		$179,034 60
Deductions during the year as follows:		
Amount used in payment of losses and claims	$1,541 54	
Amount used in purchase of surrendered policies	876 85	
Amount used in payment of dividends to policy holders	956 69	
Amount voided by lapse of policies	5,496 19	
Amount redeemed by maker in cash	388 22	
Total reduction of premium note account		9,259 49
Balance, note assets at end of the year		$169,775 11

VII. EXHIBIT OF POLICIES.

NUMBER AND AMOUNT OF POLICIES AND ADDITIONS CLASSIFIED.

	Number.	Amount.	Number.	Amount.
Policies in force at the beginning of the year:				
Endowment policies	3,171	$4,906,476		
Joint lives and survivorships	75	111,767		
Short term and irregular policies	27	49,500		
			3,273	$5,067,743
New policies issued during the year:				
Endowment policies	2,302	$4,057,483		
Joint lives and survivorships	3	561		
Short term and irregular policies	42	95,500		
			2,347	4,153,544
Old policies revived during the year:				
Endowment policies	381	$562,550		
Joint lives and survivorships	6	9,000		
Short term and irregular policies	4	15,000		
			391	586,550
Totals			6,011	$9,807,837

Deduct policies decreased and ceased to be in force				
Endowment policies	2,251	$3,626,365	......	....
Joint lives and survivorships	29	46,575	......	....
Short term and irregular policies	17	42,000	......	....
			2,297	$3,714,940
Totals at the end of the year.				
Endowment policies	3,603	$5,900,144	......	....
Joint lives and survivorships	55	74,753	......	....
Short term and irregular policies	56	118,000	......	....
			3,714	$6,092,897
Deduct policies reinsured.				
Endowment policies	......	....	48	192,670
Net numbers and amounts in force, December 31, 1872			3,666	$5,900,227

Policies ceased to be in force during the year, with mode of termination:

	No.	Amount.
By death	27	$43,611
By surrender	285	454,109
By lapse	1,338	2,154,014
Not taken	647	1,063,206
Totals	2,297	$3,714,940

Business in the state of Wisconsin, during the year 1872:

Policies issued	155	$250,940 00
Policies in force at the end of the year	168	259,577 00
Premiums received	......	11,642 37
Losses paid	......	1,000 00

MUTUAL LIFE INSURANCE COMPANY.

New York.

F. S. WINSTON, *President.* JOHN M. STUART, *Secretary.*

Attorney to accept service of process in Wisconsin, Sam'l M. Ogden, Milwaukee.

[Incorporated in 1842. Commenced business February 1, 1843.]

I. CAPITAL.

Capital authorized Capital actually paid up in cash	None.

II. ASSETS.

Loans secured by deeds of trust or mortgages on real estate		$47,002,804 87
Cash value of real estate owned by the company, unincumbered		1,314,607 57
Cash market value of bonds and stocks owned by the company		6,146,004 75
Cash in office of company and in banks		2,159,863 69
Interest accrued on cash loans and on bonds owned by the company		753,679 94
Gross premiums uncollected, not more than three months due, on policies in force Dec. 31, 1872	$112,841 43	....
Gross deferred quarterly and semi-annual prem's. on policies in force Dec. 31, 1872	1,036,158 44	....
Total	$1,148,999 87	....
Deducted to reduce the last two items, to the net value of the policies	114,899 99	....
Net amount deferred and outstanding prem's		1,034,099 88
Total admitted assets		$58,411,058 90

ITEMS NOT ADMITTED AS ASSETS.

Cash in hands of agents due the company	$24,100 53
Total unadmitted items	$24,100 53

III. LIABILITIES.

Claims for death losses and matured endowments, in process of adjustment, or adjusted and not due	$552,475 20
Net present value of the outstanding policies in force on the 31st day of December, 1872, computed according to the American Experience Table of Mortality, with four and one-half per cent. interest	51,667,250 00
Amount of any other liability, viz.: Surplus on Tontine policies, $17,562.30; post mortem dividends due, $24,000; prem's paid in advance, $29,618.38; total	71,180 68
Total liabilities as to policyholders	$52,290,905 88

IV. INCOME.

Cash received for new premiums during the year, without deductions	$4,932,185 08
Cash received for renewal premiums, without deductions for expense	9,449,228 78
Cash received for sale of annuities	5,500 00
Cash received for interest on cash loans	2,867,041 58
Cash received for interest on bonds owned and dividends on stocks	319,731 64
Cash received for interest on other debts due the company	61,359 06
Rents received for use of company's property, or under sub-lease	54,250 00
Premium on gold interest	26,848 45
Total income	$17,716,094 54

V. EXPENDITURES.

Cash paid for the company's own losses and claims, and additions thereto	$2,722,666 75
Cash paid to annuitants	17,590 02
Cash paid on account of policies lapsed, surrendered or purchased	1,555,008 72
Cash paid for dividends to policyholders	5,259,206 14
Cash paid for commissions to agents on new and renewal premiums	335,015 29
Cash paid for medical examiners' fees	38,506 80
Cash paid for salaries and other compensation of officers and employes	268,702 90
Cash paid for taxes, revenue stamps, state licenses and fees	114,638 93
Cash paid for commuting commissions	332,448 46
Cash paid for furniture, safes and fixtures for home or agency offices	1,990 20
Cash paid on any account not itemized above, viz.: exchange, postage advertising, law, printing, stationery, etc	260,408 19
Total expenditures	$10,906,181 40

VI. EXHIBIT OF POLICIES.

NUMBER AND AMOUNT OF POLICIES AND ADDITIONS CLASSIFIED.

	No.	Amount.	No.	Amount.
Policies in force at the beginning of the year:				
Whole life policies	54,647	$175,059,971 00	......	....
Endowment policies	19,053	53,472,696 00	......	....
Joint lives and survivorships	211	256,741 00	......	....
			73,911	$228,789,408 00
New policies issued during the year:				
Whole life policies	7,608	$23,824,595 00	......	....
Endowment policies	2,438	4,777,440 00	......	....
Joint lives and survivorships	8	8,187 00	......	....
			10,052	28,610,222 00
Old policies revived during the year:				
Whole life policies	1,545	$4,821,600 00	......	....
Endowment policies	586	1,506,490 00	......	....
			2,131	6,328,090 00
Old policies increased during the year:				
Endowment policies	......	....	3	13,500 00
Additions by dividends during the year	......	....	......	24,812,149 00
Totals			86,097	$288,553,369 00
Deduct policies decreased and ceased to be in force:				
Whole life policies	5,197	$16,859,195 00	......	....
Endowment policies	2,687	7,262,830 00	......	....
Joint lives and survivorships	20	52,000	......	....
			7,904	23,675,025 00
Net numbers and amounts in force December 31st, 1872:				
Whole life policies	58,603	$187,346,971 00	......	....
Endowment policies	19,391	52,507,296 00	......	....
Joint lives and survivorships	199	211,928 00	......	....
Additions by dividends	......	24,812,149 00	......	....
Totals			78,193	$264,878,344 00

Policies ceased to be in force during the year, with mode of termination:

By death	761	$2,407,625 00
By surrender and lapse	5,979	18,053,595 00
By change and old policies decreased	3	13,500 00
Not taken	1,161	8,200,305 00
Totals	7,904	$28,675,025 00

Business in the state of Wisconsin during the year 1872:

Policies issued	175	$343,315 00
Policies in force at the end of the year	2,151	4,481,280 00
Premiums received	......	173,407 45
Losses paid	......	42,830 94

MUTUAL BENEFIT LIFE INSURANCE COMPANY.

NEWARK, N. J.

LEWIS C. GROVER, *President.* EDWARD A. STRONG, *Secretary.*

Attorney to accept service of process in Wisconsin, CHAS. D. ADSIT, Milwaukee.

[Incorporated January 31st, 1845. Commenced business April, 1845.]

I. CAPITAL.

Capital actually paid up in cash	Mutual.

II. ASSETS.

Loans secured by deeds of trust or mortgages on real estate		$10,224,302 70
Premium notes and loans, taken for premiums, on policies now in force		6,854,426 31
Cash value of real estate owned by the company, unincumbered		149,062 38
Cash market value of bonds and stocks owned by the company		7,893,029 38
Cash in office of company		21,754 50
Cash deposited in banks and trust companies		481,963 44
Interest accrued on cash loans and on bonds owned by the company		329,091 88
Interest accrued on premium loans and notes		205,590 00
Gross premiums uncollected, on policies in force December 31, 1872	$393,957 72	....
Gross deferred quarterly and semi-annual premiums, on policies in force December 31, 1872	44,724 23	....
Total	$438,681 95	....
Deducted to reduce the last two items, to the net value of the policies	109,670 49	....
Net amount deferred and outstanding prem's		329,011 46
Total admitted assets		$26,488,232 05

ITEMS NOT ADMITTED AS ASSETS.

Cash in hands of agents due the company	$118,978 25
Total unadmitted items	$118,978 25

III. LIABILITIES.

Claims for death losses due and unpaid	$46,675 00
Claims for death losses and matured endowments, in process of adjustment, or adjusted and not due	552,750 00
Claims for death losses and other policy claims resisted by the company	154,800 00
Net present value of all the outstanding policies in force on the 31st day of December, 1872, computed according to the Actuaries' Table of Mortality, with four per cent. interest	22,042,372 00
Amount of all unpaid dividends of surplus, or other profits due policyholders	348,624 53
Amount of dividends declared payable in 1873, discounted to date	1,533,652 22
Total liabilities as to policyholders	$24,678,873 75

IV. INCOME.

Item	Amount
Cash received for new and renewal premiums, without deductions	$4,543,394 14
Cash received for sale of annuities	770 99
Cash received for interest on bonds owned and dividends on stocks	1,155,580 85
Cash received for interest on premium notes or loans	364,889 42
Rents received for use of company's property, or under sub-lease	3,050 00
Discount on claims paid in advance	696 41
Gross amount of notes or other obligations taken for new and renewal prem's	800,844 87
Total income	$6,869,055 68

V. EXPENDITURES.

Item	Amount
Cash paid for the company's own losses and claims, and additions thereto	$1,823,371 46
Cash paid to annuitants	1,465 70
Cash paid on account of policies lapsed, surrendered or purchased	168,835 38
Cash paid for dividends to policyholders	1,423,512 54
Cash paid for commissions to agents on first and renewal premiums	406,942 88
Cash paid for medical examiners' fees	20,882 23
Cash paid for salaries and other compensation of officers and employes	65,512 45
Cash paid for taxes, revenue stamps, state licenses and fees	84,644 00
Cash paid on any account not itemized above, viz: advertising, printing, postage, exchange, etc	95,419 85
Total cash expenditures	$4,085,586 48

PREMIUM-LOAN DISBURSEMENTS.

Item	Amount
Amount used in payment of losses and claims	128,374 87
Amount used in purchase of surrendered policies	122,189 60
Amount used in payment of dividends to policyholders	236,913 46
Total expenditures	$4,573,068 91

VI. PREMIUM-NOTE ACCOUNT.

Item		Amount
Premium notes and other prem. obligations at beginning of the year		$6,551,855 72
Premium notes and other prem. obligations received during the year		800,844 87
Total		$7,352,700 09
Deductions during the year as follows:		
Amount used in payment of losses and claims	$128,374 87	...
Amount used in purchase of surrendered policies	122,189 60	...
Amount used in payment of dividends to policyholders	236,913 46	...
Amount redeemed by maker, in cash	12,251 76	...
Total reduction of premium note account		499,729 19
Balance, note assets at end of the year		$6,852,970 90

VII. EXHIBIT OF POLICIES.

NUMBER AND AMOUNT OF POLICIES AND ADDITIONS CLASSIFIED.

	Number.	Amount.	Number.	Amount.
Policies in force at the beginning of the year:				
Whole life policies	35,665	$122,683,695	......	......
Endowment policies	2,961	10,307,387	......	......
Short term and irregular policies	42	95,860	......	......
			38,668	$133,086,942
New policies issued during the year:				
Whole life policies	2,689	$8,224,535	......	......
Endowment policies	416	1,104,555	......	......
Short term and irregular policies	16	39,600	......	......
			*3,121	9,368,690
Old policies revived during the year:				
Whole life policies	46	$146,550	......	......
Endowment policies	4	18,000	......	......
			50	164,550
Old policies increased during the year:				
Whole life policies	1	$30,600	......	......
Endowment policies	.....	9,223	......	......
			1	39,823
Old policies changed				
Whole life policies	6	$13,000	......	......
Endowment policies	3	6,500	......	......
			9	19,500
Totals			41,849	$142,679,505

Deduct policies decreased and ceased to be in force:

Whole life policies	2,094	$8,128,594	......	......
Endowment policies	295	1,295,812	......	......
Short term and irregular policies	26	62,000	......	......

Old policies changed:

Whole life policies	3	6,500	......	......
Endowment policies	6	13,000	......	......
			2,424	$9,515,336

Net numbers and amounts in force December 31st, 1872:

Whole life policies	36,810	$122,958,856	......	......
Endowment policies	3,083	10,137,358	......	......
Short term and irregular policies	32	73,460	......	......
Totals			39,425	$133,164,169

Policies ceased to be in force during the year, with mode of termination:

	Number.	Amount.
By death	506	$1,979,070
By expiry	14	47,000
By surrender	159	516,100
By lapse	991	3,039,325
By change and old policies decreased	384	2,869,741
Not taken	364	1,044,600
Totals	2,415	$9,495,836

Business in the state of Wisconsin during the year 1872:

Policies issued	69	$104,500 00
Policies in force at the end of the year	219	740,320 00
Premiums received	......	14,230 02
Losses paid	......	20,000 00

NATIONAL LIFE INSURANCE COMPANY.

CHICAGO, ILL.

BENJAMIN LOMBARD, *President.* H. G. TEED, *Secretary.*

Attorney to accept service of process in Wisconsin, J. A. PINTO, Green Bay.

[Incorporated, February 16, 1865. Commenced business, May 26, 1870.]

I. CAPITAL.

Capital authorized	$500,000 00
Capital actually paid up in cash	240,000 00

II. ASSETS.

Loans secured by deeds of trust or mortgages on real estate		$108,400 00
Loans secured by pledge of bonds, stocks, or securities, as collateral		49,656 25
Premium notes and loans, taken for prem's, on policies now in force		11,069 23
Cash value of real estate owned by the company, unincumbered		57,727 00
Cash market value of bonds and stocks owned by the company		27,000 00
Cash in office of company		10,107 68
Cash deposited in banks and trust companies		6,087 30
Postage and revenue stamps		68 70
Interest accrued on cash loans and on bonds owned by the company		14,294 00
Gross premiums uncollected, not more than three months due, on policies in force December 31, 1872	$16,960 01	......
Gross deferred quarterly and semi-annual premiums, on policies in force December 31, 1872	106,019 00	......
Total	$122,988 01	......
Deducted to reduce the last two items, to the net value of the policies	15,080 50	......
Net amount deferred and outstanding prem's		107,957 51
Total admitted assets		$392,307 62

ITEMS NOT ADMITTED AS ASSETS.

Cash in hands of officers or agents due the company	$15,000 00
Judgments for debts rendered in favor of the company	3,000 00
Value of agency supplies, printed matter and stationery on hand	5,000 00
Furniture, safes and fixtures	1,894 00
Total unadmitted items	$24,894 00

III. LIABILITIES.

Claims for death losses due and unpaid	$20,130 95
Claims for death losses and matured endowments, in process of adjustment, or adjusted and not due	42,988 00
Claims for death losses and other policy claims resisted by the company	7,000 00
Net present value of all the outstanding policies in force on the 31st day of December, 1872, computed according to the Actuaries' Table of Mortality, with four per cent. interest	76,996 22
Amount due for advances for expenses of organization	7,184 82
Total liabilities as to policyholders	$154,299 99

IV. INCOME.

Cash received for premiums on new policies, without deductions	$118,135 87
Cash received for renewal premiums, without deductions for expense	148,986 76
Cash received for interest from all sources	6,585 79
Total income	$273,708 42

V. EXPENDITURES.

Cash paid for the company's own losses and claims, and additions thereto	$116,982 42
Cash paid on account of policies lapsed, surrendered or purchased	380 18
Cash paid for commissions to agents on first premiums	36,976 36
Cash paid for salaries and expenses of managers of agencies, and agents	16,751 74
Cash paid for medical examiners' fees	4,249 60
Cash paid for salaries and other compensation of officers and employes	28,300 29
Cash paid for taxes, revenue stamps, state licenses and fees	4,591 55
Cash paid for rents	4,068 16
Cash paid for furniture, safes and fixtures for home or agency offices	2,914 78
Cash paid on any account not itemized above, viz: advertising, $6,615.07; postage, exchange and express, $5,417.46; printing, $12,852.51; law expenses, $561.55; building account, $7,204.26; incidental expenses, $6,859.82; total	39,510 67
Total cash expenditures	$254,635 75

PREMIUM-LOAN DISBURSEMENTS.

Amount voided by lapse of policies	4,616 68
Total expenditures	$259,252 43

VI. PREMIUM-NOTE ACCOUNT.

Premium notes and other premium obligations at beginning of the year		$19,720 23
Deductions during the year as follows:		
Amount voided by lapse of policies	$4,616 68	
Amount redeemed by maker in cash	4,044 32	
Total reduction of premium note account		8,661 00
Balance, note assets at end of the year		$11,059 23

VII. EXHIBIT OF POLICIES.

NUMBER AND AMOUNT OF POLICIES AND ADDITIONS CLASSIFIED.

	Number.	Amount.	Number.	Amount.
Policies in force at the beginning of the year:				
Whole life policies	6	$13,000		
Endowment policies	1	1,000		
Short term and irregular policies	5,288	6,658,000		
			5,295	$6,672,000
New policies issued during the year:				
Whole life policies	21	$37,000		
Endowment policies	39	46,000		
Short term and irregular policies	4,608	6,484,000		
			4,668	6,567,000
Old policies revived during the year:				
Whole life policies			10	14,600
Totals			9,969	$13,253,600

Deduct policies decreased and ceased to be in force:

Whole life policies	7	$9,000	......	......
Endowment policies	15	20,000	......	......
Short term and irregular policies	5,072	6,806,000	......	......
Totals			5,094	$6,835,000

Net numbers and amounts in force Dec. 31, 1872:

Whole life policies	30	$55,600	......	......
Endowment policies	25	27,000	......	......
Short term and irregular policies	4,820	6,836,000	......	......
Totals			4,875	$6,918,600

Policies ceased to be in force during the year, with mode of termination:

	Number.	Amount
By death	88	$107,000
By surrender	8	9,000
By lapse	4,646	5,649,000
Not taken	362	570,000
Totals	5,094	$6,335,000

Business in the state of Wisconsin during the year 1872:

Policies issued	308	$398,000
Premiums received		4,000
Losses paid		3,000

NATIONAL LIFE INSURANCE COMPANY OF THE U. S. OF AMERICA.

WASHINGTON, D. C.

E. A. ROLLINS, *President.* JOHN M. BUTLER, *Secretary.*

Attorney to accept service of process in Wisconsin, L. S. HANKS, Madison.

[Incorporated July 26, 1868. Commenced business Aug. 1, 1868.]

I. CAPITAL.

Capital authorized	$1,000,000 00
Capital actually paid up in cash	1,000,000 00

II. ASSETS.

Loans secured by deeds of trust or mortgages on real estate		$909,912 44
Loans secured by pledge of bonds, stocks or securities as collateral		850,000 00
Premium notes and loans taken for prem's on policies now in force		1,925 11
Cash market value of bonds and stocks owned by the company		532,320 00
Cash in office of company and deposited in bank		78,813 41
Interest accrued on cash loans and on bonds owned by the company		34,176 54
Gross premiums uncollected, not more than three months due, on policies in force December 31, 1872	$23,335 32	......
Gross deferred quarterly and semi-annual premiums, on policies in force Dec. 31, 1872	104,367 00	......
Total	$127,702 32	......
Deducted to reduce the last two items to the net value of the policies	17,274 32	......
Net amount deferred and outstanding premiums		110,428 00
Total admitted assets		$2,517,575 50

ITEMS NOT ADMITTED AS ASSETS.

Amount invested in commuting com's, or renewal com's purchased	$8,000 00
Furniture, safes and fixtures	4,771 07
Loans on personal security only	1,600 49
Suspense acct. mostly balances due from agents, secured	14,690 25
Total unadmitted items	$29,061 81

III. LIABILITIES.

Claims for death losses due and unpaid...		$200 0
Claims for death losses and matured endowments, in process of adjustment, or adjusted and not due		64,896 8
Claims for death losses and other policy claims resisted by the company....		1,000 00
Net present value of all the outstanding policies in force on the 31st day of December, 1872, computed according to the American Experience Table of Mortality, with four and one-half per cent. interest		1,664,163 00
Net present value of policies as computed by the company, with six per cent. interest	$1,844,421 00	
Total liabilities as to policyholders		$1,730,259 87

IV. INCOME.

Cash received for new and renewal premiums, without deductions	$708,296 10
Cash received for sale of annuities	5,000 00
Cash received for all other premiums	1,459 07
Cash received for interest on cash loans	123,697 35
Cash received for interest on bonds owned and dividends on stocks	32,263 50
Cash received for interest on premium notes, or loans on policies	100 44
Cash received for interest on other debts due the company	1,258 90
Discount on claims paid in advance	40 38
Cash income from other sources, viz: gold premiums	12,850 08
Total income	$884,895 82

V. EXPENDITURES.

Cash paid for the company's own losses and claims, and additions thereto....	$179,880 88
Cash paid to other companies for losses or claims on their policies reinsured by this company	10,000 00
Cash paid to annuitants	394 00
Cash paid on account of policies lapsed, surrendered or purchased	51,682 59
Cash paid for dividends to stockholders	30,000 00
Cash paid for premiums to other companies for policies reinsured	26,327 63
Cash paid for commissions to agents on first and renewal premiums	60,877 45
Cash paid for salaries and expenses of managers of agencies, and agents	27,269 97
Cash paid for medical examiners' fees	8,486 00
Cash paid for salaries and other compensation of officers and employes	38,935 95
Cash paid for United States taxes and revenue stamps, $369.80; taxes, licenses and fees in other states, $8,018.10, of which the sum of $333, was paid in the State of Wisconsin; total	8,382 90
Cash paid for rents	7,500 00
Cash paid for commuting commissions	4,500 00
Cash paid on any account not itemized above, viz: exchange and postage, $4,621.97; advertising, $8,917.78; printing and stationery, $9,612.09; sundries, $16,213.53; total	39,365 37
Total expenditures	$493,539 64

VI. EXHIBIT OF POLICIES.

NUMBER AND AMOUNT OF POLICIES AND ADDITIONS CLASSIFIED.

	Number.	Amount.	Number.	Amount.
Policies in force at the beginning of the year:				
Whole life policies...	6,586	$15,919,422	......	....
Endowment policies	1,178	2,065,826	......	....
Short term and irregular policies	139	480,224	......	....
			7,903	$18,465,472
New policies issued during the year:				
Whole life policies	2,611	$5,320,908	......	....
Endowment policies	446	616,249	......	....
Short term and irregular policies	53	260,300	......	....
			3,110	6,197,457
Additions by prems. on R. P. policies	......	......	....	655,258
Totals			11,013	$25,318,187
Deduct policies decreased and ceased to be in force:				
Whole life policies	1,485	$3,321,129	......	....
Endowment policies	294	493,550	......	....
Short term and irregular policies	44	152,900	......	....
			1,823	3,967,579
Totals at the end of the year:				
Whole life policies	7,712	$17,919,201	......	....
Endowment policies	1,330	2,188,526	......	....
Short term and irregular policies	148	587,624	......	....
			9,190	$21,350,608

Deduct policies reinsured:

Whole life policies	188	$1,098,000	......	....
			188	$1,098,000

Net numbers and amounts in force December 31st, 1872:

Whole life policies	7,529	$16,881,201	......	....
Endowment policies	1,330	2,188,525	......	....
Short term and irregular policies	148	587,694	......	....
Totals			9,007	$20,252,608

Policies ceased to be in force during the year, with mode of termination:

	Number.	Amount.
By death	71	$206,996
By surrender	55	205,956
By lapse	946	1,931,450
By change and old policies decreased	270	697,550
Not taken	481	925,697
Totals	1,823	$3,967,579

Business in the State of Wisconsin during the year 1872:

Policies issued	141	$231,971 00
Policies in force at the end of the year	247	489,707 00
Premiums received	......	15,152 38

NEW ENGLAND MUTUAL LIFE INSURANCE COMPANY.

BOSTON, MASS.

BENJ. F. STEVENS, *President.* JOSEPH M. GIBBENS, *Secretary.*

Attorney to accept service of process in Wisconsin, E. N. PUSHEE, Milwaukee.

[Incorporated April 1st, 1835. Commenced business Dec'r 1st, 1843.]

I. CAPITAL.

Capital authorized	Purely Mutual.
Capital actually paid up in cash	

II. ASSETS.

Loans secured by deeds of trust or mortgages on real estate		$1,695,342 91
Loans secured by pledge of bonds, stocks, or securities, as collateral		549,318 77
Premium notes and loans, taken for premiums, on policies now in force		2,289,271 10
Cash value of real estate owned by the company, unincumbered		600,000 00
Cash market value of bonds and stocks owned by the company		5,225,463 75
Cash deposited in banks and trust companies		195,880 65
Interest accrued on cash loans and on bonds owned by the company		164,438 43
Interest accrued on premium loans and notes		83,000 00
Rents accrued for use of company's property, or under sub-lease		8,700 71
Gross premiums uncollected, not more than three months due, on policies in force December 31, 1872	$432,186 84	....
Gross deferred quarterly and semi-annual premiums, on policies in force December 31, 1872	288,377 28	....
Total	$720,564 12	....
Deducted to reduce the last two items, to the net value of the policies	42,517 70	....
Net amount deferred and outstanding premiums		678,046 42
Total admitted assets		$11,489,462 74

III. LIABILITIES.

Claims for death losses due and unpaid	$102,730 00
Net present value of all the outstanding policies in force on the 31st day of December, 1872, computed according to the Combined Experience Table of Mortality, with four per cent. interest	10,092,462 68
Amount of all unpaid dividends of surplus, or other profits due policyholders.	75,845 58
Total liabilities as to policyholders	$10,271,038 26

IV. INCOME.

Cash received for premiums on new policies, without deductions	$284,186 52
Cash received for renewal premiums without deductions for expense	1,580,682 23
Cash received for interest on cash loans	187,564 15
Cash received for interest on bonds owned and dividends on stocks	305,181 69
Cash received for interest on premium notes or loans	163,925 46
Cash received for interest on other debts due the company	2,339 60
Rents received for use of company's property	32,900 18
Gross amount of notes or other obligations taken for new and renewal premiums	957,582 61
Total income	$3,364,282 44

V. EXPENDITURES.

Cash paid for the company's own losses and claims, and additions thereto	$787,554 58
Cash paid on account of policies lapsed, surrendered or purchased	236,626 55
Cash paid for distributions to policyholders	240,900 27
Cash paid for commissions to agents on first premiums	42,864 44
Cash paid for commissions to agents on renewal premiums	122,085 63
Cash paid for medical examiners' fees	11,633 62
Cash paid for salaries and other compensation of officers and employes	50,000 00
Cash paid for taxes, revenue stamps, state licenses and fees	23,868 18
Cash paid for commuting commissions	96,834 65
Cash paid for printing and other incidental expenses	93,678 68
Cash paid for advertising	9,558 91
Cash paid for interest accrued on the investments of the year	18,775 52
Total cash expenditures	$1,736,330 96

PREMIUM-LOAN DISBURSEMENTS.

Amount used in payment of losses and claims	84,343 47
Amount used in purchase of surrendered policies	61,311 60
Amount used in payment of distributions to policyholders	222,483 04
Amount voided by lapse of policies	154,208 54
Total expenditures	$2,208,672 63

VI. PREMIUM-NOTE ACCOUNT.

Premium notes and other premium obligations at beginning of the year		$2,494,435 33
Premium notes and other premium obligations received during the year		957,582 61
Total		$3,451,967 94
Deductions during the year as follows:		
Amount used in payment of losses and claims	$84,343 47	
Amount used in purchase of surrendered policies	61,311 60	
Amount used in payment of distributions to policyholders	222,483 04	
Amount voided by lapse of policies	154,208 54	
Amount redeemed by maker in cash	401,977 91	
Total reduction of premium-note account		874,319 56
Balance, note assets at end of the year		$2,577,648 38

VII. EXHIBIT OF POLICIES.

NUMBER AND AMOUNT OF POLICIES AND ADDITIONS CLASSIFIED.

	Number.	Amount.
Policies in force at the beginning of the year	22,893	$67,815,733
New policies made out during the year	2,128	5,065,298
Old policies revived during the year	671	1,797,720
Additions by dividends during the year	......	11,761
Totals	25,691	$74,690,506
Deduct policies decreased and ceased to be in force	3,354	8,725,981
Net numbers and amounts in force December 31st, 1872	22,337	$65,964,525

Policies ceased to be in force during the year, with mode of termination:

	Number.	Amount.
By death	262	$773,018
By expiry	24	63,200
By surrender	455	1,422,843
By lapse	2,162	5,354,698
By change and old policies decreased	......	40,000
Not taken	451	1,072,222
Totals	3,354	$8,725,981

Business in the state of Wisconsin during the year 1872:

	Number.	Amount.
Policies issued	55	$63,481 00
Policies in force at the end of the year	386	546,473 00
Premiums received	......	27,611 28
Losses paid	......	6,000 00

NEW JERSEY MUTUAL LIFE INSURANCE COMPANY.

NEWARK, N. J.

WM. E. PLUMMER, *President.* JOHN J. ANDERSON, *Secretary.*

Attorney to accept service of process in Wisconsin, WILLIAM S. GRAY, Milwaukee.

[Incorporated March 19, 1863. Commenced business January 1, 1865.]

I. CAPITAL.

Capital authorized	$100,000 00
Capital actually paid up in cash	100,000 00

II. ASSETS.

Loans secured by deeds of trust or mortgages on real estate		$464,322 84
Loans secured by pledge of bonds, stocks, or securities, as collateral		85,479 80
Premium notes and loans, taken for premiums, on policies now in force		289,527 53
Cash market value of bonds and stocks owned by the company		79,997 05
Cash in office of company		11,602 51
Cash deposited in banks and trust companies		70,304 83
Interest accrued on cash loans and bonds owned by the company		13,388 30
Interest accrued on premium loans and notes		10,339 58
Gross premiums uncollected, not more than three months due, on policies in force Dec. 31, 1872	$126,185 58	....
Gross deferred quarterly and semi-annual premiums, on policies in force December 31, 1872	102,427 21	....
Total	$228,612 79	....
Deducted to reduce the last two items to the net value of the policies	17,145 90	....
Net amount deferred and outstanding premiums		211,466 89
Due from other companies on account of reinsured risks		14,642 27
Total admitted assets		$1,251,071 60

ITEMS NOT ADMITTED AS ASSETS.

Cash in hands of agents due the company	$39,038 79
Value of agency supplies, printed matter and stationery on hand	8,504 25
Furniture, safes and fixtures	32,798 88
Total unadmitted items	$80,341 92

III. LIABILITIES.

Claims for death losses and matured endowments, in process of adjustment, or adjusted and not due	$37,000 00
Amount due and unpaid on annuity claims	13,672 00
Net present value of all the outstanding policies in force on the 31st day of December, 1872, computed according to the American Experience Table of Mortality, with four and one-half per cent. interest	1,103,159 00
Reserve on reinsured policies	26,408 00
Total liabilities as to policyholders	$1,180,297 00

IV. INCOME.

Cash received for new and renewal premiums, without deductions	$341,268 51
Cash premiums from other companies for reinsuring their risks	322,058 57
Cash received for interest from all sources	36,672 84
Discount on claims paid in advance	483 63
Gross amount of notes or other obligations taken for new and renewal pr'ms.	174,128 19
Total income	$874,611 74

V. EXPENDITURES.

Cash paid for the company's own losses and claims, and additions thereto....		$86,898 71
Cash paid to other companies for losses or claims on their policies reinsured by this company		6,750 11
Cash paid on account of policies lapsed, surrendered or purchased		23,441 52
Cash paid for dividends to policyholders		26,764 08
Cash paid for dividends to stockholders		2,000 00
Cash paid for premiums to other companies for policies reinsured		4,898 08
Cash paid for commissions to agents on first and renewal premiums....		34,159 10
Cash paid for medical examiners' fees....		5,596 85
Cash paid for salaries and other compensation of officers and employes....		14,649 60
Cash paid for taxes, revenue stamps state licenses and fees....		8,465 87
Cash paid for rents....		5,890 76
Cash paid for interest on guarantee capital....		11,250 00
Cash paid on any account not itemized above, viz: advertising, $4,785 98; expense, $7,075 12; printing, $3,429 71; postage and exchange, $2,109 02; total....		17,399 78
Total cash expenditures		$248,019 36
PREMIUM-LOAN DISBURSEMENTS.		
Amount used in payment of losses and claims....	$1,525 53	....
Amount used in purchase of lapsed and surrendered policies	8,997 07	....
Amount used in payment of dividends to policyholders....	356 58	....
Total premium note expenditures....		10,879 18
Total expenditures....		$258,898 54

VI. PREMIUM-NOTE ACCOUNT.

Premium notes and other premium obligations at beginning of the year....		$180,334 83
Premium notes and other premium obligations received during the year....		174,128 19
Total		$354,453 02
Deductions during the year as follows:		
Amount used in payment of losses and claims....	$1,525 53	....
Amount used in purchase of lapsed and surrendered policies	8,997 07	....
Amount used in payment of dividends to policyholders....	356 58	....
Amount redeemed by maker in cash....	54,046 31	....
Total reduction of premium note account....		64,925 49
Balance, note assets at end of the year....		$289,527 53

VII. EXHIBIT OF POLICIES.

NUMBER AND AMOUNT OF POLICIES AND ADDITIONS CLASSIFIED.

	Number.	Amount.
Policies in force at the beginning of the year....	3,984	$8,049,051 78
New policies issued during the year	6,162	12,893,015 00
Additions by dividends during the year....		4,925 40
Totals	10,146	$20,946,992 18
Deduct policies decreased and ceased to be in force....	1,273	2,780,325 39
Totals at the end of the year....	8,873	$18,166,666 79
Deduct policies reinsured....		260,500 00
Net numbers and amounts in force December 31, 1872	8,873	17,906,166 79
Policies ceased to be in force during the year, with mode of termination:		
By death	48	$100,800 00
By expiry....	5	23,000 00
By surrender	273	665,309 39
By lapse....	563	665,755 00
By change and old policies decreased		414,611 00
Not taken	384	910,850 00
Totals	1,273	$2,780,325 39

NEW YORK LIFE INSURANCE COMPANY.

New York.

MORRIS FRANKLIN, *President.* WILLIAM H. BEERS, *V. P & Actuary.*

Attorney to accept service of process in Wisconsin, L. S. Kellogg, Fort Atkinson.

[Incorporated 1841. Commenced business 1845.]

I. CAPITAL.

Capital authorized	Purely
Capital actually paid up in cash	Mutual.

II. ASSETS.

Loans secured by deeds of trust or mortgages on real estate		$11,890,584 26
Premium notes and loans taken for premiums on policies now in force		986,244 08
Cash value of real estate owned by the company, unincumbered		1,768,174 14
Cash market value of bonds and stocks owned by the company		4,274,225 33
Cash in office of company		17,433 40
Cash deposited in banks and trust companies, and in course of transmission.		2,225,313 24
Interest accrued on cash loans and on bonds owned by the company		68,201 97
Interest accrued on premium loans and notes		30,564 64
Rents accrued for use of company's property, or under sub-lease		18,385 73
Gross premiums uncollected, not more than three months due, on policies in force December 31, 1872	$301,517 83	
Gross deferred quarterly and semi-annual premiums, on policies in force December 31, 1872	591,405 51	
Total	$892,923 34	
Deducted to reduce the last two items to the net value of the policies	133,938 50	
Net amount deferred and outstanding premiums		758,984 84
Total admitted assets		$21,583,061 64

III. LIABILITIES.

Claims for death losses and matured endowments, in process of adjustment or adjusted and not due	$406,212 00
Claims for death losses and policy claims resisted by the company	68,000 00
Net present value of all the outstanding policies in force on the 31st day of December, 1872, computed according to the American Experience Table of Mortality, with four and one-half per cent. interest	18,089,360 00
Amount of all unpaid dividends of surplus, or other profits due policyholders	131,436 76
Total liabilities as to policyholders	$18,695,008 76

IV. INCOME.

Cash rec'd for prem's on new policies and renewal prem's, without deduct'ns	$5,948,585 76
Cash received for sale of annuities	45,101 73
Cash received for int. on cash loans	775,527 01
Cash received for interest on bonds owned and dividends on stocks	281,315 63
Cash received for interest on premium notes or loans	68,730 56
Rents received for use of company's property, or under sub lease	78,433 24
Cash income from other sources, viz: profits on sale of bonds and loans	84,074 08
Gross amount of notes or other obligations taken for new and renewal prem's	283,699 08
Total income	$7,515,407 05

V. EXPENDITURES.

Cash paid for the company's own losses and claims, and additions thereto	$1,892,350 08
Cash paid to annuitants	17,181 47
Cash paid on account of policies lapsed, surrendered or purchased	1,432,452 03
Cash paid for dividends to policyholders	635,592 04
Cash paid for premiums to other companies for policies reinsured	32,425 09
Cash paid for commissions to agents on first and renewal premiums	387,492 23
Cash paid for salaries and expenses of managers of agencies, and agents	25,000 00
Cash paid for medical examiners' fees	55,425 17
Cash paid for salaries and other compensation of officers and employes	129,423 97
Cash paid for taxes, revenue stamps, state licenses and fees	89,455 16
Cash paid for commuting commissions	51,899 72
Cash paid on any account not itemized above, viz: advertising, law, office and agency expenses	219,596 90
Total cash expenditures	$4,407,798 79

PREMIUM-LOAN DISBURSEMENTS.

Amount used in payment of losses and claims	$17,169 85	
Amount used in purchase of surrendered policies	8,941 58	
Amount used in payment of dividends to policyholders	156,010 56	
Amount voided by lapse of policies	40,395 87	
Total premium note expenditures		222,517 86
Total expenditures		$4,630,311 65

VI .PREMIUM-NOTE ACCOUNT.

Premium notes and other premium obligations at beginning of the year		$956,636 99
Premium notes and other premium obligations received during the year		283,699 03
Total		$1,240,336 02
Deductions during the year as follows:		
Amount used in payment of losses and claims	$17,169 85	
Amount used in purchase of surrendered policies	8,941 58	
Amount used in payment of dividends to policyholders	156,010 56	
Amount voided by lapse of policies	40,395 87	
Amount redeemed by maker in cash	31,574 08	
Total reduction of premium note account		254,091 94
Balance, note assets at the end of the year		$986,244 08

VII. EXHIBIT OF POLICIES.

NUMBER AND AMOUNT OF POLICIES AND ADDITIONS CLASSIFIED.

	Number.	Amount.	Number.	Amount.
Policies in force at the beginning of the year:				
Whole life policies	30,644	$90,351,019 23		
Endowment policies	8,258	22,634,030 22		
Joint lives and survivorships	5	27,160 00		
Short term and irregular policies	81	142,600 00		
			38,988	$113,154,809 45
New policies issued during the year:				
Whole life policies	6,426	$21,034,866 00		
Endowment policies	2,245	3,901,845 00		
Joint lives and survivorships	2	13,000 00		
Short term and irregular policies	36	81,340 00		
			8,709	26,031,051 00
Old policies revived during the year:				
Whole life policies	161	$471,740 00		
Endowment policies	40	82,426 28		
			201	554,166 28
Old policies increased during the year:				
Whole life policies		$56,535 00		
Endowment policies		93,708 30		
				150,243 30
Additions by dividends during the year:				
Whole life policies		$259,741 52		
Endowment policies	2	107,071 51		
			2	366,813 03
Totals			47,900	$140,257,083 06
Deduct policies decreased and ceased to be in force:				
Whole life policeies	4,710	$15,735,720 96		
Endowment policies	1,928	5,779,256 24		
Joint lives and survivorships	1	6,000 00		
Short term and irregular policies	27	113,500 00		
			6,666	21,634,477 20
Net numbers and amounts in force, December 31st, 1872:				
Whole life policies	32,521	$96,437,680 79		
Endowment policies	8,617	22,089,825 07		
Joint lives and survivorships	6	34,160 00		
Short term and irregular policies	90	110,940 00		
Totals			41,234	$118,622,605 86

Policies ceased to be in force during the year with mode of termination:

	No.	Amount.
By death	481	$1,508,006 81
By expiry	8	23,500 00
By surrender	2,612	8,492,169 24
By lapse	2,692	7,177,823 78
By change and old policies decreased		1,543,229 00
Not taken	871	2,883,748 87
Totals	6,664	$21,628,477 20

Business in the state of Wisconsin during the year 1872:

Policies issued	88	$136,500 00
Policies in force at the end of the year	919	1,650,400 00
Premiums received		55,915 94
Losses paid		4,500 00

NORTH AMERICA LIFE INSURANCE COMPANY.

NEW YORK.

N. D. MORGAN, *President.* H. C. MORGAN, *Secretary.*

Attorney to accept service of process in Wisconsin, M. L. YOUNGS, Milwaukee.

[Incorporated October 22, 1862. Commenced business October 22, 1862.]

I. CAPITAL.

Capital actually paid up in cash		Mutual.

II. ASSETS.

Loans secured by deeds of trust or mortgages on real estate		$2,996,889 95
Loans secured by pledge of bonds, stocks, or securities, as collateral		38,366 23
Premium notes and loans, taken for premiums, on policies now in force		981,776 41
Cash value of real estate owned by the company, unincumbered		299,115 43
Cash market value of bonds and stocks owned by the company		127,904 30
Cash in office of company		41,696 89
Cash deposited in banks and trust companies		52,455 64
Postage and revenue stamps		2,100 00
Interest accrued on cash loans and on bonds owned by the company		93,333 86
Rents accrued for use of company's property, or under sub-lease		4,697 96
Gross premiums uncollected, on policies in force December 31, 1872	$351,658 18	
Gross deferred quarterly and semi-annual premiums, on policies in force December 31, 1872	546,201 60	
Total	$897,859 78	
Deducted to reduce the last two items, to the net value of the policies	44,892 98	
Net amount deferred and outstanding prem's		852,966 80
Due from other companies on account of reinsured risks		25,000 00
Due from other companies for current account of premiums on risks		40,608 57
Total admitted assets		$5,556,408 93

ITEMS NOT ADMITTED AS ASSETS.

Amount invested in commuting com's, or renewal com's purchased	$146,218 42
Judgments for debts rendered in favor of the company	17,517 71
Furniture, safes and fixtures	10,662 76
Other items, viz.: suspense account	8,045 72
Total unadmitted items	$182,444 61

III. LIABILITIES.

Claims for death losses and matured endowments, in process of adjustment, or adjusted and not due	$221,690 00
Claims for death losses and other policy claims resisted by the company	5,000 00
Net present value of all the outstanding policies in force on the 31st day of December, 1872, computed according to the American Experience Table of Mortality, with four and one-half per cent. interest	5,150,764 00
Amount due to Standard Life Insurance Company	7,300 00
Amount of any other liability not included above, viz.: bills payable	52,873 20
Total liabilities as to policyholders	$5,437,627 20

IV. INCOME.

Cash received for premiums on new policies, without deductions	$122,205 07
Cash received for renewal premiums, without deductions for expense	1,150,841 98
Cash received for sale of annuities	8,600 00
Cash received for all other premiums	972 25
Cash premiums from other companies for reinsuring their risks	2,474 07
Cash received for interest on cash loans	1,962 66
Cash received for interest on bonds owned and dividends on stocks	122,772 02
Cash received for interest on premium notes or loans	56,134 94
Cash received for interest on other debts due the company	35,767 22
Rents received for use of company's property, or under sub-lease	11,692 54
Discount on claims paid in advance	5,636 49
Cash from other companies on account of losses or claims, on policies of this company reinsured	16,000 00
Cash income from other sources, viz.: gold premiums	196 42
Gross amount of notes or other obligations taken for new prem's	81,972 08
Gross amount of notes or other obligations taken for renewal premiums	198,407 50
Total income	$1,835,635 19

V. EXPENDITURES.

Cash paid for the company's own losses and claims, and additions thereto....	$1,041,779 27
Cash paid to annuitants	4,266 46
Cash paid on account of policies lapsed, surrendered or purchased	68,295 58
Cash paid for dividends to policyholders	80,681 40
Cash paid for premiums to other companies for policies reinsured	49,088 02
Cash paid for commissions to agents on first and renewal premiums	93,690 11
Cash paid for salaries and expenses of managers of agencies, and agents	87,165 50
Cash paid for medical examiners' fees	21,153 79
Cash paid for salaries and other compensation of officers and employes	44,230 06
Cash paid for United States taxes and revenue stamps, $2,841.08; state and local taxes in state where organized, $9,377.94; taxes, licenses and fees in other states, $17,364.59; total	29,583 56
Cash paid for rents	5,200 00
Cash paid on any account not itemized above, viz.: advertising, $5,716.68; general expenses, $5,492.35; claims, by accident, $202.50; profit and loss, $83,211.90; total	94,628 38
Total cash expenditures	$1,614,742 13

PREMIUM-LOAN DISBURSEMENTS.

Amount used in payment of losses and claims	$106,176 08	....
Amount used in purchase of surrendered policies	3,809 67	....
Amount used in payment of dividends to policyholders	88,425 95	....
Amount voided by lapse of policies	64,289 60	....
Total premium note expenditures		262,701 30
Total expenditures		$1,877,443 43

VI. PREMIUM-NOTE ACCOUNT.

Premium notes and other premium obligations at beginning of the year		$1,004,191 99
Premium notes and other premium obligations received during the year		245,295 66
Total		$1,249,487 65
Deductions during the year as follows:		
Amount used in payment of losses and claims	$106,176 08	....
Amount used in purchase of surrendered policies	3,809 67	....
Amount used in payment of dividends to policyholders	88,425 95	....
Amount voided by lapse of policies	64,289 60	....
Amount redeemed by maker in cash	5,009 94	....
Total reduction of premium note account		267,711 24
Balance, note assets at end of the year		$981,776 41

VII. EXHIBIT OF POLICIES.

NUMBER AND AMOUNT OF POLICIES AND ADDITIONS CLASSIFIED.

	Number.	Amount.	Number.	Amount.
Policies in force at the beginning of the year:				
Whole life policies	9,782	$26,138,884	......	....
Endowment policies	4,050	9,817,104	......	....
Joint lives and survivorships	326	896,019	......	....
Short term and irregular policies	51	216,460	......	....
			14,209	$37,068,467
New policies issued during the year:				
Whole life policies	1,582	$3,286,381	......	....
Endowment policies	617	851,106	......	....
Joint lives and survivorships	38	51,725	......	....
Short term and irregular policies	27	131,700	......	....
			2,264	4,320,912
Old policies revived during the year:				
Whole life policies	69	$190,512	......	....
Endowment policies	40	93,700	......	....
Joint lives and survivorships	2	6,000	......	....
			111	290,212
Additions by dividends during the year:				
Whole life policies	......	$6,857	......	....
Endowment policies	......	5,884	......	....
Joint lives and survivorships	......	97	......	....
			......	12,838
Totals			16,584	$41,687,429
Deduct policies decreased and ceased to be in force:				
Whole life policies	1,859	$5,021,576	......	....
Endowment policies	806	2,072,231	......	....
Joint lives and survivorships	64	172,346	......	....
Short term and irregular policies	23	65,600	......	....
			2,752	7,331,753

Totals at the end of the year:

Whole life policies	9,574	$24,596,058	......	....
Endowment policies	3,901	8,695,563	......	....
Joint lives and survivorships	302	781,495	......	....
Short term and irregular policies	55	282,560	......	....
			13,832	$34,355,676
Deduct policies reinsured	......	....	......	1,670,000
Net numbers and amounts in force December 31, 1872			13,832	$32,685,676

Policies ceased to be in force during the year, with mode of termination:

	No.	Amount.
By death	188	$564,578
By expiry	110	582,925
By surrender	61	188,107
By lapse	1,674	3,762,644
By change and old policies decreased	449	1,540,350
Not taken	270	693,149
Totals	2,752	$7,331,753

Business in the state of Wisconsin during the year 1872:

Policies issued	42	$54,000 00
Policies in force at the end of the year	224	321,600 00
Premiums received	......	11,583 74
Losses paid	......	2,000 00

PHŒNIX MUTUAL LIFE INSURANCE COMPANY.

HARTFORD, CONN.

EDSON FESSENDEN, *President.* JAMES F. BURNS, *Secretary.*

Attorney to accept service of process in Wisconsin, JOHN H. WALRATH, Milwaukee.

[Incorporated May, 1851. Commenced business May, 1851.]

I. CAPITAL.

Capital authorized	$100,000 00
Capital actually paid up in cash	16,000 00

II. ASSETS.

Loans secured by deeds of trust or mortgages on real estate		$2,975,302 46
Loans secured by pledge of bonds, stocks or securities, as collateral		101,579 13
Premium notes and loans, taken for premiums, on policies now in force		3,551,287 01
Cash market value of bonds and stocks owned by the company		588,863 75
Cash in office of company, and in bank		118,678 54
Interest accrued on cash loans and on bonds owned by the company		101,834 63
Gross premiums uncollected, not more than three months due, on policies in force December 31, 1872	$538,942 19	....
Gross deferred quarterly and semi-annual premiums, on policies in force December 31, 1872	135,904 20	....
Total	$674,846 39	....
Deducted to reduce the last two items, to the net value of the policies	77,255 57	....
Net amount deferred and outstanding premiums		597,590 82
Total admitted assets		$8,035,086 34

ITEMS NOT ADMITTED AS ASSETS.

Furniture, safes and fixtures	$12,983 16
Other items, viz.: stockholder's notes	84,000 00
Total unadmitted items	$96,983 16

III. LIABILITIES.

Claims for death losses and matured endowments, in process of adjustment, or adjusted and not due	$156,121 00
Net present value of all the outstanding policies in force on the 31st day of December, 1872, computed according to the Combined Experience Table of Mortality, with four per cent. interest	7,295,038 00
Total liabilities as to policyholders	$7,451,159 00

IV. INCOME.

Cash received for premiums on new policies, without deductions	$551,729 31
Cash received for renewal premiums, without deductions for expense	1,834,264 48
Cash received for interest on cash loans, bonds owned and dividends on stocks	257,718 14
Cash received for interest on premium notes or loans	218,544 57
Gross amount of notes or other obligations taken for new premiums	177,360 00
Gross amount of notes or other obligations taken for renewal premiums	379,136 00
Total income	$3,418,752 45

V. EXPENDITURES.

Cash paid for the company's own losses and claims, and additions thereto		$881,116 38
Cash paid on account of policies lapsed, surrendered or purchased		82,060 40
Cash paid for dividends to policyholders		943,441 71
Cash paid for dividends to stockholders		960 00
Cash paid for premiums to other companies for policies reinsured		1,272 68
Cash paid for commissions to agents on first and renewal premiums		268,874 58
Cash paid for salaries and expenses of managers of agencies and agents		100,809 65
Cash paid for medical examiners' fees		30,821 50
Cash paid for salaries and other compensation of officers and employes		84,515 52
Cash paid for taxes, revenue stamps, state licenses and fees		46,328 54
Cash paid on any account not itemized above, viz: postage, printing and sundry expenses		78,576 20
Total cash expenditures		$2,368,777 05
PREMIUM-LOAN DISBURSEMENTS.		
Amount used in payment of losses and claims	$47,383 34	
Amount used in purchase of surrendered policies	18,567 96	
Amount used in payment of dividends to policyholders	52,001 41	
Amount voided by lapse of policies	255,455 71	
Total premium note expenditures		378,408 42
Total expenditures		$2,737,185 47

VI. PREMIUM-NOTE ACCOUNT.

Premium notes and other premium obligations at beginning of the year		$3,368,674 08
Premium notes and other premium obligations received during the year		556,496 00
Total		$3,925,170 08
Deductions during the year as follows:		
Amount used in payment of losses and claims	$47,383 34	
Amount used in purchase of surrendered policies	18,567 96	
Amount used in payment of dividends to policyholders	52,001 41	
Amount voided by lapse of policies	255,455 71	
Amount redeemed by maker in cash	524 60	
Total reduction of premium note account		378,933 02
Balance, note assets at end of the year		$3,551,237 01

VII. EXHIBIT OF POLICIES.

NUMBER AND AMOUNT OF POLICIES AND ADDITIONS CLASSIFIED.

	Number.	Amount.	Number.	Amount.
Policies in force at the beginning of the year:				
Whole life policies	20,947	$50,088,435		
Endowment policies	7,755	13,461,185		
Joint lives and survivorships	5	5,000		
			28,707	$63,554,620
New policies issued during the year:				
Whole life policies	7,344	$17,563,399		
Endowment policies	3,183	4,188,335		
			10,527	21,751,734
Old policies revived during the year:				
Whole life policies	90	$207,658		
Endowment policies	73	188,919		
			163	396,577
Additions by dividends during the year:				
Whole life policies		$24,169		
Endowment policies		19,831		
				44,000
Totals			39,397	$85,746,931

Deduct policies decreased and ceased to be in force:

Whole life policies	4,320	$10,165,573	......	....
Endowment policies	2,057	3,616,091	......	....
			6,377	$13,781,664

Totals at the end of the year:

Whole life policies	24,061	$57,718,088	......	....
Endowment policies	8,954	14,242,179	......	....
Joint lives and survivorships	5	5,000	......	....
			33,020	$71,965,267

Deduct policies reinsured:

Whole life policies	......	$45,000	......	....
Endowment policies	......	10,000	......	....
			......	55,000

Net numbers and amounts in force December 31st, 1872:

Whole life policies	24,061	$57,673,088	......	....
Endowment policies	8,954	14,232,179	......	....
Joint lives and survivorships	5	5,000	......	....
Totals			33,020	$71,910,267

Policies ceased to be in force during the year, with mode of termination:

	No.	Amount.
By death	311	$763,176
By expiry	1	500
By surrender	106	276,497
By lapse	2,845	6,104,710
By change and old policies decreased	577	1,578,850
Not taken	2,537	5,057,931
Totals	6,377	$13,781,664

Business in the state of Wisconsin during the year 1872:

Policies issued	289	$500,495 00
Policies in force at the end of the year	1,489	2,219,580 00
Premiums received	......	97,390 45
Losses paid	......	9,000 00

PROTECTION LIFE INSURANCE COMPANY.

CHICAGO, ILL.

L. D. HILLARD, *President.* J. C. LAMBRITE, *Ass't Secretary.*

Attorney to accept service of process in Wisconsin, C. C. BARNES, Manitowoc.

[Incorporated, March 7, 1867. Commenced business, in Chicago, Jan'y 1, 1871.]

I. CAPITAL.

Capital authorized	$300,000 00
Capital actually paid up in cash	146,500 00

II. ASSETS.

Loans secured by deeds of trust or mortgages on real estate		$112,000 00
Prem. notes and loans, taken for prem's on policies now in force		2,621 79
Cash market value of bonds and stocks owned by the company		4,000 00
Cash in office of company		7,444 79
Cash deposited in banks and trust companies		3,140 13
Interest accrued on cash loans and on bonds owned by the company		16,863 53
Gross premiums uncollected, not more than three months due, on policies in force Dec. 31, 1872	$17,526 80	....
Deducted to reduce this item to the net value of the policies	11,813 60	....
Net amount outstanding premiums		5,713 20
Total admitted assets		$151,783 44

ITEMS NOT ADMITTED AS ASSETS.

Amount due from sundry persons	$7,875 11
Loans on personal security only	527 18
Furniture, safes and fixtures (cost)	894 03
Total unadmitted items	$9,296 32

III. LIABILITIES.

Claims for death losses due and unpaid	$12,410 00
Net present value of all the outstanding policies in force on the 31st day of December, 1872, computed according to the Combined Experience Table of Mortality, with four per cent. interest	45,644 43
Amount of any other liability not included above	8,813 30
Total liabilities as to policyholders	$66,867 73

IV. INCOME.

Cash rec'd for prem's on new policies, without deductions	$53,336 32
Cash received for annual dues	9,377 87
Cash received for interest on premium notes or loans	412 69
Rents received for use of company's property, or under sub-lease	65 00
Cash received for death assessments	46,757 67
Cash received for interest on stock notes	7,817 38
Cash income from other sources	4,594 45
Gross am't of notes or other obligations taken for new prem's	3,400 59
Total income	$125,761 92

V. EXPENDITURES.

Cash paid for the company's own losses and claims, and additions thereto	$37,804 09
Cash paid for commissions to agents on first premiums	25,441 46
Cash paid for medical examiners' fees	602 00
Cash paid for salaries and other compensation of officers and employes	13,379 06
Cash paid for United States taxes and revenue stamps, $831 35; state and local taxes in state where organized, $870 56; taxes, licenses and fees in other states, $497 97, of which the sum of 392 25 was paid in the state of Wisconsin; total	2,399 18
Cash paid for rents	987 58
Cash paid for furniture, safes and fixtures for home or agency offices	538 99
Cash paid on any account not itemized above	23,416 59
Total cash expenditures	$104,561 83

PREMIUM-LOAN DISBURSEMENTS.

Amount voided by lapse of policies	835 03
Total expenditures	$105,396 86

VI. PREMIUM-NOTE ACCOUNT.

Premium notes and other premium obligations at beginning of the year		$1,557 18
Premium notes and other premium obligations received during the year		3,400 59
Total		$4,957 77
Deductions during the year as follows:		
Amount voided by lapse of policies	$835 03	
Amount redeemed by maker in cash	1,500 95	
Total reduction of premium note account		2,335 98
Balance, note assets at the end of the year		$2,621 79

VII. EXHIBIT OF POLICIES.

NUMBER AND AMOUNT OF POLICES AND ADDITIONS CLASSIFIED.

	Number.	Amount.
Policies in force at the beginning of the year:		
Short term and irregular policies	1,593	$1,593,000
New policies issued during the year:		
Short term and irregular policies	5,039	5,039,000
Totals	6,632	$6,632,000
Deduct policies decreased and ceased to be in force:		
Short term and irregular policies	1,907	1,907,000
Net numbers and amounts in force December 31st, 1872:		
Short term and irregular policies	4,725	$4,725,000

Policies ceased to be in force during the year, with mode of termination:

	Number.	Amount.
By death	45	$45,000
By lapse	1,453	1,453,000
Not taken	409	409,000
Totals	1,907	$1,907,000

Business in the state of Wisconsin during the year 1872:

Policies issued	151	$151,000
Policies in force at the end of the year	153	153,000
Premiums received	......	1,790

RAILWAY PASSENGERS' ASSURANCE COMPANY.

HARTFORD, CONN.

JAMES G. BATTERSON, *President*. CHARLES E. WILLARD, *Secretary*.

Attorney to accept service of process in Wisconsin, HARRY BRADFORD, Milwaukee.

[Incorporated, May, 1865. Commenced business, February, 1866.]

I. CAPITAL.

Capital authorized	$1,000,000 00
Capital actually paid up in cash	300,000 00

II. ASSETS.

Loans secured by deeds of trust or mortgages on real estate	$45,000 00
Loans secured by pledge of bonds, stocks, or securities, as collateral	5,000 00
Cash market value of bonds and stocks owned by the company	374,384 75
Cash in office of company	769 81
Cash deposited in banks and trust companies	18,065 21
Interest accrued on cash loans and on bonds owned by the company	786 66
Total admitted assets	$444,006 43

ITEMS NOT ADMITTED AS ASSETS.

Cash in hands of officers or agents due the company	$6,235 35
Furniture, safes and fixtures	2,500 00
Total unadmitted items	$8,735 35

III. LIABILITIES.

Claims for death losses and matured endowments, in process of adjustment, or adjusted and not due	$6,000 00
Claims for death losses and other policy claims resisted by the company	32,000 00
Net present value of all the outstanding policies in force December 31st, 1872.	15,000 00
Amount due for salaries, rents and office expenses	125 00
Amount of any other liability, not included above, viz.: printing	500 00
Total liabilities as to policyholders	$53,625 00

IV. INCOME.

Cash received for premiums on new policies, without deductions	$130,980 26
Cash received for interest on cash loans	6,610 75
Cash received for interest on bonds owned and dividends on stocks	22,734 05
Total income	$160,325 06

V. EXPENDITURES.

Cash paid for the company's own losses and policy claims	$29,100 28
Cash paid for dividends to stockholders	30,000 00
Cash paid for commissions to agents on first premiums	40,098 37
Cash paid for salaries and expenses of managers of agencies, and agents	9,777 00
Cash paid for medical examiners' fees	3,430 88
Cash paid for salaries and other compensation of officers and employes	14,054 84
Cash paid for United States taxes and revenue stamps, $393 55; state and local taxes in state where organized, $15 00; taxes, licenses and fees in other states, $3,941 20; of which the sum of $427 00 was paid in the state of Wisconsin; total	4,349 75
Cash paid for rents	2,515 00
Cash paid for furniture, safes and fixtures for home and agency offices	386 52
Cash paid on any account not itemized above, viz: postage and expenses, $3,811 26; advertising, $6,827 74; stationery, etc., $3,755 61; agency expense, $510 09; returned prem's, $23 11; non-resident tax, $1,190 70; total	15,698 51
Total expenditures	$149,386 15

Business in the state of Wisconsin during the year 1872:

Policies issued	Unknown.
Policies in force at the end of the year	Unknown.
Premiums received	$2,330 15
Losses paid	300 00

REPUBLIC LIFE INSURANCE COMPANY.

CHICAGO, ILL.

JOHN V. FARWELL, *President.* JOHN F. COLLINS, *Secretary.*

Attorney to accept service of process in Wisconsin, J. W. McLAURY, La Crosse.

[Incorporated, March 27, 1869. Commenced business, July, 1870.]

I. CAPITAL.

Capital authorized	$5,000,000 00
Capital actually paid up in cash	848,610 00
Subscribed capital for which subscribers' notes or other obligotions are held	3,351,240 00

II. ASSETS.

Loans secured by deeds of trust or mortgages on real estate		$541,921 54
Loans secured by pledge of bonds, stocks, or securities, as collateral		62,146 07
Premium notes and loans, taken for prem's, on policies now in force		107,533 90
Cash value of real estate owned by the company, unincumbered		533,353 00
Cash market value of bonds and stocks owned by the company		122,425 00
Cash in office of company		12,120 74
Cash deposited in banks and trust companies, and with local treasurers		48,409 27
Interest accrued on cash loans and on bonds owned by the company		15,733 78
Interest accrued on premium loans and notes		1,516 01
Rents accrued for use of company's property, or under sub-lease		3,458 33
Gross premiums uncollected, not more than three months due, on policies in force December 31, 1872	$58,428 57	
Gross deferred quarterly and semi-annual premiums, on policies in force December 31, 1872	57,945 11	
Total	$116,373 68	
Deducted to reduce the last two items, to the net value of the policies	17,585 22	
Net amount deferred and outstanding prem's		98,788 46
Total admitted assets		$1,547,686 05

ITEMS NOT ADMITTED AS ASSETS.

Amount invested in commuting com's, or renewal com's purchased	$17,905 12
Loans on personal security only	14,100 65
Furniture, safes and fixtures	21,943 00
Other items, viz: suspense acc't, $8,174 48; balances of agents and other acc'ts, $19,563 92; total	27,737 40
Total unadmitted items	$81,686 17

III. LIABILITIES.

Claims for death losses and matured endowments, in process of adjustment, or adjusted and not due	$22,500 00
Net present value of all the outstanding policies in force on the 31st day of December, 1872, computed according to the American Experience Table of Mortality, with four and one-half per cent. interest	773,441 78
Amount due by the company for borrowed money	10,000 00
Amount due other companies for reinsurance	142 50
Total liabilities as to policyholders	$806,084 28

IV. INCOME.

Cash received for premiums on new policies, without deductions	$257,144 05
Cash received for renewal premiums, without deductions for expense	182,426 83
Cash premiums from other companies for reinsuring their risks	91,000 00
Cash received for interest on cash loans	30,445 59
Cash received for interest on bonds owned and dividends on stocks	8,368 12
Cash received for interest on premium notes or loans	2,045 78
Cash received for interest on other debts due the company	1,666 45
Discount on claims paid in advance	10,986 05
Cash from other companies on account of losses or claims on policies of this company reinsured	10,000 00

Gross amount of notes or other obligations taken for new premiums	$20,012 14
Gross amount of notes or other obligations taken for renewal premiums	10,775 77
Gross amount of obligations rec'd from Co's for assuming or reinsuring their risks	84,296 52
Total income	$659,164 30

V. EXPENDITURES.

Cash paid for the company's own losses and claims, and additions thereto	$127,818 10
Cash paid to other companies for losses or claims on their policies reinsured by this company	5,000 00
Cash paid on account of policies lapsed, surrendered or purchased	84,711 60
Cash paid for dividends to policyholders	7,812 04
Cash paid for premiums to other companies for policies reinsured	9,225 17
Cash paid for commissions to agents on first and renewal premiums	136,380 84
Cash paid for salaries and expenses of managers of agencies and agents	57,487 13
Cash paid for medical examiners' fees	9,715 58
Cash paid for salaries and other compensation of officers and employes	38,867 50
Cash paid for United States taxes and revenue stamps, $1,486.70; state and local taxes in state where organized, $3,125.58; taxes, licenses and fees in other states, $6.034.11, of which the sum of $408 was paid in the state of Wisconsin; total	10,646 39
Cash paid on any account not itemized above, viz: express, postage and telegrams, $4,761; advertising, $24,221 88; printing and stationery, $15,285.92; law and actuarial expense, $4,129.44; interest on mortgage on Co's building, $8,000; total	56,398 24
Total cash expenditures	$492,062 54

PREMIUM-LOAN DISBURSEMENTS.

Amount used in payment of losses and claims	$851 00	
Amount used in purchase of surrendered policies	12,402 45	
Amount voided by lapse of policies	5,473 15	
Total premium note expenditures		18,726 60
Total expenditures		$510,789 14

VI. PREMIUM-NOTE ACCOUNT.

Premium notes and other prem. obligations at beginning of the year		$25,977 24
Premium notes and other prem. obligations received during the year		115,084 43
Total		$141,061 67
Deductions during the year as follows:		
Amount used in payment of losses and claims	$851 00	
Amount used in purchase of surrendered policies	12,402 45	
Amount voided by lapse of policies	5,473 15	
Amount redeemed by maker in cash	14,501 17	
Total reduction of premium note account		33,227 77
Balance, note assets at end of the year		$107,833 90

VII. EXHIBIT OF POLICIES.

NUMBER AND AMOUNT OF POLICIES AND ADDITIONS CLASSIFIED.

	Number.	Amount.	Number.	Amount.
Policies in force at the beginning of the year:				
Whole life policies	4,970	$11,494,831 50		
Endowment policies	1,310	2,147,787 63		
Joint lives and survivorships	57	165,900 00		
Short term and irregular policies	22	81,000 00		
			6,359	$13,889,519 13
New policies issued during the year:				
Whole life policies	3,556	$9,237,891 79		
Endowment policies	843	1,512,674 16		
Joint lives and survivorships	60	136,032 00		
Short term and irregular policies	60	256,110 00		
			4,519	11,142,687 95
Old policies revived during the year:				
Whole life policies	116	$316,626 18		
Endowment policies	31	68,100 00		
Short term and irregular policies	1	3,000 00		
			148	387,726 18
Totals			11,026	$25,419,933 26

Deduct policies decreased and ceased to be in force:

Whole life policies	3,616	$8,144,938 69	......	....
Endowment policies	959	1,601,813 33	......	....
Joint lives and survivorships	43	115,300 00	......	....
Short term and irregular policies	19	65,000 00	......	....
			4,637	$9,927,052 02

Totals at the end of the year.

Whole life policies	5,026	$12,904,340 78	......	....
Endowment policies	1,225	2,126,748 46	......	....
Joint lives and survivorships	74	186,632 00	......	....
Short term and irregular policies	64	275,110 00	......	....
			6,389	$15,492,831 24

Deduct policies reinsured.

Whole life policies	......	$385,385 00	......	....
Endowment policies	....	80,000 00	......	....
Short term and irregular policies	......	42,500 00	......	....
			......	507,885 00

Net numbers and amounts in force December 31st, 1872:

Whole life policies	5,026	$12,518,955 78	......	....
Endowment policies	1,225	2,046,748 46	......	....
Joint lives and survivorships	74	186,632 00	......	....
Short term and irregular policies	64	232,610 00	......	....
Totals			6,389	$14,984,946 24

Policies ceased to be in force during the year, with mode of termination:

	No.	Amount.
By death	42	$126,318 10
By expiry	8	43,000 00
By surrender	339	585,540 00
By lapse	1,412	3,226,270 40
By change and old policies decreased	1,641	3,132,706 00
Not taken	1,195	2,813,217 52
Totals	4,637	$9,927,052 02

Business in the state of Wisconsin, during the year 1872:

Policies issued	261	$430,241 00
Policies in force at the end of the year	384	714,125 60
Premiums received	......	22,315 47
Losses paid	... ..	1,000 00

SAINT LOUIS MUTUAL LIFE INSURANCE COMPANY.

ST. LOUIS MO.

CHARLES H. PECK, *President.* ALEX. P. STEWART, *Secretary.*

Attorney to accept service of process in Wisconsin, D. R. HUNT, Madison.

[Incorporated November 18, 1857. Commenced business November 25, 1857.]

I. CAPITAL.

Capital authorized	$100,000 00
Capital actually paid up in cash	100,000 00

II. ASSETS.

Loans secured by deeds of trust or mortgages on real estate		$1,900,198 41
Loans secured by pledge of bonds, stocks or securities, as collateral		8,000 00
Premium notes and loans taken for premiums, on policies now in force		2,718,154 77
Cash value of real estate owned by the company, unincumbered		776,282 38
Cash market value of bonds and stocks owned by the company		192,777 25
Cash in office of company and in banks		64,683 11
Interest accrued on cash loans and on bonds owned by the company		90,780 58
Interest accrued on premium loans and notes		24,230 38
Premiums in due course of transmission	$82,244 57	....
Gross premiums uncollected, not more than three months due, on policies in force December 31, 1872	257,585 83	....
Gross deferred quarterly and semi-annual premiums, on policies in force December 31, 1872	200,178 15	....
Total	$540,008 55	....

Deducted to reduce the last three items, to the net value of the policies	$119,734 40	....
Net amount deferred and outstanding premiums		$420,274 15
Amounts collected by agents		154,331 38
Due from other companies on account of reinsured risks		5,023 10
Total admitted assets		$6,354,684 46

ITEMS NOT ADMITTED AS ASSETS.

Value of agency supplies, printed matter and stationery on hand	$6,000 00
Loans on bankable paper	72,844 68
Furniture, safes and fixtures	13,029 29
Other items including loans on personal security only	67,461 73
Total unadmitted items	$159,335 70

III. LIABILITIES.

Claims for death losses and matured endowments, in process of adjustment, or adjusted and not due	$141,493 00
Claims for death losses and other policy claims resisted by the company	13,000 00
Net present value of all the outstanding policies in force on the 31st day of December, 1872, computed according to the American Experience Table of Mortality, with four and one-half per cent. interest	5,881,186 00
Total liabilities as to policyholders	$6,035,679 00

IV. INCOME.

Cash received for premiums on new policies, without deductions	$237,966 44
Cash received for renewal premiums, without deductions for expense	1,363,463 95
Cash premiums from other companies for reinsuring their risks	221,605 16
Cash received for interest on cash loans	166,646 42
Cash received for interest on bonds owned and dividends on stocks	12,400 00
Cash received for interest on premium notes or loans	159,387 41
Discount on claims paid in advance	866 29
Cash from other companies on account of losses or claims on policies of this company reinsured	9,716 00
Cash income from other sources, viz: policy fees, $2,625; exchange, $424.80	3,049 80
Gross amount of notes or other obligations taken for new premiums	2,955 00
Gross am't of notes or other obligations taken for renewal premiums	427,291 53
Notes or obligations rec'd from Co's. for assuming or reinsuring their risks	409,317 85
Total income	$3,014,665 28

V. EXPENDITURES.

Cash paid for the company's own losses and claims, and additions thereto	$809,318 55
Cash paid on account of policies lapsed, surrendered or purchased	28,495 71
Cash paid for dividends to policyholders	30,668 97
Cash paid for dividends to stockholders	10,000 00
Cash paid for premiums to other companies for policies reinsured	4,220 05
Cash paid for commissions to agents on first premiums	121,020 19
Cash paid for commission to agents on renewal premiums	121,323 05
Cash paid for salaries and expenses of managers of agencies, and agents	74,558 99
Cash paid for medical examiners' fees	21,116 47
Cash paid for salaries and other compensation of officers and employes	74,926 34
Cash paid for revenue stamps, $1,609.25; state and local taxes, $28,322.55; tot'l	29,931 80
Cash paid for rents	11,785 96
Cash paid on any account not itemized above, viz: attorney's fees, $5,628.46; am't allowed Miss. Valley Life Ins. Co. on acc't of policies transferred, $8,102.48; postage and express, $9,675 05; stationery, $20,360.68; advertising, $22,787.01; losses by fire, $540.86; incidentals, $8,160.03; total	76,254 57
Total cash expenditures	$1,413,621 67

PREMIUM-LOAN DISBURSEMENTS.

Amount used in payment of losses and claims	$44,472 84	....
Amount used in purchase of surrendered policies	12,897 88	....
Amount used in payment of dividends to policyholders	94,238 97	....
Amount voided by lapse of policies	121,822 07	....
Total premium note expenditures		273,431 76
Total expenditures		$1,687,052 93

VI. PREMIUM-NOTE ACCOUNT.

Premium notes and other prem. obligations at beginning of the year	$2,154,009 00
Premium notes and other prem. obligations received during the year	839,563 86
Total	$2,993,573 86

Deductions during the year as follows:		
Amount used in payment of losses and claims	$44,472 84	...
Amount used in purchase of surrendered policies	12,897 38	...
Amount used in payment of dividends to policyholders	94,238 97	...
Amount voided by lapse of policies	121,822 07	...
Amount of short notes, etc	1,986 85	...
Total reduction of premium note account		$275,418 11
Balance, note assets at end of the year		$2,718,154 77

VII. EXHIBIT OF POLICIES.

NUMBER AND AMOUNT OF POLICIES AND ADDITIONS CLASSIFIED.

	No.	Amount.	No.	Amount.
Policies in force at the beginning of the year:				
Whole life policies	12,323	$38,656,864 34	......	......
Endowment policies	3,561	10,321,427 52	......	......
			15,884	$48,978,291 86
New policies issued during the year	......	......	6,687	19,589,115 00
Old policies revived during the year	......	......	132	352,002 00
Totals	......	......	22,703	$68,919,408 86
Deduct policies decreased and ceased to be in force		......	7,062	22,541,473 21
Totals at the end of the year:				
Whole life policies	12,329	$37,710,768 78	......	......
Endowment policies	3,255	8,464,965 87	......	......
Joint lives and survivorships	41	146,201 00	......	......
Short term and irregular policies	16	56,000 00	......	......
			15,641	$46,377,935 65
Deduct policies reinsured:				
Whole life policies	20	$120,000 00	......	......
Endowment policies	2	15,000 00	......	......
Short term and irregular policies	1	5,000 00	......	......
			23	140,000 00
Net numbers and amounts in force, December 31, 1872			15,618	$46,237,935 65

Policies ceased to be in force during the year, with mode of termination:	No.	Amount.
By death	238	$822,495 00
By surrender	75	208,226 00
By lapse	5,755	19,053,718 50
By change and old policies decreased	11	75,857 71
Not taken	983	2,386,181 00
Totals	7,062	$22,541,473 21

Business in the state of Wisconsin during the year 1872:		
Policies issued	20	$29,700 00
Policies in force at the end of the year	57	72,250 00
Premiums received	......	2,436 10
Losses paid	......	1,000 00

SECURITY LIFE INSURANCE AND ANNUITY COMPANY.

NEW YORK.

ROBERT L. CASE, *President.* ISAAC H. ALLEN, *Secretary.*

Attorney to accept service of process in Wisconsin, WALTER B. DAVIS, Madison.

[Incorporated, January 17, 1862. Commenced business, January 18, 1862.]

I. CAPITAL.

Capital authorized	$110,000 00
Capital actually paid up in cash	110,000 00

II. ASSETS.

Loans secured by deeds of trust or mortgages on real estate		$15,000 00
Premium notes and loans, taken for premiums, on policies now in force		1,978,139 28
Cash market value of bonds and stocks owned by the company		721,782 50
Cash in office of company		21,816 96
Cash deposited in banks and trust companies		56,498 30
Interest accrued on cash loans and on bonds owned by the company		11,863 31
Interest accrued on premium loans and notes		69,469 99
Gross premiums uncollected, not more than three months due, on policies in force December 31, 1872	$489,169 18	
Gross deferred quarterly and semi-annual premiums, on policies in force December 31, 1872	165,227 87	
Total	$654,397 05	
Deducted to reduce the last two items, to the net value of the policies	42,351 76	
Net amount deferred and outstanding prem's		612,045 29
Due from other companies on account of reinsured risks		21,923 68
Total admitted assets		$3,508,539 31

ITEMS NOT ADMITTED AS ASSETS.

Am't invested in commuting commissions, or renewal com's purchased	$108,275 03
Furniture, safes and fixtures	19,372 63
Total unadmitted items	$127,647 66

III. LIABILITIES.

Claims for death losses and matured endowments, in process of adjustment, or adjusted and not due	$84,500 00
Claims for death losses and other policy claims resisted by the company	12,000 00
Net present value of all the outstanding policies in force on the 31st day of December, 1872, computed according to the American Experience Table of Mortality, with four and one-half per cent. interest	3,025,998 00
Amount of unpaid dividends to stockholders	610 00
Amount due on account of salaries, rents and office expenses	933 33
Amount due on premium notes for reinsurance	3,830 32
Total liabilities as to policyholders	$3,127,871 65

IV. INCOME.

Cash received for premiums on new policies, without deductions	$168,191 86
Cash received for renewal premiums, without deductions for expense	728,089 48
Cash received for sale of annuities	6,500 00
Cash premiums from other companies for reinsuring their risks	108,204 45
Cash received for interest on bonds owned and dividends on stocks	29,845 38
Cash received for interest on premium notes or loans	91,387 09
Cash from other companies for losses on policies of this company reinsured	13,500 00
Gross amount of notes or other obligations taken for new premiums	5,013 00
Gross amount of notes or other obligations taken for renewal premiums	403,887 92
Notes or obligations rec'd from co's for assuming or reinsuring their risks	22,418 97
Total income	$1,576,538 10

V. EXPENDITURES.

Cash paid the company's own losses and claims, and additions thereto	$396,486 70
Cash paid to other companies for losses or claims on their policies reinsured by this company	70,213 18
Cash paid to annuitants	1,782 77
Cash paid on account of policies lapsed, surrendered or purchased	85,666 44
Cash paid for dividends to policyholders	83,201 34
Cash paid for dividends to stockholders	14,700 00
Cash paid for premiums to other companies for policies reinsured	27,532 87
Cash paid for commissions to agents on first premiums	36,328 28
Cash paid for commissions to agents on renewal premiums	127,563 98
Cash paid for salaries and expenses of managers of agencies, and agents	24,861 91
Cash paid for medical examiners' fees	13,909 08
Cash paid for salaries and other compensation of officers and employes	28,583 34
Cash paid for United States taxes and revenue stamps, $2,086.74; state and local taxes in state where organized, $5,205.10; taxes, licenses and fees in other states, $5,949.67; total	13,241 51
Cash paid for rents of home office and agencies	12,178 26
Cash paid for furniture, safes and fixtures for home or agency offices	608 40
Cash paid on any account not itemized above, viz.: stationery, $15,411.23; printing and advertising, $33,595.65; law, $3,116.57; postage and exchange, $5,946.10; total	58,069 55
Total cash expenditures	$994,872 50

PREMIUM-LOAN DISBURSEMENTS.

Amount used in payment of losses and claims	$28,461 58	....
Amount used in purchase of surrendered and lapsed policies	117,072 70	....
Amount used in payment of dividends to policyholders	162,487 64	....
Total premium note expenditures		$308,021 92
Total expenditures		$1,297,894 42

VI. PREMIUM-NOTE ACCOUNT.

Premium notes and other premium obligations at beginning of the year		$1,870,048 95
Premium notes and other premium obligations received during the year		431,319 89
Total		$2,301,368 84
Deductions during the year as follows:		
Amount used in payment of losses and claims	$28,461 58	....
Amount used in purchase of surrendered and lapsed policies	117,072 70	....
Amount used in payment of dividends to policyholders	162,487 64	....
Amount redeemed by maker in cash	20,202 64	....
Total reduction of premium note account		328,224 56
Balance, note assets at the end of the year		$1,973,139 28

VII. EXHIBIT OF POLICIES.

NUMBER AND AMOUNT OF POLICIES AND ADDITIONS CLASSIFIED.

	Number.	Amount.	Number.	Amount.
Policies in force at the beginning of the year:				
Whole life policies	9,353	$24,157,300	......	....
Endowment policies	2,416	4,199,188	......	....
Joint lives and survivorships	997	1,873,450	......	....
Short term and irregular policies	450	2,287,300	......	....
			13,216	$32,517,238
New policies issued during the year:				
Whole life policies	2,561	$5,981,786	......	....
Endowment policies	495	793,429	......	....
Joint lives and survivorships	100	177,641	......	....
Short term and irregular policies	52	123,600	......	....
			3,208	7,076,456
Old policies revived during the year:				
Whole life policies	49	$119,000	......	....
Endowment policies	17	32,500	......	....
Joint lives and survivorships	6	13,000	......	....
Short term and irregular policies	1	5,000	......	....
			73	169,500
Additions by dividends during the year:				
Whole life policies	......	$8,711	......	....
Endowment policies	......	5,251	......	....
Joint lives and survivorships	......	393	......	....
			......	14,355
Totals			16,497	$39,777,549
Deduct policies decreased and ceased to be in force:				
Whole life policies	2,038	$5,030,794	......	....
Endowment policies	546	1,012,342	......	....
Joint lives and survivorships	253	328,451	......	....
Short term and irregular policies	176	851,900	......	....
			3,013	7,223,487
Totals at the end of the year:				
Whole life policies	9,925	$25,236,008	......	....
Endowment policies	2,382	4,018,026	......	....
Joint lives and survivorships	850	1,736,033	......	....
Short term and irregular policies	327	1,564,000	......	....
			13,484	$32,554,062
Deduct policies reinsured			......	1,440,500
Net numbers and amounts in force December 31st, 1872			13,484	$31,113,562

Policies ceased to be in force during the year, with mode of termination:

	Number.	Amount.
By death	178	$577,075
By expiry	11	60,000
By surrender	180	561,200
By lapse	1,753	3,895,958
By change and old policies decreased	217	731,721
Not taken	674	1,397,538
Totals	3,013	$7,223,487

Business in the state of Wisconsin during the year 1872:

Policies issued	89	$118,500 00
Policies in force at the end of the year	126	168,235 00
Premiums received	......	5,736 58

TEUTONIA LIFE INSURANCE COMPANY.

CHICAGO, ILL.

I. A. HUCK, *President.* C. KNOBELSDORFF, *Secretary.*

Attorney to accept service of process in Wisconsin, HERMANN BOERNGEN, Milwaukee.

[Incorporated, March 15, 1869. Commenced business, October 1, 1869.]

I. CAPITAL.

Capital authorized	$500,000 00
Capital actually paid up in cash	194,207 00

II. ASSETS.

Loans secured by deeds of trust or mortgages on real estate		$73,764 00
Loans secured by pledge of bonds, stocks or securities as collateral		3,538 43
Prem. notes and loans, taken for prem's on policies now in force		39,289 34
Cash value of real estate owned by the company, unincumbered		68,547 30
Cash market value of bonds and stocks owned by the company		56,762 50
Cash in office of company, and Germania Bank		5,496 25
Cash deposited with the treasurer of the company		5,097 31
Interest accrued on cash loans and on bonds owned by the company		2,512 59
Interest accrued on premium loans and notes		1,999 41
Gross premiums uncollected, not more than three months due, on policies in force Dec. 31, 1872	$41,950 50	....
Gross deferred quarterly and semi-annual premiums, on policies in force December 31, 1872	55,074 89	....
Total	$97,025 39	....
Deducted to reduce the last two items to the net value of the policies	6,186 39	....
Net amount deferred and outstanding premiums		90,839 00
Total admitted assets		$347,846 13

ITEMS NOT ADMITTED AS ASSETS.

Cash in hands of officers or agents due the company	$2,530 40
Cash in hands of agents secured	2,598 88
Value of agency supplies, printed matter and stationery on hand	4,000 00
Furniture, safes and fixtures	1,869 04
Stock notes secured by 40 per cent. cash installments	305,793 00
Total unadmitted items	$316,791 32

III. LIABILITIES.

Claims for death losses and matured endowments, in process of adjustment or adjusted and not due	$10,000 00
Net present value of all the outstanding policies in force on the 31st day of December, 1872, computed according to the Combined Experience Table of Mortality, with four per cent. interest	195,399 47
Amount of all unpaid dividends of surplus, or other profits due policyholders	48 79
Amount due by the company for borrowed money	5,000 00
Total liabilities as to policyholders	$210,448 26

IV. INCOME.

Cash received for premiums on new policies, without deductions	$32,344 52
Cash received for renewal premiums, without deductions for expense	56,578 15
Cash received for all other premiums	18 75
Cash premiums from other companies for reinsuring their risks	117 85
Cash received for int. on cash loans	8,363 33
Cash received for interest on bonds owned and dividends on stocks	2,734 75
Cash received for interest on premium notes or loans	1,318 58
Cash received for interest on other debts due the company	94 96
Rents received for use of company's property, or under sub-lease	3,093 37
Discount on claims paid in advance	40 09
Cash from other companies on account of losses or claims on policies of this company reinsured	2,500 00
Cash income from other sources	155 08
Gross amount of notes or other obligations taken for new premiums	1,926 91
Gross amount of notes or other obligations taken for renewal prem's	14,288 58
Total income	$123,574 86

V. EXPENDITURES.

Cash paid for the company's own losses and claims, and additions thereto	$28,042 42
Cash paid on account of policies lapsed, surrendered or purchased	2,470 95
Cash paid for dividends to policyholders	1,485 54
Cash paid for dividends to stockholders	19 51
Cash paid for premiums to other companies for policies reinsured	482 09
Cash paid for commissions to agents on first premiums	12,104 71
Cash paid for commissions to agents on renewal premiums	3,707 15
Cash paid for salaries and expenses of managers of agencies, and agents	10,481 90
Cash paid for medical examiners' fees	5,608 54
Cash paid for salaries and other compensation of officers and employes	13,364 88
Cash paid for United States taxes and revenue stamps, $607.10; state and local taxes in state where organized, $69.23; taxes, licenses and fees in other states, $2,189.78, of which the sum of $345 was paid in the state of Wisconsin; total	2,866 11
Cash paid for rents	2,260 57
Cash paid on any account not itemized above, viz: interest, $2,313.96; advertising and printing, $6,984.48; general expenses, $4,249.59; total	13,547 28
Total cash expenditures	$96,441 65

PREMIUM-LOAN DISBURSEMENTS.

Amount used in payment of losses and claims	$653 81	
Amount used in purchase of surrendered policies	1,795 56	
Amount used in payment of dividends to policyholders	838 40	
Amount voided by lapse of policies, and redeemed	9,250 25	
Total premium note expenditures		12,538 02
Total expenditures		$108,979 67

VI. PREMIUM-NOTE ACCOUNT.

Premium notes and other premium obligations at beginning of the year		$35,611 87
Premium notes and other premium obligations received during the year		16,215 49
Total		$51,827 36
Deductions during the year as follows:		
Amount used in payment of losses and claims	$653 81	
Amount used in purchase of surrendered policies	1,795 56	
Amount used in payment of dividends to policyholders	838 40	
Amount voided by lapse of policies	9,187 77	
Amount redeemed by maker in cash	62 48	
Total reduction of premium note account		12,538 02
Balance, note assets at end of the year		$39,289 34

VII. EXHIBIT OF POLICIES.

NUMBER AND AMOUNT OF POLICIES AND ADDITIONS CLASSIFIED.

Policies in force at the beginning of the year:

	Number.	Amount.	Number.	Amount.
Whole life policies	1,028	$1,236,132 88		
Endowment policies	647	723,113 00		
Short term and irregular policies	8	122,000 00		
Joint lives and survivorships	84	8,000 00		
			1,767	$2,089,245 88

New policies issued during the year:				
Whole life policies	2,473	$2,007,901 12	......	....
Endowment policies	468	366,282 00	......	....
Joint lives and survivorships	24	32,554 00	......	....
Short term and irregular policies	4	9,000 00	......	....
			2,969	$2,415,737 12
Totals			4,736	$4,504,988 00
Deduct policies decreased and ceased to be in force:				
Whole life policies	648	$675,000 00	......	....
Endowment policies	368	339,000 00	......	....
Joint lives and survivorships	30	45,500 00	......	....
Short term and irregular policies	6	6,000 00	......	....
			1,052	1,065,500 00
Totals at the end of the year:				
Whole life policies	2,853	$2,569,084 00	......	....
Endowment policies	747	750,395 00	......	....
Joint lives and survivorships	78	109,054 00	......	....
Short term and irregular policies	6	11,000 00	......	....
			3,684	$3,439,488 00
Deduct policies reinsured:				
Whole life policies	......	$21,000 00	......	21,000 00
Net numbers and amounts in force Dec. 31, 1872:				
Whole life policies	2,853	$2,548,084 00	......	....
Endowment policies	747	750,395 00	......	....
Joint lives and survivorships	78	109,054 00	......	....
Short term and irregular policies	6	11,000 00	......	
Totals			3,684	$3,418,488 00

Policies ceased to be in force during the year, with mode of termination:

	No.	Amount.
By death	30	38,500 00
By expiry	2	2,000 00
By surrender	45	81,000 00
By lapse	383	445,500 00
By change and old policies decreased	53	54,000 00
Not taken	539	444,500 00
Totals	1,052	$1,065,500 00

Business in the state of Wisconsin during the year 1872:

Policies issued	129	$88,500 00
Policies in force at the end of the year	168	125,000 00
Premiums received	......	3,892 40

TRAVELERS' LIFE INSURANCE COMPANY.

HARTFORD, CONN.

JAMES G. BATTERSON, *President.* RODNEY DENNIS, *Secretary.*

Attorney to accept service of process in Wisconsin, D. M. BELDEN, Milwaukee.

[Incorporated June 17, 1863. Commenced business April, 1864.]

I. CAPITAL.

Capital authorized	$500,000 00
Capital actually paid up in cash	500,000 00

II. ASSETS.

Loans secured by deeds of trust or mortgages on real estate	$784,797 56
Cash value of real estate owned by the company, unincumbered	50,000 00
Cash market value of bonds and stocks owned by the company	1,102,170 00
Cash in office of company	3,063 88
Cash deposited in banks and trust companies	123,280 75
Interest accrued on cash loans and on bonds owned by the company	24,959,87

Gross premiums uncollected, not more than three months due, on policies in force Dec. 31, 1872	$106,040 03	....
Gross deferred quarterly and semi-annual premiums, on policies in force December 31, 1872	61,824 41	....
Total	$167,864 44	....
Deducted to reduce the last two items to the net value of the policies	24,790 57	....
Net amount deferred and outstanding premiums		$142,573 87
Total admitted assets		$2,230,785 93

ITEMS NOT ADMITTED AS ASSETS.

Cash in hands of officers or agents due the company	$3,446 18
Other items, viz.: non-resident tax	922 80
Total unadmitted items	$4,368 98

III. LIABILITIES.

Claims for death losses and matured endowments, in process of adjustment, or adjusted and not due	$100,625 00
Claims for death losses and other policy claims resisted by the company	38,000 00
Net present value of all the outstanding policies in force on the 31st day of December, 1872, computed according to the Actuaries' Table of Mortality, with four per cent. interest	1,292,586 00
Net present value of extra and special risks—including those on impaired lives	772 86
Amount due on account of salaries, rents and office expenses	3,125 00
Amount due to other companies for reinsurance	596 20
Reserve for accident policies in force January 1, 1873	180,267 23
Total liabilities as to policyholders	$1,615,972 29

IV. INCOME.

Cash paid for the company's own losses and claims, and additions thereto	$702,446 89
Cash received for renewal premiums, without deductions for expense	317,485 06
Cash received for all other premiums	11,549 11
Cash received for interest on cash loans	61,825 95
Cash received for interest on bonds owned and dividends on stocks	86,064 39
Rents received for use of company's property, or under sub-lease	3,118 29
Discount on claims paid in advance	517 41
Cash income from other sources, viz.: premiums on gold, $7,069 37; interest from bankers, $2,072 85; total	9,142 22
Total income	$1,192,149 32

V. EXPENDITURES.

Cash paid for the company's own losses and policy claims, and additions	$311,724 55
Cash paid to annuitants	150 00
Cash paid on account of policies lapsed, surrendered or purchased	8,006 36
Cash paid for dividends to policyholders	2,369 78
Cash paid for dividends to stockholders	50,000 00
Cash paid for premiums to other companies for policies reinsured	4,370 00
Cash paid for commissions to agents on first premiums	176,812 48
Cash paid for commissions to agents on renewal premiums	19,048 10
Cash paid for salaries and expenses of managers of agencies, and agents	66,757 77
Cash paid for medical examiners' fees	7,770 35
Cash paid for salaries and other compensation of officers and employes	35,694 72
Cash paid for United States taxes and revenue stamps, $1,089 82; state and local taxes in state where organized, $250 01; taxes, licenses and fees in other states, $9,584 89; of which the sum of $411 00 was paid in the state of Wisconsin; total	10,923 72
Cash paid for rents	21,894 62
Cash paid for furniture, safes and fixtures for home and agency offices	1,202 31
Cash paid on any account not itemized above, viz: advertising, $46,966 18; exchange and stamps, $10,074 80; express charges, $2,603 27; books and stationery, $10,088 26, expenses, $16,561 13; total	86,283 59
Total expenditures	$803,018 35

VI. EXHIBIT OF POLICIES.

NUMBER AND AMOUNT OF POLICIES AND ADDITIONS CLASSIFIED.

Policies in force at the beginning of the year:

	Number.	Amount.	Number.	Amount.
Whole life policies	5,521	$10,262,340	.....	....
Endowment policies	1,492	2,411,609	.....	....
Accident policies	36,618	80,734,349	.....	....
Short term and irregular policies	204	666,750	.....	....
			43,835	$94,075,048

New policies issued during the year:				
Whole life policies	1,906	$3,441,237	......	....
Endowment policies	459	579,768	......	....
Accident policies	32,418	105,405,716	......	....
Short term and irregular policies	2	4,500	......	....
			34,785	$109,431,221
Old policies revived during the year:				
Whole life policies	15	$24,000	......	....
Endowment policies	5	5,000	......	....
Short term and irregular policies	1	3,000	......	....
			21	32,000
Totals			78,641	$203,538,269
Deduct policies decreased and ceased to be in force:				
Whole life policies	1,203	$2,115,204	......	....
Endowment policies	395	579,423	......	....
Accident policies	26,195	85,968,850	......	....
Short term and irregular policies	44	127,800	......	....
			27,837	88,791,277
Totals at the end of the year:				
Whole life policies	6,239	$11,612,373	......	....
Endowment policies	1,561	2,416,954	......	....
Accident policies	42,841	100,171,215	......	....
Short term and irregular policies	163	546,450	......	....
			50,804	$114,746,992
Deduct policies reinsured:				
Whole life policies	22	$111,886	......	....
Endowment policies	1	5,000	......	....
Short term and irregular policies	14	61,000	......	....
			37	177,886
Net numbers and amounts in force, December 31st, 1872:				
Whole life policies	6,217	$11,500,487	......	....
Endowment policies	1,560	2,411,954	......	....
Accident policies	42,841	100,171,215	......	....
Short term and irregular policies	149	485,450	......	....
Totals			50,767	$114,569,106

Policies ceased to be in force during the year with mode of termination:

	No.	Amount.
By death	132	$306,147
By expiry	26,135	85,818,150
By surrender	51	88,522
By lapse	918	1,531,495
By change and old policies decreased	190	424,708
Not taken	411	622,255
Totals	27,837	$88,791,277

Business in the state of Wisconsin during the year 1872:

Policies issued	1,461	$4,254,950 00
Policies in force at the end of the year	1,870	4,857,442 00
Premiums received	......	40,080 77
Losses paid	......	15,330 60

UNIVERSAL LIFE INSURANCE COMPANY.

NEW YORK.

WILLIAM WALKER, *President.* JNO. H. BEWLEY, *Secretary.*

Attorney to accept service of process in Wisconsin, ALVIN B. ALDEN, Portage City.

[Incorporated February, 1865. Commenced business February 1865.]

I. CAPITAL.

Capital authorized	$200,000 00
Capital actually paid up in cash	200,000 00

II. ASSETS.

Loans secured by deeds of trust or mortgages on real estate		$147,759 37
Loans secured by pledge of bonds, stocks, or securities, as collateral		57,000 00
Premium notes and loans, taken for premiums, on policies now in force		331,088 96
Cash value of real estate owned by the company, unincumbered		8,500 00
Cash market value of bonds and stocks owned by the company		298,750 00
Cash in office of company and in banks		68,708 99
Interest accrued on cash loans and on bonds owned by the company		8,391 70
Interest accrued on premium loans and notes		12,428 42
Gross premiums uncollected, not more than three months due, on policies in force December 31, 1872	$119,341 68	
Gross deferred quarterly and semi-annual premiums, on policies in force December 31, 1872	162,452 00	
Total	$281,793 68	
Deducted to reduce the last two items, to the net value of the policies	22,550 00	
Net amount deferred and outstanding premiums		259,243 68
Due from other companies on account of reinsured risks		18,200 00
Total admitted assets		$1,195,016 14

ITEMS NOT ADMITTED AS ASSETS.

Amount invested in commuting com's, or renewal com's purchased	$20,000 00
Furniture, safes and fixtures	6,554 74
Other items, viz.: Ledger balances	33,286 63
Total unadmitted items	$59,841 37

III. LIABILITIES.

Claims for death losses and all other policy claims unpaid	$24,400 00
Net present value of all the outstanding policies in force on the 31st day of December, 1872, computed according to the American Experience Table of Mortality, with four and one-half per cent. interest	883,107 00
Total liabilities as to policyholders	$907,507 00

IV. INCOME.

Cash received for new and renewal premiums, without deductions	$560,066 52
Cash received for interest from all sources	60,830 10
Gross am't of notes or other obligations rec'd for new and renewal prem's	135,209 91
Total income	$756,106 53

V. EXPENDITURES.

Cash paid for the company's own losses and claims, and additions thereto		$195,941 98
Cash paid on account of policies lapsed, surrendered or purchased		56,165 13
Cash paid for dividends to stockholders		15,400 00
Cash paid for premiums to other companies for policies reinsured		16,504 66
Cash paid for commissions to agents on first and renewal premiums		101,861 49
Cash paid for salaries and expenses of managers of agencies, and agents		10,054 18
Cash paid for medical examiners' fees		16,288 25
Cash paid for salaries and other compensation of officers and employes		27,459 69
Cash paid for United States taxes and revenue stamps, $1,852 00; state and local taxes in state where organized, and taxes, licenses and fees in other states, $10,236 63; total		12,088 63
Cash paid for rents and office expenses		12,463 83
Cash paid for furniture, safes and fixtures for home or agency offices		4,000 00
Cash paid on any account not itemized above, viz: law expense, $2,097 59; advertising, $5,862 16; printing, stationery, express and postage, $14,616 30; total		22,576 05
Total cash expenditures		$490,738 89

PREMIUM-LOAN DISBURSEMENTS.

Amount used in purchase of surrendered policies	$47,992 46	
Amount voided by lapse of policies	37,661 80	
Total premium note expenditures		85,654 28
Total expenditures		$576,393 17

VI. PREMIUM-NOTE ACCOUNT.

Premium notes and other premium obligations at beginning of the year	$281,482 35
Premium notes and other premium obligations received during the year	135,209 91
Total	$416,692 26

Deductions during the year as follows:		
Amount used in purchase of surrendered policies	$47,992 48	
Amount voided by lapse of policies	37,661 80	
Total reduction of premium note account		$85,654 28
Balance, note assets at end of the year		$331,038 98

VII. EXHIBIT OF POLICIES.

NUMBER AND AMOUNT OF POLICIES AND ADDITIONS CLASSIFIED.

	Number.	Amount.	Number.	Amount.
Policies in force at the beginning of the year:				
Whole life policies	4,713	$12,567,779		
Endowment policies	315	700,100		
Joint lives and survivorships	129	423,000		
Short term and irregular policies	116	538,500		
			5,273	$14,229,379
New policies issued during the year:				
Whole life policies	3,021	$8,590,708		
Endowment policies	301	573,076		
Joint lives and survivorships	29	76,700		
Short term and irregular policies	180	629,000		
			3,040	9,869,482
Old policies revived during the year:				
Whole life policies	35	$72,000		
			35	72,000
Totals			8,348	$24,170,861
Deduct policies decreased and ceased to be in force:				
Whole life policies	1,834	$5,782,524		
Endowment policies	51	266,351		
Joint lives and survivorships	35	119,500		
Short term and irregular policies	77	337,500		
			2,006	6,505,875
Totals at the end of the year:				
Whole life policies	5,935	$15,447,961		
Endowment policies	565	1,006,825		
Joint lives and survivorships	123	380,200		
Short term and irregular policies	219	830,000		
			6,842	$17,664,986
Deduct policies reinsured				522,100
Net numbers and amounts in force December 31st, 1872			6,842	$17,142 886

Policies ceased to be in force during the year, with mode of termination:

	No.	Amount.
By death	66	$196,380
By expiry	1	5,000
By surrender	170	461,155
By lapse	876	2,932,297
By change and old policies decreased	153	435,700
Not taken	740	2,475,348
Totals	2,006	$6,505,875

Business in the state of Wisconsin during the year 1872:

Policies issued	133	$215,000 00
Policies in force at the end of the year	263	493,900 00
Premiums received		19,106 59
Losses paid		7,500 00

WASHINGTON LIFE INSURANCE COMPANY.

NEW YORK.

CYRUS CURTISS, *President.* WILLIAM HAXTUN, *Secretary.*

Attorney to accept service of process in Wisconsin, S. L. FULLER, Milwaukee.

[Incorporated, January, 1860. Commenced business, February 2, 1860.]

I. CAPITAL.

Capital authorized	$125,000 00
Capital actually paid up in cash	125,000 00

II. ASSETS.

Loans secured by deeds of trust or mortgages on real estate		$1,656,002 87
Loans secured by pledge of bonds, stocks, or securities, as collateral		6,107 00
Cash market value of bonds and stocks owned by the company		1,175,500 00
Cash in office of company		24,375 89
Cash deposited in banks and prem. on gold		277,241 60
Interest accrued on cash loans and on bonds owned by the company		30,170 85
Cash in course of transmission		21,805 06
Gross premiums uncollected, not more than three months due, on policies in force December 31, 1872	$56,800 00	
Gross deferred quarterly and semi-annual premiums, on policies in force December 31, 1872	189,780 00	
Total	$246,580 00	
Deducted to reduce the last two items, to the net value of the policies	26,580 00	
Net amount deferred and outstanding prem's		220,000 00
Total admitted assets		$3,411,203 27

ITEMS NOT ADMITTED AS ASSETS.

Furniture, safes and fixtures	$15,000 00
Total unadmitted items	$15,000 00

III. LIABILITIES.

Claims for death losses due and unpaid	$17,000 00
Claims for death losses and matured endowments, in process of adjustment, or adjusted and not due	42,660 00
Claims for death losses and other policy claims resisted by the company	7,000 00
Net present value of all the outstanding policies in force December 31st, 1872, computed according to the American Experience Table of Mortality, with four and one-half per cent, interest	2,914,325 00
Amount of all unpaid dividends of surplus, or other profits due policyholders	211 74
Amount of unpaid dividends to stockholders	770 00
Amount due on account of salaries, rents and office expenses	2,500 00
Total liabilities as to policyholders	$2,984,466 74

IV. INCOME.

Cash received for premiums during the year, without deductions for expense	$1,032,418 14
Cash received for interest on cash loans	99,170 37
Cash received for interest on bonds owned and dividends on stocks	68,691 64
Discount on claims paid in advance	366 58
Cash income from other sources, viz: profit on bonds sold	2,351 89
Total income	$1,202,998 62

V. EXPENDITURES.

Cash paid for the company's own losses and claims, and additions thereto	$366,090 17
Cash paid to annuitants	1,278 90
Cash paid on account of policies lapsed, surrendered or purchased	61 455 50
Cash paid for dividends to policyholders	109,095 78
Cash paid for dividends to stockholders	9,755 70
Cash paid for commissions to agents on first and renewal premiums	81,466 88
Cash paid for salaries and expenses of managers of agencies, and agents	16,338 68
Cash paid for medical examiners' fees	8,056 00
Cash paid for salaries and other compensation of officers and employes	41,359 98
Cash paid for United States taxes and revenue stamps, $447 10; taxes, licenses and fees in other states, $9,184 34, of which the sum of $339 00 was paid in the state of Wisconsin; total	9,631 44
Cash paid for rents	7,500 00
Cash paid for commuting commissions	4,766 51
Cash paid on any account not itemized above, viz: postage and exchange, $3,859 96; printing and stationery, $10,359 13; interest, $2 512 56; advertising, $12,495 71; sundry expenses, $25,771 04; total	54,998 40
Total expenditures	$671,788 84

VI. EXHIBIT OF POLICIES.

NUMBER AND AMOUNT OF POLICIES AND ADDITIONS CLASSIFIED.

	Number.	Amount.	Number.	Amount.
Policies in force at the beginning of the year:				
Whole life policies	8,214	$19,358,858	......	....
Endowment policies	2,395	4,874,785	......	....
Annuities	5	....	......	....
Short term and irregular policies	20	59,500	......	....
			10,634	$24,293,143 00
New policies issued during the year:				
Whole life policies	1,635	$4,048,119	......	....
Endowment policies	457	798,640	......	....
			2,092	4,846,759 00
Old policies revived during the year:				
Whole life policies	218	$573,500	......	....
Endowment policies	58	197,515	......	....
			276	771,015 00
Totals			13,002	$29,910,917 00
Deduct policies decreased and ceased to be in force:				
Whole life policies	1,565	$3,550,535	......	....
Endowment policies	466	1,040,425	......	....
Annuities	1	....	......	....
Short term and irregular policies	3	6,000	......	....
			2,035	4,596,960 00
Totals at the end of the year:				
Whole life policies	8,497	$20,429,942	......	....
Endowment policies	2,449	4,830,515	......	....
Annuities	4	....	......	....
Short term and irregular policies	17	53,500	......	....
			10,967	$25,308,957 00
Add outstanding additions			......	646,933 32
Net numbers and amounts in force December 31st, 1872			10,967	$25,955,890 32

Policies ceased to be in force during the year, with mode of termination:

	Number.	Amount.
By death	110	$275,690
By expiry	3	6,000
By surrender	495	1,170,265
By lapse	1,122	2,373,000
Not taken	305	772,005
Totals	2,035	$4,596,960

Business in the state of Wisconsin during the year 1872:

	Number	Amount
Policies issued	156	$195,500 00
Policies in force at the end of the year	845	1,116,805 00
Premiums received	......	39,175 85
Losses paid	......	14,000 00

WESTERN NEW YORK LIFE INSURANCE COMPANY.

BATAVIA, N. Y.

H. U. HOWARD, *President.* C. E. FISH, *Secretary.*

Attorney to accept service of process in Wisconsin, SIEGFRIED WOLFFSOHN, Milwaukee.

[Incorporated Nov. 21st, 1868. Commenced business Nov. 23d, 1868.]

I. CAPITAL.

Capital actually paid up in cash	$125,000 00

II. ASSETS.

Loans secured by deeds of trust or mortgages on real estate		$132,090 00
Premium notes and loans, taken for premiums, on policies now in force		22,529 41
Cash in office of company,		330 13
Cash deposited in banks and trust companies		5,963 15
Interest accrued on cash loans and on bonds owned by the company		9,060 71
Gross premiums uncollected, not more than three months due, on policies in force December 31, 1872	$11,394 66	....
Gross deferred quarterly and semi-annual premiums, on policies in force December 31, 1872	22,699 98	....
Total	$34,094 64	....
Deducted to reduce the last two items, to the net value of the policies	3,409 46	....
Net amount deferred and outstanding premiums		30,685 18
Total admitted assets		$200,658 58

ITEMS NOT ADMITTED AS ASSETS.

Amount invested in commuting com's, or renewal com's purchased	$1,100 00
Cash in hands of officers or agents due the company	978 05
Value of agency supplies, printed matter and stationery on hand	500 00
Bills receivable	9,605 10
Furniture, safes and fixtures	300 00
Total unadmitted items	$12,483 15

III. LIABILITIES.

Net present value of all the outstanding policies in force on the 31st day of December, 1872, computed according to the American Experience Table of Mortality, with four and one-half per cent. interest	$112,541 00
Amount of all unpaid dividends of surplus, or other profits due policyholders	1,547 21
Amount of national, state or other taxes due	1,165 18
Amount due on account of salaries, rents and office expenses	1,447 32
Amount of any other liability of the company	532 50
Total liabilities as to policyholders	$117,233 16

IV. INCOME.

Cash received for premiums on new policies, without deductions	$41,051 85
Cash received for renewal premiums, without deductions for expense	34,958 46
Cash premiums from other companies for reinsuring their risks	193 48
Cash received for interest on cash loans	5,227 75
Cash received for interest on premium notes or loans	4,085 39
Discount on claims paid in advance	90 81
Gross amount of notes or other obligations taken for new premiums	1,813 65
Gross amount of notes or other obligations taken for renewal premiums	10,815 21
Total income	$97,736 60

V. EXPENDITURES.

Cash paid for the company's own losses and claims, and additions thereto		$11,742 00
Cash paid on account of policies lapsed, surrendered or purchased		655 00
Cash paid for dividends to policyholders		1,795 64
Cash paid for premiums to other companies for policies reinsured		192 50
Cash paid for commissions to agents on first premiums		26,905 65
Cash paid for commissions to agents on renewal premiums		2,614 80
Cash paid for salaries and expenses of managers of agencies, and agents		9,609 83
Cash paid for medical examiners' fees		5,558 78
Cash paid for salaries and other compensation of officers and employes		4,046 00
Cash paid for United States taxes and revenue stamps, $376.14; state and local taxes in state where organized, $1,666.37; total		2,042 51
Cash paid for commuting commissions		100 00
Cash paid for furniture, safes and fixtures for home or agency offices		379 70
Cash paid on any account not itemized above, viz: stationery and miscellaneous expenses		2,131 02
Total cash expenditures		$67,073 43
PREMIUM-LOAN DISBURSEMENTS.		
Amount used in payment of losses and claims	$109 41	....
Amount used in payment of dividends to policyholders	6,961 43	....
Amount voided by lapse of policies	3,948 73	....
Total premium note expenditures		11,019 57
Total expenditures		$78,093 00

VI. PREMIUM-NOTE ACCOUNT.

Premium notes and other premium obligations at beginning of the year		$21,463 75
Premium notes and other premium obligations received during the year......		12,128 86
Total		$33,592 61
Deductions during the year as follows:		
Amount used in payment of losses and claims	$109 41	....
Amount used in payment of dividends to policyholders....	6,961 43	....
Amount voided by lapse of policies.........................	3,948 73	....
Amount redeemed by maker in cash.	43 63	....
Total reduction of premium note account		11,063 20
Balance, note assets at the end of the year		$22,529 41

VII. EXHIBIT OF POLICIES.

NUMBER AND AMOUNT OF POLICIES AND ADDITIONS CLASSIFIED.

	Number.	Amount.	Number.	Amount.
Policies in force at the beginning of the year:				
Whole life policies...	656	$1,234,244 35	......	....
Endowment policies	173	246,353 00	......	....
Joint lives and survivorships.......	65	89,500 00	......	....
Short term and irregular policies..........	10	35,000 00	......	....
			904	$1,605,097 35
New policies issued during the year:				
Whole life policies.........................	1,096	$1,341,278 00	......	....
Endowment policies	237	274,162 57	......	....
Joint lives and survivorships	55	67,120 00	......	....
Short term and irregular policies.	11	14,000 00	......	....
			1,399	1,696,560 57
Old policies revived during the year:				
Whole life policies........................	14	$33,500 00	......	....
Endowment policies.......................	2	4,500 00	......	....
Joint lives and survivorships..............	1	1,000 00	......	....
			17	38,500 00
Additions by dividends during the year:				
Whole life policies	......	$33 62	......	....
Endowment policies	......	27 97	......	....
			......	61 59
Totals			2,320	$3,340,219 51
Deduct policies decreased and ceased to be in force:				
Whole life policies.......	358	$558,700 00	......	....
Endowment policies	123	159,128 57	......	....
Joint lives and survivorships	35	45,500 00	......	....
Short term and irregular policies..........	4	10,000 00	......	....
			520	773,328 57
Totals at the end of the year:				
Whole life policies,.........................	1,408	$2,050,355 97	......	....
Endowment policies........................	289	365,414 97	......	....
Joint lives and survivorships..............	86	112,120 00	......	....
Short term and irregular policies....	17	39,000 00	......	....
			1,800	$2,566,890 94
Deduct policies reinsured:				
Short term and irregular policies	2	$10,000 00	......	....
			2	10,000 00
Net numbers and amounts in force December 31st, 1872:				
Whole life policies	1,408	$2,050,355 97	......	....
Endowment policies.......................	289	365,414 97	......	....
Joint lives and survivorships	86	112,120 00	......	....
Short term and irregular policies..........	15	29,000 00	......	....
Totals........................			1,798	$2,556,890 94

Policies ceased to be in force during the year, with mode of termination:

	Number.	Amount.
By death..	9	$11,700 00
By expiry......	2	3,000 00
By surrender...	27	55,628 57
By lapse..	272	395,500 00
By change and old policies decreased....................	34	61,000 00
Not taken	176	246,500 00
Totals	520	$773,328 57

DOCUMENT 3.

ANNUAL REPORT

OF THE

STATE TREASURER

OF THE

STATE OF WISCONSIN,

For the Fiscal Year ending September 30, 1873.

OFFICE OF THE STATE TREASURER,
MADISON, October 10th, 1873.

To His Excellency, C. C. WASHBURN,
Governor of Wisconsin:

SIR:—Pursuant to the requirements of law, I have the honor respectfully to submit my report, showing the transactions of this office, during the fiscal year ending September 30, 1873, and including a detailed statement of the operations of the bank department.

GENERAL FUND.

The balance in the General Fund at the commencement of the fiscal year, was............	....	$29,169 92
The receipts during the year from all sources have been............	....	1,095,872 29
Total............	....	$1,125,042 21
The disbursements have been,............	....	1,191,966 01
Leaving it overdrawn............	....	$66,923 80
The balance in the treasury at the close of the fiscal year for 1872, was............	....	$239,109 11
Distributed among the several funds, as follows:		
General Fund............	$29,169 92	....
School Fund............	5,265 65	....
School Fund Income............	19,663 63	....
Normal School Fund............	7,669 86	....
Normal School Fund Income............	38,668 87	....
University Fund............	2,837 82	....
Drainage Fund............	55,041 12	....
Agricultural College Fund............	2,483 44	....
Delinquent Tax Fund............	5,798 56	....
Commissioner's Contingent Fund............	1,311 86	....
Deposit Fund............	7,467 09	....
Sturgeon Bay Ship Canal Land Tres. F'd...	7,693 37	....
St. Croix & Lake Sup'r R. R. Co. T's F'd..	30,354 46	....
Oshkosh Normal School Building Fund..	3,845 16	....
River Falls Normal School Build'g Fund.	20,000 00	....
Allotment Fund............	1,843 30	....
Total balance in the Treasury as above..		$239,109 11
RECEIPTS AND CREDITS.		
The receipts of the Treasury during the past year, including the above balance, amount to.	....	$2,013,667 66
And the disbursements to............	....	1,798,023 14
Leaving in the Treasury the sum of............	....	$215,644 52
To the credit of the following funds:		
School Fund............	$56,341 21	....
School Fund Income............	14,289 32	....
Normal School Fund............	41,384 14	....
Normal School Fund Income............	54,669 35	....
University Fund............	2,465 43	....
Agricultural College Fund............	6,044 14	....
Drainage Fund............	23,422 19	....
Delinquent Tax Fund............	5,086 91	....
Commissioners' Contingent Fund............	1,359 61	....
Deposit Fund............	6,798 26	....
St. Croix & Lake Superior R. R. Co. T's F'd	43,864 46	....
Allotment Fund............	1,843 30	....
River Falls Normal School Build'g Fund..	25,000 00	....
	$282,568 32	....
Deduct General Fund overpaid............	66,923 80	....
		$215,644 52

The following statement exhibits the gross amount of the revenues of the state and of the several funds and of the disbursements thereof:

RECEIPTS.		
Balance in the treasury September 30, 1872		$239,109 11
For General Fund	$1,095,872 29	
School Fund	103,818 93	
School Fund Income	179,762 67	
University Fund	9,728 12	
University Fund Income	42,716 38	
Drainage Fund	93,636 46	
Normal School Fund	86,687 54	
Normal School Fund Income	71,369 10	
For Agricultural College Fund	13,560 70	
For Agricultural College Fund Income	12,558 85	
Delinquent Tax Fund	27,047 10	
Commissioners Contingent Fund	323 75	
Sturgeon Bay Ship Canal Land Trespass Fund	12,710 62	
St. Croix and Lake Superior Railroad Company Trespass Fund	18,891 04	
River Falls Normal School Build'g Fund	5,000 00	
North Wisconsin Railroad Aid Fund	875 00	
		$1,774,558 55
Total		$2,013,667 66
DISBURSEMENTS.		
From General Fund	$1,191,966 01	
School Fund	52,743 37	
School Fund Income	185,136 98	
University Fund	10,100 51	
University Fund Income	42,716 38	
Drainage Fund	125,255 39	
Normal School Fund	52,978 26	
Normal School Fund Income	55,368 62	
Agricultural College Fund	10,000 00	
Agricultural College Fund Income	12,558 85	
Delinquent Tax Fund	27,753 75	
Commissioners Contingent Fund	276 00	
Deposit Fund	668 83	
Sturgeon Bay Ship Canal Land Trespass Fund	20,403 99	
St. Croix and Lake Superior Railroad Company Trespass Fund	5,381 04	
Oshkosh Normal School Building Fund	3,845 16	
North Wisconsin Railroad Aid Fund	875 00	
		$1,798,023 14
Balance in Treasury September 30, 1873		215,644 52
		$2,013,667 66

The revenue for the year has been derived from the following sources:

State tax, including Reform School and Insane Hospital tax	$781,875 60	
Suit tax	3,805 00	
Railway companies	210,374 99	
Insurance companies	63,299 93	
Telegraph companies	3,522 00	
Plank and gravel roads	247 68	
Payments on bank bonds	410 00	
Show and pedler's licenses	7,188 29	
Penalty for nonpayment of interest on state and mortgaged lands	4,225 88	
Penalty for trespass on state lands	2,078 88	
United States, for boarding U. S. prisoners	1,420 87	
Commissioners of deeds out of state	253 00	
Ll. Breese, Secretary of State, fees collected	6,761 50	
Ll. Breese, Secretary of State, notarial fees	1,382 00	
Sale of Marathon county lands	6,498 55	
Sale of public property	409 55	
Sale of Wisconsin reports	765 00	
Sale of public documents	37 10	
Bank dept., printing and pub. bank reports	37 50	
State claim for unredeemed currency on Portage County Bank	400 00	
Refunded	879 47	
		$1,095,872 29

DISBURSEMENTS.

1. *Salaries and Permanent Appropriations*—		
Governor's office	$7,100 00	
Secretary's office	3,200 00	
Treasurer's office	3,400 00	
Attorney General's office	2,600 00	
State Superintendent's office	5,650 00	
Office of Superintendent of Pub. Property	3,200 00	
State library	1,945 36	
State Historical Society	6,300 00	
Supreme court	13,769 00	
Circuit courts	30,433 33	
Wisconsin reports	26,325 00	
		$103,922 69
2. *Legislative Expenses*		103,730 22
3. *State Prison and Charitable Institutions*—		
State Prison	$45,550 47	
Hospital for the Insane, Madison	119,438 15	
Northern Wis. Hospital for the Insane	198,677 21	
Institute for the Blind	20,875 00	
Institute for the Deaf and Dumb	23,737 25	
Industrial School for Boys	65,715 00	
Soldiers' Orphans' Home	28,193 69	
		502,186 77
4. *Interest on State Indebtedness*		157,649 67

MISCELLANEOUS.

Clerk hire, Secretary's office	$13,599 99	
Clerk hire, Treasurer's office	7,705 00	
Clerk hire, Land department	15,487 00	
		36,791 99

Disbursements—Miscellaneous—continued.

Labor about Capitol	$18,904 54	
Contingent Expenses	11,631 10	
Publishing General Laws	12,478 40	
Publishing Local Laws	1,056 40	
Publishing and advertising	1,678 00	
Printing	61,403 78	
Stationery	10,000 00	
Postage	4,006 80	
State Board of Charities and Reform	1,872 20	
Normal Institutes	2,043 16	
Militia, Military Secretary and State Armorer	2,154 57	
Protecting State Lands	5,931 92	
Immigration Commissioner	5,190 98	
Geological Survey (old)	780 00	
Geological Survey (new)	7,500 00	
Gas	5,871 75	
Fuel, 1872 and 1873	11,834 70	
Governor's Contingent Fund	600 00	
Park Fence	28,086 76	
Park Improvement	1,639 65	
Capitol Improvement	26,832 24	
County Agricultural Societies	3,600 00	
Lucius Fairchild, Fox & Wisconsin River Improvement Commissioner	2,000 00	
Bounty on wild animals	6,535 00	
Superior Harbor protection	4,229 14	
Volunteer aid	1,865 32	
C. C. Washburn, Governor, relief of sufferers by fire	7,610 16	
State Prison Commissioner, for boarding U. S. prisoners	1,420 87	
Treasury Agents per (per centum) on Pedlers' Licenses	2,477 84	
Special Appropriations	32,983 12	
Transfer to Normal School Fund Income for Normal Institutes	2,000 00	
Transfer to School Fund to correct error	20 00	
Miscellaneous	1,951 77	
		287,684 67
Total		$1,191,966 01

The amounts remaining due to the several charitable and penal institutions of this state, on account of the appropriations made to them during the year 1873, are as follows:

State Prison	$6,250 00
Hospital for Insane, Madison	13,486 75
Northern Wisconsin Hospital for the Insane	11,250 00
Institute for the Blind	5,075 00
Institute for the Deaf and Dumb	14,250 00
Industrial School for Boys	13,250 00
Soldiers' Orphans' Home	10,000 00
	$73,561 75

The following statement shows the amounts due the state, September 30, 1873, on account of the state tax:

Iowa county	$22,407 76

I am informed that owing to local difficulties growing out of a certain railroad indebtedness, the county of Iowa has failed to collect taxes of any kind during the fiscal year just closed. For this reason it has not been possible for the State Treasurer to enforce the payment of the state tax due from said county. And while I may greatly regret that the operation of the law on the subject of the assessment and collection of taxes should be defeated in any county and for any cause, yet it is a matter of just pride and satisfaction to the department under my charge, that I am able to point to the fact that never before in the history of this state has the revenue due from counties been so efficiently collected as during the last two years.

Statement of amounts due to counties from the State, September 30, 1873, on account of delinquent taxes collected during the last quarter:

Adams	$59 14
Barron	751 58
Brown	2 17
Burnett	8 04
Calumet	18 66
Chippewa	155 86
Clark	34 98
Columbia	41 20
Crawford	63 41
Dane	18 48
Dodge	47
Door	78 55
Dunn	79 85
Douglas	48 10
Eau Claire	20 92
Grant	5 79
Green Lake	12 12
Iowa	1 80
Jackson	108 27
Juneau	57 05
Kewaunee	61 64
La Crosse	10 83
La Fayette	2 88
Manitowoc	220 77
Marathon	221 18
Monroe	77 61
Marquette	14 82
Oconto	842 22
Outagamie	131 50
Pierce	813 54
Polk	201 40
Portage	90 55

Richland	$8 50
Rock	7 66
St. Croix	128 50
Sauk	16 95
Shawano	1,029 53
Trempealeau	96 85
Vernon	18 95
Waupaca	111 64
Waushara	21 49
Winnebago	11 46
Wood	300 30
	$4,994 66

STATE INDEBTEDNESS.

The debt of the State amounts to and is classified as follows:

To School Fund	$1,559,700 00	
To Normal School Fund	512,000 00	
To University Fund	111,000 00	
To Agricultural College Fund	50,600 00	
		$2,233,900 00
Bonds maturing in 1880	12,000 00	
1884	1,000 00	
1886	4,000 00	
1888	1,000 00	
1877	100 00	
		18,100 00
Currency certificates		57 00
		$2,252,057 00

SECURITIES DEPOSITED BY INSURANCE COMPANIES.

There are now on deposit in my office the following securities, viz:

From the Northwestern Mutual Life Insurance Company of Milwaukee—

U. S. registered bonds	$50,000
Bonds and mortgages upon certain real estate in the city of Milwaukee	100,000
	$150,000

From the Madison Mutual Insurance Company—

U. S. 5-20 registered bonds	$50,000
U. S. Coupon bonds	35,000
	$85,000

From the Hekla Fire Insurance Company of Madison—

Bonds and mortgages of real estate	$24,980

MUNICIPAL BONDS.

Held in Escrow by the State Treasurer.

	The following bonds, issued to the Sheboygan and Fond du Lac Railroad Company and all bearing date the 25th day of September, 1872, are now on deposit in the State Treasurer's office, viz.:		
70	Coupon bonds of the county of Marquette, numbered from 1 to 70 inclusive, of $100, each, with coupons attached..............	$7,000	....
35	Coupon bonds, of same county, numbered from 71 to 105 inclusive, of $200 each, with coupons attached..............................	7,000	....
7	Coupon bonds, of same county, numbered from 106 to 112 inclusive, of $300 each, with coupons attached..........................	2,100	
28	Coupon bonds, of same county, numbered from 113 to 140 inclusive, of $500 each, with coupons attached...	14,000	....
21	Coupon bonds, of same county, numbered from 141 to 161 inclusive, of $1,000 each with coupons attached	21,000	....
	Total.......		$51,100
6	Coupon bonds, of the village of Montello, numbered from 1 to 6, of $1,000 each with coupons attached	... .	6,000
6	Coupon bonds, of the town of Westfield, numbered from 1 to 6, of $1,000 each, with coupons attached	....	6,000
11	Coupon bonds, of the town of Harris, numbered from 1 to 11, of $500 each, with coupons attached	....	5,500
	Grand Total........................	....	$68,600

CERTIFICATES OF RAILROAD STOCK

Held in Escrow by the State Treasurer.

Certificate No. 105, issued by the Sheboygan and Fond du Lac Railroad Company to the county of Marquette, for 292 shares of $100 each, of the capital stock of said company.

Certificate No. 106, of same railroad company to same county, for 219 shares of $100 each, of said capital stock.

Certificate No. 107, of same railroad company, to the village of Montello, for 60 shares of $100 each, of said capital stock.

Certificate No. 108, of said railroad company, to the town of Westfield, for 60 shares of $100 each, of said capital stock.

Certificate No. 109, of said railroad company, to the town of Harris, for 55 shares of $100 each, of said capital stock.

All of said certificates bearing date the 27th day of September, 1872.

MISCELLANEOUS DEPOSITS.

There are also in the Treasury the following deposits, made by or on account of soldiers:

DAVID BULLEM, Co. K, 5th regiment Wis. Vol. Infantry—	
1 U. S. 10-40 bond with March 1866, and subsequent coupons.....	$100 00
DAVID BULLEM, Co. K, 5th regiment Wis. Vol. Infantry—	
1 U. S. 10-40 bond with March, 1866, and subsequent coupons.....	$50 00
Certificate of deposit of M. Von Baumbach, Milwaukee..........	50 00
Currency	42 00
CHARLES HENRICH, Co. D, 32d regiment, Wis. Vol. Infantry—	
Currency	$93 00
FRED KIRSHENBELER, Co. F, 21st regiment, Wis. Vol. Infantry—	
1 U. S. 10-40 bond, with March, 1866, and subsequent coupons....	$100 00
Currency	16 28
MARY ANN PIERSON—	
Volunteer Aid Fund, draft for..............................	$5 00
HARRIET C. KNOX—	
Volunteer Aid Fund, draft for..............................	$3 67
HEIRS OF GEO. MOREHEAD, late Co. K, 40th regiment, Wis. Vol. Infantry, deceased	$53,05
JAMES TOWLE, late Co. G, 16th regiment, Wis. Vol. Infantry, (an insane soldier)..........	$87 20

GENERAL FUND.

It is with a feeling of reluctance that I beg leave once more to direct the attention of the legislature to the condition of the general fund, which, by the first day of January next, will be again largely overdrawn, probably not less than $150,000.

The observations and suggestions submitted by me under this head in my last annual report, apply with equal force now. There is an apparent radical inconsistency between the estimates and actual appropriations, and so long as the legislature will persist in making appropriations grossly in excess of the adopted estimates, just so long will deficiencies in the general fund continue to arise.

Aside from this objectionable feature, our finances are in a healthy and satisfactory condition. The credit of the State is good at home and abroad, and its entire debt only a trifle over two and a quarter millions of dollars, or about $2.13 per capita on the United States census of 1870.

Of this debt, which was mainly incurred for the praiseworthy object of aiding the families of volunteers in our late war of the rebellion, the sum of $2,233,900 is in certificates of indebtedness to the trust funds of the State. The remaining outstanding bonds, amounting in all to $18,100, will be redeemed at any time on presentation at the State Treasury.

All of which is respectfully submitted,

HENRY BÆTZ,
State Treasurer.

RECEIPTS, PAYMENTS AND STATEMENTS

IN DETAIL.

GENERAL FUND RECEIPTS.

STATE TAX.		
Adams .... county	$2,594 82	....
Ashland .... do	980 00	....
Barron .... do	1,184 41	....
Bayfield .... do	752 58	....
Brown .... do	12,922 92	....
Buffalo .... do	4,870 79	....
Burnett .... do	769 24	....
Calumet .... do	6,684 30	....
Chippewa .... do	18,720 78	....
Clark .... do	5,534 36	....
Columbia .... do	21,519 57	....
Crawford .... do	7,428 34	....
Dane .... do	49,885 89	....
Dodge .... do	32,068 17	....
Door .... do	1,808 00	....
Douglas .... do	1,855 92	....
Dunn .... do	5,892 29	....
Eau Claire .... do	6,820 88	....
Fond du Lac ...... do	32,866 33	....
Grant .... do	29,642 37	....
Green .... do	20,214 81	....
Green Lake ...... do	8,816 48	....
Iowa .... do	74 68	....
Jefferson .... do	22,644 86	....
Jackson .... do	4,187 01	....
Juneau .... do	5,028 50	....
Kenosha .... do	12,775 68	....
Kewaunee .... do	1,498 58	....
La Crosse .... do	12,818 87	....
La Fayette .... do	16,448 45	....
Manitowoc .... do	15,905 78	....
Marathon .... do	8,378 83	....
Marquette .... do	2,843 38	....
Milwaukee .... do	102,236 49	....
Monroe .... do	8,615 78	....
Oconto .... do	11,039 42	....
Outagamie .... do	13,524 02	....
Ozaukee .... do	6,958 26	....

GENERAL FUND RECEIPTS.

State Tax—continued.		
Pepin......county	$1,615 00	
Pierce........do	7,813 92	
Polk.........do	2,362 79	
Portage.....do	5,834 16	
Racine.......do	20,809 58	
Richland....do	7,772 07	
Rock.........do	41,263 37	
St. Croix.....do	8,741 89	
Sauk.........do	17,486 96	
Shawano.....do	3,106 66	
Sheboygan....do	17,779 28	
Trempealeau..do	4,905 58	
Vernon.......do	11,281 78	
Walworth....do	27,519 91	
Washington..do	18,266 61	
Waukesha....do	26,484 63	
Waupaca.....do	7,654 18	
Waushara....do	4,032 23	
Winnebago..do	29,530 63	
Wood.......do	3,378 18	
		$781,875 60
SUIT TAX.		
Adams.....county	$15 00	
Bayfield......do	11 00	
Brown........do	35 00	
Buffalo......do	47 00	
Clark........do	68 00	
Columbia....do	87 00	
Crawford....do	51 00	
Dane.........do	809 00	
Door.........do	49 00	
Douglas......do	13 00	
Dunn........do	76 00	
Eau Claire....do	110 00	
Fond du Lac..do	51 00	
Green........do	26 00	
Green Lake...do	61 00	
Jackson......do	48 00	
Jefferson.....do	63 00	
Juneau.......do	80 00	
Kenosha......do	35 00	
Kewaunee....do	27 00	
La Crosse...do	76 00	
La Fayette....do	113 00	
Manitowoc...do	76 00	
Marathon....do	80 00	
Marquette....do	12 00	
Milwaukee...do	256 00	
Monroe......do	134 00	
Outagamie...do	103 00	
Ozaukee......do	35 00	
Pepin........do	10 00	
Pierce....... do	29 00	
Polk.........do	43 00	

Receipts, Payments and Statements—continued.

GENERAL FUND RECEIPTS.

Suit Tax—continued.		
Portage......county	$82 00	
Racine.......do	44 00	
Richland......do	86 00	
Rock.........do	145 00	
St. Croix......do	144 00	
Sauk.........do	44 00	
Shawano......do	16 00	
Sheboygan.....do	37 00	
Trempealeau...do	20 00	
Vernon.......do	48 00	
Walworth.....do	92 00	
Washington....do	89 00	
Waukesha.....do	65 00	
Waupaca......do	60 00	
Waushara.....do	12 00	
Winnebago.....do	125 00	
Wood........do	17 00	
		$3,805 00
RAILROAD TAX OR LICENSE FEE.		
*Chicago and Northwestern Railway Company	$42,683 37	
Green Bay and Lake Pepin.........do	846 02	
Mineral Point.....................do	3,315 95	
Milwaukee and Northern...........do	3,625 21	
Milwaukee and Lake Shore........do	478 21	
Milwaukee and St. Paul...........do	135,989 79	
North Wisconsin..................do	167 85	
Prairie du Chien and McGregor....do	103 62	
Sheboygan and Fond du Lac.......do	4,221 58	
Western Union...................do	10,047 40	
Wisconsin Central................do	3,506 70	
West Wisconsin..................do	5,389 29	
		210,374 99
Amounts Remaining Due and Unpaid.		
West Wisconsin Railway Company	$5,389 29	
North Wisconsin.......do	167 85	
Sheboygan and Fond du Lac Railway Company	1,887 31	
Total	$7,444 45	
INSURANCE COMPANIES.		
Fire.		
Allemannia Fire Insurance Co., Pittsburg, Pa	$688 40	
Atlantic Insurance Co., Brooklyn, N. Y	519 10	
Ætna Insurance Co., Hartford, Conn	8,187 87	
Amazon Insurance Co., Cincinnati, Ohio	600 67	
American Central Insurance Co., St. Louis, Mo	133 86	
Allemannia Fire Insurance Co., Cleveland, Ohio	157 12	
American Insurance Co., Chicago, Ill	795 62	

* The Chicago and Northwestern Railway Company has paid the second installment of its license fee ($42,683.38) immediately after the close of the fiscal year.

GENERAL FUND RECEIPTS.

Insurance Companies—Fire—continued.		
Arctic Fire Ins. Co., N. Y.	$136 03	
Atlas Ins. Co., Hartford, Conn	500 00	
Brewers' Fire Ins. Co. of America, Milwaukee	1,244 15	
Brewers' and Maltsters' Ins. Co., N. Y	223 80	
Black River Ins. Co., Watertown, N. Y	67 74	
Concordia Mut. Fire Ins. Co., Milwaukee	299 12	
Commerce Ins. Co., Albany, N. Y	81 66	
Continental Ins. Co., N. Y	870 48	
Capitol City Ins. Co., Albany, N. Y	14 13	
Commercial Union Ass. Co., London, Eng	336 50	
Connecticut Fire Ins. Co., Hartford, Conn	118 00	
Dodge Co. Mut. Ins. Co., Waupun	701 43	
Detroit Fire and Marine Ins. Co., Detroit, Mich	201 83	
Fairfield Co. Fire Ins. Co., South Norwalk, Conn	500 00	
Franklin Fire Ins. Co., Phil., Penn	820 54	
Fireman's Fund Ins. Co., San Francisco, Cal	214 20	
Farmers Ins. Co., Freeport, Ill	201 06	
Fire Association, Phil., Penn	500 00	
German Ins. Co., Erie, Penn	598 47	
Germania Fire Ins. Co., N. Y	375 43	
German American Ins. Co., N. Y	284 62	
Germantown Far. Mut. Ins. Co., Germantown, Wis	577 93	
Globe Ins. Co., Chicago, Ill	112 70	
German Ins. Co., Freeport, Ill	500 00	
Gerard Fire and Marine Ins. Co., Phil., Penn	617 14	
Herman Farmers Mut. Ins. Co., Herman, Wis	111 30	
Home Ins. Co., N. Y	2,595 25	
Hartford Fire Ins. Co. Hartford, Conn	1,818 09	
Hanover Fire Ins. Co., N. Y	375 43	
Hoffman Fire Ins. Co., N. Y	49 86	
Hekla Ins. Co., Madison, Wis	323 82	
Home Ins. Co., Columbus, Ohio	201 00	
Howard Ins. Co., New York	126 99	
Hamburg-Bremen Fire Ins. Co., Hamburg, Ger	59 15	
Hartford Steam Boiler Inspection and Ins. Co	81 16	
Humboldt Ins. Co., Newark, N. J	500 00	
Insurance Co. of North America, Phil., Penn	1,844 02	
Lancashire Ins. Co., Manchester, Eng	548 13	
London Assurance Corporation, London, Eng	650 98	
Lorillard Ins. Co., New York	84 23	
Liverpool and London and Globe Ins. Co., Liv., Eng	538 60	
Milwaukee Mechanics Mut. Ins. Co	3,001 79	
Mercantile Ins. Co., Cleveland, Ohio	129 67	
Madison Mut. Ins. Co	1,913 05	
Merchants Ins. Co., Providence, R. I	93 37	
Mechanics and Traders Fire Ins. Co., New York	283 23	
Manhattan Fire Ins. Co., New York	233 47	
Meridan Fire Ins. Co., Meriden, Conn	526 18	
Mercantile Mut Ins. Co., New York	376 17	
Milville Mut. Marine and Fire Ins. Co., N. J	500 00	
National Fire Ins. Co., Hartford, Conn	198 93	
North Western National Ins. Co., Milwaukee	2,463 29	
Niagara Fire Ins. Co., N. Y	375 43	
North Missouri Ins. Co., Macon, Mo	633 82	
North British and Mercantile Ins. Co., Lond. & Ed	843 99	

GENERAL FUND RECEIPTS.

Insurance Companies—Fire—continued.		
Narragansett F. & M. Ins. Co., Providence, R. I...	$16 46	....
New Orleans Mutual Insurance Association.......	916 67	....
National Fire and Marine Ins. Co., Phila., Pa.....	500 00	....
Orient Insurance Company, Hartford, Conn.......	166 74	....
Orient Mutual Insurance Company, New York....	314 88	....
Penn Fire Insurance Co., Phila., Pa.............	708 01	....
Phœnix Insurance Company, Hartford, Conn.....	1,097 24	....
Phenix Insurance Company, Brooklyn, N. Y......	685 62	....
Pennsylvania Fire Insurance Co., Phila., Penn....	988 19	....
Pacific Mutual Ins. Co., New York	383 27	....
Providence Washington Ins. Co., Prov., R. I......	41 63	....
Royal Insurance Co., Liverpool, Eng............	600 88	....
Republic Fire Insurance Co., New York..........	875 43	....
State Insurance Company, Hannibal, Mo..........	68 26	....
St. Paul F. & M. Insurance Co., St. Paul, Minn....	609 26	....
St. Nicholas Insurance Co., New York	74 43	....
Springfield Fire & Marine Insurance Co..........	179 98	....
Star Fire Insurance Co., New York	79 37	....
Standard Fire Insurance Co., New York..........	114 98	....
Sun Insurance Company, Cleveland, Ohio........	43 03	....
St. Joseph F. & M. Insurance Co., St. Joseph, Mo.	500 00	....
Traders' Insurance Co., Chicago, Ill............	141 15	....
Tradesman's Fire Insurance Co., New York......	151 10	....
U. S. Branch Imperial Fire Ins. Co., London, Eng.	1,012 18	....
U. S. Branch Queen Ins. Co., Liverpool, Eng......	395 54	....
Union Insurance Company, Bangor, Me..........	112 16	....
Vernon Co. Scandinavian Mut. Fire Ins. Co.......	6 12	....
Watertown Fire Insurance Co., Watertown, N. Y..	81 65	....
Williamsburg City Fire Ins. Co., Brooklyn, N. Y..	71 02	....
Western Assurance Co., Toronto, Canada.........	599 75	....
		$48,578 54
Life.		
Ætna Life Insurance Co., Hartford, Conn.........	$300 00	....
Berkshire Life Insurance Co., Pittsfield, Mass.....	300 00	....
Brooklyn Life Insurance Co., N. Y....	300 00	....
Chicago Life Insurance Co	300 00	....
Continental Life Insurance Co., New York........	300 00	....
Charter Oak Life Insurance Co., Hartford, Conn..	300 00	....
Connecticut Mut. Life Ins. Co., Hartford, Conn ...	300 00	....
Equitable Life Assur'ce Soc. of the U. States, N.Y.	300 00	....
Germania Life Insurance Co., New York.........	300 00	....
Globe Mutual Life Insurance Co., New York.....	300 00	....
Missouri Mutual Life Insurance Co., St. Louis....	375 00	....
Mutual Benefit Life Insurance Co., Newark, N. J.	300 00	....
Mutual Life Insurance Co., Chicago.............	300 00	....
Mutual Life Insurance Co., New York	300 00	....
Manhattan Life Insurance Co., New York........	300 00	....
Missouri Valley Life Ins. Co., Leavenworth, Kan..	300 00	....
Metropolitan Life Insurance Co., New York......	300 00	....
Massachusetts Mut. Life Ins. Co., Springfield, Mass.	300 00	....
National Life Insurance Co., Chicago...	300 00	....
Northwestern Mut. Life Insurance Co., Milwaukee.	4,146 89	....
New England Mutual Life Insurance Co., Boston..	300 00	....
New York Life Insurance Co., New York.........	300 00	....

GENERAL FUND RECEIPTS.

Insurance Companies—Life—continued.		
National Life Ins. Co. of U. S. A., Washington....	$300 00	....
New Jersey Mut. Life Ins. Co. of Newark, N. J...	300 00	....
North American Life Insurance Co., New York ..	300 00	....
Protection Life Insurance Company, Chicago	300 00	....
Phœnix Mutual Life Ins. Co., Hartford, Conn.....	300 00	....
Republic Life Insurance Company, Chicago......	300 00	....
Railway Passenger Assurance Co., Hartford, Conn.	300 00	....
Security Life Insurance and Annuity Co., N. Y...	300 00	....
St. Louis Mut. Life Ins. Co., St. Louis, Mo........	300 00	....
Teutonia Life Insurance Company, Chicago	300 00	....
Travelers Life Insurance Comp'y, Hartford, Conn.	300 00	....
Western New York Life Ins. Co., Batavia, N. Y...	300 00	....
Washington Life Insurance Company, New York.	300 00	....
Universal Life Insurance Company, New York....	300 00	....
		$14,721 39
PLANK AND GRAVEL ROAD TAX.		
Fod du Lac Gravel Road Company	$95 95	....
Milwaukee and Janesville Plankroad Company...	53 00	....
Milwaukee and Green Bay Plankroad Company ..	12 00	....
Milwaukee and Cedarburg Plankroad Company ..	5 93	....
Sheboygan and Calumet Plankroad Company.....	48 28	....
Mil. and Brookfield Macad. Turnpike Road Co...	32 57	....
		247 68
TELEGRAPH COMPANY LICENSES.		
Northwestern Telegraph Co.,tax of 1870 and 1871.	$2,086 00	....
Northwestern Telegraph Company, tax of 1872 ..	1,436 00	....
		3,522 00
BONDS RECEIVABLE.		
Bank of Sheboygan............................	$310 00	....
Farmers and Mechanics Bank	100 00	....
		410 00
MISCELLANEOUS.		
Sale of Marathon County Lands.................	$6,498 55	....
Income and Trespass Penalty....................	6,304 26	....
Peddlers and Show Licenses....................	7,188 29	....
U. S. Marshall boarding U. S. Prisoners..........	1,420 87	....
Llewellan Breese, Secretary of State, fees collected.	6,761 50	....
Llewellan Breese, Secretary of State, Notarial fees	1,382 00	....
Llewellan Breese, Sec'y of State, sale of documents	37 10	....
Commissioners out of State	253 00	....
A. A. Meredith, public property sold	409 55	....
Bank Dep't, printing and publish'g Bank Reports.	37 50	....
Sale of Supreme Court Reports..................	765 00	....
State claim for unre'd cur'y on Portage Co. Bank .	400 00	....
Refunded...	379 47	....
		32,337 09
Total receipts..............................		$1,095,872 29

GENERAL FUND DISBURSEMENTS.

SALARIES OF STATE OFFICERS AND CLERK HIRE.			
Executive office		$7,100 00	
Secretary of State's office		16,799 99	
State Treasurer's office		11,105 00	
Attorney General's office		2,600 00	
State Superintendents' office		5,650 00	
Office of Superintendent of Public Property		3,200 00	
Land office		15,487 00	
			$61,941 99
SUPREME COURT.			
Salaries of judges		$12,000 00	
Reporter		1,000 00	
Clerk		593 00	
Crier		176 00	
			13,769 00
CIRCUIT COURT.			
Salaries of judges			30,433 33
HISTORICAL SOCIETY.			
Annual appropriation		$3,500 00	
Secretary		1,200 00	
Librarian		1,600 00	
			6,300 00
STATE LIBRARY.			
Librarian		$1,000 00	
Books		945 36	
			1,945 36
STATE PRISON AND BENEVOLENT INSTITUTIONS.			
State Prison—			
Current expenses	$24,815 47		
Indebtedness	20,735 00		
		$45,550 47	
Hospital for the Insane, Madison—			
Expenses	58,010 25		
Assessed on counties	29,552 90		
Repairs	25,875 00		
Workshop and water supply	6,000 00		
		119,438 15	
Institute for the Blind—			
Expenses	$15,500 00		
Purchase of land	5,375 00		
		20,875 00	
Institute for the Deaf and Dumb—			
Expenses		$23,737 25	

GENERAL FUND DISBURSEMENTS.

State Prison and Benevolent Institutions—continued.			
Industrial School for Boys—			
Expenses	$35,050 00		
Assessed on counties	7,165 00		
Improvements	23,500 00		
		$65,715 00	
Soldiers' Orphans' Home—			
Expenses	$25,000 00		
Repairs	2,000 00		
Support of pupils in Normal School	939 94		
Expenses of trustees	253 75		
		28,193 69	
Northern Hospital for the Insane—			
Current expenses	$33,750 00		
Lighting, furniture and fixtures	15,000 00		
Purchase of land	2,000 00		
Water supply, ice house and fixtures	19,000 00		
Improvements on ground	5,000 00		
Artesian well	987 50		
Freight	308 83		
Heating apparatus	2,013 21		
John Davis & Co., contractors	6,337 54		
E. M. Danforth, building comm's	404 75		
Fish, Stevens, Sorenson, & Fredericksön, contractors	39,148 20		
John Fellenz, contractor	275 56		
Field, Leiter & Co., merchandise	3,051 55		
Hill & Williams, sewerage	881 16		
D. W. Maxon, building comm's	218 10		
A. M. Skeels	380 30		
McFetridge, Burchard & Co., bl'k'ts	3,053 20		
Henry Oscar, furniture	247 81		
Reynolds & Fellenz, contractors	43,047 90		
James Reynolds, drainage, pipe and cesspools	1,021 50		
Jas. Reynolds, setting steam boilers	581 01		
Jas. Reynolds, digging well	1,400 00		
S. V. Shipman, architect	2,004 85		
A. T. Stewart, mattresses	1,985 28		
James H. Walker, gasworks	2,000 00		
Wm. Walters, office rent	40 00		
Treas. Hosp., bal. of building fund	14,539 46		
		198,677 21	
			$502,186 77

AGRICULTURAL SOCIETIES.

Adams County Agricultural Society	$100 00	
Buffalo .... do	100 00	
Columbia .... do	100 00	
Crawford .... do	100 00	
Dodge .... do	100 00	
Door .... do	100 00	
Dane .... do	100 00	
Fond du Lac .... do	100 00	
Grant .... do	100 00	
Green .... do	100 00	
Green Lake .... do	100 00	

GENERAL FUND DISBURSEMENTS.

Agricultural Societies—continued.			
Iowa County Agricultural Society		$100 00	
Jefferson ......do		100 00	
Jackson ......do		100 00	
Juneau ......do		100 00	
Kenosha ......do		100 00	
La Crosse ......do		100 00	
La Fayette ......do		100 00	
Marathon ......do		100 00	
Marquette ......do		100 00	
Monroe ......do		100 00	
Outagamie ......do		100 00	
Ozaukee ......do		100 00	
Pierce ......do		100 00	
Portage ......do		100 00	
Racine ......do		100 00	
Richland ......do		100 00	
Rock ......do		100 00	
Sauk ......do		100 00	
Sheboygan ......do		100 00	
Trempealeau ......do		100 00	
Vernon ......do		100 00	
Walworth ......do		100 00	
Washington ......do		100 00	
Waukesha ......do		100 00	
Winnebago ......do		100 00	
			$3,600 00
INTEREST ON STATE INDEBTEDNESS.			
State bonds		1,020 00	
Certificates of indebtedness belonging to School Fund		109,179 00	
To Normal School Fund		35,882 00	
To University Fund		7,770 00	
To Agricultural College Fund		3,798 67	
			157,649 67
LEGISLATIVE EXPENSES.			
Senate—			
Salaries	11,625 00		
Mileage	852 00		
Employes	10,921 00		
		$23,398 00	
Assembly—			
Salaries	35,350 00		
Mileage	2,604 50		
Employes	12,745 00		
Contesting seat	408 68		
		51,108 18	
Joint expenses of legislature—			
Printing	$11,608 89		
Newspapers	2,694 10		
Gas	1,589 76		
Postage	4,124 20		
Legislative Manual	7,301 64		
Stationery	985 00		

GENERAL FUND DISBURSEMENTS.

Legislative Expenses—continued.			
Joint Expenses of Legislature—con.			
Committee on Benevolent Institutions	$500 00	....	....
Chaplains	200 00	....	....
Witnesses fees investigating committee on Dells bill	177 60	....	....
Witnesses fees investigating committee on Soldiers Orphans Home	53 40	....	....
		$29,229 09	$103,730 22
MISCELLANEOUS.			
Wisconsin reports		$26,825 00	....
Labor about capitol and park		18,904 54	....
Contingent expenses		11,631 10	....
Publishing general laws		12,473 40	....
Publishing local laws		1,066 40	....
Publishing and advertising		1,678 00	....
Printing		61,403 78	....
Stationery		10,000 00	....
Postage		4,006 30	....
State board of charities and reform		1,872 20	....
Normal institutes		2,043 16	....
Militia, military secretary and state armorer		2,154 57	....
Protecting state lands		5,931 92	....
Immigration commission		5,190 98	....
Geological survey (old)		730 00	....
Geological survey (new)		7,500 00	....
Gas		5,871 75	....
Fuel, 1872 and 1873		11,834 70	....
Governor's contigent fund		600 00	....
Park fence		28,086 76	....
Park improvement		1,639 65	....
Capitol improvement		26,332 24	....
Lucius Fairchild Fox and Wis. River Imp't Com'r		2,000 00	....
Bounty of wild animals		6,535 00	....
Superior harbor protection		4,229 14	....
Volunteer aid		1,365 82	....
C. C. Washburn, gov. relief of sufferers by fire		7,610 16	....
State Prison Commiss'r boarding U. S. prisoners		1,420 87	....
Treasury agent's per. ct., pedlars and show licenses		2,477 84	....
Examiners of state teachers		175 85	....
State board of equalization		79 00	....
Fish culture		368 30	....
Real estate returns		432 96	....
Presidential electors		296 80	....
Appraising lands		10 00	....
Wis. state horticultural society		220 50	....
Jacob Clive, ped. license money refunded		20 00	....
Refunded income penalty		44 57	....
A. J. Cramer, overpaym't of insurance tax refunded		303 79	....
Transferred to N. T. F., income for nor'l institutes		2,000 00	....
Transferred to S. F., income to correct error		20 00	....
			$277,426 55
SPECIAL APPROPRIATIONS.			
Nelson Boutin suppressing riot in Ashland co		$1,527 00	....
Thomas Kopfi, ass. surgeon 3d Wis. vol		339 00	....

GENERAL FUND DISBURSEMENTS.

Special Appropriations—continued.		
State Agricultural Society	$3,000 00	
David Taylor, compilation of laws	675 00	
W. W. Tredway, securing war claims	50 00	
Roger Spooner Assignee of E. A. Spencer, index to laws	4,000 00	
University Fund Income, chapter 82, general laws of 1867	7,808 76	
University Fund Income, chapter 100, general laws of 1872	10,000 00	
School Fund Income, chapter 79, general laws of 1866	7,068 36	
		$82,988 12
Total disbursements		$1,191,966 01

SCHOOL FUND.

RECEIPTS.			
Balance in Fund, Oct. 1, 1872		....	$5,265 65
Sales of land		$21,458 14	....
Payments on certificates		38,709 02	....
Payments on mortgages		15,314 84	....
Penalties and forfeitures		145 81	....
Penalty on taxes		133 01	....
United States, 5 per cent. on sales of public lands in Wisconsin, for 1872		27,216 01	....
Fines Received from the following Counties:			
Brown county	$100 00	....	....
Columbia.do	85 00	....	....
Clark ....do	10 00	....	....
Dunn ....do	252 00	....	....
Ozaukee..do	29 10	....	....
Richland. do	63 00	....	....
Sauk .....do	81 00	....	....
Kewaunee do	36 00	....	....
Oconto ...do	96 00	....	....
Waukesha do	70 00	....	....
		822 10	....
Transfer from General Fund, for error		20 00	....
			103,818 93
Total		....	$109,084 58
DISBURSEMENTS.			
Invested in Milwaukee water bonds		$40,000 00	....
Loaned to Madison city board of education		12,500 00	....
Refunded for overpayments		243 37	....
		$52,743 37	....
Balance, Sept. 30, 1873		56,341 21	....
			$109,084 58

SCHOOL FUND INCOME.

RECEIPTS.		
Balance in hand Oct. 1, 1872		$19,663 63
Interest on certificates and loans	$55,646 24	
Interest on certificates of indebtedness	109,179 00	
Interest per chapter 79, general laws of 1866	7,088 36	
Interest on U. S. 5.20 bonds	2,925 07	
Interest on Milwaukee waterwork bonds	3,500 00	
Commission on purchase of do., 2 per cent	800 00	
Sale of Webster's dictionaries	624 00	
		179,762 67
Total		$199 426 30

DISBURSEMENTS. *Apportionment of school money.*		
Adams......County	1,074 36	
Barron ......do	185 24	
Bayfield ......do	78 92	
Brown ......do	4,570 86	
Buffalo......do	1,897 10	
Burnett ......do	123 48	
Calumet......do	2,285 64	
Chippewa ....do	1,203 72	
Clark ......do	664 44	
Columbia ....do	4,665 78	
Crawford.....do	2,658 60	
Dane.........do	8,988 44	
Dodge ......do	7,624 26	
Door.........do	955 92	
Douglas......do	152 04	
Dunn ....do	1,664 88	
Eau Claire ...do	1,488 02	
Fond du Lac..do	8,043 42	
Grant ....do	6,514 62	
Green Lake.. do	2,161 32	
Green ....do	3,759 42	
Iowa.........do	4,370 94	
Jackson......do	1,522 06	
Jefferson .....do	6,122 84	
Juneau.......do	2,235 24	
Kenosha .....do	2,049 18	
Kewaunee....do	1,924 44	
La Crosse ....do	3,297 00	
La Fayette ...do	3,960 45	
Manitowoc ...do	6,544 02	
Marathon.....do	1,095 06	
Marquette ....do	1,457 82	
Milwaukee ...do	14,709 24	
Monroe ......do	3,009 30	
Oconto.......do	1,310 82	
Outagamie ...do	3,539 34	

SCHOOL FUND INCOME DISBURSEMENTS.

Apportionment of School Money—continued.		
Ozaukee County	3,048 36	
Pepin ......do	882 84	
Pierce ......do	1,979 88	
Polk ......do	728 70	
Portage ......do	1,859 34	
Racine ......do	4,119 78	
Richland ......do	2,845 92	
Rock ......do	6,015 24	
St. Croix ......do	1,819 02	
Sauk ......do	4,057 20	
Shawano ......do	585 90	
Sheboygan ......do	5,811 42	
Trempealeau do	1,987 46	
Vernon ......do	3,385 20	
Walworth ......do	3,964 80	
Washington ......do	4,336 92	
Waukesha ......do	4,692 36	
Waupaca ......do	2,707 74	
Waushara ......do	1,996 68	
Winnebago ......do	6,079 08	
Wood ......do	697 26	
	$181,268 79	
G. and C. Merriam, Webster's Dictionaries	3,200 00	
Refunded for over payments	668 19	
	$185,136 98	
Balance, Sept. 30th, 1878	14,289 32	
		$199,426 30

Receipts, Payments and Statements—continued.

UNIVERSITY FUND.

RECEIPTS.		
Balance in Treasury Oct. 1, 1872	....	$2,837 82
Sales of land	$3,972 56	....
Dues on certificates	4,271 00	....
Loans	1,460 50	....
Penalties on taxes	8 27	....
Penalties and forfeitures	15 79	....
		9,728 12
Total	....	$12,565 94
DISBURSEMENTS.		
Loans, comm'rs of public debt, Milwaukee water bonds	$10,000 00	....
Refunded for overpayments	100 51	....
	$10,100 51	....
Balance Sept. 30, 1873	2,465 43	....
		$12,565 94

Receipts, Payments and Statements—continued.

UNIVERSITY FUND INCOME.

RECEIPTS.		
Interest on principal due on lands	$5,448 82	....
Interest on certificates of indebtedness	7,770 00	....
Interest on Dane county bonds	1,330 00	....
Appropriation from General Fund, Chapter 82, General Laws of 1867	7,308 76	....
Appropriation from General Fund, Chapter 100, General Laws of 1872	10,000 00	....
Tuition fees of students	9,325 00	....
Material sold students from laboratory	250 00	....
Sale of products of agriculture, rent, sale of lots, etc.	1,093 80	....
Commission on purchase of Milwaukee Water Works bonds	200 00	....
Total		$42,716 38
DISBURSEMENTS.		
Henry Bætz, Treasurer of University	$42,113 85	....
Refunded for overpayments	602 53	....
		$42,716 38

AGRICULTURAL COLLEGE FUND.

RECEIPTS.		
Balance in treasury Oct. 1, 1872	....	$2,483 44
Sales of land	$7,254 98	....
Dues on certificates	4,614 80	....
Loans	1,677 67	....
Penalties	13 30	....
		$13,560 70
Total	....	$16,044 14
DISBURSEMENTS.		
Invested in Milwaukee water work bonds	$10,000 00	....
Balance, Sept. 30, 1873	6,044 14	....
		$16,044 14

AGRICULTURAL COLLEGE FUND INCOME.

RECEIPTS.		
Interest on principal due on lands	$[illegible]	....
Interest on certificates of indebtedness	3,[illegible]	....
Interest on Dane county bonds	420 [illegible]	....
Interest on U. S. 5-20 bonds	[illegible]	....
Commission on Milwaukee water work bonds	[illegible]	....
Total		$12,538 85
DISBURSEMENTS.		
Henry Betz, Treasurer of University	$12,504 32	....
Refunded for overpayments	34 53	....
Total		$12,538 85

NORMAL SCHOOL FUND.

RECEIPTS.		
Balance October 1, 1872		$7,669 86
Sales of land	$68,947 95	
Payments on certificates	6,109 00	
Loans	11,551 00	
Penalties	79 59	
		86,687 54
Total		$94,357 40
DISBURSEMENTS.		
Loan to Madison city board of education	$12,500 00	
Invested in Milwaukee water work bonds	40,000 00	
Refunded for overpayments	478; 26	
		$52,978 26
Balance September 30, 1874		41,384 14
		$94,357 40

NORMAL SCHOOL FUND INCOME.

RECEIPTS.		
Balance, October 1, 1872	....	$38,668 87
Interest on principal due on lands	$14,160 26	....
Interest on certificates of indebtedness	35,832 00	....
Tuition fees—Platteville Normal School	3,225 88	....
Whitewater .....do	2,287 36	....
Oshkosh .... do	2,832 55	....
Interest on U. S. 5-20 bonds	2,925 08	....
Interest on Milwaukee water-work bonds	3,500 00	....
Commission on....do............do	800 00	....
Interest on Troy town bonds	140 00	....
Interest on Fall River town bonds	350 00	....
Interest on Kinnickinnic..do	105 00	....
Interest on Clifton ....do	105 00	....
Transferred from General Fund for Normal Institutes	2,000 00	....
Transferred from Oshkosh Normal School Building Fund	3,105 97	....
		71,369 10
Total	....	$110,037 97
DISBURSEMENTS.		
Platteville Normal School—salaries of teachers, supplies, etc	$14,982 19	....
Whitewater Normal School—salaries of teachers, supplies, etc	16,538 22	....
Oshkosh Normal School—salaries of teachers, supplies, etc	17,363 13	....
Expenses of Regents	453 00	....
Institutes	2,538 64	....
Expenses	3,360 20	....
Refunded for overpayments	133 24	....
	$55,368 62	....
Balance, September 30, 1873	54,669 35	....
		$110,037 97

OSHKOSH NORMAL SCHOOL BUILDING FUND.

Balance, October 1, 1872	....	$3,845 16
DISBURSEMENTS.		
Bell & Rogers, building material	$739 19	....
Transfer to Normal School Fund Income	3,105 97	....
	$3,845 16	$3,845 16

RIVER FALLS NORMAL SCHOOL BUILDING FUND.

RECEIPTS.		
Balance, October 1, 1872	$20,000 00	....
Donation of Pierce county	5,000 00	....
		$25,000 00

No transactions during the past year.

DRAINAGE FUND.

RECEIPTS.		
Balance October 1, 1872	....	$55,041 12
Interest on certificates	$1,373 06	....
Sales of land	89,751 87	....
Payments on certificates	2,472 00	....
Penalties and forfeitures	37 03	....
Penalties on taxes	2 50	....
		$93,636 46
Total	....	$148,677 58
DISBURSEMENTS.		
Apportionment to Counties—		
Adams........county	$1,611 34	....
Ashland........do	8,946 23	....
Barron........do	415 96	....
Bayfield........do	700 00	....
Brown........do	366 30	....
Buffalo........do	542 26	....
Burnett........do	8,486 37	....
Chippewa........do	16,622 76	....
Clark........do	8,891 89	....
Columbia........do	724 27	....
Crawford........do	66 12	....
Dane........do	1,071 44	....
Dodge........do	148 98	....
Door........do	1,978 87	....
Douglas........do	3,504 89	....
Dunn........do	573 66	....
Eau Claire........do	538 03	....
Fond du Lac........do	189 98	....
Grant........do	153 31	....
Green........do	2 80	....
Green Lake........do	459 04	....
Jefferson........do	417 33	....
Jackson........do	8,844 46	....
Juneau........do	2,698 95	....
Kewaunee........do	352 28	....
La Crosse........do	479 87	....
Manitowoc........do	381 62	....
Marathon........do	27,683 59	....
Marquette........do	924 66	....
Monroe........do	3,720 78	....
Oconto........do	9,943 39	....
Outagamie........do	23 30	....
Pepin........do	261 82	....
Pierce........do	3 15	....
Polk........do	299 93	....
Portage........do	2,821 28	....
Rock........do	18 90	....
St. Croix........do	18 72	....

DRAINAGE FUND DISBURSEMENTS.

Apportionment to counties—continued.		
Sauk county	$136 25	
Shawano.... do	2,994 70	
Trempealeau do	787 08	
Walworth ...do	48 27	
Washington. do	3 36	
Waukesha...do	44 10	
Waupaca....do	2,054 68	
Waushara ...do	1,469 75	
Winnebago..do	1,399 53	
Wood ......do	12,222 76	
	$124,343 91	
Refunded for overpayments	911 48	
	$125,225 39	
Balance Sept. 30, 1878	23.422 19	
Total		$148,677 58

DEPOSIT FUND.

Balance October 1, 1872	....	$7,467 09
DISBURSEMENTS.		
C. B. McArthur, refunded	$141 62	....
M. McArthur......do	4 34	....
D. R. Bailey.......do	278 70	....
do...........do	249 17	....
	$668 83	....
Balance Sept. 30, 1873	6,798 26	....
		$7,467 09

DELINQUENT TAX FUND.

RECEIPTS.		
Balance October 1, 1872		$5,793 56
Taxes on state lands		27,047 10
Total		$32,840 66
DISBURSEMENTS.		
Adams .... county	$220 14	
Ashland ....do	303 90	
Barron ....do	216 06	
Bayfield ....do	643 49	
Brown ....do	155 30	
Buffalo ....do	239 68	
Burnett ....do	23 68	
Calumet ....do	133 15	
Chippewa ....do	1,307 83	
Clark ....do	759 86	
Columbia ....do	300 83	
Crawford ....do	124 93	
Dane ....do	247 61	
Dodge ....do	15 99	
Door ....do	845 72	
Douglas ....do	174 24	
Dunn ....do	346 88	
Eau Claire ....do	164 59	
Fond du Lac ....do	12 83	
Grant ....do	93 57	
Green ....do		
Green Lake ....do	142 78	
Iowa ....do	74 68	
Jackson ....do	780 87	
Jefferson ....do	14 15	
Juneau ....do	349 69	
Kewaunee ....do	381 81	
La Crosse ....do	142 68	
La Fayette ....do	66 23	
Manitowoc ....do	415 87	
Marathon ....do	2,908 02	
Marquette ....do	109 82	
Milwaukee ....do	101 10	
Monroe ....do	608 46	
Oconto ....do	1,382 84	
Outagamie ....do	993 99	
Pepin ....do	57 04	
Pierce ....do	2,008 20	
Polk ....do	1,174 10	
Portage ....do	567 09	
Richland ....do	489 10	
Rock ....do	82 73	
St. Croix ....do	2,094 82	
Sauk ....do	190 12	

DELINQUENT TAX FUND DISBURSEMENTS.

Shawano .....county	$2,385 63	....
Sheboygan......do	60 80	....
Trempealeau ...do	255 43	....
Vernon ....do	595 90	....
Waukesha ......do	40 43	....
Waupaca ....do	582 95	....
Waushara.......do	273 13	....
Winnebago......do	48 86	....
Wood ....do	2,012 64	....
	$27,621 69	....
Refunded for overpayments	132 06	....
	$27,753 75	....
Balance, September 30th, 1873	5,086 91	....
		$32,840 66

COMMISSIONERS CONTINGENT FUND.

RECEIPTS.		
Balance October 1st, 1872	....	$1,811 86
Received for diagrams, land plats, etc	....	823 75
Total	....	$1,635 61
DISBURSEMENTS.		
Seifert Gugler & Co., Maps of Wisconsin	$20 00	....
Seifert, Gugler & Co., plats and sheets	22 00	....
T. W. Gibbs, traveling expenses	34 00	....
S. S. Barlow, expenses to Washington	200 00	....
	$276 00	
Balance, Sept. 30th, 1873	$1,359 61	
		$1,635 61

ALLOTMENT FUND.

Balance October 1st, 1872	....	$1,843 30
No transactions during the year.		

NORTH WISCONSIN RAILROAD AID FUND.

Receipts	....	875 00
Disbursements	....	875 00

SOLDIERS' ORPHANS' HOME.

1872	RECEIPTS.		
Oct. 1	Balance on hand	....	$2,088 47
Oct. 7	Received from State Treasurer, on account of appropriation for 1872	$7,500 00	....
Dec. 26	Received from State Treasurer, on account of appropriation for 1872	7,500 00	....
1873			15,000 00
Apr. 17	Received from State Treasurer, appropriation for support of pupils in normal schools	....	939 94
Apr. 18	Received from State Treasurer, on account of appropriation for current expenses for 1873	$5,000 00	....
May 30	Received from State Treasurer, on account of appropriation for painting and repairs	2,000 00	....
July 21	Received from State Treasurer, on account of appropriation for current expenses for 1873	5,000 00	....
			12,000 00
	Total receipts	....	$30,028 41
1872	DISBURSEMENTS.		
Oct. 10	R. W. Burton, supt., current expenses	$1,500 00	....
Oct. 22	R. W. Burton, supt., current expenses	2,000 00	....
Nov. 16	Jas. Bintliff, for pupils in normal schools	1,000 00	....
Nov. 16	R. W. Burton, supt., current expenses	1,500 00	....
Dec. 7	........do................do..........	2,500 00	....
1873			
Jan. 7	........do................do..........	2,500 00	....
Jan. 31	........do................do..........	2,500 00	....
Feb. 20	........do................do..........	2,500 00	....
Mar. 8	........do................do..........	2,588 47	....
Apr. 17	James Bintliff, amount appropriated for pupils in normal schools	939 94	....
Apr. 18	R. W. Burton, supt., for painting and repairs	1,000 00	....
Apr. 18	R. W. Burton, supt., current expenses	2,500 00	....
May 13	........do................do..........	2,000 00	....
June 13	........do................do..........	500 00	....
July 1	........do................do..........	3,000 00	....
Aug. 11	........do................do..........	2,000 00	....
Aug. 27	........do................do..........	200 00	....
Sept. 4	........do....for painting and repairs..	1,000 00	....
	Total disbursements	$31,728 41	....
	Balance due treasurer of the Home, Sept. 30, 1873	....	1,700 00
		$31,728 41	$31,728 41

"WARD" AND "SMITH" FUNDS OF THE SOLDIERS' ORPHANS' HOME.

	RECEIPTS.		
1872 Oct. 1	Balance as stated in my last report—Ward Fund	$23,912 52	....
	Smith Fund	2,015 00	....
			$25,927 52
1873 Jan. 6	May and Nov., 1872, interest on U. S. 5-20 bonds, gold, $300; currency	$336 00	....
	June, 1872, interest on Milwaukee city bonds	250 00	....
	Dec., 1872, interest on Milwaukee city bonds	250 00	....
	Aug., 1872, interest on Albany city bonds	60 00	....
	January, 1873, interest on Pittsburgh city bonds	100 00	....
une 2	June, 1873, interest on Milwaukee city bonds	250 00	....
	May, 1873, interest on U. S. 5-20 bonds, gold, $150; currency	175 50	....
Sept. 8	Aug., 1873, interest on Albany city bonds	60 00	....
	Received from State Bank of Madison interest to Jan. 1, 1873 (credited on bank book)	45 00	....
	Do. interest to July 1, 1873, do	91 35	....
			1,617 85
	Total receipts	....	$27,545 37
	DISBURSEMENTS.		
1872 Nov. 16	Chas. E. Bross, for telegraphic instruments for the "Home."	$243 70	....
1873 Jan. 20	R. W. Burton, Supt., for Christmas gifts for the orphans	250 00	....
Apr. 14	Charles E. Bross, six month's salary for tuition in telegraphy	250 00	....
	Total disbursements	$743 70	....
	Balance, Sept. 30, 1873	26,801 67	....
		$27,545 37	$27,545 37

Bonds on deposit with treasurer	$21,000 00
Cash in State Bank of Madison, drawing 6 per cent. interest, as per bank book	5,801 67
	$26,801 67

In my last annual report I accounted, under date of July 15, 1872, for $170, "July, 1872, interest on U. S. 5.20 bonds," held by me in trust for the "Ward" fund, which was an error, such entry should have read thus:

July, 1872, interest on Ohio and Mississippi R. R. bonds............	$70 00
July, 1872, interest on Pittsburgh City bonds	100 00
	$170 00

The interest on the U. S. 5.20 bonds belonging to said fund is due on the 1st days of May and November in each year.

In this report the Ward and Smith funds are substantially treated as one fund.

This slight change became necessary, because of the money deposited in the State Bank of Madison to the credit of these funds, separate accounts have not been kept by the bank; nor has the interest accrued therefrom been accounted for to each fund separately.

Hereafter these funds will appear on my books under one head. Practically this will make no material difference, as the exact amounts originally received on account of the same can be readily ascertained by a reference to the books of the treasurer of the "Home," if such should be desired; while the principal and interest of said funds will, in the end, probably be disposed of alike in both cases.

BANKS AND BANKING.

In obedience to the requirements of law, I submit the following report of the condition and transactions of this branch of my department for the past fiscal year:

The whole number of banks doing business on the first day of October, 1872, according to my last annual report, was eighteen, with an aggregate capital of	$765,000
The whole number of banks doing business to-day is sixteen, with an aggregate capital of	715,000
Decrease	$50,000

The Bank of Eau Claire and the Sauk County Bank having been changed to National Banks.

The National Savings Bank of Hudson has changed its name to "Hudson Savings Bank."

The aggregate amount of securities held in trust for banking associations, October 1st, 1872, was	$13,653
The amount held October 1st, 1873, is	9,408
Decrease in 12 months	$4,245

The amount of circulation outstanding on the 1st day of October, 1872, and subject to redemption, was	$7,102
The amount outstanding on the 1st day of October, 1873, is	2,857
Decrease in 12 months	$4,245

During the past year the following banks wound up in accordance with the provisions of the general banking law, and have withdrawn the surplus belonging to them:

Bank of Watertown	$3,133
Bank of Sheboygan	1,111
	$4,244

Surplus is still due the following banks, the payment of which cannot be made until legal proceedings now pending, have been decided:

Bank of Columbus	$1,884 00
Bank of Prairie du Chien..................................	1,492 00
Kenosha County Bank	1,505 00
	$4,881 00

There is also due to the Exchange Bank of Darling & Co., a surplus of $2,172 00, which I deem it my duty to retain until the indebtedness of said bank to the state on account of state bonds sold to the same, amounting to about $3,655, is discharged.

The stocks of the following banks have been exchanged for United States Treasury Notes, and with them I will redeem their outstanding circulation at par, on presentation:

Names of Banks.	Circulation outstanding.	Time of redemption expires.
Hudson City Bank	$517	Not advertised.
La Crosse County Bank......................	93	.......do......
Merchants' Bank, Milwaukee	155	.......do......
Milwaukee County Bank	235	.......do......
Wisconsin Pinery Bank......................	369	.......do......
	$1,369	

Banks wound up and circulation redeemed at par in gold by this office.

Union Bank, Milwaukee, (not advertised) outstanding circulation ..	$87 00
Germania Bank, Milwaukee..................................	23 00
	$110 00

The time of redemption of the bills of the latter bank has expired, but I will redeem its circulation until the withdrawal of the securities.

The Appendix will show:

" A."—Securities, circulation and capital of banks.

" B."—Names of stockholders and the amount of stock held by each.

" C."—Names of personal bondsmen for each bank.

" D."—List of banks, their location and officers.

" E."—Bank note impressions on hand.

" F."—Bank note plates on hand.

" G."—Condition of each bank in the state at the time of the last report, July 7, 1873.

All of which is respectfully submitted.

HENRY BAETZ,
State Treasurer.

APPENDIX.

"A."

STATEMENT *in detail of the securities held in trust for each banking association and the amount of circulating notes issued and outsanding on the same on the first day of October*, 1873.

BATAVIAN BANK.

Capital $25,000.

Treasury notes	$228 00
Circulation	228 00

WISCONSIN MARINE AND FIRE INSURANCE COMPANY BANK.

Capital $100,000.

Treasury notes	$1,149
Circulation	1,149

"B."

Statement *exhibiting the names of stockholders and amount of stock owned by each in the several banks of this state, as reported to this office July* 7, 1873.

Names of Banks.	Names of Stockholders.	Residence.	Amount.	Total.
Bank of Madison	James L. Hill	Madison	....	$25,000
Batavian Bank........	G. Van Steenwyk ..	La Crosse....	$21,600	....
	E. E. Bentley	......do......	1,400	....
	J. M. Holly........	......do......	1,400	....
	E. Borreson........	......do......	300	....
	Geo. F. Gund	......do......	300	....
				25,000
Bank of Watertown ..	A. L. Pritchard	New York...	12,925	....
	Wm. H. Clark	Watertown...	8,000	....
	Linus R. Cady	......do......	4,075	....
				25,000
Bank of Commerce ..	John Black........	Milwaukee...	21,000	....
	Edward O'Neill ...	......do......	20,000	....
	G. Bremer & Co ...	......do......	5,000	....
	Nich. Hoffman	......do......	10,000	....
	C A. Koeffler......	......do......	4,500	....
	J P. Kissinger.....	......do......	5,000	....
	J.H.Rice&Friedman	......do......	2,500	....
	B. B. Hopkins	......do......	2,500	....
	Goll & Frank.......	......do......	3,000	....
	Nathan Pereles	......do......	1,000	....
	M. L. Morawetz....	......do......	2,000	....
	A. B. Geilfuss......	......do......	3,000	....
	H. Stern, Jr. & Bro.	......do......	2,000	....
	Bernard Stern......	......do......	500	....
	Geo. J. Schmidt ...	......do......	500	....
	H. Zoehrlaut.......	......do......	1,000	....
	Conrad Mayer......	......do......	500	....
	Matt. Keenan	......do......	1,000	....
	Em. Sauer	......do......	2,000	....
	Thos. Shea	......do......	1,000	....
	Wm. Bayer	......do......	1,000	....
	Ad. Winckler.......	......do......	500	....
	Jas. Ludington	......do......	2,500	....
	Wm. Zimmermann.	Thiensville ..	1,000	....
	John Dahlman	Milwaukee ..	5,000	....
	F. F. Reidel	......do......	500	....
	A. Dahlmann	......do......	500	....
	John Lipps........	......do......	1,000	....
				100,000
Columbia County B'k	John P. McGregor .	Chicago	....	25,000
Corn Exchange Bank.	Wm. Hobkirk.....	Waupun	....	25,000
German Bank........	Jas. H. Mead	Sheboygan...	15,000	....
	Geo. C. Cole.......	......do......	10,000	....
	Fr. Karste	......do......	10,000	....
				35,000

"B."—*Names of Stockholders, etc.*—continued.

Names of Banks.	Names of Stockholders.	Residence.	Amount.	Total.
Ger'n Exchange B'k..	M. Van Baumbach.	Milwaukee ..	$5,000	....
	G. Pfister	......do......	5,000	....
	Jac'b Nunnemacher	......do......	5,000	....
	Ferd Vogel........	......do......	5,000	....
	Ferd Kuehn......	......do......	5,000	....
	Rud Nunnemacher.	......do......	5,000	....
				$30,000
Hudson Savings B'k..	C. Goss	Hudson......	$5,000	....
	C. M. Goss	......do.....	1,000	....
	O. J. Goss.........	......do......	19,000	....
				25,000
Park Savings Bank...	Geo. E. Mason.....	Madison.....	$6,600	....
	James E. Baker....	......do......	6,000	....
	S. L. Sheldon......	......do......	7,000	....
	J. B. Bowen	......do......	5,000	....
	Jos. Smith.........	Waupun	7,000	....
	M. D. Miller.......	Madison.....	8,000	....
	W. W. Tredway	......do......	1,000	....
	Y. W. Hobbins.....	......do......	1,000	....
	Henry M. Lewis....	......do......	400	....
	N. W. Dean	......do......	2,000	....
	Wm. Woodward ...	Westport	1,000	....
	Dan'l G. Taylor....	St. Louis	1,000	....
	Wm. Farrell.......	Madison.....	100	....
	Sorens'n&Freders'n	......do......	500	....
	P. Hurd...........	......do......	1,000	....
	J. C. Mc'Kinney...	......do......	200	....
	Chas. A. Belden ...	......do......	1,000	....
	Susan L. Regan....	......do......	500	....
	W. J. F. Liddell....	......do.....	1,800	....
	Mary L. Roby	Greenv'eMich	1,000	....
	Chas. L. Sheldon ..	......do......	1,000	....
	Thos. Keenan......	Portage......	1,000	....
	Helen Morchead...	Madison.....	1,000	....
	Lucy A. Sheldon...	Janesville ...	1,000	....
				50,000
Peoples State Bank...	Edw. Berger.......	Burlington ..	$7,500	....
	E. N. White.......	......do......	5,000	....
	P. M. Perkins	.....do......	5,000	....
	Jac. Muth.........	......do......	5,000	....
	H. A. Sheldon	......do......	3,700	....
	Jacob Gill.........	......do......	2,000	....
	N. P. Randall	East Troy....	2,000	....
	Rufus Billings.....	Burlington...	2,000	....
	R. Wa'd......	... ..do......	1,500	....
	J. S. Crane	......do......	2,000	....
	Jac. Wambold	......do......	1,700	....
	B. Foltz & Son	......do......	1,000	....
	John P. Matther ...	......do......	1,000	....
	L. W. Conkey	Chicago, Ill..	1,000	....
	Jas. Mather........	Burlington ..	2,100	....
	J. T. Potter...	East Troy ...	1,000	....
	Palmer Gardner ...	Burlington ..	1,000	....
	F. Reuschlein	......do......	500	....
	F. Willhoft........	......do......	500	....
	H. Wagner	......do......	500	....

"B."—*Names of Stockholders, etc.*—continued.

Names of Banks.	Names of Stockholders.	Residence.	Amount.	Total.
Peoples St'e B'k—con.	T. W. Buell	Milwaukee ..	$2,500	....
	Wm. McDonald....	Dover.	500	....
	Ole Heg....	Waterford...	500	....
	Chas. Wagner	Burlington ..	500	....
				$50,000
S'nd W'd Savings B'k.	Valentine Blatz....	Milwaukee ..	25,000	....
	Jos. Schlitz.........	....do	25,000	....
	Phil. Best...........	....do	25,000	....
	W. H. Jacobs.......	....do	25,000	....
				100,000
So. Side Savings Ba'k.	G. C. Trumpff.	Milwaukee ..	12,500	....
	John B. Koeting....	....do	12,500	....
				25,000
State Bank...........	Samuel Marshall...	Milwaukee ..	25,000	....
	Lucien S. Hanks...	Madison.....	15,000	....
	J. Howard Palmer..	....do	10,000	....
				50,000
Summit Bank........	Curtis Mann.......	Oconomowoc	....	25,000
Wis. Marine & Fire Ins. Co.'s Bank.....	Alex. Mitchell.....	Milwaukee ..	....	100,000

"C."

STATEMENT *showing the names of persons who have executed bonds now on deposit in this office, as additional security for the redemption of the countersigned notes issued to their respective banks, as required by section 17 of the banking law.*

NAMES OF BANKS.	Location.	Names of bondsmen.	Penalty of bonds.
Batavian Bank................	La Crosse ...	G. Van Steenwyk ..	6,250
Wis. Marine and Fire Ins. Co..	Milwaukee ..	George Smith and	
		Alex. Mitchell	25,000

"D."

LIST OF OFFICERS *of Banks as taken from the reports made to this office on the first Monday of July*, 1873.

NAMES OF BANKS.	Location.	President.	Cashier.
Bank of Madison	Madison	J. L. Hill.........	Adrian Webster.
Batavian Bank........	La Crosse	G. Van Steenwyk .	E. E. Bentley.
Bank of Watertown...	Watertown ...	Linus R. Cady (V.P.)	W. H. Clark.
Bank of Commerce...	Milwaukee ...	Ed. O'Neill.......	A. B. Geilfuss.
Columbia County Bank	Portage	....	C. Wheeler.
Corn Exchange Bank..	Waupun......	....	Wm. Hobkirk.
German Bank.........	Sheboygan ...	Geo. C. Cole......	Jas. H. Mead.
German Exchange B'k	Milwaukee ...	Ferd. Kuchu (V.P.)	R. Nunnemacker.
Hudson Saving's Bank	Hudson	....	Alfred Goss.
Park Saving's Bank...	Madison......	Geo. A. Mason....	Jas. E. Baker (V.P.)
People's State Bank...	Burlington ...	E. N. White	Edw. Berger.
Sec'd W'd Saving's B'k	Milwaukee ...	Valentine Blatz...	W. H. Jacobs.
So. Side Saving's Bank	Milwaukee ...	G. C. Trumpff	John B. Koetting.
State Bank	Madison......	....	L. S. Hanks.
Summit Bank	Oconomowoc.	Curtis Mann......	H. K. Edgerton.
Wis.M.& F. Ins.Co. B'k	Milwaukee ...	Alex. Mitchell....	D. Ferguson.

"E."

STATEMENT *showing the number of Bank note impressions on hand October 1st, 1873.*

NAMES OF BANKS.	Location.	Denominat'n	No.
Bank of Sheboygan........................	Sheboygan ..	1,2,3,5	205
Bank of Watertown	Watertown ..	1,2,3,5	485
Batavian Bank..........................	La Crosse ...	1,5	1990
Corn Exchange Bank	Waupun	1,2,3,5	418
Milwaukee County Bank	Milwaukee ..	5,10	120
Summit Bank	Oconomowoc	2,3	716
Wisconsin Marine & Fire Ins. Co. Bank. ..	Milwaukee ..	2,3,5,5	75

"F."

LIST OF BANK NOTE PLATES *on hand, October* 1, 1873, *deposited with the Bank of Republic, New York.*

NAMES OF BANKS.	Location.	Denominat'n
State Bank	Madison	1,1,2,5
Bank of Racine	Racine	1,2,3,5
Columbia County Bank	Portage	1,1,2,5
Bank of Watertown	Watertown	1,2,3,5
Corn Exchange Bank	Waupun	1,2,3,5
Bank of Madison	Madison	1,2
Batavian Bank	La Crosse	1,5
Summit Bank	Oconomowoc	2,3
Wisconsin Marine and Fire Ins. Co. Bank	Milwaukee	2,3,5,5

"G"

Statement *of the Condition of the Banks of Wisconsin on the Morning of Monday, July 7*, 1873.

Names of Banks.	Location.	Resources.						
		Loans and Discounts.	Due from Directors.	Due from Brokers.	Over drafts.	Stocks at par value deposited with the state treasurer	Stocks not deposited with state treasurer	Promissory notes other than for loans and discounts.
Bank of Madison	Madison	$131,33 88	....	....	$815 17	....	$6,000 00	....
Batavian Bank	La Crosse	315,146 51	....	....	1,354 14	[1]$229 00	365 00	....
Bank of Watertown	Watertown	114,154 94	....	....	480 68	....	....	....
Bank of Commerce	Milwaukee	408,843 84	....	....	1,722 47	....	....	....
Columbia County Bank	Portage	63,734 41	$4,338 37	....	2,876 48	....	....	....
Corn Exchange Bank	Waupun	44,944 54	....	....	1,833 07	....	....	....
German Bank	Sheboygan	451,302 72	....	....	4,176 98	....	....	....
German Exchange Bank	Milwaukee	351,604 51	....	....	1,275 88	....	14,450 00	....
Hudson Savings Bank	Hudson	98,708 60	....	....	9,288 52	....	12,600 00	....
Park Savings Bank	Madison	106,841 28	10,000 00	....	642 99	....	....	....
Peoples' State Bank	Burlington	33,609 36	[2]31,850 00	[3]$14,504 38	....	....	....	....
Second Ward Savings Bank	Milwaukee	803,415 16	[2]162,800 00	8,192 22	17,565 42	....	....	....
South Side Savings Bank	Milwaukee	128,207 63	....	....	5,344 47	....	12,225 00	....
State Bank	Madison	236,398 97	....	....	1,174 35	....	....	....
Summit Bank	Oconomowoc	32,100 19	....	....	585 43	....	....	....
Wis. Marine & Fire Ins. Co. Bank	Milwaukee	2,150,328 95	....	....	26,815 54	1,180 00	946,489 80	....
		$5,468,675 50	$208,988 37	$22,786 66	$75,496 59	$1,409 00	$992,129 80	....

[1] U. S. Treas. Notes.

[2] And stockholders.

[3] Loans on call.

"G."—*Condition of the Banks on the Morning of Monday, July 7, 1873.*

Name of Banks.	Resources—continued.							
	Specie.	Cash Items.	Real Estate.	Loss and Expense Account.	Bills of Solvent Banks on hand.	Bills of Suspended Banks.	Due from Banks.	Total Resources
Bank of Madison	$1,127 13	$11,982 17	[1]$1,996 00	....	$29,123 35	....	$36,515 20	$218,892 90
Batavia Bank	2,700 23	2,367 94	[2]12,500 00	....	53,480 00	....	121,553 51	509,696 83
Bank of Watertown	27 05	669 93	5,829 10	....	19,335 00	....	100,959 68	241,456 39
Bank of Commerce	1,555 64	30,538 54	[3]2,200 00	....	25,306 00	....	196,866 52	667,033 01
Columbia County Bank	1,313 71	1,530 57	11,200 00	....	16,377 76	....	20,053 03	121,424 83
Corn Exchange Bank	....	158 63	[2]5,937 08	$349 51	23,013 75	....	45,162 70	121,449 28
German Bank	2,123 12	1,167 68	[2]10,000 00	....	38,600 00	....	142,312 98	649,683 48
German Exchange Bank	4,169 76	10,259 99	....	....	47,850 00	....	141,622 60	571,232 74
Hudson Saings Bank	171 00	8,596 15	7,000 00	....	28,418 37	....	83,002 94	190,780 58
Park Savings Bank	220 30	788 03	[2]20,961 60	....	23,272 10	....	20,750 06	183,476 86
People's State Bank	264 00	450 41	[3]4,368 85	[4]824 81	6,248 00	....	12,825 69	105,034 00
Send Ward Savings Bank	3,633 48	18,282 91	2,610 50	....	100,469 00	....	269,418 93	1,386,387 62
Sth Side Savings Bank	396 34	13,327 80	[3]2,573 80	....	88,492 00	....	58,544 07	304,111 11
State Bank	549 26	189 22	[5]12,000 00	....	32,428 83	....	58,593 08	336,328 71
Summit Bank	140 25	515 75	2,185 42	....	13,959 00	....	13,241 51	62,727 55
Wis. Marine & Fire Ins. Co. Bank	8,407 44	72,742 27	....	....	134,169 00	....	168,264 46	3,507,897 46
	$26,798 71	$173,567 99	$101,361 85	$1,174 32	$670,536 16	....	$1,434,686 96	$9,177,611 85

[1] Personal property. [2] And bank furniture. [3] Office furniture and fixtures. [4] And taxes. [5] $4,000 of it outfit and office fixtures.

"G."—*Condition of the Banks on the Morning of Monday, July 7, 1873.*—continued.

Names of Banks.	Liabilities. Capital.	Registered Notes in Circulation.	Due to State Treasurer.	Due to Depositors on Demand.	Due to others not included under either of the above heads.	Total Liabilities.
Bank of Madison	$25,000 00	....	....	$193,892 90	....	$218,892 90
Batavian Bank	25,000 00	$224 00	....	454,472 33	[1] $30,000 00	509,696 33
Bank of Watertown	25,000 00	....	....	215,161 07	857 74	241,456 39
Bank of Commerce	100,000 00	....	....	529.574 64	37,458 37	667,033 01
Columbia County Bank	25,000 00	....	....	90,776 73	5,647 60	121,424 33
Corn Exchange Bank	25,000 00	....	....	39,112 22	57,337 06	121,449 28
German Bank	35,000 00	....	....	220,567 11	[2] 394,116 37	649,683 48
German Exchange Bank	30,000 00	....	....	510,176 98	31,055 76	571,232 74
Savings Bank	25,000 00	....	....	152,697 18	[3] 13,083 40	190,780 58
Park Savings Bank	50,000 00	....	....	127,745 42	5,730 94	183,476 36
People's State Bank	50,000 00	....	....	52,248 24	[4] 2,785 76	105,034 00
Second Ward Savings Bank	100,000 00	....	....	1,197,408 65	88,978 97	1,386,387 62
South Side Savings Bank	25,000 00	....	....	279,111 11	....	304,111 11
State Bank	50,000 00	....	....	286,328 71	....	336,328 71
Summit Bank	25,000 00	....	....	36,908 71	[5] 818 84	62,727 55
Wisconsin Marine and Fire Ins. Co. Bank	100,000 00	1,180 00	....	1,814,365 34	1,592,352 12	3,507,897 46
	$715,000 00	$1,404 00	....	$6,200,547 34	$2,259,722 98	$9.177,611 85

[1] Surplus. [2] $24,654.56 of it surplus. [3] Profit and loss and surplus. [4] Interest, exchange, dividends and surplus. [5] Profit and loss.

SUMMARY.

Of the items of capital, circulation, deposits, specie, cash items and public securities of the banks of the state of Wisconsin, on the morning of Monday, July 7, 1873:

Capital	$715,000 00
Circulation	1,404 00
Deposits	6,200,547 84
Specie	26,798 71
Cash items	173,567 99
Public securities	1,409 00

OFFICE OF STATE TREASURER,

MADISON, July 16, A. D. 1873.

I hereby certify that the foregoing statement is an abstract of the semi-annual reports made to this office by the several banks that made reports (as far as it was practicable to arrange the items under general heads), in pursuance of the provisions of the 41st section of the act entitled "an act to authorize the business of banking." Approved April 19, 1852.

HENRY BÆTZ,
State Treasurer.

ANNUAL REPORT

OF THE

COMMISSIONERS

OF

School and University Lands

OF THE

STATE OF WISCONSIN,

For the Fiscal Year ending September 30, 1873.

STATE OF WISCONSIN,

OFFICE OF COMMISSIONERS OF SCHOOL AND UNIVERSITY LANDS,
MADISON, October 1, 1873.

To His Excellency, C. C. WASHBURN,
Governor of Wisconsin:

SIR—As required by law, we have the honor to report herewith to you our official proceedings for the year ending September 30, 1873.

The reports of the Secretary of State and State Treasurer exhibit detailed statements of the receipts and disbursements on account of tha several funds affected by our action, and to them we respectfully refer.

LANDS SOLD.

The whole amount of lands sold during the fiscal year, is 256,895.83 acres, against 350,194.42 acres sold during the fiscal year of 1872, and are classified as follows:

	Acres.
School Lands	42,055.76
University Lands	3,051.81
Normal School Lands	76,497.36
Drainage Lands	108,457.17
Agricultural College Lands	18,169.13
Marathon County Lands	8,664.60
Total	256,895.83

For a detailed statement of these sales, we respectfully refer to the accompanying tables, marked exhibit "A," "B," "C," "D," "E" and "F."

These tables show the number of acres of each class of land sold, the amount sold for, the amount of principal paid, and the amount due, on which the State is receiving seven per cent. interest.

The number of acres sold, as compared with the previous year, classified, is as follows:

	Acres, 1872.	Acres, 1873.
School Lands	63,173.56	42,055.76
University Lands	1,588.88	3,051.81
Normal School Lands	116,270 77	76,497 36
Drainage Lands	149,402.04	108,457.17
Agricultural College Lands	13,601.78	18,169.13
Marathon County Lands	6,037.89	8,664.60
Military Road Lands	120.00	(acc't closed)
Totals	350,194.42	256,895.83

FORFEITURES.

Lands held on certificate forfeited for non-payment of interest of 1872, were not offered for sale as usual, on account of the insufficiency of the notice of sale. But at this date nearly all such forfeitures have been redeemed by payment of penalties and charges.

Loans from the Trust Funds, secured by mortgages, have been forfeited during the year, as follows:

School Fund	$200 00
Normal School Fund	358 00
Total	$558 00

INCOME.

The amount of interest moneys received from the several productive trust funds, comprising certificates of sale, loans, certificates of indebtedness, and bonds, under our supervision, during the year, is as follows:

School Fund Income	$178,550 81
University Fund Income	14,743 82
Normal School Fund Income	57,967 84
Agricultural College Fund Income	12,358 85
Total Income	$263,620 32

Income from Drainage Fund	$1,373 06

PROTECTION OF STATE LANDS.

Trespasses on state lands, during the past year have been very limited, which is due in a measure to the efficiency of the agents appointed to protect the lands, and particularly on account of the effective trespass law now in force (chapter 21, Laws of 1871), which imposes large penalties on the trespasser.

The amount received during the year for principal and penalties from trespassers on account of trespasses committed and the amount paid agents for protecting lands, is as follows:

Principal collected	$1,573 00
Penalties collected	1,787 17
Total	$3,360 17

Amount paid agents	$5,931 92

LANDS HELD BY THE STATE.

The whole amount of lands held by the state at the close of the fiscal year, September 30, 1873, is 1,862,206.52 acres.

The table, marked Exhibit "G," shows the number acres of belonging to each fund, and the counties in which they are situated.

The number of acres owned by the state, classified, is as follows:

	Acres.
School Lands	245,735.52
University Lands	6,298.00
Normal School Lands	675,372.15
Drainage Lands	865,149.77
Agricultural College Lands	56,324.01
Marathon County Lands	13,327.07
Total acres	1,862,206.52

The changes in the number of acres owned by the state, as compared with the same at the close of the fiscal year of 1872, is accounted for as follows:

Number of acres owned by the state Sept. 30, 1872	2,089,715.75
Decreased by sales during the year	256,895.83
	1,832,819.92
Increased by Normal School and Drainage Lands in Wood County. not heretofore accounted for	29,386.60
Total acres owned by the state Sept. 30, 1873	1,862,206.52

PRICE AND TERMS OF SALE OF STATE LANDS.

Lands held by the state are subject to sale at private entry on the following terms: The School, University and Agricultural College Lands, are sold on ten years time, twenty-five per cent. of the purchase money being required in cash and the balance due drawing seven per cent. interest, payable annually in advance. The Normal School and Drainage Lands (swamp), and Marathon County Lands are sold for cash. The price ranges as follows:

School Lands from	$1 00	to	$1 25	per acre.
University Lands from	2 00	to	3 00	per acre.
Agricultural College Lands	1 25	..	....	per acre.
Normal School Lands (Swamp) from	75	to	1 25	per acre.
Drainage Lands (Swamp) from	75	to	1 25	per acre.
Marathon County Lands	75	..	....	per acre.

APPORTIONMENT OF DRAINAGE MONEY.

The table marked Exhibit "H" shows the amount of drainage money apportioned to the several counties, July 1, 1873, for drainage purposes, in pursuance of chapter 537, Laws of 1865.

The amount received, during the year, is $124,340.76, and is composed of the following items:

From sale of lands	$120,388 29
Payments on certificates of sale	2,202 79
Interest on certificates of sale	1,710 50
Penalty on taxes	39 18
Total	$124,340 76

INVESTMENT OF TRUST FUNDS.

Investments of the trust funds have been made during the fiscal year by purchase of Milwaukee city bonds, in pursuance of chapter 118, Laws of 1872, to the extent of $100,000, and by a loan to the board of education of the city of Madison, in pursuance of chapter 17, Laws of 1873, of $25,000—from the following funds:

BONDS.		
School Fund	$40,000	
University Fund	10,000	
Normal School Fund	40,000	
Agricultural College Fund	10,000	
Total invested in bonds		$100,000
LOANS.		
School Fund	$12,500	
Normal School Fund	12,500	
Total loaned		25,000
Total amount invested		$125,000

PRODUCTIVE TRUST FUNDS.

The total amount of the several productive funds under our supervision on the 30th day of September, 1873, is $3,870,653 71, against $3,776,185 15, for the fiscal year of 1872.

The following statements show the amount of each fund, the changes in, and increase of the same during the year:

SCHOOL FUND.		
Amount due on certificates of sale	$506,081 20	
Amount due on loans	261,449 92	
Certificates of indebtedness	1,559,700 00	
United States bonds	43,000 00	
Milwaukee city bonds	140,000 00	
Total productive fund		$2,510,181 12
UNIVERSITY FUND.		
Amount due on certificates of sale	$64,480 38	
Amount due on loans	12,039 00	
Certificates of indebtedness	111,000 00	
Dane county bonds	19,000 00	
Milwaukee city bonds	10,000 00	
Total productive fund		216,519 38
NORMAL SCHOOL FUND.		
Amount due on certificates of sale	$55,731 48	
Amount due on loans	147,312 05	
Certificates of indebtedness	512,600 00	
United States bonds	43,000 00	
Milwaukee city bonds	140,000 00	
Town bonds	20,000 00	
Total productive fund		918,643 48
AGRICULTURAL COLLEGE FUND.		
Amount due on certificates of sale	$144,823 40	
Amount due on loans	9,886 33	
Certificates of indebtedness	50,600 00	
Dane county bonds	6,000 00	
United States bonds	4,000 00	
Milwaukee city bonds	10,000 00	
Total productive fund		225,309 73
Total productive funds, Sept. 30, 1873		$3,870,653 71

DRAINAGE FUND.

This fund is comprised exclusively of certificates of sale, and is held in trust for the counties, and the receipts received therefrom is annually apportioned to the proper counties with other drainage moneys—the amount productive Sept. 30, 1873, $18,162.93.

The changes in the several classes of the productive fund, during the year, have been produced as follows:

SCHOOL FUND.

Amount of productive fund Sept. 30, 1872	....	$2,482,771 28
Decreased by payments on certificates of sale.	$38,709 02	....
Decreased by payments on loans............	15,314 84	....
Decreased by forfeiture of mortgages.........	200 00	
		54,223 86
		$2,428,547 42
Increased by new certificates of sale	$29,133 70	....
Increased by new loans.....................	12,500 00	....
Increased by Milwaukee city bonds	40,000 00	....
		81,633 70
Total productive fund, Sept. 30, 1873......	....	$2,510,181 12

Showing an increase in this fund, during the year, of $27,409.84.

UNIVERSITY FUND.

Amount of productive fund, Sept. 30, 1872....	....	$206,983 88
Decreased by payments on certificates of sale.	$4,271 00	....
Decreased by payments on loans............	1,460 50	....
		5,731 50
		$201,252 38
Increased by new certificates of sale	$5,267 00	....
Increased by Milwaukee city bonds..........	10,000 00	....
		15,267 00
Total productive fund, Sept. 30, 1873	....	$216,519 38

Showing an increase in this fund, during the year, of $9,535.50.

NORMAL SCHOOL FUND.

Amount of productive fund Sept. 30, 1872	....	$880,371 79
Decreased by payments on certificates of sale	$6,109 00	....
Decreased by payments on loans	11,551 00	....
Decreased by forfeiture of mortgages	353 00	....
		18,013 00
		$862,358 79
Increased by new certificates of sale	$3,784 69	....
Increased by new loans	12,500 00	....
Increased by Milwaukee city bonds	40,000 00	....
		56,284 69
Total productive fund Sept. 30, 1873	....	$918,643 48

Showing an increase in this fund during the year, of $38,271.69.

AGRICULTURAL COLLEGE FUND.

Amount of productive fund, Sept. 30, 1872	....	$206,058 20
Decreased by payments on certificates of sale	$4,614 80	....
Decreased by payments on loans	1,677 67	....
		6,292 47
		$199,765 73
Increased by new certificates of sale	$15,544 00	....
Increased by Milwaukee city bonds	10,000 00	....
		$25,544 00
Total productive fund, Sept. 30, 1873	....	$225,309 73

Showing an increase in this fund during the year of $19,251.53.

A comparative statement of the amounts of the several productive trust funds, September 30, 1872, and September 30, 1873:

	1872.	*1873.*
School Fund	$2,482,771 28	$2,510,181 12
University Fund	206,983 88	216,519 38
Normal School Fund	880,371 79	918,643 48
Agricultural College Fund	206,058 20	225,309 73
Totals	$3,776,185 15	$3,870,653 71

Showing a total increase in the several productive funds, during the year, of $94,468.56.

UNPRODUCTIVE FUNDS.

The unproductive trust funds are composed of unsold lands held in trust by the State for the funds, and are *estimated* as follows:

School Fund	$290,000 00
University Fund	13,000 00
Normal School Fund	810,000 00
Agricultural College Fund	70,400 00
Drainage Fund (held in trust for counties, as per chapter 537, Laws of 1865)	1,038,000 00
Total	$2,221,400 00

Ll. BREESE,
HENRY BÆTZ,
S. S. BARLOW,
Commissioners of School and University Lands.

EXHIBIT "A."

SALE OF SCHOOL LANDS *for the fiscal year ending Sept.* 30, 1873.

COUNTIES.	No. Acres.	Amount Sold for.	Principal Paid.	Interest Paid.	Balance Due.
Adams	424.31	$655 92	$436 92	$6 58	$219 00
Ashland	2,360.00	2,193 33	676 33	39 47	1,517 00
Barron	1,920.00	2,094 44	824 44	28 40	1,270 00
Bayfield	600.00	533 40	247 40	12 46	286 00
Brown		572 94	143 94	17 50	429 00
Buffalo	421.00	522 00	209 00	11 11	313 00
Burnett	1,200.00	1,129 40	475 40	22 46	654 00
Calumet	120.00	166 65	43 65	7 10	123 00
Chippewa	4,118.00	4,092 65	2,372 65	64 01	1,720 00
Clark	2,269.35	2,260 68	747 68	55 88	1,513 00
Crawford	360.00	966 78	347 78	20 18	619 00
Dodge		581 47	168 47	5 57	418 00
Door	120.00	132 21	78 21	94	54 00
Douglas	1,002.28	1,033 01	625 01	8 44	408 00
Dunn	800.00	816 46	330 46	9 70	486 00
Eau Claire	40.00	97 38	25 38	1 60	72 00
Green Lake	78.50	177 40	49 20	1 57	128 20
Jackson	1,280.00	1,593 45	619 45	32 01	974 00
Juneau	520.00	661 67	220 67	9 40	441 00
La Crosse	80.00	285 84	76 84	12 45	209 00
Manitowoc	184.47	205 90	67 90	6 11	138 00
Marathon	6,371.36	8,022 69	4,586 69	82 12	3,436 00
Marquette	40	167 69	47 69	6 14	120 00
Milwaukee		1,235 00	310 00	44 20	925 00
Monroe	520.00	720 28	268 28	9 59	452 00
Oconto	5,194.00	6,315 60	3,112 60	108 59	3,203 00
Outagamie	360.00	494 75	212 75	12 98	282 00

Ozaukee	....	85 60	22 60	14	63 00
Pepin	40.00	39 60	39 60	....	....
Polk	960.00	1,070 86	421 86	33 07	649 00
Portage	600.00	765 15	498 15	9 80	267 00
Richland	80.00	120 58	33 58	2 17	87 00
St. Croix	80.00	90 17	32 17	1 34	58 00
Sauk	120.00	131 85	40 85	1 15	91 00
Shawano	5,052.14	5,857 65	1,790 15	104 81	4,067 50
Sheboygan	240.00	657 18	146 18	18 66	511 00
Trempealeau	1,080.00	1,327 82	915 82	18 81	412 00
Vernon	240.00	335 88	122 88	7 75	213 00
Waupaca	600.00	1,951 66	908 66	34 82	1,043 00
Waushara	160.00	216 74	75 74	3 43	141 00
Winnebago	40.00	92 00	92 00	....	....
Wood	1,920.00	2,307 99	1,180 99	41 56	1,127 00
Total	42,055.76	$52,778 62	$23,644 92	$913 52	$29,133 70

EXHIBIT "B."

SALE OF UNIVERSITY LANDS *for the fiscal year ending Sept.* 30, 1873.

COUNTIES.	Number of Acres.	Amount Sold for.	Principal Paid.	Interest Paid.	Balance Due.
Chippewa	480.05	$1,387 69	$401 69	$49 38	$986 00
Clark	280.00	840 00	300 00	37 20	540 00
Door	80.00	240 00	150 00	3 51	90 00
Dunn	80.00	240 00	60 00	9 84	180 00
Eau Claire	1,306.72	3,869 51	2,026 51	100 62	1,843 00
Iowa	25.07	57 00	16 00	88	41 00
Pepin	40.00	133 84	33 84	54	100 00
Pierce	523.56	1,633 35	885 35	38 16	748 00
Portage	116.41	614 27	156 27	11 02	458 00
St. Croix	120.00	377 45	96 45	15 83	281 00
Total	3,051.81	$9,393 11	$4,126 11	$266 98	$5,267 00

EXHIBIT "C."

SALE OF NORMAL SCHOOL LANDS *for the fiscal year ending September* 30, 1873.

COUNTIES.	No. Acres.	Amount sold for.	Principal paid.	Interest paid.	Balance due.
Adams	1,885.16	$771 29	$771 29	....	....
Ashland	1,729.94	2,157 44	2,157 44	....	....
Barron	228.47	245 59	245 59	....	....
Bayfield	1,120.32	1,400 40	1,400 40	....	....
Brown	40.00	26 19	26 19	....	....
Burnett	3,394.86	3,136 05	3,136 05	....	....
Chippewa	7,618.21	8,682 10	8,682 10	....	....
Clark	1,920.13	2,298 91	2,298 91	....	....
Columbia	80.00	40 00	40 00	....	....
Dane	40.00	51 75	51 75	....	....
Dodge	120.00	111 04	111 04	....	....
Door	871.38	812 05	812 05	....	....
Douglas	2,604.35	3,255 43	3,255 43	....	....
Eau Claire	40.00	50 00	50 00	....	....
Jackson	7,005.18	5,868 02	5,498 02	$6 38	$375 00
Jefferson	40.00	50 00	50 00	....	....
Juneau	5,543.98	2,857 59	2,857 59	....	....
Kewaunee	80.00	115 09	115 09	....	....
La Crosse	54.40	75 00	57 00	1 11	18 00
Manitowoc	....	60 00	15 00	1 92	45
Marathon	13,801.53	15,990 87	15,990 87	....	....
Marquette	40.00	70 00	33 00	2 27	37 00
Milwaukee	....	475 00	194 00	14 70	281 00
Monroe	880.00	1,082 21	1,982 21	....	....
Oconto	5,660.43	6,243 90	6,243 90	....	....
Outagamie	571.96	579 52	579 52	....	....
Polk	120.00	110 00	110 00	....	....
Portage	1,920.99	1,719 35	1,719 35	....	....

EXHIBIT "C."—*Sale of Normal School Lands for the fiscal year ending September 30, 1873*—continued.

COUNTIES.	No. Acres.	Amount sold for.	Principal paid.	Interest paid.	Balance due.
Shawano	4,322.19	$6,716 30	$3,714 61	$74 19	$3,001 69
Sheboygan	40.00	55 09	55 09	....	....
Washington	40.00	39 16	39 16	....	....
Waupaca	40.00	53 22	26 22	1 82	27 00
Wood	15,643.93	8,386 38	8,386 38	....	....
Total	76,497.36	$73,584 94	$69,800 25	$102 39	$3,784 69

EXHIBIT "D."

SALE OF DRAINAGE LANDS *for the fiscal year ending September* 30, 1873.

COUNTIES.	Number of Acres.	Amount Sold for.	Principal Paid.
Adams	1,543.94	$833 44	$833 44
Ashland	2,097.60	2,622 01	2,622 01
Barron	300.03	305 04	305 04
Bayfield	1,127 92	1,409 90	1,409 90
Brown	160.00	124 48	124 48
Buffalo	495.21	384 31	384 31
Burnett	4,373.70	3,879 90	3,879 90
Chippewa	8,914.07	10,246 17	10,246 17
Clark	2,378.71	2,780 92	2,780 92
Columbia	1,680.00	840 00	840 00
Crawford	88.16	74 06	74 06
Dane	480.00	504 38	504 38
Dodge	90.90	73 06	73 06
Door	2,350.25	2,076 20	2,076 20
Douglas	2,328.38	2,910 39	2,910 39
Dunn	640.00	485 08	485 08
Eau Claire	362.24	438 47	438 47
Grant	78.25	97 51	97 51
Green Lake	441.69	448 12	448 12
Jackson	9,475.22	7,208 24	7,208 24
Jefferson	200.00	250 59	250 59
Juneau	8,064.11	4,164 27	4,164 27
Kewaunee	520.00	500 71	500 71
La Crosse	186.77	158 56	158 56
Manitowoc	160.00	209 86	209 86
Marathon	13,465.22	15.288 75	15,288 75
Marquette	563.31	346 19	346 19

EXHIBIT "D."—*Sale of Drainage Lands, for the fiscal year ending September* 30, 1873—continued.

COUNTIES.	Number of Acres.	Amount Sold for.	Principal Paid.
Monroe	4,687.57	$3,805 17	$3,805 17
Oconto	8,587.03	8,222 77	8,222 77
Polk	240.00	180 00	180 00
Portage	2,716.45	2,174 27	2,174 27
Sauk	120.00	134 51	134 51
[illegible]no	3,401.76	3,338 45	3,338 45
[illegible]u	92.81	375 66	375 66
Waupaca	1,836.57	1,887 49	1,887 49
Waushara	1,120.00	982 28	982 28
Winnebago	1,293.64	1.022 03	1,022 08
W[illegible]d	21,496.71	11,584 74	11,584 74
Total	108,457.17	$92,316 98	$92,316 98

EXHIBIT "E."

SALE OF AGRICULTURAL COLLEGE LANDS *for the Fiscal Year ending September* 30, 1873.

COUNTIES.	No. of Acres.	Amount sold for.	Principal paid.	Interest paid.	Balance due.
Chippewa	119.12	$148 90	$75 90	68	$73 00
Dunn	160.00	200 00	52 00	$2 89	148 00
Marathon	11,292.05	14,111 67	4,520 67	225 78	9,591 00
Oconto	918.85	1,149 81	408 81	28 98	741 00
Shawano	5,679.11	7,098 40	2,107 40	108 09	4,991 00
Total	18,169.13	$22,708 78	$7,164 78	$363 37	$15,544 00

EXHIBIT "F."

SALE OF MARATHON COUNTY LANDS *for the fiscal year ending Sept.* 30, 1873.

COUNTIES.	No. of Acres.	Am't sold for.	Principal paid.
Marathon	8,664.60	$6,498 25	$6,498 25

EXHIBIT "G."

LANDS HELD BY THE STATE, *September* 30, 1873.

COUNTIES.	School. No. of Acres.	University. No. of Acres.	Normal School. No. of Acres.	Drainage. No. of Acres.	Agric'l College. No. of Acres.	Marathon Co. No. of Acres.
Adams	5,775.69		11,278.11	18,889.30		
Ashland	5,820.00		44,451.52	50,541.16		
Barron	3,159.58		1,465.45	1,989.93		
Bayfield	11,585.22		10,461.29	11,807.90		
Brown			40.00	1,026.54		
Buffalo,	2,083.00			3,522.07		
Burnett	18,897.32	27.25	26,152.73	33,176.25		
Calumet			40.00	5,840.00		
Chippewa	14,541.47	599.95	40,003.22	37,439.01	78.22	
Clark	3,550.45	640.00	7,238.16	9,909.07	198.44	
Columbia	240.00			760.00		
Crawford	1,280.00	117.42		871.84		
Dane				889.00		
Dodge	40.00		1,280.00	5,256.49		
Door	2,966.25	958.05	9,050.05	20,564.88		
Douglas	12,397.77		42,870.37	43,500.21		
Dunn	1,661.33		400.00	2,053.12	720.00	
Eau Claire	3,880.00	1,249.48		674.84		
Grant	200.00		80.00			
Green Lake				838.31		
Iowa	141.33					
Jackson	10,995.86		22,564.39	34,545.49		
Jefferson				595.92		
Juneau	9,607.00		37,317.67	47,064.77		
Kewaunee			1,918.49	7,396.04		
La Crosse	629.15		283.17	3,136.05		
La Fayette	230.00					

EXHIBIT "G."—*Lands held by the State, September* 30, 1873—continued.

COUNTIES.	School. No. of Acres.	University. No. of Acres.	Normal School. No. of Acres.	Drainage. No. of Acres.	Agr'l College No. of Acres.	Marathon Co. No. of Acres.
Manitowoc	195.70	....	400.00	7,715.88	....	....
Marathon	56,892.00	960.00	205,827.95	205,145.45	30,126.11	18,327.07
Marquette	1,820.00	....	40.00	3,048.58	....	....
Monroe	3,680.00	....	1,000.00	7,683.98	....	....
Oconto	45,408.06	....	149,000.14	178,193.30	16,155.37	....
Outagamie	1,578.66	....	3,899.90	26,320.00	....	....
Pepin	720.00	156.90	....	398.52	....	....
Pierce	720.00	760.85	....	160.00	....	....
Polk	2,400.00	668.55	3,120.00	7,240.10	....	....
Portage	2,665.25	....	13,573.33	34,647.33	....	....
Racine	....	....	....	40.00	....	....
Richland	1,680.00	40.00	....	80.00	....	....
Rock	40.00	....	....	....	....	....
St. Croix	1,880.00	120.00	120.00	80.00	....	....
Sauk	1,443.03	....	....	120.00	....	....
Shawano	6,352.71	....	30,311.78	25,118.82	9,045.87	....
Sheboygan	....	....	....	36.36	....	....
Trempealeau	2,800 00	....	....	1,112.99	....	....
Vernon	2,046.45	....	440.00	1,840.00	....	....
Waukesha	76.90	....	....	440.00	....	....
Waupaca	2,478.49	....	505.43	8,834.19	....	....
Waushara	3,340.16	....	40.00	3,181.04	....	....
Winnebago	....	....	....	1,870.04	....	....
Wood	560.00	....	10,640.00	13,560.00	....	....
Totals	245,735.52	6,298.00	675,372.15	865,149.77	56,324.01	18,327.07

EXHIBIT "H."

APPORTIONMENT OF DRAINAGE MONEY, *July 1st*, 1873.

COUNTIES.	Amount Apportioned.
Adams	$1,611 34
Ashland	8,346 23
Barron	415 96
Bayfield	700 00
Brown	366 30
Buffalo	542 26
Burnett	3,486 37
Chippewa	16,522 76
Clark	3,891 89
Columbia	724 27
Crawford	66 12
Dane	1,071 44
Dodge	148 93
Door	1,978 87
Douglas	2,504 89
Dunn	573 66
Eau Claire	538 03
Fond du Lac	189 93
Grant	158 31
Green	2 80
Green Lake	459 04
Jackson	8,844 46
Jefferson	417 33
Juneau	2,698 95
Kewaunee	352 28
La Crosse	479 87
Manitowoc	381 62
Marathon	27,683 59
Marquette	924 66
Monroe	3,720 78
Oconto	9,943 39
Outagamie	23 30
Pepin	261 82
Pierce	3 15
Polk	299 93
Portage	2,821 28
Rock	18 90
St. Croix	18 72
Sauk	136 25
Shawano	2,994 70
Trempealeau	787 08
Walworth	45 12
Washington	3 36
Waukesha	44 10
Waupaca	2,054 68
Waushara	1,469 75
Winnebago	1,399 58
Wood	12,222 76
	$124,340 76

DOCUMENT 5.

ANNUAL REPORT

OF THE

SUPERINTENDENT

OF

PUBLIC INSTRUCTION

OF THE

STATE OF WISCONSIN,

FOR THE

School Year ending August 31, 1873.

SAMUEL FALLOWS,
Superintendent of Public Instruction.

MADISON, WIS.:
ATWOOD & CULVER, PRINTERS AND STEREOTYPERS.
1873.

OFFICE OF THE SUPERINTENDENT OF PUBLIC INSTRUCTION.

MADISON, December 10, 1873.

To His Excellency, C. C. WASHBURN,

Governor of Wisconsin:

SIR:—I have the honor to submit, through you, to the Legislature, the Annual Report of the Department of Instruction, for the year ending August 31, 1873.

I am, sir, very respectfully,

Your obedient servant,

SAMUEL FALLOWS,

Superintendent of Public Instruction.

ANNUAL REPORT

OF THE

SUPERINTENDENT

OF

PUBLIC INSTRUCTION

OF THE

STATE OF WISCONSIN.

Office of Superintendent of Public Instruction,
Madison, December 10, 1873.

To the Legislature of Wisconsin:

Gentlemen: In submitting my annual report for the year 1873, I will first present the statistics gathered for the year, with the usual comments and explanations, referring to the printed tables in the Appendix for details. To make room for the report on Compulsory Education, which I have prepared in obedience to a resolution of the last legislature, the first and second tables of statistics only are given, by towns, and the others by counties. The statistics of the cities are given separately.

I.—SCHOOL DISTRICTS.

The whole number of regular districts reported by the county superintendents is 4,275, an increase since last year of 80. The previous year there was an increase of 106. The number of parts of districts returned is 2,093, making, by the usual estimate of 2½ parts to a district, 930 joint districts, or 22 more than last year. The whole number of districts, therefore, not including those cities which are not under the jurisdiction of county superintendents, is 5,205. Last year the number, excluding the cities, was 5,103, so that the total increase in districts is 102. The number of cities now reporting independently is 20. The wards of a city are in some degree analogous to a school district, as each ward usually has its school. The number of wards or other divisions of territory supporting a school, is about 100.

II.—CHILDREN OVER FOUR AND UNDER TWENTY YEARS OF AGE.

The number reported is 436,002, an apparent increase from last year of 12,284. During the previous year the apparent increase was only 2,769. But after the printing of the report last year was completed, the person entrusted with the work discovered an error of 10,000 in the addition of the number of children. The real increase therefore from 1871 to 1872 was 12,769; and from 1872 to 1873, it is only 2,284. No reason can be assigned for so great a discrepancy except the unreliable character of the statistics gathered under our present system.

III.—NUMBER OF CHILDREN OF SCHOOL AGE IN THOSE DISTRICTS WHICH MAINTAINED SCHOOL FIVE OR MORE MONTHS.

The number reported under this head is 432,959, which is 3,241 less than the whole number of school age, a difference somewhat less than that exhibited last year.

IV.—TOTAL NUMBER OF PERSONS ATTENDING THE PUBLIC SCHOOLS.

The number of children between four and twenty years of age, who have attended the public schools is 281,708; the number under four years of age who have attended is 575; and the number over twenty, 1,439; making the total number, 283,722; a gain upon last year of 13,430, which is largely in excess of the addition to the school population, and therefore an encouraging sign.

The number of children reported as attending private schools in the country districts (and not registered in the public schools) is 6,396; in the independent cities, 3,185; making a total of 9,581 against 18,020 returned last year, or not much more than half the number. Twenty-three counties and eight cities, however, make no returns of the number in private schools. Tabulating all classes of pupils, the following is the result for 1872 and 1873;

	1872.	1873,
The number reported as attending public schools, is......	270,292	283,722
The number reported as attending private schools, is......	18,020	9,581
The number reported as attend'g academ's and colleges is	2,331	2,544
The number estimated for benevolent institutions, is......	1,200	1,225
Total	292,843	297,072

V.—TEACHERS AND TEACHERS' WAGES.

According to the returns made, the number of teachers required in all the schools is 4,843, and the number actually employed some part of the year was 8,903. As these figures are less than those given for the previous year, it is presumed the returns are defective. It may be hoped, however, that there is some improvement in the matter of changing teachers, reducing the number actually employed.

The average wages of male teachers, in the country districts, is $43.38 per month, and that of females, $27.52. This is is a slight increase from the average wages reported last year, which were $43.33 for males, and $27.04 for females.

In the cities, the average for male teachers has increased from $982 to $1,091 per annum, and that for female teachers from $376 to $377.

VI.—TEACHERS' CERTIFICATES.

The whole uumber granted (exclusive of those issued in the cities, and state certificates) was 7,619, which is 346 more than the number for the previous year. The items for the past two years are as follows:

	1872 1st gr.	1873 1st gr.	1872 2d gr.	1873 2d gr.	1872 3d gr.	1873 3d gr.	1872 Total.	1873 Total.
To males.......	104	107	226	250	1,936	2,059	2,266	2,416
To females	44	29	209	250	4,754	4,927	5,007	5,203
Totals........	148	136	435	500	6,690	6,986	7,273	7,619

In the cities, certificates are not issued upon a uniform basis, and cannot well be classified with those issued by county superintendents. The whole number of certificates granted in the cities, so far as returned, is 438, which, together with 6 state certificates, granted in 1873, and the number given in the foregoing table, make an aggregate of 8,063 of all grades, or 366 more than last year.

VII.—STATE CERTIFICATES.

Prof. Alexander Kerr of Madison, Miss Martha E. Hazard of Oshkosh, and I. N. Stewart, Esq. of Manitowoc, were appointed a Board of Examiners for state certificates for the year 1873. Examinations were conducted at Sparta, July 2–7, at Madison, August 20–25, and at New Lisbon, August 27–30.

Sixteen applicants were examined, of which number the following persons received first grade certificates for life:

Charles Zimmerman, Milwaukee.
Jas. T. Lunn, Sandusky.
John Nagle, Manitowoc.
Michael Kirwan, Manitowoc.

The following named persons received certificates for five years:

T. L. Cole, La Crosse.
R. B. Crandall, North Eau Claire.

VIII.—GRADED SCHOOLS.

Not including the independent cities, the number of schools with two departments is 155, an increase of 4; and the number with three or more departments is 103, or 39 less than last year. Attention is once more called to the fact that graded schools could be much more extensively introduced, in the rural districts, under the "Town System." Assuming the cities to embrace 122 graded schools, or one for each school house reported, the whole number in the state is 380, an apparent decrease of 30. From some counties, however, no returns are given under this head, and it is presumed there is an increase of both classes of schools.

IX.—SCHOOL HOUSES.

The whole number returned is 4,957. The number reported last year was 4,979, showing an apparent decrease of 22. It is presumed, however, that accurate returns would show as usual a small increase in the number. The amount expended for building and repairing was $307,934, or about $12,589 more than last year. Thirty-two different counties have one or more school houses valued from $5,000 to $30,000, aside from those embraced in the cities which do not report to the county superintendents. The number of good school houses increases every year, though building has been less active than usual, perhaps, in the country districts, during the past year. The school houses of the state will accommodate 315,111 pupils, which is 31,634 more than the whole attendance upon the public schools.

X.—RECEIPTS AND EXPENDITURES.

The sums received and expended for school purposes during the year are as follows:

RECEIPTS.		
Money on hand August 31, 1872	$428,905 80	
From taxes levied for building and repairing	246,509 22	
From taxes levied for teachers wages	1,002,628 58	
From taxes levied for apparatus and libraries	10,460 45	
From taxes levied at annual meeting	291,992 72	
From taxes levied by county supervisors	258,505 31	
From income of state school fund	168,755 34	
From other sources	220,271 11	
Total amount received		$2,628,027 98
EXPENDITURES.		
For building and repairing	$307,934 41	
For apparatus and libraries	10,143 81	
For services of male teachers	650,485 01	
For services of female teachers	766,959 87	
For old indebtedness	98,336 54	
For furniture, registers and records	41,588 40	
For all other purposes	210,816 13	
Total amount expended		$2,073,449 51
Money on hand August 31, 1873		471,091 36

XI.—SUMMARY OF GENERAL STATISTICS.

The usual summary of the most important statistics is given below, showing the increase or decrease, in the first table, as compared with the previous year, decrease being indicated by an asterisk (*).

	1879.	1878.	Increase.
Whole number of districts in the state, not including cities	5,108	5,205	102
Number of districts reported	4,989	5,130	141
Number of children over four and under twenty years of age in the state	433,717	436,001	2,284
Number of children over four and under twenty years of age in districts maintaining school five or more months	431,086	432,959	1,863
Number of children over four and under twenty years of age who have attended school	266,789	271,708	14,919
Total number of the different pupils who have attended the public school during the year	270,292	283,477	13,125
Average number of days a school was maintained	158	151	*2
Number of days' attendance of pupils over four and under twenty years of age	19,663,667	19,812,009	208,842
Total number of days' attendance of different pupils during the year	19,929,416	20,211,939	282,523
Number of days schools have been taught by qualified teachers	801,007	787,567	*13,440
Number of pupils who have attended private schools	18,020	9,581	*8,440
Number of schools with two departments	213	217	4
Number of schools with three or more departments	199	163	*89
Number of teachers required to teach the schools	5,881	4,843	*1,038
Number of different persons employed as teachers during the year	9,267	8,903	*364
Average monthly wages of male teachers in the country	$43 33	$43 38	$0 05
Average monthly wages of female teachers in the country	27 04	27 52	48
Average monthly wrges of male teachers in the cities	98 20	109 10	10 90
Average monthly wages of female teachers in the cities	37 60	37 70	10
Number of schools visited by the county superintendents	4,296	4,307	11
Number of public school houses in the state	4,979	4,957	*22
Number of pupils the school-houses will accommodate	312,612	315,111	2,499
Number of sites containing less than one acre	3,733	3,693	*40
Number of sites well enclosed	1,892	1,634	242

XI.—*Summary of General Statistics*—continued.

	1872.	*1873.*	*Increase.*
Number of school-houses built of brick or stone	656	693	37
Number of school-houses with out-houses in good condition	3,497	2,174	*1,323
Highest valuation of school-house and site	$75,000	$75,000	....

Aggregate of Values and Expenditures.

	1872.	*1873.*
Total valuation of school-houses	$3,611,607	$3,995,422
Total valuation of sites	513,089	425,788
Total valuation of apparatus	87,468	181,326
Amount expended for building and repairing	294,345	307,934
Amount expended for apparatus and libraries	9,035	10,143
Amount expended for teachers' wages	1,352,695	1,417,395
Amount expended for old indebtedness	104,838	98,336
Amount expended for furniture, registers and records	31,392	41,588
Amount expended for all other purposes	211,849	210,816
Total amount expended	$2,004,154	$2,073,660

XII.—EDUCATIONAL FUNDS AND INCOMES.

As appears by the report of the Secretary of State, the gross receipts and disbursements pertaining to the several Educational Funds and the incomes thereof, for the fiscal year ending September 30, 1872, were as follows:

	Receipts.	Disbursements
School Fund	$103,818 98	$52,793 37
School Fund Income	179,763 67	185,136 98
University Fund	9,728 12	10,100 51
University Fund Income	42,716 38	42,716 38
Agricultural College Fund	13,560 70	10,000 00
Agricultural College Fund Income	12,558 85	12,558 85
Normal School Fund	86,687 54	52,973 26
Normal School Fund Income	71,369 10	55,368 62

XIII.—APPORTIONMENT OF SCHOOL FUND INCOME.

The amount apportioned in June last, on the returns for the school year ending August 31, 1872, was $181,056.12. The ratio of apportionment was 42 cents per scholar, three cents more than for the previous year. Since the general apportionment in June, an additional sum of $225.15 has been apportioned to certain school districts, under the provisions of chapter 300, of the general laws of 1873, making the total amount apportioned, $181,281.17. No apportionment is made for those districts which do not maintain school at least five months during the preceding school year, except in some cases of peculiar hardship, which are provided for by chapter 164 of the general laws of 1872.

The apportionments from 1850 to 1873, inclusive, are as follows:

	Number of Children.	Apportionment.
1850	92,647	$8\frac{4}{10}$ cents per scholar
1851	111,481	50 do
1852	124,783	48 do
1853	138,279	45 do
1854	455,125	72 do
1855	186,960	$80\frac{4}{10}$ do
1856	213,886	70 do
1857	241,545	66 do
1858	264,977	75 do
1859	278,871	64 do
1860	288,984	64 do
1861	299,782	32 do
1862	303,656	50 do
1863	320,965	44 do
1864	329,906	47 do
1865	339,024	46 do
1866	354,517	45 do
1867	371,083	47 do
1868	361,759	48 do
1869	376,327	47 do
1870	394,837	40 do
1871	409,193	39 do
1872	418,739	39 do
1873	431,086	42 do

XIV.—TEXT BOOKS.

The number of districts reported as having "adopted a list of text books" is 1,323. For a detailed statement of the books most used in the different counties, reference is made to Table No. IX in the Appendix. This table does not include the cities.

XV.—WEBSTER'S DICTIONARY.

One hundred and four copies remained in hand at the date of the last report. The Legislature authorized the purchase of four hundred copies for the next year ensuing. Of these, one hundred and fifty-one remain on hand at this date (December 10,) and will probably be sufficient to fill all applications up to the time of the usual yearly purchase. Of the two hundred and forty-nine distributed the past year, one hundred and seventy-four have been first supplies, in part to new districts or departments, but in many cases to old districts which had previously neglected to apply for them, and seventy-five have been sold, to districts whose first supplies were worn out or lost. To meet the entire demand, for first supplies and sales, up to the usual time of purchase, in 1875, two hundred and fifty (250) copies will probably be needed. The avails of those sold go into the income of the school fund.

The general distribution of this work in our schools, is greatly to be commended, and that so many districts purchase a second copy, when the first is worn out, indicates that the book is much used and well appreciated.

XVI.—STATE TEACHER'S ASSOCIATION.

The twentieth annual meeting of this body was held in Sparta, on the 8th, 9th and 10th days of July last. The proceedings will be found among the documents appended to this report.

This yearly gathering of the principal teachers and school officers of the state is of great importance in its influence and results, and attracts more and more attention from our citizens. The next session will be held in this city.

XVII.—CONVENTION OF COUNTY SUPERINTENDENTS.

The yearly convention of county superintendents was held in the latter part of December, 1872, at Madison. A convention of principals of public schools having been called to meet at the same time and place, the bodies held a joint session. The proceedings, which were of a highly practical character, are appended to this report.

XVIII.—COLLEGES AND UNIVERSITIES.

In addition to the State Univeasity, the following institutions have reported in compliance with law: Beloit College, Galesville University, Lawrence University, Milton College, Racine College, and Ripon College.

The following table presents the usual summary of statistics for the past two years:

	1872.	*1873.*
Number of Colleges repòrted (not including State University)	8	6
Number of members of faculties	79	61
Number graduated at last commencement	66	62
Total number who have graduated	598	383
Number of students in senior classes	73	53
Number of students in junior classes	93	56
Number of students in sophomore classes	115	100
Number of students in freshman classes	153	129
Number of students not in regular classes	289	143
Number of students in preparatory departments	894	1,275
Total number in the institutions reported	2,368	1,956
Number of acres owned by the institutions	4,086	2,851
Estimated cash value of lands	$135,700 00	$66,520 00
Estimated cash value of buildings	371,000 00	302,500 00
Amount of endowment funds, except real estate	213,205 00	239,555 78
Amount of income from tuition	25,952 00	95,244 40
Amount of income from other sources	22,978 00	33,017 96

XIX.—ACADEMIES AND SEMINARIES.

Only three institutions of this class have been reported, viz: Albion Academy, German and English Academy, Milwaukee, and Rochester Seminary. The statistics of these institutions are given elsewhere.

XX.—CHARITABLE AND REFORMATORY INSTITUTIONS.

As these institutions have more or less to do with the work of education for peculiar classes, reports have again been obtained from most of them, which are to be found in their proper places, among other documents appended to this report.

XXI.—TEACHERS' INSTITUTES.

The institutes held during the past year have been conducted for the most part, by Professors Robert Graham, or Duncan McGregor and Albert Salisbury, from the three normal schools. As a report of the institute work has been made by Hon. W. H. Chandler, in be-half of the committee, I refer to that for statements as to its character and success. The report is among the documents appended to this report, where will also be found an excellent syllabus of instruction for the institutes, prepared by Prof. Graham. Table No. XIII, in the appendix, presents a summary of statistics.

Thirty-five short term institutes, of one week's duration, have been held, and twenty-one normal institutes, of from two to four weeks duration. The number of long institutes has greatly increased, which is an encouraging sign.

XXII.—THE NATURAL SCIENCES.

In my last report I briefly alluded to the importance of the study of the elements of natural sciences in the common schools, and gave it as my opinion that *every* teacher should be acquainted with such elements, and should be required to teach them on and up to January 1, 1872.

It could hardly be expected that such an important revolution in the methods of study and instruction which this requirement would necessitate, could be effected at once. Objections were made that the number of studies would be increased in the schools, while the demand was urgent for a less number; that it was almost impossible to find teachers for the country schools well informed in the branches already required, and to impose additional branches would be to make the standard still lower.

I do not consider the objections valid. It is true that we have enough of mere abstract studies in our ungraded schools. They must be taught. But these ought not to exclude studies of immediate and constant practical value.

Both classes of studies can be taught without unduly burdening the pupil's mind or distracting his attention. They are complementary not contradictory. They can be made to concentrate and not confuse the perceptive and reflective powers.

In answer to the second objection, it may be said that the legislature, two years ago, passed an act requiring the study of the Constitution of the United States and of the State of Wisconsin in addition to the studies previously required. The effect upon the teachers was beneficial. Great enthusiasm was awakened among them whenever the subject was under consideration at the institutes. County superintendents have found that a lower standing in other studies has not resulted because of the additional study required.

Hon. W. T. Harris, Superintendent of the Public Schools of St. Louis, maintains that the general efficiency and power of the teachers of that city have been increased at least fifty per cent. in a single year by the preparing and giving of one exercise of an hour per week in Natural Science.

I subjoin the testimony of Hon. Newton Bateman, Superintendent of Public Instruction for the State of Illinois, showing that the experiment of requiring Natural Sciences to be taught in the common schools of that state has thus far been a gratifying success:

"Conspicuous among the alterations made by the Twenty-seventh General Assembly in our system of public schools, is the requirement that the elements of the Natural Sciences be made a part of the common school course. It is yet too soon to speak of the practical results of this measure, in the school rooms of the State, as the plan has but just been entered upon, but there are good reasons for anticipating from it large and substantial advantages. It is believed that the measure will prove beneficial to teachers; to the schools, as such; to the pupils; to the public at large, and to the general cause of popular education and free schools.

"EFFECT ON TEACHERS.

"Our puplic school teachers themselves need the spur and inspiration of these new studies. I speak more particularly of the teachers of common district schools, weo comprise more than three-fourths of the whole number. Of these, as a class, it has often been said that dullness, listlessness, apathy, narrowness of mental vision, and a lack of spirit, enterprise and ambition, are noticeable characteristics. I once heard a shrewd observer remark that he could detect a person of this class by his very gait, bearing and speech. Without concurring in such a sweeping judgment, and repelling as false and foolish the popular caricatures of school masters and school mistresses, I ask, who are most to blame for such *tendencies* towards mental enervation, as it must be confessed do exist among elementary teachers—the young men and women themselves, or the system under which they teach? Look at the facts, as they have existed in this State from the beginning of the free school system, and for years before. What have been the studies prescribed by law?

Spelling, reading, writing, arithmetic, grammar, geography and United States history. Who first marked out this course of study, or what considerations led to its original adoption and subsequent tenacious retention, does not appear. But if the author of this common school curriculum is still living, a contemplation of its results will hardly induce him to come forth and claim the honor of his achievement. Of the seven things to be studied, the first four are indeed proper and indispensably necessary, to a certain extent, and even the last three may be profitably attended to, for a brief period, by the most advanced classes. But if it were distinctly proposed to devise a scheme whereby the schools might be rendered the least profitable, that which compels the youth of the State to spend the whole period of their school-going life upon the famous seven branches of the old Illinois law, to the proctical exclusion of everything else, must be regarded as a reasonably successful solution of the problem.

"Consider that every one of those branches may be taught in a mechanical, text-book manner (for even reading and penmanship are but partial exceptions to the statement); that every teacher who is disposed to idly drift along on the easy current of printed questions and printed answers, may do so; that after acquiring the prescribed preliminary knowledge requisite to obtaining a license, there is almost no *necessity* for further effort on the teacher's part, unless, for reasons outside of the demands of the school room, he *chooses* to exert himself; that more than one-half of the teachers of the State have been spending their time, all these years, upon three only of those branches, orthography, reading and arithmetic, living and moving and having their intellectual being, as teachers, in the spelling-book, the primer and reader, and the rudiments of numbers and calculation; that in many instances the books used are the poorest extant, while in others, the same books have been used almost from the time to which the memory of the oldest inhabitant runneth not to the contrary, till the minds of both pupils and teachers slip over their smooth familiar pages almost without a gleam of conscious thought or intelligence; that this state of things has come to be accepted and acquiesced in by the community, in a helpless kind of way, as a sort of dreary necessity from which there was no escape; that the average teacher, just like the average workman in every other pursuit, will earn his wages as easily as he can, doing no more and no better work than is required by the obligations nominated in the bond—consider all this, and then say if it be any wonder that common district school teachers, as a class, should become intellectually enervated and dwarfed, dispirited, weak and languid.

"What, then, must be the effect of the law's summons to the study of Natural Science as a condition of licensure, upon this great host of torpid and lethargic teachers? It is almost like the breath of the Lord upon the dry bones in the valley of vision. These teachers were not dead, but sleeping; they lacked not capacity, but opportunity; not ability and willingness to advance, but the obligation and necessity of advancing. And never before has such a spectacle been presented to the people of Illinois. From the time the new law was fairly promulgated in April last, till the schools opened in the autumn, the whole State became as it were one great camp of instruction. Vacation plans were everywhere cheerfully given up, and through all the unprecedentedly intense and protracted dog-day heats of the past summer, great numbers of teachers in every part of the State were assiduously engaged in preparing themselves for examination in the elements of the Natural Sciences. In many counties special Institutes were convened for the purpose, while in others, the stated Institutes were almost wholly devoted to instruction in the new branches. The President and Faculty of the State Normal University kindly consented to lend a helping hand and announced that the annual session of the State Teacher's Institute, to be held in the month of August, would be chiefly devoted to the same good work. Hundreds of teachers availed themselves of the opportunity and repaired to the University, where they were instructed by the President and the whole corps of Professors, assisted by able and experienced teachers from different parts of the State. In addition to these organized efforts, through the State and County Institutes, innumerable private classes were formed, wherever a suitable number of teachers could be assembled, and the work was diligently prosecuted, with such assistance and under such leaders as could be procured. When no one familiar with the new branches could be found to take charge of a class, the members went forward, nevertheless, and did the best they could to help and encourage one another. To all this array of means and efforts, must be added the individual exertions of teachers innumerable, who quietly pursued their studies in private. Through all those months the inquiry for suitable text-books in Natural Science was general, in every county of the State, and the limited supplies of works of that description were soon exhausted.

"Many county superintendents bore a prominent and useful part in these measures to prepare the teachers of the State for their new duties. Some of them, in addition to good service in their own counties, took part in the Institutes of other counties, and in the State Institute, and contributed in every practicable way toward the general result aimed at; and never was the value of a competent and scholarly county superintendency rendered so apparent. When the time arrived for opening the schools, in September, the teachers in those counties whose superintendents had been able and willing to lead and instruct them in the new branches, were generally ready for their work. Professional lecturers on Natural Science, college presidents and professors, private gentlemen of the requisite culture and attainments, and teachers who were already competent to give instruction in one or more of the new banches were also laid under contribution to a greater or less extent, and helped greatly to push on the work. The common school elements of society, so to speak, were profoundly stirred, everywhere, and a free-school revival, of extraordinary extent and power, was inaugurated.

"Up to Oct. 1, 1872, the number of teachers examined in the elements of of the Natural Sciences was 3,975, of whom 3,114 were successful, and 861 unsuccessful; so that in three months from the day the new law went into effect, nearly one sixth of the whole number of teachers in the state had been examined in the new branches and duly licensed to teach the same. If those be added who were previously qualified to teach the rudiments of science, the total number of teachers in line, on the new branches, the first day of the present school year, would be about one-fifth of the entire teaching force of the state. The number is constantly increasing as old certificates expire, so that by the close of the school year the elements of natural science will be taught in nearly all the common schools in the state. It is a little remarkable that of the 3114 who had passed successful examinations Oct. 1, the number of men and of women was precisely equal—1557 of each. The number of provisional certificates granted up to Oct. 1, was 1588. Nearly or quite every county in the state has already taken some part in the movement.

"Consider, now, the certain and necessary effect of all this upon the hearts, minds and purposes of the teachers of the state. Into what a new world of thought and investigation has it introduced thousands of them. How it has broken up the incrustations of old habits of routine, and lifted many and many a teacher into a new atmosphere. How it has turned thousands of young eyes from the four walls of the school-room, with its monotonous accompaniments of slates and maps and printed books, out into the wider and brighter school-room of nature. What encouragement and hope have been inspired by the successful mastery of even the merest rudiments of sciences supposed to be only for the favored few. What a mental tonic have these efforts been to all who have engaged in them, imparting freshness and vigor to the intellectual powers, with increased ability and zest in every department of instruction. With what new feelings did these teachers look forward to the resumption of their labors, when they should essay, for the first time, to teach their pupils things not written in their books, the glorified alphabet of nature, God manifest in the birds and flowers." * * *

"EFFECT UPON PUPILS.

"Passing from the consideration of the influence of the new requirements upon teachers, to note their effect upon the pupils, it is obvious that the most of what has already been said is equally applicable to this branch of the subject. For if the maxim that 'the teacher makes the school' be not absolutely true, it is more nearly so than most popular aphorisms. Nearly all the causes that have been mentioned as operating to depress and paralyze the energies and aspirations of teachers, are equally effective, in the same direction, upon scholars. If a narrow and ill-chosen course of common school studies has been steadily tending to enervate the intellect, repress the enthusiasm and dwarf the manhood of the one class, it has equally served to dampen the ardor and deaden the mental activity of the other. Like begets like, in the school room as elsewhere. Dullness and apathy in the teacher are sure to generate the same in the pupils. Nor can the opposite qualities be successfully feigned if they do not really exist. There is a spontaneity, a natural glow and force about the actions and utterances of an instructor who is deeply interested in his work, and who finds that work both congenial and exciting, which children are swift to detect and feel, and which cannot be successfully assumed.

"Children will be interested in these new studies at first, merely because they are new. They delight in change, variety, novelty. This is shown in their eagerness to advance from lesson to lesson and from book to book, and in a thousand other ways. But if this were all, it would be an insufficient reason for the introduction of the natural sciences, so far as the pupils are concerned. The novelty would be but temporary, and the clamor for change would soon become as great as before.

"The introduction of these new studies into the common schools of the state, together with oral methods of instruction therein, will be of great and lasting benefit to the school-going population of the state, because those studies and methods are in harmony with the instincts and tastes of children and with the observed facts and principles of their mental development and growth. In other words, because the studies themselves are of intrinsic and perennial interest to the youthful mind, and the proposed methods of pursuing them are in accordance with the laws of educational philosophy, and the teachings of experience.

"In declaring that the elements of the natural sciences shall be taught in the public schools, the legislature has recognized, and, as I conceive, sought to utilize the fact that the *senses* are the pioneers of all knowledge, and that their cultivation and training should be made, for several years, the chief work of education, as being the royal avenues to the brain, by which the first treasures of knowledge are garnered up.

"Children love nature with a spontaneous, enthusiastic love. Her protean forms, sweet inspirations and ever-unfolding beauties are correlated to the cravings of their own souls. The young are in close sympathy with the outward, the material—the time for ratiocinating has not yet come. These are the universal characteristics of healthy, well endowed childhood; the fundamental truths and postulates in accordance with which the early training of children should be conducted. Instead of trying to make logicians of little children, which is impossible, we should seek to make accurate observers of them, which is quite possible, and the sure foundation of future advancement in knowledge. Instead of trying to force them to a knowledge of intellectual abstractions, through books and brain work, we should first lead them forth into the magnificence and beauty of the material world, through the senses. Instead of offering them the dry formulas and abstract ideas of books and of men, we should first bid them open their eyes and ears and let the sweet wisdom of God flow in, through the omnipresent beauty of the grass-clad earth and glory-tinted skies, and the minstrelsy of twittering birds and purling waters. Instead of vainly trying to bend the child to an irrational theory of education, we should first simply follow the path indicated by the finger of God, in the unmistakable and irrepressible instincts and tendencies of the little ones whom he has made.

"The methods of instruction pursued in our most successful elementary training schools are grounded upon these principles. Their leading idea is, that the objects, facts and phenomena of the outer and material world are first to be dealt with, and that the formation of habits of close and accurate observation thereof, and discrimination therein, is the chief work of the elementary teacher. It seems to have been the object of our general assembly to bring the schools of the state into line with these approved principles. The knowledge acquired in this way is definite and positive, and it is a knowledge of things, and of their actual relations and uses, not of mere words about things. So great is the difference between passive reception and active personal search and achievement. The process of analyzing, comparing, separating and uniting different things and parts of things, by means of rightly conducted object lessons—of noting each peculiarity of shape and contour every mode of combination, adjustment and grouping; each variation of shade and tint in colors—continued from day to day, with constantly renewed materials and specimens, is to the discriminating faculties like whetstone to steel.

"The value of such a habit of quick, sharp observation, the extent and certainty of its development by proper training in early youth, the impossibility of fully securing it in after life, and the manifold benefits and pleasures accruing, all through life, from its exercise, are among the forcible arguments in favor of the method of primary training which, it is hoped and believed, will be introduced into our schools in connection with the natural sciences.

"But, says the objector, I cannot afford to allow my children to spend their time on such things; the alphabet is the only object lesson that I believe in for children who are ignorant of it; it will be time enough for the rudiments of science when the rudiments of English are mastered. The reply is at hand. It is confidently affirmed that all the valuable and curious information, and all the more valuable training of the physical senses, acquired by the study of the natural sciences in the way proposed, would be clear gain. The letters of the alphabet, and all the rudiments of the old text-book course, would be mastered in less time, and with more ease and pleasure, in connection with the new studies and methods, than without them. The reason is obvious. The child's mind is relieved and refreshed by the interest and pleasure of learning about actual material things, which can be seen and handled, and he will return to his spelling book and reader with unwonted zest, and accomplish more in five minutes than he would have done in half an hour, without the pleasurable relaxation. Thus, while the eye and hand are trained to quickness and skill, while the first principles of useful and beautiful sciences are being mastered, while the mind is pleasantly excited and interested, instead of growing tired and weary, a new life is infused into every other lesson and exercise, and better results are secured in all school work.

"To waste so much precious time in the mere effort to fix in the memory the names and shapes of the twenty-six letters of the alphabet would be ludicrous if it were not so sad. Not only one month, but several months, are often devoted, almost exclusively, to the attainment of this object. And when at last the victory is achieved, how poor and barren it is. The child can point out and call the names of twenty-six crooked and, to him, unmeaning things—that is all. No mental power has been called into exercise; no new faculty awakened; no useful information communicated; no pleasure has mingled in the task; the mind has tended to deadness and stupefaction all the time, for lack of something appropriate on which to fasten and feed, and the poor child is disgusted with his book and tired of school. Let us thank the legislature for affording us a more excellent way.

"The influence of these new studies upon pupils will be great, both directly and indirectly. They will bring into the school-room that variety, which, as has already been remarked, is so pleasing to youth, so in harmony with the ceaseless activity and vivacity of their natures. Not the least of the benefits of these studies is the opportunity they afford of meeting and satisfying this inherent craving of the juvenile spirit, while at the same time choice treasures of knowledge are gathered up day by day. The liability to a settled monotonousness of teaching is greatest in elementary schools, where the branches taught are necessarily few and simple, affording in themselves so little to excite the mind and sustain the interest of the teacher. "I can appeal to the experience of such teachers, if constant watchfulness has not been necessary, on their part, to keep from lapsing into a drowsy listlessness of manner, which would soon communicate itself to the pupils and plunge the school into a state of torpor and lethargy. In view of these familiar facts and tendencies, the placing of these new and exhaustless resources in the hands of primary teachers cannot fail to be appreciated."

XXIII.—UNIVERSITY OF WISCONSIN.

As will be seen by the catalogue, the University of Wisconsin has been enjoying signal prosperity under the faithful and energetic presidency of Rev. J. H. Twombly, D. D., and through the unwearied efforts of his laborious colleagues in the faculty. The University never stood higher in public esteem than at the present time. The standard of scholarship now demanded has never been surpassed in any previous period of its history.

Graded Schools and the University.

In my first report made to the legislature in 1870, I used the following language:

"The preparatory department ought to be abolished as speedily as possible. The high schools and academies of the state ought to do the work now done by it. I have cherished for years the conviction that the time would come when the University would be *organically* connected with our common school system. The vital bond must be the high school."

One of the principal reasons that induced me to accept the position of Superintendent of Public Instruction, was to bring the

University into its normal relations with the public schools, and as far as possible to unify our state school system.

In my report of 1871, I referred to the subject as follows:

"That the University ought to be brought into more intimate and practical relations with the public schools, none can doubt. The relation at present, to some extent at least, is one of antagonism. The preparatory school, of the University draw away students from the high school. It is supposed to be more honorable to be connected, however distant the relationship, with the University than with the high school.

"It is also claimed that some advantages accrue to the preparatory student as regards his examination for college, which are not given to other students. The latter claim is without doubt unfounded in fact. The impression, however, exists and exerts its influence.

"I think the antagonism would cease, and harmony and efficiency result if a plan like the following were adopted:

"Let the Regents and Faculty of the University furnish to all regularly organized high or graded schools of the state a list of the studies required for admission into the different collegiate departments, with the per cent. to be attained in each branch.

"Let all the graduates of such schools on the certificates of their principals, be admitted into the college classes for which they are prepared, *without further exa ination* and without *any charge for tuition* during their stay at the University. Let the names of such students and of the schools from which they graduated be published in the catalogue of the University and in the report of the Superintendent of Public Instruction.

"I think the adoption of such a plan would make the principals vie with each other, as to the *quality* and *quantity* of the students sent to the University: it would have a most healthy influence upon the patrons of the schools, awakening an interest in their prosperity never before experienced, since their children in the most impressible period of their history, could be prepared *at home* for college. It would awaken a desire to secure the best teachers for these responsible positions, and create a willingness to *pay* them as they deserve. It would bring the University to the knowledge of the people, and fasten it to their affections, and greatly increase the number of its students; it would give a needed stimulus to many boys and girls to seek a higher culture, offering them an honorable reward for their application and scholarship; it would help lift the standard of all the graded schools in the state, and complete the unity of our whole educational system; and lastly, it would have a most beneficial reactionary influence upon successive legislatures, making them not only just, but generous in their attitude toward the University."

These ideas were discussed with some of the leading educational men of the State, including principals of our public schools, the President, Faculty and Regents of the University. Nearly all

Carrie I. Bloom	Monroe Graded School.
Anson C. Prescott	Plymouth Graded School.
Fannie E. West	Milwaukee High School.
Everis H. Hayes	Waterloo Graded School.
Frank Challoner	Omro Graded School.
Emmet R. Hicks	Omro Graded School.
Ira E. Howard	Omro Graded School.
Homer S. Daniels	La Crosse Graded School.
William J. McElroy	Berlin Graded School.
Charles B. Wilcox	Berlin Graded School.
Albert S. Ritchie	Racine High School.
James B. Curtis	Portage Graded School.
William Netzer	Portage Graded School.
Charles S. Schœnmann	Horicon Graded School.
Cora L. Field	Boscobel Graded School.

Eighteen counties are represented by these forty-seven students, viz: Columbia, Dane, Dodge, Eau Claire, Grant, Green, Green Lake, Jefferson, Juneau, La Crosse, La Fayette, Milwaukee, Racine, Rock, Sauk, Sheboygan, Walworth and Winnebago.

XXIV.—CO-EDUCATION.

In my Report for 1870, I earnestly advocated the co-education of the sexes in the University, making use of the following language:

"While excellent facilities are afforded to ladies for acquiring an education in the Female College of the University, I cannot help believing that more thorough instruction would be given them, and the labor and expense of carrying on the Institution be greatly lessened if both sexes were generally to recite together.

The co-education of the sexes in the Collegiate Department, is no longer a matter of experiment. Its feasibility and success have been triumphantly demonstrated. The Iowa State University has pursued the plan for several years. I have been assured by the Professors of that University that the standard in deportment and scholarship among the gentlemen has been raised since its adoption. The Lawrence University, in our own State, has tried it with the best results. The Michigan State University the past year admitted ladies on terms of perfect equality with gentlemen in all its departments. Acting President Frieze and Professor Tyler, frankly state that the Faculty were generally opposed to their admission at the outset, but now claim that there is a revolution in sentiment among them, and that no class of students receives a more cordial welcome.

In giving utterance to these views, I am but expressing the conviction of the great majority of the friends of education, in our State and of the warmest friends of the University."

The board of regents passed the following resolutions on the subject, January 16, 1872:

"*Resolved*, That the distinctive features of a female college be maintained, by furnishing a separate education to females when preferred, but, that no student shall be debarred from electing courses of instruction or elective studies, that have been or may be established in any or all the departments of the University."

This resolution was amended January 31, 1873, so as to read as follows:

"*Resolved*, that the distinctive features of a separate female college be maintained, by furnishing a separate education to females and appropriate courses of instruction therefor; but female students, at their own request, or that of their parents or guardians, shall be allowed to enter classes in common with other students; all classes and departments being open alike to both sexes."

It will be seen by these resolutions that while a female college, as such, is maintained in the University for the education of those ladies who wish to recite exclusively with their own sex, opportunity is afforded every young woman who desires it, to recite with the opposite sex in all classes and in all departments of the University, and receive on graduation the appropriate collegiate degrees. I believe the prevailing sentiment among the young ladies is to recite with the gentlemen. This, in my judgment, is as it should be.

XXV.—SPECIAL STATISTICS.

Chapter 101 of the general laws of 1871 enacts that "it shall be the duty of the district clerk to classify those children who from defect of vision or of hearing or of intellect (under the heads of blind, deaf and dumb and idiotic), are incapacitated for instruction in the common schools, and report the same to the State Superintendent, who shall publish the same in his annual report."

Returns were received last year from fifty-eight counties. This year returns are made from all the counties except Ashland, Barron, Bayfield, Douglas and St. Croix, and all the cities except Beloit and Hudson. The figures for the two years are given below:

	1872.	*1873.*
Number incapacitated for instruction from defect of vision....	109	163
Number incapacitated for instruction from defect of hearing..	289	298
Number incapacitated for instruction from defect of intellect..	377	376

Attendance and Non-Attendance of Children of Certain Ages.

Section 2 of chapter 169 of the general laws of 1870 requires that each district clerk, in addition to the returns already provided for as to school attendance, shall report "the number of children attending school during any part of the year, between the ages of four and seven, seven and fifteen, fifteen and twenty, respectively; and to this end he shall require and instruct the teachers to enter the ages of all children attending school in the register; he shall also ascertain and report the whole number of children between the ages named, residing in the district on the last day of August previous to making such report."

The results obtained for the past two years are as follows:

	1872.	
No, of children between 4 and 7 years of age............	100,821	104,895
No. of children between 7 and 15 years of age...........	209,859	218,003
No. of persons between 15 and 20 years of age	100,482	105,927
Total number between 4 and 20 in the state..........	411,162	428,825
No. between 4 and 7 who have attended school	53,405	52,016
No. between 7 and 15 who have attended school	158,246	151,057
Number between 15 and 20 who have attended school....	64,589	45,055
Total No. between 4 and 20 attending school	276,240	248,128

As there has been an increase in the whole number attending school, the apparent decrease, as shown by these figures, must be explained on the supposition of defective or careless returns.

XXVI.—REPORTS OF PROGRESS FROM COUNTY SUPERINTENDENTS.

The following gratifying evidences of progress, are condensed from the reports of county superintendents:

In regard to schools, school-houses and school matters in general, I am able to report a steady progress. Three new creditable school-houses have been built; money has been raised in several districts with an intention of building next year; obstacles to improvements have been removed in two instances by dissolving a school district and annexing the parts to adjoining school districts re-forming new districts. My constant attention and perpetual working in such matters have everywhere accomplished at least partial and preliminary results.—L. Kessinger, *Superintendent of Buffalo County.*

We have many good, zealous and energetic teachers who are alive to the responsibilities of their profession, and strive to discharge their duties as becomes intelligent and conscientious instructors, but it cannot be denied that we have too many whose literary attainments and whose skill in the art of teaching are quite indifferent; that we have too many whose efficiency is much impaired in consequence of a slavish use of the text book in hearing recitations; that we have too many who make little or no use of such aids in teaching as the globe, outline maps, blackboard, etc. Our good teachers, however, outnumber the poor ones, and I hope the time is not far distant when Columbia county will not have an indifferent, a careless or an indolent teacher in one of her schools. * * * * We close, hoping that the coming year may prove equally fruitful in progress with the which year has closed.—L. J. BURLINGAME, *Superintendent of Columbia County.*

In regard to the work in and of the schools the past year, on the whole it has been quite satisfactory. District boards have manifested a commendable interest in securing well qualified teachers, and in sustaining them. There have been exceptions, of course, where pecuniary or personal interests have induced the employment of teachers of low grades; but in such cases the sentiment of the districts has been against the action of the boards. Teachers have exhibited a praiseworthy desire to be better instructed in the duties of their high calling, and many have made the art of teaching a careful study. —W. H. CHANDLER, *Superintendent of Dane County, 1st District.*

I am happy to say that the condition of our public schools, as a whole, is prosperous. By close attention to the examination of teachers, and an effort to raise the standard of qualification, a new stimulus has been imparted to those who were successful, by thus withdrawing unworthy competitors from the field.—Rev. A. KIDDER, *Superintendent of Eau Claire County.*

I do but simple justice to the teachers under my supervision, when I say that as a body they are faithful, earnest and conscientious workers, in what they believe to be an honorable and responsible calling. Fully conscious of the importance of the work it is theirs to do, they have been eager to learn, and prompt to adopt, any improved method of imparting instruction, and earnestly desirous of being fully up to the times; and thus I have ever found them ready and willing to receive advice and adopt my suggestions. The people of the district, as a whole, are by no means indifferent to the paramount importance of good schools, and with rare, and, I hope, decreasing exceptions, are willing to liberally support schools, when they can see an adequate return for the outlay.—W. L. O'CONNOR, *Superintendent of Fond du Lac County, 1st District.*

It is the teacher that makes the school. The employment of good teachers secures good schools; but the employment of poor teachers insures poor schools. In Grant county the people are year by year becoming more sensible of the fact, and more anxious to employ good teachers only, and to have good schools.—W. HOLFORD, *Superintendent of Grant Co.*

I think I may safely say that our teachers are growing better and better from year to year, and that some of the inefficient are giving way to a better class. A great amount of ambition is manifested on the part of the young teachers, to improve in their standing from year to year, and our high schools have adopted a commendable course in giving time to special preparation, out of the common course of study, with a view to being put in practice in the country schools.—D. H. MORGAN, *Superintendent of Green County.*

Some of our teachers are deficient in scholarship and ability to teach; a larger number fail in method rather than in a knowledge of books; a considerable number are well qualified in all respects. Nearly all are making honest efforts to improve, and it is safe to predict that in a few years this county will be as well supplied with competent teachers as many of the more populous and wealthier counties of the state.—MICHAEL KIRWAN, *Superintendent of Manitowoc County.*

The schools have not retrograded during the year. I trust they have advanced, as a great many teachers are candidates for the office of County Superintendent, which ought to be a sure sign of progression.—MAURICE MORIARTY, *Superintendent of Fond du Lac Co., 2d District*

It is a source of satisfaction to note improvements in the qualifications of our teachers, and a general disposition among them to take advantage of every opportunity offered to advance their standing and better fit them for their work.—S. D. FORBES, *Superintendent of Marquette County.*

Upon submitting this, my fourth annual school report, it affords me pleasure to state that the educational interests of this county present a far more encouraging appearance than they did four years ago.

Several elegant and commodious school buildings have been erected, which are an honor and an ornament to the communities, by whose wise, public liberality they have been built.

Our schools, generally speaking, are under the supervision of experienced and efficient teachers—teachers who seem to appreciate the responsibility of their high and holy calling.

Appropriations for school purposes are far more liberal than formerly; most of the districts maintaining school nine months during the year, while teachers' wages have advanced about 25 per cent.—H. W. GILKEY, *Superintendent of Oconto County.*

It is with pleasure I can say that good progress has been made in educational matters. Improvements have been made in buildings, better apparatus, etc., provided. Many of our best teachers are striving for higher grades of scholarship, and their work in the school-room shows a corresponding excellence.—GEO. SKEWES, *Superintendent of Racine County.*

Having thus briefly brought to your notice the condition of the different parts of the educational field, I would state, in conclusion, that while there is very much to be reformed, there is something upon which we may justly congratulate ourselves. Though the condition of the schools is far from satisfactory, there is no spot in the county so wild, so barren or so isolated that it has no school accessible to its occupants. While there are many teachers destitute of both learning and skill, there is a large number who honor the calling they have chosen. While there is a state of ignorance and indifference regarding public education that at times discourages effort and disheartens the laborer, there is yet on the other hand a degree of intelligence and wisdom that is full of promise.—J. H. TERRY, *Superintendent of Sauk County.*

XXVII.—COMPULSORY EDUCATION.

I have discussed this subject at length in my special report, to which I would call your attention. The conviction is becoming quite general among the most careful and conservative thinkers and educators in our country, from the alarming statistics of illiteracy given by the last census, that compulsory education, in some form or other, is an absolute necessity for the safety of our republican institutions. I have been compelled, from the evidence bearing upon the matter which I have been able to gather, to arrive at the conclusion that it is not only perfectly legal, but desirable, to place among our statutes a law requiring all the children of the state to be educated in the rudiments of knowledge, in the public schools *or elsewhere.*

I subjoin the opinions of some of our county superintendents:

With the statistics of the United States Commissioner of Education before them, it is a wonder how any Legislature in this age of the world can refuse to enact laws for the compulsory education in the English language of all children, white or black, Chinese or Indian, or anything else that claims to be human. This, with the moral and religious teaching that should accompany it, is the best and the only civilizing influence that will ever secure national safety and true prosperity. The great mistake of the nation has been in allowing the Indians, or any foreign tribe who make a stay in our land, to live in ignorance of our language or the advantages of schools.—Rev. A Kidder.

The safety of our free institutions demands that this evil of non-attendance shall be met, in some way. Our present school system does not do it. If a compulsory law will, let us have it by all means. Parental ignorance and indifference should not be allowed to deprive children of their most valuable inheritance, and put in jeopardy our free government. Were only the welfare of the individual at stake, we might question the propriety of interposing legal enactments, but as the worm of illiteracy is gnawing at the very foundation of our government, it becomes a proper subject for legislation. It is not expected by the most sanguine advocates of the law that it will confer the boon of education upon all, but it will do something in the right direction. The trite adage in which some objectors sum up their conclusions as to the utility of such a law:—"You may lead a horse to water, but you cannot make him drink,"—may be true as regards some, but it is no reason why those who do thirst for knowledge should not have the opportunity given them to drink.—S. D. Forbes.

XXVIII.—SUGGESTIONS OF COUNTY SUPERINTENDENTS.

I submit a few hints and suggestions from county superintendents respecting the needs, etc., of our schools.

In reporting the number of days school has been taught by a qualified teacher, clerks of joint districts have been required to report to the town clerks of all towns in which the district is situated. In a great number of cases the number of days taught in a given town are doubled, trebled, or quadrupled by incorporating all these reports, which cover the same districts, in several cases. To obviate this, district clerks might be required to report "yes" or "no" to the question "Has a school been maintained five or more months?" in all reports, except to the town clerk of the town in which the school-house is located.

In concluding this matter, I would say, that if teachers were required by law to make, he beginning of each term immediately succeeding the time of making t:e annual report by the district clerk, a roll of the scholars attending school in the district during the year, which would show their age, sex, and number of days attending during each month of school throughout the year, and each teacher employed during the year were required to add to this roll the name, age, sex, and monthly attendance of any *new*, as well as that of all scholars already enrolled, it would so facilitate the labor of the clerk in making his report, as to insure both promptness and correctness.—W. H. CHANDLER.

STATISTICS.—My statistical report, already forwarded to the department, was very unreliable in many respects. The only way to remedy this evil which every superintendent has to contend with, in my opinion, is for the legislature to pay district clerks for their labor, and then compel them to re port as they ought.—L. J. BURLINGAME.

Mostly for statistics you are referred to the annual report. As usual, the annual report is in many respects imperfect, though *much* labor has been expended upon it, and great pains taken to make it as correct as possible. The fact is, the majority of our district and town clerks make very incomplete and incorrect reports.

THE REMEDY.—It is my firm belief that the adoption of the "Township System" would secure to us much more reliable reports, as well as a great improvement in regard to school supervision, etc. I hope our legislature will take the pains to examine carefully the "Township System," and, if approved of, let them cause its adoption throughout the state, and not leave it optional with the towns. Probably it will not be adopted universally or even gener, ally by the voluntary act of the towns during the next century.—L. M. BENSON.

XXIX.—NORMAL SCHOOLS.

From the very full report submitted by the President of the Board of Regents of Normal Schools, found in another part of this report, it will be seen that the three Normal Schools are in excellent condition, ably manned and crowded with students.

Wisconsin may justly be proud of them.

XXX.—NEEDED LEGISLATION.

In my judgment the following legislation is necessary for the greater efficiency of our school system:

1. A school should be maintained for *eight* months or more, instead of *five*, as now required by law, to enable districts to draw from the income of the school fund.

2. Clerks of joint school districts should report the number of children, etc., to the town clerk only in which the school house is situated.

3. A limited State Certificate for two years should be issued to all persons graduating in the one year's course at the normal schools, said certificate to be subject to annulment as other certificates are by county superintendents.

4. A law requiring all children of the state to be instructed in the rudiments of the common English branches.

5. Compensation to District Clerks.

CONCLUSION.

During the past year I have either visited schools or delivered public addresses and attended institutes in the counties of Calumet, Columbia, Dane, 1st District; Dane, 2d District, Dunn, Grant, Jackson, Jefferson, La Fayette, Milwaukee, Monroe, Richland, Rock, 1st District; Rock, 2d District, Sauk, Sheboygan, Waukesha, Walworth and Winnebago.

I have traveled over twelve thousand miles in the discharge of my official duties. This outside work has been pleasant, though arduous.

I have endeavored, during my continuance in office, to carry out both the letter and the spirit of the law, which requires the Superintendent of Public Instruction to visit, as far as practicable, each county in the state, and awaken an interest among the people in the cause of education. I believe this to be one of the most important duties demanded of him. In this way alone can he become fully informed of the educational needs of the state, and of the best methods of meeting them.

I take occasion, in this my fourth and last report, to express my profound thanks to the friends of education in Wisconsin who have so faithfully aided me in caring for the interests of its common schools.

I would also specially express my hearty thanks to my faithful friend and co-laborer, the Rev. J. B. Pradt, Assistant Superintendent of Public Instruction, for the invaluable services he has rendered me in the laborious duties of the office.

Through the cordial co-operation of these friends, substantial progress has been made in every department of our great educational work, under my administration. The University of Wisconsin has been enjoying a greater degree of prosperity than ever before. The course of study has been extended in most of the graded schools of the State, to meet the requirements for admission into the college classes. The normal schools have increased in numbers and efficiency. The institute work has been thoroughly systematized. Many of our teachers have received State certificates after a most thorough examination. A gratifying *esprit du corps* has been observable among the rank and file of the profession, at the institutes and in the school room. A general willingness has been manifested by the people to bear the burden of taxation for the erection of new and commodious school houses, for the repair of old ones and for the payment of teachers.

To you, gentlemen, and to the people of the State, to whose common schools and University I owe a lasting debt of gratitude, I commend all our educational interests. May the blessing of God rest upon every effort put forth in their behalf.

SAMUEL FALLOWS.

SPECIAL REPORT

ON

COMPULSORY EDUCATION.

OFFICE OF SUPERINTENDENT OF PUBLIC INSTRUCTION,
MADISON, August 31, 1873.

GENTLEMEN OF THE LEGISLATURE:

In accordance with the accompanying resolution, I herewith respectfully submit my report on compulsory education.

WISCONSIN LEGISLATURE,
ASSEMBLY CHAMBER, MADISON, Feb. 27, 1873.

Hon. SAMUEL FALLOWS, *Sup't Public Instruction:*

SIR: I am directed to inform you that the Assembly has adopted Resolution No. 21, A.

WHEREAS, The general education of the masses is compatible with the advancement and the spirit that should characterize free institutions, and consequently it is the duty of the state to provide all proper means for the education of its people; therefore,

Resolved, That the Superintendent of Public Instruction be requested to make such investigations and inquiries as he may deem proper in relation to the best means, whether compulsory or otherwise, to advance the cause of education, and report the result of such investigations to the next legislature, with such recommendations as he may see fit.

I am, yours respectfully,

E. W. YOUNG, *Chief Clerk.*

From my last annual report I reprint my views on the general question of the necessity and the legality of compulsory measures:

"The alarming fact confronts us that a large number of the children of our state are not to be found in any public or private school during the year. Some are kept at home by parents on the plea that their services are needed for the sustenance of the family; others on account of the criminal indifference of their natural protectors. Neglected children are roaming the streets or playing in the alleys of our cities and larger towns, and are becoming apt scholars in all kinds of vice. Their school hereafter will be the jail and the prison. The state, for its own protection, will take care of them in their prematurely mature life of wickedness. The question arises, what shall be done with these children, soon to be the 'dangerous classes' in society? Cannot the state justly *compel* their attendance upon the *one* school as well as upon the *other?* Cannot it take measures to *prevent* as well as to *punish* crime? Is it not its solemn and imperative duty so to do? Has not every child a *right* to an education to fit it for the responsibilities and duties of good citizenship? If so, what right has the parent, through his ignorance or selfishness or indifference, to interfere with the exercise of that right? Ought not the state to step in and protect the child in his right in this respect against the parent, just as it would if the parent were to brutally ill treat the child? If the payment of taxes for educational purposes is made compulsory, should not education be compulsory? I think there can be no question on which side the *logic* of the argument is to be found. The state clearly has the right to enact a compulsory law if the penalty of the law shall fall upon the parents and not upon the children."

EDUCATION AND CRIME.

The following facts from the report of the Commissioner of Education, Gen. John Eaton, Jr., show the importance of adopting compulsory measures in *some form* or other:

"I. At least eighty per cent of the crime of New England is committed by those who have no education, or none sufficient to serve them a valuable purpose in life. In 1868, twenty per cent, of all the prisoners in the country were unable to read and write. From three to seven per cent. of the population of the United States committed thirty per cent. of all our crime, and less than one-fifth of one per cent. is committed by those who are educated.

"III. As in New England, so throughout all the country, from eighty to ninety per cent. have never learned any trade or mastered any skilled labor; which leads to the conclusion that 'education in labor bears the same ratio to freedom from crime as education in schools.'

"III. Not far from seventy-five per cent. of New England crime is committed by persons of foreign extraction. Therefore, twenty per cent. of the population furnishes seventy-five per cent. of the criminals. It is noticeable, however, that 'the immigrant coming hither with education, either in schools or labor, does not betake himself to crime.'

"IV. From eighty to ninety per cent. of our criminals connect their courses of crime with intemperance.

"V. In all juvenile reformatories, ninety-five per cent. of the offenders come from idle, ignorant, vicious homes. Almost all children are truant from school at the time of their committal; and almost all are the children of ignorant parents. These children furnish the future inmates of our prisons; for 'criminals are not made in some malign hour; they *grow*.'"

"In the face of these facts, what can be said but this:

"Ignorance breeds crime; education is the remedy for the crime that imperils us.

"The entirely uneducated man is nine times as likely to be a criminal as the average of the men who have been taught, and more than one hundred times as likely to become a criminal as he who has been thoroughly educated."

ILLITERACY IN WISCONSIN.

According to the census of 1870, the number of inhabitants of all races, ten years and over, unable to write, in Wisconsin, was 55,441, of whom 41, 328 were foreign born.

"*Age, Sex and Race of Illiterates.*—Of the 54,845 white illiterates, 9,274 were from 10 to 15 years old, of whom 5,030 were males and 4,244 females; 5,264 were from 15 to 21 years old, of whom 2,777 were males and 2,487 females; 40,307 were 21 years old and over—17,637 males and 22,670 females. Of the 360 colored illiterates 19 were from 10 to 15 years old—12 males and 7 females; 41 were from 15 to 21 years old—25 males and 16 females; 300 were 21 years old and over, of whom 185 were males and 115 females; 101 male and 135 female Indians were also reported."

As far as can be ascertained there are between forty and fifty thousand children in our state who did not attend school during the past year.

HISTORY OF COMPULSORY EDUCATION ABROAD.

I reprint from the same report a brief historical sketch of compulsory education in foreign countries:

"For a clearer understanding of this subject it is well to inquire what nations have adopted the compulsory system, and how has that system been enforced. It is not a novel expedient, nor the decree of despotic governments. It dates from the era of Solon, and is incorporated in the legislation of the most enlightened European nations. For the facts in this sketch we are indebted again to the essay of Doctor Gottschick and the report of M. Duruy

The laws prescribed 'that every man should have his son instructed in music and gymnastics.'

"In Sparta, according to the laws of Lycurgus, the state took the education of children, from their seventh year, entirely into their own hands.

"Charlemagne founded primary schools and compelled the children of all his courtiers to attend them.

"Martin Luther said, 'It is my opinion that the government ought to *compel* parents to send their children to school.' It is a characteristic of the reformers that they considered the school an essential instrument in the service of God. Attendance upon catechism was compulsory, and for every child found in the street, during the hour of religious instruction, the parents had to pay a fine, which went into the poor-box.

"In 1649, the synod of Würtemburg made attendance at school compulsory under the penalty of a fine. In 1787 this attendance was required from the sixth to the fourteenth year.

"In Saxony the law of 1778 made attendance at school compulsory from the fifth to the fourteenth year, and provided that children who went to service before their fourteenth year should attend school two hours daily at the expense of their masters. The law of 1804 was more stringent, and imposed a heavy fine upon delinquents. A similar law was enacted in Bavaria in 1802.

"In France, says M. Duruy, "Compulsory education is ancient and of noble origin." In 1795 it was ordered that all children throughout the republic should be compelled to attend school; but this regulation, like many others during that sad period, remained a dead-letter, nor was it revived by the admirable law of 1833, nor the more recent law of 1850. The attendance at school is consequently very irregular, nor was the late Emperor able to prevent it. The consequence of this has been signally exemplified by late events.

"In Prussia, compulsory education has been most efficiently enforced and its practical results can be easily computed. The first attempt at more regular attendance at school was in 1658. This was repeated in 1816. By a regulation of August 12, 1763, it was ordered that all children be sent to school from the fifth to the fourteenth year. This order was revived in 1794, and in 1819 severe penalties were imposed. The result is that in 1864, out of three million children of school age, only 130,000 did not attend school, and an officer at Potsdam, having in charge the examination of recruits for the army, received in the space of twelve years only three soldiers who could neither read nor write. In country districts where children live farther than two miles from the school, they are not obliged to attend before the completion of the sixth year; when the distance is greater, not before the seventh year. Similar laws prevail in all the German States.

"In Sweden, Norway, and Denmark, parents who do not send their children to school are subject to a fine, and either from this cause or the conviction of the value of education, out of 385,000 Swedish children in 1862, only 9,131 were uninstructed.

"In all Switzerland, except four cantons, education is obligatory. In Zurich the school-age extends from five to sixteen, inclusive. Not only parents and guardians, but also masters of trades are required to have children attend school. In the canton of Berne, young soldiers must read, write and solve ordinary examples in arithmetic, or attend school in the barracks. Ordinarily not more than three or five in a hundred are of this class. M. Baudouin, the French school commissioner to Switzerland in 1865, says: "When one travels in this country, not to admire the beauty of the landscapes, but to examine its institutions, and seek counsel in results, he has no need to look at territorial limits to know that he is passing from a canton in which education has been neglected, into another in which it has been carefully cultivated."

"In view of the amount of gross ignorance that has so far prevailed in England, the two extremes of the most stolid ignorance and the highest culture, existing in close contact, many influential Englishmen have publicly declared that the remedy is to be found in compulsory education.

Rev. Dr. Ryerson, chief superintendent of pnblic instruction for the Province of Ontario, in his annual report of 1871, comments as follows upon the compulsory features of the Ontario school law:

"3. The provison of the recent school law of Ontario on this subject is the legitimate consequence of the adoption of the principle of free schools; for if every man is to be taxed, according to his property, for the public school education of every child in the land, every taxpayer has a right to claim that every child shall be educated in the various branches of a good English education; otherwise the law is a mere pretext for raising money by taxation under false pretences.

"4. And if every man is to be taxed according to his property for the education of every child, and if every child has a right to school instruction, some provision was needful to secure both the ratepayer and the child against the oppression and wrong which might be inflicted by an unnatural guardian or parent. Society at large, no less than the parties immediately concerne requires this protection; and the protecting provision of the law, in this respect, is milder and more guarded than the corresponding one in other countries where public school education is provided for and guaranteed to every child in in the country. According to the new act, no parent or guardian is liable to punishment whose wrong against society and his youthful charge is not wilful and criminal. If such a protection in this mild and guarded form is found, on trial, to be insufficient for the purposes intended, a more stringent one will no doubt be enacted by the legislature hereafter."

METHODS OF COMPULSION.

Through the kindness of Thomas Greene, Esq., I have been enabled to procure a copy of the report of Jno. F. Moss, Esq., clerk of the Sheffield school board, England, embodying the results of his observations during an educational tour on the Continent. I quote from the report as follows:

"No one needs to be told that in Germany education is compulsory. The laws on the subject are varied in different states, and the power of compelling the attendance of children at school is not exercised uniformly.

"But something more has been achieved than the mere efficient working of compulsion. The duty of parents to attend to the education of their children has been thoroughly instilled into the minds of the people. In Prussia, people laugh at the idea of being *compelled* to send their children to school, because scarcely anyone thinks of disregarding what he knows to be a primary duty. Negligent parents are happily rare exceptions in at least the more important communities. Active intelligent citizens are to be met with in Saxony who would have difficulty in giving you the merest notion of the working of a compulsory system of education, because they have never seen compulsion applied.

"I have been astonished, on looking at registers of school attendance in some of the common schools, to note how few cases of absenteeism, without reasonable excuse, are recorded. One of the directors of a public elementary school in a populous manufacturing district, assured me that out of 2,500 scholars scarcely a score were away without proper reasons having been given, and he showed me large folio pages of the class registers with less than a dozen absences marked for which sufficient excuses had not been furnished. One instance was given in which a boy had only been absent ten times during the whole of the eight years of his school career.

"In Berlin, however, I visited a large "Gemeinde schule," where out of 900 girls nearly 50 on the average absented themselves from the girls' department three days out of the six in the week, and out of this number twenty-five were often on the delinquent list. The explanation given by the teacher was that they were the older girls, who were much wanted to assist their mothers in household duties. In the boys' department the proportion of irregular scholars did not seem so great. In this case it should be mentioned the school has not been long established, and the steady enforcement of the law is leading to a gradual diminution of absenteeism. An average attendance of 95 per cent. seems almost incredible in England; yet it is not uncommon to find such results recorded in German schools.

"The methods of dealing with delinquents are diversified, and the penalties inflicted upon negligent parents seem to be generally heavier than are provided for in England. The fine is usually doubled for a second offence, and a third conviction is in some states followed with imprisonment. Happily such extreme measures are seldom rendered necessary.

"The police in many of the communes are entrusted with the duty of enforcing the attendance of children at school during the prescribed periods; but usually complaints of neglect must in the first instance come from the school director or teacher, and only when his remonstrances or warnings prove unavailing are other measures resorted to.

"An officer called a "School Messenger," who is required to be a man of tact and judgment, is attached to each of the large schools in Saxony. His duty is to look up absentees and report to the director, who, if he deems it necessary, sends for the parent and administers a caution, which generally proves sufficient. But if a parent shows a disposition to evade the law the case is reported to the school board, of which the director is an ex-officio member, and it is afterwards taken before the magistrate. To show how seldom it became imperative that the magistrate should be appealed to, the director of the lowest elementary school in Chemnitz—and here is to be found perhaps as low a class of people as anywhere in Germany—stated, that from fifteen to twenty years' experience in that school, with about 2,000 children in attendance, he could only remember having put the law in force against negligent parents about ten or twelve times—in fact he began counting the cases on his fingers and could remember each distinctly, some of them being cases in which boys had been eventually sent to the "reformatory" because their parents could not exercise proper control.

"In some districts a child is not permitted to remove from one school to another without special permission; a proper discharge or recommendation from the school he is leaving being made a *sinequa non* before a boy can be transferred to any other school in the district. The police and district registrars supply to the various district schools the names of all children who ought to attend, and as one child after another attains school age, or is brought from another district, the names are added.

"Perhaps the best illustration of the Prussian plan of enforcing the attendance of children at school will be furnished by a brief description of the machinery employed for this purpose in Berlin. The directors of one of the public schools has considerately supplied me with a set of forms used, the object of which I will endeavor to explain. First the teacher communicates with the parent whenever he has reason to complain of a child's absence from school. This is perfectly understood as a warning of the consequences which must ensue in case of continued neglect. Should the admonition from the teacher prove ineffectual, a report is handed by the director of the school to the "Schul Commission" or School Board. Then the School Board take the case up, and three other warnings follow pretty closely one upon the other. From the Schul Commission recalcitrant parents are handed over to the "Schul Deputation"—a tribunal composed of Government Officials—who, upon neglect being duly proved, inflict the penalties imposed by law. The first offence is visited with a fine of 5 silbergroschen, and for the second offense the fine is 10 silbergroschen, the penalties being increased by 5 silbergroschen for each subsequent offense. In default of payment imprisonment follows.

"Directly a case of absenteeism or irregular attendance is reported to the Schul Commission, the name of the child must be entered by the teacher on what is called the "delinquent list," and a weekly statement of the number of attendances must be made on the prescribed form for the Schul Commission.

"It should be mentioned that when the absence of a child from school is first reported to the School Board, enquiry is immediately made as to whether he has simply been transferred to another school, and if this happens to be the case a record is made on a form provided for the purpose; all further proceedings being stayed, as it is then left for the teacher of the school to which the child has been removed to properly note the attendance, and report any irregularity in the ordinary course.

"If a child be partially exempted from the obligation to attend school, as in the case of girls of a certain age, whose parents are in need of their earnings, and who are shown to be beneficially employed in some useful occupation, a certificate is, after due consideration, granted to that effect, and attendance in the mornings only is required. Another form is provided for certificates of proficiency, which are granted to 14 or 15 years of age.

"The system necessarily involves a good deal of care and trouble on the part of the director or secretary of the school, but it appears to work very smoothly, and the results are reported to be satisfactory. I found in the case of one excellent girls' school (elementary) there were during last year about 4 per cent. of the girls attending the school on the delinquent list. But, on the other hand, 10 per cent. of the scholars never missed at all from any cause, whilst 50 per cent. attended *nearly* all the school meetings in the year.

"Other States have their peculiar plans of working, but they do not appear to differ greatly in the general features.

"In Saxony the fine imposed for a first offence amounts to about 2s. in English money, and it is increased in case of subsequent neglect; a third or fourth offence may be visited with imprisonment, without the option of pecuniary penalty. But the "reintents" are few. Through being long accustomed to the law parents have become so habituated to it that only in rare cases are the notices disobeyed which are given each Easter calling upon parents of children who may have attained the prescribed age during the preceding term to send them forthwith regularly to school. If through carelessnes the notices are disregarded by a few parents for a short time, the admonition of the teacher is usually all that is necessary to induce compliance without any necessity for recourse being had to the other authorities.

"For a little over 12½ years, Dr. E. Borneman (Königl. Sächs. Ministerial-in Schul Rath, Dresden,) formerly had charge of an important school, with about 1500 scholars in regular attendance, and during the whole period of his directorship not one case occurred in which punishment was found necessary to induce compliance with notices calling upon parents to send children to school. The learned doctor states, however, that fifty years ago, when the compulsory laws were introduced, there was considerable difficulty experienced in the mining districts before the people could be brought to see clearly the value of education; but in the towns of Saxony the change which has been fraught with such manifold benefits to the whole community was brought about.

"In the little Saxon duchies, and among the Protestants of Baden, the attendance of children at school is equally satisfactory. In Wurtumburg also the attendance is good; but in the schools of Bavaria not so regular.

"From 6 to 14 years of age is usually the period prescribed for the regular attendance of children at school 'full time,' though in some states the laws on this point have been recently extended. In some districts children from 6 to 8 or 9 years of age are only required to attend about half the time during which the older scholars are in attendance, whilst elsewhere the order of things is reversed, and children above 12 are permitted to work half time until they are 16 years of age.

"The Saxon laws on education have recently undergone revision, and now it is made imperative that a child shall have from 17 to 85 lessons per week, between the ages of 6 and 14 years, and that afterwards they shall attend school under a sort of half-time system for 6 lessons or hours per week in the evenings up to 17 years of age. The penalties for non-compliance with the laws range from 5 to 20 thalers.

"In Bavaria children must attend the ordinary school regularly up to 13 years of age, and then must follow a course of instruction in the Sunday schools or in the improvement schools, up to 17 years of age.

"Yet in the face of these stringent regulations as to school attendance—and in Germany, be it remembered, no laws are allowed to become a dead letter while they remain on the statute book—it is surprising how little one hears as to complaints by parents of hardship or irksomeness.

"The people themselves are in fact educated up to the point at which laws like these are accepted as becomes an age of enlightenment. The laws are backed up by the spirit of the nation; for more than two generations they have been thoroughly identified with the habits and thoughts of the people, and only criminals and vagabonds seem to dream of attempting evasion. Parents appear, as a rule, almost as little to think of depriving their children of physical food as of neglecting the duty of ensuring them the education which is of so much importance to them in the battle of life.

"A significant exemplification of the universality of education in Germany is furnished by the fact that out of the immense number of recruits for the united army of the Empire, enrolled in the year 1870, there were none who could not at least read or write, though some few were reported on account of 'Mangelhafte Schulbilding'—insufficient education."

COMPULSORY LAWS IN THE UNITED STATES.

I give below the text of the laws now in operation in Texas, Michigan and New Hampshire:

LEGISLATION IN TEXAS.

AN ACT to organize and maintain a system of public free schools. Approved April 24, 1871.

"SECTION 6. The board of school directors shall require the attendance on the public schools of their respective districts of all the scholastic population thereof, for a term of at least four months of each and every year; and should any of said scholastic population neglect or refuse to attend said schools, each and every parent or guardian of such child or ward neglecting or refusing to attend shall be deemed guilty of a misdemeanor, and upon trial and conviction thereof before any court of competent jurisdiction shall be fined in a sum not to exceed twenty-five dollars for each and every offense, and shall pay the costs of the prosecution; and all moneys collected for fines, under the provisions of this section, shall be paid into and become a part of the public school fund of the district where the penalty was incurred: *provided*, that when any child or ward of scholastic age may be shown to have received regular instruction from any private teacher having a proper certificate of competency, or when it may be shown that said child or ward was prevented by ill health from attending school, or that there was no public school within three miles of the residence of said child or ward, or that said absence was caused by reason of danger from hostile Indians, this shall exempt from the operation of the penalty contemplated by this section: *and provided further*, that nothing in this act shall be so construed as to compel the attendance of a child under ten years of age in the public free schools when there is no school established within one mile of the residence of said child or ward.

LEGISLATION IN MICHIGAN.

[Enacted and amended by the legislature at its session in 1871.]

AN ACT to compel children to attend school.

"SECTION 1. *The People of the State of Michigan enact*, That every parent guardian or other person in the state of Michigan, having control and charge of a child or children between the ages of eight and fourteen years, shall be required to send any such child or children to a public school for a period of at least twelve weeks in each school year, commencing on the first Monday of September, in the year of our Lord eighteen hundred and seventy-one, at least six weeks of which shall be consecutive, unless such child or children are excused from such attendance by the board of the school district in which such parents or guardians reside, upon its being shown to their satisfaction that his bodily or mental condition has been such as to prevent his attendance at school or application to study for the period required, or that such child or children are taught in a private school, or at home, in such branches as are usually taught in primary schools, or have already acquired the ordinary branches of learning taught in the public schools: *Provided*, In case a public school shall not be taught for three months during the year, within two miles by the nearest traveled road, of the residence of any person within the school district, he shall not be liable to the provisions of this act.

"SEC. 2. It shall be the duty of the director of every school district, and president of every school board within this state, to cause to be posted three notices of this law in the most public places in such district, or published in one newspaper in the township for three weeks, during the month of August in each year, the expenses of such publication to be paid out of the funds of said district.

"SEC. 3. In case any parent, guardian, or other person shall fail to comply with the provisions of this act, said parent, guardian or other person shall be liable to a fine of not less than five dollars nor more than ten dollars for the first offense, nor less than ten or more than twenty dollars for the second, and every subsequent offense; said fine shall be collected by the director of said district in an action of debt or on the case, and when collected shall be paid to the assessor of the district in which the defendant resided when the offense was committed, and by him accounted for the same as money raised for school purposes.

"SEC. 4. It shall be the duty of the director or president to prosecute any offense occurring under this act, and any director or president neglecting to prosecute for such fine within ten days after a written notice has been served on him by any tax-payer in said district, unless the person so complained of shall be excused by the district board, shall be liable to a fine of not less than twenty or more than fifty dollars, which fine shall be prosecuted for in the name of the assessor of said district, and the fine when collected shall be paid to the assessor, to be accounted for as in section three of this act."

LEGISLATION IN NEW HAMPSHIRE.

AN ACT to compel children to attend school.

SECTION 1. *Be it enacted by the senate and house of representatives, in general court convened,* That every parent, guardian, master or other person having the custody, control, or charge of any child between the age of eight and fourteen years, residing in any school district in which a public school is annually taught for the period of twelve weeks or more, within two miles of the nearest traveled road from his residence, shall cause such child to attend such public school for twelve weeks at least in each year, from and after the 1st day of September next, six weeks at least of which attendance shall be consecutive, unless such child shall be excused from such attendance by the school committee of the town, or the board of education, or the superintending school committee of such district, upon its being shown to their satisfaction that the physical condition of such child was such as to prevent his attendance at school for the period required, or that such child was instructed in a private school, or at home, for at least twelve weeks during such year, in the branches of education required to be taught in the public schools, or, having acquired those branches, in other more advanced studies.

"SEC. 2. The school committee of every town, and the board of education or superintending committee, of every district, shall cause to be posted in three of the most public places in each school district under their supervision, or to be published in some newspaper printed in the town three weeks successively, in the month of August annually, a notice of the provisions of this act, particularly calling the attention of parents, guardians, masters and others thereto. The necessary expense of posting such notice or making such publication shall be paid by the town or district whose committee incurs the same.

"Sec. 3. Any parent, guardian, master or other person violating the provisions of the first section of this act, shall forfeit and pay the sum of ten dollars for the first offense, and the sum of twenty dollars for the second and every subsequent offense, to be recovered in an action of debt in the name of the district within whose limits the penalty was incurred, by the school committee, board of education, or superintending school committee, having the supervision of the schools in such district, in any court of competent jurisdiction. All penalties recovered shall be paid to the district and added to the school money thereof.

"Sec. 4. School committees, boards of education, and superintending school committees, respectively, shall sue for all penalties incurred under the provisions of the preceding sections; and any school committee, board of education, or superintending school committee, upon whom a written notice has been served by any tax-payer, stating by whom, when, and how any such penalty has been incurred, who shall neglect for ten days after the service of such notice upon them to institute a suit for the recovery thereof, unless such penalty shall sooner be paid without a suit, or unless, upon investigation during that time, they shall be satisfied that no penalty has actually been incurred, shall forfeit and pay the sum of twenty dollars for each neglect, to be recovered by the selectmen of the town or the mayor and aldermen of the city in action of debt, in the name of the town or city, in any court of competent jurisdiction; such penalty, when recovered, to be paid to the district in which the original penalty was incurred, and added to the school money thereof.

"Sec. 5. This act shall take effect on its passage.

"Approved, July 14, 1871."

WISCONSIN.

The following bill was presented to the legislature, last winter, by Mr. Sayre, and was indefinitely postponed:

"A BILL to compel children to attend school.

"*The people of the state of Wisconsin, represented in senate and assembly, do enact as follows:*

"Section 1. That every parent, guardian, or other person in the state of Wisconsin, having control and charge of any child or children between the ages of eight and fifteen years, shall be required to send such child or children to a public school for a period of sixteen weeks in each school year, commencing on the first day of September, 1873, at least eight weeks of which shall be consecutive, unless such child or children are excused from such attendance by the board of the school district in which such parent or guardian resides, upon its being shown to their satisfaction, that his bodily or mental condition has been such as to prevent his attendance at school, or application to study for the period required, or that such child or children are taught in a private school or at home in such branches as are usually taught in primary schools, or have already acquired the ordinary branches of learning taught in the public schools. Provided in case a public school shall not be taught for four months during the year, within two miles by the nearest traveled road of the residence of any person within the school district, he shall not be liable to the provisions of this act.

"Sec. 2. It shall be the duty of the director of any school district to cause to be posted three notices of this law in the most public places in such district, one of which shall be on the door of the school house, or published in one newspaper in the township for three weeks during the month of August of each year, the expense of such publication to be paid out of the funds of said district.

"Sec. 3. In case any parent, guardian, or other person shall fail to comply with the provisions of this act, said parent, guardian or other person shall be liable to a fine of not less than five dollars, or more than ten dollars, for the first offense, nor less than ten nor more than twenty dollars for the second and every subsequent offense. Said fine shall be collected by the director of said district in the name of the district in an action of debt, or on the case, and when collected shall be paid to the treasurer of the district in which the defendant resided when the offense was committed, and by him accounted for the same as money raised for school purposes.

"Sec. 4. It shall be the duty of the director to prosecute any offense occurring under this act; and any director neglecting to prosecute for such fine for ten days after a written notice has been served upon him by any tax payer in said district, unless the person so complained of, shall be excused by the district board, shall be liable to a fine of not less than twenty dollars or more than fifty dollars, which fine shall be prosecuted for in the name of the treasurer of said district, and the fine when collected shall be paid to the treasurer to be accounted for as in section three of this act.

"Sec. 5. This act shall take effect and be in force from and after its passage and publication."

I append the views of distinguished educators in different states of the Union.

CONNECTICUT.

Hon. B. G. Northrop, Secretary of the Board of Education of the State of Connecticut, in his Annual report of 1872, says:

"Obligatory Education.—With growing faith in moral suasion as our main reliance in preventing absenteeism or reclaiming truants, I contend for the authority of the law, with its sterner sanctions to fall back upon in extreme cases. Where parental pride, interest or authority fail, and juvenile perverseness is otherwise incorrigible, legal co-ercion should be employed.

"My former objections to obligatory attendance were fully removed by observations recently made in Europe. Mingling much with plain people in Germany and other countries where attendance at school is compulsory, I sought in every way to learn their sentiments on this question. After the fullest inquiry in Prussia, especially among laborers of all sorts, I nowhere heard a lisp of objection to this law. The masses everywhere favor it. They say education is a necessity for all. They realize that the school is their privilege. They prize it and are proud of it. Attendance is voluntary in fact. Nobody seems to think of coercion. The law is operative, but it executes itself because it is right and beneficent, and commands universal approval. It is only the legal expression of the public will.

"Universal education, more than anything else, has fraternized the great German nation. It has improved her social life, ennobled her homes, promoted private virtue, comfort, and thrift, and secured general prosperity in peace. It has given her unequaled prestige and power in war. "Whatever you would have appear in a nation's life, that you must put into its schools," was long since a Prussian motto. The school has there been the prime agent of loyalty. Love of country is the germ it long ago planted in the heart of every child. The fruit now matured gladdens and enriches the whole land. Wherever that lesson is heeded, it will enrich the world. Devotion to fatherland is a characteristic sentiment of the German people. Shall such a people, with such a history, complain of compulsory attendance? This law itself has been a teacher of the nation. It has everywhere proclaimed the necessity and dignity of the public school. Kings and nobles and ministers of State have combined to confirm and diffuse this sentiment, till now it pervades and assimilates all classes.

"The absence of complaint about coercive attendance is not due, as some have supposed, to an enforced reticence or restraint. Proofs of the utmost freedom of speech abound. The Prussian military system is a grevious burden to the people. They dread it and bitterly denounce it. The law which takes every young man from his friends, his business and his home for three weary years of military service is hard, and is freely condemned. Many young families have left their fatherland for America, and thousands more are now planning to emigrate in order to escape this arbitrary conscription. But even the father who is most aggrieved by the army draft lauds the school draft.

"In various parts of Prussia and Saxony, I inquired of school directors, parents, and others, "Do you have any difficulty in executing the co-ercive law?" The answers were all substantially the same. "Many years ago," replied one, "there was some opposition. But the results of the law have commended it to all, and they obey it without complaint, and almost without exception." The present generation of parents having themselves experienced its advantages, are its advocates. Said a resident of Dresden, "A healthy child of school age can hardly be found in this city who has not attended school. Were the question of compulsory attendance to be decided to-morrow in Saxony by a plebiscite, it would be sustained by an almost unanimous verdict. Public opinion is now stronger even than the law. The people would sooner increase than relax its rigor." I nowhere learned of any recent cases of punishment for infractions of it. In many places I was assured that the penalty is practically unknown.

"8. It has been said that in some countries, without any coercive law, the attendance is as good as in Prussia or Saxony with such a law. This is simply a mistake. Holland has been cited as an illustration of this statement. But while the Dutch show commendable zeal for public schools, the attendance is not relatively as large as in Prussia, and illiteracy is by no means so rare as in Germany. But Holland *has*, indirectly, a system of compulsory attendance. It denies certain immunities and privileges and honors to the uneducated. The parents of children who are not instructed up to the required standard cannot receive relief from certain charitable institutions. The ban of legal condemnation falls upon them as truly, though not as effectively, as in Prussia.

"In Rotterdam, Hague, Amsterdam and elsewhere in Holland, I was assured that the working classes regard the school law as practically compulsory No one is permitted to teach even a private school who has not been duly "examined and approved," and the public supervision includes private as well as public schools.

"The tendency throughout all Europe is more than ever toward the recognition of the right and duty of the state to educate its entire population. Public sentiment, educated by recent events, now connects ignorance with crime, and poverty with individual and national weakness, as cause and effect. Sadowa taught Austria, and indeed all Europe, a salutary lesson. "Defeated in war, let it be our policy to excel in the arts of peace," became the national idea under the inspiration of Count Beust. There was no waste of zeal and strength in the mad cry of revenge, as now in prostrate France. Austria was not unwilling to learn from an enemy, and adopt the educational system of her conqueror. Her school system was reorganized and vitalized, and the principle of compulsory attendance made prominent. Education is obligatory in Denmark, Norway, Sweden, and also in Switzerland, except in the four small cantons of Geneva, Schwyz, Uri and Unterwalden. The total population of these four cantons is less than one seventeenth that of the whole nation. The new school law of Italy provides for both free schools and obligatory attendance, and includes the following important "civil service reform;"—"No one can be appointed to any State, Provincial or Communal office whatever, who cannot read and write."

"More than thirty years ago, Guizot, in his educational report to the French government, ably opposed obligatory education, but the recent experience of France has changed his views, and now he is its earnest advocate. That one of his advanced age, long among the foremost men of France both as a scholar and statesman, cautious yet positive in his convictions, a historian in his tastes and studies and therefore conservative, should now stoutly advocate that compulsory system which he so successfully opposed when himself the Minister of Public Instruction in 1833, is significant. The logic of events during the last forty years proves that the very system which he largely originated is unsuited to the wants of the nation and the age. M. Jules Simon, the Minister of Public Instruction, explained to me his plan for the reorganization of Primary Instruction, by making it both gratuitous and compulsory. The penalties were to be a maximum fine of one hundred francs and *loss of suffrage for three years.* After the year 1880, no citizen was to become a voter who could not read and write. But his bill is likely to fail at Versailles. While Thiers proposed an increase of eighty millions in the budget for the army, he said nothing for education. Even under Napoleon, fifteen times more was spent for the army than for education, including Primary, Secondary and Superior. The provisions for Superior education were liberal, and absorbed nearly one-half of the whole appropriation, leaving the primary schools most meager, both in quantity and quality. The Ultramontane party, now dominant, stoutly oppose both gratuitous and obligatory instruction, and little is likely to be done for the better education of the masses. The objection that obligatory instruction would challenge resistance as an act of usurpation, seems ludicrous in a land where military conscription and the most rigorous police surveillance are universal and unresisted. Gambetta as well as Guizot and the liberal republicans strongly advocate obligatory education. Even the Commune favored universal and compulsory education, as also do the majority of the Parisians still. The opposition comes from the clerical and conservative parties.

"The new school law of England *permits* all local Boards to enforce attendance. Public sentiment throughout England is now changing rapidly in favor of making compulsory attendance national and universal, instead of permissive. As one of many illustrations of this change, Rev. Canon Kingsley, formerly favoring non-compulsion, now advocates the compulsory principle. He says: "Let the public keep in mind this broad, ugly, dangerous, disgraceful fact; there are now one million three hundred and eighty thousand children in this kingdom who ought to be attending school, but who are not; 1,380,000 children growing up in ignorance, in a country which calls herself civilized, but which will be called by a very different epithet some two hundred years hence, unless she mends her ways right speedily."

He quotes a letter from Hon. O. Hosford, late Supt. of Public Instruction in Michigan, respecting the working of the compulsory law in force in that State:

"LANSING, May 31, 1872.

'Hon. B. G. NORTHROP:—

"*Dear Sir*—The compulsory law has not been in force long enough to give us any definite results. We have no *Official* reports since the law became operative, and all that I can say in reply to your inquiries will be to give the impressions I have received from personal observation and from the observations made by others.

"To your last inquiry: 'Has it increased the attendance, or the regularity of attendance, or both?' I would state that I have no doubt the next annual report will show a decided increase in attendance, and a much higher average of attendance. How great this will be can be determined only by the annual reports.

"2d. 'Has it aroused much opposition, or do the people accept it willingly?'

"I do not remember that any law, bearing upon the school interests of the State was ever received with such universal favor as this one. The press, without distinction of party, very generally commended it, and very few of the people were heard to speak against it.

"Very truly yours,
"ORAMEL HOSFORD,
"*Supt. Public Instruction.*"

IOWA.

Hon. A. L. Kissell, Superintendent of Public Instruction for the State of Iowa, in his Annual Report for 1870–71, says:

"This question has been discussed by the educationists of this country during the last decade. A law making school attendance obligatory has been enacted in some three or four states. The representative educators of the United States hold opposing views on the subject. At the National Teachers' Association that convened at Saint Louis, August, 1871, in the Superintendent's Section, the following resolutions were unanimously adopted:

"*Resolved*, That universal education is a public necessity, and the State has the full right to provide for and secure it.

"*Resolved*, That to secure universal education in this country, our present systems of voluntary school attendance should be *supplemented* by truant laws, reformatory schools, and such other compulsory measures as may be necessary to reach that class of youths now growing up in ignorance.

"This department of the Association was attended by some of the ablest educators from twelve different states. The resolutions show much unanimity on the subject in that body; and, to say the least, it was conservative, and preferred more fully to test the methods already in use to secure punctual school attendance, rather than resort to a system which has been employed in a country with different political institutions, and which was inaugurated at a period when physical force predominated more largely than at the present time. Then, indeed, comparing the Prussian compulsory system with the voluntary one of Holland, and that which prevails in some of the cantons of Switzerland, it becomes questionable whether the former has been as successful as the latter as an educational measure.

ILLINOIS.

Hon. Newton Bateman, Superintendent of Public Instruction in the State of Illinois, in his biennial report for 1871 and 1872 says:

THE SCHOOL SYSTEM ALREADY COMPULSORY.—I have said that our general free school laws, aside from the question of attendance, are themselves compulsory, They are, indeed, conspicuously so, through and through, and from beginning to end. Read the provisions contained in all state school laws, and note how largely the voluntary element is excluded; how mandatory their requirements, how absolute and peremptory the control. Note the plenary powers vested in boards of directors to make and enforce rules and regulations; their unlimited jurisdiction over the time, conduct and studies of pupils. See how these powers, armed with the authority of summary suspension or expulsion, accompany and environ the children everywhere—pursuing them through the streets; following them to their homes; dictating, even there, how a portion of their time shall be spent; penetrating the sanctuary of the domestic circle, modifying the hours of meals, and other household arrangements. Note how the state in its school laws, lays its authoritative hand upon the minds of the children dictating *what* they shall study, and what they shall not; upon their bodies, even to the infliction of stripes, for flagrant misdeeds; upon their manners and morals, by inhibitions and requirements, pains and penalties, for infractions of codes to which the assent of parents has not been asked; upon the very right to remain in school at all, authorizing suspension or expulsion at the absolute discretion of the school board, and that too, in this state, without any legal recourse or redress by action against the board.

"Notice with what surprising unanimity the supreme judiciaries of all the great states, of Massachusetts conspicuously, have sustained the maintenance and exercise, by school boards, of these extraordinary powers over the minds, bodies, time, manners, studies, rights and privileges of the youth of the country while in the public schools; how rarely the courts, supreme or inferior, have interposed against the prerogatives of teachers and school officers, declaring strict discipline and implicit obedience to be essential to the public welfare. Consider all these things, and that, with nearly equal unanimity, the people accept or acquiesce in this order of things, seeing it to be essential to the supreme end for which the schools exist, and then recall again the vehemence with which mild and considerate legislation like that to which I have referred, is assailed on account of its *compulsory* character." * * *

"Analagous Cases Cited.—The allegation that laws to secure attendance at school are unwarrantably invasive of private rights, and an abuse of the proper functions of government, is answered by reference to other notorious facts. Not to speak of the extreme war powers of the government, under order of which, husbands, fathers, sons and brothers are seized and hurried to the battle-field; property of every description taken for public uses, with or without the owner's consent; ships, railroads and telegraph lines laid under forced contributions, their rightful owners dispossessed, and government officers placed in command; the people and resources of the whole country regarded as merely so much material for the common defence—not to speak of these desperate but familiar example of coercion, there are multitudes of others, scarcely less arbitrary, which belong to times of peace:

"In periods of extreme danger or necessity, even sumptuary laws, of sweeping character, have been patiently submitted to, the right of the people, through their own constituted government, to protect themselves against imdending danger from *whatsoever* cause, not being denied. A law, denounced by some as of this odious class, is now in force in this state—a general, and stringently penal statute, concerning the sale of ardent spirits. It received a large majority of votes in each House of Assembly, notwitstanding its compulsory provisions and protests against its alleged invasions of personal liberty.

"So, let but the shadow of approaching pestilence touch our shores, and instantly the hygienic decrees of municipal legislatures and boards of health are as stern and absolute as the edicts of the Cæsars. Every incoming ship is brought-to at quarantine, as peremptorily as if she meditated a bombardment of the city; and if she should fail to respect the signal, a shot across her bows would be speedily followed by another *amidships*. The vessel may be returning from a long voyage—no taint of disease may in fact be on board—hundreds of weary people may be within a league of their homes—no heed is paid to them; *pestilence* threatens the great city, and the shall not proceed till inspected by the health-officer. Read the proclamations that ring through the city at such times, commanding all men everywhere instantly to remove every nuisance, and to cleanse and disinfect their premises. And upon the least reported neglect, see the officers and employes of the health brigade, hurrying and swarming through the city, searching the dark purlieus, entering every suspected house, breaking down doors if opposed, peering into sqalid nooks and corners, issuing peremptory orders, and *compelling* everybody, rich or poor, to obey the commands of the sanitary board—or else themselves doing what is required, and compelling the owners to pay the expense. Only last summer, when the death-rate in New York increased so frightfully under the dog-day heats of July, some twenty-five families, the papers say, were actually turned temporarily into the streets, driven out of their dwelling-places by the police, because the reeking dens in which they lived, imperiled the public health.

"So of the ordinary enactments concerning nuisances—the regulation of markets and market places—the obstruction of streets and alleys—the abuse of public parks and buildings—the erection of houses within the fire limits—rules and ordinances in respect to vaccination, and other things innumerable. They are all compulsory, sternly so; they all, in one sense, abridge the personal liberty of the individual citizen; but because the *public good demands them*, they are enforced. And now when the country is menaced by an evil which no quarantine can avert; when a malady is fastening itself upon the body politic that is beyond the skill of boards of health; when a shadow is settling down upon the country the end whereof may be political death, and the people see it and know it, and there is but one remedy, why should it not be applied?"

"An Objection Examined.—It is said that such laws cannot be enforced; that public sentiment is against them; that for a legislature to take a position a thousand moral leagues in advance of public opinion, and attempt to pull the people forward by a legal tow-line, is as chimerical as for a man-of-war to essay to take one of the islands of the sea into port, with cable and hawser—that, in the one case as surely as in the other, the lines will be snapped asunder by the strain, leaving the mass unmoved. That is partly a truism, and partly a begging of the question. So much of it as affirms that laws (admitting there may be such), to which a majority of the people are actively opposed, cannot be executed, is a truism; like saying that a pyramid cannot stand upon its apex. So much as assumes that public sentiment is hostile to such legislation, begs the question.

"It might be said that in a form of government like ours, the enactment of a law pre-supposes and implies popular approval thereof, legislation in this country being, as has already been repeated, but the crystallization of the popular will into legal forms. But, while there is not a little truth in that view, it may be considered as rather the argument of lawyers, and I do not care to press it—especially as other resources of reply are abundant. It is true, and must therefore be admitted, that measures may be introduced into legislative bodies and become laws, not only without the supporting column of the electors of the commonwealth, but in actual antagonism with the popular judgment. Instances are not wanting, indeed, where the printed statute has conveyed to the astonished masses their first knowledge of the matters contained therein. These are the laws which cannot, and some of which ought not to be enforced, having in them no vitalizing leaven of popular ideas and purposes, even if not conceived in mischief, and treason to the public weal. They belong, for the most part, to that infamous category, known in these days as 'ring legislation,' the work of rogues and demagogues, taking 'snap judgment' on the people by rushing their corrupt measures through, before even a rumor thereof can reach their outraged constituents—or else, by mercenary combinations and conspiracies, defying the people.

"But when a great public issue, intrinsically vital, far-reaching and aggressive, inviting criticism and assault, is separately and distinctly set before the people for examination aud discussion—when that issue *is* discussed, thoroughly and exhaustively, and the whole body of electors are made familiar with it, and choose their delegates to the legislature with reference to it—and when a clear majority of the known friends of that measure are elected, and the contest is transferred from the hustings to legislative halls, and is again fought triumphantly through, and promulgated as the law of the land, *that* law *is* the will of the people; intrenched in their convictions, representing their moral sentiments, and challenging their respect and support—*and it will be enforced.*"

INDIANA.

Hon. Milton B. Hopkins, Superintendent of Public Instruction of Indiana in his report for 1872, says:

"To reach these absentees, together with a large number of truants and vagrants, and bring them within the elevating and refining influence of our schools we have remaing one means, and only one—A COMPULSORY LAW. I am apprised that this word compulsory, as applied to education, grates harsh ly upon an American ear. Numerous objections are earnestly urged against it. It is asked; "Is not compulsory education incompatible with the parental and filial relations? Does not such a law interfere with the prerogatives and duties of a parent toward his child? Is there not a holy of holies within the family circle which civil authority should not enter under any pretense?" The shoes should be taken from our feet; for we are about to tread on sacred ground. Rights more precious than life belong to children. Protection, food, raiment, and an *education are inherent* rights of every child. To furnish these is the highest obligation of the parent, from which inability alone can excuse. It is no discretionary power conferred. It is a weighty obligation imposed.

"Puffendorf has well deposed upon this subject: "It is not easy to imagine or allow that a parent has conferred any considerable benefit upon his child by bringing him into the world, if he afterwards entirely neglects his *culture* and *education*, and suffers him to grow up like a mere beast, to lead a life useless to others and shameful to himself.""

"Kent says: "A parent who sends his son into the world *uneducated* and without skill in any art or science, does a great injury to mankind as well as to his own family, for he defrauds the community of a useful citizen and bequeathes to it a nuisance."

"Walker, in his American Law, also says: "There can be no doubt but this is a duty of the *highest moral obligation*. And he would be an unnatural parent that should be false to it, having the ability to perform it."

"Shall this obligation be made a *legal* duty? This question is assuming greater importance every year. It is pressing itself more closely upon the attention of the legislatures of the different states. A few have responded affirmatively; others hesitate. Indiana cannot remain silent much longer. Some moral obligations are enforced by legal sanctions, while others are not. Six of the ten moral commandments, written on tables of stone, are enforced by legal penalties in our own state; four are left with the conscince. The reason of the distinction is that when little or no public inconvenience results from the neglect of the moral obligation, the civil state will not interfere and demand obedience. The State will not interfere simply for the sake of moral obligation; but when its neglect or violation becomes the cause of great injuries and oppressive burdens to her, she will interfere for *her own sake*. It is both the right and the duty of the state to protect herself from serious mischef, and to do it by striking at the cause itself.

"Some of the most distinguished in the legal profession, and eminent educators, have fully endorsed this position. Blackstone says: 'Yet the municipal laws of most countries seem to be deficient in this point, by not constraining the parent to bestow a proper education upon his children. Perhaps they thought it punishment enough to leave the parent who neglects the instruction of his family to labor under those griefs and inconveniences which his family, so uninstructed, will be sure to bring upon him. Our laws, through their *defects* in this *particular cannot be denied*, have in one instance made wise provision for breeding up the rising generation.' He refers to the children of the very poor that are apprenticed by public law.

"Reeve, in his work on the domestic relations, says, speaking of compulsory education in reference to the poor: 'This law has by some been branded as tyranical, and as an infringement of parental rights. It is not the object of this work to enter into any defense of any particular law, but I have no doubt that this law has produced very astonishing effects; and to this is to be attributed that general knowledge of reading and writing so observable among the people of this state. For twenty-seven years of my life I was in the practice of law. During this period, in all the business which I transacted, I never found but one person that could not write and was obliged to make his mark.'"

KANSAS.

Hon. H. D. McCarty, State Superintendent of Public Instruction of the State of Kansas, in his Annual Report for 1871, says:

"For the safety of our common country; for the sake of our free institutions; for the well being and happiness of society, and for the salvation of our youth, there should be a law enacted requiring the education of every child. The people of the State expect it. Society demands it. The children of neglect and poverty, with outstretched arms and tearful eyes, plead for it. Shall the ears of our legislators be closed against these expectations, demands and entreaties? Shall the people be disappointed? Shall society continue to writhe under the curse of ignorance, and suffer gaunt poverty, and shame and villainy, unchecked, to stalk through the land, while licentiousnesss, concupiscence and debauchery only give place to open insult, violence and murder? Shall these children of neglect and poverty, for the want of an education, be forced into lives of wretchedness, shame and crime? Every ennobling, pure and holy sentiment of the heart of patriot, statesman and philanthropist revolts at the idea of such a deplorable state of affairs. And yet, is it not true? Whence comes the criminal, the highway robber, the burglar and the midnight assassin? The State must look after those hot-beds of treason, infamy and depredation, and check their growth. These children of misfortune must be schooled in youth, and taught the true objects and higher aims of life. Their hearts, affections and desires must be cultivated; honesty, frugality and temperance must be inculcated, and love of order, good government and rightful authority instilled into their wole being. They must be taught the use of the implements of industry, and that labor is honorable, that skill is profitable, and that diligence is the sure road to preferment, prosperity and happiness.

"A law compelling the daily attendance at school of every healthy boy and girl, for at least four months in the year, between the ages of seven and sixteen years, would have a most salutary effect. It is not only the imperative duty of the State to provide a full and free education, but to see that every son and daughter receive the benefit of that education. Then, and not till then, will pauperism and crime, penury and want, social discord and public strife, political perfidy and official corruption cease to distress the land."

KENTUCKY.

Hon. Z. F. Smith, Superintendent of Public Instruction of Kentucky, in his annual report of 1871, says:

"I have been somewhat surprised—I cannot say disagreeably—to find the sentiment in favor of a law of compulsory attendance of children upon the schools imposed in some form so general. I have thought the time premature, if it should ever come in our democratic country, to agitate this question, and have, therefore, ignored it so far as to consign it among the problems of the future. Public sentiment may be riper and more practical on the subject than I am aware of, and I allude to it here more in the spirit of venture and curious inquiry than to give any defined views upon the policy. Certainly, if a well prepared and conservative law compelling all parents to send their children to school, between the ages of seven and fourteen, as long as the free schools were open and accessible, were practicable to be enforced among our population, it would work great results towards diffusing and universalizing education among the masses. But our people are too impatient of the restraints of law to render such an one operative, unless it is supported by a strong approving public sentiment. Otherwise, it would be a dead letter, as many laws of our commonwealth now are. Let us have the discussion of its merits, and the expression of a ripe public sentiment, before we venture on new and untried experiments.

"But this same question has awakened inquiry, and is being agitated in other states. The policy has been fully tested in European countries, and to the great satisfaction of the friends of popular education there. It may seem somewhat harsh to enforce a law compelling parents to send their children to school. But it must be rembered that other parties have vested rights involved in the growing generations besides the parents. The children are most vitally interested, and the government to a large extent, as well as society. For the parent to neglect this fiduciary duty is a great wrong to all these, and a wrong *per se*. If the parent wishes to do right, and educate his child, the law is no terror to him. It only proposes to make the wrong-disposed do right. It is a restraint only only on the wrong intent."

LOUISIANA.

Hon. Thos. Conway, State Superintendent of Public Education of the State of Louisiana, in his report for the year 1871, says:

"How far or on what principle a parent is legally justifiable in withholding from his child the training and culture necessary to develop his higher nature, has not in this state been determined. Legal enactments, in lands whose claims to enlightenment are not so lofty as our own, make it a criminal offense. To maim the mind, to cripple the intellect, and to indurate those sensibilities which, when attuned by education, utter the grandest music of the soul, is elsewhere deemed at least as cruel as to maim the body. Dwarfed minds and imbruted hearts are considered as calamitous to a nation as deformed bodies, and the strong arm of law is extended to arrest and strike down the hand which should attempt to inflict such wrong upon the state. It is not a question of the parent's control of his child, but of the duty of a state to secure the prerequisites of intelligent citizenship to those who are to become its strength or its weakness.

"If socially no one may come between a parent's right and a child's duty, politically, no one, whatever his relation, may come between the state and its subjects. The parent and the child are alike subjects of the state, and the authority which legislates for the protection of the one is bound to do so for the protection of the other. If the law protects the parent's arm, it should protect the child's mind. If its strong arm would fall with sternest force on one who should condemn to barrenness the father's field, it should descend with equal strength on him who would consign to ignorance the mind of his child, stripping it of power, and converting its beauty into desolation."

MAINE.

Hon. Warren Johnson, State Superintendent of Common Schools of the State of Maine, in his Annual Report for 1871, says:

"COMPULSORY ATTENDANCE.—I have in previous reports urged the importance of *securing* the education of all the youth of the State. I have gone further than this, and affirmed the *right* and *duty* of the people of the State through their highest form of organization, the Legislature, to insure this result by pertinent and stringent enactments. I have based my argument upon the following points: 1st. The self duty on the part of the State to health, growth, progress, prosperity. 2d. The obligation of the State to the tax payer—the contract being that the former agrees to return educated citizens for the pecuniary consideration paid by the latter. 3d. The duty of the State to her youth, all of whom are necessarily under the bondage of their own inexperience and want of wisdom, and many of them in physical servitude to thoughtless and ignorant parents. The first announcement to the public of compulsory school attendance, excited a momentary feeling of repugnant opposition. This was very natural, as seeming to be an invasion of the immunities and sacred privileges of the family, and as being inconsistent with the established ideas of republican institutions. This first flush of thought, however, has died away largely before the second and sober convictions that prevention is better than the pestilence, knowledge better than ignorance, the school house a better institution than the jail, skilled, intelligent labor, more productive than mere brute force,—that the glory and destiny of the State are dependent upon the intellectual and moral development of the rising generations. Various other considerations are leading our people to the conclusion that every capable child in the State must be educated so as to fulfill at least the ordinary duties of citizenship. Other States are moving in the same direction. Maine has nearly 20,000 illiterates; the records of the past year show about that number of truants. The whole number of illiterates in the United States exceeds 6,000,000, or quite one-seventh of the population; while the balance of power at the last presidential election was entirely in the hands of voters who could not read the ballot deposited in the box by their own easy will. Necessarily, therefore, all the States must sooner or later turn their most thoughtful attention this matter. Will it not be better and easier for Maine to express her deteimination *now*, than hereafter, when her population shall be largely increased, especially in manufacturing centers, by the influx of a foreign and strange element?"

MARYLAND.

The school system of Maryland contains compulsory enactments. Rev. Dr. Bokkelen, Superintendent of Public Instruction, says, in his report of 1865:

"The design is to compel parents to send their children to school, and to prevent manufacturers from employing children who cannot read and write, unless they provide facilities for some moderate degree of instruction. It is only simple justice to those who are taxed to build school-houses and pay teachers that the benefit designed to be secured should reach its object. The child must be sent to school. This is the duty of parents and guardians but if they fail, it becomes the duty of the state. The law intimates no interference with parental rights. It guards the rights of the child when the parent neglects them."

The compulsory features of this law cannot have made much of an impression, for M. A. Newell, Esq., President of the Board of Education for that state, says, in his annual report for 1872, after discussing the subject of school statistics:

"Even if it should turn out to be as serious a business as we fear it is, we are not prepared to advocate a 'compulsory law,' though the current of opinion among philosophical educators seems to set in that direction just now. We have not yet done what we could to make schools attractive, interesting and useful; and until that is done, we believe that it is not prudent to use force. We would rather draw than drive; we would rather allure than compel. We do not deny the abstract right of a state to force a certain amount of intellectual food upon an unwilling stomach; but we hold that the first duty is to provide good food, and to create a healthy, natural appetite, which will render force unnecessary. Nevertheless, it is probable that, at least in Baltimore and some of the other cities and larger towns, some additional legislation is needed to provide the elements of education for 'idle, truant and neglected children.'"

The Board of Education of the State of Massachusetts, in their annual report for 1872, use the following language:

"3. Another improvement of vital importance is that which has for its object the securing of a more complete attendance at school of the children of school-age. For some years apparently not much progress has been made in that direction. Of what avail is it to build and equip commodious school-houses and employ accomplished teachers, if the children, through inability or perverseness, on their own part, or on the part of their parents and guardians, are prevented from attending the schools? The requirement of the law that every town and city shall maintain schools enough for all their children, for the period of six months in each year, certainly implies the obligation on the part of parents to send their children to school for the same period; for on no other ground could the legal requirement be justified. But it is quite certain that in practice we fall far below this standard.

"There are two ways in which this improvement might be promoted. The The one is, a more stringent system of compulsion, with the necessary agencies for its efficient administration. For want of such agencies the existing compulsory provisions are not carried into effect. Towns are required to appoint truant officers, but as there is no penalty annexed, the requirement is largely ignored. Besides, the towns and cities generally have no proper school or place of confinement and instruction to which they can send delinquents, as required by the statutes in case of conviction. The Board would therefore recommend that immediate steps be taken by the legislature to provide such schools or institutions in the localities where they may be needed. A revision and extension of the acts respecting compulsory education have been in former reports of the board recommended, and the recommendation is again renewed. The other mode referred to, of promoting the school attendance, has regard to the employment of an additional force of moral agencies."

John M. Brewster, School Superintendent of Pittsfield, Mass., in his communication to the secretary of the board, contained in the above report, says:

"PITTSFIELD.—Attendance at school, by the present law, is rendered compulsory for three months in each year for every child between the ages of eight and fourteen years, six weeks of which time shall be consecutive, with penalties for disobedience, except in certain special cases, while at the same time, the towns are required to maintain their schools at least six months in the year.

"Would it not be right and just to change the statute so as to require attendance for the whole period during which schools are required to be maintained, believing attendance upon the schools should be compulsory for the child, for the same period in which the maintenance of the schools is compulsory for the tax payers? It is in the virtuous intelligence of the citizen that the prosperity and security of the community rests. The rightfulness, then, of compulsory education cannot but be admitted. Did there not exist in almost every community a large and growing class of persons, not only ignorant themselves, but too willing to keep their children in ignorance, there would be no necessity, perhaps, of enforcing this right.

"Persistent irregularity in attendance is an injustice to the teacher, a positive injury to the school, as well as to the pupil; it shows inexcusable negtlec on the part of parents, and a disregard to cultivate in their child habits of punctuality; it tramples on the rights of school officers, who have a demand on the pupil's regular attendance, if that pupil is a member of the school at all. If the parent has any interest in the welfare of his child, any desire for his intellectual progress, any wish that he may become prompt and regular, it is hoped he will look thoroughly to this matter of irregular attendance at school and improve thereby.

"*Compulsory Education among different European Nations.*—An Italian journal, "L'Eco d'Italia," contains some interesting reports as to the educational conditions of different European nations. In Saxony, it is compulsory; all the inhabitants of the kingdom can read and write, and every child attends school. In Switzerland all can read and write, and have a good primary education. Education is obligatory, and greater efforts, in proportion to its means, are made to impart primary instruction than in any other European nation. In all the smaller states of North Germany education is compulsory and all the children attend school. In Denmark the same is true. All the Danes, with few exceptions, can read, write and keep accounts. The children all attend school until the age of fourteen.

"In Prussia almost all the children attend school regularly, except in some of the eastern districts. An officer who had charge of the military education of the Landwehr, in twelve years had only met with three young soldiers who could neither read nor write. An inquiry having been instituted, it was found that these three were the children of sailors, who had been born on the river and had never settled in any place. Instruction is obligatory.

In Sweden the proportion of the inhabitants who can neither read or write is one in a thousand. Instruction obligatory.

"In Baden every child receives instruction; and in Wurtemberg there is not a peasant, or a girl of the lowest class, or a servant in an inn, who cannot read, write and account correctly. Every child goes to school, instruction being obligatory.

"In Holland public assistance is taken away from every indigent family that neglects to send its children to school. It is estimated that the number of illiterate is three per cent.

"In Norway, almost all the Norwegians can read, write and account passably well. Instruction obligatory.

"In Bavaria, among one hundred conscripts, but seven whose education was incomplete or entirely wanting were found. Instruction also obligatory.

"France, with its twenty-three illiterate conscripts in a hundred, occupies the twelfth class. It is followed by Belgium, Italy, Austria, Greece, Spain, Portugal, Moldo-Wallachi, Russia and Turkey, in the order named. In Italy, hrwever, the conditions vary much according to the province."

Hon. John D. P. Philbrick, in the same report, makes the following statement respecting the workings of the truancy law in Boston.

"Our truant officers are expected to look after all children not attending school, who are found in the streets without any lawful occupation. From their reports, and from information derived from other sources, I had good reason for believing that they are faithful and efficient in the performance of their duty. But as I occasionally hear it said in educational speeches, or read in some newspaper communication, that there are several thousand—from ten to fifteen thousand, I think, is the number named!—vagrant urchins in the streets, growing up in ignorance, idleness and vice, I thought I would try to find where they were. Accordingly, a week or two ago, on a bright and sunny morning, taking care not to select a holiday, I set out on a voyage of discovery. I went to all the railroad stations, I drove round the marginal streets, scanning the wharves and alley-ways, keeping a sharp lookout for boys and girls of school-age. The result of this perambulatory expedition, which occupied two or three hours, was quite extraordinary in respect to the smallness of the number of children of school-age that were found at all. Every-one found was stopped and his case inquired into. The whole number found was hardly more than could be counted on one's fingers, and among them there was only one who had not a good reason for being out of school. This was a truant, who had slipped through the fingers of his teacher and escaped the vigilance of the truant officer. The next day being fine, I continued the survey, going through nearly all the streets of a densely populated section of the city. The result was about the same as that of the preceding day. The few children found, with one exception, gave good reasons for their absence from school. He was a licensed newsboy, and was generally found in school. A similar district in another part of the city was inspected on the third day. It was the same thing over again. I propose to repeat this survey of the streets when the spring opens. In my last report I presentea a tabulated report of the doings ot the truant officers during the past ten years. That report affords strong evidence of the activity of those officers, and it is no doubt largely owing to their labors that so few absentees are found in our streets."

MICHIGAN.

Hon. Oramel Hosford, Superintendent of Public Instruction of the State of Michigan, in his annual report of 1872, says:

"Notwithstanding the fact that the schools were all made free, and books furnished to those unable to purchase them, yet there were those in almost every neighborhood, so indifferent to the well-being of their children, that they would make no effort to avail themselves of the privileges offered to secure for them a good education without cost; and thousands of children were allowed to run the streets without occupation, growing up in stupid ignorance.

"Many tax payers complained of this state of things. They were taxed, they said, to pay for the school houses and to sustain the schools, to educate the children. It was claimed that the good of the state demanded the education of all the people. They admitted the claim and most willingly paid their proportion of the tax, although they had no children to educate. The school houses were built, and the schools were opened and continued, term after term, and yet many children were found in the streets, never going near the school.

"The demand was made that either the law making the schools free should be repealed, or the children should be compelled to attend them. The demand was felt to be a just one, and the law was passed, "That every parent, guardian, or other person in the state of Michigan, having control and charge of any child or children, between the ages of eight and fourteen years, shall be required to send any such child, or children, to a public school, for a period of at least twelve weeks in each school year, at least six weeks of which shall be consecutive, unless such child or children are excused from such attendance by the board of the school district in which such parents or guardians reside, upon its being shown to their satisfaction that his bodily or mental condition has been such as to prevent his attendance at school, or application to study for the period required, or that such child or children are taught in a private school or at home, in such branches as are usually taught in primary schools, or have already acquired the ordinary branches of learning taught in public school."

"The moral effect of this law was very manifest. Many children found their way to the school room, not waiting to be compelled to attend by the force of the law. The final results can only be determined by the faithfulness with which the law is executed. The law is sufficiently exacting to meet all cases; and if there is any failure, it must be in its vigorous execution. Some, in attempting to enforce the law, meet with this difficulty: parents are not only willing, but anxious to send their children to school, and do so; but the boys, particularly, are disposed to truancy, and the parents having little control over them, it is very difficult to keep them in school, and the question is asked, 'Cannot the compulsory law be supplemented with a law for incorrigible truancy?' "

"The "National Normal" for November, 1873, in commenting upon that part of the report bearing upon compulsory education, uses the following language:

"Here now is an opportunity for those conscientious seekers after knowledge in this direction. A compulsory law having been enacted in 1871, a full year has now been given in which to try the virtues of this widely recommended educational panacea. In 1870 the enrollment was 72½ per cent. of the enumeration; in 1871 *seventy-six and one-half* per cent. This increase was before the compulsory law took effect, that is, an increase of *four* per cent. was accomplished *without* that instrument. Now the per cent. is reported 78; that is, an increase of *one* and *a half* per cent. with a compulsory law. It appears then that in Michigan instead of being helpful, compulsory legislation has been hurtful. This is the more apparent when we consider that Superintendent Hosford (An. Rep., p. 146) states that his 'belief, from a survey of the whole field is, that the county superintendency has had as much to do with this increase as any other agency.' But the question is, has it been enforced? Let us look through the reports of the county superintendents and see. Barry says *nothing*. Bay says, 'Those who have had a chance to observe, know that this law has borne some (*though very few*) fruits.' Benzie says *nothing*. Berrien says, "A large majority of the districts pay no attention to it whatever.' Calhoun says *nothing*. Cass says, 'It is feared that our compulsory law is not enforced to the extent desired." Charlevoix says *nothing*. Clinton *nothing*. Eaton *nothing*. Grand Traverse *nothing*. Gratiot *nothing*. Hillsdale *nothing*. Houghton *nothing*. Ingham *nothing*. Isabella *nothing*. So Huron, Jackson, Kalamazoo, Kent, Lapeer and Lelanaw. Lenawee says, 'The compulsory act is a dead letter, and I find no one enforcing it or even paying it any attention further than to post the annual notices, and I cannot say that that has been done in all of the districts.' This is one of the best counties, educationally, in the state. Macomb says, 'There are no prosecutions, though many violations, and when prosecutions are threatened it is made or understood to be a personal quarrel.' Manistee says *nothing*. So Mason, Mecosta, Midland and Monroe. Montcalm says, 'The compulsory law seems to be a failure.' Oceana says *nothing*. So Ottawa. Saginaw says, 'It is a dead letter.' Sanilac, Shiawassee, St. Clair, Tuscola and Van Buren *nothing*. So out of this whole list there is one who ventures to assert that the law has borne some, though very few fruits. The others declare it a dead letter or say nothing which is the same thing. We hope those who quote foreign statistics will remember these home figures. It is something more than amusing to read in the Indiana report, and so in a majority of the reports, very full quotations from foreign school systems upon this subject, while it is true that, if the authors of these reports would, instead of copying what some one else has said about other countries, go into a little original investigation of the workings of the law in their own country, they would obtain the only facts that have the least bearing upon the subject—facts, too, that are sufficient in number and clearly decisive."

MINNESOTA.

Hon. H. B. Wilson, Superintendent of Public Instruction for the state of Minnesota, says, in his annual report for 1872:

"Obligatory education is a subject which is undergoing agitation among educators in every educational convention, every school report, and every educational journal and magazine in our country. However men may differ in opinion as to the best plan of preventing absenteeism, or reclaiming truants, all are impressed with the necessity of some measure to cure this almost universal evil. The most distinguished educators in our own country differ upon the question of compulsory education. Among those favoring it may be cited Newton Bateman, of Illinois, and Birdsey G. Northrop, of Connecticut. Of those opposed, the most distinguished is that of Superintendent John Wickersham, of Pennsylvania. These are all able men, good thinkers, and of very large experience. 'When doctors disagree, who shall decide?' Laws compelling attendance at school, of children between certain ages, have been adopted in Michigan, New Hampshire, Texas and California; and laws regulating the school attendance of children of certain ages, who are employed in manufactories, have been enacted in Massachusetts and Connecticut. It is believed these laws work well, are sustained and give satisfaction. In many of the European states, compulsory education laws are adopted and enforced. The fact that compulsion works well under a monarchial government is no evidence that it is adapted to a government where all power is derived from the consent of the governed. If the principle be a true one, that we so often hear reiterated, that the safety and preservation of a republican form of government lie in the virtue and intelligence of the people; and if the principle be a true one, that the power of the government can come into the home of the citizen and take thence the father, son, husband and brother, in order to preserve that government when in danger or peril, the same power can come into the family circle and force the citizen to educate his children in order that they may become qualified to exercise the rights and privileges conferred upon them by the state, and that they may be better able to preserve and defend the state when assailed by either foreign or domestic foes."

MISSISSIPPI.

Hon. H. R. Pease, Superintendent of Public Instruction for the State of Mississippi, in his annual report for 1872, says, in the conclusion of an able discussion of the subject:

"A compulsory law is not only just and feasible, and required by the highest considerations of public policy, but it is made the duty of the legislature, by the terms of the constitution, to see that every educable youth is provided with suitable facilities for elementary instruction."

NEW HAMPSHIRE.

Hon. J. W. Simonds, Superintendent of Public Instruction for the State of New Hampshire, in his annual report for 1872–3, thus speaks of the effect of the compulsory law now in operation in that state:

"A commendable effort has been made to enforce the law in the cities, especially Manchester and several of the large manufacturing villages. In many towns there has been no occasion for its enforcement, as every child that is physically able will attend school. The matter is receiving attention, and I think the effect of the law will show a good result by comparing the statistics of the non-attendance of the present with the past year."

NEW JERSEY.

Hon. Ellis A. Apgar, Superintendent of Public Instruction for the State of New Jersey, says in his Annual Report for 1871:

"Although the total attendance is satisfactory, the irregularity of attendance must be considered a great and alarming evil. Our free school law requires the schools to be kept open at least nine months during the year, but if thirty-nine per cent., or more than one-third of the total attendance during those nine months is in school less than four months, it is evident that we are not securing all the good we should from our school system. But few of our children are growing up in absolute ignorance in consequence of non-attendance, but the majority of them are evidently not receiving all the education they should because of irregular attendance. The time will undoubtedly come when some legislation will be demanded to cure this radical evil in the workings of our school system. We have passed a free school law which imposes and compels the payment of a tax sufficient to keep the schools open three-fourths of the time, and I deem it due to the tax-payer that by further enactment, a full attendance of the children should be secured during that time. It is of but little importance that the schools are required to be kept open a prescribed length of time if the children attend but a small fraction of that time."

NEW YORK.

Hon. Abram Weaver, Superintendent of Public Instruction, of the State of New York, in his annual report for 1871, says:

"Compulsory attendance is not a new expedient in education, although it has never been fully resorted to in any of the United States. The most stringent regulations of the kind, in this country, are those embraced in the laws of our own, and of some other States, relative to idle and truant children, and which authorize their arrest, and commitment to places of employment and instruction. Our own statute of 1853, upon this subject, is limited to cities and incorporated villages; but it is not enforced, and it is said that similar laws are not generally executed in the other States.

In many of the European States, obligatory attendance is an old rule, and, in some of them, a rigid one. It has been most thoroughly tested in Norway, Sweden, Denmark, in the greater part of Switzerland, in Prussia where it has been in force for a full century, and in several other German States. It has been attempted at different times in France, where it is said that "compulsory education is ancient and of noble origin," in Austria, Spain, Portugal, and Italy, but has wholly or partially failed. Even in Prussia, which is commonly cited as a model in this and in other school matters, the well nigh universal education which prevails is not, in my opinion, principally due to the stringency of the law requiring attendance.

Any such law, even when strictly enforced, in itself educates no one in anything except unquestioning obedience to superior power. It is only a police regulation to bring the bodies of children to the school-room, or to punish for their absence; whereas, the real efficiency of a system of education must depend upon what it teaches, not upon the number of its arrests and penalties; upon its adaption to the recognized wants and interests of a people, instead of its power to compel their reluctant acceptance of it; upon its moral strength and influence, rather than physical force.

"The Prussians believe in education with a unanimity and sincerity which compulsory attendance but faintly expresses. They are not only earnest in this sentiment, but are patiently and persistently thorough in the execution of it. They not only propose universal education, but provide for it in a plan that employs every known faculty, and which adopts every discovered improvement. The operation of their school system is not entrusted to undisciplined novices, to be used by them temporarily as a means to their own ulterior interests. Teachers are as thoroughly trained for their vocation, as those who enter the profession of law or the ministry, and are held to a rigid standard of qualification with reference to their natural adaptation to their work, as well as in respect to their learning. Thus prepared, their admission to their profession is a guaranty of superior attainments, and an assurance that they are worthy to become the teachers of the people. In support of all this, public sentiment dignifies the whole enterprise with the highest respectability, and contributes to its service, in teaching and supervision, the best talent of the nation. It is this thoroughness, this completeness, this unyielding pursuit of perfection in the character of the instruction given, that has chiefly done for Prussia the work which so many admire.

This opinion is confirmed by the example of Holland. In a special report, particularly devoted to the subject now under consideration, prepared by direction of the Legislature, and transmitted to that body in 1867, by my predecessor in office, the late Hon. Victor M. Rice, and in connection with an expression of the author's belief 'that in this country education can be universal without being compulsory,' it is stated that in Holland every adult citizen can read and write. Attendance at school has never been enjoined by law, but supervision has been carried to an extent which would hardly be deemed legitimate in the State of New York. Even in a private school, nobody is permitted to teach without having first been examined and licensed by the proper authorities." And further, it is recorded 'that great efforts had been made, in the debates on the clauses of the law, to procure a more decided recognition, by the State, of the principle of compulsory education. * * The usual arguments for compulsory education were adduced—that other countries had successfully established—that in China, where it reigns, all the children can read and write. It was replied that compulsory education was altogether against the habits of the Dutch people.

Here, then, we find two neighboring States, in both of which education is practically universal, but in one of which it is obligatory, and in the other voluntary. If compulsion was calculated to exert a controlling influence in the matter, we might expect to find the distinction plainly illustrated in Switzerland, in all parts of which State attendance is obligatory except in the cantons of Geneva, Switz, Uri and Unterwalden. In Geneva, however, it is authoritatively stated that education is so prevalent that, at times, a native adult who could not read and write could not be found. Thus, experience has demonstrated, that compulsory attendance is neither a certain nor an essential means to universal education.

OHIO.

Hon. Thos. W. Harvey, State Commissioner of Common Schools of the State of Ohio in his Annual Report for 1872, says:

"The influence of our public schools is not so far reaching as could be desired—not from any radical defect in the system, but from the inadequacy of the means and agencies provided for its administration. Truancy and absenteeism are evils for the cure or prevention of which no laws have been enacted. Attendance at school is entirely optional. Children unable to read or write may be employed on the farm, or in mine, workshop, or factory. The State does not interpose to protect them against the avarice of thoughtless parents or the rapacity of employers. There is, however, a growing sentiment in favor of stringent laws against truancy and the employment of illiterate youth in industries of any kind, when such employment is a virtual denial of school privileges. Our people desire to see the results of compulsory laws, although it is questionable whether they are ready to sanction their enactment.

PENNSYLVANIA.

Hon. J. P. Wickersham, Superintendent of Common Schools of the Commonwealth of Pennsylvania, in his annual report of 1871, says:

"To remedy the evil of non-attendance, many persons advocate the enactment of a law compelling children between certain ages to attend school for a certain number of months each year. Such laws, however, have not proven very effective in the countries and states where they are now in force. Prussia has such a law, but the school attendance in Prussia does not embrace a greater percentage of the school-going population than it does in other European countries that have no compulsory law. It is even doubtful whether the percentage of attendance is greater in Prussia than it is in Pennsylvania. Massachusetts has had on her statute books, for years, very rigid laws enforcing attendance at her public schools; how effective they are will be shown from the following statements taken from the last report of the Board of Education.

"'In that report, page 102, it is stated that the 'ratio of mean average attendance for the year to the whole number of persons between five and fifteen is .74.' We have no means of determining how many persons there are in Pennsylvania between the ages of five and fifteen, nor how many between those ages attend our schools, as our school statistics are compiled in a different way from that in which they are compiled in Massachusetts; but from the best estimates that can be made, attendance at school seems to be about as good here as there.

"'Abner J. Phipps, Esq., the agent of the Board of Education, says: 'It is a mournful thought that notwithstanding the very large amount expended for the maintenance of the public schools of our state, so large a proportion of children of school age fail to reap the advantage of this, and grow up in comparative ignorance. It is true we have a compulsory law with sufficient penalties, if it were enforced, but in many towns it is not only not enforced, but no disposition to enforce it is shown.'

"'Hon. Joseph White, Secretary of the Board of Education, declares, with reference to their compulsory law and the practice under it, that 'It is the weakest and least defensible part of our school system.'

"'And Gen. H. K. Oliver, the state constable, one of whose duties it is to see that the state laws concerning education are enforced, puts the case still stronger. The italics are his own. He says: 'Now, we know, indeed, that there is a compulsory statute of the commonwealth in relation to the schooling of its children, but like a great many other statutes on the books, it is paralytic, effete, dead—killed by sheer neglect. It was never enforced, and never supposed to be anybody's duty to enforce it. In fact, we are inclined to believe that it is not generally known that such a law was ever enacted, *Nobody looks after it, neither town authorities, nor school committees, nor local police, and large cities and many of the towns of the state are swarming with unschooled children, vagabondizing about the streets and growing up in ignorance and a heritage of sin. The mills all over the state, the shops in city and town, are full of children deprived of the right to such education as will fit them for the possibilities of their after life.* Nobody thinks of either enforcement or obedience in the matter, so that between those who are ignorant of the provision and those that care for none of these things, thousands of the poor younglings of the state, with all her educational boasting, stand precious small chance of getting even the baldest elements of education.'

"Waiving all question, then, as to whether a law compelling children to attend school is in consonance with the spirit of our free institutions, and whether the indisposition in this country to enforce such a law does not arise from the fact, the experience of Massachusetts teaches us that we in Pennsylvania must look in some other direction than in that of a compulsory law to find the remedy we are seeking for the evil of non attendance at school.

"After having carefully considered this delicate and difficult subject, I have about reached the conclusion that we must first do what remains to be done in the way of providing good school grounds, good school houses and good teachers for our children, and we have yet much to do in this direction, and then supplement our present voluntary system by enactments, as follows:

"1. A judicious truant law.

"2. A judicious law preventing the employment of children in mines, manufactories, &c., without some provision for their education.

"3. A law authorizing boards of directors in cities and large towns to appoint and pay, when needed, a *school missionary*, to visit the parents of children not in school or attending irregularly, and endeavor to secure their attendence.

"4. A law legalizing, if not requiring, the establishment of a home for freindless or neglected children in every county in the Commonwealth, and giving the boards of directors of the several school districts power to send to these institutions such children as the safety of Society might justify being disposed of in that way. These homes should be established, supported and managed by the same authorities that have the care of the almshouses, aided perhaps, at first, by appropriations from the State. They should provide maintenance and clothing, as well as instruction for the children. They train the children up to habits of industry, and whenever suitable opportunities presented themselves, they should place them in good families or where they could learn a useful trade.

A compulsory law, even if fully enforced, cannot bring into the schools children suffering for want of food, clothing or shelter, children who must work or steal in order to live, children who have no parents or friends to care for them; and a large proportion of those growing up in entire ignorance are of this class. The county home is just the place for them, and tens of thousands might by its means be plucked like "brands from the burning," and made good members of society. I have almost unbounded faith in the effect of good influences upon the character of the young. I believe most firmly that if all the ignorant, vicious boys and girls in Pennsylvania, could at once be brought into properly managed homes of the kind just spoken of, *nineteen out of every twenty* could be made good men and good women—good members of society. If society is ever reformed, it will be done in this way. If the evils we complain of and suffer under, are ever removed, rooted out, it will be effected by the right education of the young.

It is in favor, also, of the plan proposed, that it does not disturb the sacredness of the family—a matter so dear to the Anglo Saxon race. The State would not be called upon to over-rule or break down parental authority, but merely step in to take the parents' place where children either have no parents or none that cared for them."

RHODE ISLAND.

Hon. Thomas W. Bicknell, Commissioner of Public Schools of the State of Rhode Island, in his report of 1872, says:

"There are in Rhode Island to-day four thousand children of school age, who do not attend any school, and have no means of instruction. Some of these are in the shops, mills and factories, many of them are in the streets. To secure their education is the duty, first of the invidual; when neglected by him, it certainly falls upon the State to demand it, even by the first law of existence, namely, that of self-preservation. The annual message of the Governor calls the attention of the General Assembly to this important measure, and it is to be hoped and expected that a Joint Committee will make all necessary inquiry into the extent of the evil of youthful illiteracy and crime, and when once the magnitude of the evils is shown, the State will soon institute measures for its speedy removal."

TEXAS.

Hon. J. C. De Gress, Superintendent of Public Instruction of the State of Texas, in his annual report for 1872, says:

"Of the compulsory features of our law I can say but little. The full returns of non attendance are not yet made, and it is entirely too early to speak of the effect of the law as carried out. There is a marked tendency throughout the Union towards making the compulsory feature an accompaniment of every school law, the evil of absenteeism plainly leading to inculcation of many vices in the character of youth, through the lack of beneficial restraints of the discipline of the school room, or the absence of the moral balance of intelligence. I still hold to the opinion that the wisdom of republican government should enforce an intelligence amongst those in whom all power is centered, the people, and I believe that the later day intelligence will sanction this means used for prevention of crime, with the equal force with which it sanctions the power used in punishing crime. Laws enforce taxation as a tribute to the general welfare in supporting the powers and branches of government. Why may not the law enforce an attention to that need of education that equally underlies the foundation of our success as a government? Without taxation the material parts of the government machinery would be wanting; without education the material and vitalizing force would be lacking; and in either is foreseen a state of affairs akin to the reign of communism that affrighted a people with its red-handed career and caused brave men and wise statesmen to tremble at the furies let loose, sporting the hideous masks of ignorance."

WISCONSIN.

Successive superintendents of public instruction, in their annual reports, have called attention to the fact that several thousand children are reported as not having attended any school, publi) or private, during the year. Some of the later incumbents have evidently favored compulsory legislation, but have made no special recommendations to the legislature upon the subject.

Gov. Fairchild, in two of his messages, strenuously urged the enactment of compulsory measures. Our chief educators have been divided in opinion upon the question.

CONCLUSION.

The United States census of 1870 reveals the startling fact that out of a population of 28,238,945 ten years old and upward, 5,658,144 persons ten years old and upward were illiterate—17 per cent. of the adult males of the country.

From the facts and opinions given in the preceding pages, it will be seen,

1. That crime increases in the ratio of ignorance; that the entirely uneducated man is *nine* times as likely to be a criminal as the average of men who have been taught, and more than *one hundred* times as likely to become a criminal as he who has been thoroughly educated.

2. That those who constitute the ignorant and criminal classes of society will *not* educate their children and must therefore be *compelled* to do so.

3. That in European countries where a compulsory system is in force, the people find no fault with it, but cheerfully comply with its requisitions, and are in the main *unconscious* of the pressure which it exerts.

4. That in those countries where such a system exists the people are superior in intelligence, prowess and prosperity, to neighboring countries, where no such system prevails. Holland which has been cited to prove the opposite of this position has practically a compulsory law. (Vide quotation from Hon. B. G. Northrop's report.)

5. That many distinguished educators and statesmen abroad and at home, who were formerly opposed to sumptuary laws on education, have become convinced of the desirability of such laws, upon seeing their actual working and now are warm advocates of compulsion.

6. That the prevailing sentiment among the leading educators of our own country is that compulsory education is legal and necessary,—that each child has a right to an education, which no parent can lawfully deny—that the state should maintain that right by positive enactment, that our whole school system is compulsory. So far as the raising of taxes, the prescribing of the duties of

officers, etc., is concerned, and therefore attendance should be made compulsory.

7. That in the discussion of the subject the two questions of "compulsory attendance upon the public schools," and "compulsory education," are often confounded together. Many who are in favor of the latter, object to the former.

8. That it is yet to early to form a correct judgment concerning the workings of compulsory laws in the States which have adopted them, but that the weight of testimony thus far is in favor of such laws.

9. That prominent educators who hesitate in sanctioning compulsory education fully, yet recommend the passage of stringent truancy laws, which are half-way compulsory measures.

10. That all are in favor of making for public schools more attractive and efficient.

In my last Annual Report, after giving my view upon the legal *status* of the question, I stated that—

"The practicability of such compulsory law is another thing. Several of the states have such a law upon their statute books, but as far as I can ascertain the results are not what the friends of the measure could desire. Owing to the want of a right public sentiment the law is a dead letter, or else it execution is such a disagreeable duty that it is quietly omitted. I do not think that the sentiment is ripe enough in this state for a trial of the experiment on so large a sale as in Massachnsetts, Michigan, or Texas. The children of the rural districts do not as a rule replenish the ranks of the law breaking classes. They are to be found in school generally some portion of the year. Their education in the technical sense of the term may be very limited, but they are receiving an invaluable training in the formation of habits of industry, economy and self-reliance. The towns and cities are the recruiting places idle, the vicious, and the lawless portions of the community. As a tentative measure, I should be heartily in favor of a truancy law, which would be specially applicable to the cities and towns of the state.

"If a compulsory law should be enacted for the whole state, it should provide that the instruction required may be obtained at home, and in private schools as well as in the public schools."

The following law, relating to truant children and absentees from school, was passed by the legislature:

(*Chapter* 276—*General Laws of* 1878.)

"SECTION 1. Each of the cities in this state is hereby authorized and empowered to organize and establish truant schools for the instruction and attendance of habitual truants, wandering about in the streets or public places of any such city, having no lawful occupation or business and not attending school, between the ages of seven and sixteen years; and also to make and enforce all such ordinances, rules and by-laws, respecting such children as shall be deemed most conducive to their welfare and the good order of such city.

"SECTION 2. Any child convicted of being an habitual truant, or of wandering about in the streets or public places of any city, having no lawful occupation or business, and not attending school, between the ages of seven and sixteen years, may, in the discretion of the justice or court having jurisdiction of the case, be committed to any such truant school provided for the purpose under the authority of the next preceding section, for such time, not exceeding two years, as such justice or court may determine. And the police authorities, after such conviction and sentence, are authorized and directed to enforce the daily attendance of such children at the truant school so established; *provided*, they are found wandering in the streets.

"SECTION 3. Such justices of the peace and other judicial officers and courts as have criminal jurisdiction, shall have jurisdiction of all offences under this act, and under the ordinances and by-laws which may be passed or ordained under the authority thereof."

A truancy law to be of practical account should require the attendance of children wandering in the streets, upon schools already established, and not upon truant schools *to be* established. Few, if any, cities in which vagrant children are to be found, will incur the expense of establishing schools specially for that class. Officers also should be appointed to see that the law is enforced.

I have come to the conclusion from a careful investigation of the whole question, and specially in view of the fact that 55,441 persons 10 years old and over, in Wisconsin, are unable to write, and nearly 50,000 are not to be found in any school from year to year, that while the instructional agencies now employed should be developed to the highest degree of efficiency, the legislature should enact a law that every child within the bounds of the state, shall receive, in the public schools or elsewhere, at least the elements of a good common school education.

DOCUMENTS

ACCOMPANYING THE REPORT.

REPORTS OF COUNTY SUPERINTENDENTS.

BUFFALO COUNTY.

L. KESSINGER, SUPERINTENDENT.

By the time the reports of the town clerks should have been in my hands, I received a letter from one of them, stating that he had not received any blanks for the reports of himself and the school district clerks of his town. A similar statement was made to me, verbally, by another clerk.

DISTRIBUTION OF BLANKS.

I think the law or usage according to which the blanks are sent to the town clerks, directly from the office of the state superintendent, is, fundamentally and practically, anomalous, and ought to be changed. It seems to rest upon the supposition that the clerks report directly to the state superintendent, instead of to the county superintendent, as, in fact, they do. According to the present practice the town clerks receive the blanks several weeks before the district clerks have to report, and by the time their own reports should be in the hands of the county superintendents they are, perhaps by himself, reminded that it is too late, and then the county superintendent has to wait. If the blanks should go through the hands of the county superintendent, he would give them to the town clerks just in time, and with a verbal or written request to be prompt. This way of proceeding would also naturally induce the county superintendent to give each town clerk such advice as the case would demand, some clerks needing much, others none or but little. Even as the law now stands, such an arrangement would be no violation of it, as it does not say that the school officers should get their blanks directly. In fact, district clerks do not get them directly now, and I can see no reason why town clerks should. If I should hold my office for another term, I should very much prefer to have the blanks in question sent to my office for distribution.

Referring to the idea of a meeting of the town clerks in regard to the aforesaid blanks, a proposition I made last year, it is plain that such a meeting would, with the immediate distribution of the papers, be more effective than without it. The project of such a meeting, necessary and beneficial though it is admitted to be, will at present be nothing but a pious wish, the law failing to make an appropriation for that purpose. But I know that I could even without that meeting accomplish most of its purposes, if I had to distribute the blanks.

SCHOOLS, SCHOOL-HOUSES, ETC.

In regard to schools, school-houses and school matters in general, I able to report a steady progress. Three new cerditable school-houses have been built; money has been raised in several districts with an an intention of building next year; obstacles to improvements have been removed in two instances by dissolving a school district and annexing the parts to adjoining school districts re-forming new districts. My constant attention and perpetual working in such matters have everywhere accomplished at least partial and preliminary results.

THE INSTITUTE.

Much good has been accomplished by the Teachers' Institute conducted by Professor McGregor. The impulse given to the work of the teachers in the schools as well as in self-improvement, can scarcely be estimated. As our schools will never be better than our teachers, the path to their lasting improvement is unmistakably pointed out. Permit me to express my obligation to you for granting the just the time which I demanded for our Institute. It proved to be one of the causes of its success.

COLUMBIA COUNTY.

L. J. BURLINGAME, SUPERINTENDENT.

Columbia county is composed of twenty-one townships, embracing eight hundred square miles, and according to the last census, a total population of twenty-eight thousand eight hundred and two, (28,802), being an increase of four thousand three hundred and fifty-seven (4,357) within the last then years. There are nine thousand four hundred and sixty-one (9,461) children between the ages of four and twenty, being a decrease of one hundred and eight (108) since last year. This does not include the children of Portage city, who are reported by themselves. The names of about seventy-seven (77) per cent. of the whole number of children of school age, are found upon the teacher's records for the last year. In the county are one hundred and nine (109) entire districts, and eighty-three (83) joint districts, and one hundred and forty-nine (149) school houses. One hundred and seventy-two (172) teachers are required to teach our schools. Two hundred and ninety (290) different teachers have been employed during the year. The schools have been taught on an average of one hundred and thirty (130) days. Average wages for male teachers, $44,00; average wages for female teachers, $23,00. There has been paid for teachers wages, $32,917, being $1,179 less than we paid out last year.

GRADED SCHOOLS.

We have nine graded schools in this county, which are in the hands of competent instructors, and I think they will compare favorably with any in the state.

EXAMINATIONS.

Sixteen public and five private examinations have been held, at which four hundred and eighty (480) persons applied for certificates. Three hundred and thirty (330) certificates were granted, graded as follows: First grade, 4; Second grade, 12; Third grade, 314. Quite a large share of the summer teachers received limited certificates for six months.

TEACHERS' REPORTS.

I still continue the plan of requiring monthly reports from the teachers; by this means I am furnished with much valuable information in relation to the condition of the schools, not otherwise easily obtained. It has a very salutary effect in promoting thoroughness and system in teaching and government. If frequent visits could be made in every school, there would be no necessity for making reports, unless at the end of the term.

STATISTICS.

My statistical report already forwarded to the department, was very unreliable in many respects. The only way to remedy this evil, which every Superintendent has to contend with, in my opinion, is for the legislature to pay district clerks for their labor, and then compel them to report as they ought.

VISITATIONS.

I have made two visits to each school in the county, with the exception of ten ; four of which were not in session when I called to visit them, making in all, three hundred and thirty-four school visits during the year. It has been my intention to make my school visits thoroughly practical, and to ascertain the true condition and needs of each school. The very short time I possibly could give to each school, on account of the large number to be visited, has, in a great measure, lessened the good which might otherwise have been done. This county, in my opinion, ought to be divided into two Superintendent districts, and I have reported to the county board to that effect.

INSTITUTE.

An Institute was held at Portage City during the first of September, at which nearly ninety members were enrolled. Prof. A. Salisbury conducted it chiefly, fully sustaining his high reputation as an Institute instructor. The institute was in every respect a success, and our teachers have received a lasting good.

NORMAL SCHOOLS.

Six teachers have been nominated for admission into the Normal Schools. I have continually urged the teachers of this county to attend some of our Normal Schools. I consider them one of the most efficient means attainable for preparing our teachers for their responsible work.

TEACHERS.

We have many good, zealous and energetic teachers who are alive to the responsibilities of their profession, and strive to discharge their duties as becomes intelligent and conscientious instructors, but it cannot be denied that we have too many whose literary attainments and whose skill in the *art* of teaching are quite indifferent ; that we have too many whose efficiency is much impaired in consequence of a slavish use of the text book in hearing recitations ; that we have too many who make little or no use of such aids in teaching as the globe, outline maps, blackboard, etc. Our good teachers, however, outnumber the poor ones, and I hope that the time is not far distant when Columbia County will not have an indifferent, a careless or an indolent teacher in one of her schools.

"Next to the reading of God's Holy Word, I know of no more Godly purpose that a man goeth about, than the teaching of a School." These are the words of Roger Ascham, Preceptor of Queen Elizabeth; and three centuries, though they have modified the spelling of the words, have only made the truth more apparent. The dignity and importance of this profession is often undervalued or misunderstood. To the obscure preceptor are due those influences which produced a Shakspeare, and rendered the Queen illustruous. Many a man who has filled a large place in history, received the first impulse from his teachers. No class of persons has a more powerful influence upon our nation of the immediate future. It is questionable whether even the exception in the above quotation should be made. The teacher, five or six hours a day five days in the week, with the advantage of superior age and knowledge, is moulding the impressible minds of youth, and whether he will or not, leaving more or less distinctly, upon all his pupils the impress of his own. Teachers are a power behind the throne of public opinion, by which that throne itself is moved. No trump of fame calls to this field of humble yet effective labor. When some heroic action, some discovery in science, or some deed of patriotic valor is heralded through the land, no one thinks of the teachers by whom the virtue was encouraged and the industry stimulated by which high attainments become possible. To them, partly is often due the credit of other men's success, as on them partly rests the responsibility nf other's failures.

To fit one for this high calling, there is need of the most careful preparation and the most conscientious devotion. Yet numbers are anxious to engage in it, not only without professional training, but almost without any education; and it is surprising to see how low is the popular standard of what should be required of a teacher, and how little the value of the best talent is really appreciated. The average length of time female teachers continue in the business is from four to five years. Seventy-five per cent. of all our teachers are females. Very likely and properly this per cent. will continue to be nearly as large. For reasons beyond the control of society, and higher than human laws, their time of service will, as a rule, continue to be short. But frequent change in the corps of teachers is injurious. There should be a conservative element among them — a class permanently employed. Statistics show that the proportion of young men engaged in teaching is smaller than it was twenty years ago. But there is an army of agents urging upon the public that which is not desirable, and of persons courting success in unproductive employments for which they are not qualified. If the men of talent among these would fit themselves to be teachers, and engage in this noble work, they would become useful members of society, and in elevating humanity, find themselves ennobled and their self respect restored. The policy which has driven young men from this profession is not good. To retain in it, in sufficient numbers, those whose ability may illustrate its capacity for good, requires a change in the popular estimate of its importance.

CONCLUSION.

With sincere thanks to the school department for favors received, to the district boards, teachers and citizens, for their hearty co-operation with us in our official labors, and for their kind hospitalities which we have invariably received, we close, hoping that the coming year may prove equally fruitful in progress with the year which has closed. All of which is respectfully submitted.

DANE COUNTY — FIRST DISTRICT.

W. H. CHANDLER, SUPERINTENDENT.

In forwarding my Annnal Report for the year ending September 30, 1873, I take the opportunity of submitting a few statements, specially.

INCORRECT STATISTICS — CHANGES PROPOSED.

The reports of the town clerks have been made more promptly and more accurately than usual, indicating a disposition to comply with the law. But the difficulty in obtaining correct statistics, lies in the inaccurate reports of school district clerks, as a little study of these reports and statistics will show. For instance, the reports relating to the total receipts in the several towns, vary from the total disbursements and money on hand, from $20 to $200, while they should balance. The reports from several towns show receipts by some districts from amounts raised by vote at annual town meetings; of course if one district in the town has a revenue from such source, all would have, and one or the other class have made mistake in reporting. In reporting expenditure "for all other purposes," the amounts expended are sometimes hardly adequate for furnishing one or two school houses with wood, while the report shows six or eight thus furnished. The reports, also, concerning receipts from tax levied by county board of supervisors, indicate that district treasurers do not keep their accounts in such manner as to determine the source of revenues, or clerks are not careful in making statements.

In view of these and many like errors, which render the details valueless, it has occurred to me that a little change in the headings of the reports required would help greatly in obtaining more acurate reports. For instance, the following: "Amount on hand at date of last report;" "Amount of County School tax received;" "Amount of State School fund income received;" "Amount received from taxes levied at Annual School meeting;" "Amount received from all other sources." For expenditures: "Amount expenned for building and repairing;" "Amount expended for wages of male teachers;" "Amount expended for wages of female teachers;" "Amount expended for fuel;" "Amount expended for library;" "Amount expended for apparatus, registers, etc.;" "Amount expended for School House furniture."

In reporting the number of days school has been taught by a qualified teacher, clerks of joint districts have been required to report to the town clerks of all towns in which the district is situated. In a great number of cases the number of days taught in a given town are doubled, trebled, or quadrupled by incorporating all these reports, which cover the same districts, in several cases. To obviate this, district clerks might be required to report "yes" or "no" to the question "Has a school been maintained five or more months?" in all reports, except to the town clerk of the town in which the School House is located.

As at present arranged the blanks furnished district clerks require them to classify as male and female, the attendants upon school of pupils of certain specified ages. This is no light task, and the classification is not required in the County Superintendent's report, and so is unnecessary in the former.

In order to secure accuracy, the statistics required must be as few, distinct, and easily comprehended as possible, and I have ventured the above suggestions, after careful inquiry as to the points and cause of inaccuracies. The short time given for the compilation of these reports by county superintendents after the reception of the reports of town clerks, makes it impossible to refer them back for correction.

In concluding this matter, I would say, that if teachers were required by law to make, at the beginning of each term immediately succeeding the time of making the annual report by the district clerk, a roll of the scholars attending school in the district during the year, which should show their age, sex, and number of days attending during each month of school throughout the year, and each teacher employed during the year were required to add to this roll the name, age, sex, and monthly attendance of any *new*, as well as that of all scholars already enrolled, it would so facilitate the labor of the clerk in making his report, as to insure both promptness and correctness.

THE WORK OF THE YEAR.

In regard to the work in and of the schools the past year, on the whole it has been quite satisfactory. District boards have manifested a commendable interest in securing well qualified teachers, and in sustaining them. There have been exceptions, of course, where pecuniary or personal interests have induced the employment of teachers of low grades ; but in such cases the sentiment of the districts has been against the action of the boards. Teachers have exhibited a praiseworthy desire to be better instructed in the duties of their high calling, and many have made the *art* of teaching a careful study. Could there be secured a greater permanency in the corps of teachers, I should have more hopes of rapid and great improvement in our schools.

The attendance upon the winter sessions, was very full, taxing fully the tact of teachers and the capacity of school-houses in many instances. But that of the summer sessions was very meagre. The cultivation of many products in which juvenile labor can proftably be employed, combined with the stringency of the times, make this inevitable, as long as the present system of two terms per year is continued. It is to be hoped school districts will yet either change this arrangement, or by the adoption of the township district system, obviate the necessity of maintaining twice the number of schools during the summer that are necessary for the accommodation of those who will attend.

DODGE COUNTY—FIRST DISTRICT

L. M. BENSON, SUPERINTENDENT.

Complying with your request, I make a few statements in regard to the common schools in superintendent district No. 1 of the county of Dodge and also mention somo changes that ought, in my opinion, to made in our school laws.

IMPERFECT RETURNS.

Mostly for statistics you are referred to the annual report. As usual, the annual report is in many respects imperfect, though *much* labor has been expended upon it and great pains taken to make it as correct as possible. The fact is, the majority of our district and town clerks make very incomplete and incorrect reports.

I indulge the hope, however, that you will find the report correct in all matters of great importance.

THE REMEDY.

It is my firm belief that the adoption of the "Township System" would secure to us much more reliable reports, as well as a great improvement in regard to school supervision, etc. I hope our legislature will take the pains to examine carefully the "Township System" and, if approved of, let them cause its adoption throughout the state and not leave it optional with the towns. Probably it will not be adopted universily or even generally by the voluntary act of the towns during the next century.

INDORSING AND RENEWING CERTIFICATES.

For reasons to numerous to give here I hope our legislature at its next session will alter the laws so that the county superintendent may in his discretion indorse a certificate granted by another, and also renew those granted by himself under certain circumstances. Also I think it would be well to allow the county superintendent to grant the third grade certificate for one year, the second grade for two years and the first grade for three years.

THE SCHOOL MONTH.

The school month should be only twenty days, as school is not kept on Saturdays, except by special contract, and as one hundred days teaching will draw the public money.

Some other school laws should be modified, and I hope our legislators will in future interest themselves more in regard to the common schools than they have sometimes in the past.

EXAMINATIONS.

During the past school year, besides the private examinations, I have held ten public examinations. About 340 applications have been made for certificates, and 221, including all grades, have been granted. I have granted four of the first grade, eighteen of the second grade, and 199 of the third grade. It appears that on the average about two-thirds of the applicants succeed. I have not granted nearly as many limited third grade certificates the past year as usual. District officers, generally, are convinced that it is poor policy to expend money for second or third rate teachers There are some, however, who will hire the lowest bidder, whether he or she is well qualified or not. I hope that district boards will not, in future, petition the county superintendent to grant certificates to those who are not well qualified to teach, because much evil is likely to result from it.

Generally, the past year, as usual, each public examination, including Institute exercises, has occupied three days, making in all about thirty days spent in this way. From experience, I am satisfied that more good can be done by having the Institute exercises in connection with the examinations, though a general gathering of teachers may do much good. But very few teachers, comparatively, attend a general Institute, but nearly all attend the examinations and are therefore reached.

VISITATIONS.

In regard to visiting schools, it is my firm conviction that our system is sadly deficient. The law makes it the duty of the district officers to visit and supervise the schools in many respects, but makes no provision for remunerating them ; therefore many who are poor cannot afford to give that attention necessary to the production of good results. Again, many of our district officers feel that they are not proper judges, either of teachers or of schools, and therefore stay away.

The law makes it the duty of the county superintendent, also, to visit schools, but it must always be imperfectly done by him on account of the number he has to visit and the distance he has to travel in most counties. Again, in order to learn much about a teacher's method and management, and about the school, the superintendent should make two visits at least during the term, and remain in school each time a whole day that he may learn how all the branches are taught and what the order is, and much else. All this cannot be thoroughly and well done by the county superintendent. In my opinion we should have some one in each town to visit the schools. During the past year I have made about 140 school visits and have tried to encourage teachers in their work and stimulate pupils to make great effort, and especially to be thorough in all their studies. The time spent in school has been necessarily so short that I fear but little good has been done, as a rule.

WANT OF THOROUGHNESS.

Here I cannot refrain from expressing a deep conviction that many of our schools fall far short of what they ought to be on account of the carelessness and looseness of teachers, who, themselves, have been allowed to pass rapidly over much but have learned thoroughly but little. We have a few teachers who are very thorough in all their work, and are really great benefactors to the rising generation.

DISTRICT OFFICERS AT FAULT.

Our schools would be benefited much if district officers would take more *pains* and exercise more moral courage in hiring teachers. Relationship, friendship, religion, politics, have far too much to do with hiring teachers.

SCHOOL TERMS.

Some of our districts fail to do as much good as they might, by having school taught during the very warm and busy months of summer. The money paid for teaching during the two hottest months of the year, in most cases, especially in the rural districts, is expended very poorly indeed. In many cases, tbe teacher visits the schoolroom day after day and week after week, to find from three to ten pupils in attendance. Some districts have a winter term of four months, and divide four other months into two terms, one to be taught in the spring, and the other in early autumn. Unless the same teacher is employed for both terms or all of the terms, I think this a bad division. In case a district has nine months school in a year, I think it would be best, generally, to divide the time, so as to have a winter term and a spring term. The winter term should commence early, and there should be a short vacation of one or two weeks, commencing about the 25th of December. After the winter term there should be a short vacation, then the spring term should commence, so as to close school before very warm weather, if possible. In case the district has but eight months school during the year, there will be no need of holding school during the hottest portion of the year.

YOUNG TEACHERS.

During the past year, fewer young persons have been employed as teachers; but we have too many children teaching yet. I am glad to see some improvement in this respect, and sincerely hope our district officers will exercise great caution and judgment in hiring teachers. The people generally seem to take a lively interest in the common schools, and try to aid school officers in their efforts to improve them.

In conclusion, it gives me great pleasure to be able to state that with some exceptions, the "condition" of our schools is good, and the "prospects" very encouraging.

EAU CLAIRE COUNTY.

A. KIDDER, SUPERINTENDENT.

CONDITION OF THE SCHOOLS.

I am happy to say that the condition of our public schools, as a whole, is prosperous. By close attention to the examination of teachers, and an effort to raise the standard of qualification, a new stimulus has been imparted to those who were successful, by thus withdrawing unworthy competitors from the field.

DEFECTIVE TEACHING.

My special effort has been devoted to the organization and systematizing of methods of teaching, often spending one-half of a day in the work of teaching for an example. The great lack of teachers is, knowledge of those methods which can only be attained by witnessing a well-conducted school. Teachers do not take pains enough to visit and study the art of teaching from the best specimens of teaching we have. The privilege of doing this I think the law gives, but it ought to be compulsory. Many teachers do indifferent work who have the ability to do well, if they have only visited a model school and learned how to keep and teach the same. The great drawback is the entire lack of appreciation by the mass of the people of the work and qualifications of a County Superintendent, and the unwillingness properly to compensate him for his fidelity or talent for the work. But as "virtue has its own reward," so there is some pay in the consciousness of having accomplished a good work.

GRADED SCHOOLS.

The three graded schools in this city are well manned (with women mostly), and we have many model teachers and departments.

THE INSTITUTE.

The Institute held last April was one of great interest. It was conducted by Prof. Graham. A large number attended, and a new impetus was given to the cause of education in this county. Institute work by the State I regard as indispensable to progress in our school system. The object of the law should be to make them more effectual by a compulsory attendance of the teachers. Eighty names were enrolled as members of the Institute.

COMPULSORY EDUCATION.

With the statistics of the United States Commissioner of Education before them, it is a wonder how any Legislature in this age of the world can refuse to enact laws for the compulsory education in the English language of all children, white or black, Chinese or Indian, or anything else that claims to be human. This, with the moral and religious teaching that should accompany it, is the best and the only civilizing influence that will ever secure national safety and true prosperity. The great mistake of the nation has been in allowing the Indians, or any foreign tribe who make a stay in our land, to live in ignorance of our language or the advantages of schools.

But this is not the time for a lengthy dissertation, so I stop.

FOND DU LAC COUNTY—SECOND DISTRICT.

MAURICE MORIARTY, SUPERINTENDENT.

As my annual report contains the financial statement of interest regarding the schools, I do not deem it necessary to repeat those statements here, but shall confine myself to a few brief matters of statements regarding the present condition of the schools in this district. During the past year, I have held two examinations at Fond du Lac City, which were attended with a better result than if in three different places in said district, as heretofore, it being the means of bringing them all together in one place. A legislative act passed last winter entitled me to do so, and had the desired effect. These examinations were attended by 200 applicants. Of this number, 9 received second grade, 156 third grade certificates, and 35 were rejected. The schools have not retrograded during the year. I trust they have advanced, as a great many teachers are candidates for the office of County Superintendent, which ought to be a sure sign of progression.

THE COUNTY SUPERINTENDENCY.

This office, under our republican form of government, is based on the will of the people, and, under the political programme of caucuses and conventions, a superintendent must be a politician to secure the office, and will sometimes be forced to do some unpleasant work in order to hold the position, with politics running as high as they are at present. I think, therefore, some legislative reforms are needed before this system will be comprehended and rendered capable of its utmost good.

The question has been repeatedly asked me, if, in my opinion, the schools were more likely to progress, or had done any better under the system of county superintendents than that of town superintendents. I could notice no great difference, but that the county created a bigger office for one man, costing the district $1,000 per annum instead of $250, under town government, allowing $25 for each of the ten towns comprising the eastern district, and I think there are men in each of the towns capable of doing justice to the office, and that they would be more independent as representing one town than ten, as the applicants would probably be not inhabitants of their town.

Certainly, we may understand that it is not the design of our common school system to rear up a race of professional gentlemen to worry the world by their wits, or a superfluous class of accomplished women with no capacities for the domestic accomplishments of life; but the design of the system is rather to rescue the race especially its helpless offspring, from ignorance and vice and start them fairly onward in life, with improved capabilities of usefulness and enjoyment. If the public does this duty well, it may fold its arms complacently. It is all that nature or the law may rightfully demand. I think it would be an improvement and a benefit to our schools, if the official term of district officers was limited to one year; for sometimes they fail in that harmony among them that should exist at all times and under all circumstances. If annually elected, the strife would end sooner, and, I think, would lead to better results.

GRANT COUNTY.

W. H. HOLFORD, SUPERINTENDENT.

Grant County is in the south-western part of the State and is bounded on almost three sides by the Wisconsin and Mississippi rivers, and its land is much broken by the valleys of some nine or ten small rivers flowing into these large ones. Being that much of it is prairie, the county contains much good land but far more that is poor. It is one of the older and wealthy (not wealthier) parts of Wisconsin. This county contains nearly 1200 square miles, and contains about 250 school districts, and employs nearly 300 teachers.

But many of these districts are too feeble to support good teachers; others are distracted and rendered almost powerless for good by quarrels of one locality with another locality, and jealousies of one part of the district against another part of it. Such evils have caused the division and sub-division of districts that once contained as parts those districts now so feeble. And a few other districts fully able seem too stingy to keep up good schools. On an average during this last year, about two-fifths of the schools have been very poor. The causes were: in some cases, incompetent teachers; in other cases, ruinous old school-houses: in others still, school through the last of June, in July and August; again, school-houses destitute of apparatus even to being without a blackboard; in other instances, very inconvenient school-houses with out-houses, if any, in shameful condition; and in others, district quarrels and frequent change of teachers.

About two-fifths of the districts had fair average schools that did passably good work; but these could be improved in many respects. The causes of fair schools were: teachers of fair ability, school-houses more or less convenient and in good repair; School begun by the first of September and continued till Christmas week, had two weeks' vacation, then had school—not till any stated fixed time, but—till the "breaking up" of winter, the muddy time, came, at which time they had another vacation of about three weeks, then as soon as the roads were dry, came all the remainder of the school for that school year; a fair supply of apparatus in passably clean school-houses; harmony in the districts; no change of teachers during the year.

About one-fifth of the districts had first-class schools. The causes were, the employment of first-class teachers for one, two or more years in succession; school houses and out-houses kept in good repair and thoroughly clean by a person hired for that purpose, thus leaving the teachers free to devote their whole time to rendering the school a complete success; the schools were held between the 25th of August and the 20th of the next June; an abundant supply of blackboard, programme clock and good seats and desks; liberal pay to teachers and harmonious action in the districts. Two districts of the one-fifth had nearly all these things except the first-class teachers. Of course these districts had poor schools.

Perhaps no village of its size in the state has a better school nouse and grounds than Lancaster. Probably in our state no village of its size has a better high school, or trains more or better teachers in a common school than the city of Boscobel; and Platteville high schools would be and do about the same, but that the normal school relieves both of these village schools of all their most advanced pupils. Also, the villages of Bloomington, Muscoda and Cassville have had good schools, and they expect to have better next year than they had this last year.

SCHOOL HOUSES.

There are several school houses that are in a ruinous condition in more than one sense. They are not only old, worn out, and dangerous to the physical health of the pupils, but they are equally dangerous to their moral health, as it is impossible to keep the rooms warm in a windy day, and as obscene cuts mar the outside of the doors and walls, and nearly all parts of the out-houses, where they have any, belonging to such school houses. Of course these are exceptional cases, and I have urged the district board and teachers to remedy such things.

Most of the village and some of the country schools are provided with school furniture. Comparatively few are well seated; and there is a great lack of good, sufficient and low enough blackboard. As these matters have been much agitated for the past four years at least, they will be remedied to a great extent during the next two or three years, if county superintendent and teachers continue to urge it upon school boards.

SCHOOL SUPERVISION.

I visited 101 different schools, and made 147 visits to schools, besides several short calls in passing. In a county so large it takes much more travel to visit 100 schools, situated in the many localities, and to reach the extreme parts, than it does in a county containing from 45 to 125 schools.

During these visits I have done all I could in so short a time to help teachers and to incline pupils to correct existing evils and errors, and to advise with teachers, district boards and patrons concerning schools and how to improve them. In this way I have gathered much valuable matter in the line of excellencies and that of defects, those relating to how to cause improvements and to avoid difficulties. What I have collected in this manner in each six months, I have incorporated into my next set of examination questions, thus rendering all of my questions full of suggestions.

EXAMINATIONS AND TEACHERS.

By far the most important duty of the county superintendent is the examination, supervision and inspection of teachers by judicious, searching and suggestive written and oral questions, by advice, by encouragement, by suggestions and by criticisms averse and commendatory. For our common schools the widest and best provision in the school law, all of which is good, is, that it provides for the *examination* of teachers and makes *no* provision for the "renewal of certificates" that have expired. But there is great need that the state superintendent should urge county superintendents to examine *all* who would teach but do not hold certificates that are in force. Many teachers in the state who, judging from their total lack of progress before the examination became an unavoidable and surely occurring thing (it is such in some counties), would never have been able to merit third grade certificates, now hold first grade county certificates, and are preparing to take third grade state certificates. Not only are their certificates of a higher grade than before, but their stock of common sense, judgment, tact and skill in managing schools, is more than equally as much improved. And I am confident that these improvements would not have been made had there been any possibility of avoiding the examinations; and to the fact that they cannot be avoided, the normal schools are indebted for many of their best students. Yet, because not one county superintendent in five, and aside from these, not one person in a thousand, presents these things in this light, many ministers of the Gospel, professors in our higher institutions of learning, physicians, rich merchants and persons of influence in all other positions in life—join in *urging* and often in begging or commanding the county superintendents to grant certificates to those who *cannot* pass. Hence, permit me to say to you that county superintendents are sorely in need of sympathy, support and commands from the state superintendent in this particular. The only effectual method of securing prompt and regular attendance at teachers' institutes, is to have it understood by all that teachers cannot teach in any county in the state without meriting certificates under a judicious searching and suggestive examination; and that the *only* way to renew a certificate when it has legally expired, is by passing an examination; except that it may be extended by the endorsement of the county superintendent for not more than two months preceding any of the next public examinations for his county that the teacher may desire to attend. At present this seems to be not generally but very limitedly understood.

It is the teacher that makes the school. The employment of good teachers secures good schools; but the employment of poor teachers insures poor schools. In Grant county the people are year by year becoming more sensible of the fact, and more anxious to employ good teachers only, and to have good schools.

INSTITUTES.

A two weeks' Institute was held at Lancaster, conducted by Prof. W. D. Parker, assisted by me. It was attended by 64 teachers, and was profitable and interesting. Several teachers have written me substantially as follows: Please tell the State Superintendent that "I would not take one hundred dollars for what I learned there." I am glad of this on their account, but much *more* so on the account of their present and future pupils. And the teachers are very anxious to have Mr. Parker come again. Besides this, I conducted six two day Institutes and twenty-two half-day Institutes in connection with my examinations.

TIME FOR ANNUAL SCHOOL MEETING.

Many school-houses are sadly out of repair and will remain so all winter, not because the school board does not want to repair them, but because the annual school meeting, whether held in either the very busy time, the last Monday in August, or the equally busy time, the last Monday in September,—was held too late to give sufficient time for securing workmen and getting the work done before it will become too cold. Of course they will not be repaired next spring, and the neglect will be repeated next fall. For *many* reasons the annual school meeting in rural districts should be held the *first* Monday in *July*, between "corn plowing" and "haying."

GREEN COUNTY.

D. H. MORGAN, SUPERINTENDENT.

TOWNSHIP SYSTEM.

In connection with what you may find in my report, I would say, that I am more and more convinced of the necessity of resorting to the "Township System of School Government." Almost all of the town clerk's reports are defective in one or more particulars—not on account of any neglect of their own, but because there are so many men acting as district clerks who have no idea of the proper manner of preparing their reports. In very few instances have the aggregate of those between the ages of four and seven, seven and fifteen, fifteen and twenty, equalled the whole number returned, and the same error will apply, only with a greater difference, to the different divisions of those who have attended school.

The district reports, unamended, would be absolutely valueless, except as to the number of children.

Had we a board of education in each town, whose business it should be to meet on a given day, to transact whatever business is required of them, all these statistical errors might be avoided. The legislature of the State did not see fit to make it optional with the people whether we should have county instead of town superintendents, but made it absolute, and those that have interest enough in educational matters to observe, feel satisfied that the legislature never did a wiser thing than the establishing of the system of county supervision; and I can see no good reason for our legislature refusing to give us the township system, simple and pure, without any provisos.

OUR TEACHERS.

I think I may safely say that our teachers are growing better and better from year to year, and that some of the inefficient are giving place to a better class. A great amount of ambition is manifested on the part of the young teachers, to improve in their standing from year to year, and our High Schools have adopted a commendable course in giving time to special preparation, out of the common course of study, with a view to being put in practice in the country schools.

THE INSTITUTE.

Our Institute, though held during the warmest week of the season, was largely attended, and Mr. Salisbury succeeded in making the work both entertaining and instructive. So much are our teachers impressed with the value of Institute work, that I shall hold three short term Institutes in different parts of the country, during the fall, and before the commencement of winter schools. We have made arrangements to hold monthly teachers' meetings during the winter.

MANITOWOC COUNTY.

MICHAEL KIRWAN, SUPERINTENDENT.

I. STATISTICS.

The statistics of my annual report are not all correct. Town clerks are careless, or worse, in compiling their reports, and the data furnished them by district clerks is often an almost unintelligible mass of contradictions, of little value to any one, and of less credit to the maker of the reports. To decipher, interpret, compare and correct the conflicting statements requires more patience, higher regard for accuracy, and, sometimes, better ability than the average town clerk is endowed with. He is anxious to be well rid of the whole matter, and a feeling of relief comes over him when he has mailed or handed it to the county superintendent. He seldom accepts the superintendent's offer to return it for correction, and often dextrously avoids compromising his own fame as a mathematician by sending the report to the superintendent without setting down the footings; leaving it for the latter to satisfy the state superintendent that 5+4=6+7.

Reports of the clerks of joint districts give rise to multitudinous errors. The number of children reported between 4 and 7, 7 and 15, and 15 and 20 years of age, in a town, should equal the whole number of children over 4 and under 20 years of age in that town; but under the present system of reporting, this cannot be the case, when the town embraces part of a joint district, even though the officers report as required correctly. The clerk of a joint school district is instructed to report to the clerk of the town in which the school-house is situated, the number of children over 4 and under 20 years of age, residing in that part of the district which lies within said town. He also reports to the same town clerk the whole number of children in the district between 4 and 7, 7 and 15, and 15 and 20 years of age. The town clerk's report then shows the sum of these three columns to be more than the whole number of children in the town; for a part cannot be made to equal the whole. The statistics showing the attendance of pupils set forth the same discrepencies, and for like reasons.

The clerk of a joint district reports to each town clerk whose town embraces a part of the district the number of days that school has been taught. Usually, this item is embodied in the report of each town clerk to whom it is sent, and each of two or more towns is credited with what properly belongs to only one, thus making the aggregate for the county appear much greater than it is.

The report of the district clerk often gives testimony of wonderful financial ability on the part of the treasurer—ability which, had Jay, Cooke & Co., possessed it, would have averted their recent disaster and the consequent panic which is felt throughout the country—the ability to disburse seems largely in excess of the total receipts.

I. TEACHERS.

Number, Age, Experience, Wages, etc.—One hundred and twenty-seven teachers are required to teach the schools in this county. During the last school year, 140 persons have been licensed to teach. The average age of those persons is 22¼ years; 21 were without experience in teaching; 29 are not residents of this county, and six of the number licensed did not teach. The average wages per month for male teacher is $48.48; for females, $31.50. The average number of days each district has maintained school the past year is about 145.

2. *Qualifications and Progress.*—Some of our teachers are deficient in scholarship and ability to teach; a larger number fail in method rather than in a knowledge of books; a considerable number are well qualified in all respects. Nearly all are making honest efforts to improve, and it is safe to predict that in a few years this county will be as well supplied with competent teachers as many of the more populous and wealthier counties of the state.

3. *From other Counties.*—At present we are compelled to send abroad for a limited number of teachers who, thanks to the educators who aid us in the matter, generally prove to be all that we can reasonably expect. But this mode of obtaining teachers has this disadvantage: the teacher who comes here from another county seldom proposes to remain longer than one or two terms; the reputation he makes during his stay may never reach his home, and the incentives to exertion are, therefore, fewer in his case than in that of the resident teacher. If he is not strictly conscientious he may, by carelessness in his work, do wrong to his pupils and to the

friends who recommend him. Teachers in the county are anxious to gain reputation and careful to maintain it; because upon these conditions depend their chances of future employment.

II. ASSOCIATIONS.

Two Teachers' Associations were organized last winter, and regular meetings were held for several months. Informal meetings were also called in several localities and were largely attended by the citizens generally, as well as teachers. Messrs. Viebahn, I. N. Stewart, Walker, and J. C. Smith were especially active and efficient in convening and instructing these assemblages, and their labors have greatly benefited their fellow-teachers. In some of the inspection districts of the county each of the late examinations occupied four days; of which two days were given, in each place, to oral exercises conducted by Mr. Viebahn and myself.

III. INSTITUTE.

An Institute was held at at Manitowoc, from July 21 to August 15, under the charge of Professor Graham and Mr. Viebahn. This was our first long-term institute, and we are well satisfied with its results. 103 members were enrolled; the average daily attendance was 71. Hard work was a characteristic feature of the session. There was no hedging on the part of the instructors, and no pupil was allowed to shirk his duty. The discipline maintained was nearly perfect. The conductors required, and, by the character of their work, commanded and secured, the closest attention. Instances of communication, even under the comprehensive definition of that word given by Professor Graham — anything calculated to draw the attention of a member of the institute from the work in hand — were few. Teachers who deprecate communication in their schools, were thus afforded an opportunity to illustrate by example the advantage of their theory. The papers written at the examination which took place at the close of the institute, were much better, on the whole, than those of any previous examination which I have held.

IV. THE NORMAL SCHOOL AT OSHKOSH.

is exercising a slutary influence upon our schools. This county is quite largely represented in the school, and we have 18 of its pupils teaching here now. Judging by the progress its students make, the school is doing thorough work; and I have not yet met one of its returned pupils who does not regret the necessity which compelled him to leave it, or who does not feel that the instruction there given has made him stronger both educationally and morally.

V. LENGTH OF SCHOOL TERM.

As stated elsewhere in this report, the average number of days each district in this county has maintained school the past year is about 145. This leaves too long an interval between the terms of school, during which teachers must seek employment in other pursuits, and pupils are likely to forget much that has just been taught them. Teachers can hardly become enthusiastically devoted to a calling which affords them employment half the year only. Ought not the law to require that districts maintain school eight or ten months each year, instead of five months? Can we ever have a full corps of efficient teachers in our schools unless the present law be so amended? Many districts now provide for five months school for no other reason than that the law obliges them to do so. Remove the constraint and the provision will not be made. In stipulating that a district shall maintain five months school each year, the law recognizes the fact that it will not do to leave this matter of education wholly at the option of the people. Were it to do so, intelligent communities might protect their school interests; but those interests would languish in localities whose inhabitants are indifferent to education, or hostile to the present system. The suggested amendment could not be considered oppressive in spirit unless the existing law is so; and the consequent increase of taxes would be too insignificant to be seriously felt. If a state assumes to educate its citizens the means should be adapted to the end. The present provisions are neither adequate nor economical. The work is incomplete because sufficient time is not given to insure its completion; it is not well done because the best facilities which the state can obtain for its performance are not obtained. Time is wasted because school is not maintained during the pleasantest months of the year; opportunities are lost when children cannot go to school at any time they wish to do so; money is thrown away in being paid to incompetent teachers whose places could as well be filled by capable persons if steady service were guaranteed; and it is also wasted in paying teachers to teach again what was taught before, and has been forgotten in the long intervals of mental inactivity. Persons are constantly abandoning teaching for other occupations; but how can it be otherwise? What man is willing to sacrifice his own interests for the aggrandizement of another; to live in obscurity and poverty when a happier lot is attainable? Establish the profession of teaching on a solid basis, and there will no longer be any foundation for this charge. If an individual were to pursue the same policy in his business that states adopt toward their common schools he would be derided for his mismanagement and bankruptcy would be inevitable. Wretched school houses, bare walls, rickety benches without desks, and half educated teachers are not elements which a great commonwealth should tolerate in a system of which it boasts. It may be impossible to remove these evils at once, but immediate measures ought to be taken with a view to their eradication. Let us have an educational system in fact as well as in name; the term as applied to our mixed schools at this time is a misnomer.

VI. EXAMINATIONS AND CERTIFICATES.

It is to be regretted that there is so little uniformity among county superintendents in the examination of applicants for certificates. In some counties applicants are required to devote two days to an examination in third grade branches, and three or four days to an examination in the subjects named in a certificate of the first grade; in other counties they are hurried, in a single day, through all the branches required for a certificate of the first grade. How an examiner can form a correct estimate of the qualifications of a teacher who is forced to write on fifteen subjects between the hours of 9 A. M. and 4 or 5 P. M., must ever be beyond the comprehension of ordinary mortals. It would seem that under this mode of proceeding a good deal must be taken for granted. Applicants who fail to obtain limited certificates in one county migrate to an adjoining county and are immediately classed with the elect; thus proving to the satisfaction of their friends, if not to their own, the injustice and severity practiced in the county to which their valuable services are lost.

Certificates of the higher grades are sometimes granted as mere matters of compliment and not in pursuance of any examination. What assurance is given by a certificate obtained in this manner that its holder is able to teach the branches named therein? The school officer who accepts it as evidence of qualifications is likely to be deceived; the teachers of the county in which it is given are wronged by a favoritism which substitutes conjecture, or personal regard, or political considerations, for proved merit; and the superintendent who issues the paper must be lowered in the estimation of those who are cognizant of the act. Such proceedings are but too frequent in this State; but an incident may be related to show that we are not alone unfortunate in this regard: Yesterday a certificate, issued by a county superintendent in Missouri, was handed to me by a teacher who remarked that he wished to teach in Manitowoc County, and presumed this certificate would furnish satisfactory proof of his scholarship. The certificate represented his standing to be 4 on a scale of 5 in all subjects required in our State for a county certificate of the first grade, (Algebra and Constitutions excepted), and in addition thereto Mental and Moral Philosophy, and Rhetoric. Yet this teacher declined to be examined here for a third grade certificate, frankly admitting that he doubted his ability to obtain it on his merits! When he learned that I would not license him unless he wrote satisfactory papers, he assured me that a certificate is no evidence of a teacher's ability, and that it is generally given as a mark of favor. He seemed sincere in making this assertion, and it could not be disputed that, in at least one instance, he knew whereof he affirmed. The Missouri certificate shows that in that State an applicant for a county certificate of the first grade is examined in all the branches above designated, and also in Algebra, Chemistry, Plane Trigonometry, and surveying.

Cannot more uniformity in examining applicants, and stricter honesty in licensing them, be secured in our own State by discussing these points at the annual meetings of the Superintendents at Madison?

VII. COUNTY SUPERINTENDENTS.

1. *Time of Election.*—The law fixing the time for the election of these officers should be so amended that they shall be chosen when the excitement of local or State politics cannot influence or bias the electors. The only issues that should be raised in the election of a Superintendent are integrity, willingness to do his duty, and fitness for the position to which he aspires. These considerations are often disregarded, for nominations are mainly controlled

by caucuses and politicians, and electors vote for a ticket or party rather than for candidates. If Superintendents were elected in May or June, voters would be more likely to be guided by proper than by partisan motives; and a candidate for re-election, if beaten at the polls, might secure a school, should he wish to do so, in a short time after his defeat, instead of being forced to wait nearly a year for a situation, as he must now do.

2. *Manner of Choosing.*—Many good educators think the elective system but a hazardous one, at best, for the office of Superintendent, and hold that an appointing power, properly vested, would be preferable. But it is not easy to determine to whom this power can be safely entrusted. A superior officer, who is elevated to place by party machinery, is expected to be solicitous for the preservation and strengthening of the ropes and pulleys by which he was hoisted; and, although his appointments might not ignore ability, it is to be feared that fealty to party might be no insignificant claim if pointedly urged. Something ought to be done to protect the office against designing politicians and their dupes, who have the same means of forcing themselves upon the people for this as for other offices.

3. *Qualifications.*—The law relating to this office ought to be further amended so as to make moral character and scholarship conditions of eligibility. A teacher is required to have these qualifications, but the man who examines him is often devoid of both. A judge who is impeached and convicted is not allowed to retain his seat upon the bench and sentence others for offenses similar to that which he has committed; a man can not teach what he does not know; how, then, can a superintendent that daily allows himself to become fuddled refuse to license a teacher who does the same thing; or mark the latter's standing in a subject of which the examiner himself has no knowledge? Some persons may regard these questions as absurd, others will admit that they are very perinent and deserve a statutory answer.

MARATHON COUNTY.

THOS. GREENE, SUPERINTENDENT.

I have the pleasure to report that very great improvement made during the year, in all the schools in the county, is evident.

Our Institute for the year was held in September, 1872. It was conducted by Professor Graham, of Oshkosh, and was productive of much good.

Examinations of teachers have been conducted as heretofore. The average attainments of scholarship of the applicants is somewhat in advance of that of last year.

There are 14 towns in this county; but one (the town of Wien), has adopted the township system of school government.

There are 55 districts in the county, and 54 school houses. Four large frame school houses have been built during the year. They will soon be occupied. Also, two log houses have been put up. One district only has failed to comply with the legal requisition of maintaining a school for five months during the year — owing to the fact that the board did not receive the money necessary to complete their school house until the month of June, 1873. The board hope that the State Superintendent will permit them to draw from the state fund.

I have visited 53 schools; some twice, some three times. My visits were as unexpected and as informal as it was possible to make them. A day passed in each school enabled me to ascertain the progress the pupils were making in their studies, and the fitness of the teachers for the very important positions they occupy.

MARQUETTE COUNTY.

S. D. FORBES, SUPERINTENDENT.

UNRELIABLE STATISTICS.

I have experienced the same difficulty this year as last in obtaining reliable statistics from the several districts of the county; an with my best efforts directed to harmonize the inconsistency of reports, they are but an approximation to the true state of matters to which they relate. The value of the "general statistics," if they have any, depends upon their accuracy; but the possibility of overcoming the carelessness and negligence of unpaid district clerks, renders them extremely unreliable. I repeat my opinion, that a law allowing district clerks a fair compensation for their services, payable on certificate of the completeness and accuracy of their reports, would go far to remedy the evil.

This year I report only 3,364 pupils of school age in the county, or 107 less than last year. I am certain there has been no such falling off in the actual number of school children in the county, and that the discrepancy arises from incorrect reports.

SCHOOL ATTENDANCE.

The proportion who have attended school is nearly the same as last year, or about 60 per cent. of the whole number of school age in the county. The per cent. of non-attendance is largest in those localities mainly inhabited by foreigners, in some towns amounting to nearly 70 per cent. In many districts the school is a mere farce, kept up only for the purpose of "drawing the public money," and accomplishing none of the ends for which free schools are established. Would it not have a beneficial effect to apportion the public fund on the number who attend school, or rather upon the aggregate days attendance of the preceding year.

The safety of our free institutions demands that this evil of non-attendance shall be met, in some way. Our present school system does not do it. If a compulsory law will, let us have it by all means. Parental ignorance and indifference should not be allowed to deprive children of their most valuable inheritance, and put in jeopardy our free government. Were only the welfare of the individual at stake, we might question the propriety of interposing legal enactments, but as the worm of illiteracy is gnawing at the very foundation of our government, it becomes a proper subject for legislation. It is not expected by the most sanguine advocates of the law that it will confer the boon of education upon all, but it will do something in the right direction. The trite adage in which some objectors sum up their conclusions as to the utility of such a law:—"You may lead a horse to water but you cannot make him drink,"—may be true as regards some, but it is no reason why those who do thirst for knowledge should not have the opportunity given them to drink.

SCHOOL-HOUSES.

I am able to note but few improvements in school buildings during the past year. Owing to the general failure of crops for the two preceding years the people have felt too poor to make investments of this kind, beyond actual necessities. Only one new school-house has been built the past year, but several are in contemplation for the year to come. Forty buildings are reported in "good condition." This, in the opinion of the 'average district clerk,' means that at least three-fourths of the roof is rain proof, the floor open to nothing larger than rats, the walls half covered with plaster, and not above one-fourth the window lights broken. Perhaps one-half the school-houses of the county are fit for use as such. Not more.

APPARATUS.

It would seem strange that there should be such a lamentable deficiency in that cheapest and yet most important appendage of the school room — blackboard. Yet I have in mind but one school house in the country with a sufficient supply of this essential article. About eight feet in length is the average, whereas fifty is none too much for an average school of 35 pupils. But what the parents had when they were young is good enough for their children.

The statistics show ten school houses in the county supplied with outline maps, or four more than last year, which does not speak very well for the appreciation of these important aids to the teacher; and this in spite of the law authorizing district boards to purchase apparatus without a vote of the district. But says the wise economistt: "They never had no such things when I went to school, and got along just as well"!

SURROUNDINGS.

The crying evil of insufficient and ill-conditioned outhouses presents itself almost everywhere, a shame to patrons and teachers, and a prolific source of demoralization to pupils. Our schools cannot be propagators of healthy moral sentiment until all the pure influences are brought to bear there that prevail in the houses of the best families. This evil can be reached only through a general education of public sentiment, which is a slow process.

Eight school house sites are reported as "well enclosed"; the remainder lie out to the common, many of them staring upon the public highway without shade or shelter from sunshine or storm, the most desolate, dreary, and unattractive sights that meet the eye of the traveler.

TEACHERS.

It is a source of satisfaction to note improvements in the qualifications of our teachers, and a general disposition among them to take advantage of every opportunity offered to advance their standing and better fit them for their work.

I have issued during the year one hundred and seven certificates, viz: One first grade, eight second grade, and ninety-eight third grade; of which twenty-four were to males, and eighty-three to females. Of this number eleven of the third grade were duplicates. A number of six-month licenses have been issued, mostly to those who had never taught.

INSTITUTES.

Two Institutes have been held during the year, one in the spring, of a week's duration, and one in the fall of four weeks. At the former about forty teachers were in attendance, at the latter fifty-seven. Both were conducted by Prof. A. Salisbury as principal, and gave general satisfaction. The influence of the first was apparent in our summer schools, and the latter will, I am sure, be seen in the greater efficiency of our coming winter schools. Our teachers are entitled to credit for the time and money thus spent in trying to improve their qnalifications. The expense was indeed considerable compared with the meager wages paid teachers in the county.

In obedience to the law of change, I resign the duties of the of the office of County Superintendent on the first of January. During the two years of my supervision I have accomplished but a small part of what I had hoped for at the outset, but am gratified in the belief that the schools of the county have not degenerated; on the contrary, have advanced a step in efficiency and usefulness, and that the duties of the position will devolve upon a competent person, from whose labors greater results may be expected.

OCONTO COUNTY.

H. W. GILKEY, SUPERINTENDENT.

Upon submitting this, my fourth annual school report, it affords me pleasure to state that the educational interests of this county present a far more encouraging appearance than they did four years ago.

Several elegant and commodious school buildings have been erected, which are an honor and an ornament to the communities, by whose wise public liberality they have been built.

Our schools, generally speaking, are under the supervision of experienced and efficient teachers — teachers who seem to appreciate the responsibility of their high and holy calling.

Appropriations for school purposes are far more liberal than formerly; most of the districts maintaining school nine months during the year, while teachers' wages have advanced about 25 per cent.

Term-time and vacations are generally regular; indeed we might say they are reduced to a uniform calendar — the schools commencing about September 1st, and closing before the first of July; thus avoiding the unprofitable schools during the hot and sultry weather of midsummer.

The wide-spread dissatisfaction which prevailed throughout the county, on account of poor teachers and inefficient school supervision, has gradually disappeared, and school patrons delight in speaking in terms of praise and commendation of their teachers, and extend a cordial welcome to the supervisor while upon his tour of duty.

I have labored to make my school visits thorough, effective and frequent. I visit each school twice a term, with few exceptions, and improve my time while there. Efficient school visitation is among the most active means employed to promote the interests of the school. The teacher is stimulated to renewed exertion, and the pupils are encouraged to increase their diligence; while parents are led to place a higher appreciation upon common school instruction, and district officers can be reminded of their duties in relation to providing for the wants and comforts of the school room, which are so essential to the school.

But while much has been accomplished in different directions, to promote the welfare and prosperity of our schools, there remains much more yet to be done. Constant and unremitting exertion and well directed effort are still requisite to overcome the remaining obstacles and keep the educational machinery in successful operation.

POLK COUNTY.

CHARLES E. MEARS, SUPERINTENDENT.

Father Time has brought us to the close of another school year. It has been a year of general prosperity to the schools in Polk county. Not that they have attained to perfection, but much improvement has been noticed in the work performed.

TEACHERS AND WAGES.

My report for this year, as well as the one for 1872, contains the names of new teachers. Some of our older teachers are retiring from the work, and there being a constant increase in the number of districts, it is necessary that new teachers should be licensed each year. Better work being performed, higher wages are demanded and received.

SCHOOL CHILDREN.

The number of school children in the county over the age of four and under the age of twenty, as per the town clerk's reports, is 2,006; an increase of 295 over the number reported in the year 1872. The number of different children who have attended school during the year is 1,301, which leaves the large number of 705 who are not reported as having attended school. This is an increase of 141 over the number of the same class reported last year.

The benefit to be derived from our schools is not to be estimated by the amount in dollars and cents that they cost, but in the attendance of the children and the work there performed. The per cent. of attendance can and ought to be increased. Will not a compulsory school law help us?

SCHOOL HOUSES.

Eight new school houses have been built in the county during the year; four of logs and four frame buildings. Many improvements have been commenced on school grounds. New fences and repairs in the school room are to be seen in many districts.

REPORTS OF TEACHERS AND DISTRICT OFFICERS.

The teachers, with occasionally a little negligence, report at the end of each school month. I cannot understand how a teacher, with a right understanding of the meaning of that word, can be negligent in the performance of *any* duty. But, "as the twig is bent so is the tree inclined," and if a child is taught to be negligent while young, it will always be so, with, perhaps, an occasional exception.

My statistical report is not correct, but it is the best we can do. These reports can never be made strictly accurate so long as one district or town clerk is negligent or inefficient. Let us have the township system of school government, then, with a competent secretary of the town board of directors, we may hope for better and more correct reports. I hope that the next legislature may amend the township law so that *it will be a law*, instead of leaving it for the town to adopt. Our school law is the source of many evils, from the fact that it *permits* almost every thing and obliges very little to be done. Then let us pay all town school officers $2.00 per day for their work.

TEACHERS' CERTIFICATES.

The total number of certificates issued during the year is sixty-eight. Two second grade, and sixty-six third grade. There is considerable improvement in the standing of our teachers, and next spring I expect to report a better result in the matter of certificates. To ten applicants I refused to grant certificates. The rules governing examinations are the same as those reported two years ago.

INSTITUTE AND ASSOCIATION.

No better evidence of improvement and progress is needed, than is seen in the general attendance of our teachers at the meetings of the Institute and Association.

A second Normal Institute was held at Osceola Mills, August 19th to September 18th, 1872, conducted by Professor Albert Earthman, of Reedsburg.

Henry B. Dike is President, and Laura W. Mears Secretary of the Polk County Teachers' Association. Its annual meetings are held holiday week in each year.

At the annual meeting of 1871 the Association resolved to publish a second edition of the *Educational Record*, said *Record* to contain, when published, a summary of the educational work in Polk county, for the years 1872 and 1873. Henry B. Dike was elected to edit the *Record*, with the addition of Miss Ella Walker and Willis Scott to assist in its publication.

PORTAGE COUNTY.

W. R. ALBAN, SUPERINTENDENT.

According to the reports of town clerks, there has been received received from all sources, the sum of $20,167.39. The city of Stevens Point, reports nothing received from the tax levied by the county supervisors. The town of Stevens Point reports nothing received from county, and nothing received from the state school fund. Assuming that both have received their proper proportion of each of these funds, about $300 should be added to the amount first above named.

The disburements for all purposes, during the year were $25,145.00, leaving a balance in the several district treasuries of $4,022.39. Of the sum expended, there was $5,970.28 paid to male teachers, and $12,988.12, paid to female teachers. There are 81 school houses in the county, comprising 91 departments. Of these houses, 58 are reported in good condition; 52 with out-houses in good condition; 17 furnished with out-line maps, and only 6 reported to have sufficient blackboard—an article really indispensable to every well regulated school.

PUPILS.

The whole number of childred over four and under twenty years of age, is 4,630. The whole number who have attended the public schools, 3,272; leaving 1,358 who have either been taught at home attended private schools or are growing up in ignorance. The most favorable view that can be taken of it, will leave over one thousand children of school age, who have during the past year received no instruction in school. Of these reported, the average attendance has not been over 60 days each, which gives an actual full attendance of 1,958 children, during the school year of 100 days.

From the above statement, is deduced the conclusion, that from absenteeism alone, to say nothing of tardiness, uncomfortable school rooms, and want of a sufficient number of text books, all of which exist to a considerable extent—of the $25,145 expended, 40 per cent. has been thrown away. If we take into the account the whole number of children of school age, the showing will be still more unfavorable. One hundred days to each child will give an attendance of 463,000 days.' The actual number of days as reported by the town clerks is only 236,518, being an average of 50¼ days to each scholar. Deducting $\frac{1}{16}$ an account of sickness, inclement weather and other unavoidable causes, and another $\frac{1}{16}$ on account of private schools, there will still remain 197,582 days lost by non-attendance, which is equal to 100 days for 1,975 scholars. The actual cost of conducting our schools as reported, was $5.43 for each child of school age. Multiplying this by 1,975, the number of non-attendants, we have the sum of $10,724.28, totally lost to the purposes for which it was appropriated—more than ⅖ of the whole amount paid during the year for the support of schools. I might stop to inquire, is this just to our children? Is it just to the tax payers from whose pockets we wrest the money to support these schools? What wonder that compulsory education has many advocates among earnest men, to whom the acknowledged principle, that "the safety of the State depends upon the proper education of the youth," is not a stale platitude, but an eternal vital truth which republics cannot safely ignore. Upon the school children of to-day, will soon devolve the multifarious interests, the responsible duty of conducting our national and State government—whether civil, military, naval or domestic. And as we are all, to a great extent, creatures of circumstances, as our characters are formed by influences which surround us in youth, so the future of these children will be determined. Whether when they arrive at mature years, they shall be prepared to wield the ballot intelligently, to fill places of honor and trust properly, to be in their turn the guides of youth and blessings to the community in which the live, or whether they are reckless, ignorant, intemperate, vicious, preying upon the best interests of society, are questions we are helping to solve now, by the proper or improper appliance of the means of their education; by our earnestness or laxity in guarding them from immoral influences, and immoral and corrupting practices, both at home and at school.

Meager attendanee is sometimes caused by keeping the school in session at a season of the year when the necessities of parents appear to render it necessary for them to have the labor of their children at home. This is particularly the case in the rural districts. A few districts have adopted the plan of having a four months winter term, two months during April and May, and two months, from the middle of August to the middle of October. This plan appears to work well, and I am satisfied that schools so kept have a much better average attendance than the two term plan; yet, notwithstanding the well-known fact that corn-hoeing, potatoe bugging and berry picking thins the school to a sixth part of the proper attendance, the large majority of our schools continue through this season of the year, as though the principal aim of its continuance were to put in circulation, through the agency of the school ma'am, the few dollars that may remain in the hands of the district treasurer.

TEACHERS.

Since teaching has passed so largely into the hands of women, and according to the signs of the times, is destined to be still more exclusively the profession of that sex, it is unavoidable that a large part of our teaching be done by comparatively young teachers. This has been, and still is the case in this county, and perhaps will continue to be the case for an indefinite time in the future. Other counties in the State being similarly situated, there is no possibility of remedying the matter by drawing from them. Few female teachers expect to continue in that calling longer than the existence of unwedded life. Our schools are mainly conducted by teachers from 16 to 21 years of age. While their average qualifications are on the advance, so far as book learning and theory of teaching is concerned—still the want of a greater number of more experienced teachers is severely felt. Experience not only has a tendency to increase the facility of communicating instruction, but what is of equal importance, it increases the governing power. In this last, many of our teachers are sadly deficient. To remedy this state of things, I would suggest that school boards should be more faithful in the discharge of their duties and the exercise of the powers which the law very properly arms them with. To suppose that a diffident girl in her teens is competent to govern a house full of rude, thoughtless, uncultured boys and girls, without the earnest and well directed co-operation of the school board, is a supposition void of any substantial foundation. The power to make and enforce rules for the general management of the school, should be carefully and wisely but vigorously exercised. For want of the exercise of this power, not only unnecessary disorder exists in many schools, but profanity, vulgarity and general rudeness, exist to too great an extent. If we believe that good morals, as well as intelligence is necessary to form the good citizen, then the school and its purlieus should be carefully guarded against all these evils. The prevalence of these evils causes many of our citizens to withdraw their children from such influences and send them to private schools; a thing much to be deplored, because it weakens and degrades the public schools. They should be, and with all their faults are, the pride of our State. They should, and can be made so good, that every child of Wisconsin may receive such culture of mind and morals, as will fit him for any position. But this will not come by chance. It can be effected only by the united action of school officers, parents and teachers.

LABORS OF COUNTY SUPERINTENDENT.

During the year I have held two Institutes, one of two weeks duration at Stevens Point, in September, 1872; the other of four days, at Amherst, in April, 1873. Both these Institutes were poorly attended, as had been before intimated. Both were well conducted, and much valuable information was gained by the few who were in attendance.

I held nine public examinations, at which 200 persons were present for examination. The examinations were to a great extent written, making the examination by me of over 2,000 papers necessary in order to determine the standing of the applicants. One hundred and sixteen certificates were issued as the result of these examinations. I issued nine certificates on private examinations. One hundred and forty-four visits were made by me during the year, exclusive of a number of informal visits to Stevens Point and Plover schools.

Our teachers, in general, have been faithful to their trusts during the year. The irregularity of the attendance of scholars and the non-attendance of some have not been ou account of disartisfaction with teachers as a general thing, but have resulted from other causes, some of which have been alluded to. In conclusion, permit me to say, the people need a thorough waking up in relation to the duty of sending their children to school regularly, and it does appear that it would be eminently fitting and just, that parents who will make no effort to keep their children in school, when that school is, by the munificence of the State, free as air, should in some way have a little of the coercive power of the government applied to them to bring them to a sense of their obligations to their children and to community.

RACINE COUNTY.

GEO. SKEWES, SUPERINTENDENT.

It is with pleasnre I can say that good progress has been made in educational matters. Improvements have been made in buildings, better apparatus, etc., provided. Many of our best teachers are striving for higher grades of scholarship, and their work in the school-room shows a corresponding excellence.

SCHOOL-HOUSES.

Many of our school-houses are getting old, and the worse for wear. Preparation for building should be made at an early day in several of these districts. Most of our school-houses are destitute of good blackboards, outline maps, charts, etc., which are essential to the successful working of the schools. Another drawback is the rude construction of benches and desks, as well as their improper arrangement, and want of means for needed ventilation, altogeth- making the school-room, which should be made as cheerful and attractive as possible, a very undesirable place for children.

One new building has been completed within the past year and three were erected the year preceding. These buildings have cost from $700 to $1500 each, arranged and furnished in modern style, and are a credit, not only to their respective districts, but to the county.

SCHOOL GROUNDS.

It is to be regretted that so many of our schools have not sufficient room for play grounds, etc., only nine in seventy-six reported as having one acre.

It is to be hoped that school districts in preparing to build, will see to it that an eligible site is secured, and of sufficient size to afford room for exercise and amusement without trespassing on adjoining fields or the public highway. And I would heartily recommend that the school-yard be neatly enclosed with a good, substantial fence and ornamented with shade trees. These things can be had with but little trouble and cost and will add very much to the attractiveness of the ground. In visiting schools on our prairies during warm summer weather I have often been reminded of the want of a little grateful shade to relieve the excessive heat of the mid-day hour.

OUTBUILDINGS.

A few of our districts with commendable foresight have provided wood sheds for storage of wood, saving more in the cost of fuel than the outlay on building, besides greatly improving the appearance of school grounds. With regard to outhouses, let every parent and every district board examine the matter fairly, and then remedy the evils that must be glaringly apparent to every thinking mind.

ASSOCIATIONS.

The county is divided into two association districts — the eastern and western.

Associations have been held every three weeks in each division while the schools have been open. These meetings are of great advantage to the teachers attending them, as methods of teaching are discussed, class exercises introduced, defects noted, and improvements suggested. But our associations are not so largely attended as they should be, and those who most need the benefit of these meetings are the last to be reached by them.

I would urge upon school officers to see that teachers of their respective districts be encouraged and aided to attend our associations.

INSTITUTES.

While associations are helps, our greatest aid in advancing the cause and raising the *standing*, as well as the *standard* of teachers, is in our institute work.

Here we have time not only to present the best methods of teaching, but to secure the drill in and review of the branches taught, and stimulate teachers with new zeal to educate in the highest and best sense of the word. A four week's institute was held at Rochester in October of last year, with an attendance of seventy teachers. A short institute, with examinations, was held at Union Grove during the first week of last April, with an enrollment of fifty names. Again this fall there has been held an institute of three weeks in Burlington, with an attendance of eighty teachers, most of them in regular attendance throughout. These institutes have been attended with most excellent results, and their good effects have been apparent in the increased efficiency of teachers in their school work, and experience has proved that it has been a good outlay of time and money.

I secured the services of some of the best educators and institute workers in the State to aid in this work, and our teachers will gratefully remember their labors among us, as lecturers, as teachers, as educators.

EXAMINATIONS.

Thirteen examinations have been held during the past term. It has been my constant aim to select questions that would test the knowledge of applicants fairly and thoroughly on the several branches, as well as to be suggestive in leading to thought and study of principles rather than mere wordy repetition of rules and definitions.

There are now five holding first grade, twenty second grade, and one hundred third grade certificates. As there are several always leaving as well as coming into the ranks of teachers, and quite a number holding certificates not desirous of teaching, the demand and supply are very nearly equal. But very few limited certificates have been granted, and these by request of district boards. If an applicant's standing is low on one or more branches, or on the general average, a certificate has been granted for six months, in order that such teacher may be subject to frequent examinations, and it has been found a stimulus to more careful study.

SCHOOL VISITATIONS.

All of the schools have, on the average, been visited four times, and many of them five and more times. Most all of the time, when schools were open, has been spent in school visitation. I have found it impossible to spend one-half day in every school each term, as special cases required a second visit, and teachers' associations had to be reached, occasioning loss of time.

For the greater part of the term, when possible, a day has been spent in visiting but two schools, spending what time could be given, allowing for traveling, &c.

I have found that after becoming acquainted with our teachers and their work, that it was not necessary to remain one half of a day in the schools of our better teachers and have endeavored to spend more time where I could be of greater service.

But it requires two months to visit all of the schools, even without loss of time, and as our school terms are very irregular in opening and closing, it would sometimes happen that a school would be closed before it could be reached by visiting in rotation. And I would respectfully recommend that more time be given to the fall schools. During the months of July and August all of the schools should be closed, for I find a smaller per cent. of the children in attendance during these months than at any other portion of the year — besides the excessive heat renders some of our school houses almost intolerable.

During the past two years I have watched with interest the growth of our teachers. Most of them have improved their standing and shown themselves worthy of their profession. We have had comparatively few failures, some of these arising from young and inexperienced teachers crowding into the larger and more difficult schools to manage, and not proving sufficient to meet the emergencies.

Very much depends upon the judgment of district boards in engaging teachers, as all holding certificates are not suitable for every school.

As 60 per cent. is the minimum average for a third grade certificate, it some times happens that inferior teachers may work themselves up to the required standing, and by right claim certificates which cannot be denied unless there has been previous proof of their inefficiency as teachers. Certificates for applicants for schools should be carefully examined by district boards before engaging them.

RICHLAND COUNTY.

WM. J. WAGGONER, SUPPERINTENDENT.

The report I this day forward you is, as a whole, nearer correct than that of last year, personal knowledge enabling me to make some corrections in the reports I receive. But few persons possess the necessary qualifications, or have the practice, to discharge such clerical duties without mistakes, and as few will be offered pay for the service, accurate district reports are things very far in the future. Simplicity will tend to greater accuracy, and if there is anything in them that can be omitted without detracting from its general usefulness, it would seem well to do so. I encounter the feeling that they are useless, and as a result attention is only given to what is necessary to secure the public money.

A number of districts have changed the time of holding the annual meeting from September to August, (which should be made the time by legislative enactment), which, when it becomes universal, will insure more accurate financial statements.

The report shows an increased attendance of 5 per cent., and in those over 20 years of age an increase of 15 per cent., while there is a decrease of 36 per cent. of those under four.

The reported receipts of the year are $32,677.50 against $30,034.-48 last year. There have been paid for building and repairs $3,-508.21 against $1,349.90 last year. There were paid to male teachers $246.47 less than last year, and to females $1,035.44 more

The expenditures of the year are $25,904.54, being $3,492.39 more than last year, and leaves in the treasuries $8,464.20, a little more than was reported last year.

PROGRESS.

As evidence of progress I would instance the building of comfortable houses, many efforts to provide for the regular attendance of the children, more visits by officers and parents, frequent inquiries concerning the qualifications and success of teachers before hiring them, a higher appreciation of the service of live teachers, and a better comprehension of the theory of teaching with more thorough work on the part of nearly all engaged, are unmistakable evidences.

By doing a large amount of "field-work," giving my time and whatever ability I possess to the study and discharge of the duties of the office, I think, a healthy, growing interest has been secured. As useful means to this end I would note: 1st. The use of a column in the *Richland County Republican*, in which I published thoughts and suggestions for the benefit of teachers, pupils and patrons, tabulated statements from teachers' reports, short communications from the same, other educational intelligence, and brief accounts of my school visits; 2nd, The close communication and confidence secured by the monthly reports of the teachers, which enables them to lay before me the condition and needs of their schools, for more effective operations when visiting. These monthly reports show the number of pupils enrolled, the average daily attendance, cases of tardiness, number of families whose children were tardy, whether communications are allowed, if text books are needed, if written examinations are had, the number of pupils with habits that would make them bad members of society, visits by board, parents and teacher, the wages, the names of pupils satisfactory in deportment, those neither absent nor tardy, and those that have studied faithfully, and any other items that they might desire to communicate.

In July I prepared and forwarded the following circular:

OFFICE OF COUNTY SUPERINTENDENT OF SCHOOLS,
RICHLAND CENTER, Wis., July 30, 1878.

To the Citizens assembled at Annual School Meeting:

GENTLEMEN: To convey you information on the progress and condition of our schools, and to offer some suggestions for your consideration at this meeting, is the object of this circular.

In section 92 of the School Law, which describes the powers and duties of the county superintendent, you will find him charged with the following: "To visit and examine all the schools and school-districts within his jurisdiction as often in each year as shall be practicable; to inquire into all matters relating to the management, the course of study and mode of instruction, and the text-books and discipline of such schools, sites, outbuildings and appendages, and of the district district generally; to advise with and counsel the district boards in relation to their duties, and particularly in relation to the construction, warming and ventilation of school-houses, and the improving and adorning of the school grounds connected therewith, and to recommend to school officers and teachers the proper studies, discipline and management of the schools."

In the prosecution of those duties it has been my good fortune to visit 118 schools in the county, most of them twice, and many three times. I find some imperative demands that cannot be neglected without districts losing money or endangering the health of the children, saying nothing of the loss sustained in not securing their proper development.

I find a large number of teachers are conscientiously working to honor the calling, by giving their time and talents to the work of instruction. I find others who apparently labor under protest, not loving the profession well enough to strive for greater excellence in the work. There are still others who have "mistaken their calling," or lack the mental qualifications, the skill, judgment or energy necessary to do what is expected of them.

I find the country schools in various degrees of advancement, some very backward, most middling, while a few are working under a reasonably "high pressure."

I find a few good, comfortably furnished houses, a large number that answer the purpose of a school room, an equal number that, with repairs and re-seating, would answer quite well, while there are about twenty that are almost unfit for the purpose.

That you are impressed, in some degree, with the value and necessity of our common school system is evident from the large sums willingly paid to erect school houses and furnish them, to repair others, provide fuel and pay teachers—aggregating not less than twenty thousand dollars a year. Also evidenced by frequent inquiries for energetic, well qualified teachers, and in the universal anxiety for more substantial progress in the schools, giving better returns for the time and money expended. I am desirous that you become still more interested, and have been laboring to acquaint every one with our present educational condition, that such action will be taken as will insure you larger and quicker returns for the investment.

SCHOOL HOUSES.

After selecting honest, capable, unselfish men to administer the affairs of the district, and providing means to pay the necessary expenses of the year, your attention is called to the necessity of making your school houses comfortable. This is done by making them warm by clapboarding, if log, by daubing or pointing, supplying glass, banking up the sides even to or above the floor, providing a good, large stove and plenty of pipe, then a supply of dry wood, and you will have done all that can be done in the way of warmth, but do not for a moment entertain the thought of not doing anything to make the house warm because it is sold and you expect soon to build. If you are going to use the house, patch and bank up in such a manner as will keep out the cold, otherwise you make a draft on the vitality of those who look to to you for protection, and in many ways will the school prove unprofitable. The difficulty of keeping the feet warm, a necessary condition of good health and a well ordered school, would be greatly obviated, if every school house were carefully banked up to prevent the circulation of air under the floor. Where the house is comfortable, though badly seated, it would be a good investment to make or buy some properly constructed, substantial seats and desks, which could be used in a new house, and almost the comfort and convenience of a new house be at once obtained, besides it would divide the tax of furnishing and building. As your children are expected to spend nearly six hours a day, from five to nine months each year on the seats of the school room, their health and comfort depend largely on the construction of these seats. But few school rooms in the county are supplied with suitable ones; badly constructed, or improperly arranged seats and desks, are a constant source of deformity, disease and disorder among the children.

SURROUNDINGS OF THE SCHOOL HOUSE.

Of the 123 school houses in the county, only 22 have grounds enclosed. They should all be fenced, and a live, practical teacher will see to having trees and shrubbery set out and have flowers growing—all sources of proper education.

The gate, a constant expense if not allowed to lay on the ground, should be strongly made, and the most durable hinges I have noticed consist of ¾ inch square iron, one piece with an eye and the other with what might be called a hook; most blacksmiths have made them. Where hogs and sheep are not running in the road, a good obstruction to other stock can be made by taking some posts six or eight inches in diameter and six feet long, dress smooth, place three feet in the ground, and make of them three parallel rows in front, or inside, of the gateway and parallel with the fence; they must be close enough to prevent cattle walking through, and placed diagonally from the first row.

Of out-houses in good condition, 50 were reported. I should be happily disappointed to find even that number in "good condition." True modesty and decency demand that each district should have at least one; let them be properly cleaned before school commences, and, if necessary, specially charge the teacher to adopt measures to keep them decent. I know it can be done.

CHARTS, MAPS, APPARATUS, ETC.

Every school-house should have a blackboard extending across the end opposite the door and on both sides between the windows. It should be five feet wide and come within 2½ feet of the platform or floor. If your house is old and you intend building soon, for the present make one 5 by 12 feet; by all means get one without delay, and the larger the better. Many blackboards are now so glazed that they cannot be used; plane and paint them, using oil, lampblack and a little emery. Two coats now and another occasionally will keep it in fair condition. Probably the most satisfactory thing to use is liquid slating, which can be had of the dealers in school furniture, maps, etc., here. Knowing the needs and value of this article makes me thus explicit, that no excuse can be given for not having one suitable for use. Chalk, or crayons, register, pail, dipper, broom, shovel, wash-basin, sheepskin for rubbers, all are necessary articles that you will not fail to supply. A chair, a small table with a drawer, are valuable additions to the school-room, and should take the place of the clumsy, uncomfortable, book-destroying teacher's desk in many rooms.

No district can afford to do without some kind of Reading Charts or Cases for the beginners, their progress is much greater where they are used. A map of Wisconsin, one of the United States, one of the World, some writing charts and phonetic charts are articles you should obtain. A copy of the late law and the names of dealers in these articles you have received from the State Superintendent. A few districts have lost their dictionaries. It is the book of the school room, and should be secured without delay. After first supply, it is furnished at cost ($8) by the State. I have the necessary blanks to make out for it.

Whatever of these articles you have or may get, make the necessary preparation for their preservation, and when delivered to the teacher hold him or her strictly responsible for their careful use and protection. Teachers who cannot use, or fail to exercise a proper oversight over the property of the district while under their charge, lack essential qualifications of the true teacher.

SCHOOL TERMS.

Over one thousand dollars are wasted every year in this county by dragging out summer schools through July and August. During these hot months few children go to school, and in a large majority of cases learn very little. For truth of this, examine your registers and compare the attendance in July with May. There are two or three weeks in the spring when the roads are wet and muddy that it is not well to have school. Another vacation might be had between Christmas and New Years. You will also observe that neither teachers nor pupils can do complete justice to more than a three months' term without vacation, and that all high or graded schools hold their sessions from the month of September in one year till the fifteenth of June of the next, and that vacations occur as often as once in three months.

The graded schools in this county are conducted on this plan, and a number of the country schools have tried it, and I trust nearly all will soon adopt it. In arranging the terms, something like the following divisions will be found applicable:

FOR A FIVE MONTHS' SCHOOL.

First. 2 months fall, 3 winter; commence the middle of September, and have a short vacation between the terms.

Second. 3 months winter, 2 spring; commence last of November, and the spring term as soon as the roads are dry.

Third. Five months term to commence early in October and have a Christmas vacation.

FOR A SIX MONTHS' SCHOOL.

First. 2 months fall, 4 winter; commence early in September, have one week's vacation, then another during the holidays.

Second. 4 months winter, 2 spring; commence first of November, a week's vacation during the holidays; as soon as the roads are passable commence the spring term.

FOR A SEVEN MONTHS' SCHOOL.

First. 2 months fall, 3 winter and 2 spring; commence early in September and observe about the same order of vacations already given.

Second. 5 months winter, 2 spring; commence early in October and observe vacations as before.

FOR AN EIGHT MONTH'S SCHOOL.

First. 2½ Fall, 3½ Winter, and 2 Spring; commence early in September, and give such vacations as are already noticed.

Of these plans the first in each is considered best. With a little calculation the above arrangement may be adapted to any district in the county. If you get a good teacher you can keep him, or her, for the whole term greatly to your profit. It is better to pay $50 to an intelligent manager and worker, than $5 to a drone. While some of the time included in these arrangements may include "sugar-making," "corn planting" and husking, I submit, whether they will keep as many from school and for as long a time, as "corn hoeing," garden work, and harvest. The published Monthly Reports I receive from teachers will give you something of an idea of the attendance at different seasons, also a knowledge of other matters.

HIRING TEACHERS.

The most responsible duty of all is hiring a teacher. Unless he, or she, is a good one, the money is thrown away, the time of your children squandered, and your expense and efforts of no avail. The safest plan is to hire one of whose success in teaching you have personal knowledge, or on the recommendation of some one that possesses such knowledge. So important is your interest in this matter that I would urge every citizen, when passing a school in any section of the county to stop, and walk quietly in and spend a little time while yourself or team is resting, in taking observations on the work that is being done. Such is your privilege, and the importance of the teacher's work all parents recognize, and I know of no one thing that would do more to render teachers thoughtful and diligent, and as a consequence efficient, than to have their school work in shape for a visitor at any moment.

While much is expected of teachers, without your cooperation little can be done. Make it a point to assist them in all things, and when they propose measures or do acts that you deem impracticable or unnecessary, have a confidential talk with them on the subject but let no word or act of yours convey to your children the idea that the teacher is wrong. The complete progress of the school largely depend on your countenance and support, and when teachers' are hired because you know they are qualified to teach and govern your school, it should prove a success.

So far as I possess the ability to discern, I will not shrink from the delicate task of requiring every teacher to stand on his or her merits as exhibited to me at examination and school visits, and to sift out the absolutely incompetent; and I hope to receive your cordial support in the effort.

In marking certificates, 8 is considered very good, 7 fair, while 6 is passable. It is designed that these numbers show the person's knowledge of that branch, and not that they answered so many questions out of ten. The marking for "Ability to Teach" is made after seeing the candidate teach and embraces, knowledge, ability, and will use it, the mental discipline secured, tact to instruct, ability to govern, etc. Always get the best teachers you can for the money you have to pay, remembering that it is better to have a shorter school and a better teacher if you can not have both. And there are many female teachers in the county that with your support, will successfully teach any of the Winter schools, and as men can earn more money in other employments, you can hire a well qualified woman for what you may pay an inefficient man. Boys and girls are seldom profitable teachers; the work needs a maturity of mind that youth can not possess, hence other things being equal a person over 18 years of age is always to be preferred.

Come to the Institutes and Examinations and judge yourselves of the character and ability of our teachers; and it would save running, and writing, and disappointment, if district officers would engage teachers at these places.

ATTENDANCE AND INSTRUCTION.

Nearly all of the Winter schools are well attended, and in a few cases, beyond the capacity of the houses to accommodate. Where a school is full it would be better to keep the youngest pupils out, that the oldest ones who may be going for the last time may have nothing to interrupt them in securng the greatest improvement possible. With the increased opportunities of each year, the younger ones may gain the loss of a term.

There is yet a great deal of irregular attendance on the schools that needs a remedy. If the people are very earnest about the progress of their children, a "course of instruction" might be adopted in many districts that would require almost daily attendance to prosecute, which would materially improve it and be of great benefit. Let us look forward to something of this kind.

ANNUAL MEETING.

Section 17 of the School Code provides for changing the annual meeting from the last Monday in September to the last Monday in August. Many districts have made the change and all should do it. If it could be held still a month earlier it would be all the better. By law, the school year ends the 31st of August, and the District Clerk's report is made up to that time. If the meeting were held before, the same report of the condition, finances, etc., of the district, made to the meeting, could be made to the Town Clerk, which would insure greater accuracy. It also gives more time for making repairs, getting fuel, and hiring a teacher.

NEW BUILDINGS.

As each year witnesses the erection of new school houses, in order that they may be adapted to their use, I wish to offer some suggestions, and they are not founded in fancy but are the result of careful observation, study, and experience. Suit yourselves in the material and the quality of the work, but for the purposes of a school observe the following:

Make it as near square as possible, (the teacher has a better view of the school(, of good size and height, put a door in the *south end* and no windows in the north, let the bottom of the windows be high from the floor, and if they can be let down from the top by letting down on one side and raising from the bottom at the other, good ventilation will be had; if not ceiled throughout with lumber, wainscot up to the blackboard and windows; the blackboard should be part of the wall, about five feet wide and come within two and a half feet of the floor or platform, extended entirely across the north end, and down the sides between the windows—a projection four inches wide should be made at the bottom to hold the crayons and rubbers; a platform six inches high and five feet wide should extend entirely across the north end; hooks for clothing, etc., should be placed on the south end and in the corners make two or three shelves; the stove should stand near the door and the pipe run to a chimney in the opposite end. As this matter of heating is of prime importance, every school house should be heated by furnace, similnr to the stores in Richland Center. Take this matter into consideration before building, and you may be assured that the health and comfort of the children will soon repay the extra cost, which is only first cost, as the after expense is less than to use a stove in the room. Warming the house in this way would secure the children against sitting all day with wet feet and do something towards stopping the inroads of fever and consumption.

Before determining the size of the house calculate the amount of room required for seats, desks and aisles. It should be arranged so that not more than two pupils occupy the same desk. If you wish to get the improved seats and desks, Messrs. Downs & Co., Richland Center, and Thomas Lewis

Esq. of Richland City, are agents for their sale in this county. As they are used in Richland Center, Lone Rock, Sextonville, Woodstock, Richland City, the Young, and Hallen schools, you can examine and measure them and make as near like them as possible. Lest all cannot do so I will give a few directions. The seat should be twelve inches wide, the front edge one inch higher than the back, and be from 12 to 16 inches high to suit different sized pupils; the back which will be the front of the desk, should incline three or more inches from a perpendicular, the desk should not be less than 18 inches wide and 40 long and be inclined not to exceed one inch from a horizontal, and under it should be a rack or shelf for holding books, &c.; when placed, the desk *must* project over the front edge of the seat; remember that a desk is to be used by a person sitting there, and should not be made for the convenience of men and women getting in and out of it.

Now to obtain the size of the school-house, consider how many pupils you wish to accommodate and find the space that the seats and desks, allowing about two feet for each aisle, and always having one up the center of the room under the stove pipe; then you can arrange to have four rows of double desks with aisles between each, and aisles on each side next to the wall; or two rows of double desks, and one row of single desks, the latter arranged along the wall.

The platform across the north end will take off 5 feet, and there should be 4 feet more in front of this for recitation seats. A table with a drawer, and a chair should be provided for the use of the teacher. From these statements you can calculate the size of what will prove to be a convenient and valuable school room. I shall be happy to render any assistance in preparing plans for building you desire.

Hoping these suggestions will aid somewhat in the work, on the prosperity of which depends the perpetuity of the free institutions that are America's pride and boast,

I am, zealously your servant,

Wm. J. Waggoner,
County Superintendent of Schools.

N. B.—*To District Clerks and Treasurers*:—I would ask that you give special attention to making your reports this fall that they may give an accurate condition of affairs. The clerk will obtain from the treasurer such items as are needed for the financial statement. (If the annual meetings were held in August, the treasurer's report would contain this.) The clerk of a joint district should receive one small blank from *each* town clerk, and *also*, a large one from the clerk of the town in which the school house is located. He will see by an explanation on the small blank that he should not insert *anything* in items 1 and 17 of the *large*. By carefully observing this, no serious error need occur.

I hope town clerks will see that the district clerks are promptly provided with blanks as above. If the State Superintendent does not send enough, write to him for what you need. W. J. W.

INSTITUTES.

Two successful Institutes were held in Richland Center during the year. The one in April, conducted by Prof. Duncan McGregor, was of four and a half days' duration, in which we enrolled 101 members, and averaged four days' attendance for each. The two weeks' Institute, in August, was conducted by Prof. Warren D. Parker, assisted by Prof. A. Salisbury. Sixty-five members were enrolled, who went away feeling well paid for the time and expense, and resolving to co-operate with the superintendent in his efforts to raise the standard of qualifications. Essays were read by Mrs. Eastland and Mrs. Baker, and the Misses Daggett, Holden and Pierce. Lectures were delivered by Rev. L. Leonard, and Profs. Parker aud Salisbury.

THE EXAMINATIONS.

I have secured much valuable improvement, and the commendation of the people, by rigidly requiring each candidate to depend on his or her already acquired knowledge. Some work has been suggestive of what should be known. In the oral exercises I aim at three things: 1st. To impart instruction. 2d. To indicate methods for school exercises. 3d. To ascertain the knowledge and power of the applicant. By fearlessly pursuing the above course, and classifying as practiced here, and indicated in the accompanying circular, headed "Examinations," etc., it has aroused the ambition of many teachers who have sought the means necessary to secure rank among the best in this county.

CIRCULAR IN REGARD TO EXAMINATIONS.

All who have attended my former examinations must have learned that no effort will be spared to make them practical, and have the result a fair and truthful exponent of the candidate's knowledge. I trust that you have been making good use of your time in securing that culture that promises success. If your leisure hours from school-room duties have been thus employed, you can confidently anticipate the result. Should you fail at this examination, you can attend all the others, if you choose. Permit me to advise you not to seek knowledge for the purpose of getting a certificate, but for the value its acquisition is to yourself and associates, and the examinations will be nearly shorn of their terrors.

As a certificate in the lowest, or third grade, includes a range of subjects such, that a proficient in them is unquestionably a fair scholar, justice to this class requires grading, which is being practised in this as well as other counties with good success. Each year witnesses the addition of a new force from our schools and a retirement of others from the service. It does not seem just that the inexperienced should take rank with those who have spent years in fitting themselves for the profession, hence we have decided on the following regulations, contained in our report to the county board, as likely to secure the best reeults:

Class A includes those who have taught one year, are not less than six in any branch, and are known to be successful in governing schools.

Class B includes those of less experience, or fall below the standard in some branches, or have indifferent success in governing.

Class C embraces beginners and all others.

"Theory and Art" is divided on the certificates into "Theory and Teaching," and "Ability to Teach." The marking for the latter is made after seeing the holder in charge of different schools. This embraces knowledge, the ability and will to use it, the necessary tact to impart information, secure mental discipline, and rightly govern a school. The certificate tells the number of months the holder has taught, and the days' attendance on Institutes for the two preceding years.

By the above distinctions school offices can judge with some certainty of a candidates fitness to teach their school, and it is hoped that they will prove an incentive to better qualifications and better work on the part of teachers, which will secure the cordial appreciation of the friends of the public schools.

SUGGESTIONS ABOUT KEEPING THE "ROLL OF HONOR."

In order that the published reports of teachers may represent a uniform standard of merit, each teacher should require the observance of the following rules before placing a pupil's name on the "Roll of Honor:" 1. *Must not commit acts demanding reproof.* 8. *No communication without leave.*

For numerous reasons I hope to see these two rules complied with in sending me names. I know my teachers require more than the above, and I think none should be satisfied with less.

Believe me zealously your friend,

WM. J. WAGGONER,
County Superintendent.

RICHLAND CENTER, April 2d, 1873.

CERTIFICATES.

During the school year ending August 3, 1873, 372 applicants attended the examinations, of which there were seventeen public public ones, and 30 private, granted to individuals after the class of the public examinations. Of these 245 received certificates, 56 of them being limited on account of failure in some branches, a majority of whom taught one term satisfying their patrons. If they pursue the vocation I expect them to take full time certificate when they next attend. To draw the division line of qualifications where so few have an abiding interest in the work, or a thorough comprehension of the subjects taught, is very difficult, and mistakes liable to be made. I find those not qualified in knowledge who possess that character of mind that enables them to perform the duties better than others of superior acquirements. This will serve to explain why so many limited certificates are issued when there would be teachers enough without them. And when we consider that nearly all of the 372 applicants thought they could pass a suitable examination, to them, the officer's action appears quite arbitrary.

By as faithfnl a supervision of the schools as is possible with the number, and in this broken country, a wholesome rivalry and greater exertion have been secured between schools and teachers, and I anticipate a less number of failures by future applicants. They should be partially prepared for the work by frequent written examinations in school, where time can be taken to explain the points of failure.

SCHOOL HOUSES.

It is a pleasure to again record the building of new houses, the number this year being eight—all frame but one, which is log, the old one having been destroyed by fire about the middle of the winter term. I have not seen these houses but know that an effort has been made to render them convenient and comfortable, some receiving the improved furniture. The houses range in cost from $400 to $1,200.

VISITING—CONCLUSION.

Owing to the prevalence of the epizootic, and the severity of the winter, I made a less number of visits than in the same time last year. The work of the superintendent here is not more needed in the school room than outside, in the dissemination of such information as will tend to the upbuilding of a sentiment that will sustain zealous thinking teachers in their efforts to progress, and thereby secure their active co-operatiou in all measures that tend toward improvement.

In conclusion I will say that the people of this county are moving slowly forward, her educational interests and facilities keeping pace with the development of those resources on which material prosperity depends.

SAUK COUNTY.

J. H. TERRY, SUPERINTENDENT.

The following extract from my annual report to the County Board of Supervisors, exhibits the condtion of public education in this county during the past year:

A correct view of the existing condition of the educational work of the county necessitates the presentation in detail of the state of each separate agency that forms a part of the system. The first in importance is the

UNGRADED DISTRICT SCHOOL.

Of these schools the county has 151. Individually considered, they occupy but a humble station among the educational forces; regarded as a whole they constitute the instrumentality that must be relied on to secure the principal part of the results to accrue from the whole system. To them the majority of all the children are indebted for whatever literary culture they have acquired. For their maintenance more than that of any other class of institutions is a school fund provided, and burdensome taxation submitted to. Hence the necessity of increasing their efficiency to the highest possible standard. That they have at this time scarcely attained this anywhere, and in many parts of the county they are so far from it that they will not in years, if ever, reach it, may be easily accounted for; but the remedy for this state of affairs is not easily prescribed. To popular indifference, and a low popular estimate of the worth of the school, is attributable the greater part of all the defects and the positive evils that belong to this part of the system. Yet deficient as these schools are, little as they benefit those who attend them, there is satisfaction in the thought that the last year has been productive of results quite as good as those of any previous year, if not better. A prominent source of their weakness is the inexperience and incapacity of their teachers. There is no remedy for this, so long as many districts are unable to appropriate for teachers' wages an amount sufficient to secure better qualifications. The efforts made by many weak districts in the county to place their schools in charge of competent teachers are such as to command the admiration of all who witness them; yet with other occupations offering better inducements to skill and culture, even such efforts are often but partially successful. The number of teachers who have acquired little skill in their work, must, so long as the present financial obstacles remain in some of the districts, and the present ideas of public education prevail in others, be largely in excess of the other class. Yet it is believed that the proportion of teachers who have chosen this work for their occupation has never been greater than during the past year. Other evils than that of poorly qualified teachers have afflicted this class of schools, and the attention of the people has been called to the principal ones through a circular issued to the annual meetings.

THE GRADED SCHOOLS.

Of schools belonging to this class, using the term loosely, there are nine in the county. They represent all degrees of efficiency, from that of the average country school to that of the best high schools of the state. As there are large interests at stake in this class of schools, the usual tendency of public sentiment in regard to them is toward a higher standard, both of scholarship and discipline, than is demanded for the ungraded schools. An important purpose is served by many of them aside from that constituting the prime object in establishing them, viz., the preparation of teachers for the lower class of schools. As no institutions nearer than the state normal schools are designed expressly to meet this want, it is most desirable that it should be met, even to the present limited extent, by this agency. Even where no direct instructions are given as to methods of teaching, the superior skill manifested in the management of these schools is a good model for those who are to become teachers, and is quite frequently imparted in some measure to the schools of neighboring districts. It is highly creditable to them, that while carrying their respective courses of study somewhat beyond that of most country schools, their work in the elementary branches is, in most instances, far more thorough and satisfactory than in the latter class.

THE SUPERINTENDENCY

Is another part of the school system which not only deserves, but during the last few years has received, no inconsiderable share of attention from the people; and, although there is a wide diversity of opinion as to the necessity of this branch of the service, all will probably agree in the desire to know that it is serving the purpose for which it was instituted, and that the money which it costs is fairly earned. The work which engrosses most of the time of the superintendent may be stated in four general divisions: 1st, the examination and licensing of teachers; 2d, the holding of teachers' institutes; 3d, increasing the interest of the people in their schools by writing and addresses; 4th, supervision of the schools.

EXAMINATIONS.

During the year more than 300 applicants for certificates have been examined, and 235 of these have been licensed. The number of certificates in force at any one time has not been largely in excess of the number of schools. Any regard for either the letter or the spirit of the law that provides for these examinations, renders it impossible that it should be otherwise. In fact, at no time is there a sufficient number of teachers in the county, qualified as the law evidently contemplates, to take charge of all the schools. Hence, upon the principle that poorly qualified teachers are better than none, has come the necessity for fixing a standard of qualification so low that nothing but the exigencies of the public interests would justify it. To go still lower than this and issue a still larger number of certificates would not only be the height of folly; it would be an outrage upon the schools—the surest way to impair their usefulness. More than this, it would defeat the most important end sought in the passage of the law, viz., the exclusion of incompetent teachers from the schools.

INSTITUTES.

Eight weeks of the year have been spent holding institutes, as follows: one week at Delton, one at Spring Green, two at Logansville, and four at Prairie du Sac. The good results of work of this kind are doubted only by those who know nothing of the condition of the schools and the needs of the teachers. Nearly 200 different teachers received a greater or less amount of benefit from these gatherings. It is hoped that the long term or Normal Institute has become in Sauk county an established part of the educational machinery. If this be the case, the people and the teachers are to be congratulated upon their good fortune in securing an advantage that is enjoyed by but a small part of all the counties of the State. Until that happy era arrives when the county shall have within its borders some institution of its own devoted to the preparation of teachers, the teachers' institute will be the only source of professional training available to the greater number.

AWAKING POPULAR INTEREST.

Considerable time has been spent in preparing circulars and articles for the press, having in view the increase of public interest. At five different points meetings have been held to address the people, and confer with them regarding their schools. Although it is impossible accurately to measure the influence of efforts of this kind, there is no reason to suppose they have not wrought good. Work of this kind is far from being least in importance. Upon the amount of interest felt by the people in their schools depends almost their entire value; reform in the sentiment of the district must precede all other reforms. In this connection may also be mentioned the organization of a County Teachers' Association, which it is believed, will be an effective instrumentality, not only in educating public sentiment, but also in increasing the zeal and ability of the teachers.

SUPERVISION.

This part of the duties of the office, popularly supposed to be the principal part, both as regards the superintendent's time and the people's equivalent for the cost to them of the office, must necessarily, in a county as large as ours, be of secondary importance. If the schools are all to be visited in the year, the visits must be so short as to become nearly worthless. If a sufficient length of time is to be used at each school to ascertain its character and suggest the remedies for its most obvious faults, then a large number must be ignored during a long interval. Yet, imperfectly as this work must be done, good results flow from it. With a number of schools about one-third as great, this would become the most potent means for the improvement of the schools at the command of the superintendent. Even with our present large number it is essential, as affording the only sure method for obtaining that acquaintance with the teachers necessary for an intelligent exercise of the superintendent's judgment in certain cases. It is also essential for affording that acquaintance with the people that must precede the exercise of a beneficial influence. During the year, 129 visits have been made. During the last twenty months, with eleven exceptions, all the schools in the county have been visited.

CONCLUSION.

Having thus briefly brought to your notice the condition of the different parts of the educational field, I would state, in conclusion, that while there is very much to be reformed, there is something upon which we may justly congratulate ourselves. Though the condition of the schools is far from satisfactory, there is no spot in the county so wild, so barren or so isolated that it has no school accessible to its occupants. While there are many teachers destitute of both learning and skill, there is a large number who honor the calling they have chosen. While there is a state of ignorance and indifference regarding public education that at times discourages effort and disheartens the laborer, there is yet on the other hand a degree of intelligence and wisdom that is full of promise.

WASHINGTON COUNTY.

F. REGENFUSS, SUPERINTENDENT.

IMPROVEMENT.

I am happy to state that I find a marked improvement in the schools of our county generally for the year, and especially in those districts where the school officers and the parents take a lively interest in the cause of education. The theory and practice of teaching is beginning to interest our teachers more and more, and the old system is passing away before the improvements of the present; and, as one of its consequences, a more regular attendance is secured, as shown by the statistical report. The people generally manifest a growing interest in their schools, as is indicated by the annual school meetings. So far as I have heard from those meetings, appropriations have been made in many districts for improvements, by way of building new school-houses, repairing, painting, enclosing school grounds, purchasing apparatus, etc. We have already five districts in this county that have graded schools; one with four, two with three and two with two departments.

VISITATIONS.

In regard to visiting schools I have to report that I had somewhat to neglect this part of my duty on account of the severe winter and blocked roads and especially on account of a painful sickness that confined me to my bed and room for nearly eight weeks. All the schools visited, with but a few exceptions, showed a stisfactory improvement.

AMENDMENTS OF SCHOOL LAW.

The amendments to the and the alterations of the school law, made by the last legislature are just and sound, particularly that portion which makes twenty days a school month, and gives the power of hiring a teach iuto the hands of the board, as a whole, instead of the clerk.

Generally, we have every reason to be encouraged and engage in the work with renewed vigor and energy for the ensuing year, for there is every prospect of making the schools in this county equal to those of any other county, since we have the talent and good will among us; and I have so much faith in the good will and moral intelligence of my fellow citizens that we will reach very soon the standing we are aiming at; and although some think we are working *slowly*, let them understand that we are working *sure*.

WAUSHARA COUNTY.

THEO. S. CHIPMAN, SUPERINTENDENT.

As the general plan of school work in this county has been much the same as in preceding years, no lengthy special report seems to be necessary.

NORMAL INSTITUTES

Have been held as follows: At Plainfield, September and October, 1872, attendance 33, term seven weeks, and at Auroraville in March and April, 1873, term of seven weeks, with an attendance of 98, closing with the State Institute of four days, conducted by Robt. Graham, attendance 113. Much good work was done. At the spring institute no no tuition was charged; heretofore it has been customary to charge tuition at the county, long-term institutes.

CERTIFICATES.

Of the 163 certificates of all grades issued, two have been given to persons 15 years of age; ten to persons 16 years of age; fifteen to persons 17 years of age, and 134 to persons 18 or more years of age; 31 have been to residents of other counties, thus leaving 132 as the number of all grades in this county, who have received certificates. Three 1st grade, thirteen 2d grade, one hundred and twenty-six 3d grade, twenty of which were limited to six months' time, and twenty-one limited 3d grade were issued.

At the fall examinations, 19 failed to receive certificates, and at the spring examination, 70. Six were withheld on account of the age of the applicants, and 83 failed to reach the required standing in the different branches.

There have been required 89 teachers to teach the schools, and 159 different persons employed.

SCHOOL HOUSES.

Have been erected as follows: At Coloma, a large frame house, well seated and provided with sufficient black-boards, capable of seating 60 pupils, and well adapted to the wants of the district; in school district, No. 5, in the town of Wautoma, known as the Webb district—a good, substantial frame house, capable of seating about 50 pupils, furnished with patent, improved seats; the first school-house in the county to adopt the modern improvements in seats and desks. School houses are in process of construction in joint district No. 4, town of Hancock, known as the Yout District, and in Warren, at Hamilton's Mill, both to be ready for the next winter term of school.

The school-house at Mt. Morris has been painted and otherwise refited with a "leanto" built for wood house and well. The plan adopted here of having the well in a small room built for that purpose and the room under lock and key and in charge of the teacher during a session of school, is a plan that would be well to adopt in many other districts.

TEACHERS' ASSOCIATION.

One meeting of the Teachers' Association of Green Lake, Marquette and Waushara counties, was held at Auroraville in the winter, as this was the first meeting, and one of the coldest days of the winter, few were in attendance. It is hoped that these meetings of the Association may be continued.

APPARATUS.

A large number of districts—35 according to the reports of districts—have been furnished through agents with Mitchell's outline Maps at an expense of $22 per set. A few districts have purchased Chapman's Sectional Map of Wisconsin, and a few others, writing charts, A. B. C. charts, and Globes.

VISITATIONS.

In visiting schools during the winter, all but seven were visited once. All the districts were visited once and some twice, but of seven no school was in session at time of visit, owing, in some cases, to adjournment on account of sickness of pupils or teacher, or vacation, want of teacher, or close of session. Of the Summer Schools all but six were visited once; these six were all closed before I was able to visit the districts, (owing in some cases to short terms of school) except one visited before and after session of school. Every district visited once. Some schools have been visited twice during a term. 120 visits were made to schools in the winter and 116 in the summer.

*FOND DU LAC COUNTY—FIRST DISTRICT.

W. L. O'CONNOR, SUPERINTENDENT.

The First Superintendent District of this county consists of the towns of Alto, Eldorado, Friendship, Fond du Lac, Lamartine, Metomen, Oakfield, Ripon, Rosendale, Springvale and Waupun, comprising ninety-one (91) school districts, in each of which a school has been maintained for five or more months, during the past year.

SCHOOL HOUSES.

Two school houses have been built in my jurisdiction, during the year; one in district No. 3, in the town of Friendship, and the other in district No. 6, in the town of Waupun. The former is a wooden structure, costing about $1,000; the latter is of brick, and was erected at an expense of something over $1,600. Both are well built houses, conveniently seated, properly ventilated, and are highly creditable both to the towns in which they are located and to the districts that erected them. Most of the school houses, in my district, are now comfortable and convenient structures, and the out-buildings are generally in good repair.

APPARATUS.

Comparatively few of the school-houses are supplied with anything in the shape of apparatus, excepting a blackboard, which, I am happy to say, has come to be regarded as nearly as much of a necessity in a school-room as a teacher, and I look forward to a time, not far in the future, I hope, when a much more extensive apparatus will be regarded as a necessity even in our smaller district schools. A few of the schools are supplied with maps, charts and globes, but none are supplied with all the appliances that our best instructors regard as necessary to the successful prosecution of the work of education.

TEACHERS.

I do but simple justice to the teachers under my supervision,

* Not received in season for insertion in its proper place.

when I say that as a body they are faithful, earnest and conscientious workers, in what they believe to be an honorable and responsible calling. Fully conscious of the importance of the work it is theirs to do, they have been eager to learn, and prompt to adopt, any improved method of imparting instruction, and earnestly desirous of being fully up to the times; and thus I have ever found them ready and willing to receive advice and adopt my suggestions. The people of the district, as a whole, are by no means indifferent to the paramount importance of good schools, and with rare, and, I hope, decreasing exceptions, are willing to liberally support schools, when they can see an adequate return for the outlay.

EXAMINATIONS.

There were present at the examinations held during the year, 300 candidates, of whom 236 received certificates. Second grade certificates were given to sixteen candidates and third grade to two hundred and twenty. I have granted eight special certificates, generally upon application from school boards for such license. Thus there is, at this time, an excess of 132 teachers, in the district over the number required to teach the schools. The examinations have been part, oral and partly written. The questions have been fair test questions free from quibbles and catches.

INSTITUTES.

Believing that the most effective way to improve our schools, is by improving the teachers, I established institutes at three points, Ripon, Waupun, and Fond du Lac. These institutes were well attended, and I believe productive of good results, both to the teachers and the schools of the district. At each meeting of the institute class exercises were held by one or more departments of different schools in the district. The classes introduced commendable drill, and acquirements creditable alike to the scholars, their teachers, and the districts to which they belonged. The teachers furnishing classes were, Miss Belle Smith, of Lamartine, Mrs. E. B. Richards, of Ripon, E. M. Millard, of Waupun; John Ingalls, of Ripon; Kirk Spoor and Miss Hattie L. Simpson, of Brandon; and great credit is due these teachers not only for the excellence of the class exercises exhibited, but for their assistance in making the institutes interesting and profitable. The principal object of these institutes was to secure, as far as practical, a uniformity in the methods of conducting school exercises in the different schools in the district so that in case of a teacher changing frōm one school district to another, his or her method of teaching might not be altogether new to the new school. Much of the usefulness of our schools is lost by the time spent by scholars having to become acquainted with the new methods of teaching introduced by the new teacher. The great variety of school books in use, adds to the loss, and by the time the new teacher or scholar becomes acquainted with the new books and new ways of teaching, the term is usually nearly half gone.

COMPULSORY ATTENDANCE.

It is conceded by every candid thinker, that the great safeguard of republican institutions is in the intelligence of the masses. A nation, the great bulk of whose people are ignorant, never has, and never can succeed in an experiment of self-government. Acting upon the theory that the success of our republican institutions depends upon the education and intelligence of the people, the states of the Union, almost without exception, have established the free school system. Since the state has thus made ample provision for the education of all classes, putting the rich and the poor on the same footing as to school privileges, I sincerely hope for another step in advance, and that speedily; one that I regard as a duty, not only to our free institutions, but to the youth of the land, in whose hands they must, ere many years, be left to be strengthened or to fail, as we shall prepare this rising generation for the discharge of the trust to devolve upon them. The step forward in our educational system that I hope to see, is the compulsory attendance at school, of each child up to a certain age, for a certain portion of each year. I am aware that to very many, compulsory education may seem arbitrary, but you, gentlemen, may, many of you, remember the time when the levying a tax for the support of a free school was deemed equally arbitrary, and when the "taking of the money of the rich to educate the poor" was denounced more bitterly than is to-day the proposition to compel all classes to accept and improve the privileges secured to them. Nor do we believe, should such a law be enacted and enforced, that those, who by the stupidity, ignorance or cupidity of parents, are now kept from school, who under such a law would be fairly educated, would in future years find fault with such requirements. They would recognize in it more of an act of justice, than an arbitrary enactment. It is a fact, worthy of our serious consideration, that in this first superintendent district, inhabited by people who pride themselves upon their intelligence and enterprise, there were reported 2,259 ceildren of school age, who were not registered at any school in the district during the past year, and that we may safely say that more than one-half of this number should have been at school.

If the education of the masses be regarded as the safeguard of our free institutions, and a preventive of vice and crime, and if, to secure this end the property of the nation is to be taxed, then we claim that it is the duty of the state to use its power to compel all to avail themselves of the privileges thus secured. Such a measure would neutralize the complaints against our school system. The rich would be more willing to be taxed to educate the poorer classes if they were certain they would accept the boon thus conferred.

"DISTRICT QUARRELS."

Several "School District Quarrels," as they are called, have taken place in my Superintendent district during the past year. It has been said that these quarrels are a good thing: that they impart life to an otherwise dull and uninteresting school meeting, and by exciting an interest in school matters, accomplish a certain amount of good. It may be so, but I have failed to see it. These disturbances may be traced to innumerable sources. The hiring of a teacher without a certificate is one of them. But the most fruitful source of these annoying disturbances is in the district boards employing a relative of either of the board to teach the school. This almost always "kicks up a muss," especially if some one else in the district has a relative or friend who wants the school. It matters not how competent the teacher may be, if the best in the county, it would make no difference; jealousies *will* arise; the other party *will* find fault, and, in a little while, there is an outbreak, and a "school district quarrel" is started that may last a generation. My advice to school boards is not to employ a relative of one of the board to teach the school, under any circumstances: better to take an entire stranger. Peace and harmony in the management of our school affairs should be cultiveted, and if neighbors disagree, it would be the part of wisdom to drop their differences and have nothing but harmony at the school meeting.

REPORTS OF CITY SUPERINTENDENTS.

GREEN BAY.

A. H. ELLSWORTH, SUPERINTENDENT.

It affords me pleasure in reporting the past school year as a successful and prosperous one in our city. By the liberal course adopted by our school commissioners, seconded by our citizens, our schools are increasing in popularity and strength. With the number now in daily attendance, we are enabled to make a successful grading, and with a popular principal and efficient corps of teachers, we look for still better results the ensuing year.

OCONTO.

H. W. GILKEY, SUPERINTENDENT.

Upon assuming the duties of this office, five months ago, I found several of the departments of our schools in charge of young teachers of limited experience, and very defective educational qualifications. The people had clamored long and loud for a class of teachers of experience and ability; but their petitions had been disregarded, and a deaf ear turned to their entreaties, until fault-finding and dissatisfaction had given way to disgust and indifference. Under this state of affairs, the common council were forced to interpose and remove the principal cause of complaint; since which time, our schools have enjoyed a tolerable degree of prosperity. Still there are several obstacles to educational progress in our midst yet, to contend with; the principal of which are jealousy, partizan strife and private ambition.

Our school accommodations are wholly inadequate for the number of pupils in attendance, aside from those who would like to attend, but are debarred therefrom for want of room. The people stand ready to meet any appropriations, by taxation, looking forward to the erection of school houses of sufficient capacity to accommodate their children for instruction; but those in authority are not disposed to act, thus effectually excluding many from the privilege of public instruction. Aside from this, may be mentioned a lack of school apparatus to illustrate the different branches taught; also a revision of the course of study adopted, to be pur- and a more thorough gradation of all the departments.

Notwithstanding these hindrances, our new school year has commenced under very favorable auspices, and the present indications are, a more successful, harmonious, and prosperous school year than heretofore enjoyed since the organization of our city.

Our teachers' meetings, which we hold monthly, are well attended, and the exercises are participated in with an apparent relish.

In conclusion, I would state, that it shall be my earnest endeavor, while connected with the schools, to labor for their success, for around them cluster our fondest hopes of future safety and prosperity.

REPORT OF CONVENTION OF SUPERINTENDENTS AND PRINCIPALS.

MADISON, December 26, 1872.

Agreeably to notice, a convention of Superintendents and Principals, assembled at the capitol, at 10 o'clock, A. M. The meeting of Superintendents was called to order by Samuel Fallows, Superintendent of Public Instruction, and the Principals present were invited to participate, in a joint session. Gen. Fallows was chosen President of the joint convention, and I. N. Stewart, of Manitowoc, Secretary.

TOWNSHIP SYSTEM.

The convention proceeded to discuss the question—"Should the Town System be made Obligatory?"—and Mr. A. F. North, Superintendent of Waukesha county, who was to open the discussion, not being yet present, Rev. J. B. Pradt, Assistant State Superintendent, was requested to take his place.

Mr. Pradt said a school system should be uniform, and that such a degree of confidence should be inspired in legislative action as that laws should be passed, if passed at all, without a "permissory" feature. The chief obstacle to the immediate adoption of the town system was the prejudice of the people, who have been accustomed to a different one. All the State Superintendents, however, had recommended a town system, and the time ought to be near when it could be introduced generally. The County Superintendents should bring about a fair trial of the system, which would lead to its more general adoption. Making the system compulsory at present, was of doubtful expediency.

Superintendent Holford, of Grant county, found it impracticable to get a trial; people were adverse to change. Villages with graded schools of three departments should not be exempt from the town system, as is now provided. We needed effectual town supervision as well as state and county supervision; if we could have this with a town system, he would favor the change.

Superintendent North thought the system the better one in *theory*, but would it give us any better teachers? What was the experience in Massachusetts, Pennsylvania, Iowa? In his own town its adoption heretofore would have resulted in poorer teachers and schools, on the average. Did not think it should yet be made compulsory; wanted more light; how many towns had adopted it?

The President said but few, and was sorry to add that some of those had gone back on it.

Mr. Pradt had had some experience with the system as a county superintendent in northern Pennsylvania, where the country was then new and the population mixed, as in Wisconsin, and thought the system there secured better teachers, as it tended to more permanence in their employment.

Mr. Stewart said local jealousies stood in the way. The system should be recommended and inaugurated by our leading educators; was willing to see it tried as a general system; we could go back to the old one if it proved unsuccessful.

Major A. J. Cheney said it worked well in Massachusetts (where it was made obligatory after three or four years), and would work well in Wisconsin or any other State further west. He thought section 36 of the township law, in regard to villages, a great defect, as it prevents many thickly settled towns, with villages, from adopting the system. This should be changed.

Superintendent Chandler, of Dane County, said people were opposed to the system because they thought it would be more expensive; we could have good schools under the present system; to make the town system obligatory at present would excite opposition of which little demagogues would take advantage to its injury. We must introduce it gradually. Hereafter it would be demanded.

Mr. Holford said we must have Town Superintendents, who are professional teachers; we would then have some assurance of qualified teachers and proper teaching, but not without; County Superintendents could not exercise a close supervision of the schools and teachers.

The President said the main popular objection was the supposed expense of the system. Really, it was cheaper. We could not go in advance of public sentiment. He agreed with Major Cheney, that section 36 should be repealed. Successful examples of the working of the system would remove popular prejudice.

W. D. Parker, of Janesville, moved the appointment of a committee to report to-morrow, at 11 o'clock, and Messrs. Parker, Pradt and Stewart were appointed. At Mr. Parker's request Gen. Fallows was put in his place.

REPORTS OF JOINT DISTRICTS.

Supt. Chandler opened the discussion on a "Change in the report of Joint School Districts." The school reports, generally, were unreliable, and a prolific source of errors was the reports from joint-districts, which duplicated and triplicated numbers, or worse—made five months schooling into twenty months, etc. Only one report should be made from a joint-district, and that to the clerk of the town containing the school-house.

Supt. North thought the school reports not so very unreliable; there was "a Providence shapes our ends"—[Mr. Chandler—"Rough"]—and if there was too much on one side, there was too little on the other; and so it averaged about right. He would have the school taxes levied by the county, based like other taxes, on the valuation of property in the towns, without regard to the apportionment of the school fund income.

On motion, a committee was appointed by the chair, consisting of Messrs. Chandler, North and Holford, to report on the subject to-morrow, at 11 o'clock.

FRIDAY, 9 A. M., Dec. 28.

NATURAL SCIENCE IN COMMON SCHOOLS.

The first topic for discussion was, "Shall a knowledge of Natural Sciences be required for a second grade certificate?"

A. Salisbury, of Brodhead, supposed the discussion was started by the example of Illinois, which now required Natural Science to be taught in her common schools, and borrowed the idea from St.

Louis, where, however, it occupies but one hour a week. He did not believe the plan practicable at present, and yet he would have the teacher know more than he was called on to teach. It was hardly worth while to disturb our present system until we "could sustain something really philosophical and rational."

O. R. Smith, of Sparta, said but a very small proportion of teachers now obtained second grade certificates, and to increase the requirements would diminish the number, and not advance the qualifications of the teachers. As such a law would be inoperative at present, like that requiring the constitutions to be taught, he would be opposed to its enactment.

Mr. Pradt thought that to follow St. Louis and Illinois in this matter would be only another instance of attempting to pluck the fruit before it is ripe.

Mr. Chandler said some cram a little and get a second grade, to influence school boards. He thought county superintendents should have discretionary power to require more studies for this grade. The place to begin the reform was at the Normal School.

J. K. Purdy, of Fort Atkinson, thought the influence of second grade certificates with school boards on the wane. Teachers themselves cared little for them.

Supt. Holford agreed with Mr. Purdy, but if the law *required* more studies for even a third grade, teachers would be prepared rather than not teach. Half the country schools did not teach geography, and less grammar.

Mr. Chandler asked if teachers did not know more about the "constitutions" since the new law.

Mr. Holford said they did, but gave some amusing specimens of their blunders.

E. Marsh, of Waterloo, said teachers could not control the studies pursued in school, but if the law required the natural sciences, teachers would find out something about them, as they have about the constitutions. He would require them even for a third grade.

Mr. Smith knew of a board which required a second grade—the teachers got them—and knew as little of the additional studies as they did of Hebrew. Most of the teachers have no means of studying natural science; some superintendents could not examine them in it. Even now there is great difficulty in supplying the schools with teachers. Natural science should be taught through the Institutes, as far as possible.

Mr. Chandler said that the law proposed would affect only 400 teachers. The State was now expending $100,000 per annum to funish the means for obtaining this instruction.

President Albee, of the Oshkosh Normal School, thought it not more difficult to supply teachers than before the enactment of the law requiring the Constitutions. Costly apparatus was not necessary to teach the elements of natural sci ence. Any one can pluck a leaf and find out its classification—what tree it belongs to.

Mr. Salisbury thought such a law would not improve the real qualifications of teachers. A little show of algebra gives a fictitious standing; so it would be in this matter.

Mr. Cheney had seen the working of the law in Illinois, and found it a farce. One superintendent, in examination, asked one question in physiology, and one in natural philosophy. In one school he found classes in natural philosophy, chemistry and geology, and none in grammar, geography or history—hadn't time for both—must obey the new law!

Prof. Graham said the the law should apply to third grade as well as second; the elements of science should be taught in common schools. Superintendents in Illinois didn't do their duty—the fault was not in the law; the subject should be taught orally.

Mr. Chase, of Madison, did not see how teachers who know nothing about it, could teach it orally; but too much time was given to geography; we could save some for natural science; could give at least an appetite first; teachers should be brought upon a higher plane.

Mr. North said that Tyndall could give this appetite for these studies because he was a master, but let a *tyro* attempt to teach them, and he creates only disgust.

Superintendent Fallows regretted that his knowledge of these sciences had not been more thorough. The tendency of education is science-ward, and this direction is right. He thought that a knowledge of natural science ought to be required of every teacher in the State. It was pertinently remarked that the law requiring the Constitution to be taught had not diminished the number of teachers, nor did he think that the proposed measure would have this effect. He thought our common school education not practical enough. We spend too much time upon grammar, geography, etc., and too little upon science. One great difficulty is, there are no text books adapted to district schools. He wished he could cajole Tyndale and Huxley into writing text books for Wisconsin an Illinois.

Mr. North stated that such books had been published in England.

Superintendent Fallows said that by next year it would be safe to put this law upon the statute book, and the requirement would bring teachers to the sufficient knowledge.

Prof. Pickard stated that Miss Youmans had published a text book in botany; Kingsley on geology, and Balfour on physics.

On motion of Mr. Reynolds, the whole subject was referred to a committee of three, and Messrs. Marsh, Barnes and Chase were appointed on tho committee.

APPOINTMENTS TO NORMAL SCHOOLS.

The next topic was "Changes Required in Appointment of Students to Normal Schools."

W. D. Parker, in opening the discussion, said that many students in our normal schools ought to be in common schools. There was a large and constantly growing class who, for some reason or other, cannot attend the public school, and so drift into the academic department of the normal school; and although the law points directly towards teaching, nobody supposes that these persons will ever make teachers; they do not even propose it to themselves. They are there simply because it is not convenient to go to public schools.

Mr. Purdy stated that this discussion showed that there was some dissatisfaction with the material now in our normal schools. This dissatisfaction is felt by the teachers in these schools as well as by the public. The law provides that our normal schools shall be restricted to the instruction of teachers, but the fact is, a great proportion of the pupils do not propose teaching, and are simply acquiring a good common education. It was the business of the normal school to hunt out those persons who give promise of making good teachers. Under the present law county superintendents appoint without any such knowledge, merely appointing the first applicants.

Mr. Albee said the regents had prescribed the duties of the superintendents and of the normal school teachers. One of the points in the county superintendent's certificate of appointment is that the applicant is of good moral character. A person who w ie is not of good moral character. Every student upon entering the normal school must sign a declaration that he intends to teach in the schools of Wisconsin. He did not think the material was above the average, but about the average in intellect. Many are driven, by being refused a certificate, to enter the normal school, to prepare themselves for teaching. He thought there was a far greater earnestness in the normal schools than in the public schools. He did not think the declaration was ever signed lightly. It was carefully read and its purport noted.

Superintendent Dale, of Oshkosh, said that it was a delicate matter for a superintendent to decide, as to the moral character of an applicant. He objected to being made a police officer. He knew, however, of cases in which persons had been rejected, but in such cases the mortal enmity of the rejected applicant and all his family would be incurred. The superintendents should be supported by some board of examiners, or by the teachers. As it now is, the whole burden rests upon the superintendent.

Mr. Chandler said that the certificate of the county superintendent was only a certificate that, in his opinion, the person recommended was a proper person to be examined by the faculty for admission. If a superintendent makes one mortal enemy by rejecting one applicant of immoral character, he ought to have made a hundred firm friends by his course. He believed that normal schools ought to restrict their efforts to the instruction of teachers, and yet, practically, they have to furnish some rudimentary instruction. He cited the case of an applicant at Whitewater, who had taught and held a third grade certificate, and yet who never studied grammar a single hour.

Mr. Parker said he was glad to see a disposition upon all hands to bring all our educational interests into harmony. This was the first good natured discussion he had ever attended, when the Normal Schools were under discussion. He thought the Regent present (Mr. Chandler) had struck the key-note, when he said that teachers and superintendents must work together. He knew a case, in which a boy was expelled from the schools of a city, for want of moral character, and yet that boy is in one of the Normal Schools, without any recommendation.

Prof. D. McGregor, of Platteville Normal School said that they had uniformly rejected applicants that proved themselves unfit either in scholarship or character, whether they had a recommendation or not. The academic department was a drag, and the great question is how can we get rid of it. He thought that in most cases, the declaration was signed in good faith.

On motion of Mr. Reynolds, the subject was referred to a committee of three, consisting of Messrs. Reynolds, Purdy and Dale.

Superintendent Fallows, in behalf of the committee on "Compulsory Township System," made the following report:

Your committee, to whom was referred the matter of Compulsory Township System, beg leave to report by resolution, as follows:

Resolved, That in the opinion of this Convention section 36 of chapter 182, G. L. 1869, should be so amended as not to exclude villages having schools of not less than three departments from the operation of said chapter.

Resolved, That in the opinion of this Convention, county superintendents and educators generally should urge the adoption of the township system by towns, that it may have a fair and impartial trial.

SAMUEL FALLOWS,
I. N. STEWART.

The resolutions were adopted.

THE DEAF AND DUMB.

At this point, Mr. George L. Weed, Principal of the Institute for the Deaf and Dumb, located at Delavan, appeared before the conuention with Miss Addie Rutherford, of Lake Mills, a member of his graduating class, and gave an illustration of their methods of instruction.

Mr. Weed said that he was glad that the Deaf and Dumb Institute was recognized as belonging to the educational system of the state. In one sense it was a benevolent institution, and to a certain degree under the control of the Board of Chrrities, and yet it is in the main educational. He wished to bring out four points: 1st. What is the condition of the deaf and dumb before they come to the Institute. 2d. What are the means of reaching the deaf and dumb. In the first place, there is the method of articulation. In most cases this is impracticable, but yet in some cases possible. Next, finger-spelling, or dactylology. 3d. Sign language. 4th. Written language.

Miss Rutherford then recited in the sign language "The Angel's Song," "It Came upon the Midnight Clear," with a most thrilling effect. Prof. Weed then told a story in the sign language, which Miss Rutherford wrote out upon the blackboard. The persons present witnessed these exercises with intense interest, and the thanks of the convention were voted to Prof. Weed and Miss Rutherford.

FRIDAY, P. M., 2 o'clock.

B. M. Reynolds, of Monroe, offered the following resolution:

Resolved, That in the opinion of this convention, persons holding normal school diplomas and state certificates granted by competent authority in other states, should be entitled to all the privileges enjoyed by those holding diplomas from our normal schools, and state certificates granted by competent authority in this state of corresponding grades and courses of study, on having such diplomas and certificates approved and countersigned by the Superintendent of Public Instruction.

The resolution was discussed by Prof. Reynolds, Miss Stetson, Col. Chase, Mr. Salisbury, Mr. Little, Prof. Graham and Mr. Wright.

The subject was referred to a committee consisting of Messrs. Chandler, Delamatyr and Reynolds.

INSTITUTE WORK.

The subject of Institute work for 1873 was taken up. Gen. Fallows made pertinent remarks upon the subject, and suggested that the Institute work be connected with the Normal School, and that the conductors of Institutes be members of the Faculty of Normal Schools.

The subject was subdivided, and the topic of the relation of Institute to Normal Schools taken up, Prof. Graham spoke at some length upon the subject and also upon the compulsory attendance of teachers upon the Institutes. He advocated the division of the State into sections, and each Normal School to do the work for that section. Remarks were made by Messrs. Salisbury, Chandler, Rev. J. B. Pradt, Mr. Holford, Prof. McGregor, Mr. I. N. Stewart, Mr. Barnes, Prof. Albee, Mr. Delamatyr and Supt. Wright, after which the subject was referred to a committee of five to report in the evening, consisting of Messrs. Smith, Wright, Stewart, Salisbury and Barnes.

The subject of compulsory attendance upon Teachers' Institutes was then discussed at some length by Supts. Holford, Terry, Shaw and Maguire, and Miss Stetson, when the matter was referred to a committee, consisting of Supt. Little, of Sheboygan county, E. H. Sprague, of Stockbridge, and Supt. Burlingame, of Columbia county.

Messrs. Parker and Barnes spoke in favor of short institutes.

The convention then adjourned, and Prof. Graham appeared for the purpose of conducting a class drill of those wishing to engage in institute work for 1873.

FRIDAY EVENING, 7½ o'clock.

THE UNIVERSITY AND GRADED SCHOOLS.

The "Relation of the State University to the Graded Schools" was taken up for discussion. Mr. Reynolds opened the discussion. He believed the State University was doing the best possible under the circumstances. and that the Preparatory Department was a necessity, as the most of the pupils come from rural district schools, where it is impossible for them to get such instruction as is given in that department.

The discussion was continued by President Twombly, of the University, who detailed the present organization of the institution, and called attention to the progress made during the last few years; in requisites for admission and extension of course of study in college of letters and college of arts; in establishment of agricultural engineering and mining departments, and in the female college. He made sundry suggestions relating to the practical operation of the law of last winter, remitting tuition fees to pupils entering the University upon graduating from graded schools of the state.

A spirited discussion followed. in which Messrs. Reynolds, Smith, Carpenter, Fallows, President Twombly and Chandler participated, and reference was made to a feeling against the University in some quarters. The result of the discussion was to show that the dangers and evils connected with the University to which attention was called, could be averted only by perfecting a state system of instruction.

The whole subject was then referred to a committee consisting of President TWOMBLY, Supt. FALLOWS, and Messrs. CHANDLER, GRA-

HAM, SHAW and DELAMATYR, who were instucted to make make a report at the next meeting of the State Teachers' Association, on "A System of Education for the State."

Miss STETSON, a teacher of elocution from Milwaukee, was then introduced, who recited several humorous selections in verse, and briefly unfolded her system of teaching reading.

O. R. SMITH, in behalf of the committe on Institutes, presented the following report, which was adopted:

The Committee to whom was referred the subject of Teachers' Institutes have had the same under consideration, and respectfully report as follows:

In the opinion of your committee the institutes should be conducted primarily with the view to better fit teachers for their work in the common schools of the state, and they are of the opinion that this may be best accomplished as follows:

1st. There shall be State Director of Institutes, who shall have full control of all institute work in the state, being respnosible only to the Board of Normal Regents, and unconnected with any school or other office.

2d. He shall have three or more District Assistants, who shall be attached to the faculties of the Normal Schools, in addition to the force already provided, but subject to the control of the Director whenever in his judgment, their services are required for institute work.

3d. Such additional force may be employed as, in the judgment of the Director, is necessary, subject to the regulations of the Normal Board.

O. R. SMITH.
A. O. WRIGHT,
I. N. STEWART,
ALBERT SALISBURY,
HOSEA BARNES,
Committee.

Mr. Chandler, in behalf of the committee on "Reports from Joint Districts," made the following report, which, on motion, was laid on the table for further consideration:

The committee, to which was referred the subject of "Change in Reports of Joint School Districts," would report, that having given the matter consideration, they have concluded that the evils desired to be obviated, may be obviated by either of the following methods, viz:

1st. By such a change in the reports required of district and town clerks by the State Superintendent, as to do away with the partial reports of clerks of joint school districts to the clerks of all towns, parts of which are embraced in the joint districts, and in lieu thereof, a requirement of reports from clerks of joint school districts to the clerk of the town in which the school house is located only, which shall show the whole number of children of school age residing in the district, and also the town in which such children reside, and a collation of these reports by the town clerks, to show the actual number residing in each town represented in the several districts, entire or partial, in the reports received by him. The reports of the county superintendent should also be so arranged as to finally tabulate these reports of town and district clerks in such a manner as to afford a correct basis for the apportionment of the school fund.

2d. By such a change in the law, as to require the apportionment of the school money, to counties and by them to towns, in the same manner as now provided, and, the apportionment of such a county tax, as is required, to entitle towns to participate in the apportionment, upon the whole property of the county, and authorizing the apportionment of the funds thus obtained, in the same manner as the public school fund is now distributed. If to this provision was added one authorizing the town treasurers to pay over to the treasurers of adjoining towns the amounts to which parts of joint school districts were entitled to receive from them, and by such treasurers paid over to the treasurers of joint school districts entitled to receive the same, the great inconvenience of district treasurers of joint school districts in obtaining the small sums due them from several different town treasurers might be avoided.

W. H. CHANDLER,
A. F. NORTH,
W. H. HOLFORD,
Committee.

Mr. Ed. Marsh made a report upon "Requiring the Natural Sciences in Common Schools," which was laid on the table.

O. R. Smith submitted the following preamble and resolution, which, on motion, was adopted:

Whereas, We believe it to be the duty of the State to provide for the education of every child in its borders; and,

Whereas, There is a large class of children who, through imperfect development, are incapacitated to receive instruction in the public schools; therefore

Resolved, That it is the sense of this convention that it is the duty of the legislature to immediately establish a school for the education of the idiotic and feeble-minded children of the State.

Saturday, 10 A. M.

Miss Stetson presented the subject of Elocution.

The report of the committee on Requiring a Knowledge of the Natural Sciences for a Second Grade certificate, was taken up, and after discussion, the following substitute was adopted:

Resolved, That this convention fully believes in the importance of a knowledge of the elements of Natural Sciences to entitle a candidate to receive a certificate of any grade, and urge that the measure be enacted into a law as soon as practicable.

The report on the charge of reports of joint districts was called up, and the first method there suggested was adopted, changing the blanks so that the report shall be made by the clerk of the district to the clerk of the town only in which the school house is located, specifying the number of children from each town, so that the town clerk receiving the report can certify them to the other town clerks.

A further report, through W. H. CHANDLER, recommending the apportionment of money to counties and by counties to towns, was adopted.

ATTENDANCE AT INSTITUTES.

The committee on Compulsory Attendance upon Institutes made the following report:

Your committee, to whom was referred the matter of recommending legislation compelling teachers to be in attendance upon Institutes, beg leave to report as follows:

While we deeply deplore the existing state of affairs in some of the counties of the state, regarding the attendance of teachers upon Institutes, under present circumstances we see no great good to be derived from a law compelling teachers to attend, or from a law compelling or permitting superintendents to refuse certificates for non-attendance. We can offer the following:

Resolved, That teachers who willfully or through neglect absent themselves from teachers' institutes held in their county, thereby refusing to accept the advantages offered them by the state and county, should meet with the universal censure of all true teachers, and as fast as practicable should be eliminated from the teaching force.

E. A. LITTLE,
E. H. SPRAGUE,
L. J. BURLINGAME.
Committee.

Mr. Glazier thought the resolution unnecessarily harsh. The great difficulty in the way of a more general attendance was the fact that there was no fixed time for holding institutes. An institute was held within a few miles of his school, of which he had no notice until two weeks after his school had commenced.

Prof. S. H. Carpenter thought that in this matter, as in every other, men would be governed by their interests. If it could be shown to be for the interest of teachers to attend, they would attend. It should be the duty of the county superintendent to bring this matter to the attention of the teachers.

Mr. Chandler thought that some discretionary power of withholding a certificate for such non-attendance would be useful.

Mr. Pradt thought of the old adage about leading the horse to water, etc. You may compel teachers to attend, but it will be of no use. First make the institutes regular and attractive, then let their benefits be known to teachers, then most of those who will be benefited will attend.

Mr. De La Matyr said all the teachers in Walworth county had attended the institutes, save three or four, and they were the ones who needed it most.

Mr. Bashford said that many superintendents were not fit to exercise this discretion. When they do their part, the teachers will do the rest. He knew a case where the Board ordered a school closed, and requested the teachers to attend the session, and then requested them to make up lost time. Make it profitable for teachers; let them be paid for time, or a portion of it.

Mr. Chandler remarked that only those superintendents who are interested in the work complain of non-attendance.

Mr. North did not like to hear all this talk about low wages. The teachers in his county got all they were worth, and the poor ones ten times more than they were worth.

Mr. Holford said we lacked system, which we must have before we can compel attendance.

Prof. Smith could see nothing of practical utility in the report.

On a vote being taken the resolution was lost.

STATE NORMAL SCHOOLS.

Mr. Albee reported the condition of the Normal School at Oshkosh.

Last year the total registration was 158; average membership, 82; average attendance, 78; number in attendance during the whole year, 17; over 6 and less than 10 months, 52; over 3 and less than 6 months, 60; less than 3 months, 29. This term there were enrolled and present, 158, besides in preparatory classes, 58. There were 112 applicants, and 88 admitted, and 28 counties are represented in the school. The great difficulty is that the purse is slender. They try to fit pupils for the third grade during the first year. During the last term or two of the year, special attention is given to interpreting the methods inculcated in the instructions given. There are 70 out teaching, and 69 of these are in the mixed schools, one in the graded.

Mr. E. H. Sprague then presented the following statement as to the Platteville Normal School:

The Platteville School has graduated four classes: in 1869, eight; in 1870, fifteen; in 1871, twelve; in 1872, eight—total, 43. Of these, three-fourths are teaching in the State. The present senior class numbers 27; whole number admitted into the normal department since its establishment in 1866 is 435. Present number in various departments, normal, 135; academic, 110; model, 50—total, 295.

UNIFORM TEXT BOOKS.

Mr. Wright presented a paper upon the question "Shall the State of Wisconsin adopt a Uniformity of Text Books?" The paper proposed that the State should adopt a series of books for a long term of years; that the books should be selected by a competent commission; that arrangements should be made to procure the books at the lowest wholesale rates. Referred to a committee consisting of O. R. Smith, I. N. Stewart and J. W. Bashford.

Mr. Shaw, for committee on term of office of county superintendent, reported as follows:

Your committee, to whom was referred the subject of election and term of office of county superintendents, would respectfully recommend to this convention that the law should be so amended as to bring the election in the spring, and that the term should expire on the 30th of June.

S. SHAW,
T. H. TERRY,
O. J. TAYLOR,
Committee.

After a short discuision, the report was adopted.

Superintendent Terry offered the following resolution, which was adopted:

Resolved, That in the opinion of this body, the law relating to teachers' certificates should be so amended as to make the time during which a certificate of the second grade shall remain in force, two years, and that for the certificate of the first grade, three years.

Sup't North presented this resolution, which was adopted:

Resolved, That in the opinion of this convention, twenty days should constitute a school month.

Superintendent Fallows stated that he wished photographs of the school houses of the State, to be put into a portfolio and sent to the world's exhibition at Vienna.

On motion of Mr. Parker the State Superintendent was requested to take such steps as in his judgment may be necessary, to secure the representation of the educational interests of this State at the International Exhibition at Vienna.

After a vote of thanks to Superintendent Fallows for his courtesy as presiding officer, the convention adjourned.

I. N. STEWART,
Secretary.

WISCONSIN STATE TEACHERS' ASSOCIATION.

SPARTA, Wis., July 8, 1873.

Pursuant to call, the Twenty-First Annual Session of the Wisconsin Teachers' Association commenced at Sparta, July 8, 1873. After the singing of "Hail, Festive Day," by the Glee Club of Sparta, the members of the Association were welcomed by T. B. Tyler, Esq., President of the School Board, in the following words:

Mr. President, Ladies and Gentlemen of Wisconsin Teachers' Association:

As the representative of the people of the village of Sparta, I am charged with the pleasing duty of extending to you a cordial, hearty welcome. We welcome you because you are energetic in educating the masses—a boundless, glorious work; and we desire to cheer you on by kind words and generous deeds. I trust ample accommodations have been made for your personal comfort and convenience during your brief stay among us. Had I the requisite time and ability, and it were proper on this occasion, I might endeavor to convince you that the people honor your profession; that the common school teacher is no longer regarded as a pedagogue, but is recognized socially and intellectually as the peer of the best and wisest in the land.

This proud eminence you have fairly won by patient, persistent toil. I should also express the hope that your labors on this occasion may tend to improve and perfect methods of teaching that will result in giving the country better men and women. Men and women with all the faculties, moral, mental and physical, trained for the practical duties of life. Not mere money making mercenaries, but noble, virtuous, high-minded men and women; for such only will be able to organize and maintain what we call good society; such only can perpetuate our free institutions. But my duty ends when I again greet you as the honored guests of our people, and welcome you as friends and fellow-workers in the great cause of universal education.

President McGregor responded as follows:

"On behalf of the Wisconsin Teachers' Association, I thank you, sir, for your real welcome and kindly wishes. The trouble you have taken, the expense you have incurred, the admirable facilities you have placed at our disposal for this meeting, testify to us, in a manner far stronger than words can, the interest you take in our work. To-night we appear before you to celebrate the twenty-first anniversary of this association. To-night we attain our majority, and we trust our deliberations may be such as become men and women of our profession. On our programme of exercises you find names of men who who are acknowledged leaders in the educational work of the United States; others leaders in our own State, and others, though less widely known, no less earnestly working, making our profession honored as well as honorable. We have come from all parts of the State to compare the results of another year's work, and to gather strength and enthusiasm for our future labors. We come for work, for profit and for pleasure. We cordially invite you, sir, and the citizens of Sparta, to meet with us, to participate in our exercises; and we hope to show you that we are thoroughly in earnest, working for what appears to us the best interest of the schools of our State, and that though actively engaged in the work of teaching, we are still, as every successful teacher must be, constant students, striving to keep pace with the demands of the times for better qualified teachers, and for more efficient schools."

After the singing of "All is Well," by the choir, led by Mr. A. Earthman, of Reedsburg, President McGregor introduced the Rev. Dr. Fowler, of the Northwestern University, Evanston, Ill., who delivered an able and forcible lecture the "Teacher and his Work."

After the announcement of programme for Wednesday, and a quartette by male voices, the meeting was adjourned.

WEDNESDAY, A. M., July 9th. The opening exercises were in the following order: Anthem by the choir. Prayer by the Rev. Mr. Carmichael, and singing an appropriate selection.

Samuel Shaw, of Berlin, was called to the chair, and the President delivered his address.

On motion of W. D. Parker the address was referred to a committee consisting of R. Graham, Oshkosh; A. J. Hutton, Eau Claire B. M. Reynolds, Monroe.

The following committees were announced:

Enrollment: A. Earthman, Reedsburg; L. W. Briggs, Green Bay; Wm. E. Anderson, Waukesha.

On Finance: H. C. Howland, Eau Claire; Miss Mattie Hazzard, Oshkosh; J. M. Rait, Sheboygan.

Reports were made of educational matters in matters in their respective places, by: L. W. Briggs, Green Bay; M. T. Park, Racine; E. M. Bowen, Wausau; W. D. Parker, Janesville; E. H. Sprague,

Stockbridge; J. T. Lunn, Richland County; J. M. Rait, Sheboygan; H. C. Howland, Eau Claire; J. C. Pickard, Milwaukee; C. E. Mears; Polk Co., J. H. Twombly, State University, Madison; J. H. Terry, Sauk Co.; A. F. North, Waukesha; A. A. Spencer, Green Lake Co.; L. J. Burlingame, Columbia Co.; J. J. Fruit, La Crosse; M. H. Holden, Monroe Co.

After a recess of ten minutes State Superintendent Fallows made an address on the "Unity of the School System."

A paper on "Extent, Nature and Value of Supervision in Graded Schools," was read by B. M. Reynolds, of Monroe.

J. Q. Emery followed with a paper on the same subject.

R. Graham, chairman of committee in the president's address, made the following report of committees, which was adopted:

On that part which refers to Compulsory Education.—W. D. Parker, Rev. A. Kidder, Rev. Gilliland.

School Houses and Grounds.—I. N. Stewart, J. H. Terry, Miss Cordelia Potter.

Frequency of Change of Teachers.—H. C. Howland, J. Q. Emery, D. E. Gardiner.

Efficiency of Primary Instruction.—G. S. Albee, J. C. Pickard, Miss Martha Kidder.

Drawing.—D. McGregor, J. B. Thayer, Miss Ellen Merriam.

County Associations and Educational Columns.—A. F. North, A. O. Wright, J. W. Rait.

Reform in Spelling.—Alex. Kerr, Amos Whiting, L. W. Briggs.

Libraries.—O. R. Smith, J. C. Pickard, Samuel Shaw.

R. GRAHAM,
A. J. HUTTON,
B. M. REYNOLDS,
Committee.

After the announcement of programme for the afternoon, and the singing of "Float Away, the meeting adjourned."

HIGH SCHOOL SECTION.

OPERA HALL, WEDNESDAY, P. M., July 9, 1873.

The High School Section was called to order by Samuel Shaw, chairman, at 2 o'clock. Prof. Putnam, of Boston, was introduced, and occupied the first half hour in a lecture on drawing. He urged the teachers to do more work in this branch. Gave an account of the work in Massachusetts, and the benefits arising from the study. His remarks were appropriate and suggestive.

Prof. Rockwood, of Whitewater, addressed the teachers on reading, discussing the subject under the following heads: first, relation to the teacher; second, how to read; necessary preparation—special and general; necessity of literary culture—a love for *what* you read, etc.

A. J. Hutton, West Eau Claire, read a paper on "Arithmetic."

Miss Florence Bush, of Berlin, read an essay on the "Moral Influence of the Teacher."

Recess.

After recess, the teachers gave good attention to O. R. Smith's paper on "Training."

Prof. G. A. Weed, of State Institution for the Deaf and Dumb, made a "Familiar Talk" on the work being done for this class of unfortunates. Gave methods of instruction, and several illustrations of sign language. Made strong appeals to the teachers to notify him of any cases of deaf and dumb children, and assist him in bringing them to be educated.

O. R. Smith moved the following, which was passed: "The appointment of a committee to take into consideration the education of all children not capable of receiving instruction in our common schools."

The chair appointed O. R. Smith, Alex. Kerr and A. F. North as such committee.

After the reading of a paper on "School Exhibitions," by Miss Carrie Battell, of Berlin, the association adjourned till 7:30 P. M.

INTERMEDIATE SECTION.

High School, Wednesday, P. M., July 9, 1873.

This part of the association was called to order at 2:15, by A. Salisbury, chairman. 1st. An essay by Mrs. I. N. Stewart, on the Primary School. 2d. Penmanship, by Prof. Hinman, of St. Louis. 3d. Class drill in physical exercises, by Miss Agnes Goodwin, who presented a class of twenty-four children, who had been drilled but one week. The exercise showed good work, and gave much pleasure to the large number who saw it.

J. B. Holbrook read a paper on Grammar.

After recess, the teachers listened to papers by C. F. Viebahn, on "Pestalozzi and Froebel;" on "Language Lessons," by Miss Catharine Lilly and H. E. Hoard; on "Methods, Inductive and Deductive," by J. B. Thayer. The association then adjourned.

WEDNESDAY, Evening, July 9th.

Opened with music by the choir.

R. Graham, chairman of committee on "Mixed Schools," made the following report, which was adopted:

The committee to whom was referred the subject of "Mixed Schools," ask leave to report as follows:

More than one-half of the citizens of this commonwealth are educated in the mixed schools. It is imperative, therefore, that these schools should be properly cared for.

The school-house should be pleasantly situated in a healthy locality, with sufficient grounds for recreation. It should be substantially built, neat, but not expensive, well ventilated, comfortably seated, and supplied with some simple apparatus, as globe, outline maps, and such geometrical forms as may be easily constructed by any teacher, plenty of blackboard, and books for reference.

The teacher should be intelligent, truthful and healthy.

The pupils should be trained to habits of punctuality, thought, obedience and labor, with a due regard to health, morals and manners.

The teacher, if at all efficient, should be retained a sufficient time to allow him to work out his plan. The school board should adopt a course of study, and insist that the teacher prosecute diligently this course. Classes should be consolidated, so far as may be done without injury to the advancement of pupils.

Branches to be studied: Reading, spelling, penmanship, arithmetic, geography and grammar.

The teacher should acquaint himself with the habits of his pupils out of school in relation to sleep, food, dress and amusement, and seek a reform where needed.

The parents and teacher should be in full sympathy with each other in the work, and should mutually visit and consult at *home* and at the school-room. The rights respectively of pupil, parent, teacher, school board and county superintendent should be the subject of careful thought, each by the other.

Respectfully submitted,

R. GRAHAM, *Chairman.*

G. S. Albee made the following report on "Teaching Forces," which was adopted:

Your committee appointed to consider the means of increasing the teaching forces of the State, would suggest that the efficiency of our work may be increased either by putting to it more strength, or improving the means by which the existing power is applied.

For the former, it is needful that the people so realize how the education of our youth is interwoven with all immediate and future happiness, that money shall not weigh against worth, or time against culture. Ignorance must not suffer formal incompetence to lull conscience into the lethargy of satisfaction. School work must be sternly judged by present needs, not tolerated because of precedents.

All this requires a degree of foresight and sense of moral obligation in the direction of this paramount work, which the present generation does not possess.

For present, immediate growth in the work, therefore, we must look to the improvement of our appliances for progress and reform.

Statistics, industriously gathered by our State Department, are confessedly so imperfect, and so little heeded, save to point a paragraph in a speech, that the good results which might be felt in every district, directing energies, arousing consciences to a realization of what duties have not been done, what privileges left unimproved and not secured.

The limited supervision of the country schools can be improved, by the Superintendent having a plan of correspondence with each teacher and school, involving a free interchange of thought, regarding doubts and difficulties, successes and failures; competitive or illustrative *work* of pupils. Let this be conducted so carefully and persistently that the Superintendent is felt as if present in each school every day.

The lack of permanence in the profession with its train of ills, can best be remedied by the Superintendent, through an unflinching and outspoken recognition of merit, making itself felt in tangible reward, which shall encourage the better preparation for this high calling.

The teacher needs truer conceptions of the work which ought to be done by him, than is apparent to-day; not *higher*, it may be, but *truer*. He needs to scan carefully, and ponder deeply the reason why each and every branch taught by him, is made part of the pupil's labor. He must not rest content with this alone. It must not only be made clear in his mind that it is *a* useful thing, but *the* useful branch for *this* pupil. There should be a selection thus discriminatingly made. Who can so wisely, so *forcibly* aid these young men and maidens to judge aright as their lawful director? If his power be not alone sufficient, let him call in the aid of associate discussion, that to their willingness they may add wisdom.

The teacher too often disregards the many forces which the Creator has placed ready to his hand, because experience has not given him a distinct view of the mainsprings in the child's nature, nor any adequate knowledge of the bearings which school life, school culture and school habits of the children must have upon the life work of the man.

The boat, perchance, was headed up stream when he entered and took the oars, and he pulls manfully, day after day, without question whether it is the true course, or wisest expenditure of energy. This waste of force, or misdirected effort is gradually but surely being diminished through the wide-spread influence of Institutes and Institute workers. It is believed that this agency is second to none in the State for the reformation of this greatest existing evil; and that this work here begun, and afterwards impressed by superintendents, will, before long, so impress patrons with their good fruits that every teacher will be impelled to seek this guidance in their work.

It is felt that the wide-spread belief that there is, in the higher courses of instruction, a better culture than that afforded by the study of those directly connected with daily labor and life, too often weakens the teacher and pupil in this work.

In the opinion of your committee it is due to a truer culture of the great mass of the people that the high and normal schools of the State make strenuous efforts to counteract this pernicious impression by all means in their power.

Hon. W. T. Harris, Superintendent of Schools in St. Louis, then delivered a forcible, logical lecture, on "The Relation of Education to the Individual, Society and the State," after which the Association adjourned to Thursday morning.

THURSDAY MORNING, July 10.

The opening exercises consisted of prayer, by Rev. A. KIDDER, and music by the choir.

J. H. Twombly made some general remarks on the State University, closing with a report on State System of Education, which, on motion of G. S. Albee, was accepted.

The committee on "State System of Education" present the following report:

The duty of the State to provide for the education of the people, its right to levy taxes for that purpose, and the vital importance of education to the individual and to the State, are, with us, universally acknowledged. These facts admitted, it is evidently the duty of the State to see that the education furnished is the right of the quality, breadth and aim, and likewise to adopt such a system and employ such methods as will secure to pupils and to the commonwealth, the highest possible benefits.

Let instruction be thoroughly philosophic, constantly adapted to the laws of mind, and the pupil will make rapid advance in knowledge, attain to a high degree of accuracy in his mental processes, and to such confidence in himself and in appropriate methods as will give him unfaltering persistency in the search after truth. Consciousness of power to do is an attainment of inestimable value. "I can," "I cant," are brief expressions, but they indicate the difference between conquerors and slaves.

Precision, vigor, harmony are important—wise direction more so. Teachers, then, must apprehend the true end of life—life's grand possibilities.

Public education should provide for the training of the physical and moral powers, as certainly as for the mental. From the time the pupil enters the primary school till he graduates at the university, attention should be given to his physical development.

Moral culture claims high consideration.

Heathen nations acknowledge fealty to their gods, and Christian States should ever recognize, particularly in the department of instruction, claims of that religion from which they derive their purest civilization and vital force.

A state school system implies grades of schools, classification of scholars and courses of study. These necessarily depend somewhat upon the density of population, the intellectual development of the people, the time which youth can or will devote to study, and the character of the prominent occupations. To present an ideal system of education, suited to a highly perfected state of society, might be interesting, and, in some respects, useful, for a perfect picture has power to awaken and inspire, and it is wise frequently to lift our thoughts from the defective to the perfect; but a brief business paper must deal with the practical, the immediately possible, rather than the ideal and the distant. As an association, we can only promulgate ideas; but if these ideas ultimately receive legislative sanction and are embodied in law, they will be influential in systematizing our school work, in securing the adoption of better methods, and in the attainment of a higher and broader culture. The time has fully come when the nine thousand teachers and the five thousand schools of this State should cease to work without a general plan, and should make available to the young and to the commonwealth, all the advantages to be derived from comprehensive system and cordial co-operation.

There are three recognized departments of education—Elementary, Secondary and Higher. In each of these departments there are different schools. In the Elementary Department—Primary and Grammar schools. In the Secondary Department—High Schools and Academies. In the Higher Department—Colleges, also Polytechnic and Professional Schools, or Universities embracing all these. In some of these schools there must of necessity be two classes of studies. First. A portion of those which constitute a complete and thorough course from the alphabet up to the highest post graduate studies of the University. Second. Those studies which are necessarily taught for the benefit of children and youth having but limited opportunities to acquire an education.

In every town there are many youth whose schooling is comprised in a very limited number of weeks or months, and justice to them and the public, requires that they have instruction in branches not belonging to the grade of school school which they attend. Provision in such cases must be left to the several schools and the local authorities; yet there should be a general course of study recognized by all the teachers in the State, and a section of that course should constitute the central programme of each school. Carrying out such a plan, the teachers of the State would feel that they are, in one sense, instructors in the University, and are as certainly represented by the graduate from that institution as the professor who gives the final lesson. A due appreciation of this fact would give many teachers stimulus to greater diligence and thoroughness.

The want of proper secondary education in this state is keenly felt by those who conduct the higher institutions. The multiplication of high schools should receive the early attention of the legislature and of the public. They are necessary for the colleges and equally so for the lower schools.

The highest state of educational development requires colleges, and above these technical and professional schools; but for the present we may group all these under the comprehensive title of University.

The State University should embrace the following colleges and departments; 1. A classical college, having the courses of ancient and modern languages. 2. An industrial college, in which should be organized the following departments, viz: Agriculture, Civil Engineering, Mining, Mechanism Architecture, Journalism and Pedagogics.

Many of the courses of study indicated are already established in the Uni sity, and some others ought to be at an early day. The departments of Mechanism and Architecture should be added immediately. Journalism would soon be required, and Pedagogics—the highest science of teaching—could be provided for, as a department of the University, with much less expense than in an independent institution. Besides this, there is a culture acquired by contact with young men who fitting themselves for the various higher callings, which is of intrinsic value to the teacher.

The connection recently formed between the State University and the graded schools is operating well for the University, and accomplishing *much* for the schools. The definite requisitions, made for admission to the colleges and the sub-Freshman class, shows precisely the work to be done in the public schools to effect this connection.

Normal Schools.—These institutions do not stand in the regular line, but they bear an instructive relation to the prosperity of the schools of every grade. Whether they should have preparatory departments or not is a question which we do not propose, at present, to discuss. That their connection with the University should be intimate and cordial can not be doubted.

Compulsory Attendance.—The right to maintain public schools, and especially the fact of taxing the people for their support, implies the right to require by law such attendance as will give youth an opportunity to obtain a sufficient education for an honorable discharge of the duties of citizens

We recommend the subject of compulsory attendance to the careful consideration of the people of this state. We would not rely wholly or mainly upon law, for the school must be a centre of attraction and controlled chiefly by love and hope, yet it is more than possible that wise legislation might secure the attendance of many who now swell the ever-to-be-dreaded column of absentees.

In conclusion, the committee presented the following recommendation:

1. That a uniform course of study be fixed by law for the graded schools of the State.

2. That all high schools be required by law to arrange their courses of study so that they shall correspond with the standard for admission to the University.

3. That the course of study in the normal schools be so extended that graduates of those schools shall be thoroughly prepared to enter the junior class of the college of arts in the University of Wisconsin, and that they be admitted without examination.

4. That a department of pedagogics be established in the University, embracing substantially the studies of the junior and senior classes of the college of arts, and such instruction in the principles and methods of teaching as may be necessary to qualify teachers for the highest grades of schools, and for the important duties of school supervision.

5. That for the successful completion of the university course in pedagogics, an appropriate degree as bachelor or doctor of pedagogics be given. This would do much to secure for teaching a public recognition as a profession. A profession must have its collegiate degrees.

6. That a committee be appointed to carry into effect, as soon as practicable, the foregoing recommendations.

Respectfully submitted.

J. H. TWOMBLY,
ROBERT GRAHAM.
W. H. DE LA MATYR,
Committee.

H. C. Howland, Chairman of Committee on "Frequency in Change of Teachers," made the following report, which was adopted:

"The committee to whom was referred that part of the President's address relating to 'Frequency in Change of Teachers,' respectfully submit the following: Among the causes which lead to such changes may be mentioned: deficiency in the qualifications of teachers; want of purpose on the part of many who teach of making teaching a permanent business; low wages paid to teachers; prevailing opinion in many places that such frequency of change is beneficial; cynical nature of patrons, and delays of school boards to re-engage competent teachers. Better qualified teachers, and the adoption of the township system of school government, would produce greater permanency.

H. C. HOWLAND,
J. Q. EMERY,
D. E. GARDINER,
Committee.

Rev. A. Kidder read the following on "Compulsory Education:"

Resolved, That the progress of virtue and morality, as well as the safety of the nation, depends upon the compulsory education, if not otherwise secured, of all children of our country in the English language; and that it is the duty of educators to make special efforts to form public sentiment in its favor, and of our legislature to enact laws for its accomplishment as soon as they can be sustained.

The resolution was discussed by Messrs. Albee, Smith, Parker, North, Kerr, Earthman and Mears. It was finally referred to a committee, consisting of Messrs. Albee, Kerr and Parker, to report at the annual meeting of the Association in July, 1874.

The Committee on County Associations and Educational Columns reported as follows:

The Committee on "County Teachers' Associations and Educational Columns" report as follows: That as an earnest, intelligent and progressive spirit on the part of the teacher is essential to his success, the county superintendents are recommended to hold frequent Teachers' Meetings, and to encaurage the formation of Teachers' Associations in each county.

That a column in the local newspaper, for school intelligence, is desirable, and it is recommended wherever practical, to have such, to be made up to a considerable extent of what the superintendent finds praiseworthy in the work of teachers, in the school buildings and surroundings, with such pertinent communications on educational matters as teachers may be induced to make.

ALEX. F. NORTH,
A. O. WRIGHT,
J. M. RAIT,
Committee.

On motion of G. S. Albee, the report was adopted.

The following committees, not being ready to report, were, on motion, authorized to report at the session, July, 1874:

Committee on Deficiencies of Primary Instruction, and Committee on reform in Spelling.

A. Earthman, Chairman of Committee on Honorary Membership, reported as follows:

Your committee on honorary membership would recommend that the following gentlemen be chosen honorary members of this association: Hon. W. T. Harris, St. Louis; Dr. C. H. Fowler, Evanston; the president and the members of the school board of Sparta.

A. EARTHMAN,
H. E. HOARD,
R. SPOOR,
Committee.

Report adopted.

The committee appointed to give aid to teachers in securing situations, and school officers in obtaining teachers, through the chairman, G. S. Albee, made the following report:

Your committee appointed to aid teachers in securing situations, and school offieers in obtaining teachers, herewith submit their report of the year's work:

Circulars containing a scheme of questions regarding needful information, have been printed and distributed among the teachers, superintendents and press of this state.

The number of applications on file from teachers desiring situations, is about eighty.

The number of applications on file from school officers desiring teachers is about sixty.

From the failure on the part of many applicants to give information when situations or teachers have been secured, your committee are unable to make a reliable statement on this point.

Most of the applications from teachers have been for positions in graded schools, while fully one-half those from school officers have been from mixed schools.

This being the first year of this committee's work, its existence even was known to but few until situations for the past school year had nearly all been filled, but the considerable number entering into correspondence with the committee indicate that there is a need of some intermediate agency between the teachers and school boards of the state.

G. S. ALBEE,
J. Q. EMERY,
A. EARTHMAN,
Committee.

The report was accepted, and the committee continued for another year.

S. Shaw read a paper entitled "Machinery."

After recess, O. R. Smith reported briefly on "Uniformity of

Text-books." The committee was continued, and asked to report at the December meeting of teachers and superintendents.

A paper on "Drawing" was read by W. H. Chase, of Madison.

After which, I. N. Stewart, chairman of committee on school-houses and grounds, made the following report, which was adopted:

Your committee, to whom was referred that portion of the president's address relative to the condition of school-houses and grounds, would respectfully report:

We recommend that all teachers use every means of personal influence and example to secure improvement in the care and ornamentation of school-houses and grounds; that conductors of institutes be asked to give this subject special attention; that county superintendents use the press for calling attention to improvements in any district, as well as any notable deficiency. Teachers should use every possible influence on parents, as well as pupils, which may tend to remedy the evil existing. In many districts, a day's voluntary work on the part of parents, setting out trees, repairing and clearing the grounds, could be secured. The pupils themselves, under suitable direction, can make a good beginning.

We would call special attention, in behalf of health, decency and morals, to the deplorable condition of out-buildings, which too frequently exists. No true teacher should hold his peace, day nor night, till the nuisance is abated.

I. N. STEWART,
J. H. TERRY,
CORDELIA POTTER,
Committee.

Report on "Methods Increasing the School Fund," was read by A. O. Wright. Accepted.

The following resolution, introduced by W. Parker, was passed:

Resolved, That when the association adjourns, it adjourns to meet in Madison, on the second Wednesday in July, 1874.

The association then proceeded to ballot for president, with the following result:

Whole number of votes cast, 162; of which B. M. Reynolds received 112; H. C. Howland, 47; scattering, 3.

B. M. Reynolds having received a majority over all, was declared elected.

In a few well chosen remarks he thanked the members of the association for the honor conferred upon him.

S. Shaw then reported for the committee on nominations as follows:

For Vice Presidents.—H. C. Howland, Eau Claire; S. S. Rockwood, Whitewater; Miss Mattie Hazzard, Oshkosh.

For Secretary.—L. W. Briggs, Green Bay.

For Treasurer.—C. F. Viebahn, Manitowoc.

Executive Committee.—D. McGregor, Platteville; W. D. Parker, Janesville; Alex. Kerr, Madison; G. S. Albee, Oshbosh; A. Earthman, Reedshurg.

S. SHAW,
R. GRAHAM,
H. C. HOWLAND,
MRS. I. N. STEWART,
MISS FLORENCE BUSH,
Committee.

The report was accepted, and the ballot being cast by the secretary for the association, the above named persons were declared elected.

O. R. Smith made the following report, which was adopted:

The committee to whom was referred the subject of the relation of our public schools to the institutions for special instruction of those who are incapacitated for the modes of the common schools, have had the same under consideration and respectively report as follows:

We find in the report of the Superintendent of Public Instruction for 1872, 636 children reported as being disqualified to be subjected to the public schools; 93, blind; 204, deaf and dumb; 339, idiotic.

Inasmuch as statisticians have found that it is impossible to secure accuracy in the reports of this class, and as experience has shown that about one-third only are reported, it may safely be concluded that we have at least 2,000 children in this state to be put in the above classes.

The state has recognized its duty to educate every child in its borders, no matter how low or unfortunate. It is dictated by self preservation. It has munificent funds for this purpose, the income of which is sacredly appropriated to accomplish the end for which they were originally constituted.

Fine, special schools have been established for the blind, at Janesville, and the deaf and dumb, at Delavan. They are doing a valuable work and doing it well. No provision has yet been made for the idiotic, who number at least 1,000. These children draw public money and cannot be excluded from our schools, where they are an inconvenience and danger. It has been demonstrated in Illinois, New York, Pennsylvania, Massachusetts, Kentucky, Ohio, and in foreign countries, where are established flourishing institutions for their training, that these children can be educated and made self sustaining. It is no longer an open question. Indeed, to the methods employed in the training of idiots are we indebted for the improved methods of instruction which have been adopted in our schools in the last twenty years.

The state cannot safely longer neglect to provide for this unfortunate class; therefore,

Resolved, That the Wisconsin Teachers' Association hereby reaffirms its conviction that it is the duty of the state to immediately provide a school for the special training of the feeble minded children of the state.

O. R. SMITH,
A. F. NORTH,
A. KERR,
Committee.

The commitee on Obituaries, consisting of O. R. Smith, J. C. Pickard and S. Shaw, reported through the chairman, as follows:

WHEREAS, in the dispensation of Divine Providenee, we have lost from our roll of members our honored President, Prof. J. K. Purdy, Prof. M. Montague and Prof. Jackson Bushnell; therefore,

Resolved, That we bow in submission to Him who doeth all things well.

Resolved, That by the death of our President, J. K. Purdy, the Association has lost an efficient officer, our profession an untiring and progressive student, a patient instructor, and true teacher; the state a citizen of character prominence; society a type of the highest manhood, and the church a devout and consistent Christian. We mourn his loss as a friend and brother, and a wise and safe counselor in every educational enterprise.

Resolved, That in the death of Prof. M. Montague, Superintendent of Schools for Walworth county, the state has been deprived of the valuable service of an able and high-minded educator; this Association of the prudent counsel and dignified presence of one of its most eminent members; the people of Walworth county of an official whose whole heart was in the work pertaining to his position; the teachers under his supervision of a sympathizing friend and adviser, and the Christian ministry of one of its purest and most diligent workers in the cause of Christ.

Resolved, That by the death of Prof. Jackson, of Beloit College, the state of Wisconsin has lost a noble and public spirited citizen the institution whose prosperity he had ever at heart one of its main supports, and our educational interests a distinguished teacher and sincere friend.

Resolved, That we tender to the friends of the deceased our heartfelt sympathy in their affliction.

The report was adapted.

After reading the report, Mr. Smith addressed the teachers, and was followed by Professors Kerr, Rockwood and Salisbury, after which the association adjourned till evening.

THURSDAY EVENING, July 10, 1873.

Association called to order by President McGregor, listened to the following report of the Finance committee:

Received of C. M. Treat, former Treasurer	$71 59
Paid orders drawn in 1872	12 05
Balance on hand July 8, 1873	$59 54
Received from tickets on membership	81 00
Amount	$140 54
Deduct bills, current expenses 1873	115 15
Leaving on hand	$25 39

Respectfully submitted,
MISS M. E. HAZZARD,
H. C. HOWLAND,
J. M. RAIT,
Committee.

J. C. Pickard, chairman of Committee on Resolutions, reported as follows:

WHEREAS, The harmonious development of all the faculties of our being should be the aim of our educational system; and

WHEREAS, We recognize in the human mind an inate love of order, symmetry and beauty, whether in nature or art, an inborn craving for noble architecture, perfect machinery, tasteful houses, and becoming dress; and find in the development of this æsthetic faculty, according to the rules of correct taste, an element greatly conducive to the intellectual, moral and religious welfare of the community; therefore,

Resolved, That a comprehensive plan of drawing should be introduced into our school system, beginning in the lowest, progressing through every grade, and finding its culmination in a thoroughly equipped art department of the State University.

That Wisconsin, now abreast of the foremost States in whatever is designed, through the public school, to secure intellectual development, ought not to suffer herself to fall behind in æsthetic culture.

Resolved, That the members of this Association appreciate most heartily the welcome they have received at the hands of the citizens of Sparta. In the ample accommodations furnished for our meetings, in the tasteful decorations of this hall, in the arrangements made for our social enjoyment, in the open-hearted way in which all doors have stood open that we might enter, not as guests, but as part of each household, we recognize the spirit which fosters free schools and gives them life and power: which looks upon the teacher not as a Modoc Chief, busy with the scalps of the innocent, but as a "man and brother," God-appointed to stand by the parent's side, or in his place, in the training of the children.

Our thanks (a feeble word) are given from full hearts, to one and all, to those especially who have had the hard work to do, and have done it so well. Henceforth the name of Sparta shall suggest not so much Spartan valor and firmness, as Spartan generosity and hospitality.

Resolved, That our thanks are due to Rev. Dr. Fowler, of Evanston, Illinois, President N. W. University, and Hon. W. T. Harris, of St. Louis, for the lectures delivered before the association, and that the president be requested to solicit of Mr. H. a copy of his lecture for publication in the *Journal of Education*.

Resolved, That we gratefully acknowledge the courtesy extended to us by those railway companies and steamboat lines that have reduced their fares for our accommodation.

Resolved, That the sweet singers who have done so much to add the agreeable to the useful, deserve the hearty thanks which are hereby tendered.

Resolved, That it has been good to be here; if any one returns hence to his work without a deeper sense of its importance, and a settled purpose to labor to make his profession such that it cannot be justly styled "unprofessional," he must have culpably failed to catch the earnest spirit of the occasion.

J. C. PICKARD,
A. J. HUTTON,
J. J. FRUIT,
Committee.

The resolutions were adopted.

There being no further business the Twenty-first Annual Session of the Wisconsin State Teachers' Association adjourned *sine die*.

DUNCAN McGREGOR, *President*.

M. T. PARKS, *Secretary*.

Reports of the State Charitable and Reformatory Institutions.

REPORT OF THE WISCONSIN INDUSTRIAL SCHOOL FOR BOYS.

A. D. HENDRICKSON,
SUPERINTENDENT.

(*Extracts from the Annual Report.*)

Smallest number in the school at any time during the year.............	259
Largest number at any time during the year..........................	282
Average during the year..	271
Whole number in school since July, 1860	966

EMPLOYMENT.

Eight hours of each day in winter and nine in summer, are devoted to school and work. During the winter, the time devoted to school is four hours, and to work four hours. In summer the school time is four hours per day, and the work five. Each half day, except Saturday afternoon and Sunday, has its work session and school session, with a recess intervening. Saturday afternoon of each week is devoted to recreation, writing letters, receiving visits of friends, and other miscellaneous duties. The small boys' work-time is one hour less per day than the above.

HOMES.

We have, as at date of last report, six families in as many buildings. These we call family buildings, each of which is in charge of a man and woman. The man, as the father or elder brother, looks after the comfort, conduct and health of his boys. His duties require him to be in the building or in the yard, night or day, when his boys are there. The internal arrangement of the home is managed by a woman. She is expected to care for the inmates' wearing apparel and extend to the boys of her family such attention as a good mother should to her own children.

EDUCATION.

It will be difficult to give any extended report of the educational facilities and workings of our school, without repeating the substance of former reports. It may not be a matter of interest to the board of managers to be told from year to year that the majority of our boys have taken the first lessons of education in the streets and the saloons; that the cultivation of their minds, manners and morals have been sadly neglected; that the training of the hand, head and heart, which should have received attention at home, at school, and in the church, has been left undone; yet, these are the facts which force themselves upon our minds in working out the problem of reform.

The bent twig has grown up an inclined tree. It now resists the hand put forth to straighten it. It is not difficult for the sculptor to bring forth images of beauty from the native marble; but his task is a difficult one, when required to produce symmetrical figures from the deformed and mutilated blocks upon which unskilled hands have wasted their energies.

Very much like this is the task assigned to us. We are expected by the friends of our inmates and other well meaning people (not by the board of managers) to do in a twelvemonth what parents and teachers failed to do in so many years. We cannot manufacture brains, change the heart or perform miracles. We need time first to help the boy unlearn what he has learned amiss, and then to teach him what he ought to know as he should know it.

Our Institution is a school in more than an ordinary sense. Ordinarily, children learn in the family, they learn in their intercourse in society, they are instructed in the lecture room and in the church as well as in the school proper; but it devolves upon the officer of a reformatory to perform all these duties. Our families are places of instruction, our workshops are schools of learning, our assembly room to us is the lecture hall and church.

SCHOOL.

This department of our Institution differs in no essential respect from the public or graded schools of the towns and cities of the state, except, perhaps, we have a less number pursuing higher branches of English education. The common branches of English education are taught. Special attention is given to reading, writing and the art of computation.

ASSEMBLY ROOM.

For the first time in the history of this Institution we have an assembly room which is not a school room. Here we gather at the close of each day, pupils, teachers and all connected with the Institution. This is properly classified as one of the means of education. Probably no portion of the day is productive of greater mental and moral improvement than the half hour spent in the assembly room. It is a daily reunion of all the families, a time of pleasant emotions, when face answers to face, and voice unites to voice in song. We here review the day's proceedings, calling attention to the defects and awarding commendation for that which is honorable and praiseworthy. The occurrences of the day, any matter of general interest found in the journals of the times, whatever may furnish a theme of useful information is here presented. These exercises are conducted by the teacher, the superintendent, or others, frequently by some visitor who may chance to favor us with his presence. Here, also, vocal music is cultivated. All are requested to join in the songs. Aided by a leading voice and the instrument, a large portion of our boys acquire much practical knowledge of vocal music.

An hour of each Sabbath morning is spent in the assembly room, in reading and studying. A service is conducted at half past ten o'clock. Sunday School at half past two. All assemble again in the evening, and listen to select reading or a brief lecture. These exercises are adapted to the capacity of children, and generally prove seasons of interest to most in the assembly. In other words, briefly, we assemble four times on Sunday, spending in all about five hours of the day in exercises calculated, as we believe, to make us all wiser, better and happier.

LIBRARY.

Forty-one volumes have been added this year, making in all 881 volumes. Some of them are too much worn for circulation. We find difficulty in keeping our library books in good repair. This results, first and principally, from the fact that the books of these times are poorly bound. With even careful handling they soon loosen from the cover and fall to pieces. Secondly, from the rough usage to which they are subjected in the hands of boys. Some 200 or more volumes are circulated weekly. Many of the boys read these books with marked attention. The periodicals are so distributed and interchanged from family to family that all can have opportunity to read them.

WISCONSIN INSTITUTION FOR THE EDUCATION OF THE BLIND.

JANESVILLE, October 1, 1873.

HON. S. FALLOWS, *Superintendent of Public Instruction:*

DEAR SIR: During the year that has now closed, this Institution has been conducted very much as in previous years. Its doors have been open, free of charge, to the blind children of the state, just as the district schools are to their more fortunate brothers and sisters. Seventy-seven of them have availed themselves of its privileges. In literature, they have studied reading, spelling, writing (by two systems—one for correspondence with the seeing and the other legible by the touch), geography, arithmetic, English literature and physiology. A few individuals have also attended to other studies. In the evening the school, divided into suitable classes, has listened to reading. The examinations show a degree of knowledge acquired that is proof of hard work on the part of both teachers and scholars.

So far, our work corresponds very nearly with that of the ordinary schools, though carried on mainly by different methods. The condition of the blind requires us to supplement this work by giving such a knowledge of the art of music or of some handicraft as may enable the graduates of the Institution to do something for their future support.

In music, therefore, two teachers have been constantly employed. The piano, cabinet organ, violin and various other instruments have been taught; two choirs, an orchestra and a class in theory of music have had daily exercises; and many scholars have had private training of the voice.

The broom shop has been carried on energetically by Mr. Stephen, on a system that has developed good results. Cane-seating has been taught to a few—mostly girls. All the girls have had instruction in one or more branches of feminine industry, such as sewing, knitting, bead-work or crocheting.

Ten pupils have been discharged this year. Of these, three have opened broom shops, with good promise of success; one other is competent to do so, whose plans are not known; one has entered Evanston Theological Seminary; one has commenced teaching music, under encouraging circumstances; three girls have returned to their families, having gained the education here that their misfortune prevented them from getting in the schools of their neighborhoods; and the other left school on account of ill health, after too short a stay for much improvement.

During the summer I had opportunity to study the operations of the Institutions for the Education of the Blind in Great Britain. They bestow a vast deal of labor upon training in various branches of handicraft—training the hand well but greatly neglecting the mind. The results, as ascertained by conference with numerous persons intimately acquainted with the facts, are much less satisfactory than those attained by American institutions, which, without neglecting the hand, have striven to cultivate the mind. Intelligent labor is always more valuable and more remunerative than unintelligent, even in the case of those who have all their senses. The loss of the sense of vision affects the use of the hand directly and disastrously. If it were not the chief seat of the sense of touch it could not be profitably employed in labor, when it is no longer guided by the eye. The mind, however, is far less injuriously affected by the loss of sight, and the more thoroughly that of the blind man is cultivated, the better is he equipped for the encounters of life. Superior natural powers, well cultivated, will enable him to devote himself to intellectual pursuits altogether, or, as an employer, to direct the labor of others. Musical ability, well cultivated, will enable him to gain his living in the fields of sound, where light is not required. If he has only the degree and kind of mental ability possessed by most men, he must rely upon his hands, impeded though they are by the absence of their natural director, the eye; and here he will find that there is no substitute for the eye equal to a well trained mind. Aided by it, he will perform his work more easily and produce a better article; and, in addition to this, will be able to dispose of it to better advantage than if ignorant.

It is gratifying to find that the system of education adopted in this Institution is supported by the fact that the opposite system, when tried elsewhere most thoroughly, has produced much less desirable results.

The operation of that part of the school law which requires the annual enumeration of the children of each school district who cannot see to go to school, continues to be favorable to the efficiency of the Institution. I desire to express here my thanks to many town and district officers who have rendered special assistance in procuring the education of blind children before the suitable time for instruction has passed. It is to be regretted that many parents of such children are so negligent of their interests as to allow them to pass the time of childhood and youth in idleness and ignorance. We have had several applications this year for the admission of young men who have thus spent their youth. When it is too late they have begun to see the value of the opportunities offered by the state. Whoever contributes to prevent such cases by assisting in sending a blind child to school at the proper age, confers an incalulable benefit upon him and a favor upon the community. The Institution enters upon a new year under favorable auspices.

Very respectfully,

THOMAS H. LITTLE,

Supt. of Wisconsin Institution for the Education of the Blind.

INSTITUTE FOR THE EDUCATION OF THE DEAF AND DUMB.

The intellectual progress of the school is worthy of special record, inasmuch as the year is believed to have been one of the most successful in the history of the Institute.

The whole number of pupils, in twenty-one years, is three hundred and seventy-seven, of whom one hundred and forty-eight are present at this date.

The following table exhibits the relation of the school to the future, so far as it can be determined by data necessarily uncertain, but believed to be sufficiently accurate to warrant action. Taking as a basis the present number in school, the average admissions for the last three years, and the number of deaf mutes reported, ten years of age, but not in school, the table shows the prospects of the Institute for three years to come. The "Prospective Dismissions" (in the table) represent those pupils whose time will have expired in the respective years indicated. The "Prospective Admissions" are based on the average admissions during the last three years, increased by five. The "Expected Attendance" is the result after deducting the Prospective Dismissions and adding the Prospective Admissions. The "Non-attendance" refers to those who have been reported as deaf mutes between ten and twenty years of age, and not now in school. This number is uniform in the table because the number who *become* of age each year is equal to the prospective admissions. The sum of the Expected Attendance and of the Non-attendance gives what the school should number each year.

Year.	Prospective Dismissions.	Prospective Admissions.	Expected Attendance.	Non-Attendance.	Should be Attendance.
1873			150	100	250
1874	30	30	150	100	250
1875	15	30	165	100	265
1876	5	30	190	100	290

This table does not take into account increase of population. Should it appear—which is not unlikely—that some of the one hundred non-attendants are not proper subjects, it is probable that the list would be kept good by the addition of proper subjects. The decrease of Prospective Dismissions within three years is owing to the fact that a very large proportion of those now in school have been here a comparatively short time. A rate of increase, proportionate to the number of deaf mutes in the state, would double the school in three years.

These calculations are based on the supposition that children be received at ten years of age. This has been the custom here for many years. It is a practical question among instructors of deaf mutes, whether ten or twelve is the proper age for admission. The true solution depends on a variety of circumstances, such as the natural capacity of the child. the degree of physical development, home influences, and the probable time it will be allowed in the Institute. Hitherto, I have not rejected any applicants over ten years of age, though there are instances in which it has become evident that delay in entry would have proved advantageous to the pupil.

Experience in deaf-mute instruction has demonstrated the fact that there are three classes of these unfortunate children and youth for whom special and specific provision should be made, according to their natural capacity and their attainments. The first of these classes is composed of those who should be retained five years, within which the Institute will accomplish all that can be expected for them in education and general training. A second class includes those whose progress warrants their continuance in school two additional years. For these two classes, your action of a year ago is all that can be asked. There is a third class, by far the smallest, worthy of a higher department, which would furnish opportunity for a yet fuller development, and qualify its members for special positions of labor and usefulness, evermore presenting an elevated standard of attainment to the departments below it whose members would be stimulated thereby. During the past two years, we have had in fact, though not in name, a "High Class," whose studies have been equal to, if not in advance of, those of similar classes in the first institutions for deaf-mutes in the country. Should not such a department, as early as practicable, be recognized as an established part of this Institute?

There is a misapprehension in many minds respecting the time allowed in the Institute, as compared with that in public schools generally. A moment's thought should correct the error. The relative time in the Institute is really shorter. A child comes to us ten years of age. It is true, he has had an existence of ten years, during which his physical being has had a corresponding development. But in almost every other respect, there has been no maturing process. The phrase, "ten years," applied to an ordinary child, includes much besides mere age and physical development. If this be all, we pronounce his condition abnormal. With that decade of years, we associate knowledge—of men, of things, of Deity—knowledge acquired by *language*, understood in its simpler forms from infancy; language *spoken*, almost from infancy and *heard* through ten years of hourly communication with hundreds of others from whom he receives constant instruction. At ten years of age, that child has been in the school of life nearly the whole period. Now let him spend five hours a day in a school house, under special teachers, for two years; and through life, it will be said of him that he had only two years of schooling, though practically he had four times that number. His education was in progress, though his school period in its technical sense, was very limited.

So then, it is a most serious error to compare, as equivalent, a term of years in the Institute with a term of corresponding number in a hearing and speaking school. To place the deaf-mute on an equality with his more fortunate companions, would require an extension of the institute school-period beyond the limit which the noblest generosity of the state could be expected to exercise towards its unfortunate children, who, after all that can be done for them, must remain the children of misfortune still. But notwithstanding this, there has been solved, again and again, within the twenty-one years of the history of this Institute, what was once a problem—whether deafness is an insurmountable barrier to mental improvement and general training; whether isolation must be the perpetual condition of the deaf-mute; whether the ordinary relations between man and man could exist between the deaf-mute and his fellow; whether he could be made to understand the true aims of life and immortality, and effectually aided in securing them.

SOLDIERS' ORPHANS' HOME.

Hon. Samuel Fallows:

Dear Sir—At your suggestion I respectfully submit a brief report:

The schools of the Soldiers' Orphans' Home are in a prosperous condition. They are three in number, containing 144 pupils. In respect to order and discipline, throroughness and progress in studies, our schools compare favorably with any of similar grades. The course of study has been extended since last report by the introduction of Word Analysis and Civil Government. Elementary Algebra will soon be added.

This year four pupils have been admitted to the normal department, and two to the preparatory class of our state normal schools. The Home has now nine pupils in these state institutions; one at Platteville, five at Whitewater and three at Oshkosh.

Creditable reports reach me from all parties.

Respectfully,

R. W. BURTON.

STATE PRISON.

CHAPLAIN'S REPORT.

I present the following as my annual report of the moral, religious and educational departments of the Wisconsin State Prison, for the year ending Sept. 30, 1873:

In regard to the moral and religious departments of this institution, I can safely say it has been a year of prosperity, and more than usual success has attended our efforts to promote the welfare of our prison population—to lead them to a better mind, and to establish in them the principles of a higher life.

The inmates of this institution seem pleased at the return of the Sabbath Day, and as cheerfully attend its religious services, and conduct themselves with as much propriety as any outside congregation. No violation of the rules of strict propriety has ever occurred in our public meetings during the seven years of my official connection with the Prison, and, had I no other means of knowing, judging from the deportment of my congregation, I should say that while all were interested, many were profited by our Sabbath services. We have public religious service every Sabbath morning at 10½ o'clock, at which all the convicts in the institution are required to be present; also, we have a social meeting from 3½ to 4½ o'clock, Sabbath evening. To this meeting, none are admitted but such as are members of the prison church, or such as express a desire to lead a new life by faith in Jesus Christ.

Our social meetings are conducted by the convicts themselves, and they are truly interesting and profitable, and they make them sometimes very affecting. Many Christian people from the outside give us their influence and encouragement, by attending our afternoon exercises, and contribute largely to the interest of the meetings by discoursing to us beautiful music, and interspersing the exercises with inspiring songs and hymns. Many strong men, unaccustomed to weep, are frequently seen bathed in tears, as some touching strain speaks of home and childhood's innocence, and the hopes of other years, now perished forever.

Since the organization of what is know as the prison church, in 1867, there have been admitted to membership, and received the rites of Christian fellowship, 183 persons. The whole number honorably discharged during the same time is 101. Of these I am happy to say that but one has ever been returned to this or any other prison, as far as I have been able to ascertain, but on the contrary, many, if not *all*, are laboring to rebuild, by honest industry and Christian fidelity, a manly character ruined by a life of crime.

Since my last report, I have received into society 25 persons, and have honorably discharged 17, which leaves me with a present membership of 32, in good standing and with unabated interest, and more encouraging prospects than at any time since my connection with the prison.

The prison school is in successful operation, and doing a good work. There have been admitted to the school, since its establishment, 303 scholars. I have discharged from the school in the same time, 266, leaving a present membership of 34 scholars, besides officers and teachers, classed according to the different degrees of improvement found in the school. In regard to the order and deportment of the school, I can only say what I said in my last report, "It is truly remarkable, that for the whole term of six years that this school has been in operation, with a membership of from 40 to 70 scholars and teachers, not one solitary breach of good order has occurred, but all have behaved with propriety." This department has made a greater impression for good in the prison this year than any previous year since its institution.

Our library is doing a good work in the institution, and is highly appreciated by all the prisoners—which they demonstrate by the careful manner in which they treat all books committed to their care. Not a single book has in any manner been disfigured by them, since the opening of the library, one year ago. The library is in a good working condition and in a good state of preservation. The number of books is the same as last year, none having been lost or destroyed.

These benevolent, humane and Christian provisions made by the state for the improvement and comfort of the unfortunate convicts of this prison, are, in my judgment, greater preventives of crime in the future of these men and women than the sentence of the law that confines them here.

It is a well attested truth that nothing of importance can be accomplished in the reformatory departments of our penal institutions without the cheerful co-operation of the commissioners, wardens and their subordinate officers, and I most cheerfully acknowledge that the unusual results, which have attended my efforts as Chaplain in this institution, have been more the result of the cheerful co-operation of the officials of the prison than the feeble efforts I have been able to make myself.

Our worthy Commissioner, Hon. G. F. Wheeler, and his faithful deputy, Hon. Benj. Bettis, have cheered me in my work, not only by a hearty "God speed," but have at all times given me the whole weight of their influence, both official and personal; and, what I have said of the first officers of the Prison, I can say as truthfully of all the subordinate officers; and, for their uniform kindness to me, and for the valuable assistance they have so cheerfully rendered me in the discharge of my duties, I return to them my sincere thanks.

Respectfully submitted,

HENRY DREW,
Chaplain.

REPORTS OF UNIVERSITIES AND COLLEGES.

UNIVERSITY OF WISCONSIN.

Annual Report of the President of the Board of Trustees of the University of Wisconsin, for the year ending August 31, 1873.

1. Corporate name of the institution, University of Wisconsin.
2. Name of the place where the institution is located, Madison, Wisconsin.
3. Year when the institution was founded, 1848.
4. Names of members of the Faculty, with their respective salaries:

Names.	Departments of Instruction.	Salary.
J. H. Twombly, D. D....	President and Professor of Mental and Moral Philosophy..........................	$3,500
John W. Sterling, Ph. D.	Vice-President and Professor of Natural Philosophy and Astronomy............	2,000
William F. Allen, A. M..	Professor of Latin and History............	2,000
S. H. Carpenter, LL. D..	Professor of Logic, Rhetoric and English Literature	2,000
Alexander Kerr, A. M...	Professor of Greek Language and Literature, and Principal of Preparatory Department.	2,000
John B. Feuling, Ph. D.	Professor of Modern Languages and Comparative Philology	2,000
Col. W. J. L. Nicodemus	Professor of Military Science and Civil Engineering	2,000
John B. Parkinson, A. M.	Professor of Mathematics, and Lecturer on Civil Polity and International Law	2,000
J. E. Davies, A. M., M. D.	Professor of Natural History and Chemistry	2,000
W. W. Daniells, M. S. ..	Professor of Agriculture and Analytical Chemistry	2,000
Roland Irving, A.M., E.M.	Professor of Geology, Mining and Metallurgy, and Curator of Cabinet...........	2,000
Hon. L. S. Dixon, LL. D.	Chief Justice of the Supreme Court of Wisconsin, and Professor of Law..........	......
Hon. Orsamus Cole, LL.D.	Associate Justice of the Supreme Court of Wisconsin, and Professor of Law	......
Hon. W. P. Lyon, LL. D.	Associate Justice of the Supreme Court of Wisconsin, and Professor of Law........	......
Hon. P. L. Spooner	Dean of Law Faculty	......
Hon. H. S. Orton, LL. D.	Professor of Law............................	......
J. H. Carpenter, Esq.....	Professor of Law............................	......
William F. Vilas, LL. B.	Professor of Law............................	......
R. B. Anderson, A. M...	Instructor in Languages..................	$1,200
Elmer H. Craig, A. B. ..	Instructor	700
Robert H. Brown, Ph. B.	Instructor	700
Mrs. D. E. Carson	Preceptress..................................	900

University of Wisconsin—continued.

Names.	Departments of Instruction.	Salary.
Miss Josephine Magoon.	Assistant Preceptress	700
Miss L. S. Spencer, Ph. B.	Instructress	600
Miss Augusta Buttner	Instructress in French and German	600
*Miss Ella F. Sage	Teacher of Instrumental Music	......
*Miss Mary C. Woodworth	Teacher of Vocal Music	......
*Miss Annie Cushman	Teacher of Drawing and Oil Painting	......

	Male.	Female.	Total.
5. Total number who have graduated—			
From colleges	176	9	185
From law department	......	......	92
			279
6. Number who graduated at last commencement—			
From colleges	22	......	22
From law department	......	......	24
			46
7. Number of students in the senior class	22	......	......
8. Number of students in the junior class	31	13	......
9. Number of students in the sophomore class	31	12	......
10. Number of students in the freshman class	21	21	......
11. Number of students not in the regular classes	41	54	......
12. Number of students in the preparatory department.	157	35	......

13. Number of acres of land owned by the institution, 234 in the farm; total	82,000
14. Estimated cash value of land owned by the institution	$141,892 00
15. Estimated cash value of buildings owned by the institution.	145,000 00
16. Amount of endowments and funds except real estate	......
17. Amount of income for the current year from all sources except tuition	45,318 17
18. Amount received for tuition during the current year	9,825 00
19. Rates of tuition in collegiate department per annum, not including board	18 00
20. Rates of tuition in preparatory department per annum, not including board	18 00
21. Amount paid on account of expenses of the institution, exclusive of building and repairs, during the year ending August 31, 1878	54,688 64

C. S. HAMILTON,
President of the Board of Trustees.

By J. H. TWOMBLY.

*Income of Department.

BELOIT COLLEGE.

Annual Report of the President of the Board of Trustees of Beloit College for the year ending August 31, 1873.

1. Corporate name of the Institution. The Board of Trustees of Beloit College.
2. Name of the place where the institution is located, Beloit.
3. Year when the institution was founded, 1847.
4. Names of members of the faculty, with their respective salaries:

Names.	Departments of Instruction.	Salary.
Aaron L. Chapin, D. D.	History and Civil Politics	$1,800
Rev. Joseph Emerson, M.A.	Greek Language and Literature	1,500
Jackson J. Bushnell, M.A.	Mathematics and Natural Philosophy	1,500
Rev. Wm. Porter, M. A.	Latin Language and Literature	1,500
Rev. Jas. J. Blaisdell, M.A.	Mental and Moral Philosophy	1,500
James H. Eaton, M. D.	Chemistry and Natural Science	1,500
Rev. H. M. Whitney, MA.	Rhetoric and English Literature	1,500
Peter Hendrickson, M. A.	Modern Languages	1,200
Ira W. Pettibone, M. A.	Principal of Preparatory School	1,500
Thomas D. Christie, B.A.	Assistant in Preparatory School	800

	Male.	
5. Total number who have graduated	201	......
6. Number who graduated at last commencement	18	......
7. Number of students in the Senior Class	18	......
8. Number of students in the Junior Class	10	......
9. Number of students in the Sophomore Class	14	......
10. Number of students in the Freshman Class	20	......
11. Number of students not in the Regular Classes	......	......
12. Number of students in the Preparatory Department	121	......

13. Number of acres of land owned by the institution		1,648
Site	20	
Other lands in Wisconsin	601	
In other states	1,027	
14. Estimated cash value of land owned by the institution		$34,500 00
Site	$20,500	
Other lands	14,500	
15. Estimated cash value of buildings owned by the institution		55,500 00
16. Amount of endowments and funds except real estate		118,907 65
17. Amount of income for the current year from all sources except tuition		11,970 82
18. Amount received for tuition during the current year		4,239 76
19. Rates of tuition in collegiate department per annum, not including board		36 00
20. Rates of tuition in preparatory department per annum, not including board		26 00
21. Amount paid on account of expenses of the institution, exclusive of building and repairs, during the year ending August 31, 1873		16,477 77

A. L. CHAPIN,
President of the Board of Trustees.

GALESVILLE UNVIERSITY.

Annual Report of the President of the Board of Trustees of Galesville University, for the Year ending August 31, 1873.

1. Corporate name of the institution, The Board of Trustees of Galesville University.
2. Name of the place where the institution is located, Galesville, Wis.
3. Year when the institution was founded, chartered 1854—opened 1859.
4. Names of members of the faculty, with their respective salaries:

Names.	Departments of Instruction.	Salar's.
Rev. H. Gilliland, D. D..	Mental and Moral Philosophy	$1,200
Rev. D. S. Howes, B. S..	Natural Science.........	......
Miss F. F. Luce, A. M...	Ancient Languages......................	300
Miss E. L. French, M.E.L	Mathematics	300
Miss A. P. Bruce	Music and German..........................	......

	Male.	Female
5. Total number who have graduated......................	10	8
6. Number who graduated at last commencement...........	2	......
7. Number of students in the Senior Class	2	......
8. Number of students in the Junior Class	2	......
9. Number of students in the Sophomore Class	13	......
10. Number of students in the Freshman Class	18	......
11. Number of students not in the Regular Classes...	......	......
12. Number of students in the Preparatory Department......	103	......

13. Number of acres of land owned by the institution	600
14. Estimated cash value of land owned by the institution..........	$10,000
15. Estimated cash value of buildings owned by the institution.....	12,000
16. Amount of endowments and funds, except real estate...........	3,000
17. Amount of income for the current year from all sources except tuition	1,060
18. Amount received for tuition during the current year............	1,340
19. Rates of tuition in collegiate department per annum, not including board..	27
20. Rates of tuition in preparatory department per annum, not including board.....	21
21. Amount paid on account of expenses of the institution, exclusive of building and repairs, during the year ending Aug. 31, 1873.	2,450

H. GILLILAND,
President of the Board of Trustees.

LAWRENCE UNIVERSITY.

Annual Report of the President of the Board of Trustees of Lawrence University for the year ending August 31, 1873.

1. Corporate name of the institution, Lawrence University.
2. Name of place where the institution is located, Appleton.
3. Year when the institution was founded, 1847.
4. Names of members of the faculty, with their respective salaries:

NAMES.	Departments of Instruction.	Salary.
G. M. Steele, D. D.	Claflin Professor of Ethics and Civil Polity.	$1,500
Hiram A. Jones, A. M.	Professor of Ancient Langurges	1,000
James C. Faye, A. M.	Professor of Chemistry and Physics	1,000
....	*Professor of Mathematics and Astronomy.	......
Wilbur F. Yocum, A. M.	Professor of Natural History.	1,000
†James H. Wormer, A. M.	Non-resident Professor of Modern History and Languages	350
O. P. De Land	Principal of Commercial School	1,000
Miss M. J. Evans	Preceptress and teacher of Latin and German	700
Miss L. M. Hodgkins	French and Botany	650
Miss S. A. Clark	Drawing and Painting	......
Mrs. S. S. Fitch	Vocal and Instrumental Music	......

	Male.	Female.
5. Total number who have graduated	103	52
6. Number who graduated at last commencement	7	4
7. Number of students in the Senior Class	10	2
8. Number of students in the Junior Class	12	2
9. Number of students in the Sophomore Class	9	9
10. Number of students in the Freshman Class	22	8
11. Number of students not in regular classes	31	28
12. Number of students in the Preparatory Department	136	86

13. Number of acres of land owned by the institution	....
14. Eestimated chash value of land owned by the institution	$4,880 00
15. Estimated cash value of buildings owned by the institution and ‡lot on which they stand	98,000 00
16. Amount of endowments and funds except real estate	67,523 13
17. Amount of income for the current year from all soures except tuition	8,288 58
18. Amount received for tuition during the current year	1,559 64
19. Rates of tuition in collegiate department per annum, not including board	21 00
20. Rates of tuition in preparatory department per annum, not including board	15 00
21. Amount paid on account of expenses of the institution, exclusive of building and repairs, during the year ending August 31, 1873	10,292 70

GEO. M. STEELE,
President of the Board of Trustees.
By H. A. JONES.

* The duties of this chair are at present performed by Prof. Yocum.
† Present one term in the year.
‡ Lot estimated at $50,000.

MILTON COLLEGE.

Annual Report of the President of the Board of Trustees of Milton College, for the year ending August 31, 1873.

1. Corporate name of the institution, Milton College.
2. Name of the place where the institution is located, Milton.
3. Year when the institution was founded as an academy, 1844; as a college, 1867.
4. Names of members of the faculty, with their respective salaries:

Names.	Departments of Instruction.	Salar's.
Rev. W. C. Whitford, A.M.	Natural, Mental and Moral Sciences	$1,000
Edward Searing, A. M.	Latin Language	800
Albert Whitford, A. M.	Mathematics	800
Jairus M. Stillman	Vocal and Instrumental Music	500
Miss Mary F. Bailey, L.A.	German and English Languages	350
Miss Jane C. Bond, L. A.	English Language and Mathematics	350
Miss R. Mintie Howard	Instrumental Music	300
Lucius Heritage	Tutor in Latin	180
E. D. Squires	Penmanship and Bookkeeping	180

	Male.	Female	Total.
5. Total number who have graduated	42	50	92
6. Number who graduated at last commencement	2	5	7
7. Number of students in the Senior Class, College	2	2	4
8. Number of students in the Junior Class, College	6	3	9
9. Number of students id the Sophomore Class, College.	16	10	26
10. Number of students in the Freshman Class, College.	25	14	39
11. Number of students not in the regular classes	40	30	70
12. Number of students in the Preparatory Department.	35	20	55

13. Number of acres of land owned by the institution	73
14. Estimated cash value of land owned by the institution	$3,700
15. Estimated cash value of buildings owned by the institution.	$30,500
16. Amount of endowments and funds except real estate	$4,225
17. Cabinets, apparatus, libraries and furniture	$4,900
18. Amount of income for the current year from all sources except tuition	$225
19. Amount received for tuition during the current year	$2,830 49
20. Rates of tuition in collegiate department per annnm, not including board	$27 to $33
21. Rates of tuition in preparatory department per annum, not including board	$24 to $27
22. Amount paid on account of expenses of the institution, exclusive of building and repairs, during the year ending August 31, 1873	$3,797 49

W. C. WHITFORD,
President of the Board of Trustees.

RACINE COLLEGE.

Annual Report of the Warden of Racine College, for the year ending August 31, 1873.

1. Corporate name of the institution, Racine College.
2. Name of the place where the institution is located, Racine.
3. Year when the institution was founded, 1852.
4. Names of members of the faculty, with their respective salaries:

Names.	Departments of Instruction.	Salary.
Rev. J. De Koven, D. D.	Warden	$2,500
Rev. E. B. Spalding, A.M.	Acting Prof. of Political Economy and History, Acting Dean of Scientific School, and Head Master	2,000
Rev. H. Wheeler, B. D.	Professor of Mathematics	1,800
Rev. A. Falk, Ph. D.	Professor of Greek	1,800
Rev. J. J. Elmendorf, D.D.	Professor of Belles Lettres and Moral Philosophy	1,800
Rev. R. G. Hinsdale, B. D.	Professor of Chemistry and Geology	1,800
Rev. I. H. Converse, A. M.	Professor of Latin	1,800
Rev. F. S. Luther, A. M.	Rector of the Grammar School	1,100
Geo. S. Meade, A. M.	Masters	1,100
Watson B. Hall, A. M.		1,200
Rev. A. Piper, A. M.		1,100
Sam'l L. Hudson, A. M.		800
Henry C. Dillon, A. B.		800
J. Holmes Converse		1,000
Edw'd C. Gould, A. M.		800

	Male.	Female
5. Total number who have graduated about	70	......
6. Number who graduated at last commencement	17	......
7. Number of students in the Senior Class	10	......
8. Number of students in the Junior Class	11	......
9. Number of students in the Sophomore Class	9	......
10. Number of students in the Freshman Class	18	......
11. Number of students in the Scientific School	14	......
12. Number of students in the Preparatory Department	139	......

13. Number of acres of land owned by the institution	90
14. Estimated cash value of land owned by the institution	$9,000 00
15. Estimated cash value of buildings owned by the institution	100,000 00
16. Amount of endowments and funds, except real estate	....
17. Amount of income for the current year, from all sources except tuition	....
18. Amount received for tuition during the current year	75,329 04
19. Rates of tuition in collegiate department, per annum, including board	427 00
20. Rates of tuition in preparatory department, per annum, including board	412 00
21. Amount paid on account of expenses of the institution, exclusive of building and repairs, during the year ending August 31, 1873	....

JAMES DE KOVEN,
Warden of Racine College.

RIPON COLLEGE.

Annual Report of the President of the Board of Trustees of Ripon College, for the year ending August 31, 1873.

1. Corporate name of institution, Ripon College.
2. Name of the place where the institution is located, Ripon, Wis.
3. Year when the institution was founded (as a college), 1863.
4. Names of members of the Faculty, with their respective salaries:

Names.	Departments of Instruction.	Salar's.
Rev. W.E.Merriman,A.M.	Mental and Moral Science	$1,200
Rev. E. H. Merrell, A. M.	Greek	1,000
Joseph M. Geery, A. M.	Rhetoric and English Literature	1,000
C. A. Kenaston, A. M	Mathematics and Astronomy	950
Rev. John H. Haire, A.M	Latin	850
Moses M. Barrett, A. M	Chemistry and Natural History	850
John C. Fillmore, A. M.	German and Music	.....
Mrs. C. T. Tracy	Botany and Mathemttics	480
Miss L. H. Adams, A. M.	Greek and Mathematics	480
Miss Kate Bushnell	Higher English Studies	500
Miss C. M. Nettleton	Music and Vocal Culture	700

	Male.	Female	Total.
5. Total number who have graduated	28	19	47
6. Number who graduated at last commencement	8	4	12
7. Number of students in the senior class	8	4	12
8. Number of students in the junior class	6	4	10
9. Number of students in the sophomore class	14	6	20
10. Number of students in the freshman class	6	3	9
11. Number of students not in regular classes 12. And in the preparatory department	......	......	334

13. Number of acres of land owned by the institution	440 00
14. Estimated value of land owned by the institution	$4,440 00
15. Estimated cash value of buildings owned by the institution	6,500 00
16. Amount of endowments and funds except real estate	45,900 00
15. Amount of income for the current year from all sources except tuition	8,700 00
18. Amount received for tuition during the current year, about	3,500 00
19. Rates of tuition in collegiate department per annum, not including board	24 00
20. Rates of tuition in preparatory department per annum, not including board	21 00
21. Amount paid on account of expenses of the institution, exclusive of building and repairs, during the year ending August 31, 1873	....

W. E. MERRIMAN,
President of the Board of Trustees.

REPORTS OF ACADEMIES AND SEMINARIES.

ALBION ACADEMY.

Annual Report of the President of the Board of Trustees of Albion Academy and Normal Institute for the year ending August 31, 1873.

1. Corporate name of the institution, Albion Academy and Normal Institute.
2. Name of the place where the institution is located, Albion, Dane Co., Wis
3. Year when the institution was founded, 1854.
4. Names of members of the faculty, with their respective salaries:

Names.	Departments of Instruction.	*Salaries.
Rev. A. R. Cornwall, A. M	Prof. Latin and Metaphysics	......
Prof. Jos. Beardsley, A M.	Prof. Greek and Higher Mathematics	......
Prof. Thure Kumlien, A.M	Curator Cabinet	......
Mrs. E. M. Dennison	Preceptress	......
Mrs. A. L. Cornwall, L. P.	German, French, Botany	......
Lemuel West	Teacher of Arithmetic	......
N. R. Doan	Physiology and History	......
G. S. Maxson	Teacher in English Branches	......
G. W. Latta	Penmanship	......
Augusta Head	Instrumental Music	......

	Male.	Female.	
5. Total number who have graduated	47	83	......
6. Number who graduated at last commencement	2	1	......
7. Number of students in the —— Class	......	......	......
8. Number of students in the —— Class	......	......	......
9. Number of students in the —— Class	......	......	......
10. Number of students in the —— Class	......	......	......
11. Number of students in the Regular Classes	......	......	181
12. Number of students in the Preparatory Department	......	......	......

*The salary of teachers is proportioned to the income, which is irregular—according to the number of students.

13. Number of acres of land owned by the institution............. 162
14. Estimated cash value of land owned by the institution...... ... $1,500
15. Estimated cash value of buildings owned by the institution..... 50,006
16. Amount of endowments and funds except real estate............ 5,000
17. Amount of income for the current year from all sources except tuition ....
18. Amount received for tuition during the current year..................
19. Rates of tuition in academical department per term, not including board.. $6 to $8
20. Rates of tuition in preparatory department per term, not including board ....
21. Amount paid on account of expenses of the institution, exclusive of building and repairs, during the year ending August 31, 1873..

C. R. HEAD,
President of the Board of Trustees.

GERMAN AND ENGLISH ACADEMY.

Annual Report of the President of the Board of Trustees of German and English Academy of Milwaukee, for the year ending August 31, 1873.

1. Corporate name of the institution, German and English Academy.
2. Name of the place where the institution is located, Broadway.
3. Year when the institution was founded, 1853.
4. Names of members of the faculty, with their respective salaries:

Names.	Departments of Instruction.	Salary.
P. Engelmann..........	Mathematics and Botany	$1,000
W. Shleif..............	Ancient and Modern Language	1,000
C. Choinsky	German	800
J. Brucker	German and English.....................	700
Ed. Vogel	Music..................................	800
Wm. Stapleton	Arithmetic and Geography	900
G. Brosius	Gymnast	180
Dr. T. Brendesse........	Chemist................................	120
Miss Chapman	English	700
Miss Clark	English branches	600
Miss Kupper	German and English.....................	600
Miss Baison............	German and French	600
Miss Brown............	English Branches.......................	600
Mrs. Baker.............	Drawing.	312
Mrs. Derflinger... ... / Mrs. Rohde..........	Industry...............................	120

		Male.	Female
5. Total number who graduated		......	2
6. Number who graduated at last commencement		......	4
7. Number of students in the —— class	Element't Higher, and Y'g Ladies Departments.	216	104
8. Number of students in the —— class			
9. Number of students in the —— class			
10. Number of students in the —— class			
11. Number of students not in the regular class.			
12. Number of students in Preparatory Departm't			

13. Number of acres of land owned by the instution	....
14. Estimated cash value of land owned by the institution.	....
15. Estimated cash value of buildings owned by the institution..	$42,000
16. Amount of endowment and funds except real estate	
17. Amount of income for the current year from all sources except tuition	4,000
18. Amount received for tuition during the current year	10,000
19. Rates of of tuition in academical department per annum, not including board	46
20. Rates of tuition in preparatory department per annum, not including board, respectivly.	28 and 34
21. Amount paid on account of expenses of the institution, exclusive of bnilding and repairs, during the year ending August 31, 1871	12,000

P. ENGELMANN & W. SCHLEIF,
Principals of German and English Academy.

ROCHESTER SEMINARY.

Annual Report of the President of the Board of Trustees of Rochester Seminary, for the Year ending August 31, 1873.

1. Corporate name of the institution, Rochester Seminary.
2. Name of the place where the institution is located, Rochester, Racine county, Wisconsin.
3. Year when the institution was founded, 1866.
4. Names of members of the faculty, with their respective salaries:

Names.	Departments of Instruction.	Salar's.
J. H. Gould, Principal..	Latin, Nat. Sciences and Normal Instruction	$1,000
Geo. F. Newell, M. D...	Lectures on Anat. Phys. and Hygiene......	gra't's
Mrs. Mary A. Gould	Preceptress and Teacher of Mathematics and Higher English	400
Mrs. Florence Jackson..	Instrumental and Vocal Music	.....
Ozro G. Augir..........	Geography	.....

	Male.	Female
5. Total number who have graduated........................	2	1
6. Number who graduated at last commencement................	.....	1
7. Number of students	55	32
8. Number of students in the —— Class......................	......	......
9. Number of students in the —— Class......................	......	......
10. Number of students in the —— Class......................	......	......
11. Number of students not in the Regular Classes.............	......	......
12. Number of students in the Preparatory Department........	......	......

13. Number of acres of land owned by the institution............	1½
14. Estimated cash value of land owned by the company........	$500
15. Estimated cash value of buildings owned by the institution...	6,000
16. Amount of endowments and funds, except real estate.........	None yet.
17. Amount of income for the current year from all sources, except tuition	$615
18. Amount received for tuition during the current year..........	1,000
19. Rates of tuition in academical department per annum, not including board..	$21 to $24
20. Rates of tuition in preparatory department per annum, not including board..	18
21. Amount paid on account of the expenses of the institution, exclusive of buildings and repairs, during the year ending August 31, 1873..	215

REV. O. D. AUGIR,
President of the Board of Trustees.

STATE CERTIFICATES.

The following studies and regulations have been prescribed, in accordance with the provisions of the law bearing upon the subject, for the procuring of these important certificates:

For a state certificate of five years, a successful examination in the studies now required for a first grade county certificate, with the addition of English literature and the *rudiments* of mental philosophy. The applicant must present satisfactory evidence of success in teaching for at least *three* terms, of three months each.

For a state certificate for life, of the *second grade*, a successful examination in orthoepy and orthography, arithmetic, penmanship, English grammar, reading, geography, United States history, elementary algebra, plane geometry (six books), natural philosophy, physiology, English literature, constitutions of United States and of state of Wisconsin, theory and practice of teaching and the *rudiments* of botany and mental philosophy.

For a state certificate for life, *first grade*, a successful examination in the studies requirrd for a second grade certificate, and in the *rudiments* of zoology, chemistry, geology and political economy.

Applicants for either grade of life certificates must present satisfactory evidence of successful teaching for at least *nine* terms, of three months each. All stationery needed will be furnished by the examiners.

Evidence must be furnished to the state superintendent, at Madison, of success in teaching, previous to the examination.

Applicants who fail in any of the studies required for either of the above certificates, limited or unlimited, may present themselves for examination in such studies within one year from previous examination. A re-examination in the studies in which they were successful will not be demanded.

The questions used at the examinations held during 1873 are given in order to indicate more definitely the scope of the examitions.

QUESTIONS.

ORTHOEPY AND ORTHOGRAPHY.

1. A list of words to be pronounced, in the writing of which the following conditions are to be observed:

(1.) List to be written.

(2.) Vowels in accented syllables to be marked according to Webster's Dictionary.

(3.) Words to be placed under the rules of spelling.

(4.) Derivative words to be separated into root, prefix and suffix.

(5. Parts of speech to be indicated.

(6.) Primitive words to be defined.

2. Define Word, Prefix, Suffix. Distinguish between derivative and compound words. Write correctly the following words, designating derivative and compound words. (List of words to be pronounced.)

3. Form, by prefix and suffix, as many words as possible from the following roots: tract, ducé or duct, tain, vert, plicate.

ANALYTICAL ARITHMETIC.

(First five, answers only; of the last five, write complete analysis.)

1. How is the value of a proper fraction affected by adding the same number to both its terms?

2. If $3\frac{3}{5}$ yards of cloth cost $\$5\frac{1}{2}$, whas will $6\frac{1}{4}$ yards cost.

3. How many square feet in a board 12.6 ft. long and 8 inches wide?

4. If to my age you add its half, its third, and 28 years, the sum will be three times my age? what is my age?

5. A makes a shoe in $\frac{2}{3}$ of a day; B makes one in $\frac{3}{5}$ of a day; how many shoes can both make in a day?

6. $\frac{2}{3}$ of the price for an article is equal to $\frac{3}{4}$ its cost; what is the gain per cent.?

7. A and B rented a pasture for $72; A puts in 40 sheep, and B 8 cows; if 4 sheep eat as much as one cow, how much ought each to pay?

8. If $\frac{2}{9}$ of A's money is equal to $\frac{4}{7}$ of B's, and both together have $340, how much has each?

9. What fraction is as much greater than $\frac{4}{5}$ as $\frac{5}{8}$ is less?

10. What number is that to which, if you add $\frac{4}{7}$ of $\frac{8}{11}$ of itself, $\frac{1}{3}$ of the sum will be 101?

ARITHMETIC.

(Analyze all Solutions.)

1. What is the difference between simple addition and compound addition? In what respect are the processes alike?

2. In what three ways may a fraction be divided by a fraction? Illustrate.

3. What is the difference between a divisor and a multiple of a number?

4. Required the quotients of 1169, divided by the two prime factors next larger than 1.

5. How many square feet in the four walls of a room 36 feet long, 30 feet wide, and 10½ feet high?

6. What is the difference between *the unit of a fraction* and *a fractional unit?*

7. In what time, at 12 per cent., will $240 amount to $720?

8. A merchant sold goods for $600, and gained 25 per cent.; he invested the proceeds in flour, on which he lost 20 per cent.; did he gain or lose by the transaction, and how much?

9. If 8 men cut 24 cords of wood in 12 days, working 7 hours a day, how many men will cut 150 cords in 10 days, working 5 hours a day?

10. If 4,096 men are formed into an oblong, with 4 times as many men in rank as in file, how many will there be in rank and file?

PENMANSHIP.

1. Define penmanship.
   What constitutes a system of Penmanship?
   What is a principle in Penmanship?

2. Write and name, in their order, the principles employed in the system which you understand, naming the system. Write four letters illustrating each.

3. What is meant by slant?
   Illustrate by a diagram, the manner in which it is obtained.

4. In forming letters, how are lines combined?
   Illustrate each by example.

5. What is the standard of measurement?
   What letter is the standard height?
   What letter is the standard width?

6. According to the standard of measurement, name the classes into which small letters are divided.
   Write the letter of the class in which *a* belongs.

7. Place, within parallel horizontal lines, the letters of the second class.

8. Write the capital letters *in order of their classification*, analyzing the first one in each class.

9. Analyze the following small letters, stating the height of each, and the class to which it belongs: *p*, *i*, "long *s*," *k*, *s*.

(1.) What is the height of capitals?

(2.) What exceptions to this rule?

(3.) Analyze the word "Examination."

10. At what time should the study of penmanship begin?

What is the benefit to be derived from black board exercises?

State the manner in which you would give a class the first three lessons.

ENGLISH GRAMMAR.

1. What classes of words are used as connectives? What peculiarities belong to each class?

2. Analyze: "Behold him proudly view some pompous pile, whose high dome swells to emulate the skies, and smile, and say, 'My name shall live with this, till Time shall be no more,' while at his feet the crumbling dust of the fallen fabric preaches the solemn lesson."

3. Correct the following: (a) He sent me the books, which he had promised. (b) He laid out to have had a fine garden.

4. Define two Grammatical figures; two Rhetorical figures.

5. Parse the italicised words: *I wish to know what is sought so* vigorously by those *petitioning?*

6. Write the poss. sing., and poss. plural, of the following words: valley; man; calf; Davis.

7. Write the plural of the following: son-in-law; mouthful; 2; pea; halo; fowl.

8. What are the rules for the use of *shall* and *will*?

9. Give synopsis of the verb *have*, in progressive form, second per., sing., solemn style.

10. How are the tenses in the Indicative formed?

GEOGRAPHY.

1. Describe one route through to Boston, with reference to (a) principal cities, (b) railroads, (c) general natural features, (d) special points of interest.

2. Which is generally the shorter passage, that from New York to Liverpool, or the return? Give reasons.

3. What countries of Europe are crossed by the parallel of Chicago?

4. Locate and describe (a) Mecca, (b) Mauritius, (c) Yukon, (d) Odessa.

5. What gives mountain chains their direction with reference to oceans and continents?

6. Name the chains comprising the great mountain system, which extends from the Bay of Biscay to the China Sea.

7. What physical conditions make Sahara a desert?

8. Trace the Isotherm of Sparta (45°) across the continent, mentioning the causes of its deflections.

9. Describe the Japan current.

10. Draw an outline map of Wisconsin and locate (a) three railroad lines, (b) five principal cities, (c) three different mineral regions.

UNITED STATES HISTORY.

1. Give an account of the plan and object of Burgoyne's campaign and the causes which led to his defeat.

2. What are the leading facts respecting Shay's Rebellion?

3. Why is the name of John Paul Jones famous in history?

4. Specify the acquisitions of territory made by the United States since the first treaty with England.

5. Name, with dates, the successive Administrations from 1837 to 1861.

6. What war occurred during Polk's Administration? Name and describe three battles of that war.

7. When, where and by whom was Wisconsin first settled? When admitted into the Union?

8. Name the seceding States in the late Rebellion.

9. Give an account of that battle which you consider the decisive one, in the late Rebellion, with your reasons for so considering it.

10. Give the date of (a) the settlement of Pennsylvania, (b) the treaty of peace closing the war of 1812, (c) the battle of Gettysburg, (d) the surrender of Lee.

ALGEBRA.

1. Find the value of $\left(\frac{1}{m}+\frac{1}{n}\right)(a+b)-\left(\frac{a+b}{m}-\frac{a-b}{n}\right)$.

2. Expand $\left(\frac{2x}{3}+5a\right)^6$ by the binominal formula.

3. Given: $27(7-x)^2-43=77-(7-x)^2$, to find x.

4. Given: $yx=24$, and $x^3+y^3 : x^3-y^3 :: 35 : 19$, to find x and y.

5. There are three numbers in geometrical progression; their sum is 42, and the difference of the first and second subtracted from the difference of the second and third is 6. Required the numbers.

6. Show that x^2 multiplied by $x^3=x^5$; state the result in the form of a principle.

7. Divide $(a^5-b^2)\sqrt{a+b}$ by $(a+b)\sqrt[4]{a+b}$.

8. Define, (*a*) surd; (*b*) root; (*c*) logarithm.

9. What is the value of the finite quantity, *a*, divided by 0? Demonstrate it.

10. A man rode a certain distance at the rate of 12 miles an hour and walked back at the rate of 3½ miles per hour; the time occupied in going and returning was 2 hours. How far did he ride?

PLANE GEOMETRY.

1. Theorem.—If a regular hexagon be inscribed in a circle, any side will be equal to the radius of the circle.
2. Classify and define the different quadrilaterals.
3. Theorem.—The area of a square circumscribed about a circle is double the area of a square inscribed in the same circle.
4. Theorem.—Three straight lines which bisect the three angles of a triangle meet in the same point.
5. Problem.—To describe a circle through three given points.
6. Similar triangles are to each other as the squares of their homologous sides.
7. Define: (a) *equal* figures; (b) *equivalent* figures; (c) *similar* figures.
8. What is the sum of the angles of a hexagon?
   Of a decagon?
9. Theorem.—Parallelograms on equal bases, and between the same parallels, are equal in area.
10. Theorem.—The angle formed by a tangent and a chord is measured by one-half the intercepted arc.

NATURAL PHILOSOPHY.

1. Define specific gravity; how is it ascertained?
2. Explain the principle of the screw; give the ratio of power to weight.
3. What is a Voltaic battery? A Bunsen battery?
4. Upon what principle in Optics does the construction of the Spectroscope depend?
5. Show that heat will melt a solid. What is meant by the melting-point?
6. Give the law of universal gravitation. What is the law of weight?
7. Define acoustics; sound. How is sound produced?
8. Explain the laws of motion, in a liquid escaping from an orifice beneath its surface.
9. How is elevation ascertained by means of the pendulum? What is a compensation pendulum?
10. What is the theory of magnetism?

PHYSIOLOGY AND HYGIENE.

1. Mention five important distinctions between animals and plants.
   Define physiology.
2. Name the tissues of the human body.
3. How many bones are there in the body?
   Classify the bones.
   Name and number of those in each class.

4. Why do the joints suffer most in rheumatism?
   Why should seats in school be of such height as to permit the feet to rest on the floor?
   Why should the erect position in sitting and standing be strictly observed?
5. What are the muscles?
   Give their use.
   What joint in the system has the greatest range of movement, and why?
6. Why should recesses for small or feeble pupils be frequent?
   What effect have pure air and light on the muscles?
7. Name the circulatory organs.
   Give, in full, the anatomy of the heart.
8. What is the Medulla Oblongata?
   Name the membranes of the brain.
9. Where does the sense of touch reside?
   If one side of the brain is injured, why is the *opposite* side of the body affected?
10. Give the anatomy of the teeth.

ENGLISH LITERATURE.

1. What constitutes the literature of a country? With whom does the history of English literature begin?

2. What were the characteristics of the Elizabethan Age? Who was the chief poet of this age? Name prominent writers of philosophy and prose belonging to this period.

3. What was the origin of the Drama? When and where was Shakspeare born?

4. When did Milton live? Name his principal poetical works. Who was the author of "The Ode on St. Cecilia's Day?"

5. Classify the Plays of Shakspeare as regards their character. What benefits are to be derived from the study of his works?

6. What was the origin of journalism in England? Who is the founder of the English novel? Who wrote The Letters of Junius?

7. Mention the chief poetical works of Scott; also five of his prose works.

8. Name poetical works of each of the following authors: Byron, Moore, Campbell and Coleridge.

9. Compare the writings of Dickens and Thackeray.

10. Has England any prominent novelist at present? Name the chief historians, essayists and poets of England now living.

GOVERNMENT.

1. What is a constitution?
2. In what cases has the Supreme Court original jurisdiction?
3. What is an *ex post facto* law? What is a writ of *habeas corpus*?
4. Give the processes by which a bill may become a law.
5. What are the limits to the number of members in the Senate and Assembly of Wisconsin?
6. What is the usual method of making treaties?
7. From what constitutional resources are the educational resources of the State derived?
8. What is meant by "common law?" Has it any force in our State?
9. What rights are reserved to the States? or, in what matters is the State supreme?

How may a bill become a law in this State?

THEORY AND PRACTICE.

Write upon the following topics, giving your views as derived from your own experience or observation:

1. Assigning Lessons.
2. Conducting Recitations.
3. Order in the school-room.
4. Discipline.
5. Prizes.
6. Punishments.
7. Self-reporting System.
8. Examinations.
9. Exhibitions.
10. The Teacher's Profession.

BOTANY.

1. Discuss the four stages of plant life.
2. Name the Floral Envelopes.

   Name the Essential Organs of the Flower.

   What is the office of the Flower?
3. Define Pappus; Pollen; Ovule; Dehiscence.
4. What is the Fruit? Define Pericarp.

   Define the following forms of the Pericarp, and give one example of each: Achenium; Pome; Caryopsis; Nut.

   What terms are properly applied to the pericarps of the following plants: Bean, Grape; Maple; Peach?

5. Describe, by the proper term, the roots of the following plants: Beet, Turnip; Grasses, Dahlia, Solanum Tuberosum.

Define the following terms, and give familiar examples: Sucker; Stolon; Runner.

6. What is the Leaf? From what is it derived?

Name and define the parts of a complete leaf.

7. Define Venation. Name the three characteristic modes of Venation.

Define briefly the following forms of the leaf, and illustrate each by a drawing: Ovate, Lanceolate; Cordate; Linear.

8. What is the inflorescence of the following plants: Currant; Lilac; Clover; Onion; Oak?

Place in their respective orders, the Tomato, Indian Corn, Sun Flower, Plum, and Tulip.

9. Name five deciduous trees, and five flowering plants indigenous to the locality in which you live.

State the nature of the soil most favorable to the growth of such trees as you mention.

10. What is your method of teaching Botany?

MENTAL PHILOSOPHY.

1. Define Consciousness, Attention, Conception.
2. What conditions are involved in an act of Memory?
3. How do you distinguish Classification from Generalization?
4. Name the more prominent Benevolent affections.
5. Use and abuse of Imagination.
6. Why have children little idea of time?
7. What do you mean by Intuition?
8. Distinguish between *taste* and *good taste*.
9. Define Resentment, Revenge.
10. What is implied in an act of choice?

ZOÖLOGY.

1. Divide the Class Mammalia into Orders. Give the characteristics of each order.

2. What are the peculiarities of respiration in Birds? In what respect do the lungs of birds differ from the same organs in Mammals?

3. Describe Vultures. Give their character. Their use. Name a famous bird of this tribe found in South America. Also, one common in the Southern States.

4. Assign to its particular Order each of the following birds: Woodpecker, Partridge, Thrush, Stork, Penguin.

5. Which of the other Classes of animals do Reptiles most closely resemble in their general form? From what circumstance do they derive their name?

6. Mention an animal belonging to each of the four great natural divisions of Reptiles.

7. What is meant by the metamorphosis of an Insect? Illustrate by examples.

8. Give the anatomy of the Grasshopper.

9. How are Crustaceans characterized?
Mention three animals of this class.

10. What is essential to the successful study of Zoology?

CHEMISTRY.

1. By what means may the spontaneous changes of animal and vegetable matter be arrested? Illustrate.

2. What is hard water? How are stalactites formed?

3. Give the explanation of the formation of ether, sometimes called sulphuric ether. Its properties and uses.

4. What are the names and symbols of the lead oxides?

5. What is carbolic acid? What are its uses?

6. How is cast iron made? How converted into wrought iron?

7. How was the soda-ash of commerce formerly made? Give the history of the modern method.

8. What is a deodorizer? a disenfectant? an antiseptic?

9. In what crops is sulphuric acid an important constituent? How may it be applied?

10. Describe methods of making vinegar.

GEOLOGY.

1. Define the term Rock.
Name the principal stratified rocks.
Name the principal unstratified rocks.

2. Define the terms, laminæ, strata, joint, fault, dip.

3. What is a Fossil?
Name, in order, the Fossiliferous Rocks, beginning with the oldest.
What is the oldest record of animal life?

4. What was the Age of Fishes? of Reptiles?
What place is most noted for fossil footprints?

5. Where are the most extensive coal-fields in the world?
Name the coal-fields of the United States.
Distinguish between anthracite and bituminous coal.

6. What is a Glacier? Name and define the three forms of Moraines.
What large river of Asia has its origin in a glacier?

7. Distinguish between Drift and Modified Drift. Give proofs that the action of Drift has been from the North.
8. State the difference between Granite and Gneiss.
9. To what systems do the rocks of Wisconsin belong?
   Locate the mineral wealth of the state.
   Mention the rocks in the section where you live.
   What fossils have been found in the state, of special interest, and where?
10. What portions of the state are free from Drift?
   Why is no coal found in Wisconsin?
   Where is the limestone region of Wisconsin?

POLITICAL ECONOMY.

1. What is the difference between price and value?
2. What determines the rate of wages?
   Why are the wages of women lower than those of men?
3. On what does the value of money depend?
4. Arguments for and against direct taxation.
5. Why are both profits and wages high in a new country?
6. What do you say of credit as a substitute for money?
7. What do you understand by unproductive labor? Illustrate.
8. What effect has the extension of machinery upon laborers?
9. Is competition pernicious?
10. Would the good of society be promoted by the social independence of women?

UNIVERSITY OF WISCONSIN.

In the absence of an official report, various items of importance are taken from the last annual catalogue.

RE-ORGANIZATION.

Chapter 144—General Laws of 1866.

SECTION 1. The object of the University of Wisconsin shall be to provide the means of acquiring a thorough knowledge of the various branches of learning connected with scientific, industrial and professional pursuits; and to this end it shall consist of the following colleges, to-wit: 1st. The College Arts; 2d. The College of Letters; 3d. Such professional and other colleges as from time to time may be added thereto or connected therewith.

SECTION 2. The College of Arts shall embrace courses of instruction in the mathematical, physical and natural sciences, with their application to the industrial arts, such as agriculture, mechanics and engineering, mining and metallurgy, manufactures, architecture and commerce; in such branches included in the College of Letters as shall be necessary to a proper fitness of the pupils in the scientific and practical courses for their chosen pursuits; and in military tactics; and as soon as the income of the University will allow, in such order as the wants of the public shall seem to require, the said courses in the sciences and their application to the practical arts, shall be expanded into distinct colleges of the University, each with its own faculty and appropriate title.

SECTION 3. The College of Letters shall be co-existent with the College of Arts, and shall embrace a liberal course of instruction in languages, literature and philosophy, together with such courses or parts of courses in the College of Arts as the authorities of the University shall prescribe.

Amendment of 1867.

SECTION 4. The University shall be open to female as well as male students, under such regulations and restrictions as the Board of Regents may deem proper; and all able-bodied male students of the University, in whatever college, shall receive instruction and discipline in military tactics, the requisite arms for which shall be furnished by the State.

BOARD OF REGENTS.

STATE SUPERINTENDENT OF PUBLIC INSTRUCTION,
Ex-officio Regent.

Term expires first Monday in February, 1874.

6th Congressional District....	AUG. L. SMITH.......	Appleton.
6th ....do...........	JACOB S. BUGH......	Wautoma.
1st ....do...........	B. R. HINKLEY......	Oconomowoc.
3d ....do...........	H. H. GRAY..........	Darlington.

Term expires first Monday in February, 1875.

7th Congressional District....	ANGUS CAMERON...	La Crosse.
5th .... do...........	C. S. HAMILTON.....	Fond du Lac.
2d ....do...........	J. C. GREGORY	Madison.

Term expires first Monday in February, 1876.

State-at-Large................	N. B. VAN SLYKE...	Madison.
8th Congressional District....	H. D. BARRON	St. Croix Falls.
4th ....do...........	J. R. BRIGHAM	Milwaukee.

OFFICERS.

C. S. HAMILTON,
PRESIDENT.

JOHN S. DEAN,
SECRETARY.

STATE TREASURER,
EX-OFFICIO TREASURER.

EXECUTIVE COMMITTEE,
N. B. VAN SLYKE, J. C. GREGORY, B. R. HINKLEY.

FARM COMMITTEE,
B. R. HINKLEY, H. H. GRAY.

FARM SUPERINTENDENT,
JOHN PERRY.

The faculty and instructors are given in the report of the president, on page 189.

SUMMARY OF STUDENTS.

Attendance for the year 1872–3, and the Fall Term of 1873–4, inclusive:

POST GRADUATES, 1872–3	2	....
		2
Graduating Classes of 1873.		
COLLEGE OF ARTS	14	....
Department of Civil Engineering	3	....
COLLEGE OF LETTERS	5	....
Law Department	26	....
		48
COLLEGE OF ARTS—		
Department of General Science—		
Senior Class	17	....
Junior Class	13	....
Sophomore Class	39	....
Freshman Class	61	....
		130
Department of Civil Engineering—		
Senior Class	2	....
Junior Class	6	....
		8
COLLEGE OF LETTERS—		
Course in Ancient Classics—		
Senior Class	6	....
Junior Class	15	....
Sophomore Class	10	....
Freshman Class	9	....
		40
Course in Modern Classics—		
Freshman Class	6	....
		6
Students in college studies—not regularly classified		40
Sub-Freshman Class		47
Preparatory Students		114
FEMALE COLLEGE—		
Senior Class	14	....
Junior Class	12	....
Sophomore Class	20	....
Freshman Class	23	....
		69
Students in college studies—not regularly classified		67
Preparatory Students		55
Law Department		23
College and Law Students		425
Sub-Freshman Class		47
Preparatory Students		169
Total		641

Attendance, Fall Term, 1873–74.

College of Arts—		
Department of General Science—		
Senior Class	17	....
Junior Class	12	....
Sophomore Class	33	....
Freshman Class	58	....
		120
Department of Civil Engineering—		
Senior Class	2	....
Junior Class	3	....
		5
College of Letters—		
Course in Ancient Classics—		
Senior Class	6	....
Junior Class	14	....
Sophomore Class	9	....
Freshman Class	9	....
		38
Course in Modern Classics—		
Freshman Class	6	....
		6
In College Studies—not regularly classified		25
Sub-Freshman Class		26
Preparatory Students		42
Female College—		
Resident Graduate		1
Senior Class	14	....
Junior Class	9	....
Sophomore Class	17	....
Freshman Class	19	....
		59
In College Studies—not regularly classified		33
Preparatory Students		30
Law Department		23
College and Law Students		310
Sub-Freshman Class		26
Preparatory Students		72
Total		408

THE COLLEGES.

I. COLLEGE OF ARTS.

The College of Arts is organized under the following section of the General Laws of 1866, Ch. CXIV:

Section 2. The College of Arts shall embrace courses of instruction in the mathematical, physical and natural sciences, with their application to the industrial arts, such as agriculture, mechanics and engineering, mining and metallurgy, manufactures, architecture and commerce, in such branches included in the College of Letters as shall be necessary to a proper fitness of the pupils in the scientific and practical courses for their chosen pursuits and in military tactics; and as soon as the income of the University will allow, in such order as the wants of the public shall seem to require, the said courses in the sciences and their application to the practical arts, shall be expanded into distinct colleges of the University, each with its own faculty and appropriate title.

The plain object of this section is to provide, not only for a general scientific education, but also for such a range of studies in the *applications of science* as to meet the wants of those who desire to fit themselves for agricultural, mechanical, commercial, or strictly scientific pursuits. The courses of study are such as to provide a sound education in the elements of science, and at the same time to give great freedom in the selection of studies according to the choice of the individual student. As higher demands are made they will be met by adding to the list of elective studies, and by the enlargement of the Faculty of Arts so as to form distinct colleges, as provided for in the act of re-organization.

This College embraces the Departments of General Science, Agriculture, Civil Engineering, Mining and Metallurgy, and Military Science.

DEPARTMENT OF GENERAL SCIENCE.

FRESHMAN YEAR.

First Term.

Mathematics—Higher Algebra. Loomis.
English—Mulligan's Structure of the English Language.
French—Otto's Conversation Grammar, or
German—Comfort's German Course.
Optional—Scandinavian.

Second Term.

Mathematics—Solid Geometry. Loomis.
English—Carpenter's English of the XIV Century.
French—Otto's Grammar and Reader, or
German—Comfort's German Course.
Optional—Scandinavian.

Third Term.

Mathematics—Plane and Spherical Trigonometry.
Botany—Gray's Manual.
French—Otto's Grammar and Reader, or
German—Comfort's Grammar and Whitney's Reader.
Themes and Declamations throughout the course; also, French and German Composition.

SOPHOMORE YEAR.

First Term.

Surveying, Navigation.
Conic Sections and Analytical Geometry—Loomis.
Crystallography.
English Literature—Shaw's Complete Manual.
French—Select Prose and Poetry; or
German—Whitney's Grammar and Reader.

Second Term.

Zoology—Nicholson.
Analytical Geometry—Loomis.
French—Select Prose and Poetry; or
German—Whitney's Grammar and Reader.

Third Term.

Calculus—Loomis.
Zoology—completed.
French—Racine—Oeuvres choisies; or
German—Schiller's William Tell.
Lectures—History.

JUNIOR YEAR.

First Term.

Mechanics—Snell and Lectures.
Chemistry—Elliot and Storer, Lectures.
Rhetoric—Bain and Lectures.

Second Term.

General Physics—Snell and Lectures.
Chemistry—Fownes and Lectures.
History—Hallam's Middle Ages.

Third Term.

Astronomy—White.
Mineralogy.
Analytical Chemistry.

SENIOR YEAR.

First Term.

Mental Philosophy—Porter and Lectures.
Political Economy—Walker and Lectures.
Logic—Inductive, Fowler.
Æsthetics—Bascom and Lectures.
Lectures—Science of Language.
Optional—Metallurgy, Assaying.

Second Term.

Moral Philosophy—Hopkins.
Logic—Deductive, Jevons and Lectures.
Geology—Dana and Lectures.
Lectures—International Law.

Third Term.

Natural Theology.
Constitutional Law—Story and Lectures.
Paleontology.
Lectures—History of Civilization.
Optional—Economic Geology.

DEPARTMENT OF AGRICULTURE.

It is the design of the University to give in this Department a thorough course of scientific instruction, in which the leading studies shall be those that relate to agriculture. The instruction in this course will be thorough and extensive, and will be given with constant reference to its practical applications, and the wants of the farmer.

The University farm is used to aid this department in conducting experiments in Agriculture and Horticulture.

Students can enter this, as all other departments of the University, at any time upon examination, can pursue such studies as they choose, and receive a certificate of attendance.

The analytical laboratories are connected with this department.

FRESHMAN YEAR.

Same as the course in the Department of General Science.

SOPHOMORE YEAR.

In addition to the studies of the course in the Department of General Science, candidates for this course will take drawing two hours a week.

Agriculture.—General farm economy; employment of capital, etc. Mixed husbandry. Special farming—by sections.

Drawing.—Mapping farm.

Chemistry.—Fownes and Lectures.

Rhetoric.—Bain and Lectures.

Second Term.

Agriculture.—Natural History; breeding and care of farm animals; characteristics of different breeds. Beneficial and injurious insects.

Materials used in Building.

General Physics.—The application of the laws of light and heat to vegetable growth.

Chemistry.—Fownes and Lectures.

Third Term.

Agricultural Botany.—Botanical characteristics and geographical distribution of the natural orders, with their relative importance. The genera and species having agricultural value; those having commercial or medical value; those having ornamental value, and those which are noxious or detrimental—as weeds or poisonous plants.

Horticulture.—Hot beds, their construction and use. Methods of propagation of plants by layers, by cuttings, by budding or grafting, etc. Transplanting. Varieties of small fruits and the best means of cultivating them. General management of orchards and nurseries. Landscape Gardening. Forestry.

Veterinary Science.

Analytical Chemistry.

Astronomy.—White.

Architecture.—Drafting Farm Buildings.

SENIOR YEAR.

First Term.

Analytical Chemistry—Quantitative.

Mental Philosophy—Porter and Lectures.

Political Economy—Walker and Lectures.

History of Agriculture.

Second Term.

Agricultural Chemistry—Soils, etc.
Geology—Dana and Lectures.
Logic—Deductive, Jevons and Lectures.
International Law—Lectures.

Third Term.

Agricultural Chemistry—Food, etc.
Road Building.
Draining and Draining Engineering.
Economic Geology.

Two original papers, each on the relation of some branch of science to agriculture, will be required during the senior year.

DEPARTMENT OF CIVIL ENGINEERING.

The object of this department is to give students such instruction in the theory and practice of engineering as to fit them, after a moderate amount of practice in the field, to fill with credit the most responsible positions in the profession of the civil engineer.

During the vacation at the close of the Junior year, students are required to prepare a memoir on some selected subject; that for 1874 is: "Water supply for the city of Madison, Wisconsin."

The following is given as a specimen of the projects required for the degree of civil engineer: "Project for the location and building of a railroad." The road to begin at the East Madison depot, in the city of Madison, and run to the depot in the town of Oregon, distance, 10 miles. No gradient greater than $\frac{1}{250}$, and no radius of curvature less than 600 feet. Double track with a guage of 3 feet. Distance between tracks 5 feet, and 5 feet between outside rail of track and the sides of the excavation or embankment. Slopes of embankments 2 to 1, and cuttings 1½ to 1. Ballast of broken stone. Proper provision made for the passage of public and private roads and water courses.

Full specifications and estimates for each class of work.

Suitable profile and cross-section drawings of the road.

The memoir, by reference to the specifications, estimates and drawings will give a complete history of the work from its beginning to its completion.

Valuable instruments and models have been added during the past year.

The requirements for commencing the course are the same as those for entering the Junior class of the department of general science.

JUNIOR YEAR.

First Term.

Descriptive Geometry—Church.
Rhetoric—Bain and Lectures.
Analytical Mechanics—Snell and Lectures.
Chemistry—Lectures.
Drawing—Topographical.

Second Term.

Mechanics of Engineering—Rankine.
General Physics—Snell and Lectures.
Building Materials—Lectures.
Chemistry—Lectures.
Drawing—Geometrical.

Third Term.

Mechanics of Engineering—Rankine.
Mineralogy—Determinative.
Astronomy—White.
Analytical Chemistry—Qualitative.
Drawing—Machines.

Vacation Work.

Memoir on some selected subject.

SENIOR YEAR.

First Term.

Prime Movers—Rankine and Lectures.
Mental Philosophy—Porter and Lectures.
Geodesy—Rankine.
Metallurgy—Lectures.
Drawing—Steam Engine and other Prime Movers.

Second Term.

Structures—Rankine.
Logic—Jevons.
Bridges—Haupt and Lectures.
Geology—Lectures.
Drawing—Bridges.

Third Term.

Water Engineering—Bresse and Lectures.
Economic Geology—Lectures.
Constitutional Law—Story and Lectures.
Railroad Engineering—Henck and Field Practice.
Drawing—Maps of Hydrographical Surveys and Plans. Profiles and Sections of railroad surveys.

Practical exercises with the use of the instruments and the preparation projects of machines and structures continue through the entire course.

These are required for graduation.

DEPARTMENT OF MINING AND METALLURGY.

This department was established by the Regents at their annnal meeting in June, 1871.

The object of this department is to furnish instruction in those branches of science, a thorough knowledge of which is essential to the intelligent worker, either in Mining or Metallurgy.

To render the instruction as practicable as possible, visits will be made by the students with the professor in charge to various Mining and Metallurgical works, and during the long vacation the students will be required to prepare a memoir on some selected subject.

Laboratories completely equipped are provided for practical instruction in Analytical Chemistry, Assaying, Determinative Mineralogy, etc. Collections of Minerals, Ores, Rocks, Fossils, etc., are available to the student, and will be added to from time to time. In some particulars, and especially in the Large Assay Laboratory, just fitted up, this department of the University has advantages not possessed by any other western institution.

Students will be allowed to take any part of the course for which they are fitted.

The requirements for beginning the studies of this department are the same as for the Civil Engineering course.

JUNIOR YEAR.

First Term.

Descriptive Geometry—Church.
General Chemistry—Lectures.
Crystallography—Lectures.

Drawing—Topographical and Geometrical.
Analytical Mechanics—Snell and Lectures.
Rhetoric—Bain and Lectures.

Second Term.

Metallurgy—Lectures.
Mechanics of Engineering—Rankine.
Analytical Chemistry—Lectures and Laboratory Practice.
General Chemistry—Lectures.
Drawing—Shades and Shadows and Perspective.

Third Term.

Mineralogy—Lectures and Laboratory Practice.
Analytical Chemistry—Laboratory Practice.
Metallurgy—Lectures.
Mechanics of Engineering—Rankine.
Drawing—Furnaces, Machines, etc.

Vacation Work.

Memoir on some selected subject.

SENIOR YEAR.

First Term.

Mineralogy—Determinative.
Assaying—Laboratory Practice.
Quantitative Analysis—Laboratory Practice.
Prime Movers—Rankine.
Mental Philosophy—Porter and Lectures.
Drawing—Furnaces, etc.

Second Term.

Geology—Lectures.
Mining Engineering—Lottner and Lectures.
Quantitative Analysis—Laboratory Practice.
Drawing—continued.

Third Term.

Geology—Lectures.
Mining Engineering—Continued.
Economic Geology—Lectures.
Railroad Engineering—Henck and Field Practice.
Dawing—Continued.

DEPARTMENT OF MILITARY SCIENCE.

The object of this department is to fit its graduates to perform the duties of subaltern officers in the Regular Army.

The following are the text books used in this department, viz:

Smith's Topography.
Mahan's Military Engineering.
Mahan's Advanced Guards, Outposts, etc.
Benet's Military Law and Practice of Courts Martial.
Benton's Ordnance and Gunnery.
Upton's Infantry Tactics.
United States Tactics for Field and Garrison, Artillery and Cavalry.
United States Manual of Signals.
United States Army Regulations.

The Board of Regents at its Annual Sessions will forward to the Governor of the State, the names of five students who have gone through the above course, standing first on the list according to merit in their studies and military deportment, who shall be recommended to the War Department as proper persons to receive the appointment of Second Lieutenants in the Regular Army.

All graduates of this course receive a suitable diploma.

Military drill is required of all able-bodied male members of the Sophomore and Freshman Classes, who must provide themselves with the prescribed uniform. This uniform is cheap, neat and suitable for ordinary wear. It is expected that many students not connected with these classes will join the Battalion. This is earnestly recommended as furnishing a most healthful exercise.

Those joining the Battalion will be subject to all the Rules and Regulations; and cannot withdraw without special action of the Faculty.

II. COLLEGE OF LETTERS.

COURSE IN ANCIENT CLASSICS.

This course embraces the Ancient Classics, Mathematics, Natural Science and English Literature, and is intended to be fully equivalent to the regular course in the best classical colleges in the country.

While great care is taken by the authorities of the University to furnish young men with the means of obtaining a thorough preparation for the various departments of business, those studies which enable the student to secure the treasures of ancient wisdom and bring him into sympathy with the great thinkers of past ages will receive a requisite share of the time of instructors and students.

FRESHMAN YEAR.

First Term.

Mathematics—Higher Algebra. Loomis.
Latin—Livy and Latin Composition.
Greek—Homer's Iliad, Grammar and Composition.
Optional—Scandinavian.

Second Term.

Mathematics—Solid Geometry. Loomis.
Latin—Cicero de Officiis. Composition.
Greek—Herodotus. Grammar and Composition.
Optional—Scandinavian.

Third Term.

Mathematics—Plain and Spherical Trigonometry.
Botany—Gray's Manual.
Greek—Thucydides. Grammar and Composition.
Themes and Declamations throughout the course.

SOPHOMORE YEAR.

First Term.

Surveying and *Navigation.*
Conic Sections.—Loomis.
Crystallography.
English Literature.—Shaw's Complete Manual.
Latin.—Horace.
German.—Comfort's Second Course.

Second Term.

Zoology.—Nicholson.
Latin.—Horace.
German.—Comfort's Course.

Third Term.

Latin.—Tacitus.
Greek.—Æschylus, Prometheus, Goodwin's Moods and Tenses.
German.—Comfort's Course.
German Composition throughout the year.
History.—Lectures.

JUNIOR YEAR.

First Term.

Mechanics.—Snell and Lectures.
Chemistry.—Elliott and Storer, Lectures.
Rhetoric.—Bain and Lectures.
Greek.—Demosthenes on the Crown. Greek Syntax.
Optional.—Historical Geography.

Second Term.

General Physics.—Snell and Lectures.
History.—Hallam's Middle Ages.
Greek.—Plato, Apology and Crito.

Third Term.

Astronomy.—White.
Latin.—Quintilian or Juvenal.
Comparative Philology.—Whitney and Lectures.
Optional.—The Roman Constitution. Deutsche Literaturgeschichte.

SENIOR YEAR.

First Term.

Mental Philosophy—Porter and Lectures.
Political Economy—Walker and Lectures.
Logic, Inductive—Fowler.
Æsthetics—Bascom and Lectures.

Second Term

Moral Philosophy—Hopkins.
Logic, Deductive—Jevons and Lectures.
Geology—Dana and Lectures.
International Law—Lectures.

Third Term.

Natural Theology—Chadbourne.
Constitutional Law—Story.
Rhetoric—Day's Art of Discourse (Invention).
History of Civilization—Lectures.

COURSE IN MODERN CLASSICS.

In this course German and French take the place of Greek. The studies are so arranged as to give students a good knowledge of literature and such acquaintance with the language as will fit them to engage in the duties of instruction, or to prosecute, to advantage, professional studies.

FRESHMAN CLASS.

First Term.

Mathematics—Higher Algebra, Loomis.
Latin—Literary and Latin Composition.
German—Comfort's Course, or
French—Otto's Conversation Grammar.
Optional—Scandinavian.

Second Term.

Mathematics—Solid Geometry, Loomis.
Latin—Cicero de Officiis. Composition.
German—Comfort's Course, or
French—Otto's Grammar and Reader.
Optional—Scandinavian.

Third Term.

Mathematics—Plane and Spherical Trigonometry.
Botany—Gray's Manual.
German—Comfort's Grammar, Whitney's Reader, or
French—Otto's Grammar and Reader.

Themes and declamations throughout the course, also French and German Composition.

SOPHOMORE YEAR.

First Term.

Surveying, *Navigation.*
Conic Sections—Loomis.
Crystallography.
English Literature—Shaw's Complete Manual.
Latin—Horace.
German—Whitney's Grammar and Reader, or
French—Select Prose and Poetry.

Second Term.

Zoology—Nicholson.
German—Whitney's Grammar and Reader, or
French—Select Prose and Poetry.
Latin—Horace.

Third Term.

Latin—Tacitus.
Anglo-Saxon—March.
German—Schiller's William Tell, or
French—Racine.
History—Lectures.

JUNIOR YEAR.

First Term.

Mechanics—Snell and Lectures.
Chemistry—Elliot & Storer. Lectures.
Rhetoric—Bain and Lectures.
German—Lessing's Minna von Barnhelm, or
French—Moliere, Le Misanthrope,
Optional—La Litterature Francaise Classique.

Second Term.

Ge. eral Physi s—Snell and Lectures.
History—Hallam's Middle Ages.
German—Goethe's Faust, or
French—La Litterature Francaise Classique.

Third Term.

Astronomy—White.
Latin—Quintilian or Juvenal.
Comparative Philology—Whitney and Lectures.
Optional –The Roman Constitution, Deutsche Literaturgeschichte, or La Grammaire Historique de la Langue Francaise.

SENIOR YEAR.

First Term.

Mental Philosophy—Porter and Lectures.
Political Economy—Walker and Lectures.
Logic, Inductive—Fowler.
Æsthetics—Bascom and Lectures.

Second Term.

Moral Philosophy—Hopkins.
Logic, Deductive—Jevons and Lectures.
Geology—Dana and Lectures.
International Law—Lectures.

Third Term

Natural History—Chadbourne.
Constitutional Law—Story and Lectures.
Rhetoric—Day's Art of Discourse. Invention.
History of Civilization—Lectures.

III. FEMALE COLLEGE.

The course of study in this college is the same as that in the department of general science, college of arts, with the following substitutes allowed:

In place of surveying, navigation, agriculture, analytical Geometry, and the calculus, of the sophomore year; and in place of chemistry and analytical chemistry of the junior year, Latin or drawing may be substituted.

Ladies are permitted to pursue any course or elective study in the University, when preferred, and the same degree is conferred upon them as upon the gentlemen for the satisfactory completion of any course of study.

Students who do not desire to graduate may enter at any time, and take any study of the term which they are prepared to prosecute to advantage.

The ladies' hall, erected by the munificence of the state, is an elegant and commodious building. It contains a chapel, teachers' rooms, recitation rooms, study and lodging rooms for about eighty students, and ample accommodations for boarding.

Students' rooms are neatly carpeted and furnished with heavy furniture. Occupants will be expected to provide the toilet sets needed in their rooms; also, towels, napkins, sheets, pillow-cases, blankets and counterpanes, all of which should be plainly marked with the name of the owner.

Students occupying this building are under the immediate charge of the preceptress, who, with her associate teachers, gives constant attention to the manners and general conduct of the pupils.

Competent and successful teachers give instruction in instrumental and vocal music.

The department of boarding is under the direction of an experienced and efficient matron, whose excellent character, business tact, and kind attention to the young ladies evince peculiar fitness for her position. Ladies occupying rooms in the building are required to board with the matron.

It is the design of the regents and faculty of the University to furnish young ladies with the means of securing an education as thorough and finished as can be obtained at any other institution in the country. To accomplish this object all available resources will be employed.

SUB-FRESHMAN CLASS.

For the purpose of securing a thorough preparation for the course in Ancient Classics, College of Letters, the following course has been arranged in Latin and Greek;

First Year.

Latin—Leighton's Lessons, Allen and Greenough's Grammar and Selections, (Cæsar, Curtius, Nepos and Sallust. 184 pages).
Greek—Leighton's Lessons, Goodwin's Grammar and Reader (Xenophon.)
History—Thalheimer's Ancient History.

Second Year.

Latin—Cicero's Select Orations (8), Virgil's Æneid (6 books), Allen's Composition (35 lessons), Grammar.

Greek—Goodwin's Reader (Xenophon and Herodotus, 155 pages). Homer's Iliad (2 books), Arnold's Composition (33 exercises), Grammar.

PREPARATORY DEPARTMENT.

The studies of this department are arranged with special reference to the accommodation of students who desire a suitable preparation, in English, to enter the College of Arts, the Female College, or the Sub-Freshman Class of the College of Letters.

Those who enter this Department are subject to the same rules as college students.

First Term.

History of England—Anderson.
Sentential Analysis—Greene.
Elementary Algebra.

Second Term.

Physical Geography.
Natural Philosophy.
Elementary Algebra—continued.

Third Term

Physiology.
Higher Algebra—Loomis.
Plane Geometry—Loomis.

POST-GRADUATE COURSE.

Bachelors of Art, Science and Philosophy will be admitted to the University as candidates for an appropriate degree. They must devote two years to study under the direction of the President and Faculty, and pass a satisfactory examination before the Board of Examiners appointed by the Regents.

The studies are optional; but they must be selected from at least two sections, and the studies in some one section must be continued during the whole course.

The object of this course is to secure a higher grade of scholarship in Literature and Science than it seems possible to attain in the present state of our colleges, under the ordinary class-system.

COURSE OF INSTRUCTION.

SECTION I. *Philosophy and History.*

History of Philosophy.
History and Archæology.
International Law and Jurisprudence.
Critical Study of English Literature.

II. *Philology.*

Sanskrit—Anglo-Saxon.
Ancient and Modern Classic Languages.
Comparative Grammar.
Science of Language.

III. *Mathematics and Physics.*

Calculus of Variations.
Analytical Mechanics.
Dynamical Theory of Heat, Light, etc.
Practical Astronomy and Geodesy.

IV. *Natural History.*

Botany.
Zoology.
Comparative Anatomy.

V. *Natural Sciences.*

Mineralogy.
Geology.
Chemical Philosophy and Analysis.

VI. *Applied Sciences.*

Mining Engineering.
Civil Engineering.
Mechanical Engineering.
Architecture.
Chemical Technology.
Metallurgy.
Economic Geology.

LECTURES.

In addition to the lectures given in connection with the recitations, some subjects are taught entirely by lectures, the students being required to take notes, and to recite upon the lectures as from a text-book.

The following are the regular courses of lectures:

To the Senior Class, on Mental and Moral Philosophy, by the President; on English Literature, Rhetoric and Logic, by Prof. Carpenter; on History, by Prof. Allen; on Political Economy, Civil Polity and International Law, by Prof. Parkinson; on Geology and Economic Geology, Mining Engineering, and on Metallurgy, by Prof. Irving.

To the Junior Class, on Chemistry, by Prof. Davies; on History, by Prof. Allen; on Mechanics, Physics and Astronomy, by Prof. Sterling; on Rhetoric and English Composition, by Prof. Carpenter; on Analytical and Applied Chemistry, by Prof. Daniells; on Metallurgy and Assaying, by Prof. Irving; and on Comparative Philology, by Prof. Feuling.

To the Sophomore Class, on Comparative Anatomy and Physiology, by Prof. Davies; on History, by Prof. Allen; on Agriculture, by Prof. Daniells.

To the Freshman Class, on the Laws of Health and Methods of Study, by the President; on Structural and Systematic Botany, by Prof. Davies.

In addition to these courses, other lectures are delivered on special subjects by members of the faculty and other scientific gentlemen.

DEPARTMENT OF LAW.

The Faculty in this department is given on page 189, and is also indicated in connection with the following:

COURSE OF INSTRUCTION.

First Term.

P. L. Spooner, Esq.,	Real Estate.
Judge Orton,	Personal Property.
J. H. Carpenter, Esq.,	Criminal Law.
Judge O. Cole,	Domestic Relations.
W. F. Vilas, Esq.,	Constitution and Jurisdiction of Courts.
	Common Law Pleadings.

Second Term.

P. L. Spooner, Esq., -	Real Estate.
Judge Orton, - - -	The Law Merchant, covering Negotiable Paper, Suretyship and Guaranty. Insurance. Fixtures.

Third Term.

J. H. Carpenter, Esq., -	Contracts.
Judge Lyon, - - -	Practice.
W. F. Vilas, Esq., -	Equity Pleading. Pleading under the Code.
P. L. Spooner, Esq., - -	Real Estate.
Judge Orton, - -	Partnership Sales.
J. H. Carpenter, Esq., -	Bailment and Agency.
Judge Dixon, - -	Equity Jurisprudence.
W. F. Vilas, Esq., - -	Law of Evidence.
S. U. Pinney, Esq., -	Corporations.

REMARKS.

The Law Department of the University of Wisconsin was organized and put into practical operation in the year 1868, and its success has been gratifying in the highest degree. The great advantage of professional schools for the rapid and thorough elementary training of professional men has been long since completely demonstrated, and no profession has more entirely accepted and heartily acknowledged the benefits of such schools than the legal profession.

The learning of this profession embraces almost all the relations of life, and as it is the result of the experience of many ages, is scattered through very numerous volumes of treatises, reports, statutes and digests. To obtain the mastery of the numerous topics embraced within the limits of the body of the law in such degree of perfection as marks the learned lawyer, requires many years of diligent study and practical experience.

This result is not to be attained by any mere student. What the beginner wants is to gain a comprehensive, general view and analysis of the whole system; then to learn, without the careful reading which would occupy a lifetime, what the books contain and where to search for more particular and detailed information; and to acquire the habits and modes of legal study and thought.

Superadd to this an acquaintance with the rules and principles of practice in the Courts, and the Student is prepared to begin the work of life.

This degree of attainment can be reached in the professional school in at least half the time that the student can otherwise acquire it, and with the additional advantage that there is no incumbrance of obsolete ideas or mistaken impressions, which are so difficult for any but a lawyer to distinguish from living doctrine among the great mass of legal writings.

To afford to the young men of Wisconsin and the northwest ready facilities for such acquirements, this department has been established.

THE METHOD OF INSTRUCTION

Is for the most part by lectures, and by reading under the direction of the professors, with moot court practice. The lecture system is peculiarly adapted to the study of law. Few text books are written for students. The most elementary works are designed as exhaustive treatises for the use of lawyers and embrace not only the history of the growth of the doctrines, but also a discussion of the subject in far more detail than the student can advisably pursue so early. The lectures give a clear analysis of the subject under discussion, not involved with that which is obsolete or too minute.

The practising lawyer, acting as instructor, can refer the student to just such parts of the text books and to such adjudications in the reports, as present in the best manner the principles which it is important to know. This system of reading cases in connection with text books is of the first importance.

The Moot Court will be held weekly; and here the students are taught to perform, as students, just what they will be required to do as lawyers. The preparation of pleadings and the argument of questions—all selected from actual cases occurring in practice and designed to illustrate the subjects discussed in the lectures—under the direction of the Dean of the Faculty, will afford to the student unsurpassed facilities for acquiring a practical familiarity with the modes of administering the law. To those who know the difficulty with which the young lawyer acquires the easy confidence necessary to successful practice, this part of the school will especially commend itself.

An additional means to the same end consists in the forming of Clubs by the Students themselves, for which the Instructors will afford every assistance, and the use of the lecture-room is granted.

A certificate of graduation from this Department will entitle the student to admission to practice, in all the courts of the State.

The peculiar advantages which the City of Madison, as the capital of the State, affords to the student of law, deserve mention.

All sessions of the Supreme Court are held here, and also one term of the United States Circuit and District Courts annually. The Circuit Court for the County of Dane holds three terms annually; so that there is almost constantly some court in session.

The Law Library of the State, which is probably the largest collection of the kind in the Northwest, is at all times accessible to the Students. The advantage of this library to the Student can hardly be overestimated. He can here become familiarized with series of reports and with many treatises which are rarely found in private libraries.

The Miscellaneous Library of the State Historical Society, numbering over 50,000 volumes, is also open to the Students of this school.

Admission.—Students will be admitted at any time; but those who are not Collegiate graduates must be 20 years of age to enter this Department.

Candidates will be examined in the ordinary English branches.

Credentials of good moral character must be furnished.

Every candidate for graduation is required to "prepare and read before the class and Faculty, within six weeks before the close of the collegiate year, a dissertation on some legal subject or on some subject connected with the history, science or practice of the Law which shall be approved by the Faculty."

LIBRARIES.

The University library contains about 5,000 volumes, and is open to the Students every day for taking out books, and two hours every afternoon for consultation. A few of the best American and Foreign periodicals are taken, and it is the intention to increase the number of these as largely as possible.

Students also have opportunity, free of expense, to consult the

State Historical and State libraries, the former numbering over fifty thousand volumes, the latter comprising a choice selection of miscellaneous works and a very complete law library. Each is furnished with commodious rooms kept comfortable at all hours of the day. These are library privileges unsurpassed in the west and equalled in very few institutions in the country.

The students, by a special arrangement, are enabled to take out books from the Circulating library of the Madison Institute, at a very low rate. This is a very well selected collection of about 3,500 volumes.

APPARATUS, CABINETS, ETC.

The University is provided with extensive and valuable geological and mineralogical cabinets and collections in natural history; also with well selected philosophical and chemical apparatus.

There are also chemical, mineralogical and assay laboratories well supplied with apparatus and chemicals, affording excellent facilities for the prosecution of studies in their respective departments of science.

The Regents have recently made liberal appropriations for apparatus in the several departments of natural science.

TERMS OF ADMISSION.

Candidates for admission to the University will be examined on Thursday and Friday preceding the Annual Commencement; also on the Tuesday and Wednesday of the first week of each term.

Preparatory Department.—Candidates for admission will be examined in the following studies: reading, spelling, penmanship, arithmetic, civil and descriptive geography, English grammar, and history of the United States.

Candidates must not be under twelve years of age.

Sub-Freshman Class of the College of Letters.—Candidates will be examined in the studies required for admission to the Preparatory Department, and in elementary algebra and plane geometry (Loomis, five books).

College of Arts and Female College.—Candidates for admission to the Freshman Classes of these colleges will be examined in all the studies required for admission to the Preparatory Department, and in elementary algebra, plane geometry (five books), history of England, physical geography, physiology and Green's English Grammar and Analysis. In 1875, candidates will also be examined in the elements of natural philosophy.

College of Letters.—*Course in Ancient Classics.*—Candidates for admission to this course will be examined in all the studies required for admission to the Sub-Freshman Class, and in the following:

Latin.—Allen & Greenough's Grammar, Allen's Composition (35 lessons), Allen's Selections (to p. 134), six books of Virgil's Æneid and eight orations of Cicero.

Greek.—Goodwin's Grammar, Arnold's Composition (33 exercises), Goodwin's Reader (155 pages) and two books of Homer.

History.—Thalheimer's Ancient History.

Equivalents for any of the above named studies will be accepted.

College of Letters.—*Course in Modern Classics.*—Candidates will be examined in the studies required for admission to the College of Arts, and in

Latin.—Allen & Greenough's Grammar, Allen's Composition (35 lessons), Allen's Selections (to p. 134), six books of Virgil's Æneid and eight of Cicero's Select Orations.

History.—Thalheimer's Ancient History.

Ladies are admitted to the Preparatory Classes on the same terms as gentlemen.

Candidates for advanced standing in any college must, in addition to the studies named above, pass examination in those previously pursued by the class which they propose to enter, or in those equivalent to them.

No one can be admitted to the Freshman Class under the age of fifteen years, nor to an advanced standing without a proportional increase of age.

Technical Courses.—The requirements for commencing the Engineering or any Technical Course are the same as those for entering the Junior class of the College of Arts.

Applicants for admission from other colleges must present certificates of honorable dismission.

The University is open to students from other states.

GRADUATES OF GRADED SCHOOLS.—The Law of March, 1872, provides that "all *graduates* of any *graded school* of the State who shall have passed an examination at such graded school satisfactory to the Faculty of the University for admission into the Sub-Freshman class and College classes of the University, shall be at once and at all times entitled to free tuition in all the colleges of the University."

For the examination, under this law, the following regulations have been adopted by the Faculty:

1. The examination shall be in writing.

2. In preparing a paper let the candidate (1) write on but one side; (2) leave one or more lines blank after each answer; (3) number answers to correspond with questions; (4) write with ink.

3. The number of questions submitted shall be, in Arithmetic, 20; English Grammar, 10; Civil and Descriptive Geography, 20; Physical Geography, 20; United States History, 10; History of England, 10; Sentential Analysis, 10; Elementary Algebra, 10; Plane Geometry, 10.

4. Orthography and Penmanship shall be determined and marked from the papers.

5. The Principal shall examine the papers and mark them on a scale of one hundred. Candidates must obtain at least 75 per cent. in each study, and an average of 85 per cent.

6. It shall be the duty of the Principal to forward to the President of the University the Questions, the Examination Papers of the candidate, and a certificate of the following form:

—— GRADED SCHOOL, —— County, Wis.
——, 187—.

This is to certify that —— ——, a graduate of this School, has prepared the accompanying papers under my supervision, and that to the best of my knowledge and belief, the examination has been fairly conducted.

Signed,

—— ——, *Principal.*

EXPENSES.

LAW DEPARTMENT.—Matriculation fee, $25.00. Tuition per term, $10.00.

To "one suitably qualified pupil from each Assembly district, to be nominated by the representative of such district, whenever a vacancy shall occur, who, other things being equal, shall prefer an orphan of a soldier who has died in defense of his country," and to all graduates of any graded school of the State, who are admitted to the University under the law of March, 1872, *tuition* is free.

Blank forms for nomination can be had on application to the Secretary of the Board of Regents, or the President.

Tuition for all, except Law and free students	$6 00
Room rent in North and South (gentlemen's) Halls	2 00
Heating University Halls, 1st and 2d terms	2 00
....do..........do...... 3d term	1 00
Room rent in Ladies' Hall, furnished	5 00
First and 3d terms, heating and lighting public rooms in Ladies' Hall.	2 00
Second term, heating and lighting public rooms in Ladies' Hall	4 00
First....do... .do.........do... students' rooms	5 00
Second..do.....do.........do..........do	8 00
Third...do.....do.........do..........do	4 00
Board in Ladies Hall, including washing of bedding, towels and napkins, per week	3 00
Personal washing, per dozen	60
Instrumental music, 20 lessons	10 00
Use of instrument per term	2 00
Vocal music, 20 lessons	10 00

The rooms in Ladies' Hall are in suits to accommodate four students, *if unnecessarily* occupied by a less number, the additional expense of fuel, light and room-rent will be charged to the occupants *pro rata.*

Students will be charged for not less than one term, and no deduction will be made for voluntary absence.

Students are allowed twelve and a half cents, per hour, for work on the University farm.

Payment of all University charges for tuition, room rent, heating, etc., is required strictly *in advance.*

NOTE,—$3.00 is charged for each Diploma.

GENERAL INFORMATION.

POLICY.

It is the aim of the University to meet the educational wants of of every student in the State. The courses of study as laid down are intended to be the mere outlines of work. In the optional studies and post-graduate course there is provision for all the demands of higher scholarship which are now made upon the Institution. And it is confidently expected that by the sale of lands and in other ways, provision will be made for the constant growth of the University as greater demands are made upon it.

It is advisable that students should pursue the prescribed courses if possible, adding to them as they are able, from the optional studies; but, by special vote of the Regents, the Faculty may excuse a student from any study in either course and substitute for it any other of equal educational value, such action of the Faculty being a matter of record.

The whole policy of the Institution is determined by the Regents, who, as a body, represent the people and no particular sect or party.

GOVERNMENT.

Students are held responsible only for good order and the diligent use for their time. Those who fail to conform to this simple requirement are at once dismissed. The University is no place for idlers, for disorderly persons or for those who do not propose to give their *whole time* to the work prescribed for them by the Faculty. The loss of a single recitation is not only injurious to the student, but those connected with him.

Leave of absence will not be granted except in cases of absolute necessity.

Each Faculty has special care of its own Collge or Department, but all the instructors teach wherever their services are required. Weekly reports are made by each Professor to the Faculty of the work in his own department and of all cases of delinquency.

The students and Faculty are assembled for prayers daily fifteen minutes before the morning hour for commencing recitations. At this time all public announcements are made and the President also gives directions and instruction to the students in regard to all their general duties as members or the University.

No student is required to attend any religious exercises of any kind, but all directions in regard to this matter, given by parents or guardians, will be cheerfully followed.

GROWTH AND PROSPECTS.

Since the re-organization of the University, in 1867, it has had constant prosperity. The Gymnasium and Ladies' Hall have been erected, Laboratories fitted up, and the Instructional force greatly increased. The requirements for admission have been increased, the courses of study improved and extended, and the Normal School developed into a Female College with a complete four years' course. A Law Department has been established, which has already gained a high reputation among the law schools of the country; and the University has been placed in immediate connection with the graded schools of the State. The prospects of continued growth are of a most cheering character.

EXAMINATIONS.

At the close of the first and second terms there is a public examination of all the classes of the University in the studies of the term.

During the week preceding the Commencement, the several classes are examined, in presence of a Board of Visitors, in the studies of the year.

Promotion from class to class is made to depend on these examinations.

DEGREES.

Students who complete the course in Ancient Classics, in the College of Letters, are entitled to the degree of Bachelor of Arts, and, after the expiration of three years from the time of graduation, upon application to the Faculty, accompanied with evidence of satisfactory proficiency are recommended to the Regents to receive the degree of Master of Arts.

Students who complete the course in the department of General Science, in the College of Arts, are entitled to the degree of Bachelor of Science, and after the expiration of three years from the time of graduation, on recommendation of the Faculty to the Regents, as in case of Master of Arts, receive the degree of Master of Science.

Students who complete the prescribed course of study in the Law Department, upon examination and recommendation of the Law Faculty, are entitled to the degree of Bachelor of Laws.

Students who complete the course in Agriculture, are entitled to the degree of Bachelor of Agriculture.

Students who complete the course in Civil Engineering, are entitled to the degree of Bachelor of Civil Engineering, and after the expiration of one year from the conferring of this degree, upon the presentation of a suitable Project, are entitled to the degree of Civil Engineer. Residence at the institution will not be required during this last year.

Students who complete the course in Mining and Metallurgy, will, under the same condition, be entitled to the degrees of Bachelor of Mining and Mining Engineer.

Students who complete the course in Mechanical Engineering, will, under the same condition, be entitled to the degrees of Bachelor of Engineering and Mechanical Engineer.

Graduates of the Female College, receive the same degree as graduates of the other colleges for the same course of study.

LITERARY SOCIETIES.

The Literary Societies—Athenæan, Hesperian and Castalian—are sustained with great interest, and furnish valuable aid in the intellectual training of the student. Each society has a library.

These societies admit to membership only students connected with the regular classes.

ROOMS.

Private rooms, under certain restrictions, can be secured by gentlemen on application to the locating officer at the opening of each term.

No student will be allowed to occupy a room until his bills for the term are settled.

Those in the regular classes are allowed the choice of rooms, and in the order of the classes.

Regular students, in previous occupancy, if on the ground at the opening of the term, are permitted to retain their rooms, unless needed for those in higher classes.

Rooms for gentlemen are furnished, except stoves, at the expense of the students, who should bring their own bedding, towels, etc. Other furniture can be obtained here second-hand, or new, at moderate prices.

Students will not be allowed to board themselves, except in the North Hall.

Occupants of rooms are held responsible for all damages to the same.

Students not accommodated in the University, and not residing with their parents in Madison, will lodge and board in town, under regulations as the Faculty may prescribe.

CALENDAR.

'73-'74.

Fall Term begins Wednesday, September 3, and closes Wednesday, December 17.

Winter Term begins Wednesday, January 7, and closes Wednesday, March 25.

Spring Term begins Wednesday, April 1, and closes Thursday, June 18.

Anniversaries of Literary Societies, Tuesday evening before Commencement.

Alumni Address, Wednesday evening before Commencement.

Commencement, Thursday, A. M., June 18.

'74-'75.

Fall Term begins Wednesday, September 2, and closes Wednesday, December 16.

Winter Term begins Wednesday, January 7, and closes Wednesday, March 24.

Spring Term begins Wednesday, March 31, and closes Thursday, June 17.

It is intended to print a Triennial Catalogue for 1875, and graduates will confer a favor by communicating to the President of the University, full information in respect to the titles they have received, the offices they have held and other matters of importance suitable for publication.

RFPORT

OF THE

President of the Board of Regents of Normal Schools.

Hon. Samuel Fallows,

Superintendent of Public Instruction:

Sir: In accordance with the requirements of law, I have the honor to submit herewith an annual report of the doings of the Board of Regents of Normal Schools, of receipts and expenditures, and of the prospect, progress and condition of the normal schools for the school year ending August 31, 1873.

MEETINGS.

Two meetings of the board have been held during the year, the semi-annual meeting in January and the annual meeting in July.

Besides the usual and necessary routine business, the following subjects were considered and acted upon:

CLAIMS AND BALANCES.

The old claim of M. M. Leahy, for balance due on heating apparatus at Whitewater, has been settled by mutual agreement and paid.

The town of Platteville has been notified of the nature and amount of claim for clearing up the title to the Platteville Academy site, and payment demanded.

The town, by a popular vote, last spring, refused to make provision for payment, but it is hoped that better counsels will prevail, and that the town will not forfeit its excellent reputation for generosity and public spirit, and compel the board to enforce the collection of a just and equitable demand.

A committee has been directed and empowered to settle all claims for tuition and book-rent at Platteville, which, it is hoped, may be accomplished as soon as the next meeting of the board.

The president having reported an unexpended appropriation for apparatus, it was ordered to be disbursed for expenses of committees, on audit of bills by executive committee.

INSURANCE.

The president was instructed to renew insurance on the buildings as it expires. Two Babcock fire extinguishers have been placed in the building at Platteville.

IMPROVEMENTS.

At Platteville an important addition to the building, giving better facilities for the natural science department, and additional cloak rooms, has been ordered, at a cost not to exceed twelve hundred dollars, and is now being completed under the immediate direction of Regent Evans.

The furnaces at Platteville have been ordered to be thoroughly repaired, or replaced with new ones, which will be necessarily done before winter.

The heating apparatus at Whitewater has been thoroughly overhauled, the boiler placed in a small structure outside the main building, and the pipes and fixtures so changed and remodeled, as to ensure, it is believed, ample heating capacity in all parts of the building.

One of the vacant attic rooms over the cabinet has been neatly fitted up, under the immediate supervision of Regent Weeks, for a text book library.

CABINETS.

Additions are being made from time to time, as opportunity offers, to the cabinets, so that the students may have specimens at hand, aiding them to make such acquaintance with nature, in her varied forms, as to become intelligent observers and competent instructors of the little ones, who are to be, either blighted by their ignorant neglect, or quickened by their intelligent guidance.

For the same purpose, it has been our study to furnish such needed

APPARATUS

and appliances, as will enable our professors to demonstrate such of the known laws of light, heat, electricity, motion, chemical action, etc., as shall awaken an interest in each student, and send them into the great field of public education as observers, thinkers and discoverers in the realm of practical science, and fit them in a measure to stimulate and direct the activities and energies of our Young America.

It has not been forgotten either, that in this research and march of progress, the gathered wisdom of the *past* and *present* is accumulated power to move, and keep moving, the wheels of progress; therefore, our

LIBRARIES

Are being carefully and continuously added to, so that our Faculties and students may keep abreast of recorded knowledge and fresh discoveries, and go forth fitted to advise all earnest seekers among our youth to such a course of reading, and such an appreciation of *good* books as may counteract, in some degree, the flood of trashy reading which threatens to deluge our land, and overwhelm our youth with its sickly, vapory emanations.

DIPLOMA.

A new form of diploma has been adopted, and the President instructed to procure its engravement with suitable device.

SALARIES.

By resolution of the board, and after consultation with the Secretary of State and State Treasurer, the monthly payment of teachers' salaries is now made by one warrant for each school, drawn and disbursed by the local regent, he taking each teacher's receipt therefor on a pay roll. This method will simplify and shorten the records necessarily made each month in the offices of the Secretar of the Board, Secretary of State and State Treasurer, on salary accounts.

COURSE OF STUDY.

The course of study has been somewhat modified to meet practical wants, and an elementary course of one year adopted, with a recommendation and request for such legislation as shall make the certificate of having completed such course equivalent to a state certificate of third grade, good for two years from the date thereof.

It is also in contemplation to establish—as soon as the number desiring it may warrant—a more extended course, in connection with, and as a supplement to, the present three years' course, that still higher professional culture may be attainable in our schools.

At the same time, the necessity is deeply felt, of making provision for the highest possible training of that large and vastly preponderating class of our common school teachers, who can, in the *hurried* march of our civilization, devote but little time—a term—a year, or two years to preparation for such teaching, as they only expect to be the transition phase towards some other avocation or life-work.

It would of course be desirable, that *all* our *public school teachers* should be *thoroughly* trained and fitted in the best methods for their work *as* teachers; but since this is impracticable and unattainable in our nation, it has been, and shall be our endeavor, while not neglecting the giving of opportunities for high professional culture and training, to such as desire, or can be induced to seek them—yet, to provide the best possible training to that numerous host of undisciplined and transient teachers, whose crude culture must, in the very nature of things, be the controlling and moulding influence in a large majority of our common schools.

For this purpose, we gladly welcome all who come to our normal classes, even if only for a term, hoping to hold them longer.

For this purpose also, special attention is given to our

INSTITUTES.

This branch of our work has been thoroughly revised and organized. An Institute course of two weeks, or more (as circumstances may require), under the advice and general direction of the committee on Institutes, has been established at each school.

The state has been districted into three institute districts, and a teacher from each school detailed in special charge of the work in each district.

These, with the aid of such occasional help as can be obtained from the best teachers in the state, are enabled to reach every teacher who will come to the institute. These institutes are so arranged and timed, as to reach and accommodate every section.

The whole work is under the general direction of the committee on Institutes, and the director designated by them, who is expected to unify and harmonize the work, and to whose report, submitted herewith, attention is invited for more particular statements of work and results in this very important auxiliary branch of our labor.

VISITATIONS AND EXAMINATIONS.

Important action has been had during the year, revising and extending such visitations of the schools by committees, and reports thereon, as shall bring the board in close sympathy with the schools and give a more perfect understanding of their routine work, their difficulties and the remedies, their successes and the uses.

Provision has been made for an examination of the progress of classes, and for a special examination of candidates for graduation, by a committee of the board. To still further provide for critical knowledge, from all standpoints, of the condition and progress of our schools, the board has required the president of each school to make annual report at the close of each school year, to the president of the board, to be considered and placed upon our files.

ABSTRACT OF PROCEEDINGS.

To keep fresh in recollection the whole work and transactions, the secretary has been required to make, print, and forward to each member, an abstract of the proceedings of each meeting, immediately after the adjournment thereof.

FOURTH NORMAL SCHOOL.

Considerable delay has been had in obtaining satisfactory chain of title to any site selected by the committee appointed for the purpose of selecting a site for the Fourth Normal School at River Falls, but at our last annual meeting, the site known as the "Brackett site" was selected, the abstract of title subjected to the scrutiny of the Attorney General of the State, and the transfer made to the board.

The executive committee will proceed, under instructions, to employ an architect to procure plans, and to submit them to the board for adoption; in time, it is hoped, to let the contract during the coming winter, for the erection of the building, and its completion in the summer of 1875.

MEMBERS, OFFICERS AND COMMITTEES.

The following is a list of the members, officers and standing committees of the board; the president having, by resolution, been placed at the head of the "executive committee," the committee on "employment of teachers" and the "committee on supplies:"

BOARD OF REGENTS.

His Exellency, Governor C. C. WASHBURN, *ex officio* ...... Madison.

Hon. SAMUEL FALLOWS, Supt. Public Inst., *ex officio*.... Madison.

Terms expire February 1, 1874.

W. H. CHANDLER.. Sun Prairie.
T. D. WEEKS.. Whitewater.
A. H. WELD... River Falls.

Terms expire February 1, 1875.

W. C. WHITFORD... Milton.
J. H. EVANS.. Platteville.
WM. STARR.. Ripon.

Terms expire February 1, 1876.

WM. E. SMITH... Milwaukee.
JAMES I. LYNDES.. La Crosse.
SAMUEL P. GARY... Oshkosh.

OFFICERS OF THE BOARD.

President	WM. STARR	Ripon.
Vice President	WM. E. SMITH	Milwaukee.
Secretary	SAMUEL FALLOWS	Madison.
Treasurer, ex officio	HENRY BÆTZ	Madison.

STANDING COMMITTEES.

Executive Committee—President, Chandler, Gary.
Finance Committee—Lyndes, Washburn, Whitford.
Employment of Teachers—President, Smith, Weld.
Committee on Institutes—Fallows, Chandler, Smith.
Comitttee on Supplies—President, Evans, Weeks, Gary.
Committee on Course of Study and Text Books—Weeks, Whitford, Weld.
Visitation of Normal Schools—Evans, Weeks, Gary.
Examination of Senior Classes—Chandler, Whitford, Weld.

TERMS OF ADMISSION.

The following rules governing admission of students are given for general information and reference:

REGULATIONS FOR ADMISSION,

Adopted by the Board of Regents.

1. Each Assembly District in the State shall be entitled to six representatives in the Normal School, and in case vacancies exist in the representatives to which any Assembly District is entitled, such vacancies may be filled by the President and Secretary of the Board of Regents.

2. Candidates for admission shall be nominated by the superintendent of the county, (or if the county superindendent has not jurisdiction, then the nomination shall be made by the city superintendent of the city), in which such candidate may reside, and shall be at least sixteen years of age, of sound bodily health, and good moral character. Each person so nominated, shall receive a certificate settieg forth his name, age, health and character, and a duplicate of such certificate shall be immediately sent by by mail, by the superintendent, to the secretary of the board.

3. Upon the presentation of such certificate to the president of a normal School, the candidate shall be examined, under the direction of said President, in branches required by law for a third grade certificate, except History and Theory and Practice of Teaching, and if found qualified to enter the Normal School in respect to learning, he may be admitted, after furnishing such evidence as the president may require, of good health and moral character, and after subscribing the following declaration:

I, ——— ———, do hereby declare that my purpose in entering this state normal school is to fit myself for the profession of teaching, and that it is my intention to engage in teaching in the public schools in this state.

4. No person shall be entitled to a diploma who has not been a member of the school in which such diploma is granted, at least one year, nor who is less than nineteen years of age; but a certificate of attendance may be granted by the president of a normal school to any person who shall have been a member of such school for one term, provided, that in his judgment such certificate is deserved.

CONDITION OF FUNDS.

The following synopsis of the condition of the Normal School Fund, the Income Fund and the Building Fund, at the close of the fiscal year ending September 30th, is compiled from the books of the state treasurer and secretary of state.

Normal School Fund.

This fund is composed of the proceeds of the sale of lands set apart for the support of normal schools, by chapter 537, Laws of 1865.

RECEIPTS.		
Sales	$68,947 95	....
Dues	6,109 00	....
Loans	11,551 00	....
Penalties	79 59	....
	$86,687 54	....
DISBURSEMENTS.		
Milwaukee water bonds, purchased	....	$40,000 00
Madison City Board of Education, loan	....	12,500 00
Refunded for overpayment	....	473 26
	$86,687 54	$52,973 26
Balance, September 30, 1872	7,069 86	....
Balance, September 30, 1873	....	41,884 14
	$94,357 40	$94,357 40

The amount of productive funds on the 30th day of September, 1772 and 1773, respectively, was as follows:

	1872.	1873.
Amount due on certificates of sales	$58,055 74	$55,731 43
Amount due on mortgages	146,716 05	147,312 05
Certificates of indebtedness	512,600 00	512,600 00
United States bonds	43,000 00	43,000 00
Milwaukee city water bonds	100,000 00	140,000 00
Town bonds	20,000 00	20,000 00
	$880,371 79	$918,643 48

Amount of productive fund Sept. 30, 1872	....	$880,371 79
Decreased by payments on certificates of sale	$6,109 00	....
Decreased by payments on loans	11,551 00	....
Decreased by forfeiture of mortages	358 00	....
		18,018 00
		$862,358 79
Increased by new certificates of sale	$3,784 69	....
Increased by new loans	12,500 00	....
Increased by Milwaukee city bonds	40,000 00	....
		56,284 69
Total productive fund Sept. 30, 1873	....	$918,643 48

Showing an increase in this fund during the year, of $38,271.69.

Normal School Fund Income.

RECEIPTS.		
Balance, October 1, 1872	....	$38,668 87
Interest on principal due on lands	$14,160 26	....
Interest on certificates of indebtedness	35,882 00	....
Tuition fees—Platteville Normal School	3,225 88	....
Whitewater......do	2,237 36	....
Oshkosh ....do	2,832 55	....
Interest on U. S. 5-20 bonds	2,925 08	....
Interest on Milwaukee water-work bonds	3,500 00	....
Commission on... do......... ..do	800 00	....
Interest on Troy town bonds	140 00	....
Interest on Fall River town bonds	350 00	....
Interest on Kinnickinnic..do	105 00	....
Interest on Clifton....... do	105 00	....
Transferred from General Fund for Normal Institutes	2,000 00	....
Transferred from Oshkosh Normal School Building Fund	3,105 97	....
		71,369 10
Total	....	$110,037 97
DISBURSEMENTS.		
Platteville Normal School—salaries of teachers, supplies, etc	$14,982 19	....
Whitewater Normal School—salaries of teachers, supplies, etc	16,538 22	....
Oshkosh Normal School—salaries of teachers, supplies, etc	17,363 18	....
Expenses of Regents	453 00	....
Institutes	2,538 64	....
Expenses	3,360 20	....
Refunded for overpayments	133 24	....
	$55,368 62	....
Balance, September 30, 1873	54,669 35	
		$110,037 97

The Oshkosh Normal School Building Fund has been closed, and the balance therein transferred to the Normal School Fund Income.

The following is the condition of the River Falls Normal School Building Fund:

River Falls Normal School Building Fund.

RECEIPTS.		
Balance, October 1, 1872	$20,000 00	
Donation of Pierce county	5,000 00	
		$25,000 00

No transactions during the past year.

For receipts from various sources, and summary of expenditures during the fiscal year ending September 30th, see foregoing table of "Normal School Fund Income."

A detailed statement of expenditures is herewith submitted:

STATEMENT OF EXPENDITURES.

Date.	No.	To whom and for what paid.	Amount.
1872			
Sep. 4	1024	A. Salisbury, institute expenses........	$110 00
Sep. 4	1025	C. Viebahn, inititute expenses	119 00
Sep. 4	1026	A. J. Hutton, institute expenses..................	120 00
Sep. 4	1027	J. H. Holbrook, institute expenses..............	69 00
Sep. 4	1028	J. Burnham, institute expenses..................	28 50
Sep. 4	1029	R. Gaaham, institute expenses..................	270 25
Sep. 4	1030	A. Salisbury, institute expenses	74 20
Sep. 4	1031	Hosea Barnes, institute expenses................	113 95
Sep. 4	1032	S. P. Gary, supplies, W. Water St. S	46 25
Sep. 5	1033	Wm. Starr, expenses for regents	134 95
Sep. 5	1035	G. S. Albee, supplies for Oshkosh N. S..........	15 05
Sep. 5	1035	S. P. Gary, furniture, Oshkosh N. S.............	83 41
Sep. 11	1036	Chas. H. Allen, expenses as egent..............	203 00
Sep. 14	1037	W. Starr, for cabinets normal schools............	800 00
Sep. 14	1038	Chas. H. Allen, expenses as agent...............	107 00
Sep. 14	1039	S. Maria Chapman, note and mortgage..........	591 81
Sep. 23	1040	H. E. Ward, expenses as institute conductor.....	61 65
Sep. 23	1041	D. McGregor, work in institute.................	120 40
Sep. 23	1042	Martha A. Terry, work in institute.............	116 30
Sep. 23	1043	E. H. Sprague, services in institute:	117 55
Sep. 23	1044	O. R. Smith, institute expenses	150 00
Sep. 23	1045	W. D. Parker, institute expenses	139 55
Sep. 23	1046	A. O. Wright, institute expenses	113 90
Sep. 23	1047	W. A. De LaMatyr, institute expenses...........	64 00
Sep. 28	1958	Ivison Blakeman, T. & Co., books Oshkosh N. S.	83 40
Sep. 28	1049	Seifert, Gugler & Co., views of..........do......	20 00
Sep. 30	1050	J. S. Lippincott & Co., books...........do......	12 60
Oct. 3	1051	W. DeWolf, hardware, Whitewater N. S	126 29
Oct. 3	1052	A. Eastman, institute expenses.........	159 65
Oct. 3	1053	C. E. Mears, institute expenses..................	32 65
Oct. 4	1054	G. A. Libbey, heating apparatus W. W. N. S.....	432 38
Oct. 4	1055	Hoffman, Billings & Co........do...............	70 59
Oct. 4	1057	T. Wilkinson, expenses as inspector W.W. N. S..	70 05
Oct. 7	1057	J. H. Evans, repairs in Platteville N. S.........	382 69
Oct. 8	1058	M. Montague, instructing in Whitewater N. S....	200 00
Oct. 10	1059	G. A. Libbey, work and materials....do.........	316 80
Oct. 18	1060	R. Graham, institute expenses	34 65
Oct. 18	1061	W. H. Holden, institute expenses	20 00
Oct. 18	1062	Geo. Root & Son, books, Oshkosh N. S........	132 90
Oct. 18	1063	W. D. Parker, institute expenses................	36 00
Oct. 18	1064	A. F. North, institute expenses.................	35 00
Oct. 19	1065	Miss E. Carle, institute expenses................	20 00
Oct. 22	1066	Mason & Hamlin's organs (3) State normal sch'ls	400 00
Oct. 30	1067	Sam'l Fallows, salary as Sec'y Bd. R. N. S	87 50
Oct. 31	1068	Allen & Hicks, printing for Oshkosh N. S.......	104 50
Nov. 7	1069	M. Montague, institute expenses	52 00
Nov. 11	1070	T. C. Chamberlin, institete expenses............	15 00
Nov. 30	1071	J. K. Hoffman, institute expenses	26 15
Nov. 30	1072	Geo. Skewes, institute expenses......	53 50
Nov. 30	1073	R. Graham, salary and expenses as agent	315 30
Dec. 5	1074	T. V. Maguire, institute expenses	50 00
Dec. 5	1075	J. Nelligar & Co., apparatus Oshkosh N. S.......	637 89
Dec. 11	1076	G. A. Libbey, heating apparatus W. Water N. S..	97 51
Dec. 14	1077	J Nelligar & Co., philosophical appar. Oshk.N.S	233 18
Dec. 14	1078	Wilson, Hinkle & Co., books, Oshkosh N. S	9 30
Dec. 14	1079	Ivison, Blakeman T. & Co.........do...........	38 00
Dec. 14	1080	Ginn Bro., books Oshkosh N. S.....	47 00

Statement of Expenditures—continued.

Date.	No.	To whom and for what paid.	Amount.
1872.			
Dec. 21	1081	S. P. Gary, wood, Oshkosh N. S.	$272 50
Dec. 21	1082	S. P. Gary, supplies, Oshkosh N. S.	324 47
Dec. 21	1083	Winchester & Partridge, grate, etc., Whitewater N. S	85 92
Dec. 21	1084	Iverson, Blakeman, T., & Co., books, Oshkosh N. S.	15 00
Dec. 23	1085	N. M. Littlejohn, building materi'l, Whitewat'r N. S.	74 44
Dec. 23	1086	A. Y. Chamberlin, ...do..........do.	111 70
Dec. 28	1087	O. J. Taylor, institute expenses	47 25
Dec. 28	1088	J. W. Bashford, institute expenses	15 00
1873.			
Jan. 2	1089	Bell & Rogers, building material, Oshkosh N. S.	739 19
Jan. 2	1090	W. Lynch, institute expenses	87 00
Jan. 6	1091	Sam'l Fallows, salary as Sec'y of B'd Reg'ts N. S.	37 50
Jan. 9	1092	R. Graham, expenses as agent	15 45
Jan. 29	1093	Day & O'Connor, supplies, Whitewater N. S.	263 00
Jan. 29	1094	E. J. Redington, coal, ...do	660 10
Jan. 29	1095	O. M. Sikes, drayage, ...do	133 27
Jan. 29	1096	T. D. Weeks, supplies, ...do	265 68
Jan. 29	1097	F. D. Mills, institute expenses	18 35
Jan. 29	1098	J. H. Evans, cabinet, N. S.	105 98
Jan. 29	1099	J. B. Pradt, institute expenses	21 75
Jan. 30	1100	W. Starr, committees expenses	65 78
Jan. 31	1101	W. DeWolf, building material, Whitewater N. S.	34 49
Jan. 31	1102	J. H. Goodearle, ...do..........do.	74 45
Jan. 31	1103	Coats & Thompson, ...do..........do.	160 02
Jan. 31	1104	Tattle & Shaffee, ...do..........do.	39 23
Jan. 31	1105	J. H. Evans, supplies, Platteville N. S.	915 72
Jan. 31	1106	H. H. Greenman, music teacher, Whitewater N. S.	240 00
Jan. 31	1107	O. Arey, supplies, ...do	318 27
Jan. 31	1108	A. H. Weld, expenses as regent	48 00
Jan. 31	1109	W. P. Whitford, ...do	13 45
Jan. 31	1110	J. I. Lyndes, ...do	31 50
Jan. 31	1111	J. W. Evans, ...do	28 60
Jan. 31	1112	T. D. Weeks, ...do	16 20
Jan. 31	1113	W. H. Chandler, ...do	15 00
Jan. 31	1114	R. Graham, expenses as agent	25 95
Jan. 21	1115	S. P. Gary, ...do	28 95
Jan. 31	1116	W. Starr, ...do	35 00
Jan. 31	1117	M. E. & G. B. Carter, in care of Mrs. Chapman	50 73
Jan. 31	1118	W. E. Smith, expenses as regent	19 50
Feb. 1	1119	Journal of Education, advertising	37 50
Feb. 1	1120	Sam'l Fallows, telegraphing for B'd of Reg. N. S.	5 38
Feb. 1	1121	Harper & Bros., books, Oshkosh N. S.	12 80
Feb. 1	1122	Ivison, Blakeman, T. & Co., books, Oshkosh N. S.	41 87
Feb. 1	1123	Rounds & Morley, printing, Oshkosh N. S.	2 75
Feb. 17	1124	Goodell & Drinkall, supplies, Platteville N. S.	6 90
Feb. 17	1125	Devidorf & Co., ...do..........do.	51 73
Feb. 27	1126	H. C. Bowen, ...do..........do.	30 00
Feb. 26	1127	S. P. Gary, ...do..........do.	111 00
Feb. 26	1128	S. P. Gary, ...do..........do.	442 41
Feb. 26	1129	S. P. Gary, ...do..........do.	170 83
Feb. 26	1130	L. Stadt Miller, cabinet, Whitewater N. S.	100 00
Feb. 28	1131	G. A. Libbey, heating apparatus, Whitewater N. S.	92 88
Mar. 10	1132	S. P. Gary, wood, Oshkosh N. S.	319 17
Mar. 20	1133	P. B. Hulse, books, ...do	31 50
Mar. 20	1134	Mason & Hamlin, organ, Oshkosh N. S.	166 67
Mar. 24	1135	Jno. H. Rolfe, books, Oshkosh N. S.	20 00
Apr. 3	1136	Sam'l P. Gary, wood, ...do	215 00

Statement of Expenditures—continued.

Date.	No.	To whom and for what paid.	Amount.
Apr. 12	1137	B. M. Reynolds, Institute Expenses	$29 50
Apr. 16	1138	A. H. Conkey, Institute expenses	20 00
Apr. 16	1139	Salary as Secretary Board of Regents N. S	87 50
Apr. 16	1140	E. Baker, back pay as janitor Oskosh Nor'l Sch'l	125 00
Apr. 22	1141	Geo. Mathews, fire extinguishers, Platteville N.S.	80 00
Apr. 23	1142	W. Starr, reference libraries, Normal Schools	550 63
Apr. 23	1143	T. C. Chamberlin, institute expenses	8 00
Apr. 24	1114	J. Nellegar, apparatus, Whiteater, Normal School	20 69
Apr. 28	1145	A. Salisbury, institute expenses	46 82
Apr. 28	1146	A. Salisbury ....do......do	45 80
Apr. 29	1147	Ivison B. T. & Co., books, Oshkosh Normal Sch'l	6 27
Apr. 29	1848	Ivison B. T. & Co.,....do....do..........do....	85 34
Apr. 29	1149	MacMillan & Co .....do....do..........do....	24 00
May 5	1150	R. Graham, services as institute conductor	272 85
May 5	1151	Geo. Skewes, institute expenses	11 50
May 5	1152	O. R. Smith....do.......do	25 55
May 5	1153	W. J. Button, books, Oshkosh Normal School	82 01
May 5	1154	A. Ethridge....do.....do..........do	14 04
May 5	1155	Ivison, B.T.&Co.do.....do..........do	41 67
May 5	1156	A. H. Andrews, furn'g. do..........do	240 24
May 5	1157	L. C. Cooley, apparatus.do..........do	110 00
May 5	1158	J. Nellegar & Co., apparatus, Platteville N. Sch'l	168 86
May 14	1159	Geo. Williams, wood, Oshkosh Normal School	549 56
May 24	1160	A. Salisbury, institute expenses	88 90
May 24	1161	D. McGregor, institute expenses	68 20
May 27	1162	J. Nellegar, apparatus, Oshkosh Normal School	9 46
May 27	1163	F. S. Belden books.... ...do.........do	52 44
June 12	1164	C. M. Treat, institute expenses	20 00
July 8	1165	Geo. Williamson, wood, Oshkosh Normal School	225 00
July 8	1166	Ivison, B. T. & Co., books..do.........do	6 88
July 9	1166	T. D. Weeks, supplies, Whitewater Normal Sch'l	257 42
July 9	1167	G. W. Hersee, piano rep'g....do.........do	8 00
July 9	1168	Day & O'Connor, supplies ...do.........do	58 07
July 10	1169	M. M. Leahy, settlem't of acc't for h't'g W. N. S.	650 00
July 10	1170	J. H. Evans, supplies, Platteville Normal School.	1,139 85
July 11	1171	W. C. Whitford, expenses as regent	9 80
July 11	1172	W. Starr, to defray expenses of committees	1,000 00
July 11	1173	W. H. Chandler, expenses on com. of institute	125 55
July 11	1174	Atwood & Culver, printing	80 00
July 11	1175	W. J. Park, stationery for institutes	75 82
July 11	1176	Sam'l Fallows, expenditures for the B'd	10 45
July 11	1177	Journal Education, advertising	87 50
July 11	1178	Seifert & Gugler, diplomas, State Normal School	25 80
July 11	1179	E. A. Charlton, supplies, Platteville ....do	53 25
July 11	1180	J. H. Evans, text books......do........do	590 14
July 11	1181	J. H. Evans, expenses as regent	22 60
July 11	1182	W. H. Chandler.do.......do	6 50
July 11	1183	J. J. Lyndes ....do.......do	21 10
July 11	1184	W. Starr........do.......do	27 00
July 11	1185	Sam'l Fallows, exp's as visit'r to Platteville N S.	10 15
July 11	1176	T. D. Weeks, expenses as regent	13 70
July 11	1186	A. H. Webb .. do........do	42 00
July 11	1188	W. E. Smith....do........do	14 00
July 11	1189	Sam'l P. Gary ..do....... do	20 70
July 11	1190	J. Nellegar & Co., apparatus, Platteville N. S.	88 88
July 11	1191	Oliver Avey, supplies, Whitewater Normal Sch'l	207 14
July 12	1192	A. Salisbury, institute expenses	285 25
July 12	1193	Sam'l Fallows, salary as Sec'y B'd of R. of N. S.	75 00

Statement of Expenditures—continued.

Date.	No.	To whom and for what paid.	Amount.
1873.			
July 22	1194	B. M. Reynolds, institute expenses	$13 50
July 24	1195	T. D. Weeks, supplies Whitewater N. School	190 00
July 24	1196	D. McGregor, Institute expenses	220 30
July 24	1197	H. Greenman, services as teacher, vocal, W. N. S.	240 00
July 29	1198	J. A. Terry, Institute expenses	9 60
July 30	1199	J. H. Evans, addition to Platteville building	500 00
July 31	1200	W. D. Parker, Institute expenses	16 90
Aug. 4	1201	E. D. Coe, printing, Whitewater Normal School	170 00
Aug. 4	1202	J. D. Wilder, slating, Oshkosh Normal School	43 48
Aug. 7	1203	E. S. Redington, coal, Whitewater Normal S	1,206 16
Aug. 11	1204	R. Graham, expenses and service conducting Inst.	161 00
Aug. 16	1205	Stedman, Brown & Co., 4 copies Gray's Alas, S.N.S	48 00
Aug. 18	1206	A. Salisbury, services as Institute conductor	117 35
Aug. 26	1207	Hosea Barnes, Normal Institute expenses	152 90
Aug. 26	1208	J. H. Evans, addition Platteville school building.	700 00
Aug. 27	1209	W. H. Chandler, expenses Institute conductor	77 20
Aug. 28	1210	S. P. Gary, supplies Oshkosh Normal School	175 98
Aug. 28	1211	S. P. Gary, supplies and repairs, Oshkosh N. S.	428 68
Aug 28	1212	S. P. Gary, new roof, Oshkosh school building	166 95
Aug. 28	1213	O. R. Smith, services as Normal Inst. conductor.	100 00
		Total	$21,544 88
		SALARIES OF TEACHERS AND JANITORS.	
Sep. 4	446	Edwin Baker, salary as janitor in Oshkosh N. S.	$50 00
Sep. 7	447	L. L. Goodell.........do....... Platteville N. S.	50 00
Sep. 17	448	G. S. Albee, salary as teacher in Oshkosh N. S.	250 00
Sep. 17	449	R. Graham........do.............do	180 00
Sep. 17	450	H. C. Bowen......do.............do	150 00
Sep. 17	451	Anna W. Moody...do.............do	100 00
Sep. 17	452	Mary H. Ladd ....do.............do	80 00
Sep. 17	453	M. E. Hazard .....do.............do	70 00
Sep. 17	454	M. A. Hill ....do.............do	80 00
Sep. 17	455	R. C. Swart........do.............do	70 00
Sep. 17	456	F. E. Albee........do.............do	60 90
Sep. 17	457	M. Hosford, salary as librarian.....do	10 00
Sep. 17	458	Edwin Baker, salary as janitor .....do	50 00
Sep. 19	459	O. Arey, salary as teacher in Whitewater N. S.	250 00
Sep. 19	460	T. C. Chamberlin .do.............do	180 00
Sep. 19	461	S. S. Rockwood ...do.............do	100 00
Sep. 19	462	H. E. G. Arey......do.............do	100 00
Sep. 19	463	M. A. Terry.......do.............do	80 00
Sep. 19	464	C. H. Lilly ....do.............do	70 00
Sep. 19	465	S. E. Eldridge.....do.............do	70 00
Sep. 19	466	Mary DeLaney....do.............do	50 00
Sep. 19	467	S. D. Vincent, salary as janitor .....do	50 00
Sep. 26	468	E. A. Charlton, as teacher in Platteville N. S.	250 00
Sep. 26	469	D. M. McGregor ..do.............do	150 00
Sep. 26	470	Geo. Beck ....do.............do	150 00
Sep. 26	471	D. G. Purman.....do.............do	150 00
Sep. 26	472	C. E. Adams ......do.............do	80 00
Sep. 26	473	E. Curtis..........do.............do	70 00
Sep. 26	474	E. M. Mills ......do.............do	70 00
Sep. 26	475	T. J. Colburn .....do.............do	25 00
Sep. 26	476	L. L. Goodell.....do.............do	50 00
Sep. 30	477	S. S. Rockwood ...do.............do	50 00
Oct. 26	478	G. S. Albee, salary as teacher in Oshkosh N. S.	250 00

Statement of Expenditures—continued.

Date.	No.	To whom and for what paid.	Amount.
		Salaries of Teachers, etc.—continued.	
1873			
Oct. 26	479	R. Graham, salary as teacher in Oshkosh, N. S....	$180 00
Oct. 26	480	H. C. Bowen.................do......	150 00
Oct. 26	481	A. W. Moody.................do..............	100 00
Oct. 26	482	M. H. Ladd..................do..............	80 00
Oct. 26	483	M. E. Hazard ....do..............	70 00
Oct. 26	484	M. S. Hill..................do..............	80 00
Oct. 26	485	R. C. Swart.................do..........	70 00
Oct. 26	486	F. E Albee..................do..............	60 00
Oct. 26	487	M. Hosford, salary as librarian, Oshkosh N. S....	10 00
Oct. 26	488	E. Baker, salary as janitor.............do.......	50 00
Oct. 26	489	H. E. Bateman, salary as teacher ......do........	80 00
Oct. 26	490	E. A. Charlton, salary as teacher, Platteville N. S..	250 00
Oct. 26	491	D. McGregor.................do..............	150 00
Oct. 26	492	George Beck ....do..............	150 00
Oct. 26	493	D. G. Purman ....do..............	150 00
Oct. 26	494	C. E. E. Adams..............do..............	80 00
Oct. 26	495	E. Curtis...................do..............	70 00
Oct. 26	496	E. M. Mills ....do..............	70 00
Oct. 26	497	T. J. Colburn...............do..............	25 00
Oct. 26	498	L. L. Goodell, salary as janitor, Platteville N. S...	50 00
Oct. 31	499	O. Arey, salary as teacher, Whitewater N. S......	250 00
Oct. 31	500	T. C. Chamberlin............do..............	180 00
Oct. 31	501	S. S. Rockwood ....do..............	150 00
Oct. 31	502	H. E. G. Arey ....do..............	100 00
Oct. 31	503	M. A. Terry.................do..............	80 00
Oct. 31	504	C. A. Lilly ....do...	70 00
Oct. 31	505	S. E. Eldridge..............do..............	70 00
Oct. 31	506	Mary De Lany................do..............	50 00
Oct. 31	507	J. D. Vincent, salary as janitor, Whitewater N. S...	50 00
Nov. 21	508	G. S. Albee, salary as teacher, Oshkosh N. S......	250 00
Nov. 21	509	R. Graham...................do..............	180 00
Nov. 21	510	A. W. Moody ....do..............	100 00
Nov. 21	511	M. Hosford, salary as librarian, Oshkosh N. S.....	10 00
Nov. 21	512	M. H. Ladd, salary as teacher, Oshkosh N. S......	80 00
Nov. 21	513	Helen E. Bateman............do..............	80 00
Nov. 21	514	F. E. Albee ....do..............	60 00
Nov. 21	515	M. S. Hill..................do..............	80 00
Nov. 21	516	M. E. Hazard ....do..............	70 00
Nov. 21	517	H. C. Bowen ....do..............	150 00
Nov. 21	518	R. C. Swart ....do..............	70 00
Nov. 21	519	E. Baker, salary as janitor, Oshkosh N. S	50 00
Nov. 22	520	E. A. Charlton, salary as teacher in Platteville N. S.	250 00
Nov. 22	521	D. McGregor.................do.....	150 00
Nov. 22	522	D. G. Purman ....do..............	150 00
Nov. 22	523	Geo. Beck...................do..............	150 00
Nov. 22	524	E. M. Mills ....do..............	70 00
Nov. 22	525	E. Curtis...................do..............	70 00
Nov. 22	526	T J. Colburn................do..............	25 00
Nov. 22	527	L. L. Goodell, salary as janitor, Platteville N. S...	50 00
Nov. 26	528	O. Arey, salary as teacher, Whitewater N. S.	250 00
Nov. 26	529	T. C. Chamberlin............do..............	180 00
Nov. 26	530	S. S. Rockwood ....do..............	150 00
Nov. 26	531	M. A. Terry.................do..............	80 00
Nov. 26	532	H. E. G. Arey ....do..............	100 00
Nov. 26	533	S. E. Eldridge..............do..............	70 00
Nov. 26	534	Mary De Lany................do..............	50 00

Statement of Expenditures—continued.

Date.	No.	To whom and for what paid.	Amount.
		Salaries of Teachers, etc.—continued.	
1878.			
Nov. 26	535	J. D. Vincent, salary as janitor, Whitewater......	50 00
Dec. 4	536	C. H. Lilly, salary as teacher in Whitewater.....	70 00
Dec. 18	537	G. S. Albee, salary as teacher in Oshkosh, N. S....	250 00
Dec. 18	538	R. Graham..............do....................	180 00
Dec. 18	539	R. C. Swart ....do....................	70 00
Dec. 18	540	M. H. Ladd ....do....................	80 00
Dec. 18	541	M. E. Hazard ....do....................	70 00
Dec. 18	542	A. W. Moody ....do....................	100 00
Dec. 18	543	M. L. Hill ....do....................	80 00
Dec. 18	544	F. E. Albee ....do....................	60 00
Dec. 18	545	H. E. Bateman ....do....................	80 00
Dec. 18	546	H. C. Bowen ....do....................	150 00
Dec. 18	547	E. Baker, salary as janitor in Oshkosh N. S......	50 00
Dec. 18	548	M. Hosford, salary as librarian in Oshkosh N. S..	10 00
Dec. 18	549	E. A. Charlton, salary as teacher, Platteville N. S.	250 00
Dec. 18	550	D. McGregor............do....................	150 00
Dec. 18	551	D. G. Purman ....do....................	150 00
Dec. 18	552	Geo. Beck...............do....................	150 00
Dec. 18	553	E. Mills................do....................	70 00
Dec. 18	554	C. Adams................do....................	80 00
Dec. 18	555	E. Curtis...............do....................	70 00
Dec. 18	556	T. J. Colburn ....do....................	25 00
Dec. 18	557	L. L. Goodell, salary as janitor in Platteville N. S.	50 00
Dec. 24	558	O. Arey, salary as teacher in Whitewater N. S....	250 00
Dec. 24	559	T. C. Chamberlin........do....................	180 00
Dec. 24	569	S. S. Rockwood ....do....................	150 00
Dec. 24	561	H. E. G. Arey...........do....................	100 00
Dec. 24	562	M. A. Terry.............do....................	80 00
Dec. 24	563	S. E. Eldridge..........do....................	70 00
Dec. 24	554	C. H. Lilly.............do....................	70 00
Dec. 24	565	W. J. Shower ....do....................	50 00
Dec. 24	566	M. DeLany ....do....................	50 00
Dec. 24	567	J. D. Vincent, salary as janitor in Whitewater N. S.	50 00
1878.			
Jan. 18	568	O. Arey, salary as teacher in Whitewater N. S....	250 00
Jan. 18	569	T. C. Chamberlin ....do....................	180 00
Jan. 18	570	S. S. Rockwood..........do....................	150 00
Jan. 18	571	H. E. G. Arey ....do....................	100 00
Jan. 18	572	M. A. Terry ....do....................	80 00
Jan. 18	573	C. H. Lilly.............do....................	70 00
Jan. 18	574	S. E. Eldridge..........do....................	70 00
Jan. 18	575	M. De Lany ....do....................	50 00
Jan. 18	576	J. D. Vincent, salary as janitor in Whitewater N. S.	50 00
Jan. 24	577	E. A. Charlton, salary as teacher in Platteville N. S.	250 00
Jan. 24	578	D. McGregor.............do....................	150 00
Jan. 24	579	G. Beck.................do....................	150 00
Jan. 24	580	D. G. Purman ....do....................	150 00
Jan. 24	581	C. Adams ....do....................	80 00
Jan. 24	582	E. Curtis ....do....................	70 00
Jan. 24	583	Eva Mills ....do....................	70 00
Jan. 24	584	T. J. Colburn...........do....................	25 00
Jan. 24	585	L. L. Goodell, salary as janitor in Platteville N. S.	50 00
Jan. 28	586	G. S. Albee, salary as teacher in Oshkosh N. S....	250 00
Jan. 28	587	H. C. Bowen ....do....................	150 00
Jan. 28	588	R. Graham ....do....................	180 00
Jan. 28	589	M. H. Ladd ....do....................	80 00
an. 28	590	M. L. Hill..............do....................	80 00

Statement of Expenditures—continued.

Date.	No.	To whom and for what paid.	Amount.
		Salaries of Teachers, etc.—continued.	
1878.			
Jan. 28	591	R. C. Swart, salary as teacher, Oshkosh	$70 00
Jan. 28	592	F. E. Albee........do...........do............	60 00
Jan. 28	593	H. E. Bateman.....do...........do............	80 00
Jan. 28	594	M. E. Hazard ......do...........do............	70 00
Jan. 28	595	A. W. Moody ......do...........do............	100 00
Jrn. 28	596	E. Baker, salary as janitor.........do............	50 00
Jan. 28	597	M. Hosford, salary as librarian ....do............	10 00
Feb. 26	598	G. S. Albee, salary as teacher......do............	250 00
Feb. 26	599	H. E. Bowen.......do...........do............	150 00
Feb. 26	600	R. Graham.........do...........do............	180 00
Feb. 26	601	A. M. Moody.......do...........do............	100 00
Feb. 26	602	H. E. Bateman .....do...........do............	80 00
Feb. 26	603	M. H. Ladd........do...........do............	80 00
Feb. 26	604	M. S. Hill ....do...........do............	80 00
Feb. 26	605	M. E. Hazard ......do...........do............	70 00
Feb. 26	606	R. C. Swart........do...........do............	70 00
Feb. 26	607	F. E. Albee ....do...........do............	60 00
Feb. 26	608	M. E. Hosford, salary as librarian...do............	10 00
Feb. 26	609	E. Baker, salary as janitor.........do............	50 00
Feb. 28	610	E. A. Charlton, salary as teacher, Platteville N, S.	250 00
Feb. 28	611	D. McGregor.......do...........do............	150 00
Feb. 28	612	D. G. Purman ......do...........do	150 00
Feb. 28	613	Geo. Beck..........do........... do............	150 00
Feb. 28	614	C. E. Adams ....do...........do............	80 00
Feb. 28	615	E. Curtis...........do...........do............	70 00
Feb. 28	616	E. A. Mills.........do...........do............	70 00
Feb. 28	617	T. J. Colburn.......do...........do............	25 00
Feb. 28	618	L. L. Goodell, salary as janitor ....do............	50 00
Mar. 4	619	D. Arey, salary as teacher in Platteville N. S	250 00
Mar. 4	620	T. C. Chamberlin...do........... do.......... ..	180 00
Mar. 4	621	S. S. Rockwood ....do...........do	150 00
Mar. 4	622	S. E. Eldridge......do...........do............	70 00
Mar. 4	623	H. E. G. Arey ......do...........do............	100 00
Mar. 4	624	C. H. Lilly.........do...........do............	70 00
Mar. 4	625	M. A. Terry ....do...........do........ ...	80 00
Mar. 4	626	Mary DeLany......do...........do............	50 00
Mar. 4	627	J. D. Vincent. salary as janitor ....do...........	50 00
Mar. 26	628	G. S. Albee, salary as teacher in Oshkosh N. S....	250 00
Mar. 26	629	H. C. Bowen ....do...........do............	150 00
Mar. 26	630	R. Graham..........do...........do............	180 00
Mar. 26	631	A. W. Moody.......do...........do............	100 00
Mar. 26	632	M. S. Hill..........do...........do............	80 00
Mar. 26	633	R. C. Swart ....do...........do............	70 00
Mar, 26	634	F. E. Albee ....do...........do............	60 00
Mar. 26	635	Helen Bateman.....do...........do........ ...	80 00
Mar. 26	636	M. H. Ladd ....do...........do............	80 00
Mar. 26	637	M. E. Hazard.......do...........do............	70 00
Mar. 26	638	M. E. Hosford, salary as librarian .do............	10 00
Mar. 26	639	E. Baker, salary as janitor ....do............	50 00
Mar. 26	640	E. A. Charlton, salary as teacher in Platteville N. S	250 00
Mar. 26	641	D. McGregor.......do...........do............	150 00
Mar. 26	642	D. G. Purman......do...........do............	150 00
Mar. 26	643	Geo. Beck .... do... ....do............	150 00
Mar. 26	644	Eva Mills..........do ....do............	70 00
Mar. 26	645	C. E. Adams ....do...........do............	80 00
Mar. 26	646	E. Curtis...........do............do............	70 00

Statement of Expenditures—continued.

Date.	No.	To whom and for what paid.	Amount.
		Salaries of Teachers, etc.—continued.	
1873.			
Mar. 26	647	T. J. Colburn, salary as teacher, Platteville.......	$94 00
Mar. 26	648	L. L. Goodell, salary as janitor, Platteville	50 00
Apr. 2	649	O. Arey, salary as teacher in Whitewater N. S....	250 00
Apr. 2	650	S. S. Rockwood ....do............do............	150 00
Apr. 2	651	A. Salisbury ....do............do............	90 00
Apr. 2	652	S. E. Eldridge......do........... do............	70 00
Apr. 2	653	H. E. G. Arey ......do............do............	100 00
Apr. 2	654	M. DeLany ....do .. ..do............	50 00
Apr. 2	655	C. H. Lilly.........do............do............	70 00
Apr. 2	656	T. C. Chamberlin...do........... do...	180 00
Apr. 2	657	M. A. Terry........do.... ......do............	80 00
Apr. 2	658	J. D. Vincent, salary as janitor ....do............	50 00
Apr. 26	659	E. A. Charlton, salary as teacher, Platteville N. S.	250 00
Apr. 26	660	D. McGregor.......do... ....do...........	150 00
Apr. 26	661	D. G. Purman......do........... do...........	150 00
Apr. 26	662	Geo. Beck..........do.... ....do...........	150 00
Apr. 26	663	E. Mills............do............do	70 00
Apr. 26	664	C. Adams ....do...........do...........	80 00
Apr. 26	665	E. Curtis...........do............do...........	70 00
Apr. 26	666	T. J. Colburn ......do............do...........	48 00
Apr. 26	667	L. L. Goodell, salary as janitor ....do...........	50 00
Apr. 26	668	O. Arey, salary as teacher, Whitewater N. S......	250 00
Apr. 26	669	T. C. Chamberlin...do............do...........	180 00
Apr. 26	670	H. E. G. Arey ......do... .... do....... ...	100 00
Apr. 26	671	S. S. Rockwood ....do............do...........	150 00
Apr. 26	672	S. E. Eldridge......do......... ...do........ ...	70 00
Apr. 26	673	M. A. De Lany.....do............do...........	50 00
Apr. 26	674	C. H. Lilly.........do............do........ ...	70 00
Apr. 26	675	J. D. Vincent, salary as janitor ....do...........	50 00
Apr. 26	676	M. I. Burt, salary as teacher.......do...........	33 50
May 1	677	G. S. Albee ....do........Oshkosh N. S.....	250 00
May 1	678	R. Graham.........do............do...........	180 00
May 1	679	A. W. Moody.......do....... ....do.....	100 00
May 1	680	R. C. Swart ....do............do...........	70 00
May 1	681	M. Ladd ....do............do...........	80 00
May 1	682	M. S. Hill ....do............do...........	80 00
May 1	683	M. E. Hazard ......do............do...........	70 00
May 1	684	H. C. Bourn........do............do...........	150 00
May 1	685	F. E. Albee ....do............do...........	60 00
May 1	686	H. E. Bateman .....do............do...........	80 00
May 1	687	M. S. Hosford, salary as librarian..do...........	10 00
May 1	688	E. Baker, salary as janitor.........do...........	75 00
May 3	689	A. Salisbury, salary as teacher, Whitewater N. S..	120 00
May 24	690	O. Arey............do............do...........	250 00
May 24	691	T. C. Chamberlin...do............do...........	180 00
May 24	692	A. Salisbury........do............do...........	120 00
May 24	693	S. S. Rockwood ....do............do...........	150 00
May 24	694	H. E. G. Arey ......do............do...........	100 00
May 24	695	S. E. Eldridge......do......... .. do...........	70 00
May 24	696	M. I. Burt ....do.... ....do...........	65 00
May 24	697	C. H. Lilly.........do............do...........	70 00
May 24	698	M. De Lany........do............do...........	50 00
May 26	699	J. D. Vincent, salary as janitor ....do...........	50 00
May 27	700	E. A. Charlton, salary as teacher, Platteville N. S.	250 00
May 27	701	D. McGregor.......do............do...........	150 00
May 27	702	Geo. Beck..........do............do...........	150 00

Statement of Expenditures—continued.

Date.	No.	To whom and for what paid.	Amount.
		Salaries as Teachers, etc.—continued.	
1873			
May 27	703	D. Y. Purman, salary as teacher, Platteville.......	$150 00
May 27	704	E. Curtis.............do.............do.........	70 00
May 27	705	C. E. Adams..........do.............do.........	80 00
May 27	706	Eva Mills............do.............do.........	70 00
May 27	707	T. J. Colburn ....do.............do.........	48 00
May 27	708	L. L. Goodell, salary as Janitor, Platteville N. S ..	50 00
May 29	709	M. A. Terry, sal. as tch'r in Whit'r N.S., 2 w'ks in Apr	40 00
May 31	710	G. S. Albee, salary as teacher in Oshkosh N. S....	250 00
May 31	711	H. C. Brown..........do............do.........	150 00
May 31	712	R. Graham............do............do.........	180 00
May 31	713	A. W. Moody ....do............do.........	100 00
May 31	714	M. S. Hill ....do............do.........	80 00
May 31	715	M. H. Ladd ....do............do.........	80 00
May 31	716	T. E. Albee...........do............do.........	60 00
May 31	717	M. E. Hazard ....do............do.........	70 00
May 31	718	H. E. Bateman ....do............do.	80 00
May 31	719	R. C. Swart ....do............do.........	70 00
May 31	720	M. Hosford, salary as librarian ....do.........	10 00
May 31	721	E. Baker, salary as janitor............do.........	75 00
June 17	722	G. S. Albee, salary as teacher. ......do.........	250 00
June 17	723	R. Graham............do............do.........	180 00
June 17	724	A. W. Moody ....do............do.........	100 00
June 17	725	M. S. Hill ....do............do.........	80 00
June 17	726	R. C. Swart ....do............do.......	70 00
June 17	727	H. C. Bowen..........do............do.........	150 00
June 17	728	M. E. Hazard ....do............do.........	70 00
June 17	729	M. H. Ladd...........do............do.........	80 00
June 17	730	H. E. Bateman........do....... ...do.........	80 00
June 17	731	F. E. Albee ....do............do.........	60 00
June 17	732	M. Hosford, salary as librarian ....do.......	10 00
June 17	733	E. Baker, salary as janitor............do.........	75 00
June 20	734	O. Arey, salary as teacher in Whitewater N. S....	250 00
June 20	735	S. S. Rockwood ....do............do.........	150 00
June 20	736	S. E. Eldridge ....do............do........	70 00
June 20	737	A. Salisbury..........do............do.........	120 00
June 20	738	T. C. Chamberlin .....do............do.........	180 00
June 20	739	H. E. G. Arey ....do............do.........	100 00
June 20	740	M. I. Burt ....do............do.........	65 00
June 20	751	C. H. Lilly............do............do.........	70 00
June 20	742	M. DeLany............do............do.........	50 00
June 20	743	J. D. Vincent, salary as janitor.........do.........	50 00
June 24	744	E. A. Charlton, salary as teacher, Platteville N. S..	250 00
June 24	745	D. McGregor.. ......do........ do.........	150 00
June 24	746	D. G. Purman.........do............do.........	150 00
June 24	747	Geo. Beck ....do............do.........	150 00
June 24	748	E. Curtis..............do............do.........	70 00
June 24	749	C. E. Adams..........do........... do.... ...	80 00
June 24	750	E. Mills ....do............do.........	70 00
June 24	751	T. J. Colburn ....do............do.........	48 00
June 24	752	L. L. Goodell, salary as janitor ....do.........	50 00
July 8	753	M. J. Showers, salary as librarian ....do.........	50 00
July 11	754	A. E. Charlton, salary as teacher .....do.........	250 00
July 11	755	S. H. Shellenger, salary as librarian ..do.........	100 00
July 26	756	M. DeLany, extra pay as teacher in Whitew'r N. S.	50 00
Aug. 12	757	E. Baker, salary as janitor, Oshkosh N. S........	75 00
Aug. 12	758	L. L. Goodell, salary as janitor, Platteville N. S ..	50 00

Statement of Expenditures—continued.

		Salaries as Teachers, etc—continued.	
Aug. 12	759	T. D. Weeks, for janitors salary, Whitewater N. S.	$50 00
Aug. 27	760	T. D. Weeks....do...............do..........	50 00
		Salaries..................................	$33,050 00
		Buildings, supplies, institute expenses, etc., brought forward..........................	21,544 88
		Total....................................	$54,594 88

ACCOMPANYING REPORTS.

Some changes have taken place in the several faculties, for which and for the present composition of the faculty of each school, reference is made to the presidents reports to me, submitted herewith, to which also your careful attention is invited for detailed information concerning the organization and work of each school, its prospect, progress and condition, its individuality, its generalization, its accomplishments in the past, and its aims in the future.

All of which is respectfully submitted,

WILLIAM STARR,
President of Board of Regents.

REPORT OF THE PRESIDENT OF THE PLATTEVILLE NORMAL SCHOOL.

To the Hon. WM. STARR,

President of the Board of Regents of Normal Schools:

DEAR SIR: It is with pleasure that I submit my annual report of the condition, progress and prospects of the State Normal School at Platteville.

The past year has been a period of steady growth and prosperity. Unmarked by any striking events, it has witnessed faithful work from day to day. The attendance for the scholastic year ending June 26, 1873, was as follows:

NORMAL DEPARTMENT.

Ladies	92	....
Gentlemen	90	...
Total	—	182

Classified as follows:

Senior class	27	....
Middle class	43	....
Junior class	112	....
Total as above	—	182

PREPARATORY AND ACADEMIC DEPARTMENT.

Ladies	68	....
Gentlemen	93	....
Total	—	161
MODEL SCHOOL		65
Whole number enrolled		408

The enrollment for the present term (fall of 1873), has been large, amounting in the aggregate to three hundred and twenty. Every desk in the school rooms has been occupied, and some students have been seated in one of the recitation rooms. This large attendance is gratifying to the teachers, but the faithful work of our students is still more gratifying. Their excellent deportment, based as it seems to be, upon a sincere regard for the right, gives promise to even better results in the future. Indeed, if those who have entered this school with the professed purpose of fitting themselves for the profession of teaching, fail, while students, to acquire habits of self control, if they lack a nice sense of honor, if they act from impulse rather then from principle, it bodes ill for the schools that may come under their charge.

Of the work accomplished during the several terms of the year, I need not speak in detail. The Board of Visitors appointed by the Superintendent of Public Instruction, consisting of Prof. W. D. Parker, of Janesville; Supt. C. M. Treat of Clinton, and Prof. Alexander Kerr, of Madison, visited us on different occasions, as did also the various committees of the Board of Regents. To all these gentlemen we endeavored to give full opportunity to learn the true condition of the school.

The exercises of the anniversary week were conducted according to the following

PROGRAMME:

EXAMINATIONS—Monday, Tuesday and Wednesday A. M., June 23d, 24th and 25th.

CLASS DAY EXERCISES.—Wednesday evening, June 25th.

ADDRESS BY HON. S. FALLOWS, Wednesday, June 25th.

FIFTH ANNUAL COMMENCEMENT—Thursday, June 26th, 9½ o'clock, A. M.

MEETING OF ALUMNI ASSOCIATION—Thursday evening, June 26th.

Messrs. Chandler, Weld and Whitford, the committee appointed to examine the graduating class, were present during the week and having performed their duty, admitted the following persons to the honors of graduation, in accordance with the recommendation of the Faculty:

GRADUATES.

Names.	Post Office.	County.
Charles Bradon	Georgetown	Grant.
Michael Joseph Casey	Portage City	Columbia.
Charles Warren Lemont	Wiota	La LaFayette
Charles M. Long	Richland City	Richland.
James Oliver Luce	Georgetown	Grant.
Joseph E. Luce	Georgetown	Grant.
David E. Morgan	Spring Green	Sauk.
James William Murphy	Plattville	Grant.
Henry David Neely	Plattville	Grant.
John J. Roche	Darlington	LaFayette.
Silas Henry Schellenger	Platteville	Grant.
Paine T. Stephens	Mifflin	Iowa.
Walter Thurtell	Jamestown	Grant.
Nathan E. Utt	Platteville	Grant.
Edwin A. Williams	Bassett's Station	Kenosha.
Ella C. Aspinwall	Oregon	Dane.
Nora Lois Bayley	Platteville	Grant.
Carrie A. Edwards	Galena, Ills	
Johanna B. George	Mineral Point	Iowa.
Ada Grindell	Platteville	Grant.
Nellie A. Hill	Platteville	Grant.
Anna Potter	Platteville	Grant.
Ella Dora Sylvester	Mifflin	Iowa.
Velma Sylvester	Castle Rock	Grant.
Alice E. Tracy	Platteville	Grant.
Emma Watkins	Lancaster	Grant.

The graduating exercises were held Thursday, June 26, with the following:

PROGRAMME.

MUSIC.—*Anthem*—"O, Father Almighty."

PRAYER, BY REV. A. P. JOHNSON.

ORATION—Men of Principle hold the Scales of Justice, - Joseph E. Luce.
ORATION—The True end of Life, - - - Charles M. Long.
ESSAY—A Nation's Dependence on her Schools, - - Alice Tracy.
ORATION—Tendencies to Republicanism, - - Nathan E. Utt.
ESSAY—We are all Painters, - - - - - - Ada Grindell.
ORATION—The Cost of Ideas, - - - - David E. Morgan.

MUSIC—*Quartette*—"Sweet Night, be Calm."

ESSAY—The Power of Words, - - - - Nellie A. Hill.
ESSAY—Under the Rose, - - - - - Ella C. Aspinwall.
ORATION—The Necessity of Political Virtue, - - Charles Brandon.
ORATION—Success in Life, - - - - Edwin A. Williams.
ORATION—"All some Force Obey," - - Michael Joseph Casey.

ESSAY—"Know Thyself," - - - - Carrie A. Edwards.
ORATION—A Leaf from History, - - - John A. Roche.

MUSIC.

ORATION—"I will find a way or make one," - Charles Warren Lemont.
ESSAY—Fossils, - - - - - - Velma Sylvester.
ORATION—The Body the Mirror of the Mind, - James William Murphy.
ESSAY—Crucibles, - - - - - - Emma Watkins.
ORATION—The Departed Great and Good, - - Henry David Neely.
ESSAY—Shoddy, - - - - - - Johanna B. George.
ORATION—Our Moral Being, our first Care, - Silas Henry Schellenger.

MUSIC—*Quartette*—"List, the Evening Breeze is Stealing."

ESSAY—Thorns, - - - - - - Ella Dora Sylvester.
ORATION—Light, - - - - - - James Oliver Luce.
ORATION—Blessings in Disguise, - - - - Oliver Thurtell.
ESSAY—Individuality, - - - - - - - Anna Potter.
ESSAY—The Dew on Hermon. - - - - Nora Lois Bayley.
ORATION—Spectrum Analysis, - - - - Paine T. Stephens.

MUSIC—*Anthem*—"Hear My Cry, O God."

PRESENTATION OF DIPLOMAS.

GRADUATES' PARTING SONG.

BENEDICTION.

The number of graduates of the school, with their occupations, is as follows:

Class of 1869	8
1870	15
1871	12
1872	8
1873	26
Total	69

	Gentlemen.	Ladies.	Total.
Teaching in Wisconsin	28	22	50
Teaching in other States	1	3	4
Students in higher institutions	5	1	6
Clergyman	1	....	1
Lawyers	2	....	2
Merchant	1	....	1
U. S. mail agent	1	....	1
Married, and left the profession	....	1	1
Not teaching at present	....	2	2
Deceased*	1	....	1
Total	40	29	69

*George D. Utt, of the Class of 1871, died Oct. 18, 1873, at Marinette, Wis., where he was engaged as Principal of the public school. Mr. Utt was a young man of sterling worth, of excellent promise as a teacher.

Of the last graduating class, twenty-four are teaching, one is studying elocution in the College of Oratory of the Boston University, and one has entered the University at Madison. Several of the gentlemen reported as "teaching," not having been able to secure permanent positions, have taken district schools of four or five months. I believe all of them would gladly have engaged for the year, had opportunity been given.

The prospects of the school are encouraging. I have already mentioned the attendance of the present term. The senior class is not large—probably ten will graduate—but it is composed of students who will, I am confident, do credit to themselves and to the school. The middle and junior classes are quite full, and comprise a large number of students who intend to complete the course of study. The preparatory and academic department is full to overflowing, and a large proportion of those students intend, in due time, to enter the Normal.

Little interest seems to be manifested in the "Elementary Course" of one year. Those who are ambitious to complete a course of study desire something more than can be included in a single year. It is my opinion that it would be well to establish an elementary course of two years, and to make the advanced course four years instead of three, as now.

As it seems undesirable to have an "institute course," in connection with the regular work of the school, I repeat the suggestion made in my last report, to the effect that an institute be held here during the summer vacation for the special benefit of this and the adjoining counties. The school building, apparatus and fixtures, so far as needed, could be devoted to the use such an institute, and a competent teaching force could be readily secured.

The extensive repairs and improvements in our school building authorized by the board of regents, are now nearly completed They will add very much to our facilities for work, and provide for the increasing wants of the school. The *suite* of rooms for the the department of the Natural Sciences, consisting of a large recitation room, a room for apparatus and a laboratory, is especially convenint and attractive. The new heating apparatus, though not yet fully tested, bids fair to do away with one great source of discomfort in past years.

In this connection, too much credit cannot be given to Hon. J. H. Evans, Resident Regent, who has devoted a large part of his time for several months past to the interests of the school. By his untiring exertions and his watchful care, the work has been thoroughly done, and every needed provision made to promote the comfort and convenience of teachers and students.

The geological and mineralogical cabinet is in good condition. Valuable contributions have been received from Amherst W. Barber, Esq., of Yankton, Dakota, and from others. The private collection of Regent Evans, which is freely used for the benefit of the school, has also been largely increased during the year.

I am happy to hear emphatic testimony to the zeal, energy and efficiency of my associate teachers. The prosperity of the school is owing in a great degree to their faithful labors. They have not only performed the work of their respective departments, but they have also heartily seconded all plans to promote the general interests of the school.

At the close of the summer term, Miss Eva M. Mills, who has been a teacher of geography and history for three years, resigned her position to the regret of all connected with the school. Miss Carolyn E. Adams, for two years principal of the academic and preparatory department, was transferred to the normal, and Mr. C. H. Nye, for many years the efficient principal of one of the public schools of this village, was appointed in her place. Miss P. A. Knight, of Lockport, N. Y., was also appointed an assistant in the normal department.

FACULTY.

EDWIN A. CHARLTON, A. M.,
President and Professor of Mental and Moral Science.

DUNCAN McGREGOR, A. M.,
Professor of Mathematics, and Conductor of Institutes, 1st District.

D. GRAY PURMAN, A. M.,
Professor of English Language and Literature.

GEORGE BECK, M. S.,
Professor of Natural Sciences.

CAROLYN E. ADAMS, Ph. B.,
Teacher of Reading and History.

PHILA A. KNIGHT,
Teacher of Arithmetic and Geography.

CHARLES H. NYE,
Principal of Academic Department.

EMELINE CURTIS,
Principal of Primary Department.

T. J. COLBURN.
Teacher of Vocal Music.

CALENDAR, 1874.

WINTER TERM, 12 weeks. From Tuesday, January 6th, to Friday, March 27th, 1874.

VACATION, one week.

SPRING TERM, 12 weeks. From Tuesday, April 7th, to Thursday, June 25th, 1874.

CLASS DAY, Wednesday, June 24th, 1874.

GRADUATING EXERCISES, Thursday, June 25th, 1874.

MEETING OF ALUMNI ASSOCIATION, Thursday eve., June 25th.

VACATION, nine weeks.

FALL TERM, 16 weeks. From Tuesday, September 1st, to Friday, December 18th, 1873.

VACATION, two weeks.

With profound gratitude to yourself and your associates in the Board of Regents, for the generous support you have given me, and for the confidence you have reposed in me,

I remain, with great respect,
Your obedient servant,
EDWIN A. CHARLTON.

REPORT OF THE PRESIDENT OF THE WHITEWATER NORMAL SCHOOL.

To the Hon. WILLIAM STARR,

President of the Board of Regents of Normal Schools:

The State Normal School at Whitewater has passed through another year of uninterrupted prosperity. The students in attendance as candidates for the teachers' work have numbered two hundred and twenty-four. The moral character of these students has been all the state can reasonably demand, and equal to that found anywhere in similar institutions. Their intellectual status is quite equal to those in attendance in former years. Whenever the institution, in the administration of its affairs, has called upon them for their support, they have responded as students ought in whose hands the state places such important trusts. In the discharge of their daily duties they have manifested an appreciation of their work by their earnestness and devotion to it.

FACULTY.

It gives me great pleasure to state that the Faculty are devoted to their work. No sacrifice in behalf of the institution seems too great for any of them to make. Thoroughly in earnest in promoting its welfare, they meet honestly and promptly the duties required of them. While the instution and its friends felt deeply the loss of Prof. T. C. Chamberlin, nevertheless it is a satisfaction to know that his services are not lost to the state. His place has been filled by Prof. H. E. Copeland, a young gentleman thoroughly prepared for his work. The addition of Prof. Albert Salisbury to the faculty has increased its efficiency, while his labors in the institutes must render valuable aid in the state work of instruction. Miss M. A. Terry, a thorough teacher in the training department, has been called to a responsible position in the Janesville High School. Miss Annie M. Green, a graduate of 1871, is filling acceptably Miss T.'s place.

An additional teacher is needed to take charge of penmanship and to assist in the general work of the school.

The following is the present organization of the

FACULTY.

OLIVER AREY, A. M.,
President, and Professor of Mental and Moral Philosophy.

H. E. COPELAND,
Professor of Natural Sciences.

S. S. ROCKWOOD, A. M.,
Professor of Mathematics and Elocution.

ALBERT SALISBURY, A. B.,
Professor of History and Conductor of Institutes.

MRS. H. E. G. AREY, A. M.,
Preceptress and Teacher of English Literature and Drawing.

MISS CATHERINE H. LILLY,
Teacher of Latin, German and Grammar.

MISS MARY DE LANY,
Teacher of Geography and Civil Government.

MISS ANNIE M. GREEN,
Principal and Critic in Academic Department.

HARVEY H. GREENMAN, D. D. S.,
Professor of Vocal Music.

MISS S. E. ELDREDGE,
Principal and Critic in Primary Department.

MISS VIRGINIA DEICHMAN,
Teacher of Instrumental Music.

WM. J. SHOWERS,
Librarian.

GRADUATES.

With two exception, the graduates are employed in their appropriate work. Some are holding important positions in State institutions. Some are laboring in the schools of the rural disiricts, others are in the ward and high schools in the cities and villages, and so far as I have knowledge of their work it is acceptable to those employing them.

GRADUATES' CALENDAR.

Names.	*Where teaching.*
Samuel Rockwell Alden	Buffalo, N. Y.
William E. Anderson	Waukesha, Wis.
George Morgan Bowen	Wausau, Wis.
Antoni Cajori	Milwaukee, Wis.
James Walter Congdon	Palmyra, Wis.
Andrew Jackson Steele	Tougaloo, Miss.
Charles Lewis Brockway	Not teaching.
Franklin Hiram King	Pursuing post graduate course.
Winnie Cole	Milwaukee, Wis.
Jennie Louise Fowler	Milwaukee, Wis.
Sarah E. Edwards	Madison, Wis.
Mary Colton	Chippewa Falls.
Margaret McIntyre	Delavan, Wis.
Mary McCutchan	Horicon, Wis.
Dora O'Connor	Elkhorn, Wis.
Hannah Stackpole	Married.
Eva Kinney	Cold Spring, Wis.
Annie Marie Green	Neenah, Wis.

Names.	*Where engaged.*
Mary De Lany................................	Whitewater, Wis.
Celia Almira Taylor..........................	Brodhead, Wis.
Helen Underwood Sturtevant....	Delavan, Wis.
Elmina Rice................................	Farmington, Wis.

GRADUATES, JUNE, 1878.

William J. Showers..........................	Blind Asylum, Wis.
Walter Allen................................	....
Foland P. Fowler............................	....
James Larkin................................	....
William McGoorty............................	....
Lyman C. Wooster............................	....
Jennie Church...............................	Lancaster, Wis.
Lilla C. Redington..........................	....
Margaret E. Conklin	Madison, Wis.
Caroline B. Weir............................	....
Alice Lacy	....
Ellen F. O'Connor	....
Marie L. Lewis	....
Ada H. Stone	....

UNDERGRADUATES.

The demand for the services of undergraduates has been unusually large, beyond the power of the school to supply. The labors of these students are not always successful. Some of them fail to accomplish the duties they attempt to perform, since all who present themselves as candidates for the teacher's profession cannot take upon themselves the responsibilities of the teacher's life, without giving more time to the labor of preparation than they think reasonable. But no more fail than fail among those following the other avocations of life. Others are successful and their services are much sought after and satisfactorily remunerated.

BUILDING.

The building in its general plan, is good, but in some of its special departments it is neither philosophical in its arrangement, nor sufficiently commodious to afford the best results. In the training department, studying and teaching are done in the same room, at the same time. Under such circumstances, neither teaching nor studying can be done as it ought. Waste of intellectual power must occur daily, since constant antagonisms exist between the efforts of the teacher before her class, and those of the pupil at his studies. The teacher, when occupied in the discussion of the subject of the lesson is the controlling current of thought in the room, and seriously disturbs the weaker mind of the pupil in the prosecution of his work. This confusion ought not to exist. The persistent flow of the youthful mind is feeble, and should not be turned from its purpose by any such unphilosophical arrangement of school room. A school room so planned divides the purpose of the school against itself, and may be compared to a train of cars with an engine attached at each end, steaming in opposite directions.

Should an engineer be so foolish as to perform an act like the above, he would be promptly dismissed, but teachers and school officers in the discharge of their duties, do as foolish an act daily, and are tolerated.

The rooms of the department of natural science are inadequate. The work done there requires more commodious rooms. A room larger than the present one, and more remote from the laboratory, is necessary, that the apparatus may be protected from the action of corroding gases. The laboratory is too small and inconvenient to admit of efficient instruction in the department of experimental chemistry. The lecture room is ample, and affords all needful facilities.

The members of the Board are respectfully invited to consider these points.

The grounds have been gradually improved since the opening of the school, but much remains to be done. The interests of the schools in the rural districts demand that the grounds of the normal schools should be cultivated to their highest practical point, since their educational force is as direct in the development of the ennobling powers of the mind, as any force connected with the institutions. It is very rare that the destructive nature, even of school boys, cannot be brought under pleasant control when they are introduced among well kept shrubs and flowers, while on the other hand, the hard trampled and offensive looking yards which surround many school-rooms, are well calculated to bring this nature into most active exertion. To let them lie uncared for, is to disregard the silent means which Providence has placed in the hands of men for the promotion of youthful welfare.

REPAIRS.

The room over the cabinet has been neatly fitted up for a text book library, which will afford accommodations for this department.

Rubber moulding has been put upon the stairs, preventing the further wear of them, and at the same time so deadening sound that the general movements of the school are made without inconvenience.

The heating apparatus, which has been the source of such discomfort, is now competent to warm the building in the coldest weather. The basement laboratory has been furnished with shelves tables, chairs and other conveniences suitable for dissecting, investigating and classifying such zoological specimens as it may be desirable for students to examine.

Attention has been called to this work because the public mind is manifesting a lively interest in it, and it would seem important that the teachers should cultivate this field to some extent that their intelligence may be abreast of public sentiment. What has been done in this direction has awakened considerable interest among the thoughtful students and the outlook is altogether encouraging.

CITIZENS OF WHITEWATER.

The citizens of Whitewater have ever given a hearty support to the school. They have opened their doors to the student, furnishing them with comfortable homes at the lowest possible rates. When the institution has needed moral or other support, it has not been wittheld. Willing hearts and willing hands have ever been extended to all connected with the school. They have thus shown their earnest desire to further the interests of the institution which the state has located in their midst, and they deserve the confidence placed in them.

CONCLUSION.

In conclusion, allow me to congratulate the board for the skill and efficiency with which the important trusts confided to them by the state have been managed, and to thank them for the many acts of official and personal kindness to the members of the school at Whitewater.

Very respectfully,

OLIVER AREY.

REPORT OF THE PRESIDENT OF THE OSHKOSH NORMAL SCHOOL.

HON. WM. STARR,

President Board of Regents of Normal Schools:

DEAR SIR: I herewith submit the report of the condition and organization of the Oshkosh Normal Schools for the school year ending June 18, 1873:

Total enrollment in the Normal Department........................ 261

	Gentlemen.	Ladies.	Total.
Fall term..	55	100	155
Winter term....................................	36	90	126
Spring term	46	97	143
Institute class (fall term).....................	15	22	37

No. of different pupils, exclusive of Institute class....................	224
Average membership..	127
Average daily attendance..	122.2
Applicants examined during the year..................................	170
Applicants admitted upon examination	132

Of the above enrollment—

13 have attended this school two years.

79 have attended this school one year, and less than two years.

50........do ....do..two terms........do .. three terms.

60........do..........do.. one.............do....two terms.

22........do..........do..less than one term.

36 taught winter terms of school during the year.

41 taught summer terms of school during the year.

70 are known to be teaching at the present writing.

31 counties of the state were represented in the department during the year.

During the present term 185 have been enrolled.

223 applicants have been examined.

103...........do......admitted.

ENROLLMENT IN MODERN SCHOOL.

	Boys.	Girls.	Total.
Grammar department	31	63	99
Intermediate department	26	32	58
Primary department	23	33	56
Total	85	128	213

The following extract from the last annual catalogue will show the present *Organization and Aims of the School.*

The school comprises two departments—the Normal and the Model school.

For the purpose of carrying into effect the provisions of the law under which normal schools were established, two courses for the normal department have been provided by the Board of Regents.

I. An Elementary Course.

II. A Higher Course.

The first is intended to fit teachers for work in grades below the the high school, whether graded or mixed, and consists of the first year of the subjoined higher course, with the addition of Botany, Physiology, Natural Philosophy, Physical Geography and Constitutions of the United States and of Wisconsin.

Pupils who take Latin, or other branches than those indicated in the higher course, are obliged to devote an additional amount of time.

It is earnestly recommended that four years be devoted to the work, that a better culture may be gained than is possible in the shorter time.

COURSE OF STUDY.

	Preparatory Class.	First Year.			Second Year.			Third Year		
	One to Three Terms.	Fall Term, 17 Weeks.	Winter Term 10 Weeks.	Spring Term, 13 Weeks.	Fall Term, 17 Weeks.	Winter Term, 10 Weeks.	Spring Term, 13 Weeks.	Fall Term, 17 Weeks.	Winter Term, 10 Weeks.	Spring Term, 13 Weeks.
Mathematics	Arithmetic.	Arithmetic.	Arithmetic.		Algebra.	Alegebra.	Geometry.	Geometry and Plane Trigonom'y.	Astronomy.	
Language.	Reading. Grammar.	Spelling. Reading.	Analysis of Words, Reading.	Grammar, (Et'y and (Syntax.)	English Analysis.	Rhetoric.	Criticism.			
Nat. Science	Geography.	Geography.	Lectures upon Laws of Health.		Botany (six weeks), Nat. Philosophy.	Nat. Philosophy, Physiology.	Botany.	Chemistry, Zoology.	Chemistry.	Physical Geography.
History and Science.				History of U. S.	Civil Government.	Civil Government.		Political Economy.	Mental Philosophy, General History.	Mental Philosophy, General History.
Gen'l Drills	Spelling. Penmanship.	Penmanship (half term), Vocal Music (half term.)	Vocal Music.	Vocal Music. Penmanship and Drawing.			Drawing.			Reviews.
Profession'l Instruction			Practice Teaching.	Practice Teaching.						
		Lectures, School Management, and Art of Teaching.			Class Work in Training School.			Lectures	Philosophy of Education.	School Laws of Wisconsin, School System.

ANALYSIS OF THE FIRST YEAR'S WORK.

First Term.

ARITHMETIC.—Principles and processes through compound numbers; fractions, with analysis of processes.

READING.—Elementary sounds, with marking of letters, and principles of pronunciation, according to Webster's Dictionary. Analysis of thought as a basis of *intelligent* reading.

SPELLING.—Rules for spelling, with applications; spelling (oral or written), of selected lists, with their Orthoepy. Methods of teaching.

GEOGRAPHY.—General view of the World with reference to form; comparison of Grand Divisions in location, contour, elevation, and the causes affecting climate. Outline Map—United States, North and South America and Europe. Special study of Wisconsin and United States. Chief islands, seas, lakes, cities and countries compared in respect to dimensions, direction and distance, orally and by diagrams. Methods of teaching.

PENMANSHIP.—Principles, their combination in *small* letters, with special attention to *shape*, *slant*, *height* and *space*. Methods in teaching.

MUSIC.—Drill upon rythm, reading and singing of scale, and reading plain music at sight.

OBSERVATION.—The pupils of the "first year class" are required to visit the different departments of the model school to examine, under specific directions, the methods of instruction, class and school management, and to present to the teacher of methods a written report of his observations.

Second Term.

ARITHMETIC.—Ratio and proportion; percentage, developent of its formulas and application to business. Business forms. Methods of teaching.

READING.—Critical analysis of thought, and drill upon expression. Methods of teaching.

WORD ANALYSIS.—Prefixes, suffixes and derivation of words.

Vocal Music.—Transposition of scale, reading in different keys, modulation; singing exercises.

Practice Teaching.—During the winter and spring terms class exercises are conducted by members of the "first year class," each in turn, in the presence of classmates and the teacher of methods. These exercises, involving the discussion of each elementary branch, are intended not only to be a close test of the pupil's executive ability and aptness to teach, but also to serve as practical illustrations of the directions given in lectures upon methods of instruction and class management.

Third Term.

Grammar.—Etymological forms; parsing of words in prose construction; correction of false syntax.

United States History.—Discoveries, and claims based upon them; chief settlements; revolution, causes, immediate and remote; development of the Union in territory and civilization. Method of teaching.

Drawing.—Linear—straight lines and angles. The training of the judgment in the determination of direction, distance and proportion, as well as giving facility to the hand and eye, is the leading feature of this half term course; simple designing of familiar objects, with methods of teaching young pupils.

Theory and Art of Teaching.—1. Organization and classification of schools. Programmes of recitation and study, their arrangement and utility.

Warming, ventilation and care of school-room.

2. Recitation—objects, methods, errors to be avoided, relative time occupied.

Study—objects, correct habits of study, adaptation to age and mental growth. Incentives to thought and observation.

Instruction—formal and informal.

3. Culture in manners and morals. Rights and duties of parents, pupils and teachers. Teacher's employment of time out of school hours, *rest*, *recreation*, *mental* and *social* culture.

Preservation of health and vigor, the teacher's duty. Requisites to efficient mental effort.

4. School Government—its *moral* aspect; authority, whence

derived; power, how exercised. Relative influence of different modes upon the present and future character of the pupil. Causes of disobedience. Peculiar *obstacles* and *aids* to school government considered. Teacher's *mental* and *moral* character, its controlling influence; enthusiasm, honesty and foresight.

5. Development of perception, memory, reasoning.—Order of studies adapted to mental growth, in accordance with the laws of mind.

Training of the senses, memory, judgment. Influence of habits of correct observation, upon memory and judgment. How correct the prevalent misuse of memory, and induce the better use of the senses and reason in the pupils work? Culture, through close attention, accurate statement, habits of association and illustration.

6. Specific methods of teaching each elementary branch.

MODEL AND TRAINING SCHOOL.

This school, consisting of three departments, Primary, Intermediate and Grammar, presents a well defined gradation of classes. Each room is under the constant charge of an experienced teacher, and the whole under the close supervision of the director.

These departments are intended:

1. To present to the pupils of the Normal Department, models of the methods best adapted to the management and instruction of pupils in the different stages of progress.

2. To afford opportunity for testing more fully the ability of each candidate for graduation, in systematic class work.

The course of oral instruction in Botany, Zoölogy aud Natural Philosophy, is intended to cultivate habits of close and intelligent observation of the facts and laws intimately connected with our daily life.

SCHEDULE OF STUDY.

SEVEN GRADES—THREE ROOMS.

Department	Grades	
PRIMARY—Grades,	1. 2.	Each grade requires one year's work.
INTERMEDIATE—Grades,	3. 4. 5.	
GRAMMAR—Grammar,	6. 7.	

Primary Department.

FIRST GRADE—SECTION B.

1. Reading from blackboard, 30 minutes each day.
2. Printing or Writing } On slate, 25 minutes each day.
3. Oral instruction on familiar objects, also instruction in morals and manners. Animals wild and tame. 30 minutes each day.
4. Drawing, lines and angles, 15 minutes each day.
5. Recess, extra, 30 minutes each day.
7. Music, 12 minutes each day.
7. Physical exercises, 15 minutes each day.
8. Opening exercises, 15 minutes each day.

General recesses, and music exercise, 30 minutes each day.

Total, 3 hours each day.

FIRST GRADE—SECTION A.

1. Reading, 1st Reader, 30 minutes each day.
2. Writing, on slate, with arm movement, 25 minutes each day.
3. Oral instruction, familiar objects, botany, summer, 30 minutes each day.
4. Numbers, count backwards and forwards, and write to 100, Roman and Arabic, 15 minutes each day.
5. Drawing, combination of straight lines and angles, 15 minutes each day.
6. Recess, extra, 30 minutes each day.
7. Physical exercises, 15 minutes each day.
8. Music, 12 minutes each day.

SECOND GRADE.

1. Reading, 2d Reader, 15 minutes each one-half day.
2. Writing, simple analysis, 25 minutes each day.
3. Oral instruction, in connection with map and globe, comparing objects not familiar with those known, 30 minutes each day.
4. Arithmetic (oral and written), without book, from slate and blackboard, with numbers not to exceed 3 orders, 15 minutes each day.
5. Drawing, curves, 15 minutes each day.
6. Spelling, from reading book, 15 minutes each half day.
7. Music, 15 minutes each day.
8. Physical exercises, 15 minutes each day.

[Remark. The above schedule leaves 40 minutes for teacher to render judicious aid to pupils in regard to *difficulties*, and how to study.]

Intermediate Department.

THIRD GRADE.

1. Reading, 2d Reader begun, 40 minutes each day.
2. Writing, general, 25 minutes each day.
3. Oral instruction, in connection with geography, outline maps, general, 30 minutes each day.
4. Arithmetic, with book, 25 minutes each day; 10 mental, 15 written.
5. Language, parts of speech, beginning of composition, how to talk, general, 25 minutes each day.
6. Drawing, design begun, general, 15 minutes each day.
7. Spelling, 15 minutes each day.
8. Music, general, 15 minutes each day.
9. Physical exercises, 10 minutes each day.
10. Opening exercises, recess, music, 45 minutes each day.

FOURTH GRADE.

1. Reading, 3d completed and 4th begun, 20 minutes per half day.
2. Writing or drawing, 25 minutes each day.
3. Oral instruction, in connection with geography, outline maps, morals and manners, general, 30 minutes each day.
4. Arithmetic, 25 minutes each day.
5. Language, general, 25 minutes each day.
6. Spelling, 15 minutes each day.
7. Music, 12 minutes each day.
8. Physical exercises, 10 minutes each day.

This schedule for Room 2 leaves three-quarters of an hour for assistance.

Grammar Department..

FIFTH GRADE.

1. Reading, 4th Reader completed, 25 minutes each day.
2. Writing or Drawing, general, 30 minutes each day.
3. Oral Instruction, Natural History or Botany, General, 20 minutes each day.
4. Geography, 25 minutes each day.
5. Aritmetic, 25 minutes each day.
6. Grammar, Etymology, 25 minutes each day.
7. Spelling, 15 minutes each day.
8. Music, general, 15 minutes each day.
10. Opening Exercises, Recesses, general Music exercise, 45 minutes each day.

By receiving aid from Normal Department for 50 minutes reading, and 25 minutes geography, the teacher of 5 and 6 grades has three-quarters of an hour to render assistance.

SIXTH GRADE.

1. Reader, 5th Reader begun, 25 minutes each day.
2. Writing (Correspondence), or Drawing, general, 30 minutes each day.
3. Oral Instruction, Natural History or Botany, 25 minutes each day.
4. History and Geography, 25 minutes each day.
5. Arithmetic, 25 minutes each day.
6. Grammar, syntax, 40 minutes each alternate day.
7. Spelling, rules, 15 minutes each day.
8. Music, general, 15 minutes each day.
9. Physical exercises, 10 minutes each day.

SEVENTH GRADE.

1. Reading, 5th Reader, 25 minutes each day.
2. Writing, book-keeping or drawing, 40 minutes each day.
3. Oral instruction, biography and natural philosophy, 20 minutes each day.
4. History and geography, 20 minutes each day.
5. Arithmetic, 40 minutes each day.
6. Grammar, analysis and false syntax, 40 minutes each day.
7. Spelling, rules, lists and analysis of words, 20 minutes each day.
8. Music, general, 15 minutes each day.
9. Physical exercises, 10 minutes each day.

AIMS OF THE SCHOOL.

The foregoing outline of study gives an imperfect idea of the school work. The fact that it is knowledge *acqaired*, rather than learning *imparted*, which gives mental grasp and power, shapes the method in every exercise.

In giving the needful academic culture, a correct method of dealing with mind, is impressed by a careful unfolding of mental processes, in the pupil's experience with each branch, so as to substitute habits of correct and definite thinking, for thoughtless memorizing.

Certain branches are dwelt upon, until a clear understanding of the processes by which they are built up is gained, while others, because of limited time, are treated more briefly, and with especial reference to the information which they contain.

In the former class are the elementary, or "common school" branches; those natural sciences which most nearly concern daily work and life, and those branches which tend most directly to cultivate logical thought and definite expression.

RECORDS OF STUDENTS.

A record of each pupil's standing in recitations and written examinations is kept, and the pupil's fitness to pass from any branch is determined by the combined average of his class-standing and final examination.

DISCIPLINE AND SUPERVISION.

Experience has proved that knowledge and method in instruction are of little worth without prompt and close attention to school duties, on the part of every pupil.

The discipline of the school is, therefore, closely observant of all departures from needful regulations. The student is expected to exhibit in his deportment all those qualities which he would have displayed bv pupils in his own school. His character for courtesy, industry and integrity, will, beyond mere scholarly attainments, mark his fitness for the teacher's work.

ADMISSION.

Pupils are admitted at any time, but it is very desirable that they enter at the beginning of the fall or spring term, as new classes are organized then. Those who may not be able to enter until the middle of the fall term will find it best to enter at the earliest date possible, as no advantage will be gained in waiting until the winter term.

EXPENSES.

1. Tuition in the Normal Department is *free* to all students who sign the declaration of intention to teach.

2. All text-books needed by the pupil are furnished by the state, for a rent of $1 term.

3. Board, including furnished room, fuel and lights, costs from $3 to $3.50 a week. Rooms for self-boarding can be had at low rates, many pupils bringing the expense for board and room within $2 a week.

4. Pupils desiring the discipline of the school, but not wishing to teach, are admitted to classes upon the payment of tuition.

5. Pupils who fail to enter the Normal Department upon examination, are fitted in the Grammar Department of the Model School.

TERMS OF TUITION IN MODEL SCHOOL.

Grammar Department, - - -	50 cents a week.
Intermediate " - - -	40 " "
Primary " - - -	30 " "

LIBRARY AND READING ROOM.

An excellent reference library is furnished for the use of the students, including the standard works in history, biography, science, professional and general literature, so that the student may readily carry his investigations beyond the text-book.

The students and faculty have organized a reading-room, where the leading periodicals are furnished at a nominal cost to each pupil.

CABINET AND APPARATUS.

A cabinet of minerals, shells and corals is already formed, which, with additions soon to be made, will afford much aid in illustration.

An excellent philosophical apparatus has been furnished during the past year.

LITERARY SOCIETY.

A lyceum, organized by the students, holds regular sessions each week. These exercises are a most profitable auxiliary to the school work, in training to habits of independent thought and expression.

The departments of the Model School have proved an efficient auxiliary in developing methods of teaching. The school is now fully organized and conducted by teachers who have brought the work to a high degree of excellence. All methods employed are intended to be thoroughly practicable for teachers in mixed schools; and, to this end, neither extensive apparatus nor books are permitted to usurp the province of the teacher who is the center and inspirer of the work.

All needless formality is excluded as constituting a stumbling block to the young teacher; yet class discipline is maintained at all points, that the student may become imbued with a high ideal in class and school management.

The "practice work" of the normal students is conducted under critical supervision of a teacher, and a daily record is made of the merits and defects in each students's work. In the work, much attention is paid to methods of primary instruction, since they constitute the basis of all teaching, and are so imperfectly understood by most teachers. Frequent class exercises are conducted by pupil teachers in presence of the normal students.

FACULTY.

The following is the present organization of the Faculty of the school:

GEORGE S. ALBEE, *President*,
Teacher of Mental and Social Science, and School Management.

ROBERT GRAHAM,
Teacher of Music and Reading, and Conductor of Institutes.

HENRY C. BOWEN,
Teacher of Natural Science.

MISS ANNA W. MOODY,
Teacher of History, Rhetoric and Composition.

MISS MARY H. LADD,
Teacher of Mathematics.

MISS MARTHA E. HAZARD,
Teacher of Drawing, Penmanship and Calisthenics.

MRS. HELEN A. BATEMAN,
Teacher of Reading and Grammar.

Model School.

ROBERT GRAHAM,
Director.

MISS MARIA S. HILL,
Teacher in Grammar Department.

MISS FRANCES E. ALBEE,
Teacher in Intermediate Department.

MISS ROSE C. SWART,
Teacher in Primary Department.

By reference to the tabular statement of attendance, you will observe that more than one-half of the pupils attended less than one year. This disproportion is the greater because of the fact that this is but the second year since the opening of the school, and the enrollment greatly in excess of the preceding year. There is an increasing tendency among the pupils to devote more time to preparation before entering upon permanent work; but until greater wealth furnishes the means, or greater permanence stronger inducements, a large part of the work here must be for the first-year class. From this class must nearly all the mixed, and many departments of the graded schools, obtain whatever supply is furnished by normal schools. Yet with the present grade of culture possessed by candidates, one year does not suffice to impress the subject matter of the elementary branches and give definite shape to their methods of instruction.

If the excellent "elementary course," framed by the Board of Regents last winter, could be made, by law, the basis of a limited state certificate, after due examination by a competent committee, it would, in my opinion, afford a stronger incentive to culture than the full diploma of the school; since it would be *attainable* by the great majority of those who intend to teach but a few years. It is true, that to complete this course worthily, will require nearly or quite two years discipline, but the tangible reward of a certificate, good throughout the state for three or five years, would in most cases add the second year's work to the culture possessed by the teachers of this state.

Each term's experience but deepens the conviction that our chief efforts should be directed to firmly establishing pupils in a knowledge of the elements which they are to teach, rather than in attempting a wider range of study, to leave them weak and timid in their daily duties. It shall be our earnest endeavor to train pupils to an intimate sympathy with this work.

Very respectfully yours,

G. S. ALBEE.

REPORT OF THE COMMITTEE ON INSTITUTE WORK.

HON. WM. STARR,
President Board of Regents of Normal Schools:

SIR: The undersigned, having been designated by the committee on institutes to become associated with the state superintendent in the arrangement, supervision and management of the institute work, and having been instructed to report to the board, I have the honor to submit the following:

Under instructions from the board, the committee proceeded, immediately after the last semi-annual meeting, to divide the state into institute districts, and to designate Profs. R. Graham, D. McGregor and A. Salisbury as institute conductors in the districts thus designated. These gentlemen were able to conduct personally nearly the entire number of institutes held in the spring, and the work performed was reported much more satisfactory and valuable than that which was practicable under the system of one agent to direct, with such assistance in managing as it was possible to extemporize.

The same may be said of the institutes held this fall—the universal testimony being in favor of the new arrangement, which insures the presence of a conductor of experience and skill during the entire term, and by the saving of time in passing from point to point during the institute season, renders it possible to do much more work with no increase of expense. The policy of your committee, in affording aid in conducting short term institutes, has been to co-operate with county superintendents, furnishing a conductor and paying such incidental necessary expenses as were not properly chargeable to the county by the county superintendent. It is hoped one of the incidental benefits which will result from this course will be the help it has afforded the county superintendents to a more critical and effective discharge of their important duties. The demand for this and longer institute work is increasing from year to year, involving more and more expenditure of money and greater impression upon teachers and their work, and it becomes a matter of vital importance to so guide and control it, that the means thus expended shall not be squandered or perverted to impress the teachers and teaching of the state for evil rather than for good.

In preparing for the normal institutes to be held, it was thought best by your committee to appoint, at Sparta, for one week immediately preceding the meeting at that place of the State Teachers' Association, an institute for institute conductors. A programme was arranged, topics and class work were assigned to various individuals, and essays and exhibitions of practical institute work were subjected to the careful scrutiny and close criticism of the very best teachers in the state. The results fully vindicated the wisdom of the measure. Uniformity of plan, precision and order in method, unity and definiteness of purpose, were clearly and greatly promoted, while much that would otherwise have crept in, which was not only of doubtful utility, but positively useless, if not harmful, was prevented. A syllabus, which embodied the results and conclusions of this work, was prepared by Prof. Graham, and issued by the committee for the guidance of conductors. It proved a great help, and a decided improvement upon anything hitherto attempted in the state. In visiting the institutes in Dunn, Juneau, Grant, Sauk, Wood, Waupaca, Racine and Dane counties, I found the different conductors closely following the syllabus, and uniformly testifying that the more it was studied and comprehended, the better was it liked for itself and for its adaptation to the purpose intended.

It is a matter of congratulation that this important element in our educational forces has now become systematized; that it is now not only recognized as a force, but assigned its proper place, and thus brought into harmonious co operation with academic normal school collegiate and university instruction. There ought to be, and there is, no real antagonism between any of these parts of our whole educational system. Their spheres of operation are distinct, but point to a single end. The eminent workers in one department are often found of the highest use in other departments.

When all the parts of the educational work are as distinctly classified, it may be dignified by the name of a system.

I refer to the report of the State Superintendent for statistics showing the number of institutes held, and the number attending them, remarking only in passing, that in all these points they have exceeded those of any previous year largely, while the aggregate amount expended in the work, has not been largely increased.

One further point remains to be noticed. That concerns the

effect upon the normal schools, of appointing an active professor in the faculty, to be a conductor of institutes, and thus withdrawing a teacher, during term time, from each of the schools, for a part of two terms.

The effect of this arrangement upon the institute work is certainly happy,—good, and only good. The effect upon the schools has been made the subject of careful inquiry, and I have visited the schools at Platteville and Whitewater during the absence of teachers there for this purpose, in order to ascertain by observation, as well as inquiry, the facts. That it somewhat interrupts the regular work, cannot be denied. But this interruption is far less than at first thought would seem probable, and not, in the judgment of all interested and consulted, so detrimental as to affect the advantages of the plan, which brings the normal school into such vital and close relations with the common schools of the State, as to enable them to labor more intelligently in the furnishing of teachers for their work in them, as well as acquaints the teachers, actual and embryo, with the work and province of the normal schools. I would recommend that authority be given the Presidents to employ, during the absence of professors in institute work, students who are qualified to conduct recitations, at such compensation as will be just and reasonable.

In closing this report, I desire to add my testimony thus publicly to that of the teachers among whom they have been employed, of the great service and eminent ability displayed by the conductors of institutes appointed by the committee from the Normal Schools, and also by Prof. Parker, of Janesville; Barnes, of Kenosha; Thayer, of Menominee; North, of Waukesha, and Hutton, of Eau Claire. The work of these coming under my own observation, I speak advisedly and unqualifiedly in its praise.

Respectfully submitted,

W. H. CHANDLER,
Committee.

SUN PRAIRIE, Oct. 20, 1873.

REPORTS OF EXAMINING COMMITTEES.

PLATTEVILLE NORMAL SCHOOL.

To Hon. Samuel Fallows,
State Superintendent of Public Instruction.

Sir:—Agreeable to section 34 of chapter 151 of the General Laws of 1869, the Committee appointed to visit Platteville Normal School, begs leave to report as follows, for the year ending August 31, 1873.

Two members of the Committee visited the Normal School together, January 8 and 9, and again June 15 and 16—the third member visited alone, July 23, 24, 25 and 26.

The Committee submits the following general opinions upon which their judgment of the Platteville School is based.

An organization designed for the special training of men and women as teachers, implies more than the Academy, more than the High School, in its faculty, it demands the power to train, to drill in methods upon matter. No pouring in, no drawing out, no mere teaching will in any good degree give the youth command of his capabilities as a teacher. No mere good nature, no cheerful address, nor ambition of the student can accomplish this result. A trainer is as necessary for each position in the Normal School, as are students with special adaptability necessary for teachers. No person who simply hears recitations, no mere school-master can be tolerated in any position in a training school. He whose business it is to teach thoroughly and to train systematically, must not only be full of the subjects to be taught, but he must be conscious of ability to train others to his own plan of thought and action. Normal students should be thoroughly trained in the principles which underlie whatever they are to teach in the future; and the application of those principles should be so broad and numerous that students will never fail to recognize them wherever found, and however disguised or related.

The supervisor of the various departments of school,—or of any other work having a single objective point,—must be so positive as to stamp the product of that work with the manner of the supervisor. The trainer must make an indelible impress as to matter, if the product of his labor, in turn, is to make a positive impression.

Judged by this standard, it is the opinion of this committee that the Platteville Normal School does not represent the possibilities of such an organization under reasonable management. This committee is unable to say that the school is as efficient as it should be, in view of the numerical strength of the teachers and students. Your committee believes that the school is not so strong as desirable in its general supervision, and in the supervision of practice teaching; and that in certain branches it measurably fails to impress its students with the force of ideas, in contradistinction to language, considered simply as language. There seems to be a want of power in directing the work promptly and certainly to objective points, as shown in the class movements and in some recitations.

The effort to work the school to the course of study implies superficial instruction, and, in fact, accounts for the want of intense application to particular topics, and for the habit of mental ease rather than intellectual strength. The limited time and great range of thought imposed by the course of study, and the effort made by the faculty to meet these demands, can only defeat the aims which the educator has in view. The course of study shows that only one term and eight weeks are given to such important branches as geometry and natural philosophy, and but one term is given to each of such branches as English grammar, physiology, physical geography, local geography, United States history, and chemistry.

This committee respectfully objects to any attempt "to furnish well qualified teachers for the public schools of the State of Wisconsin," by completing any of these studies in the time specified. Every teacher understands how subjects must continually grow upon students, and how time is necessary for the development of the understanding; and it is believed that, for the average mental power, little can be done in such limited periods, especially when the catalogue of 1872–3 specially states that, in addition to instruction in three ponderous branches throughout the course, "students will receive instruction and drill in reading, penmanship, vocal music, drawing, composition, declamation and physical exercises through the course." It seems to this committee that normal students, before all others, should give so much thought to all topics which elicit any special training, as to create a *habit* of thought on these topics, rather than to cram for spcial recitations; and it is believed that no average normal student can do himself lasting credit, or his pupils any permanent, essential service, by spending only the time specified in the course, in any of the subjects mentioned. This committee considers the lack of adjustment of time for training and amount of work required, so serious an obstacle to the formation of proper *habits* of thought and action in the normal student, that the opinion takes form, and it is therefore, recommended that the Regents and Faculties of the Normal Schools adjust the course of study to the capabilities of the average normal student.

This committee believes that the Platteville Normal School is already wielding a broad and beneficent influence, and that it deserves the moral support of the citizens of the state; yet the committee is of the opinion that if there is wisdom in the law providing for annual visitation by other persons than the Board of Normal School Regents, it is the duty of such visitors to criticise with discrimination; and this committee would be understood by these comments, as simply endeavoring to do an ultimate service to general education in the state.

All of which is respectfully submitted.

W. D. PARKER,
ALEX. KERR,
C. M. TREAT,
Committee.

AUGUST 31, 1873.

WHITEWATER NORMAL SCHOOL.

HON. SAMUEL FALLOWS,
Superintendent of Public Instruction:

DEAR SIR: As chairman of your committee appointed to visit the Whitewater Normal School, I beg leave to present the following report:

Agreeable to your wishes, the committee visited the school twice during the year, and were pleased to find it in excellent running order. From the opening exercises to the closing at night, no exceptions could be taken tn the general good order that prevailed· President Arey is a master workman, ably assisted by Mrs. Arey and a corps of first class teachers. The class drill is good; the physical exercises are superior, and the moral character of the school is above reproach.

Thus much I am warranted in saying for the entire committee; but having been called to a different field of labor, I have not been able to meet the committee and consult as to a general report. I have written them to make any suggestions to the state superintendent that they may see fit, believing this to be better than to longer delay my report. As a member of the committee I may be allowed to express my opinion upon one feature of the normal schools, which I do not remember to have seen discussed by any committee. It seems to me that there are many students now attending who are physically or otherwise unfit to become successful teachers. It appears to me that a more rigid examination, as to natural ability, should be instituted. In the report of the committee of '72, the teachers are spoken of as being over-worked, and more teachers needed. I have no doubt of the truth of this statement, but if a critical examination could be made by the president of the school and members of the Normal Board of Regents, and all be rejected who are evidently incapacitated to meet the demands of a successful teacher, there would be less cause for complaint in this direction. No doubt, the drill received would make better citizens of this class of young men and women, and in that way the state be benefited.

Respectfully submitted,

W. A. De LA MATYR.

OSHKOSH NORMAL SCHOOL.

Hon. Samuel Fallows,

State Superintendent of Public Instruction:

Your committee appointed to visit the Oshkosh Normal School, beg leave respectfully to report as follows:

In accordance with your request, we visited the school twice during the year.

Our first visit was near the close of the fall term, when the school was full and in the pursuit of its regular work. Our second visit was in the spring term. We found much in the organization, management and working of the several departments of the school, that met our hearty approval. The discipline seemed most excellent. The earnestness of the pupils in the pursuit of their studies, was very remarkable, and worthy of imitation by every school in the state. We have never seen their diligence and industry surpassed by the pupils of any other institution which it has been our privilege to visit.

We saw recitations conducted by every teacher employed in the school, and we are convinced by our observations that the effort of faculty, is to make independent thinkers, and fit the pupils for the special work of teaching as well as for that of good and useful citizens.

At our first visit we had some fear lest there was a tendency to over work, but at our second, we thought we saw an improvement in this respect. Pupils in all our schools should be trained to put forth continuous, concentrated mental effort, but relaxation and recreation should be judiciously intermingled with all school work. In this respect the "normal" should be a model, as well as in all other things regarding public education.

The discipline of the school in all its departments is such as to give personal culture and to inculcate good morals, and yet seemed to us as incidental to the work of mental training. Special attention is given to position in standing, in walking and sitting, and no clownish or boorish conduct was observed.

In reference to these matters, we never saw better training with results so good, and we would commend it to the notice of all teachers as well worthy of ther strict imitation.

We were highly pleased with the results exhibited in vocal music; it is a prominent exercise in all the departments, and we never saw better evidences of good instruction in this most important department of education than in this institution. We never heard the singing equaled in any public school.

The modes of instruction pursued in the model departments we heartily commend to the attention of all who have charge of primary schools. If they were more generally pursued, the results obtained in our public schools would be far more satisfactory, a large amount of time and expense would be saved, and so much physical and mental effort would not be misdirected, and far better scholars would be the result.

In the normal department there seemed to be perfect freedom of action on the part of pupils during recesses, pleasant conversation was carried on, and yet there was no boisterous language and no rules of propriety and decorum were infringed upon.

It is an interesting question as to what shall be the character of our normal schools. What they should aim to be there is no doubt.

We think that all who have given the subject careful attention, will admit that a large share of the work must be academic for a long time to come. Didactics must receive attention more or less, and the more the better. Schools of practice must be established as rapidly as possible, still, at present, academic and primary work must claim paramount attention. The normal school cannot be transplanted full-grown to our soil, but must grow up with and out of our school system, and give it direction. We must not be impatient for great results. They will come by and by under a good administration of our normal affairs. We are led to these observations by what we have seen of the material which the normal teachers have to work upon. It is crude, and when received is unfit to enter upon didactics as a speciality. As our school system develops in all its parts, the true normal work will be entered upon. For so desirable a thing we must labor and wait.

We feel ourselves unfitted to enter upon any general criticism, so far as the programme of studies is concerned, or as to the general policy of the Oshkosh school in reference to its scheme of work.

There is, we are aware, much difference of opinion among our educators in regard to the functions of the normal school. We have some opinions upon the subject, but they may be mere theory. There may be a differerence of opinion as to the length and character of the course of study, as to whether the pupils entering the school qualified merely for a third grade certificate, should be put upon a course of study having reference merely to the work of teaching, whether such a curriculum does not tend to a narrowness of view and not toward mental development, whether the common or the higher branches should receive most attention, whether the curriculum should be purely English or English and classic combined, and also in reference to other important questions affecting the interest of our public education.

We do not propose to discuss in this report these points, interesting as they are, but commend them to the careful and judicious consideration of our Normal Regents, believing they will abate no efforts to make the "Normal" all that we have a right to expect.

We think, however, that the so called common branches, alone, do not give culture and breadth of thought. They deal too much with particular facts, and not enough with general principles to secure so desirable a result.

It is remarked in our colleges that thorough and real culture are not developed until the student enters upon what may be called the intellectual studies of the course. If the students in our normal schools are trained mainly in the common branches, the tendency will be to narrowness and bigotry. It seems to us that if the students enter the "Normal" with the qualifications required by law, they should enter at once upon the pursuit of some one of the higher branches. We think, too, that if Latin forms a part of the programme, as it should, it ought to be commenced at the very outset. Most of our graded schools require instruction in Latin, and if it be placed so late in the course, the young men will not have time fit themselves to give instruction in this branch. A thorough training in Latin gives discipline that cannot be surpassed by that derived from any other study. It includes grammar, rhetoric, cultivation of taste, judgment and a general knowledge of language.

It should be the aim of all schools not only to impart information and give instruction to the student but to train him to work out his processes independently of the teacher, and to give him that desire for knowledge that shall impel him to study even after he leaves the school. We think the Oshosh school is laboring faithfully to accomplish this desirable end. The student is required not only to state the fact, but to point out all its relations and bearings; not only to recite, but rigidly demonstrate the propositions laid down.

Respectfully submitted,

A. O. WRIGHT,
J. C. PICKARD,
B. M. REYNOLDS,
Committee.

La Crosse, Wis, Nov. 10, 1873.

INSTITUTE WORK,

1873.

To those Persons who Conduct and those who Attend Institutes:

The work of training the youth of this state to habits of thought, industry and usefulness is one of grave importance.

Properly to lay the foundation of true greatness, broad and deep, so that good citizenship shall result, is worthy of careful attention.

Considerable time and money are being expended by the state in order to prepare teachers for their duties.

A meeting of gentlemen interested in the work was called at Sparta, July 2–8, to mature a plan of institute work for the state, that there might, if possible, be unity of effort. After careful consideration, the accompanying schedule has been prepared to guide you in your duties.

While considerable time ought to be given to methods of presentation and detail of plan, yet much *class work* is needed, so that the subject taught, as well as the *manner* of *teaching*, shall be well understood. In this a *clear comprehension* of a subject does not necessarily involve minuteness of detail.

The *quality* and not the *quantity* should be the aim, in the short time allowed. To accomplish this, the institute must be, as far as possible, a *model school.*

The recitations should be models; the *manners*, *deportment*, *punctuality*, models. Thus the spirit emanating from these meetings will permeate the subsequent life of each teacher.

As a great amount of work is laid out, it is recommended that the class be numbered, and divided into two sections by the even and and numbers.

No. 1 reciting one day in *Reading*, *Geography*, *Grammar*, and No. 2 listening; the same day, No. 2 reciting in *Arithmetic*, *Spelling* and *History*, while No. 1 is listening. The next day, No. 1 recites in *Arithmetic*, *Spelling* and *History*, and No. 2 in *Reading*, *Geography* and *Grammar*.

In this manner a healthy competition will secure in recitations a fair standard of perfection, while the pupils will not be overburdened with so *much* work as not to do *any well*.

It is recommended that the *conductor* and *assistant*, shall prepare each day a scheme of the work they wish to accomplish, so that there may be *point* and *freshness* in the recitation.

Also that but one evening lecture per week be given, as the evenings should be devoted to study and preparation for the daily work.

Also that *one* daily exercise in class work be conducted as a *model*, by a pupil, to be followed by criticism from critics previously appointed.

Each conductor shall cause a full record of *attendance*, *deportment* and *daily plan of work* to be made, and at the close of the institute, forwarded to the state superintendent at Madison.

To this schedule is appended a programme of *study* and *recitations* in mixed schools, not as a pattern but as suggestive. Also a scheme for the study of botany for one term.

SYLLABUS.

SCHEDULE OF DAILY WORK.

				h. m.	
2. Reading	45	min.	per day—	3.45	per week.
2. Arithmetic	45	"	"	3.45	"
3. Geography	35	"	"	2.55	"
4. Spelling and Analysis of words	25	"	"	2.50	"
5. Penmanship and Drawing	20	"	"	1.40	"
6. Grammar	35	"	"	2.55	"
7. History and Constitution	40	"	"	3.20	"
8. Opening Exercises, Roll Call	15	"	"	1.15	"
Recesses	30	"	"	2.30	"
Physical exercises	10	"	"	0.50	"
9. Critical Class Drill, Criticism	30	"	"	2.30	"
10. Methods of Teaching Theory and Art, Lecture or Discussion	30	"	"	2.30	"

Morning session begin at 9 o'clock.
Afternoon session at 1.30 o'clock.

READING.

Time 45 minutes—divided into two parts—(*a*) first part 25 minutes, (*b*) second part 20 minutes.

FIRST WEEK.

Second Day. First Part.—Lecture on importance of Reading, and on the manner of treating cases of *Defective Articulation.*

Second Part.—*Powers* and *Markings* of *a.*

Third Day. First Part.—Method of conducting recitations in *Primary Reading* (1) with reference to *beginners;* (2) with reference to first and second Reader Classes.

Second Part.—*Powers* and *Markings* of *e* and *i.*

Fourth Day. First Part.—Continuation of third day's work.

Second Part.—*Powers* and *Marking* of *o* and *u.*

Fifth Day. First Part.—Drill in *Spelling* by sound.

Second Part.—Written review of above second part work, with *five* words to illustrate each vocal element.

SECOND WEEK.

First Part.—During the remainder of the term give attention in every exercise to *analysis of thought*, and let that be followed by reading with reference to the *laws of expression.* Confine the reading this week to *one descriptive* or *narrative*, selection, with special attention *Pitch.*

Second Part.—The letters representing *Vocal Sounds*, called *Vocal Substitutes* with *five* illustrative words for each sound.

THIRD WEEK.

First Part.—Read an *argumentative* piece giving attention to *Rate* and *Force.*

Second Part.—Classification of consonants, *Powers* and *Markings.*

FOURTH WEEK.

First Part.—Read *one* piece in Verse or in Dialogue, giving attention to *Qualities* of *Voice* and to manner of breathing, *Effusive, Expulsive* and *Explosive*, with written Review of the whole.

Second Part.—Powers of *vowels* in *unaccented* syllables, with drill on *accent*, with written Review of the whole.

ARITHMETIC.

Forty-five minutes daily to be devoted to it. Fifteen minutes at the beginning of each exercise for the first two weeks, to be given in illustration of methods used in *oral teaching* This part of the time for the last *two* weeks, to be given to *Mental Arithmetic.* The remaining half hour for whole sessions as follows;

FIRST WEEK.

1. *Decimal Scale*—local value of figures.
2. *Decimal Scale*—with reduction, numeration and notation.
3. *Addition* and *Subtraction.*
4. Multiplication.
5. Division.

SECOND WEEK.

1. Factoring:—(1) Any factor. (2) Greatest. (3) Two nearest equal (4) Groups by two. (5) Prime. (6) Roots.
2. Least Common Multiple.
3. Greatest Common Divisor.
4. General Principles and Reduction of Fractions.
5. Addition and Subtraction of fractions.

THIRD WEEK.

1. Multiplication af Fractions.
2. Division of Fractions.
3. Complex Forms.
4. Relation to Decimals.
5. Denominate numbers.

FOURTH WEEK.

1.
2. } Percentage, with its different cases.
3.

4. Percentage: Applications.
5. Business papers.

GEOGRAPHY.

Time daily 35 minutes. Acquaint the class with the elements of *Geographical description: known objects.*

FIRST WEEK.

a. Kinds of land, as *hilly, level, prairie, rolling.*
b. Kinds of water, as lake, brook, river.
c. Productions: 1. Mineral—Soil, rocks. 2. Vegetable—Plants, Trees. 3. Animal—Wild, tame.
d. Direction, } School Room—School Grounds—developing the idea of foot
e. Distance, } yard, rod, mile.

Compare the above respectively with *unknown* objects.

SECOND WEEK.

1. With Globe and Map of the World show the necessity of a common starting point of Measurement: *Equator* and *Meridian.*
2. Shape of the Earth. Reasons.
3. Line, Points, Circles (great and small), Zones.
4. Variable length of a Degree of Longitude.
5. Definitions—illustrating land and water—(Black-board work.)

THIRD WEEK.

1. Day and Night; Change of Sesasons. Causes.
2. Outline Map—North America: (1.) Indentations, as Capes, Bays. (2.) Mountain Systems. (3.) Rivers. (4.) Political Divisions. (5.) Cities. Same for Europe.

FOURTH WEEK.

1. Represent on Blackboard (on scale of 20 miles to an inch) a square of 50 inches on each side and draw with reference to area Islands, States, Lakes, and with reference to distance, cities.
2. Map Drawing and description of.
3. 4. Wisconsin, as follows: (1.) Indentations. (2.) Elevations. (3.) Waters. (4.) Climate. (5.) Soil. (6.) Mineral Products. (7.) Civilization. (8.) Productions, exports, imports. (9.) Cities. (10.) Railroads and navigable rivers. (11.) Counties, Towns, Townships. (12.) Comparative areas, comparing Texas, N. Y., Va., Mass.

SPELLING.

Time, 25 minutes each day.

FIRST WEEK.

Lists of twenty-five words each day not spelled by rule, but frequently misspelled.

SECOND WEEK.

Two rules of spelling, with words to illustrate *rules* and *exceptions*.

THIRD AND FOURTH WEEKS.

Word Analysis by prefix and suffix (holding closely to this work, as it is invaluable to the pupil.)

NOTE.—*One exercise* during the last week on *method* of using the *Spelling Book*, and *one* in *Oral Spelling* by the whole class,

PENMANSHIP.

Daily Exercise, 20 minutes (2 weeks).

First Day.—Specimen of penmanship secured from each member of Institute. Attention given to positions of hands, feet, body, and manner of holding pen. Movement drill, 5 minutes. (Note.) This movement drill for 5 minutes should precede each day's work.

Second Day.—*Slant*—Make lines 1, 2 and 3 units in length, a portion of class at the board. Write on board and paper. Criticisms confined to slant.

Third Day.—*Height*—Comparative height of letters; *u* taken as the standard. Scale formed. Writing on board and paper. Criticisms confined to slant and height.

Fourth Day.—*Form*—Small letter principles and manner of combining. Special attention to angles, turns and points of intersection.

Fifth Day.—Analysis of small letters to *m*.

Sixth Day.—Analysis of remaining small letters.

Seventh Day.—Capital principles and analysis of capitals.

Eighth Day.—Right and wrong forms of letters. Tests applied to specimens presented the first day. Methods of criticism applied.

Ninth Day.—Preparatory drill with reference to class work. Lecture on materials and care of them.

Tenth Day.—Regular school work, 10 minutes. Questions answered.

Eleventh Day.—Epistolary forms.

Twelfth Day.—Written review.

DRAWING.

To succeed Penmanship—20 minutes daily.

Thirteenth Day.—(1) Idea of line—*beginning Point, ending Point.* (2) Direction—*vertical, horizontal, oblique.* (3) Dimension of lines—(1) Undetermined. (2) Specific. Linear standard to be taught.

Fourteenth Day.—Combination of lines to form *angles.* (1) Right angle. (2) 2 Right Angles. (3) 4 Right Angles. (4) *Acute* and (5) *Obtuse* angles in like manner. (1) *Undetermined* and (2) specific lines to be used.

Fifteenth Day.—Combinations of 3 lines—*triangles.* (1) Right-angled, *Isosceles*, Equilateral, Scalene.

Sixteenth Day.—Combinations of 4 lines—quadrilaterals. Same manner as (15).

Seventeenth Day.—Combinations of more than 4 lines.

Eighteenth Day.—Formation of Roman Capital Letters, using straight lines.

Nineteenth Day.—Applications, familiar objects, as ladder, rake, window.

Twentieth Day.—Outline of work in curved lines, to teachers.

NOTE.—Each daily lesson should open with a review.

GRAMMAR.

DAILY EXERCISE THIRTY-FIVE MINUTES.

First Day.—State the province of Grammar; show *what* may be taught to to younger pupils, and *how* to teach it.

Second Day.—Analysis of the simple sentence: (1) declarative, (2) interrogative, exclamatory; the class having been directed to bring *four* examples of each kind.

Third Day.—Introduce the *noun.* Class write lists of nouns, *proper* and *common*, on the blackboard, giving equivalents of one class in those of the other. Here and always require strict attention to spelling, capital letters, penmanship, and orderly arrangement.

Fourth Day.—Introduce the *verb* in connection with the nouns used the day previous, so as to form sentences. Analyze sentences thus made.

Fifth Day.—Introduce the *pronoun*, showing the necessity for it. Have the pupils give numerous sentences in which the pronoun is properly used. Place these upon the board and substitute nouns for the pronouns.

Sixth Day.—Introduce the *adjective*, showing the necessity for it. Let the pupils make numerous sentences containing all the parts of speech now known. Analyze. Here recognize the adjective phrase and clause.

Seventh Day.—Introduce the *adverb*, requiring the class to provide sentences illustrative of the various kinds. Here recognize adverbial *words*, *phrases* and *clauses*.

Eighth Day.—Illustrative lesson showing how the detached sentences already made may be combined into a composition. Connections to be developed here.

Ninth Day.—Compare and contrast *adjective* and *adverbial* modifiers.

Tenth Day.—Have the class bring in a composition, " What I have learned about Grammar." Those to be retained for exercises on false syntax.

Eleventh Day.—Properties of noun and pronoun.

Twelfth Day.—Pupils to furnish sentences, showing these properties. Parse.

Thirteenth Day.—Declension of personal pronouns, showing changes made for *Gender*, *Person*, *Number*, *Case*.

Fourteenth Day.—Pronouns continued. Compare and contrast *Personal* with the other classes of pronouns. Pupils to furnish sentences for this purpose.

Fifteenth Days.—Properties and classes of verbs.

Sixteenth, Seventeenth and Eighteenth Days.—Conjugation of verb (developing law.)

Nineteenth Day.—Correction of false syntax noticed during the Institute.

Twentieth Day.—Review the work. Bring to the notice of the class any difference of treatment, which the subjects may require in school, from that in the Institute.

HISTORY.

Time. 40 minutes daily for two weeks.

First Day.—Spanish claims.

Second Day.—French claims.

Third Day.—English claims.

Fourth Day.—Dutch claims.

Fifth Day.—Kinds of Colonies. (Royal, Proprietary, Charter.)

Sixth Day.—French and Indian War and results.

Seventh Day.—Causes of Revolution.

Eighth Day.—Campaigns of Revolution. (Leaders, Battles.)

Ninth Day.—Treaties and results.

Tenth Day.—Written Review.

CONSTITUTIONS.

Time, same as History.

Eleventh Day.—The Confederation; its *origin*, *peculiarities* and *defects*.

Twelfth Day.—The Constitution; points of improvement on confederation. Preamble, things taught by it.

Thirteenth Day.—Representation in government; (1) what share of the people meet for law making; (2) who are counted as the people; (3) what are the qualifications of a legislator; (4) manner of electing; (5) privileges and emoluments. The two branches of Legislative Department being treated separately or comparatively.

Fourteenth Day.—Continuation of the same; *powers* and *duties* of the two houses.

Fifteenth Day.—The President; manner of election and duties.

Sixteenth Day.—The Cabinet; powers and duties of heads of departments.

Seventeenth Day.—Citizenship; naturalization; state electorship.

Eighteenth Day.—Compare critically the legislative department of State government with United States.

Nineteenth Day.—In like manner compare the Executive departments. Vice President and Lieutenant Governor.

Twentieth Day.—Written Review.

ALGEBRA.

Time of recitation 45 minutes, outside of regular institute work.

First Day.—Connection of Algebra and Arithmetic. Illustrations.

Second Day.—Connection of Algebra and Arithmetic. Illustrations.

Third Day.—General Definitions—Classify Symbols.

Fourth Day.—Review—Idea of *Positive and Negative Quantities.*

Fifth Day.—Addition—Relation to Arithmetic. Cases. Axioms or Principles.

Sixth Day.—Subtraction—Cases, law of signs, Axioms or Principles.

Seventh Day.—Multiplication, law of signs, relative to Arithmetic.

Eighth Day.— do law of Exponents.

Ninth Day.— do of Binomials.

Tenth Day.— do Theorems I. II. III.

Eleventh Day.—Division, law of signs.

Twelfth Day.—Division, laws of Exponents.

Thirteenth Day.—Theorem $x^0=1$.

Fourteenth Day.—Theorem $\frac{1 \quad -2}{x^2 \quad x.}$

Fifteenth Day.—Factoring, Monomials, Binomials.

Sixteenth Day.—Factoring, Binomials.

Seventeenth Day.—Greatest Common Divisor and Least Common Multiple.

Eighteenth Day.—Fractions, Reduction, ascending, descending.

Nineteenth Day.—Symbols of 0, ∞, $\frac{0}{0}$.

Twentieth Day.—Review.

GEOMETRY.

First Day.—Introduction; idea of line, surface, solid.

Second Day.—Definition and classification of lines and angles, and formation of polygons, especially trirngles.

Third Day.—Review; axioms.

Fourth Day.—Theorem treating of straight lines and their intersections.

Fifth and Sixth Days.—Same subject.

Seventh Day.—Triangles and their classification.

Eighth, Ninth, Tenth, Eleventh and Twelfth Days.—The orems (1 per day) re lating to triangles.

Thirteenth Day.—Quadrilaterals; classification.

Fourteenth, Fifteenth, Sixteenth and Seventeenth Days.—Theorems relating to quadrilaterals.

Eighteenth Day.—Polygons; classifications and theorems.

Nineteenth Day.—Theorem or problem.

Twentieth Day.—Review.

APPENDIX.

NATURAL SCIENCES.

In view of the difficulty attending the introduction of new branches of study into the mixed schools of the state, it is recommended that work be done upon Botany and Physiology only; the former in the summer months and the latter in the winter.

PLAN OF WORK FOR BOTANY.

(1.) *Leaves.*—
- (1) Parts.
- (2) Form.
- (3) Venation.
- (4) Margin.
- (5) Kinds.
- (6) Arrangements on stem.
- (7) Use.

(2.) *Flowers.*—
- (1) Parts. (*a*) Sepals. (*b*) Petals. (*c*) Stamens. (*d*) Pistils. (Seed vessel.)
- (2) Form, color.
- (3) Arrangement on stem.
- (4) Purpose of.
- (5) Adaptation of parts to purposes.

(3) *Stem.*—
- (1) Parts.
- (2) Modes of growth.
- (3) Kinds.
- (4) Uses.

(4) *Roots*—
- (1) Parts.
- (2) Kinds.
- (3) Uses.

(NOTE.) In nearly every advance step in *term* or *classification*, let the specimen be in the pupil's hand. Let a constant *review* be kept up by a description of leaves and flowers previously presented by the pupil, naming the plant described, where known: *e. g.* "The leaf of the elm is ovate, doubly serrate, rough," etc.

PROGRAMME FOR MIXED SCHOOLS.

STUDY.

Time	Study
9.00 to 9.10.	Opening exercises.
9.10 to 9.20.	Gen. Ex. (Oral.) Fundamental Operations. Arithmetic.
9.20 to 9.30.	"A" Arith. 1st, 2d and 3rd Readers.
9.30 to 9.40	" " 2d and 3d Readers, Primer Print.
9.40 to 9.50	" " 3d Reader.
95.0 to 10.05	" " 2d " Recess.
10.05 to 10.25.	"B" " 2d " 1st Reader Copy Numbers.
10.25 to 10.45.	
10.45 to 11.00.	
11.00 to 11.15.	"A" Geography, "B" Arithmetic.
11.15 to 11.35.	" "
11.35 to 11.45.	"B" Spelling, "A" Geography.
11.45 to 12.00.	"B" Spelling, 1st Reader Drawing Objects
1.10 to 1.20.	"A" Reading, "B" Geography, 2d Reader.
1.20 to 1.35.	" " " "
1.35 to 1.55.	"B" Geography. 1st and 2d Reader Drawing Objects.
1.55 to 2.15.	"A" Grammar. "B" Geography.
2.15 to 2.20.	" "
2.20 to 2.45.	
2.45 to 3.00.	
3.00 to 3.20.	"B" Spelling.
3.20 to 3.35.	"A" Spelling. 2d Reader Study Map.
3.35 to 3.50.	"B" Spelling. 2d Reader Study Map.
3.50 to 4.00.	Gen. Ex. on Outline Map.

This programme is suggested as a guide, not a pattern. Circumstances will modify the number of exercises. The order and relative amount of time have been carefully considered. The General Exercise is deemed an important part of the school work, and earnestly commended to the attention of teachers. Considering the variety of matter to be presented, it is thought advisable that several branches be presented in a weekly series, as suggested for 3d Gen. Ex., or in proportionate parts of a term.

"A" and "B" classes in Arithmetic and Geography are considered as nearly corresponding to the 4th and 3d Reader classes; "B" Spelling to include after the 3d and 2d Reader classes, wholly or in part.

PROGRAMME FOR MIXED SCHOOLS.

RECITATION.

9.20 to 9.10. Opening Exercises.
9.10 to 9.20. General Exercises.—Numbers; fundamental operations.
9.20 to 9.30. Primer.
9.30 to 9.40. 1st Reader.
9.40 to 9.50. 2d Reader.
9.50 to 10.05. 3d Reader.
10.05 to 10.25. "A" Arithmetic.
10.25 to 10.45. Penmanship.
10.45 to 11.00. Recess.
11.00 to 11.15. "C" Arithmetic.—Rudiments (oral.)
11.15 to 11.35. "B" Arithmetic (text-books.)
11.35 to 11.45. Primer.
11.45 to 12.00 "A" Geography.
12.00 to 1.00. Recess.
1.00 to 1.10. General Exercise; *Music or Language.*
1.10 to 1.20. 1st Reader.
1.20 to 1.35. 2d Reader.
1.35 to 1.55. 4th Reader.
1.55 to 2.05. Primer.
2.05 to 2.20. "B" in Geography.
2.20 to 2.45. General Exercise.—*History* 2 days, *Biography* 1 day, *Constitution* 1 day, *Physiology* or *Botany* 1 day.
2.45 to 3.00. Recess.
3.00 to 3.20. "A" Grammar.
3.20 to 3.35. "B" Spelling.
3.35 to 3.50. "A" Spelling.
3.50 to 4.00. General Exercise on Outline Maps of Wisconsin or United States.

POINTS OF THEORY AND PRACTICE.

(1.) Mixed schools; organizing and classifying.
(2.) Programme; study and recitation.
(3.) School records and regulations.
(4.) Time of teacher out of school, how employed.
(5.) Care of pupils; in relation to food, dress, recreation, sleep, labor.
(6.) School discipline; opening exercises, movements of classes, recesses, communications, punishment.
(7.) Relative rights and duties of pupils, teacher, patrons, school board, superintendent.
(8.) Examination of teachers; contract.

(9.) Recitations, manner of conducting, end in view, written and oral; review, examination.

(10.) Rhetorical exercises.

(11.) Oral instruction.

(12.) Manner and habits of teacher and pupil.

(13.) Sanitary regulations of school room and grounds.

(14.) Care of school building and property.

The above Syllabus has been prepared by Prof. ROBT. GRAHAM, at our request.

SAMUEL FALLOWS, *Supt. Pub. Ins.*,
W. H. CHANDLER,
WM. E. SMITH,
Committee on Institutes.

APPENDIX.

STATISTICAL TABLES.

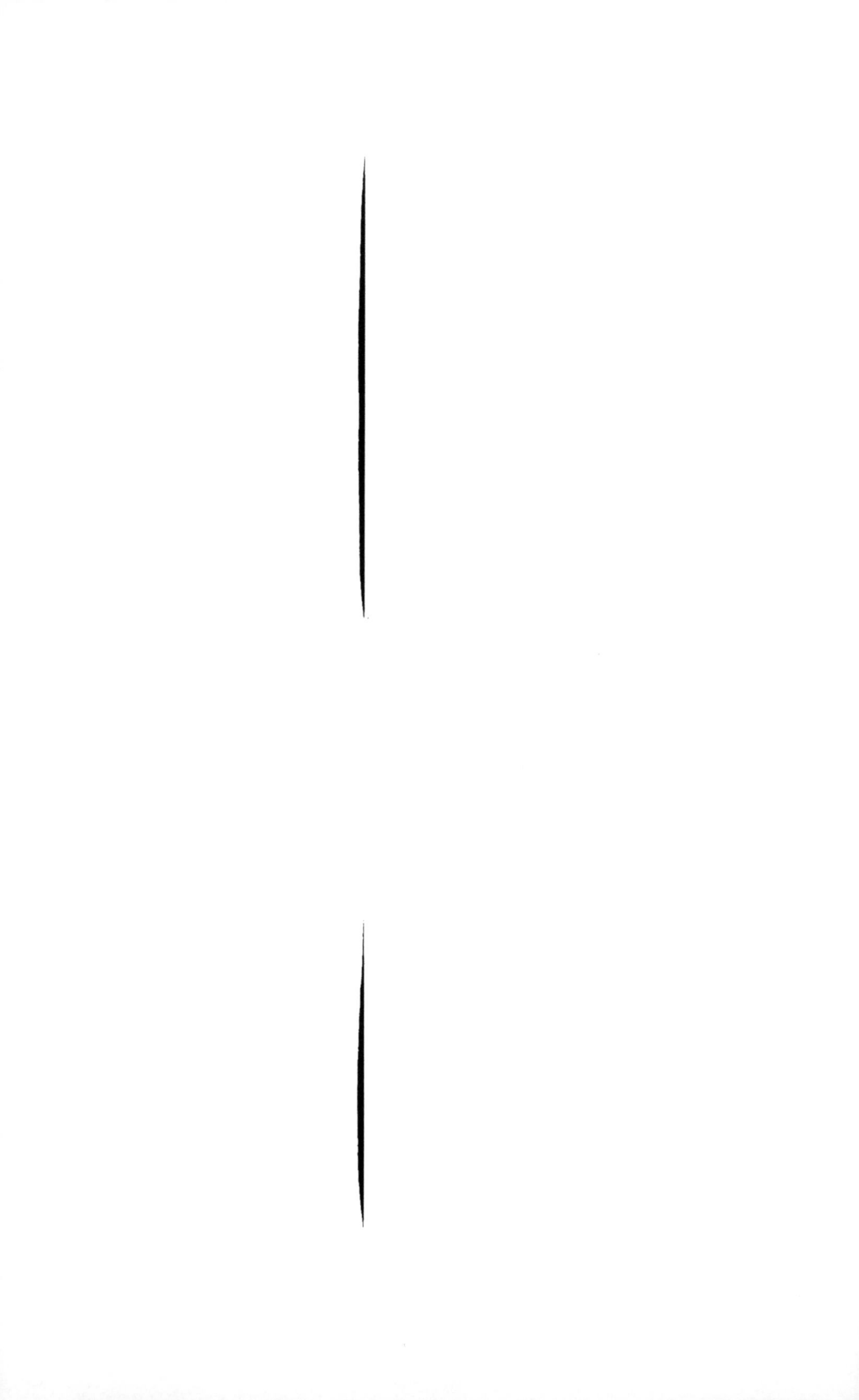

TABLE No. I.

APPORTIONMENT OF SCHOOL FUND INCOME

FOR 1873.

Counties and Towns.	No. of Children.	Apportionment.
ADAMS COUNTY.		
Adams	172	$72 24
Big Flats	26	10 92
Dell Prairie	166	69 72
Easton	117	49 14
Jackson	212	89 04
Leola	57	23 94
Lincoln	198	83 16
Monroe	155	65 10
New Chester	142	59 64
New Haven	383	160 86
Preston	70	29 40
Quincy	97	40 14
Richfield	105	44 10
Rome	62	26 04
Springville	138	57 96
Strong's Prairie	380	159 60
White Creek	78	32 76
Totals	2,558	$1,074 36
BARRON COUNTY.		
Barron	322	$135 24
BAYFIELD COUNTY.		
Bayfield	176	$73 92
BROWN COUNTY.		
Bellevue	322	$135 24
Depere	251	105 42
Depere, village	588	246 96
Eaton	1,182	76 44
Fort Howard	1,136	477 12
Glenmore	301	126 42

TABLE I.—*Apportionment of School Fund Income*—continued.

COUNTIES AND TOWNS.	No. of Children.	Apportionment.
BROWN COUNTY—continued.		
Green Bay	386	162 12
Green Bay, city	1,781	748 02
Holland	704	295 68
Howard	531	223 02
Humbolt	298	125 16
Lawrence	290	121 80
Morrison	542	227 64
New Denmark	353	148 26
Pittsfield	259	108 78
Preble	551	231 42
Rockland	350	147 00
Scott	618	259 46
Suamico	370	155 40
West Depere	422	177 24
Wrightstown	648	272 16
Totals	10,883	$4,570 86
BUFFALO COUNTY.		
Alma	180	$75 60
Alma, village	225	94 50
Belvidere	229	96 18
Buffalo	199	83 58
Buffalo, city	115	48 30
Canton	284	119 28
Cross	277	116 34
Dover	135	56 70
Fountain City	351	147 42
Gilmanton	143	60 06
Glencoe	269	112 98
Lincoln	183	76 86
Maxville	191	80 22
Milton	142	59 64
Modena	305	128 10
Montana	204	85 68
Naples	396	166 32
Nelson	541	227 22
Waumandee	386	162 12
Totals	4,755	$1,997 10
BURNETT COUNTY.		
Grantsburg	294	$123 48
CALUMET COUNTY.		
Brillion	329	138 18
Brothertown	682	286 44
Charlestown	526	220 92
Chilton	635	266 70
Harrison	724	304 08

TABLE I.—*Apportionment of School Fund*—continued.

COUNTIES AND TOWNS.	No. of Children.	Apportionment.
CALUMET COUNTY—continued.		
New Holstein	764	$320 88
Rantoul	407	170 94
Stockbridge	840	352 80
Woodville	535	224 70
Totals	5,442	$2,285 64
CHIPPEWA COUNTY.		
Anson	99	$41 58
Bloomer	690	289 80
Chippewa Falls	684	287 28
Eagle Point	600	252 00
Edson	133	55 86
La Fayette	323	135 66
Sigel	87	36 54
Wheaton	250	105 00
Totals	2,866	$1,203 72
CLARK COUNTY.		
Beaver	105	$44 10
Eaton	123	51 66
Grant	189	79 38
Levis	92	38 64
Loyal	226	94 92
Lynn	50	21 00
Mentor	155	65 10
Pine Valley	384	161 28
Weston	258	108 36
Totals	1,582	$664 44
COLUMBIA COUNTY.		
Arlington	361	$151 62
Caledonia	500	210 00
Columbia	952	399 84
Courtland	512	215 04
Dekorra	539	226 38
Fort Winnebago	310	130 20
Fountain Prairie	492	206 64
Hampden	390	163 80
Leeds	462	194 04
Lewiston	442	185 64
Lodi	583	244 86
Lowville	302	126 84
Marcellon	336	141 12
Newport	653	274 26
Otsego	651	273 42
Pacific	112	47 04
Portage City	1,539	646 38

TABLE I.—*Apportionment of School Fund Income*—continued.

COUNTIES AND TOWNS.	No. of children.	Apportionment.
COLUMBIA COUNTY—continued.		
Randolph	449	$188 58
Scott	334	140 28
Springdale	322	135 24
West Point	348	146 16
Wyocena	479	201 18
Totals	11,068	$4,648 56
CRAWFORD COUNTY.		
Clayton	684	$287 28
Eastman	585	245 70
Freeman	542	227 64
Haney	251	105 42
Marietta	212	89 04
Prairie du Chien	446	187 32
Prairie du Chien, city	1,532	643 44
Scott	381	160 02
Seneca	565	237 30
Union	153	64 26
Utica	523	219 66
Wauzeka	456	191 52
Totals	6,330	$2,658 60
DANE COUNTY—1st District.		
Albion	463	$194 46
Blooming Grove	426	178 92
Bristol	494	207 48
Burke	388	162 95
Christiana	650	273 00
Cottage Grove	494	207 48
Deerfield	427	179 34
Dunkirk	407	170 94
Dunn	495	207 90
Medina	529	222 18
Pleasant Springs	459	192 78
Sun Prairie	328	137 76
Sun Prairie, village	227	95 34
Stoughton, village	335	140 70
Windsor	466	195 72
York	362	152 04
Totals	6,950	$2,919 00
DANE COUNTY—2d District.		
Berry	490	$205 80
Black Earth	358	150 36
Blue Mounds	500	210 00
Cross Plains	659	276 78
Dane	426	178 92
Fitchburg	490	205 80

TABLE 1—*Apportionment of School Fund Income*—continued.

COUNTIES AND TOWNS.	No. of Children.	Apportionment.
DANE COUNTY—*2d District*—continued.		
Madison	326	$136 92
Madison, city	3,963	1,664 46
Mazomanie	666	279 72
Middleton	717	301 14
Montrose	447	187 74
Oregon	541	227 22
Perry	454	190 68
Primrose	441	185 22
Roxbury	556	233 52
Rutland	416	174 72
Springdale	467	196 14
Springfield	615	258 30
Vermont	480	201 60
Verona	429	180 18
Vienna	395	165 90
Westport	496	208 32
Totals	14,332	$6,019 44
DODGE COUNTY—*1st District*.		
Beaver Dam	666	$279 72
Beaver Dam, city	1,352	567 84
Calamus	509	213 78
Clyman	545	228 90
Elba	618	259 56
Emmett	524	220 08
Fox Lake	675	283 50
Lowell	1,010	424 20
Oak Grove	719	301 98
Portland	571	239 82
Randolph, village	109	45 78
Shields	464	194 88
Trenton	714	299 88
Westford	435	182 70
Totals	8,911	$3,742 62
DODGE COUNTY—*2d District*.		
Ashippun	608	$253 26
Burnett	366	153 72
Chester	308	129 36
Herman	745	312 90
Hubbard	1,371	575 82
Hustisford	708	297 36
Lebanon	679	285 18
LeRoy	672	282 24
Lomira	923	387 66
Rubicon	781	328 02
Theresa	828	347 76
Waupun, village	367	154 14
Williamstown	891	374 22
Totals	9,242	$3,881 64

TABLE 1—*Apportionment of School Fund Income*—continued.

COUNTIES AND TOWNS.	No. of Children.	Apportionment.
DOOR COUNTY.		
Bailey's Harbor	125	$52 50
Brussells	251	105 42
Clay Banks	178	74 76
Egg Harbor	87	36 54
Forestville	207	86 94
Gardner	94	39 48
Gibralter	197	82 74
Jacksonport	40	16 80
Liberty Grove	135	56 70
Nasewaupa	156	65 52
Sevastopol	159	66 78
Sturgeon Bay	310	130 20
Union	199	83 58
Washington	138	57 96
Totals	2,276	$955 92
DOUGLAS COUNTY.		
Superior	362	152 04
DUNN COUNTY.		
Colfax	82	34 44
Dunn	358	150 36
Eau Galle	373	156 66
Elk Mound	152	63 84
Grant	276	115 92
Lucas	155	65 10
Menomonie	875	367 50
New Haven	115	48 30
Peru	77	32 34
Red Cedar	286	120 12
Rock Creek	114	47 88
Sheridan	46	19 32
Sherman	178	74 76
Spring Brook	511	214 62
Stanton	158	66 36
Taintor	65	27 30
Weston	143	60 06
Totals	3,964	1,664 88
EAU CLAIRE COUNTY.		
Bridge Creek	492	206 64
Brunswick	203	85 26
Eau Claire	1,483	622 86
Lincoln	375	157 50
Otter Creek	372	156 24
Pleasant Valley	130	54 60
Seymour	63	26 46
Union	201	84 42
Washington	212	89 04
Totals	3,531	$1,483 02

TABLE I.—*Apportionment of School Fnnd Income*—continued.

COUNTIES AND TOWNS.	No. of Children.	Apportionment.
FOND DU LAC COUNTY—1st District.		
Alto	584	$245 28
Eldorado	711	298 62
Fond du Lac	577	242 34
Fond du Lac, city	5,441	2,285 22
Friendship	457	191 94
Lamartine	586	246 12
Metomen	593	249 06
Oakfield	465	195 30
Ripon	447	187 74
Ripon, city	1,008	423 36
Rosendale	437	183 54
Springvale	493	207 06
Waupun	466	195 72
Waupun, village	371	155 82
Totals	12,636	5,307 12
FOND DU LAC COUNTY—2d District.		
Ashford	801	336 42
Auburn	768	322 56
Byron	550	231 00
Calumet	654	274 68
Eden	663	278 46
Empire	422	177 24
Forest	614	257 88
Marshfield	786	330 12
Osceola	572	240 24
Taycheedah	685	287 70
Totals	6,515	2,736 30
GRANT COUNTY.		
Beetown	751	315 42
Bloomington	486	204 12
Blue River	315	132 30
Boscobel	660	277 20
Cassville	571	239 82
Clifton	441	185 22
Ellenboro	349	146 58
Fennimore	745	312 90
Glen Haven	428	179 76
Harrison	406	170 52
Hazel Green	855	359 10
Hickory Grove	365	153 30
Jamestown	442	185 64
Lancaster	1,121	470 82
Liberty	496	208 32
Lima	399	167 58
Little Grant	361	151 62
Marion	294	123 48

TABLE I.—*Apportionment of School Fund Income.*—continued.

COUNTIES AND TOWNS.	No. of Children.	Apportionment.
GRANT COUNTY—continued.		
Millville	81	$34 02
Mount Hope	297	124 74
Muscoda	374	157 08
Paris	374	157 08
Patch Grove	321	134 82
Platteville	1,336	561 12
Potosi	1,119	469 98
Smelser	498	209 16
Waterloo	393	165 06
Watterstown	283	118 86
Wingville	351	147 42
Woodman	271	113 82
Wyalusing	328	137 76
Totals	15,511	$6,514 62
GREEN COUNTY.		
Adams	446	$187 32
Albany	532	223 44
Brooklyn	537	225 54
Cadiz	578	242 76
Clarno	615	258 30
Decatur	794	333 48
Exeter	345	144 90
Jefferson	660	277 20
Jordan	492	206 64
Monroe	1,481	622 02
Mount Pleasant	475	199 50
New Glarus	415	174 30
Spring Grove	490	205 80
Sylvester	345	144 90
Washington	298	125 16
York	448	188 16
Totals	8,951	$3,759 42
GREEN LAKE COUNTY.		
Berlin	382	$160 44
Berlin, city	1,067	448 14
Brooklyn	499	209 58
Green Lake	494	207 48
Kingston	340	142 80
Mackford	507	212 94
Manchester	436	183 12
Marquette	409	171 78
Princeton	592	248 64
St. Marie	259	108 78
Seneca	161	67 62
Totals	5,146	$2,161 32

TABLE I.—*Apportionment of School Fund Income*—continued.

COUNTIES AND TOWNS.	No. of Children.	Apportionment.
IOWA COUNTY.		
Arena	926	$388 92
Clyde	307	128 94
Dodgeville	1,559	654 78
Highland	1,370	575 40
Linden	750	315 00
Mifflin	598	251 16
Mineral Point	675	283 50
Mineral Point, city	1,362	572 04
Moscow	487	204 54
Pulaski	587	246 54
Ridgeway	1,086	456 12
Waldwick	400	168 00
Wyoming	300	126 00
Totals	10,407	$4,370 94
JACKSON COUNTY.		
Albion	705	$296 10
Alma	444	186 48
Garden Valley	374	157 08
Hixton	446	187 32
Irving	491	206 22
Manchester	162	68 04
Melrose	426	178 92
Northfield	209	87 78
Springfield	367	154 14
Totals	3,624	$1,522 08
JEFFERSON COUNTY.		
Aztalan	427	179 54
Cold Spring	273	114 66
Concord	584	245 28
Farmington	1,171	491 82
Hebron	487	204 54
Ixonia	647	271 74
Jefferson	1,421	596 82
Koshkonong	1,156	485 52
Lake Mills	560	235 20
Milford	618	259 56
Oakland	405	170 10
Palmyra	601	252 42
Sullivan	704	295 68
Sumner	191	80 22
Waterloo	458	192 36
Waterloo, village	229	96 18
Watertown	1,012	425 04
Watertown, city	3,633	1,525 86
Totals	14,577	$6,122 34

TABLE I.—*Apportionment of School Fund*—continued.

COUNTIES AND TOWNS.	No. of Children.	Apportionment.
JUNEAU COUNTY.		
Armenia	95	$39 90
Clearfield	85	35 70
Fountain	252	105 84
Germantown	219	91 98
Kildare	294	123 48
Lemonweir	442	185 64
Lindina	390	163 80
Lisbon	136	57 12
Lyndon	200	84 00
Marion	126	52 92
Mauston	369	154 98
Necedah	526	220 92
New Lisbon	465	195 30
Orange	136	57 12
Plymouth	372	156 24
Seven Mile Creek	447	187 74
Summit	339	142 38
Wonewoc	429	180 18
Totals	5,322	$2,235 24
KENOSHA COUNTY.		
Brighton	493	$207 06
Bristol	394	165 48
Paris	317	133 14
Pleasant Prairie	512	215 04
Randall	228	95 76
Salem	516	216 72
Somers	489	205 38
Wheatland	364	152 88
Kenosha, city	1,566	657 72
Totals	4,879	$2,049 18
KEWAUNEE COUNTY.		
Ahnepee	649	$272 58
Carlton	580	243 60
Casco	372	156 24
Franklin	457	191 94
Kewaunee	863	362 46
Lincoln	324	136 08
Montpelier	320	134 40
Pierce	617	259 14
Red River	400	168 00
Totals	4,582	$1,924 44

TABLE I.—*Apportionment of School Fund Income*—continued.

Towns and Counties	No. of Children.	Apportionment.
LA CROSSE COUNTY.		
Bangor	476	$199 99
Bums	380	159 60
Campbell	233	97 86
Farmington	687	288 54
Greenfield	301	126 42
Hamilton	894	375 48
Holland	392	164 64
La Crosse, city	3,256	1,367 52
Onalaska	605	254 10
Shelby	246	103 32
Washington	380	159 60
Totals	7,850	$3,397 00
LA FAYETTE COUNTY.		
Argyle	455	191 10
Belmont	500	210 00
Benton	717	301 14
Blanchard	189	79 38
Darlington	1,141	479 22
Elk Grove	369	154 98
Fayette	474	199 08
Gratiot	689	289 38
Kendall	397	166 74
Monticello	238	99 96
New Diggings	750	315 00
Seymour	412	173 04
Shullsburg	1,217	511 14
Wayne	434	182 28
White Oak Springs	216	90 72
Willow Springs	427	179 34
Wiota	761	319 62
Totals	9,386	$3,942 12
MANITOWOC COUNTY.		
Cato	796	$334 32
Centerville	662	278 04
Cooperstown	741	311 22
Eaton	672	282 24
Franklin	776	325 92
Gibson	776	325 92
Kossuth	968	406 56
Liberty	657	275 94
Manitowoc	511	214 62
Manitowoc, city	2,441	1,025 22
Manitowoc Rapids	820	344 40
Maple Grove	605	254 10
Meeme	698	293 16
Mishicott	727	305 34
Newton	888	372 96

TABLE I.—*Apportionment of School Fund Income*—continued.

COUNTIES AND TOWNS.	No. of Children.	Apportionment.
MANITOWOC COUNTY—continued.		
Rockland	480	201 60
Schleswig	776	325 92
Two Creeks	223	$93 66
Two Rivers	1,364	572 88
Totals	15,581	6,544 02
MARATHON COUNTY.		
Bergen	35	$14 70
Berlin	380	159 60
Jenny	52	21 84
Knowlton	48	20 16
Maine	304	127 68
Marathon	189	79 38
Mosinee	154	64 68
Stettin	275	115 50
Texas	100	42 00
Wausau	165	69 30
Wausau, city	490	205 80
Weston	159	66 78
Wien	42	17 64
Totals	2,393	$1,005 06
MARQUETTE COUNTY.		
Buffalo	323	$135 66
Crystal Lake	257	107 94
Douglas	273	114 66
Harris	196	82 32
Mecan	318	133 56
Montello	391	164 22
Moundville	172	72 24
Neshkoro	165	69 30
Newton	261	109 62
Oxford	241	101 22
Packwaukee	254	106 68
Shields	263	110 46
Springfield	110	46 20
Westfield	247	103 74
Totals	3,471	$1,457 82
MILWAUKEE COUNTY.—*1st District.*		
Franklin	734	$308 28
Greenfield	898	376 16
Lake	1,444	606 48
Oak Creek	920	386 40
Totals	3,996	$1,678 32

TABLE I.—*Apportionment of School Fund Income*—continued.

COUNTIES AND TOWNS.	No. of Childeen.	Apportionment.
MILWAUKEE COUNTY—*2d. District.*		
Granville	919	$385 98
Milwaukee	1,430	600 60
Milwaukee, city	27,359	11,490 78
Wauwatosa	1,318	553 56
Totals	31,026	$13,030 92
MONROE COUNTY.		
Adrian	259	$108 78
Angelo	198	83 16
Clifton	208	87 36
Glendale	354	148 68
Greenfield	223	93 66
Jefferson	379	159 18
La Fayette	196	82 32
Leon	284	119 28
Lincoln	500	210 00
Little Falls	253	106 26
Oak Dale	300	126 00
Portland	290	121 80
Ridgeville	402	168 84
Sheldon	315	132 30
Sparta	1,190	499 80
Tomah	760	319 20
Wellington	280	117 60
Wilton	444	186 48
Wells	330	138 60
Totals	7,165	$3,009 30
OCONTO COUNTY.		
Gillett	93	$39 06
Little Suamico	212	89 04
Marinette	556	233 52
Oconto	275	115 50
Oconto, city	1,102	462 84
Pensaukee	268	112 56
Peshtigo	471	197 82
Stiles	144	60 48
Totals	3,121	$1,310 82
OUTAGAMIE COUNTY.		
Appleton	1,986	$796 32
Black Creek	281	118 02
Bovina	166	69 72
Buchanan	406	170 52
Center	521	218 82
Cicero	56	23 52

TABLE 1—*Apportionment of School Fund Income*—continued.

COUNTIES AND TOWNS.	No. of Children.	Apportionment.
OUTAGAMIE COUNTY—continued.		
Dale	473	$198 60
Deer Creek	85	35 70
Ellington	526	220 92
Freedom	651	273 42
Grand Chute	693	291 06
Greenville	600	252 00
Hortonia	441	185 22
Kaukauna	659	276 78
Liberty	196	82 32
Maine	34	14 28
Maple Creek	320	134 40
Osborn	188	78 96
Seymour	174	73 08
Totals	8,366	$3,513 72
OZAUKEE COUNTY.		
Belgium	977	$410 34
Cedarburg	1,147	481 74
Fredonia	888	372 96
Grafton	796	334 32
Mequon	1,302	546 84
Port Washington	1,205	506 10
Saukville	943	396 06
Totals	7,258	$3,048 36
PEPIN COUNTY.		
Albany	166	$69 72
Durand	373	156 66
Frankfort	153	64 26
Lima	246	103 32
Pepin	476	199 92
Stockholm	211	88 62
Waterville	392	164 64
Waubeek	85	25 76
Totals	2,102	$882 84
PIERCE COUNTY.		
Clifton	187	$78 54
Diamond Bluff	210	88 20
Ellsworth	378	158 76
El Paso	174	73 08
Gilman	196	82 32
Hartland	368	154 56
Isabelle	92	38 64
Maiden Rock	245	102 90
Martell	387	162 54
Oak Grove	333	139 86

TABLE 1—*Apportionment of School Fund Income*—continued.

COUNTIES AND TOWNS.	No. of Children.	Apportionment.
PIERCE COUNTY—continued.		
Prescott	410	172 20
River Falls	525	220 50
Rock Elm	259	108 78
Salem	110	46 20
Spring Lake	194	81 48
Trenton	181	76 02
Trimbelle	311	130 62
Union	154	64 68
Totals	4,714	$1,979 88
POLK COUNTY.		
Alden	164	$68 88
Balsam Lake	102	42 84
Black Brook	138	57 96
Farmington	289	121 38
Lincoln	186	78 12
Luck	85	35 70
Milltown	65	27 30
Osceola	274	115 08
St. Croix Falls	278	116 76
Sterling	154	64 68
Totals	1,735	$728 70
PORTAGE COUNTY.		
Almond	282	$118 44
Amherst	422	177 24
Belmont	193	81 06
Buena Vista	254	106 68
Eau Plaine	109	45 78
Grant	75	31 50
Hull	241	101 22
Lanark	165	69 30
Linwood	125	52 50
New Hope	371	155 82
Pine Grove	130	54 60
Plover	377	158 34
Sharon	386	162 12
Steven's Point	21	8 82
Steven's Point, City	799	335 58
Stockton	477	200 34
Totals	4,427	$1,859 34
RACINE COUNTY.		
Burlington	1,000	$420 00
Caledonia	1,234	518 28
Dover	424	178 08
Mt. Pleasant	827	347 34

TABLE I.—*Apportionment of School Fund Income*—continued.

COUNTIES AND TOWNS.	No of Children.	Apportionment.
RACINE COUNTY—continued		
Norway	379	$159 18
Racine, city	3,916	1,644 72
Raymond	560	235 20
Rochester	350	147 00
Waterford	569	238 98
Yorkville	550	231 00
Totals	9,809	4,119 78
RICHLAND COUNTY.		
Akan	301	$126 42
Bloom	510	214 20
Buena Vista	388	162 96
Dayton	399	167 58
Eagle	549	230 58
Forest	360	151 20
Henrietta	355	149 10
Ithaca	532	223 44
Marshall	378	158 76
Orion	284	119 28
Richland	613	257 46
Richwood	591	248 22
Rockbridge	430	180 60
Sylvan	377	158 34
Westford	382	160 44
Willow	327	137 34
Totals	6,776	2,845 92
ROCK COUNTY—1st District.		
Avon	343	144 06
Center	414	173 88
Fulton	863	362 46
Janesville	352	147 84
Janesville, city	3,553	1,492 26
Magnolia	454	190 68
Newark	426	178 92
Plymouth	548	230 16
Porter	502	210 84
Spring Valley	472	198 24
Union	760	319 20
Totals	8,687	3,648 54
ROCK COUNTY—2d District.		
Beloit	271	113 82
Beloit, city	1,492	626 64
Bradford	307	128 94
Clinton	671	281 82
Harmony	431	181 02

TABLE I.—*Apportionment of School Fund Income.*—continued.

COUNTIES AND TOWNS.	No. of Children.	Apportionment.
ROCK COUNTY—*Second District*—continued.		
Johnstown	384	$161 28
La Prairie	305	128 10
Lima	379	150 18
Milton	614	257 88
Rock	374	157 08
Turtle	407	170 94
Totals	5,635	$2,366 70
ST. CROIX COUNTY.		
Cady	33	$13 86
Cylon	170	71 40
Eau Galle	128	53 76
Emerald	107	44 94
Erin	545	228 90
Hammond	375	157 50
Hudson	159	66 78
Hudson, city	614	257 88
Kinnickinnick	166	69 72
Pleasant Valley	165	69 30
Richmond	368	154 56
Rush River	202	84 84
St. Joseph	137	57 54
Somerset	216	90 72
Springfield	97	40 74
Stanton	217	91 14
Star Prairie	148	62 16
Troy	292	122 64
Warren	192	80 64
Totals	4,331	$1,819 02
SAUK COUNTY.		
Baraboo	1,134	$476 28
Bear Creek	378	158 76
Dellona	248	104 16
Delton	339	142 38
Excelsior	331	139 02
Fairfield	304	127 68
Franklin	375	157 50
Freedom	319	133 98
Greenfield	301	126 42
Honey Creek	452	189 84
Ironton	567	238 14
Lavalle	394	165 48
Merrimack	351	147 42
Prairie du Sac	839	352 38
Reedsburg	652	273 84
Spring Green	424	178 08
Sumpter	300	126 00
Troy	412	173 04

TABLE I.—*Apportionment of School Fund*—continued.

COUNTIES AND TOWNS.	No. of Children.	Apportionment.
SAUK COUNTY—continued.		
Washington	404	$169 68
Westfield	417	175 14
Winfield	298	125 16
Woodland	421	176 82
Total	9,660	$4,057 20
SHAWANO COUNTY.		
Angelica	61	$25 62
Bell Plain	228	95 76
Grant	100	42 00
Hartland	220	92 40
Herman	87	36 54
Lessor	26	10 92
Maple Grove	88	36 96
Pella	157	65 94
Richmond	58	24 36
Seneca	28	11 76
Shawano	62	26 04
Shawano, village	124	52 08
Washington	47	19 74
Waukechon	109	45 78
Totals	1,395	$585 90
SHEBOYGAN COUNTY.		
Greenbush	759	$318 78
Herman	980	411 60
Holland	1,179	495 18
Lima	885	371 70
Lyndon	653	274 26
Mitchell	497	208 74
Mosell	447	187 74
Plymouth	939	394 38
Rhine	789	331 38
Russell	215	90 30
Scott	599	251 58
Sheboygan	603	253 26
Sheboygan, city	2,420	1,016 40
Sheboygan Falls	824	346 08
Sheboygan Falls, village	545	228 90
Sherman	715	300 30
Wilson	576	241 92
Totals	13,625	$5,722 50
TREMPEALEAU COUNTY.		
Albion	91	$38 22
Arcadia	777	326 34
Burnside	286	120 12

TABLE I.—*Appropriation of School Fund Income*—continued.

Counties and Towns.	No. of Children.	Apportionment.
Trempealeau County—continued.		
Caledonia	209	$87 78
Ettrick	536	225 12
Gale	655	275 10
Hale	272	114 24
Lincoln	347	145 74
Preston	374	157 08
Sumner	255	111 30
Trempealeau	801	336 42
Totals	4,613	$1,937 46
VERNON COUNTY.		
Bergen	333	$139 86
Christiana	668	280 56
Clinton	368	154 56
Coon	326	136 92
Forest	302	126 84
Franklin	512	215 04
Genoa	234	98 28
Greenwood	344	144 48
Hamburg	419	206 22
Harmony	408	171 36
Hillsborough	347	145 74
Jefferson	459	192 78
Kickapoo	454	190 68
Liberty	206	86 52
Stark	314	131 88
Sterling	425	178 50
Union	249	104 58
Viroqua	748	314 16
Webster	350	147 00
Wheatland	248	104 16
Whitestown	274	115 08
Totals	8,060	$3,385 20
WALWORTH COUNTY.		
Bloomfield	382	160 44
Darien	508	213 36
Delavan	816	342 72
East Troy	530	222 60
Elkhorn	352	147 84
Geneva	689	289 38
La Fayette	359	150 78
La Grange	535	224 70
Linn	321	134 82
Lyons	456	191 52
Richmond	464	194 88
Sharon	668	280 56
Spring Prairie	415	174 30
Sugar Creek	348	146 16
Troy	401	168 42

TABLE I.—*Apportionment of School Fund Income*—continued.

COUNTIES AND TOWNS.	No. of Children.	Apportionment.
WALWORTH COUNTY—continued.		
Walworth	512	$215 04
Whitewater	1,535	644 70
Totals	9,291	$3,902 22
WASHINGTON COUNTY.		
Addison	909	381 78
Barton	569	238 98
Erin	548	230 66
Farmington	788	330 96
Germantown	775	325 50
Hartford	1,114	467 88
Jackson	815	342 30
Kewaskum	531	223 02
Polk	749	314 58
Richfield	697	292 74
Schliesingerville	153	64 26
Trenton	850	357 00
Wayne	862	362 04
West Bend	460	193 20
West Bend, village	506	212 52
Totals	10,326	$4,336 92
WAUKESHA COUNTY.		
Brookfield	973	$408 66
Delafield	545	228 90
Eagle	415	174 30
Genesee	574	241 08
Lisbon	502	210 84
Menomonee	924	388 08
Merton	696	292 32
Mukwanago	505	212 10
Muskego	632	265 44
New Berlin	723	303 66
Oconomowoc	637	267 54
Oconomowoc, village	635	266 70
Ottawa	401	168 42
Pewaukee	732	307 48
Summit	506	212 52
Vernon	460	193 20
Waukesha	1,098	461 16
Totals	10,958	$4,002 36
WAUPACA COUNTY.		
Bear Creek	213	$89 46
Caledonia	363	152 46
Dayton	334	140 28
Dupont	57	23 94

TABLE I.—*Apportionment of School Fund Income*—continued.

COUNTIES AND TOWNS.	No. of Children.	Apportionment.
WAUPACA COUNTY—continued.		
Fannington	271	$118 82
Fremont	267	112 14
Helvetia	73	30 66
Iola	345	144 90
Larrabee	183	76 86
Lebanon	286	120 12
Lind	391	164 22
Little Wolf	342	143 64
Matteson	125	52 50
Mukwa	279	117 18
New London, village	490	205 80
Royalton	422	177 24
St. Lawrence	310	130 20
Scandinavia	468	196 56
Union	117	49 14
Waupaca	697	292 74
Weyauwega	414	173 88
Totals	6 447	$2,707 74
WAUSHARA COUNTY.		
Aurora	437	$183 54
Bloomfield	532	223 44
Coloma	88	36 96
Dakota	146	61 32
Deerfield	90	37 80
Hancock	181	76 02
Leon	381	160 02
Marion	246	103 32
Mount Morris	264	110 88
Oasis	292	122 64
Plainfield	381	160 02
Poysippi	299	125 58
Richford	149	62 58
Rose	154	64 68
Saxville	277	116 34
Springwater	187	78 54
Warren	320	134 40
Wautoma	330	138 60
Totals	4,754	$1,996 68
WINNEBAGO COUNTY.		
Algoma	294	$123 48
Black Wolf	385	161 70
Clayton	527	221 34
Menasha	1,284	539 28
Neenah	1,334	560 28
Nepeuskun	421	176 82
Nekimi	584	245 28
Omro	1,151	483 42
Oshkosh	215	90 30

TABLE I.—*Apportionment of School Fund Income*—continued.

COUNTIES AND TOWNS.	No. of Children.	Apportionment.
WINNEBAGO COUNTY—continued.		
Oshkosh, city	4,605	$1,934 10
Poygon	389	163 38
Rushford	814	341 88
Utica	405	170 10
Vineland	437	183 54
Winchester	624	262 08
Winneconne	776	325 92
Wolf River	229	96 18
Totals	14,474	$6,079 08
WOOD COUNTY.		
Centralia	308	$129 36
Grand Rapids	209	87 78
Grand Rapids, city	458	192 36
Lincoln	96	40 32
Rudolph	166	69 72
Saratoga	152	63 84
Seneca	130	54 60
Sigel	141	59 22
Totals	1,660	$697 20

TABLE I—*Apportionment of School Fund Income*—continued.

RECAPITULATION.

COUNTIES.	No. of Children.	Apportionment.
Adams	2,558	$1,074 8
Barron	322	135 24
Bayfield	176	73 92
Brown	10,883	4,570 86
Buffalo	4,755	1,997 10
Burnett	294	123 48
Calumet	5,442	2,285 64
Chippewa	2,866	1,203 72
Clark	1,582	664 44
Columbia	11,068	4,648 56
Crawford	6,330	2,658 60
Dane, 1st district	6,950	2,919 00
Dane, 2d district	14,332	6,019 44
Dodge 1st district	8,911	3,742 62
Dodge 2d district	9,242	3,881 64
Door	2,276	955 92
Douglas	362	152 04
Dunn	3,964	1,664 88
Eau Claire	3,531	1,483 04
Fond du Lac, 1st district	12,636	5,307 12
Fond du Lac, 2d district	6,515	2,736 30
Grant	15,511	6,514 62
Green	8,951	3,759 42
Green Lake	5,146	2,161 32
Iowa	10,407	4,370 94
Jackson	3,624	1,522 08
Jefferson	14,577	6,122 34
Juneau	5,322	2,235 24
Kenosha	4,879	2,049 18
Kewaunee	4,582	1,924 44
La Crosse	7,850	3,297 00
La Fayette	9,386	3,942 12
Manitowoc	15,581	6,544 02
Marathon	2,393	1,005 06
Marquette	3,471	1,457 82
Milwaukee, 1st district	3,996	1,678 32
Milwaukee, 2d district	31,026	13,030 92
Monroe	7,165	3,009 30
Oconto	3,121	1,310 82
Outagamie	8,366	3,513 72
Ozaukee	7,258	3,048 36
Pepin	2,102	882 84
Pierce	4,714	1,979 88
Polk	1,735	728 70
Portage	4,427	1,859 34
Racine	9,809	4,119 78
Richland	6,776	2,845 92
Rock, 1st district	8,687	3,648 54
Rock, 2d district	5,635	2,366 70
St. Croix	4,331	1,819 02
Sauk	9,660	4,057 20
Shawano	1,395	585 90
Sheboygan	13,625	5,722 50

TABLE I.—*Apportionment of School Fund Income*—continued.

RECAPITULATION—continued.

COUNTIES.	No. of Children.	Apportionment.
Trempealeau	4,613	$1,937 46
Vernon	8,060	3,385 20
Walworth	9,291	3,902 22
Washington	10,326	4,336 92
Waukesha	10,958	4,002 36
Waupaca	6,447	2,707 74
Waushara	4,754	1,996 68
Winnebago	14,474	6,079 08
Wood	1,660	697 20
Grand total	431,086	$181,056 12

TABLE No. II.

DISTRICTS, CHILDREN AND SCHOOL ATTENDANCE.

ADAMS COUNTY.

Towns.	Whole number of School Districts in the town.	Number of districts which have reported.	Whole number of parts of Districts in the town.	Number of parts of Districts which have reported.	Number of Male children, over 4 and under 20 years of age.	Number of Female children over 4 and under 20 years of age.	Whole number over 4 and under 20 years of age in town.	Number over 4 and under 20 years in Districts maintaining school 5 or more months.	Number of days school has been taught by qualified teachers during the year.	Number over 4 and under 20 years who have attended school.	Number under 4 years who have attended school.	Number over 20 years who have attended school.	Total number of different pupils who have attended school during the year.	Number of days attendance of pupils over 4 and under 20 years.	Number of days attendance of pupils under 4 years.	Number of days attendance of pupils over 20 years.	Total number of days attendance of different pupils during the year.
Adams	3	3	2	2	74	96	170	146	557	145	....	4	149	10,365	....	143	10,508
Big Flats	1	1	....	....	20	13	33	33	120	22	....	3	25	1,630	....	....	1,630
Dell Prairie	2	1	5	5	78	84	162	153	821	127	3	...	130	7,62	...	43	7,715
Easton	3	3	....	....	54	55	109	109	405	98	1	....	99	6,45	6	....	6,491
Jackson	3	3	5	5	110	100	210	210	990	177	....	2	179	9,51	....	60	9,811
Leola	2	2	1	1	39	31	70	54	318	54	...	1	58	1,52	....	49	1,811
Lincoln	3	3	3	3	99	92	191	191	805	190	1	4	195	10,68	2	138	10,818
Monroe	3	3	1	1	84	85	169	169	704	95	....	....	95	7,48	....	....	7,048
New Chester	2	2	3	3	72	55	127	127	636	94	....	....	94	4,57	....	....	4,517
New Haven	4	4	4	4	188	180	368	368	1,165	289	....	1	290	18,445	....	52	18,497
Preston	1	1	3	3	35	28	63	63	508	41	....	....	41	2,057	....	....	2,057
Quincy	3	3	1	1	60	44	104	104	516	87	2	....	89	6,80	....	....	6,870
Richfield	1	1	6	6	67	60	127	127	746	75	....	....	75	5,067	....	....	5,067
Rome	3	3	....	....	50	35	85	85	1,408	65	....	....	65	4,560	....	....	4,560

TABLE No. II.—*Districts, Children and School Attendance*—continued.

ADAMS COUNTY—county.

Towns.	Whole number of School Districts in the town.	Number of Districts which have reported.	Whole number of parts of Districts in the Town.	Number of parts of Districts which have reported.	Number of Male children over 4 and under 20 years of age.	Number of Female children over 4 and under 20 years of age.	Whole number over 4 and under 20 years of age in town.	Number over 4 and under 20 years in Districts maintaining school 5 or more months.	Number of days school has been taught by qualified teachers during the year.	Number over 4 and under 20 years who have attended school.	Number under 4 years who have attended school.	Number over 20 years who have attended school.	Total number of different pupils who have attended school during the year.	Number of days attendance of pupils over 4 and under 20 years.	Number of days attendance of pupils under 4 years.	Number of days attendance of pupils over 20 years.	Total number of days attendance of different pupils during the year.
Springville	3	3	4	4	63	59	122	106	908	100	....	....	100	5,556	....	....	5,556
Strong's Prairie	5	5	2	2	231	184	415	415	974	285	....	8	293	10,184	....	80	10,264
White Creek	1	1	1	1	42	40	82	82	308	44	....	....	44	3,574	....	....	3,574
Totals	43	43	41	41	1,366	1,241	2,607	2,542	10,890	1,988	7	23	2,021	116,221	8	565	116,794

BARRON COUNTY.

Towns.	Whole number of School Districts in the town.	Number of Districts which have reported.	Whole number of parts of Districts in the Town.	Number of parts of Districts which have reported.	Number of Male children over 4 and under 20 years of age.	Number of Female children over 4 and under 20 years of age.	Whole number over 4 and under 20 years of age in town.	Number over 4 and under 20 years in Districts maintaining school 5 or more months.	Number of days school has been taught by qualified teachers during the year.	Number over 4 and under 20 years who have attended school.	Number under 4 years who have attended school.	Number over 20 years who have attended school.	Total number of different pupils who have attended school during the year.	Number of days attendance of pupils over 4 and under 20 years.	Number of days attendance of pupils under 4 years.	Number of days attendance of pupils over 20 years.	Total number of days attendance of different pupils during the year.
Barron	20	20	....	....	312	256	568	385	2,245	327	2	....	350	19,208	55	....	11,408

BAYFIELD COUNTY.

Towns.	Whole number of School Districts in the town.	Number of Districts which have reported.	Whole number of parts of Districts in the Town.	Number of parts of Districts which have reported.	Number of Male children over 4 and under 20 years of age.	Number of Female children over 4 and under 20 years of age.	Whole number over 4 and under 20 years of age in town.	Number over 4 and under 20 years in Districts maintaining school 5 or more months.	Number of days school has been taught by qualified teachers during the year.	Number over 4 and under 20 years who have attended school.	Number under 4 years who have attended school.	Number over 20 years who have attended school.	Total number of different pupils who have attended school during the year.	Number of days attendance of pupils over 4 and under 20 years.	Number of days attendance of pupils under 4 years.	Number of days attendance of pupils over 20 years.	Total number of days attendance of different pupils during the year.
Bayfield	1	1	....	....	72	81	153	153	....	60	....	1	61	....	....	....	....

BROWN COUNTY.

Ashwaubenon	1	1	....	....	63	49	112	112	200	71	....	....	71	2,485	....	....	2,485
Bellevue	3	3	....	....	192	188	380	380	500	185	....	....	185	23,194	....	....	23,194
Depere	5	5	1	1	117	127	299	299	682	138	....	....	138	29,116	....	....	29,116
Depere, village	1	1	....	....	279	391	620	620	200	325	....	....	325	35,000	....	....	35,000
Eaton	2	2	1	1	95	87	182	64	540	182	....	....	182	6,393	....	....	6,393
Glenmore	4	4	....	....	155	147	302	302	596	217	....	....	217	20,587	....	....	20,587
Green Bay	2	2	1	1	191	195	386	386	440	386	....	....	386	12,146	....	....	12,146
Holland	4	4	....	....	367	367	734	734	626	400	....	....	400	23,788	....	....	23,788
Howard	5	5	....	....	219	256	475	475	774	271	....	....	271	29,975	....	....	29,975
Humbolt	4	4	....	....	190	179	369	369	660	165	4	....	169	11,154	....	....	11,154
Lawrence	7	7	....	....	140	132	272	272	281	182	....	....	182	16,354	....	....	16,354
Morrison	6	6	....	....	279	263	542	542	863	324	5	....	329	13,183	66	....	13,199
New Denmark	6	6	....	....	202	196	398	398	888	221	....	....	221	19,624	....	....	19,624
Pittsfield	3	3	....	....	138	119	257	257	585	108	....	....	108	9,350	....	....	9,350
Preble	4	4	1	1	301	259	560	560	608	460	....	....	460	24,040	....	....	24,040
Rockland	5	5	....	....	180	170	350	350	838	350	....	....	350	15,772	....	....	15,772
Scott	6	6	2	2	337	299	636	636	789	366	....	....	366	24,242	....	....	24,242
Suamico	3	3	....	....	195	204	399	399	441	200	....	....	200	15,000	....	....	15,000
West Depere	2	1	1	....	262	268	530	278	288	178	....	....	178	45,320	....	....	45,320
Wrightstown	7	7	1	....	379	320	699	699	1,119	400	....	....	400	25,808	....	....	25,808
Totals	80	79	8	6	4,281	4,166	8,447	8,327	12,080	4,879	9	....	4,888	391,760	....	....	391,826
City of Fort Howard	....	....	....	....	494	475	969	969	198	629	....	....	629	55,337	....	....	55,337
City of Green Bay	....	....	....	....	1,024	1,094	2,118	2,118	200	993	....	....	993	100,418	....	....	100,418
Grand Total	80	79	8	6	5,799	5,785	11,534	11,414	12,478	7,101	9	....	7,110	547,515	....	....	547,581

TABLE No II.—*Districts, Children and School Attendance*—continued.

BUFFALO COUNTY.

Towns.	Whole number of School Districts in the town.	Number of Districts which have reported.	Whole number of parts of Districts in the town.	Number of parts of Districts which have reported.	Number of Male children over 4 and under 20 years of age.	Number of Female children over 4 and under 20 years of age.	Whole number over 4 and under 20 years of age in town.	Number over 4 and under 20 years in Districts maintaining school 5 or more months.	Number of days school has been taught by qualified teachers during the year.	Number over 4 and under 20 years who have attended school.	Number under 4 years who have attended school.	Number over 20 years who have attended school.	Total number of different pupils who have attended school during the year.	Total number of days attendance of different pupils during the year.	Number of days attendance of pupils under 4 years.	Number of days attendance of pupils over 20 years.	Number of days attendance of pupils over 4 and under 20 years.
Alma	3	2	....	....	88	92	180	180	296	85	....	....	85	5,699	....	....	5,699
Alma, village	1	1	....	....	97	100	197	197	220	153	....	....	153	21,441	....	....	21,441
Belvidere	4	4	....	....	133	116	249	249	450	142	....	....	142	9,861	....	....	9,861
Buffalo	3	3	1	....	80	96	176	176	377	94	....	....	94	5,904	....	....	5,904
Buffalo, city	1	1	....	....	55	57	112	112	162	72	....	....	72	5,454	....	....	5,454
Canton	5	5	2	2	151	147	298	298	973	173	....	....	173	13,848	....	....	13,848
Cross	4	4	....	....	141	151	292	292	450	161	....	....	161	11,677	....	....	11,677
Dover	4	4	....	....	93	93	186	141	399	85	....	1	86	3,794	....	....	3,794
Fountain City	1	1	....	....	194	208	402	402	198	290	....	1	291	33,264	....	....	33,264
Gilmanton	4	4	....	....	91	71	162	162	540	142	....	3	145	9,467	....	110	9,557
Glencoe	5	5	1	1	162	157	319	319	744	264	....	....	264	13,161	....	....	13,161
Lincoln	3	3	3	....	94	105	199	199	300	105	....	....	105	4,429	....	....	4,429
Maxville	3	3	3	3	103	85	188	188	420	92	....	4	96	2,255	....	....	2,255
Milton	2	2	2	2	65	89	154	154	220	58	....	....	58	3,124	....	....	3,124
Modena	4	4	....	....	188	123	311	311	616	155	....	....	155	13,267	....	....	13,267
Montana	3	3	....	....	108	101	209	209	320	82	....	....	82	4,150	....	....	4,150
Naples	7	4	1	1	194	164	358	358	706	282	2	2	286	13,841	7	99	14,017
Nelson	6	6	2	2	285	245	530	530	1,059	357	3	1	361	20,363	....	26	20,389

Waumandee	4	4	3	3	199	196	395	395	980	318	....	1	319	23,745	....	100	23,845
Totals	67	63	19	15	2,521	2,396	4,917	4,872	9,428	3,060	5	13	3,078	215,744	7	335	216,086

BURNETT COUNTY.

Grantsburg	4	4	....	....	187	175	362	362	442	176	3	11	190	7,156	5	268	7,429

CALUMET COUNTY.

Brillion	6	6	....	....	212	166	378	378	795	236	....	....	236	12,787	....	....	12,787
Brothertown	9	9	1	1	359	329	688	688	1,332	312	....	....	312	16,468	....	....	16,468
Charlestown	8	8	....	....	266	259	525	525	1,014	330	....	....	330	23,361	....	....	23,361
Chilton	7	7	2	2	340	342	682	682	1,307	486	....	1	487	37,796	....	11	37,807
Harrison	10	10	2	2	378	363	741	741	1,562	363	....	1	364	2,530	....	68	2,598
New Holstein	6	6	3	3	367	393	760	760	1,410	370	....	....	370	39,504	....	....	39,504
Rantoul	4	4	3	3	257	206	463	463	838	220	2	....	222	7,353	4	....	7,357
Stockbridge	8	8	1	1	405	381	786	786	1,319	481	1	6	488	39,506	20	311	39,837
Woodville	6	6	1	1	272	264	536	536	898	273	....	....	273	17,998	....	....	17,998
Totals	64	64	13	13	2,856	2,703	5,559	5,559	10,475	3,071	3	8	3,082	215,303	24	390	215,717

CHIPPEWA COUNTY.

Anson	4	4	....	....	42	38	80	80	526	57	1	1	59	4,333	41	19	4,393
Auburn	5	5	....	....	142	99	241	241	475	117	....	....	117	5,553	....	....	5,553
Bloomer	6	6	....	....	171	167	338	338	881	236	....	....	236	18,221	....	....	18,221
Chippewa Falls	1	1	....	....	357	320	677	677	200	390	....	2	392	43,800	....	110	43,910
Eagle Point	15	15	....	....	368	351	719	719	2,172	450	....	....	450	27,098	....	....	27,098

Table No. II.—*Districts, Children and School Attendance*—continued.

Chippewa County—continued.

Towns.	Whole number of School Districts in the town.	Number of Districts which have reported.	Whole number of parts of Districts in the town.	Number of parts of Districts which have reported.	Number of Male children over 4 and under 20 years of age.	Number of Female children over 4 and under 20 years of age.	Whole number over 4 and under 20 years of age in town.	Number over 4 and under 20 years in Districts maintaining school 5 or more months.	Number of days school has been taught by qualified teachers during the year.	Number over 4 and under 20 years who have attended school.	Number under 4 years who have attended school.	Number over 20 years who have attended school.	Total number of different pupils who have attended school during the year.	Number of days attendance of pupils over 4 and under 20 years.	Number of days attendance of pupils under 4 years.	Number of days attendance of pupils over 20 years.	Total number of days attendance of different pupils during the year.
Edson	4	4	....	....	82	88	170	170	571	104	1	....	105	6,416	5	....	6,421
La Fayette	7	6	2	1	192	186	378	378	991	246	1	....	247	13,434	12	....	13,446
Sigel	3	2	1	1	42	26	69	69	396	39	....	....	39	1,659	....	....	1,659
Wheaton	6	6	1	....	145	121	266	266	710	175	....	....	175	8,543	....	....	8,543
Totals	51	49	4	2	1,542	1,396	2,938	2,938	6,872	1,826	3	8	1,830	129,057	58	129	129,844

CLARK COUNTY.

Towns.	Whole number of School Districts in the town.	Number of Districts which have reported.	Whole number of parts of Districts in the town.	Number of parts of Districts which have reported.	Number of Male children over 4 and under 20 years of age.	Number of Female children over 4 and under 20 years of age.	Whole number over 4 and under 20 years of age in town.	Number over 4 and under 20 years in Districts maintaining school 5 or more months.	Number of days school has been taught by qualified teachers during the year.	Number over 4 and under 20 years who have attended school.	Number under 4 years who have attended school.	Number over 20 years who have attended school.	Total number of different pupils who have attended school during the year.	Number of days attendance of pupils over 4 and under 20 years.	Number of days attendance of pupils under 4 years.	Number of days attendance of pupils over 20 years.	Total number of days attendance of different pupils during the year.
Beaver	7	3	1	....	87	87	74	66	454	58	....	....	58	3,816	....	....	3,816
Eaton	5	5	....	....	85	71	156	156	758	114	....	....	114	7,087	....	....	7,087
Grant	3	3	1	1	99	95	194	194	453	98	2	....	100	6,426	42	....	6,468
Hixton	....	....	1	1	12	8	20	20	160	14	....	....	14	956	....	....	956
Levis	3	3	....	....	44	43	87	87	320	74	....	....	74	4,074	....	....	4,074
Loyal	5	5	1	1	66	78	144	92	541	98	....	....	98	4,968	....	....	4,968
Lynn	3	3	....	....	24	42	66	66	398	83	....	....	83	1,733	....	....	1,733
Mentor	2	2	2	2	87	77	164	164	355	84	....	....	84	6,120	....	....	6,120

Pine Valley	4	4	2	2	287	212	449	449	995	....	....	....	305	17,086	....	....	17,086
Sherman	3	3	1	1	62	35	97	81	481	80	....	....	80	2,980	....	....	2,980
Washburn	....	....	....	....	....	....	....	....	....	....	....	....	....	....	....	....	....
Weston	3	3	2	2	73	72	145	132	530	115	....	....	115	5,925	....	....	5,925
York	1	1	1	1	65	57	122	122	370	77	....	....	77	7,525	....	....	7,525
Totals	39	25	12	11	891	827	1,718	1,629	5,810	840	....	....	1,147	63,144	42	....	63,186

COLUMBIA COUNTY.

Arlington	6	6	3	3	181	196	377	377	1,329	214	....	....	214	15,242	....	....	15,242
Caledonia	6	6	2	2	240	230	470	470	1,145	338	....	1	339	23,552	....	126	23,678
Columbus	7	7	5	5	467	469	936	936	1,719	684	6	10	700	53,007	....	118	53,125
Courtland	3	3	5	5	2·3	262	495	495	....	....	....	....	....	....	....	....	....
Dekorra	7	7	4	4	268	237	505	505	1,520	447	2	9	458	35,712	50	308	36,070
Fort Winnebago	4	4	3	3	154	150	304	304	1,040	259	....	3	262	16,010	....	177	16,187
Fountain Prairie	5	5	5	5	276	245	521	521	1,717	336	....	....	336	32,186	....	....	32,168
Hampden	4	4	6	6	176	189	365	365	1,120	310	....	1	311	7,020	....	50	7,070
Leeds	6	6	2	2	236	214	450	450	1,189	275	1	2	278	20,755	5	14	20,771
Lewiston	10	10	....	....	234	236	470	470	1,302	335	....	2	337	19,610	....	24	19,634
Lodi	5	5	5	5	322	314	636	636	1,326	474	2	2	478	43,421	....	105	43,526
Lowville	5	5	3	3	144	148	292	292	1,181	325	1	6	332	26,799	1	301	27,101
Marcellon	4	4	7	7	167	140	307	307	2,003	265	....	1	266	20,010	....	65	20,075
Newport	4	4	3	3	323	322	645	645	977	526	....	11	537	40,862	....	507	41,369
Otsego	4	4	4	4	340	286	626	626	1,188	313	....	4	316	15,680	....	185	15,865
Pacific	2	2	3	3	43	40	83	83	490	76	....	3	79	4,648	....	82	4,731
Randolph	3	3	6	6	257	229	486	486	1,244	305	4	4	312	37,483	29	25	37,537
Randolph, village	....	....	1	1	16	23	39	39	198	39	....	....	39	7,722	....	....	7,722
Scott	8	8	2	2	182	151	333	333	1,573	283	....	1	284	22,479	....	54	22,533
Springdale	3	3	6	6	162	130	292	292	1,250	....	....	....	....	....	....	....	....
West Point	6	6	3	2	197	175	372	372	1,172	276	1	2	279	22,645	32	67	22,744
Wyocena	7	7	5	5	240	217	457	457	1,106	396	....	1	397	....	....	....	....
Totals	109	109	83	83	4,858	4,608	9,461	9,461	25,999	6,476	17	62	6,555	464,823	117	2,208	467,148

Table No. II.—*Districts, Children and School Attendance*—continued.

Columbia County—continued.

Towns.	Whole number of School Districts in the town.	Number of Districts which have reported.	Whole number of parts of Districts in the town.	Number of parts of Districts which have reported.	Number of Male children over 4 and under 20 years of age.	Number of Female children over 4 and under 20 years of age.	Whole number over 4 and under 20 years of age in town.	Number over 4 and under 20 years in Districts maintaining school 5 or more months.	Number of days school has been taught by qualified teachers during the year.	Number over 4 and under 20 years who have attended school.	Number under 4 years who have attended school.	Number over 20 years who have attended school.	Total number of different pupils who have attended school during the year.	Number of days attendance of pupils over 4 and under 20 years.	Number of days attendance of pupils under 4 years.	Number of days attendance of pupils over 20 years.	Total number of days attendance of different pupils during the year.
Portage City	....	....	....	....	738	700	1,438	1,438	199	965	....	....	965	108,008	....	.....	108,008
Grand totals	109	109	83	83	5,596	5,303	10,899	10,899	26,198	7,441	17	63	7,520	567,831	117	2208	570,156

CRAWFORD COUNTY.

Towns.	Whole number of School Districts in the town.	Number of Districts which have reported.	Whole number of parts of Districts in the town.	Number of parts of Districts which have reported.	Number of Male children over 4 and under 20 years of age.	Number of Female children over 4 and under 20 years of age.	Whole number over 4 and under 20 years of age in town.	Number over 4 and under 20 years in Districts maintaining school 5 or more months.	Number of days school has been taught by qualified teachers during the year.	Number over 4 and under 20 years who have attended school.	Number under 4 years who have attended school.	Number over 20 years who have attended school.	Total number of different pupils who have attended school during the year.	Number of days attendance of pupils over 4 and under 20 years.	Number of days attendance of pupils under 4 years.	Number of days attendance of pupils over 20 years.	Total number of days attendance of different pupils during the year.
Bridgeport	1	1	2	2	58	66	119	119	490	58	2	....	60	4,295	50	.....	4,345
Clayton	11	11	3	3	363	354	717	671	300	....	....	1	301	26,699	....	.....	26,742
Eastman	9	9	3	3	320	292	612	612	1,530	480	4	....	484	27,781	39	.....	27,820
Freeman	7	7	7	7	309	251	560	560	980	403	....	3	406	18,649	....	92	18,741
Haney	8	8	6	6	117	102	219	219	780	196	....	3	194	10,198	....	148	10,346
Marietta	4	4	1	1	96	108	204	204	573	130	....	1	131	7,727	....	60	7,789
Prairie du Chien	3	3	3	3	156	126	282	282	882	191	....	..	191	15,824	....	.....	15,824
Prairie du Chien, city	2	2	2	2	525	558	1,083	1,083	688	557	....	....	557	41,958	....	.....	41,958
Scott	6	6	5	5	211	182	393	393	720	323	....	....	323	18,269	....	.....	18,269
Seneca	8	8	3	3	272	296	568	568	1,400	417	7	....	424	23,687	41	.....	23,728
Union	4	4	2	2	90	86	177	178	776	....	....	....	....	....	....	.....	....

Utica	7	7	5	2	292	289	581	581	1,332	380	....	....	380	16,500	....	.....	16,500
Wauzeka	8	8	3	3	247	229	476	425	1,423	295	....	4	299	18,207	....	128	18,330
Totals	78	73	45	42	3,051	2,941	5,992	5,895	13,257	3,730	13	12	3,755	229,994	130	466	230,390

DOUGLAS COUNTY.

Superior	2	2	....	....	166	175	341	341	180	234	....	....	234	32,773	....	.....	37,773

DANE COUNTY—*First District.*

Albion	6	6	6	6	231	175	406	406	1,018	257	....	1	258	17,201	....	74	17,275
Blooming Grove	5	5	4	4	219	191	410	410	880	180	....	3	183	8,214	....	75	8,289
Bristol	4	4	7	7	237	254	491	491	495	254	2	5	261	13,149	40	125	13,315
Burke	9	9	2	2	210	201	411	411	1,244	281	....	....	281	9,941	....	32	9,973
Christiana	10	9	2	1	288	293	581	527	1,174	359	....	7	366	23,117	....	106	23,224
Cottage Grove	9	9	2	2	225	237	462	462	1,283	331	....	....	331	19,175	....	.....	19,175
Deerfield	5	5	7	7	199	185	384	384	602	204	1	3	208	11,184	8	57	11,249
Dunkirk	10	10	....	....	263	222	485	485	1,310	385	....	3	388	24,837	....	105	24,942
Dunn	6	6	4	4	218	233	451	451	923	308	....	3	311	19,814	....	90	19,894
Medina	7	7	2	2	279	261	540	540	1,022	352	....	2	354	17,665	....	20	17,685
Pleasant Springs	6	6	4	4	224	192	416	416	708	240	1	7	284	13,401	15	129	13,545
Stoughton, village	1	1	....	....	152	132	284	284	180	160	....	3	163	21,041	....	64	21,105
Sun Prairie	5	5	6	6	182	148	330	330	699	194	....	1	199	11,136	....	53	11,189
Sun Prairie, village	1	1	....	....	111	118	229	229	188	242	....	....	242	20,434	....	.....	20,434
Windsor	7	7	4	4	251	214	465	465	991	262	....	1	266	15,330	....	60	15,390
York	8	8	2	2	205	172	377	377	1,053	202	....	1	203	13,057	....	.....	13,057
Totals	99	98	52	51	3,494	3,228	6,722	6,722	14,180	4,211	4	40	4,262	242,436	62	991	259 742

TABLE No. II.—*Districts, Children and School Attendance*—continued.

DANE COUNTY—*Second District*.

Towns.	Whole number of School Districts in the town.	Number of Districts which have reported.	Whole number of parts of Districts in the town.	Number of parts of Districts which have reported.	Number of Male children over 4 and under 20 years of age.	Number of Female children over 4 and under 20 years of age.	Whole number over 4 and under 20 years of age in town.	Number over 4 and under 20 years in Districts maintaining school 5 or more months.	Number of days school has been taught by qualified teachers during the year.	Number over 4 and under 20 years who have attended school.	Number under 4 years who have attended school.	Number over 20 years who have attended school.	Total number of different pupils who have attended school during the year.	Total number of days attendance of different pupils during the year.	Number of days attendance of pupils under 4 years.	Number of days attendance of pupils over 20 years.	Number of days attendance of pupils over 4 and under 20 years.
Berry	5	5	3	3	274	236	510	510	943	176	....	....	176	9,318	....	.....	9,818
Black Earth	3	3	2	2	200	179	379	379	442	221	....	1	222	28,546	....	63	28,609
Blue Mounds	4	4	1	1	233	244	477	477	540	247	....	5	252	13,402	....	99	13,501
Cross Plains	5	5	2	2	357	320	677	677	973	299	2	2	303	17,167	20	.....	17,187
Dane	4	4	8	8	227	213	440	440	1,010	239	....	2	241	19,630	....	33	19,663
Fitchburg	8	8	5	5	258	238	496	496	1,550	300	....	....	300	32,040	....	.....	32,040
Madison	2	2	4	4	158	159	317	317	917	195	....	....	195	16,107	....	.....	16,107
Mazomanie	2	2	3	3	337	344	681	681	347	483	....	14	497	49,599	....	1015	50,614
Middleton	8	8	2	2	384	347	731	731	1,460	484	....	....	484	35,243	...	.....	35,243
Montrose	4	4	3	3	217	213	430	430	868	181	....	....	181	14,827	....	.....	14,827
Oregon	8	8	4	4	262	279	541	541	1,436	455	....	2	457	34,539	....	90	34,629
Perry	3	3	6	6	259	197	456	456	1,083	258	....	4	262	11,242	...	126	11,368
Primrose	4	4	6	6	211	201	412	412	1,296	296	....	6	302	20,612	....	141	20,753
Roxbury	4	4	3	3	231	236	467	467	925	195	1	2	198	11,281	....	.....	11,281
Rutland	6	6	7	7	220	200	420	420	1,250	330	....	3	333	22,527	....	340	22,867
Springdale	5	5	2	2	210	227	437	437	1,009	289	....	5	294	16,602	....	163	16,765
Springfield	6	6	3	3	299	275	574	574	1,328	315	1	1	317	19,531	8	20	19,559
Vermont	6	6	.....	.....	252	239	491	491	844	303	....	....	......	16,558	....	.....	16,558
Verona	6	6	2	2	211	191	402	402	1,061	329	5	1	335	26,681	12	.....	26,693

Vienna	2	2	6	6	172	164	336	336	1,129	319	....	7	326	18,558	....	222	18,780
Westport	6	6	5	5	263	254	517	517	1,540	276	....	....	276	13,005	....	....	13,005
Totals	101	101	78	78	5,235	4,956	10 191	10,191	21,943	6,170	9	55	6,234	457,110	40	2312	459,562
City of Madison	....	....	....	....	1,751	1,866	3,617	3,617	185	2,211	....	....	2,211	168,772	....	....	168,772
Grand total	101	101	78	78	6,986	6,822	13,808	13,808	22,128	8,381	9	55	8,445	625,882	40	2312	628,334

DODGE COUNTY—*First District.*

Ashippun	5	5	7	7	313	313	626	626	1,589	362	1	1	364	22,754	6	19	22,779
Burnett	3	3	4	4	175	173	348	348	....	257	....	....	257	20,687	....	....	20,687
Chester	4	4	5	5	137	155	292	292	1,523	182	....	....	182	13,009	....	....	13,009
Herman	8	7	3	3	389	363	752	752	1,119	267	....	....	267	14,220	....	....	14,220
Hubbard	6	6	4	4	637	605	1,242	1,242	1,391	807	....	....	807	64,323	....	....	64,323
Hustisford	4	4	5	5	388	315	703	703	1,130	348	....	....	348	24,075	....	....	24,075
Lebanon	3	3	3	2	341	349	690	690	523	121	....	....	121	5,445	....	....	5,445
LeRoy	7	7	2	2	359	307	666	666	1,258	320	1	....	321	19,240	1	....	19,241
Lomira	10	10	2	2	469	415	884	884	1,693	541	....	1	542	29,748	....	50	29,798
Rubicon	6	6	5	5	385	395	780	780	1,501	395	....	3	398	21,344	....	138	21,482
Theresa	3	3	5	5	407	415	822	822	992	256	....	....	256	14,175	....	....	14,175
Waupun, village	....	....	2	2	131	158	289	289	360	307	....	....	307	29,035	....	....	29,035
Williamstown	6	6	3	3	441	444	885	885	1,223	312	....	....	312	28,575	....	....	28,575
Totals	65	64	50	49	4,572	4,407	8,979	8,979	14,332	4,475	2	5	4,482	306,630	7	207	306,844

DODGE COUNTY—*Second District.*

Beaver Dam	7	7	4	4	300	286	586	586	1,408	367	....	....	367	15,366	....	....	15,366
Calamus	7	7	3	3	273	212	485	485	1,213	285	....	....	285	14,934	....	....	14,934
Clyman	4	4	6	6	279	237	516	516	1,537	318	....	2	320	23,273	....	23	23,296

TABLE No. II.—*Districts, Children and School Attendance*—continued.

DODGE COUNTY—*Second District.*

TOWNS.	Whole number of School Districts in the town.	Number of Districts which have reported.	Whole number of parts of Districts in the Town.	Number of parts of Districts which have reported.	Number of Male children over 4 and under 20 years of age.	Number of Female children over 4 and under 20 years of age.	Whole number over 4 and under 20 years of age in town.	Number over 4 and under 20 years in Districts maintaining school 5 or more months.	Number of days school has been taught by qualified teachers during the year.	Number over 4 and under 20 years who have attended school.	Number under 4 years who have attended school.	Number over 20 years who have attended school.	Total number of different pupils who have attended school during the year.	Number of days attendance of pupils over 4 and under 20 years.	Number of days attendance of pupils under 4 years.	Number of days attendance of pupils over 20 years.	Total number of days attendance of different pupils during the year.
Elba	6	6	3	3	329	336	665	665	1,311	561	11	....	572	41,028	96	....	41,124
Emmett	8	8	1	1	243	213	456	456	1,176	240	....	1	241	14,537	....	....	4,537
FoxLake	2	2	9	9	327	296	623	623	1,745	575	....	....	575	55,400	....	....	55,400
Lowell	9	9	7	7	533	492	1,025	1,025	2,358	730	2	3	735	50,722	6	76	50,806
Oak Grove	7	7	7	7	416	367	783	783	2,273	493	....	4	497	38,946	....	143	39,089
Portland	6	6	5	5	273	282	555	555	1,562	373	2	4	379	23,693	....	....	23,693
Randolph, village	....	....	1	1	41	58	99	99	198	....	....	....	....	....	....	....	....
Shields	4	4	2	2	244	213	457	457	864	224	....	....	224	15,186	....	....	15,186
Trenton	8	8	8	8	360	302	662	662	2,487	489	7	10	506	36,177	35	249	36,461
Westford	4	4	4	4	191	198	389	389	1,235	205	3	30	238	7,407	65	....	7,472
Totals	72	72	60	60	3,809	3,492	7,301	7,301	19,367	4,860	25	54	4,939	336,621	202	491	337,314
City of Beaver Dam	....	....	....	....	647	753	1,400	1,400	200	813	....	....	813	....	....	....	....
Grand totals	72	72	60	60	4,456	4,245	8,701	8,701	19,567	5,673	25	54	5,752	336,621	202	491	337,314

DOOR COUNTY.

Bailey's Harbor	1	1	....	..	64	69	133	133	160	94	....	....	94	6,157	....	....	6,157
Brussells	2	2	....	....	134	128	262	262	210	210	....	....	210	5,387	....	....	5,387
Clay Banks	2	2	....	....	108	103	211	140	303	140	....	....	140	6,705	....	....	6,705
Egg Harbor	3	3	....	....	39	44	83	84	381	83	....	....	83	3,899	....	13	3,912
Forestville	3	3	....	....	118	129	247	247	852	105	....	....	105	5,487	....	....	5,487
Gardner	3	3	....	....	72	73	145	145	375	71	21	....	92	18,750	200	....	18,950
Gibraltar	4	3	....	....	98	89	187	187	343	140	....	....	140	7,986	....	....	7,986
Jacksonport	1	1	....	....	20	23	43	43	123	24	....	....	24	1,370	....	....	1,370
Liberty Grove	3	3	....	....	88	77	165	165	315	91	....	....	91	1,177	....	....	1,777
Nasewaupee	3	3	1	1	85	70	155	155	501	104	4	1	109	8,326	34	74	8,434
Sevastopol	4	4	....	....	99	81	180	180	591	132	....	....	132	7,515	....	....	7,515
Sturgeon Bay	5	5	1	1	159	166	325	217	491	195	1	2	198	21,122	7	125	21,254
Union	2	2	....	....	99	94	193	193	308	87	....	....	87	5,658	....	....	5,658
Washington	1	1	....	....	61	69	130	130	180	93	....	1	94	4,741	....	10	4,751
Totals	37	76	2	2	1,244	1,215	2,459	2,280	4,633	1,569	26	4	1,599	104,280	241	222	104,743

DUNN COUNTY.

Colfax	2	2	1	1	44	38	82	82	274	254	....	....	254	2,696	....	....	2,696
Dunn	7	7	2	2	171	178	349	349	1,447	262	....	....	262	18,185	....	....	18,185
Eau Galle	8	8	2	2	237	212	449	449	1,052	290	....	....	290	20,023	....	....	20,023
Elk Mund	3	3	1	1	72	70	142	142	300	90	....	....	170	3,236	....	....	3,236
Grant	6	6	2	2	154	155	309	309	614	194	....	3	197	2,964	....	....	3,040
Lucas	3	3	1	1	94	69	163	163	530	130	....	1	131	4,947	....	....	4,947
1 Mnie	6	6	1	1	522	490	1,012	1,012	800	740	....	14	754	51,227	....	1573	52,800
Nw Haven	3	2	....	....	64	63	127	86	217	74	....	....	74	2,341	....	....	2,341
Peru	3	2	....	....	27	20	47	47	252	47	....	....	47	2,656	....	....	2,656
Red Cedar	5	5	2	2	131	130	261	216	582	184	....	2	186	8,809	....	....	8,809
Rock Creek	4	4	....	....	81	67	148	148	552	105	....	....	105	7,234	....	....	7,234
Sheridan	2	2	....	....	21	29	50	50	238	85	....	....	85	2,410	....	....	2,410

TABLE No. II.—*Districts, Children and School Attendance*—continued.

DUNN COUNTY—continued.

TOWNS.	Whole number of School District.	Number of Districts which have reported.	Whole number of parts of Districts in the Town.	Number of parts of Districts which have reported.	Number of Male children over 4 and under 20 years of age.	Number of Female children over 4 and under 20 years of age.	Whole number over 4 and under 20 years of age in town.	Number over 4 and under 20 years in Districts maintaining school 5 or more months.	Number of days school has been taught by qualified teachers during the year.	Number over 4 and under 20 years who have attended school.	Number over 4 years who have attended school.	Number over 20 years who have attended school.	Total number of different pupils who have attended school during the year.	Number of days attendance of pupils over 4 and under 20 years.	Number of days attendance of pupils under 4 years.	Number of days attendance of pupils over 20 years.	Total number of days attendance of different pupils during the year.
Sherman	6	6	....	....	118	101	219	200	717	175	....	1	176	8,386	....	50	8,436
Spring Brook	8	8	....	....	252	264	516	516	976	371	....	5	376	22 395	....	142	22,533
Stanton	4	4	....	....	91	97	188	188	400	60	....	....	60	1,353	....	....	1,353
Taintor	2	2	1	1	63	63	126	126	272	103	....	2	105	5,071	....	....	5,071
Weston	3	3	....	....	77	76	153	153	518	96	1	...	97	4,841	....	....	4,841
Total	75	74	13	13	2,219	2,122	4,341	4,236	9,741	3,010	1	28	3,039	168,774	....	1665	170,439

EAU CLAIRE COUNTY.

TOWNS.	Whole number of School District.	Number of Districts which have reported.	Whole number of parts of Districts in the Town.	Number of parts of Districts which have reported.	Number of Male children over 4 and under 20 years of age.	Number of Female children over 4 and under 20 years of age.	Whole number over 4 and under 20 years of age in town.	Number over 4 and under 20 years in Districts maintaining school 5 or more months.	Number of days school has been taught by qualified teachers during the year.	Number over 4 and under 20 years who have attended school.	Number over 4 years who have attended school.	Number over 20 years who have attended school.	Total number of different pupils who have attended school during the year.	Number of days attendance of pupils over 4 and under 20 years.	Number of days attendance of pupils under 4 years.	Number of days attendance of pupils over 20 years.	Total number of days attendance of different pupils during the year.
Bridge Creek	4	4	4	4	296	243	539	539	1,098	456	....	1	457	43,514	....	5	43,519
Brunswick	5	5	1	1	132	127	259	259	670	169	....	2	168	10.901	....	93	16,994
Eau Claire	3	3	....	....	943	973	1,916	1,916	517	1,331	....	17	1,348	120,166	....	489	120,654
Lincoln	4	4	1	1	214	175	389	389	522	202	....	....	202	12,212	....	....	12,212
Otter Creek	5	5	4	4	172	191	363	363	1,152	270	....	3	273	17,378	....	126	17,505
Pleasant Valley	2	2	1	1	36	39	75	75	352	44	....	....	44	2,443	....	....	2,443
Seymour	2	2	1	1	36	37	73	73	266	58	....	....	58	3,686	....	....	3,686

Union..............	5	5	....	....	95	106	201	201	710	152	....	....	152	11,498	....	....	11,490
Washington	8	8	....	....	112	92	204	204	913	160	3	1	164	8,294	116	32	8,442
Totals..........	38	38	12	12	2,036	1,983	4,019	4,019	6,194	2,839	3	24	2,866	230,091	116	745	236,953

FOND DU LAC COUNTY—*First District.*

Alto..............	9	9	4	4	186	280	566	566	1,756	454	1	5	455	34,013	10	15	35,028
Eldorado	6	6	3	3	430	349	779	779	1,264	343	....	3	346	21,529	....	12	21,541
Fond du Lac........	8	8	6	6	306	271	577	577	1,280	306	1	....	365	27,666	7	....	29,672
Friendship	5	5	4	4	256	201	457	457	747	298	...	2	300	19,816	....	50	19,866
Lamartine	9	9	4	4	309	288	597	597	1,822	484	....	2	486	31,920	....	....	40,601
Metomen	11	11	6	6	309	291	600	600	2,330	521	1	3	535	42,668	10	36	45,869
Oakfield	7	7	3	3	277	193	470	470	2,007	303	....	2	305	22,204	....	40	22,244
Ripon	8	8	6	6	209	191	400	400	1,805	256	1	3	260	19,541	54	124	19,819
Ripon, city	2	2	2	2	452	463	916	916	824	659	....	1	660	53,081	....	8	53,139
Rosendale.	8	8	5	5	248	231	479	479	1,613	239	1	....	340	19,402	1	....	19,403
Springvale..........	8	8	5	5	244	234	478	478	1,915	324	....	6	330	23,549	....	171	23,578
Waupun............	8	8	6	6	254	257	511	511	2,214	304	....	1	305	20,346	....	56	20,402
Waupun, village....	1	1	1	1	168	151	319	319	360	302	....	....	304	30,483	....	....	30,483
Totals	90	90	55	55	3,749	3,400	7,149	7,149	19,947	4,893	5	28	4,991	370,219	82	556	380,632
City of Fond du Lac	....	....	....	....	2,601	2,868	5,469	5,469	200	3,475	....	6	3,481	600,472	....	500	600,972
Grand Total	90	90	55	55	6,350	6,268	12,618	12,618	20,147	8,368	5	34	8,472	970,691	82	1056	981,604

FOND DU LAC COUNTY—*Second District.*

Ashford	8	8	3	3	430	384	814	814	1,434	500	....	....	500	28,83	....	....	28,834
Auburn	10	10	2	2	445	347	792	792	1,535	480	....	1	481	24,993	....	1	24,994
Byron.............	11	11	3	3	263	255	518	518	1,740	436	9	7	453	27,501	9	108	27,996

TABLE No. II.—*Districts, Children and School Attendance*—continued.

FOND DU LAC COUNTY—*Second District*—continued.

Towns.	Whole number of School Districts in the town.	Number of Districts which have reported.	Whole number of parts of Districts in the town.	Number of parts of Districts which have reported.	Number of Male children over 4 and under 20 years of age.	Number of Female children over 4 and under 20 years of age.	Whole number over 4 and under 20 years of age in town.	Number over 4 and under 20 years in Districts maintaining school 5 or more months.	Number of days school has been taught by qualified teachers during the year.	Number over 4 and under 20 years who have attended school.	Number under 4 years who have attended school.	Number over 20 years who have attended school.	Total number of different pupils who have attended school during the year.	Total number of days attendance of different pupils during the year.	Number of days attendance of pupils under 4 years.	Number of days attendance of pupils over 20 years.	Number of days attendance of pupils over 4 and under 20 years.
Calumet	5	5	....	....	343	291	684	684	864	267	2	....	327	27,646	20	....	27,666
Eden	10	10	4	4	340	347	687	687	1,546	500	....	....	500	23,884	....	....	23,824
Empire	8	8	1	1	228	207	435	435	1,259	372	....	....	372	27,618	....	....	27,618
Forest	9	9	4	4	338	359	697	697	1,482	313	1	2	316	24,749	....	103	24,852
Marshfield	1	1	6	6	458	350	808	808	875	358	....	....	358	54,986	....	....	54,986
Osceola	8	8	2	2	268	300	568	568	1,266	404	....	....	404	30,509	....	....	40,509
Taycheedah	8	8	2	2	328	278	606	606	831	297	....	....	297	13,878	....	....	13,878
Totals	78	78	33	33	3,441	3,118	6,559	6,559	11,832	3,922	12	10	4,004	289,548	29	207	100,847

GRANT COUNTY.

Towns.	Whole number of School Districts in the town.	Number of Districts which have reported.	Whole number of parts of Districts in the town.	Number of parts of Districts which have reported.	Number of Male children over 4 and under 20 years of age.	Number of Female children over 4 and under 20 years of age.	Whole number over 4 and under 20 years of age in town.	Number over 4 and under 20 years in Districts maintaining school 5 or more months.	Number of days school has been taught by qualified teachers during the year.	Number over 4 and under 20 years who have attended school.	Number under 4 years who have attended school.	Number over 20 years who have attended school.	Total number of different pupils who have attended school during the year.	Total number of days attendance of different pupils during the year.	Number of days attendance of pupils under 4 years.	Number of days attendance of pupils over 20 years.	Number of days attendance of pupils over 4 and under 20 years.
Beetown	12	12	3	3	382	367	749	749	1,456	533	....	1	534	30,190	....	44	30,234
Bloomington	12	10	7	5	238	256	494	494	1,588	338	....	3	341	29,971	....	138	30,109
Blue River	6	6	2	2	171	164	335	335	696	181	....	4	185	10,033	....	135	10,168
Boscobel	1	1	....	....	336	340	676	676	198	567	....	14	581	62,318	....	840	63,158
Cassville	5	5	....	....	299	278	577	577	729	351	....	6	357	26,867	37	261	27,165

Clifton	12	12	5	5	210	210	420	420	1,579	356	....	7	363	20,906	....	332	21,238
Ellenboro	9	8	3	2	176	166	842	842	1,025	290	....	4	294	11,300	....	99	11,399
Fennimore	17	17	5	5	408	365	773	773	2,395	531	1	2	534	24,006	27	19	24,052
Glen Haven	7	7	2	2	223	218	441	441	1,172	325	5	1	331	22,274	150	137	22,561
Harrison	8	8	....	....	207	179	386	386	1,065	282	....	....	282	14,894	....	....	14,894
Hazel Green	8	8	1	1	412	416	828	828	1,310	616	....	3	619	44,537	....	148	44,685
Hickory Grove	9	9	4	4	201	185	386	386	1,176	251	2	6	259	13,602	15	215	13,832
Jamestown	8	8	....	....	233	214	447	447	1,002	296	....	....	296	17,083	....	....	17,083
Lancaster	16	14	6	6	551	531	1,082	1,082	2,071	698	....	1	699	61,407	....	2	61,409
Liberty	8	8	2	2	204	185	389	389	1,221	342	4	1	347	20,468	48	81	20,547
Lima	9	9	5	5	214	200	414	414	1,151	293	....	....	293	15,447	....	....	15,447
Little Grant	8	8	3	3	165	170	335	335	1,035	202	....	....	202	11,527	....	....	11,527
Marion	8	8	4	4	144	153	297	297	1,058	140	....	2	142	7,521	....	14	7,535
Millville	3	3	2	2	36	33	69	69	362	53	....	....	53	3,902	....	....	3,902
Mount Hope	6	6	4	4	188	186	374	374	896	278	....	....	278	12,343	....	....	12,343
Muscoda	5	5	....	....	202	206	408	408	610	249	....	....	249	3,798	....	....	3,798
Paris	7	7	3	3	181	163	344	344	930	227	....	2	229	12,530	....	29	12,559
Patch Grove	10	10	8	8	169	154	323	305	1,280	275	....	....	275	10,166	....	....	10,166
Platteville	10	10	2	2	712	699	411	411	1,428	953	....	1	954	66,252	....	56	66,308
Potosi	10	10	2	2	622	547	1,169	1,169	1,309	561	....	4	565	38,442	....	153	38,595
Smelser	8	8	2	2	284	223	507	507	1,188	320	....	....	320	17,012	....	....	17,012
Waterloo	8	8	....	....	204	181	385	385	1,016	288	....	2	290	11,089	....	186	11,275
Watterstown	5	5	....	....	140	112	252	252	677	219	1	1	221	10,424	10	41	10,475
Wingville	8	8	3	3	227	180	407	407	1,092	296	....	1	297	9,930	....	36	9,966
Woodman	7	7	4	4	151	124	275	275	983	204	....	1	205	10,828	....	42	10,865
Wyalusing	8	8	4	4	175	181	356	356	1,065	307	....	....	307	16,959	....	....	16,959
Totals.	258	253	86	83	8,065	7,586	15,651	15,544	34,863	10,822	13	67	10,902	668,021	287	2,958	671,266

GREEN COUNTY.

Adams	6	6	1	1	205	207	412	412	867	286	....	....	286	12,270	....	....	12,270
Albany	7	7	2	2	258	270	528	528	1,323	422	12	4	444	28,512	....	129	28,641
Brooklyn	5	5	5	5	227	250	477	477	1,431	446	....	....	448	23,710	....	102	23,812

TABLE No. II.—*Districts, Children and School Attendance*—continued.

GREEN COUNTY—continued.

TOWNS.	Whole number of School Districts in the town.	Number of Districts which have reported.	Whole number of parts of Districts in the Town.	Number of parts of Districts which have reported.	Number of Male children over 4 and under 20 years of age.	Number of Female children over 4 and under 20 years of age.	Whole number over 4 and under 20 years of age in town.	Number over 4 and under 20 years in Districts maintaining school 5 or more months.	Number of days school has been taught by qualified teachers during the year.	Number over 4 and under 20 years who have attended school.	Number under 4 years who have attended school.	Number over 20 years who have attended school.	Total number of different pupils who have attended school during the year.	Number of days attendance of pupils over 4 and under 20 years.	Number of days attendance of pupils under 4 years.	Number of days attendance of pupils over 20 years.	Total number of days attendance of different pupils during the year.
Cadiz	9	9	3	3	303	272	575	575	1,226	453	1	2	456	26,361	3	100	26,464
Clarno	9	9	1	1	294	300	594	594	1,446	......	....	....	......	19,246	....	.....	19,246
Decatur	7	7	4	4	383	406	789	789	2,584	636	....	9	645	35,500	....	388	35,888
Exeter	6	6	3	3	192	181	373	373	1,409	295	3	1	299	18,708	45	....	18,753
Jefferson	6	6	4	4	295	356	651	651	1,484	418	....	3	421	26,499	....	90	26,589
Jordan	5	5	3	3	242	205	447	447	999	400	....	1	401	21,842	....	43	21,885
Monroe	5	5	5	5	763	760	1,523	1,523	3,770	1,122	3	1	1,126	116,148	50	71	116,269
Mt Pleasant	9	9	2	2	230	231	461	461	1,161	400	1	4	405	17,718	4	85	17,807
New Glarus	3	3	6	6	197	162	359	359	668	218	....	....	218	16,262	...	...	16,262
Spring Grove	8	8	1	1	274	249	523	523	1,272	411	2	1	414	20,780	22	82	20,884
Sylvester	7	7	3	3	168	187	355	355	1,594	306	....	9	315	25,871	....	.....	25,871
Washington	5	5	4	4	216	186	402	402	1,268	319	2	3	324	15,819	10	79	15,918
York	4	4	2	2	208	186	394	394	850	325	....	....	325	9,487	....	.....	9,487
Totals	101	101	49	49	4,445	4,408	8,863	8,868	23,652	6,323	24	40	6,527	483,683	144	1,119	484,946

GREEN LAKE COUNTY.

Berlin	2	2	8	7	192	147	339	339	1,257	278	....	2	280	20,532	....	70	20,602
Brooklyn	3	3	7	7	257	224	481	481	1,261	364	....	1	365	23,421	....	40	23,461
Green Lake	7	7	9	9	304	261	565	565	2,387	427	....	1	428	41,075	....	33	41,018
Kingston	2	2	5	5	173	163	336	336	1,103	324	....	3	327	10,057	...	50	10,107
Mackford	3	3	3	3	276	158	534	534	1,769	395	1	3	499	22,573	61	....	22,634
M[illegible]er	3	3	7	7	243	221	464	464	1,193	250	1	5	256	21,681	10	100	21,791
Marquette	2	2	4	4	160	159	319	317	869	191	....	....	191	14,253	....	....	14,253
Princeton	5	5	2	2	360	358	718	718	829	492	....	....	492	18,836	....	....	18,836
St. Marie	2	2	6	6	163	140	303	303	1,005	150	....	1	151	8,388	....	2	8,390
Seneca	2	2	4	4	85	84	169	169	802	112	....	....	112	7,512	....	....	7,512
Totals	36	36	55	54	2,218	2,015	4,228	4,228	12,475	2,983	2	16	3,001	188,328	71	295	188,694
City of Berlin	....	....	....	....	532	950	1,091	1,091	200	669	....	....	960	86,582	....	....	86,582
Grand Total	36	36	55	54	2,745	2,574	5,319	5,319	12,675	3,652	2	16	3,670	274,910	71	295	275,276

IOWA COUNTY.

Arena	12	12	3	3	512	449	951	951	2,087	687	2	2	691	39,875	90	34	39,999
Clyde	4	4	2	1	146	149	297	297	556	184	....	....	184	8,287	....	....	8,287
Dodgeville	12	12	4	4	761	763	1,524	1,524	2,273	1,143	2	....	1,145	76,507	....	64	76,571
Highland	11	11	3	3	709	661	1,891	1,391	1,657	801	4	4	809	42,138	5	81	42,224
Linden	9	9	3	3	372	363	735	725	1,482	598	....	....	598	31,411	....	....	31,411
Mifflin	9	9	2	2	319	292	611	611	1,548	....	....	....	427	22,341	....	....	22,341
Mineral Point	12	11	2	2	363	289	652	652	1,596	400	....	6	406	23,630	....	224	23,850
Moscow	4	4	3	3	239	243	481	481	....	....	....	....	....	....	....	....	....
Pulaski	6	6	1	1	338	272	610	610	1,014	389	1	....	390	36,507	37	....	36,544
Ridgeway	14	14	4	4	539	536	1,165	1,165	....	....	....	....	....	....	....	....	....
Waldwick	5	5	1	1	203	217	420	420	....	....	....	....	....	....	....	....	....
Wyoming	6	6	2	2	124	164	288	288	862	183	....	....	183	18,799	....	....	18,799
Totals	105	104	27	29	4,615	4,387	8,902	8,902	13,355	4,385	7	14	4,399	257,495	132	408	258,030

TABLE No. II.—*Districts, Children and School Attendance*—continued.

IOWA COUNTY—continued.

TOWNS.	Whole number of School Districts in the town.	Number of Districts which have reported.	Whole number of parts of Districts in the town.	Number of parts of Districts which have reported.	Number of Male children over 4 and under 20 years of age.	Number of Female children over 4 and under 20 years of age.	Whole number over 4 and under 20 years of age in town.	Number over 4 and under 20 years in Districts maintaining school 5 or more months.	Number of days school has been taught by qualified teachers during the year.	Number over 4 and under 20 years who have attended school.	Number under 4 years who have attended school.	Number over 20 years who have attended school.	Total number of different pupils who have attended school during the year.	Number of days attendance of pupils over 4 and under 20 years.	Number of days attendance of pupils under 4 years.	Number of days attendance of pupils over 20 years.	Total number of days attendance of different pupils during the year.
City of Mineral Point	....	....	....	....	609	741	1,350	1,350	160	567	....	10	577	69,449	....	118	69,567
Grand Total	105	104	27	29	5,224	5,128	10,2q2	10,252	13,515	4,952	7	24	4,976	326,944	132	521	327,597

JACKSON COUNTY.

TOWNS.	Whole number of School Districts in the town.	Number of Districts which have reported.	Whole number of parts of Districts in the town.	Number of parts of Districts which have reported.	Number of Male children over 4 and under 20 years of age.	Number of Female children over 4 and under 20 years of age.	Whole number over 4 and under 20 years of age in town.	Number over 4 and under 20 years in Districts maintaining school 5 or more months.	Number of days school has been taught by qualified teachers during the year.	Number over 4 and under 20 years who have attended school.	Number under 4 years who have attended school.	Number over 20 years who have attended school.	Total number of different pupils who have attended school during the year.	Number of days attendance of pupils over 4 and under 20 years.	Number of days attendance of pupils under 4 years.	Number of days attendance of pupils over 20 years.	Total number of days attendance of different pupils during the year.
Albion	5	5	2	2	341	348	689	689	942	502	....	2	504	52,148	....	160	52,308
Alma..........	3	3	5	5	206	184	390	390	1,179	378	....	....	378	28,880	....	....	20,880
Garden Valley	5	5	4	4	204	162	366	366	1,182	155	....	2	157	7,436	....	49	7,485
Hixton	8	8	2	2	245	214	459	459	1,271	291	....	....	291	15,495	....	....	15,495
Irving..........	8	8	1	1	288	255	493	493	1,172	299	2	2	306	17,810	25	110	17,445
Manchester	5	5	1	1	98	101	199	199	752	129	2	....	131	8,171	6	....	8,187
Melrose..........	8	8	2	1	212	205	417	417	1,130	333	1	1	335	21,134	10	17	21,161
Northfield	4	4	1	1	135	112	247	219	495	111	3	1	115	7,087	48	50	7,185
Springfield	7	7	3	3	224	174	398	398	1,384	309	....	2	311	12,869	....	44	12,913
Totals	53	53	21	20	1,903	1,755	3,658	3,630	9,407	2,502	8	10	2,520	162,521	89	430	163,050

JEFFERSON COUNTY.

Aztalan	11	11	5	5	274	261	535	535	1,461	247	....	2	249	12,014	....	8	12,022
Cold Spring	6	6	2	2	175	166	841	841	918	270	....	...	270	9,285	....	.....	9,285
Concord	12	12	8	8	325	305	630	630	1,308	476	....	....	476	23,346	....	.....	23,346
Farmington	11	11	3	3	494	488	982	982	1,225	456	....	....	456	15,977	....	.....	15,977
Hebron	7	7	2	2	259	218	495	495	1,117	338	4	4	346	27,598	85	100	27,773
Ixonia	13	13	6	6	367	381	748	748	1,633	339	....	....	339	20,383	....	.....	20,338
Jefferson	15	15	4	4	924	834	1,758	1,758	1,903	877	....	....	877	64,698	....	75	64,773
Koshkonong	10	10	6	6	585	543	1,101	1,101	1,460	790	....	....	790	77,373	....	.....	77,378
Lake Mills	11	11	9	9	258	261	517	517	1,542	416	...	1	417	11,688	...	18	11,706
Milford	10	10	4	4	312	310	622	622	1,415	400	1	4	405	27,000	1	141	27,142
Oakland	13	13	6	6	202	163	365	365	1,827	206	....	1	261	18,767	....	31	18,798
Palmyra	11	11	6	6	332	295	627	627	1,628	377	....	1	378	37,806	....	34	37,840
Sullivan	10	10	6	6	327	307	634	634	1,510	469	....	1	470	31,549	....	56	31,605
Sumner	5	5	4	4	93	91	183	183	784	114	....	...	114	6,940	....	.....	9,940
Waterloo	10	10	5	5	238	228	462	462	1,238	280	....	....	280	9,237	..	.....	9,237
Waterloo, village	1	1	....	....	124	117	241	241	200	177	....	5	182	23,514	....	273	24,887
Watertown	12	12	4	4	496	491	987	987	1,608	511	....	....	511	40,956	....	.....	40,956
Totals	168	168	80	80	5,755	5,455	11,210	11,210	22,772	6,817	5	19	6,841	458,231	36	736	459,003
City of Watertown	....	...	....	....	1,850	1,792	3,642	3,642	200	1,294	....	...	....	176,167	....	.....	176,167
Grand Total	168	168	80	80	7,605	7,247	14,852	14,852	22,972	8,111	5	19	6,841	634,398	36	736	635,170

JUNEAU COUNTY.

Armenia	3	3	....	....	47	50	97	97	317	79	....	2	81	2,877	....	2	2,879
Clearfield	3	3	1	1	54	35	89	85	362	74	....	....	74	3,967	....	....	3,967
Fountain	6	6	1	1	135	120	255	255	795	171	...	2	173	10,059	...	77	10,136
Germantown	6	5	1	1	113	117	230	153	747	165	....	....	165	14,786	..	.....	14,786
Kildare	4	4	3	3	160	130	290	290	789	266	..	....	266	11,728	..	.....	11,728
Lemonweir	6	6	6	6	200	214	414	414	1,668	263	1	....	664	15,689	15	.....	15,704

Table No. II.—*Districts, Children and School Attendance*—continued.

Juneau County—continued.

Towns.	Whole number of School Districts in the town.	Number of districts which have reported.	Whole number of parts of Districts in the town.	Number of parts of Districts which have reported.	Number of Male children, over 4 and under 20 years of age.	Number of Female children over 4 and under 20 years of age.	Whole number over 4 and under 20 years of age in town.	Number over 4 and under 20 years in Districts maintaining school 5 or more months.	Number of days school has been taught by qualified teachers during the year.	Number over 4 and under 20 years who have attended school.	Number under 4 years who have attended school.	Number over 20 years who have attended school.	Total number of different pupils who have attended school during the year.	Number of days attendance of pupils over 4 and under 20 years.	Number of days attendance of pupils under 4 years.	Number of days attendance of pupils over 20 years.	Total number of days attendance of different pupils during the year.
Lindina	4	4	4	4	260	232	492	492	1,178	324	1	2	327	21,378	36	80	21,389
Lisbon	2	2	2	2	81	74	155	155	564	141	....	2	143	9,242	....	....	9,242
Lyndon	3	3	2	2	106	97	203	142	613	128	1	....	129	6,387	20	....	6,407
Marion	4	4	....	....	67	53	120	120	550	111	....	2	113	7,020	....	210	7,230
Mauston	1	1	....	....	193	173	366	366	180	312	....	47	359	43,200	....	470	43,670
Necedah	2	2	2	2	240	290	530	508	460	442	1	....	443	81,600	5	....	81,605
New Lisbon	1	1	....	....	241	252	493	493	190	393	2	3	398	38,124	23	96	38,243
Orange	3	3	....	....	89	78	167	167	426	93	....	....	93	6,530	....	....	6,530
Plymouth	5	5	2	2	212	203	415	415	916	325	....	1	326	21,490	....	138	21,628
Seven Mile Creek	6	6	4	4	204	183	387	387	1,077	286	....	....	286	18,662	....	....	18,662
Summit	5	5	4	4	183	159	342	342	1,154	250	4	2	256	18,483	13	23	18,519
Wonewoc	6	6	4	4	238	231	469	469	1,404	417	....	1	418	18,444	....	13	18,475
Totals	70	69	36	36	2,823	2,691	5,514	5,350	13,390	4,240	10	64	4,814	289,662	112	1127	290,901

KENOSHA COUNTY.

Towns.	Whole number of School Districts in the town.	Number of districts which have reported.	Whole number of parts of Districts in the town.	Number of parts of Districts which have reported.	Number of Male children, over 4 and under 20 years of age.	Number of Female children over 4 and under 20 years of age.	Whole number over 4 and under 20 years of age in town.	Number over 4 and under 20 years in Districts maintaining school 5 or more months.	Number of days school has been taught by qualified teachers during the year.	Number over 4 and under 20 years who have attended school.	Number under 4 years who have attended school.	Number over 20 years who have attended school.	Total number of different pupils who have attended school during the year.	Number of days attendance of pupils over 4 and under 20 years.	Number of days attendance of pupils under 4 years.	Number of days attendance of pupils over 20 years.	Total number of days attendance of different pupils during the year.
Totals	7	7	6	6	236	239	473	473	1,876	216	....	3	219	13,794	....	130	13,924

Bristol	7	7	3	3	192	201	393	393	1,095	290	....	4	294	24,032	....	200	24,243
Paris	10	10	3	3	193	187	370	370	1,753	257	....	....	257	18,194	....	....	18,194
Pleasant Prairie	11	11	3	2	243	229	472	472	1,589	316	....	....	316	21,075	....	....	12,526
Randall	3	3	2	2	113	96	209	209	849	157	....	....	157	12,526	....	....	12,526
Salem	9	0	1	1	267	248	515	515	1,582	303	....	10	313	32,294	....	78	33,691
Somers	8	8	6	5	284	225	509	509	1,858	288	1	8	248	21,845	21	277	22,143
Wheatland	6	6	....	....	185	180	365	365	773	204	....	....	204	13,114	....	....	13,114
Totals	61	61	24	23	1,713	1,605	3,306	3,306	11,295	2,081	1	25	2,057	156,874	21	685	157,580
City of Kenosha	....	....	....	....	910	2,002	1,912	1,912	109	575	10	5	595	107,350	800	700	108,850
Grand totals	61	61	24	23	2,623	2,607	5,218	5,218	11,404	2,606	11	30	2,652	264,224	831	1885	266,430

LA CROSSE COUNTY.*

Bangor	7	7	2	2	243	258	501	501	1,210	354	7	4	365	32,969	235	186	33,390
Burns	9	9	1	1	211	180	391	391	1,257	326	3	1	330	30,889	72	60	31,021
Campbell	4	4	1	1	143	128	271	271	598	187	....	....	187	33,086	....	....	33,086
Farmington	9	9	3	3	344	322	666	666	1,502	390	....	....	393	24,390	....	198	24,577
Greenfield	4	4	2	2	143	117	260	200	572	125	....	....	125	8,056	....	....	8,056
Hamilton	10	10	5	5	546	442	888	888	2,055	579	....	2	599	54,956	....	87	55,043
Holland	4	4	2	2	170	148	318	318	748	265	25	2	292	10,666	....	38	10,704
Onalaska	7	7	1	1	308	287	595	595	1,141	356	3	5	364	21,537	2	95	21,634
Shelby	3	3	2	2	147	121	268	268	603	155	....	1	156	9,062	....	31	9,093
Washington	4	4	1	1	218	177	395	395	434	171	....	....	177	8,254	....	....	8,254
Totals	61	61	20	20	2,373	2,180	4,533	4,493	10,120	2,932	38	18	2,988	238,794	309	695	234,798
City of La Crosse	....	....	..	....	1,600	1,765	3,365	3,365	200	1,752	....	10	1,763	177,768	....	420	178,188
Grand totals	61	61	20	20	3,973	3,945	7,918	7,858	10,320	4,684	38	28	4,750	411,562	309	1115	412,986

*No report received from Kewaunee county at the date of printing this table.

Table No. II.—*Districts, Children and School Attendance*—continued.

LA FAYETTE COUNTY.

Towns.	Whole number of School Districts in the town.	Number of Districts which have reported.	Whole number of parts of Districts in the town.	Number of parts of Districts which have reported.	Number of Male children over 4 and under 20 years of age.	Number of Female children over 4 and under 20 years of age.	Whole number over 4 and under 20 years of age in town.	Number over 4 and under 20 years in Districts maintaining school 5 or more months.	Number of days school has been taught by qualified teachers during the year.	Number over 4 and under 20 years who have attended school.	Number under 4 years who have attended school.	Number over 20 years who have attended school.	Total number of different pupils who have attended school during the year.	Total number of days attendance of different pupils during the year.	Number of days attendance of pupils under 4 years.	Number of days attendance of pupils over 20 years.	Number of days attendance of pupils over 4 and under 20 years.
Argyle	6	6	3	3	221	211	432	432	1,167	285	....	6	291	18,728	....	155	18,888
Belmont	4	4	3	3	274	256	530	530	1,077	416	1	1	418	26,872	20	22	26,914
Benton	6	6	4	4	381	354	735	735	1,420	409	....	1	410	24,461	...	15	24,476
Blanchard	1	1	3	3	128	98	226	226	547	179	....	2	181	12,465	...	139	12,604
Darlington	7	7	3	3	540	548	1,088	1,088	1,475	916	1	9	926	62,115	1	489	62,605
Elk Grove	6	6	2	2	180	191	371	359	794	262	....	....	262	16,961	....	....	16,961
Fayette	8	8	....	....	228	218	446	446	1,109	350	....	....	350	24,170	....	....	24,170
Gratiot	10	10	7	7	358	343	701	701	2,582	520	1	....	521	30,122	30	....	30,152
Kendall	4	4	6	6	198	188	381	381	1,286	189	....	2	191	7,204	....	41	7,235
Monticello	3	3	4	4	108	112	220	220	905	260	....	....	260	15,555	....	....	15,555
New Diggings	3	4	1	1	393	384	777	777	578	384	....	....	384	28,175	...	....	28,175
Seymour	4	4	4	4	220	205	425	425	1,279	332	....	1	333	19,284	....	41	19,325
Shullsburg	6	6	1	1	522	583	1,095	1,095	1,121	748	....	....	748	51,571	....	.....	51,571
Wayne	7	7	3	3	225	218	443	443	1,518	354	....	4	358	21,594	...	174	21,768
White Oak Spring	2	2	1	1	96	93	189	189	475	102	2	....	104	2,437	88	.....	2,525
Willow Springs	8	8	2	2	239	217	456	456	1,283	318	....	2	320	19,059	....	108	19,169
Wiota	8	8	5	5	361	317	678	678	1,517	462	4	...	466	24,735	41	.....	24,776
Totals	94	94	52	52	4,672	4,521	9,198	9,181	6,498	6,486	9	28	6,523	405,508	180	1179	406,867

MANITOWOC COUNTY.

Cato	6	6	5	5	366	382	748	748	1,088	484	....	3	487	32,664	....	161	32,825
Centerville	5	5	....	....	338	314	652	652	726	272	....	....	272	35,946	....	....	35,946
Cooperstown	6	6	....	....	365	374	739	739	808	281	....	....	289	36,413	....	....	36,413
Eaton	4	4	4	4	318	300	618	618	689	353	....	1	354	17,069	....	18	17,087
Franklin	5	5	4	4	415	418	853	853	1,191	324	....	....	324	18,268	....	....	18,268
Gibson	7	7	2	2	394	382	776	776	960	411	....	1	412	30,027	....	24	30,051
Kossuth	5	5	2	2	518	484	1,002	1,002	868	315	....	....	315	24,997	....	....	24,997
Liberty	4	4	5	5	247	252	499	447	564	325	1	1	327	12,345	....	24	12,369
Manitowoc	1	1	5	5	281	290	571	571	394	156	....	....	156	10,539	....	....	10,539
Manitowoc, city	1	1	3	3	1,206	1,265	2,471	2,471	737	1,311	1	6	1,318	149,869	30	360	150,259
Manitowoc Rapids	6	6	....	....	453	406	859	859	937	433	....	2	435	30,061	....	92	30,153
Maple Grove	4	4	3	3	312	259	571	571	700	331	12	....	343	11,021	40	....	11,061
Meeme	6	6	....	....	366	362	728	728	907	358	4	....	362	21,305	10	....	21,315
Mishicott	6	6	2	2	381	349	730	730	1,265	482	1	....	483	33,409	85	....	33,494
Newton	6	6	1	1	457	447	904	904	811	309	1	1	311	15,602	1	1	15,604
Rockland	2	2	3	3	239	194	433	433	363	105	....	....	105	5,209	....	....	5,209
Schleswig	6	6	1	1	406	426	832	832	1,009	394	....	....	393	28,485	....	....	28,485
Two Creeks	2	2	....	....	130	122	252	252	321	126	....	....	126	10,923	....	....	10.923
Two Rivers	6	6	1	1	676	702	1,378	1,378	1,078	739	....	....	739	58,809	....	....	58,809
Totals	88	88	41	41	7,888	7,728	15,616	15,564	14,432	7,508	20	15	7,551	582,961	166	680	553,807

MARATHON COUNTY.

Bergen	2	2	....	....	15	11	26	26	287	21	....	....	21	2,515	....	....	2,515
Berlin	10	9	1	1	199	220	419	419	1,118	243	....	....	243	16,394	....	....	16,394
Jenny	2	1	....	....	61	33	94	94	198	59	....	....	59	....	....	....	....
Knowlton	1	1	....	....	30	37	67	67	180	35	....	....	35	3,247	....	....	3,247
Maine	5	4	1	1	113	129	242	242	520	174	....	....	174	9,212	....	....	9,212

Table No. II.—*Districts, Children and School Attendance*—continued.

Marathon County—continued.

Towns.	Whole number of School Districts in the town.	Number of Districts which have reported.	Whole number of parts of Districts in the town.	Number of parts of Districts which have reported.	Number of Male children over 4 and under 20 years of age.	Number of Female children over 4 and under 20 years of age.	Whole number over 4 and under 20 years of age in town.	Number over 4 and under 20 years in Districts maintaining school 5 or more months.	Number of days school has been taught by qualified teachers during the year.	Number over 4 and under 20 years who have attended school.	Number under 4 years who have attended school.	Number over 20 years who have attended school.	Total number of different pupils who have attended school during the year.	Total number of days attendance of different pupils during the year.	Number of days attendance of pupils under 4 years.	Number of days attendance of pupils over 20 years.	Number of days attendance of pupils over 4 and under 20 years.
Marathon	4	3	....	....	87	112	199	199	348	129	....	....	129	8,045	....	....	8,405
Mosinee	6	6	....	....	81	66	147	147	731	128	1	....	129	5,910	26	....	5,936
Stettin	6	6	....	....	155	162	317	317	600	174	....	....	174	1,661	....	....	1,661
Texas	6	6	....	....	61	83	144	144	888	102	....	....	102	7,364	....	....	7,364
Wausau	6	6	1	....	92	103	195	195	634	118	....	1	114	7,535	....	36	7,565
Wausau, city	1	1	....	....	333	330	663	663	178	400	....	2	402	42,548	....	....	42,548
Weston	3	2	1	1	70	72	142	142	400	109	....	....	109	5,655	....	....	5,655
Wien	2	2	....	....	48	16	64	64	209	84	....	....	84	2,083	....	....	2,083
Totals	54	49	4	3	1,345	1,374	2,719	2,719	6,286	1,721	1	3	1,725	112,164	26	30	112,220

MARQUETTE COUNTY.

Towns.	Whole number of School Districts in the town.	Number of Districts which have reported.	Whole number of parts of Districts in the town.	Number of parts of Districts which have reported.	Number of Male children over 4 and under 20 years of age.	Number of Female children over 4 and under 20 years of age.	Whole number over 4 and under 20 years of age in town.	Number over 4 and under 20 years in Districts maintaining school 5 or more months.	Number of days school has been taught by qualified teachers during the year.	Number over 4 and under 20 years who have attended school.	Number under 4 years who have attended school.	Number over 20 years who have attended school.	Total number of different pupils who have attended school during the year.	Total number of days attendance of different pupils during the year.	Number of days attendance of pupils under 4 years.	Number of days attendance of pupils over 20 years.	Number of days attendance of pupils over 4 and under 20 years.
Buffalo	5	5	5	5	156	158	314	314	1,436	256	....	2	258	19,279	....	59	19,338
Crystal Lake	3	3	2	2	141	124	265	265	545	115	....	2	117	4,275	....	160	4,434
Douglas	5	5	....	....	147	133	280	280	668	218	....	3	221	10,120	....	200	10,320
Harris	2	2	2	2	87	99	186	186	680	119	....	....	123	6,613	....	....	6,613

Mecan	3	3	....	....	153	175	328	328	330	107	....	....	107	4,763	....	....	4,763
Montello	3	3	4	4	197	184	381	381	900	260	....	....	268	17,552	....	155	17,707
Moundville	3	3	....	....	95	80	175	175	416	143	....	2	151	17,765	....	80	11,845
Neshkoro	2	2	2	2	98	69	167	167	460	87	....	....	87	3,724	....	....	3,724
Newton	3	3	1	1	121	115	236	236	451	69	....	3	72	4,606	....	84	4,690
Oxford	4	4	2	2	106	130	236	236	785	161	....	1	162	13,919	....	86	14,005
Packwaukee	4	4	3	3	143	122	265	249	921	183	....	....	183	11,339	....	....	11,339
Shields	1	1	3	3	94	84	178	178	446	139	1	1	156	8,034	....	....	8,034
Springfield	2	2	4	4	61	54	115	115	709	65	....	....	65	4,405	....	....	4,405
Westfield	1	1	5	5	129	109	238	238	789	195	....	....	195	16,325	....	....	16,325
Totals	41	41	33	33	1,728	1,636	3,364	3,348	9,536	2,117	1	14	2,165	136,719	....	824	137,542

MILWAUKEE COUNTY—*First District.*

Franklin	5	5	5	5	394	405	799	799	1,767	305	....	1	306	23,473	....	27	23,500
Greenfield	7	7	7	7	459	455	914	914	2,138	498	....	....	498	31,505	....	....	31,505
Lake	7	7	2	2	744	749	1,493	1,493	1,430	675	....	....	675	66,976	....	....	66,976
Oak Creek	8	8	2	2	460	450	910	910	1,582	499	....	....	499	34,948	....	....	34,948
Totals	27	27	16	16	2,057	2,059	4,116	4,116	6,917	1,977	....	1	1,978	156,902	....	27	156,929

MILWAUKEE COUNTY—*Second District.*

Granville	11	11	1	1	469	453	922	922	1,606	465	....	....	465	23,926	....	....	23,926
Milwaukee	10	10	....	....	747	685	1,432	1,432	1,649	647	....	....	647	48,476	....	....	48,476
Wauwatosa	10	10	3	3	640	680	1,320	1,320	2,123	649	5	....	654	47,895	333	....	48,228
Totals	31	31	4	4	1,856	1,818	3,674	3,674	5,378	1,761	5	....	1,766	120,297	333	....	120,630
City of Milwaukee	....	....	....	....	14,259	14,896	29,155	29,155	196	11,224	....	....	11,224	1,233,192	....	....	1,233,192
Grand Total	31	31	4	4	16,115	16,714	32,829	32,829	5,574	12,985	5	....	12,990	1,353,489	333	....	1,353,822

TABLE No. II.—*Districts, Children and School Attendance*—continued.

MONROE COUNTY.

Towns.	Whole number of School Districts in the town.	Number of Districts which have reported.	Whole number of parts of Districts in the Town.	Number of parts of Districts which have reported.	Number of Male children over 4 and under 20 years of age.	Number of Female children over 4 and under 20 years of age.	Whole number over 4 and under 20 years of age in town.	Number over 4 and under 20 years in Districts maintaining school 5 or more months.	Number of days school has been taught by qualified teachers during the year.	Number over 4 and under 20 years who have attended school.	Number under 4 years who have attended school.	Number over 20 years who have attended school.	Total number of different pupils who have attended school during the year.	Number of days attendance of pupils over 4 and under 20 years.	Number of days attendance of pupils under 4 years.	Number of days attendance of pupils over 20 years.	Total number of days attendance of different pupils during the year.
Adrian	8	8	8	8	154	135	289	289	627	192	....	8	195	12,055	....	186	12,241
Angelo	1	1	4	8	77	97	174	174	370	156	....	....	156	9,342	....	....	9,342
Clifton	4	4	1	1	163	126	289	289	520	139	....	....	139	8,673	....	....	8,673
Glendale	4	4	2	2	180	153	333	333	748	238	....	....	238	17,130	....	....	17,130
Greenfield	8	2	2	2	122	102	224	224	886	177	....	5	182	7,708	....	98	7,806
Jefferson	5	5	2	2	218	174	392	392	562	215	....	1	216	9,960	....	40	10,000
La Fayette	3	2	2	2	89	72	161	161	402	144	....	....	144	12,137	....	....	12,137
Leon	2	2	7	7	118	157	275	275	431	140	...	6	146	11,242	....	100	11,342
Lincoln	12	12	2	2	269	251	520	520	1,784	421	2	4	427	22,420	46	100	22,566
Little Falls	7	7	1	1	144	114	258	248	914	192	1	....	193	12,910	19	....	12,929
Newtime	2	2	1	....	12	8	20	10	173	20	....	....	20	1,459	....	....	1,459
Oak Dale	5	5	1	1	187	167	354	354	630	212	....	....	212	9,773	....	....	9,773
Portland	4	4	3	3	165	134	299	299	669	182	....	....	182	9,204	....	....	9,204
Ridgeville	4	4	2	2	258	202	460	460	844	460	1	....	461	28,538	57	....	28,595
Sheldon	3	3	3	3	168	143	311	311	420	169	....	....	169	9,909	....	....	9,009
Sparta	7	7	5	5	621	653	1,274	1,274	1,729	1,122	1	3	1,126	106,229	7	124	106,360
Tomah	6	5	5	5	423	361	784	784	1,234	602	4	6	612	51,237	213	420	51,870
Wellington	5	5	3	3	208	154	362	362	769	236	....	1	237	18,263	....	20	18,283
Wells	8	8	6	6	133	126	264	264	910	250	5	4	259	13,889	42	123	14,054

Wilton	5	5	4	3	206	192	398	398	1,042	382	....	5	387	21,488	....	463	21,951
Totals..........	88	85	59	56	3,920	3,521	7,441	7,421	16,174	5,649	14	38	5,701	388,565	384	1,780	390,629

OCONTO COUNTY.

Gillett	3	3	....	....	43	45	88	88	388	55	....	....	55	4,471	....	....	4,471
Little Suamico......	3	3	....	....	128	118	246	246	360	134	....	....	134	5,260	....	....	5,260
Maple Valley.......	1	1	....	....	16	29	45	45	110	14	....	....	14	1,095	....	....	1,095
Marinette	1	1	....	....	323	297	620	620	180	259	2	....	261	34,866	12	....	34,878
Oconto............	6	6	....	....	190	145	335	335	999	235	....	....	235	15,632	....	....	15,632
Pensaukee..........	4	4	....	....	130	132	262	262	697	206	....	....	206	16,816	....	....	16,816
Peshtigo	7	7	....	....	339	196	635	617	1,003	424	..	4	428	27,669	....	135	27,804
Stiles	2	2	....	....	72	71	143	143	320	90	....	1	91	6,538	....	8	6,546
Totals..........	27	27	....	....	1,217	1,020	2,374	2,356	4,007	1,410	....	....	1,415	112,347	12	143	112,502
City of Oconto	....	....	....	....	512	477	989	989	202	833	....	....	833	....	....	....	63,978
Grand Total....	27	27	....	....	1,729	1,497	3,363	3,345	4,209	2,243	2	5	2,248	176,325	12	143	176,480

OUTAGAMIE COUNTY.

Black Creek.......	5	5	....	....	161	144	305	305	588	206	....	....	206	10,764	....	....	10,764
Bovina	5	5	....	....	101	112	213	213	634	123	2	....	125	5,650	....	....	5,650
Buchanan	4	4	....	....	194	203	397	397	572	228	....	....	228	12,250	....	....	12,250
Center	6	6	2	2	337	268	605	605	923	315	....	....	315	16,175	....	....	16,175
Cicero	3	3	....	....	42	30	72	72	364	30	....	....	30	2,214	....	....	2,214
Dale	5	5	2	2	207	192	399	399	926	340	....	....	340	24,127	....	....	24,127
Deer Creek.	1	1	....	....	44	44	88	88	132	60	....	....	60	5,275	....	....	5,275
Ellington	7	7	1	1	279	285	564	564	1,203	391	....	....	391	33,750	....	....	33,750
Freedom	4	4	3	3	334	301	635	635	921	400	....	....	400	22,561	....	....	22,561

TABLE No. II.—*Districts, Children and School Attendance*—continued.

OUTAGAMIE COUNTY—continued.

TOWNS.	Whole number of School Districts in the town.	Number of Districts which have reported.	Whole number of parts of Districts in the Town.	Number of parts of Districts which have reported.	Number of Male children over 4 and under 20 years of age.	Number of Female children over 4 and under 20 years of age.	Whole number over 4 and under 20 years of age in town.	Number over 4 and under 20 years in Districts maintaining school 5 or more months.	Number of days school has been taught by qualified teachers during the year.	Number over 4 and under 20 years who have attended school.	Number under 4 years who have attended school.	Number over 20 years who have attended school.	Total number of different pupils who have attended school during the year.	Number of days attendance of pupils over 4 and under 20 years.	Number of days attendance of pupils under 4 years.	Number of days attendance of pupils over 20 years.	Total number of days attendance of different pupils during the year.
Grand Chute	9	9	1	1	356	343	699	699	1,507	385	....	....	385	25,200	....	.....	25,200
Greenville	7	7	3	3	336	324	660	660	1,462	458	....	....	458	39,285	....	.....	39,235
Hortonia	4	4	2	2	252	238	490	490	702	365	....	....	365	24,983	33	.....	25,016
Kaukauna	6	6	....	....	374	332	706	706	1,042	447	....	....	447	35,360	....	.....	35,360
Liberty	3	3	1	1	98	110	208	208	569	117	....	....	117	4,418	....	.....	4,418
Maine	1	1	....	....	18	22	40	40	110	30	....	....	30	1,997	....	.....	1,997
Maple Creek	3	3	....	....	157	178	335	385	416	176	....	....	176	10,658	....	.....	10,658
Osborn	2	2	3	3	115	108	223	162	547	97	....	....	97	4,850	....	.....	4,850
Seymour	3	3	1	1	151	101	252	252	573	189	2	....	191	10,839	113	.....	10,952
Totals	78	78	19	19	3,556	3,335	6,891	6,830	13,199	4,357	4	....	4,361	290,306	146	.....	290,452
City of Appleton	....	....	....	....	1,090	1,000	2,090	2,090	185	1,003	....	....	1,003	87,253	....	.....	87,253
Grand Total	78	78	19	19	4,646	4,335	8,981	8,920	13,384	5,360	4	....	5,364	377,559	146	.....	377,705

OZAUKEE COUNTY.

Belgium	8	8	....	....	506	528	1,034	1,034	994	520	....	...	520	42,775	....	.....	42,775
Cedarburg	6	6	3	3	599	571	1,170	1,170	1,236	430	1	....	350	22,021	20	.....	22,041
Fredonia	7	7	3	3	474	426	900	900	1,524	478	2	..	480	35,208	92	.....	35,300
Grafton	5	5	2	2	419	371	790	790	1,034	347	10	....	357	26,440	408	.....	26,848
Mequon	12	12	1	1	680	613	1,293	1,293	1,951	608	....	....	608	42,825	....	.....	42,825
Port Washington	6	6	1	1	580	645	1,225	1,225	1,059	701	12	....	758	46,885	160	.....	47,045
Saukville	5	5	5	5	533	474	1,007	1,007	1,492	356	....	....	356	21,050	....	.....	21,050
Totals	49	49	15	15	3,791	3,628	7,419	7,419	9,290	3,360	25	...	3,409	237,204	670	.....	237,884

PEPIN COUNTY.

Albany	3	3	....	....	66	65	131	131	408	105	....	....	117	4,972	....	.....	4,972
Durand	1	1	3	3	204	204	408	408	632	265	....	....	285	27,789	....	.....	29,570
Frankfort	2	2	1	1	89	75	164	164	472	128	....	....	128	4,060	....	.....	4,060
Lima	4	4	4	3	109	94	203	203	892	171	....	....	171	6,048	....	.....	6,048
Pepin	6	6	....	....	203	201	404	404	690	300	....	6	306	20,864	....	294	21,158
Stockholm	3	3	....	....	100	92	192	192	349	116	....	4	120	5,392	....	61	5,453
Waterville	6	6	1	1	214	209	423	423	858	319	....	2	321	17,476	....	78	17,679
Waubeek	1	1	2	2	44	48	92	92	428	88	....	....	88	3,346	....	.....	5,967
Totals	26	26	12	9	1,029	988	2,017	2,017	4,724	1,492	....	12	1,492	89,917	....	433	394,919

PIERCE COUNTY.

Clifton	3	2	1	....	51	47	98	98	160	90	....	3	93	4,005	....	118	4,123
Diamond Bluff	2	2	3	3	130	79	209	209	631	166	....	....	166	14,396	....	.....	14,396
Ellsworth	5	5	....	....	217	177	394	394	554	240	....	....	240	5,585	....	.....	5,585

TABLE No. II.—*Districts, Children and School Attendance*—continued.

PIERCE COUNTY—continued.

Towns.	Whole number of School Districts in the town.	Number of Districts which have reported.	Whole number of parts of Districts in the town.	Number of parts of Districts which have reported.	Number of Male children over 4 and under 20 years of age.	Number of Female children over 4 and under 20 years of age.	Whole number over 4 and under 20 years of age in town.	Number over 4 and under 20 years in Districts maintaining school 5 or more months.	Number of days school has been taught by qualified teachers during the year.	Number over 4 and under 20 years who have attended school.	Number under 4 years who have attended school.	Number over 20 years who have attended school.	Total number of different pupils who have attended school during the year.	Number of days attendance of pupils over 4 and under 20 years.	Number of days attendance of pupils under 4 years.	Number of days attendance of pupils over 20 years.	Total number of days attendance of different pupils during the year.
El Paso	5	5	1	1	94	86	180	180	672	97	....	....	97	9,044	...	.....	9,044
Gilman	4	4	3	3	125	187	262	253	720	143	....	2	145	5,808	....	18	5,826
Hartland	5	5	3	3	223	193	416	416	1,133	339	....	2	341	13,866	....	13	13,879
Isabelle	1	1	2	2	48	52	100	100	400	88	....	....	88	2,106	....	.....	2,106
Maiden Rock	4	4	3	3	151	138	289	289	....	......	....	....	....	2,709	....	.....	2,709
Martell	5	5	2	2	220	212	432	432	767	248	....	1	249	10,326	....	30	10,356
Oak Grove	4	4	3	3	184	178	357	357	850	......	....	....	258	17,668	....	.....	17,668
Prescott	....	....	1	1	193	215	408	408	155	265	....	...	265	27,328	....	.....	27,328
River Falls	6	6	4	4	332	306	638	638	1,379	252	....	1	253	14,719	....	...	14,719
Rock Elm	7	7	2	2	143	147	290	250	948	123	15	5	143	11,747	67	371	12,186
Salem	3	3	2	1	48	57	105	105	536	64	....	1	65	4,109	....	48	4,155
Spring Lake	7	7	2	2	116	106	222	172	771	182	....	4	174	10,111	....	274	10,385
Trenton	2	2	2	2	81	69	150	99	388	99	....	....	99	3,510	....	.....	3,510
Trimbelle	6	6	2	2	191	150	341	341	....	269	....	....	269	16,151	....	.....	16,151
Union	5	5	....	...	70	76	146	166	580	86	....	1	87	7,222	....	12	7,234
Totals	74	73	36	34	2,617	2,420	5,037	4,916	9,644	2,695	15	20	2,782	180,360	67	384	181,811

POLK COUNTY.

Men	5	5	....	....	155	111	266	266	588	161	....	....	116	6,632	....	....	6,632
Balsam Lake	5	5	....	....	59	49	108	62	490	70	1	....	71	4,617	7	....	4,625
Blk Brk.	3	3	....	....	87	77	164	164	863	119	....	2	121	5,561	....	52	5,613
Farmington	5	5	....	....	172	163	335	335	646	225	....	....	225	15,716	....	....	15,716
Lincoln	4	4	....	....	105	81	186	191	549	131	1	....	132	2,600	1	....	2,601
Loraine	2	2	....	....	15	13	28	12	100	9	....	....	9	655	....	....	655
Luck	3	3	....	....	44	41	85	69	220	33	....	....	33	1,483	....	....	1,483
Milltown	1	1	1	1	44	25	69	69	345	41	....	....	41	2,513	....	....	2,513
Ola	5	5	2	2	164	150	314	314	1,078	247	4	2	253	18,736	10	13	18,759
St. Gix Falls	6	6	3	3	154	136	290	283	982	171	....	....	171	10,866	....	....	10,866
Sterling	4	4	1	1	83	86	169	169	540	94	....	....	94	2,169	....	....	2,169
Totals	43	43	7	7	1,062	932	2,014	1,921	5,901	1,301	6	4	1,311	71,550	18	65	71,633

PORTAGE COUNTY.

Al ond	2	2	6	6	119	116	235	235	1,082	193	....	4	197	7,398	....	108	7,506
Amherst	7	7	4	4	226	181	407	370	1,338	324	....	2	324	22,228	....	121	22,346
Belmont	6	6	....	....	98	107	205	205	873	184	....	....	184	11,304	....	....	11,304
Buena Vista	6	6	2	2	143	105	248	248	1,123	217	....	3	220	10,270	....	....	10,270
Eau Plaine	4	4	....	....	62	55	117	117	521	89	....	....	89	5,664	....	....	5,664
Grant	2	2	....	....	42	39	81	81	230	60	....	....	60	5,133	....	....	5,133
Hull	4	4	1	1	119	82	201	201	747	110	....	....	110	5,839	....	....	5,839
Lanark	3	3	4	4	83	72	155	155	857	170	....	1	171	11,790	....	....	11,791
Linwood	2	2	1	1	64	72	136	136	461	110	....	....	110	5,638	....	....	5,638
New Hope	5	5	....	....	197	204	401	401	505	216	....	1	217	8,784	....	5	8,789
Pine Grove	1	1	4	4	77	70	147	147	694	96	....	....	96	4,914	....	....	4,914
Plover	7	7	2	2	204	213	417	408	1,238	311	....	2	313	25,473	....	26	25,499
Sharon	5	5	....	....	222	206	428	428	618	134	....	....	134	7,842	....	....	7,842
Steven's Point	1	1	....	....	10	6	16	16	200	15	....	....	15	1,614	....	....	1,614

TABLE No. II.—*Districts, Children and School Attendance*—continued.

PORTAGE COUNTY—continued.

Towns.	Whole number of School Districts in the town.	Number of districts which have reported.	Whole number of parts of Districts in the town.	Number of parts of Districts which have reported.	Number of Male children, over 4 and under 20 years of age.	Number of Female children over 4 and under 20 years of age.	Whole number over 4 and under 20 years of age in town.	Number over 4 and under 20 years in Districts maintaining school 5 or more months.	Number of days school has been taught by qualified teachers during the year.	Number over 4 and under 20 years who have attended school.	Number under 4 years who have attended school.	Number over 20 years who have attended school.	Total number of different pupils who have attended school during the year.	Number of days attendance of pupils over 4 and under 20 years.	Number of days attendance of pupils under 4 years.	Number of days attendance of pupils over 20 years.	Total number of days attendance of different pupils during the year.
Steven's Point, city..	1	1	1	1	471	520	991	991	870	785	....	1	786	81,056	....	....	81,056
Stockton	7	7	4	4	195	230	425	425	1,474	808	1	1	810	21,633	....	14	21,647
Totals..........	68	68	29	20	2,333	2,278	4,610	4,559	12,777	3,272	1	15	3,288	236,516	....	274	236,790

RACINE COUNTY.

Towns.	Whole number of School Districts in the town.	Number of districts which have reported.	Whole number of parts of Districts in the town.	Number of parts of Districts which have reported.	Number of Male children, over 4 and under 20 years of age.	Number of Female children over 4 and under 20 years of age.	Whole number over 4 and under 20 years of age in town.	Number over 4 and under 20 years in Districts maintaining school 5 or more months.	Number of days school has been taught by qualified teachers during the year.	Number over 4 and under 20 years who have attended school.	Number under 4 years who have attended school.	Number over 20 years who have attended school.	Total number of different pupils who have attended school during the year.	Number of days attendance of pupils over 4 and under 20 years.	Number of days attendance of pupils under 4 years.	Number of days attendance of pupils over 20 years.	Total number of days attendance of different pupils during the year.
Burlington	4	4	5	5	505	509	1,014	1,014	1,316	446	....	1	447	38,498	....	4	38,502
Caledonia	8	8	7	7	575	539	1,114	1,114	2,244	725	....	....	725	57,017	....	....	57,017
Dover	6	6	5	5	213	178	391	351	1,514	206	....	....	206	19,578	....	....	19,578
Mt. Pleasant........	10	10	9	9	438	401	839	839	1,887	484	4	6	494	44,079	10	228	44,317
Norway	3	3	3	3	197	181	378	378	934	214	....	2	216	10,616	....	76	10,692
Raymond...........	7	7	6	6	304	280	584	584	1,885	326	....	....	326	22,022	....	....	22,022
Rochester	3	3	3	3	165	145	310	310	787	234	....	....	234	28,604	....	....	28,604
Waterford	7	7	3	3	304	271	575	575	1,582	339	1	....	340	33,671	32	....	33,703
Yorkville	8	8	6	6	283	263	546	546	2,245	436	1	1	438	32,936	11	76	33,023
Totals..........	56	56	47	47	2,984	2,767	5,751	5,711	14,394	3,410	6	10	3,426	289,016	58	384	289,458

Racine, city	....	....	....	....	1,926	2,187	4,063	4,063	200	2,299	....	3	2,302	299,546	....	315	299,861
Grand Total	56	56	47	47	4,910	4,904	9,814	9,774	14,594	5,709	6	13	5,728	581,562	53	699	582,314

RICHLAND COUNTY.

Akan	9	9	1	1	145	157	302	302	951	228	....	....	228	13,281	....	....	13,281
Bloom	6	6	4	4	288	228	516	516	960	396	....	....	396	19,440	....	....	19,440
Buena Vista........	7	7	1	1	177	178	355	355	1,007	323	....	10	333	24,728	....	427	25,155
Dayton.............	6	6	4	4	220	193	413	375	776	310	3	2	315	15,996	40	54	16,090
Eagle	8	8	1	1	244	260	504	504	1,078	396	....	...	396	18,163	...	....	18,163
Forest	9	9	4	4	192	156	348	348	1,046	342	1	2	345	14,917	15	86	15,018
Henrietta	5	5	4	4	183	195	378	378	616	272	....	3	275	17,090	....	28	17,122
Ithaca	5	4	5	5	250	262	512	476	1,052	394	....	1	395	22,507	....	11	22,518
Marshall	6	6	2	2	198	187	385	385	1,066	356	1	5	362	26,605	8	249	26,857
Orion	6	5	1	1	150	149	299	282	622	224	....	1	225	11,658	...	47	11,705
Richland	5	5	5	5	306	320	626	626	1,528	549	7	27	583	39,728	169	2113	42,010
Richwood	8	8	2	2	325	295	620	620	1,198	484	1	2	487	23,420	101	89	23,610
Rockbridge	6	6	7	7	240	186	426	426	966	340	1	3	344	19,487	4	147	10,638
Sylvan	9	9	....	....	194	198	392	392	1,073	368	....	3	371	19,568	....	113	19,681
Westford	5	5	2	2	200	179	379	379	813	287	....	....	287	9,902	....	....	9,902
Willow.............	5	5	4	4	174	161	335	335	869	232	7	2	241	12,774	66	118	12,958
Totals	105	103	47	47	3,486	3,304	6,790	6,737	15,621	5,501	21	61	5,583	309,268	398	3482	313,148

ROCK COUNTY—*First District.*

Avon	7	7	4	4	167	167	334	320	1,392	224	1	1	226	15,726	21	18	15,765
Center	2	2	12	12	214	202	416	116	2,242	332	...	1	330	16,907	21	7	16,935
Fulton	7	7	6	6	388	357	745	745	1,971	634	1	4	495	49,090	9	139	49,189
Janesville	7	7	4	4	194	153	347	347	1,614	240	1	1	242	14,964	31	48	15,043

Table No. II.—*Districts, Children and School Attendance*—continued.

Rock County—*First District*—continued.

Towns.	Whole number of School District.	Number of Districts which have reported.	Whole number of parts of Districts in the Town.	Number of parts of Districts which have reported.	Number of Male children over 4 and under 20 years of age.	Number of Female children over 4 and under 20 years of age.	Whole number over 4 and under 20 years of age in town.	Number over 4 and under 20 years in Districts maintaining school 5 or more months.	Number of days school has been taught by qualified teachers during the year.	Number over 4 and under 20 years who have attended school.	Number over 4 years who have attended school.	Number over 20 2ears who have attended school.	Total number of different pupils who have attended school during the year.	Number of days attendance of pupils over 4 and under 20 years.	Number of days attendance of pupils under 4 years.	Number of days attendance of pupils over 20 years.	Total number of days attendance of different pupils during the year.
Magnolia	6	6	5	5	210	199	409	409	1,591	283	....	2	275	20,063	....	111	20,174
Newark	8	8	1	1	205	219	424	424	1,258	361	1	4	366	22,824	5	164	22,993
Plymouth	5	5	8	8	275	252	257	257	1,931	367	1	3	387	16,346	50	.....	16,397
Porter	4	4	9	9	243	213	456	456	1,882	331	....	4	332	23,424	....	117	23,541
Spring Valley	5	5	5	5	238	228	466	466	1,362	378	....	1	379	25,640	....	48	25,688
Union	10	10	2	2	369	369	738	738	1,945	628	2	10	640	52,210	29	498	52,732
Totals	61	61	56	56	2,508	2,359	4,862	4,862	4,848	17,183	7	31	3,672	257,194	166	1145	258,505
City of Janesville	....	....	....	....	1,674	1,860	3,534	3,534	168	1,674	....	....	1,674	148,681	....	....	148,681
Grand Total	61	61	56	56	4,177	4,219	8,396	8,382	17,851	5,452	7	31	5,346	495,875	166	1145	407,186

Rock County—Second District.

Towns.	Whole number of School District.	Number of Districts which have reported.	Whole number of parts of Districts in the Town.	Number of parts of Districts which have reported.	Number of Male children over 4 and under 20 years of age.	Number of Female children over 4 and under 20 years of age.	Whole number over 4 and under 20 years of age in town.	Number over 4 and under 20 years in Districts maintaining school 5 or more months.	Number of days school has been taught by qualified teachers during the year.	Number over 4 and under 20 years who have attended school.	Number over 4 years who have attended school.	Number over 20 2ears who have attended school.	Total number of different pupils who have attended school during the year.	Number of days attendance of pupils over 4 and under 20 years.	Number of days attendance of pupils under 4 years.	Number of days attendance of pupils over 20 years.	Total number of days attendance of different pupils during the year.
Beloit	6	6	4	4	143	121	264	264	1,326	157	....	....	157	10,743	....	.....	10,743
Bradford	4	4	9	9	160	167	327	327	1,986	246	....	....	246	20,465	26	.....	20,491
Clinton	4	4	8	8	332	320	652	652	1,786	308	....	2	310	24,158	....	25	24,183

Harmony	8	8	3	3	238	185	423	423	1,475	289	....	1	290	19,776	....	27	19,803
Johnstown	6	6	5	5	308	188	396	396	1,367	77	....	....	77	6,684	....	76	6,684
La Prairie	4	4	11	11	182	186	368	368	2,223	391	....	1	392	27,907	...	123	27,983
Lima	5	5	3	3	161	115	276	276	2,155	234	....	2	236	19,684	....	....	19,806
Milton	5	5	7	7	320	268	588	588	1,817	436	....	....	436	44,276	....	....	44,276
Rock	6	6	6	6	207	165	372	372	1,808	358	....	....	358	20,064	....	....	20,064
Turtle	6	6	5	5	240	190	430	430	1,705	427	....	....	427	26,843	....	....	26,843
Totals	54	54	65	65	2,191	1,905	4,096	4,096	17,648	2,918	3	6	2,924	220,570	26	250	220,846
City of Beloit	....	....	....	....	752	753	1,505	1,505	197	923	....	1	924	112,367	....	....	112,367
Grand total	54	54	65	65	2,943	2,658	5,601	5,601	17,845	3,841	3	7	3,848	332,937	26	250	333,213

ST. CROIX COUNTY.

(Report not received in season for insertion here.)

SAUK COUNTY.

Barabo	4	4	7	7	680	545	1,175	1,175	1,648	1,052	....	12	1,064	89,680	....	165	89,795
Bear Creek	2	3	1	1	168	195	363	363	1,512	316	....	2	318	17,098	....	74	17,172
Dellona	4	4	5	5	117	115	232	226	1,104	216	....	....	216	10,149	....	....	10,149
Delton	5	5	4	4	163	163	326	305	1,121	289	....	....	289	19,461	....	....	19,461
Excelsior	6	6	4	4	152	161	313	282	1,190	243	....	....	243	16,196	....	....	16,196
Fairfield	6	6	2	1	151	127	278	278	876	239	....	2	241	15,339	....	55	15,394
Franklin	5	5	5	5	181	185	366	246	1,083	227	....	....	227	9,233	....	....	9,233
Freedom	6	6	1	1	180	176	356	356	750	241	....	1	242	12,628	....	54	12,682
Greenfield	4	4	3	3	169	131	300	300	952	228	....	3	231	15,339	....	70	15,409
Honey Creek	6	6	4	4	267	240	507	507	975	329	....	3	332	22,316	....	20	22,336
Ironton	3	3	4	4	243	252	495	495	1,388	387	....	3	390	22,980	....	39	23,019
La Valle	7	6	5	5	150	124	274	354	1,435	238	....	1	239	16,318	....	....	16,318
Merrimack	4	4	4	4	148	147	295	295	1,148	272	....	....	272	14,479	....	....	14,479
Prairie due Sac	4	4	4	1	384	395	779	779	802	548	....	5	553	56,174	....	524	56,698
Reedsburg	6	6	3	3	300	315	615	615	1,160	392	....	....	392	30,857	....	....	30,857

TABLE No. II.—*Districts, Children and School Attendance*—continued.

SAUK COUNTY—continued.

Towns.	Whole number of School Districts in the town.	Number of Districts which have reported.	Whole number of parts of Districts in the town.	Number of parts of Districts which have reported.	Number of Male children over 4 and under 20 years of age.	Number of Female children over 4 and under 20 years of age.	Whole number over 4 and under 20 years of age in town.	Number over 4 and under 20 years in Districts maintaining school 5 or more months.	Number of days school has been taught by qualified teachers during the year.	Number over 4 and under 20 years who have attended school.	Number under 4 years who have attended school.	Number over 20 years who have attended school.	Total number of different pupils who have attended school during the year.	Number of days attendance of pupils over 4 and under 20 years.	Number of days attendance of pupils under 4 years.	Number of days attendance of pupils over 20 years.	Total number of days attendance of different pupils during the year.
Spring Green	5	5	1	1	225	244	469	469	824	322	....	....	322	23,015	....	....	23,015
Sumpter	4	4	4	4	144	148	292	292	1,087	211	....	2	213	15,081	....	....	15,081
Troy	6	6	5	5	211	207	418	418	1,366	300	....	2	302	18,466	....	78	18,544
Washington	8	8	2	2	206	171	377	377	1,241	290	1	3	294	13,683	6	145	13,834
Westfield	6	6	1	1	248	240	488	488	998	232	....	2	234	15,189	...	166	15,355
Winfield	6	6	3	3	172	136	307	307	1,114	255	....	....	255	10,916	....	....	10,916
Woodland	7	7	2	2	242	203	445	445	1,098	336	....	4	340	21,222	....	131	21,353
Totals	125	124	74	70	4,851	4,619	9,470	9,366	24,871	7,163	1	45	7,209	485,719	6	1,521	487,246

SHAWANO COUNTY.

Towns.	Whole number of School Districts in the town.	Number of Districts which have reported.	Whole number of parts of Districts in the town.	Number of parts of Districts which have reported.	Number of Male children over 4 and under 20 years of age.	Number of Female children over 4 and under 20 years of age.	Whole number over 4 and under 20 years of age in town.	Number over 4 and under 20 years in Districts maintaining school 5 or more months.	Number of days school has been taught by qualified teachers during the year.	Number over 4 and under 20 years who have attended school.	Number under 4 years who have attended school.	Number over 20 years who have attended school.	Total number of different pupils who have attended school during the year.	Number of days attendance of pupils over 4 and under 20 years.	Number of days attendance of pupils under 4 years.	Number of days attendance of pupils over 20 years.	Total number of days attendance of different pupils during the year.
Angelica	1	1	....	....	44	34	78	78	68	44	...	....	44	1,574	....	....	1,574
Bell Plain	7	7	....	....	107	113	220	220	40	127	1	1	128	5,546	....	....	5,546
Grant	1	1	1	1	45	56	101	101	90	....	....	....	....	....	....	....	....
Green Valley	1	1	....	....	13	14	27	27	60	....	....	....	13	262	....	....	262
Hartland	4	4	....	....	131	138	269	269	20	89	....	....	....	1,390	....	....	1,390

Herman	3	3	.....	.....	48	45	93	62	210	33	.....	.....	33	2,029	.....	.....	2,029
Isor	1	1	.....	.....	9	20	29	29	100	.....	.....	.....	19	1,236	.....	.....	1,236
Maple G ro	1	1	.....	.....	46	43	89	89	174	.....	.....	.....	29	.....	.....	.....	.....
Pella	1	1	.....	.....	92	80	172	172	110	.....	.....	.....	61	2,386	.....	.....	2,386
Richmond	1	1	1	1	41	30	71	71	44	.....	.....	.....	31	2,092	.....	.....	2,092
Seneca	1	1	.....	.....	21	18	39	39	100	.....	18	1	19	.....	.....	.....	.....
Shawano	1	1	.....	.....	36	28	64	64	240	.....	.....	.....	42	1,810	.....	.....	1,810
[illegible]o, village	.....	.....	1	1	89	77	166	166	300	.....	.....	.....	110	18,072	.....	.....	18,072
Washington	1	1	.....	.....	31	20	51	51	60	.....	14	.....	14	830	.....	.....	830
Waukechon	3	3	.....	.....	65	42	107	107	426	.....	.....	.....	71	4,448	.....	.....	4,448
Totals	27	24	3	3	818	758	1,576	1,555	2,812	243	33	2	620	41,276	.....	.....	41,276

SHEBOYGAN COUNTY.

[illegible]bush	7	7	5	5	431	390	821	821	1,817	642	.....	2	644	45,093	.....	136	45,139
Herman	7	7	.....	.....	452	483	935	935	1,066	387	.....	.....	387	28,883	.....	.....	28,883
Holland	12	12	1	1	606	545	1,151	1,151	2,339	812	.....	2	814	66,002	.....	62	66,064
Lima	6	6	6	6	459	443	900	900	1,984	604	.....	.....	604	41,794	.....	.....	41,794
Lyndon	8	8	8	8	314	301	615	615	2,454	491	.....	3	494	47,301	.....	151	47,452
Mitchell	5	5	4	4	274	237	511	511	1,235	[illegible]34	2	1	437	24,845	8	43	24,896
Mosell	3	3	.....	.....	220	247	467	467	436	136	.....	.....	136	13,451	.....	.....	13,451
Plymouth	6	6	4	4	194	472	966	966	1,568	549	.....	15	564	42,017	.....	817	42,834
Rhine	7	7	2	2	401	431	832	832	1,106	337	1	.....	338	14,648	2	.....	14,650
Russell	2	2	2	2	155	131	286	286	419	116	.....	.....	116	9,273	.....	.....	9,273
Scott	8	8	1	1	321	283	604	604	1,390	389	1	5	395	19,384	16	247	19,647
Sheboygan	5	5	2	2	350	289	639	639	1,002	236	.....	.....	236	15,074	.....	.....	15,074
Sheboygan Falls	6	6	5	5	413	394	807	807	1,494	446	2	.....	448	28,226	25	.....	26,251
Sheboygan Falls, vil	.....	.....	1	1	250	298	548	548	220	303	.....	.....	303	25,814	.....	.....	25,814
Sherman	6	6	5	5	370	352	722	660	1,483	414	.....	.....	414	21,244	.....	.....	21,244
Wilson	5	5	2	2	261	266	527	527	1,076	315	6	.....	321	11,110	30	.....	11,140
Totals	93	93	48	48	5,769	5,562	11,331	11,269	21,089	6,011	12	28	6,651	462,069	81	1,456	463,606

Table No. II.—*Districts, Children and School Attendance*—continued.

Sheboygan County—continued.

Towns.	Whole number of School Districts in the town.	Number of Districts which have reported.	Whole number of parts of Districts in the Town.	Number of parts of Districts which have reported.	Number of Male children over 4 and under 20 years of age.	Number of Female children over 4 and under 20 years of age.	Whole number over 4 and under 20 years of age in town.	Number over 4 and under 20 years in Districts maintaining school 5 or more months.	Number of days school has been taught by qualified teachers during the year.	Number over 4 and under 20 years who have attended school.	Number under 4 years who have attended school.	Number over 20 years who have attended school.	Total number of different pupils who have attended school during the year.	Number of days attendance of pupils over 4 and under 20 years.	Number of days attendance of pupils under 4 years.	Number of days attendance of pupils over 20 years.	Total number of days attendance of different pupils during the year.
Sheboygan city	....	....	....	....	1,174	1,226	2,400	2,400	195	1,071	....	...	1,071	158,548	....	.....	158,548
Grand Total	93	93	48	48	6,943	6,788	13,731	13,669	21,284	1,682	12	28	7,722	620,617	81	1,456	622,154

TREMPEALEAU COUNTY.

Towns.	Whole number of School Districts in the town.	Number of Districts which have reported.	Whole number of parts of Districts in the Town.	Number of parts of Districts which have reported.	Number of Male children over 4 and under 20 years of age.	Number of Female children over 4 and under 20 years of age.	Whole number over 4 and under 20 years of age in town.	Number over 4 and under 20 years in Districts maintaining school 5 or more months.	Number of days school has been taught by qualified teachers during the year.	Number over 4 and under 20 years who have attended school.	Number under 4 years who have attended school.	Number over 20 years who have attended school.	Total number of different pupils who have attended school during the year.	Number of days attendance of pupils over 4 and under 20 years.	Number of days attendance of pupils under 4 years.	Number of days attendance of pupils over 20 years.	Total number of days attendance of different pupils during the year.
Albion	3	3	1	1	69	66	135	104	270	56	....	....	56	3,188	....	.....	3,188
[illegible]ia	10	9	3	3	430	448	884	884	1,572	310	....	....	310	12,188	....	.....	12,188
Burnside	4	4	....	....	181	144	325	325	527	89	....	....	89	9,415	....	.....	9,415
Caledonia	2	2	2	2	108	87	195	195	574	172	....	2	174	10,717	....	18	10,785
Ettrick	3	2	5	3	270	257	527	527	620	206	....	3	208	11,359	....	76	11,435
Gale	7	7	4	4	341	361	702	702	1,517	517	....	3	520	34,327	....	111	34,488
Hale	4	4	....	....	143	141	284	284	504	163	..	1	163	7,784	....	7	7,734
Lincoln	5	5	2	2	188	172	355	355	859	190	....	1	191	11,582	....	12	11,594
Preston	5	4	1	1	174	171	345	286	467	182	....	....	182	5,148	....	...	5,148
Sum[illegible]er	6	6	1	1	140	125	265	265	882	236	1	2	239	14,780	14	44	14,[illegible]31

Trempealeau	9	9	3	3	382	396	778	778	1,688	598	...	....	593	42,225	....	.....	42,225
Totals.	58	54	22	22	2,427	2,368	4,795	4,705	9,540	2,713	1	11	2,751	162,630	14	269	162,882

VERNON COUNTY.

Bergen	5	4	3	3	202	177	379	379	919	180	....	5	185	7,950	....	189	8,139
Christiana..........	4	4	2	2	311	350	670	670	440	341	....	4	345	14,370	....	79	13,449
Cbn	7	7	1	1	193	177	370	370	1,040	263	1	3	267	17,004	33	73	17,110
Coon	3	3	1	1	175	146	321	321	468	160	....	....	160	5,155	....	.....	5,155
Forest.............	6	6	1	1	153	162	315	315	903	260	....	1	261	20,683	....	24	20,707
Franklin	9	9	....	....	261	212	473	473	1,132	330	1	4	335	19,121	....	42	19,163
Genoa..............	4	4	4	4	129	154	283	283	882	194	....	...	194	11,282	....	.. ..	11,282
hhwood...... ..	6	6	1	1	180	164	344	344	968	245	2	....	247	13,887	36	....	13,923
Hamburg	6	6	2	2	281	230	511	511	900	287	....	1	288	13,687	....	47	13,734
Harmony	5	5	2	2	223	191	413	413	850	226	....	3	229	14,622	....	122	14,744
Hillsborough.......	5	5	3	3	273	241	514	514	1,212	372	1	2	375	30,839	17	20	30,876
Jefferson	6	6	3	3	342	193	435	435	1,019	328	....	3	331	13,430	....	43	13,473
Kickapoo	7	7	....	....	227	242	169	469	865	350	....	1	351	15,854	....	25	15,879
Liberty	2	2	6	6	121	91	212	212	980	166	....	4	170	8,189	....	183	8,372
Stark	6	6	3	3	174	153	327	327	1,070	214	3	7	224	10,810	60	227	11,097
Sterling	7	7	4	4	240	217	457	457	1,491	350	....	....	350	16,805	...	.....	16,805
Union.............	5	5	....	....	148	100	248	248	8,704	150	....	3	153	8,463	....	171	8,634
Vqua..........	8	8	4	4	383	355	738	738	1,775	511	1	27	539	34,790	27	1136	35,953
Wer	4	4	5	5	187	167	354	354	1,063	176	....	2	178	7,897	....	83	7,980
Wheatland	2	2	5	5	143	145	288	288	900	173	3	1	179	3,040	26	18	3,084
Whitestown	3	3	3	3	123	100	223	223	747	216	....	6	222	12,102	....	215	12,317
Tals	110	100	53	53	4,368	8,976	8,344	8,344	28,328	5,494	12	77	5,583	299,980	199	2697	302,876

Table No. II.—*Districts, Children and School Attendance*—continued.

WALWORTH COUNTY.

Towns.	Whole number of School Districts in the town.	Number of Districts which have reported.	Whole number of parts of Districts in the Town.	Number of parts of Districts which have reported.	Number of Male children over 4 and under 20 years of age.	Number of Female children over 4 and under 20 years of age.	Whole number over 4 and under 20 years of age in town.	Number over 4 and under 20 years in Districts maintaining school 5 or more months.	Number of days school has been taught by qualified teachers during the year.	Number over 4 and under 20 years who have attended school.	Number under 4 years who have attended school.	Number over 20 years who have attended school.	Total number of different pupils who have attended school during the year.	Number of days attendance of pupils over 4 and under 20 years.	Number of days attendance of pupils under 4 years.	Number of days attendance of pupils over 20 years.	Total number of days attendance of different pupils during the year.
Bloomfield	6	6	3	3	198	169	367	367	1,291	149	....	....	149	8,111	....	....	8,111
Darien	5	5	7	7	258	233	491	489	1,686	384	....	3	387	25,754	....	94	25,848
Delavan	6		4	4	415	417	832	832	1,495	644	....	141	920	70,122	....	1180	71,302
East Troy	5	5	8	3	248	271	519	519	1,246	387	....	3	390	36,029	....	161	36,190
Elkhorn	1	1	....	....	161	195	356	356	180								
Geneva	4	4	6	6	479	439	918	918	1,555	627	....	6	633	19,411	....	223	79,634
La Fayette	7	7	1	1	216	205	421	421	1,223	303	....	....	303	23,543	....	....	23,543
La Grange	4	4	6	6	267	258	525	513	1,508	379	....	1	380	33,708	....	80	33,788
Linn	8	8	2	2	44	155	290	299	1,527	290	....	....	290	17,788	....	....	17,788
Lyons	7	7	3	3	244	205	449	449	1,355	351	....	3	354	24,396	7	87	24,490
Richmond	6	6	5	5	96	198	394	394	1,634	332	....	2	334	21,352	....	100	21,452
Sharon	8	8	6	6	333	307	640	640	2,110	590	....	....	590	27,265	....	....	27,265
Spring Prairie	8	8	3	3	202	179	381	338	1,437	285	2	1	288	25,670	9	79	25,758
Sugar Creek	5	5	4	4	196	174	370	570	979	284	....	2	286	24,173	....	123	24,326
Troy	5	5	6	6	201	173	374	374	1,514	281	....	2	283	23,815	....	76	23,891
Walworth	7	7	8	3	246	242	488	488	1,525	336	....	2	338	26,444	....	19	26,463
Whitewater	6	6	7	7	668	770	1,438	1,423	1,599	792	....	...	792	79,056	....	....	79,056
Totals	98	98	69	69	4,672	4,590	9,262	9,190	23,864	6,414	2	166	6,717	746,684	16	2222	548,902

WASHINGTON COUNTY.

Addison	7	7	4	4	427	447	874	874	2,298	205	....	....	295	17,257	....	....	17,257
Barton	4	4	5	5	266	264	530	530	1,224	251	....	....	251	13,622	....	....	13,622
Erin	10	10	1	1	286	261	547	547	1,443	334	....	....	334	17,164	....	....	17,164
Farmington	6	6	6	6	393	391	784	784	1,818	510	1	2	513	42,287	40	106	42,433
Germantown	9	9	2	2	414	367	781	781	1,476	874	3	....	877	21,059	17	....	21,076
Hartford	6	6	5	5	577	509	1,086	1,086	1,473	679	1	5	685	64,623	2	251	64,876
Jackson	9	9	3	3	421	397	818	818	1,455	239	2	....	241	18,116	50	....	18,246
Kewaskum	6	6	....	....	290	271	561	591	842	229	....	....	229	13,932	....	....	13,932
Polk	11	11	....	....	408	359	767	767	1,881	376	....	....	376	26,358	....	....	26,358
Richfield	7	7	4	4	372	342	714	714	1,189	386	....	....	386	15,097	....	....	15,097
Schleisingerville	1	1	....	....	76	63	139	139	180	76	....	....	76	6,603	....	....	6,603
Trenton	8	3	10	10	424	438	862	862	404	494	....	....	494	38,566	....	....	38,566
Wayne	5	5	4	4	430	435	865	865	1,045	441	....	....	441	21,842	....	....	21,843
West Bend	5	5	4	4	232	223	455	455	1,282	209	....	....	209	782	....	....	46,720
West Bend, village	1	1	....	....	265	271	536	536	200	363	....	....	383	46,720	....	....	46,720
Totals	90	90	48	48	5,281	5,038	10,819	10,819	18,855	5,276	7	7	5,290	364,108	109	357	364,594

WAUKESHA COUNTY.

Brookfield	9	9	5	5	459	444	903	903	2,000	490	....	2	492	34,733	....	....	34,783
Delafield	8	8	2	2	299	247	546	546	1,703	483	1	3	487	36,055	18	54	36,127
Eagle	5	5	3	3	224	224	468	468	669	319	....	6	325	23,599	1	357	23,957
[illegible]ec	7	7	5	5	275	243	518	518	1,960	373	....	....	373	34,674	....	....	34,674
Lisbon	7	7	4	4	266	263	529	529	1,126	318	....	....	318	18,833	....	....	18,833
[illegible]c	9	9	2	2	467	494	961	961	1,769	576	....	3	579	40,618	....	66	40,684
Merton	7	7	5	5	285	290	575	575	1,414	447	....	....	447	34,134	....	....	34,134
Mukwanago	7	7	2	2	251	275	526	526	1,347	419	....	....	419	30,824	....	....	30,824
Muskego	7	7	4	4	310	283	593	593	1,681	395	2	1	398	26,062	6	25	26,093
New Berlin	8	8	6	6	367	334	701	701	1,115	371	....	2	373	25,520	....	36	25,556
[illegible]oc	6	6	8	8	313	256	569	537	3,061	308	3	3	314	25,305	22	41	25,368

Table No. II.—*Districts, Children and School Attendance*—continued.

Waukesha County—continued.

Towns.	Whole number of School Districts in the town.	Number of Districts which have reported.	Whole number of parts of Districts in the town.	Number of parts of Districts which have reported.	Number of Male children over 4 and under 20 years of age.	Number of Female children over 4 and under 20 years of age.	Whole number over 4 and under 20 years of age in town.	Number over 4 and under 20 years in Districts maintaining school 5 or more months.	Number of days school has been taught by qualified teachers during the year.	Number over 4 and under 20 years who have attended school.	Number under 4 years who have attended school.	Number over 20 years who have attended school.	Total number of different pupils who have attended school during the year.	Number of days attendance of pupils over 4 and under 20 years.	Number of days attendance of pupils under 4 years.	Number of days attendance of pupils over 20 years.	Total number of days attendance of different pupils during the year.
Oconomowoc, village	3	3	....	....	214	201	415	415	367	375	....	....	375	32,128	....	....	32,128
Ottawa	5	5	5	5	213	201	414	414	1,584	285	....	3	288	15,911	....	186	16,097
Pewaukee	9	9	3	3	386	381	767	767	1,901	537	5	1	543	45,892	290	69	46,251
Summit	6	6	4	4	244	216	460	460	1,608	268	....	....	268	24,276	....	....	24,276
Vernon	7	7	1	1	228	211	439	439	1,198	300	1	....	301	20,896	60	....	20,956
Waukesha	11	11	3	3	622	615	1,237	1,237	2,118	904	....	....	904	62,348	...	....	62,348
Totals	121	121	62	62	5,423	5,198	10,621	10,589	25,641	7,204	12	24	7,168	531,808	397	834	533,039

WAUPACA COUNTY.

Towns.	Whole number of School Districts in the town.	Number of Districts which have reported.	Whole number of parts of Districts in the town.	Number of parts of Districts which have reported.	Number of Male children over 4 and under 20 years of age.	Number of Female children over 4 and under 20 years of age.	Whole number over 4 and under 20 years of age in town.	Number over 4 and under 20 years in Districts maintaining school 5 or more months.	Number of days school has been taught by qualified teachers during the year.	Number over 4 and under 20 years who have attended school.	Number under 4 years who have attended school.	Number over 20 years who have attended school.	Total number of different pupils who have attended school during the year.	Number of days attendance of pupils over 4 and under 20 years.	Number of days attendance of pupils under 4 years.	Number of days attendance of pupils over 20 years.	Total number of days attendance of different pupils during the year.
Bear Creek	4	4	....	....	101	110	212	212	293	124	....	....	124	389	....	....	389
Caledonia	3	3	3	3	170	160	330	330	721	128	....	....	128	6,627	....	....	6,627
Dayton	8	3	6	6	181	144	325	325	1,250	274	....	....	274	20,522	....	....	20,522
Dupont	2	2	....	....	28	20	48	48	230	16	3	....	19	771	15	....	786
Farmington	7	7	3	3	176	144	320	320	1,876	207	....	1	208	14,048	....	30	14,078
Fremont	3	3	2	2	143	125	268	268	658	185	3	....	188	9,108	50	....	9,158

Helvetia	2	1	1	1	34	34	68	68	220	35	....	....	35	2,567	....	....	2,567
Iola	5	5	1	1	188	147	335	335	680	198	....	3	201	10,609	....	133	10,742
Larrabee	4	4	1	1	114	111	225	225	577	147	3	1	151	7,727	73	13	7,814
Ldn	5	5	....	....	128	135	263	263	700	220	....	1	221	14,193	....	100	14,293
Lind	5	5	4	4	208	179	387	387	960	252	....	4	256	12,040	....	220	12,260
Little Wolf	5	5	2	2	178	174	352	352	960	210	....	....	210	16,442	....	....	16,442
Matteson	2	2	1	....	63	63	126	126	250	25	....	8	33	1,728	....	72	1,800
Mukwa	4	4	3	3	187	174	361	321	795	198	....	....	198	12,828	....	....	12,828
New London, village	1	1	1	1	238	250	488	488	280	333	1	1	335	35,389	15	40	35,444
Royalton	5	4	3	3	166	160	326	326	960	145	....	....	145	16,183	....	....	16,183
St. Lawrence	2	2	2	2	156	155	311	311	484	232	....	1	282	1,441	....	....	6,937
Scandinavia	5	5	3	3	258	216	474	474	840	279	....	....	279	15,372	....	....	15,372
Union	1	1	2	2	64	64	128	128	375	68	....	1	69	5,244	....	43	5,287
Wica	2	2	6	6	381	440	821	821	1,148	615	....	5	620	50,891	....	250	51,141
Weyauwega	4	4	2	2	239	220	459	439	716	391	....	2	393	47,406	....	113	47,419
Totals	74	72	46	45	3,402	3,225	6,627	6,567	14,473	4,281	10	28	4,319	301,527	153	1014	308,191

WAUSHARA COUNTY.

Aurora	4	4	5	5	211	215	426	426	1,318	309	....	1	310	21,369	....	12	21,381
Bloomfield	7	7	....	....	305	274	579	579	880	279	2	3	284	9,397	18	....	9,430
Coloma	1	1	2	2	49	51	100	100	224	76	....	1	77	4,717	....	56	4,773
Dakota	2	2	6	6	102	70	172	172	985	88	....	....	88	4,564	....	....	4,564
Deerfield	2	2	3	3	31	35	66	66	637	66	....	....	66	4,443	....	....	4,443
Hancock	2	2	3	3	87	91	178	178	124	....	....	....	124	6,404	....	....	6,404
Leon	4	4	5	5	205	183	388	388	1,328	341	....	....	341	22,624	....	....	22,624
Marion	3	3	6	6	145	124	269	269	1,286	285	1	1	287	17,252	....	140	17,422
Mount Morris	2	2	6	6	145	125	270	279	1,069	162	....	....	162	10,842	....	....	10,842
Oasis	5	5	3	3	151	136	287	287	1,030	232	....	1	233	11,069	....	50	11,119
Plainfield	5	5	4	4	208	195	403	403	1,298	312	....	2	314	18,803	....	25	18,828
Poysippi	2	1	4	4	148	110	258	258	684	164	....	2	166	8,558	....	141	8,699
Richford	3	3	3	3	69	73	142	142	808	103	....	2	105	5,770	....	63	5,833
Rose	3	3	3	3	89	100	198	198	601	97	....	2	99	6,087	....	46	6,183

TABLE No. II.—*Districts, Children and School Attendance*—continued.

WAUSHARA COUNTY—continued.

Towns.	Whole number of School Districts in the town.	Number of Districts which have reported.	Whole number of parts of Districts in the town.	Number of parts of Districts which have reported.	Number of Male children over 4 and under 20 years of age.	Number of Female children over 4 and under 20 years of age.	Whole number over 4 and under 20 years of age in town.	Number over 4 and under 20 years in Districts maintaining school 5 or more months.	Number of days school has been taught by qualified teachers during the year.	Number over 4 and under 20 years who have attended school.	Number under 4 years who have attended school.	Number over 20 years who have attended school.	Total number of different pupils who have attended school during the year.	Total number of days attendance of different pupils during the year.	Number of days attendance of pupils under 4 years.	Number of days attendance of pupils over 20 years.	Number of days attendance of pupils over 4 and under 20 years.
Saxville	4	4	3	3	159	131	290	290	979	162	2	1	165	8,911	37	60	9,008
Springwater	4	4	3	3	82	101	183	183	905	180	1	4	135	5,927	43	274	6,244
Warren	4	4	4	4	158	166	324	324	843	246	....	....	246	16,600	....	....	16,600
Wautoma	2	2	4	4	179	172	351	351	760	255	....	2	257	25,140	....	104	25,244
Totals	59	58	67	67	2,523	2,361	4,884	4,884	16,299	3,421	6	22	3,450	208,479	98	986	2.0,593

WINNEBAGO COUNTY.

Towns.	Whole number of School Districts in the town.	Number of Districts which have reported.	Whole number of parts of Districts in the town.	Number of parts of Districts which have reported.	Number of Male children over 4 and under 20 years of age.	Number of Female children over 4 and under 20 years of age.	Whole number over 4 and under 20 years of age in town.	Number over 4 and under 20 years in Districts maintaining school 5 or more months.	Number of days school has been taught by qualified teachers during the year.	Number over 4 and under 20 years who have attended school.	Number under 4 years who have attended school.	Number over 20 years who have attended school.	Total number of different pupils who have attended school during the year.	Total number of days attendance of different pupils during the year.	Number of days attendance of pupils under 4 years.	Number of days attendance of pupils over 20 years.	Number of days attendance of pupils over 4 and under 20 years.
Algoma	4	4	2	2	152	155	307	307	804	200	....	3	203	13,788	....	135	13,923
Black Wolf	5	5	1	1	176	194	370	370	737	205	....	....	205	12,152	....	....	12,152
Clayton	10	10	3	3	291	255	546	546	1,842	405	3	5	413	27,203	24	138	27,366
Menasha	6	6	2	2	614	680	1,294	1,294	1,124	624	....	....	624	93,513	....	....	93,513
Neenah	4	4	3	3	118	116	234	195	1,009	109	1	....	110	6,330	4	....	6,344
Neenah, city	2	2	2	2	641	634	1,275	1,275	702	681	....	6	687	72,250	....	509	72,759
Nekimi	7	7	4	4	290	269	559	559	1,556	351	....	1	352	23,352	....	....	23,352
Nepeuskun	7	7	5	5	216	221	437	373	1,644	260	....	....	260	15,556	....	....	15,556

Omro	8	8	6	4	596	578	1,173	1,173	1,793	895	....	...	895	29,319	....	.....	29,319
Oshkosh	3	2	2	2	74	84	158	158	615	.....	....	....	.....	....	....	.....	....
Poygan	6	6	...	....	212	180	392	392	734	262	....	....	262	15,112	....	.....	15,112
Rushford	9	9	4	4	402	419	821	821	2,036	619	....	7	626	59,630	....	.....	59,630
Utica	7	7	4	4	176	168	344	344	1,331	285	....	2	287	21, 92	....	41	21,953
Vinland	8	8	2	2	210	204	414	414	1,160	377	....	4	381	30,195	....	54	20,249
Winchester	4	4	5	5	248	229	477	477	533	238	....	4	242	13, 64	....	49	13,658
Winneconne	6	6	1	1	376	353	729	729	1,068	518	3	2	518	48, 40	63	06	48,899
Wolf River	6	6	3	2	204	172	376	376	903	252	....	....	252	15, 17	....	.....	15,771
Totals	102	101	51	46	4,995	4,911	9,906	9,808	17,701	6,276	7	34	6,317	501,440	92	1022	495,514
City of Oshkosh	....	....	....	....	2,271	2,370	4,641	4,641	200	2,938	....	....	2,938	....	....	....	....
Grand Total	....	....	....	....	7,266	7,281	14,547	14,444	17,901	9,214	7	34	9,255	501,440	92	1022	495,514

WOOD COUNTY.

Centralia	4	3	1	1	179	177	356	356	611	323	15	....	338	21,908	....	.....	21,908
Grand Rapids	4	3	....	....	123	104	227	227	418	132	....	....	132	....	....	.....	4,380
Grand Rapids, city	1	....	....	....	234	223	457	457	200	210	....	....	210	34,557	....	.....	34,557
Lincoln	3	3	3	3	99	100	199	199	420	.....	....	....	.....	....	....	.....	....
Remington	1	....	....	....	26	32	58	58	105	24	....	....	24	988	....	.....	988
Rudolph	3	3	....	....	84	97	181	181	667	129	....	....	129	....	....	11	11,972
Saratoga	8	4	....	....	71	70	141	141	550	120	....	....	120	6,984	....	1	7,430
Seneca	4	4	....	....	55	74	129	129	585	101	1	....	120	8,604	....	.....	8,604
Sigel	3	3	....	....	39	36	75	75	385	52	...	....	52	....	....	.....	....
Totals	31	23	4	4	910	913	1,823	1,823	3,941	1,091	16	....	1,106	73,041	...	12	89,839

TABLE No. II.—*Districts, Children and School Attendance*—continued.

RECAPITULATION BY COUNTIES.

COUNTIES.	Whole number of School Districts in the county.	Number of Districts which have reported.	Whole number of parts of Districts in the county.	Number of parts of Districts which have reported.	Number of Male children over 4 and under 20 years of age.	Number of Female children over 4 and under 20 years of age.	Whole number over 4 and under 20 years of age in the county.	Number over 4 and under 20 years in Districts maintaining school 5 or more months.	Number of days school has been taught by qualified teachers during the year.	Number over 4 and under 20 years, who have attended school.	Number under 4 years who have attended school.	Number over 20 years who have attended school.	Total number of different pupils who have attended school during the year.	Total number of days attendance of different pupils during the year.	Number of days attendance of pupils under 4 years.	Number of days attendance of pupils over 20 years.	Number of days attendance of pupils over 4 and under 20 years.
Adams	43	43	41	41	1,366	1,241	2,607	2,542	10,890	1,988	7	23	2,021	116,221	8	565	116,704
Barron	20	20	....	....	312	256	568	385	2,245	327	2	....	550	19,208	55	.....	11,403
Bayfield	1	1	....	....	72	81	53	153	....	60	....	1	61	....	....	.....	....
Brown	80	79	8	6	5,799	5,735	11,534	11,414	12,478	7,101	9	....	7,110	547,515	....	5	47,531
Buffalo	67	63	19	15	2,521	2,896	4,872	4,872	9,428	3,060	5	13	3,078	215,744	7	385	216,086
Burnett	4	4	....	....	187	175	362	362	442	176	3	11	190	7,156	5	268	7,420
Calumet	64	64	13	13	2,856	2,703	5,559	5,559	10,475	3,071	3	8	3,082	215,303	24	390	215,717
Chippewa	51	49	4	2	1,542	1,396	2,938	2,938	6,872	1,826	3	3	1,880	129,059	58	129	129,844
Clark	87	23	12	11	891	827	1,718	1,629	5,810	840	....	....	1,147	63,144	42	.....	63,186
Columbia	109	109	83	83	5,596	5,303	10,899	10,899	26,198	7,441	17	62	7,520	567,831	117	2,208	570,156
Crawford	62	62	42	39	2,688	2,557	5,275	5,224	11,574	3,430	13	11	3,454	203,095	130	423	203,648
Dane, 1st dist.	99	98	52	51	3,494	3,228	6,722	6,722	14,180	4,211	4	40	4,262	242,436	62	991	259,742
Dane, 2d dist.	101	101	78	78	6,986	6,822	13,808	13,808	22,128	8,381	9	55	8,445	325,882	40	2,812	628 834
Dodge, 1st dist.	65	64	50	49	4,572	4,407	8,979	8,979	14,332	4,475	2	5	4,482	806,680	7	207	806,844
Dodge, 2d dist.	72	72	60	60	4,456	4,245	8,701	8,701	19,567	5,073	25	54	5,752	836,621	202	491	837,814
Door	87	76	2	2	1,244	1,215	2,280	2,280	4,633	1,569	26	4	1,599	104,280	241	222	104,743
Douglas	2	2	....	....	166	175	341	341	180	234	....	....	234	82,773	....	.....	82,773
Dunn	75	74	13	13	2,219	2,122	4,341	4,286	9,741	3,010	1	28	3,089	168,774	....	1,065	170,489
Eau Claire	38	38	12	12	2,036	1,983	4,019	4,019	6,194	2,899	3	24	2,936	230,091	116	745	236,953

Fond du Lac, 1st dist.	90	90	55	55	6,350	6,268	12,618	12,618	20,147	8,368	5	34	8,472	970,691	83	1,056	981,604
Fond du Lac, 2d dist.	78	78	33	33	3,441	3,118	6,559	6,559	11,832	3,922	12	10	4,004	289,548	29	207	100,347
Grant	258	253	86	83	8,065	7,586	15,651	15,544	34,863	10,822	13	67	10,902	668,021	287	2,958	671,266
Green	101	101	49	49	4,455	4,408	8,863	8,863	23,652	6,463	24	40	6,527	433,683	144	1,119	434,946
Green Lake	36	36	55	54	2,745	2,574	5,319	5,319	12,675	3,652	2	16	3,670	274,910	71	295	275,276
Iowa	105	104	27	29	5,224	5,128	10,352	10,352	13,515	4,952	7	24	4,976	326,944	132	521	327,597
Jackson	53	53	21	20	1,903	1,755	3,658	3,630	9,407	2,502	8	10	2,520	162,531	89	430	163,050
Jefferson	168	168	80	80	7,605	7,247	14,852	14,852	22,972	8,111	5	19	6,841	634,398	36	736	635,170
Juneau	70	69	36	36	2,823	2,691	5,514	5,350	13,390	4,240	10	64	4,314	289,662	112	1,127	290,901
Kenosha	61	61	24	23	2,623	2,607	5,218	5,218	11,404	2,606	11	30	2,652	264,224	821	1,385	266,430
Kewaunee	45	45	9	9	2,715	2,576	4,291	5,291	6,471	2,606	37	4	3,643	208,162	192	142	208,496
La Crosse	61	61	20	20	3,973	3,945	7,918	7,858	10,820	4,684	38	28	4,750	411,562	309	1,115	412,986
La Fayette	94	94	52	52	4,672	4,521	9,193	9,181	6,493	6,486	9	28	6,523	405,508	180	1,179	406,867
Manitowoc	88	88	41	41	7,888	7,728	15,616	15,564	14,432	7,508	20	15	7,551	582,961	166	680	553,807
Marathon	54	49	4	3	1,345	1,374	2,719	2,719	6,286	1,721	1	3	1,725	112,164	26	30	112,220
Marquette	41	41	33	33	1,728	1,636	3,364	3,348	9,536	2,117	1	14	2,165	136,719	....	824	137,542
Milwaukee, 1st dist.	27	27	16	16	2,057	2,059	4,116	4,116	6,917	1,977	....	1	1,978	156,902	....	27	156,929
Milwaukee, 2d dist.	31	31	4	4	16,115	16,714	32,829	32,829	5,574	12,985	5	....	12,990	1,353,489	333	.....	1,353,822
Monroe	88	85	59	56	3,920	3,521	7,441	7,421	16,174	5,649	14	38	5,701	388,565	384	1,780	390,629
Oconto	27	27	....	....	1,729	1,497	3,226	3,226	4,209	2,243	2	5	2,248	176,325	12	143	176,480
Outagamie	78	78	19	19	4,646	4,335	8,981	8,920	13,384	5,360	4	....	5,364	377,559	146	.....	377,705
Ozaukee	49	49	15	15	3,791	3,628	7,419	7,419	9,290	3,560	25	...	3,409	237,204	670	.....	237,884
Pepin	26	26	12	9	1,029	988	2,017	2,017	4,724	1,492	....	12	1,492	89,917	...	433	894,919
Pierce	74	73	36	34	2,617	2,420	5,037	4,916	9,644	2,695	15	20	2,782	180,360	67	884	181,311
Polk	43	43	7	7	1,082	932	2,014	1,921	5,901	1,301	6	4	1,311	71,550	18	65	71,633
Portage	63	63	29	29	2,332	2,278	4,610	4,559	12,777	3,272	1	15	3,288	236,516	....	274	236,799
Racine	56	56	47	47	4,910	4,904	9,814	9,774	14,594	5,709	6	13	5,728	581,562	53	699	582,314
Richland	105	103	47	47	3,486	3,304	6,790	6,737	15,621	5,501	21	61	5,583	309,268	398	3,482	313,148
Rock, 1st dist	61	61	56	56	4,177	4,219	8,396	8,382	17,351	5,452	7	31	5,346	455,875	166	1,145	407,186
Rock, 2d dist	54	54	65	65	2,943	2,658	5,601	5,601	17,845	3,841	3	7	3,848	332,937	26	250	333,213
St. Croix	73	73	20	20	2,215	1,879	4,094	4,094	11,201	2,867	12	51	3,465	163,371	702	345	164,418
Sauk	125	124	74	70	4,857	4,619	9,470	9,366	24,871	7,163	1	45	7,209	485,719	6	1,521	487,246
Shawano	27	24	3	3	818	758	1,576	1,606	2,812	243	33	2	620	41,276	....	.....	41,276
Sheboygan	93	93	48	48	6,943	6,788	13,731	13,669	21,284	7,682	12	23	7,722	620,617	81	1,456	622,154

TABLE No. II.—*Districts, Children and School Attendance*—continued.

RECAPITULATION BY COUNTIES—continued.

TOWNS.	Whole number of School Districts in the town.	Number of districts which have reported.	Whole number of parts of Districts in the town.	Number of parts of Districts which have reported.	Number of Male children, over 4 and under 20 years of age.	Number of Female children over 4 and under 20 years of age.	Whole number over 4 and under 20 years of age in town.	Number over 4 and under 20 years in Districts maintaining school 5 or more months.	Number of days school has been taught by qualified teachers during the year.	Number over 4 and under 20 years who have attended school.	Number under 4 years who have attended school.	Number over 20 years who have attended school.	Total number of different pupils who have attended school during the year.	Number of days attendance of pupils over 4 and under 20 years.	Number of days attendance of pupils under 4 years.	Number of days attendance of pupils over 20 years.	Total number of days attendance of different pupils during the year.
Trempealeau	58	54	22	22	2,427	2,368	4,795	4,705	9,540	2,713	1	11	2,751	162,630	14	269	62 ,82
Vernon	110	109	53	53	4,368	3,976	8,344	8,344	28,328	5,494	12	77	5,583	299,980	199	2697	62 ,86
Walworth	98	98	69	69	4,672	4,590	9,262	9,190	23,864	6,414	2	166	6,717	746,634	16	2222	58 ,92
Washington	90	90	48	48	5,281	5,038	10,319	10,319	18,855	5,276	7	7	5,270	364,108	109	357	84 ,94
Waukesha..........	121	121	62	62	5,423	5,198	10,621	10,589	25,641	7,168	12	24	7,204	531,808	397	834	53 ,69
Waupaca	74	72	46	45	3,402	3,225	6,627	6,567	14,473	4,281	10	28	4,319	301,527	153	1014	68 ,91
Waushara	59	58	67	67	2,523	2,861	4,884	4,884	16,299	3,431	6	22	3,459	208,479	98	986	99 ,93
Winnebago.........	102	101	51	46	7,365	7,182	14,547	14,444	17,701	6,276	7	34	6,317	501,440	92	1022	85 ,54
Wood	31	23	4	4	910	913	1,823	....	3,941	1,091	16	...	1,106	73,041	....	12	89,80
Totals	4275	4218	2093	2059	222,590	213,411	436,001	432,959	787,567	261,708	575	1439	263,477	10,842,000	7929	46707	19711939

TABLE No. III.

SCHOOLS, TEACHERS, WAGES, LIBRARIES, ETC.

COUNTIES.	SCHOOLS, TEACHERS, WAGES, ETC.									LIBRARIES.			
	Number of Schools with two Department.	Number of School with three or mor Departments.	Number of Teachers required to teach the Schools.	Number of different persons employed as teachers during the year.	Average wages of Male Teachers per month.	Average wages of Female Teachers per month.	Number of Schools visited by County Superintendent during the year.	Number of different visits made.	Number of addresses or lectures delivered by him.	Number of volumes added during ye r.	Amount expended for books during the year.	Whole number of volumes in District Library.	Cash value of the Library.
dlas	2		65	110	$37 74	$21 18	64	131					
Barron			20	29	32 51	30 97	20	72					
Byld			1	1	60 00		1						
Brn	2	1	74	103	42 42	28 13	77	31	243				
Bo	2	1	77	100	43 71	30 19	73	25			$2 50	202	173 00
Burnett			4	2	45 66	35 00	4	6					
Calumet	3		68	101	47 44	25 76	61	65					
Chippewa	1	2	38	72	51 19	35 30	49	83	35			389	55 00
Clark	1		40	73	34 17	31 30	4	1	1	19	25 40	216	30 40
Columbia	6	3	63	84	44 64	23 86	149	90	06	46	28 98	442	49 50
Crawford	4	1	79	29	38 35	25 50	62	89	80				
Dane, 1st district	1	2	110	87	41 95	26 28	104	14		3	8 25	337	36 00
sDe, 2d lrict	1	3	58	28	42 50	29 00	134	90	4	101	107 67	747	85 65
Dodge, 1st listrict	4	2	10	84	39 07	22 77	100	142	107	5	5 75	625	95 00
Dodge, 2d district	3	3	92	5[illegible]	46 60	25 27	87	96	91			960	1,132 57
Door	1		37	55	39 18	31 99	37	94	58				

TABLE III—*School Teachers, Wages, etc.*—continued.

COUNTIES.	SCHOOLS, TEACHERS, WAGES, ETC.									LIBRARIES.			
	Number of Schools with two Departments.	Number of Schools with three or more Departments.	Number of Teachers required to teach the Schools.	Number of different persons employed as teachers during the year.	Average wages of Male Teachers per month.	Average wages of Female Teachers per month.	Number of Schools visited by County Superintendent during the year.	Number of different visits made.	Number of Addresses or Lectures delivered by him.	Number of volumes added during the y'r.	Amount expended for books during the year.	Whole number of volumes in District Library.	Cash value of the Library.
Douglas	1	1	6	8	112 50	35 00	2	18	......	......	......	......	......
Dunn	1	1	79	155	38 80	30 80	70	122	7	......	......	......	......
Eau Claire	......	4	60	105	59 31	32 48	58	167	117	85	100 00	107	301 00
Fond du Lac, 1st dist	10	4	104	179	44 23	28 75	94	129	......	10	19 00	300	347 00
Fond du Lac, 2d dist.	3	......	71	121	41 67	24 00	79	2	......	......	......	103	100 00
Grant	6	7	247	373	42 97	27 97	101	127	13	20	1	212	216 50
Green	6	2	150	241	33 10	24 44	140	152	......	......	12 75	438	238 50
Green Lake	6	......	74	126	33 23	23 17	70	143	19	6	16 00	216	172 00
Iowa	9	1	115	169	38 00	22 00	79	81	......	......	......	66	70 00
Jackson	4	1	72	120	42 12	28 58	......	......	......	......	......	25	23 00
Jefferson	10	5	153	228	41 08	28 92	123	131	......	1	6 00	550	631 00
Juneau	1	3	100	162	48 61	24 70	92	108	16	......	......	279	318 00
Kenosha	1	......	61	103	39 96	30 46	61	133	......	11	10 00	676	522 00
Kewaunce	......	2	53	63	39 02	26 62	41	......	......	......	......	9	1 50
La Crosse	3	1	71	107	38 00	31 00	64	118	......	9	......	33	36 00
La Fayette	4	2	137	228	39 25	23 14	115	181	6	56	......	308	197 50
Manitowoc	1	4	127	158	48 49	31 50	97	124	3	21	25 00	780	1,288 00
Marathon	......	1	56	74	51 00	36 91	56	87	27	111	113 28	180	193 22
Marquette	3	......	50	91	28 40	20 50	52	94	......	4	5 00	184	62 00
Milwaukee, 1st dist	1	1	41	54	48 76	28 80	85	84	......	......	......	904	811 20
Milwaukee, 2d dist.	3	......	87	53	47 21	32 64	32	90	......	......	......	101	69 00

	Col. 1	Col. 2	Col. 3	Col. 4	Col. 5	Col. 6	Col. 7	Col. 8	Col. 9	Col. 10	Col. 11	Col. 12	Col. 13
Monroe	.....	1	129	224	35 80	24 04	99	126	.....	.....	.....	.....	.....
Oconto	2	2	84	50	57 75	35 24	32	85	2	.....	.....	.....	.....
Outagamie	1	.....	93	151	38 18	27 72	91	165	111	16	10 00	94	75 00
Ozaukee	5	1	65	72	44 92	26 79	58	74	36	11	8 85	848	898 81
Pepin	1	1	36	50	33 27	28 26	26	32	33	.....	.....	.....	.....
Pierce	1	1	99	150	36 80	30 10	132	239	29	37	25 00	331	203 00
Polk	.....	.....	45	64	42 50	30 75	73	74	20	39	50 00	47	85 00
Portage	4	1	91	142	43 55	27 90	82	144	.....	6	8 00	99	201 80
Racine	2	1	81	118	37 72	27 08	76	159	.....	.....	.....	941	486 00
Richland	.....	2	126	217	29 44	21 57	81	106	1	1	5 00	105	82 50
Rock, 1st dist.	1	2	90	167	42 86	24 06	81	138	.....	221	194 56	657	653 00
Rock, 2d dist.	5	2	92	171	37 76	27 21	80	181	.....	30	40 00	845	305 00
Sauk	5	4	178	277	40 00	26 25	115	129	5	32	24 50	1,148	1,112 00
Shawano	1	3	19	20	39 00	27 80	11	.....	.....	10	5 00	21	35 00
Sheboygan	4	8	127	188	43 09	26 53	103	150	.....	7	11 25	755	448 28
Trempealeau	1	1	72	113	37 30	30 10	70	118	.....	2	1 50	139	168 00
Vernon	2	1	135	222	31 04	23 30	104	136	136	.....	.....	4	17 00
Walworth	5	6	159	250	49 45	27 85	125	153	.....	6	10 00	252	355 25
Washington	2	3	113	146	44 18	20 20	86	99	1	.....	.....	325	308 00
Waukesha	8	3	142	223	50 00	26 60	120	.....	.....	.....	.....	180	85 00
Waupaca	1	3	109	183	45 23	25 90	61	91	5	16	96 00	42	135 50
Waushara	3	.....	89	159	35 75	20 65	87	190	.....	.....	.....	26	80 00
Winnebago	3	4	133	213	48 60	27 60	127	275	.....	.....	.....	98	195 00
Wood	3	.....	29	87	55 30	29 60	.....	24	.....	.....	1 50	6	15 00
Totals	155	103	5,295	8,350	$43 38	$27 52	4,307	6,736	1,511	932	$978 24	16,302	$16,053 68

TABLE No. IV.

SCHOOL HOUSES, SITES, APPARATUS, ETC.

COUNTIES.	No. of school houses in the county.	No. of pupils school houses will accommodate.	No. of sites containing less than one acre.	No. of sites well enclosed.	No. of school houses built of stone or brick.	No. of school houses in good condition.	No. with out houses in good condition.	No. of school houses properly ventilated.	No. of districts which have adopted text books.	No. furnished with outline maps.	No. furnished with sufficient black board.	No. of joint districts (with school houses in a certain town.)
Adams	64	2,565	53	3	....	42	34	29	13	9	46	20
Barron	18	600	....	....	....	....	10	....	20	1	....	....
Bayfield	1	100	1	1	1	1	1	1	1	1	1	1
Brown	77	5,922	42	25	10	58	49	55	16	22	28	10
Buffalo	71	3,741	41	13	3	58	42	48	16	12	63	11
Burnett	3	310	2	2	....	3	3	3	....	2	8	....
Calumet	64	3,767	53	20	2	51	45	32	9	14	7	10
Chippewa	51	2,538	43	34	....	40	30	46	19	19	27	2
Clark	38	1,481	32	10	....	36	24	29	9	6	36	5
Columbia	150	8,509	114	44	27	106	95	97	65	58	25	40
Crawford	75	4,026	48	19	5	46	23	44	46	19	23	16
Dane, 1st district	104	5,386	73	54	27	72	67	61	19	39	1	41
Dane, 2d district	137	7,494	94	45	33	100	85	73	26	44	....	87
Dodge 1st district	101	6,087	86	23	12	76	62	69	24	17	2	80
Dodge, 2d district	89	5,885	80	20	16	69	57	71	15	23	....	28
Door	38	1,799	19	6	....	27	16	30	12	9	12	1
Douglas	3	296	2	1	....	3	3	3	2	1	3	....
Dunn	76	3,475	47	10	....	48	24	8	8	9	6	10
Eau Claire	45	3,443	38	13	2	36	28	3	12	12	13	6

Fond du Lac, 1st dist	92	5,708	82	51	8	69	65	68	36	42	22	51
Fond du Lac, 2d dist	78	5,095	71	18	10	60	53	76	15	41	64	24
Grant	216	13,644	123	59	42	166	96	155	39	86	....	44
Green	133	8,327	88	38	30	90	63	72	30	28	29	29
Green Lake	68	3,234	55	19	7	48	23	31	7	11	28	30
Iowa	121	6,369	85	13	13	79	44	66	19	17	19	17
Jackson	63	2,980	85	12	1	44	33	38	20	12	....	11
Jefferson	129	8,313	110	35	64	95	82	82	27	27	41	40
Juneau	87	4,156	67	16	....	58	43	72	36	18	10	19
Kenosha	60	2,764	47	26	3	39	38	44	10	24	39	13
Kewaunee	47	3,395	36	77	....	40	26	44	6	....	5	15
La Crosse	68	3,506	40	21	8	40	37	35	19	24	10	12
La Pointe	120	7,489	76	45	22	85	59	94	31	32	26	....
Manitowoc	107	10,244	85	29	6	90	74	69	15	51	11	20
Marathon	54	2,420	34	16	....	44	21	29	12	41	20	4
Marquette	56	2,851	44	8	....	40	28	39	13	10	1	15
Milwaukee, 1st dist	35	2,850	34	19	9	31	27	26	26	23	14	7
Milwaukee, 2d dist	30	2,264	30	17	7	27	26	32	11	26	6	2
Monroe	119	5,985	93	30	1	80	57	42	20	23	6	27
Oconto	28	1,410	20	7	....	25	23	15	6	11	13	....
Outagamie	89	4,845	78	40	....	72	73	56	43	31	41	12
Ozaukee	58	4,933	54	31	32	50	40	44	10	28	30	20
Pepin	31	1,590	20	3	4	25	13	26	8	3	8	5
Pierce	91	4,477	67	14	2	58	37	41	11	18	3	19
Polk	45	1,715	16	9	....	33	21	27	6	8	4	4
Portage	61	4,140	65	16	....	57	54	48	10	17	6	16
Racine	76	4,121	71	36	19	55	50	39	14	30	15	20
Richland	122	6,361	108	23	1	73	54	80	38	13	36	22
Rock, 1st dist	83	4,805	60	29	37	66	57	64	32	17	73	24
Rock, 2d dist	84	3,636	61	39	14	64	61	49	33	38	43	30
St. Croix	78	3,301	48	28	1	39	51	55	14	25	3	17
Sauk	160	8,260	121	34	13	39	87	111	42	50	23	55
Shawano	29	1,197	16	....	....	10	5	18	6	3	17	2
Sheboygan	114	8,182	106	31	6	78	86	75	35	47	9	21
Trempealeau	73	3,495	81	16	2	57	44	54	11	14	8	13
Vernon	134	6,754	109	43	2	91	59	92	66	30	61	29

TABLE No. IV.—*School Houses, Sites, Apparatus, etc.*—continued.

COUNTIES.	No. of school houses in the county.	No. of pupils school houses will accommodate.	No. of sites containing less than one acre.	No. of sites well enclosed.	No. of school houses built of stone or brick.	No. of school houses in good condition.	No. with out-houses in good condition.	No. of school houses properly ventilated.	No. of districts which have adopted text books.	No. furnished with outline maps.	No. furnished with sufficient black board.	No. of joint districts (with school houses in a certain town.)
Walworth	130	8,018	105	60	26	189	818	94	45	46	....	316
Washington	103	8,315	95	22	36	78	75	78	82	21	77	31
Waukesha	121	8,285	95	43	37	37	89	88	91	88	....	47
Waupaca	98	5,214	80	30	3	66	59	68	26	53	....	22
Waushara	84	3,806	54	14	1	52	53	61	38	35	....	37
Winnebago	110	7,615	96	53	18	81	67	64	33	46	34	35
Wood	26	1,359	24	10	......	19	16	12	4	5	5	3
Totals	4,835	286,821	3,693	1,523	623	3,517	2,863	3,182	1,323	1 451	1,156	1,168

TABLE No. V.

SCHOOL HOUSE PROPERTY.

Counties.	Highest valuation of the school house and site.	Cash value of school houses in the town.	Cash value of sites.	Cash value of apparatus, etc.
Adams	$1,050	$16,310	$1,002	$49,950
Barron	350	4,950	....	....
Bayfield	3,000	....	....	....
Brown	3,300	41,075	2,010	1,354
Buffalo	6,600	35,955	2,492	1,385
Burnett	....	2,800	30	10
Calumet	6,000	20,320	3,133	793
Chippewa	6,000	25,440	6,266	1,562
Clark	2,200	12,210	1,190	254
Columbia	17,000	92,599	9,325	2,867
Crawford	2,600	25,600	2,525	619
Dane, 1st dist	6,000	57,775	4,518	1,597
Dane, 2d dist	4,300	75,765	5,406	2,691
Dodge, 1st dist	6,000	44,287	5,937	1,559
Dodge, 2d dist	12,000	65,045	7,650	1,518
Door	4,500	12,555	2,685	91,177
Douglas	7,000	11,500	3,300	80
Dunn	14,000	36,287	3,590	606
Eau Claire	22,000	57,222	9,622	999
Fond du Lac, 1st district	2,050	57,929	7,592	1,285
Fond du Lac, 2d district	2,780	36,555	3,530	1,488
Grant	7,650	168,670	14,360	3,340
Green	2,500	96,295	8,875	1,440
Green Lake	3,256	26,506	2,207	340
Iowa	3,000	44,543	5,153	1,503
Jackson	3,500	50,180	6,489	457
Jefferson	9,000	139,488	10,681	3,189
Juneau	8,000	32,588	3,746	918
Kenosha	2,550	26,784	6,499	1;207
Kewaunee	1,000	16,835	1,602	981
La Crosse	4,500	28,890	3,120	684
La Fayette	26,000	91,920	8,106	3,827
Manitowoc	40,000	95,490	16,063	3,541
Marathon	7,000	26,872	2,824	1,768
Marquette	2,600	18,529	1,051	584
Milwaukee, 1st dist	14,175	36,900	5,885	3,599
Milwaukee, 2d dist	7,500	25,075	2,405	1,617
Monroe	30,000	57,080	5,182	1,142
Oconto	13,365	21,410	3,385	569
Outagamie	1,175	33,980	3,619	1,321
Ozaukee	9,650	38,910	6,802	2,427
Pepin	3,000	14,834	1,262	450
Pierce	3,900	30,694	3,073	1,243

TABLE No. V.—*School-House Property*—continued.

COUNTIES.	Highest valuation of the school house and site.	Cash value of school houses in the town.	Cash value of sites.	Cash value of apparatus, etc.
Polk	2,750	16,590	1,254	323
Portage	3,800	34,037	4,300	752
Racine	3,650	45,440	4,671	1,262
Richland	4,500	37,236	3,315	1,052
Rock, 1st dist	16,300	66,106	3,694	1,123
Rock, 2d dist	10,000	50,900	4,985	1,268
St. Croix	1,750	33,105	1,385	444
Sauk	34,000	94,875	10,499	2,507
Shawano	3,100	7,370	1,574	215
Sheboygan	10,000	62,334	4,222	3,132
Trempealeau	6,050	29,748	2,661	446
Vernon	8,000	46,235	2,995	830
Walworth	20,500	129,750	12,980	3,107
Washington	7,000	79,605	6,611	2,779
Waukesha	15,000	94,375	10,932	3,342
Waupaca	8,000	46,910	4,860	2,067
Waushara	2,200	23,549	2,232	1,053
Winnebago	8,400	82,260	11,176	2,339
Wood	4,500	10,155	1,140	363
Totals	40,000	2,847,582	297,188	181,326

TABLE No. VI.

PRIVATE SCHOOLS, NOT INCORPORATED.

COUNTIES.	Number of such schools in the town.	Number which are denominational or parochial.	No. of teachers engaged in such schools.	Average number of days such schools have been taught.	No. of pupils registered who have not attended district school during year.	Average number in daily attendance.
Adams	......	......	......	......	......	...
Barron	......	......	......	......	......	...
Bayfield	......	......	......	......	......	...
Brown	6	6	13	980	860	880
Buffalo	2	2	4	400	125	110
Burnett	......	......	......	......	......	...
Calumet	4	4	5	666	112	99
Chippewa	......	......	......	......	......	...
Clark	......	......	......	......	......	...
Columbia	3	3	1	84	1	48
Crawford	6	4	14	220	320	300
Dane, 1st dist	11	11	12	411	21	198
Dand, 2d dist	12	10	12	588	185	66
Dodge, 1st dist	......	......	......	......	......	...
Dodge, 2d dist	28	27	31	580	918	102
Door	......	......	......	......	......	...
Douglas	......	......	......	......	......	...
Dunn	......	......	......	......	......	...
Eau Claire	3	3	6	352	11	25
Fond du Lac, 1st dist	6	5	7	......	......	...
Fond du Lac, 2d dist	16	16	26	1,153	40	447
Grant	7	5	20	266	185	110
Green	4	2	5	144	40	31
Green Lake	......	......	......	......	......	...
Iowa	4	2	6	148	20	116
Jackson	4	2	4	247	27	29
Jefferson	16	15	16	1,110	564	400
Juneau	......	......	......	......	......	...
Kenosha	3	3	4	200	53	....
Kewaunee	2	2	3	185	249	210
La Crosse	6	5	5	166	41	76
La Fayette	......	......	......	......	......	...
Manitowoc	16	14	20	176	399	58
Marathon	2	2	3	60	18	36
Marquette	5	2	2	66	64	25
Milwaukee, 1st dist	15	15	25	137	300	34
Milwaukee, 2d dist	7	6	7	182	165	110
Monroe	1	......	1	......	......	...
Oconto	2	1	3	190	90	70
Outagamie	2	2	2	......	......	...
Ozaukee	16	1	17	985	568	460
Pepin	......	......	......	......	......	...
Pierce	2	......	4	......	......	...
Polk	......	......	......	......	......	...

TABLE No. VI.—*Private Schools, etc.*—continued.

COUNTIES.	Number of such schools in the town.	Number which are denominational or parochial.	No. of teachers engaged in such schools.	Average number of days such schools have been taught.	No. of pupils registered who have not attended district school during year.	Average number in daily attendance.
Portage	....	....	....	....	....	....
Racine	9	6	11	591	425	273
Richland	1	....	1	66	10	25
Rock, 1st dist.	4	2	4	25	15	11
Rock, 2d dist.	1	....	1	140	6	20
St. Croix	....	....	....	....	....	....
Sauk	6	4	4	....	....	....
Shawano	....	....	....	....	....	....
Sheboygan	12	10	10	1,176	200	132
Trempealeau	....	....	....	....	....	....
Vernon	2	2	2	229	104	....
Walworth	5	3	4	80	92	75
Washington	9	2	20	161	251	31
Waukesha	16	14	17	196	644	54
Waupaca	11	5	18	....	58	....
Waushara	3	2	3	200	72	30
Winnebago	3	2	3	82	48	50
Wood	3	....	....	....	....	....
Totals and averages.	296	206	309	12,671	6,396	70

TABLE No. VII.

FINANCIAL STATISTICS.

RECEIPTS.

Counties.	Money on hand, August 31, 1878.	From taxes levied for building and repairing.	From taxes levied for Teachers' wages.	From taxes levied for apparatus and library.	From taxes levied at annual town meeting.	From taxes levied by County supervisors.	From Income of State School Fund.	From all other sources.	Total amount received during year.
Adams	$2,499 29	$949 97	$6,680 40	$19 50	$139 89	$916 55	$991 27	$1,143 94	$13,345 31
Barron	1,903 07	....	....	....	....	....	135 44	....	....
Bayfield	....	....	....	....	....	....	....	....	....
Brown	6,670 05	1,929 00	10,548 43	186 28	5,736 03	2,526 04	4,468 47	1,031 30	30,506 36
Buffalo	7,768 15	3,182 58	14,933 30	236 03	435 00	1,863 47	1,495 40	4,340 82	33,466 74
Burnett	....	103 94	950 00	....	100 13	100 00	123 48	262 71	1,640 26
Calumet	2,855 24	2,005 34	12,386 02	59 29	....	1,948 16	2,260 85	1,419 57	28 034 47
Chippewa	12,011 87	2,868 52	7,592 05	130 11	8,610 77	717 58	812 65	1,912 53	34,831 72
Clark	7,895 86	3,296 35	6,784 41	310 00	2,002 54	2,400 04	428 77	1,391 48	25,078 28
Columbia	6,351 22	3,531 35	28,402 53	90 82	1,972 22	3,321 79	3,354 89	8,177 04	55,201 86
Crawford	5,469 88	1,637 42	13,199 41	28 75	596 06	1,607 59	2,046 76	1,022 08	25,607 95
Dane, 1st district	4,076 18	3,201 59	15,340 97	94 60	503 70	2,435 70	2,597 68	3,775 17	32,203 14
Dane, 2d district	4,951 85	4,160 87	22,247 78	222 85	3,256 14	3,539 43	4,318 09	4,181 64	46,716 42
Dodge 1st district	4,695 77	3,549 48	19,251 81	188 21	1,121 20	2,581 47	2,996 77	830 82	35,215 53
Dodge, 2d district	3,673 43	4,989 83	18,977 80	148 80	1,287 06	2,985 65	3,615 91	934 78	36,378 57
Door	3,082 02	698 59	8,121 48	50 00	140 00	597 86	955 76	2,245 88	16,532 02
Douglas	1,771 03	2,765 93	6,500 00	500 00	....	....	145 14	....	8,653 10
Dunn	4,557 12	6,674 26	13,752 08	1,497 30	681 00	1,303 62	1,388 39	603 94	30,457 71
Eau Claire	8,217 14	13,370 62	19,762 45	120 72	10 00	1,080 93	1,393 28	3,769 81	44,211 67

TABLE No. VII.—*Financial Statistics—Receipts*—continued.

COUNTIES.	Money on hand, August 31, 1873.	From taxes levied for building and repairing.	From taxes levied for Teachers' wages.	From taxes levied for apparatus and library.	From taxes levied at annual town meeting.	From taxes levied by County Supervisors.	From Income of State School Fund.	From all other sources.	Total amount received during year.
Fond du Lac, 1st dis.	$4,380 54	$2,622 20	$21,486 14	$346 00	$520 53	$1,663 38	8,615 26	2,404 03	88,583 08
Fond du Lac, 2d dis.	2,965 90	1,767 08	11,102 85	58 32	149 56	2,477 75	2,802 24	795 11	22,820 29
Grant	18,475 99	4,872 46	46,193 00	229 10	6,285 87	5,569 13	6,236 07	2,833 99	85,195 61
Green	4,816 56	2,546 11	27,637 78	165 00	756 92	3,372 26	3,694 24	4,473 11	47,461 92
Green Lake	3,516 08	2,027 88	9,694 65	10 00	298 84	1,399 46	1,322 28	1,686 29	19,949 98
Iowa	3,241 27	1,208 07	12,023 71	202 64	3,367 36	149 13	3,086 19	913 44	24,414 24
Jackson	4,645 65	2,196 13	15,912 12	23 75	1,985 86	886 85	1,386 04	3,873 72	30,910 12
Jefferson	5,592 37	5,265 66	27,844 91	80 36	482 27	3,682 29	4,449 15	6,190 96	53,676 79
Juneau	4,164 08	1,494 35	17,099 07	38 50	698 95	2,170 79	2,204 68	1,367 46	29,282 88
Kenosha	1,962 78	1,527 57	11.430 52	10 00		4,682 10	1,343 35	822 07	19,908 01
Kewaunee	2,612 77	2,741 20	6,696 20	147 25	1,350 87	1,376 97	1,689 38	4,489 42	22,206 45
La Crosse	4,202 45	1,164 52	13,301 80		869 96	1,376 41	1,613 83	1,414 49	23,943 46
La Fayette	6,299 33	7,256 22	26,785 20	25 00	1,995 78	3,532 71	1,924 05	6,489 56	56,307 85
Manitowoc	31,415 74	19,138 92	22,007 46	178 00	1,848 77	11,563 21	3,924 05	6,159 44	98,912 45
Marathon	20,093 11	5,818 02	8,547 20	270 93	2,140 55	2,538 75	6,511 35	11,127 81	48,266 74
Marquette	1,353 39	1,055 69	7,768 26	98 72	48 95	1,148 06	729 88	465 49	13,211 27
Milwaukee, 1st dis.	3,368 40	13,516 94	5,264 69		939 11	3,796 50	1,361 90	1,915 00	30,476 30
Milwaukee, 2d dis.	2,368 46	2,120 12	6,904 98			2,887 27	1,675 57	2,099 81	17,722 38
Monroe	7,314 58	3,535 61	22,651 81	337 50	277 22	2,365 86	1,484 71	3,910 96	43,082 93
Oconto	2,808 54	6,088 22	5,506 00	55 00	1,470 03	446 78	2,689 30	3,971 60	20,807 96
Outagamie	6,166 40	4,931 35	14,023 38	84 66	1,660 50	3,167 40	476 83	1,481 98	34,098 62
Ozaukee	3,735 54	1,820 45	11,675 47	89 98	2,047 94	2,860 13	2,508 81	908 03	26,039 08
Pepin	2,411 75	2,399 14	4,720 54	84 00	623 20	444 52	3,067 40	768 69	12,650 92
Pierce	3,979 74	3,225 94	15,068 82	261 65	628 00	756 59	687 67	1,543 96	28,046 16
Polk	3,959 43	2,692 81	7,280 44	29 05	989 51	446 41	643 87	1,425 64	17,227 86

Portage	5,425 92	2,084 43	15,446 84	187 61	1,456 09	1,191 11	1,694 78	1,681 61	29,167 39
Racine	8,701 68	2,255 63	17,483 43	47 90	....	2,127 10	2,256 93	842 53	29,059 93
[illegible]ld	8,168 94	4,204 31	13,573 85	108 00	584 12	3,135 92	2,424 96	1,614 69	33,855 98
Rock, 1st dist	5,257 70	3,211 64	14,002 34	273 00	834 36	2,821 72	1,939 64	6,906 92	35,247 82
Rock, 2d dist	6,238 02	4,998 43	15,083 83	158 00	1,952 88	3,320 01	1,481 20	4,569 00	34,340 74
St. Croix	4,810 99	1,197 32	10,770 94	....	2,725 48	349 04	581 02	2,194 88	19,481 89
Sauk	7,104 20	5,084 22	32,045 84	337 44	1,485 05	3,482 19	3,732 49	1,945 96	55,221 39
[illegible]ho	1,890 12	1,571 75	1,913 02	15 01	1,168 73	596 41	553 90	58 83	7,047 34
[illegible]an	6,191 66	2,966 72	19,677 97	70 69	2,024 43	4,303 33	4,487 81	2,620 02	43,462 96
[illegible]au	3,487 95	2,476 00	10,478 77	38 73	634 85	1,112 86	1,719 79	2,699 14	24,928 71
Vernon	6,188 66	3,476 69	18,064 78	466 53	645 93	3,113 06	3,140 70	1,615 83	36,812 27
Walworth	9,879 69	11,534 03	39,345 89	542 50	622 76	3,991 48	3,913 29	4,642 63	74,716 18
Washington	3,876 00	5,041 53	13,719 42	25 00	2,506 64	5,229 39	4,276 86	4,201 60	39,014 99
Waukesha	5,860 61	5,292 87	31,848 69	151 19	400 00	3,830 57	4,524 04	2,191 67	52,165 25
Waupaca	6,517 61	2,803 08	16,854 06	122 00	234 42	2,298 85	2,070 92	2,901 01	33,553 87
Waushara	3,392 36	1,531 01	11,848 34	10 00	113 66	2,301 50	1,658 14	1,143 21	21,493 23
Winnebago	8,635 77	4,815 49	27,763 68	485 25	552 14	3,948 75	3,772 44	5,799 25	54,417 11
Wood	756 87	818 53	3,921 61	26 00	1,148 23	382 65	445 95	1,042 15	10,580 65
Totals	$335,689 97	$227,304 48	$914,395 22	$9,780 45	$87,109 00	$142,221 98	$137,902 17	$159,189 92	$1,996,985 12

TABLE No. VIII.

FINANCIAL STATISTICS.

DISBURSEMENTS.

COUNTIES.	For building and re pairing.	For apparatus and library.	For services of male teachers.	For services of female teachers.	For old indebtedness.	For furniture, register and records.	For all other purposes.	Total amount paid out during year.	Money on hand August 31, 1873.
Adams	$1,234 11	$42 25	$2,053 09	$6,520 04	$513 97	$67 08	$731 22	$11,165 70	$2,179 52
Barron	1,889 60	....	883 73	2,233 17	663 00	....	466 73	6,168 23	....
Bayfield	....	....	....	....	....	....	....	....	....
Brown	2,628 69	186 25	9.444 38	7,387 67	686 85	515 01	1,855 90	24,342 06	7,014 05
Buffalo	4,427 60	89 21	9,656 35	6,796 34	1,182 59	1,024 07	1,956 00	25,482 40	8,921 72
Burnett	116 00	5 05	595 00	235 00	66 79	5 40	104 18	761 32	248 48
Calumet	1,982 57	85 95	6,975 25	7,497 42	1,119 48	129 20	1,457 21	19,247 28	3,787 19
Chippewa	3,446 34	164 74	7,238 98	8,915 32	893 60	116 05	2,279 98	23,055 01	11,776 71
Clark	4,096 88	87 60	2,413 55	5,645 00	501 72	254 06	795 51	14,309 25	10,769 03
Columbia	2,693 12	89 03	15,247 89	20,669 17	3,536 70	686 83	5,946 90	48,869 64	6,832 22
Crawford	1,698 69	46 75	1,641 90	8,693 55	732 86	291 87	1,511 47	19,617 09	5,990 86
Dane, 1st dist	3,536 79	125 97	10,208 01	10,419 51	304 04	219 74	3,563 41	28,527 51	4,296 44
Dane, 2d dist	3,813 76	205 57	24.086 12	15,886 35	1,734 71	1,664 06	4,482 16	41,169 91	6,490 28
Dodge, 1st dist	3,248 56	90 35	11,000 03	11,994 36	625 78	211 53	3,236 85	3,507 46	4.708 07
Dodge, 2d dist	4,900 69	119 80	10,778 83	12,184 07	1,063 67	646 10	3,551 60	32,950 70	3,968 32
Door	2,055 61	74 64	3,996 01	3,787 62	541 16	296 40	1,033 34	11,155 58	4,446 83
Douglas	1,647 99	46 25	2,300 00	1,187 50	....	803 40	510 60	6,495 84	2,156 26
Dunn	5,267 45	95 30	6,310 50	9,647 80	802 47	346 85	2,621 68	25,092 05	5,365 66
Eau Claire	4,408 64	179 80	6,874 00	18,790 62	5,964 10	833 47	4,176 02	35,625 23	9,473 49

Fond du Lac, 1 dist.	$3,694 16	$656 37	$11,398 09	$18,113 15	$597 69	$1,086 59	3,337 28	85,418 24	4,528 75
Fond du Lac, 2 dist.	828 15	39 00	5,395 77	7,582 59	746 47	111 77	1,489 31	17,445 89	4,736 68
Grant	7,364 03	250 57	20,177 00	82,186 84	5,102 53	863 22	6,664 55	72,608 74	12,586 87
Green	4,049 86	75 90	12,620 76	16,913 75	3,194 44	403 71	5,486 70	42,745 12	4,717 80
Green Lake	2,890 16	....	4,332 88	7,876 50	390 80	385 03	1,616 06	17,591 43	3,164 42
Iowa	1,513 84	44 55	8,448 43	9,467 55	2,002 19	71 12	2,648 07	22,963 39	1,831 15
Jackson	2,304 34	42 27	4,230 60	11,446 83	2,953 95	156 60	2,105 05	23,239 64	7,670 48
Jefferson	7,168 16	219 91	13,678 86	17,612 57	3,310 98	809 40	6,207 78	49,221 32	5,296 83
Juneau	1,941 89	32 61	8,143 05	11,541 76	479 06	266 20	2,432 17	24,836 74	4,502 18
Kenosha	871 58	104 05	5,861 58	9,064 55	1,460 60	225 92	1,930 89	19,315 89	1,900 55
Kewaunee	3,334 68	27 99	5,089 50	3,789 56	730 94	485 23	1,264 85	15,582 71	6,308 13
La Crosse	2,001 88	20 47	8,925 54	6,615 83	585 79	284 45	1,472 82	19,906 83	4,036 63
La Pointe	7,543 34	85 15	15,379 70	15,407 98	4,607 29	932 20	4,999 40	48,953 14	7,354 71
Manitowoc	35,045 55	188 14	24,779 38	14,376 57	2,117 28	1,403 19	4,820 05	79,155 91	20,019 51
Marathon	5,415 03	420 77	8,548 11	5,532 25	1,298 95	865 78	7,778 08	31,864 16	19,373 57
Marquette	967 82	59 25	2,981 25	5,456 98	746 06	176 10	1,094 47	11,341 69	1,803 53
Milwaukee, 1st dist	3,536 78	45	3,447 55	6,504 92	693 52	728 02	1,824 54	26,235 68	4,244 62
Milwaukee, 2d dis.	836 13	17 00	5,678 20	4,872 20	925 20	174 70	1,602 13	14,131 17	3,079 00
Monroe	3,672 19	452 68	9,398 50	17,740 64	779 97	202 98	4,566 07	36,813 73	6,270 20
Oconto	5,508 05	51 75	2,580 00	6,104 15	60 00	324 00	840 06	16,721 86	4,566 10
Outagamie	5,692 22	68 18	6,381 48	12,143 27	396 27	296 38	1,910 17	26,888 37	7,288 88
Ozaukee	1,943 45	79 45	12,622 08	4,777 23	758 54	211 27	1,255 24	22,141 27	4,101 85
Pepin	2,740 81	22 65	2,544 00	4,459 65	413 81	175 43	887 91	11,407 95	1,566 97
Pierce	4,056 10	163 11	7,204 00	9,715 00	916 64	406 58	2,223 09	25,762 76	6,291 17
Polk	2,349 69	92 80	3,237 50	5,141 84	762 73	101 98	939 38	12,627 92	4,599 94
Portage	2,287 72	129 40	5,970 23	12,988 12	621 92	150 31	2,997 28	25,145 00	4,022 30
Racine	2,643 65	28 55	4,619 80	13,964 75	284 54	389 70	3,090 03	24,968 24	4,163 45
Richland	3,508 21	37 59	8,004 55	10,681 05	721 00	325 31	2,197 54	25,904 54	8,464 20
Rock, 1st dist.	2,566 95	324 76	7,390 42	11,844 79	1,751 27	477 46	4,957 90	29,293 55	5,953 77
Rock, 2d dist	5,703 53	265 45	4,539 35	14,771 51	1,792 54	611 05	4,311 28	31,591 85	5,306 71
St. Croix	1,705 10	....	6,434 50	7,857 10	420 23	376 24	1,780 79	16,843 97	4,386 96
Sauk	2,876 29	185 52	14,451 16	22,698 21	2,137 31	844 25	4,068 64	48,161 38	7,060 01
Shawano	554 04	55 55	1,124 00	1,972 50	3,669 94	32 17	428 78	693 57	6,092 56
Sheboygan	2,920 32	96 21	13,460 74	15,213 01	897 74	1,208 13	2,858 50	35,627 78	6,530 25
Trempealeau	2,589 54	103 94	5,831 75	7,653 00	792 05	269 31	3,141 56	20,646 45	4,165 53
Vernon	3,101 67	105 31	10,411 13	12,208 88	1,731 39	442 59	2,443 67	30,444 64	6,267 63

TABLE VIII.—*Financial Statistics—Disbursements*—continued.

COUNTIES.	For building and repairing.	For apparatus and library.	For services of male teachers.	For services of female teachers.	For old indebtedness.	For furniture, register and records.	For all other purposes.	Total amount paid out during the year.	Money on hand, Aug. 31, 1872.
Walworth	$9,374 56	$493 69	$15,821 62	$27,306 57	$2,307 24	$710 40	$7,956 37	$64,719 48	$12,456 26
Washington	7,252 20	24 10	15,601 72	8,859 82	616 58	539 09	2,820 55	34,908 88	4,097 16
Waukesha	4,548 45	100 85	13,366 60	22,963 80	991 79	814 15	4,855 97	47,493 20	6,284 85
Waupaca	2,536 13	680 66	6,975 04	18,276 28	1,133 04	291 55	3,(77 03	28,472 30	6,338 91
Waushara	2,044 82	179 00	4,258 18	9,586 06	210 01	433 54	1.532 28	18,154 82	3,934 39
Winnebago	3,612 04	103 52	14,735 84	19,295 85	3,459 17	265 90	6,308 25	47,525 09	7,688 02
Wood	2,292 48	....	2,740 00	3,211 56	78 15	68 00	2,925 66	11,009 20	1,176 38
Totals	$231,880 67	$7,863 68	$500,095 08	$649,275 03	$77,480 79	$29,307 12	$174,418 07	$1,643,975.65	$353,150 08

TABLE No. IX.

TEXT BOOKS.

NUMBER OF DISTRICTS USING THE DIFFERENT BOOKS MENTIONED.

Counties.	Spellers.						Readers.					Arithmetics.				History of U. S.			
	Sander's.	Sander's Union.	National.	Wilson.	McGuffey.	Town.	Sanders.	Sanders.	National.	Wilson.	McGuffey.	Thomson.	Davies.	Ray.	Robinson.	Willard.	Wilson.	Goodrich.	Barnes' Brief.
Adams	21	40					21	39			1		2	26	37		4	30	
Barron		20						20						20				20	
Bayfield	1						1								1			1	
Brown	12	2												8	2	2			
Buffalo			62		1		4	1	62				58	1					
Burnett			4						4				4						
Calumet	24	4	33				17	2	33		5	11	30		9	12		6	3
Chippewa	7		35						39			2	36		3			13	
Clark		25			11			14	20		2		26	1	8			2	
Columbia	100	21		96				27				52		9	76			96	3
Crawford		59			11			61			11			46	26			23	
Dane, 1st dist	77		10				76		8		4	34	9	33	8	7	6	26	
Dane, 2d dist	106		15		9		103		28		3	1	33	88				97	
Dodge, 1st dist	83		5	6			73		7		9		9	46	10			53	
Dodge, 2d dist	70		16		4		50		17		17	43	8	23			1	18	9
Door	17			4	9		12			3	15		1	21	8			8	
Douglas			2	2										2				2	
Dunn	55	5	12				55	5	13			4	15	53		9	6	3	1

TABLE No. IX—*Text Books*—continued.

COUNTIES.	SPELLERS.						READERS.					ARITHMETICS.				HISTORY OF U. S.			
	Sanders.	Sanders Union.	National.	Wilson.	McGuffey.	Town.	Sanders.	Sanders' Union.	National.	Wilson.	McGuffey.	Thompson.	Davies.	Ray.	Robinson.	Willard.	Wilson.	Goodrich.	Barnes' Brief.
Eau Claire	19	....	....	13	....	....	....	....	6	19	....	11	2	24	....	....	....	3	....
F. du Lac, 1st dis.	56	....	18	1	....	....	47	....	80	7	....	....	20	6	27	....	....	36	....
F. du Lac, 2d dis.	82	....	....	....	....	....	80	....	3	....	....	57	14	11	....	....	....	13	....
Grant	23	4	....	2	111	....	31	....	....	....	127	6	....	159	10	....	23	42	....
Green	40	20	....	....	69	....	25	22	....	....	79	....	....	130	3	....	....	33	....
Green Lake	....	....	....	....	....	....	....	67	....	....	....	25	1	26	....	....	....	37	1
Iowa	....	12	22	....	74	....	....	26	13	....	79	....	14	87	13	....	....	53	....
Jackson	24	2	22	....	4	....	6	4	32	....	7	....	6	47	3	....	2	4	2
Jefferson	66	....	35	....	....	....	47	3	50	....	....	27	60	....	17	....	....	33	....
Juneau	23	57	....	....	4	....	12	63	....	....	7	....	....	44	....	....	....	34	....
Kenosha	40	....	24	....	....	....	21	....	24	....	....	7	34	....	9	....	....	18	....
Kewaunee	16	1	....	....	24	....	23	2	....	....	....	4	....	34	3	....	4	15	....
La Crosse	....	26	....	....	31	....	....	87	....	12	17	....	14	48	3	....	....	14	....
La Fayette	40	15	....	29	25	18	14	....	....	17	58	2	8	91	13	....	15	....	....
Manitowoc	81	14	2	....	7	....	81	13	14	....	9	1	11	81	8	2	3	35	3
Marathon	16	....	31	....	3	....	14	....	28	....	7	....	38	3	....	4	....	6	....
Marquette	88	17	....	....	2	....	87	13	....	....	6	5	....	8	40	....	....	27	....
Milw'kee, 1st dis.	8	....	3	....	20	....	7	....	5	....	20	3	6	20	....	....	....	17	....
Milw'kee, 2d dis.	12	....	2	....	16	....	....	....	9	1	19	4	1	23	6	....	....	21	....
Monroe	95	....	....	....	7	....	82	....	....	....	11	....	....	91	18	....	1	33	10
Oconto	....	....	....	7	10	....	....	....	....	7	18	....	2	23	2	....	6	....	....

Outagamie	14			58	12			7		68	12	11	9		64	4		4	25
Ozaukee	37			5	15		37			5	12	5	14	20	18		6	18	
Pepin	4		5				4		5			3			5		1	1	
Pierce	70	1		10			14			78		3	1		68			20	
Polk	2		41						41		2		34		5		4	3	3
Portage	45	22					20		51			25	43	25		2	2	34	5
Racine	50	5	15		2		33	11	21		2	16	39	1	7			32	1
Richland		104	3		11			104	2				3	33	86			44	
Rock, 1st dist.		10	2	8	32		25	11		21	19	1		43	35		6	12	
Rock, 2d dist.		40	3	3	30			43	9	14	43	13	4	37	25			8	2
St. Croix																			
Sauk		95	30	1	4			94	37	7	1		67	15	46	22		48	2
Shawano	6		6									1	10						
Sheboygan		88	19		3			72	24			2	78	5	22	1		51	2
Trempealeau	9		48				2		62			3	49	5			2	4	
Vernon		64	8		53			63	8		53		1	126				97	
Walworth	54	66	5		3		1	94				15	1	1	99		5	44	
Washington	83	3			15		78	5			11		23	32	34			63	
Waukesha																			
Waupaca	51	13		4	6						6	54	12	5	5	4	5	10	
Waushara	26	55					25	54						29	36			52	
Winnebago	32	19			37		23	31			31		17	17	51		6	33	
Wood	20		2				28						8		4				
Totals	1,655	996	538	249	675	18	1,227	1,006	705	254	728	451	855	1,713	923	69	108	1,451	73

TABLE No. IX.—*Text Books*—continued.

COUNTIES.	GEOGRAPHY.						GRAMMAR.						PHYSIOLOGY.		ALGEBRA.		
	Monteith.	McNally and Monteith.	Cornell.	Mitchell.	Guyot.	Warren.	Clark.	Green.	Harvey.	Pinneo.	Kerl.	Brown.	Jarvis.	Cutter.	Davies.	Robinson.	Ray.
Adams	7	22		30			40		4		10	1		1		7	
Barron							20										
Bayfield																	
Brown											2					1	1
Buffalo	45	12			1		43	2					1	2		7	2
Burnett	4							3									
Calumet	32						15		7		2		1		2	1	
Chippewa	32		4				11		13								
Clark	8	26					22				6						
Columbia				74			50				33	35		12	8	18	
Crawford	1			55		16				30	37			2		8	
Dane, 1st district	16		10	39			31	5		7	22			7		4	9
Dane, 2d district	83	21	23				61			37	18			1		2	8
Dodge, 1st district		58	18	4			14				33			9			12
Dodge, 2d district	14	12	36	6		2	65				5		1	1	6	6	2
Door	19	7	4				4				15			1			1
Douglas			2					2				1					3
Dunn	46		28				58				8	1			5		
Eau Claire	4		30		3		14		7		7					4	
Fond du Lac, 1st dist		25	20			2	9				45	2		14		16	2
Fond du Lac, 2d dist			89	42					22		35						

Grant	51		18	92		4	8		6	82	54		8	5		8	7
Green	5	4							5	71	4					5	9
Green Lake	28	37	17				51			1	13			25		38	
Iowa	54	11		35			48			39				8			1
Jackson	24	9		4	1		19		1	6	2				2	1	
Jefferson	37	37	20				74	6						4	9		
Juneau	6	4		66			11				36	2		4	1	8	8
Kenosha	80			15			17	23			9		2	8		8	6
Kewaunee	10	10	14							14	7						
La Crosse	84	15	6				24			16				2		6	
La Fayette	73	15		12			15	1	10	54	29			2	2	4	5
Manitowoc	19	9		45		2	9	1	4	29	19			8	1	7	1
Marathon	25	16			2		17		12						7		
Marquette	4		10	33			32			8				2		6	
Milwaukee, 1st district	21	4		2			2		2	9	5			1	6	1	
Milwaukee, 2d district	5		5	21	1		8				5	1		2	2	3	2
Monroe	44	43		15			8	16	8	22	26			8	8		5
Oconto	8	1	19				12			16				1		2	
Outagamie	31			41		4	35		26								
Ozaukee	31		8	13			17			10	13				2		1
Pepin	2						4									1	
Pierce	14	20		2			10		8	4	28					8	
Polk	23							2	2					1			
Portage	59		9	6			86		5	18				4			12
Racine		72	1			8	82	30		1	16			1	1	1	1
Richland		13	1	80			5			12	72			2		3	
Rock, 1st district	5		47	10		5	20	13	4	2	4			2	2	3	3
Rock, 2d district		9	41			9	19	9	2	17	9			1	4	9	8
St Croix		51			4		10					32		1	5		
Sauk	35			12	3	4	67		15	2	33			3	9	3	1
Shawano				8			5	1	1								
Sheboygan		48	2	39			22		8		32		1	1	3	6	
Trempealeau	47		3				38							1	1	3	
Vernon	84	22	34		2						77			3	8		
Walworth	58	22	11		25		22	18	2		62			4		19	
Washington	62		3	24			48				7						10

Table No. IX.—*Text Books*—concluded.

Counties.	Geography.						Grammar.						Physiology.		Algebra.		
	Monteith.	McNally and Monteith.	Cornell.	Mitchell.	Guyot.	Warren.	Clark.	Green.	Harvey.	Pinneo.	Kerl.	Brown.	Jarvis.	Cutter.	Davis.	Robinson.	Ray.
Waukesha																	
Waupaca	13	20	14	20			38				13		4	4	3	4	
Waushara	56	19					51				13		1			9	
Winnebago	15	1		32			28	1	2		41					11	
Wood		4					2										
Totals	1,324	699	492	877	48	51	1,321	128	161	507	893	75	19	138	92	236	109

Table No. X.

SPECIAL STATISTICS OF SCHOOL ATTENDANCE.

Required by section 2, chapter 163, and by chapter 101, general laws of 1871.

Counties.	Number of children between 4 and 7 years of age in the county.	Number of children between 7 and 15 years of age in the county.	Number of persons between 15 and 20 years of age in the county.	Number of children between 4 and 7 years of age who have attended school.	Number of children between 7 and 15 years of age who have attended school.	Number of children between 15 and 20 years of age who have attended school.	Number incapacitated for instruction from defect of vision.	Number incapacitated for instruction from defect of hearing.	Number incapacitated for instruction from defect of intellect.
Adams	585	1,247	666	368	1,138	418	3	5	2
Barron	150	287	131	97	185	33	1	......	......
Bayfield	39	77	37	......	......	......	......	......	......
Brown	2,068	3,207	1,340	940	2,144	637	4	6	2
Buffalo	1,309	2,514	985	672	557	......	......	3	3
Burnett	109	194	59	37	119	20	......	1	......
Calumet	1,601	2,677	1,281	796	1,889	386	1	1	5
Chippewa	924	1,447	567	453	1,146	225	4	5	1
Clark	400	659	336	156	484	160	......	2	1
Columbia	1,903	4,211	2,106	1,218	3,581	1,319	6	9	6
Crawford	1,267	2,607	1,183	815	1,981	608	2	2	3
Dane, 1st district	1,476	2,998	1,699	732	2,432	885	3	6	4
Dane, 2d district	2,298	4,963	2,646	1,224	3,369	1,499	6	10	9
Dodge, 1st district	1,583	3,244	1,850	908	2,692	1,001	4	3	9
Dodge, 2d district	2,040	4,066	2,320	957	2,437	755	4	5	10
Door	645	1,030	405	323	878	140	2	1	7
Douglas	121	135	85	76	115	43	1	......	......
Dunn	1,056	2,392	1,066	748	1,689	443	......	4	11
Eau Claire	1,050	2,072	830	702	1,768	487	3	4	3

TABLE No. X.—*Special Statistics of School Attendance*—continued.

Counties.	Number of children between 4 and 7 years of age in the county.	Number of children between 7 and 15 years of age in the county.	Number of persons between 15 and 20 years of age in the county.	Number of children between 4 and 7 years of age who have attended school.	Number of children between 7 and 15 years of age who have attended school.	Number of persons between 15 and 20 years of age who have attended school.	Nu'ber incapacitated for instruction from defect of vision.	Nu'ber incapacitated for instruction from defect of hearing.	Nu'ber incapacitated for instruction from defect of intellect.
Fond du Lac, 1st dist	1,952	2,970	1,820	1,007	2,619	1,113	4	3	8
Fond du Lac, 2d dist	1,573	2,855	1,713	894	2,324	689	6	2	1
Grant	3,554	7,251	4,000	2,133	6,661	2,377	6	13	9
Green	1,761	3,676	2,838	1,232	3,308	1,546	11	7	5
Green Lake	914	2,004	947	565	1,543	590	2	1	5
Iowa	1,343	2,738	1,647	678	2,149	889	......	3	4
Jackson	979	1,814	865	496	1,443	563	6	3	6
Jefferson	2,411	5,320	2,821	1,324	3,915	1,327	4	11	10
Juneau	1,2[illegible]7	2,955	1,322	848	2,865	916	4	4	3
Kenosha	750	1,513	848	395	1,195	494	......	2	4
Kewaunee	1,539	2,426	1,191	687	1,542	285	3	5	7
La Crosse	1,065	2,472	1,144	479	1,828	568	......	1	3
La Fayette	2,087	4,425	2,402	1,276	3,760	1,450	3	4	4
Manitowoc	4,260	7,338	3,511	1,811	4,959	762	3	9	13
Marathon	825	1,322	551	414	1,122	184	1	4	5
Marquette	832	1,705	784	399	1,262	462	1	4	5
Milwaukee, 1st dist	1,123	2,035	958	470	1,239	244	......	2	3
Milwaukee, 2d dist	876	1,797	774	343	1,125	163	2	3	8
Monroé	1,862	3,755	1,632	1,213	3,812	1,032	4	7	8
Oconto	680	1,017	494	391	717	144	......	......	4
Outagamie	2,008	3,192	1,621	1,035	2,598	759	......	1	6
Ozaukee	1,962	3,446	1,956	927	2,289	400	2	3	1
Pepin	495	1,015	388	288	805	281	1	2	......

[illegible]rce	1,159	2,228	949	584	1,760	433	1	6	4
Polk	496	984	356	240	786	181	1	2	1
Portage	1,076	2,294	1,021	622	1,838	561	1	8	9
Racine	1,316	2,720	1,400	582	2,018	603	1	8	6
Richland	1,647	3,375	1,724	1,134	3,104	1,233	3	10	10
Rock, 1st district	931	2,301	1,307	656	2,063	857	2	4	8
Rock, 2d district	813	1,912	1,000	603	1,504	509	3	2	2
St. Croix	828	1,734	772	582	1,564	543	......	......	......
Sauk	2,238	4,903	2,512	1,366	4,066	1,731	3	4	20
Shawano	422	664	288	131	360	67	1	......	......
[illegible]gan	2,724	5,481	2,840	1,368	4,017	1,047	3	4	15
[illegible]u	1,148	2,213	918	447	1,644	446	2	2	6
Vernon	2,160	3,454	2,730	1,276	2,442	1,776	......	1	......
Walworth	1,788	4,465	2,587	1,039	3,671	1,315	3	7	7
[illegible]ington	2,498	2,968	2,591	1,114	3,389	768	......	9	3
Waukesha	2,289	5,139	2,639	1,312	4,425	1,292	......	4	11
Waupaca	1,521	3,108	1,431	828	2,558	851	1	8	11
[illegible]a	1,071	2,639	1,180	724	1,844	715	1	4	5
Winnebago	2,167	4,626	2,616	1,002	3,382	1,266	2	6	5
Wood	273	412	220	......	......	......	......	......	......
Totals	87,305	174,838	86,340	46,234	130,812	42,947	140	240	321

Table No. X—*Special Statistics of School Attendance*—continued.

Required by section 2. chapter 169, general laws of 1871.

CITIES.

Cities.	No. of children between 4 and 7 years of age in the city.	No. of children between 7 and 15 years of age in the city.	No. of persons between 15 and 20 years of age in the city.	No. of children between 4 and 7 years of age who have attended school.	No. of children between 7 and 15 years of age who have attended school.	No. of persons between 15 and 20 years of age who have attended school.	No. incapacitated for instruction from defect of hearing.	No. incapacitated for instruction from defect of vision.	No. incapacitated for instruction from defect of intellect.
[illegible]	546	931	613	167	755	71	......	1	1
Beaver Dam	342	692	366	166	469	178	1	......	......
Beloit	338	716	447	157	648	118	......	......	......
Berlin	341	586	264	72	472	125	......	......	4
Fond du Lac	1,238	2,633	1,598	......	......	......	5	5	1
Fort Howard	291	440	229	125	453	51	......	......	1
Green Bay	548	1,195	375	180	780	33	......	2	1
Hudson	142	330	144	70	279	114	......	......	......
Janesville	767	1,377	1,190	215	1,422	37	4	4	4
Kenosha	446	961	500	152	436	117	1	1	1
La Crosse	977	1,609	779	358	1,222	162	1	2	2
Madison	837	2,064	896	......	......	......	2	2	2
Milwaukee	6,398	15,212	7,545	2,832	8,028	364	3	25	15
[illegible] Point	308	729	313	100	609	136	......	......	1
Oconto	301	547	141	249	417	167	1	......	1
[illegible]sh	1,243	2,358	1,045	......	......	......	1	1	2
Portage	327	772	339	210	645	110	1	......	2
Racine	836	7,087	1,140	468	1,605	226	......	3	5
Sheboygan	482	1,206	712	261	743	67	2	5	5
Watertown	980	1,716	946	......	1,262	32	1	2	3
Totals	17,588	43,165	19,587	5,782	20,245	2,108	23	53	50

Table No. XI.—STATISTICS OF CITIES.

SCHOOLS, CHILDREN AND ATTENDANCE.

Cities.	No. of public schools in city.	No. of male children over 4 and under 20 years of age.	No. female children over 4 and under 20 years of age.	Whole No. children over 4 and under 20 years of age in city.	No. under 4 yr's who h'v' at'dec.	No. over 20 yr's who h'v' at'dec.	No. over 4 and under 20 years who have att'd school.	Total No. diff't pupils who h'v attend'd school during year.	No. days' at'dce pup. un. 4 yrs.	No. days' att'ce pup. over 20 yrs.	No. of days attendance of pupils over 4 and under 20 years.	Whole No. days' attendance of different pupils during year.	No. days school been taught by qualified teach.	Pr ct. enrol't on No. res't in city.	Pr ct. of at'ance on No. enroll'd.	No. of days lost by absence.
Appleton	13	1,090	1,000	2,090			1,003	1,003			78,722	87,253	185	48	47	98,302
Beaver Dam	11	646	753	1,400			813	813					200			
Beloit	18	752	753	1,505		1	923	924			112,367	112,367	197		98	8,848
Berlin	13	532	559	1,091			669	669			86,582	86,582	200	61	80	16,120
Fond du Lac	45	2,601	2,868	5,469		6	3,475	3,481		500	600,472	600,972	200	64	86	45,500
Fort Howard	7	494	475	969			629	629			55,339	55,339	198	65	44	
Green Bay	12	1,024	1,094	2,118			993	994			100,418	100,418	200	46	50	13,746
Hudson	7	313	308	616			463	463			42,179	42,179	180	91	75	11,677
Janesville	25	1,674	1,860	3,534			1,674	1,674			148,681	148,681	168	47	59	11,251
Kenosha	12	910	1,002	1,912	10	5	575	595	800	700	107,350	107,350	109	31	86	115
La Crosse	24	1,600	1,765	3,365		10	1,752	1,762		420	177,768	178,188	200	52	55	17,835
Madison	23	1,842	1,955	3,797			3,797	3,797			168,772	168,772	185			
Milwaukee	152	14,259	14,896	29,155			11,214	11,224			1,233,192	1,233,192	196	38	86	152,138
Mineral Point	11	609	741	1,350		10	567	577			43,729	43,729	160	54	87	50
Oconto	8	512	477	989			833	333			63,978	63,978	202	83	45	28,595
Oshkosh	56	2,271	2,370	4,641			2,938	2,938					200	63	91	
Portage	11	738	700	1,438			965	965			103,008	103,008	199	36	67	18,543
Racine	26	1,926	2,137	4,063		3	2,299	2,302		315	299,546	299,861	200	56	65	17,879
Sheboygan	16	1,174	1,226	2,400			1,071				158,548	158,548	195	40	97	4,360
Watertown	18	1,850	1,792	3,642			1,294	1,294			176,167	176,167	200	35	95	8,813
Totals	508	36,818	38,726	75,544	10	35	37,957	38,936	800	1,935	3,156,818	3,756,598	3,774	50	72	453,262

Table No. XI—*Statistics of Cities*—continued.

TEACHERS, SALARIES, LIBRARIES.

Cities.	TEACHERS, SALARIES, ETC.								LIBRARIES.							
	No. teachers required to teach sch'ls.	No. male tc'rs emp. dur. yr.	No. fem. tch's emp. during year.	Whole No. of t'chers emp. during year.	Highest sal'y paid to male t'ch's during year (per annum).	Av. sal. p'd to male t'chers during year (per annum.)	Highest sal'y paid female t'chrs during yr. (per ann.)	Av. sal's paid fem. t'rs dur. yr. (per ann.)	No. sep. sch'l lib's in city.	Whole No. v'ls ad'd dur. yr.	Whole am'nt exp. for b'ks during year.	No. volumes loaned during year.	No. vols. lost during year.	Whole No. of vols. in all libraries.	Av. No. vols. in each library.	Cash value of all the libraries.
Appleton	12	4	8	13	$900	$630	$450	380	....	....	....	....	....	....	....	....
Beaver Dam	11	2	9	11	1,400	1,000	400	248	....	....	....	....	....	....	....	....
Beloit	16	1	15	16	1,600	1,600	800	418	1	....	....	....	....	....	....	....
Berlin	13	2	13	13	1,500	975	500	327	1	....	....	....	....	200	....	....
Fond du Lac	47	3	44	47	1,500	800	650	361	....	....	....	....	....	....	....	....
Fort Howard	9	4	7	11	1,080	900	450	334	....	....	....	....	....	....	....	....
Green Bay	13	1	12	13	1,500	1,500	500	500	1	....	....	....	....	250	250	100
Hudson	7	....	7	7	....	....	720	456	1	....	....	....	....	60	....	200
Janesville	28	1	27	28	1,650	1,650	509	334	1	....	....	....	....	50	50	100
Kenosha	13	2	10	12	1,600	1,025	700	367	1	....	....	....	....	100	100	200
La Crosse	33	6	27	33	1,200	1,133	450	394	....	....	....	....	....	....	....	....
Madison	24	1	23	24	1,500	1,500	585	450	1	50	....	....	....	....	....	300
Milwaukee	165	38	127	165	2,500	1,312	1,200	520	....	....	....	....	....	....	....	....
Mineral Point	10	2	8	10	1,100	820	860	360	1	....	....	....	....	100	....	100
Oconto	12	4	8	12	1,200	900	450	431	....	....	....	....	....	....	....	....
Oshkosh	56	5	51	56	2,000	960	500	335	1	....	....	....	....	125	....	....
Portage	13	1	12	13	1,200	1,200	450	329	1	....	....	80	....	230	....	345
Racine	31	5	27	32	2,000	1,360	800	367	1	....	....	500	....	1,300	....	1,000
Sheboygan	16	3	13	16	1,400	866	400	332	1	....	....	....	....	200	200	100
Watertown	19	6	13	21	1,350	600	500	300	1	34	70	....	....	450	....	988
Totals	548	91	459	553	$2,500	$1,001	1,200	377	13	84	$70	1,300	....	3,065	175	3,433

Table No. XI.—*Statistics of Cities*—continued.

SCHOOL HOUSES AND SITES.

Cities.	No. public school houses in the city.	No. school houses yet required.	No. now being built.	Whole No. school children resident in city.	Whole No. school houses will accommodate.	No. of school house sites own'd by city.	No. sites contain'g only one lot.	No. sites contain'g more than one lot.	No. of sites suitably enclosed.	No. school houses b'lt stone or brick.	Highest valuation of school house and site.	Cash value of all the public school houses in the city.	Cash value of sites.	No sch. ho's properly ventilated.	No. sch. ho'es with separate out-ho'ses for the sexes.	No. sch. ho'ses out-ho's good condi'n.
Appleton	4	2	....	2,090	1,000	4	....	4	4	2	12,000	$35,000	$8,000	3	4	4
Beaver Dam	4	....	....	....	....	4	....	4	4	3	15,000	30,000	300	3	4	....
Beloit	3	....	....	....	....	3	....	3	3	3	35,000	50,000	700	1	3	3
Berlin	2	....	....	1,091	900	2	....	2	2	....	35,000	47,000	7,000	2	2	2
Fond du Lac	16	7	....	5,469	2,600	17	1	16	16	2	50,000	95,565	21,000	16	16	16
Fort Howard	5	....	....	969	700	4	1	3	2	2	20,000	22,000	6,700	4	5	4
Green Bay	4	....	....	2,118	840	4	....	4	4	3	30,000	50,000	12,000	....	4	4
Hudson	5	1	....	616	400	3	....	3	2	3	8,000	14,000	3,500	....	5	5
Janesville	5	1	....	3,534	1,140	5	....	5	5	5	50,000	100,000	1,000	4	5	5
Kenosha	3	1	....	1,833	550	2	....	2	2	2	10,000	20,000	3,000	3	3	3
La Crosse	5	1	....	3,365	1,600	5	....	5	5	3	20,000	45,000	8,000	5	5	5
Madison	7	1	1	3,797	1,400	8	1	7	6	7	20,000	96,000	....	7	7	7
Milwaukee	21	3	2	29,155	9,000	22	3	19	38	19	45,000	308,775	....	....	19	21
Mineral Point	2	....	....	1,350	660	2	....	2	2	2	10,000	15,000	1,500	2	2	2
Oconto	5	3	....	989	400	5	2	3	1	....	2,000	8,000	1,300	....	5	5
Oshkosh	10	1	....	4,641	2,500	11	1	10	....	3	75,000	125,000	25,000	10	10	10
Portage	5	2	1	1,438	950	4	....	4	3	1	10,000	10,500	5,500	3	3	3
Racine	6	2	....	4,063	1,600	6	....	6	6	5	15,000	44,000	15,000	....	6	2
Sheboygan	4	....	1	2,400	800	3	....	3	2	2	9,000	12,000	4,000	3	4	4
Watertown	6	1	....	3,642	1,250	5	2	3	4	3	19,000	20,000	5,100	4	6	6
Totals	122	26	5	72,560	28,290	119	11	108	111	70	$75,000	$1,147,840	$128,600	70	118	111

Table No. XI.—*Statistics of Cities*—continued.

FINANCIAL STATISTICS—RECEIVED.

Counties.	Money on ha'd Aug. 31, 1872.	From taxes levied for building and repairing.	From taxes levied for teachers wages.	Tax lev'd for apparatus and library.	From taxes levied at the annual meeting.	From taxes levied by the county supervisors.	From income of state school fund.	From all other sources.	Total amount received during the year.
Appleton	$1,133 45	$2,100 00	$5,225 00	100	$1,496 50	$424 36	$1,051 91	$3,835 90	$15,358 12
Beaver Dam	1,015 13	1,000 00	4,000 00	....	....	525 33	525 83	1,850 00	8,815 99
Beloit	3,086 03	....	....	....	14,000 00	1,097 13	626 64	810 05	19,569 85
Berlin	2,062 47	....	....	....	7,000 00	375 86	448 14	550 00	8,874 10
Fond du Lac	2,826 91	....	....	....	....	37,338 88	2,285 22	24,508 72	66,959 78
Fort Howard	3,630 87	1,754 74	3,800 00	....	1,585 00	366 99	477 12	1,337 00	12,951 72
Green Bay	8,544 62	....	7,500 00	....	1,500 00	553 14	748 02	14 75	18,861 05
Hudson	470 92	....	....	80	3,885 00	250 38	245 38	....	4,351 68
Janesville	....	....	....	....	15,000 00	2,250 00	1,499 94	838 36	19,588 30
Kenosha	2,760 00	500 00	5,950 00	....	5,600 00	1,600 00	589 00	400 00	8,625 00
La Crosse	4,777 90	7,850 00	16,050 00	500	80,538 83	1,185 21	1,367 52	58 51	87,927 97
Madison	7,813 24	....	12,622 94	....	....	....	1,677 83	25,379 55	46,993 56
Milwaukee	48,123 71	....	....	....	69,977 61	47,252 62	11,400 78	....	176,844 78
Mineral Point	....	1 000 00	3,461 41	....	....	538 59	572 04	....	5,572 04
Oconto	....	....	8,773 96	....	....	331 05	462 84	....	9,567 85
Oshkosh	4,000 00	5,000 00	20,250 00	....	18,000 00	12,000 00	1,934 10	....	81,184 10
Portage	800 30	....	....	....	5,000 00	609 96	664 38	518 14	7,092 81
Racine	....	....	....	....	15,000 00	5,000 00	1,644 72	757 50	22,402 22
Sheboygan	3,742 29	....	....	....	5,417 32	1,000 00	1,016 40	822 71	11,498 72
Watertown	1,477 49	....	....	....	11,383 45	3,588 83	1,525 86	....	17,970 68
Totals	$93,215 33	$19,204 74	$87,633 81	680	$204,883 72	$116,283 33	$30,853 17	$61,081 19	$550,510 17

TABLE No. XI.—*Statistics of Cities*—continued.

FINANCIAL STATISTICS—PAID.

CITIES.	For building and repairing.	For apparatus and libraries.	For services of male teachers.	For services of female teachers.	For old indebtedness.	For furniture, registers and records.	For all other purposes.	Total amount paid out during the year.	Money on hand August 31, 1873.
Appleton	$2,953 91	$116 00	$2,238 72	$3,545 38	$1,368 86	$13 30	$1,965 05	$12,201 22	$8,156 70
Beaver Dam	1,000 00		1,800 00	2,900 00	1,000 00	110 36	895 07	7,705 43	1,110 36
Beloit			1,600 00	6,272 00	6,500 00	367 85	3,718 05	18,457 90	1,111 95
Berlin			1,950 00	3,500 00				8,386 57	2,050 00
Fond du Lac	30,776 91		2,160 00	16,738 50	540 00	3,281 65	6,380 71	59,877 77	7,081 96
Ft. Howard	3,918 19		1,805 00	2,176 76	840 00	43 05	1,803 53	10,586 53	2,365 19
Green Bay	1,175 72		1,500 00	5,812 50		1,361 08	48 75	9,898 05	8,963 00
Hudson	2,400 00			2,385 00		25 00	500 00	5,310 00	
Janssville	4,000 00		1,650 00	10,000 00	2,000 00	1,000 00	938 30	19,588 30	
Kenosha	500 00		1,750 00	4,200 00		100 00	2,100 00	6,900 00	1,725 00
La Crosse	8,042 84	36 85	6,665 00	9,601 25		1,775 34	4,210 15	30,331 43	10,819 49
Madison	12,282 09	79 40	1,500 00	10,349 95		150 00	6,605 06	30,966 50	16,027 06
Milwaukee	684 70	1,904 18	101,167 11			1,039 75	162 00	122,404 01	54,440 72
Mineral Point	375 62		1,640 00	2,148 00	500 60		571 33	5,235 45	
Oconto			3,280 00	3,290 00	1,693 78	20 00			1,284 07
Oshkosh	5,231 21		4,500 00	15,750 00		1,600 00		28,373 21	2,810 89
Portage	350 00		1,200 00	3,950 00			974 17	6,474 12	500 64
Racine	2,098 58	108 70	6,800 00	7,505 00		587 76	3,302 18	22,402 22	
Sheboygan	113 99		2,600 00	3,740 00		745 09	1,374 03	8,574 01	2,924 71
Watertown	150 08	85 00	4,474 10	3,819 50	6,412 51	60 15	849 68	15,801 09	2,169 54
Totals	$76,053 74	$2,280 13	$150,339 93	$117,682 84	$20,855 75	$12,281 28	$36,398 06	$429,473 86	$118,541 28

CERTIFICATES.

Counties.	Male Teachers.			Female Teachers.			Total.
	1st Gr.	2d Gr.	3d Gr.	1st Gr.	2d Gr.	3d Gr.	
Adams	....	4	3	....	1	60	68
Barron	....	....	8	....	....	21	29
Bayfield	....	....	1	....	....	....	1
Brown	3	20	25	....	....	....	48
Buffalo	4	9	48	2	4	48	115
Burnett	....	....	2	....	....	2	4
Calumet	....	4	32	....	3	64	103
Chippewa	....	....	40	....	....	109	149
Clark	....	4	15	....	2	38	59
Columbia	4	4	56	....	4	112	180
Crawford	5	2	23	1	3	53	86
Dane, 1st district	7	9	70	....	10	126	222
Dane, 2d district	8	3	83	1	4	180	249
Dodge 1st district	4	10	75	....	8	124	221
Dodge, 2d district	3	4	40	1	4	79	131
Door	....	....	15	....	....	30	45
Douglas	....	....	....	....	....	5	5
Dunn	2	6	29	....	7	103	147
Eau Claire	1	1	12	3	1	49	67
Fond du Lac, 1st dist	....	10	60	....	6	160	236
Fond du Lac, 2d dist	....	5	28	....	4	128	165
Grant	5	7	85	3	4	294	398

Green	7	5	38	2	2	124	178
Green Lake	1	4	28	2	12	65	112
Iowa	....	5	52	....	7	134	198
Jackson	....	4	16	....	14	64	98
Jefferson	4	4	64	....	6	135	213
Juneau	7	2	33	2	3	103	150
Kenosha	2	2	17	....	15	41	75
Kewaunee	....	....	24	....	....	32	56
La Crosse	....	3	29	....	....	40	72
La Fayette	3	10	69	2	19	137	240
Manitowoc	2	3	62	....	1	72	140
Marathon	1	5	28	....	1	23	58
Marquette	1	4	19	....	4	79	107
Milwaukee, 1st dis	....	3	13	1	1	35	52
Milwaukee, 2d dis	1	1	15	....	1	22	40
Monroe	2	4	44	1	18	133	202
Oconto	1	....	7	....	....	51	59
Outagamie	....	5	30	....	3	83	121
Ozaukee	1	12	33	....	....	33	79
Pepin	1	1	18	....	2	38	60
Pierce	....	....	55	....	....	55	110
Polk	....	1	18	....	1	48	68
Portage	1	1	24	....	2	88	116
Racine	1	6	27	1	9	99	143
Richland	1	3	60	1	3	121	245
Rock, 1st dist	1	4	51	1	4	137	198
Rock, 2d dist	4	....	28	1	2	100	135
St. Croix	....	....	....	....	....	....	....
Sauk	2	5	65	....	....	157	229
Shawano	....	9	....	....	14	....	23
Sheboygan	4	3	36	3	1	113	160
Trempealeau	....	2	24	....	4	59	89
Vernon	2	8	45	....	1	86	142
Walworth	....	6	50	....	4	166	226
Washington	3	8	48	....	2	57	118

TABLE No. XII.—*Certificates*—continued.

COUNTIES.	MALE TEACHERS.			FEMALE TEACHERS.			Total.
	1st Gr.	2d Gr.	3d Gr.	1st Gr.	2d Gr.	3d Gr.	
Waukesha	2	3	55	......	7	122	189
Waupaca	2	4	35	1	6	132	180
Waushara	3	3	16	......	10	110	142
Winnebago	1	5	34	......	6	99	145
Wood	......	......	......	......	......	......	......
Totals	107	250	2,059	29	250	4,927	7,619

TABLE No. XIII.

TEACHERS' INSTITUTES.

COUNTIES.	Where held.	By whom conducted.	T'chrs Pres.	No. of days inst. cont.	When held.
[illegible]	Friendship and White Creek	R. Graham and J. M. Higbee	60	18	Oct. 28, '72 & Apr. 24, '73
[illegible], jt. with Dunn	[illegible]	A. Salisbury and J. B. Thayer	8	20	July 28; Aug. 22, 1873.
Buffalo	Alma	D. McGregor	50	5	Aug. 25; Jan. 21, 1873.
Brown	Depere	R. [illegible]	78	5	Oct. 13, 17, 1873.
[illegible]	Chilton	B. M. Reynolds and E. H. Sprague	60	19	[illegible]. 4, 28, 1873.
Chippewa	Chippewa Falls	Jno. A. McDonald & D. [illegible]	69	9	Oct., 1872, and Seps., '73
Clark	Neillsville	R. Graham	15	5	Oct. 6–11, 1873.
Columbia	Portage City	A. [illegible]	83	5	Sept. 1–8, 1873.
[illegible]	Mt. [illegible]	F. D. Mills	28	3	Sept., 1873.
[illegible], 1st [illegible]	Sun [illegible]	D. McGregor and N. H. Chandler	65	5	[illegible], 1873.
[illegible], 2d [illegible]	Oregon, Belleville and Middleton	B. M. Reynolds, Morgan, Taylor and [illegible]	285	12	[illegible] 30, Apr., Sept. and Oct., 1873.
Dodge, 1st district	Places of [illegible]	[illegible] Supt., John A. Barney	200	12	Apr. and Sept., 1873.
Dunn	Menomonie	A. Salisbury and J. B. Thayer	53	20	July 29–22, 1873.
Eau Claire	Eau Claire	R. Graham	80	5	April 1–8, 1873.
Grant	Georgetown, Hazel Green, Mont-[illegible], Washburn, Platteville, [illegible] and [illegible]	W. H. Holford, D. McGregor, C. H. Nye and W. D. Parker.	189	22	Nov. and Dec., 1872; Jan., Feb., March and Aug., 1873.
[illegible]	Monroe, Belville	A. Salisbury and B. M. Reynolds	100	6	Jan. 24–28, & Sept. 1-2, '73
[illegible] Lake	Dartford	R. Graham	53	5	Sept. 22, Oct. 4, 1 [illegible]
Iowa	Mineral Point	D. McGregor	48	8	[illegible]. 6, 10, 1873.
Jackson	[illegible] River [illegible]	D. McGregor	40	4½	Sept. 8, 12, 1873.
Jefferson	Jefferson	D. McGregor	52	4	Apr. 7, 1873.
Juneau	[illegible] and New Lisbon	A. O. Wright and Hosea Barnes	115	26	Oct. 15–20, '72, Aug. 4-30 '73
Kenosha	Wilmot	T. V. Maguire	64	12	Oct. 1–15, 1872.
Kewaunee	Kewaunee	A. Salisbury	47	4	Apr. 15–18, 1873.

TABLE No. XIII.—*Teachers' Institutes*—continued.

COUNTIES.	Where held.	By whom conducted.	T'chrs. pres't.	No. of days Inst. con.	When held.
La Crosse	West Salem	A. Salisbury	83	10	March 12–27, 1873.
La Fayette	Shullsburg	D. McGregor	35	4½	April 21–25, 1873.
Manitowoc	Manitowoc	R. Graham, Viebahn, and Kirwan	103	20	July 21, Aug. 15, 1873.
Marathon	Wausau	R. Graham	36	4	Sept. 27, 1873.
Marquette	Oxford	A. Salisbury and W. F. Johnson	40	5	April 28, 1873.
Milwaukee, 1st dist	Hales' Corner	R. Graham	81	3	Sept 12, 1873.
Milwaukee, 2d dist	Wauwatosa	R. Graham and A. F. North	55	3	Sept. 9–11, 1873.
Outagamie	Appleton	R. Graham	119	10	April and Sept., 1873.
Ozaukee	Grafton	A. Salisbury	34	5	October 6–12, 1873.
Pepin	Arkansaw	D. McGregor	25	4½	September, 1873.
Pierce	River Falls	E. T. Case	25	2	Nov, 25–26, 1872.
Polk	Osceola Mills	A. Earthman and Chas. E. Mears	26	18	Aug. 19—Sept. 18, 1872.
Portage	Stevens Point	R. Graham and W. R. Alban	30	14	April, 1873.
Racine	Rochester and Union Grove	M. Montague, A. F. North, B. F. Anderson, Hosea Barnes	120	24	Oct., 1872, April, 1873.
Richland	Richland Center	McGregor, Parker and Salisbury	166	13½	Apr. 14, and Aug. 18, '73.
Rock, 1st dist	Janesville	W. D. Parker	56	5	Sept. 23–30, 1872.
Rock, 2d dist	Janesville and Clinton Junction	W. D. Parker and D. McGregor	......	9	Sept. 26–Oct. 1, 1872, and April 28–May 3, 1873.
Sauk	Delton, Spring Green, Logansville and Prairie du Sac	J. H. Terry, A. Salisbury and A. F. North	215	38	Sept. 21–26, and Sept. 30–Oct. 16, 1872; April 1-12, and Aug. 4–30, '73.
Sheboygan	Plymouth	I. N. Stewart and C. W. Clinton	56	10	Aug. 4–18, 1873.
Trempealeau	Trempealeau and Coral City	Amos Whiting	45	4	Apr. 2–3, and 9–10, 1873.
Walworth	Delavan	Geo. Beck	55	9	Aug. 12–22, 1873.
Washington	At places of Examinations	Chauncey Gray	19	......	April, June, 1873.
Waukesha	Waukesha	North, Skewes, and Anderson	255	20	April and Sept., 1873.
Waupaca	Weyguwega	Graham, Hutton and McGregor	82	24	May 6 and Aug. 4, 1873.
Waushara	Plainfield and Auroraville	R. Graham	110	35	Sept. and Oct., 1873.
Winnebago	Oshkosh	G. S. Albee	39	10	Aug. 11–23, 1873.

Table No. XIII.—*Institutes*—continued.

Counties.	No. of Schools in the County, or Supt. dist't.	No. of Teachers Holding Certificates. Male. 1st gr.	2d gr.	3d gr.	Female. 1st gr.	2d gr.	3d gr.	Whole No. Attending the Institute. Males.	Females.	Total.	No. of days the Institute was in Session.	No. Attending. 1 day only.	2 days only.	3 days only.	Full Term.	No. who have Received Instructions in Common Schools. M.	F.	Graded Schools. M.	F.	Academies. M.	F.	Colleges or Universities. M.	F.	Normal Schools. M.	F.
Buffalo	77	4	9	48	2	4	48	26	24	50	5	2	4	10	84	....	....	....	....	....	....	....	....	....	....
Calumet	68	....	4	8	....	2	47	17	43	60	19	2	5	2	19	15	45	8	19	2	....	2	2	1	1
Chippewa	56	....	....	17	....	....	33	4	25	29	5	....	....	....	20	....	....	....	....	....	....	....	....	....	....
Clark	40	1	....	....	....	1	6	1	14	15	4	1	1	2	11	1	4	1	3	1	....	....	....	....	....
Columbia	180	2	6	26	1	4	147	66	20	86	5	....	2	4	80	66	20	25	18	8	8	1	1	1	4
Dane, 1st dist.	108	....	....	....	.	....	....	25	42	67	5	1	6	4	56	25	42	9	22	6	10	11	13	3	6
Dunn	79	2	6	24	1	6	61	18	40	43	20	1	....	6	46	13	40	9	25	1	2	3	3	1	1
Eau Claire	45	1	2	6	3	2	50	15	47	82	5	....	5	8	69	15	67	11	46	13	4	4	4	1	4
Grant	250	....	....	....	....	....	....	16	49	65	10	....	....	....	27	14	25	4	15	8	16	2	1	11	11
Green	144	3	....	17	3	3	48	26	64	90	4	33	64	90	60	26	64	15	40	3	2	5	2	2	3
Jackson	64	1	2	4	...	4	24	8	32	40	5	....	5	15	20	8	32	2	23	3	8	2	5	....	1
Jefferson	187	4	2	9	....	2	31	18	34	52	4	5	18	11	17	18	33	8	23	6	10	4	9	3	3
La Crosse	67	....	5	40	....	2	65	33	50	83	8	2	5	1	75	33	50	20	36	16	18	7	4	3	1
La Fayette	119	6	10	69	5	19	137	10	25	35	5	6	5	12	12	9	19	7	18	5	14	1	....	1	1
Marathon	....	....	....	....	....	....	....	27	35	62	8	5	14	....	43	9	11	9	7	2	4	2	2	2	3
Marquette	59	2	4	9	1	4	52	5	35	40	5	....	....	8	37	....	....	....	5	....	4	1	....	1	6
Oconto	32	4	2	8	....	2	21	5	26	31	...	11	20	....	20	11	40	8	19	2	3	2	1	....	4
Outagamie	85	1	2	16	....	2	28	25	50	75	5	6	4	10	55	19	36	14	31	8	7	13	23	8	5
Ozaukee	58	1	12	43	....	...	30	18	15	33	5	20	25	30	33	18	15	4	6	6	3	10	3	6	5
Pepin	32	1	1	9	....	1	22	4	18	22	5	....	2	....	18	68	62	32	35	....	....	....	....	....	....
Polk	47	1	1	20	....	1	40	6	28	34	19	....	1	1	2	6	28	1	9	3	7	1	....	....	2
Portage	83	1	2	10	....	1	60	10	38	48	5	....	4	1	43	....	....	8	20	1	....	....	1	1	1
Racine	77	1	2	....	1	15	....	19	61	80	15	....	...	1	79	18	56	10	30	6	18	1	4	1	3

TABLE No. XIII.—*Institutes*—continued.

Counties.	No. of Schools in the County or Supt. dist't.	No. of Teachers holding Certificates. — Male. 1st gr.	Male. 2d gr.	Male. 3d gr.	Female. 1st gr.	Female. 2d gr.	Female. 3d gr.	Whole No. attending the Institute. Males.	Females.	Total.	No. of days the Institute was in Session.	No. Attending. 1 day only.	2 days only.	3 days only.	Full Term.	No. who have received Instruction in Common Schools M.	Common Schools F.	Graded Schools. M.	Graded Schools. F.	Academies. M.	Academies. F.	Colleges or Universities. M.	Colleges or Universities. F.	Normal Schools. M.	Normal Schools. F.
Richland	129	2	2	36	....	5	118	20	81	101	5	2	4	5	68	17	71	17	51	1	6	....	8	1	1
Rock, 1st dist.	83	1	4	46	1	4	117	29	34	63	4	9	9	15	31	24	15	4	10	21	16	3	7	2	1
Rock, 2d dist	93	1	....	11	....	4	45	23	56	79	4	....	4	39	36	14	58	13	37	5	12	4	13	1	....
Sauk	180	5	5	75	....	....	150	19	60	79	19	....	2	1	21	....	....	....	....	....	....	....	....	....	....
Sheboygan	113	1	1	3	2	1	26	3	53	56	10	1	16	....	11	3	53	1	21	1	2	1	1	1	2
Vernon	115	3	2	65	....	5	80	19	23	42	4	1	2	9	30	19	23	15	16	9	10	8	....	2	1
Walworth	140	4	2	8	1	....	72	11	44	54	9	5	5	1	11	11	41	3	31	5	15	1	....	1	10
Waukesha	121	2	3	57	....	7	140	35	80	115	15	35	....	....	80	15	20	30	25	4	2	9	7	2	1
Waupaca	96	2	3	18	2	1	72	14	57	71	5	....	....	....	....	63	14	56	12	2	1	....	....	2	5
Winnebago	123	3	6	40	....	7	106	5	34	89	10	....	....	....	....	....	....	....	....	....	....	....	....	....	....
Wood	50	....	....	....	....	....	....	7	31	88	5	2	4	11	21	7	14	4	13	1	2	....	1	....	....
Totals	3144	60	100	677	23	109	1876	482	1358	1840	256	150	236	292	1194	565	993	265	666	149	189	93	110	58	86

TABLE No. XIV.

DISTRIBUTION OF DICTIONARIES.

STATEMENT *showing the counties, towns and districts which have been supplied with Dictionaries, during the year ending December 10, 1873.*

COUNTIES.	TOWNS.	No. of Districts.	No. of Copies.
Ashland	Ashland	1, 2	2
Barron	Barron	11 sub-dis.	11
Brown	Ashwaubenon	1	1
	Depere	7, 3 Deps.	3
	Lawrence	5	1
	Morrison	6	1
	Pittsfield	1, 4	2
Buffalo	Alma, village	1, 1 Dep.	1
	Naples	2, 1 Dep.	1
	Waumandee	3, jt.	1
Calumet	Harrison	10	1
	New Holstein	3	1
Clark	Beaver	5, 6	2
	Eaton	3, 5	2
	Loyal	9	1
	Sherman	2	1
	Weston	2	1
Columbia	Fort Winnebago	7	1
	Lodi	1, 2 Deps.	2
Crawford	Clayton	19	1
	Seneca and Freeman	8	1
	Wauzeka	8	1
Dane	Stoughton, village	3, 1 Dep.	1
Dodge	Beaver Dam	10	1
	Emmett	8	1
	Oak Grove	7, 1 Dep.	1
Door	Forestville	2, 3	2
	Sturgeon Bay	5	1
Dunn	Eau Galle, Rock Elm, Pierce Co.	7	1
	Grant	1, 4	2
	New Haven	3	1
	Sherman	5	1
	Spring Brook	7, 8, New.	2
Eau Claire	Eau Claire, city	4 Deps.	4
Fond du Lac	Eldorado and Lamartine	6	1
	Fond du Lac, city	21 Deps.	21
Grant	Bloomington	4	1
	Liberty	9	1
Green	Cadiz	13	1
	Jefferson	10, 1 Dep.	1
	Monroe, village	1 Dep.	1

TABLE XIV.—*Distribution of Dictionaries*—continued.

COUNTIES.	TOWNS.	No. of Districts.	No. of Copies.
Green Lake	Brooklyn	1,13	2
Iowa	Ridgway	14	1
	Dodgeville	5	1
	Pulaski	1	1
Jackson	Alma	8	1
	Irving and Springfield	2	1
	Manchester	1	1
	Springfield	9	1
Juneau	Necedah	4	1
Kenosha	Paris	1	1
Kewaunee	Ahnepee	1,2 Deps.	2
La Crosse	La Crosse, city	10 Deps.	10
La Fayette	Belmont and Elk Grove	5	1
	Elk Grove	4	1
	Elk Grove, Benton, New Diggings	8	1
Manitowoc	Franklin	4	1
Marathon	Bergen	2	1
	Hull and Beaver	1	1
	Wausau	5	1
Milwaukee	Lake	1,4 Deps.	4
	Milwaukee, city	1 Dep.	1
Monroe	Oakdale	5	1
	Sparta and Angelo	1	1
	Ridgeville	5	1
	Wilton and Tomah	10	1
Oconto	Maple Valley	5	1
Outagamie	Appleton city	4, 1 Dep.	1
	Buchanan	1	1
	Kaukauna	1	1
	Seymour	4	1
Pepin	Frankfort	3	1
	Pepin	3, 5	2
Pierce	Clifton	7	1
	Rock Elm	4	1
	Spring Lake	7	1
Polk	Balsam Lake	4, 5	2
	Loraine	2	1
	Luck	4	1
	Sterling	5	1
Portage	Amherst	8	1
	Amherst*	3	1
	Plover	9	1
Richland	Richland	3	1
Rock	Johnstown	2, 1 Dep.	1
	Union	10	1
St. Croix	Cady	3	1
	Somerset	4	1
	Troy	10	1
Sauk	Spring Green	2, 1 Dep.	1
	Washington	5	1
Shawano	Angelica	1	1
	Hartland	3	1
	Lessor	2	1
Sheboygan	Lyndon and Sherman	9	1
Vernon	Jefferson	2	1

*Joint with Scandinavia, Waupaca County.

TABLE IV.—*Distribution of Dictionaries*—continued.

COUNTIES.	TOWNS.	No. of Districts.	No. Copies.
Walworth	Bloomfield	10,2 Deps.	2
	Richmond....................	11	1
	Sharon....................	11, 1 Dept.	1
	Whitewater..........	1,2 Deps.	3
Waukesha........	Delafield	4	1
	Waukesha (Industrial School) ..	1, 5 Deps.	5
	Wauwatosa....................	1,1 Dept.	1
Waupaca.........	Dayton....................	8	1
Winnebago.......	Clayton and Winchester........	14	1
	Nekimi	7,2 Deps.	2
	Nepeuskun	9	1
Wood	Saratoga	4	1

STATEMENT *showing the Districts to which Dictionaries have been sold during the year ending December* 10, 1873.

COUNTIES.	TOWNS.	No. of District.	No. Copies.
Adams	Strong's Prairie...	1	1
Brown	Green Bay, city...	1 Dep.	1
Dane............	Fitchburg	7	1
	Mazomanie....................	2,1 Dep.	1
	Stoughton....	3,1 Dep.	1
Dodge	Beaver Dam and Oak Grove....	2	1
	Chester and Trenton......	3	1
Dunn	Dunn	4	1
Eau Claire........	Eau Claire, city	2, 3 Deps.	2
Fond du Lac	Friendship	5	1
	Metomen....................	9	1
	Osceola	1	1
Grant	Fennimore, H. Grove & Marion.	1	1
	Lancaster	8	1
Green	Exeter and Mt. Pleasant........	8	1
	Jefferson and Sylvester.........	8&9	1
	Monroe	5	1
Grern Lake	Green Lake, Manchester and Markesan	17	1
	Mackford	2	1
	Princeton and St. Marie.......	3	1
Jackson	Hixton....................	2	1
	Melrose	1, 3	1
Kenosha	Paris	5	1
	Somers....................	2, 11	2
	Somers and Paris *	15	1
Kewaunee........	Lincoln	3	1
	Pierce	4	1
La Crosse	Burns....................	2	1
	Farmington	1	1
La Fayette........	Fayette	5	1
Manitowoc	Cato	10	1
	Maple Grove	1	1

* Joint with Mt. Pleasant and Yorkville, Racine county.

TABLE XIV.—*Dictionaries Sold*—continued.

COUNTIES.	TOWNS.	No. of District.	No. of Copies.
Marquette	Westfield	3	1
	Little Falls	3	1
Monroe	Sparta and Angelo	1,6 Deps.	6
Oconto	Pensaukee	2	1
	Peshtigo	1,3 Deps., 3	4
Outagamie	Greenville	5	1
Pierce	Clifton	4	1
	Farmington	2	1
Polk	Sterling	3	1
Racine	Caledonia	4	1
	Mt. Pleasant	5	1
Rock	Bradford	2	1
	Lima	9	1
Sauk	Ironton and Lavalle	3	1
	Dellona and Winfield	3	1
Sheboygan	Lyndon and Plymouth	1	1
	Plymouth	5	1
Walworth	Darien and Sharon	6	1
	Sugar Creek	7	1
Washington	Erin	3	1
Waukesha	Mukwanago	5	1
Waupaca	Farmington	1	1
	Iola	1	1
	Union	3	1
Waushara	Springwater	2	1
	Wautoma	1	1
Winnebago	Algoma	1	1
	Neenah	1, 1 Dep.	1
	Omro	3, 5, 6	3

TABLE No. XV.

COUNTY SUPERINTENDENTS IN THE STATE,

Elected for 1874-5.

County.	Name.	Post Office.
Adams	J. M. Higbee	Plainville.
Ashland	John W. Bell	La Pointe.
Barron	A. B. Finley	Prairie Farm
Bayfield	Edwin Leehy	Bayfield.
Brown	Martin H. Lynch	Depere.
Buffalo	Lawrence Kessinger	Alma.
Burnett	John G. Fleming	Grantsburg.
Calumet	W. B. Minaghan	Chilton.
Chippewa	Jas. A. Bate	Chippewa Falls.
Clark	R. J. Sawyer	Neillsville.
Columbia	LeRoy J. Burlingame	West Point.
Crawford	Thos. L. Redlon	Wheatville.
Dane, 1st dist	W. H. Chandler	Sun Prairie.
Dane, 2d dist	M. S. Frawley	Black Earth.
Dodge, 1st dist	John T. Flavin	Watertown.
Dodge, 2d dist	Arthur K. Delaney	Hustisford.
Door	Chris Daniels	Sturgeon Bay.
Douglas	J. S. Graham	Superior.
Dunn	Geo. Tonnar	Menominie.
Eau Claire	Joseph F. Ellis	Eau Claire.
Fond du Lac, 1st dist	W. L. O'Connor	Rosendale.
Fond du Lac, 2d dist	Jas. J. Kelley	Osceola.
Grant	Geo. M. Guernsey	Platteville.
Green	Daniel H. Morgan	Monroe.
Green Lake	A. A. Spencer	Berlin.
Iowa	Wm. H. Peck	Mineral Point.
Jackson	T. P. Marsh	Pole Grove.
Jefferson	S. A. Craig	Fort Atkinson.
Juneau	Geo. P. Kenyon	New Lisbon.
Kenosha	Jas. P. Briggs	Kenosha.
Kewaunee	John M. Read	Kewaunee.
La Crosse	Sherman W. Leete	West Salem.
La Fayette	Jas. G. Knight	Darlington.
Manitowoc	Michael Kirwan	Manitowoc.
Marathon	Thomas Greene	Wausau.
Marquette	Henry M. Older	Packwaukee.
Milwaukee, 1st dist	Thos. O. Herrin	Milwaukee.
Milwaukee, 2d dist	James L. Foley	Butler.
Monroe	A. E. Howard	Sparta.
Oconto	A. T. Stearns	Oconto.
Outagamie	Patrick Flanagan	Appleton.
Ozaukee	Edward H. Janssen	Cedarburg.
Pepin	M. B. Axtell	Pepin.

County Superintendents in the State—continued.

County.	Name.	Post Office.
Pierce	Martin E. Cady	River Falls.
Polk	Charles E. Mears	Osceola Mills.
Portage	Jas. O. Morrison	Plover.
Racine	Thomas Malone	Rochester.
Richland	Wm. J. Waggoner	Richland Center.
Rock, 1st dist	Edson A. Burdick	Janesville.
Rock, 2d dist	J. B. Tracy	Emerald Grove.
St. Croix	Frank P. Chapman	New Richmond.
Sauk	Jas. T. Lunn	Ironton.
Shawano	Chas. R. Klebesadel	Shawano.
Sheboygan	M. D. L. Fuller	Plymouth.
Trempealeau	Jas. B. Thompson	Trempealeau.
Vernon	Orvis B. Wyman	Viroqua.
Walworth	S. P. Ballard	Sharon.
Washington	Fred. Regenfuss	West Bend.
Waukesha	Isaac N. Stewart	Waukesha.
Waupaca	Justus Burnham	Waupaca.
Waushara	Theo. S. Chipman	Berlin, Green Lake Co.
Winnebago	H. A. Hobart	Winneconne.
Wood	Clarence L. Powers	Grand Rapids.

Lightning Source UK Ltd.
Milton Keynes UK
UKHW020015181218
334174UK00006B/161/P